# Brief Contents

# Writing
## Ten Core Concepts

**Second Edition**

## Robert P. Yagelski
University at Albany, State University of New York

 CENGAGE

Australia • Brazil • Mexico • Singapore • United Kingdom • United States

***Writing: Ten Core Concepts,* 2nd Edition**
Robert P. Yagelski

Product Director: Monica Eckman

Product Manager: Laura Ross

Content Developer: Lynn Huddon

Senior Content Developer: Leslie Taggart

Associate Content Developers:
  Claire Branman and Jacqueline Czel

Product Assistant: Shelby Nathanson

Marketing Manager: Kina Lara

Content Project Manager: Rebecca Donahue

Senior Art Director: Marissa Falco

Manufacturing Planner: Betsy Donaghey

IP Analyst: Ann Hoffman

IP Project Manager: Erika Mugavin

Production Service/Compositor:
  Christian Arsenault, SPi Global

Text Designer: Bill Reuter

Cover Designer: Roycroft Design

Cover Image: Don Mason/Stockbyte/Getty
  Images

For product information and technology assistance, contact us at
**Cengage Customer & Sales Support, 1-800-354-9706**

For permission to use material from this text or product,
submit all requests online at **www.cengage.com/permissions.**

Further permissions questions can be emailed to
**permissionrequest@cengage.com.**

Library of Congress Control Number:

Student Edition:
ISBN: 978-1-305-95676-6

Loose-leaf Edition:
ISBN: 978-1-337-09175-6

**Cengage**
20 Channel Center Street
Boston, MA 02210
USA

Cengage is a leading provider of customized learning solutions with employees residing in nearly 40 different countries and sales in more than 125 countries around the world. Find your local representative at **www.cengage.com.**

Cengage products are represented in Canada by Nelson Education, Ltd.

To learn more about Cengage platforms and services, register or access your online learning solution, or purchase materials for your course, visit **www.cengage.com.**

Printed at CLDPC, USA, 08-19

# Contents

## Chapter 4   A Student Writer Applies the Core Concepts

## PART 2  Writing to Analyze

### Chapter 5  Understanding Analytical Writing

### Chapter 6  Examining Causes and Effects

## Chapter 9  Analyzing Literary Texts

## Chapter 10  Evaluating and Reviewing

## PART 3  Writing to Persuade

### Chapter 11  Understanding Argument

### Chapter 12  Making Academic Arguments

## PART 4 Writing to Narrate and Inform

### Chapter 15 Understanding Narrative Writing

### Chapter 16 Writing Personal Narratives

## Chapter 17  Writing Informative Essays

## Chapter 18  Digital Storytelling

# PART 5  Essential Skills for Contemporary Writers

## Chapter 19  Working with Ideas and Information

## Chapter 20    Designing Documents

## Chapter 21    Finding Source Material

## Chapter 22  Evaluating Sources

## Chapter 23  Using Source Material

## Chapter 24  Citing Sources Using MLA Style

# Readings by Theme

# Preface

Writing is a way to understand and participate in the world around us. It is a vehicle for learning—a way to make sense of our experiences and convey what we learn to others. Writing is a powerful means of individual expression and social interaction that has the capacity to change us. As the National Commission on Writing in America's Schools and Colleges put it, "At its best, writing has helped transform the world."

Composition teachers know all this, of course. They understand the power of writing, and they know that writing well is necessary for students to succeed in college and beyond. But instructors also know that a one-semester course is never quite enough to help students develop the sophisticated skills they will need to write effectively in their college classes and in their lives outside school. Research indicates that students need their entire college careers to develop those skills. First-year writing courses can lay the foundation for that process.

To make the most of the composition course, *Writing: Ten Core Concepts* focuses on the most important skills and knowledge that students must develop to be able to write the kind of sophisticated prose expected in college. It teaches the foundational lessons that students need to develop their competence as writers.

## A Focus on Important Aspects of Writing

Research underscores what composition instructors well know: most college students tend to have difficulty with a few crucial aspects of writing. Among these are:

- addressing an audience effectively
- focusing on a main idea and developing it sufficiently
- organizing texts appropriately
- adopting an appropriate register or "voice" in writing
- supporting assertions or arguments
- identifying and using appropriate sources
- revising effectively
- applying the conventions of academic writing

For the most part, these difficulties apply across disciplines and forms of writing. Significantly, research reveals that most of these problems arise from three main sources:

- students' lack of understanding of the rhetorical nature of writing
- students' inexperience with different rhetorical tasks across the college curriculum
- students' misunderstanding of how to manage the process of writing

In other words, these problems arise from a basic misunderstanding of the rhetorical and social nature of writing and inexperience with managing the writing process *in the context of varied rhetorical tasks*, especially the kind of writing tasks typical of academic work in college.

Consequently, *Writing: Ten Core Concepts* rests on three central ideas about writing:

- *Writing is a rhetorical act.* Writing is fundamentally an interaction between a writer and a reader within a specific social context. In this sense, writing is always a social activity, and effective writing connects writers and readers in complex and powerful ways.

- *Writing is a way to participate in the conversations that shape our lives.* Through writing, writers and their readers collaborate in knowledge-making and share information and opinions about issues that matter to them. Writing enables us to take part in the many ongoing conversations about important matters that affect how we live and how we understand ourselves and the world we inhabit. In the most basic way, writing is a way to *construct* the world by participating in these complex conversations.

- *Writing is a means of inquiry.* Writing is an intellectual activity that can lead to a deeper understanding of ideas, experiences, and information. It is a means of understanding ourselves and the world we share. Writing can engage students in careful, critical thinking about themselves and the world around them. Writing is a unique and powerful vehicle for learning.

These ideas inform both the content and structure of *Writing: Ten Core Concepts*. As students are guided through various writing tasks and learn to manage the process of writing efficiently, they also gain a fuller understanding of the nature of writing as rhetoric, conversation, and inquiry. This book will help composition instructors meet a central challenge in working with student writers: helping students develop a sophisticated understanding of writing and gain experience as writers acting on that understanding.

*Writing: Ten Core Concepts* emphasizes what is essential in writing at the college level and guides students as they apply that knowledge to various writing tasks. It trains students to think rhetorically and helps them manage the fundamental characteristics of effective academic writing. In this regard, the Ten Core Concepts serve as a framework for understanding writing and a practical, step-by-step guide for negotiating the demands of academic writing tasks.

## Ten Core Concepts

The Ten Core Concepts distinguish this textbook from other writing guides. Most composition textbooks try to cover every conceivable aspect of writing in college and beyond, presenting far more material than students could ever grasp and retain in a single semester. That approach ultimately waters down the most important lessons that student writers must learn. *Writing: Ten Core Concepts* is different. It emphasizes what students must really learn to become effective writers.

These Core Concepts are not basic skills, nor are they procedures for completing specific kinds of writing tasks. Rather, they are fundamental insights into the nature of writing that students must enact as they complete varied writing tasks. These Core Concepts boil down what has been learned through research and practice into key ideas about what writing is and how effective writing works. For example, Core Concept #4—"a writer must have something to say"—emphasizes the need for a piece of writing to convey a clear main point or idea. Studies indicate that college writing instructors identify the lack of a clear main idea as one of the most common weaknesses in student writing. This concept helps students understand why effective writing in most genres is characterized by a focus on a main idea; it also helps them understand how the different expectations in various academic disciplines can shape a writer's main idea and how that main idea is presented and developed in specific kinds of texts. Most importantly, the concept guides students through a process that enables them to identify, refine, and articulate the main idea of any writing project they are working on. In this way, the Core Concepts can deepen students' understanding of key insights about writing at the same time that students practice applying those insights in their own writing.

The Ten Core Concepts are not prescriptive. They are not step-by-step instructions for writing in specific genres. Instead, they are fundamental but flexible guidelines for writing; they serve as a set of heuristics that students can apply to *any* writing task. *Writing: Ten Core Concepts* is informed by the basic idea that practice is essential in developing writing competence. In a sense, this idea is the 11th Core Concept. Only through sustained, guided practice in writing different kinds of texts for various rhetorical situations can students develop the understanding and ability to write effectively for different purposes. Accordingly, *Writing: Ten Core Concepts* relies in part on the repetition of the Ten Core Concepts to give students the practice they need to make these Concepts part of their repertoire as writers.

## The Structure of *Writing: Ten Core Concepts*

*Writing: Ten Core Concepts* is organized into five parts. Part 1 introduces students to the Core Concepts. Parts 2, 3, and 4 guide students through the most common forms of three main categories of writing: analysis, argument, and narrative. The focus in these three sections is on helping students understand the uses of various genres *within rhetorical contexts*. Through contemporary examples and engaging exercises, students learn how various forms of writing enable them to address specific audiences and effectively accomplish various rhetorical purposes; moreover, these chapters give students sustained practice in applying the Ten Core Concepts to different kinds of writing and rhetorical situations. Finally, Part 5 addresses research skills and the conventions of writing. A brief description of each of these main sections follows:

**Part 1: A Guide to Writing Effectively.** The four chapters in this section introduce students to the essential insights into writing that they must acquire if they are to be able to apply their writing skills effectively in different contexts. In this section, students explore the fundamental ideas about writing described above: writing as rhetoric, as conversation, and as inquiry. Most important, they learn and practice the Ten Core Concepts that form the heart of this textbook. Chapter 2 explains these concepts, using examples to illustrate the lessons as well as exercises to help students understand how to apply the concepts in their own writing. Chapter 3 is an interactive, visual guide students can use to apply the Ten Core Concepts to any piece of writing. Chapter 4 presents a case study of a first-year student writer as she applies the Ten Core Concepts to complete a writing assignment.

**Part 2: Writing to Analyze.** The six chapters in Part 2 help students acquire competence in the most common forms of analytical writing in college. Chapter 5 introduces important features of analysis. Each of the other chapters explores the purposes and features of a different form of analytical writing and, using the Ten Core Concepts, guides students through an analytical writing project. The chapters also include practice in some of the key intellectual tasks associated with analysis, such as using a theoretical framework, that often challenge students.

**Part 3: Writing to Persuade.** In this section, students gain an understanding of the principles of effective argumentative writing, and they work through writing projects representing three main kinds of argument. Using the Ten Core Concepts as a guide for their writing, students explore the nature and purposes of argument in various contexts and practice applying the essential elements of argumentation for different rhetorical purposes.

**Part 4: Writing to Narrate and Inform.** The chapters in this section help students learn how to write effective narratives for different rhetorical purposes and also appreciate the important uses of narrative in academic contexts. Like the chapters in Parts 2 and 3, the chapters in this section guide students in applying the Ten Core Concepts so that they produce effective narrative writing that meets the needs of various rhetorical situations.

**Part 5: Essential Skills for Contemporary Writers.** This section provides students with practical advice about working with source material, conducting research for their various writing projects, and mastering and applying the conventions of written English. Chapter 19 focuses on essential intellectual skills that are important to the work that students do throughout college, including reading academic texts; responding to texts; and summarizing, paraphrasing, and synthesizing texts. Chapter 20 guides students in understanding an increasingly important aspect of effective writing today: document design. Chapters 21, 22, and 23 provide an up-to-date guide for finding, evaluating, and using source material in an interconnected world characterized by access to overwhelming bodies of information. Chapters 24 and 25 help students understand and apply the guidelines for citing sources recommended by the MLA and the APA. Chapter 26 guides students in developing an effective writing style, with specific attention to the stylistic conventions of academic writing, which often confuse students. Finally, Chapter 27 helps students craft effective, engaging prose and avoid errors that can weaken their writing. Rather than trying to reproduce a comprehensive handbook, this chapter focuses on the most common problems in student writing, including the formal errors that research shows are typical of college student writing.

Throughout *Writing: Ten Core Concepts* students encounter varied examples of effective writing in different genres and different media. They see how other writers, including student writers, meet the challenges of contemporary writing in college and beyond, and they are given an assortment of opportunities to practice what they learn, all the while using the Ten Core Concepts as their framework for writing.

## Integrated Coverage of Digital Literacy Practices

*Writing: Ten Core Concepts* focuses on the contemporary student who lives in an increasingly technological, globalized age. To write well today requires students to manage many different rhetorical tasks using various technologies, including constantly evolving digital media that have become essential tools for communication. Rather than addressing "digital literacy" as a separate skill or topic, *Writing: Ten Core Concepts* incorporates emerging digital technologies and literacy practices into the advice and practice it provides students for all their writing tasks. Throughout this textbook, students encounter examples and exercises that reflect various uses of communications technologies, and they receive advice for taking advantage of these technologies to meet the needs of the rhetorical situations within which they are writing.

## More Than 50% New Reading Selections and a New Genre

■ **New Professional and Student Reading Selections.** Twenty-one new, full-length readings offer new models for using various forms and genres of writing and also offer new topics for discussion. New selections feature work by well-known contemporary authors such as Deborah Tannen, Maria Konnikova, Lindy West, Sherry Turkle, and John Tierney, and touch on issues such as how current technologies have impacted our abilities to have meaningful conversation with one another, the ways that trigger warnings can work to expand freedom of expression rather than hinder it, and why current recycling practices aren't as effective and successful as we want to believe they are.

■ **New Coverage of Summary-Response Essays.** Chapter 19 includes a new section on summary-response writing that uses the Ten Core Concepts to guide students through the process of creating this common and important genre.

## New "Talking About This Reading" Dialogue with Students

Most reading selections in this edition are accompanied by a unique, new feature called "Talking About This Reading," in which real students comment on challenging or inspiring aspects of the reading and pose questions that the reading raised for them. In response to these comments and questions, I offer advice and strategies to help students understand the reading and meet the challenges it might present to them.

## New Strategies for Academic Reading

Chapter 19 includes a new section on reading challenging academic texts. Like the accessible step-by-step approach used to guide students through the main composing assignments in Parts 2, 3, and 4, this new guide to reading offers seven distinct strategies that students can use to understand any text. In this chapter, students learn to: skim a text to understand the big picture; read the introduction or preface of a text; examine the rhetorical context of a text; identify key terms; understand the structure or organization of a text; review a text's bibliography; and take effective notes while reading a text.

## New Student Case Study

Chapter 4 features a new project that enables students to see how a student writer, Chloe Charles, applied the Ten Core Concepts to a real writing assignment. The chapter follows Chloe through the process of composing an essay for an assignment in her college writing course, from generating a timely topic and developing a guiding thesis statement, to revising in response to feedback from her peers and her instructor, to preparing her final submitted essay.

## New Research and 2016 MLA  Documentation Guidelines

- **Revised Discussion of Finding Digital Sources.** Chapter 21 offers students up-to-date guidance for finding digital source materials when conducting research and developing research projects.
- **Updated MLA Guidelines.** Chapter 24 has been extensively revised to reflect the new 2016 MLA guidelines for documenting sources, including many new model citations and new digital examples to help students cite sources accurately.

## MindTap® English for Yagelski's *Writing: Ten Core Concepts,* 2nd Edition

MindTap® English engages your students to become better thinkers, communicators, and writers by blending your course materials with content that supports every aspect of the writing process. Interactive activities on grammar and mechanics promote application in student writing, and an easy-to-use paper management system allows for electronic submission, grading, and peer review while tracking potential plagiarism. A vast database of scholarly sources with video tutorials and examples supports each step of the research process, and professional tutoring guides students from rough drafts to polished writing. Visual analytics track student progress and engagement with seamless integration into your campus learning management system that keeps all your course materials in one place.

MindTap® English now comes equipped with the diagnostic-guided JUST IN TIME PLUS learning module for foundational concepts and embedded course support. The module features scaffolded video tutorials, instructional text content, and auto-graded activities designed to address each student's specific needs for practice and support to succeed in college-level composition courses.

## Acknowledgments

Writing a textbook can be a daunting undertaking, but it is made less so by the inherently collaborative nature of the work. This book is not mine; rather, it is the result of the sustained efforts of many people, whose ideas, dedication, and hard work helped make *Writing: Ten Core Concepts* a reality. It is impossible to thank them enough.

I am extremely grateful to Lyn Uhl for identifying this project as an important one and providing the support necessary to realize the vision that informed this project from the beginning. Special thanks to Monica Eckman, who provided leadership and support for this project from its very beginnings and whose knowledge and energy helped me manage the pressure of this work. I am also deeply grateful to Laura Ross, the editor for this project, whose expert guidance in refining it for this new edition have been integral to its success. Laura made this book a better one, and she always made the work fun and fulfilling. I am truly thankful for her dedication to this project and feel fortunate to be able to work with her.

My sincerest gratitude goes to Leslie Taggart, the senior development editor for this project, whose insight, patience, good humor, and constant support not only were essential in keeping the project moving forward but also made it possible for me to find the wherewithal to finish the work. The quality of this textbook is in so many ways a result of Leslie's dedication, expert advice, and exceptional judgment.

My thanks also to Vanessa Coloura for her terrific work on the MindTap version of the first edition of this book.

I am truly blessed to have had Lynn Huddon as the development editor for this edition. Lynn is as diligent and insightful as any editor I have worked with in more than 15 years of writing textbooks, and there is no doubt that the quality of this new edition is in large part a function of her hard work and keen eye for detail. She kept the project on track in the face of countless unexpected challenges, and she was always ready with excellent suggestions for improvements and refinements. Lynn was also exceedingly patient with this sometimes frustrated author and ever available to solve the many problems, large and small, that arise in the development of a composition textbook. I am extremely grateful to her and consider myself truly fortunate to have had the opportunity to work with her on this project.

My thanks, too, to Andy Fogle, of Bethlehem High School in Bethlehem, New York, who helped with the research for several chapters during the development of the first edition, and Tony Atkins, of the University of North Carolina at Greensboro, who not only provided invaluable insight about the treatment of technology throughout the book but also helped develop the chapter on document design.

I gratefully acknowledge the important role of my terrific colleagues in the Program in Writing and Critical Inquiry at the State University of New York at Albany. Their expertise and dedication as teachers of writing have not only inspired me but also helped deepen my own understanding of effective writing pedadogy. Their influence has shaped this new edition in both subtle and profound ways. In particular, I thank Susan Detwiler and Joe Creamer, superb colleagues and wonderful teachers whose feedback has enriched my thinking about writing instruction in general and about this textbook in particular. Susan and Joe were always willing to help me test ideas and review student writing as I developed this new edition. Also, my sincere thanks to Chloe Charles, a student of Joe Creamer's at SUNY-Albany and the author of the essay that appears in Chapter 4. Chloe is a hard-working, dedicated, and curious student who was cheerfully willing to put in a great deal of time and effort to meet our deadlines for this edition. I am very proud to be able to include her essay in this book, and I am blessed to have had the chance to work with her and learn from her.

I am also deeply grateful to the students who took the time to read and comment on the various selections included in this textbook. Their thoughtful questions and comments have enriched the readings and provided additional avenues of inquiry for their many peers who will eventually read this book.

It should go without saying that my students over the years have been perhaps the most important influence on my work as a teacher and a writer. They have taught me so much of what I know about writing, and they have enriched my life and work. I am grateful to all of them for allowing me to be part of their learning and their lives. They truly do make this work worthwhile.

My colleagues and friends in the Capital District Writing Project (CDWP), including Aaron Thiell, Christopher Mazura, Amy Salamone, Molly Fanning, Alicia Wein, and Christine Dawson, have been my supporters and teachers for many years now. I rely on them much more than they know, and their influence infuses this text. I am especially grateful to Carol Forman-Pemberton, my co-director at CDWP, who has become my most trusted colleague and wonderful friend over the dozen or so years we have been working together. I have learned from her more about writing and teaching than I could ever include in a single textbook, and her wisdom as a professional has guided my own work. I am truly fortunate to have her as a colleague and friend.

The many experts at Cengage who helped with the design, production, and marketing of this textbook also deserve a special thanks: Marissa Falco, Rebecca Donahue, Samantha Ross Miller, Kina Lara, Jacqueline Czel and Elizabeth Cranston. I especially wish to acknowledge Erin Parkins, whose tireless work on behalf of this textbook helped make the first edition a success.

I greatly benefited from the advice of many insightful instructors who provided thoughtful reviews and other kinds of feedback that helped shape this edition. My sincerest thanks to all the following instructors: Lauryn Angel, Collin College; Jennifer Atkins-Gordeeva, University of Central Arkansas; Emily Beard-Bohn, Saginaw Valley State University; Geralynne Berg, Lac Courte Oreilles Ojibwe Community College; Laura Carroll, Abilene Christian University; Carole Ann Chapman, Ivy Tech Community College of Indiana; Thomas Chester, Ivy Tech Community College; Jaclyn Chupeck, Saint Francis University; Aaron Clark, Brookhaven College; Heather M. Clark, Ivy Tech Community College; Sheilah R. Craft, Ivy Tech Community College; Brittany Cuenin, Lander University; Renee DeLong, Minneapolis Community and Technical College; Sharon Graham, Fort Hays State University; Sarah Guerrettaz, Ivy Tech Community College; John Hansen, Mohave Community College; Janice Hartman, Juniata College; Troy Hickman, Ivy Tech Community College; Martha M. Holder, Wytheville Community College; Aaron D. Hoover, Ivy Tech Community College; Lauri Humberson, St. Philip's College; Karen Keaton Jackson, North Carolina Central University; Valerie Jahns, University of Wisconsin Fox Valley; Andrea Jefferson, Ivy Tech Community College; Nancy Lee-Jones, Endicott College; Gerald Maki, Ivy Tech Community College; Christina Marty, University of Wisconsin Fox Valley; John Moran, St. Philip's College; Jeff Paschke-Johannes, Ivy Tech Community College; Jared M. Riddle, Ivy Tech Community College; Nancy Riecken, Ivy Tech Community College; Michael A. Schwartz, Moreno Valley College; Charlotte Smith, Ivy Tech Community College; Elizabeth Starr, Ivy Tech Community College; Jaclyn Sullivan, Saint Francis University; Jessica Thompson, Mississippi State University; Dayle K. Turner, Leeward Community College; Marsha Turner-Shear, Ivy Tech Community College-Bloomington; Stephanie L. Webster, Ivy Tech Community College; Debbie J. Williams, Abilene Christian University; and Susan Wright, William Paterson University.

Finally, I very grateful for the support of my family, without whom I could never have completed this work and whose patience with me and confidence in me sustained me through many challenging moments. My parents—Ron and Joan Yagelski—and my siblings—Mary Cooper, Gary Yagelski, and Dianne Yagelski—support me in ways they never really see, and their presence in my life reinforces my belief in myself. My mother-in-law, Charlotte Hafich, is always there to offer encouragement and check in on my progress; I can never thank her enough for her love and support. My sons, Adam and Aaron, who light up my life in ways they can never realize, are always ready to share and debate ideas with me, and I am energized by their pride in what I do; they help me see the world in ways that shape my writing and keep me going. And most of all, Cheryl, my wife of 35 years and the love of my life, is the best partner any writer could ever hope to have. Her love, constant support, and boundless confidence in me are the foundation that make it possible for me to undertake a task as big as a textbook and see it through. I am so deeply blessed to be able to share this work—and my life—with her. She always provides safe harbor.

*Robert P. Yagelski*

**In this chapter, you will learn to**

1. Identify many purposes for writing both inside and outside of the classroom.

2. Reflect upon your own diverse writing experiences to consider the most appropriate strategies for a specific audience and purpose in future writing situations.

3. Describe new and different ways to think about your own and others' writing.

**MindTap**®

Understand the goals of the chapter and complete a warm-up activity.

1950    1970    1990    2010    2030?

# Why We Write   1

**WRITING IS A POWERFUL MEANS** of communicating ideas and information across time and space. It enables us to participate in conversations and events that shape our lives and helps us make sense of the world. In fact, writing can change the world. Consider these examples:

- Adam Smith's economic theories, presented in his 1776 book *The Wealth of Nations*, continue to influence government economic policies today, which in turn affect the lives of almost every person on earth.
- *The Art of War*, believed to have been written in the 6th century B.C.E. by Chinese military strategist Sun Tzu, is still widely read by military leaders, politicians, and business leaders.
- Betty Friedan's *The Feminine Mystique*, published in 1963, is considered by many to have begun the women's rights movement that has reshaped American social, cultural, political, and economic life in the past half century.
- Charles Darwin's *On the Origin of Species*, published in 1859, revolutionized scientific thinking about life on earth and laid the foundation for the modern field of biology.
- *Silent Spring*, by Rachel Carson, which was published in 1962, helped spark the modern environmental movement and influenced the creation of laws to protect wildlife and the environment.
- Al Gore's 2006 book *An Inconvenient Truth* and the film based on it convinced millions of people that global climate change is a grave threat to human life that must be addressed by all nations.
- Messages posted on Facebook and Twitter during the so-called "Arab Spring" in 2011 helped provoke protests in Egypt and Tunisia that led to new governments in those nations.

These are only the most dramatic examples of the capacity of writing to transform our world.

For many college students, however, writing is mostly a requirement. Most students don't seem to mind writing, but few would choose to write the kinds of essays and reports usually assigned in school. Students consider such assignments necessary, but they don't necessarily enjoy them. For many students, writing in school can be tedious and dull. Maybe you feel the same way.

Yet students write all the time, for all kinds of reasons:

- They send text messages, post to Instagram and Facebook, and tweet to stay in touch with friends, share information, let others know what they think, and keep informed about events or issues that matter to them.

- They respond to their favorite blogs or maintain their own blogs.
- They keep journals or diaries.
- They circulate petitions to support causes on their campus or in their town.
- They rap and participate in poetry slams to express their feelings about important issues in their lives.
- They write essays to gain admission to college or graduate school.
- They create resumes to land jobs.

Whether they realize it or not, students regularly use writing to live their lives, to accomplish tasks that they have to do or choose to do, and to participate in their communities.

If these kinds of writing don't seem as important as, say, a book like *An Inconvenient Truth* or *Silent Spring*, they should. For if a book can be said to have changed the world, the same is true of tweets and texts and blogs and essays and letters written by ordinary people, including students. A job application letter can change your life. A petition can change a policy on your campus that affects hundreds or thousands of students (see Sidebar: "How a Student Changed a College Policy on Free Speech"). An essay can inspire your classmates, change their minds about an issue, or move them to take action. A tweet or Facebook post can help spark a social or political movement. In 2013 a young woman from California named Alicia Garza posted a message to her Facebook page about the death of a young black man in Florida named Trayvon Martin. Her message became the hashtag #BlackLivesMatter, which in turn became an important national movement that helped shape discussions about race relations in the United States and even influenced the presidential election in 2016. Sometimes such ordinary kinds of writing can result in even more extraordinary change: in Egypt, in February, 2011, tweets, email messages, texts, blog posts, and Facebook entries from ordinary citizens played a key role in the protest movement that led to the resignation of Egypt's president, who had ruled that nation for more than three decades. In other words, writing by ordinary citizens helped change the government of that country—a change that has touched the life of every Egyptian and many people outside Egypt.

JASON REDMOND/AFP/Getty Images

## SIDEBAR    HOW A STUDENT CHANGED A COLLEGE POLICY ON FREE SPEECH

In September 2013, a student named Vincenzo Sinapi-Riddle at Citrus College in Glendora, California, was soliciting signatures for a petition about the surveillance of American citizens by the United States government as part of its so-called "war on terror." Sinapi-Riddle was a member of a national student organization called Young Americans for Liberty, whose mission, according to its website, is "to identify, educate, train, and mobilize young people" who are committed to its Libertarian political views. As the following account reveals, Sinapi-Riddle was standing outside the student center on the Citrus College campus talking about his petition with another student when an administrator threatened to remove him from campus for violating the college's policy on free speech. Sinapi-Riddle was told that he was standing outside the designated area for protest and therefore could not continue advocating for his petition. With the help of an organization called the Foundation for Individual Rights in Education, or FIRE, Sinapi-Riddle filed a lawsuit against Citrus College, arguing that the college's free speech policy violated students' constitutional right to free speech. He won his suit, and Citrus College revised its policy. As Sinapi-Riddle wrote on his blog, we "launched our initiative to raise awareness about warrantless government spying with great success. In the end we gathered over 300 signatures for our petition asking student government to denounce NSA spying, but in the process of protesting one egregious violation of our rights we stumbled upon another."

This case provides a compelling example of how students can use writing to effect change. Sinapi-Riddle and his fellow students in Young Americans for Liberty used writing to raise awareness about an issue (government surveillance of citizens) that concerns them, but writing was also an essential tool in his lawsuit against Citrus College. In addition to the various legal documents required in the case, Sinapi-Riddle used blog posts, social media, and news reports to support his position and take action against a policy that he believed was wrong.

### Citrus College Stand Up For Speech Lawsuit

On September 17, 2013—Constitution Day—Citrus College (Glendora, California) student Vincenzo Sinapi-Riddle was threatened with removal from campus by an administrator for asking a fellow student to sign a petition protesting NSA surveillance of American citizens. His crime? Sinapi-Riddle was petitioning outside of the college's tiny "free speech area." Sinapi-Riddle is president of the Citrus College chapter of Young Americans for Liberty and is passionate about his political beliefs, but he has curtailed his expressive conduct on campus in light of this incident and Citrus College's speech-repressive policies. . . .

In addition to challenging Citrus College's "free speech area," which comprises just 1.37% of campus, Sinapi-Riddle is challenging two other policies: (1) the college's "verbal harassment policy," which prohibits a wide range of speech protected by the First Amendment, including "inappropriate or offensive remarks"; and (2) the college's elaborate permitting requirements for student group speech, which

*Continued*

require student groups wishing to express themselves on campus to wait two weeks and obtain the permission of four separate college entities prior to doing so.

## College that Suppressed Anti-NSA Petition Settles Lawsuit

LOS ANGELES, December 3, 2014—Today, Citrus College in California agreed to settle a student's free speech lawsuit for $110,000, marking the Foundation for Individual Rights in Education's (FIRE's) second victory for the First Amendment in 24 hours.

Student Vincenzo Sinapi-Riddle filed the federal lawsuit in July as part of FIRE's Stand Up For Speech Litigation Project. Sinapi-Riddle was threatened with removal from campus for soliciting signatures for a petition against domestic surveillance by the National Security Agency (NSA) outside of Citrus's tiny "free speech area."

In addition to the monetary settlement for Sinapi-Riddle's damages and attorneys' fees, Citrus has revised numerous policies, agreed not to impede free expression in all open areas of campus, and adopted a definition of harassment that complies with the First Amendment.

"Citrus College agreed to eliminate its restrictive 'free speech zone' in the face of a FIRE lawsuit back in 2003, but later reinstated its speech quarantine when it thought no one was watching," said FIRE President Greg Lukianoff. "But FIRE was watching, and we'll continue to do so. If the speech codes come back again, so will we."

To hold Citrus to today's settlement, the U.S. District Court for the Central District of California will retain jurisdiction over the case for one year, allowing Sinapi-Riddle to enforce the agreement without filing a new lawsuit.

The incident leading to the lawsuit took place on September 17, 2013—Constitution Day. Sinapi-Riddle had gone to Citrus's designated free speech area to collect signatures for a petition urging the college's student government to condemn the NSA's surveillance program. Then, as Sinapi-Riddle took a break to go to the student center, he began a discussion about the petition with another student. An administrator put a stop to the conversation, claiming that a political discussion could not take place outside of the free speech area and threatening to eject Sinapi-Riddle from campus for violating the policy.

In addition to restricting student free speech to an area comprising just 1.37 percent of the campus, Citrus maintained a lengthy approval process for registered student organizations seeking to engage in expressive activity. Sinapi-Riddle, president of Young Americans for Liberty at Citrus, had given up on organizing events because of a burdensome process that included review by four different college entities and a requirement of 14 days' advance notice. The process was so complex that the Student Handbook had to include a flowchart illustrating it.

The lawsuit against Citrus College was one of four suits filed on July 1, marking the public launch of FIRE's Stand Up For Speech Litigation Project. Attorneys Robert Corn-Revere, Ronald London, and Lisa Zycherman of the law firm Davis Wright Tremaine represented Sinapi-Riddle. FIRE has coordinated seven lawsuits to date, with more on the way. Citrus is the third that has been settled in favor of students' free speech rights; each of the remaining four suits is ongoing.

"I feel that free speech and the ability to express oneself freely is a very important right for all students," said Sinapi-Riddle. "I'm very grateful for FIRE's help in making sure that limitations on free speech are a thing of the past at Citrus College."

Sources: "Citrus College Stand Up For Speech Lawsuit." *Foundation for Individual Rights in Education*, www.thefire.org/cases/citrus-college-stand-up-for-speech/. Accessed 8 May 2016.

"Second Victory in 24 Hours: College that Suppressed Anti-NSA Petition Settles Lawsuit." *Foundation for Individual Rights in Education*, 3 Dec. 2014, www.thefire.org/second-victory-24-hours-college-suppressed-anti-nsa-petition-settles-lawsuit/.

## Questions for Discussion

1. Identify the various ways in which writing was used in this case (e.g., petitions, social media). What role did each of these kinds of writing play? (You can visit the website of the Foundation for Individual Rights in Education for more information about the case. Also, search the web for additional news reports.)

2. What do you think the uses of writing in this case reveal about writing as a tool for political action? Do you think Sinapi-Riddle and the other students involved in this case could have accomplished their goals without using writing as they did? Why or why not? What advantages (or disadvantages) do you see in the way students used writing in this situation? What alternatives did the students have?

3. Write a brief essay about a time when you used writing to voice a concern, lodge a complaint, or try to change something. Then, in a group of classmates, share your essays. What similarities and differences do you see in the writing that is described in these essays? What conclusions might you draw from these essays about the role of writing in your lives?

As a college student you will probably do most of your writing for your classes. This textbook will help you learn to manage college writing assignments effectively. But writing well can also help you live your life in ways that extend far beyond the classroom. So in this chapter—and throughout this textbook—we will examine some of the many different situations in which you might be asked to write.

# Understanding Writing

This textbook has another important goal: to help you understand what writing is. One reason that so many people struggle with writing is that they don't sufficiently understand the nature of writing. They believe writing is a matter of following arcane rules that are often difficult to remember or grasp. They think writing is a matter of inspiration and creativity, which they believe they lack, or they assume they can't write well because they don't have a large enough vocabulary. These beliefs are based on common misconceptions that can lead to frustration and prevent students from becoming successful writers. Yes, writing well *does* require knowing rules, and having a large vocabulary doesn't hurt. But writing is more than rules or inspiration or vocabulary. Writing should be understood in four important ways:

- Writing is a powerful means of expression and communication.
- Writing is a way to participate in ongoing conversations about ideas, events, and issues that matter in our lives.
- Writing is a unique form of thinking that helps us learn.
- Writing is a way to understand ourselves and the world around us.

For students who come to understand writing in these four ways, learning to write effectively can be a much more satisfying and successful process. *Abandoning common misconceptions and appreciating the complexity, power, and joy of writing are the first steps to learning to write well and feeling confident about writing.* This textbook will introduce you to the most important ideas—the Core Concepts—that you need to know in order to write well. It is also designed to give you practice in the most common forms of writing for a variety of audiences and purposes—in college, in your community, in the workplace, and in your life in general.

---

**FOCUS**   **THINK DIFFERENTLY ABOUT YOUR WRITING**

What were the most important pieces of writing you have ever done in your life? Under what circumstances did you write them? What form did they take (e.g., were they conventional essays, letters, blog posts, Prezi presentations)? Why were they important? In what ways did they affect your life? What do these pieces of writing suggest about the role of writing in your life? Jot down brief answers to these questions and consider what your answers reveal about the role of writing in your life. You might do many kinds of important writing without really be aware of them.

---

# Writing in College

Let's face it: Students have to write well if they expect to do well in school. Whether it's a lab report in a biology class, a research paper in a sociology course, a proposal in a business class, or a literary analysis essay in an English course, writing effectively means better learning and better grades. In this regard, **writing in college serves three main purposes:**

- It is a way for you to demonstrate what you know.
- It helps you learn.
- It enables you to join important conversations about the subjects you are studying.

## Write to Demonstrate What You Know

Writing is a way for you to show your instructors what you have learned. An essay exam in history, for example, helps your instructor decide whether you have understood a particular concept (say, manifest destiny) or learned about historical events that are part of the course syllabus. Similarly, your economics professor might assign an essay requiring you to analyze a market trend, such as the popularity of smartphones, to determine whether you and your classmates have grasped certain economic principles. For this reason, college students are asked to write many different kinds of assignments: reports, research papers, analytical essays, arguments, synopses, creative writing like poems, personal narratives, reflective essays, digital stories, multimedia presentations, and more.

---

**FOCUS** | **THINK DIFFERENTLY ABOUT YOUR WRITING**

Think about a recent essay exam or assignment that you wrote for one of your classes. First, describe the writing you did. What was the assignment? What exactly did you write? What do you think was most important about that piece of writing? What did it reveal about what you know about the subject? What do you think it suggests about you as a writer?

When writing essay exams, reports, or research papers for your classes, keep in mind that you are writing to demonstrate what you have learned. Have confidence that your writing reflects what you know. And remember that your writing can also help you identify what you still need to learn.

---

## Write to Learn

Writing an essay exam or a research paper isn't just a way to demonstrate learning; it is also a means of learning in itself. As you will see in the next chapter, writing is a form of intellectual inquiry, and it is essential to student learning, no matter the subject. To write an ethnographic analysis of a culture for an anthropology class, for example, is to learn not only about that culture but also about ethnography as a way of understanding how we live together. It's true that students can learn a great deal by reading, but writing engages the mind in ways that reading does not. Reading about ethnography can help students understand what ethnography is; writing an ethnographic report about a culture enables students to *apply* that understanding, which can lead to a deeper learning of the subject matter.

This idea that writing is learning can be easy to forget when you are trying to meet deadlines and follow detailed guidelines for an assignment. But if you approach your writing assignments as a way to learn about your subject matter, the process of writing can be more satisfying and can lead to more effective essays. And remember that every writing assignment is also an opportunity to learn about writing itself. The more you write, the better you understand the power and joy of writing and the better able you will be to meet the challenges of writing.

And one last point about the power of writing as a way to learn: The more you write, especially when you write as a way to explore your subject matter, the more you learn about *yourself* as a writer and thinker. Knowing your strengths as a writer enables you to take advantage of them; knowing your weaknesses is essential if you are to improve your writing. That understanding will help you become a better writer.

Describe a writing assignment you did for a college or high school class that was especially challenging for you. Explain why you found the assignment challenging. Now consider what you learned by doing the assignment. What did you learn about the subject matter? What did you learn about writing? Did anything surprise you about doing that assignment? What surprises you now as you look back on it? What do you think you learned about yourself as a writer?

If you approach writing assignments as opportunities to discover new information, explore new ideas, and enhance your understanding of your subject, writing can be more satisfying, and you might find you learned more than you think you learned. You might also find that your writing improves.

## Write to Join Academic Conversations

Writing is the primary way that experts in all academic disciplines do their work and share their ideas:

- Mathematics professors may work mostly with numbers and formulas, but they also write articles about current problems in mathematics that other mathematicians read.
- Historians study ancient artifacts to help them understand past events, and they share their understanding in the articles and books they write for other historians and for the general public.
- Scientists might spend long hours in their labs, but they test each other's theories by sharing and debating the results of their experiments in papers they write for scientific journals and professional meetings.
- Scholars in all fields regularly share information and debate ideas by posting messages to professional online discussion forums and blogs.

In all these cases, writing is the main vehicle by which scholars discuss the central questions in their fields. They cannot do their work without it.

Writing for a college class, whether it be psychology or business or chemistry, is a way for students to enter these same conversations about the ideas, information, and ways of thinking that define academic fields. Part of what students learn when they write in college, then, is how to use writing as a tool for discovering and sharing knowledge in various academic disciplines. In this sense, writing an assignment for a college class is a process of learning to write like a scholar in that academic discipline. When you are asked to write a research paper in a psychology course or a lab report in a biochemistry class, you are learning to do the kind of intellectual work that psychologists or biochemists do. You are learning to see the world as they do. You are learning to participate in the conversations about important topics in those academic fields. And by doing so you are using writing to expand and deepen your knowledge about those fields as well as about the world in general.

| FOCUS | THINK DIFFERENTLY ABOUT YOUR WRITING |
|---|---|

Take two or more assignments you wrote for different college (or high school) classes. For example, take a literary essay you wrote for an English class, a report you did for a biology class, and a research paper for a history class. List the similarities and differences that you notice among them. Look at the writing style you used in each paper, the structure of each paper, and the language you used. What stands out about each paper? In what ways are the papers different or similar? How can you explain the similarities and differences you see in these papers? What do you think the similarities and differences among these papers suggest about the writing you are asked to do in college?

Of course, writing in college also serves another purpose: it gives students genuine practice that helps them become better writers, which can benefit them in their lives outside of school as well.

### EXERCISE 1A

Read the three excerpts included here. Each excerpt is taken from an article or book in a different academic subject. The first is from a marketing textbook, the second from an education journal, and the third from a scientific journal. After reading the excerpts, compare them by addressing these questions:

- What do you notice about the writing in these three pieces?
- What do you think are the purposes of the writing in each case?
- What similarities or differences do you see in the writing style, language, and structure of these excerpts? What might these similarities and/or differences suggest about writing in different disciplines?
- What does your comparison of these three excerpts suggest about writing in general?

### 1. What Is Marketing?

What does the term *marketing* mean to you? Many people think it means the same thing as personal selling. Others think marketing is the same as personal selling and advertising. Still others believe marketing has something to do with making products available in stores, arranging displays, and maintaining inventories of products for future sales. Actually, marketing includes all of these activities and more.

Marketing has two facets. First, it is a philosophy, an attitude, a perspective, or a management orientation that stresses customer satisfaction. Second, marketing is activities and processes used to implement this philosophy.

The American Marketing Association's definition of marketing focuses on the second facet. Marketing is the activity, set of institutions, and processes for creating, communicating, delivering, and exchanging offerings that have value for customers, clients, partners, and society at large.

Marketing involves more than just activities performed by a group of people in a defined area or department. In the often-quoted works of David Packard,

*(Continued)*

cofounder of Hewlett-Packard, "Marketing is too important to be left only to the marketing department." Marketing entails processes that focus on delivering value and benefits to customers, not just selling goods, services, and/or ideas. It uses communication, distribution, and pricing strategies to provide customers and their stakeholders with the goods, services, ideas, values, and benefits they desire when and where they want them. It involves building long-term, mutually rewarding relationships when these benefit all parties concerned. Marketing also entails an understanding that organizations have many connected stakeholder "partners," including employees, suppliers, stockholders, distributors, and society at large.

Source: Lamb, Charles, et al. *Essentials of Marketing.* 7th ed., Cengage Learning, 2012.

### 2. Brain-Based Teaching Strategies for Improving Students' Memory, Learning, and Test-Taking Success

Decades ago, my high school chemistry teacher slowly released hydrogen sulfide (which produces a smell like rotten eggs) from a hidden container he opened just before we entered his classroom. A few minutes after we took our seats and he began his lecture, a foul odor permeated classroom. We groaned, laughed, looked around for the offending source. To an outside observer entering our class at that time, we would have appeared unfocused and definitely not learning anything. This demonstration, however, literally led me by the nose to follow my teacher's description of the diffusion of gases through other gases. It is likely that during that class I created two or three pathways to the information about gas diffusion that I processed through my senses and ultimately stored in my long-term memory. Since then, that knowledge has been available for me to retrieve by thinking of an egg or by remembering the emotional responses as the class reacted to the odor permeating the room. Once I make the connection, I am able to recall the scientific facts linked to his demonstration.

Event memories, such as the one that was stored that day in chemistry class, are tied to specific emotionally or physically charged events (strong sensory input) and by the emotional intensity of the events to which they are linked. Because the dramatic event powers its way through the neural pathways of the emotionally preactivated limbic system into memory storage, associated scholastic information gets pulled along with it. Recollection of the academic material occurs when the emotionally significant event comes to mind, unconsciously or consciously. To remember the lesson, students can cue up the dramatic event to which it is linked.

Source: Willis, Judy. "Brain-Based Teaching Strategies for Improving Students' Memory, Learning, and Test-Taking Success." *Childhood Education*, vol. 83, no. 5, 2007, p. 310.

### 3. Screening for Depression

Depression is the second most common chronic disorder seen by primary care physicians.[1] On average, 12 percent of patients seen in primary care settings have major depression.[2] The degrees of suffering and disability associated with depression are comparable to those in most chronic medical conditions.[3] Fortunately, early identification and proper treatment significantly decrease the negative impact of depression in most patients.[4] Most patients with depression can be effectively treated with pharmacotherapeutic and psychotherapeutic modalities.[5]

Depression occurs in children, adolescents, adults, and the elderly. It manifests as a combination of feelings of sadness, loneliness, irritability, worthlessness, hopelessness, agitation, and guilt, accompanied by an array of physical symptoms.[6] Recognizing depression in patients in a primary care setting may be particularly challenging because patients, especially men, rarely spontaneously describe emotional difficulties. To the contrary, patients with depression who present to a primary care physician often describe somatic symptoms such as fatigue, sleep problems, pain, loss of interest in sexual activity, or multiple, persistent vague symptoms.[7]

### References

1. Wells KB. Caring for depression. Cambridge, Mass.: Harvard University Press, 1996.

2. Spitzer RL, Kroenke K, Linzer M, Hahn SR, Williams JB, deGruy FV 3d, et al., Health-related quality of life in primary care patients with mental disorders. Results from the PRIME-MD 1000Study. *JAMA*. 1995;274:1511–7.

3. Hays RD, Wells KB, Sherbourne CD, Rogers W, Spritzer K. Functioning and well-being outcomes of patients with depression compared with chronic general medical illnesses. *Arch Gen Psychiatry*. 1995;52:11–9.

4. Coulehan JL, Schulberg HC, Block MR, Madonia MJ, Rodriguez E. Treating depressed primary care patients improves their physical, mental, and social functioning. *Arch Intern Med*. 1997;157:1113–20.

5. Elkin I, Shea MT, Watkins JT, Imber SD, Sotsky SM, Collins JF, et al., National Institute of Mental Health treatment of Depression Collaborative Research Program. General effectiveness of treatments. *Arch Gen Psychiatry*. 1989;46:971–82.

6. Diagnostic and statistical manual of mental disorders: DSM-IV-TR. 4th ed, text rev. Washington, D.C.: American Psychiatric Association, 2000.

7. Suh T, Gallo JJ. Symptom profiles of depression among general medical service users compared with specialty mental health service users. *Psychol Med*. 1997;27:1051–63.

---

Source: Sharp, Lisa K., and Martin S. Lipsky "Screening for Depression Across the Lifespan: A Review of Measures for Use in Primary Care Settings." *American Family Physician*, vol. 66, no. 6, 15 Sept. 2002, www.aafp.org/afp/2002/0915/p1001.html.

# Writing in the Workplace

In almost any job or career you can think of, you will be expected to use writing in some way to do your work. Consider these anecdotes:

- A few years ago a student planning to attend law school asked me what he could do now to prepare himself for law school. I called an old friend who is a lawyer to ask what I should tell my student. My friend offered two bits of advice: (1) get good grades, and (2) take as many writing courses as possible. Writing, my friend said, is the most important thing lawyers do.

- A college friend of mine has worked for many years as a management trainer for a large insurance company. Almost every aspect of her job involves some kind of writing: training materials, memos, reports, multimedia presentations, and formal email messages. Effective writing is a central reason she is an effective manager.
- One of my colleagues teaches nursing. Her students spend a lot of time as interns in hospitals learning how to take a patient's pulse and blood pressure, obtain blood samples, set up IVs, and administer medication. They also learn to write. Writing accurate and thorough reports, my colleague says, is as important as anything else a nurse does. Communicating with doctors and other nurses is one of the most crucial aspects of a nurse's job, and much of it is done through writing. Without good writing skills, she says, nurses could not care for their patients effectively.

These anecdotes underscore the importance of writing in different work environments and illustrate the different ways that writing enables people to do their jobs well. Professionals already recognize this fact. In one recent survey, 97% of business executives listed the ability to write clearly and persuasively as "absolutely essential" or "very important" for success in college and the workplace.[1] And because the modern workplace is changing rapidly, you are more likely than ever to be expected to communicate effectively in writing in a number of different media, including traditional print reports, proposals, letters, and memos as well as email, PowerPoint, blogs, wikis, and other social media and digital formats. This is the nature of the workplace today, one that already places a great premium on communication and especially on writing—and one that is being reshaped by new media. To succeed in the workplace, you must know how to write well.

---

**FOCUS** | **THINK DIFFERENTLY ABOUT YOUR WRITING**

Examine a piece of your own writing that you finished recently. What do you notice about your writing? What strengths or weaknesses do you see? What might this piece of writing suggest about you as a writer? Now think about how you might present yourself as a writer to a potential employer. What would you say to that employer about your writing? What have you learned about writing that might appeal to an employer?

Think of any writing assignment as career training. The better you can write, the more likely you are to succeed in your chosen career. Use your college writing assignments to develop your writing skills in preparation for the writing you will do in your future career. And if you have other kinds of writing experience, such as writing for your school newspaper or developing promotional materials for a student organization, put them on your resume.

---

[1] *The MetLife Survey of the American Teacher: Preparing Students for College and Careers.* Metropolitan Life Insurance Company, 2011, p. 21.

EXERCISE 1B

Talk to a few people you know about the writing they do for their jobs. Try to find people who work in different kinds of jobs. For example, maybe you have a relative who is a salesperson, a friend who is a physical therapist, or a neighbor who manages a restaurant. Ask them to describe any writing they do in their jobs and the media they regularly use, such as websites, email, and social media. Ask them about the challenges they face as writers in their workplaces. Also ask them for their advice about preparing for workplace writing. If you have had a job or hold one now, consider asking your co-workers about the writing they do for their jobs and think about any writing you have been asked to do in your job. Then write a brief report for your classmates in which you share what you learned from this exercise about workplace writing—or about writing in general.

# Writing as a Citizen

The idea that citizens must be educated in order for democracy to work is deeply embedded in American culture. It is known as the Jeffersonian ideal, which imagines a free and thriving society based on a productive, educated citizenry. Today, "educated" also means "literate," and it's hard to imagine being an active part of society without writing. In fact, we write to participate in our society in many different ways, from political campaigns to consumer advocacy. Consider these examples:

> ❯ BECAUSE of a growing budget deficit, your state legislature is considering a tuition increase as well as large cuts in funding for state colleges and universities. Members of your college community, including students, have written letters and emails to legislators urging them to vote against the funding cuts and the tuition hike. Some students have written editorials for the school newspaper expressing opposition to the budget cuts. To organize a rally at the state capitol, students use Twitter, Facebook, email, and blogs, all of which provide information about the rally and background information about the proposed state budget.

Carlo Allegri/REUTERS

❯ A developer has proposed building a giant new retail store in your town. Some local businesspeople are concerned that businesses on the town's main street will suffer if the new store is built. Residents opposed to the new store have organized a citizens' group and created a Facebook page to advocate for their position. They post information about the proposed store and share opinions about its potential impact on the town. They also write letters to the local newspaper and distribute flyers to local businesses. Other residents, concerned about the town's slow economic growth, support the new store and have expressed their support on a blog and in articles and letters they have written for local publications. They also circulate a YouTube video to explain their support for the new store.

❯ THE owners of a major league sports team in your city have threatened to leave the city if a new stadium is not built to replace the aging stadium that the team currently plays in. The team is popular and important to the city, and many residents support the proposal for a new stadium. Other residents oppose the plan on the grounds that it will increase taxes without creating new jobs. These residents form a community organization to publicize their concerns. They use social media to explain what they believe will be the impact of a new stadium. They also write letters to government officials and send press releases to local TV stations.

These scenarios illustrate how we can use writing to participate directly in important discussions, decisions, and events that affect our lives. Writing is a way for individual citizens to express their opinions and share information; it is a way for citizens to take action as members of their communities. Through writing, whether in a traditional print form such as a letter to an editor or in emerging new forms of social media, citizens can shape the ideas, opinions, and actions of others involved in the situation at hand. In all these instances, writing helps transform the world.

---

**FOCUS** | **THINK DIFFERENTLY ABOUT YOUR WRITING**

Have you ever written a letter to a politician or business leader to express your opinion or voice a concern? Have you ever written a response to a blog or tweeted to share your perspective on an issue or controversy? Have you ever written a letter to the editor of a newspaper or magazine or sent an email message in response to an article or editorial? If so, what prompted you to do so? Why did you choose to write in that situation? To what extent do you think your writing made a difference—to you or to anyone else who might have read what you wrote?

A well-written letter, a carefully crafted blog post, or even a provocative tweet can often be more effective than a phone call to express a concern, request an action, or raise awareness about an issue.

---

Think about an issue that concerns you. Maybe there is a controversy on your campus or in your town that affects you somehow. (On my campus, for example, because of concerns about alcohol abuse and vandalism, the university president canceled a popular student picnic, which led to an outcry among students and some faculty.) Or you might have a special interest in an issue in your state or in the nation, such as standardized testing in schools or the creation of wind farms in rural or wilderness areas. Now consider how you might best make your opinion heard in public discussions about this issue. Could you write a letter to someone in authority who is involved in the situation,

such as a politician or business leader? What about a letter to the editor of your local paper or school newspaper? A blog post? A Facebook page? A brochure or newsletter? Maybe a formal proposal intended for someone in a position of authority? Decide what kind of writing you think would work best in this situation and explain why. Then write it.

Alternatively, if you have ever written out of concern about an issue that was important to you, write a brief essay describing that situation and explaining what you wrote. To what extent did your writing in that situation make a difference to you or others involved?

# Writing to Understand Ourselves

A few years ago my family threw a surprise party to celebrate my father's 70th birthday. Many friends and relatives would attend, and we wanted to do something special to celebrate my father's life. I decided to create a video that would be a kind of documentary about him. (See Chapter 18, "Composing Digital Stories.") With help from my siblings, I spent several months collecting old photographs and memorabilia, gathering facts about my father's childhood and working life, and interviewing friends and relatives about their experiences with him. Using this material, I created a 20-minute video that focused on the important aspects of his life, including his military service and his family. As I composed that video, certain themes began to emerge about my father. I learned a lot about him that I hadn't previously known. More important, I gained a deep appreciation for the impact he had on many other people. Eventually, I screened the video at the surprise party, but composing it gave me a better understanding of my father and the world he grew up in; it also helped me learn about myself and my relationship with him.

My video about my father's life illustrates how writing can help us understand ourselves and the world around us. Here are two other examples:

> A student of mine was a veteran of military service in Iraq during the most intense fighting there between 2004 and 2006. For one assignment, he wrote a graphic and disturbing essay, in which he struggled to understand what he had experienced in Iraq. His essay revealed that he had deeply conflicted feelings about the war, because in the midst of the horror he saw, he also developed very special bonds with his fellow soldiers and witnessed profound acts of love and bravery. His essay was one of the most compelling pieces of writing I have ever received from a student—not because it was about war but because it was such a heartfelt effort by the student to understand some very difficult experiences.

> ONE of my students was hired by the university's office for international students to help write a newsletter. She was a good writer who earned good grades, but she found writing for international students much more challenging than she expected. Her supervisor constantly required her to revise her articles. Little by little, however, she began to see that her problems with these articles had little to do with her writing skill but arose from her lack of familiarity with that audience. The more she learned about the international students and their experiences in the U.S., the better she appreciated their needs as readers of the newsletter. Her articles improved, and in the process of writing them, she learned a great deal about the international students on our campus and the challenges they face as students in the U.S. She also learned something valuable about writing and about herself as a writer—and a person.

Writing is a powerful way not only to describe but also to examine, reflect on, and understand our thoughts, feelings, opinions, ideas, actions, and experiences. This capacity of writing is one of the most important reasons we write. In many college classes, you may be asked to write assignments that are designed to help you understand yourself and the world around you in the same way that my student's essay helped him understand his experiences in Iraq. But all of the writing you do in college, whether or not it is directly about your own experiences, presents opportunities for you to learn about yourself.

## FOCUS    THINK DIFFERENTLY ABOUT YOUR WRITING

Think about a time you wrote about an experience or issue that was important to you in some way—in a journal, a letter, or a school essay, or even on Facebook. Why did you choose to write about that experience? Thinking back on it now, what difference did it make to you to write about the experience? What do you think you learned by writing in that situation?

If you approach every writing assignment as an opportunity to learn not only about your subject but also about yourself, you will find that even the most tedious writing assignment can turn out to be a more rewarding experience.

## EXERCISE 1D

Write a brief essay about an important experience that helped make you the person you are today. Write the essay for an audience of your classmates, and tell your story in a way that conveys to them why the experience was important to you.

Now reflect on your essay. Did you learn anything—about the experience itself or about yourself—as a result of writing your essay? Did writing about your experience change your view of the experience in any way? What did writing this essay teach you about yourself? What did it teach you about writing?

MindTap®
Reflect on your learning and writing process.

### In this chapter, you will learn to

1. Identify the ten core concepts for effective writing.

2. Apply the ten core concepts to analyze texts written by others.

3. Describe your own beliefs about writing and how that can affect what and how you write.

## MindTap®

Understand the goals of the chapter and complete a warm-up activity.

# Ten Core Concepts for Effective Writing

**2**

**WHEN I FIRST LEARNED** to rock climb, an experienced climber gave me some advice: always climb with your eyes. That may sound strange, but it actually makes good sense. The key to climbing a vertical rock face is finding the right holds for your hands and feet, which is not always as straightforward as it sounds. To keep moving safely and efficiently up the cliff, climbers have to link together handholds and footholds. So even before starting up the cliff, climbers examine it carefully and identify a possible route to the top. Climbers call this process "seeing the line" up a cliff or a mountain. Once on the cliff, they are always looking ahead to the next handhold or foothold. That simple statement—"always climb with your eyes"—turned out to be some of the best advice about climbing I ever received. It was a way to boil down the complicated act of climbing into a single, simple, basic idea.

This chapter does the same thing with writing: It boils down the complex, powerful, wonderful, and sometimes challenging activity of writing into ten essential ideas, or Core Concepts. There's much more to learn about writing than these concepts, just as in climbing you have to learn more than how to "climb with your eyes," and Part II of this textbook goes into much more detail so that you can apply these concepts to various writing tasks. But these concepts are fundamental insights that every writer must learn in order to write effectively. Students who incorporate these insights into their writing process will become better writers, no matter what kind of writing they are doing.

Learning to write effectively also requires developing a certain kind of attitude toward writing. Some climbers talk about "conquering" a mountain, but many climbers reject that way of thinking. For them, the point of climbing is not about defeating a mountain but about respecting it, adapting to it, and experiencing it. That attitude influences their decisions about which routes to follow up a mountain, when to start a climb, when to abandon it. It also affects the meaning of climbing: For them, climbing is about appreciating the experience of being in the mountains and meeting their challenges.

In the same way, the experience of writing can depend a great deal on a writer's attitude toward writing. Students who believe that writing is mostly about following certain rules tend to see writing as a process of learning and applying those rules, which can make writing tedious and diminish the joy of writing. If, on the other hand, you think of writing as a process of discovery, then each writing task can become a way to learn—about your subject, about yourself, and about the world around you. Students who approach writing in this way are open to the possibilities of writing and better able to harness its power. For them, writing isn't primarily about applying rules; it's about understanding and engaging the world and communicating effectively with others.

The ten Core Concepts discussed in this chapter, then, are not rules to learn or directions to follow. They are insights into how to write more effectively. Learning these concepts is a matter of experiencing the variety, complexity, and power of writing so that you can harness that power. Learning to write more effectively is partly a process of learning how to think differently about writing and about yourself as a writer.

This chapter asks you to examine your beliefs about writing and adopt a certain attitude about writing—an attitude that might differ from what you have learned about writing in the past. It encourages you to shift your focus as a writer from remembering and applying rules to exploring your subject, addressing your readers, and accomplishing your rhetorical goals. That shift can change your entire experience as a writer. In learning and applying these Core Concepts, you will, I hope, feel more like a rock climber who is fully engaged in the arduous yet exhilarating act of moving toward a mountain summit.

# The Ten Core Concepts for Effective Writing

The ten Core Concepts are based on what research and experience tell us about writing effectively. Each concept is based on a fundamental insight that student writers can learn in order to write effectively in a variety of situations—in school, in the workplace, and in the community. Understanding these concepts doesn't guarantee that you will always write effectively, but you cannot learn to write effectively without applying these ten essential insights about writing:

1. Writing is a process of discovery and learning.
2. Good writing fits the context.
3. The medium is part of the message.
4. A writer must have something to say.
5. A writer must support claims and assertions.
6. Purpose determines form, style, and organization in writing.
7. Writing is a social activity.
8. Revision is an essential part of writing.
9. There is always a voice in writing, even when there isn't an I.
10. Good writing means more than good grammar.

# Core Concept 1 Writing is a process of discovery and learning.

A few years ago, a student in one of my classes decided to write an essay about her relationship with her parents. Writing that essay turned out to be a much more involved—and important—experience than she expected.

In the first draft of her essay, Chelsea, who was twenty-two years old, described how her relationship with her parents was changing now that she was an adult. Her draft was lighthearted and full of fond memories and funny anecdotes about her parents that revealed how much she enjoyed her new relationship with them. But something was missing from the draft. For one thing, Chelsea mentioned briefly that her parents had recently divorced after more than twenty years of marriage, but she wrote almost nothing about the divorce. That seemed strange to Chelsea's classmates, who asked her about the divorce during a workshop of her draft. The more we discussed her draft, the clearer it became that there was a lot more to the story than Chelsea had revealed in her draft.

As Chelsea revised her draft, her essay began to change. It was no longer a lighthearted story about what it was like to have an adult relationship with her parents; it was now a more complicated essay that revealed Chelsea's conflicted feelings about what had happened to her parents' marriage and how it affected her (see "Changes"). There was still humor in the essay, but it was bittersweet, tempered by her realization that her changing relationship with her parents was accompanied by loss as well as gain.

Chelsea's essay became a journey of discovery through which she learned a lot about herself, her parents, and the experience she was describing in her essay. She also learned a valuable lesson about writing. When she began the essay, she thought it would be a simple narrative about her changing relationship with her parents. But the process of writing took her deeper into her experience and the complexities of human relationships. It helped Chelsea gain insight into an important period in her life and, maybe, understand something important about relationships (and life) in general.

Writing her essay also enabled Chelsea to communicate something interesting about relationships to her readers, but what she communicated was knowledge and insight that she gained *through the act of writing*, which enabled her to examine and reflect deeply on her experience. This capacity of writing to help writers learn about and understand something is part of what makes writing so powerful—and so important.

## Changes

I didn't know how to handle the fact that my parents were actually two separate people who had ceased to exist as one entity, two people who had other interests and other desires besides just solely being parents. With three grown children they felt that it was their time to move on and become separate people. The combination "Momanddad" that I had once imagined as this real thing suddenly transformed into a Mom and a Dad who were pursuing their own separate lives and their own interests.

And I had to choose. My brother moved out and found an apartment to hide in, away from the crumbling walls of our family. I was torn—torn between moving out and moving on from the only thing I ever knew, from this Momanddad that was suddenly becoming non-existent. *But we can't leave Dad alone.* And so it was decided that I would live with Mom and my sister would live with Dad. How do you choose? Is who you live with the one you side with, because in that case, it would change everything. Changing. Everything was changing.

—excerpt from "Changes" by Chelsea

As Chelsea discovered, writing is much more than a step-by-step procedure for organizing ideas into a specific form, such as a lab report or a narrative. Writing effectively requires understanding that you are on a journey of discovery that enables you to understand something better and to convey what you discovered to others. That journey sometimes takes you to places that you didn't expect, and it is rarely a straightforward, linear process from start to finish. If you approach a writing task as such a journey, it won't always be easy, but it can be much more satisfying—not to mention more successful.

**LEARNING BY WRITING**

The Irish singer-songwriter Conor O'Brien revealed during an interview that his songwriting has been influenced by post-modern poetry. O'Brien says that he developed a deep appreciation for the poetry of John Ashberry in a college English literature course. "I remember having to write an essay about John Ashberry and I absolutely despised his words," O'Brien said. "I thought they were really elitist. But then by the end of my essay, I actually fell in love with it and I thought the complete opposite about it. . . . It was very rhythmic and very beautiful."

Redferns/Getty Images

*Any* writing task can be a surprising journey that leads to new learning and insight, no matter what your topic is or what kind of assignment you're working on:

- When you write a narrative about an experience, as Chelsea did, you might understand that experience more fully.
- When you write an analysis of someone else's words or ideas, as singer-songwriter Conor O'Brien did (see Sidebar: "Learning by Writing"), you can develop a deeper appreciation for those words or ideas.
- When you write a blog post about a political campaign, you engage the ideas of others who might disagree with you, which can help you examine the basis for disagreement.
- When you write an argument about a problem, you might understand that problem better so that you are able to see solutions that were invisible to you before you began writing.
- When you write a lab report about an experiment you did for a chemistry class, you might gain a better grasp of the experimental process and the specific research question you were examining.

This kind of discovery and learning is possible because writing engages your intellect in a way that goes beyond reading or listening. If you have ever been so immersed in a writing task that the time seems to fly by, then you have experienced this capacity of writing to engage your mind fully.

## What This Means for You as a Writer

- **Approach every writing task with curiosity.** Don't assume you already know exactly what you want to say or where your writing will end up, even when you're writing about something you know very well. Don't expect to know at the beginning exactly how everything will turn out in the finished text. Be open to unexpected possibilities as you work through an assignment. Even when your assignment is very specific and has rigid rules to follow (for example, a chemistry lab report with explicit directions for format or a persuasive essay in which you're required to provide exactly three arguments for and against your position), remember that you can't know everything at the start. That's why you're writing in the first place: to learn something new or deepen your understanding of something you thought you knew.

- **Be patient.** Because writing is rarely straightforward, it shouldn't be reduced to a step-by-step procedure. You can't do everything in a single draft. To engage in writing as a process of discovery and learning almost always involves working through several drafts as you explore your subject, gather information, develop ideas, consider your audience, learn more about your subject, and refine what you thought you wanted to say. This process can be messy and even frustrating at times, but it can also be illuminating. Forcing this process into a step-by-step procedure will not only make it more difficult (as you probably already know) but also prevent it from becoming a worthwhile journey of discovery. And it will usually result in less effective writing. If, on the other hand, you have a little patience as you engage in this process of discovery and learning, you might be surprised by where your writing can take you.

- **Don't try to make your writing perfect as you work through an assignment.** Early drafts of any assignment are opportunities to explore your subject and learn more about it. Avoid the impulse to make everything perfect the first time. Rough drafts are just that: drafts. They can be changed and improved. Sometimes you have to allow yourself to write messy drafts, especially in the early stages of an assignment. You can even temporarily ignore rules of usage and style in your early drafts and focus instead on exploring your subject matter and discovering what you want to say in your piece, as Chelsea did. You will go back later to correct errors, tighten up your sentences, develop ideas, or clarify a point. (See Core Concept #10.)

- **Allow yourself sufficient time to write.** Writing at the last minute forces students to rush, which undercuts the process of discovery and learning that writing should be. It is also stressful and less enjoyable. Allowing sufficient time to move through the process deliberately and patiently will result not only in greater learning but also greater enjoyment—and more effective writing.

## PRACTICE THIS LESSON

Keep an informal journal or a private blog as you work on your next piece of writing. Each time you work on your writing, describe in your journal or blog what you did. If you read something and take notes for your writing, describe that. If you make an outline or jot down some ideas for your introduction, describe that. If you get an idea while taking a shower or riding a bus, describe that. If you share a draft with a friend or roommate, describe that. Also record any questions, concerns, or problems that arise as you work on this piece of writing, and explain how you addressed those questions, concerns, or problems. Describe how you feel as you work on the piece. What seems to be going well and what doesn't? Keep a record of *everything* you did and thought as you completed the writing task. Once you're finished with the writing task, go back and review your journal or blog. What does it reveal about how you write? What does it suggest about writing in general? What surprises you about your descriptions of what you did to complete your writing task? What do you think you can learn from this journal about writing? About yourself as a writer?

If possible, interview someone who is a professional writer or who writes regularly in his or her work, and ask that person what he or she does when writing. What steps or activities does the person engage in when completing a writing task? How does this person explain what he or she does when writing? After you finish your interview, describe in a paragraph or two what you learned about writing from this writer and compare what he or she does to what you do.

# Core Concept 2 · Good writing fits the context.

If writing is a journey of discovery, how do we know when that journey produces writing that is good? The answer is, It depends.

Consider the expression, "Today was a very good day." People say this all the time, but what exactly does it mean? A student who earned a good grade on a test could say it was a good day. Someone receiving a raise at work might consider that a good day, but quitting a job could also make for a good day. Winning the lottery would be a very good day for most people. So would getting married. But getting divorced might also be considered a good day. You get the point: What counts as a good day depends on the person and the circumstances.

The same goes for writing. Students generally believe they know what an instructor means by "good writing," but **what counts as good writing can only be determined by examining the specific context of the writing.**

When it comes to writing, *context* is often understood as the *rhetorical situation*, which traditionally includes the writer, the subject of the writing, and the audience (see Focus: "The Rhetorical Situation"). These components determine what constitutes effective writing in a given situation. For example, a lab report that earns an A in a biology class might not qualify as a good report in a pharmaceutical company, because the biology instructor and the lab supervisor in a pharmacy might have different expectations for lab reports; moreover, the purpose of the writing differs in each case. Writers have to determine the expectations for each writing situation. They must consider their audience and make decisions about content, form, and style that they believe will most effectively meet the expectations of that audience. Good writing is writing that meets the needs of the rhetorical situation—which often means meeting the specific criteria for an assignment (see Sidebar: "Grades vs. Good Writing" on page 30).

---

**FOCUS    THE RHETORICAL SITUATION**

Writer

Subject          Audience

In classical rhetorical theory, the rhetorical situation is represented as a triangle:

The metaphor of a triangle illuminates the relationships among the writer, reader, and subject matter in a particular act of writing. The writer and the audience have a specific relationship to the subject matter in the form of their shared knowledge about the subject, their opinions about it, their respective experiences with it, their stake in it, and so on. In addition, the writer has some kind of relationship to the audience, even if he or she doesn't actually know that audience. For example, a historian writing an article for a

*(Continued)*

professional journal assumes that she is writing as a member of the community of professional historians, with whom she will share certain values, knowledge, and expectations when it comes to the subject of the article and to history in general. To write well requires understanding your audience and its relationship to your subject—and to you—so that you can adapt your writing appropriately to achieve your goals in that rhetorical situation.

The rhetorical situation is an essential concept that helps writers better understand the social nature of writing and thus create more effective texts. Most instructors use the term to highlight the observable elements of the writing situation, especially the intended audience and the writer's purpose in addressing that audience. (In this textbook, I generally use the term in this basic way.) Some theorists, however, have illuminated how other factors can influence writing within a rhetorical situation. These factors might include the writer's identity (including race, gender, ethnicity, and so on), the cultural context of the writing, the historical moment, and the reader's background, among other such factors. These factors can shape not only what and how a writer writes but also how the writer's text is given meaning within the rhetorical situation. (See Chapter 8 for a more thorough discussion of analyzing the rhetorical situation.)

To write effectively, then, requires assessing the rhetorical situation. Writers should consider **four key dimensions of the rhetorical situation** to guide their decisions as they complete a writing task:

- **Purpose.** *Why* you are writing helps determine *what* to write and whether your writing is appropriate and effective in a particular context. A high school guidance counselor might praise your college admissions essay because it is clear and well organized, but can that essay really be considered "good" writing if it does not convince the college admissions officer to admit you to the college? And what if you are rejected by one college but accepted by another? Does that make your essay "good writing" or not? Writing can never really be evaluated without considering the writer's purpose: Are you trying to persuade an admissions officer that you are a good student? Are you attempting to solve a problem by analyzing it carefully? Do you want to share an insight about love by telling the story of a relationship? Good writing accomplishes the writer's goals in a specific rhetorical situation.

- **Form or genre.** Each rhetorical situation demands a specific form or genre—that is, a specific kind of text: an argument, a report, a blog post, a multimedia presentation, a poem. And each form is governed by specific criteria regarding structure and style. A lab report will usually be written in a formal, objective style, whereas a blog post might have a less formal, more provocative style. Writers select the appropriate form for the rhetorical situation and adapt their writing to that form. Certain forms of writing are appropriate for specific rhetorical situations, and no one style is appropriate for every kind of writing.

Understanding and using various forms for different rhetorical situations is essential for effective writing.

- **Audience.** Good writing meets the expectations of the intended audience. That college admissions essay is "good" if it resonates with the college admissions officer who reads it. To write effectively, then, requires anticipating the expectations of your audience and adapting your text to those expectations in that rhetorical situation. Sometimes that's a straightforward task: In a job application letter, you adopt a formal writing style and avoid irrelevant personal tidbits, knowing that such language and information would be considered inappropriate by the person reviewing job applications. Usually, though, analyzing your audience is more complicated, even when you know the audience. That's because there is always a subjective element to writing. Readers can agree on the general characteristics of good writing but disagree on whether a specific piece of writing is good. For example, they might agree that an editorial is well organized and clearly written—characteristics usually associated with good writing—but disagree about whether that editorial is "good" because one reader finds the writer's style too glib whereas another finds it engaging. Readers react to a piece of writing on the basis of their backgrounds, age, gender, experiences, and personal preferences as well as their reasons for reading that piece. So different audiences might judge the same piece of writing very differently. Writers must understand the challenge of anticipating such differences and adapt their writing as best they can to achieve their purposes with their intended audience.

- **Culture.** The dimensions of context described so far are all shaped by the broader cultural context. *Culture* can be defined as your sense of identity as it relates to your racial and ethnic backgrounds, your religious upbringing (if any), your membership in a particular social class (working class, for example), and the region where you live (for example, central Phoenix versus rural Minnesota or suburban Long Island). Not only does culture shape how readers might react to a text but it also shapes basic aspects of a rhetorical situation such as the subject matter and language. An important issue (for example, gender equality) might be understood very differently by people from different cultural backgrounds. Writers can't be expected to address all the complex nuances of culture that might influence a specific rhetorical situation, but to write effectively requires being sensitive to these nuances and understanding how a factor such as religious background or ethnic identity might shape readers' reactions.

In addition, the rhetorical context for any writing task includes **the medium**, which can significantly affect what and how a writer writes in a given situation (see Core Concept #3).

So the question of whether the writing is "good" is really beside the point. What matters is whether the writer accomplished his or her purposes with a specific audience in a specific rhetorical situation. The important question, then, is not whether a piece of writing is "good" but whether the writing is appropriate and effective for the rhetorical situation.

## What This Means for You as a Writer

- **Consider your purpose.** What do you hope to accomplish with a specific piece of writing? Answering that question, even in a general way, can guide your writing and make it more likely that your text is effective for your rhetorical situation. For college writing assignments, avoid the temptation to think of your purpose as simply getting a good grade. Instead, identify your purpose in terms of the specific characteristics of the assignment and what the instructor expects you to learn or do. If your instructor doesn't provide such information, try to obtain it so that you have a clearer idea of the expectations or guidelines that will help determine what counts as good writing for that assignment. Have a clear sense of purpose that matches the expectations for the assignment.

- **Consider your audience.** The decisions writers make about matters like content, form, and style should be driven by their sense of what will work best for their intended audience. Even when writing for a general audience (for example, when writing a letter to the editor of a newspaper read by thousands of people with very different backgrounds and expectations), try to identify basic characteristics of your audience and their likely expectations about a given subject (for example, readers of a regional newspaper are likely to be familiar with a local political controversy or be generally supportive of a local industry). One of the first things you should always do when you begin a piece of writing is think carefully about your audience.

- **Consider the form of the writing.** Form does matter when it comes to determining whether a piece of writing is effective. A research paper for a sociology class will be very different from a letter to the editor of your campus newspaper, yet both pieces of writing might be considered "good." The form of your writing will shape your decisions about style, organization, and length as well as the content of a piece. For each writing task, use an appropriate form and identify the standards for organization, style, length, etc., for whatever form of writing you are using.

- **Study good writing.** Although there is no single definition of "good writing," students can learn a lot by paying attention to what others—including their instructors—consider good writing. What counts as good writing in each of your classes? What is different or similar about how different instructors evaluate their students' writing? What is it about a specific piece of writing that certain readers like or dislike? Exploring such questions can lead to insights into what features of writing readers value in different situations.

---

**PRACTICE THIS LESSON**

Find a short piece of writing that you think is good. (You might select one of the readings included in this textbook.) Share that piece of writing with two or three friends or classmates and ask them their opinion of it. What do they like or dislike about the piece of writing? What did they find especially effective or ineffective about it? Ask them to explain their opinions as clearly as they can. Then write a brief reflection on what you learned about "good" writing from this activity. In your essay, compare the reactions of your friends or classmates to the piece of writing you chose, and draw your own conclusions about the role of audience in writing.

---

## Core Concept 3  The medium is part of the message.

Good writing depends on context, and that context includes the medium—that is, the tools or technology the writer uses. Writing a blog entry about a controversial parking policy on your campus will be different from writing an analysis of that parking policy for a business course or a letter of complaint to the campus parking office. Different media place different demands on writers. Effective writing means adjusting to the medium.

Students today are fortunate to be living in an age of astonishing technological developments that open up countless opportunities for writers. Using widely available technologies, students exchange ideas and information in ways that were unimaginable even a few years ago. They can communicate easily and widely through social media. They can use cell phones to send text messages, take and share photos, update websites, or download music and videos. They can participate in online discussions with their professors and classmates without leaving home. They can use computers to produce sophisticated documents that only a decade ago would have required a professional printing service. They can easily create multimedia presentations incorporating sound, image, and text.

These technologies are dramatically changing how we communicate and may be changing the very act of writing itself. When I create a website for one of my classes, I write differently than when I create a printed syllabus for the same class, even though most of the content is the same. I organize the website differently, because students will use it differently from the syllabus. I change some of the content, because my students don't access content on the website in the same way they find it on the syllabus. I include images as well as links to other online resources. Even my writing style changes a bit. In short, the medium changes my writing.

Think about creating a Prezi presentation as compared to, say, writing a report for an economics class. The audience and purpose might be the same, but the form and the content will differ. More to the point, the tools for composing are different. Prezi enables you to create documents that include much more than text. All these factors can influence both *what* and *how* writers write. For example, you will probably use less text in a Prezi presentation, which will affect your decisions about the content of your presentation. In addition, you will likely incorporate images and even audio and video clips into your Prezi document but not in your report. You also adjust your writing style: for the report you will use a formal academic style and probably complex sentences and lengthy paragraphs, whereas the Prezi presentation will require more concise language, bulleted lists, and titles for most slides. All these differences might seem obvious, but because writers today often have several choices for the medium they will use, they need to be aware of the ways in which the medium shapes what they write and how they write in that medium to accomplish a specific purpose.

Although most essays, reports, and research papers assigned in college courses still require students to write in conventional formats, increasingly students are asked or choose to write in other media. More and more students are asked by their instructors to participate in online discussions about course topics and use multimedia programs to make presentations, sometimes in place of traditional papers. In each case, the medium can shape the writing task in important ways. The medium can also affect your relationship to your audience (see Sidebar: "Blogging vs. Writing a Newspaper Column"). Part of your task as a writer, then, is to understand how different media might affect your writing and to adapt to the medium you're using.

| SIDEBAR | BLOGGING VS. WRITING A NEWSPAPER COLUMN |

Political writer Andrew Sullivan, a columnist for the *Sunday Times of London*, has written numerous books on politics and culture as well as articles for magazines and newspapers, including *Time*, the *New Republic*, and the *Atlantic*. In 2000 he began writing a blog called *The Dish*. These different media, he says, influence his writing style, choice of subject matter, and interactions with his readers. According to Sullivan, blogging "is instantly public. It transforms this most personal and retrospective of forms into a painfully public and immediate one." It also calls for "a colloquial, unfinished tone." Here's part of how he describes the differences between these two kinds of writing:

> A blogger will air a variety of thoughts or facts on any subject in no particular order other than that dictated by the passing of time. A writer will instead use time, synthesizing these thoughts, ordering them, weighing which points count

iStockphoto.com/Cameron Whitman

more than others, seeing how his views evolved in the writing process itself, and responding to an editor's perusal of a draft or two. The result is almost always more measured, more satisfying, and more enduring than a blizzard of [blog] posts.

Source: Sullivan, Andrew. "The Years of Writing Dangerously." *The Dish*, 6 Feb. 2015, dish. andrewsullivan.com/2015/02/06/the-years-of-writing-dangerously/.

Although Sullivan was one of the earliest proponents of blogging and helped popularize the medium among political writers, he stopped blogging in 2015 in part because of health concerns. In a post on his blog in which he announced his retirement from blogging, Sullivan described blogging as "a genuinely new mode of writing" and identified its essential characteristics: "its provisionality, its conversational essence, its essential errors, its ephemeral core, its nature as the mode in which writing comes as close as it can to speaking extemporaneously."

## What This Means for You as a Writer

- **Know the medium.** For most college writing assignments, student use computers to write conventional papers or reports. Such assignments place familiar demands on writers when it comes to organization, style, etc. Other media, such as blogs, wikis, or Prezi, call for different strategies regarding organization, style, and even content. In many cases, what and how you write may be similar in different media, but not always. Be familiar with the characteristics of the medium in order to use it effectively for the task at hand.

- **Choose an appropriate medium.** If given a choice, consider which medium would enable you to create the most effective document for that rhetorical situation. A Prezi presentation with embedded audio and video clips might be the best choice for an assignment in which your audience will be your classmates or students attending a presentation about extracurricular activities on your campus. For other writing situations, a blog or even a Facebook page might be more effective, depending upon the your message and the audience you hope to reach. Consider the medium carefully as you decide how best to achieve your intended purpose with your intended audience.

- **Adjust your writing process to the medium.** All writing tasks require planning, developing ideas, drafting, revising, and editing. But those activities can differ depending upon the medium, so effective writers adjust their writing process accordingly. Obviously, you will organize a research paper for a history course differently than you would a blog entry or video script, but sometimes the differences between one medium and another aren't so obvious. For example, many students make the mistake of writing a PowerPoint or Prezi presentation as if it were a conventional report. As a result, they include too much text in the presentation and use too few visual elements. The outcome can be an ineffective document that may be tedious for an audience to follow. It is better to consider the characteristics of the medium *as you are creating your document* and move through the writing process with the medium in mind.

## Core Concept 4 · A writer must have something to say.

Having a clear, valid main point or idea is an essential element of effective writing—not only in college but also in the workplace and other settings. In most cases, college instructors expect students to have a clearly defined main point or idea that is appropriate for the assignment, no matter what kind of writing the assignment calls for. (Research shows that college instructors identify the lack of a clearly defined main idea as one of the biggest problems they see in their students' writing.) If you describe a favorite book or movie to a friend, you will very likely be explaining what you see as its main idea or point. In the same way, readers expect writers to have something to say; as a writer, you should oblige them. (See Focus: "So What?" on page 35)

This is not to say that the main point or idea is always simple or easily boiled down to a one-sentence summary or thesis statement. Much college writing is about complex subjects, and students are often required to delve into several ideas or bodies of information in a single assignment. A 20-page research paper for an information science course about how new digital technologies are affecting the music industry will include many complicated points, kinds of information, and key ideas. So will a critique of the major arguments about the existence of God for a philosophy course. But even such involved pieces of writing, if they are to be effective, will be focused on a main idea and will convey a clear main point. That critique of major philosophical arguments about the existence of God, for example, might focus on the central point that all those arguments reflect the human desire to understand why we exist or that most philosophers equivocate when it comes to this basic question.

Remember, though, that you when you're beginning a writing assignment, you won't always know exactly what your main point will be. Sometimes, the assignment will determine your main idea or point. For example, in an anthropology class you may be asked to write an essay defining *culture* as anthropologists generally understand that concept. In such a case, you will be expected to convey a main point based on what you are learning in the course about how anthropologists understand culture. Sometimes, however, identifying your main point or idea will be more complicated. A student of mine once wrote a research paper about being a vegetarian. She started out thinking that she would write about the pros and cons of being a vegetarian to show that vegetarianism is not practical for most people. But as she wrote, she learned more about the subject and began to shift her focus to the environmental destruction caused by eating meat. In the end, her main point changed: she argued in favor of a vegetarian diet as an ethical response to the environmental destruction caused by the standard American diet. As she explored her subject, she was guided by a sense of her main idea, which evolved as she wrote. Her final paper had a clearly articulated main point but not the one she started with.

©iStockphoto.com/MsLightBox

---

**FOCUS**    **SO WHAT?**

One useful way to help identify and refine your central idea or the main point in a piece of writing is to ask, So what? Suppose you've written a personal narrative about your first job. So what? Why should readers care about that experience? What's in it for them? What will you say *about* that experience that might matter to others? Answering such questions can help ensure that you are telling your story in a way that conveys a *relevant* main idea or point to your readers. The same applies to just about any kind of writing you will do in college. For an economics class you might write an analysis of tax cuts as a way to generate jobs. So what? To answer that question requires you to decide whether your analysis is relevant in the field of economics. Why analyze tax cuts now? What makes that topic something that will interest others in the field? Is your main point something that economists would consider relevant and important? Asking this question about your topic also ensures that you are thinking about your audience and connecting your main point or idea to their interests as well.

---

## What This Means for You as a Writer

- **Identify your main idea.** Every kind of writing—even the most formulaic lab report in a biology or chemistry class—should have a main point. But it is important to distinguish between your *subject* and your main idea or point. The subject of a biology lab report might be osmosis, but the main point might be that osmosis doesn't occur with a certain type of membrane. Similarly, for an American history course you might write an analysis of the impact of the Civil Rights movement on race relations in the U.S. Your subject would be the impact of the Civil Rights movement on race relations, but your main point would be what you have to say *about* that impact on the basis of your analysis—for example, that race relations were changed in specific ways as a result of the Civil Rights movement.

- **Have something relevant to say.** Having something to say is one thing; having something *relevant* to say is another. Whenever you write, you are participating in a conversation (see Core Concept #7), and what counts as relevant or appropriate depends on the nature of that conversation. In college, what counts as relevant usually depends on the academic subject. For example, in an analysis of the social importance of Hip Hop music for a sociology class, you might conclude that Hip Hop became popular because it expressed the discontent young people of certain social and racial groups felt. For a paper in a music appreciation class, by contrast, you might argue that certain musical qualities, such as rhythm, account for Hip Hop's popularity, an argument that might be considered irrelevant in a sociology course. Part of what makes writing effective is not only having something to say but also knowing what is relevant or appropriate to say in a specific context.

- **Make sure that your main idea or point is clear to your readers.** Don't assume that because something is clear to you, it will also be clear to your readers. Sometimes, students can become so deeply immersed in their writing that they lose perspective. They think they have made their points clearly, but their readers may have trouble seeing the main idea. This is especially true when the assignment is complicated and lengthy. So it's important to share your drafts to get a sense of whether readers are understanding your main idea (see Core Concept #7) and then to revise with your audience in mind to make sure your main idea comes through clearly (see Core Concept #8).

- **Don't try to say too much.** A clear main point is partly a result of what the writer *doesn't* say. Including too many ideas or too much information in a piece of writing can obscure the main point, even if the ideas and information are relevant. Because most college writing assignments address complicated subjects, it can sometimes be a challenge for students to decide what to include in their writing. So it's important to decide whether an idea or piece of information is *essential* in an assignment. If not, consider removing it.

---

### PRACTICE THIS LESSON

Post a draft of an assignment you are working on to your Facebook page or to an online forum for sharing documents, such as GoogleDocs. Ask your friends to summarize the main idea of your paper. Compare their summaries to your own sense of your main idea. Do their summaries match your idea? If not, consider revising your draft so that your main idea is clear to other readers.

Alternatively, reread an assignment you wrote for a previous class and see whether you can identify the main point.

# Core Concept 5  A writer must support claims and assertions.

"Winters are warmer than they used to be around here."

"Most people would rather text than talk face-to-face."

"The average person doesn't pay attention to politics."

In casual conversation we usually don't expect people making statements like these to provide supporting arguments or facts to prove the point. In most college writing, however, appropriate support for claims and assertions is essential.

As we saw in Chapter 1, a central purpose of writing in college is to understand and participate in conversations about the topics and questions that define each academic discipline. To participate in those conversations requires knowing how to make a case for a particular point of view and support conclusions about a relevant topic. In other words, not only must writers have something relevant to say, but they must also be able to back up what they say.

Students sometimes fail to support their ideas or assertions effectively because they are unfamiliar with the expectations for doing so in a specific academic subject. The important point to remember is that *all* academic disciplines have such standards, though different disciplines might have different conventions regarding what counts as appropriate support or evidence for a claim or assertion:

- In an English literature class, you might cite passages from a poem or quote from critical reviews of that poem to support a claim about the work of a particular poet. Your claim would be more or less persuasive depending upon whether readers consider those passages or quotations to be sufficient support for your claim.

- In economics, some kinds of statistical information carry more weight than other kinds when drawing conclusions about economic trends or developments.

- In a biochemistry lab, data from experiments might be the main evidence for conclusions or claims.

In each case, an important element of effective writing is using evidence that is considered appropriate and persuasive by readers familiar with that discipline. The same holds true outside of school, though the standards for supporting your statements tend to be less well-defined and less rigorous in most popular writing than in academic or workplace writing (see Focus: "Supporting a Claim").

---

**FOCUS    SUPPORTING A CLAIM**

The need for writers to support their claims or assertions applies to any kind of writing, including newspaper and magazine articles, business proposals, legal documents, government reports, petitions, blogs, and many other kinds of documents. The following examples are taken from various sources: a government report on higher education, an excerpt from a

*(Continued)*

book on women and careers, and a newspaper column about fair pay for baseball stadium vendors. As you read them, notice how each writer backs up his or her statements and consider how that support affects your reaction as a reader:

> There is a troubling and persistent gap between the college attendance and graduation rates of low-income Americans and their more affluent peers. Similar gaps characterize the college attendance rates—and especially the college completion rates—of the nation's growing population of racial and ethnic minorities. While about one-third of whites have obtained bachelor's degrees by age 25–29, for example, just 18 percent of blacks and 10 percent of Latinos in the same age cohort have earned degrees by that time.

Source: *A Test of Leadership: Charting the Future of Higher Education*. United States Department of Education, 2006, p. 11.

. . . . . . . . . . . . . . . . . . . . . . . . . . . . . . . . . . . . . . . . . . . . .

> When I arrived at college in the fall of 1987, my classmates of both genders seemed equally focused on academics. I don't remember thinking about my future career differently from the male students. I also don't remember any conversations about someday balancing work and children. My friends and I assumed that we would have both. Men and women competed openly and aggressively with one another in classes, activities, and job interviews. Just two generations removed from my grandmother, the playing field seemed to be level.
>
> But more than twenty years after my college generation, the world has not evolved nearly as much as I believed it would. Almost all of my male classmates work in professional settings. Some of my female classmates work full-time or part-time outside the home, and just as many are stay-at-home mothers and volunteers like my mom. This mirrors the national trend. In comparison to their male counterparts, highly trained women are scaling back and dropping out of the workforce in record numbers. In turn, these diverging numbers teach institutions and mentors to invest more in men, who are statistically more likely to stay.

Source: Sandberg, Cheryl. *Lean In: Women, Work, and the Will to Lead*. Alfred A. Knopf, 2013, p. 1414.

. . . . . . . . . . . . . . . . . . . . . . . . . . . . . . . . . . . . . . . . . . . . .

> The Angels are one of the richest and most successful franchises in Major League Baseball—in fact, in all pro sports.
>
> They're valued by Forbes at $554 million (up 6% from a year ago), carry the fourth-largest player payroll in the major leagues, and at this point in the season rank fifth in per-game attendance. As they're very much in the hunt for their division lead, it's quite possible that lucrative post-season games will be added to the schedule.

So why are they trying to nickel-and-dime their stadium ushers, ticket sellers and janitors? . . .

The Angel Stadium employees are the worst paid among all California ballpark workers in their job classifications, the SEIU says. Here are some comparisons provided by the union, which also represents some of the workers at the other parks:

Angel Stadium ushers (the lowest paid among the affected employees) earn $11.21 an hour. At Dodger Stadium the rate is $12.77, and at the Oakland Coliseum it's $14.03. Janitors in Anaheim receive $11.50 an hour; at Chavez Ravine it's $12.31, in Oakland $17.50 and at the San Francisco Giants' AT&T Park $15.15. Ticket sellers at Angel Stadium get $13.65 an hour, but at the San Diego Padres' Petco Park they get $16.43.

Source: Hiltzik, Michael. "Angel Baseball, Paying the Little Guy Peanuts." *Los Angeles Times*, 7 Aug. 2011, articles.latimes.com/2011/aug/07/business/la-fi-hiltzik-20110807.

## What This Means for You as a Writer

- **Provide sufficient support.** First and foremost, make sure you have adequately supported your main points, claims, and assertions. Regardless of your subject or the kind of writing you are doing, readers expect that you make a case for what you have to say. Review your drafts to be sure you have provided the necessary support for your ideas.

- **Provide relevant and appropriate support.** What counts as appropriate and effective support for a claim depends upon the subject, the academic discipline, and the rhetorical situation. The kind of evidence used to support a claim in a history course, for example, won't necessarily work in a psychology course; similarly, readers of newspaper editorials have different expectations for relevant support than, say, economists who read professional journals. As a writer, part of your task is to understand the expectations for evidence and support for the kind of writing you're doing. You should be able to anticipate readers' expectations so that the support you provide for your claims will be persuasive and appropriate for the rhetorical situation.

- **Evaluate your sources.** Citing relevant sources to support or illustrate a point is a crucial part of effective academic writing, but not all sources are created equal. A self-help blog might not suffice as an appropriate source in an essay about teen depression for a psychology course, whereas a study published in a professional journal would. Having information from a source to support a claim or assertion is not the same as having information from a credible source. Make sure the sources you cite are not only appropriate for the writing task at hand, the course, and the rhetorical situation but also trustworthy. (Chapters 21 and 22 provide detailed discussions of finding and evaluating sources.)

Compare how the authors of the following two passages support their statements or arguments. The first passage is from a report by an economist examining the impact of poverty on educational achievement. The second is an excerpt from an analysis by an economist about how the American public's misconceptions about economics affect their voting habits. First, write a brief summary of each passage, identifying its main assertions or points. Then identify the supporting evidence or arguments for each main point. What kinds of evidence or support does each author use? What sources do they use to support their points? Finally, discuss the differences and similarities in how these authors support their points. What are the main similarities and differences? How might you explain these similarities and differences?

1. The impact of education on earnings and thus on poverty works largely through the labour market, though education can also contribute to productivity in other areas, such as peasant farming (Orazem, Glewwe & Patrinos, 2007: 5). In the labour market, higher wages for more educated people may result from higher productivity, but also perhaps from the fact that education may act as a signal of ability to employers, enabling the better educated to obtain more lucrative jobs. Middle-income countries—which frequently have well developed markets for more educated labour—are particularly likely to see the benefits of education translated into better jobs and higher wages. In Chile, for instance, between one quarter and one third of household income differences can be explained by the level of education of household heads (Ferreira & Litchfield, 1998, p. 32).

Source: van der Berg, Servaas. *Poverty and Education.* UNESCO / International Institute for Educational Planning, 2008, p. 3.

2. Consider the case of immigration policy. Economists are vastly more optimistic about its economic effects than the general public. The Survey of Americans and Economists on the Economy asks respondents to say whether "too many immigrants" is a major, minor, or non-reason why the economy is not doing better than it is. 47% of non-economists think it is a major reason; 80% of economists think it is not a reason at all. Economists have many reasons for their contrarian position: they know that specialization and trade enrich Americans and immigrants alike; there is little evidence that immigration noticeably reduces even the wages of low-skilled Americans; and, since immigrants are largely young males, and most government programs support the old, women, and children, immigrants wind up paying more in taxes than they take in benefits.

Given what the average voter thinks about the effects of immigration, it is easy to understand why virtually every survey finds that a solid majority of

Americans wants to reduce immigration, and almost no one wants to increase immigration. Unfortunately for both Americans and potential immigrants, there is ample reason to believe that the average voter is mistaken. If policy were based on the facts, we would be debating how much to increase immigration, rather than trying to "get tough" on immigrants who are already here.

Source: Caplan, Brian. "The Myth of the Rational Voter." *Cato Unbound*, 6 Nov. 2006, www.cato-unbound.org/2006/11/05/bryan-caplan/myth-rational-voter.

2

## Core Concept 6 Purpose determines form, style, and organization in writing.

A resume is a carefully structured record of the writer's work history and qualifications; a cover letter for a job application is a statement of the writer's suitability for the job. Each document has familiar conventions regarding content, organization, and style, which the reader (usually a person involved in hiring for the job) expects the writer to follow. A resume shouldn't be organized in the narrative format that might be used for a report on an internship, nor should a cover letter be written in the informal style and tone of a text message or Facebook post.

The conventional forms of a resume and cover letter serve very specific purposes for both reader and writer. These forms convey relevant information efficiently within the rhetorical situation. They are functional. That's one reason that they have become standard. Writing an effective resume and cover letter, then, is partly a matter of knowing how to use a well-established *form* to accomplish a specific purpose (to get a job interview) within a specific rhetorical situation (the job application process). The same is true of *any* kind of writing, including academic writing. Every kind of text—a lab report, a research paper, a personal narrative, a blog entry, a proposal, a review—

is governed by expectations regarding form. For some forms, such as resumes, these expectations can be very specific and rigid; for others, such as personal narratives, the expectations tend to be much more flexible. (See Focus: "What Is *Form* in Writing?") A writer must be familiar with expectations of the form in which he or she is writing if the text is to be rhetorically effective.

Core Concept Six **41**

You have probably heard teachers refer to *form* when discussing writing assignments, but what exactly is *form*? Generally, *form* refers to the way a piece of writing is organized as well as to any features that determine the shape or structure of the document, such as subheadings or footnotes. *Form* also includes the introductory and concluding sections of a piece of writing. *Form* is often used interchangeably with *genre*; for example, you might hear an instructor refer to *narrative* as both a form and a genre of writing. But *genre* generally refers to a type of writing, such as narrative or short story, rather than to the form of the writing. *The Merriam-Webster Dictionary* defines *genre* as "a category of artistic, musical, or literary composition characterized by a particular style, form, or content." In other words, a specific genre can appear in several different forms.

Often, terms such as *design* and *layout* are used to describe features of documents that include visual elements, such as graphs or photographs; design and layout can therefore be considered part of the *form* of a document. In many kinds of digital texts—including multimedia documents and online media such as web pages—design, layout, and related components can be as important as the text itself. The alignment of the text or the contrast in font sizes and colors can influence how the text is received by an audience (see Chapter 20).

For most traditional college writing assignments, *form* is generally used in two ways: (1) to refer to the general kind of writing expected for that assignment (research paper, narrative, argument, etc.); and (2) to describe the relevant conventions regarding the style and structure of the document for a specific kind of writing.

Notice that *purpose* drives *form*. For example, a writer structures a narrative in a certain way to tell a story effectively. In this sense, it is helpful to think of the form of a piece of writing as a tool to help you achieve your purpose in a specific rhetorical situation.

For many students, the problem isn't learning rules or guidelines for specific kinds of writing, such as lab reports or books reports; the problem is that they learn *only* rules and guidelines for specific kinds of texts without understanding the *purposes* of those rules and guidelines and without considering the rhetorical situation—that is, how their intended readers will likely read that text. As a result, students often approach writing as a matter of creating a certain kind of document rather than adopting a specific form that serves a specific purpose for a specific rhetorical situation. Think again about a resume. An effective resume requires more than proper format. It must also include appropriate information about the job applicant that is presented in carefully chosen language. An employer reviews a resume quickly, looking for specific information to determine whether the writer is a suitable candidate for the job. A resume is designed to present that information clearly and efficiently. Knowing that, the applicant must select and present relevant information strategically so that the qualifications match the requirements of the job. A successful resume is one in which the writer uses the form to present his or her qualifications effectively to an employer. Form follows function.

The same principle applies to the writing that students commonly do in college. The format of a lab report in chemistry, for example, enables a reader (the course instructor, other students, or perhaps other chemists) to find relevant information about a lab experiment quickly and easily. A literary analysis essay has less rigid guidelines for form, but readers still expect the writer to follow a generally recognizable pattern when presenting an analysis of a poem or novel. The same is true of analytical writing in philosophy or psychology. The specific forms might differ, but in each case, the form serves certain purposes within the academic discipline. Writers in each discipline learn to use the form to achieve their rhetorical purposes.

Many students focus only on *form* (on the rules and guidelines for a specific kind of text) and neglect *function* (the purpose of the text within the rhetorical situation). Good writers learn the rules and guidelines for the forms of writing they do, whether those forms are business letters or lab reports or blog posts, but they also understand the *purposes* of those forms of writing and apply the rules to accomplish their purposes.

## What This Means for You as a Writer

- **Determine the appropriate form for the rhetorical situation.** In many situations, the form will be obvious: a resume and cover letter for a job application; a lab report for a chemistry class. For most college writing assignments, instructors will specify the genre (argument, analysis, review, report, etc.) and provide guidelines for the form (organization, style, length, and so on). When the form of writing isn't clear or specified, assess the rhetorical situation to determine which form would be most appropriate and effective. What is the purpose of the writing? Who is the intended audience? What form of writing would mostly likely reach that audience and communicate your message effectively? Answering these questions will help you decide on the best form of writing for the task at hand. Remember that the form is a rhetorical choice: select the form that will enable you to accomplish your purpose with your intended audience.

- **Become familiar with the conventions of the form of writing you are doing.** Writers should follow the conventions governing form for well-established genres (e.g., lab reports) to meet their readers' expectations. But *there are no universal rules governing either forms or genres of writing that apply to all situations.* In many instances, writers have a great deal of choice regarding organization, style, length, and similar features of a document. Digital texts such as web pages and social media offer writers great flexibility, and even very specialized kinds of writing, such as resumes and cover letters, can appear in many acceptable variations of format, style, and even content. As a writer, your task is not only to learn the basic expectations for a specific kind of writing but also *to adjust your style and tone according to the specific rhetorical situation and to organize your text accordingly.* In most academic disciplines, there are established conventions for form, style, etc., but sometimes instructors do not make those conventions clear. If you're not sure about those conventions—for example, how to organize an assignment, whether the style must be formal, and so on—ask your instructor.

- **Pay attention to organization.** How a document is organized is one of the most important elements of form in writing. It is also one of the most challenging for many students. Studies show that college instructors consider the inability to organize texts appropriately to be one of the biggest problems in their students' writing. So it's important to learn how to organize an essay or report or digital document appropriately for the specific academic subject. In some cases, the general structure will be provided. For example, lab reports usually require specific sections in a specific sequence. Following the guidelines for such assignments will essentially organize the report for you. However, other forms allow for more flexibility in organizing the text. Ask your instructor about the expectations for organizing writing assignments, and if possible, find examples of that form or genre to see how they are organized.

## PRACTICE THIS LESSON

Visit a job search website, such as Monster.com, and read several advertisements for jobs that interest you. Then write a resume and cover letter for two or three such advertisements. (For this exercise, you might write a "fictional" resume and cover letter, inventing appropriate job experiences and relevant background information. Or you can use your own work experience and background.) Alter your resume and cover letter for each job. Then consider the differences in your resumes and letters. What changes did you make? What remained the same? Why did you make those changes? Now consider what this exercise might suggest about the conventions for the form and style of resumes and cover letters.

Monster.com

# Core Concept 7 Writing is a social activity.

We tend to think of writing as a solitary activity. The image of the writer working alone in a quiet room is a popular one. But this image is incomplete and even misleading. In fact, **writing is an inherently social act in at least three ways:**

- **First, writers write for an audience.** Unless you are writing an entry in a personal diary that you plan never to share with anyone or a note to remind yourself to take out the trash, your writing is almost always intended to be read by someone else. And as we saw earlier, your audience significantly influences what you write, how you write, and even *whether* you write. Whether the audience is a course instructor, classmates, a friend, co-workers, or a larger audience, writers write with their reader or readers in mind, even if they're not always aware of it. In this sense, writing is always a social transaction between writer and reader, a way to connect writers and readers. In addition, the reason for writing something usually arises from a social situation: a paper assigned in a college class; a problem in your town that prompts you to write a post to an online discussion board; an essay commemorating an important anniversary; a blog post about a current controversy. Writing happens because our interactions with others give us reasons to write. (See Focus: "The Rhetorical Situation" on page 27.)

- **Second, writers often involve others in the process of writing.** Writers regularly receive advice or suggestions from trusted readers as they develop a piece of writing. In class, students often engage in peer review—that is, sharing drafts with classmates and commenting on their classmates' writing. College instructors offer their students suggestions for improving their drafts. Digital media such as blogs enable writers to receive feedback from their readers. Wikis allow writers to collaborate directly. In these ways, the act of writing is social rather than solitary. In fact, in business settings and in many other situations outside of school, collaborative writing is the norm, not the exception.

- **Third, the rules, conventions, and forms of writing are socially constructed.** These rules, conventions, and forms have evolved over time as a result of the way people have used writing to communicate, to share ideas and information, to learn, and to accomplish a variety of other purposes. Familiar forms of writing, such as narratives and business letters and research reports, have developed because people needed these forms in order to accomplish specific purposes in writing. Research reports, for example, help make it easier for scientists to share the results of their experiments and to collaborate in answering important scientific questions. Resumes are efficient forms for conveying information about a job candidate's qualifications. By the same token, certain rules for writing style, such as the rule that you shouldn't use the first person in scientific writing, have evolved to fit the purposes of that kind of writing. Even *what* writers choose to write about is shaped by what others have written. The topics considered relevant in, say, a course on business ethics are determined in large part by what others in that field are saying. So both *what* and *how* we write are shaped by social factors.

The notion that writing is social is important because it undercuts the myth that writing ability is innate or exclusively the result of individual effort. This myth leads many students to believe that they don't have the ability to write well or that writing is something that they have to figure out exclusively on their own. Neither belief is true. In fact, many social factors shape an act of writing. Individual skill and experience along with effort and motivation do matter, but many other influences outside a writer's individual control affect writing. In this sense, writing ability is as much a function of how writers respond to specific rhetorical situations, which are inherently social, as it is a result of individual effort. So your effectiveness as a writer depends not only on the effort you put into a writing task but also on the way you fit in and respond to the social situations in which you are completing that task. Learning to respond to those situations effectively begins with understanding the social nature of writing.

## What This Means for You as a Writer

- **Place your writing in context.** As we saw earlier (Core Concept #2), all writing takes place in a rhetorical context, which shapes what and how the writer writes. Make it a habit to analyze the rhetorical situation for *every* writing task. Students tend to think of writing assignments as a matter of producing a certain kind of text rather than responding to the rhetorical situation. That kind of thinking can lead to ineffective writing because it tends to focus only on the *what* (the subject matter and form) rather than the *why* (the rhetorical purpose) of the writing task. Focusing instead on the rhetorical situation, which is inherently social in nature, can help you adapt successfully to the different kinds of writing tasks you are likely to face as a college student; moreover, emphasizing the *purpose* (that is, the *why*) of your writing rather than focusing only on creating a specific kind of text (the *what*) is more likely to engage you in inquiry and learning about your subject (see Core Concept #1).

- **Remember the larger context.** Even when you write for a college course, you are part of larger conversations about important issues in specific academic fields and in the society at large. For example, an analysis of U.S. involvement in the Vietnam War for a history course can be shaped by current debates about the U.S. military efforts in Afghanistan and Iraq. Broader social, cultural, and historical factors can influence what you write, giving it a sense of immediacy and significance. Being aware of these larger contextual forces can lend a sense of relevance to your writing.

- **Seek the input of others.** Even if you do most of your writing by yourself, at some point it will be helpful to get advice or feedback from others. In your writing course you may be required to engage in peer review and share your writing with your classmates or to revise in response to your instructor's feedback. But even if you aren't, you can benefit by asking a trusted friend, classmate, or co-worker to read your work-in-progress and consider their reactions to what you've written. Many online sites enable writers to share drafts and ideas and seek advice about their writing. Listening carefully to what others say about your writing can help you decide how to revise to make your writing more effective. (Much more discussion about getting and using feedback appears later in this textbook.)

- **Write for your readers.** When you're in the midst of creating a document and perhaps struggling with matters such as organization or style, you can easily forget that you are writing for a reader. Reminding yourself that your text is being created for an audience can often help make the task clearer. Instead of focusing on whether a sentence is correct, for example, consider how a reader might respond to it. That shift in perspective can help you keep the purpose of your writing in view and avoid getting bogged down in rules and procedures. The rules and conventions are important, but following rules and conventions doesn't result in good writing if the writing does not effectively address the intended audience and meet the needs of the rhetorical situation (see Core Concept #10).

2

---

**PRACTICE THIS LESSON**

Take a piece of writing you did recently and, in a brief paragraph or two, explore the social aspects of that text:

1. Consider the topic. What made you decide to write about that topic? Was your decision influenced in any way by others? Is the topic of interest to others?

2. Think about your audience. What do you know about that audience? What was your purpose in writing to that audience? What kind of reaction did you hope your writing would provoke?

3. Describe any advice or input you received as you completed this piece of writing. Did you share your drafts with anyone? Did you consult an instructor or post a draft on social media?

4. Examine the broader relevance of what you wrote. For example, if you wrote an analysis of a poem or short story, consider what might make that analysis relevant beyond the course and the assignment. Does the analysis focus on subjects that concern people other than your classmates in that course? If so, in what ways? What makes the analysis relevant to your life outside that course? What might make it relevant to others?

5. Consider what your experience with this piece of writing suggests about the social nature of writing.

---

## Core Concept 8 Revision is an essential part of writing.

The famous American writer Ernest Hemingway once told an interviewer that he revised the ending of his novel *A Farewell to Arms* 39 times. The interviewer asked, "Was there some technical problem there? What was it that had stumped you?" Hemingway replied, "Getting the words right."

"Getting the words right" doesn't mean fixing a "technical problem." It means writing and rewriting until the meaning is clear and the message comes through for the audience. Sometimes, that requires tinkering with words and phrases, but often it means much larger changes: adding new material, deleting sentences or paragraphs, moving them from one place to another in the draft, or completely rewriting entire passages. Such rewriting is an integral part of the writing process.

Creating an effective text is rarely so simple that a writer can move from beginning to end in a straight line and then go back to "fix" things. Writing is more often a circuitous, recursive process in which the writer stops and starts, goes back, jumps ahead, changes something, adds or deletes something, starts over, and maybe even writes the ending first (as the best-selling novelist John Irving says he does). It is through this process that writers explore their subjects and make meaning for their readers. Rarely does a writer know at the beginning exactly what his or her text will finally look like or what it will say. The shape of the text and its meaning emerge from the process of writing, and revising is central to that process.

Inexperienced writers often make the mistake of believing they can get everything right in a single draft, which they can quickly review to correct minor errors. This belief arises from a lack of practice with the various kinds of sophisticated writing required in college. Eventually students learn that writing an effective text can't be squeezed into a single draft. In most college writing assignments (and most other kinds of writing as well), there are simply too many things going on for a writer to attend to all of them at once. For example, if you are struggling to describe a complicated concept in an analytical essay for a political science course, you are probably not going to be thinking much about spelling and punctuation. By the same token, if you are focused on spelling and punctuation, you are probably not thinking in depth about how to explain that concept.

So most experienced writers divide each writing assignment into manageable tasks. When writing rough drafts, they mostly ignore matters like spelling and punctuation, knowing they can address those matters later, and focus instead on larger matters: Is my paper complete? Are the ideas clearly presented? Are there unnecessary passages that can be eliminated? Is the piece well organized? Have I addressed my intended audience appropriately? Does this piece achieve my rhetorical goals? As they revise each draft, they don't just "fix" mistakes; rather, they pay attention to how well they've explored their subject, how effectively they've addressed their audience, and how successfully they've accomplished their purpose. And they "listen" to their draft to see what meaning begins to emerge from it, learning more about their subject as they write and revising accordingly. Only after they have addressed these larger issues do they focus on improving sentences and correcting errors. (See Focus: "Revising versus Editing.") Writers who understand revising in this way usually find writing easier—and their writing becomes more effective.

---

**FOCUS**     **REVISING VS. EDITING**

Inexperienced writers tend to confuse revising with editing. Revising is the process of working with a draft to make sure it explores the subject adequately, addresses the intended audience effectively, and meets the needs of the rhetorical situation. It is not simply correcting spelling or punctuation errors, adjusting capitalization, and eliminating usage problems. Those activities are *editing*. Editing means making sure that your writing is correct and that you've followed the appropriate rules for form and usage. It is usually the very last step before a piece of writing is finished. (See Core Concept #10.)

# What This Means for You as a Writer

- **Understand revision as a process of discovery and meaning-making.** The British writer E. M. Forster is reputed to have said, "How do I know what I think until I see what I say?" I take that to mean that Forster never began a piece of writing knowing exactly what he was thinking or what he wanted to say. He found out through the process of writing. His statement can serve as advice for all writers. If you believe that writing is simply a matter of putting down on paper what's already in your head, you'll be frustrated and your writing will never feel right. But approaching writing as a process of discovery opens up possibilities, and revising is how writers find and realize those possibilities. It is the process of making the meaning of writing clear—both to the writer and to readers. (In this sense, this Core Concept is an extension of Core Concept #1.)

- **Don't try to do everything at once.** Approach every writing task as a series of smaller tasks, each of which is more manageable than the whole. Write a *first* draft without trying to make it a *final* draft. Once you have a first draft, work on it in stages, focusing on specific issues or problems in each stage. Start with larger issues, such as whether you have developed your main idea sufficiently or supported your main argument adequately, and then revise for organization or structure. Later, revise to make sure your tone is right for your intended audience, and then attend to your word choice and sentence structure to make sure your sentences are clear. Finally, edit for correctness. Working through a draft in this way will make revision easier and more effective.

- **Leave the editing for last.** Focusing on matters like spelling and punctuation while you're writing a first draft will divert your attention away from your subject and make it harder to focus on the ideas you are trying to convey to your readers. The best way to avoid this problem is to ignore minor errors of spelling, punctuation, grammar, and usage until you are just about finished with your text. At that point, after you have worked through your drafts and developed your ideas sufficiently, you can run your spellchecker, look for punctuation mistakes, attend to usage or grammar problems, and make sure that you have followed the basic rules of standard English. Leaving the editing for last will make your writing go more smoothly.

---

**PRACTICE THIS LESSON**

Using a wiki or a site like GoogleDocs, share a draft of your writing with two or three classmates or friends. Be sure to explain the assignment and purpose of your draft. Ask each person to identify the strengths and weaknesses of your draft and suggest at least one revision for each weakness. Then compare the suggestions for revision provided by your classmates or friends. In what ways do their suggestions overlap? Do they disagree about what needs to be changed in your draft? How might their suggestions help you revise so that your text will achieve your rhetorical purpose? Now consider what their various suggestions might indicate about the process of revision. (You can do this exercise without using a wiki or GoogleDocs by simply having your readers comment on the same copy of your draft.)

# Core Concept 9 There is always a voice in writing, even when there isn't an I.

When I was in graduate school I took a course in sociolinguistics. As someone who knew little about sociolinguistics, I found the assigned readings slow and difficult. But one book by a famous anthropologist named Clifford Geertz stood out. Geertz pioneered a research technique called "thick description," by which he would describe in very rich detail the rituals and common beliefs of a culture in order to understand the culture from an insider's perspective. His research profoundly influenced the fields of anthropology and sociolinguistics. What really struck me about Geertz's work, though, was his writing style. Although his work was scholarly, specialized, and theoretical, it was also engaging to read, even for someone who knew little about anthropology and sociolinguistics. When I praised Geertz's writing during a discussion with my professor, he smiled and acknowledged that students often reacted as I did to Geertz. Geertz's writing, he said, was seductive. His comment surprised me, because I had never heard anyone describe academic writing as "seductive." (You can judge for yourself: An excerpt from an essay by Geertz appears in Focus: "The Voice of a Scholar.")

My professor was really talking about *voice* in writing. Voice is difficult to define, but it has to do with what we "hear" when we read a text, how the writing "sounds." Voice is partly a technical matter of word choice and sentence structure, but it is also a function of the writer's confidence and authority (or lack of it). It is that nebulous quality that makes a piece of writing distinctive. It's what enables a reader to say, "That sounds like Stephen King." Or Clifford Geertz. As I learned in my sociolinguistics course, it isn't only popular writers like Stephen King whose writing can be said to have a distinctive voice. Even the most conventional scientific research report or philosophical treatise can have a distinctive voice. In fact, a strong, distinctive voice is one of the key elements of effective writing.

---

**FOCUS    THE VOICE OF A SCHOLAR**

Here are the opening two paragraphs from "Thick Description: Toward an Interpretive Theory of Culture," by Clifford Geertz, one of the most influential essays ever written in the field of anthropology. As you read, consider which features of Geertz's writing contribute to his voice:

> In her book, *Philosophy in a New Key*, Susanne Langer remarks that certain ideas burst upon the intellectual landscape with a tremendous force. They resolve so many fundamental problems at once that they seem also to promise that they will resolve all fundamental problems, clarify all obscure issues. Everyone snaps them up as the open sesame of some new positive science, the conceptual center-point around which a comprehensive system of analysis can be built. The sudden vogue of such a *grande idée*, crowding out almost everything else for a while, is due, she says,

---

"to the fact that all sensitive and active minds turn at once to exploiting it. We try it in every connection, for every purpose, experiment with possible stretches of its strict meaning, with generalizations and derivatives."

After we have become familiar with the new idea, however, after it has become part of our general stock of theoretical concepts, our expectations are brought more into balance with its actual uses, and its excessive popularity is ended. A few zealots persist in the old key-to-the-universe view of it; but less driven thinkers settle down after a while to the problems the idea has really generated. They try to apply it and extend it where it applies and where it is capable of extension; and they desist where it does not apply or cannot be extended. It becomes, if it was, in truth, a seminal idea in the first place, a permanent and enduring part of our intellectual armory. But it no longer has the grandiose, all-promising scope, the infinite versatility of apparent application, it once had.

Source: Geertz, Clifford. "Thick Description: Toward an Interpretive Theory of Culture." *The Interpretation of Cultures: Selected Essays*, Basic Books, 1973, p. 3.

Many students believe that academic writing is supposed to be dull and "voice-less." But they're confusing voice with style or tone (see Focus: "Voice vs. Tone"). A scientific paper might be written in an objective style, but that doesn't mean it will have no voice. Moreover, college instructors usually expect students' writing to have voice, even when they don't allow students to use the first person in course writing assignments. Being aware that you always have a voice in your writing and that voice is an element of effective writing is an important step toward developing your voice in your writing.

## FOCUS    VOICE VS. TONE

Trying to define voice in writing is like trying to describe the color blue: You can't quite say exactly what it is, but you know it when you see it. Still, it's important to be able to talk about voice, because it is a key element of effective writing. It's also important to understand how voice differs from other aspects of writing, especially *tone*. If *voice* is the writer's personality that a reader "hears" in a text, then *tone* might be described as the writer's attitude in a text. The tone of a text might be emotional (angry, enthusiastic, melancholy), measured (such as in an essay in which the author wants to seem reasonable on a controversial topic), or objective or neutral (as in a scientific report). Tone is kind of like your tone of voice when speaking: you can be upset, sad, happy, uncertain, or concerned, and the tone of your voice (how loud or soft it is, how you inflect your speech, how you emphasize certain words—for example, stretching out *told* in a statement like this: "I *told* you not to go outside in the rain!") reflects your mood. In writing, tone is created through word choice, sentence structure, imagery, and

(*Continued*)

similar devices that convey to a reader the writer's attitude. Voice in writing, by contrast, is like the sound of your spoken voice: deep, high-pitched, nasal, etc. It is the quality that makes your voice distinctly your own, no matter what tone you might take. In some ways, tone and voice overlap, but voice is a more fundamental characteristic of a writer, whereas tone changes depending upon the subject and the writer's feelings about it. Consider, for example, how you would describe Clifford Geertz's voice as compared to his tone (see Focus: "The Voice of a Scholar" on page 50).

## What This Means for You as a Writer

- **Recognize and develop your own writerly voice.** Part of every writer's challenge is to refine his or her voice and use it effectively. The first step is to recognize that you always have voice in writing, even in academic writing. Many of the exercises in this textbook will help you develop and strengthen your voice. It takes practice. Listen for the voice in the assigned texts in your classes. Try to get a sense of what makes them distinctive. Listen for your voice in your own writing as well. When revising a draft, pay attention to the "sound" of the writing—not only to make sure your writing is clear and understandable but also to give it the "sound" of confidence and authority. Adjust your style and tone so that they are appropriate for the kind of writing you are doing (for example, avoiding vivid descriptive language in a lab report but using description to convey emotion in a narrative or argument), but always strive to write with a strong voice. A strong voice is more likely to make your writing effective.

- **Remember that *all* writing has voice.** Although you might have been taught that some kinds of academic writing, such as lab reports or science research papers, should be "objective" and therefore do not have a voice, the truth is that good writing will always have voice. That does not mean you should use "creative" language in every kind of writing you do. It *does* mean that you should follow the appropriate conventions for style and tone and use them as effectively as you can to bring out your own distinctive voice.

- **Don't fake it.** If you are unsure of your main idea or if you are confused about the assignment you are working on, your writerly voice is likely to reflect that. Often when students are unfamiliar with a subject or learning something for the first time, they try to "sound" academic by writing convoluted sentences, using inflated language, or substituting wordy phrases for more common words (for example, using "due to the fact that" instead of "because"). Such strategies usually make the writing less clear and weaken the writer's voice. And it's usually easy for an instructor to see that students are "padding" their writing because they aren't sure they have anything valid to say or they're confused about the assignment or subject (as Calvin does in the comic strip). So one way to have a strong, effective voice is to explore your subject sufficiently (Core Concept #1), do appropriate research if necessary (Core Concept #5), and have a clear sense of your main idea or argument (Core Concept #4). These can lead to confidence, which is an essential element of voice.

I USED TO HATE WRITING ASSIGNMENTS, BUT NOW I ENJOY THEM.

I REALIZED THAT THE PURPOSE OF WRITING IS TO INFLATE WEAK IDEAS, OBSCURE POOR REASONING, AND INHIBIT CLARITY.

WITH A LITTLE PRACTICE, WRITING CAN BE AN INTIMIDATING AND IMPENETRABLE FOG! WANT TO SEE MY BOOK REPORT?

"THE DYNAMICS OF INTERBEING AND MONOLOGICAL IMPERATIVES IN *DICK AND JANE*: A STUDY IN PSYCHIC TRANSRELATIONAL GENDER MODES."

ACADEMIA, HERE I COME!

**2**

## PRACTICE THIS LESSON

Compare the three excerpts below. Each excerpt is the introductory passage from an academic article published in a scholarly journal. How would you describe the voice in each passage? What differences and similarities do you see in the voices of these passages? What specific features of the writing do you think accounts for the voice in each passage (e.g. word choice, sentence structure, use of first or third person, etc.)? Which do you like best? Why? What do you think your reaction to these passages suggests about voice in writing?

1. Writing represents a unique mode of learning—not merely valuable, not merely special, but unique. That will be my contention in this paper. The thesis is straightforward. Writing serves learning uniquely because writing as process-and-product possesses a cluster of attributes that correspond uniquely to certain powerful learning strategies.

    Although the notion is clearly debatable, it is scarcely a private belief. Some of the most distinguished contemporary psychologists have at least implied such a role for writing as heuristic. Lev Vygotsky, A. R. Luria, and Jerome Bruner, for example, have all pointed out that higher cognitive functions, such as analysis and synthesis, seem to develop most fully only with the support system of verbal language—particularly, it seems, of written language. Some of their arguments and evidence will be incorporated here.

    Here I have a prior purpose: to describe as tellingly as possible how writing uniquely corresponds to certain powerful learning strategies. Making such a case for the uniqueness of writing should logically and theoretically involve establishing many contrasts, distinctions between (1) writing and all other verbal languaging processes—listening, reading, and especially talking; (2) writing and all other forms of composing, such as composing a painting, a symphony, a dance, a film, a building; and (3) composing in words and composing in the two other major graphic symbol systems of mathematical equations and scientific formulae. For

    *(Continued)*

the purposes of this paper, the task is simpler, since most students are not permitted by most curricula to discover the values of composing, say, in dance, or even in film; and most students are not sophisticated enough to create, to originate formulations, using the highly abstruse symbol system of equations and formulae.

Source: Emig, Janet. "Writing as a Mode of Learning." *College Composition and Communication*, vol. 28, no. 2, May 1977, p. 122.

2. Over the past two decades, the presence of computers in schools has increased rapidly. While schools had one computer for every 125 students in 1983, they had one for every 9 students in 1995, one for every 6 students in 1998, and one for every 4.2 students in 2001 (Glennan & Melmed, 1996; Market Data Retrieval, 1999, 2001). Today, some states, such as South Dakota, report a student to computer ratio of 2:1 (Bennett, 2002).

Just as the availability of computers in schools has increased, their use has also increased. A national survey of teachers indicates that in 1998, 50 percent of K–12 teachers had students use word processors, 36 percent had them use CD ROMS, and 29 percent had them use the World Wide Web (Becker, 1999). More recent national data indicates that 75 percent of elementary school-aged students and 85 percent of middle and high school-aged students use a computer in school (U.S. Department of Commerce, 2002). Today, the most common educational use of computers by students is for word processing (Becker, 1999; inTASC, 2003). Given that, it is logical to ask: Do computers have a positive effect on students' writing process and quality of writing they produce?

As is described more fully below, the study presented here employs meta-analytic techniques, commonly used in fields of medicine and economics, to integrate the findings of studies conducted between 1992–2002. This research synthesis allows educators, administrators, policymakers, and others to more fully capitalize on the most recent findings regarding the impact of word processing on students' writing.

Source: Goldberg, Amie, et al. "The Effect of Computers on Student Writing: A Meta-analysis of Studies from 1992 to 2002." *The Journal of Technology, Learning, and Assessment*, vol. 2, no. 1, 2003, p. 3.

3. Cognitive, or executive, control refers to the ability to coordinate thought and action and direct it toward obtaining goals. It is needed to overcome local considerations, plan and orchestrate complex sequences of behavior, and prioritize goals and subgoals. Simply stated, you do not need executive control to grab a beer, but you will need it to finish college.

Executive control contrasts with automatic forms of brain processing. Many of our behaviors are direct reactions to our immediate environment that do not tax executive control. If someone throws a baseball toward our face, we reflexively duck out of the way. We have not necessarily willed this behavior; it seems as if our body reacts and then our mind "catches up" and realizes what has happened. Evolution has wired many of these reflexive, automatic processes into our nervous systems. However, others can be acquired through practice because learning mechanisms gradually and thoroughly stamp in highly familiar behaviors.

For example, consider a daily walk to work. If the route is highly familiar and if traffic is light, our mind can wander. Before we know it, we may have gone a considerable distance and negotiated street crossings and turns with little awareness of having done so. In these cases, the control of our behavior occurs in a "bottom-up" fashion: it is determined largely by the nature of the sensory stimuli and their strong associations with certain behavioral responses. In neural terms, they are dependent on the correct sensory conditions triggering activity in well-established neural pathways.

Source: Miller, E. K., and J. D. Wallis. "Executive Function and Higher Order Cognition: Definition and Neural Substrates." *Encyclopedia of Neuroscience*, edited by Larry R. Squire, vol. 4, Academic Press, 2009.

## Core Concept 10 — Good writing means more than good grammar.

When I was a brand-new professor of English, I submitted a grant proposal in which I misspelled the name of Christopher Columbus in the very first sentence. (I spelled it "Columbis.") I learned of the error only after one of the members of the review committee told me about it. It was extremely embarrassing, but it wasn't disastrous. My proposal was selected as a finalist for the grant competition. The reviewers obviously saw the error, but they nevertheless selected my proposal. Why? Despite such a blatant error, they considered the proposal good enough to make the first cut in the grant competition. The error didn't mean that the writing was poor.

I sometimes tell this story to illustrate the point that a correct paper isn't necessarily an effective one—or that an incorrect paper isn't necessarily *ineffective*. Following the rules and conventions of standard written English is important, but good writing is much more than good grammar. A perfectly correct essay can also be a perfectly lousy piece of writing if it does not fulfill the expectations of the intended audience and meet the needs of the rhetorical situation. An error-free history paper won't earn a good grade if it does not meet the instructor's guidelines for historical analysis or if it includes erroneous information, superficial analysis, and unsupported assertions. By the same token, a brilliant historical analysis that also includes numerous misspelled words, punctuation errors, inappropriate word choice, and convoluted sentences is not likely to earn an A+. Those errors will probably distract your instructor and might even suggest that you were unwilling to devote adequate time and attention to the assignment. For better or worse, "grammar," good or bad, makes an impression upon readers, even if it is only one element of effective writing.

As Chapter 27 explains, student writers tend to make the same errors, and for most students, errors of spelling, punctuation, and usage are not a very serious problem. Sometimes, these kinds of errors *do* constitute a serious challenge for a student writer and require time, attention, and effort to overcome. Nevertheless, many students spend too much time worrying about correctness and far too little time attending to larger issues that make writing effective. As this chapter makes clear, effective writing encompasses many things, "good grammar" among them. It is essential that you apply the rules of usage and follow the conventions of written English, because those rules are part of what makes writing effective. However, if you learn the rules and conventions of standard written English but little else about writing, you will most likely not be a very good writer.

## What This Means for You as a Writer

- **Learn and apply the appropriate rules for standard written English.** By the time they reach college, most students know most of what they need to know about the rules for correct writing. They may not always be able to explain those rules, but they have learned many of them intuitively. So recognize that you already know a great deal about the rules for correct writing, but also be aware of what you don't know. When you're unsure about a matter of usage or punctuation, consult your instructor, your campus writing center, an online writing resource, or a textbook such as this one.

- **Recognize that few rules apply in every instance.** Many of the rules for correct writing are clear and well established, but some aren't. There is often disagreement among grammarians and writing teachers about specific points of usage and style. As a writer, you have to be aware that such differences occur and that the rhetorical context determines what rules apply. So learn the accepted conventions for the kind of writing you are doing. Remember, too, that these conventions can change from one academic subject to another, so make it a point to become familiar with the conventions for writing in the different courses you take.

- **Always edit your writing for correctness.** Don't be obsessive about minor errors as you're working through early drafts of a piece of writing (see Core Concept #8), but make sure you edit carefully and thoroughly before submitting your work. It usually doesn't take very long to review a finished draft for minor errors, to reread it for clarity, and to make corrections to words or sentences, and it doesn't take much effort to run the spell check on your word processing program. Editing for minor problems and ensuring that you have followed the conventions of standard English should become a regular part of your writing process.

- **Focus on the errors you regularly make.** Identify the mistakes you regularly make and review the appropriate rule for each one. For example, maybe you often forget to include a comma after an introductory clause (e.g., "When he woke up the next morning, his wallet and keys were missing."). If you're not sure about the rule, talk to your writing instructor or someone at your campus writing center, or review Chapter 27 of this textbook. Studies show that most students tend to make the same kinds of minor errors. If you focus attention on the errors you tend to make, you will learn to look for these errors when you edit your assignments. Eventually, most of those errors will disappear from your writing.

---

**PRACTICE THIS LESSON**

Make a list of the five most common errors of spelling, punctuation, or usage that you tend to make. For each one, consult Chapter 27 to identify the appropriate rule. (You may have to review several past writing assignments to develop this list of common errors.) Use this list when you edit your writing future assignments.

---

MindTap®
Reflect on your learning and writing process.

In this chapter, you will learn to

1. Apply the ten core concepts in your own writing to create effective texts.

2. Engage in writing as a process of inquiry.

MindTap®

Understand the goals of the chapter and complete a warm-up activity.

# The Ten Core Concepts in Action

**WRITING GROWS OUT OF A NEED** to answer a question, make a decision, or solve a problem. For college students, that need is usually created by course assignments—but not always. Sometimes it grows out of a situation that calls for writing of some kind:

- a problem on your campus that affects you;
- a tweet or news editorial that you want to respond to;
- an event that raises questions for members of your community;
- an important anniversary that evokes memories you want to share with others;
- a controversial online video that you want to comment on;
- a project that you believe might improve your workplace.

In each of these examples, circumstances prompt you to create a document intended for a specific audience for a specific purpose. In other words, the need to write grows out of a rhetorical situation (see page 27 in Chapter 2). Sometimes, too, writing grows out of a writer's simple desire to understand something better.

Whatever your motivation for writing, this chapter takes you through the process of creating an effective text for your specific rhetorical situation:

- *If your assignment specifies a topic and genre*, then follow the guidelines your instructor has provided and adjust each of the following steps to fit those guidelines.
- *If your assignment doesn't specify a topic and genre and gives you free choice about what to write*, then develop a project that enables you to answer a question, make a decision, or solve a problem on an issue that interests you; develop your project so that it fits your specific rhetorical situation.

This chapter uses the Ten Core Concepts described in Chapter 2 to help you identify a relevant topic, explore that topic thoroughly, and write an effective document on that topic that is appropriate for your rhetorical situation.

Think of this chapter as a guide rather than a set of step-by-step instructions for completing a writing project. Parts II, III, and IV of this textbook provide specific guidance for analytical, argumentative, and narrative writing. Those later chapters examine different genres in detail; this chapter shows how to put the Ten Core Concepts in action. Use this chapter in conjunction with the chapters in Parts II, III, and IV to guide you through the process of effective writing for a specific kind of text.

The ten steps in this chapter correspond to the Ten Core Concepts described in Chapter 2. As you work through this chapter, you might find that you do not need to complete each step or that you need to repeat a step. You might also move through the steps out of sequence. Some steps may take a few moments to complete; others will take much longer. That's OK. Writing is a process of exploration that can lead to insights into complicated issues that matter for you and your readers, and the process will not be exactly the same for every writer or writing task. So use this chapter to learn about your topic and create a project that engages your readers.

## Step 1   Discover and explore a topic.

### Begin with a Question

Identify something you are wondering about, something that intrigues or puzzles you, something that calls for a decision or solution.

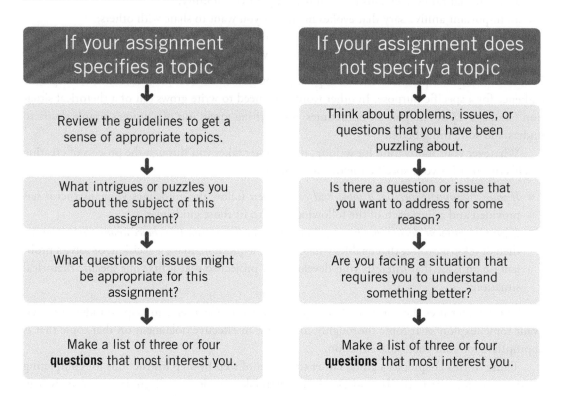

| If your assignment specifies a topic | If your assignment does not specify a topic |
|---|---|
| Review the guidelines to get a sense of appropriate topics. | Think about problems, issues, or questions that you have been puzzling about. |
| What intrigues or puzzles you about the subject of this assignment? | Is there a question or issue that you want to address for some reason? |
| What questions or issues might be appropriate for this assignment? | Are you facing a situation that requires you to understand something better? |
| Make a list of three or four **questions** that most interest you. | Make a list of three or four **questions** that most interest you. |

## Explore Your Questions

Write a brief paragraph for each question, explaining why it might be worth exploring for this project. In each paragraph:

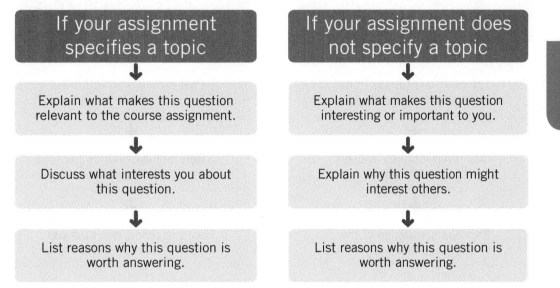

**If your assignment specifies a topic**

→

Explain what makes this question relevant to the course assignment.

↓

Discuss what interests you about this question.

↓

List reasons why this question is worth answering.

**If your assignment does not specify a topic**

→

Explain what makes this question interesting or important to you.

↓

Explain why this question might interest others.

↓

List reasons why this question is worth answering.

3

## Select a Working Topic

Review your paragraphs and select one of the questions from your list as your working topic for your project. (This question might change as you learn more about your topic, but for now it is the question that will serve as your working topic.)

## Identify What You Know about Your Topic

Jot down what you already know about your working topic, including:

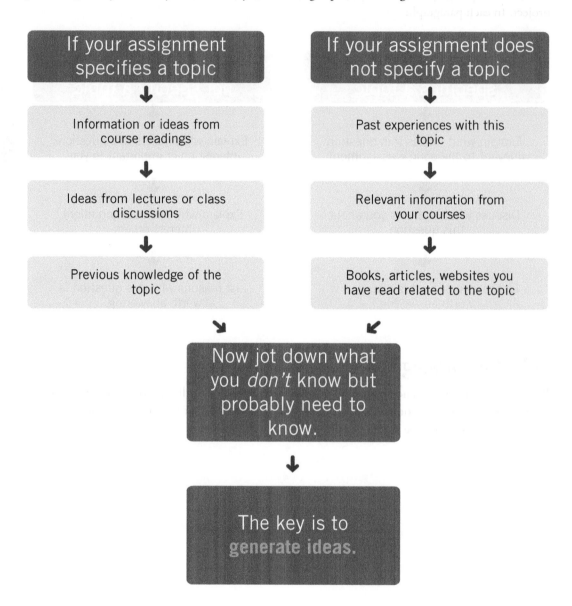

If your assignment specifies a topic

↓

Information or ideas from course readings

↓

Ideas from lectures or class discussions

↓

Previous knowledge of the topic

If your assignment does not specify a topic

↓

Past experiences with this topic

↓

Relevant information from your courses

↓

Books, articles, websites you have read related to the topic

↘  ↙

Now jot down what you *don't* know but probably need to know.

↓

The key is to generate ideas.

## Adjust Your Question

Review your notes to determine whether you should amend your question and working topic.

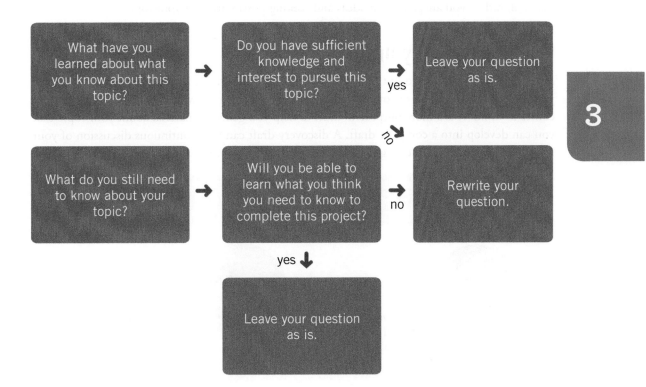

3

## Use Technology to Generate Ideas and Gather Information

Explore your question with digital tools:

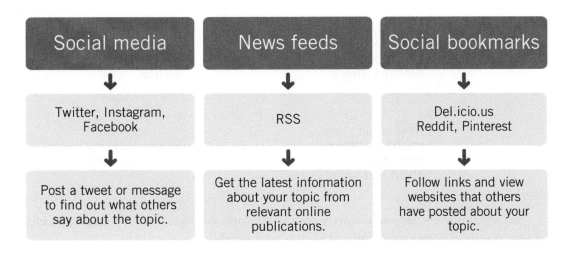

Hearing what others say or think about a topic can help you generate ideas and identify questions you will need to address. These tools provide a fast and easy way to tap into ideas, information, and conversations about your topic. Keep in mind that you are not looking for source material; rather, you are generating ideas and seeking possibilities for your topic.

## Write a Discovery Draft

A discovery draft is focused but informal and open-ended writing intended to help you explore your topic. It is not a first or rough draft, nor is it freewriting, in which you just write whatever comes to mind. It is a more purposeful draft to help you generate material about your topic that you can develop into a complete draft. A discovery draft can be a continuous discussion of your topic or it can be pieces and fragments, some of which are more developed than others.

To write a discovery draft

**Do**

Begin writing, using ideas and information you have.

Write as much as you can about your topic.

Make notes about questions to be explored later.

Keep writing until you have nothing more to write about your topic.

**Don't**

Try to write a finished essay.

Focus on organization or coherence.

Worry about the quality of your writing.

Leave anything out at this stage.

You will eventually use your discovery draft to develop a complete draft of your project, but for now you are exploring your topic and identifying possibilities.

## Step 2 | Examine the rhetorical context.

### Identify Your Audience

Briefly describe your intended audience for your project:

---

### Describe who you expect or hope will read your project.

| If your assignment specifies an audience, describe that audience. | If you have no assignment, identify the audience you would most like to reach. |

### Be as specific as possible.

| If your assignment does not specify an audience, assume that your instructor and/or your classmates are your audience. | If your intended audience is general (e.g., readers of a national newspaper like *USA Today* or people interested in politics), say so. If you are writing for a more specialized audience (e.g., students on your campus, people who snowboard, or video gamers), identify that audience as clearly as you can. |

### Explore your audience.

| Jot down your sense of your instructor's expectations for this assignment. Refer to the assignment guidelines to understand additional audience expectations for the assignment. | Anticipate what your intended audience might know about your topic. Write down what you think they will expect from your project. Consider relevant special circumstances (e.g., video gamers will likely be familiar with online gaming sites). |

## Consider the Context

Examine how the specific circumstances under which you are writing might influence your project:

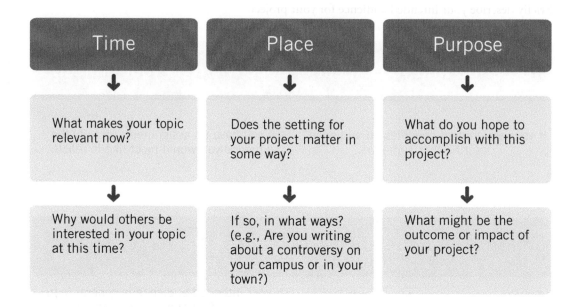

| Time | Place | Purpose |
|------|-------|---------|
| What makes your topic relevant now? | Does the setting for your project matter in some way? | What do you hope to accomplish with this project? |
| Why would others be interested in your topic at this time? | If so, in what ways? (e.g., Are you writing about a controversy on your campus or in your town?) | What might be the outcome or impact of your project? |

## Review Your Question

Adjust the question you developed for Step #1 in view of what you have learned about your audience and the context for your project:

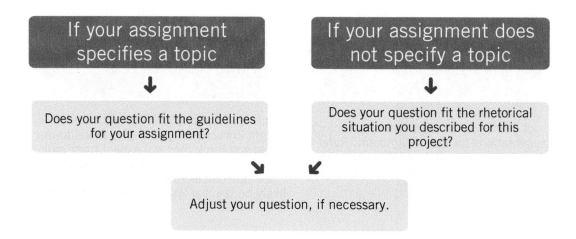

| If your assignment specifies a topic | If your assignment does not specify a topic |
|------|------|
| Does your question fit the guidelines for your assignment? | Does your question fit the rhetorical situation you described for this project? |

Adjust your question, if necessary.

## Develop Your Discovery Draft

Review your discovery draft in light of what you have learned so far about your audience and your rhetorical situation:

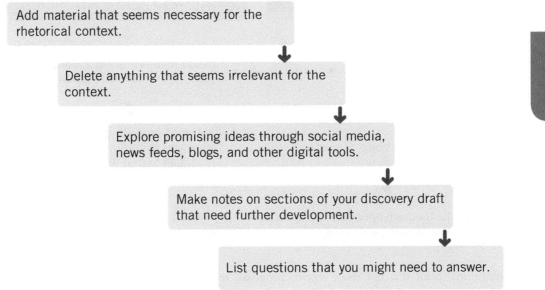

Add material that seems necessary for the rhetorical context.

Delete anything that seems irrelevant for the context.

Explore promising ideas through social media, news feeds, blogs, and other digital tools.

Make notes on sections of your discovery draft that need further development.

List questions that you might need to answer.

Remember that at this point you are still exploring your topic in a way that will make it effective for your intended audience.

## Step 3    Select an appropriate medium.

Most college assignments call for conventional academic essays, which are usually submitted either electronically (as a Word or PDF file) or in hard copy. In such cases, the medium is traditional print text, and you should follow appropriate conventions for standard academic writing. (Assignments that call for conventional writing for non-academic forums, such as newspapers, magazines, or newsletters, might follow slightly different conventions but are still print texts.) However, writers today have access to many different media, including digital and online media.

## Select a Medium

Identify a medium that would be appropriate for your rhetorical context:

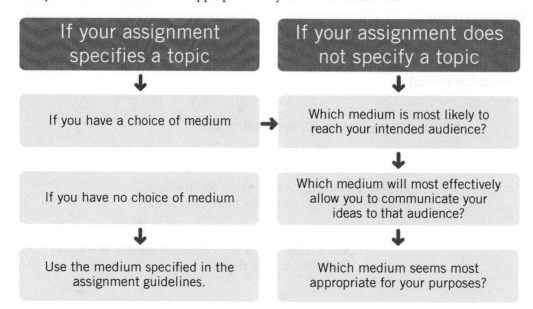

A traditional print text (an essay, report, proposal, research paper) might be the best way to achieve your rhetorical purpose and adhere to the guidelines of the assignment, but consider other media through which you can present your ideas:

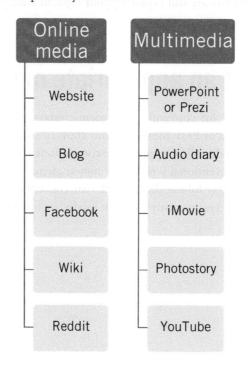

# Consider How the Medium Might Shape Your Project

Your choice of medium can significantly affect the way you present your ideas to your audience:

| Structure | • Does this medium require you to organize your project in a specific way?<br>• What options for structuring your project does this medium provide? |
|---|---|
| Length | • Does this medium place any length restrictions on your project? (For example, an essay written to be read as part of an audio diary may need to be shorter than a traditional print essay.)<br>• If so, how will these restrictions affect the depth of your exploration of your topic? |
| Image and sound | • Does this medium enable you to incorporate sound and/or visual elements?<br>• If so, what kinds of images and/or sound are appropriate?<br>• How will you incorporate these elements? |
| Style | • What are the expectations for writing style in this medium?<br>• Will you have to adopt any specific stylistic conventions for this medium? (For example, blogs usually call for shorter sections, or "chunks," of texts to help readers scroll more easily through the post.) |

# Return to Your Discovery Draft

Make notes about how the medium you have chosen might affect the development of your project.

Consider whether the medium will make it necessary to eliminate, add, or change material you have already generated.

Revise your main question to fit the medium, if necessary.

## Step 4  Have something to say.

At this point you have a topic, but you must determine what you will *say* about that topic. What will the main point of your project be?

## Revisit Your Main Question

Reread your Discovery Draft and then return to the question you developed for Step #1:

| If your assignment specifies a topic | If your assignment does not specify a topic |
|---|---|
|  |  |
| **How does your main question relate to the subject of the course?** (E.g., if you are analyzing the causes of high rates of suicide among teens in the U.S. for a psychology class, consider what makes this question relevant in the field of psychology.) | **How does your question relate to larger conversations about your subject?** (E.g., a question about whether charter schools help minority students improve their chances of going to college is part of a longstanding debate about education reform in the U.S.) |
|  |  |
| **Consider these questions:**<br>• In what ways is your topic important in this academic field?<br>• How will your project contribute to an understanding of this topic?<br>• What will your project say to your readers about this topic?<br>• What do you think you want to say about the topic, based on what you know at this point? | **Consider these questions:**<br>• Why is your topic important? What makes it relevant now?<br>• What might your project contribute to ongoing discussions about this issue?<br>• Why would your intended audience find your topic interesting or important?<br>• What do you have to say, based on what you know at this point, that will be interesting and relevant to your audience? |

## Write a Guiding Thesis Statement

On the basis of your notes from Step #1 and your revised Discovery Draft, write a brief paragraph explaining your main point and the purpose of your project as you understand it at this point. Include your main question and a brief explanation of why it is important to your intended audience.

This paragraph is your Guiding Thesis Statement, a working summary of the main idea for your project. Your Guiding Thesis Statement may change as you develop your project, but you can use it to guide your work as you explore your topic. Revise your Guiding Thesis Statement as often as necessary as you gain a clearer sense of the main point of your project.

## Review Your Discovery Draft

Use your Guiding Thesis Statement to review your discovery draft:

**Identify ideas, issues, or questions that seem important to your main point as described in your Guiding Thesis Statement:**
- Which sections of your discovery draft seem especially important to your main point?
- Which sections need more development, given your main point?

↓

**Identify gaps in your Discovery Draft:**
- Does anything seem to be missing that is relevant to your main point?
- What questions about your topic remain to be addressed?
- What more do you need to know about this topic to address the main point described in your Guiding Thesis Statement?

↓

**Consider the Rhetorical Situation:**
- Is your main point relevant to your intended audience?
- Does your Discovery Draft clearly present your main point in a way that addresses your intended audience?
- What might be missing from your draft that your audience will expect?

## Revise Your Guiding Thesis Statement

On the basis of your review of your Discovery Draft, revise your Guiding Thesis Statement so that it clearly explains the nature and purpose of your project and accounts for audience expectations. You now have a working statement of the main point of your project.

## Step 5 Back up what you say.

Most college writing assignments require students to support their claims, assertions, and positions. Even in narrative writing, writers provide support (often in the form of anecdotes or descriptions rather than factual evidence) for the ideas they want to convey to readers. As you develop your project and learn about your topic, be sure to support your main points or claims.

**Remember** that at this point in the process you are still exploring your topic, developing your ideas, and gathering information. "Backing up what you say" is as much a process of learning and exploring as it is a matter of identifying evidence or support, so be open to possibilities.

**Begin** by referring back to your Guiding Thesis Statement to remind yourself of your main question and the main purpose of your project.

## Identify Your Main Claims or Assertions

On the basis of your Guiding Thesis Statement identify and explore the major points you will make in support of your main point:

| List your major claims or assertions. | |
|---|---|
| List any claims or assertions that seem relevant at this stage. | Be as specific as possible, knowing you will adjust your list as you explore your topic. |

↓

| Explore each claim or assertion. | |
|---|---|
| Write a sentence explaining why each claim is relevant to your main point. | Write a sentence describing what you need to know to support each claim or assertion. |

↓

| Prioritize your list of claims or assertions. | |
|---|---|
| Which claims or assertions seem most important? | Which claims or assertions might be secondary to other claims or assertions? |

↓

| Identify potential sources. | |
|---|---|
| What kinds of information or evidence do you need to support your claims or assertions? | Where might you find the information or evidence you need? (See Chapter 21.) |

↓

| Begin exploring each claim. | |
|---|---|
| Develop your ideas for each major claim or assertion. | Find information or evidence to support each claim or assertion. |

## Review Your Discovery Draft

Return to your Discovery Draft and be sure it includes the major claims and assertions you identified in Step #1.

## Write a Complete Draft

At this point, you should be ready to write a draft of your project. If so, write as complete a draft as you can based on what you have learned so far about your topic and using the information you have gathered for this exercise. Use your Discovery Draft as the basis for your Complete Draft, or simply refer to your Discovery Draft for ideas to be included in your Complete Draft.

3

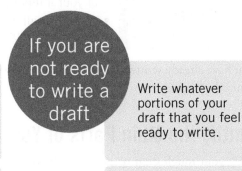

If you are ready to write a draft

Keep in mind that this is a rough draft.

Make your draft as complete as possible but don't worry about making it polished.

If you are not ready to write a draft

Write whatever portions of your draft that you feel ready to write.

Continue exploring your topic and move on to Step 6.

## Step 6 Establish a form and structure for your project.

The form of your project should present your ideas and information clearly and effectively to your readers. In deciding on an appropriate form for your project, consider:

| | |
|---|---|
| **Genre** | • Follow the conventions governing form for the genre (argument, analysis, narrative) in which you are writing.<br>• Parts II, III, and IV of this textbook will guide you in developing a proper form for specific genres (e.g., proposals, public argument, etc.). |
| **Medium** | • The medium can shape the form and even the content of your project.<br>• Multimedia and online projects will influence how you structure your project. |
| **Rhetorical situation** | • The form of a project will be shaped in part by your sense of your intended audience.<br>• The form will also be influenced by your sense of the purpose of your project. |

If you have already written your rough draft, use this exercise to determine whether your draft is organized effectively.

## Identify the Main Parts of Your Project

Review your rough draft or use your Discovery Draft as well as your notes to make a list of the main sections or components of your project.

## Develop an Outline

Use your list to create a basic outline for your project (refer to chapters in Parts II, III, and IV for more detailed guidance on organizing specific kinds of texts):

**If you have written a rough draft**

Create an outline on the basis of your draft.

Make sure to include the main sections from your list.

**If you have not yet written a rough draft**

Use your Discovery Draft and your list to develop an outline.

Make your outline as detailed or general as is helpful at this point.

## Refine Your Outline

Review your outline to determine whether it effectively meets the needs of your rhetorical situation:

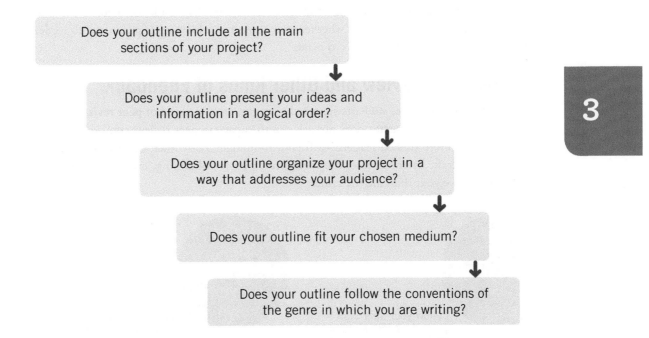

Does your outline include all the main sections of your project?

Does your outline present your ideas and information in a logical order?

Does your outline organize your project in a way that addresses your audience?

Does your outline fit your chosen medium?

Does your outline follow the conventions of the genre in which you are writing?

## Write or Revise Your Draft

Using your outline as a guide, write a rough draft of your project or revise the rough draft you have already written so that you have strengthened the structure of your project.

## Step 7 Get feedback.

At this point it makes sense to involve others in the process of developing your project to help you determine whether your draft is effective and to identify potential problems to address in your revisions. The goal is to get a sense of whether your project is achieving its purpose with readers and to help you decide which revisions to make.

## Consider Peer Review and Other Kinds of Feedback

In most college writing classes students are asked to engage in some kind of **peer review** of drafts with classmates. If your instructor does not ask you to engage in peer review, you can seek feedback from one or more trusted readers—a friend, roommate, co-worker, or relative—who can respond to your draft. In either case, the main principles for obtaining, evaluating, and using feedback to improve your draft are the same.

**If you have peer review in your class**

- Follow your instructor's procedure for providing and receiving feedback on drafts.
- Be sure you understand what you are expected to do during peer review.
- Listen carefully to your classmates' feedback on your draft.
- Take your classmates' comments seriously.
- Ask questions to clarify their comments or to encourage them to give you feedback on specific questions or concerns you have about your draft.
- Use the lists of questions below to guide your readers and evaluate their feedback.

**If you seek feedback on your own**

- Identify one or more readers whom you trust to read your draft thoughtfully.
- Consider finding readers online through a discussion forum for writers or a writing center, or post your draft on Facebook to share it with friends.
- Make sure your readers understand the nature of your assignment or project.
- Explain your rhetorical situation (especially your intended audience and your purpose for this project).
- Use the lists of questions below to help guide your readers and evaluate their feedback.

**Remember** that it takes practice to learn how to give and receive useful feedback on writing-in-progress. Think of it as part of the process of inquiring more deeply into your subject and making your project more effective.

## Ask Your Readers to Respond to Your Draft

Use the following sets of questions to guide your readers' responses:

| Topic | <ul><li>How interesting and relevant is the topic?</li><li>Is the purpose of the project clear? Is it worthwhile?</li><li>Is the main point or idea clear? Does the writer have something to say?</li><li>How well does the draft explore the topic? Is anything missing or unnecessary?</li><li>What are the main claims or assertions? Are they adequately supported?</li><li>What questions are left unanswered for readers?</li></ul> |
|---|---|
| Medium and Form | <ul><li>Does the medium work for this topic? Does it address the intended audience effectively? How does the writer take advantage of the capabilities of the medium?</li><li>How is the project organized? In what ways can the writer organize it more effectively?</li><li>How well does the introduction introduce the topic and main ideas? How well does it draw readers into the project? How can it be more engaging or focused?</li><li>How well does the conclusion sum up the project? Does it emphasize the writer's main ideas?</li></ul> |
| Style | <ul><li>Is the writing generally clear and readable? Is the prose engaging?</li><li>Which passages are confusing or difficult to follow? How can they be improved?</li><li>Where in the draft do problems with usage or grammar impede meaning? How can those problems be corrected?</li><li>Does the writer's voice come through clearly and effectively?</li></ul> |

In addition, ask your readers to jot down any other questions or comments they might have about your draft.

**Remember** that the more specific your readers' comments, the more useful they are likely to be. So ask your readers to elaborate on their responses to specific sections of your draft.

## Identify Common Themes in Your Readers' Responses

If you engaged in peer review with several classmates or you had more than one person outside of class read your draft, you will need to consider their feedback carefully and evaluate the usefulness of their responses as you consider the need for specific revisions. (If you had only one reader respond to your draft, pay special attention to that reader's strongest reactions.)

First, look for similarities in your readers' responses.

| | |
|---|---|
| If your readers agree that something in your draft is working well, → | That part of your draft likely needs little (if any) revision. |
| If your readers all cite the same problems, → | You should probably address those problems in your revisions. |

## Consider Conflicting Advice in Your Readers' Responses

Different readers might have different reactions to your project. Such disagreements might indicate sections of your draft that need revision, though not always. Sometimes disagreements can simply be matters of personal preferences among your readers. Nevertheless, carefully consider disagreements among your readers as you decide upon specific revisions:

| | |
|---|---|
| If your readers disagree about specific aspects of your draft | • Review the readers' comments to understand their disagreements.<br>• Consider each reader's perspective about that part of your draft.<br>• As you review disagreements among your readers' responses to your draft, consider which feedback seems to take your rhetorical situation into account. |
| If you agree with one reader and disagree with others | • Consider why you agree or disagree.<br>• Review the relevant sections of your draft to see whether your readers' comments might have changed your mind.<br>• If possible, ask readers to explain or clarify their reactions.<br>• Keep in mind that not all feedback will necessarily be relevant or helpful. |

## Identify Possible Revisions on the Basis of Your Readers' Feedback

On the basis of your review of your readers' responses to your draft, make notes about possible revisions you should make:

Identify elements of your draft that your readers agree are working well.

↓

List the main areas of concern on which your readers agree.

↓

Identify specific comments from one or more readers that suggest a need for specific revisions.

↓

Make a list of revisions that you should probably consider on the basis of this feedback.

**Remember** that *you* must decide which revisions are best, based on your assessment of the rhetorical situation and your own purposes for your project.

## Step 8 Revise.

Revision is part of the process of discovery and learning. It is also a rhetorical process by which you craft your project so that it effectively reaches your intended audience and achieves your rhetorical purposes. As you revise, keep in mind that you will continue to learn about your topic even as you improve your draft.

As you proceed, refer to your list from Step #7 as well as to your Guiding Thesis Statement to decide on specific revisions.

# Focus First on Content

Review your draft to determine whether you have sufficiently developed your ideas and effectively made your main point:

| Main idea | • What is your main point in this project?<br>• Does that point come through clearly?<br>• What makes your project relevant? Is the relevance of your topic evident? |
|---|---|

| Focus | • Does your project stay focused on your main idea?<br>• Do you get off track at any point? If so, should you rewrite or eliminate those sections? |
|---|---|

| Development | • Have you developed your ideas sufficiently? Which sections need further development?<br>• Have you presented enough information to support your claims or assertions? Where are your claims or evidence weak or insufficient?<br>• Have you gone into too much detail in any sections? If so, should you condense or eliminate those sections? |
|---|---|

Consult your list of potential revisions from Step #7 to make sure it includes any issues related to content that you have identified. If necessary, add to or revise that list.

# Focus Next on Form

Reread your revised draft from beginning to end to determine whether you need to reorganize it or strengthen its form or structure (refer to your outline and your notes from Step 6):

| Organization | • Have you presented your ideas in a sensible order?<br>• Which sections should be moved so that your ideas are more logically presented to your readers?<br>• Which sections might be combined to make your project tighter? |
|---|---|
| Transitions | • What are the main sections of your project? Do you make clear transitions between these sections? Where might transitions be missing?<br>• Do your transitions help your readers follow your discussion?<br>• Which transitions might confuse readers? |
| Medium | • Have you followed the conventions for your medium?<br>• If you are working in a digital medium, have you structured your project so that readers/viewers can follow it easily?<br>• For multimedia projects, have you placed visual or audio elements effectively? |

Consult your list of potential revisions from Step #7 to make sure it includes any issues related to form that you have identified. If necessary, add to or revise that list.

## Consider Your Rhetorical Situation

Review your revised draft to be sure you have addressed your intended audience effectively and fulfilled the needs of your rhetorical situation:

Use the questions from Step #2 to review your draft in view of the rhetorical situation.

Consult your list from Step #7 to identify potential revisions related to your rhetorical situation.

If necessary, add to or revise that list to include revisions that will help your draft better meet the expectations of your intended audience.

## Revisit Your Introduction and Conclusion

Return to your introduction and conclusion to make sure they effectively introduce and conclude your project in view of your rhetorical situation:

| Introduction | • How clearly does your introduction describe your topic?<br>• How well does it draw your readers into your project?<br>• What compelling reason does your introduction give your intended audience for reading your project?<br>• Does it convey the purpose of your project? |
| --- | --- |
| Conclusion | • What main ideas are emphasized in your conclusions? Is this the appropriate emphasis in view of your rhetorical purpose?<br>• Does your conclusion do more than simply restate your main idea?<br>• How does it leave your readers with a sense that you have fulfilled the purpose of your project? |

Return to your list of potential revisions from Step #7 to make sure it includes any revisions you now think you should make to your introduction or conclusion.

## Prioritize Your List of Potential Revisions

Now review the list of potential revisions that you developed for Step #7. No matter how long or short that list is, you will need to decide which revisions are most important and which might be most challenging. Organize your list of potential revisions according to the following four broad categories:

# 1. List revisions related to content

Do you need to develop any sections of your draft? Do you need to do additional research or develop additional ideas?

Do you need to condense or eliminate sections that are too lengthy or unnecessary?

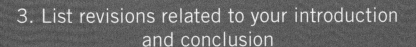

# 2. List revisions related to form and medium

Does your project need to be reorganized in any way?

Which sections of your project need to be moved? Which transitions need to be revised, added, or eliminated?

# 3. List revisions related to your introduction and conclusion

Do you need to make any revisions to your introduction?

Do you need to revise your conclusion?

# 4. List any changes needed to address your rhetorical situation

Do you need to make changes to your draft to address your readers' expectations more effectively?

Do you need revisions to make sure your project fits your rhetorical situation?

Your list of potential revisions amounts to a **revision plan**. Begin revising your draft according to this plan, moving from the first item on your list to the last. Keep in mind that this process might take more than one sitting, and you might find a need to write new sections of your draft and then revise again. That's OK. As we noted earlier, revision is a recursive, sometimes circuitous process, and the goal is to explore your subject fully while you bring your draft into line with the expectations of your rhetorical situation.

Once you work through your revision plan, you should have a revised draft that is close to finished. All the main pieces should be in place: a focused, sufficiently developed project that presents your main ideas effectively and clearly to your intended audience; a sound structure; an engaging introduction; and an effective conclusion.

## Step 9 | Strengthen your voice.

No matter the rhetorical situation, effective writing has a strong voice that reflects the writer's command of his or her subject matter. Your voice will give your readers confidence that your project is worth reading.

### Consider Your Rhetorical Context

Review the rhetorical context for your project to gain a better sense of how your voice might meet the expectations of your readers and help you achieve your purpose:

> Are there any specific expectations or restrictions regarding voice, tone, and writing style in this rhetorical context? (For example, a business proposal should not be written in a conversational style.)

> Do your voice, tone, and writing style fit the form or genre of your project? (For example, a lab report should have an objective voice and formal writing style.)

> Does your draft speak with a voice that fits your rhetorical context? If not, what changes should you make so that your voice and writing style fit the rhetorical context?

### Consider Whether You Should Use the First Person

Determine whether the use of first person is appropriate for this project:

If first person is appropriate → Decide whether using the first person will make your project more effective. → If so, revise accordingly.

If first person is inappropriate → Review your draft to eliminate any uses of "I."

## Strengthen Your Voice

Reread your draft out loud to "listen to" your voice and consider the following questions to guide your revisions:

> Does your voice sound authoritative and confident? Does it convey a sense that your project is valid and worthwhile?

> Is your voice consistent throughout your project? If not, where is it weakest? What changes might make it stronger in those sections?

## 3

At this stage, assume that your project is complete and appropriately structured and try to ignore those aspects of your project as you review your draft for voice and style.

## Step 10 Make it correct.

Edit your draft for clarity and correctness.

| Make your sentences clear | • Revise sentences that are unclear.<br>• Eliminate wordiness.<br>• Restructure sentences that are difficult to follow.<br>• Refer to Chapter 26 for advice on style. |
|---|---|
| Use sources correctly | • Integrate source material smoothly into your prose.<br>• Check quotations for accuracy.<br>• Make sure sources are cited correctly (see Chapters 24 and 25).<br>• Format your bibliography correctly (if appropriate). |
| Correct errors | • Correct errors of usage and punctuation.<br>• Refer to Chapter 27 for guidance in correcting errors. |

MindTap®
Reflect on your learning and writing process.

### In this chapter, you will learn to

1. Apply the Ten Core Concepts to a specific writing assignment.

2. Demonstrate how an idea for a piece of writing develops through the use of the Ten Core Concepts.

## MindTap

Understand the goals of the chapter and complete a warm-up activity.

# A Student Writer Applies the Core Concepts

4

**CHLOE CHARLES** was a first-year student at the State University of New York at Albany when she wrote the following essay for her introductory writing course. As a psychology major and someone who had taken advanced English courses in high school, Chloe well understood the importance of writing. When she received an assignment requiring her "to develop an in-depth, informed argument that reflects an understanding of an issue," she was already exploring an issue that mattered to her.

Chloe Charles

## Step 1   Discover and explore a topic.

### Begin with a Question

Chloe's idea for her essay began to take shape a few months before she received the assignment to write an argument. For an earlier assignment, Chloe had written an essay describing her stepfather's struggles to find work after losing his job during the Great Recession that began in 2007. Although her stepfather had a college degree and many years of work experience, he was unable to find a new job in his field. After many months of trying and failing to find work, he decided to change careers, and at the age of 36 he returned to college to earn a certificate that would enable him to become a high school teacher.

Writing about her stepfather's experience raised questions for Chloe about the widespread belief in American society that college is the best choice for every student. Her essay about her stepfather suggested that the issue is more complicated than she had previously thought. So when her writing instructor gave an assignment asking students "to examine a question related to the purpose of college," Chloe already had a question:

*Is college for everyone?*

Chloe had always believed it is, but her stepfather's experience made her wonder. Her great-grandfather had never gone to college, yet he had become a successful businessman and led a comfortable life. Her stepfather, by contrast, had gone to college—twice—and was struggling to make ends meet. As a new college student herself committed to pursuing a career as a lawyer, Chloe wanted to understand the implications of her own choice and learn more about why Americans seem to place such a high value on attending college. She needed to examine these issues more carefully if she was going to make "an in-depth informed argument," as her assignment required.

## Explore the Question

Chloe's instructor, Joe, had given his students several assignments that encouraged them to explore the question of the purpose of education. One of those assignments required students to read and interpret several essays about education. One of those essays was "Knowledge Its Own End," written in 1852 by the influential 19th Century thinker John Henry Newman. Chloe was intrigued by Newman's claim that higher learning is a basic human need. In a draft for the assignment she wrote,

> Newman states that knowledge is not good or bad but depends on how we treat it. Even in ancient Greece and Rome, he says, most people had the will to look outside their own perceptions to find out what was happening around them. Newman acknowledges that some people are better suited for manual labor or serving in the military, but they still need knowledge to do their jobs well. He knows that people everywhere in the world, not just a few, want to know and understand what is going on in the world.

Reading and writing about Newman acquainted Chloe with important philosophical ideas about the role of knowledge in human society. She also read more recent scholarly essays, including one published in 2015 by Charles Murray, a controversial political thinker, who argued that not everyone is suited for college. Although Chloe believed she disagreed with Murray, she found some of his arguments persuasive, especially in view of her stepfather's and grandfather's experiences. Wrestling with these scholarly perspectives began to inform Chloe's own thinking about whether college is for everyone, and when Joe finally assigned the argument essay, Chloe was immersed in this topic.

## Select a Working Topic

Chloe knew she would focus her essay on the broad question of whether college is appropriate for everyone, but at this early stage of her assignment she wasn't entirely sure what specific direction her project would take. Joe asked his students to submit a one-page proposal in which they described their topics, stated the main research question they would address, and identified an appropriate audience for their arguments. As a result of her preliminary exploration, Chloe began to wonder how college had become such a powerful expectation in American society and how that expectation affects young people today. In her proposal she wrote, "Not everyone gets the opportunity to go to college, and I want to look at the history of higher education in the U.S.

and its importance in American society." At this point, her primary interest was in examining the history of higher education in the U.S. to understand why college has become such an important expectation.

## Identify What You Know About Your Topic

Because Chloe had been writing about her topic for most of the semester, she already had a lot of relevant material and she knew some important things about her topic. For example, writing about her stepfather gave her insight into some of the factors, such as the economic situation, that can affect one's career choices and success. Chloe also began to understand how complicated her topic was. For example, the lack of a college degree didn't seem to be a disadvantage for her great-grandfather, who established his business in very different economic circumstances from those her stepfather faced. But a college degree seemed to be a mixed bag for her stepfather: His degree in English helped him establish a career in journalism, but when he lost his job as a journalist, his degree didn't seem to help him find a new job. These cases suggested that there are no easy answers to the question of whether college is a good choice for everyone and helped Chloe understand that she needed to examine the historical context in order to address the issue sufficiently.

Chloe's reading of scholarly essays, such as those by John Henry Newman and Charles Murray, also helped her become familiar with longstanding philosophical questions about the purpose of education and the ongoing debates about education in Western culture. At the same time, Chloe was aware of extensive coverage in the mass media about the high rates of college loan debt among American students today, a problem that is often cited in debates about the value of college.

Chloe's efforts to explore the question of the purpose of college encouraged her to learn more about the history of higher education in the U.S. and about the advantages and disadvantages of a college degree in contemporary American society. As a new college student herself, the question she was trying to answer was directly relevant to her own life as well as to that of her classmates.

## Adjust Your Question

On the basis of her exploration, Chloe felt confident in focusing her project on the following questions, which she included in the proposal she submitted to her instructor:

> *Why is it expected in American society that everyone should pursue a college education? Where does this expectation come from?*

## Use Technology to Generate Ideas and Gather Information

Chloe was working on her essay at a time (in 2015) when the question of whether college is worthwhile was getting a great deal of attention in the press and on social media. One of the candidates running for U.S. president at the time, Senator Bernie Sanders, had proposed making college free for all students, a proposal that provoked much debate. Concerns about high levels of student debt prompted many Americans to question whether college was really worth the seemingly high cost. Chloe could follow these debates online to learn more about the various perspectives on these issues, and she could use social media platforms like Twitter to follow key figures in these debates and to share ideas with her peers.

# Write a Discovery Draft

Because Chloe had already been writing about her topic by the time her instructor assigned the argument essay, she had a lot of material to work with. So instead of writing a Discovery Draft from scratch, she pulled together material from her essay about her stepfather and her essay about the assigned readings by John Henry Newman and Charles Murray. These various writings, which focused on different aspects of her topic, amounted to a Discovery Draft that included key ideas and information that Chloe could use to build her argument in her new essay. Here's part of what she wrote in her essay about her stepfather:

> Most people think of college as a resource to obtain a degree so that later on when they are entering the job force, they will receive a higher paying job. However, this is not true for everyone, especially in my family. When I was young, my stepfather had a job at my hometown news station. He was a journalist and an editor. He loved his job and was one of the most qualified people there, having earned a Bachelor's degree in English with a minor in communications. But all of this was not enough for him to keep his job during the recession in 2007. After many months with no success finding a job, he had to go back to school to get a new degree, so he could get a new job to support our family—one he could keep.

In this excerpt Chloe examines her own family's experience in a way that raises important questions about the value of a college degree today. She continued to explore these questions in her essay about John Henry Newman and Charles Murray:

> Many Americans in past decades could live relatively successful lives without earning college degrees, but now times have changed. Many people today question the value of a college degree and wonder why college has become the expected path for high school graduates. One reason is that college became much more accessible after World War I. Before that war, there was little fluctuation in college attendance rates, but after the Great Depression ended in the 1940s, more Americans began to go to college. This increase happened partly because many people believed that they could earn more money in the long run if they obtained a college degree. That was true. In 1975, a person with a bachelor's degree earned about 1.5 times more in yearly pay than

did someone with only a high school diploma (Brock 111). There are also many social and intellectual benefits of attending college that students can take advantage of to create successful careers. Having a college education can lead to better health, living arrangements, and lifestyle (Brock 110).

Another important factor that helps explain the increase in the number of Americans attending college was changing societal norms in the United States. Prior to 1965 mostly white men, usually from upper-middle or upper classes, were seen and welcomed on college campuses (Brock 111). African Americans and women were not encouraged to attend college. College was also a financial hardship for many families. Then in 1965 Congress passed the Higher Education Act, which helped the general population obtain financial aid to attend the college of their choice. As well, federal aid for higher education increased from $655 million in 1955 to $3.5 billion in 1965 (Brock 111). This increase in funding made tuition prices affordable for many. And as societal norms began to change, so did the demographics in college populations. Many universities were more open to diversity due to the Civil Rights Act, which was passed in 1964, and attitudes about gender began to change as well. Colleges all over the country began to welcome students of any race, culture, gender, etc. (Brock 111). This made attending "an institution of higher learning for virtually anyone who possessed a high school diploma and the necessary financial resources" possible (Campbell and Siegel 488).

In these excerpts Chloe is not only continuing to explore her main questions about the value of college but also strengthening her own understanding of her topic. In addition to writing about her own experience, she is drawing on materials she found through her search of scholarly articles. (Some of this material ended up in the final version of her argument. See page 117.)

In her proposal for her argument assignment, Chloe pursued these ideas that she had been writing about for her previous assignments. Here's an excerpt from her proposal:

For my argument I want to look at what happened historically that made acquiring a higher education a necessity in the U.S. I want to learn when and why this became the norm since historically most people did not need a college degree to live a successful life. I want to see what national events shaped this view. Understanding what makes people believe that college is so important will help me answer the question that we have been asked frequently in our class: Is college worth it for me?

Chloe's Discovery Draft, then, included materials from previous assignments as well as new ideas, and writing the draft gave her a clearer sense of her topic. At this stage, she still had a lot of research to do, but her main idea for her argument was already beginning to take shape.

## Step 2 Examine the rhetorical context.

### Identify Your Audience

Chloe's immediate audience for her essay was her writing class. She had shared her previous assignments with some of her classmates, all of whom were also writing about topics related to education. In this way, the class became a community of scholars who were working together on their writing to gain a better understanding of important questions, issues, and problems in education. Chloe also knew that her topic was relevant to her classmates, because, like her, they all had to make the decision to attend college and would therefore likely be interested in understanding the implications of that decision. In her proposal for this assignment, she wrote,

> Students will be interested in my topic because I'm sure they want to know why there is a societal expectation that everyone should attend college. I can assume that students might want to know their own role in the history of higher education. How have we, as college students, affected the institutions we attend, and how have we ourselves benefited from attending those institutions?

In posing such questions, Chloe was trying to anticipate the expectations of her primary audience, which could ultimately help her make her argument more relevant and therefore more persuasive.

Chloe's assignment also called for her to write an argument that would be relevant to a broader audience, including scholars and experts interested in education. She believed her questions were relevant to such an audience because colleges have had to make adjustments as the number of Americans who attend college has increased. And although Chloe's assignment called for an academic paper, she selected a topic that actually had wide appeal outside academic settings. At the time she was writing in 2015, questions about the value of college were being intensely debated not only by college students and their families but also by politicians and educators. So although Chloe was writing most directly to an audience of her classmates and other college students, her argument was also relevant to an audience that went beyond her class.

### Consider the Context

**Time:** As already noted, Chloe's topic was timely because of recent economic and political developments that potentially affected the decisions of many Americans about whether or not to attend college. These developments helped intensify the debates about the high cost of college, student loan debt, and related issues that were occurring at the time Chloe was writing. In fact, though, Chloe was addressing questions that Americans have been wrestling with for many decades—questions that had taken on a new urgency because of these recent developments.

**Place:** In New York state, where Chloe was a college student, the tuition increases at state universities stirred controversy at the time Chloe was writing her essay. And what was happening in New York was happening in many other states as well. So Chloe was addressing issues that were relevant to college students and others throughout the U.S.

**Purpose:** As she indicated in her proposal, Chloe wanted to gain a better understanding of American attitudes about higher education so that she would have a more informed perspective on her own decisions. But she also saw her essay as part of a larger conversation about higher education in the U.S., and she believed that other students would benefit from understanding how American attitudes about college had changed over time.

## Review Your Question

In thinking about the rhetorical context, Chloe felt confident that her topic was relevant to her intended audience, but her preliminary work on her essay prompted her to adjust her working question slightly:

*Is college worthwhile for everyone?*

This version of her question encompassed the current debates about college as well as the larger issue of the purpose of college better than her earlier version ("Is college for everyone?").

## Develop Your Discovery Draft

After reviewing the rhetorical context, Chloe could now return to her Discovery Draft to identify important ideas that she needed to explore further. She knew that her historical analysis might be unfamiliar to some readers, and she wanted to make sure she explained key historical developments clearly and thoroughly. For her earlier essay about the assigned readings by John Henry Newman and Charles Murray, she learned about important scholarly perspectives on the purpose and value of college, and she had done some research on federal policies, such as the Higher Education Act of 1965, and social movements, such as the Civil Rights movement, that helped increase the number of Americans attending college. Now she wanted to learn more about the current debate surrounding the value of college and the economic and social pressures facing students today as they decide whether college is the right choice for them. She also wondered whether there were other government policies that she should consider in her effort to understand how college came to be so valued in American society.

## Step 3 Select an appropriate medium.

### Select a Medium

Like most college assignments, Chloe's called for a conventional academic essay to be submitted electronically (as a Word or PDF file) or in hard copy. So she did not have to select a medium for her project. However, she knew that she would have to follow the conventions for academic writing, and part of the purpose of the assignment was to help her learn how to take advantage of those conventions to make an effective argument.

## Consider How the Medium Might Shape Your Project

The structure and style of Chloe's paper would be shaped by the conventions of academic writing, as you'll see later. As a student who had taken advanced English classes in high school, she was generally familiar with these conventions and kept them in mind as she proceeded with her project. In addition, Joe, Chloe's instructor, had certain expectations for how his students would use source material in making their arguments. For example, he wanted to make sure that students consulted scholarly sources in addition to sources from popular media so that they might gain a broader perspective on their topics. Chloe had already found several scholarly articles, and she would supplement her research with other kinds of sources as well, such as statistical data from the U.S. Department of Education. In this way, the conventions for an academic essay influenced not only the form of her essay but also her decisions about the kind of material she should look for as she explored her topic.

## Step 4  Have something to say.

As you can probably tell, Chloe had a genuine interest in her topic and wanted to learn more about it. As she wrote in her proposal, "This topic matters to me because I have always been taught how important it is to receive a college education so that I can be successful in the rest of my life." So she had a stake in answering her question, "Is college worthwhile for everyone?" She also knew that her question mattered to thousands of other students. Moreover, because of her work on her previous essays and her preliminary research for this essay, she already had a strong sense that college has value beyond a career—all of which gave Chloe a good start on a main point or claim.

## Revisit Your Main Question

Here is Chloe's main question after she adjusted it in Step #2:

> *Is college worthwhile for everyone?*

For her proposal she had already begun to identify how this question is both timely and relevant to her intended audience—which included her classmates, other college students, and a much larger audience interested in issues related to higher education—and she had already begun to formulate a main point or thesis.

## Write a Guiding Thesis Statement

Here is the Guiding Thesis Statement that Chloe developed as a result of her work on her proposal and Discovery Draft:

> Various social and economic developments along with government policies in the past century have resulted in a dramatic increase in the number of Americans who attend college, and today many students feel pressure to go to college. However, many students might be attending college because of this societal pressure rather than pursue other career paths that would be right for them.

## Review Your Discovery Draft

After reviewing her Discovery Draft and other materials she had gathered through her preliminary research, Chloe realized that her Guiding Thesis Statement did not really encompass the larger question of the value of college, a question she explored in her essay on John Henry Newman and Charles Murray and one that is central to the ongoing debates about college in the U.S.

## Revise Your Guiding Thesis Statement

Here is Chloe's revised Guiding Thesis Statement:

> Various social and economic developments along with government policies in the past century have resulted in a dramatic increase in the number of Americans who attend college. Today many students feel pressure to go to college rather than pursue other career paths that would be right for them, believing that college will lead to a better-paying job. However, in view of a challenging job market, some students are questioning whether college is worth the increasing tuition and high rates of student debt. But the question of whether college is worthwhile is more than a matter of money; college has value that goes beyond the salary a college graduate might earn.

This statement captured the main point Chloe expected to make in her essay. However, as she conducted research, learned more about her topic, and developed her argument, she would find that she had to refine this statement.

## Step 5 Back up what you say.

As we have seen, Chloe had begun her research for this assignment long before developing her Discovery Draft. Previously, she had written essays on related topics and had already identified some relevant sources. But she knew she had more to learn about her topic. In other words, Chloe wasn't just finding relevant sources to support her thesis or back up her claims; she was delving more deeply into her topic to understand it better so that she could make a more informed, compelling argument. That's the process of inquiry that writing should be, and she was fully engaged in that process.

## Identify Your Main Claims or Assertions

Using her Guiding Thesis Statement as a starting point, Chloe could begin identifying some of the claims she expected to make in her essay:

- College has become an expectation for many students today.
- Federal education policies as well as social and political developments over the past century have led to an increase in the number of Americans who attend college.
- The pressure to attend college might prevent some students from pursuing other career opportunities that are right for them.

- Recent economic developments have made attending college much more challenging for many students.
- College generally leads to better jobs.
- College has value that goes beyond getting a better job.

Reviewing this list, Chloe realized that she could reorganize the list into two main claims and several supporting claims:

1. College has become an expectation for many students in the U.S.

   a) Federal education policies as well as social and political developments over the past century have led to an increase in the number of Americans who attend college.

   b) The pressure to attend college might prevent some students from pursuing other career opportunities that are right for them.

   c) Recent economic developments have made attending college much more challenging for many students.

2. College is worthwhile in several different ways.

   a) College generally leads to better jobs.

   b) College has value that goes beyond getting a better job.

Obviously, Chloe had already been exploring some of these claims for her previous assignments and her proposal, and as a result of Step #4 she identified questions and subtopics that she needed to learn more about. Her ongoing research led her to some new information, including a scholarly study that examined how the demand for access to college in the U.S. changed between 1919 and 1964. This material related directly to the first main claim listed above.

Through this process, Chloe continued to find supporting evidence for her claims, which deepened her understanding of her topic. In fact, what she was learning about the history of higher education in the U.S. was beginning to influence her own opinion about whether college is the best choice for everyone.

## Review Your Discovery Draft

Chloe's Discovery Draft already included some of her key claims, and her ongoing research generated additional material to support those claims as well as new ideas about her main point. She now had a lot of relevant material for her historical analysis, a rough idea for organizing her essay, and a clear sense of the direction of her argument. She felt confident that she was ready to write a complete rough draft.

## Write a Complete Draft

Here's Chloe's first full draft of her essay. As you read, you'll notice that Chloe incorporated into this draft much of the material she included in her Discovery Draft. In addition, her main idea is essentially the same as in the Discovery Draft. She includes an in-depth and complicated historical analysis to explain the rise in college attendance over the past 100 years and to provide some insight into why students today feel such pressure to attend college. But you might also notice that Chloe's main argument isn't always clear and that she doesn't fully address all the main claims she identified in Step 5. There are other problems in the draft as well. That's OK. This is a rough draft on a complex topic, and Chloe was still developing her argument. The goal at this stage was to write as complete a draft as possible; Chloe would develop and refine that draft in subsequent steps.

**DRAFT**

### The Ever-Changing Norms About College in the United States

My great-grandfather never attended college and he led what I believe is a very successful life. He owned a sports shop in Syracuse, New York where many high school and even some college athletes bought their equipment. My great-grandfather only had a high school education. He never once took a business course, or had to even take a general education course, so why do I? Today, it is very common for students graduating high school to receive a higher education. "In the fall of 2015 some 20.2 million students are expected to attend American colleges and universities" ("Back to School Statistics"). So what changed? Why have so many people in the past five or six decades lived a nice life without any form of college education, but today those who don't are struggling to make ends meet. Today, students that are thinking about attending college or a university are asking many why questions. Why were they so influenced to attend college when they can go into many other careers, some their recent ancestors have taken? Why has our society decided that a higher education is needed for the majority of United States citizens? Many factors have caused a change in our nation's attitudes about the acceptability of going to college. These factors include social movements, laws, even the availability of jobs over time. Since the World Wars, and specifically World War I, the social norm among Americans has changed from a view that a college degree was not needed to succeed to a view that people needed one to survive in our fragile economic infrastructure.

One of the main reasons it is so common for people to attend college today is that it is a lot more accessible than it was before World War I. Before WWI there was no actual fluctuation in the number of individuals attending a college or university in the United States. After the war the rate of students attending college actually declines, but this was due to the Great Depression, when many people had to focus on making money instead of spending it on college tuition. However, after World War II the economy righted itself, and college attendance increased rapidly (Campbell and Siegel 487). This increase was due to two main reasons: the approach to investment in education and household income. After WWII many individuals believed that they would be able to make more money in the long run if they obtained a college degree. In 1975, a person who had a bachelor's degree earned about 1.5 times more in yearly pay than did someone with only a high school diploma (Brock 111). There are also many social and intellectual benefits of attending college that a student can use to create a successful career for themselves and/or their families, after they graduate from college. Having a higher education can lead to better health, living arrangements, life style choices, etc. (Brock 110). The second reason was the wealth of families of students wanting to pursue a degree. Years ago it was hard for someone in the working or lower-middle class to go to college because the family could not pay tuition in full (Campbell and Siegel 484). Today, many families can afford to send their children to college because of the financing opportunities colleges now have to offer.

Another important factor to help explain the increase in population size at colleges was the changing societal norms in the United States. Prior to 1965 only white men, usually from the upper or middle class, were seen and welcome on college campuses (Brock 111). African Americans and women were not seen as candidates for attending college due to their status in society and because of the hardship in receiving financial aid from universities. Then in 1965, the "Higher Education Act of 1965" was passed which helped the general population to receive federal aid to attend any college of their choosing. As well, federal aid for higher education increased from $655 million in 1955 to $3.5 billion in 1965 (Brock 111). This helped colleges budget more of their money towards scholarships, so more students from lower income households, many of whom were Black or Hispanic, had a higher chance of attending. Later on in 1972, the Pell Grant program was initiated to "focus on the circumstances and needs of recent high school graduates from low-income families" (Baum 24). Even though the amount of students attending a higher education institution was growing, the United States numbers were still low compared to other nations' averages. This program was intended to increase those numbers so it targeted people who could not attend college. Along with these new and growing programs, the government started to target more community colleges. These institutions were seen as "developing institutions"; if the government could focus on making this form of higher education better, then more students could be put into classrooms for slightly lower prices than that of a four-year private or public university. This overall increase in funding also made tuition prices affordable for many, especially those who had a lower income.

The government overall ended up changing the mind sets of many individuals; they made people believe that "young people should not have to be born to affluent or educated parents in order to be able to expect a college education" (Baum 23). With this new mind set, more and more students of many different backgrounds were able to attend the college of their choice. This gave people who did not think they were right for college an incentive to work hard, since they now had more to look forward to in the future. Since the norms of society started to change, the demographics in colleges started to change as well. Many universities were now more open to diversity because of the Civil Rights Act, and views about women in society were changing. Colleges all over the country started to welcome those of any race, culture, gender, etc. (Brock 111). This made attending "an institution of higher education for virtually anyone who possessed a high school diploma and the necessary financial resources" possible because of this national view of acceptance to others, no matter who they are (Campbell and Siegel 488). This long-awaited access was just what people were looking for to obtain a degree, which in turn bettered their lives.

Even though technology is a smaller factor that led to the increase of college students, and did not come around until later on, it has played a tangible role. Today, more colleges are able to reach out to high school graduates or people seeking to go back to school who are looking for information on that certain college. Many campuses have even changed their curriculum to better fit the newest advancements that have come out over the past forty years. One of those is online courses. The University of Phoenix in 2005 enrolled more than 117,000 students, many of whom need to have flexible schedules and cannot attend an actual campus (Brock 113). Numerous community colleges have reached out to students looking to stay close to home. A community college is a safe decision for those who have many specific needs and are looking for an affordable higher education. Over the years community colleges, through the help of the media, have targeted the "non-traditional" college student, the one who may have a job, want to save money, or is not quite ready to take the big step to attend a large private or public university (Brock 114). Whatever the reason, community colleges and online courses have expanded and become popular to many seeking a higher education due to what technology has given them.

All of these factors have positively encouraged more and more United States citizens to believe that a degree is what they must receive in order to do well throughout their lives, especially in today's society. So many people seem to grow up thinking after they graduate they must go to college. This is not a bad concept to believe. However, many students are still asking the question: Why must I go to college when there are other jobs out there for me? This question has been answered as the U.S. has grown over the past decades.

The norm in the 1960's was that women stayed at home, African Americans worked lower-end jobs, white men with a high school diploma got trade/labor jobs, and those with a college degree landed jobs that enabled them to enter the comfortable middle and upper classes. However, things have changed since then. Now many of the jobs that get you into the middle class require a college degree. Even in the 1990's, the *Chicago Tribune's* listing of the 100 best jobs included accountant, engineer, computer programmer, teacher, dentist, paramedic, and pilot (Kleiman). Today some of the top jobs are "dentist, nurse practitioner, software developer." All of these jobs have one thing in common: They all require a college

4

degree, whether it is an associates, bachelors, masters, or even a doctorate. The lower ranking jobs, including social worker, preschool teacher, and architect, also require some form of schooling ("100 Best Jobs"). This is one of the reasons that so many people have gone to college: There are barely any jobs that allow a person to live comfortably today, or even in the past twenty years, that do not require a college degree. In an earlier economy people could "make it" without a degree, but many economic factors, such as job security and fluctuating job markets, have caused this to change.

As our nation has changed socially, economically, and even politically, one of the major views that have changed is our basic ideas about receiving a college degree or higher education. Before the World Wars the number of students attending college was low and only encompassed one primary group of people. Many believed that they did not need to attend college after high school, and some who wanted to were not allowed. As the years have gone by, many programs have been established, grants have been proposed, and systems have changed on campuses. Each of these factors has helped to change the bias about those who can attend a college or a university. Today, people cannot live the life they want without having a good-paying job, which they cannot have without a degree. This is why it is of dire importance that everyone be eligible and have the resources to attend college. We still have not accomplished as much as other nations have, but as a country we are doing the best we can to help fulfill the needs of students, so they can live a full and comfortable life.

## Works Cited

"Back to School Statistics." *Fast Facts*, National Center for Educational Statistics / Institute of Educational Science, nces.ed.gov/fastfacts/display.asp?id=372. Accessed 30 Nov. 2015.

Baum, Sandy. "The Federal Pell Grant Program and Reauthorization of the Higher Education Act." *Journal of Student Financial Aid*, vol. 45, 2015, pp. 23-34.

Brock, Thomas. "Young Adults and Higher Education: Barriers and Breakthroughs to Success." *The Future of Children*, vol. 20, no. 1, Spring 2010, futureofchildren.org/ futureofchildren/publications/docs/20_01_06.pdf.

Campbell, Robert, and Barry M. Siegel, "The Demand for Higher Education in the United States, 1919-1964." *The American Economic Review*, vol. 57, no. 3, June 1967, pp. 482-494. *JSTOR*, www.jstor.org/stable/1812115.

Kleiman, Carol. "Best Jobs for the 90's: From Cook to Cop." *Chicago Tribune*, 31 May 1992, articles.chicagotribune.com/1992-05-31/news/9202180452_1_new-jobs-carol-kleiman-career-counselors.

"The 100 Best Jobs." *US News & World Report*, money.usnews.com/careers/best-jobs/ rankings/the-100-best-jobs. Accessed 30 Nov. 2015.

## Step 6 · Establish a form and structure for your project.

Chloe's assignment called for a conventional academic paper, but the guidelines for organizing the paper were vague. Like many college instructors, Chloe's instructor did not impose a specific structure but left it up to students to decide how to organize their individual projects. For Chloe, deciding how to organize her essay was not straightforward, since her argument included a complicated historical analysis and several subclaims. In reviewing her draft, she considered the following:

**Genre:** Chloe's assignment called for "an in-depth, informed argument that reflects your understanding of the issue." Those instructions didn't give Chloe much to go on, but she decided her best strategy was to organize her paper according to the two main claims she identified in Step #5, incorporating her analysis and evidence into her discussion of each claim. (See Chapter 5 for advice about organizing an analytical essay and Chapter 11 for advice about organizing arguments.)

**Medium:** Chloe would follow the conventions for writing an academic paper, which meant that she would present supporting evidence for each claim and cite her sources using MLA style (which her instructor required). However, there is no standard method for organizing an academic essay, so she had to rely on her sense of her rhetorical situation in making her decisions about the structure of her essay.

**Rhetorical Situation:** Chloe had two primary concerns: (1) informing her audience about why college has become such a powerful expectation in American society, and (2) persuading her audience that college is worthwhile though not necessarily the best choice for every student today. She decided to retain the structure of her rough draft, which was organized roughly around these two main purposes.

Chloe determined that her draft was generally well organized, with the first half devoted to her historical analysis of American attitudes about college and the second half focused on her main argument about whether college is appropriate for everyone. However, each of these two main sections of her essay was not as clearly focused and well organized as they could be, and the transition between them was weak. Part of her challenge was to clarify her argument and integrate her analysis (the first half of her essay) more effectively into that argument (the second half of her essay). So her task at this point was to improve the organization of each section so that her analysis supported her argument and her main claims were clear to her audience.

## Identify the Main Parts of Your Project

As we have seen, Chloe began her draft with a clear sense of her main claims. She was making two central claims and several supporting claims. So the basic organization of her draft around her two central claims was sound. Now she could focus on clarifying and organizing her supporting claims in each of those two main sections.

# Develop an Outline

Chloe learned to use outlines in high school, and she continued to use a basic outline format for most of her college assignments. However, for this assignment she did not create an outline before completing her rough draft. She found that working on an outline at this stage of her project distracted her from exploring her ideas and developing her analysis. Instead, she made notes to herself about the main ideas she would incorporate into her essay. She also had her list of claims from Step #5, which functioned as a kind of outline for her essay. This approach made sense, because Chloe was still trying to understand some of the reasons for the increase in college attendance and the developments that helped make college such a highly valued experience in American society. But now she had to improve the organization of her draft so that her claims were more clearly conveyed to her audience.

The basic organization of her draft looked like this:

I. Introduction.

    A. Great-grandfather's experience

    B. Main question: How did attending college become a norm in American society?

II. College Attendance in the U.S. Increased after WWI.

    A. A college degree brought financial, social, and intellectual benefits.

    B. College became more affordable for many families.

    C. Changing societal norms meant that more women and minorities were able to attend college after 1965.

    D. Government policies also helped increase college attendance.

        1. Higher Education Act of 1965

        2. Pell Grants

        3. Support for community colleges

III. Attitudes Toward College in the U.S. Changed after WWII.

    A. Government policies made colleges more accessible to more Americans.

    B. College welcomed a more diverse student population.

IV. Technology Played a Role in Increased College Attendance.

    A. Online courses gave many people access to college.

    B. Community colleges used media to increase student access.

V. Is College Right for Every Student?

    A. Societal norms encourage more people to attend college.

    B. Many of the most sought-after jobs require a college degree.

    C. It is difficult to make it in society today without a college degree.

If you compare this outline of Chloe's rough draft with her list of claims from Step #5, you can easily see that her draft was out of balance. Most of her essay is devoted to her analysis of how attending college has become a norm in the U.S., and she did not focus sufficient attention on making her argument about whether college is worthwhile for everyone; only her second-to-last paragraph directly takes up her argument (which is reflected in Part V of her outline).

This outline also reveals that some sections of Chloe's essay might not be necessary. For example, Part IV is devoted to a discussion of technology, which her instructor suggested might not strengthen her analysis (see below under Step #7). So in addition to developing Part V, she might need to condense or even eliminate some of Part IV.

## Write or Revise Your Draft

Reviewing her draft, Chloe identified some weaknesses in its structure, but before revising it, she decided to wait and see what her peer reviewers and her instructor would have to say about the essay's structure.

**Step 7** Get feedback.

## Ask Your Readers to Respond to Your Draft

Chloe received both written and verbal feedback on her draft from classmates during in-class peer review. Her instructor provided students with specific questions to address as they reviewed each other's drafts, but Chloe was also eager to see whether her argument was convincing to her peers. Later, she met with her instructor to discuss possible revisions to her draft.

## Identify Common Themes in Your Readers' Responses

Chloe's classmates identified two main strengths of her draft: (1) they generally found her topic interesting and relevant, and (2) they found her anecdote about her great-grandfather engaging and effective. Several classmates offered their own perspectives on Chloe's main question of whether college is worthwhile. One classmate wrote that although many careers require a college degree, he could "off the top of my head think of many stories of people I know who didn't need a degree" to be successful. So Chloe knew that the question of whether college is worthwhile resonated with her audience.

But her classmates also identified two main concerns: (1) her analysis was sometimes hard to follow, and (2) she didn't adequately represent alternative perspectives on the value of college. Chloe's instructor, Joe, agreed with those concerns and added a third one: a lack of complexity in her discussion of some of her key points. He noted that her draft "sometimes explores the topic in depth and sometimes oversimplifies the issues." Specifically, he felt that her discussion of women and minority students in her third paragraph was oversimplified, in part because she neglected to mention the existence of all-women's colleges and Historically Black Colleges (HBCs). Similarly, he felt that her discussion of jobs in her second-to-last paragraph did not sufficiently account for the significant changes that have occurred in the American economy in the past several years.

Despite these concerns, Joe felt that Chloe's draft was generally strong:

- He noted that her topic was especially relevant to her audience.
- He described her historical analysis as "excellent."
- He praised her use of source material.

To address these concerns, Joe suggested that Chloe find alternative perspectives on the value of college; specifically, he noted that Charles Murray, about whom she had written for a previous assignment, represented an alternative viewpoint that she could incorporate into her argument. He also wondered why she did not incorporate into her essay the ideas of John Henry Newman, whom she also wrote about for her previous assignment. Finally, he encouraged Chloe to bring out her own voice more clearly rather than rely so heavily on source material; doing so would likely make her argument more persuasive to her audience.

Here are sections of Chloe's draft with comments by her instructor, Joe, and three of her classmates (Ashley, Bart, and Bethany):

My great-grandfather never attended college and he led what I believe is a very successful life. He owned a sports shop in Syracuse, New York where many high school and even some college athletes bought their equipment. My great-grandfather only had a high school education. He never once took a business course, or had to even take a general education course, so why do I? Today, it is very common for students graduating high school to receive a higher education. "In the fall of 2015 some 20.2 million students are expected to attend American colleges and universities" ("Back to School Statistics"). So what changed? Why have so many people in the past five or six decades lived a nice life without any form of college education, but today those who don't are struggling to make ends meet. Today, students that are thinking about attending college or a university are asking many why questions. Why were they so influenced to attend college when they can go into many other careers, some their recent ancestors have taken? Why has our society decided that a higher education is needed for the majority of United States citizens? Many factors have caused a change in our nation's attitudes about the acceptability of going to college. These factors include social movements, laws, even the availability of jobs over time. Since the World Wars, and specifically World War I, the social norm among

**Bart:** I like the way you start your essay with your great-grandfather's successful experiences and then move to the question of why you should attend college.

**Bethany:** I especially like how you begin with the anecdote about your great-grandfather. It makes the topic seem more personal and more real.

**Joe:** Is this your thesis?

Americans has changed from a view that a college degree was not needed to succeed to a view that people needed one to survive in our fragile economic infrastructure.

One of the main reasons it is so common for people to attend college today is that it is a lot more accessible than it was before World War I. Before WWI there was no actual fluctuation in the number of individuals attending a college or university in the United States. After the war the rate of students attending college actually declines, but this was due to the Great Depression, when many people had to focus on making money instead of spending it on college tuition. However, after World War II the economy righted itself, and college attendance increased rapidly (Campbell and Siegel 487). This increase was due to two main reasons: the approach to investment in education and household income. After WWII many individuals believed that they would be able to make more money in the long run if they obtained a college degree. In 1975, a person who had a bachelor's degree earned about 1.5 times more in yearly pay than did someone with only a high school diploma (Brock 111). There are also many social and intellectual benefits of attending college that a student can use to create a successful career for themselves and/or their families, after they graduate from college. Having a higher education can lead to better health, living arrangements, life style choices, etc. (Brock 110). The second reason was the wealth of families of students wanting to pursue a degree. Years ago it was hard for someone in the working or lower-middle class to go to college because the family could not pay tuition in full (Campbell and Siegel 484). Today, many families can afford to send their children to college because of the financing opportunities colleges now have to offer.

Another important factor to help explain the increase in population size at colleges was the changing societal norms in the United States. Prior to 1965 only white men, usually from the upper or middle class, were seen and welcome on college campuses (Brock 111). African Americans and women were not seen as candidates for attending college due to their status in society and because of the hardship in receiving financial aid from universities. Then in 1965, the "Higher Education Act of 1965" was passed which helped the general population to receive federal aid to attend any college of their choosing. As well, federal aid for higher education increased from

**Joe:** Chloe, I'm having a little trouble following your discussion here. Is this paragraph really about access to higher education? You seem to have several key points to make here, but your discussion could be more coherent.

**Bart:** I think your historical approach helps us understand the issue. I like the fact that you look at how norms are changing, and I think it's good that you look back into the early 1900's.

**Joe:** But my mom graduated from college in 1960.

**Joe:** Yes, that's true. But what about women's colleges and Historically Black Colleges? Women and African Americans could attend those, right? Your statements here oversimplify the situation at the time.

$655 million in 1955 to $3.5 billion in 1965 (Brock 111). This helped colleges budget more of their money towards scholarships, so more students from lower income households, many of whom were Black or Hispanic, had a higher chance of attending. Later on in 1972, the Pell Grant program was initiated to "focus on the circumstances and needs of recent high school graduates from low-income families" (Baum 24). . . .

The government overall ended up changing the mind sets of many individuals; they made people believe that "young people should not have to be born to affluent or educated parents in order to be able to expect a college education" (Baum 23). With this new mind set, more and more students of many different backgrounds were able to attend the college of their choice. This gave people who did not think they were right for college an incentive to work hard, since the now had more to look forward to in the future. . . .

Even though technology is a smaller factor that led to the increase of college students, and did not come around until later on, it has played a tangible role. Today, more colleges are able to reach out to high school graduates or people seeking to go back to school who are looking for information on that certain college. Many campuses have even changed their curriculum to better fit the newest advancements that have come out over the past forty years. One of those is online courses. The University of Phoenix in 2005 enrolled more than 117,000 students, many of whom need to have flexible schedules and cannot attend an actual campus (Brock 113). Numerous community colleges have reached out to students looking to stay close to home. A community college is a safe decision for those who have many specific needs and are looking for an affordable higher education.  Over the years community colleges, through the help of the media, have targeted the "non-traditional" college student, the one who may have a job, want to save money, or is not quite ready to take the big step to attend a large private or public university (Brock 114). Whatever the reason, community colleges and online courses have expanded and become popular to many seeking a higher education due to what technology has given them.

All of these factors have positively encouraged more and more United States citizens to believe that a degree is what they must receive in order to do well throughout their lives, especially

**Joe:** Good! These two important government programs affected college attendance. But were there others that were as important? I know the G.I. Bill helped many Americans go to college after WWII.

**Joe:** Yes. Good point. And you use the quotation very effectively to make your point.

**Ashley:** I found this point a little hard to follow. Specifically, why exactly would lowering the cost of college make people work harder? And what are they looking forward to in the future? I think I get what's you're trying to say, but your point will be stronger if you are a bit clearer here.

**Joe:** It's true that technology might increase access to college, but this does not add much to your analysis, since by the time online courses were developed, the main trends you discuss earlier in your essay had already resulted in higher college attendance. Do you need this material?

**Joe:** Yes, community colleges have targeted non-traditional students, but they have not expanded only because of technology, as you suggest in this paragraph. You're oversimplifying matters.

in today's society. So many people seem to grow up thinking after they graduate they must go to college. This is not a bad concept to believe. However, many students are still asking the question: Why must I go to college when there are other jobs out there for me? This question has been answered as the U.S. has grown over the past decades.

**Joe:** How? you need to explain.

## Consider Conflicting Advice in Your Readers' Responses

The students who reviewed Chloe's draft generally agreed on the main strengths and weaknesses in the draft, and their feedback was consistent with some of Joe's comments. There were no significant disagreements among her reviewers, and their comments helped Chloe see that her main argument was not getting through to her readers. She also could see that her historical analysis was strong but needed to be clarified and more fully developed in some sections; moreover, she needed to integrate that analysis more effectively into her main argument.

4

## Step 8 Revise.

Using her classmates' and instructor's comments as a guide, Chloe had a clear plan for revision, and she worked through several drafts, each time addressing more specific issues to strengthen her essay. In addition, she was still exploring her topic, refining her analysis, and strengthening her argument.

## Focus First on Content

Chloe focused her revisions on two main areas: developing her main argument and integrating her analysis more effectively into that argument. These two main areas included the following related concerns:

- **Clarify the main argument.** During their conference about her rough draft, Chloe's instructor described her thesis as "squishy," and her classmates told her that they weren't always clear on the main point of her essay.
- **Include alternative viewpoints.** Her instructor and several classmates suggested that Chloe could add depth and complexity to her argument by incorporating the ideas of John Henry Newman as well as alternative viewpoints about the value of college, especially the arguments of Charles Murray.
- **Clarify the historical analysis.** Chloe realized from her classmates' comments that she needed to explain several key points in her analysis more clearly.

- **Avoid oversimplifying.** Chloe's instructor pointed out several places in her drafts where she seemed to oversimplify important developments, such as the increase in the numbers of women and minorities who attend college.

Here are some of the revisions Chloe made to address these concerns:

- She revised her opening paragraph to establish her focus more clearly and introduce her main point:

Draft: My great-grandfather never attended college and he led what I believe is a very successful life. He owned a sports shop in Syracuse, New York where many high school and even some college athletes bought their equipment. My great-grandfather only had a high school education. He never once took a business course, or had to even take a general education course, so why do I? Today, it is very common for students graduating high school to receive a higher education. "In the fall of 2015 some 20.2 million students are expected to attend American colleges and universities" ("Back to School Statistics"). So what changed? Why have so many people in the past five or six decades lived a nice life without any form of college education, but today those who don't are struggling to make ends meet. Today, students that are thinking about attending college or a university are asking many why questions. Why were they so influenced to attend college when they can go into many other careers, some their recent ancestors have taken? Why has our society decided that a higher education is needed for the majority of United States citizens? Many factors have caused a change in our nation's attitudes about the acceptability of going to college. These factors include social movements, laws, even the availability of jobs over time. Since the World Wars, and specifically World War I, the social norm among Americans has changed from a view that a college degree was not needed to succeed to a view that people needed one to survive in our fragile economic infrastructure.

> The latter half of this paragraph poses an important question about why college has become such a powerful expectation for American students, but it does not convey a sense of Chloe's main argument about the value of college today.

Revised version: My great-grandfather never attended college, and he led what I believe is a very successful life. He owned a sports shop in Syracuse, New York, where many high school and even some college athletes bought their equipment. He never once took a business course to learn how to run a business or even a general education course, so why do I? Today, it is common for students graduating high school to pursue a

> Chloe kept her reference to her great-grandfather, which her readers found engaging and effective.

higher education. 20.2 million students were expected to attend American colleges and universities in the 2015-2016 academic year ("Back to School Statistics"). In the 1940's only 8% of men and 5% of women between the ages of 20 and 24 attended college. By 1991 almost 31% of men and 29% of women attended college (Snyder 16-17). So what changed? Why did so many people in my great-grandfather's generation live a nice life without any form of college education, yet today those without college degrees can struggle to make ends meet?

Students today face very different challenges from those my great-grandfather faced. Even with a college degree, many people entering the job market cannot find the jobs in their majors. My stepfather is a good example. Even with a college degree, he struggled to find work in his field of study. And the average student now leaves college with more than $35,000 in loan debt (Sparshott). Not surprisingly, many students now question whether college is worth the time, effort, and cost. They wonder whether they really need a degree to be successful, despite the pressure they feel to go to college. Although many people see numerous benefits to college, many others argue that a college degree is no longer the best path to being successful. The decision about whether to attend college is not a simple one, but I still believe college offers great benefits in addition to a possible career path. And everyone should at least have the opportunity to go to college if they choose to.

■ She revised passages in which her claims were oversimplified:

**Draft:** Another important factor to help explain the increase in population size at colleges was the changing societal norms in the United States. Prior to 1965 only white men, usually from the upper or middle class, were seen and welcome on college campuses (Brock 111). African Americans and women were not seen as candidates for attending college due to their status in society and because of the hardship in receiving financial aid from universities.

**Revised version:** Prior to the 1940's usually white men from the upper or middle class populated college campuses (Brock 111). Fewer African Americans and women attended college partly due to social norms and also because of the difficulty of obtaining financial aid. Although there were all-black and all-women colleges, those institutions often did not have the resources that the larger universities had.

Chloe added facts to help support her claim about how common attending college has become.

Chloe divided her original introductory paragraph into two, making it easier for readers to follow her discussion and also enabling her to give emphasis to her questions about how things have changed by ending the paragraph with them (highlighted in blue).

Chloe expanded her discussion of the situation facing students today. She also added new material about her stepfather to illustrate that situation.

The paragraph now ends with a clear statement of Chloe's main argument (highlighted in orange).

Chloe's instructor questioned her claim about the lack of access to college among African Americans and women, noting that there were women's colleges and Historically Black Colleges that they could attend.

Chloe revised this sentence to make her point clearer.

This new sentence (highlighted in orange) adds complexity to Chloe's point by acknowledging women's and Historically Black Colleges but noting an important limitation facing those institutions.

- She incorporated new material to address alternative perspectives on the value of college and to add depth to her argument:

**Draft:** The norm in the 1960's was that women stayed at home, African Americans worked lower-end jobs, white men with a high school diploma got trade/labor jobs, and those with a college degree landed jobs that enabled them to enter the comfortable middle and upper classes. However, things have changed since then. Now many of the jobs that get you into the middle class require a college degree. Even in the 1990's, the *Chicago Tribune's* listing of the 100 best jobs included "accountant, engineer, computer programmer, teacher, dentist, paramedic, pilot" (Kleiman). Today some of the top jobs are "dentist, nurse practitioner, software developer." All of these jobs have one thing in common: They all require a college degree, whether it is an associates, bachelors, masters, or even a doctorate. The lower ranking jobs, including social worker, preschool teacher, and architect, also require some form of schooling ("100 Best Jobs"). This is one of the reasons that so many people have gone to college: There are barely any jobs that allow a person to live comfortably today, or even in the past twenty years, that do not require a college degree. In an earlier economy people could "make it" without a degree, but many economic factors, such as job security and fluctuating job markets, have caused this to change.

> In this passage Chloe uses source material to support the claim that college is necessary today for having a successful career. She offers no additional supporting arguments, nor does she acknowledge counter-arguments.

**Revised version:** As time went on, more and more people in American society realized the economic benefits of a degree. In 1975, a person who had a bachelor's degree earned about 1.5 times more in yearly pay than did someone with only a high school diploma (Brock 111). In 2013 median annual earnings for young adults (ages 25-34) with a bachelor's degree were $48,500 as compared to $30,000 for those with a high school diploma ("Income"). There are also many social and intellectual benefits of attending college. Having a higher education can lead to better health, living arrangements, life style choices, etc. (Brock 110). Before World War I few people would have believed that statement, because people could do okay without a degree. Today, so many people grow up thinking that they must go to college to have a successful life. But does a college degree guarantee success? Are too many students going to college because of societal expectations when college might not be the right path for them? . . .

> Chloe retains some material from her rough draft (orange) and adds new material (blue) to show how a college degree can affect income.

Charles Murray, author of *Are Too Many People Going to College?*, believes that college is not worth it for everyone.

> Chloe retains her point about the connection between college and a successful life (orange), but she adds important questions (blue) that complicate her point.

He states that not everyone is prepared for the strenuous intellectual challenge of a liberal education (Murray 237). One study Murray cites shows that only 10% of high school students who take the SAT score in the percentile that would lead them to get at least a 2.7 GPA in college (Murray 238). If students are not going to do well, then what? Many drop out and attempt to find a full-time job; others return home to figure out a new plan, but overall this is affecting graduation rates. Murray points out that only those who are interested in getting a liberal education should attend school (Murray 240). Many who do not want to go to college can do well in other fields, such as trade jobs.

> This new paragraph introduces an alternative perspective on whether college is worthwhile and adds complexity to Chloe's discussion. Acknowledging important counter-arguments not only reflects a better understanding of the issue but also strengthens her own position.

Chloe made many other revisions to

- elaborate on, develop and refine her analysis,
- clarify important points,
- support her claims, and
- strengthen her main argument about the value of college.

You can see these revisions in her finished version on page 117.

## Focus Next on Form

Reviewing her instructor's and classmates' comments as well as her outline helped Chloe recognize the need for the following revisions:

- Reorganize the supporting claims in her analysis about why Americans have come to place such a high value on attending college.
- Eliminate unnecessary material.
- Add or strengthen transitions, especially from her introduction into her analysis.

These revisions, which addressed problems with how Chloe's rough draft was organized, also helped integrate her analysis into her main argument, which was one of the two main concerns she needed to address (see Step #8). In other words, strengthening the structure of her essay also strengthened her main argument.

Here are some of her revisions to strengthen the form and structure of her essay:

**Draft:** One of the main reasons it is so common for people to attend college today is that it is a lot more accessible than it was before World War I. Before WWI there was no actual fluctuation in the number of individuals attending a college or university in the United States. After the war the rate of students attending college actually declines, but this was due to the Great Depression, when many people had to focus on making money instead

> The second paragraph of Chloe's rough draft jumped directly into her analysis of how college attendance increased in the U.S. after the World Wars without explaining why that analysis is important.

of spending it on college tuition. However, after World War II the economy righted itself, and college attendance increased rapidly (Campbell and Siegel 487). This increase was due to two main reasons: the approach to investment in education and household income. After WWII many individuals believed that they would be able to make more money in the long run if they obtained a college degree. In 1975, a person who had a bachelor's degree earned about 1.5 times more in yearly pay than did someone with only a high school diploma (Brock 111). There are also many social and intellectual benefits of attending college that a student can use to create a successful career for themselves and/or their families, after they graduate from college. Having a higher education can lead to better health, living arrangements, life style choices, etc. (Brock 110). The second reason was the wealth of families of students wanting to pursue a degree. Years ago it was hard for someone in the working or lower-middle class to go to college because the family could not pay tuition in full (Campbell and Siegel 484). Today, many families can afford to send their children to college because of the financing opportunities colleges now have to offer.

Chloe moved most of the material in this second paragraph to paragraph 6 in her revised essay, where it fit more logically. This move was part of her effort to reorganize her analysis so that it was clearer to her readers.

**Revised version:** To understand the situation facing students today, it helps to know how we got here. As my great-grandfather knew, it wasn't always the case that young people were expected to go to college. During the 20th Century a number of important developments helped make attending college a societal norm and influenced how Americans think about the importance of a college degree. One of those developments was increased government financial aid. Prior to the 1960's it was hard for someone in the working or lower-middle class to afford college tuition (Campbell and Siegel 484). Today, many families can afford to send their children to college because of numerous government programs. For example, the Higher Education Act of 1965 helped the general population receive federal aid to attend any college of their choosing. Federal aid for higher education increased from $655 million in 1955 to $3.5 billion in 1965 (Brock 111), which enabled colleges to budget more money for scholarships. As a result, more students from lower income households had a better chance of attending college. One of the most important government programs was the Servicemen's Readjustment Act of 1944, commonly known as the GI Bill, which helped soldiers returning from World War II pay for college. By the end of 1947 almost half

These two new sentences (blue highlight) provide a transition from the introductory paragraphs to the historical analysis and explain the reason for that analysis.

Chloe retained these sentences (orange) from her rough draft but she replaced the vague phrase "years ago" with the more specific phrase "prior to the 1960's."

This material (green) was moved from paragraph 2 of her rough draft to this paragraph in her revised draft, where it helped her tell the story of the impact of government programs on college attendance in the U.S.

Chloe added information about the GI Bill (blue) to provide more support for her claim about the government role in increasing college attendance.

of the students attending colleges in the U.S. were benefitting from this bill ("History and Timeline"). Later programs such as the Pell Grant program, which was initiated in 1972, would "focus on the circumstances and needs of recent high school graduates from low-income families" (Baum 24). All these programs affected not only how many Americans attended college but also which Americans could attend.

The final sentence (orange) sums up the main point of the paragraph and sets up the transition to the next paragraph.

These are careful revisions that not only strengthen Chloe's analysis but also make it easier for her readers to understand.

## Consider Your Rhetorical Situation

All the revisions described so far were intended to clarify key points or develop Chloe's main ideas in response to feedback from classmates and her instructor. She interpreted that feedback not only as suggestions for improving her essay but also as clues to how her essay was being received by readers and how well she was reaching her intended audience.

For example, Chloe knew that her readers reacted positively to her references to her great-grandfather in her opening paragraph, so she not only retained those references but she also added references to him later in her essay. In addition, because her use of her family's experience seemed effective in conveying her ideas to her readers, she added a brief reference to her stepfather's experience. These revisions were undertaken specifically with her audience in mind.

Chloe also considered her larger rhetorical purpose. As noted earlier, she understood her essay as part of a much larger, ongoing conversation about education in the U.S., and her historical analysis reinforced the idea that the issues she was writing about have long interested Americans. But she also knew that these issues had special relevance to her classmates. She wanted her essay to resonate with readers who shared her concerns about access to college and who, like her, might have wondered about their own decision to attend college.

With this in mind, in her revised essay Chloe decided to add more up-to-date facts and figures to convey a better sense of the situation facing students today. She also incorporated the perspectives of experts who had more recently been writing about the question of the value of college, something she had not included in her rough draft. These revisions, she felt, gave her essay currency as well as greater relevance to other college students.

## Revisit Your Introduction and Conclusion

We have already seen the significant revisions Chloe made to her introduction (page 108), which were part of her effort to clarify the focus of her essay and establish her main argument. In addition to the new material she added to that introduction, she made careful changes to strengthen successful elements that her readers had identified in their comments. For example, in the opening paragraph of her rough draft she posed several questions, which didn't clearly establish her focus; her revised version, by contrast, includes a more carefully worded question that points more clearly to the main issue she will address in her essay, which is whether college is worthwhile today:

**Draft:** So what changed? Why have so many people in the past five or six decades lived a nice life without any form of college education, but today those who don't are struggling to make ends meet? Today, students that are thinking about attending college or a university are asking many why questions. Why were they so influenced to attend college when they can go into many other careers, some their recent ancestors have taken? Why has our society decided that a higher education is needed for the majority of United States citizens?

> This passage from the rough draft actually poses three related but separate questions. Chloe will address all these questions in her essay, but the way they are introduced here is confusing.

**Revised version:** . . . So what changed? Why did so many people in my great-grandfather's generation live a nice life without any form of college education, yet today those without college degrees can struggle to make ends meet?

> This question, placed at the end of the first paragraph, leads effectively into the second paragraph.

Students today face very different challenges from those my great-grandfather faced. Even with a college degree, many people entering the job market cannot find jobs in their majors. My stepfather is a good example. Even with a college degree, he struggled to find work in his field of study. And the average student now leaves college with more than $35,000 in loan debt (Sparshott). Not surprisingly, many students now question whether college is worth the time, effort, and cost. They wonder whether they really need a degree to be successful, despite the pressure they feel to go to college. Although many people see numerous benefits to college, many others argue that a college degree is no longer the best path to being successful. The decision about whether to attend college is not a simple one, but I still believe college offers great benefits in addition to a possible career path. And everyone should at least have the opportunity to go to college if they choose to.

> This new material about Chloe's stepfather (green) helps establish the contrast between the situation facing students prior to WWI and the one facing students today.

> Chloe has turned the questions from her previous draft into statements (orange) that clearly identify the problem she will address in her essay.

> Chloe has added two sentences (blue) that clearly state her main argument (her thesis), which was missing from her rough draft.

Chloe also substantially revised her conclusion. Her original version unnecessarily restated several main points and did not convey a clear sense of what she was advocating. Her revised version, however, is more succinct and ends with a more forceful statement about the need to make college available to Americans:

**Draft:** As our nation has changed socially, economically, and even politically, one of the major views that have changed is our basic ideas about receiving a college degree or higher education.

Before the World Wars the number of students attending college was low and only encompassed one primary group of people. Many believed that they did not need to attend college after high school, and some who wanted to were not allowed. As the years have gone by, many programs have been established, grants have been proposed, and systems have changed on campuses. Each of these factors has helped to change the bias about those who can attend a college or a university. Today, people cannot live the life they want without having a good-paying job, which they cannot have without a degree. This is why it is of dire importance that everyone be eligible and have the resources to attend college. We still have not accomplished as much as other nations have, but as a country we are doing the best we can to help fulfill the needs of students, so they can live a full and comfortable life.

> These three sentences (orange) unnecessarily restate main points from the essay.

> The last two sentences (blue) are a weak ending that seem to contradict one another and don't clearly state Chloe's position.

**Revised version:** As our nation has changed throughout the years, attitudes about college have changed as well. Today, people cannot live a comfortable lifestyle without having a well paying job, which can be difficult to receive until they get a degree. This is why it is of such great importance that everyone be eligible and have the resources to attend college. Charles Murray stated that "we should not restrict the availability of a liberal education to a rarefied intellectual elite" (Murray 234). We still need universities that are available to the majority of students who want to attend and who are willing to put in the work to succeed. Our country and our universities have done a lot for their students, but now they need to do more.

> Chloe retains her point that college can lead to a good job (orange), but she adds three new sentences (blue) that reinforce her main argument and leave her readers with a strong statement of her position.

Chloe did not make all these revisions at once. Rather, she worked through multiple drafts, beginning with the larger issues and eventually focusing on more minor issues until she was satisfied that her essay was adequately developed and her argument well supported.

## Step 9 Strengthen your voice.

Chloe felt that the revisions she made to strengthen her argument also strengthened her voice. Specifically, her use of her own family's experience and her effort to keep her classmates in mind as she revised helped make her voice more personal without losing a sense of authority.

## Consider Your Rhetorical Context

Chloe's main goal was to write an essay that conveyed her analysis and argument clearly to her readers, who, she hoped, shared her interest in her topic. In fact, Chloe's own intense curiosity about the questions she addressed in her essay energized her research as well as her writing, and her voice in her essay reflects that. She developed a serious, informed, yet engaging voice that, she hoped, contributed to the effectiveness of her argument. She wanted her readers to sense her genuine interest in the topic and to see her as a credible writer with something worthwhile to say about a topic that was timely and of great interest to many Americans, including her classmates. In this sense, her voice emerged from her constant attention to the rhetorical context.

## Consider Whether You Should Use the First Person

Chloe used the first person in the earliest draft of her essay and retained it in the final version. She did so partly because her instructor did not prohibit its use. The assignment guidelines stated that students should write in an appropriate academic style but that doing so "does not mean that you cannot use the first person (you can) or create a voice that engages your readers (you should)." Chloe took those instructions to heart and believed that using the first person was a good rhetorical strategy for her essay, given the nature of the assignment and her own sense of her purpose.

## Strengthen Your Voice

We've already seen some of the most important revisions that Chloe made to strengthen her voice:

- adding material about her own family's experiences
- using the first person strategically
- clarifying confusing passages in language that was more straightforward
- strengthening her conclusion by emphasizing her own heartfelt and informed perspective

With these revisions, her voice in the final version of her essay was much stronger than in her rough draft.

## Step 10 | Make it correct.

Chloe's early drafts had numerous minor errors of punctuation, spelling, and usage, and in those drafts she also failed to cite some sources properly. Chloe addressed these problems in her final set of revisions, editing carefully to correct errors and make her prose clearer and more concise.

Here's Chloe's finished essay:

Chloe Charles

Prof. Joseph Creamer

Seminar in Writing and Critical Inquiry

1 March 2016

Why Is College So Important in the United States?

My great-grandfather never attended college and he led what I believe is a very successful life. He owned a sports shop in Syracuse, New York, where many high school and even some college athletes bought their equipment. He never once took a business course to learn how to run a business or even a general education course, so why do I? Today, it is common for students graduating high school to pursue a higher education. 20.2 million students were expected to attend American colleges and universities in the 2015-2016 academic year ("Back to School"). In the 1940's only 8% of men and 5% of women between the ages of 20 and 24 attended college. By 1991 almost 31% of men and 29% of women attended college (Snyder 16-17). So what changed? Why did so many people in my great-grandfather's generation live a nice life without any form of college education, yet today those without college degrees can struggle to make ends meet?

Students today face very different challenges from those my great-grandfather faced. Even with a college degree, many people entering the job market cannot find the jobs in their majors. My stepfather is a good example. Even with a college degree, he struggled to find work in his field of study. And the average student now leaves college with more than $35,000 in loan debt (Sparshott). Not surprisingly, many students now question whether college is worth the time, effort, and cost. They wonder whether they really need a degree to be successful, despite the pressure they feel to go to college. Although many people see numerous benefits to college, many others argue that a college degree is no longer the best path to being successful. The decision about whether to attend college is not a simple one, but I still believe college offers great benefits in addition to a possible career path. And everyone should at least have the opportunity to go to college if they choose to.

To understand the situation facing students today, it helps to know how we got here. As my great-grandfather knew, it wasn't always the case that young people were expected to go to college. During the 20th Century, a number of important developments helped make attending college a societal norm and influenced how Americans think about the importance of a college degree. One of those developments was increased government financial aid. Prior to the 1960's, it was hard for someone in the working or lower-middle class to afford college tuition (Campbell and Siegel 484). Today, many families can afford to send their children to college because of numerous government programs. For example, the Higher Education Act of 1965 helped the general population receive federal aid to attend any college of their choosing. Federal aid for higher education increased from $655 million in 1955 to $3.5 billion in 1965 (Brock 111), which enabled colleges to budget more money for scholarships. As a result, more students from lower income households had a better chance of attending college. One of the most important government programs was the Servicemen's Readjustment Act of 1944, commonly known as the GI Bill, which helped soldiers returning from World War II pay for college. By the end of 1947, almost half of the students attending colleges in the U.S. were benefitting from this bill ("History and Timeline"). Later programs such as the Pell Grant program, which was initiated in 1972, would "focus on the circumstances and needs of recent high school graduates from low-income families" (Baum 24). All these programs affected not only how many Americans attended college but also which Americans could attend.

These government programs also influenced American attitudes about higher education and encouraged the belief that "young people should not have to be born to affluent or educated parents in order to be able to expect a college education" (Baum 23). As a result, students of many different backgrounds were able to attend the college of their choice. Prior to the 1940's, usually white men from the upper or middle class populated college campuses (Brock 111). Fewer African Americans and women attended college partly due to social norms and also because of the difficulty of obtaining financial aid. Although there were all-black and all-women colleges, those institutions often did not have the resources that the larger universities had. But that began to change as a result of the Civil Rights and Women's Movements in the 1960's and 1970's. Many universities were now more open to diversity due to these movements, and colleges began to welcome students of any race, culture, gender, etc. (Brock 111). This growing national acceptance of diverse groups made attending "an institution of higher education [possible] for virtually anyone who possessed a high school diploma and the necessary financial resources" (Campbell and Siegel 488).

In addition to these earlier programs, the government began supporting community colleges as far back as the 1990's. A community college can be a safe decision for students with specific needs who are looking for an affordable education. Over the years, community colleges, through the use of media, have targeted the "non-traditional" college student: the one who may hold a job, cannot afford the tuition at a university, or is not quite ready to attend a large private or public university (Brock 114). These benefits of a community college are what interested government policymakers most. If community college could improve and grow, then more students could attend college for a lower price than that of a four-year private or public university. This option was appealing to many students, especially those who had financial troubles but still wanted to get a degree, and helped increase overall college attendance.

These various factors all contributed to the idea that college is a path to a better life. After the U.S. pulled out of the Great Depression and World War II ended, college attendance increased rapidly (Campbell and Siegal 487). As time went on, more and more people in American society realized the economic benefits of a degree. In 1975, a person who had a bachelor's degree earned about 1.5 times more in yearly pay than did someone with only a high school diploma (Brock 111). In 2013, median annual earnings for young adults (ages 25-34) with a bachelor's degree were $48,500 as compared to $30,000 for those with a high school diploma ("Income"). There are also many social and intellectual benefits of attending college. Having a higher education can lead to better health, living arrangements, life style choices, etc. (Brock 110). Before World War I, few people would have believed that statement, because people could do okay without a degree. Today, so many people grow up thinking that they must go to college to have a successful life.

But does a college degree guarantee success? Are too many students going to college because of societal expectations when college might not be the right path for them? My stepfather earned a college degree in English and then landed a job as a journalist. He did everything society expected him to do, but it wasn't enough. In 2007, during the Great Recession, he lost his job like many others in the country, and after months of trying, he couldn't find work in his field. Because of that, he returned to college to try to find a new career. He is not alone. According to the Economic Policy Institute, "Unemployment of young graduates is extremely high today," 7.2% as compared to 5.5% in 2007; in addition, "wages of young high school and college graduates have failed to reach their pre-recession levels, and have in fact stagnated or declined for almost every group since 2000" (Davis et al.). So now many college graduates are asking, Was my degree even worth it in the first place?

Charles Murray, author of *Are Too Many People Going to College?*, believes that college is not worth it for everyone. He states that not everyone is prepared for the strenuous intellectual challenge of a liberal education (Murray 237). One study Murray cites shows that only 10% of high school students who take the SAT score in the percentile that would lead them to get at least a 2.7 GPA in college (Murray 238). If students are not going to do well, then what? Many drop out and attempt to find a full-time job; others return home to figure out a new plan, but overall this is affecting graduation rates. Murray points out that only those who are interested in getting a liberal education should attend school (Murray 240). Many who do not want to go to college can do well in other fields, such as trade jobs.

The other major factor students must consider when deciding whether to go to college is the cost. In the United States many top ranked public universities cost $20,000 to $30,000 per year in tuition, fees, room and board, and additional personal costs, while at most private colleges a student pays from $50,000 to $65,000. In an article titled "College Calculus: What's the Real Value of Higher Education?" John Cassidy quotes Professor Peter Cappelli, who discusses the burden many families face when attempting to send their children to school. Cappelli reveals that students in college are paying almost four times as much as other students around the world (Cassidy). With the help of financial aid some or most of these costs can be taken care of, but that is just for the select few. Everyone else must either hope to receive local/private scholarships or take out loans. If you are a person from a lower income family, it is nearly impossible to pay for college by yourself. In 2013 the average debt college students graduated with was $27,670 (Snider), and in 2015 it was more than $35,000, the highest ever (Sparshott). If graduates cannot find a job, this serious debt cannot be paid off, which leaves them in more debt due to the interest (Snider). It is a deadly cycle that students do not want to get sucked into.

Even though the cost of college and student debt are major concerns, college has much more to offer than just a degree. In a response to Charles Murray, Kevin Carey argues that college not only exposes students to the skills they will need for the workplace but also helps them better understand the world we live in and how they will fit into it. Carey states that "higher education exposes students to our intellectual and cultural inheritance, to hard-won wisdom and works of surpassing beauty" (Carey). College is grueling for many students, but the benefits of getting a degree today are extremely rewarding. Especially when students can reflect on how much effort they put into learning and see how it helped them become successful. Also, students benefit from many valuable opportunities to grow intellectually that they can only receive by going to a university. The influential 19th Century education philosopher John Henry Newman believed that after our basic human needs are covered, we are destined to go out and seek a higher form of knowledge. We have to discover the beauty of knowledge and how it affects our own world. Since everyone has this God-given capability, we just need the motivation to act on it.

The high cost of college and the high rates of student loan debt should not prevent students from taking advantage of these many benefits of attending college. Government policies can be adopted to help students pay for college and reduce student debt. Programs like the Higher Education Act and Pell Grants, which helped millions of Americans attend college during the 20th Century, can be implemented today to make sure that college remains an option for any student who chooses to attend.

As our nation has changed throughout the years, attitudes about college have changed as well. Today, people cannot live a comfortable lifestyle without having a well paying job, which can be difficult to receive until they get a degree. This is why it is of such great importance that everyone be eligible and have the resources to attend college. Charles Murray stated that "we should not restrict the availability of a liberal education to a rarefied intellectual elite" (Murray 234). We still need universities that are available to the majority of students who want to attend and who are willing to put in the work to succeed. Our country and our universities have done a lot for their students, but now they need to do more.

4
MLA

Works Cited

"Back to School Statistics." *Fast Facts*, National Center for Educational Statistics / Institute of Educational Sciences, nces.ed.gov/fastfacts/display.asp?id=372. Accessed 15 Feb. 2016.

Baum, Sandy. "The Federal Pell Grant Program and Reauthorization of the Higher Education Act." *Journal of Student Financial Aid*, vol. 45, 2015, pp. 23-34.

Brock, Thomas. "Young Adults and Higher Education: Barriers and Breakthroughs to Success." *The Future of Children*, vol. 20, no. 1, Spring 2010, futureofchildren.org/futureofchildren/publications/docs/20_01_06.pdf.

Campbell, Robert, and Barry M. Siegel. "The Demand for Higher Education in the United States, 1919–1964." *The American Economic Review*, vol. 57, no. 3, June 1967, pp. 482-494. *JSTOR*, www.jstor.org/stable/1812115.

Carey, Kevin. "The Best of American Opportunity." *Cato Unbound*, 13 Oct. 2008, www.cato-unbound.org/2008/10/13/kevin-carey/best-american-opportunity.

Cassidy, John. "College Calculus: What's the Real Value of Higher Education?" *The New Yorker*, 7 Sept. 2015, www.newyorker.com/magazine/2015/09/07/college-calculus.

Davis, Alyssa, et al. *The Class of 2015*. Economic Policy Institute, 27 May 2015, www.epi.org/files/2015/the-class-of-2015-revised.pdf.

"History and Timeline." *U.S. Department of Veterans Affairs*, www.benefits.va.gov/gibill/history.asp. Accessed 14 Feb. 2016.

"Income of Young Adults." *Fast Facts*. National Center for Education Statistics / Institute of Education Sciences, nces.ed.gov/fastfacts/display.asp?id=77. Accessed 15 Feb. 2016.

Murray, Charles. "Are Too Many People Going to College?" *"They Say/I Say": The Moves That Matter in Academic Writing, with Readings,* edited by Gerald Graff and Cathy Birkenstein, 3rd ed., W. W. Norton, 2015, pp. 234-53.

Newman, John Henry. "Knowledge Its Own End." *Reading the World: Ideas That Matter,* edited by Michael Austin, 2nd ed., W. W. Norton, 2010, pp. 53-59.

Snider, Susannah. "10 Colleges That Leave Graduates with the Most Student Loan Debt." *US News & World Report,* 17 Feb. 2015, www.usnews.com/education/best-colleges/the-short-list-college/articles/2015/02/17/10-colleges-that-leave-graduates-with-the-most-student-loan-debt.

Snyder, Thomas D., editor. *120 Years of American Education: A Statistical Portrait.* National Center for Educational Statistics, 1993, nces.ed.gov/pubs93/93442.pdf.

Sparshott, Jeffrey. "Congratulations, Class of 2015. You're the Most Indebted Ever (For Now)." *The Wall Street Journal,* 8 May 2015, blogs.wsj.com/economics/2015/05/08/congratulations-class-of-2015-youre-the-most-indebted-ever-for-now/.

4
MLA

MindTap
Reflect on your learning and writing process.

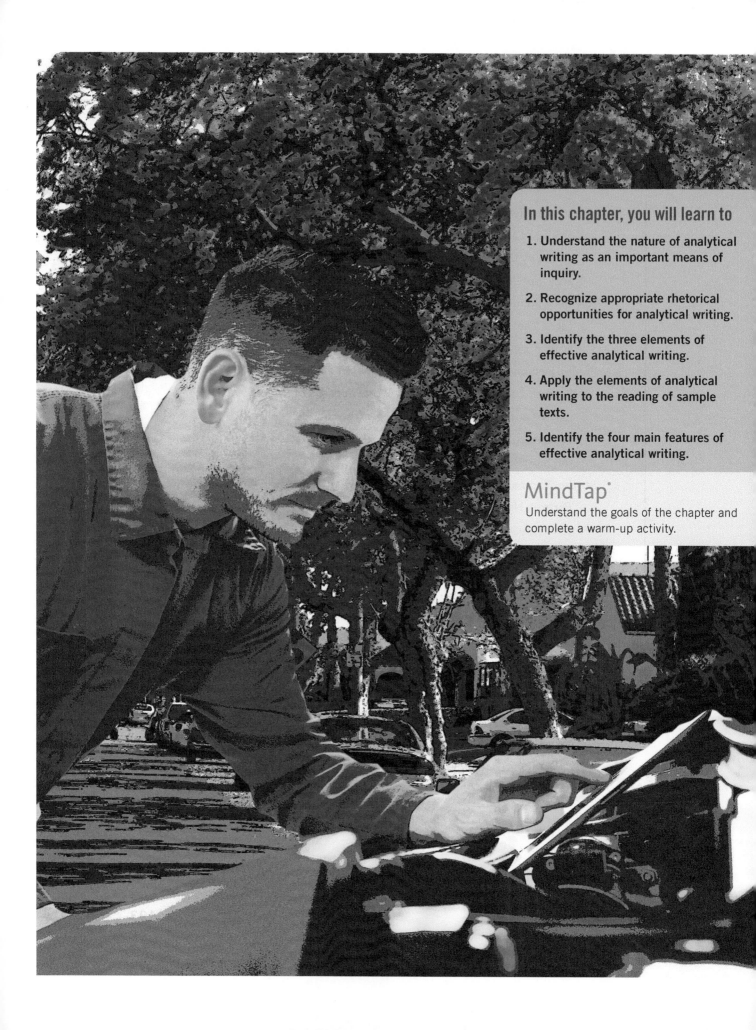

In this chapter, you will learn to

1. Understand the nature of analytical writing as an important means of inquiry.

2. Recognize appropriate rhetorical opportunities for analytical writing.

3. Identify the three elements of effective analytical writing.

4. Apply the elements of analytical writing to the reading of sample texts.

5. Identify the four main features of effective analytical writing.

MindTap®

Understand the goals of the chapter and complete a warm-up activity.

# Understanding Analytical Writing 5

**FOR MANY YEARS** *Car Talk* was one of the most popular shows on American radio. Each week listeners would call in for help solving problems with their cars. Usually, after listening to a caller's description of the problem—say, the car stalls unexpectedly—the *Car Talk* hosts, Tom and Ray, would ask questions: What kind of car is it? How old is it? How many miles are on it? How long has it been stalling? When exactly does it stall? When you're idling at a traffic light? When you first start it up? After you've been driving it for a while? Does it stall in all kinds of weather? Does anyone else drive it? Then Tom and Ray would propose an explanation for the problem. Sometimes they would disagree on the reasons for the problem, and each would present his own explanation based on how he interpreted the information provided by the caller. Their back-and-forth was usually funny, and their efforts to solve their listeners' car troubles were intended to be entertaining. But Tom and Ray didn't just make jokes about car problems to keep their audience engaged; they also used sophisticated analysis to solve problems that matter to their audience. That is, they tried to understand how or why something was happening by carefully examining the situation and considering relevant information.

We use analysis every day to make decisions and solve problems. Even something as mundane as deciding which roads to drive home from school or which bus route to take to campus involves analysis. In making such a decision, we consider many factors, such as time, weather, cost, and circumstances like road construction or traffic. More complicated matters—for example, deciding which college to attend or whether to borrow money to buy a car—might require more sophisticated analysis. But all analysis involves carefully examining an issue, phenomenon, or situation so that you can understand it sufficiently to decide on an appropriate action or draw reasonable conclusions about it. Analysis is an important part of how we live in a complicated world, and it is central to college studies.

## Occasions for Analytical Writing

Analytical writing grows out of a writer's need to understand something better. Effective analytical writing communicates clearly to readers who share the writer's interest in the question or problem being analyzed. A main purpose of all analytical writing is to help interested readers better understand the topic at hand. In a sense, then, analytical writing is a kind of collaborative problem solving by which writers and readers explore questions or problems in their quest for answers or solutions. Consider the following scenarios, in which circumstances prompted students to engage in analytical writing:

❯ AFTER learning in an environmental policy class about the potentially harmful environmental and health impacts of large-scale agriculture, a few students at a college near a large city became concerned about the campus policy to purchase foods from large distributors that transport produce hundreds of miles. When the students approached the food service coordinator about the possibility of buying produce from farms located just outside the city, they were told that such a policy would be too expensive and difficult to implement. The students understood these objections, but they were not convinced that buying food from local farms was not feasible. So they decided to investigate. If such a policy did not save money, would it nevertheless help make the campus "greener"? Would it help the local economy? Would local food be healthier or taste better? Would students be unhappy with changes to the dining hall menus? The students discussed these questions with their instructor and did some research; they also talked to other students about the issue. Their investigation eventually led them to write a letter to their college president proposing a new policy to purchase more locally produced foods for the campus dining hall. Their letter included an analysis of the advantages and disadvantages of such a policy, including a breakdown of potential costs and a discussion of how other students on the campus felt about such a policy.

. . . . . . . . . . . . . . . . . . . . . . . . . . . . . . . . . . . . . . . . . .

❯ JIM, a student at a large state university, began following a discussion on Facebook about the value of college after a classmate informed his Facebook friends that he was leaving college because he could no longer afford it. Jim's classmate did not think borrowing more money to pay for his final few semesters was a good idea. His comment provoked a debate about whether a college degree is worth the cost. Some students wondered whether their degrees would lead to good-paying jobs, which prompted other students to argue that the purpose of college isn't just to prepare students for careers but to educate them as citizens as well. A few students posted links to articles about the rising costs of college tuition as well as average salaries of college graduates compared with those of workers without degrees. Jim followed the discussion closely because of his own concerns about paying for college. To save money, Jim enrolled in a less-expensive community college for two years before transferring to a four-year university. After he posted a message about his decision, someone asked whether Jim received the same quality of education at the community college as he would have had he enrolled for all four years at the university. Jim wasn't sure. As he followed the discussion, he also read the articles that others had posted, found more information about the advantages and disadvantages of two-year college degrees, and posted links to relevant articles on his social media accounts. Eventually, his investigation helped him understand some benefits and costs of attending a two-year college, which he shared on his Facebook page. One of his friends suggested that Jim write an essay about the issue for his old high school newspaper, which Jim did, using his Facebook post as his starting point.

⟩ AMBER, a part-time college student who serves in the National Guard, took a leave of absence from classes because her unit was deployed to Afghanistan for six months. Part of the unit's mission was to build roads and an irrigation system for farmers in a remote region of Afghanistan. Amber was excited about this mission, which she believed would improve the lives of Afghans and relations between Afghans and Americans. However, during her months there, Amber began to realize that the situation was more complicated than she first believed. Many residents feared reprisals from insurgents if they accepted American help. Others worried that new roads would mean more military vehicle traffic. Also, the new irrigation system didn't reach some of the smaller farmers. Cultural and religious differences between Afghans and Americans exacerbated misunderstandings about these projects. All these problems caused Amber to wonder whether the Americans' humanitarian efforts created more problems than they solved. Amber talked to other soldiers about these concerns. She read articles and online discussions to learn more about the complexities of humanitarian aid in Afghanistan. When she returned to the United States, she continued writing a blog that she began in Afghanistan, focusing on her own analysis of the difficulties faced by American units engaged in humanitarian efforts. Her blog attracted many readers, some who shared her concerns and others who challenged her conclusions.

5

In each of these situations, complex questions prompted students to investigate further. In each case,

- **the need to understand an important issue** motivated the students to engage in analysis
- **the desire to communicate what they learned** through their analysis with others motivated the students to write up their analysis in some form

All three of these scenarios illustrate the importance of the rhetorical situation not only in creating a reason for analytical writing but also in shaping the writing itself. The most effective analytical writing addresses the needs of a particular rhetorical situation and communicates to an interested audience what the writer learned as a result of his or her analysis (see Sidebar: "One Writer's Motives for Analytical Writing " on page 128).

Charles C. Mann's award-winning book *1491* examines the state of scientific knowledge about the people who were living in the Americas before Christopher Columbus arrived in 1492. Mann's curiosity about the history of indigenous cultures in North and South America led him to explore a complicated, ongoing controversy about how many people inhabited these continents before Columbus arrived, who they were, and the civilizations they created. His book is an extended analysis of that controversy and how scientists use available archaeological evidence to understand life in the Americas before 1492. In the preface to his book, Mann explains how he came to his subject:

> My interest in the peoples who walked the Americas before Columbus only snapped into anything resembling focus in the fall of 1992. By chance one Sunday afternoon I came across a display in a college library of the special Columbian quincentenary issue of the *Annals of the Association of American Geographers.* Curious, I picked up the journal, sank into an armchair, and began to read an article by William Denevan, a geographer at the University of Wisconsin. The article opened with the question, "What was the New World like at the time of Columbus?" Yes, I thought, what *was* it like? Who lived here and what could have passed through their minds when European sails first appeared on the horizon? I finished Denevan's article and went on to others and didn't stop reading until the librarian flicked the lights to signify closing time.

Source: Mann, Charles C. *1491.* Vintage Books, 2006, p. x.

**EXERCISE 5A**    **EXPLORING OCCASIONS FOR ANALYTICAL WRITING**

1. Think about a decision you had to make about an important situation or problem in your life. For example, perhaps you had to decide whether to renew the lease on your apartment or move to a less expensive apartment with new roommates. Or maybe you decided to change your major or take a semester off to volunteer for an organization like Habitat for Humanity. Write a brief essay in which you describe the situation and explain how you came to your decision. Discuss the factors you considered as you arrived at your decision. Did you do any research—for example, by talking to others for advice or by looking for information on the Internet? What information did you gather? How did you use this information? In other

© Helga Esteb/Shutterstock.com

words, what did you do to analyze this situation? On the basis of this experience, draw conclusions about how you use analysis in your life.

2. Examine an article or essay in a publication you like to read (online or in print) that analyzes a problem or issue of interest to you. Why do you think the writer chose the topic? What kind of analysis did he or she conduct to understand the question or problem at hand? In what ways does the writer address his or her readers with this analysis? Draw conclusions about how useful the analysis is in this case. What makes it worthwhile? What problems do you see?

3. Think about an issue or problem on your campus that interests you. What do you know about the issue or problem? What do you need to know? Now imagine that you were to write an analysis to address that issue or problem. Who would be your audience? What outcome would you hope for if you were to write such an analysis? Write a paragraph describing the problem, the analysis you would write about it, and the audience for that analysis.

# Understanding Analytical Writing in College

Analytical writing is perhaps the most common kind of writing assigned in college classes. The familiar *research paper* is usually an analytical project in which the writer examines an issue or problem and, using appropriate sources, analyzes that issue or problem in a way that is appropriate for that course. For instance, in a psychology course, you might write a paper about gender differences in interpersonal relationships, and part of your task would be to analyze the role of gender in relationships, much as a psychology researcher might do. Your analysis would involve reviewing appropriate sources, such as relevant psychological studies, to understand better how gender plays a role in relationships; it would also involve using psychological concepts or theories to help make sense of interpersonal relationships. Ideally, your paper would demonstrate that you understand those concepts and can apply them to your topic. In this sense, analytical writing is an effective way to learn because, in analyzing a subject like interpersonal relationships, you are likely to think more carefully (and perhaps differently) about that subject and understand it better.

Effective analytical writing in college begins with the desire to understand. Usually, this desire is focused on a complex issue or problem involving a number of different considerations. Analytical writing requires delving into the complexity of a topic by examining available evidence carefully, looking for patterns or trends in that evidence, and drawing reasonable, well-supported conclusions on the basis of the evidence.

In the following sections, we will examine three examples of analytical writing to illustrate these **three elements of effective analytical writing:**

- a desire to understand
- a careful examination of the evidence
- well-reasoned conclusions

All three readings focus on the same general subject—education—but the specific topics are different.

# A Desire to Understand

This first example is from an essay by a distinguished professor who examines the impact of the increasing competition that American students face as they try to get accepted to college. In this excerpt from the beginning of his essay, Mark C. Taylor notices a problem with his students that leads him to a question, which in turn leads to the beginnings of an analysis of the problem:

> Several years ago I was teaching a course on the philosophical assumptions and cultural impact of massive multi-user online games at Williams College. The students in the course were very intelligent and obviously interested in the topic.
>
> But as the semester progressed, I began to detect a problem with the class. The students were working hard and performing well but there was no energy in our discussions and no passion in the students. They were hesitant to express their ideas and often seemed to be going through the motions. I tried to encourage them to be more venturesome with tactics I had used successfully in the past but nothing worked.
>
> One day I asked them what was or, perhaps better, was not going on. Why were they so cautious and where was their enthusiasm for learning? They seemed relieved to talk about it and their response surprised me. Since pre-kindergarten, they explained, they had been programmed to perform well so they could get to the next level. They had been taught the downside of risk and encouraged to play it safe. What mattered most was getting into a good elementary school, middle school and high school so that they would finally be admitted to a top college. Having succeeded beyond their parents' wildest expectations, they did not know why they were in college and had no idea what to do after graduation.
>
> In today's market-driven economy we constantly hear that choice is the highest good and that competition fuels innovation. But this is not always true. Choice provokes anxiety and competition can quell the imagination and discourage the spirit of experimentation that is necessary for creativity. In a world obsessed with ratings, well-meaning parents all too often train their children to jump through the hoops they think will lead to success.

Source: Taylor, Mark C. "The Perils of Being Perfect." *The New York Times*, 12 Sept. 2010, www.nytimes.com/roomfordebate/2010/09/12/why-are-colleges-so-selective/the-perils-of-being-a-perfect-student.

This excerpt reveals that Taylor's analysis of his students' lack of motivation began with his desire to understand something he noticed in his class.

We all have these moments of wondering, driven by a desire to understand something that interests, puzzles, or concerns us:

- Why do my friends prefer Snapchat to Facebook?
- How can parking be made more convenient on campus?
- What makes my dog so afraid of thunder but not of loud noises from the street?
- Why do more students seem to have trouble with math than with history or English?

Such wondering can lead to a kind of informal analysis: talking with friends, reading relevant newspaper articles, seeking information online. In academic writing, however, such wondering is usually shaped by the academic subject being studied, so that certain questions are considered important or relevant and certain ways of exploring those questions are expected. Psychologists, for example, are interested in certain questions about human behavior (Why are some people shy while others are not? How do children learn concepts? What is depression, and what causes it?), while economists are interested in others (Why do some people buy things they don't need? What factors affect the decisions people make about whether to save or spend money? How does family income influence investment decisions?). In this sense, Taylor's question about his students can be viewed as part of a larger conversation among scholars and policymakers in the field of education, and his analysis of that question will be influenced by what others in his field have said about the topic.

## A Careful Examination of the Evidence

The next example also begins with a desire to understand something. Authors Michael McPherson and Morton Schapiro want to know why some Americans are more likely to attend college than others. This question of access to education has been widely studied in the United States, and experts know that several factors, such as family income, affect the ability of different groups of Americans to go to college. Therefore, McPherson and Schapiro can assume that readers of their report, who are likely to be other education researchers or policymakers, are familiar with the idea that family income affects access to college. But because this issue is so complicated, they also know that one factor, such as family income, can't entirely explain the problem, so they have to look more closely at the issue. Here's part of their analysis:

> There are certainly significant financing constraints that contribute to differential higher education access. But there are equally important differences in pre-college preparation. Table 5 looks at college enrollment by family income and mathematics test scores. It shows that students scoring in the top third in math are quite likely to go on to college, especially if they come from families above the 25th percentile in income. Even for students in the lowest quartile, the enrollment rate is 82 percent. However, as test score performance declines, enrollment rates plummet. The decrease is especially large for students from lower income backgrounds—for example, the 82 percent rate for

**TABLE 5** Postsecondary enrollment rates of 1992 high school graduates by family income and math test scores

| Math Test Scores | Lowest Income | Second Quartile | Third Quartile | Highest Income |
|---|---|---|---|---|
| Lowest Third | 48 | 50 | 64 | 73 |
| Middle Third | 67 | 75 | 83 | 89 |
| Top Third | 82 | 90 | 95 | 96 |

Source for table: *Education Pays 2004*, p. 30

those with the highest test scores mentioned above falls to 48 percent when math test scores are in the lowest third. Income clearly plays a role here, but scholastic performance also contributes to explaining college entry.

---

Source: McPherson, Michael S., and Morton Owen Schapiro. "Opportunity in Higher Education." *Reflections on College Access and Persistence*, Advisory Committee on Student Financial Assistance, 2006, www.ed.gov/acsfa.

In this excerpt, McPherson and Schapiro carefully review math test scores of high school graduates from different family income levels, looking for patterns in the scores to explain why some students are more likely to attend college than others. But they don't jump to easy conclusions. Although they acknowledge that family income is a key factor, their analysis indicates that even low-income students who have high math scores are likely to attend college. Obviously, the issue is more complicated than just a matter of family income. Most questions worth analyzing are more complicated than they seem at first glance.

## Well-Reasoned Conclusions

In this next example, education researchers Linda Darling-Hammond and George Wood examine another complicated education issue: determining which government policies are likely to improve education in the United States. They draw conclusions from test scores and other statistical information about students. Like McPherson and Schapiro, Darling-Hammond and Wood also review test scores and family income, but in this case, they compare U.S. students to students from other nations, using scores from the Programme for International Student Assessment (PISA). Notice how they move from an examination of their data to conclusions about the most effective government policies:

> Of nations participating in PISA, the U.S. is among those where two students of different socio-economic backgrounds have the largest difference in expected scores. On this measure of equity, the U.S. ranked 45th out of 55 total countries, right above Brazil and Mexico. On the PISA assessments in reading, math, and science, for example, the distance between the average score for Asian and white students, on the one hand, and Hispanic and Latino students, on the other, is equal to the distance between the United States average and that of the highest scoring countries.
>
> In all these content areas, U.S. students from all groups do least well on the measures of problem-solving. These data suggest, first, that the United States' poor standing is substantially a product of unequal access to the kind of intellectually challenging learning measured on these international assessments. In addition, U.S. students in general, and historically underserved groups in particular, are not getting sufficient access to the problem-solving and critical thinking skills needed to apply this knowledge in a meaningful way.
>
> The reason for these disparities is not a mystery. The United States not only has the highest poverty rates for children among advanced nations with the fewest social

supports, it also provides fewer resources for them at school. America is still at risk in large measure because we have failed to ensure access to education and basic family supports for all of our children.

---

Source: *Democracy at Risk: The Need for a New Federal Policy in Education.* Forum for Education and Democracy, 2008, www.forumforeducation.org/sites/default/files/u48/FED%20FINAL%20 REPORT.pdf.

In the first paragraph of this excerpt, the authors review data that reveal inequities in test performance among U.S. students of different socio-economic and racial backgrounds. In the second and third paragraphs, they conclude from their analysis that many American students do poorly on international tests because their family income prevents them from having access to high-quality education.

Because most topics for analysis in academic subjects are so complex, writers rarely offer easy answers or simple solutions. Instead, they reach conclusions that are well supported by their analysis of available data—and sometimes they raise new questions.

# Doing Analysis

So far we have explored reasons for conducting an analysis, and we have looked at examples of analysis in academic work. But what exactly does it mean to analyze something? This section gives you practice in three important kinds of intellectual tasks that are usually part of the process of analysis:

- using a framework to analyze something
- making reasonable claims on the basis of available data or information
- supporting claims

## Using a Framework to Analyze Something

Analysis often involves applying some kind of framework—a theory, a principle, or a set of criteria—to help explain or understand a problem, event, trend, or idea. For example, in psychology a writer might use the theory of behaviorism to explain the actions of children in a school lunchroom. An economist might use the principle of supply and demand to analyze prices of iPhones. For a theater arts class, students might use specific technical criteria to analyze the cinematography of chase scenes in action films. (See the flowchart on the next page.)

The use of a framework helps illuminate what is being analyzed by focusing attention on specific elements, questions, or issues. For example, using technical criteria to analyze chase scenes in action films can help us understand how a director used camera angles, lighting, and editing to provoke certain reactions in viewers.

To be effective, frameworks must be applied appropriately. Students sometimes simply refer to a theory or principle rather than actually use it for analysis. For example, in this excerpt from an

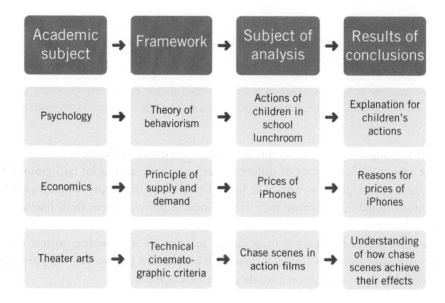

essay about teaching philosophies, the student attempts to apply a theory of teaching (proposed by education scholars Gerald Grant and Christine Murray) to explain the philosophy of a specific teacher (Ms. Jones):

> Ms. Jones' teaching philosophy stresses the importance of being connected with her students and the community. "When I first started teaching, I didn't understand my students' behavior or home life. I still don't," she said. "The more I learn about my students, the better idea I have of how I can relate to them." Living in the urban community where her school is located has given Ms. Jones certain insights about her students. For example, she is aware that her students are regularly exposed to gangs, drugs, and violence as well as rich cultural traditions. Her first-hand experience with the community has given Ms. Jones an opportunity to learn about her students. "Teachers must be part detective and part researcher, shifting clues children leave, collecting data, testing hypothesis and looking unblinkingly at the way children really are . . . in order to fill out and make credible the story of their growth and development." (Grant & Murray, 1999, p. 35)

In this case, the student refers to Grant and Murray's theory of effective teaching but does not use it to help readers understand Ms. Jones' teaching philosophy. To *apply* Grant and Murray's theory, the student writer should have used each of the key ideas of that theory (e.g., the teacher as detective and the teacher as researcher) to explain why Ms. Jones teaches as she does. To be helpful, a theory should be used as a "lens" to help readers see more clearly whatever is being analyzed.

Here's an example in which a student analyzes a writer's experience as a biracial woman by using a psychological theory. In an article published in a scholarly journal in psychology, Carmen Braun Williams describes her struggles with her own sense of identity as a woman whose mother is white and whose father is African American. In the following excerpt, the student uses a theory of racial identity development developed by a scholar named W. S. Carlos Poston to explain part of Williams' experience:

> In her article, Carmen Braun Williams suggests that race is a socially constructed category that has been misconstrued as biological (Williams 34). She explains how a biracial person such as herself is confronted by the problem of not fitting neatly into the socially constructed racial categories of "White" and "Black." Williams describes her experience as a child, when she was unself-conscious and unaware of these racial categories, after her family moved to the U.S. in the 1950s: "I was around eight years old when I first started noticing that my parents were often subjected to intense scrutiny by passers-by. I started hearing ugly words kids shouted at us from their porches as we walked past" (33). These incidents led to Williams realizing that her "entire being was reduced to one thing: 'not White'" (33).
>
> Williams' experience is consistent with W. S. Carlos Poston's first stage in his model of racial identity development. According to Poston, during this first stage, which he calls "Personal Identity," "The child will tend to have a sense of self that is somewhat independent of his or her ethnic background" (Poston 153). This was the case for Williams. "As a child," she writes, "I was blissfully unaware of my difference"; however, her "innocence . . . was shattered by racism" (Williams 33). As Poston notes, "Individuals at this stage are often very young, and membership in any particular ethnic group is just becoming salient" (Poston 153). Accordingly, Williams' awareness of her own biracial identity was "just becoming salient" as a result of her experiences after her family moved to the U.S.

Notice how this student applies the framework—in this case, Poston's theory of racial identity development—directly to Carmen Braun Williams' experiences as a biracial woman in order to explain those experiences. Poston's theory becomes a way for us to better understand Williams' experiences, which is what a framework should do.

---

### EXERCISE 5B | USING FRAMEWORKS FOR ANALYSIS

The following passage is an excerpt from a 2015 report titled "Social Media Usage: 2005–2015" from the Pew Research Center:

> Across demographic groups, a number of trends emerge in this analysis of social media usage:
>
> - **Age differences: Seniors make strides**. Young adults (ages 18 to 29) are the most likely to use social media—fully 90% do. Still, usage among those 65 and older has more than tripled since 2010 when 11% used social media. Today, 35% of all those 65 and older report using social media, compared with just 2% in 2005.
> - **Gender differences: Women and men use social media at similar rates**. Women were more likely than men to use social networking sites for a number of years, although since 2014 these differences have been modest. Today, 68% of all women use social media, compared with 62% of all men.

*(Continued)*

- **Socio-economic differences: Those with higher education levels and household income lead the way**. Over the past decade, it has consistently been the case that those in higher-income households were more likely to use social media. More than half (56%) of those living in the lowest-income households now use social media, though growth has leveled off in the past few years. Turning to educational attainment, a similar pattern is observed. Those with at least some college experience have been consistently more likely than those with a high school degree or less to use social media over the past decade. 2013 was the first year that more than half of those with a high school diploma or less used social media.
- **Racial and ethnic similarities:** There are no notable differences by racial or ethnic group: 65% of whites, 65% of Hispanics and 56% of African-Americans use social media today.

Source: Perrin, Andrew. *Social Media Usage: 2005-2015*. Pew Research Center, 8 Oct. 2015, www.pewinternet.org/2015/10/08/social-networking-usage-2005-2015/.

Using this report as a framework, analyze the way a specific group of people—for example, your family members, students who live in your dormitory, or members of a club to which you belong—use social media. Try to explain their uses of social media in terms of the research on different demographic groups that is cited in this article.

# Making Reasonable Claims on the Basis of Available Information

Analysis requires examining and interpreting information in a way that leads to reasonable claims or assertions. One of the most common mistakes students make in analysis is going too far in making claims on the basis of available information—that is, making assertions that are not supported by the evidence at hand. Here's one example of a student making that mistake:

> According to one study, boys tend to associate their academic performance with skills and effort while girls associate it with luck (Grossman and Grossman, 1994). My concern is with the implications of such research. Other studies suggest that American students attribute academic success to ability and intelligence, whereas in other nations, such as Japan, students attribute academic success to effort (Kitayama and Cohen, 2007). Therefore, either there was a paradigm shift in the effort by American boys and girls or the data are false.

In this excerpt, the writer reviews two bodies of research that seem to contradict each other. The student draws two possible conclusions from this apparent contradiction: (1) that there must have been a change (a "paradigm shift") in the way American boys and girls perceive the role of effort in academic success, or (2) that the data are somehow incorrect. Neither conclusion is necessarily supported by the available information. It is possible that the attitudes of American students did change, but we can't know for certain on the basis of the two studies cited. Nor does it follow that the apparent contradiction in the two studies means that the results of the studies were incorrect. In fact, there are many possible explanations for the contradiction between the studies. For example, the studies might have examined very different student populations, or they might have used different methods (surveys, interviews, and so on). In addition, the studies might have treated gender differences differently. Given the information provided in this excerpt, we have no way of knowing whether the two studies were even examining the same thing. (For example, one study might have focused on gender differences in a specific subject area such as math, whereas the other study might have investigated student attitudes in general.)

All these possibilities suggest that the matter is too complex and the available information too limited for the claims the student makes. Given the limited information provided, the student should revise these claims. For example, it is reasonable to claim that student attitudes about the reasons for academic success seem to vary by gender as well as by nation. Such a limited claim is supported by the information provided.

The point is that you should make only those claims that reasonably emerge from your information or that can be clearly supported by your data. Here's an example of a writer doing just that. In this excerpt from a book about diet and health, the author reviews the evidence for the widespread belief that a lack of fiber in one's diet can be a factor in developing diseases of the digestive tract, including colon cancer:

> Over the past quarter-century . . . there has been a steady accumulation of evidence refuting the notion that a fiber-deficient diet causes colon cancer, polyps, or diverticulitis, let alone any other disease of civilization. The pattern is precisely what would be expected of a hypothesis that simply isn't true: the larger and more rigorous the trials set up to test it, the more consistently negative the evidence. Between 1994 and 2000, two observational studies—of forty-seven thousand male health professionals and the eighty-nine thousand women of the Nurses Health Study, both run out of the Harvard School of Public Health—and a half-dozen randomized control trials concluded that fiber consumption is unrelated to the risk of colon cancer, as is, apparently, the consumption of fruits and vegetables. The results of the forty-nine-thousand-women Dietary Modification Trial of Women's Health Initiative, published in 2006, confirmed that increasing the fiber in the diet (by eating more whole grains, fruits, and vegetables) had no beneficial effect on colon cancer, nor did it prevent heart disease or breast cancer or induce weight loss.

Source: Taubes, Gary. *Good Calories, Bad Calories: Challenging the Conventional Wisdom on Diet, Weight Control, and Disease.* Alfred E. Knopf, 2007, pp. 132–33.

5

The author's purpose is to determine whether a high-fiber diet has specific health benefits, as many health care professionals and researchers have long claimed. Notice that he emphasizes that the best available studies do not support prevailing conclusions about the health benefits of eating fiber; moreover, he limits his claim to what he can reasonably support on the basis of the few available studies, asserting only that the hypothesis about specific health benefits of a high-fiber diet, such as lower rates of colon cancer, is not borne out by these studies. He does not say that eating fiber isn't beneficial; rather, he concludes that eating fiber does not lead to lower colon cancer rates and similar health benefits.

Remember to say only what your information allows you to say. Make sure your claims and assertions are reasonable given the information you have.

---

## EXERCISE 5C   MAKING REASONABLE CLAIMS

These charts present data on income and wealth distribution in the United States. For each of the following claims, determine whether the claim can be made on the basis of the data reflected in the charts; if not, revise the claim so that it is supported by the data in the charts:

1. In the past three decades, the rich have become richer while the poor have become poorer.
2. Since 1980, the incomes of the wealthiest Americans have risen more rapidly than those of other Americans.
3. College has become less affordable for all but the wealthiest Americans.
4. Economic recessions don't significantly affect income growth in the United States.

### Income gains at the top dwarf those of low- and middle-income households

Percent change in real after-tax income since, 1979

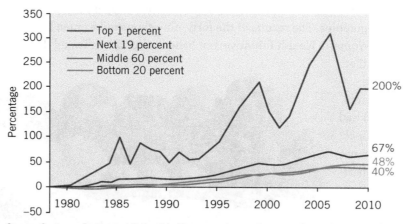

Source: Center on Budget and Policy Priorities, www.cbpp.org/income-gains-at-the-top-dwarf-those-of-low-and-middle-income-households-0.

*(Continued)*

---

## Tuition growth has vastly outpaced income gains

Inflation-adjusted average tuition and fees at public four-year institutions and income for select groups (1973 = 100%)

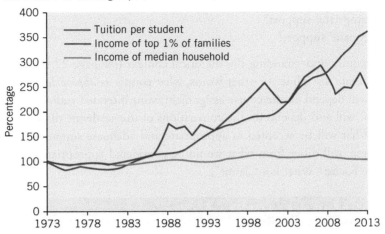

Source: Center on Budget and Policy Priorities, www.cbpp.org/tuition-growth-has-vastly-outpaced-income-gains.

## Nonfarm business sector: Real compensation per hour

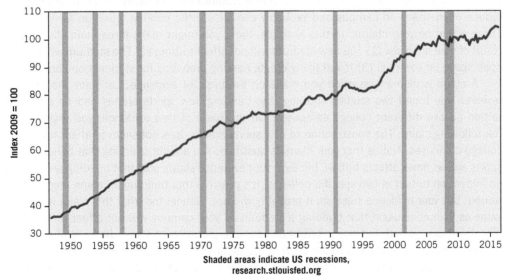

Shaded areas indicate US recessions,
research.stlouisfed.org

Source: United States, Bureau of Labor Statistics. *Nonfarm Business Sector: Real Compensation Per Hour* [COMPRNFB]. FRED, Federal Reserve Bank of St. Louis, research.stlouisfed.org/fred2/series/COMPRNFB. Accessed March 4, 2016.

# Supporting Claims

When it comes to supporting claims in analytical writing, writers must consider two important questions:

- What is "appropriate" support?
- What is "adequate" support?

Both questions require understanding the rhetorical context (see page 27 in Chapter 2), which includes the academic discipline. In other words, what counts as *appropriate* and *adequate* support for a claim will depend on the course assignment, your intended audience, and the purpose of your project; it will also depend on the conventions of the academic discipline within which you're writing. What will be accepted as appropriate and adequate support in a chemistry lab report, for example, will differ from what would be considered appropriate and adequate for a history paper (see Focus: "What Is a Claim?").

---

**FOCUS    WHAT IS A CLAIM?**

A claim in analytical writing is a statement or assertion you make as a result of your analysis. For example, if you are analyzing the impact of a proposed new football stadium on your campus, you might examine whether the cost of the new facility will affect tuition, increase traffic on campus, complicate parking, or reduce open space that students currently use for various activities. Your research might reveal that a new stadium will not likely affect tuition but will reduce open space on campus and probably complicate the parking situation for students. Those would be your claims. In this example, then, you might make three main claims as a result of your analysis: (1) The new stadium will not affect tuition; (2) The stadium will reduce open space on campus; (3) It will likely create parking problems for students on campus.

A claim is also an assertion you make on the basis of evidence. Let's say that in your research you found two studies showing that building new sports arenas had no effect on tuition on two different college campuses. On the basis of that evidence, you might make the following claim: The construction of new sports arenas does not seem to affect tuition on college campuses. Notice that your claim is qualified: You are not claiming that building new sports arenas *never* affects tuition, because your evidence shows only that building arenas had no impact on tuition at two specific colleges. It's possible that building an arena *might* affect tuition, but your evidence suggests it probably will not. Notice, too, that this claim is not the same as your conclusion that building a stadium on your campus will not affect tuition. The two claims are related, but one is based on your interpretation of a specific body of evidence (two studies) and the other is based on your overall analysis of various kinds of evidence.

One last point: A claim is not the same thing as an opinion. In this case, you are making a *claim* about the possible impact of building a sports stadium on tuition at your college. Your *opinion* might be that building the stadium is a bad idea, but for this analysis, that opinion might not be relevant. What matters is what your analysis reveals as you try to address the research question about what effect building the stadium might have on your campus in general. You make your claims on the basis of that analysis. Although your analysis might influence your opinion, your claims and your opinion are not the same thing.

Consider the following criteria as you decide whether your support for a claim is appropriate and adequate:

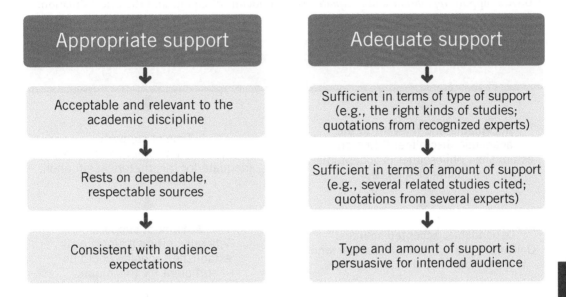

| Appropriate support | Adequate support |
|---|---|
| Acceptable and relevant to the academic discipline | Sufficient in terms of type of support (e.g., the right kinds of studies; quotations from recognized experts) |
| Rests on dependable, respectable sources | Sufficient in terms of amount of support (e.g., several related studies cited; quotations from several experts) |
| Consistent with audience expectations | Type and amount of support is persuasive for intended audience |

To some extent, the decision about whether support for a claim is appropriate and adequate is subjective. Not all readers will agree that a writer has sufficiently supported a claim, even when those readers have similar backgrounds and expectations, but you can try to anticipate whether your support is sufficient by considering the expectations your audience is likely to have for your rhetorical situation.

Let's look at a political scientist supporting a claim effectively in an essay, written for a scholarly journal, about the value of civility in modern society:

> Because we are all members of the same political community, interacting on grounds of civic equality, we have an obligation to be polite in our everyday interactions with our fellow citizens. In the linguistic analogy developed by the philosopher Michael Oakeshott, civility is a kind of "adverbial" restraint on the civic language we speak with one another. In the same way that one is enjoined to speak politely, modestly or temperately, the adverbial condition of civility modifies and qualifies conduct without specifying its content. We can communicate our wishes or injunctions to fellow citizens—whatever those wishes may be—so long as we agree to subscribe to common conditions on the means we may legitimately use in the pursuit of those self-chosen ends (Oakeshott, 1990, pp. 120–121, 126 and 128; see also Boyd, 2004a). Membership is defined in terms of this common moral relationship and it is this relationship that in turn gives rise to our responsibility to be civil to others.

Source: Boyd, Richard. "The Value of Civility?" *Urban Studies*, vol. 43, no. 5–6, May 2006, p. 864.

The author, Richard Boyd, states his claim in the first sentence of this excerpt. To support his claim, he refers to an analogy by an influential philosopher (Michael Oakeshott). To what extent is Boyd's support *appropriate* and *adequate* for his academic discipline and rhetorical situation?

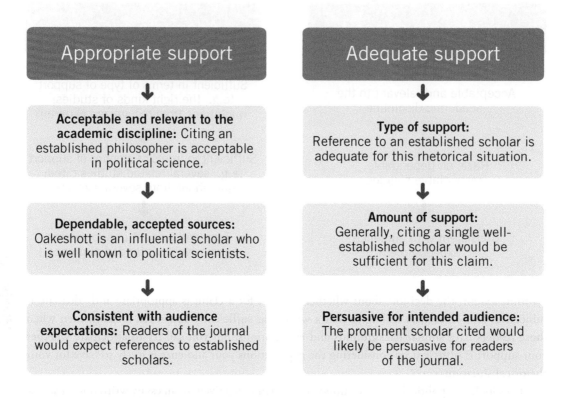

| Appropriate support | Adequate support |
|---|---|
| ↓ | ↓ |
| **Acceptable and relevant to the academic discipline:** Citing an established philosopher is acceptable in political science. | **Type of support:** Reference to an established scholar is adequate for this rhetorical situation. |
| ↓ | ↓ |
| **Dependable, accepted sources:** Oakeshott is an influential scholar who is well known to political scientists. | **Amount of support:** Generally, citing a single well-established scholar would be sufficient for this claim. |
| ↓ | ↓ |
| **Consistent with audience expectations:** Readers of the journal would expect references to established scholars. | **Persuasive for intended audience:** The prominent scholar cited would likely be persuasive for readers of the journal. |

This example illustrates the importance of the rhetorical context in supporting claims. Although some readers might disagree, it is likely that most readers in Boyd's discipline (political science) would find his support for his claim reasonable.

Deciding what kind of information you need to support a claim and how much support is enough can be confusing. In the following excerpt from an essay written for a general writing course, the student tries to make a claim about the reasons for a certain community's economic struggles. In the beginning of the paragraph the student provides statistical data to support a claim that the community's economic status might be the result of its "low educational achievement." But then she makes a further claim about additional causes of the community's economic struggle. The assignment called for an analysis that would be appropriate for a general audience (for example, readers of the local newspaper):

One could argue that because of the low educational achievement in this community, the socioeconomic status is relatively low. Thirty-two percent of the adults in the area did not complete secondary education. Twenty-three percent of the population in this district are below poverty level and 35.7% make under $25,000 (the per capita income is $15,272, according to the U.S. Census Bureau, 2000). However, other factors cause this village to struggle economically. First, there are not many high-paying job opportunities.

This area's industry consists primarily of manufacturing (17.2%); education, health and social services (19.9%); and recreation and accommodation (16.6%) (U.S. Census Bureau, 2000). There are four main institutions that provide jobs for this community: the Big Mountain Resort, a state prison, the school district, and a regional hospital. A small percentage of the population (3.6%) owns private businesses (U.S. Census Bureau, 2000).

The statistical evidence the student provides in the second and third sentences of this paragraph is insufficient to support the claim in the first sentence (that low educational achievement is the cause of the community's low economic status). That statistical evidence indicates that significant percentages of the residents have not finished high school and have low incomes, but the evidence does not show that the high rate of high school incompletion explains or causes low income. So the writer looks to other statistical evidence to try to explain the community's economic struggles—for example, the kinds of jobs available there and the percentage of the population that own private businesses. But do the figures actually support her claim about the likely causes of the community's economic status? For one thing, the percentage of specific kinds of jobs (manufacturing, service, and so on) tells us nothing about the number of "high-paying" jobs. For another, the small percentage of people who own private businesses does not necessarily mean low-paying jobs. Jobs in a private business can be low-paying or high-paying, and jobs in the public sector, such as in education, can also be both. In the end, although the writer provides a lot of statistical information that seems appropriate, it is not exactly relevant to her claim nor is it sufficient to support that claim:

5

| Appropriate support | Adequate support |
|---|---|

**Acceptable and relevant to the academic discipline:** The kind of support seems acceptable for the rhetorical situation but not relevant to the claim.

**Type of support:** Statistical information on jobs, income, and education is appropriate, but the specific information is inadequate for the claim.

**Dependable, accepted sources:** Census Bureau is a dependable source.

**Amount of support:** Too little support that is directly relevant to the claim is provided.

**Consistent with audience expectations:** A general audience would likely expect more relevant information for the specific claim.

**Persuasive for intended audience:** Although the kind of data is likely persuasive for a general audience, readers might not find the data sufficient to support the claims.

**EXERCISE 5D** | **SUPPORTING A CLAIM WITH APPROPRIATE AND ADEQUATE INFORMATION**

Use the criteria described in this section to identify sufficient support for each of the following claims. For each claim, list two or three kinds of evidence or information that you think would provide appropriate support (for example, a specific kind of statistical information, a certain kind of study, the views of a certain kind of expert, etc.). The basic rhetorical situation is described in parentheses after each claim.

1. The economic benefits of a college degree outweigh the costs of tuition. (letter to the editor of the campus newspaper)

2. Religion is an important component of American politics. (analytical paper for a political science course)

3. Popular films suggest that racist attitudes persist in the United States. (review for a film class)

# Features of Analytical Writing

The examples earlier in this chapter illustrate **four main features of effective analytical writing:**

1. **A relevant topic worthy of analysis.** Academic fields are defined by certain bodies of knowledge (for example, the periodic table in chemistry, the nature of human emotion in psychology) and by the kinds of questions or problems that experts in those fields examine (What happens when two substances from the periodic table are combined? Why are some people more likely to suffer from depression than others?). So identifying a worthy topic for analysis requires knowing what kinds of questions are relevant in a specific field and what is known about those questions. The best analytical writing grows out of questions that are genuinely interesting to the writer and relevant to readers. Considering whether your topic might interest other students in your class or other readers familiar with that academic subject is an important step toward determining whether the topic is worthy of analysis.

2. **Complexity.** Rarely are interesting questions or problems as straightforward as they might seem. Good analysis, therefore, is about exploring complexity and trying to understand a question, problem, trend, event, or idea more fully by examining it in depth. Good analytical writing requires a measure of objectivity and even skepticism to avoid oversimplified explanations. It should help readers appreciate and grasp the complexity of a topic.

3. **Sufficient and appropriate evidence and support.** Effective analytical writing involves finding sufficient information about a topic and gathering appropriate evidence to support claims and conclusions. How much information is *sufficient* depends on the topic, the rhetorical situation, and the depth of analysis. Similarly, what counts as *appropriate* evidence depends on the subject, the expectations of the audience, the purpose of the analysis, and the field of study. The right kind of information and evidence can lead to more effective analysis.

4. **Reasonable conclusions.** Because most topics in academic writing are complex, writers must interpret the information they find and draw reasonable conclusions supported by relevant evidence. In good analytical writing, writers resist the temptation to settle on seemingly obvious conclusions. Instead, they examine possibilities and draw conclusions that their readers should find reasonable on the basis of available information and evidence.

All good analytical writing shares these characteristics. Let's look at how one writer employs these features of analysis effectively.

In the following essay, well-known sociolinguist Deborah Tannen examines why hairstyles seem to be such a point of contention among mothers and their daughters. Tannen's essay was published in 2015 in *The American Prospect*, a magazine devoted to politics and culture. It demonstrates strategies that are widely used in any analytical writing.

## MindTap®

Read this analysis. Highlight and take notes online. Additional readings are also available online.

· · · · · · · · · · · · · · · · · · · · · · · · · · · · · · · · · · ·

### Talking About This Reading

**Mark Fenlon (student):** This essay includes many concepts and definitions from linguistics and other fields. It's hard to make sense of the main point when I'm struggling to keep up with all this new information. How can I keep track of the analysis and the terms being defined?

**Bob Yagelski:** Mark, you have begun to answer your own question. Your challenge is following the author's analysis at the same time you are learning unfamiliar terms and concepts. So separate your reading into steps. First, try to get an overall sense of the author's main point by skimming the article. Second, identify and define unfamiliar terms. (Take notes for both steps.) Once you have done so, reread the article more carefully. (Chapter 19 describes this strategy in more detail.)

· · · · · · · · · · · · · · · · · · · · · · · · · · · · · · · · · · ·

## Why Mothers and Daughters Tangle Over Hair
### by Deborah Tannen

1   "Do you like your hair that long?" my mother asked soon after I arrived for a visit. I laughed. Looking slightly hurt, she asked why I was laughing. "I've been interviewing women for the book I'm writing about mothers and daughters," I explained, "and so many tell me that their mothers criticize their hair." "I wasn't criticizing," my mother said, and I let it drop. Later in my visit I asked, "So Mom, what do you think of my hair?" Without missing a beat, she replied, "I think it's a little too long."

2    I wasn't surprised by any of this, because my mother always thought my hair was too long. I'd taken to getting a haircut shortly before visiting my parents, sometimes the very morning before I boarded a plane to Florida. But that never made a difference. I could count on her telling me my hair was too long.

3    While talking to women for the book *You're Wearing THAT?: Understanding Mothers and Daughters in Conversation*, I collected a cornucopia of mothers' remarks on their daughters' hair. Many of these comments were more overtly critical than my mother's, such as "Comb your hair. The birds will make a nest in it." Some were both overt and indirect: "You did that on purpose?" Sometimes the wolf of criticism came dressed in the sheep's clothing of a compliment: "I love your hair when it's pushed back off your face," said when her daughter's hair was falling forward onto her face, or "I'm so glad you're not wearing your hair in that frumpy way anymore."

4    Sometimes it wasn't criticism that frustrated women so much as the focus on hair instead of matters the daughters thought more important. During a presidential campaign season, a journalist interviewed both candidates for president. When her mother asked, "How did it go?" she began an enthusiastic account of the interviews. "No," her mother interrupted, "I mean at the hair salon. What style did you settle on? Did you put it up or leave it down?" Another woman told me that after she appeared on television standing behind the president of the United States in a bill-signing ceremony, her mother's comment was, "I could see you didn't have time to cut your bangs."

5    I came to think of the subjects about which mothers (and daughters) were critical as the big three: hair, clothes, and weight. I always thought of them in that order, because hair was the subject of the largest number of remarks repeated to me, and, it seemed, the most unnerving.

6    Why? Why so much preoccupation with hair? I first asked myself this question years ago, while taking part in a small academic conference at which each participant—eight men and four women—gave a brief presentation. As I listened to one of the women give her talk, I was distracted by her hair, which seemed intentionally styled to render her half-blind. When she looked down to read her paper, thanks to a side part and no bangs, a curtain of hair fell clear across her face, completely covering one eye. As she read aloud, she kept reaching up to push the hair off her face, but it immediately fell right back, a result she ensured by stopping short of hooking it behind her ear. She must have believed that pinning her hair behind her ear would spoil its style.

**A Relevant Topic Worthy of Analysis**
In the opening paragraphs, Tannen poses a question that she believes her readers will find worth analyzing: Why is there such preoccupation with women's hair? Her question, which grows out of her own experience as well as her observations of other women, leads to her analysis, which can be seen as part of a larger conversation about the role of gender in contemporary life.

7    After catching myself concentrating on the speaker's hair rather than her talk, I scanned the room to check out the other two women's

hairstyles. One, the youngest among us, had long, frosted blond hair that cascaded over her shoulders—an effect she enhanced by frequently tossing her head. The third woman had dark brown hair in a classic style that, I thought to myself, was a cross between Cleopatra and Plain Jane.

8    Then I wondered why I was scrutinizing only the women; what about the men? A glance around the room made the answer obvious: Every one of the men had his hair cut short, in no particular style. There could have been a man with a ponytail or a thick wavy mane or long hair falling below his ears. But there wasn't. All the men had chosen neutral hairstyles. What, I asked myself, would be a comparably neutral hairstyle for a woman? Then I realized: There's no such thing.

9    I came to think of this contrast in terms of a concept from linguistics, my academic field: The men's choices were "unmarked," but any choice a woman makes is "marked"; that is, it says something about her. Here's how linguistic markedness works. The "unmarked" forms of most verbs in English communicate present tense. To communicate past tense, a speaker "marks" a verb by adding something. For example, you can take the verb *visit* and mark it for *past* by adding -*ed* to make *visited*. Similarly, the unmarked forms of most nouns in English are singular, such as *toy*. To make the word plural, you add -*s* to get *toys*. Like a present-tense verb or a singular noun, a man can have a hairstyle that is "unmarked"—that is, neutral; it doesn't tell you anything about him except that he's male. But any choice a woman makes carries extra meaning: It leads observers to conclude something about the type of person she is. That's why I titled an essay on this subject "There Is No Unmarked Woman."

10    The concept of markedness helps explain many mothers' seemingly excessive concern with so apparently superficial a topic as their daughters' hair. They are thinking of how others will interpret their daughters' character. That concern was explicit in one mother's warning that no one would take her daughter seriously if she didn't style her hair more carefully: "If they see someone with loose ends in their hair, they'll think you have loose ends in your life."

11    Mothers aren't the only ones who are inclined to be critical of women's hair (as well as their clothes and weight). Because the range of hairstyles from which a woman must

**Complexity**
In **paragraphs 7, 8, and 9**, Tannen begins to delve into the complexity of her seemingly straightforward question about hairstyles, indicating that the question really has to do with gender. She also introduces the concept of "linguistic markedness," which she uses as a framework for her analysis.

**Sufficient and Appropriate Evidence and Support**
In **paragraph 10** and elsewhere in her essay, Tannen relies on experiences that we all share to explore and support her main assertion. She is essentially asking her readers to think carefully about their own experiences with and views about hairstyles as evidence for her claims. Using experience in this way is not unusual in analytical writing and can be an effective way for a writer to help readers understand the analysis and to persuade them of the validity of the writer's claims.

5

choose is vast, the chances that anyone—especially another woman—will think she made the best choice are pretty slim. How often do you look at a woman and think, She would look better if her hair were longer, shorter, curlier, straighter, pushed back, pulled forward, colored, not colored, dyed a different color, highlighted or not, more fashionably styled, just differently styled? We think these things but we don't say them. A mother, however, often feels that she has a right if not an obligation to say something, because it's her job to ensure that things go as well as possible for her daughter.

12    There is yet another layer to all this: Women's and girls' hair (as well as clothes and weight)—indeed, the preoccupation with women's appearance more generally—is inextricably intertwined with sex. Our very notion of "woman" entails sexuality in a way that our notion of "man" does not. A woman who is not attractive is dismissed, and being deemed attractive requires being sexy—but not too sexy, because that would lead to her being dismissed in a different way. Furthermore, the line between too sexy and not sexy enough is a fine one and is located differently by different observers, so there is no way a woman can be certain of getting it just right. This criterion drives many, if not all, fashion choices: how short or long a skirt or dress should be; how tight-fitting and shape-showing slacks, tops, or dresses should be; how much skin is revealed, what body parts are glimpsed or displayed. And hair is an essential element in this sexual equation.

> **Complexity**
> In **paragraphs 11 and 12**, Tannen adds "another layer" to her analysis of our preoccupation with hairstyles: the role of sex, which complicates how people react to women's hairstyles. In this way, Tannen explores her subject's complexity and avoids oversimplified explanations.

> **Sufficient and Appropriate Evidence and Support**
> In **paragraph 12**, Tannen uses an example from the Orthodox Jewish tradition (and her own family history) to support her claim about "the connection between exposing hair and seeking to attract men."

13    Hair, in short, is a secondary sex characteristic: Like breasts and the distribution of body fat that gives women a curvy shape, more head hair (and less facial hair) is one of the physical features distinguishing the sexes that begin to appear during puberty, signaling sexual maturity. Enhancing and drawing attention to secondary sex characteristics can be a way of emphasizing sexual attractiveness. Thus, hair so abundant that it partially covers a woman's face can be sexy, and more hair can be sexier than less. That is the aesthetic that drives "big hair," and the anxiety that underlies the concept of a "bad-hair day." And that is the reason why many societies require women to cover, hide, or remove their hair. The connection between exposing hair and seeking to attract men is explicit in the Orthodox Jewish tradition by which women cut off their hair when they marry, as my grandmother did in the early 1900s Hasidic Jewish community of Warsaw. (My father was told that when his mother was having her head shaved in preparation for her wedding, her younger sisters, who had abandoned orthodoxy, pounded on the door, begging her not to let them do it; she later regretted having acquiesced and let it grow back.)

14    This tradition came to mind when I asked an Arab woman whether mothers in her country comment on their daughters' appearance. She replied that a common mother-to-daughter remonstrance would be, "I can see hair"—a way to admonish a daughter to tighten her headscarf. Though the requirement to wear headscarves might seem at first very different from the "freedom" to expose hair, these seemingly opposite customs are really two sides of the same coin, divergent ways of managing men's responses to this secondary sex characteristic: on one hand, precluding it by hiding hair; on the other, capitalizing on it by displaying hair in as alluring a style as possible.

15    While I was working on this essay, my phone rang. It was my cousin Elaine calling. "I'm visiting my mother," she began. I was concerned, because I knew that her mother had recently been discharged from the hospital after a life-threatening illness. Elaine continued, "'What do you think was the first thing she asked me?" Still living in this essay, I offered, half-joking, "Was it about your hair?" "Yes!" she exclaimed. "That is what she asked! I had been here maybe ten minutes when she said, 'Don't you think you need a haircut?'"

16    "You won't believe this," I said, and then read her the first paragraph of this essay.

17    After we both laughed at the uncanny similarity, Elaine continued, "I'm trying to assert myself now that I'm 60, so I told her, 'I just had it cut!'" She explained that she'd made sure to do that because her mother always thinks her hair is too long. At that I read her the second paragraph of this essay.

18    After more shared laughter, Elaine resumed her account. Her mother kept returning to the topic: "Are you sure you don't think it would be better shorter?" and "We have to go to my hairdresser." Elaine capitulated: "I was in her house for less than half an hour before she was whisking me off, walker and all, to her hair salon!" But Elaine drew the line at cutting her hair; she submitted only to having it blow-dried. Then she questioned her own sanity when, upon hearing her mother say, "Now you're a pleasure to look at," she heard herself say: "Maybe it would have been better shorter."

**Sufficient and Appropriate Evidence and Support**
In **paragraphs 14 through to 17**, Tannen uses an anecdote support her claims about the importance women place on their hair. Anecdotes can be appropriate evidence in academic writing, but usually academic audiences expect other kinds of evidence, such as statistical data or quotations from scholarly texts (see "Supporting Claims" on pages 140–144). In this case, however, because Tannen was writing for a more general audience, she did not cite scholarly sources, which would be expected for a scholarly journal.

5

**Reasonable Conclusions**
In **paragraph 18**, Tannen interprets what she has learned through her analysis. She concludes that the desire for acceptance is an important part of the reason for women's preoccupation with their hair. In analytical writing, conclusions and interpretations must be supported by available evidence.

19    After we laughed together, our conversation turned serious. Wondering aloud why her mother's concern with her hair bothered her so much, Elaine said, "It's a symbol of lack of acceptance." Without doubt, that's part of why we all react so strongly to perceived criticism, no matter how subtle, from our mothers—and why many of us are so quick to perceive criticism in any comment or, for that matter, gesture (like reaching out to brush hair off our faces) or facial expression ("I didn't say anything"; "But you had that look"). There is an exquisite irony—a perfect relationship storm, you might say—between daughters and mothers. Because girls and women are judged by appearance, mothers want their daughters to look as attractive as possible. But any suggestion for improvement implies criticism. And therein lies the irony: For mothers, the person to whom you most want to offer helpful suggestions is the one most likely to resist and resent them; for daughters, the person you most want to think you're perfect is the one most likely to see your flaws—and tell you about them.

20    My cousin then told me something I hadn't known: Her mother hated her own hair, because her mother had told her it was ugly. Indeed, Elaine's mother had gone to medical school to ensure she'd be able to support herself, because her mother had led her to believe she was too unattractive to count on getting married. How, Elaine wondered, could her mother not see that she was doing to her daughter just what her own mother had done to her? There are many ways to answer that question. One is that Elaine's mother wanted to make sure her daughter didn't suffer the same fate, by making sure she was attractive. Another is that she was doing what many women do: Both mothers and daughters often regard each other as reflections of themselves and consequently look at each other with a level of scrutiny that they otherwise reserve for themselves. For mothers, especially, that isn't entirely irrational: They are held responsible for their daughters in a way that fathers are not. Someone who disapproves of a girl's appearance will often think, Why did her mother let her go out looking like that?

**Complexity**
Tannen's analysis focuses on how gender norms influence attitudes about appearance in general and hairstyles in particular. In **paragraph 19** she examines another factor: relationships between mothers and daughters. By showing that mothers "are held responsible for their daughters in a way that fathers are not" Tannen avoids oversimplifying her analysis and shows that differences in how men and women think about hairstyles have to do with gender roles, sexuality, and familial relationships.

**Reasonable Conclusions**
In her final three paragraphs Tannen concludes her essay with speculation about what her analysis means for women. Notice that although she offers some advice, she qualifies it by using adverbs such as "maybe" (paragraph 20) and "perhaps" (paragraph 21), and in her brief concluding paragraph (paragraph 22) she leaves her readers with a somewhat ambiguous statement regarding her mother's criticisms of her own hairstyle (which she relates in her opening paragraph). Such ambiguity can result when a writer has carefully analyzed a complex topic and has reached no straightforward conclusions.

21    Maybe it doesn't matter what mothers' motives are. The challenge for daughters is deciding how to respond. I always chuckle when recalling the woman who told me she silenced her mother by saying, "My lifetime interest in the topic of my hair has been exhausted."

22    Or perhaps more important than figuring out what to say in response to perceived criticism is how to stop feeling bad about it. Women tell me it helps to realize that criticizing and caring are expressed in the same words. That way, a daughter can shift her focus from the criticizing to the caring. This often happens automatically after our mothers are gone, or when we fear losing them. One woman told me of getting a call that her mother had been hospitalized. Full of worry and fear, she caught a plane and rushed to the hospital right from the airport. Distressed to see her mother with an IV bag attached to her arm and an oxygen tube in her nose, she approached the bedside and leaned over to give her a kiss. Her mother looked up at her and said, "When's the last time you did your roots?" Rather than reacting with her usual annoyance, the daughter heaved a sigh of relief: Her mother was OK.

23    As for me, it is now nearly a decade since my mother died. Several years ago, I began getting my hair cut shorter. My mother was right: It does look better this way.

5

## Questions to Consider:

1. How well do you think Tannen's analysis answers her main question about why women are preoccupied with hairstyles? What main factors does she identify in her analysis to help explain this preoccupation? Does her analysis sufficiently explain it, in your view? Why or why not? What might your answer to these questions suggest about you as an audience for this essay?

2. Assess Tannen's use of evidence in this essay. What kinds of evidence does she use to examine women's preoccupation with hairstyles? Why do you think she chose these specific kinds of evidence? Do you find her use of evidence persuasive? Why or why not? What other kinds of evidence might she have cited to support her claims and further her analysis?

3. What conclusions does Tannen draw from her analysis about the importance of hairstyles among women? Do you think her analysis sufficiently leads to these conclusions? Explain, citing specific passages from her essay to support your answer.

4. Tannen uses the concept of "linguistic markedness" as a framework for her analysis (see paragraph 9). What advantages do you think this framework offers her in her analysis? What conclusions about hairstyles does she draw from her use of this framework? How effective do you find her use of this framework in explaining our preoccupation with hairstyles?

MindTap®
Reflect on your understanding of analytical writing.

## In this chapter, you will learn to

1. Define causal analysis and understand its purpose and uses.

2. Identify appropriate rhetorical opportunities for writing causal analysis.

3. Identify and apply the four main features of analytical writing to sample causal analyses.

4. Create a causal analysis essay, applying the four main features of causal analysis and using the Ten Core Concepts from Chapter 3.

## MindTap®

Understand the goals of the chapter and complete a warm-up activity.

# Examining Causes and Effects

6

**WE ROUTINELY ENCOUNTER** situations in our daily lives that raise questions about causes or effects. For example, maybe you've noticed that you seem to have more energy during pick-up basketball games if you've eaten a light lunch. You wonder, Is there a connection between what you eat and how you feel during exercise? So you pay attention to what you eat on days when you play basketball, you ask a friend about her eating habits before exercising, and you look online for information about the impact of diet on exercise. You are trying to determine the effect of your diet on your exercising so that you can decide what and when to eat on the days you work out. Analyzing causes and effects in this way can help us make decisions and solve problems.

In more formal causal analysis, the purpose is usually to identify possible causes or effects in order to understand an event, phenomenon, or trend; to explain a social, economic, or political development; or to develop a solution to a complex problem:

- An economist examines whether a certain federal policy affects how people invest their money.
- A biologist studies the side effects of a new medication.
- A psychologist analyzes the impact of social media on peer-group relationships among teens.
- A political scientist measures the effect of negative ads on the outcome of a political campaign.

Such analyses rarely boil something down to a single cause or effect, but they can help explain a phenomenon, event, trend, development, or outcome. Because of this capacity to illuminate complex matters, causal analysis is essential in academic work.

## Occasions for Causal Analysis

In *Born to Run*, a book about the physiology, history, and practice of running, author Christopher McDougall tells his readers that the book began with a single question: "Why does my foot hurt?" As a life-long runner, McDougall was frustrated by chronic running-related injuries and began to investigate why he—and most other avid runners—suffer so many injuries. His book is an investigation into the causes of injuries among runners and the effects of various approaches to running. McDougall's inquiry led him to discover the practice of barefoot running, which some studies suggested results in fewer injuries than running with modern running shoes. After examining those studies and the barefoot running movement, he concluded that running with shoes is a primary cause of injury among avid runners.

Circumstances or an experience can trigger a question that points to causes or effects about something that matters to the writer and to others. McDougall wondered what caused his running injuries, and his analysis was of great interest to the thousands of other runners who shared his worries about injury. In this sense, causal analysis can be a means of solving problems. McDougall wanted to avoid injury, but he first had to understand what was causing his injuries. His analysis was driven by his need to understand something; that understanding became the basis for his decisions about how best to run.

The need to answer a question about why something happens is often the starting point for effective causal analysis. In addition, college writing assignments often provide opportunities to analyze causes or effects:

- A biology lab report might describe an experiment that examines the effects of a specific hormone on the growth pattern of tadpoles.
- For a business class, students might investigate whether low-interest loans to small businesses help create jobs in their communities.
- A paper for a psychology class might examine the impact of bullying on self-esteem among teens.
- An assignment in an art history class might ask students to explore the factors that led to the Impressionist movement.

Like McDougall's book about barefoot running, such assignments usually begin with a relevant question about why something happens. The analysis is driven by the writer's curiosity about the causes or effects of something that matters.

---

### EXERCISE 6A   OCCASIONS FOR CAUSAL ANALYSIS

1. Make a list of four or five questions that seem to point to causes and effects. For example, does drinking coffee really keep me up at night? Why does college tuition increase faster than inflation? The questions on your list should be about issues or activities that matter to you.

2. Select one or two questions from your list and try to identify the possible causes and effects implied by the question.

3. For each question on your list, identify an audience who might be interested in the answer to the question. Write a sentence or two explaining why that audience would care about the answer to the question.

---

# Understanding Causal Analysis

Identifying causes and effects demands care to avoid simplistic explanations. In many cases, causes or effects might seem obvious, but often there is greater complexity than meets the eye. For example, many people believe that the widespread use of text messaging has caused students' spelling skills to erode. At first glance, texting does seem to be a reasonable explanation for poor spelling among young people, but a closer look reveals that many other factors—including the schools students attend, the nature of the writing instruction they receive, students' socio-economic backgrounds, their early experiences with reading and writing—can influence how well (or how poorly) a student spells.

Analyzing causes or effects requires exploring a topic sufficiently in order to determine whether a cause-effect relationship is real. In order to pinpoint texting as a cause of poor spelling, for example, a writer would have to establish, first, that spelling skills have in fact diminished as texting has increased. The writer would also have to find out how widespread texting is among students and how much time most students spend texting as compared to other kinds of writing, making sure that the evidence is trustworthy and convincing. In addition, other possible causes would have to be investigated: for example, the kind of writing instruction students usually receive; how much attention spelling is given in schools; whether students' experiences with reading and writing outside schools have an impact on spelling; and so on. All these factors complicate the picture and make it likely that texting alone does not explain poor spelling in student writing.

---

**FOCUS** | **CAUSATION VS. CORRELATION**

Perhaps the most common mistake in causal analysis is confusing correlation for causation. For example, some studies have shown that children who watch a lot of television are more likely to have behavior problems in school. Some people might conclude from such studies that watching too much TV causes children to act out. But in fact the studies did not establish that watching TV for so many hours a day actually causes behavior problems; rather, the studies identified a *correlation* between watching a certain amount of TV and certain kinds of behaviors. The *causes* of those behaviors were not identified. It's possible that the children who watched a lot of TV had other factors in common that might have contributed to their behaviors, such as less adult supervision, fewer opportunities to interact with other children, or even a certain kind of diet. Correlation might *suggest* the causes of something, but it doesn't *prove* them.

6

---

**EXERCISE 6B** | **UNDERSTANDING CAUSE AND EFFECT**

1. Identify an issue that interests you involving causes or effects. For example, you might be concerned about an increase in the ticket prices of sporting events at your school and wonder why those prices have risen. In a brief paragraph, describe the issue or situation and identify what you believe are the main causes or effects involved. Explain why you believe specific causes or effects are significant in this case. Describe any evidence you might have for your views about those causes and effects.

2. In a group of classmates, share the paragraphs you wrote for Question #1. Discuss each person's views about causes and effects in the issue they examined. Do you agree with each person's list of possible causes and effects? Why or why not? As a group, try to identify in each case possible explanations that the writer might have missed. What conclusions about causal analysis might you draw from this exercise?

*(Continued)*

3. Identify a current controversy that seems to involve disagreements about causes and effects. (For example, the debate about gun control in the U.S. often focuses on the question of whether stricter gun ownership regulations will reduce gun violence.) Find several articles or editorial essays about the controversy and examine how the writers discuss causes and effects by addressing the following questions: Do the writers discuss specific causes and effects? Do they oversimplify the issue in identifying specific causes and effects? Do they mistake causation for correlation? In a brief paragraph, describe the controversy and the articles or essays you examined and draw conclusions about the usefulness of causal analysis in addressing such controversies.

# Reading Causal Analysis

This section includes several examples of causal analysis that illustrate **the four main characteristics of effective analytical writing** as discussed in Chapter 5:

| | |
|---|---|
| A relevant topic worthy of analysis | • How does the writer establish this topic as worthy of analysis?<br>• What is the writer's purpose in examining these causes and effects?<br>• Why should readers want to understand the causes and effects examined by the writer? |
| Complexity | • How thoroughly does the writer explore each possible cause or effect?<br>• What possible alternative explanations for the phenomenon being analyzed does the writer consider, if any?<br>• Does the analysis avoid oversimplifying the subject? |
| Sufficient information and appropriate analysis | • How does the writer's causal analysis explain the phenomenon being analyzed? Does this analysis sufficiently explain the phenomenon?<br>• What evidence does the writer present? Is this evidence appropriate for this topic? Does it support the writer's claims and conclusions sufficiently? |
| Reasonable conclusions | • What conclusions about the phenomenon does the writer reach through this causal analysis?<br>• Do these conclusions grow logically out of the analysis?<br>• How persuasive are these conclusions in explaining the phenomenon? |

## The Flight From Conversation
### by Sherry Turkle

*As the use of technologies like smartphones has increased in recent years, scholars, educators, policymakers, and others have debated the impact of these technologies on everything from how adolescents spell to how people date to the nature of privacy. In this essay, which was published in the* New York Times *in 2012, Sherry Turkle, one of the world's foremost experts on the impact of technology on human relationships, joins the debate. During her career as a researcher, Turkle, the Abby Rockefeller Mauzé Professor of the Social Studies of Science and Technology at the Massachusetts Institute of Technology, has studied not only how people use technology to conduct their social lives but also how these technologies affect the way we relate to each other and even how we understand ourselves. In particular, Turkle has examined how social media and various forms of online interactions have affected our very sense of identity as human beings. Like most aspects of human life, communication is extremely complicated, and identifying specific cause-and-effect relationships between, say, social media and identity is difficult at best. However, Turkle's extensive research has led her to conclude that some of the effects of our uses of mobile devices like smartphones to manage our social lives are detrimental. As you'll see in this essay, she uses her own causal analysis of such devices to raise concerns about how humans relate to each other. Her essay illustrates how causal analysis can be a tool for addressing some of the most challenging human problems.*

### Talking About This Reading

**Nisha Bell (student):** "I found this article interesting because I just wrote an essay on texting. I think it's ridiculous the way that most of us have avoided face-to-face conversation."

**Bob Yagelski:** Our own experiences and perspectives influence how we respond to a writer's ideas. In this case, Nisha's own views about the impact of social media helped make Turkle's essay more engaging and relevant. But even when we don't have strong feelings about the subject of a reading, we can see its broader relevance. Turkle's essay is about important technological and social developments that affect all of us, which makes her essay worth considering carefully. It can help us understand the world we live in today.

We live in a technological universe in which we are always communicating. And yet we have sacrificed conversation for mere connection.

At home, families sit together, texting and reading e-mail. At work executives text during board meetings. We text (and shop and go on Facebook) during classes and when we're on dates. My students tell me about an important new skill: it involves maintaining eye contact with someone while you text someone else; it's hard, but it can be done.

Over the past 15 years, I've studied technologies of mobile connection and talked to hundreds of people of all ages and circumstances about their plugged-in lives.

*(Continued)*

I've learned that the little devices most of us carry around are so powerful that they change not only what we do, but also who we are.

We've become accustomed to a new way of being "alone together." Technology-enabled, we are able to be with one another, and also elsewhere, connected to wherever we want to be. We want to customize our lives. We want to move in and out of where we are because the thing we value most is control over where we focus our attention. We have gotten used to the idea of being in a tribe of one, loyal to our own party.

Our colleagues want to go to that board meeting but pay attention only to what interests them. To some this seems like a good idea, but we can end up hiding from one another, even as we are constantly connected to one another.

A businessman laments that he no longer has colleagues at work. He doesn't stop by to talk; he doesn't call. He says that he doesn't want to interrupt them. He says they're "too busy on their e-mail." But then he pauses and corrects himself. "I'm not telling the truth. I'm the one who doesn't want to be interrupted. I think I should. But I'd rather just do things on my BlackBerry."

A 16-year-old boy who relies on texting for almost everything says almost wistfully, "Someday, someday, but certainly not now, I'd like to learn how to have a conversation."

In today's workplace, young people who have grown up fearing conversation show up on the job wearing earphones. Walking through a college library or the campus of a high-tech start-up, one sees the same thing: we are together, but each of us is in our own bubble, furiously connected to keyboards and tiny touch screens. A senior partner at a Boston law firm describes a scene in his office. Young associates lay out their suite of technologies: laptops, iPods and multiple phones. And then they put their earphones on. "Big ones. Like pilots. They turn their desks into cockpits." With the young lawyers in their cockpits, the office is quiet, a quiet that does not ask to be broken.

In the silence of connection, people are comforted by being in touch with a lot of people—carefully kept at bay. We can't get enough of one another if we can use technology to keep one another at distances we can control: not too close, not too far, just right. I think of it as a Goldilocks effect.

Texting and e-mail and posting let us present the self we want to be. This means we can edit. And if we wish to, we can delete. Or retouch: the voice, the flesh, the face, the body. Not too much, not too little—just right.

Human relationships are rich; they're messy and demanding. We have learned the habit of cleaning them up with technology. And the move from conversation to connection is part of this. But it's a process in which we shortchange ourselves. Worse, it seems that over time we stop caring, we forget that there is a difference.

We are tempted to think that our little "sips" of online connection add up to a big gulp of real conversation. But they don't. E-mail, Twitter, Facebook, all of these have their places—in politics, commerce, romance and friendship. But no matter how valuable, they do not substitute for conversation.

Connecting in sips may work for gathering discrete bits of information or for saying, "I am thinking about you." Or even for saying, "I love you." But connecting in sips doesn't work as well when it comes to understanding and knowing one another. In conversation we tend to one another. (The word itself is kinetic; it's derived from words that mean to move, together.) We can attend to tone and nuance. In conversation, we are called upon to see things from another's point of view.

Face-to-face conversation unfolds slowly. It teaches patience. When we communicate on our digital devices, we learn different habits. As we ramp up the volume and velocity of online connections, we start to expect faster answers. To get these, we ask one another simpler questions; we dumb down our communications, even on the most important matters. It is as though we have all put ourselves on cable news. Shakespeare might have said, "We are consum'd with that which we were nourish'd by."

And we use conversation with others to learn to converse with ourselves. So our flight from conversation can mean diminished chances to learn skills of self-reflection. These days, social media continually asks us what's "on our mind," but we have little motivation to say something truly self-reflective. Self-reflection in conversation requires trust. It's hard to do anything with 3,000 Facebook friends except connect.

As we get used to being shortchanged on conversation and to getting by with less, we seem almost willing to dispense with people altogether. Serious people muse about the future of computer programs as psychiatrists. A high school sophomore confides to me that he wishes he could talk to an artificial intelligence program instead of his dad about dating; he says the A.I. would have so much more in its database. Indeed, many people tell me they hope that as Siri, the digital assistant on Apple's iPhone, becomes more advanced, "she" will be more and more like a best friend—one who will listen when others won't.

During the years I have spent researching people and their relationships with technology, I have often heard the sentiment "No one is listening to me." I believe this feeling helps explain why it is so appealing to have a Facebook page or a Twitter feed—each provides so many automatic listeners. And it helps explain why—against all reason—so many of us are willing to talk to machines that seem to care about us. Researchers around the world are busy inventing sociable robots, designed to be companions to the elderly, to children, to all of us.

One of the most haunting experiences during my research came when I brought one of these robots, designed in the shape of a baby seal, to an elder-care facility, and an older woman began to talk to it about the loss of her child. The robot seemed to be looking into her eyes. It seemed to be following the conversation. The woman was comforted.

And so many people found this amazing. Like the sophomore who wants advice about dating from artificial intelligence and those who look forward to computer psychiatry, this enthusiasm speaks to how much we have confused conversation with connection and collectively seem to have embraced a new kind of delusion that accepts the simulation of compassion as sufficient unto the day. And why would we want to talk about love and loss with a machine that has no experience of the arc of human life? Have we so lost confidence that we will be there for one another?

We expect more from technology and less from one another and seem increasingly drawn to technologies that provide the illusion of companionship without the demands of relationship. Always-on/always-on-you devices provide three powerful fantasies: that we will always be heard; that we can put our attention wherever we want it to be; and that we never have to be alone. Indeed our new devices have turned being alone into a problem that can be solved.

When people are alone, even for a few moments, they fidget and reach for a device. Here connection works like a symptom, not a cure, and our constant, reflexive impulse to connect shapes a new way of being.

Think of it as "I share, therefore I am." We use technology to define ourselves by sharing our thoughts and feelings as we're having them. We used to think, "I have a

*(Continued)*

feeling; I want to make a call." Now our impulse is, "I want to have a feeling; I need to send a text."

So, in order to feel more, and to feel more like ourselves, we connect. But in our rush to connect, we flee from solitude, our ability to be separate and gather ourselves. Lacking the capacity for solitude, we turn to other people but don't experience them as they are. It is as though we use them, need them as spare parts to support our increasingly fragile selves.

We think constant connection will make us feel less lonely. The opposite is true. If we are unable to be alone, we are far more likely to be lonely. If we don't teach our children to be alone, they will know only how to be lonely.

I am a partisan for conversation. To make room for it, I see some first, deliberate steps. At home, we can create sacred spaces: the kitchen, the dining room. We can make our cars "device-free zones." We can demonstrate the value of conversation to our children. And we can do the same thing at work. There we are so busy communicating that we often don't have time to talk to one another about what really matters. Employees asked for casual Fridays; perhaps managers should introduce conversational Thursdays. Most of all, we need to remember—in between texts and e-mails and Facebook posts—to listen to one another, even to the boring bits, because it is often in unedited moments, moments in which we hesitate and stutter and go silent, that we reveal ourselves to one another.

I spend the summers at a cottage on Cape Cod, and for decades I walked the same dunes that Thoreau once walked. Not too long ago, people walked with their heads up, looking at the water, the sky, the sand and at one another, talking. Now they often walk with their heads down, typing. Even when they are with friends, partners, children, everyone is on their own devices.

So I say, look up, look at one another, and let's start the conversation.

Source: Turkle, Sherry. "The Flight from Conversation." *The New York Times*, 21 Apr. 2012, nyti.ms/1wTAafi.

## EXERCISE 6C    ANALYZING THE FLIGHT FROM CONVERSATION

1. What, specifically, is the problem or phenomenon Turkle is analyzing? How does she establish this problem or phenomenon as a relevant topic for analysis? Do you find her analysis relevant? What might your answer to that question suggest about you as a member of Turkle's audience for this essay?

2. In the third paragraph of this essay Turkle writes that as a result of her own research she has learned that mobile devices like smartphones "are so powerful that they change not only what we do, but also who we are." What does she mean by that statement? What evidence does she present to support that claim? Do you find this evidence persuasive? Why or why not?

3. In Turkle's view, what are the implications of the ways in which contemporary humans communicate through social media and mobile devices? Why is she worried about these developments? Do you think her analysis gives her reason to be worried? Explain.

## Everyone's Gone Nuts:
## The Exaggerated Threat of Food Allergies
### by Meredith Broussard

*Many people have questions about the effects of eating certain foods and the causes of food-borne illnesses. In the following piece, writer Meredith Broussard examines the apparent increase in food allergies in the U.S. She asks a common question: What causes food allergies? Broussard's strategy for presenting her analysis is uncommon. Her "essay," which appeared in 2011 as a two-page spread in* Harper's *magazine, is actually a series of annotations to a pamphlet from an organization called The Food Allergy and Anaphylaxis Network (FAAN). Each annotation is in effect an analysis of one aspect of the issue of food allergies, with the annotation on the top-left serving as the introduction and the one on the lower-right as the conclusion. Broussard's essay illustrates the importance of the medium (Core Concept #3) and also reminds us that form is driven by the writer's purpose (Core Concept #6).*

. . . . . . . . . . . . . . . . . . . . . . . . . . . . . . . . . . . . . . . . .

### Talking About This Reading

**Katie Foss (student):** "I found this reading very interesting, because so many parents are concerned about food allergies today. However, the acronym "FAAN" shows up very frequently, and it started to sound repetitive."

**Bob Yagelski:** "FAAN" is an acronym for "Food Allergy and Anaphylaxis Network," a long name that can easily cause a reader to stumble. Writers often use acronyms to make their prose easier for readers. In this case, "FAAN" is much less distracting than "Food Allergy and Anaphylaxis Network," but Katie is probably noticing the acronym because it is so unfamiliar. In such cases, try to ignore it and focus instead on the writer's ideas. That strategy might seem simple, but it can help you get past the distraction.

**6**

---

**EXERCISE 6D**    **ANALYZING EVERYONE'S GONE NUTS**

1. What conclusions does Broussard reach about the causes of food allergies? Do you find these conclusions surprising? Why or why not? How well do you think her conclusions are supported by her analysis?

2. What kinds of information does Broussard rely on to support her claims? How persuasive do you find her support?

3. How effective do you find Broussard's strategy for presenting her analysis? What are the advantages and disadvantages of annotating a pamphlet to analyze it? Do you think her analysis would be more or less effective if it were presented in a conventional essay format? Explain.

# EVERYONE'S

## The exaggerated threat of food

Of little concern to most parents or educators only a generation ago, food allergies are now seen as a childhood epidemic. The American Academy of Pediatrics recently began recommending that peanuts be withheld until a child turns three; hundreds of food-allergy nonprofits and local parents groups have formed; and six states have passed laws requiring food-allergy safety measures in their schools, with similar legislation currently being considered in Congress. Children are even being recruited to help battle this supposed threat, as in this Food Allergy & Anaphylaxis Network (FAAN) brochure, which enjoins young students to "Be a PAL" and protect the lives of their classmates. But the rash of fatal food allergies is mostly myth, a cultural hysteria cooked up with a few key ingredients: fearful parents in an age of increased anxiety, sensationalist news coverage, and a coterie of well-placed advocates whose dubious science has fed the frenzy.

One of the first and most influential of the food-allergy nonprofits, FAAN has successfully passed off as fact its message that food allergies have become more prevalent and dire. Since 2005, more than 400 news stories have used FAAN's estimates that allergic reactions to food send 30,000 Americans to emergency rooms each year and that 150 to 200 ultimately die. The group derived these figures from a 1999 study of a rural Minnesota community, in which 133 people over a five-year period were determined to have suffered anaphylaxis—an allergic reaction that can mean everything from going into shock to developing an itchy mouth. Yet only nine people in the study ever required hospitalization for anaphylaxis from any cause. As for the death estimate, just one person died of anaphylactic shock, prompted not by food allergies but by exercise. The Centers for Disease Control and Prevention, in its most up-to-date figures, recorded only 12 deaths from food allergies in all of 2004. When asked about these statistical discrepancies, FAAN founder and CEO Anne Muñoz-Furlong said focusing on any number misses the point: "One child dying from food allergies is too many."

In 2005, every major American media outlet covered the story of a teenager who died after kissing a boy who earlier in the day had eaten a peanut-butter sandwich. This "kiss of death" confirmed for countless nervous parents their worst fears: food-allergic children were in constant danger—they could "even die!" as FAAN warns here—from any sort of secondhand exposure to certain foods. (In a press release soon after the girl's death, FAAN instructed food-allergic teens to tell "that special someone that you can die.... Don't wait for the first kiss.") But there is simply no evidence that a food allergen can do serious harm if not ingested. Nicholas Pawlowski, an allergist at Children's Hospital of Philadelphia, says he occasionally has to spread peanut butter on a patient's arm to demonstrate to parents that their child will not die from casual contact with a nut. In the case of the peanut-butter kiss, a coroner later ruled, to no fanfare, that the girl had smoked pot soon before the embrace and actually died from an asthma attack.

No one knows exactly why, but more and more kids are becoming allergic to certain foods. Especially peanuts, tree nuts, milk, eggs, soy, wheat, fish, and shellfish.

Sometimes, if they eat even a tiny amount of the food they're allergic to, they can become very ill ... even die!

That's why kids who have food allergies need all of us to help keep them safe. You too can help, and if you do a good job, you could become a PAL Hero and receive a special certificate.

Here are some of the ways you can Be a PAL: Protect A Life

Be a PAL

A PAL Hero is someone whose
allergic reaction, or even save a life.
Allergy & Anaphylaxis Network (F
Heroes with special recognition an
might be you!
Just looking out for our frien
however, makes us all heroes. Som
forget how to be a PAL... and P

BE

Prote
From F

For more Informa
The Food Alle
17... Les Jackson Me
(800) 929-

# GONE NUTS

llergies, *by Meredith Broussard*

In addition to offering certificates to "PAL Heroes," FAAN presents individuals and businesses with a service award named after Muñoz-Furlong's daughter, a former food-allergic child who, like most people, grew out of her allergies. Anne Muñoz-Furlong says she founded FAAN when her community didn't seem to believe the threat to her child was real. Her organization and others have certainly helped to change the perception of food allergies. (A recent *Newsweek* cover showing a pigtailed girl in a gas mask with a carton of milk in one hand and a peanut-butter sandwich in the other is typical of much recent coverage.) But all we know for certain now is that more parents *think* their children suffer from food allergies. Indeed, even the best allergy tests produce high rates of false positives, and most studies of childhood prevalence interview no one under the age of eighteen. Ken Kochanek, a CDC statistician, says there are far too few recorded incidents of anaphylactic shock triggered by food allergies to draw any sound epidemiological conclusions: "We can't find any hard data that supports the severity."

These hugging forms evoke a better world in which we all look out for our food-allergic friends. Such chumminess already exists within the world of food-allergy advocacy. The FAAN children's website was built using a donation from Dey, the distributor of the EpiPen adrenaline injector; Dey and Verus Pharmaceuticals, the maker of EpiPen's chief competitor, sponsor FAAN's major annual fundraising event. (As part of its safety guidelines, FAAN suggests carrying an adrenaline injector at all times and regularly renewing the prescription.) Just about all the leading food allergists also have ties to FAAN or the Food Allergy Initiative (FAI), an organization prone to even more extreme rhetoric. This intimacy helps explain why suspect statistical findings get published. For instance, the coauthors of an oft-cited study on the dangers facing food-allergic children at restaurants were Anne Muñoz-Furlong's husband, who serves as a top FAAN executive, and a FAAN medical-board member whose research is funded in part by FAI. The latter is also an editor at the leading allergy journal where the study appeared; the journal's editor-in-chief is head of FAI's medical board.

There is no question that food allergies are real. Yet instead of creating the healthy, happy children shown here, exaggerating the threat may actually do as much harm as the allergies themselves. The peril is now perceived as so great that psychosomatic reactions to foods and their odors are not uncommon. Recent surveys have also shown that children thought to have food allergies feel more overwhelmed by anxiety, more limited in what they believe they can safely accomplish, than even children with diabetes and rheumatological disease. One study documented how food-allergic youths become terror-stricken when inside places like supermarkets and restaurants, since they know that allergens are nearby. Such psychological distress is exacerbated by parents, who report keeping their children away from birthday parties and sending them to school in "No Nuts" T-shirts. Having been fed a steady diet of fear for more than two decades, we have become, it appears, what we eat. ∎

*Meredith Broussard is a writer living in Philadelphia.*

ANNOTATION   65

Source: Broussard, Meredith. "Everyone's Gone Nuts: The Exaggerated Threat of Food Allergies." *Harper's*, Jan. 2008, pp. 64–65.

## The Reign of Recycling
### by John Tierney

*In the opening sentence of the following essay,* New York Times *columnist John Tierney writes, "If you live in the United States, you probably do some form of recycling." But although recycling is generally thought to be a good thing, how many Americans really think about its impact? Tierney asks us to do just that. He wants us to consider whether recycling actually helps our communities and protects the environment, as proponents claim. To answer that question, he presents a careful analysis of the both the costs and benefits of recycling and, drawing on statistical data, he examines the social, economic, and environmental effects of recycling. You won't read too far into this essay before realizing that Tierney is making an argument against recycling as a way to protect the natural environment. In that regard, his essay, which was published in the* New York Times *in 2015, is a good example of how a writer can use careful, in-depth causal analysis to support a position and make a case for a particular approach to a complex problem. In this case, Tierney advocates a special garbage tax as a better way to reduce waste and lower carbon emissions into the atmosphere. His analysis provides a compelling rationale for such a tax as an alternative to recycling programs. Whether you agree with him or not, his analysis raises important questions about environmental protection and exposes the complexity of something (recycling) that many of us might take for granted.*

. . . . . . . . . . . . . . . . . . . . . . . . . . . . . .

### Talking About This Reading

**Coreen Christel (student):** "This essay was very interesting, but I feel that the author neglected the topic of single-stream recycling. Does this practice make any difference in cost effectiveness, carbon footprints, etc.?"

**Bob Yagelski:** Coreen's question underscores how important it is for a writer to define his or her terms. In this case, Tierney does not distinguish among different methods of recycling. When a reading raises a question like this, reread the text to see whether you missed something. In paragraph 23, for example, Tierney writes that "[r]ecyclers have tried to improve the economics by automating the sorting process. . . . The more types of trash that are recycled, the more difficult it becomes to sort the valuable from the worthless"—which might refer to single-stream recycling. Coreen can decide whether that passage addresses her concern.

. . . . . . . . . . . . . . . . . . . . . . . . . . . . . .

If you live in the United States, you probably do some form of recycling. It's likely that you separate paper from plastic and glass and metal. You rinse the bottles and cans, and you might put food scraps in a container destined for a composting facility. As you sort everything into the right bins, you probably assume that recycling is helping your community and protecting the environment. But is it? Are you in fact wasting your time?

In 1996, I wrote a long article for *The New York Times Magazine* arguing that the recycling process as we carried it out was wasteful. I presented plenty of evidence that recycling was costly and ineffectual, but its defenders said that it was unfair to rush to judgment. Noting that the modern recycling movement had really just begun just a few years earlier, they predicted it would flourish as the industry matured and the public learned how to recycle properly.

So, what's happened since then? While it's true that the recycling message has reached more people than ever, when it comes to the bottom line, both economically and environmentally, not much has changed at all.

Despite decades of exhortations and mandates, it's still typically more expensive for municipalities to recycle household waste than to send it to a landfill. Prices for recyclable materials have plummeted because of lower oil prices and reduced demand for them overseas. The slump has forced some recycling companies to shut plants and cancel plans for new technologies. The mood is so gloomy that one industry veteran tried to cheer up her colleagues this summer with an article in a trade journal titled, "Recycling Is Not Dead!"

While politicians set higher and higher goals, the national rate of recycling has stagnated in recent years. Yes, it's popular in affluent neighborhoods like Park Slope in Brooklyn and in cities like San Francisco, but residents of the Bronx and Houston don't have the same fervor for sorting garbage in their spare time.

The future for recycling looks even worse. As cities move beyond recycling paper and metals, and into glass, food scraps and assorted plastics, the costs rise sharply while the environmental benefits decline and sometimes vanish. "If you believe recycling is good for the planet and that we need to do more of it, then there's a crisis to confront," says David P. Steiner, the chief executive officer of Waste Management, the largest recycler of household trash in the United States. "Trying to turn garbage into gold costs a lot more than expected. We need to ask ourselves: What is the goal here?"

Recycling has been relentlessly promoted as a goal in and of itself: an unalloyed public good and private virtue that is indoctrinated in students from kindergarten through college. As a result, otherwise well-informed and educated people have no idea of the relative costs and benefits.

They probably don't know, for instance, that to reduce carbon emissions, you'll accomplish a lot more by sorting paper and aluminum cans than by worrying about yogurt containers and half-eaten slices of pizza. Most people also assume that recycling plastic bottles must be doing lots for the planet. They've been encouraged by the Environmental Protection Agency, which assures the public that recycling plastic results in less carbon being released into the atmosphere.

But how much difference does it make? Here's some perspective: To offset the greenhouse impact of one passenger's round-trip flight between New York and London, you'd have to recycle roughly 40,000 plastic bottles, assuming you fly coach. If you sit in business- or first-class, where each passenger takes up more space, it could be more like 100,000.

Even those statistics might be misleading. New York and other cities instruct people to rinse the bottles before putting them in the recycling bin, but the E.P.A.'s life-cycle calculation doesn't take that water into account. That single omission can make a big difference, according to Chris Goodall, the author of "How to Live a Low-Carbon Life." Mr. Goodall calculates that if you wash plastic in water that was heated by coal-derived electricity, then the net effect of your recycling could be more carbon in the atmosphere.

To many public officials, recycling is a question of morality, not cost-benefit analysis. Mayor Bill de Blasio of New York declared that by 2030 the city would no longer send any garbage to landfills. "This is the way of the future if we're going to save our earth," he explained while announcing that New York would join San Francisco, Seattle and other cities in moving toward a "zero waste" policy, which would require an unprecedented level of recycling.

*(Continued)*

6

The national rate of recycling rose during the 1990s to 25 percent, meeting the goal set by an E.P.A. official, J. Winston Porter. He advised state officials that no more than about 35 percent of the nation's trash was worth recycling, but some ignored him and set goals of 50 percent and higher. Most of those goals were never met and the national rate has been stuck around 34 percent in recent years. "It makes sense to recycle commercial cardboard and some paper, as well as selected metals and plastics," he says. "But other materials rarely make sense, including food waste and other compostables. The zero-waste goal makes no sense at all—it's very expensive with almost no real environmental benefit."

One of the original goals of the recycling movement was to avert a supposed crisis because there was no room left in the nation's landfills. But that media inspired fear was never realistic in a country with so much open space. In reporting the 1996 article I found that all the trash generated by Americans for the next 1,000 years would fit on one-tenth of 1 percent of the land available for grazing. And that tiny amount of land wouldn't be lost forever, because landfills are typically covered with grass and converted to parkland, like the Freshkills Park being created on Staten Island. The United States Open tennis tournament is played on the site of an old landfill—and one that never had the linings and other environmental safeguards required today.

Though most cities shun landfills, they have been welcomed in rural communities that reap large economic benefits (and have plenty of greenery to buffer residents from the sights and smells). Consequently, the great landfill shortage has not arrived, and neither have the shortages of raw materials that were supposed to make recycling profitable.

With the economic rationale gone, advocates for recycling have switched to environmental arguments. Researchers have calculated that there are indeed such benefits to recycling, but not in the way that many people imagine.

Most of these benefits do not come from reducing the need for landfills and incinerators. A modern well-lined landfill in a rural area can have relatively little environmental impact. Decomposing garbage releases methane, a potent greenhouse gas, but landfill operators have started capturing it and using it to generate electricity. Modern incinerators, while politically unpopular in the United States, release so few pollutants that they've been widely accepted in the eco-conscious countries of Northern Europe and Japan for generating clean energy.

Moreover, recycling operations have their own environmental costs, like extra trucks on the road and pollution from recycling operations. Composting facilities around the country have inspired complaints about nauseating odors, swarming rats and defecating sea gulls. After New York City started sending food waste to be composted in Delaware, the unhappy neighbors of the composting plant successfully campaigned to shut it down last year.

The environmental benefits of recycling come chiefly from reducing the need to manufacture new products—less mining, drilling and logging. But that's not so appealing to the workers in those industries and to the communities that have accepted the environmental trade-offs that come with those jobs.

Nearly everyone, though, approves of one potential benefit of recycling: reduced emissions of greenhouse gases. Its advocates often cite an estimate by the E.P.A. that recycling municipal solid waste in the United States saves the equivalent of 186 million metric tons of carbon dioxide, comparable to removing the emissions of 39 million cars.

According to the E.P.A.'s estimates, virtually all the greenhouse benefits—more than 90 percent—come from just a few materials: paper, cardboard and metals like the aluminum in soda cans. That's because recycling one ton of metal or paper saves about three tons of carbon dioxide, a much bigger payoff than the other materials analyzed by the E.P.A. Recycling one ton of plastic saves only slightly more than one ton of carbon dioxide. A ton of food saves a little less than a ton. For glass, you have to recycle three tons in order to get about one ton of greenhouse benefits. Worst of all is yard waste: it takes 20 tons of it to save a single ton of carbon dioxide.

Once you exclude paper products and metals, the total annual savings in the United States from recycling everything else in municipal trash—plastics, glass, food, yard trimmings, textiles, rubber, leather—is only two-tenths of 1 percent of America's carbon footprint.

As a business, recycling is on the wrong side of two long-term global economic trends. For centuries, the real cost of labor has been increasing while the real cost of raw materials has been declining. That's why we can afford to buy so much more stuff than our ancestors could. As a labor-intensive activity, recycling is an increasingly expensive way to produce materials that are less and less valuable.

Recyclers have tried to improve the economics by automating the sorting process, but they've been frustrated by politicians eager to increase recycling rates by adding new materials of little value. The more types of trash that are recycled, the more difficult it becomes to sort the valuable from the worthless.

In New York City, the net cost of recycling a ton of trash is now $300 more than it would cost to bury the trash instead. That adds up to millions of extra dollars per year—about half the budget of the parks department—that New Yorkers are spending for the privilege of recycling. That money could buy far more valuable benefits, including more significant reductions in greenhouse emissions.

So what is a socially conscious, sensible person to do?

It would be much simpler and more effective to impose the equivalent of a carbon tax on garbage, as Thomas C. Kinnaman has proposed after conducting what is probably the most thorough comparison of the social costs of recycling, landfilling and incineration. Dr. Kinnaman, an economist at Bucknell University, considered everything from environmental damage to the pleasure that some people take in recycling (the "warm glow" that makes them willing to pay extra to do it).

He concludes that the social good would be optimized by subsidizing the recycling of some metals, and by imposing a $15 tax on each ton of trash that goes to the landfill. That tax would offset the environmental costs, chiefly the greenhouse impact, and allow each municipality to make a guilt-free choice based on local economics and its citizens' wishes. The result, Dr. Kinnaman predicts, would be a lot less recycling than there is today.

Then why do so many public officials keep vowing to do more of it? Special interest politics is one reason—pressure from green groups—but it's also because recycling intuitively appeals to many voters: It makes people feel virtuous, especially affluent people who feel guilty about their enormous environmental footprint. It is less an

*(Continued)*

ethical activity than a religious ritual, like the ones performed by Catholics to obtain indulgences for their sins.

Religious rituals don't need any practical justification for the believers who perform them voluntarily. But many recyclers want more than just the freedom to practice their religion. They want to make these rituals mandatory for everyone else, too, with stiff fines for sinners who don't sort properly. Seattle has become so aggressive that the city is being sued by residents who maintain that the inspectors rooting through their trash are violating their constitutional right to privacy.

It would take legions of garbage police to enforce a zero-waste society, but true believers insist that's the future. When Mayor de Blasio promised to eliminate garbage in New York, he said it was "ludicrous" and "outdated" to keep sending garbage to landfills. Recycling, he declared, was the only way for New York to become "a truly sustainable city."

But cities have been burying garbage for thousands of years, and it's still the easiest and cheapest solution for trash. The recycling movement is floundering, and its survival depends on continual subsidies, sermons and policing. How can you build a sustainable city with a strategy that can't even sustain itself?

Source: Tierney, John. "The Reign of Recycling." *The New York Times*, 3 Oct. 2015, nyti. ms/1PVYvv6.

---

### EXERCISE 6E    ANALYZING THE REIGN OF RECYCLING

1. What are the main effects of recycling, according to Tierney's analysis? What kinds of evidence does he present to support his conclusions about recycling? How does Tierney contrast his evidence with that of people who support recycling?

2. Tierney's analysis is the basis for his argument against recycling as an effective way to protect the environment. Do you think his analysis makes his argument stronger? Why or why not?

3. Did you find Tierney's analysis of recycling surprising in any way? Explain. Do you think Tierney intended to surprise his readers with his analysis? Why or why not?

# Writing Causal Analysis

As this chapter makes clear, we constantly encounter situations—not only in school but also in our daily lives—that might lead to causal analysis. Like Christopher McDougall, whose question about his own running injuries led to an in-depth analysis of the effects of different styles of running (see page 153), you might have a question that could be answered with causal analysis. For example, you might wonder about policies being implemented at the high school you attended to address parents' concerns about an increase in bullying: What impact might such policies have? Writing an effective causal analysis on this or any other compelling topic requires examining your subject in depth and thoroughly investigating possible causes and effects. Use

**the four main features of effective analytical writing** (described in Chapter 5) to guide your causal analysis:

1. **A relevant topic worthy of analysis.** Establish why it is important to understand the causes or effects of the event, trend, or phenomenon you are examining:
   - Why would readers want to understand causes or effects when it comes to this topic?
   - What's at stake for them—and for you—in trying to explain causes or effects in this case?
   - What can be gained by identifying causes and effects in this case?

2. **Complexity.** Explore possible explanations and avoid settling for easy or obvious explanations:
   - How well do the causes or effects you have identified explain the phenomenon, trend, or event you are analyzing?
   - Do the causes or effects you have identified potentially oversimplify the phenomenon, trend, or event you are analyzing?
   - Have you ruled out other possible causes or effects?
   - Have you avoided the trap of mistaking correlation for causation? (See Focus: "Causation vs. Correlation," page 155.)

3. **Sufficient Information and Appropriate Evidence.** Gather enough information about possible causes or effects to explain the event, trend, or phenomenon you are analyzing and to rule out other possible explanations:
   - Have you investigated possible causes sufficiently to explain the effects you have identified?
   - Have you learned enough about the subject you are studying to rule out other possible causes or effects?
   - How confident are you that your sources are valid and trustworthy and your evidence is adequate to explain the causes and effects you have identified?

4. **Reasonable Conclusions.** Present well reasoned and persuasive conclusions about the causes or effects of the phenomenon, event, or trend you are analyzing:
   - Do your conclusions about causes or effects of the event, trend, or phenomenon you have analyzed grow logically out of the evidence you have presented?
   - Do your conclusions present readers with a sound explanation that does not oversimplify the topic?

This section will help you develop a writing project based on causal analysis by taking you through the Ten Core Concepts. Each step described here corresponds to a step described in Chapter 3.

## Step 1 Identify a topic for causal analysis.

Begin with a question that interests or puzzles you about why something happens or whether one thing causes another:

Does the gas- or oil-drilling technique called hydraulic fracturing contaminate groundwater?
What impact is my major likely to have on my future economic status?
Does illegal sharing of digital music files lead to higher music prices for consumers?

Start with a question provided by your instructor for a course assignment or a question about something that happened in your life, an important trend, or a controversial issue:

| Something happening in your life | • Will a proposed new tuition plan at your school mean that some students will not be able to afford college?<br>• Is a new superstore in your town hurting local businesses? |
|---|---|
| An important trend | • How do social media affect dating habits among college students?<br>• Are new anti-bullying policies in high schools effective? |
| A controversial issue | • Do charter schools improve graduation rates among poor and minority students?<br>• Does illegal immigration hurt the U.S. economy? |

Develop this question using Step #1 in Chapter 3.

## Step 2  Place your topic in rhetorical context.

Your question should be interesting to you but also relevant for your intended audience or your course assignment. Consider your audience or your course assignment guidelines and address the following questions:

- Why would this question matter to your intended audience? What makes this question important?
- In identifying the causes and effects reflected in this question, what's at stake for your audience? For you?

Using your answers to these questions as a guide, follow the steps for Step #2 in Chapter 3.

## Step 3  Select a medium.

An effective causal analysis can be presented in any medium, although most academic causal analyses will be presented in the form of a conventional paper.

| If your assignment specifies a medium | Use the medium specified in the assignment guidelines. | Focus on how this medium enables you to present your analysis effectively. |
| --- | --- | --- |
| If you have a choice of medium | Consider which medium best addresses your intended audience. | Focus on how your choice of medium best accomplishes your rhetorical goals. |

For example, imagine that you want to analyze the causes of bullying to help educate teens about the problem. Your intended audience might include teens as well as parents and school officials. In such a case, you might consider several different media that are likely to reach that audience and enable you to present your analysis clearly and provocatively, such as a brochure, a video posted on YouTube, or a letter to the editor of a newspaper or news website.

Step #3 in Chapter 3 provides additional advice to help you decide on an appropriate medium for your causal analysis.

## Step 4  Identify your main claim.

In causal analysis, the writer makes a claim about the causes or effects of the event, trend, or development being analyzed. For example,

**Question:** Will higher sales of hybrid cars reduce greenhouse gas emissions?

↓

**Analysis:** Hybrid cars use less fuel and have lower emissions than conventional cars; hybrid cars might encourage people to drive more; hybrid cars require significant energy to produce.

↓

**Claim:** Hybrid cars might help reduce greenhouse gas emissions but not enough to make a significant difference without other measures to reduce the use of hydrocarbon fuels.

**Question:** Are e-readers making print books obsolete?

↓

**Analysis:** E-readers are replacing books among some readers; e-readers might actually lead to the purchase of print books; some readers continue to prefer print books for a variety of reasons.

↓

**Claim:** E-readers are likely to reduce the demand for print books but not eliminate print books.

6

In each of these examples the writer's task is to explore possible causes and effects to try to answer the main question. To put it differently, the writer develops a causal analysis that leads to a main claim (conclusion) about hybrid cars and greenhouse gases or e-readers and print books.

At this point in the development of your project, you probably won't know exactly what your main claim (or claims) will be because you are still investigating your topic and examining various causes and effects. But your main question should suggest possible claims, and you probably have some idea of what you might find as you investigate your topic. So begin there:

- What claim do you expect to make about your main question?
- What do you expect to find as you investigate causes and effects related to your question?
- What are the possible answers to your main question, based on what you know at this point?

Complete Step #4 in Chapter 3 to develop a Guiding Thesis Statement, which is essentially a statement of the main claim(s) you will make in your causal analysis. As you develop your Guiding Thesis Statement, address the following questions:

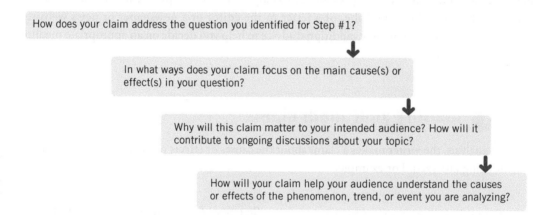

How does your claim address the question you identified for Step #1?

In what ways does your claim focus on the main cause(s) or effect(s) in your question?

Why will this claim matter to your intended audience? How will it contribute to ongoing discussions about your topic?

How will your claim help your audience understand the causes or effects of the phenomenon, trend, or event you are analyzing?

## Step 5    Support your claim(s).

At this point, you should be deep in the process of researching your topic to examine possible causes and effects. Support for your claim or claims will grow out of what you learn by examining the potential causes and effects of whatever you are analyzing.

Let's say you are analyzing the possible effects of a proposed state law based on the idea of "zero tolerance" for bullying. The law would require schools to suspend students who bullied other students. Your main question is,

*Do zero-tolerance policies reduce bullying?*

After investigating the issue, you develop your main claim:

*Zero-tolerance policies will probably not significantly reduce bullying in schools.*

This claim is based on what you learned through your research about why bullying occurs, who engages in it, how prevalent it is, and what steps have been taken to reduce it. You might have found, for example, that students who engage in bullying do so for complicated reasons and are not necessarily discouraged from bullying by rules or punishments. Moreover, zero-tolerance policies have had unintended consequences in schools where they have been adopted; in some cases, students who have had relatively minor disagreements were labeled "bullies" and suspended from school. All of these points provide support for your main claim. Inquiring into causes and effects thus helps you identify specific evidence to support your claim(s).

As you research your topic, look for information that will help you understand the causes and effects you are analyzing and support your claims about those causes and effects. Don't settle for easy answers or simply explanations. Complete the following exercise:

| 1. List what you have learned about causes and effects. | <ul><li>Bullies were usually bullied themselves.</li><li>Peer groups can encourage bullying behavior.</li><li>Bullies usually have low self-esteem.</li><li>Zero-tolerance policies have had mixed results and unintended consequences.</li><li>Some anti-bullying programs can help reduce bullying.</li></ul> |
|---|---|
| 2. Determine whether each item on your list helps support your main claim(s); eliminate items that don't. | <ul><li>*Bullies were usually bullied themselves.* This item seems to support the main claim by showing that the reasons for bullying are complex and have little to do with policies, rules, and punishments.</li><li>*Bullies usually have low self-esteem.* This item also helps explain the causes of bullying.</li><li>*Some anti-bullying programs can help reduce bullying.* This item identifies successful alternatives to zero-tolerance policies.</li></ul> |
| 3. Identify the reasoning, information, and/ or source that supports each item on your list. | <ul><li>Several psychological studies indicating that low self-esteem seems to lead to bullying.</li><li>An essay by a school psychologist arguing that zero-tolerance policies may also undermine efforts to help bullies overcome low self-esteem.</li><li>Report about success of one anti-bullying program.</li></ul> |
| 4. Determine whether your information, reasoning, and sources are sufficient for each item. | <ul><li>Is a single essay enough support for the claim that zero-tolerance policies haven't worked? Is it possible that in this case there was a flaw in the policy itself or that it was not enforced properly? What other information can you find about the impact of such policies?</li><li>Do the studies you found reflect a consensus among researchers and other experts that bullying is correlated with low self-esteem?</li></ul> |

6

Expect to make adjustments in your claims as you learn more about the causes and effects you are examining. If necessary, **revise your main claim**. That's part of the process of inquiry:

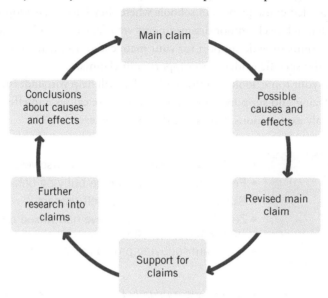

The more thoroughly you explore your topic by examining specific causes and effects and identifying support your claims, the more likely the next steps in the process will lead to an effective piece of writing.

At this point you are probably ready to write a complete draft of your project. If not, move to the next step before completing your draft.

## Step 6 Organize your causal analysis.

How you organize an analysis of causes and effects depends on what you determine is the most logical and effective way of presenting your topic and your claims to your intended audience. Here we will consider two approaches to organizing a causal analysis:

- according to causes and/or effects
- according to your main claims

### Organizing Your Causal Analysis Around Causes and/or Effects

Organize your causal analysis according to the specific causes or effects you have identified through your research. For example, author John Tierney organizes his article, "The Reign of Recycling" (which is included in this chapter), according to the different effects of recycling that he has identified through his research. He presents his analysis of each effect in turn: environmental, economic, and social. As he analyzes each of these kinds of effects, he draws conclusions about whether recycling is actually a benefit or a drawback and uses his evidence to call into question the claims made by supporters about the benefits of recycling. In this way Tierney takes readers in a step-by-step way through his complex analysis as he moves toward his main claim that recycling does not advance the cause of environmental protection.

You can employ a similar strategy to organize your causal analysis. To do so, follow these steps:

1. List the main causes or effects you have identified through your research. (You can use the list you developed for Step #5 above.)

2. Identify your evidence or the key points of support for each cause or effect on your list.

3. Arrange the list in the order that makes the most sense. Consider: What order will present your analysis most clearly to your readers? What order seems to be most logical?

4. Identify the main claims you will make on the basis of your analysis of each cause or effect on your list. (These claims will probably be placed near the end of your analysis.)

5. Use your list to develop an outline for your causal analysis.

For example, let's say you have identified three main causes of bullying:

- Bullies often engage in bullying because they were bullied themselves.
- Peer groups can encourage and reinforce bullying behavior.
- Low self-esteem sometimes prompts children to engage in bullying.

Let's say you have also identified two main effects of zero-tolerance policies:

- Zero-tolerance policies have not significantly reduced bullying behavior.
- These policies have often had serious unintended consequences.

Your analysis of these causes and effects leads to your main claim that zero-tolerance policies should not be implemented in schools; instead, certain kinds of anti-bullying programs that have been shown to be effective in reducing bullying behavior should be developed. Using the five steps above, you might develop a rough outline like this:

   I.  Introduction
       A.  The growing incidence of bullying both in person and online
       B.  Why bullying must be addressed now

  II.  Background
       A.  The complexity of bullying as a social problem
       B.  The development of zero-tolerance policies

6

III. Causes of Bullying
   A. Bullies being bullied themselves
   B. The problem of low self-esteem
   C. The influence of peer groups

IV. Effects of Zero-Tolerance Policies
   A. Lack of success in reducing bullying
   B. Unintended consequences

V. Anti-Bullying Programs
   A. Description of specific kinds of anti-bullying programs
   B. Impact of these programs in addressing bullying

VI. Main Claims
   A. Zero-tolerance policies should not be implemented in schools
   B. Anti-bullying programs should be developed

VII. Conclusion

For each subheading in this outline, you would include the specific evidence or support you found in your research.

## Organizing Your Causal Analysis Around Claims

A second option is to organize your project around the main claims you are making about the causes and/or effects you have identified. Returning to the example of bullying, begin with the two main claims that have emerged from your analysis:

- Zero-tolerance policies in schools have not been shown to reduce bullying significantly among teens.
- The most effective approach to reducing bullying seems to be educational programs that help teens understand and respond to bullying.

You can structure your project around these two main claims. Follow these steps:

1. For each main claim, list your supporting claims.

↓

2. Identify your evidence for each supporting claim.

↓

3. Arrange the list in the order that makes the most sense. Consider: What order will present your analysis most clearly to your readers? What order seems most logical?

↓

4. Create an outline with each main section of your project devoted to one of your main claims.

Such an outline might look like this:

I. Introduction (why bullying is an important problem to address)
   A. The growing incidence of bullying both in person and online
   B. Why bullying must be addressed now

II. Background
   A. The complexity of bullying as a social problem
   B. The development of zero-tolerance policies

III. Main Claims
   A. Zero-tolerance policies should not be implemented in schools.
      1. Causes of bullying are complex.
      2. Effects of zero-tolerance policies have been mixed.
      3. Zero-tolerance policies have had unintended consequences.

   B. Anti-bullying programs should be developed.
      1. Anti-bullying programs address the root causes of bullying.
      2. Anti-bullying programs have been shown to reduce bullying behavior.
      3. Anti-bullying programs avoid unintended consequences.

IV. Conclusion

These are two common approaches to organizing a causal analysis, but they are not the only options. Refer to your rhetorical situation to guide your decisions about form. Step #6 in Chapter 3 provides additional guidance for organizing your project.

If you have already written a rough draft, revise it according to your outline. If you have not yet written a rough draft, do so, using your outline as a guide. Remember that as you write your draft, you might need to do additional research and adjust your claims accordingly (see Step #5 on page 172).

## Step 7 Get feedback.

Use the following sets of questions to focus on the feedback you receive on the main characteristics of analytical writing (a worthy topic, complexity, sufficient support, and reasonable conclusions) and on specific aspects of causal analysis.

Ask your readers to consider addressing these questions:

| A relevant topic worthy of analysis | • What is the main point of the analysis? Is it clear?<br>• What are the cause(s) or effect(s) of the event, trend, or phenomenon being analyzed? Are they clearly identified?<br>• What rationale does the writer provide for examining causes and effects for this topic? |
| --- | --- |
| Complexity | • Is the topic examined in sufficient depth?<br>• What important factors or issues might need to be more fully examined? What alternative explanations might be explored?<br>• Does the analysis sufficiently explain the cause(s) and effect(s) you have identified? |
| Appropriate and sufficient support | • What evidence is presented to support the main claims?<br>• How does this evidence support the causes and effects identified in the analysis?<br>• Are the sources appropriate for this rhetorical situation?<br>• What evidence or support might be unnecessary or redundant? |
| Reasonable conclusions | • What conclusions does the writer draw from the analysis?<br>• Do these conclusions grow logically from the analysis of specific causes and effects?<br>• Are the conclusions presented clearly and persuasively?<br>• Does the conclusion adequately sum up the analysis and emphasize the main points of the project? |

Step #7 in Chapter 3 provides additional guidance for getting helpful feedback on your draft.

## Step 8 Revise.

The preceding steps helped you delve more deeply into your topic to expose its complexity. Now you have to manage that complexity—for yourself and for your readers. At this point, then, your primary task is twofold:

1. Determine what you have learned from your analysis.
2. Sharpen the focus of your project so that your analysis is presented appropriately for your intended audience.

In analytical writing, revision is largely a matter of refining your analysis and making it understandable to your readers without sacrificing complexity. That process might also mean clarifying for yourself what your analysis reveals and identifying more clearly the implications and importance of your analysis in view of your rhetorical situation.

Address the following questions about your draft as you work through Step #8 in Chapter 3:

| A relevant topic worthy of analysis | • What is the purpose of your analysis? How might you refine the questions you are addressing with your analysis?<br>• What makes your analysis relevant? What are you trying to say as a result of your analysis?<br>• What are your main claims? Are they clearly presented? |
|---|---|
| Complexity | • How does your analysis address the question(s) you pose in your project?<br>• Have you explored causes and effects in a way that does not oversimplify your topic? What sections of your analysis might need further explanation?<br>• Which sections of your draft might be unnecessary? |
| Appropriate and sufficient support | • What evidence do you offer to support your main claims?<br>• Which claims might need additional evidence?<br>• Which evidence or support can you eliminate without weakening your analysis, if any?<br>• What makes your sources appropriate for your topic and rhetorical situation? |
| Reasonable conclusions | • What conclusions do you present as a result of your analysis? Do your conclusions address your main question?<br>• How do your conclusions relate to the causes and effects you have analyzed?<br>• Which key issues might you have overlooked in your conclusions? |

6

Review your draft with these sets of questions in mind and revise accordingly.

## Step 9  Refine your voice.

The readings in this chapter illustrate some of the different ways that writers can establish their voices in analyses that focus on causes and effects. For example, notice the differences in the voices of Sherry Turkle (see page 157) and John Tierney (see page 164). Consider how each writer's voice might contribute to the effectiveness of his or her analysis and the persuasiveness of his or her main conclusions.

Your goal at this point is to revise your draft in a way that strengthens your distinctive voice and insures that it is appropriate for this project. The advice provided in Step #9 in Chapter 3 will help you do so. Keep in mind that your voice helps establish your credibility and therefore is a factor in making your causal analysis persuasive to your intended audience. In addition, your voice can be strengthened by your own confidence in your analysis. If you feel confident that you have sufficiently explored the cause(s) and effect(s) of the event or phenomenon you have analyzed, your voice is likely to reflect that confidence and make your project more effective.

## Step 10 | Edit.

Complete Step #10 in Chapter 3. For an analysis of this kind, be especially careful about syntax problems that can result from your efforts to explain complicated ideas or summarize complicated studies. (See Chapter 27 for more information about syntax problems.)

---

**WRITING PROJECTS | CAUSAL ANALYSIS**

1. Identify a controversial proposal in your region. For example,

   - Your governor has proposed a new tax cut that has provoked controversy among politicians and voters.
   - Your local government has proposed a ban on skateboarding in public areas such as parks and library parking lots.
   - Your college is considering a proposal for a new general education curriculum that would affect all students.

   Write an analysis of the potential impact of the proposal. Identify an appropriate audience for your analysis (e.g., students on your campus) and a medium that would best reach that audience.

2. If you have made an important decision recently, analyze the effect of that decision in your life. For example, perhaps you decided to attend a two-year college instead of a four-year college. Or you might have joined the U.S. military before attending college. Maybe you chose to move to a new apartment or a different town. For an audience of your classmates, write an essay in which you analyze the factors that led to your decision and the effects of that decision on important aspects of your life. Consider presenting your analysis in a medium other than a conventional essay that might be appropriate for your intended audience.

3. In November, 2011, campus police at the University of California at Berkeley removed students who were demonstrating on that campus as part of the Occupy Wall Street movement. At one point the police used pepper spray on some of the demonstrators, and several videos and well as photos such as this one were widely circulated after the event:

BRIAN NGUYEN/REUTERS

The images provoked criticism of the Berkeley campus police and administration. James Fallows, a correspondent for the *Atlantic Monthly*, described "the moral power" of those images, and compared it to other iconic images, such as the Chinese protestor in Beijing's Tiananmen Square in 1979:

AP Images/Jeff Widener

Examine the reaction to either of these images (or another image that you believe was important). Then write an essay analyzing the impact of the images.

Alternatively, examine the controversies that led to the Black Lives Matter movement that emerged in 2013 after several widely publicized shootings of Black men—specifically, Eric Garner in New York City and Michael Brown in Ferguson, Missouri. Find videos related to these cases and examine the reaction to those videos in the mainstream press as well as on social media. Then write an essay about the effects of these videos. Identify an appropriate audience that you believe would be interested in your analysis.

6

## MindTap®

Request help with these Writing Projects and feedback from a tutor. If required, participate in a peer review, submit your paper for a grade, and view the instructor's comments online.

## In this chapter, you will learn to

1. Define comparative analysis and understand its purpose and uses.

2. Understand how comparison and synthesis can function as tools for analysis.

3. Identify appropriate rhetorical opportunities for writing analysis that involves comparison and synthesis.

4. Apply the two important characteristics of analytical writing that involves comparison and synthesis.

5. Identify and apply the four main features of comparative analysis to examples of analytical writing.

6. Create a comparative analysis essay, applying the four main features of analytical writing and using the Ten Core Concepts from Chapter 3.

## MindTap®

Understand the goals of the chapter and complete a warm-up activity.

# Comparing and Synthesizing

**SOMETIMES,** the most effective way to analyze something is by comparing it with something else. Often, we can better understand something that is unfamiliar by comparing it to something we already understand. A mechanic might help you grasp a problem with a car's transmission by comparing it to the gears on a bicycle, which might be more familiar to you. In the same way a writer can use the familiar to help explain something new by comparing the two. For example, an economist might explain a recent development, such as the crash of the U.S. housing market during the so-called Great Recession of 2008, by comparing it to a similar event, such as the Great Depression of the 1930's, which has been studied for many years. Comparing two things can expose insights that might not be evident otherwise. In this way, comparison enables a writer illuminate a complicated issue.

In most academic analysis, however, simply comparing two or more things isn't usually sufficient to complete an analysis that adequately explains a complicated event, development, trend, idea, or problem. In comparative analysis, writers often examine several events, trends, developments, or bodies of data in order to understand or explain something adequately. Such analysis usually requires not only comparing but also *synthesizing* ideas or information. *Synthesis is the combining of two or more separate ideas, themes, or elements into a coherent new idea.* The previous example of an economist using comparison to explain a recent economic event illustrates the importance of synthesis in analytical writing. In that case, the writer might compare a recent recession to the Great Depression of the 1930's, but because these events are so complex, the writer will probably also have to examine a number of different perspectives on these two events. The writer will identify common themes or arguments from those different perspectives and bring them together to make a new argument or draw a new conclusion about the recent recession. In doing so, the writer synthesizes ideas and information from different sources to help explain the event or phenomenon that is the focus of his or her analysis.

Understanding complex matters, then, usually requires bringing together several distinct but related ideas, positions, or perspectives. In this sense, a writer must look for connections as well as contrasts or contradictions in an effort to explain something:

- A historian compares three different explanations for the rise of the women's suffrage movement in the U.S. in the 1920's and draws on all three explanations to present a new explanation.
- An ecologist examines several contradictory studies of the impact of hydrofracturing, or "fracking," which is a technique for extracting natural gas or oil from underground, to determine whether fracking is likely to affect drinking water.

- A psychologist reviews a number of studies of the use of social media by college students to draw conclusions about the influence of social media on study habits.

Comparative analysis does not always require synthesis, but very often the two go hand in hand as writers explain complicated subjects. In this chapter, *comparative analysis* is understood to include synthesis unless otherwise noted.

# Occasions for Comparing and Synthesizing

We routinely engage in informal comparative analysis, probably without realizing it:

- A customer choosing a new rain jacket from among several different brands compares them to determine which one has the right features, fit, quality, and price.
- A high school student deciding which college to attend compares tuition, financial aid packages, programs, and the quality of campus life at several different schools.
- A voter sees several tweets reflecting different positions on proposed changes in federal tax laws that will affect her own tax bill and then reviews several editorials on the same subject to determine whether to support the changes.
- Students review three studies of the impact of buying local foods and they develop a proposal for their campus food service to support local farmers.

These examples suggest that comparative analysis, like most analytical writing, grows out of a need to understand something better in order to make a decision or solve a problem. In each case, people consider several different perspectives or kinds of information to help them make a decision or determine their positions on issues of importance to them.

Notice, too, that these examples reflect shared concerns. In each case, a number of different people potentially have an interest in the issues or questions that lead to comparison or synthesis. This shared interest connects writers and readers and provides a foundation for effective comparative analysis. The students preparing a proposal for their campus dining service, for example, will synthesize the studies they found not only to explain the impact of using local foods in the dining halls but also to make a more persuasive case to their readers (the dining service administrators and students who use the dining halls). In this sense, comparative analysis is a **rhetorical tool** with which writers can present their ideas more effectively to interested readers.

Comparison and synthesis are essential components of much analytical writing in college, even if the focus of the assignment is not explicitly to compare or synthesize. For example, an assignment for an atmospheric science course might ask students to investigate the implications of severe weather for a region's economic productivity. For such an assignment, a student might compare several major hurricanes to illuminate differences and similarities in the economic impact of such storms. The student might then synthesize data from several different analyses to draw conclusions about the overall economic impact of severe weather. In the end, the focus of the student's paper is not a comparison of the hurricanes' economic impact or a synthesis of several economic studies of severe weather, but comparison and synthesis are crucial components of the overall analysis.

Comparison and synthesis can lead to a more in-depth understanding of a topic of importance to a writer and his or her readers. The desire to understand should drive a writer's decisions when comparing or synthesizing ideas or information.

Dennis K. Johnson/Lonely Planet Images/Getty Images

---

### EXERCISE 7A  OCCASIONS FOR COMPARATIVE ANALYSIS

1. Think of a recent experience in which you had to make a decision involving two or more distinct options. For example, you might have had to decide which college to attend after being accepted by three different schools. Or you might have purchased a digital tablet from among several different choices. In a brief paragraph, describe this experience and discuss how you made your decision after considering your options. What conclusions might you draw from this experience about the purposes of comparative analysis?

2. Find a newspaper article, essay, blog post, or other kind of text in which several items are compared—for example, an editorial essay comparing two political candidates or a website comparing consumer items such as smartphones. In a brief paragraph, describe the purpose of the comparison and its relevance to a specific audience.

3. Think of an activity you are involved in that requires regular use of specific equipment or services. For example, you might fish, which requires specialized equipment. Or you might cook, which requires certain equipment but also supplies, such as produce or spices. Describe the activity, and identify the equipment or services you need for that activity. Discuss how a comparative analysis of that equipment or service might influence your engagement in that activity. For example, if you cook, you might examine how a comparison of several sources of produce could not only help you decide which sources you should use but also help you better understand those food sources.

7

# Understanding Comparison and Synthesis

The preceding section underscores **two important characteristics of analytical writing that involves comparison and synthesis:**

1. A reason for comparison
2. A basis for comparison

# A Reason for Comparison

Comparison for the sake of comparison may be an interesting intellectual exercise—for example, you might compare two breeds of dogs to decide which is more attractive—but such comparisons won't usually help address an issue or solve a problem. Effective comparison or synthesis is based on *purposeful* analysis. Writers should have a compelling reason for comparing or synthesizing two or more things, and readers should share that sense of purpose. For example, a comparison of different breeds of dogs to determine which ones make the best pets for small apartments might appeal to readers considering whether to have a pet. Similarly, dog owners visiting a veterinary clinic might be interested in a pamphlet that synthesizes information about several different kinds of flea and tick protection to help dog owners decide which protection is best for their pet. In such cases, the comparison or synthesis arises from the writer's need to understand or explain something that is important to both the writer and the intended readers:

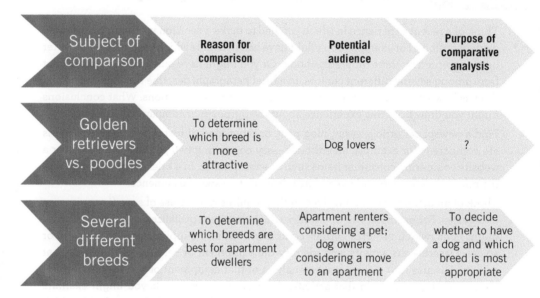

| Subject of comparison | Reason for comparison | Potential audience | Purpose of comparative analysis |
|---|---|---|---|
| Golden retrievers vs. poodles | To determine which breed is more attractive | Dog lovers | ? |
| Several different breeds | To determine which breeds are best for apartment dwellers | Apartment renters considering a pet; dog owners considering a move to an apartment | To decide whether to have a dog and which breed is most appropriate |

# A Basis for Comparison

I once overheard two people debating whether evaluating teachers on the basis of student test scores will actually improve schools. One person argued that if a teacher's students don't meet a certain score on standardized tests, the teacher should be fired. That approach, he argued, works for businesses: Employees who don't perform are fired. The other person responded, "You're comparing apples to oranges."

©iStockphoto.com/JAIME L. RIVERA

You've probably heard that saying—or used it yourself—in casual conversation. Usually, it is used to dismiss a comparison—or an argument based on a comparison—as invalid or specious.

This common saying actually refers to a fallacy described in formal logic, usually called *false comparison* or *false analogy*. In this example, the first person compares schools and businesses to argue for the use of standardized test scores to evaluate teachers. But as the other person realized, the comparison is problematic in several ways. For one thing, schools and businesses are very different kinds of institutions with different purposes, so what might work for one won't necessarily work for the other. In addition, the job of a teacher is very different from most jobs in businesses, whose primary purpose is to make money; teachers aren't hired to produce a product for profit but to educate children. Finally, students' test scores might be one kind of information used to evaluate a teacher's effectiveness, but low student test scores don't necessarily mean that the teacher has been ineffective, just as falling sales might not mean that the salesperson is doing a poor job, because there are many factors outside the teacher's control or the salesperson's control that might have influenced the test scores or sales. Therefore, the first person's implied point—that because businesses fire employees who don't perform, schools can improve by firing teachers whose students don't perform well on tests—is illogical.

This example illustrates that *a valid comparison requires a sound basis for the comparison.* It is possible to compare schools and businesses, but the basis for that comparison must be valid. For example, both schools and businesses are complicated organizations that can benefit from being more efficient. On that basis, we might compare the management policies of a school and a business to determine whether one functions more effectively than the other in managing routine operations, such as payroll, scheduling, etc. Similarly, we might compare how schools and businesses implement various strategies for saving money on expenditures such as supplies or utilities. In such comparisons, the basis for comparison (efficiency) can lead to useful analysis.

Writing effective comparative analysis, then, requires writers to identify compelling reasons and a sound basis for comparison; moreover, when synthesizing ideas or information, writers must be careful to identify similarities and account for differences or distinctions. (For more advice about synthesizing, see Chapter 19.)

**7**

### EXERCISE 7B  PRACTICING COMPARISON AND SYNTHESIS

1. For each of the following items, identify a **reason** and a **basis** for comparison. Also, describe a specific audience for analysis in each case.

   - Compare the views of the candidates in a current political election on a specific issue (e.g., immigration).
   - Compare different brands of smartphones.
   - Compare several different exercise programs.
   - Compare the work of two or more artists (filmmakers, musicians, etc.).

2. Select one of the items in Question #1. Find two or more reviews or essays about those items. In a brief paragraph, synthesize those reviews so that you present to your intended audience (which you identified for Question #1) several key points about or criticisms of the items being compared.

# Reading Comparative Analysis

The following selections illustrate several different ways in which writers use comparison and synthesis to explore a topic in order to understand it better. As you read, consider how each selection addresses the four main features of analytical writing discussed in Chapter 5:

| A relevant topic worthy of analysis | • How does the writer establish the topic as one that is worthy of analysis?<br>• How does the writer establish that the comparison he or she is making is relevant?<br>• What is the purpose of that comparison? Why should readers care about the comparison at this point in time? |
|---|---|
| Complexity | • What is the basis for comparison?<br>• What claims does the writer make on the basis of the comparison?<br>• How does the comparison reveal the complexity of the topic?<br>• How does the writer avoid oversimplifying the topic through comparison and/or synthesis? |
| Sufficient information and appropriate analysis | • What kinds of evidence does the writer provide to support his or her claims?<br>• Is the evidence sufficient? Is it appropriate for the rhetorical situation?<br>• How does the comparative analysis illuminate the topic? |
| Reasonable conclusions | • What conclusions does the writer draw from the comparison?<br>• Does the comparison lead logically to these conclusions?<br>• How are the conclusions supported by his analysis?<br>• Are the conclusions persuasive? Are they presented effectively? |

## MindTap

Read these comparative analysis examples. Highlight and take notes online. Additional readings are also available online.

# Move Over, Millennials, Here Comes Generation Z
## by Alex Williams

*In the following essay, which was published in the* New York Times *in 2015, reporter Alex Williams presents a detailed description of Generation Z, which he defines roughly as people who were born between 1996 and 2011. His essay addresses the question, Who is Generation Z? But in answering that question, Williams delves into social, economic, political, financial, and historical trends in a way that might help us better understand American culture at this point in time. His comparison between the Millennial Generation and Generation Z actually encompasses other generations, including the so-called "Silent Generation," which came of age after World War II. In this regard, his analysis includes both comparison and synthesis. As you'll see, Williams does not settle for identifying straightforward similarities and differences among these groups; instead, he examines the characteristics of these groups in the context of larger historical forces, and he consults various kinds of data and multiple perspectives so that the picture of Generation Z that emerges reflects the complexity of that generation and the world it inhabits. In these ways, although his writing style is journalistic style and might not sound academic, Williams employs strategies that are common in academic analysis.*

. . . . . . . . . . . . . . . . . . . . . . . . . . . . . . . . . . . . . . . .

### Talking About This Reading

**Gordon Cheney (student):** The organization of this article confused me slightly. I got mixed up with the comparisons between different generations. Sometimes the author seemed to say that the generations were nothing like each other, and then he would seem to identify a difference without stating it as a difference.

**Bob Yagelski:** This article includes both comparison and synthesis, and your confusion probably occurs in sections where you expected comparison but actually encountered synthesis. Reread those passages, keeping in mind that the author's main focus is on Millennials, which he compares to the other generations. Remembering that should help you follow the author's analysis more easily.

. . . . . . . . . . . . . . . . . . . . . . . . . . . . . . . . . . . . . . . .

Hear the word "millennial," and plenty of images spring to mind.

There's Facebook's Mark Zuckerberg, in his hoodie, earning his first billion by the age of 23.

There's Miley Cyrus, preening for the cameras in a flesh-baring act that recalls a Snapchat sexting session.

There's Lena Dunham, TV's queen of overshare, spiraling into navel-gazing soliloquies that seem scripted from the therapist's couch.

They're brash, they're narcissistic, they're entitled. Or so the cliché goes.

But what about "Generation Z," the generation born after millennials that is emerging as the next big thing for market researchers, cultural observers and trend forecasters? With the oldest members of this cohort barely out of high school, these tweens and teens of today are primed to become the dominant youth influencers of tomorrow. Flush with billions in spending power, they promise untold riches to marketers who can find the master key to their psyche. No wonder the race to define, and market to, this demographic juggernaut is on. They are "the next big retail disrupter," according to *Women's Wear Daily*. They have "the weight of saving the world and fixing our past mistakes on their small shoulders," according to an article on Fast

*(Continued)*

Company's Co.Exist site by Jeremy Finch, an innovation consultant. Lucie Greene, the worldwide director of the Innovation Group at J. Walter Thompson, calls them "millennials on steroids."

While it is easy to mock the efforts of marketers to shoehorn tens of millions of adolescents into a generational archetype, à la the baby boomers, it is also clear that a 14-year-old in 2015 really does inhabit a substantially different world than one of 2005. Millennials, after all, were raised during the boom times and relative peace of the 1990s, only to see their sunny world dashed by the Sept. 11 attacks and two economic crashes, in 2000 and 2008. Theirs is a story of innocence lost. Generation Z, by contrast, has had its eyes open from the beginning, coming along in the aftermath of those cataclysms in the era of the war on terror and the Great Recession, Ms. Greene said. "If Hannah Horvath from 'Girls' is the typical millennial—self-involved, dependent, flailing financially in the real world as her expectations of a dream job and life collide with reality—then Alex Dunphy from 'Modern Family' represents the Gen Z antidote," Ms. Greene said. "Alex is a true Gen Z: conscientious, hard-working, somewhat anxious and mindful of the future."

Generational study being more art than science, there is considerable dispute about the definition of Generation Z. Demographers place its beginning anywhere from the early '90s to the mid-2000s. Marketers and trend forecasters, however, who tend to slice generations into bite-size units, often characterize this group as a roughly 15-year bloc starting around 1996, making them 5 to 19 years old now. (By that definition, millennials were born between about 1980 and 1995, and are roughly 20 to 35 now.)

Steve Sands/Getty Images Entertainment/Getty Images

Eric McCandless/ABC via Getty Images

| | Millennials (born 1980-1995) | Generation Z (born 1996-2010) |
|---|---|---|
| TV ICON | Hannah Horvath, "Girls" | Alex Dunphy, "Modern Family" |
| MUSIC | Lady Gaga | Lorde |
| SOCIAL MEDIA | Facebook | Snapchat, Whisper |
| WEB STAR | PewDiePie, YouTube | Lele Pons, Vine |
| STYLE INFLUENCER | Olsen twins | Tavi Gevinson |
| CLOTHES | American Apparel | Shop Jeen |
| FIRST GADGET | iPod | iPhone |

Even accepting those rather narrow boundaries, Generation Z still commands attention through its sheer size. At approximately 60 million, native-born American members of Generation Z outnumber their endlessly dissected millennial older siblings by nearly one million, according to census data compiled by Susan Weber-Stoger, a demographer at Queens College. The fact that some are still in their post-toddler years, however, makes it difficult for marketers trying to distill their generational essence. Among the 5-year-olds, cultural tastes do not reach much further than "Shaun the Sheep" and "Bubble Guppies." As for the older end of the Generation Z spectrum, some demographers still lump them in with the millennials, but increasingly, many marketers see them as a breed apart.

So, who are they? To answer that question, you have to take a deeper look at the world in which they are coming of age. "When I think of Generation Z, technology is the first thing that comes to mind," said Emily Citarella, a 16-year-old high school student in Atlanta. "I know people who have made their closest relationships from Tumblr, Instagram and Facebook." Sure, millennials were digital; their teenage years were defined by iPods and MySpace. But Generation Z is the first generation to be raised in the era of smartphones. Many do not remember a time before social media. "We are the first true digital natives," said Hannah Payne, an 18-year-old U.C.L.A. student and lifestyle blogger. "I can almost simultaneously create a document, edit it, post a photo on Instagram and talk on the phone, all from the user-friendly interface of my iPhone." "Generation Z takes in information instantaneously," she said, "and loses interest just as fast." That point is not lost on marketers. In an era of emoji and six-second Vine videos, "we tell our advertising partners that if they don't communicate in five words and a big picture, they will not reach this generation," said Dan Schawbel, the managing partner of Millennial Branding, a New York consultancy.

So far, they sound pretty much like millennials. But those who study youth trends are starting to discern big differences in how the two generations view their online personas, starting with privacy. While the millennial generation infamously pioneered the Facebook beer-bong selfie, many in Generation Z have embraced later, anonymous social media platforms like Secret or Whisper, as well as Snapchat, where any incriminating images disappear almost instantly, said Dan Gould, a trend consultant for Sparks & Honey, an advertising agency in New York. "As far as privacy is concerned, they are aware of their personal brand, and have seen older Gen Y-ers screw up by posting too openly," Mr. Gould said. That point was driven home in a 2013 Mashable article titled "I'm 13 and None of My Friends Use Facebook," in which Ruby Karp, a New York teenager, wrote: "Let's say I get invited to a party and there's underage drinking. I'm not drinking, but someone pulls out a camera. Even if I'm not carrying a red Solo cup, I could be photographed behind a girl doing shots."

But the difference between generations goes much deeper than choosing Snapchat over Facebook. Between 2000 and 2010, the country's Hispanic population grew at four times the rate of the total population, according to the Census Bureau. The number of Americans self-identifying as mixed white-and-black biracial rose 134 percent. The number of Americans of mixed white and Asian descent grew by 87 percent. Those profound demographic shifts are reflected at the cultural level, too. Attitudes on social issues have shifted, in some cases seismically, in the decade since

*(Continued)*

millennials were teenagers. Same-sex marriage, for example, has gone from a controversial political issue to a constitutional right recognized by the Supreme Court. For today's 14-year-olds, the nation's first African-American president is less a historic breakthrough than a fact of life. "America becomes more multicultural on a daily basis," said Anthony Richard Jr., a 17-year-old in Gretna, La. "It's exponential compared to previous generations."

This vision of a generation with wired brains, making their way in an ethnic-stew society of the future, makes them sound like the replicants from "Blade Runner." But the parents of Generation Z teenagers play an equally powerful role in shaping their collective outlook. Millennials, who are often painted, however unfairly, as narcissistic brats who expect the boss to fetch them coffee, were largely raised by baby boomers, who, according to many, are the most iconoclastic, self-absorbed and grandiose generation in history. Think: Steve Jobs. (To be more charitable, maybe it's no surprise that a *New York Times* article from last year called millennials "Generation Nice," and lauded their communal spirit, given that their parents were save-the-world boomers.)

By contrast, Generation Z tends to be the product of Generation X, a relatively small, jaded generation that came of age in the post-Watergate, post-Vietnam funk of the 1970s, when horizons seemed limited. Those former latchkey kids, who grew up on Nirvana records and slasher movies, have tried to give their children the safe, secure childhood that they never had, said Neil Howe, an economist and the co-author of more than a dozen books about American generations. "You see the mommy blogs by Generation X-ers, and safety is a huge concern: the stainless-steel sippy cups that are BPA-free, the side-impact baby carriages, the home preparation of baby food," said Mr. Howe, who runs Saeculum Research, a Virginia-based social trends consultancy. (As a historian who takes the long view, however, Mr. Howe defines the cohort quite differently; he has called it the "Homeland Generation" because they grew up in post-9/11 America, and argues that it did not begin until around 2004.)

Part of that obsession with safety is likely due to the hard times that both Generation Z members and their parents experienced during their formative years. "I definitely think growing up in a time of hardship, global conflict and economic troubles has affected my future," said Seimi Park, a 17-year-old high school senior in Virginia Beach, who always dreamed of a career in fashion, but has recently shifted her sights to law, because it seems safer. "This applies to all my friends," she said. "I think I can speak for my generation when I say that our optimism has long ago been replaced with pragmatism."

That sober sensibility goes beyond career, it seems. A Sparks & Honey trend report called "Meet Generation Z: Forget Everything You Learned About Millennials" asserted that the cohort places heavy emphasis on being "mature and in control." According to a survey of risky behavior by the Centers for Disease Control and Prevention, the percentage of high school students who had had at least one drink of alcohol in their lives declined to about 66 percent in 2013, from about 82 percent in 1991. The number who reported never or rarely wearing a seatbelt in a car driven by someone else declined to about 8 percent, compared with about 26 percent in 1991.

Put it all together—the privacy, the caution, the focus on sensible careers—and Generation Z starts to look less like the brash millennials and more like their grandparents (or, in some cases great-grandparents), Mr. Howe said. Those children of the late 1920s through the early '40s, members of the so-called Silent Generation, were shaped by war and the Depression and grew up to be the diligent, go-along-to-get-along careerists of the '50s and '60s—picture Peggy from "Mad Men." "The parallels with the Silent Generation are obvious," Mr. Howe said. "There has been a recession, jobs are hard to get, you can't take risks. You've got to be careful what you put on Facebook. You don't want to taint your record." Those children of the New Deal, epitomized by the low-key Warren Buffett, "didn't want to change the system, they wanted to work within the system," Mr. Howe said. "They were the men in the gray flannel suits. They got married early, had kids early. Their first question in job interviews was about pension plans."

That analogy only goes so far for a generation predisposed to making Vine videos of themselves doing cartwheels over their cats. (Let's not forget that the Silents, too, had no shortage of mavericks who made noise on the world stage—Martin Luther King Jr., Elvis Presley and Andy Warhol, to name but a few.) As for the gray flannel suits, parents may not want to send their teenagers off to the tailor just yet. The Sparks & Honey report argued that "entrepreneurship is in their DNA." "Kids are witnessing start-up companies make it big instantly via social media," said Andrew Schoonover, a 15-year-old in Olathe, Kan. "We do not want to work at a local fast-food joint for a summer job. We want to make our own business because we see the lucky few who make it big."

Which leads to a final point worth mentioning about the Silent Generation: As Mr. Howe pointed out, it was not just the most career-focused generation in history. It was also, he said, the richest.

Source: Williams, Alex. "Move Over, Millenials, Here Comes Generation Z." *The New York Times*, 18 Sept. 2015, nyti.ms/1UZOjDg.

---

## EXERCISE 7C    COMPARING MILLENNIALS AND GENERATION Z

7

1. How would you describe the purpose of Williams' comparison between Millennials and other generations, especially Generation Z? What issue, problem, or trend is he trying to understand? What makes his comparison relevant today? What do you think his analysis reveals about American culture? What does it suggest about social and economic change in the U.S.?

2. How does Williams support his claims about attitudes each generation? What forms of evidence does he provide? Do you find this evidence sufficient and persuasive? Why or why not?

3. Williams makes numerous references to pop culture and celebrities (for example, he mentioned the TV shows *Girls* and *Modern Family*, Facebook founder Marc Zuckerberg, and singer Miley Cyrus) . What purposes do these references serve in his analysis? What do you think these references suggest about Williams' assumptions about his audience? Did you find these references helpful or effective? Explain. What do you think your answer to that question suggests about you as a reader?

## The Whole Truth
by Julian Baggini

*Is lying always wrong? In the following essay, British philosopher Julian Baggini addresses that question by examining what several other philosophers have said about lying and truth in human affairs. Baggini's essay illustrates how a writer can draw on the ideas of others to explore a complicated question, synthesizing the perspectives of other philosophers and ultimately drawing his own conclusions about lying. Notice that the focus of the essay isn't the comparison of various perspectives but the question of whether lying is always wrong. A casual reader might not even realize that Baggini is comparing and synthesizing the ideas of other writers, yet he uses comparison and synthesis to strengthen his analysis without calling attention to the comparisons he is making.*

*Because Baggini was originally writing for a British audience, some of his references might be unfamiliar to you. For instance, British readers would recognize Lake Buttermere (located in the Lake District, a popular vacation destination in northwest England). Baggini also assumes his readers are familiar with prominent philosophers from the past, such as David Hume and St. Augustine, as well as with more recent historical events, such as President Bill Clinton's affair with a White House intern in the 1990s. Consider what these references suggest about Baggini's intended audience: readers of* Prospect *magazine, in which this essay first appeared in 2011.*

· · · · · · · · · · · · · · · · · · · · · · · · · · · · · · · · · · ·

### Talking About This Reading

**Carol Moore (student):** The organization was confusing to me. The author bounced back and forth on references, and I couldn't grasp the organization of the essay.

**Bob Yagelski:** Carol, you've identified a common source of difficulty in reading a complex academic analysis: following an author's references to other scholars or texts. Baggini cites a variety of scholarly and popular sources, which you obviously found confusing. One helpful strategy is to identify the focus (or topic sentence) of each paragraph. (Notice that Baggini usually discusses only one source in a paragraph.) Doing so can help you keep track of Baggini's main point and make sense of any reference he makes in a paragraph.

· · · · · · · · · · · · · · · · · · · · · · · · · · · · · · · · · · ·

There is nothing more common than inconsistency and confusion over the imperative not to tell a lie. While "liar" is universally a term of opprobrium, almost everyone accepts that the social world would cease turning without a good scattering of white lies, half-truths and evasions.

In his new book *Born Liars: Why We Can't Live Without Deceit* (Quercus), Ian Leslie is the latest writer to try to work out some of what might follow from the simple realisation that lying is not always wrong. As I see it, the key is to recognise that lying is a problem because of what it is not: telling the truth. And if lying is a complex matter that is because truth is too. So once we get to the truth about lying, we're already in a dizzying tangle of ideas. To give one example, I could promise right now to tell the truth, the whole truth and nothing but the truth. The problem is that sometimes telling the truth is not the point, telling the whole truth is impossible, and there may be things other than the truth that matter too. So even if I went on without a single further lie, the promise itself would have been one.

The problem with telling "the truth" starts with the definite article, because there is always more than one way to give a true account or description. If you and I were to each describe the view of Lake Buttermere, for example, our accounts might be different but both contain nothing but true statements. You might coldly describe the topography and list the vegetation while I might paint more of a verbal picture. That is not to say there is more than one truth in some hand-washing, relativistic sense. If you were to start talking about the cluster of high-rise apartment blocks on the southern shore, you wouldn't be describing "what's true for you," you'd be lying or hallucinating.

So while it is not possible to give "the truth" about Lake Buttermere, it is possible to offer any number of accounts that only contain true statements. To do that, however, is not enough to achieve what people want from truth. It is rather a prescription for what we might call "estate agent truth." The art of describing a home for sale or rent is only to say true things, while leaving out the crucial additional information that would put the truth in its ugly context. In other words, no "false statement made with the intention to deceive"—St Augustine's still unbeatable definition of a lie—but plenty of economy with the truth.

This is also the truth of many lawyers, who always instruct their clients to say only true things, but to leave out anything that might incriminate them. This exposes the difference between a truly moral way of thinking and a kind of legalistic surrogate. Legalistic thinking asks only "what am I permitted to do?" whereas truly moral thinking asks "what would be the right thing to do?" As I have argued in my book *Complaint: From Minor Moans to Principled Protest*, moral ways of thinking are increasingly being replaced with legalistic ones. We think more of our entitlements, rights and strict legal obligations and less of what is required to be a good person.

Moral codes that stress the avoidance of telling lies are more legalistic than moral because they ultimately focus on the technical issue of whether a claim is true or false, not on the moral issue of whether one is being appropriately truthful. Not telling lies becomes a virtue in itself when, as the philosopher Bernard Williams argued in *Truth and Truthfulness*, there are two positive virtues of truth, and each is somewhat complex. The first of these he calls accuracy, the second sincerity. People who claim we should never lie not only neglect the second, they also have an impoverished understanding of the first. To say that the truth requires accuracy does not mean simply that everything you say must be 100 per cent correct, but that it must include all the relevant truths. So, for instance, the estate agent may technically be accurate when she describes a property as being 307 metres from the local shop, but it would even more accurate, in Williams's sense, to point out that the direct route is blocked and so it's about half an hour's walk away. Accuracy requires us to say enough to gain an accurate picture; not telling lies only requires us to make sure what we do say is not false.

The second virtue of truth, sincerity, is not required at all by lie-avoiders. Sincerity concerns the earnest desire to say what you truly think and describe what is truly there. That helps explain why one of the most famous "lies" of recent decades is not a lie at all, but objectionable nonetheless: Bill Clinton's famous "I did not have sexual relations with that woman, Miss Lewinsky." As many people have pointed out, to a Southern Baptist, this could indeed be interpreted as being strictly true. "Sexual relations" is, in many parts, a euphemism for coitus, not any other sexual acts between two people. If this is so, then Clinton was accurate only in the legal sense, not in Williams's. Even more clearly, he was not sincerely trying to convey the truth of his situation.

*(Continued)*

7

Williams's stress on the virtues of truth is therefore much more valuable than the legalistic stress on the vices of lying. It shows that truthfulness—the whole truth if you like—requires more than just true things being said, while acknowledging that there really is no such thing as "the whole truth" anyway. Full disclosure is never possible. Truthfulness is largely a matter of deciding what it is reasonable to withhold.

Nevertheless, even Williams's account leaves out something else which is very important: the question of whether or not truth always trumps other virtues. "Nothing but the truth" is the wrong maxim if things other than truth matter more. The most obvious examples are of courtesy and concern for people's feelings, where kindness matters more than revealing the full, naked truth. Even here, however, we need to be careful. There is a risk of second guessing what is best for people or what we think they are able to deal with. Normally, it is better to allow people to make up their own minds on the basis of facts. Withholding truth for someone's own benefit is sometimes justified but often it simply diminishes their autonomy. This is what Kant got right when he claimed that lying violates the dignity of man.

We might sometimes be justified in lying to others for our own dignity too. Bill Clinton lied, for sure. But he only did so only because a zealous prosecutor brought to public light what should probably have remained private. If what you did is nobody else's business, aren't you entitled to lie to preserve your privacy?

Even when it comes to matters that truly belong in the public domain, we should ask ourselves whether we would really prefer politicians to simply speak the truth. Would it really be wise for a prime minister to announce, when a crisis breaks, that no one really knows what's going on yet or has a clue what to do next? Leadership in a crisis may require projecting more calm and control than one really has behind closed doors. More honesty in politics would certainly be a good thing; complete honesty most probably disastrous.

But perhaps the most interesting counter-example to the twin virtues of sincerity and accuracy was proposed by the sociologist Steve Fuller, who has been widely condemned for suggesting that intelligent design theory merits a hearing. Many of Fuller's colleagues know he is a smart guy and can't understand why he persists with this kind of argument. The answer is perhaps to be found in a piece he wrote in the spring 2008 edition of *The Philosopher's Magazine* explaining his modus operandi. The idea that one should always say what one truly believes is narcissistic nonsense, he argued. The role of the intellectual is to say what they think needs saying most at any given time in a debate, not to bear testimony to their deepest convictions. Although this might involve some dissembling, it serves the cause of establishing truth in the long run better than simply saying the truth as you see it. What matters is how what one says helps build and expand the widest, most expansive truth—not whether as a distinct ingredient it is more or less true than another.

I find Fuller's argument very persuasive. Indeed, it fits with my own tendency to want to talk more about the virtues of religion around atheists than with believers, or to question the value of philosophy with philosophers. The quest for truth requires a constant critical edge. In the case of intelligent design, I think Fuller is sharpening the wrong blade, and a dangerous one at that. But the idea that the contemporary consensus needs some shaking from its dogmatic slumber is not such a stupid one, and may justify a suspension of sincerity in the name of furthering debate.

There are, then, numerous reasons why lying is not always wrong, and why telling the truth is not always the main priority. Nevertheless, it is vital to remember that—ultimately—truth matters. You could concoct a hypothetical situation in which we had to choose between lying or creating misery for all humankind, but until and unless we ever come against such scenarios, most of us value truth, even to the detriment of some happiness. That is why we should develop the habit of telling truth, and distaste for lies. Truth should be the default; lying an exception that requires a special justification.

In *Born Liars*, Ian Leslie rightly points out that lying is deeply connected to what makes us human. We may not be the only creatures who have a "theory of mind"— the ability to see the world from the point of view of others—but we are certainly the species in which that capacity is most developed. It is precisely because of this that the possibility of lying emerges. We can lie only because we understand that others can be made to see the world other than as we know it to be.

But theory of mind is also connected to another human capacity: empathy. As Adam Smith and David Hume argued long before modern psychology strengthened their case, our ability to understand how other people feel is what makes morality possible. Emotional insight is what drives the golden rule: simply by imagining what it would be like to suffer a wrongdoing shows us why it is indeed wrong. So it is with being lied to. In that way, our ability to take up the viewpoint of another is both what makes lying possible and gives us a reason not to do it—usually, at least.

Source: Baggini, Julian. "The Whole Truth." *Prospect*, 20 Apr. 2011, www.prospectmagazine.co.uk/magazine/philosophy-of-lying-truth-ian-leslie/.

---

### EXERCISE 7D    ANALYZING THE WHOLE TRUTH

1. What is the occasion for Baggini's analysis of lying? What justification does he give to establish the importance of this topic?

2. What, specifically, does Baggini compare in this essay? How is his comparison relevant to his main question? How does his comparison help him answer that question?

3. What answer does Baggini give to his main question about lying? How convincing did you find his answer? Do you think his comparative analysis makes his answer more or less persuasive? Explain.

## Sherlock Holmes Can Teach You to Multitask
### by Maria Konnikova

*Sometimes a writer uses comparison in surprising ways that can illuminate an issue or address a problem. In the following essay, which was published in* Wired *magazine in 2013, writer Maria Konnikova, who holds a Ph.D. in psychology, compares the fictional characters of Sherlock Holmes and his assistant Watson to help explain a phenomenon that many experts see as a growing problem today: multitasking. Multitasking is, quite simply, doing several things at once. It isn't really new, but the rapid development and widespread availability of digital technologies have given rise to a new kind of multitasking. For example, many people today routinely watch TV while surfing the Internet with a digital tablet and texting friends*

*(Continued)*

*with a smartphone at the same time. Students can open multiple windows on a web browser at the same time and click rapidly from one to another while checking their email or posting a tweet. You probably multitask in these ways without even realizing it. But as Konnikova suggests, studies show problems with multitasking, and many psychologists, education researchers, and other experts advise against it. In fact, the adoption of laws in many states in recent years that prohibit texting while driving, which is a potentially dangerous form of multitasking, reflects a growing concern about multitasking.*

*Konnikova wonders what we can do about our tendency to multitask. Her answer lies in her comparison of Holmes and Watson and their different styles of processing information. Her essay is a good example of how a seemingly simple comparison can reveal the complexity of something (in this case, paying attention to what is around you). Her essay also illustrates the usefulness of comparison in analyzing a phenomenon (multitasking) and finding a solution to a problem.*

. . . . . . . . . . . . . . . . . . . . . . . . . . . . . . . . . . . . . . . . . . .

## Talking About This Reading

**Jacquelyn Hicks (student):** While the explanations of Holmes and Watson were well stated, the author's viewpoint is different from my own. Yes, these days it is hard to avoid multitasking, but if you're willing to put the technology aside, you can learn to concentrate.

**Bob Yagelski:** Jacquelyn, sometimes our disagreement with an author can influence our response to a text. That's OK. Your response to Konnikova reflects your genuine engagement with her analysis. But you can disagree with an author and still see validity in her analysis. In this case, acknowledge that disagreement, but try not to let your own viewpoint obscure the insights you might gain from Konnikova's analysis.

. . . . . . . . . . . . . . . . . . . . . . . . . . . . . . . . . . . . . . . . . . .

A phone heralds the arrival of a text message with a fabulous buzzing. The computer dings when an email has hit your inbox. Your Facebook page pops up a new red alert. Your Twitter feed does whatever it is that Twitter feeds do, drawing your mind to any number of stories and announcements in the course of a second. What is it you were saying again? Or thinking or working on?

In a world as loud as ours, it's hard not to get distracted. Although the problem is far from new—even the Benedictine monks complained of not being able to focus—the modern environment plays into our brain's predilection for mind-wandering in uncanny fashion. Neurologist Marcus Raichle has spent most of his career looking at our brain's so-called resting state—and what he has discovered is that, in that default state, the last thing our minds are doing is resting. Instead, they remain suspended in a state of ever-ready engagement, a baseline activation that constantly gathers information from the environment, flitting from stimulus to stimulus to see which might be important enough to warrant our attention. In other words, our minds are made to wander.

Nothing plays into that propensity more than our predilection for multitasking. It's as if the modern world has realized how best to capture our brain's constant willingness to engage in whatever salient thing comes along. But not only is such constant attentional wandering counterproductive—recent studies have shown that heavy media multitaskers are actually worse at the very thing they should be good at, task switching—it also makes us unhappy. An engaged mind is a happy mind; a wandering one, not so much. In feeding the multitasking frenzy, not only are we less productive, but we become less satisfied.

What to do? How to manage it all and still be at our best, our most alert and engaged? The answer comes from an unlikely-seeming source: Sherlock Holmes. Early on in the Holmes stories, the detective distinguishes the process of seeing from that of observing: he and Watson might experience the exact same stimuli, but they don't actually process them in the same fashion. Where Watson just sees, without actually engaging his attention in any meaningful fashion, Holmes observes: he chooses, mindfully and deliberately, where to direct his attention—or not, as the case may be. Watson lets the default network do whatever it is that it does; Holmes has trained it to respond to very specific stimuli, in very specific fashion.

The result? Watson doesn't actually take note of much of anything in his environment, not the flow of his thoughts nor the way that a pretty face or a sunny day might be affecting his thinking. Instead, he floats superficially from stimulus to stimulus, letting each input passively affect his brain with little knowledge on his part of what is happening or why. Holmes, on the other hand, knows exactly what the multiple demands on his attention are, and consciously chooses to attend to some stimuli and not to others. He knows exactly what is affecting him, and how, and is able to recall where he was looking, what he was thinking, what he was experiencing, and what it all means.

The difference between Holmes and Watson is that of mindfulness versus mindlessness, engagement versus disengagement. Watson's path is the natural one, the one our brain takes if we are passive. Holmes's is the more effortful—the active decision to engage with certain elements of the environment and not with others. Our untrained brain is Watsonian. It sees, but does not observe. It registers, but does not process. It multitasks, without getting the richness of experience in any of the single tasks that makes up its multitasking.

Successful thought is about more than taking in and processing information. It is also about learning to pay attention, choosing what to pay attention to and how deeply to pay attention to it. The world won't quiet down. If anything, it will get louder. But maybe we can learn to quiet ourselves down instead, controlling our attention and our environment instead of letting it control us.

Source: "Sherlock Holmes can teach you to multitask [Wired Magazine 2/17/2013]", adapted from MASTERMIND: HOW TO THINK LIKE SHERLOCK HOLMES by Maria Konnikova, copyright © 2013 by Maria Konnikova. Used by permission of Viking Books, an imprint of Penguin Publishing Group, a division of Penguin Random House LLC.

**7**

## EXERCISE 7E    ANALYZING SHERLOCK HOLMES AND MULTITASKING

1. What specific problem associated with multitasking is Konnikova attempting to address with her comparison between Sherlock Holmes and Watson? Why is this problem relevant? What makes it worth addressing? Does her comparison between Holmes and Watson sufficiently address the problem? Why or why not? Cite specific passages from the essay in your answer.

2. On what basis does Konnikova compare Sherlock Holmes and Watson? Is this basis a reasonable one for the comparison she is making? Explain.

3. What conclusions does Konnikova draw from her analysis? How does her comparison of Holmes and Watson lead to those conclusions? Do you find her analysis persuasive? Why or why not? Do you think your answer to that question has anything to do with your own views about or experiences with multitasking?

# Writing Analysis Involving Comparison and Synthesis

You might have noticed that in the past few years more and more businesses and homeowners in many parts of the United States are installing solar panels and wind turbines. If you have ever wondered how someone might decide between those two means of generating electricity, you have begun to think in terms of comparative analysis. This section will help you develop a project based on such analysis. Read this section in tandem with Chapter 3; each step described here corresponds to a step described in Chapter 3. Also, use the four features of effective analytical writing (Chapter 5) to guide your comparison and synthesis:

1. **A relevant topic worthy of analysis.** Establish why it is important or relevant to compare the ideas, events, trends, or phenomena you are comparing:

   - Why would readers want to understand similarities or differences among the things you are comparing?
   - What's at stake for them—and for you—in explaining similarities or differences in these things?
   - What makes your reasons for comparing or synthesizing valid or relevant in this rhetorical situation?

2. **Complexity.** Explore the ideas, events, trends, or phenomena you are comparing or synthesizing in sufficient depth; avoid superficial comparisons or oversimplified synthesis:

   - Have you explored the ideas, events, trends, or phenomena you are comparing sufficiently to explain the similarities or differences among them?
   - How sound and reasonable is your basis for comparison in this case?
   - How does your synthesis of ideas, information, or perspectives contribute to your analysis without oversimplifying?

3. **Sufficient information and appropriate evidence.** Gather enough information about the ideas, events, trends, or phenomena you are comparing or synthesizing to understand and explain them:

   - What have you learned about the ideas, events, trends, or phenomena you are comparing that enables you to explain them sufficiently?
   - Are your comparisons based on enough information to make them valid?
   - To what extent are your sources trustworthy and your evidence adequate to explain the ideas, events, trends, or phenomena you are comparing?

4. **Reasonable conclusions.** Present reasonable and convincing conclusions on the basis of your comparison or synthesis:

   - How do your conclusions relate to the main purpose of your comparison or synthesis?
   - How does your synthesis of different ideas or perspectives lead your readers to your conclusions?
   - In what ways do your conclusions present readers with a sound explanation that does not oversimplify your topic?

## Step 1   Identify a topic for comparative analysis.

Comparative analysis doesn't necessarily begin with comparison; it usually happens because comparison (and synthesis) can help the writer answer a question or solve a problem. This question or problem can arise from your own experience, a trend, or an issue of current interest. So start with a question or problem that calls for or leads to comparison:

| Your own experience | <ul><li>What are the advantages and disadvantages of attending a two-year college as compared to a four-year college?</li><li>Is renting a better financial decision than purchasing a home?</li></ul> |
| --- | --- |
| A social or cultural trend | <ul><li>Why are more young people living together rather than getting married?</li><li>How do college students use different social media platforms such as SnapChat and Twitter?</li><li>What advantages do digital tablets have over laptops or smartphones?</li></ul> |
| An issue of current interest | <ul><li>Is universal health care a better system than the one currently in place in place in the U.S.?</li><li>Are online classes better than traditional face-to-face classes?</li><li>Is solar or wind power a better alternative to fossil fuels?</li></ul> |

Develop this question using Step #1 in Chapter 3.

## Step 2   Place your topic in rhetorical context.

The question you developed for Step #1 should point to a comparison of two or more things. For example, you might begin with this question: Is wind or solar power a better alternative to fossil fuels? Obviously, answering such a question requires comparing wind and solar power with fossil fuels. Now consider why such a comparison might matter—not just to you but to others:

7

| Who might also be interested in your question? | • People interested in environmental issues<br>• Homeowners or business owners<br>• Other students in your class<br>• People involved with the energy business |
|---|---|

| Why would this comparison matter to them? | • Alternatives to fossil fuels is a topic of general interest.<br>• Debates about climate change direct attention to alternative energy.<br>• Many people, including homeowners and business owners, are concerned about energy costs. |
|---|---|

| What's at stake for them in such a comparison? | • A better understanding of the relevant issues<br>• The ability to make a more informed decision about energy use<br>• A potential change of mind about current controversies |
|---|---|

In addressing these questions, you are identifying key elements of your rhetorical context that might shape your comparative analysis. Obviously, if your course assignment specifies an audience and purpose, adhere to the assignment guidelines as you examine the rhetorical context.

Using your answers to these questions as a guide, complete Step #2 in Chapter 3.

## Step 3  Select a medium.

If you have a course assignment, use the medium specified in the assignment guidelines. If you have a choice of medium, consider, as always, which medium might best address your intended audience and which might enable you to present your comparative analysis most persuasively.

Depending upon your audience and the purpose of your analysis, a website or perhaps a brochure might be a better way to convey the results of your comparison or synthesis than a traditional paper or essay. For example, if you wanted to participate in a debate in your town about new state policies that would encourage homeowners to use alternative energy sources, you might present your comparative analysis in a brochure, in a video, or on a local social media site so that you might reach your audience most effectively:

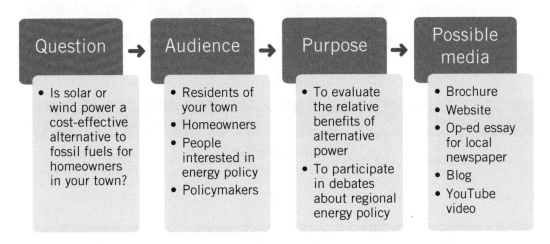

| Question | Audience | Purpose | Possible media |
|---|---|---|---|
| • Is solar or wind power a cost-effective alternative to fossil fuels for homeowners in your town? | • Residents of your town<br>• Homeowners<br>• People interested in energy policy<br>• Policymakers | • To evaluate the relative benefits of alternative power<br>• To participate in debates about regional energy policy | • Brochure<br>• Website<br>• Op-ed essay for local newspaper<br>• Blog<br>• YouTube video |

Step #3 in Chapter 3 will help you decide on the most appropriate medium for your comparative analysis.

## Step 4  Identify your main claim.

Your comparison of two or more ideas, trends, viewpoints, or products should lead to one or more claims about whatever you're analyzing—claims that address your main question from Step #1.

For example, in an analysis of solar and wind power as alternatives to fossil fuels, your comparison might reveal that one is better than the other, so your **main claim** might be that solar is a more cost effective and practical alternative to fossil fuels than wind power. However, it's possible that your comparative analysis will lead to a more complicated finding. You might have discovered, for example, that solar power is less efficient than wind power but wind turbines have more serious environmental consequences than solar panels; moreover, you might have learned that solar power is more practical in certain locations, whereas wind power cannot be used at all in neighborhoods where homes are close together. So your analysis might not lead to the conclusion that one is better than the other but that several key factors must be considered in deciding which to use. In that case, your main claim might be something like this:

*Neither wind nor solar power can feasibly be used on a large scale in all regions of the U.S.; therefore, both should be used where they are practical.*

7

As this example illustrates, a comparison involving a complicated question might lead to several different claims:

### Question

Which is a better alternative to fossil fuels: solar or wind power?

### Comparative Analysis

| Cost-effectiveness | Environmental consequences | Geographical considerations |

### Possible Claims

| One is better than the other. | No clear choice; each has advantages and disadvantages. |

Because you probably don't yet know what your analysis will reveal, you might not be able to identify your main claim with certainty at this point. So tentatively identify your main claim now, but be open to the possibility that it could change as you learn more through your analysis. Your main purpose at this point is to delve into your comparison and gain a better understanding of your topic so that you can address your question from Step #1.

Follow Step #4 in Chapter 3 to develop a **Guiding Thesis Statement**, which is a brief statement of the main claim(s) you expect to make in your comparative analysis. In addition, address the following questions:

Does your claim adequately address the question you identified for Step #1?

↓

How does the comparison you are making lead to your main claim?

↓

What makes your claim relevant to your rhetorical situation?

↓

How will your claim help your readers understand the ideas, phenomena, trends, or events you are comparing?

## Step 5  Support your claim(s).

At this stage you should be well into your research. As you explore your topic, keep in mind that you are trying to understand what you are comparing so that you can address your main question and meet the needs of your rhetorical situation. Your claims and your support for them will develop through this process of inquiry.

In addition to your main claim, your comparative analysis will likely result in several supporting claims. These claims might change as you explore your topic and find support for each claim.

Let's return to the example of solar power versus wind power. As you research the topic, you should gain a better understanding of some of the considerations related to alternative energy, and as a result you should have developed several supporting claims:

| Main claim | • In most cases solar power is a better alternative to fossil fuels than wind power. |
|---|---|
| Supporting claims | • Solar is less expensive than wind power.<br>• Wind power has significant environmental consequences.<br>• Neither solar nor wind power is feasible in all regions, but solar is more flexible. |

7

These supporting claims essentially build your case for your main claim. But for each of these claims you will need to provide evidence or reasoning. To do so, complete Step #5 in Chapter 3, supplementing it with the following steps:

| 1. List what you have learned through your comparison. | • Solar is generally less expensive than wind power.<br>• Wind power has some significant possible environmental consequences.<br>• Neither solar nor wind is feasible in all geographic locations.<br>• Wind power has a longer history than solar electric power. |
| --- | --- |
| 2. Determine whether each item on your list helps support your main claim(s); eliminate items that don't. | • Relative costs, environmental impact, and geographical feasibility are relevant to main claim.<br>• History of wind vs. solar power seems irrelevant to main claim. |
| 3. Identify the reasoning, information, and/or source that supports each item on your list. | • Cost analyses by economists of solar and wind power<br>• Articles and essays about the environmental impact of wind power and the controversies surrounding wind projects<br>• Studies of feasibility of solar and wind power for specific regions |
| 4. Determine whether your information, reasoning, and sources are sufficient for each item. | • Do cost analyses compare alternative power to fossil fuels?<br>• Are feasibility studies current and credible<br>• Are there other important considerations not addressed by available sources? |

As you continue to research your topic, keep the following in mind:

- **You are not only comparing but also synthesizing ideas or information.** As a result, you might develop claims that don't necessarily grow out of a direct comparison. For example, your comparison of wind and solar power might lead to a claim that neither is clearly preferable to the other in all cases but both can help reduce the environmental impact of fossil fuels. Your support for this claim will likely be based on synthesizing several different studies or perspectives about different aspects of energy—such as cost, equipment size, weather—rather than just citing studies that show that one is better than the other.

- **Comparative analysis can lead to unexpected insights that require you to adjust your claims.** For example, you might have learned that many states have special programs to help homeowners pay for solar panels, making solar panels less expensive than wind turbines in those states. That knowledge complicates your claim that solar power is more cost effective than wind power. As a result, you might have to adjust your claim, as in this example:

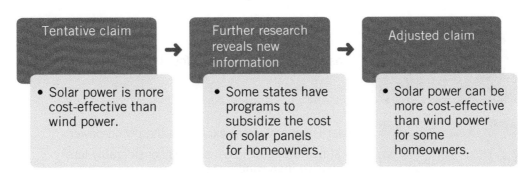

As you continue your inquiry, then, don't hesitate to revise your main claims or adjust your supporting claims.

If you have followed Steps 1 through 5 in Chapter 3, you are probably ready to write a complete draft of your project. Or you can move onto the next step before completing your draft.

7

## Step 6 | Organize your comparative analysis.

There are many ways to organize a comparative analysis. Here we will describe two conventional approaches: (1) a point-by-point comparison; and (2) main claims. The first approach works best when the focus of your project is a comparison of two things; often, if your research leads to complicated claims, or if you are synthesizing several ideas, the second approach can work well. Here's how these approaches might work for our example of a comparative analysis of solar vs. wind power as alternatives to fossil fuels:

### Organizing Your Comparative Analysis According to a Point-by-Point Comparison

In this approach, organize your project according to the criteria or principles that formed the basis for your comparison. Let's say that your research has led to the conclusion that there are three main considerations when it comes to determining whether solar power is preferable to wind power as an alternative to fossil fuels: cost, efficiency, and geographical considerations. You can organize your project by comparing solar and wind power on each of these three considerations:

| Basis for comparison | • Feasibility of alternatives to fossil fuels. |
|---|---|
| Cost | • Solar is generally less expensive than wind power.<br>• In states with subsidies, solar is considerably less expensive than wind power.<br>• Both solar and wind remain more expensive than most fossil fuels; however, costs for solar are decreasing. |
| Efficiency | • Solar panels are less efficient than wind turbines.<br>• Efficiency of both solar and wind power is improving with new technologies. |
| Geography | • Solar power is most feasible in regions with sunny, dry weather but also useful in other climates.<br>• Wind turbines are not feasible for homes in urban and many suburban neighborhoods but is preferable in open areas. |

A basic outline for this project would look like this:

I.   Introduction

II.  Background on alternative energy
     A. The need for alternative energy sources
     B. Solar and wind as the best available alternatives to fossil fuels

III. Comparison of solar and wind power as alternatives to fossil fuels
     A. Cost
     B. Efficiency
     C. Geography

IV.  Conclusion

To organize your comparative analysis in this way, follow these steps:

> 1. List the main points of comparison—that is, the criteria or principles on which you based your comparison.

> 2. Arrange the list in a way that would be effective for your readers: What order will present your analysis most clearly to those readers? What order seems to make the most logical sense?

> 3. Use this list to adjust the outline you developed for Step #6 in Chapter 3.

## Organizing Your Comparative Analysis According to Your Main Claims

You might decide that a point-by-point comparison does not effectively present what you found through your analysis and might even oversimplify your topic, especially if you found yourself synthesizing ideas and information from very different perspectives. In that case, consider organizing your project around your main claims

Let's imagine that your analysis of solar and wind power led to three main claims: (1) In most cases, solar power is more cost-effective than wind power; (2) the feasibility of solar and wind power depends on several key factors, especially geographical location; and (3) both solar and wind power remain impractical for most homeowners. You might organize your project as follows:

I.    Introduction

II.   Background on alternative energy

III.  Main claim #1: Cost-effectiveness of solar and wind power

IV.   Main claim #2: Feasibility of solar and wind power

V.    Main claim #3: Practicality of alternative energy

VI.   Conclusion

For each main claim, you would include your supporting claims. To organize your project in this way, follow this procedure:

**1. List the main claims you are making as a result of your comparative analysis.**

↓

**2. Identify your support and sources for each claim.**
Organize your main points of support for each claim from most persuasive to least persuasive.

↓

**3. Arrange the list in the order that makes the most sense.**
Consider: What order will present your claims most effectively to your readers? What order seems to make the most logical sense?

↓

**4. Create an outline** with each main section of your project devoted to one of your main claims.

Keep these possibilities in mind as you complete Step #6 in Chapter 3 to organize your project.

## Step 7  Get feedback.

Follow Step #7 in Chapter 3 to receive useful feedback on your comparative analysis, but have your readers also focus on the main characteristics of analytical writing (as described earlier above in this chapter):

| A relevant topic worthy of analysis | • What are the writer's reasons for comparison?<br>• Does the writer have something relevant to say? Does he or she show why this comparison matters?<br>• What makes this comparison relevant to the rhetorical situation? |
| --- | --- |
| Complexity | • What key ideas has the writer compared and/or synthesized? Does the analysis avoid oversimpifying the topic?<br>• What is the basis for comparison? Is it a reasonable basis for comparison?<br>• How thorough is the comparison? |
| Appropriate and sufficient support | • What support does the writer provide for main claims?<br>• Which sections of the essay need more support or stronger evidence?<br>• How appropriate are the sources for this topic and rhetorical situation?<br>• Is any of the evidence or support unnecessary? |
| Reasonable conclusions | • What conclusions does the writer reach as a result of the analysis? Do these conclusions grow logically from the comparison?<br>• How does the writer's synthesis of various perspectives lead to his or her conclusions? Are these conclusions reasonable? |

7

## Step 8 | Revise.

Follow the steps for Step #8 in Chapter 3 to revise your draft. Also use the following questions to guide your revisions:

| A relevant topic worthy of analysis | • How does your comparison fit the needs of your assignment or rhetorical situation?<br>• What is the purpose of your analysis? Should you refine the questions you are trying to answer with your analysis?<br>• Do you have something relevant to say as a result of your analysis? |
| --- | --- |
| Complexity | • What question(s) do you pose in your project? Have you developed your analysis sufficiently to answer these questions?<br>• Which sections of your analysis might need further explanation to address your topic sufficiently?<br>• Have you avoided oversimplifying your topic? |
| Appropriate and sufficient support | • What evidence do you provide to support your main claims? Is this evidence sufficient?<br>• Which sections need additional or stronger evidence? Can you eliminate any evidence or support without weakening your analysis?<br>• Are your sources appropriate for the rhetorical situation? |
| Reasonable conclusions | • In what ways do your conclusions address your main question? Do they grow logically out of your comparison?<br>• Do you present your conclusions clearly and persuasively?<br>• Have you neglected any key issues in your conclusons? |

Review your draft with these sets of questions in mind and revise accordingly.

## Step 9 | Refine your voice.

Sometimes in comparative analysis the writing can become repetitive or confusing because the comparison is presented in a way that repeats information about each thing being compared. (See "Talking About This Reading" on page 194.) As you follow the steps for Step #9 in Chapter 3, be alert for passages in your draft that might sound repetitive and revise them accordingly.

## Step 10   Edit.

Complete Step #10 in Chapter 3.

---

**WRITING PROJECTS**   **COMPARISON AND SYNTHESIS**

1. Identify a current controversy that interests you but about which you have no strong opinion. This controversy could be political (the debate about gun control), cultural (online privacy), economic (income inequality in the U.S.), or something else. Identify the main positions or perspectives on that controversy and write a comparative analysis of them. Be sure to have a clear basis for your comparison of these ideas or perspectives. Draw conclusions about the controversy on the basis of your analysis of the competing positions or perspectives and your own inquiry into the issues.

2. Imagine that you have been asked to be part of a campus committee charged with examining the relative benefits and drawbacks of living on campus as compared to living off campus. Focusing on your own campus and community, write a comparative analysis in which you explore the pros and cons of different student living arrangements. Assume that your campus administration is your primary audience for your report.

3. Identify a technological development that is changing the way we live. For example,

   - Social media have influenced many different aspects of our social and political lives.
   - Wireless devices such as smartphones have changed how we communicate and conduct business.
   - Online shopping has affected what goods we buy and how we buy them.
   - Computers have changed the way we write.

   Analyze such a technological development, comparing how we do things now as a result of this development to how we did them in the past. For your project, identify a specific audience and select a medium that would most effectively reach that audience.

---

## MindTap®

Request help with these Writing Projects and feedback from a tutor. If required, you may also participate in peer review, submit your paper for a grade, and view instructor comments online.

7

### In this chapter, you will learn to

1. Define rhetorical analysis and understand its purpose and uses.

2. Identify appropriate opportunities for rhetorical analysis.

3. Define the three main frameworks for rhetorical analysis and understand their different features and uses.

4. Apply three frameworks for rhetorical analysis to appropriate texts.

5. Write a rhetorical analysis of a written or visual text using an appropriate framework for analysis and the Ten Core Concepts.

### MindTap®

Understand the goals of the chapter and complete a warm-up activity.

# Conducting Rhetorical Analysis

**IN JUNE 2015** Donald J. Trump announced his candidacy for the Republican Party's nomination for President of the United States. Trump's speech, which he delivered at Trump Tower in New York City, was widely criticized as rambling, pompous, and full of inaccuracies, and many critics dismissed the speech as well as the candidate. Yet Trump soon emerged as the leading Republican candidate in a controversial campaign. His speeches, which offended many Americans and shocked many political experts, nevertheless seemed to resonate with many voters and energize his supporters. Political commentators in both the Republican and Democratic parties continued to point out numerous flaws and errors in Trump's speeches, while supporters often praised the candidate for telling it like it is. Scholars and political experts tried to explain these very different reactions to Trump's speeches. Why did the candidate's words appeal so forcefully to some voters yet infuriate others? How can we account for such different reactions? And what effect did his speeches ultimately have?

To answer such questions requires a specialized kind of analysis called *rhetorical analysis*, which explains *how* a text works within a certain set of circumstances. Rhetorical analysis illuminates the impact of a speech, image, video, song, advertisement, or essay by examining the characteristics and strategies that make a text persuasive (or not) within the rhetorical situation. Through rhetorical analysis, we can better understand why the statements of a controversial politician resonate with many voters and explain how elements such as language and imagery lend persuasive power to a speech. We can also examine the historical and political context to illuminate how a speech might play a role in an election.

Because rhetorical analysis explains how a text affects an audience, it can be a powerful tool, not only for academic assignments but also in our lives as consumers, citizens, and workers.

## Occasions for Rhetorical Analysis

If you have ever thought about what makes a particular television commercial so popular, a hit song so catchy, or a movie so engrossing, you have engaged in a kind of rhetorical analysis. For instance, you might have discussed with some friends why you find a certain scene in a popular horror movie so memorable. Examining how camera angles, music, and plot twists make the scene frightening helps you appreciate the director's expertise and better understand filmmaking in general. Such informal analysis can enhance the aesthetic enjoyment of a movie or song.

But you might also have reason for more formal rhetorical analysis:

> A well-known actor delivers a speech about protecting the world's oceans on a university campus. His speech is widely praised, but some students find his main argument questionable. They believe the positive response to his speech is based on his fame as an actor rather than on the strength of his argument. After rereading the speech, which was published in the campus newspaper, one student writes a letter to the editor explaining why the speech was appealing to so many students and pointing out the flaws in the speaker's argument.

. . . . . . . . . . . . . . . . . . . . . . . . . . . . . . . . . . . . . . . . . .

> A non-profit organization that collects and distributes food to low-income families has had difficulty recruiting student volunteers. Few students have responded to its flyers to volunteer to help with food distribution for an upcoming holiday. The organization's leaders have appointed a committee to look into recruitment. As part of its work, the committee analyzes recruiting materials for other successful organizations, including U.S. military recruiters, to see what makes them persuasive and how they might be adapted for social media to reach potential student volunteers.

---

**EXERCISE 8A    OCCASIONS FOR RHETORICAL ANALYSIS**

1. Find an essay, blog post, YouTube video, flyer, or letter to an editor about a controversy that interests you. The document might reflect your own views about the issue or it might be something with which you disagree. Write a paragraph explaining why you find the essay, blog post, video, flyer, or letter persuasive or not. Identify specific features, such as the use of language or images, that you believe help explain the document's effect on you.

2. Identify a film or television show that is popular with your friends. Write a paragraph explaining what makes the film or show appealing. Identify specific characteristics, such as the themes or filmmaker's style, that appeal to you and your friends.

3. Think of a time when a document of some kind seemed to have an impact on someone you know. For example, perhaps your parents were persuaded to vote for a political candidate by certain television ads supporting that candidate. Or maybe your roommate decided to buy a certain kind of device, such as a tablet or smartphone, after reading promotional materials about it. In a brief paragraph, describe that situation and examine how an understanding of the persuasiveness of the text might have been useful.

---

Both these scenarios call for rhetorical analysis. In each case, the analysis, which grows out of the need to understand why a text (a speech or a recruiting flyer) seems effective in addressing an audience, becomes a tool for solving a problem, making a decision, or developing a course

**Take A Closer Look.**

www.nd.gov/dhs/prevention

North Dakota Department of Human Services
North Dakota Prevention Resource and Media Center
The Office of Juvenile Procedural Safeguarding Prevention

of action. For example, understanding how military recruitment materials use certain images to appeal to students' sense of adventure can help a non-profit organization design more effective recruitment materials of its own. In this way, rhetorical analysis can help you identify and use appropriate strategies to create persuasive documents of your own.

# Understanding Rhetorical Analysis

Rhetorical analysis goes beyond describing the features of a text—for example, the writer's style or use of images—to explaining *how* a text works. You might see a poster like this one and notice the provocative words on the left side that form the shape of a beer bottle: *poison, depression, brain damage.* You might also notice the red color of the web address, the stark black background, and the bold white words, "Take A Closer Look." Describing such features calls attention to *what* is in the text, but it doesn't explain *why* the creators of the poster included those features or *how* those features might influence a viewer's response. Why use red, for example? What does that color signify? Why make the background black? What effect are the creators of the poster trying to achieve through these features? Would the effect be different with, say, a yellow or pink background? And who is the intended audience for this poster? Young people? Casual drinkers? How might the features of the poster—the beer bottle, the red words, the white command—speak to those audiences?

Such questions point to the rhetorical choices made by the poster's creators to reach a specific audience. Rhetorical analysis illuminates how a text reflects a rhetorical purpose and whether that text is likely to be persuasive to that audience. In this regard, **rhetorical analysis addresses three main questions:**

- **What** are the main features of the text?
- **How** do those features affect the intended audience?
- **Why** did the writer include those features and craft the text in specific ways?

Notice that in rhetorical analysis, you are not evaluating the message itself but how the message is conveyed. *The point of rhetorical analysis is not to agree or disagree with the message but to examine how effectively the message is conveyed to an audience.*

There are a variety of methods for conducting a rhetorical analysis. What follows is a discussion of three main methods, or frameworks, for rhetorical analysis.

8

# Basic Rhetorical Analysis

In its most basic form, rhetorical analysis is a matter of explaining a text in terms of the main elements of the rhetorical triangle: writer, audience, and purpose (see page 27 in Chapter 2). To do so, you must take the following steps:

1. **Identify the intended audience:** For whom is the text intended? What is the nature of the intended audience(s)? What characteristics might affect the audience's response to this message? (Would the gender or age of the audience matter?) What are the audience's expectations in this situation? (Is the text part of a special occasion, such as a graduation ceremony, that might influence what the audience expects from the speaker or writer?)

2. **Determine the author's purpose:** Why is the author addressing this particular audience? Does he or she have special expertise or authority on the topic? Does he or she have a special connection to the intended audience? What has prompted the author to address this topic at this time?

3. **Explain the rhetorical situation:** What are the circumstances surrounding the creation of this text? Are there specific factors that might affect how it is received by an audience? (Is the topic related to a current controversy? Are there economic or social conditions that might affect how the audience responds to the text?) Does the situation place any constraints on the author or the audience? (Is there a set of conventions that must be followed—as in a commencement address?)

4. **Examine the components of the text:** What is the author's message? What strategies are used to convey that message? What features of the text (word choice, style, arrangement) are most important in conveying that message?

5. **Evaluate the author's decisions:** How well has the author crafted the message to reach the intended audience? How well do the specific features of the text convey the message in this situation? How do those features reflect the author's intentions? How effectively do the strategies communicate the message to the audience? How well has the author accounted for important components of the rhetorical situation?

Library of Congress Prints and Photographs Division Washington, D.C. [LC-US262-15178]

For example, let's imagine you are analyzing President Abraham Lincoln's famous Gettysburg Address, delivered in November, 1863, a few months after that pivotal battle in the American Civil War. Here's the full text of the speech:

Four score and seven years ago our fathers brought forth on this continent a new nation, conceived in liberty, and dedicated to the proposition that all men are created equal.

Now we are engaged in a great civil war, testing whether that nation, or any nation, so conceived and so dedicated, can long endure. We are met on a great battle-field of that war. We have come to dedicate a portion of that field, as a final resting place for those who here gave their lives that that nation might live. It is altogether fitting and proper that we should do this.

But, in a larger sense, we can not dedicate, we can not consecrate, we can not hallow this ground. The brave men, living and dead, who struggled here, have consecrated it, far above our poor power to add or detract. The world will little note, nor long remember what we say here, but it can never forget what they did here. It is for us the living, rather, to be dedicated here to the unfinished work which they who fought here have thus far so nobly advanced. It is rather for us to be here dedicated to the great task remaining before us—that from these honored dead we take increased devotion to that cause for which they gave the last full measure of devotion—that we here highly resolve that these dead shall not have died in vain—that this nation, under God, shall have a new birth of freedom—and that government of the people, by the people, for the people, shall not perish from the earth.

- **Identify the intended audience:** The main goal is to identify (as much as possible) the relevant characteristics of the audience for which the speech was originally composed. Lincoln's immediate audience was the group of 15,000–20,000 people gathered for the dedication of the National Cemetery in Gettysburg on November 19, 1863. That audience included other politicians and dignitaries as well as ordinary citizens. But his broader audience was the American people as well as soldiers in the Union army.

- **Determine the writer's purpose:** Lincoln likely had several purposes in giving his speech. He intended not only to honor the soldiers who had given their lives at Gettysburg but also to reassure Americans—and especially the Union soldiers—that their great sacrifices were worthwhile. He hoped to convince them that their cause was worthy and that they must continue fighting, despite the costs.

- **Explain the rhetorical situation:** Identify the important features of the rhetorical situation that gave rise to the speech and shaped the impact of the speech. Lincoln's address was delivered at a ceremony dedicating the Gettysburg National Cemetery, an important event honoring the thousands who died there. At that point, the Civil War had been going on for two and a half years, with a horrific toll in lives lost and disrupted and no end in sight. Lincoln knew his words would be scrutinized not only by those present for the dedication but also by the nation as a whole. Also, he was not the main speaker at the ceremony, which might have prompted him to give such a short speech.

- **Examine the text:** Analyze how the important elements of Lincoln's speech—including his language and the structure of his speech—convey his message and affect his audience. The brevity of Lincoln's speech suggests that he chose his words carefully. His language is appropriately somber for the occasion, and he honors those who fell at that great battle. The structure of the speech emphasizes the larger cause for which the soldiers who died in that battle fought. He begins with a direct reference to the Declaration of Independence ("all men are created equal") and ends with a now-famous phrase that might be seen as a reference to the U.S. Constitution. His simple but careful word choices underscore a sense of the importance of the cause ("nobly advanced"; "great task"). His final statement that the government "shall not perish from the earth" emphasizes both the cost of the war and the importance of the cause.

8

- Evaluate the writer's decisions: Assess the overall rhetorical effectiveness of the speech. Lincoln's speech, now considered one of the great orations ever delivered, was widely praised at the time. Its simple but profound words conveyed both a sense of humility and the gravity of the moment and reassured Americans that their suffering was justified because their cause was right. His speech was appropriately solemn for the occasion but also resolute in the face of such great sacrifice.

Basic rhetorical analysis relies on key concepts—writer, audience, purpose, rhetorical situation—to explain how a text works in a given situation. As this example shows, this kind of analysis can be detailed and in-depth, enabling you to focus on elements that seem most important in a specific rhetorical situation.

---

**FOCUS**    **EXAMINING THE RHETORICAL SITUATION**

One helpful approach to analyzing the rhetorical situation was developed by a professor of communications named Lloyd Bitzer. Bitzer argued that understanding the specific rhetorical situation is essential for creating a text that is persuasive in that situation. Bitzer identified three main elements of the rhetorical situation:

**Exigence:** a situation that creates a need for communication or a problem that calls for persuasion; an urgency created by a situation in which something must change.

**Audience:** those who have an interest in the problem or situation and can be influenced by the writer or speaker; the audience is somehow involved in the situation such that it can help change that situation.

**Constraints:** factors that might place limits on the writer, including the time and place, the people involved, and social factors such as race, age, and gender. According to Bitzer, these factors "have the power to constrain decision and action needed to modify the exigence."

These terms are tools for closely examining how a rhetorical situation might shape a text and the impact of that text on an audience. Bitzer uses the example of Abraham Lincoln's Gettysburg Address to illustrate how an effective text fits the rhetorical situation:

- In that situation, the *exigence* was created by the horrible toll of dead and wounded in the Battle of Gettysburg, which was understood to be a crucial victory for the Union but at a terrible price. Lincoln saw a need to comfort the nation and justify the battle.

- His *audience*, the citizens of the Union states, had the power to support or reject his cause. Lincoln's speech spoke directly to their concerns.

- Finally, Lincoln negotiated important *constraints*, including the fact that he was delivering a eulogy for the Union dead. He was also addressing a nation deeply scarred and exhausted by the war. Those factors no doubt shaped his choice of words and even the short length of his speech.

# Using Classical Rhetorical Theory for Rhetorical Analysis

In Aristotle's famous definition, rhetoric is the art of identifying the available means of persuasion—in other words, understanding what makes a speech or text persuasive. Because of this focus on understanding persuasion, classical rhetorical theory can be a useful framework for examining how texts work and evaluating their impact on audiences.

Classical theory describes two sets of "proofs" that can be used for persuasion: artistic proofs and inartistic proofs.

1. **Artistic proofs.** These refer to the means of persuasion created by the writer or speaker. There are three kinds of artistic proofs, or "appeals":

   ***Ethical appeals (ethos).*** Appeals based on the character of the writer or speaker, which encompasses the background, expertise, integrity, and status of the writer/speaker; also, appeals based on the character of the subject of a text:

   - Who is the author (or subject of the text)? What is his or her reputation?
   - What kind of persona does the author convey? How does he or she relate to the audience?
   - What authority does this person have to address the topic? Does he or she have special training, expertise, or experience related to the topic?

   ***Logical appeals (logos).*** Appeals based on reasoning:

   - What logical arguments does the author present in support of his or her position?
   - Are these arguments well supported and carefully reasoned?

   ***Emotional appeals (pathos).*** Appeals based on emotion:

   - How does the writer use emotion in presenting his or her position?
   - What emotional response does the writer try to elicit from the audience? (For example, does the writer try to incite anger or evoke sympathy?)

2. **Inartistic proofs.** Existing evidence that a speaker or writer can use to make a text persuasive, such as facts, videos, scientific studies, and witness testimony:

   - What evidence does the writer present to support his or her claims?
   - How credible is that evidence? Is it appropriate for the topic?
   - Is the evidence used appropriately, fairly, and logically?

   (See "Making a Persuasive Appeal" and "Appraising and Using Evidence" in Chapter 11 for more information about persuasive appeals and the use of evidence.)

8

To illustrate how these categories help explain a text's effect on an audience, let's apply a classical framework to a famous speech on women's rights delivered in 1995 by Hillary Clinton. Clinton, who was then the U.S. First Lady, was speaking at the United Nations 4th World Conference on Women in Beijing. Here is an excerpt from her speech:

I would like to thank the Secretary General for inviting me to be part of this important United Nations Fourth World Conference on Women. This is truly a celebration, a celebration of the contributions women make in every aspect of life: in the home, on the job, in the community, as mothers, wives, sisters, daughters, learners, workers, citizens, and leaders.

**Emotional appeal:** Clinton evokes solidarity with her audience and offers praise for women, which helps establish an emotional bond with her audience.

It is also a coming together, much the way women come together every day in every country. We come together in fields and factories, in village markets and supermarkets, in living rooms and board rooms. Whether it is while playing with our children in the park, or washing clothes in a river, or taking a break at the office water cooler, we come together and talk about our aspirations and concern. And time and again, our talk turns to our children and our families. However different we may appear, there is far more that unites us than divides us. We share a common future, and we are here to find common ground so that we may help bring new dignity and respect to women and girls all over the world, and in so doing bring new strength and stability to families as well.

By gathering in Beijing, we are focusing world attention on issues that matter most in our lives—the lives of women and their families: access to education, health care, jobs and credit, the chance to enjoy basic legal and human rights and to participate fully in the political life of our countries. . . .

Earlier today, I participated in a World Health Organization forum. In that forum, we talked about ways that government officials, NGOs, and individual citizens are working to address the health problems of women and girls. Tomorrow, I will attend a gathering of the United Nations Development Fund for Women. There, the discussion will focus on local—and highly successful—programs that give hard-working women access to credit so they can improve their own lives and the lives of their families.

What we are learning around the world is that if women are healthy and educated, their families will flourish. If women are free from violence, their families will flourish. If women have a chance to work and earn as full and equal partners in society, their families will flourish. And when families flourish, communities

**Logical Appeal:** This logical argument in favor of supporting women's rights is likely to appeal to conservative members of her audience.

and nations do as well. That is why every woman, every man, every child, every family, and every nation on this planet does have a stake in the discussion that takes place here.

Over the past 25 years, I have worked persistently on issues relating to women, children, and families. Over the past two and a half years, I've had the opportunity to learn more about the challenges facing women in my own country and around the world.

I have met new mothers in Indonesia who come together regularly in their village to discuss nutrition, family planning, and baby care. I have met working parents in Denmark who talk about the comfort they feel in knowing that their children can be cared for in safe and nurturing after-school centers. I have met women in South Africa who helped lead the struggle to end apartheid and are now helping to build a new democracy. I have met with the leading women of my own hemisphere who are working every day to promote literacy and better health care for children in their countries. I have met women in India and Bangladesh who are taking out small loans to buy milk cows, or rickshaws, or thread in order to create a livelihood for themselves and their families. I have met the doctors and nurses in Belarus and Ukraine who are trying to keep children alive in the aftermath of Chernobyl.

The great challenge of this conference is to give voice to women everywhere whose experiences go unnoticed, whose words go unheard. Women comprise more than half the world's population, 70% of the world's poor, and two-thirds of those who are not taught to read and write. We are the primary caretakers for most of the world's children and elderly. Yet much of the work we do is not valued—not by economists, not by historians, not by popular culture, not by government leaders.

At this very moment, as we sit here, women around the world are giving birth, raising children, cooking meals, washing clothes, cleaning houses, planting crops, working on assembly lines, running companies, and running countries. Women also are dying from diseases that should have been prevented or treated. They are watching their children succumb to malnutrition caused by poverty and economic deprivation. They are being denied the right to go to school by their own fathers and brothers. They are being forced into prostitution, and they are being barred from the bank lending offices and banned from the ballot box.

Those of us who have the opportunity to be here have the responsibility to speak for those who could not. As an American,

**Ethical Appeal:** Here and in the following paragraph, Clinton cites her own experience, which gives her credibility as someone who understands women's issues.

**Emotional Appeal:** These images of caring, hard-working women evoke sympathy and admiration to help persuade the audience that supporting women is a worthwhile cause.

**Inartistic Proof:** Clinton cites facts to support her claim about the need to address women's issues.

**Emotional Appeal:** These images can provoke in the audience a sense of outrage and reinforce the idea that women must be protected from harm.

8

I want to speak for those women in my own country, women who are raising children on the minimum wage, women who can't afford health care or child care, women whose lives are threatened by violence, including violence in their own homes. . . .

If there is one message that echoes forth from this conference, let it be that human rights are women's rights and women's rights are human rights once and for all. Let us not forget that among those rights are the right to speak freely—and the right to be heard.

Women must enjoy the rights to participate fully in the social and political lives of their countries, if we want freedom and democracy to thrive and endure. It is indefensible that many women in nongovernmental organizations who wished to participate in this conference have not been able to attend—or have been prohibited from fully taking part.

> **Logical Appeal:** Clinton uses deductive reasoning (see "Deductive Reasoning" in Chapter 11) to convince her audience of the need to support women's rights.

Let me be clear. Freedom means the right of people to assemble, organize, and debate openly. It means respecting the views of those who may disagree with the views of their governments. It means not taking citizens away from their loved ones and jailing them, mistreating them, or denying them their freedom or dignity because of the peaceful expression of their ideas and opinions.

In my country, we recently celebrated the 75th anniversary of Women's Suffrage. It took 150 years after the signing of our Declaration of Independence for women to win the right to vote. It took 72 years of organized struggle, before that happened, on the part of many courageous women and men. It was one of America's most divisive philosophical wars. But it was a bloodless war. Suffrage was achieved without a shot being fired.

> **Inartistic Proof:** These facts support Clinton's inductive reasoning that securing women's rights is difficult but achievable

But we have also been reminded, in V-J Day observances last weekend, of the good that comes when men and women join together to combat the forces of tyranny and to build a better world. We have seen peace prevail in most places for a half century. We have avoided another world war. But we have not solved older, deeply-rooted problems that continue to diminish the potential of half the world's population.

Now it is the time to act on behalf of women everywhere. If we take bold steps to better the lives of women, we will be taking bold steps to better the lives of children and families too.

Using a classical framework in this way enables you to identify specific persuasive appeals, analyze the writer's choices, and evaluate the potential effect of those choices on a given audience.

Pau Barrena/Bloomberg/Getty Images

Ethical appeals are based on the character of the speaker or writer, referred to as *ethos* in rhetorical theory, but the strength of such an appeal can be affected by other factors, including the rhetorical situation, the audience, and the speaker's purpose. To account for the role of such factors in shaping an ethical appeal, we can identify two versions of *ethos*: invented ethos and situated ethos.

**Invented ethos** refers to a speaker's (or writer's) attempt to construct a particular kind of persona that might be persuasive for a specific rhetorical situation. For example, business leaders and political candidates sometimes try to present themselves as "regular" citizens to make themselves appear more likeable and appealing to their customers or constituents, as in this photograph of Mark Zuckerberg, founder and CEO of the social media company Facebook.

In formal settings, business leaders, especially those of large companies like Facebook, usually wear business suits. In this image, Zuckerberg, who was photographed while delivering a keynote address at the Mobile World Congress in Barcelona, Spain, in 2016, wears a T-shirt, tennis shoes, and casual pants. What message about Zuckerberg do you think this image conveys? What message do you think Zuckerberg intends to send to the audience at his address or to users of Facebook?

**Situated ethos** is a function of a speaker's reputation or standing in a specific community or context. For example, a physician will have a certain credibility not only in a professional setting, such as a hospital, but also in the community at large, because of the social standing of medical doctors.

You can use these concepts to lend greater depth to your rhetorical analysis.

## Stylistic Analysis

Sometimes looking closely at figures of speech, diction (word choice), rhythm, and syntax (sentence structure) can illuminate how a writer's language achieves a certain effect on an audience. This kind of analysis is often called *stylistic analysis*.

Here, for example, is an excerpt from the beginning of the famous address that President Franklin Delano Roosevelt gave to Congress on December 8, 1941, a day after the attack on Pearl Harbor by Japanese military forces, an event that drew the U.S. into World War II. Stylistic analysis enables us to examine Roosevelt's diction and syntax to assess its potential impact on his audience:

> Yesterday, December 7th, 1941—a date which will live in infamy—the United States of America was suddenly and deliberately attacked by naval and air forces of the Empire of Japan.

8

The seriousness of the situation called for a forceful yet somber speech. Roosevelt accomplishes that goal in part through his syntax and diction. He begins with three short elements separated by commas ("Yesterday, December 7th, 1941") followed by a parenthetical clause that is set off by dashes ("a date which will live in infamy"), creating a slow, somber pace to emphasize the importance of that fateful date. He uses the passive voice to emphasize the phrase *the United States of America* and to ensure that it will appear in the sentence before the phrase *the Empire of Japan*. Consider how different his statement would sound in the active voice: The Empire of Japan attacked the United States of America. The emphasis would shift away from the phrase *the United States of America*. Finally, his diction reinforces the emphasis created by his syntax. Two adverbs (suddenly and deliberately), for example, highlight the calculated nature of the surprise attack on the U.S. and reinforce the fact that the U.S. was the victim.

Stylistic analysis also enables us to examine how writers use various **figures of speech** to create certain effects to achieve their rhetorical purpose. For example, President Roosevelt used anaphora (see Focus: "Common Figures of Speech for Stylistic Analysis") to underscore the grave threat that the U.S. faced from Japan and to highlight the fact that the attack on Pearl Harbor was part of a larger, dangerous pattern:

> Yesterday, the Japanese government also launched an attack against Malaya.
> Last night, Japanese forces attacked Hong Kong.
> Last night, Japanese forces attacked Guam.
> Last night, Japanese forces attacked the Philippine Islands.
> Last night, the Japanese attacked Wake Island.
> And this morning, the Japanese attacked Midway Island.

The repetition of the phrase *last night* at the beginning of four successive sentences highlights the pattern of attack by Japan and creates a sense of doom. Notice, too, that the repetition of sentence structure (an introductory element followed by the subject, verb, and direct object) with the same subject (the Japanese) and verb (attacked) maintains emphasis on the perpetrators of the aggression (Japan) and reinforces the belligerence of Japan's actions. This repetitive syntax along with *anaphora* also maintains the strong but somber tone of the speech as well as its plodding rhythm, which helps underscore the seriousness of the occasion and conveys a sense of danger that might encourage Roosevelt's audience to agree that a declaration of war against Japan was not only justified but also necessary.

In this way, stylistic analysis illuminates how careful choices about language make a text more likely to accomplish the author's rhetorical goals. At the same time, practicing stylistic analysis can help you become a more sophisticated reader as well as a more successful writer.

---

**FOCUS    COMMON FIGURES OF SPEECH FOR STYLISTIC ANALYSIS**

Linguists have identified dozens of figures of speech, but this list includes the most common ones, which can be useful tools in stylistic analysis (and in your own writing):

**Alliteration:** Repetition of the consonant sound at the beginning of a word: "We buy our blankets at Bed, Bath & Beyond."

**Anaphora:** Repetition of the same word or phrase at the beginning of successive phrases, clauses, or sentences: "Never give in to pessimism. Never give in to defeatism. Never give in to nihilism."

**Antithesis:** Juxtaposition of contrasting words, phrases, or ideas for emphasis: "We are here to serve our citizens, not our ambitions."

**Epistrophe:** Repetition of the same word at the end of successive phrases, clauses, or sentences: "government of the people, by the people, for the people, shall not perish from the earth."

**Hyperbole:** Exaggeration used for emphasis: "I received a billion tweets about the election."

**Irony:** Using a word or phrase to mean the opposite of its literal meaning or conveying a meaning that is opposite of what appears to be the case: "You'll just *love* waiting in the long lines at the airport."

**Metaphor:** An implied comparison between two seemingly unrelated things: "Life is a journey."

**Oxymoron:** Putting two contradictory terms together: "The senator's affair was an *open secret* around the Capitol."

**Personification:** Assigning human qualities or abilities to inanimate objects or abstractions: "Fear raises its ugly head."

**Rhetorical Question:** A leading question whose answer is obvious. Example: "Are we going to just give up and let the other team win?"

**Simile:** A comparison between two fundamentally different things, using "like" or "as": "The brothers were like two peas in a pod."

These three main frameworks for rhetorical analysis can be combined to examine a text in great detail. For example, a stylistic analysis of Hillary Clinton's address about women's rights could enrich a classical analysis of her persuasive appeals.

---

**EXERCISE 8B**    **UNDERSTANDING RHETORICAL ANALYSIS**

1. Find an essay, blog post, flyer, web page, video, or other document you created in which you present an opinion or point of view. In a brief paragraph, identify what you think are the main features that might make your document persuasive to your intended audience. Explain why you included these features.

2. Using one of the frameworks discussed in this section, analyze the document you selected for Question #1 (or a different document). What did you learn about the effectiveness of the document as a result of your analysis? What changes might you make to the document on the basis of your analysis?

3. Find an essay, speech, blog post, or similar kind of text that presents an opinion on a topic that interests you. Analyze the rhetorical situation, using the concepts of a basic rhetorical analysis.

4. Using the same text you analyzed for Question #3 (or a different text), identify the persuasive appeals used in the text and evaluate the effectiveness of those appeals for the intended audience.

8

# Analyzing Images

Rhetorical analysis is not limited to written documents. You can also analyze the rhetorical effectiveness of advertisements, websites, videos, photographs, brochures, and similar visual or multimedia texts. In fact, as digital technologies enable us to use images and sound in increasingly sophisticated ways, the ability to understand the rhetorical impact of visual elements—what is sometimes called *visual literacy*—becomes ever more important.

For example, consider this photograph of the Snake River and Grand Teton mountain range in Wyoming made by Ansel Adams:

Such an image dramatically conveys a sense of the majesty of the American landscape in a way that is challenging to do with words alone. Some scholars believe that images like this one influenced the way Americans think about wilderness and helped spark the environmental movement in the 20th century.

Or consider this anti-smoking public service announcement:

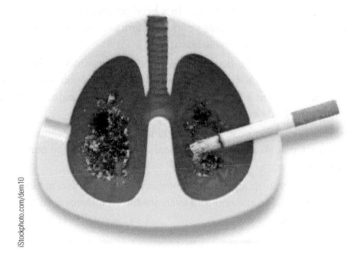

Using familiar items in a surprising way, this image provocatively communicates an anti-smoking message without words.

Finally, consider how combining words and images opens up additional possibilities for conveying a message, as in this advertisement from Amnesty International, a human rights organization:

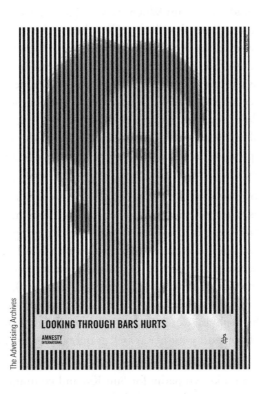

The ad presents the partially obscured image of Burmese human rights activist Aung San Suu Kyi, a Nobel Peace Prize laureate, who was held under house arrest in her native Burma from 1989 to 2010. The tagline ("Looking through bars hurts") has a double meaning: being imprisoned hurts, and so does looking at this ad, in which the vertical bars create an optical effect that can be physically uncomfortable for the viewer.

Visual analysis enables us to examine how texts like this advertisement convey their messages. Like the rhetorical analysis of a written document, visual analysis begins with an examination of the rhetorical situation: author, audience, purpose, and context. You can use the frameworks for rhetorical analysis described earlier in this chapter to analyze images and multimedia documents. For example, a **basic rhetorical analysis** of the Amnesty International advertisement would include an examination of the elements described on page 218:

- **Identify the intended audience:** Since Amnesty International (AI) is a global organization, we can assume an international audience for this advertisement. But AI was probably especially interested in reaching two main audiences: (1) the citizens and leadership of Burma, and (2) citizens and leaders in nations, such as the U.S. and France, that could pressure the Burmese government.

- **Determine the writer's purpose:** Amnesty International's main goal was to achieve the release of Aung San Suu Kyi from house arrest. To achieve that purpose, AI hoped to influence international opinion and pressure the Burmese government. This ad was intended to remind its audience of Suu Kyi's plight and evoke sympathy for her.

- **Explain the rhetorical situation:** When she was first arrested, Suu Kyi was a leader of the democratic opposition to Burma's military rulers during the national elections of 1990. In 1991 Suu Kyi was awarded the Nobel Peace Prize while still under arrest, and she remained imprisoned for 15 years of the next 23 years (until her release in 2010). Her case became an international cause as nations encouraged the Burmese government to release her and end its suppression of political opposition. While other nations in southeast Asia enjoyed economic development and close ties with western nations, Burma became more isolated, largely because of its refusal to release Suu Kyi. AI's ad campaign during those years can be seen as an effort to keep pressure on Burma by directing worldwide attention on Suu Kyi's case. This ad was published in 2010 just before Suu Kyi was released by the Burmese government.

- **Examine the components of the text:** The ad has three main features: the image of Suu Kyi, the vertical bars, and the phrase "Looking through bars hurts." Together, these three features convey a stark sense of imprisonment and evoke sympathy for the prisoner. Part of the ad's impact rests on the audience's familiarity with Suu Kyi, who was a sympathetic figure for most of the intended audience (citizens and leaders around the world) and a source of concern for part of that audience (the Burmese government). The ad's impact also rests on the vertical bars, which are literally difficult to look at because of the optical effect they create. Finally, the brief phrase explicitly reminds the audience of Suu Kyi's imprisonment and can provoke both sympathy for her as well as outrage against the Burmese government.

- **Evaluate the writer's decisions:** The simple design of the ad employs visual and textual elements effectively to evoke sympathy for Suu Kyi and communicate its message that her imprisonment is wrong and should be ended. The visual discomfort of looking at the vertical bars symbolizes Suu Kyi's physical discomfort, dramatically reminding the audience of Suu Kyi's situation. Even the likeness of Suu Kyi, with her slightly bowed head, conveys a sense of her situation and contributes to the effort to evoke sympathy in the audience.

You can also use **a classical approach** (see page 221) to analyze a visual text like this advertisement, focusing on the three kinds of artistic appeals:

- **Ethical appeal:** As a respected human rights organization, Amnesty International has international credibility. As a Nobel laureate, Aung Suu Kyi also has widespread credibility and respect.

- **Emotional appeal:** The image of Suu Kyi partially obscured by vertical bars is clearly intended to evoke sympathy as well as outrage. The tagline strengthens the emotional appeal by calling attention to the physical reality of Suu Kyi's situation. Moreover, the visual effect literally causes discomfort in the viewer, which is likely to enhance the emotional appeal.

- **Logical appeal:** The implicit logic of this ad focuses on the physical discomfort of Suu Kyi, which is highlighted by the visual effect of the vertical bars and the tagline. The reasoning of the ad might be stated as follows: Because incarceration is painful, we should be concerned about the imprisonment of Suu Kyi. The ad also suggests that this imprisonment is morally wrong or illegal. Viewers who recognize the likeness of Suu Kyi will know that she suffered greatly in promoting human rights for the citizens of her nation. Imprisoning someone with such integrity, the ad suggests, is wrong. Such a logical appeal relies on the cultural meaning of the image of Suu Kyi as a champion of human rights as well as the meaning of the vertical lines (which signify prison bars).

As this example suggests, images encompass various design features, such as color and layout, to create their effects. Examining these technical components can result in a more sophisticated rhetorical analysis (see Focus: "Principles of Visual Design ).

## FOCUS  PRINCIPLES OF VISUAL DESIGN

Artists and graphic designers create visual texts according to five established principles of composition—balance, proportion, emphasis, contrast, and movement—which you can use to illuminate the effect of specific components of an image. For example, imagine that this photograph is part of a public relations campaign to promote sailing vacations in a certain location. Here's how we might apply these principles to evaluate the rhetorical impact of the photograph:

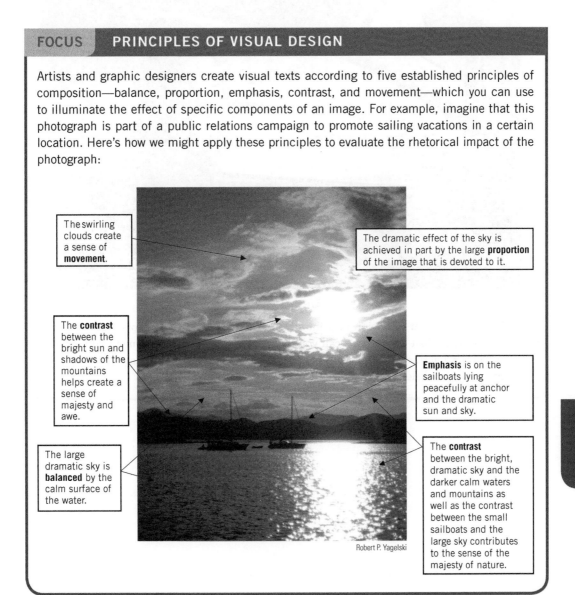

The swirling clouds create a sense of **movement**.

The dramatic effect of the sky is achieved in part by the large **proportion** of the image that is devoted to it.

The **contrast** between the bright sun and shadows of the mountains helps create a sense of majesty and awe.

**Emphasis** is on the sailboats lying peacefully at anchor and the dramatic sun and sky.

The large dramatic sky is **balanced** by the calm surface of the water.

The **contrast** between the bright, dramatic sky and the darker calm waters and mountains as well as the contrast between the small sailboats and the large sky contributes to the sense of the majesty of nature.

Robert P. Yagelski

8

1. Using the tools for visual analysis discussed in this chapter, analyze an image, such as a photograph circulated via social media, that you find compelling.

2. Use the concepts discussed in this section to analyze the effectiveness of this public service announcement:

Distraction

3. Analyze a popular television or print advertisement using the concepts discussed in this section. What conclusions can you draw about how the advertisement addressed its intended audience? What conclusions can you draw from your analysis about the impact of visual elements on an audience?

# Reading Rhetorical Analysis

What follows are three examples of rhetorical analysis, illustrating the four main characteristics of effective analytical writing and the frameworks for rhetorical analysis described in this chapter. Consider these questions as you read:

| A relevant topic worthy of analysis | • How does the writer establish that the text is relevant and worthy of analysis?<br>• What is the writer's purpose in analyzing this text? |
| --- | --- |

| Complexity | • Has the writer examined the main features of the text?<br>• How has the writer explained the impact of the text on the intended audience? |
| --- | --- |

| Sufficient information and appropriate analysis | • What analytical framework has the writer applied to this text? How does this analysis illuminate the effectiveness of the text?<br>• What evidence does the writer use to support the analysis? Is this evidence appropriate? |
| --- | --- |

| Reasonable conclusions | • What conclusions does the writer draw from the analysis?<br>• Does the analysis lead logically to these conclusions?<br>• How persuasive are the conclusions? How effectively are they presented? |
| --- | --- |

## MindTap

Read these rhetorical analysis examples. Highlight and take notes online. Additional readings are also available online.

8

# Obama's Graceful Pause in Charleston
### by Peter Manseau

*On the evening of June 17, 2015, a dozen or so people were attending a prayer meeting at the historical Emanuel African Methodist Episcopal Church in Charleston, South Carolina. In the midst of a discussion of Scripture at that meeting, a young man named Dylann Roof pulled a gun from his backpack and began shooting the other participants. Nine people were killed, including Clementa Pinckney, the pastor of the church who was also a state senator in South Carolina. A few days later, then-President Barack Obama delivered the eulogy at Reverend Pinckney's funeral. The shootings in Charleston were among several other mass shootings in the U.S. in 2015, and many Americans were intensely interested in what President Obama would say. In remarks that lasted approximately 30 minutes, he praised Rev. Pinckney, acknowledged the other victims of the shooting, condemned the violence, and called for reforming the nation's gun laws to help prevent more such shootings. His eulogy was widely praised and described as stirring, rousing, electrifying, and frank.*

*But the moment that received the most attention from journalists, political observers, and politicians occurred near the end of Obama's speech, when he paused for several seconds and then began singing the traditional Christian hymn "Amazing Grace." In the following essay, writer Peter Manseau focuses on that moment from President Obama's eulogy. Although Manseau does not present a traditional rhetorical analysis, his careful examination of that one moment in the speech relies on the rhetorical concepts discussed in this chapter, especially the role of rhetorical context. As you'll see, Manseau's essay, which appeared in* The Atlantic *in June 2015, shows that a carefully timed silence can be as important as a speaker's carefully chosen words in determining the impact of a speech on an audience.*

· · · · · · · · · · · · · · · · · · · · · · · · · · · · · · · · · · · ·

## Talking About This Reading

> **Colin Roberts (student):** "This author's interpretation of President Obama's speech makes sense, but it also made me wonder whether prolonged moments of silence, like the one in Obama's speech, will continue to have such an impact with future generations that are becoming increasingly less patient in such a fast-paced society."

> **Bob Yagelski:** Colin, your thoughtful comment underscores the importance of examining the rhetorical context when analyzing a speech such as the one President Obama delivered in South Carolina in 2015. We can't know how future generations might respond to a pause like the one in his speech, but we can carefully analyze the audience to assess the potential impact of such a strategy. We can also be aware of how social and technological developments might influence an audience's response.

· · · · · · · · · · · · · · · · · · · · · · · · · · · · · · · · · · · ·

Coverage of the memorial service held for Reverend Clementa Pinckney in Charleston last week focused largely on the surprising moment when the leader of the free world broke into song. That song, of course, was "Amazing Grace" and the president sang it distinctly in the style of the black church.

For all the attention Obama's unexpected performance received, though, it's worth taking another look at the "Amazing Grace" clip, this time watching for the silence. His singing seems to be a release of the collective tension that had been building for a week after the Emanuel A.M.E. shooting. But the preceding pause seems to hold its hearers captive. Though he is frequently interrupted with cheers and amens throughout his eulogy for Reverend Pinckney, the pause he takes 35 minutes into the speech is easily the longest break from the text before him.

Between the second time he speaks the words "Amazing Grace" and the first time he sings them, 13 full seconds pass. Thirteen seconds with thousands hanging on his next words: grieving church members, a phalanx of purple-robed clergy, and a church band that had until then had been all too ready to accompany him with organ trills and guitar licks.

During those 13 seconds, Obama looks out over the crowd, then down at his notes, then he shakes his head slightly. Watch behind him; the assembled clergy seem momentarily unsure what will happen next. They sit still, watching him. The only movement comes from Bishop Julius H. McAllister, seated just to the left, who closes his eyes and sways as if he can already hear the music. Throughout the eulogy, the president's words had been met with call-and-response encouragements, but for every one of those thirteen seconds there is only silence.

Obviously, Obama knows how to work a crowd. He's familiar with the rhythms of worship in the black church; he usually rides them effortlessly. But this long pause was different. What did it mean?

"Silence is to sermons what space is to magazines," Mark Galli, a former pastor and current editor of the evangelical magazine *Christianity Today*, has written. "If an article simply begins in the upper left-hand corner of a page (or fails to use columns or uses all of the page for words), we're less likely to read it." White space not only provides a frame; if used well, it also focuses attention, raises expectations, and heightens the encounter with plain text on a page. An unexpectedly quiet moment in the midst of intense preaching attempts to do the same. As Richard L. Eslinger, another evangelical writer, put it, "Without a necessary silence, the power of words decays."

"Some preachers use a pause at the beginning of a sermon to establish mutual 'presence'" with their congregations, the Lutheran-minister-turned-Catholic-priest Richard John Neuhaus once wrote. "Similarly, a brief pause in the middle of the sermon or at some other point along the way can effectively reestablish presence and purpose."

This was a homiletic gambit particularly favored by Martin Luther King Jr. When called to the pulpit, Neuhaus remembered, King would often stand and wait—sometimes ten seconds or more—but it would be "a very active kind of waiting," in which he would look out over the congregation, "establishing his identity to them, and theirs to him. "And in those accumulating seconds, it would become clear "something important was about to happen."

Silence isn't necessarily associated with black churches in the popular imagination. The notion of religious silence may evoke thoughts of Trappists using monastic sign language to avoid disturbing the contemplative calm of the cloister, or a meetinghouse full of Quakers patiently listening to the clock tick until someone has something to say.

*You can listen to this eulogy being delivered by President Obama by searching for the video of it on YouTube, using the phrase *Clementa Pinckney eulogy*.

(Continued)

Yet long pauses like the one Obama used in Charleston are an overlooked part of worship in many black churches. In his 1995 book, *The Hum: Call and Response in African American Preaching*, Evans Crawford suggested that silence—what he called the "sermon pause"—often becomes a third partner to the familiar pairing of the preacher's questions and the congregation's affirmative replies.

"It is not a 'dead silence' but a 'live silence,'" Crawford writes. "It is a silence that organizes time, that invites us to think of time not as something passed but as something plotted."

In the introduction to his classic 1927 collection of poems emulating African American sermons, *God's Trombones*, James Weldon Johnson said silence is one of the essential stylistic elements by which congregations instantly know one preacher from another.

Some prominent preachers—such as the mid-20th century giant of the black church, Howard Thurman—were known for pausing for minutes on end during their preaching and public prayer. In churches crowded with people eager to shout and sing, such lingering silences became more tension-filled the longer they wore on. "These periods of silence induced a sense of awkwardness initially," the Baptist minister Jerry M. Carter writes of Thurman's pauses. "But the climate produced by silence, when coupled with relevant content, is what makes for a powerful preaching moment."

Creating such moments is a high-wire act. "This takes a degree of confidence," Neuhaus said of drawn-out, intentional sermon pauses. "The uncertain preacher is eager to get through it, lest he lose the point or the people's attention." If most preachers were to try it, the *Christianity Today* editor Galli adds, "people would likely fidget, wondering if we had simply forgotten what we were going to say."

But for experienced preachers, silence can be used in exactly the opposite way: to demonstrate full control over the moment and the craft. Obama's eulogy is an indication of the confidence he seems to feel midway through his second term. This speech, through responding to tragedy, may be remembered as one of the most triumphant of his presidency. Singing certainly has something to do with that, but so does silence.

Source: Manseau, Peter. "Obama's Graceful Pause in Charleston." *The Atlantic*, 30 June 2015, www.theatlantic.com/politics/archive/2015/06/obamas-graceful-pause-in-charleston/397223/.

---

## EXERCISE 8D    ANALYZING A EULOGY

1. Manseau's analysis focuses on only a few seconds of a speech that lasted more than 30 minutes. Do you think his analysis sufficiently explains those few moments and their role in the entire speech? Why or why not? (Cite specific passages from the essay to support your answer.)

2. Manseau tells his readers that pauses during speeches, such as the one President Obama made during his eulogy, are part of the oral tradition in black churches. Why is that information important to Manseau's analysis? What does it contribute to our understanding of the choices President Obama made in delivering that speech?

3. Find a video of President Obama's eulogy online and watch it. Consider how well Manseau's analysis explains your own reaction to the speech. After viewing the video, do you find yourself more or less convinced by Manseau's analysis? Explain.

## Rhetorical Analysis of a National Health Service of England Public Service Advertisement

*Public service announcements (PSAs) typically provide information intended to promote the public good. Often, PSAs emphasize positive feelings. The famous U.S. Forest Service ad campaign to prevent forest fires, for example, featured the friendly cartoon character of Smokey the Bear, who was meant to appeal to children as much as to adults. Sometimes, however, PSAs are intended to be provocative and even disturbing, such the anti-smoking PSA from the National Health Service of England analyzed in the following essay. As you read, notice how the analysis, which appeared on the website writinghood.com in 2009, relies on a traditional classical framework and places the PSA in broader rhetorical context to explain its purpose.*

### Talking About This Reading

**Malik King (student):** The author used a lot of terms such as *pathos* that to an ordinary person would be difficult to understand. That made the text hard to understand at times.

**Bob Yagelski:** Malik, your comment reminds us that writers make assumptions about what their readers know, especially if the intended audience is a specialized one. This essay was published on a website intended for people interested in writing, and the author reasonably assumed that readers of that website would understand terms like *pathos*. If you're "an ordinary person" who is not part of that intended audience, you might have to learn the definitions of such terms (which are explained in this chapter!) so that you can follow the author's analysis.

The average smoker needs over five thousand cigarettes a year.
Get unhooked. Call 0800 169 0 169 or visit getunhooked.co.uk

NHS

SMOKEFREE

The Advertising Archives

Advertisements often use a variety of techniques to convince viewers of the argument they are presenting. This anti-smoking advertisement by National Health Service (NHS) of England is no exception. It employs pathos and embeds an ethical argument in its visual appeal. It also makes a logical appeal through the text of the ad and its imagery. To understand this advertisement it is also important to consider the point of view, since the advertisement was created by a government program that deals with health care and is funded by the citizens of England.

This National Health Service of England advertisement makes a very strong appeal to pathos, or emotion. The image provokes a strong sense of shock. The young woman, who is understood to be a smoker, is shown with a hook protruding from her mouth, like a fish that has been caught. The NHS intends to shock viewers with this graphic, if metaphoric, depiction of just how addictive smoking can be. The text below the image

*(Continued)*

reinforces the emotional appeal. Like the image, the text is intended to shock the viewer with an alarming statistic—5000 cigarettes per year—that underscores the addictive nature of smoking. The word choice is deliberate. The ad does not read, "The average smoker smokes five thousand cigarettes in a year"; instead, it states that "the average smoker *needs*" that many cigarettes. Using that term ("needs") reinforces the addictiveness of smoking.

The ethical appeal in this advertisement is made implicitly through the image of the young woman, who is being pulled by a fishing line and hook that is painfully embedded in her lip. This image can evoke sympathy as well as shock, enhancing the emotional appeal, but the NHS is also using the image to suggest that this is what companies that produce and sell cigarettes are doing to their customers. The NHS seems to want viewers to be taken aback and to see just how serious a smoking addiction is and thus to consider what tobacco companies do unethical. The ad is also largely intended to appeal to smokers. Most smokers might not consider their addiction serious, but through this ad the NHS seems to be trying to prevent such a complacent attitude. The agency wants the smokers themselves to realize just how badly they are "hooked" not only by the cigarettes they are smoking but also by the companies that produce cigarettes.

The advertisement's logical appeal rests on the implicit reasoning that an addiction is painful and therefore bad and should be avoided. Using the image of the "hooked" woman in combination with the fact, which is conveyed by the text, that a smoker "needs" 5000 cigarettes each year, the ad makes a logical argument: Addiction is painful, destructive, and obviously bad for people (an idea conveyed by the image); cigarette smoking is an addiction (a point made by the text); therefore, smoking is bad for people. The logical conclusion to be drawn is that smokers should quit smoking.

Point of view can also help explain the message conveyed by this advertisement. The argument made by the ad reflects the point of view of the National Health Service of England, which is a publicly funded health care system in England. As a publically funded agency, NHS is supported by taxes, which the NHS uses to fund its healthcare services. At first glance it might appear that the NHS ad is being produced for the sole purpose of showing just how devastating a smoking addiction can be, but the ad might reflect a larger purpose. The more people who become sick under the care of the National Health Service, the more tax money the government must provide to the agency. Since smoking can lead to lung cancer and other illnesses such as cardiovascular disease and chronic obstructive pulmonary disease, more smokers means more money that the NHS can expect to spend caring for these patients. So the more people the NHS can prevent or stop from smoking, the more money they will be able to spend on other patients. It seems reasonable to conclude, then, that part of the purpose of the NHS in developing this ad was to reduce the amount of tax revenue that will ultimately be spent on patients with self-inflicted and preventable illnesses.

This advertisement attempts to persuade viewers through strong emotional and ethical appeals, but the larger meaning of the advertisement can be seen by considering the point of view of the ad's creator, National Health Service of England.

Source: "A Great Example of a Rhetorical Analysis." *Writinghood*, 27 Dec. 2009, writinghood.com/writing/a-great-example-of-a-rhetorical-analysis/.

1. What is the author's purpose in analyzing this public service announcement? Why do you think readers should be interested in such an analysis?

2. What is the context for the public service announcement? How does the author account for that context in explaining the PSA's persuasive appeals?

3. How well do you think this analysis explains the PSA? Do you find the PSA persuasive? Why or why not? What might your response to the PSA suggest about rhetorical analysis?

## A Rhetorical Analysis of the Declaration of Independence: Persuasive Appeals and Language
### by Jim Stover

*Jim Stover, an English teacher at the Baylor School in Chattanooga, Tennessee, takes an unusual approach in this analysis of the Declaration of Independence, one of the most famous and important documents ever written. Stover combines a stylistic analysis with a classical approach to examine the arguments forwarded in the Declaration. But instead of a conventional essay, Stover presents his analysis in a "two-column" format, using different colors to identify and explain the different persuasive appeals and stylistic devices in the document. The substance of Stover's analysis is traditional, but its form is not. Stover produced this analysis for his high school students. As you read, decide whether this format makes his analysis more or less effective for his intended audience.*

. . . . . . . . . . . . . . . . . . . . . . . . . . . . . . . . . . . . . . .

### Talking About This Reading

**Tamara Lopez (student):** My first impression was that this was going to be very difficult, but the writer's color-coded analysis actually made it a lot easier to understand. However, I didn't know the meanings of some of the words in the Declaration itself: usurpations, abdicated, magnanimity, consanguinity, acquiesce.

**Bob Yagelski:** Tamara, reading an old text such as the Declaration of Independence often means confronting unfamiliar terms and stylistic features. In this case, you have taken the first step toward making sense of such terms: You have identified them. Now you can look them up (and use the strategies for reading unfamiliar texts described in Chapter 19). As for Stover's approach to presenting his analysis, his use of visual design features (as described in this chapter and Chapter 20) obviously worked for you.

. . . . . . . . . . . . . . . . . . . . . . . . . . . . . . . . . . . . . . .

8

## Color key

**Persuasive appeals**

Green: appeal to ethos (the standing of the writer or speaker).

Magenta: appeal to pathos (emotion).

Blue: appeal to logos (reason): deductive reasoning (navy blue) and inductive reasoning (dark blue).

**Language analysis**

Light blue: diction (word choice).

Orange: syntax (sentence structure).

Dark green: images (figurative language, imagery, and the like).

••••••••••••••••••••••••••••••••••••••••••••••

IN CONGRESS, July 4, 1776.

### The unanimous Declaration of the thirteen united States of America,

1   When in the Course of human events, it becomes necessary for one people to dissolve the political bands which have connected them with another, and to assume among the powers of the earth, the separate and equal station to which the Laws of Nature and of Nature's God entitle them, a decent respect to the opinions of mankind requires that they should declare the causes which impel them to the separation.

In the long first sentence of the declaration, the writers set their revolution in the context of human history ("the Course of events"). They also establish their ethical standing—that they are men of good sense, good character, and good will—first, by acknowledging that they need to explain to the world the reasons for their actions.

2   We hold these truths to be self-evident, that all men are created equal, that they are endowed by their Creator with certain unalienable Rights, that among these are Life, Liberty and the pursuit of Happiness.—That to secure these rights, Governments are instituted among Men, deriving their just powers from the consent of the governed, —That whenever any Form of Government becomes destructive of these ends, it is the Right of the People to alter or to abolish it, and to institute new Government, laying its foundation on such principles and organizing its

In the first sentence of the second paragraph, the parallel structure and repetition of *that* enable the writers to enunciate with great clarity their fundamental beliefs, which become the major premise in a deductive argument:

Major premise: the role of government is to protect the rights of the people; when government fails to do so, the people have the right to change it.

powers in such form, as to them shall seem most likely to effect their Safety and Happiness. Prudence, indeed, will dictate that Governments long established should not be changed for light and transient causes; and accordingly all experience hath shewn, that mankind are more disposed to suffer, while evils are sufferable, than to right themselves by abolishing the forms to which they are accustomed. But when a long train of abuses and usurpations, pursuing invariably the same Object evinces a design to reduce them under absolute Despotism, it is their right, it is their duty, to throw off such Government, and to provide new Guards for their future security.—Such has been the patient sufferance of these Colonies; and such is now the necessity which constrains them to alter their former Systems of Government. **The history of the present King of Great Britain is a history of** repeated injuries and usurpations, all having in direct object the establishment of an absolute Tyranny over these States. To prove this, let Facts be submitted to a candid world.

He has refused his Assent to Laws, the most wholesome and necessary for the public good.

He has forbidden his Governors to pass Laws of immediate and pressing importance, unless suspended in their operation till his Assent should be obtained; and when so suspended, he has utterly neglected to attend to them.

He has refused to pass other Laws for the accommodation of large districts of people, unless those people would relinquish the right of Representation in the Legislature, a right inestimable to them and formidable to tyrants only.

Minor premise: the British government has usurped the rights of the colonists.

Conclusion: the colonists have a right to overthrow that government.

The personification of prudence emphasizes how reasonable the writers are. But logic drives them to conclude that they have no choice but to overthrow a tyrannous government. The negative diction about the actions of the British king and his subjects begins in this paragraph—and carries an emotional appeal.

What follows in the body of the document is an inductive proof of the minor premise above: a list of ways in which the British government (and especially the King) has stripped the colonists of their rights.

8

Through most of the document, the writers appeal to pathos through the words they use in their list of the King's wrongs: check out all the negative words in this section of the document.

He has called together legislative bodies at places unusual, uncomfortable, and distant from the depository of their public Records, for the sole purpose of fatiguing them into compliance with his measures.

He has dissolved Representative Houses repeatedly, for opposing with manly firmness his invasions on the rights of the people.

He has refused for a long time, after such dissolutions, to cause others to be elected; whereby the Legislative powers, incapable of Annihilation, have returned to the People at large for their exercise; the State remaining in the mean time exposed to all the dangers of invasion from without, and convulsions within.

He has endeavoured to prevent the population of these States; for that purpose obstructing the Laws for Naturalization of Foreigners; refusing to pass others to encourage their migrations hither, and raising the conditions of new Appropriations of Lands.

He has obstructed the Administration of Justice, by refusing his Assent to Laws for establishing Judiciary powers.

He has made Judges dependent on his Will alone, for the tenure of their offices, and the amount and payment of their salaries.

He has erected a multitude of New Offices, and sent hither swarms of Officers to harrass our people, and eat out their substance.

He has kept among us, in times of peace, Standing Armies without the Consent of our legislatures.

He has affected to render the Military independent of and superior to the Civil power.

He has combined with others to subject us to a jurisdiction foreign to our constitution, and unacknowledged by our laws; giving his Assent to their Acts of pretended Legislation:

**The long list of grievances reads like hammer blows** because of the parallel structure and anaphora, the vilifying verbs, and the choice of other words that arouse the emotion of the audience.

For Quartering large bodies of armed troops among us:

For protecting them, by a mock Trial, from punishment for any Murders which they should commit on the Inhabitants of these States:

For cutting off our Trade with all parts of the world:

For imposing Taxes on us without our Consent:

For depriving us in many cases, of the benefits of Trial by Jury:

For transporting us beyond Seas to be tried for pretended offences

For abolishing the free System of English Laws in a neighbouring Province, establishing therein an Arbitrary government, and enlarging its Boundaries so as to render it at once an example and fit instrument for introducing the same absolute rule into these Colonies:

For taking away our Charters, abolishing our most valuable Laws, and altering fundamentally the Forms of our Governments:

For suspending our own Legislatures, and declaring themselves invested with power to legislate for us in all cases whatsoever.

He has abdicated Government here, by declaring us out of his Protection and waging War against us.

He has plundered our seas, ravaged our Coasts, burnt our towns, and destroyed the lives of our people.

He is at this time transporting large Armies of foreign Mercenaries to compleat the works of death, desolation and tyranny, already begun with circumstances of Cruelty & perfidy scarcely paralleled in the most barbarous ages, and totally unworthy the Head of a civilized nation.

The list climaxes with "He is"—the only phrase other than "He has" in the list. The present tense lends urgency to the need for revolution; otherwise, only "death, desolation, and tyranny" await.

8

He has constrained our fellow Citizens taken Captive on the high Seas to bear Arms against their Country, to become the executioners of their friends and Brethren, or to fall themselves by their Hands.

He has excited domestic insurrections amongst us, and has endeavoured to bring on the inhabitants of our frontiers, the merciless Indian Savages, whose known rule of warfare, is an undistinguished destruction of all ages, sexes and conditions.

The emotional language reaches a crescendo in the final paragraphs citing the King's actions. He has shown "Cruelty & perfidy scarcely paralleled in the most barbarous ages," and he is "totally unworthy [to be] the Head of a civilized nation."

3  In every stage of these Oppressions We have Petitioned for Redress in the most humble terms: Our repeated Petitions have been answered only by repeated injury. A Prince whose character is thus marked by every act which may define a Tyrant, is unfit to be the ruler of a free people.

The two paragraphs following the list of grievances are packed with effective rhetorical devices that only heighten the ethical appeal: the writers are intelligent and eloquent men.

4  Nor have We been wanting in attentions to our Brittish brethren. We have warned them from time to time of attempts by their legislature to extend an unwarrantable jurisdiction over us. We have reminded them of the circumstances of our emigration and settlement here. We have appealed to their native justice and magnanimity, and we have conjured them by the ties of our common kindred to disavow these usurpations, which, would inevitably interrupt our connections and correspondence. They too have been deaf to the voice of justice and of consanguinity. We must, therefore, acquiesce in the necessity, which denounces our Separation, and hold them, as we hold the rest of mankind, Enemies in War, in Peace Friends.

Again, the writers assure the world of their honest efforts to avoid independence. But the King, whose injustices they have just listed, has given them no choice. The colonists have made every appeal, not only to the King, but to "our Brittish brethren." Again—to no avail. They too "have been deaf to the voice of justice and of consanguinity."

5  We, therefore, the Representatives of the united States of America, in General Congress, Assembled, appealing to the Supreme

In the concluding paragraph, the writers (and signers) of the Declaration appeal to God ("the Supreme Judge

Judge of the world for the rectitude of our intentions, do, in the Name, and by Authority of the good People of these Colonies, solemnly publish and declare, That these United Colonies are, and of Right ought to be Free and Independent States; that they are Absolved from all Allegiance to the British Crown, and that all political connection between them and the State of Great Britain, is and ought to be totally dissolved; and that as Free and Independent States, they have full Power to levy War, conclude Peace, contract Alliances, establish Commerce, and to do all other Acts and Things which Independent States may of right do. And for the support of this Declaration, with a firm reliance on the protection of divine Providence, we mutually pledge to each other our Lives, our Fortunes and our sacred Honor.

of the world") and rely "on the protection of divine Providence." God, they argue, is on their side. Furthermore, they are men willing to pledge "our Lives, our Fortunes and our sacred Honor" for the principles enunciated in the declaration.

Like the second paragraph, the concluding paragraph relies on parallel structure and repetition of that in declaring the colonies "Free and Independent States." The climax of the last line effective portrays the signers as heroes: men who will risk everything to support the rights of man established by God. **Thus the writers of the declaration appeal in a most effective way to** ethos (they are reasonable and honorable men), **pathos** (they have proven emphatically the outrages of the King and Parliament), **and logos** (they state their beliefs and prove that the King has trampled on their rights).

Stover, Jim. "The Declaration of Independence: An Analysis of the Three Persuasive Appeals." mail.baylorschool.org/~jstover/technology/techfair04/DecofIndappeals.htm. Accessed 30 Apr. 2013.

---

### EXERCISE 8F     ANALYZING THE DECLARATION OF INDEPENDENCE

1. Stover does not explicitly provide a reason for his analysis of the Declaration of Independence. What do you think makes his analysis relevant? Do you find it relevant? Why or why not?

2. How effectively do you think Stover uses design and format to present his analysis? Do you think his analysis would be more or less effective in a more traditional essay format? Explain.

3. What can you learn from Stover's analysis? In what ways does his analysis influence your understanding of the Declaration of Independence?

8

# Writing Rhetorical Analysis

Political speeches can have a lasting impact long after they are delivered, as several examples in this chapter illustrate, including Abraham Lincoln's Gettysburg Address and Barack Obama's speech in Charleston, South Carolina in 2015. That's one reason they are so often the focus of rhetorical analysis, which is a powerful tool for understanding how a speech or other kind of text achieves its potential effect on an audience. But whatever kind of text you are analyzing, effective rhetorical analysis involves the careful examination of how the text's specific features might contribute to its impact on an audience. Use the **four features of effective analytical writing** (Chapter 5) to guide your rhetorical analysis:

1. **A relevant topic worthy of analysis.** Establish why the text you have selected is important or relevant:

   - Why would readers want to understand the effectiveness of the text you are analyzing? What makes the text relevant or important?

   - What's at stake for them—and for you—in understanding this text?

   - What are your reasons for selecting this text?

2. **Complexity.** Explore the text you are analyzing in sufficient depth:

   - How carefully have you examined the main features of the text and their potential impact on an audience?

   - How fully have you analyzed the rhetorical situation? Have you considered the various potential audiences for this text?

3. **Sufficient information and appropriate evidence.** Gather sufficient information to explain the text you are analyzing; apply one or more frameworks to develop sufficient evidence to support your analysis:

   - What information have you gathered about the author and the circumstances surrounding the creation of this text for readers to understand the author's intentions?

   - How carefully have you explained the rhetorical situation?

   - What analytical framework(s) have you chosen? How appropriate is this framework for your evaluation of the text?

   - Have appropriate and trustworthy sources been used to support the analysis?

4. **Reasonable conclusions.** Present convincing conclusions on the basis of your rhetorical analysis:

   - How do the key concepts and technical terms of your analytical framework(s) help you reach your conclusions?

   - Do your conclusions grow logically out of your analysis?

   - Do your conclusions present readers with a persuasive explanation of the effectiveness of this text?

This section will help you develop a rhetorical analysis using the Ten Core Concepts described in Chapter 3. (Keep in mind that the generic term *text* can refer to a written text such as an essay or speech as well as visual or multimedia texts such a films, advertisements, photographs, or websites.)

## Step 1  Identify a topic for rhetorical analysis.

Rhetorical analysis often arises from

- a **reaction** to a text, or
- a **question** about a text.

For example, you might be moved by a political speech or shocked by a public service announcement. You might wonder why an old film remains popular or a certain book is controversial. Reactions and questions like these can lead to rhetorical analysis, so begin there:

| Reactions to a text | Questions about a text |
|---|---|
| Have you read an essay or seen an ad that provoked a strong, emotional response? | Is there a film, song, book, or ad whose popularity puzzles or surprises you? |
| Have you seen or read something that influenced your views about an issue or topic? | Does a famous speech, image, or essay seem especially relevant today? |
| Have you heard or read a speech that aroused your passions about an issue? | Does a controversy about a film, ad, photo, speech, or tweet interest you? |

8

1. **Using these questions, make a brief list of possible texts for rhetorical analysis.** Briefly explain what interests you about each text and why each might be worth analyzing. (If you have a course assignment that specifies a text to analyze, skip to Step #3.)

2. **Select a text from your list that seems most promising or relevant for a rhetorical analysis.** (Keep your list, though. As you work through the next few steps, you might change your mind and decide to analyze a different text.)

3. **Explore your reactions to or questions about the text.**

   - What is your initial reaction to the text? What interests you about it? Is there a section or aspect of it that appeals to you for some reason?

   - What emotions, if any, does it provoke in you?

   - What questions does the text raise for you? Why are these questions worth pursuing?

   - What might make this text relevant—or provocative or persuasive—to others?

   Using these questions to guide you, make notes about your reactions to or questions about this text.

4. **Formulate a question about the text.** Use your notes from Step #3 to develop a general question about the text to guide your examination of it. For example, let's say you became very interested in the controversies surrounding the political candidates during the 2016 American presidential election (which is referred to at the beginning of this chapter), and you want to know more about important political speeches that seem to have influenced the outcome of recent elections. One such speech is an address given during the 2008 American presidential election by then-candidate Barack Obama. Obama gave his speech, which is now referred to as the "More Perfect Union" speech, in the midst of a controversy surrounding his former pastor, Reverend Jeremiah Wright. In that speech, which he delivered in Philadelphia, Obama called on Americans of all races to acknowledge their shared "history of racial injustice" but also to work together to "move beyond some of our old racial wounds . . . to continue on the path of a more perfect union." At the time, the speech was praised and criticized, but today some experts believe that it helped Obama become the first American president of color. If you want to analyze the speech more closely to understand its impact, you might ask, What made that particular speech so important among hundreds of campaign speeches? How might it have influenced the 2008 election?

This question is a starting point for your analysis. You will refine the question as you explore the text and develop your analysis. Develop this question using Step #1 in Chapter 3.

## Step 2 Place your topic in rhetorical context.

An important component of rhetorical analysis is examining the rhetorical context of the text you're analyzing, but your own essay also has a rhetorical context. So it's important to examine what might interest others about the text you have chosen and identify the relevance of your analysis for a potential audience:

1. **Identify an audience that might be interested in an analysis of this text.** Your course assignment might specify an audience, such as your classmates, but you might also have a broader, less immediate audience for your analysis. For example, in identifying a potential audience for your analysis of Barack Obama's "More Perfect Union" speech, **consider these questions:**

| Who might have a general interest in the text you are analyzing? | • American citizens<br>• Voters<br>• People interested in political history |
| --- | --- |
| **Who might have a more specialized interest in that text?** | • Obama's political supporters or opponents<br>• People interested in race relations in U.S. |
| **Who might be interested in a rhetorical analysis of this text?** | • People interested in politics<br>• Students studying oratory<br>• Students interested in writing or rhetoric<br>• Voters concerned about the current political climate |

Note that you could address several distinct audiences that share certain interests or characteristics. So it might be useful to think of a **primary audience** and **secondary audiences** for your analysis. In this example, your primary audience might be your classmates and your secondary audiences might include student voters and people interested in politics and political oratory.

8

2. **Examine the relevance of the text for your audience.** Having a sense of why an audience would be interested in the text you are analyzing can shape your analytical approach. For example, knowing that your readers might be interested in how then-candidate Obama tried to address the divergent concerns of different races in his 2008 speech might lead you to focus your analysis on his use of language specifically related to race. **Consider these questions:**

| What makes the text you are analyzing relevant? | • It is an important speech by a presidential candidate.<br>• It addresses a complex issue of enduring relevance in the U.S.<br>• It represents a significant moment in recent history. |
| --- | --- |
| Why would an audience care about an analysis of this text? | • It can illuminate the oratorical skills of an important person.<br>• It could shed light on contemporary political discourse.<br>• It can illuminate what is considered an important factor in the 2008 U.S. presidential election. |

3. **Identify your purpose in analyzing this text.** The general purpose of any rhetorical analysis is to explain how the text conveys a message to an intended audience, but your analysis can also have a more specific purpose. For example, political analysts examined Obama's "More Perfect Union" speech for insight into Obama's policies. You might seek to analyze the speech in order to gain insight into the difficulties of talking about race in the U.S. or to examine the role of race in U.S. presidential politics. Addressing the questions in Steps #1 and #2 will help you identify a purpose for your rhetorical analysis.

With these considerations in mind, complete Step #2 in Chapter 3.

## Step 3 Select a medium.

Although rhetorical analysis essays are often written in conventional print format, other media can be used. For example, analyses of political speeches now routinely appear on blogs and YouTube. Multimedia presentation sites such as Prezi might also be appropriate, depending upon your rhetorical situation.

If the text you are analyzing is a visual text or includes sound or images, it might make sense to select a medium that easily incorporates those elements. For example, an analysis of Obama's "More Perfect Union" speech might be more effective if it included video or audio clips from the speech rather than simply quotes from the transcript—especially if you wish to analyze Obama's use of voice, rhythm, and pacing. However, if such a multimedia format is unlikely to reach your intended audience, a more conventional medium might be more appropriate.

In selecting a medium for your rhetorical analysis, follow your assignment guidelines (if any), but if you have a choice, consider a medium that will enable you to present your analysis most effectively to your intended audience. **Address these questions:**

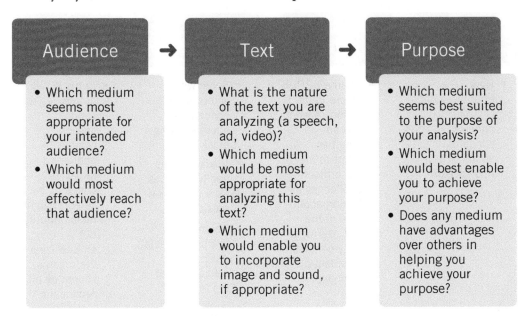

Step #3 in Chapter 3 provides additional guidance for selecting an appropriate medium for your rhetorical analysis.

## Step 4  Identify your main claim and develop your analysis.

In examining the rhetorical effectiveness of the text you are analyzing, you will make one or more main claims about that text. These claims should be related to the purpose of your analysis. For example, if you are analyzing Barack Obama's "More Perfect Union" speech to highlight the challenges of talking about race in the U.S., your main claim might be that Obama adopted strategies intended to celebrate racial diversity but also to find common ground among Americans of all racial identities. Your task would then be to develop your analysis so that it elaborates on and supports that claim.

If you're not yet sure what your main claim will be, use your question from Step #1 to develop a tentative claim for your rhetorical analysis. For example, let's say your question about then-candidate Obama's 2008 speech was this:

*How effectively did Obama address concerns about race in this speech?*

Your purpose in analyzing this speech is to examine the challenges of talking about race in the U.S., so you might state your tentative main claim as follows:

*Obama's 2008 "More Perfect Union" speech was a risky effort on the part of a presidential candidate to meet the difficult challenge of talking about race in the U.S.*

8

As you examine the speech, you will develop a more in-depth understanding of the strategies Obama used, the rhetorical situation, historical factors, and the response to the speech. That inquiry might lead you to refine your claim:

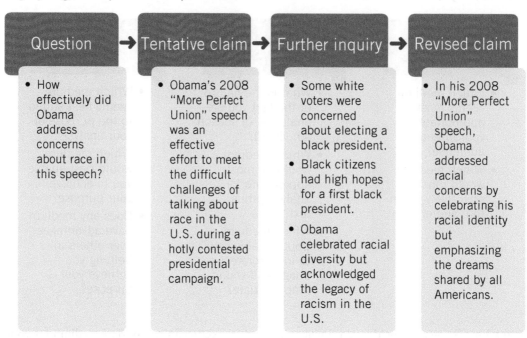

| Question | Tentative claim | Further inquiry | Revised claim |
|---|---|---|---|
| • How effectively did Obama address concerns about race in this speech? | • Obama's 2008 "More Perfect Union" speech was an effective effort to meet the difficult challenges of talking about race in the U.S. during a hotly contested presidential campaign. | • Some white voters were concerned about electing a black president.<br>• Black citizens had high hopes for a first black president.<br>• Obama celebrated racial diversity but acknowledged the legacy of racism in the U.S. | • In his 2008 "More Perfect Union" speech, Obama addressed racial concerns by celebrating his racial identity but emphasizing the dreams shared by all Americans. |

Remember that your claim is tentative. It will guide your inquiry, but as you pursue your analysis, you might need to revise your claim again.

Now, starting with your tentative claim, develop your analysis of the text you have selected by identifying the context of that text and selecting a framework for analysis.

## Identify the Rhetorical Context of the Text You are Analyzing

Examine the circumstances surrounding the creation of this text to identify key factors that can help you understand the text, the strategies used, and its impact.

For example, Obama's speech came after the pastor of his church, Jeremiah Wright, made controversial remarks that many Americans interpreted as racist (anti-white), anti-American, and even violent. The intense response to those remarks hurt Obama's presidential campaign. In addition, Obama chose to deliver his speech in Philadelphia, which is known as the "City of Brotherly Love," a decision that seems to reflect his main themes.

Now address the three main questions for rhetorical analysis:

- **What are the main features of the text?** Identify the key themes, images, language, figures of speech, and other features of the text that seem to make it persuasive (or not). If you are analyzing a visual text, use the tools for visual analysis described in this chapter (pages 228–232).
- **How do those features affect the intended audience?** Describe the possible impact of the main features of the text on the intended audience. Identify as best you can how the intended audience(s) might (or did) react to the specific features you have identified.

- **Why did the writer include those features and craft the text in specific ways?** Explain the reasons that the author might have included specific features. Consider how those features and their potential impact help the author of the text achieve his or her rhetorical purposes.

### Select a Framework for Your Analysis

Your analysis so far has considered the main elements of the rhetorical situation. Now choose one (or more) of the frameworks for rhetorical analysis described in this chapter: basic analysis, classical analysis, stylistic analysis (see pages 218–227) and analyze the text using that framework. (Follow the guidelines for each framework presented in this chapter.) Select your framework with your purpose in mind:

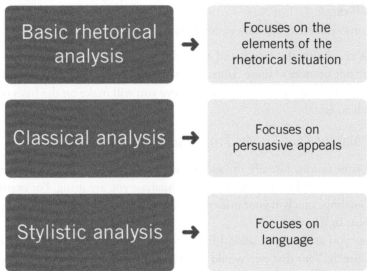

Basic rhetorical analysis → Focuses on the elements of the rhetorical situation

Classical analysis → Focuses on persuasive appeals

Stylistic analysis → Focuses on language

As you proceed, adjust your main claim accordingly. Step #4 in Chapter 3 provides additional guidance for developing your analysis.

## Step 5  Support your analysis.

Most of the evidence you use to support your claims and assertions will likely be passages from the text you are analyzing (or features of the images or sound, if the text is a visual or multimedia text). For example, the primary evidence for your claims about the strategies used by then-candidate Obama in his "More Perfect Union" speech will be sections from the speech where those strategies are used. So as you develop your analysis for Step #4, you are also gathering evidence to support your analysis. However, you might also find a need to consult outside sources to understand

- the rhetorical situation,
- the background of the author of the text, and
- the response to the text.

8

In addition, you might use other analyses of the text to support your claims. Let's explore each of these sources of support for your analysis.

## List Your Main Claims

First, identify the claims you expect to make as a result of your analysis. For example, in analyzing the impact of Obama's "More Perfect Union" speech, you might have developed the following tentative claims:

- Obama's speech was a brave and honest but risky effort to address the challenge of race relations in the U.S.
- The effectiveness of the speech rested on Obama's appeals to common ground among people of all races.
- Obama's most effective appeals were ethical and emotional appeals.

As you continue examining the speech and research its impact, you might need to adjust, refine, or even eliminate one or more of these claims, and you might find a need to add others. But at this point it is necessary to identify the claims you believe you will make on the basis of your analysis and your research so far.

## Identify Evidence for Your Claims From Your Analysis

As you develop your claims, identify the specific evidence that supports each claim. The nature of that evidence will depend on the framework for analysis you are using. For example, if you are doing a stylistic analysis, much of your evidence is likely to be figures of speech and other language devices that appear in the text.

Let's imagine you are using a classical framework (see page 221) to analyze Obama's "More Perfect Union" speech. Your first step would be to identify the three kinds of appeals (emotional, ethical, and logical) in the speech. For example, here's a passage in which Obama makes an ethical appeal, showing that his own racial identity and family history lend him credibility as someone who understands the complexity of race relations:

> I am the son of a black man from Kenya and a white woman from Kansas. I was raised with the help of a white grandfather who survived a Depression to serve in Patton's Army during World War II and a white grandmother who worked on a bomber assembly line at Fort Leavenworth while he was overseas. I've gone to some of the best schools in America and lived in one of the world's poorest nations. I am married to a black American who carries within her the blood of slaves and slaveowners—an inheritance we pass on to our two precious daughters. I have brothers, sisters, nieces, nephews, uncles and cousins, of every race and every hue, scattered across three continents, and for as long as I live, I will never forget that in no other country on Earth is my story even possible.

If you were making the claim that Obama relies on his own family history to make an ethical appeal and to persuade his audience that his argument is valid, you could cite this passage as evidence to support that claim.

You should find evidence to support each main claim in your analysis. For some claims, you might need more than one piece of evidence, especially if the claim is central to the main point of your analysis.

## Consult Relevant Outside Sources

Outside sources can strengthen your rhetorical analysis in four ways:

- They can help explain the rhetorical context.
- They provide information about the author.
- They enable you to document reactions to the text.
- They can provide examples of other analyses of the text.

For instance, to learn more about the controversy surrounding the remarks of Obama's pastor, Jeremiah Wright, which were an important part of the rhetorical situation for the speech, you could review newspaper accounts, editorials, and videos of Wright's remarks as well as television news reports about them. Those sources could also provide support for a claim that Obama tried to use the controversy to his advantage.

Similarly, you can use the reaction to the speech to support claims about the impact of specific persuasive strategies used in the speech. For example, you could cite polls taken about the speech, news stories describing public reaction, and editorials written in response to the speech.

Finally, citing other analyses of the text can reinforce your own analysis. For example, if you were making a claim that the power of the speech lies in Obama's effort to speak to both blacks and whites, you could bolster your claim by citing a critic such as journalist Roy Peter Clark, who wrote that "Obama's patriotic lexicon is meant to comfort white ears and soothe white fears." (Clark, Roy Peter. "Why It Worked: A Rhetorical Analysis of Obama's Speech on Race." *Poynter*, 1 Apr. 2008, www.poynter.org/2008/why-it-worked-a-rhetorical-analysis-of-obamas-speech-on-race/88009/.)

Remember that in this kind of analysis, there is no "proof" that your claims are true; rather, you are providing evidence so that your analysis persuades your audience. Step #5 in Chapter 3 provides additional guidance for developing support for your analysis.

At this point, you should be ready to write a complete draft of your project. If not, move onto the next step before completing your draft.

## Step 6  Organize your rhetorical analysis.

There is no conventional structure for a rhetorical analysis, but you can follow one of **two basic patterns for organizing your analysis:**

- according to your main claims
- according to an analytical framework

## Organizing Your Analysis According to Your Claims

In any rhetorical analysis, you will make claims about the features of the text you are analyzing, the strategies or appeals used in the text, the impact of those features or strategies on the intended audience, and the effectiveness of the text in achieving the rhetorical goals. To develop an outline based on your claims, follow these steps:

### 1. List your main claims.

| Obama's speech was a brave and honest effort to address the challenge of race relations in the U.S. | The effectiveness of Obama's speech rests on his appeals to common ground among the races. | Obama's most effective appeals are ethical and emotional appeals. |

### 2. For each claim, list any supporting claims.

| Obama directly addresses the controversy over Rev. Wright to demonstrate his sincerity. | Obama celebrates diversity but emphasizes commonality. | Obama presents himself as an example of racial diversity. He invokes a sense of connection to all Americans. |

### 3. Identify your evidence or support for each claim.

| Relevant passages from text; news accounts; editorials about the controversy | Relevant passages from the text | Relevant passages from the text; other analyses of the speech |

### 4. Arrange your claims in a logical order that makes sense for your audience.

Begin with the broadest claim (Obama's speech was a brave effort to address race relations) and move to more specific claims (the nature of each of his appeals).

Now use your list to develop an outline:

I. Introduction (the importance of Obama's "More Perfect Union" speech)

II. Background

    A. Historical context of race relations in U.S.

    B. Political context for the speech

    C. Controversy over Rev. Wright's remarks

III. Main Claims

    A. Obama's speech was a brave and honest effort to address the challenge of race relations in U.S.

        1. Obama directly addressed Rev. Wright controversy

        2. Obama acknowledges the difficulty of race relations in U.S.

    B. The effectiveness of the speech rests on Obama's appeal to common ground

        1. Obama celebrates diversity but emphasizes commonality

        2. Obama connects citizens of all racial identities to common American goals and dreams

    C. Main persuasive appeals were ethical and emotional

        1. Ethical appeals

            a) Obama's personal story

            b) Obama's record

        2. Emotional appeals

            a) Obama's personal story

            b) stories of other Americans

            c) sense of patriotism

IV. Conclusion

For each main heading and subheading, include the specific evidence you are using to support the claim. Notice that the technical analyses (e.g., the specific kinds of appeals; the rhetorical situation) are woven into the essay where appropriate. So, for example, you might include your analysis of the rhetorical situation in section II and section IIIa.

## Organizing Your Analysis According to Your Analytical Framework

You can also organize on the basis of the analytical framework you are using: a basic rhetorical analysis (see page 218), a classical framework (see page 221), or a stylistic analysis (see page 225). In this approach, structure your essay around the main concepts associated with each framework. For example, if you are using a basic rhetorical framework, organize your essay using the steps described on page 218. Following those steps, you might produce an outline like this:

I. Introduction

    (Explain main purpose of your rhetorical analysis.)

II. Context

    A. Background information about the text being analyzed

    B. Description of original rhetorical context for the text

8

III.  Analysis of Rhetorical Situation

    A.  Author's purpose

    B.  Examination of audience characteristics and expectations

IV.  Analysis of Text

    A.  Main features of text

    B.  Main persuasive strategies

V.  Evaluation of Author's Rhetorical Decisions

    A.  Effectiveness of main rhetorical strategies

    B.  Impact on intended audience

VI.  Conclusion

(Overall assessment of effectiveness of text)

Notice that in this approach, you would incorporate your main claims into the appropriate section of your essay. For example, a claim about Obama's use of emotional appeals would likely appear in section IVb, Va, or Vb.

If you are using a classical framework, you might follow a simple outline like this:

I.  Introduction

II.  Description of Rhetorical Situation

III.  Emotional Appeals

IV.  Ethical Appeals

V.  Logical Appeals

VI.  Conclusion

In this case, each main section would contain discussion of:

- the specific appeals of that kind in the text
- the impact of those appeals
- how they advance the speaker's purpose
- evidence to support your claims about each appeal.

The order in which you discuss each kind of appeal would depend upon which ones you found to be most important or effective.

More sophisticated analyses that include stylistic or visual analysis would call for more detailed versions of these outlines. Of course, you should always consider the intended audience and the purpose of your rhetorical analysis in deciding how best to organize it.

Follow Step #6 in Chapter 3 for additional guidance.

## Step 7 Get feedback.

The main purpose for getting feedback on your draft is to determine whether your rhetorical analysis is persuasive to your readers. But you also want to determine whether your evaluation of the text you are analyzing matches your readers' reactions to that text.

For example, if you are making a case that Barack Obama's 2008 "More Perfect Union" speech was effective in addressing the challenges of race relations in the U.S., to what extent do your readers share your sense of the effectiveness of the speech? Do one or more of them find the speech unpersuasive? If so, why? By posing such questions, you can use readers of your draft to test your analysis. If they disagree with your conclusions, it's possible that you might need to re-examine them, or maybe you simply haven't made your case effectively. Either way, you can use your readers' reactions to the original text to guide your revisions.

Follow **Step #7 in Chapter 3** to obtain useful feedback. In addition, be sure your readers address the four main characteristics of analytical writing:

| A relevant topic worthy of analysis | • Has the writer provided persuasive reasons for analyzing the selected text?<br>• Does the writer explain the relevance of the text and the purpose of a rhetorical analysis of it? |
|---|---|
| Complexity | • How thorough is the analysis? Has the writer explained the text sufficiently?<br>• Has the writer examined the rhetorical situation sufficiently?<br>• In what ways does the analytical framework illuminate the text being analyzed? |
| Appropriate and sufficient support | • What support does the writer provide for his or her claims?<br>• Is the evidence sufficient? Does the writer use outside sources appropriately?<br>• Is there sufficient background information about the text?<br>• Does the writer use technical terms appropriately? |
| Reasonable conclusions | • Do the writer's conclusions grow logically from the analysis? Are the conclusions presented clearly and persuasively?<br>• Do the conclusions provide a persuasive explanation for the rhetorical effectiveness of the text? |

8

## Step 8  Revise.

The advice for Step #8 in Chapter 3 will guide you as you revise your draft. Supplement that advice with the questions listed in Step #7 in this chapter. In addition, make sure your draft addresses the three main questions for rhetorical analysis (see page 217):

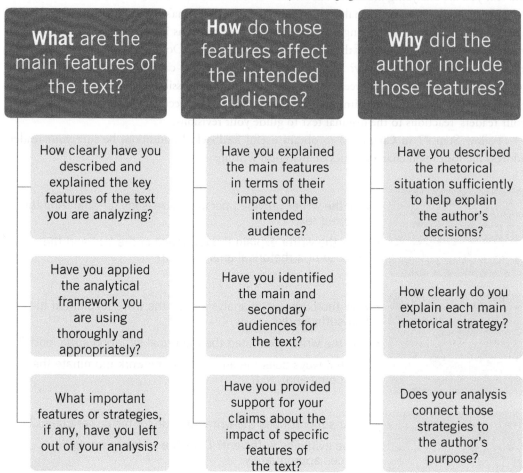

**What** are the main features of the text?

- How clearly have you described and explained the key features of the text you are analyzing?

- Have you applied the analytical framework you are using thoroughly and appropriately?

- What important features or strategies, if any, have you left out of your analysis?

**How** do those features affect the intended audience?

- Have you explained the main features in terms of their impact on the intended audience?

- Have you identified the main and secondary audiences for the text?

- Have you provided support for your claims about the impact of specific features of the text?

**Why** did the author include those features?

- Have you described the rhetorical situation sufficiently to help explain the author's decisions?

- How clearly do you explain each main rhetorical strategy?

- Does your analysis connect those strategies to the author's purpose?

## Step 9  Refine your voice.

Many essays of rhetorical analysis follow the conventions of traditional academic writing. If your assignment calls for such an essay, make sure your voice is appropriately formal. (See Chapter 26 for advice on developing an academic writing style.) But as the readings in this chapter suggest, the writer's voice can vary widely in rhetorical analyses, depending upon the intended audience and purpose for the analysis as well as the medium. An analysis intended for a blog, for example, is likely to be less formal than one written as a conventional academic essay. Similarly, your voice will likely be less formal in an analysis presented in multimedia format. As you review your draft, decide what kind of voice and style are most appropriate for your own rhetorical context and revise accordingly. In addition, follow Step #9 in Chapter 3.

## Step 10   Edit.

Complete **Step #10 in Chapter 3.**

---

**WRITING PROJECTS**    **RHETORICAL ANALYSIS**

1. Select a classic speech, such as Abraham Lincoln's Gettysburg Address or Martin Luther King, Jr.'s "I Have a Dream" speech, and write a rhetorical analysis of it. Use one of the frameworks described in this chapter for your analysis. Assume your audience to be your classmates or others who might be interested in rhetoric and oratory. (You can easily find lists of famous speeches by searching online.)

2. Alternatively, analyze a contemporary speech you have heard, such as an address given on your campus by a guest speaker or a speech from a current political campaign. (Such speeches are often available on YouTube or news websites.)

3. Do a rhetorical analysis of promotional materials from an organization or agency that is involved in some kind of public advocacy—for example, on public health or environmental issues, social issues such as bullying, or a similar issue that interests you. The document you select for your analysis might be a flyer, direct-mail campaign letter, a public service announcement, a website, or an advertisement. For your analysis, conduct research to learn more about the organization and the issue it addresses. Select a framework for analysis that you think is most appropriate for the kind of text you are analyzing—or use a combination of frameworks. On the basis of your analysis, make recommendations to the organization or agency about how they might make their materials more persuasive.

4. Recreate the rhetorical analysis you wrote for Question #1 or #2 in a different medium. For example, convert your analysis for Question #1 into a Prezi presentation, podcast, or video.

5. Do a rhetorical analysis of your college or university website (or one section of that website). On the basis of your analysis, make recommendations for revising the website to make it more appealing to students and other potential audiences.

6. Analyze several different television or Internet advertisements for the same kind of product, identifying which are most effective in addressing their intended audiences. For example, select several ads for different brands of cars or smartphones. On the basis of your analysis, draw conclusions about what rhetorical strategies, especially visual strategies, work best in this kind of advertisement.

8

---

## MindTap®

Request help with these Writing Projects and feedback from a tutor. If required, participate in peer review, submit your paper for a grade, and view instructor comments online.

**In this chapter, you will learn to**

1. Define literary analysis and understand its purpose and uses.

2. Identify appropriate rhetorical opportunities for literary analysis.

3. Apply the four main features of effective analytical writing to sample literary analysis writings.

4. Identify and apply the four important features of literary analysis to examples of literary texts.

5. Write a literary analysis essay, applying the four main features of literary analysis and using the Ten Core Concepts from Chapter 3.

## MindTap®
Understand the goals of the chapter and complete a warm-up activity.

# Analyzing Literary Texts

**OUR LIVES ARE FILLED WITH TEXTS:** newspaper and magazine articles, books, billboards, tweets, Facebook posts, films, brochures. Many of these texts are utilitarian. For example, we read the manual for a bluetooth device to learn how to program it; we visit Weather.com to find out if rain is predicted. But we use some texts—stories, novels, poems, films, comics, plays—to help make sense of who we are. These texts might entertain and inform us, but they also help us explore important questions about how we live, what we do, and why things are the way they are. Writers analyze these texts to understand what they have to say and how they say it:

■ A television critic tries to explain what the discussions of characters in the popular TV shows *Transparent* and *Orange is the New Black* reveal about changing attitudes regarding transgendered people.

■ A historian examines letters written by George Washington to understand his decisions as the commander of the Continental Army.

■ A sociologist analyzes Hip Hop music to explain its appeal among specific demographic groups.

Although analyzing texts is a specialized form of analytical writing that is most common in certain academic disciplines, especially English, it occurs in popular culture as well. If you've ever disagreed with someone about what a book, a song, or a film means, you've engaged in a kind of informal textual analysis. Debates about the merits of popular books and films can also involve textual analysis. A 2016 episode of the television series *black-ish*, for example, became part of an ongoing debate in the United States about race relations. The episode focused on a conversation among the main characters, an upper-middle-class African American family, about police brutality. Although some viewers complained that the show portrayed police unfairly, many critics praised the episode, in which the parents advised their teenage son and daughter and their 6 year old twins how to conduct themselves around police, for confronting a controversial subject in an honest and thoughtful way. These varied discussions about the episode amounted to efforts by both viewers and professional critics to interpret the episode and draw conclusions about what the show might tell us about a complex and important subject like race relations. In other words, people were analyzing the show to understand it and interpret the significance of its themes.

In academic writing, textual analysis, which is usually called *literary analysis*, is a careful, in-depth examination of a text's themes as well as the techniques and strategies the author used to convey ideas and explore themes. Often, this kind of analysis involves the use of theories to help explain a text. For example, a writer might apply the principles of a sociological theory to illuminate racial stereotypes in a television show like *black-ish* (see Focus: "Theoretical Frameworks for Literary Analysis" on page 267). In this way, analysis of the text goes beyond a description of what the text might say or mean and leads to a sophisticated interpretation of the text.

If you wrote essays about poems, novels, or short stories for your high school English classes, you have an idea of what literary analysis is. This kind of analytical writing is part of the age-old conversations about the importance and meaning of literary art. In effect, writers analyze works of literature to participate in those conversations and contribute to our collective understanding of literary art and its role in cultural life. For students, literary analysis is a way to engage more deeply with works of literature in order to understand them and explore the ideas they present.

---

**FOCUS**   **EXPLICATION VERSUS THE SEARCH FOR HIDDEN MEANING**

Students sometimes complain that literary analysis is really a process of finding the "hidden meaning" in a work of literature. Although it's true that literary analysis often leads to conclusions about meanings in a novel or poem that aren't obvious, it is misleading to think in terms of "hidden meanings" when writing essays of literary analysis. Instead, literary critics tend to focus on explication, the process of carefully examining aspects of a literary work as a way to understand that work in greater depth, to see its richness, and to appreciate the complexity of its ideas, techniques, and themes. As a writer of literary analysis, your goal is to explain what you see in a work of literature and to help your readers appreciate that work. You develop an interpretation of the text to illuminate its ideas and techniques for your readers. The meaning isn't "hidden"; instead, you are making meaning by presenting the understanding you have gained through your own careful analysis of the text.

---

# Occasions for Analyzing Texts

Textual analysis, like all analysis, arises from a desire to understand something—in this case, a text. It can begin with a question that leads a writer to an interpretation of the text: What does this poem mean? Why does this play end as it does? What does this film suggest about free will? What does this advertisement reveal about contemporary attitudes toward environmental protection? Such questions prompt a writer to look more closely at a text, and in turn analyzing the text enables the writer to illuminate it for other readers.

Textual analysis can also arise from controversy or disagreements about what a text means, why it is significant, or even whether it should be read (see Focus: "Revising *Huck Finn*"). In such cases, the social and cultural importance of literature becomes evident. As noted earlier, literary texts are a way for people to make sense of human life, so it isn't surprising that disagreements can arise as different readers offer different interpretations of novels, plays, films, and other works of literary art. Such controversies indicate that literary analysis is a way for writers not only to present interpretations of literary texts but also to participate in the broader social and cultural discourse about literature and art.

In 2011, a publisher named NewSouth Books released a new edition of Mark Twain's classic novel *The Adventures of Huckleberry Finn*. In the new edition the word *nigger* in the original novel was replaced with the word *slave*. The publication of this edition ignited great controversy. Some critics charged the publisher with censoring a great American literary work; others hailed the new edition as a way to attract new readers who might otherwise have been offended by its original language. The controversy prompted some writers to re-examine the book and analyze Twain's intentions. Some critics explored the book's meaning in the context of contemporary attitudes about race, which are different from attitudes at the time of the book's original publication in 1884. In a sense, the controversy prompted many writers to ask, What does this novel really mean? Why is it important? Many essays of literary analysis grow out of the need to address these questions.

As a college student, you will most likely write textual analysis for specific course assignments. In such cases, your analysis can be seen as part of an inquiry into the texts you are reading for that course. Your classmates' shared interest in understanding those texts gives your analysis a purpose that extends beyond your own desire to understand a text. And that sense of purpose can energize your analysis.

Even when a course assignment specifies the poem, story, novel, or other text you will analyze, you will still have to develop your own interpretation of the text. That means that no matter how specific an assignment might be, the focus of your analysis will probably arise from your own questions about a text. And because other students in your class are likely to have similar questions about the assigned texts, your analysis is likely to be more effective and more engaging if it focuses on a question or questions about the text that are interesting not only to you but also to your classmates.

## EXERCISE 9A    OCCASIONS FOR TEXTUAL ANALYSIS

1. Think of a thought-provoking film you have seen or a novel you have read. Write a list of three or four questions that the film or novel raised for you.

2. In a group of classmates, identify a recent book, film, television show, song, or similar text that is popular or controversial. Have each person in the group write a few sentences explaining the main theme or point of the text. Be careful not to simply write your opinion or evaluation of the text; focus instead on the ideas in that text. Then compare what you wrote. What similarities and differences are there in your respective interpretations of the text? What do you think these similarities and differences suggest about the nature of textual interpretation?

3. Identify a film, book, or other text that you enjoy and find several reviews of that text. Are there similarities and differences in the interpretations of the text presented in those reviews? Do you agree or disagree with the reviewers' interpretations? Did they change your opinion about the text in any way? If so, how? In a brief paragraph describe what you learned about the text from these reviews.

9

# Understanding Textual Analysis

Effective literary analysis usually includes **four important features**:

- a thought-provoking interpretation
- evidence to support the interpretation
- strategic summary of the text
- appropriate literary concepts and terms

## Interpretation

Effective literary analysis engages readers with a thought-provoking interpretation that helps them understand a text, perhaps in a new way. Such analysis might include evaluation, but effective literary analysis is much more than a judgment about whether or not a text is "good" or whether the writer liked it. There is not much use for readers in a textual analysis whose primary purpose is to tell them whether the writer did or didn't like a play or novel or poem. Instead, readers are interested in whether the writer has insight into what a play means, the way a novel explores a theme, a poet's use of imagery, or the significance of a text.

## Evidence

A writer's interpretation should be supported by persuasive evidence and reasoning. It is one thing to say, for example, that Hamlet had a moral responsibility to avenge his father's death, and it is another to build a case for that interpretation by citing passages from the play, referring to other plays by Shakespeare that explore similar themes, and quoting from critics who have analyzed the play. In the end, readers might disagree with the writer's interpretation, but they should feel that the writer has presented a thoughtful, well-supported case for that interpretation.

## Summary

Effective literary analysis almost always includes some summary of the whole text or parts of it. Usually, a writer summarizes key passages or scenes to help readers understand the writer's interpretation. Sometimes, students fall into the trap of simply retelling a novel's plot or restating the content of a poem. Such summaries do not advance an interpretation and therefore don't help readers understand the text. Good textual analysis moves beyond summary but uses summary strategically to explain and support the interpretation.

## Terminology

In your high school English classes, you probably encountered terms like *imagery, theme, symbol, point of view, setting,* and *motif.* These terms relate to important concepts in literary analysis that help writers explain a text. Many of these terms focus on technique. For example, you might discuss how a poet uses images to create a certain mood in a poem. In the same way that scientific terms help scientists explain the subjects they study, literary terminology helps writers explain sophisticated aspects of a text that might be difficult to explain in common language. *Motif*, for example, describes a specific kind of pattern in a poem, novel, story, or film; a writer can use the term in analyzing a pattern in a poem or story without having to explain the pattern itself. ("The motif of the hero's journey is consistent throughout the *Harry Potter* novels.") Sometimes, writers apply theoretical frameworks in their analysis of a text; such frameworks often include their own specialized concepts and terms (see Focus: "Theoretical Frameworks for Literary Analysis").

---

**FOCUS   THEORETICAL FRAMEWORKS FOR LITERARY ANALYSIS**

Professional literary critics often adhere to certain theoretical perspectives, sometimes called schools of criticism, such as feminism or Marxism, which represent different methods or approaches to studying literary texts. Explaining the many available literary theories is beyond the scope of this textbook, but it is important to be aware that such theories can be useful in textual analysis. Among the most well-established such theories are psychoanalytical theory, reader-response, postcolonial theory, deconstruction, formalism, and structuralism in addition to feminism and Marxism. These various theories can be useful interpretative tools for examining texts in specific ways. Feminist literary theory, for example, which focuses on issues of gender, can illuminate gender roles in a text; using feminist theory, a writer might examine the way male-female relationships are portrayed in a film or play. Similarly, a Marxist critic might explore the role of social class in the plot of a novel. For some assignments, you might be asked to apply a literary theory in analyzing a text. If so, follow your instructor's guidelines in using that theory, keeping in mind that the theory is a tool for developing your interpretation of that text.

---

**EXERCISE 9B   UNDERSTANDING TEXTUAL ANALYSIS**

1. Identify a film, television show, book, or similar text that is currently popular. Write a brief paragraph describing what you think makes that text popular. Your description might focus on the plot, the characters, the technique, the text's themes or subject matter, or whichever elements of the text seem most noticeable or important to you. On the basis of your description, what conclusions might you draw about what this text means to you and to others?

2. In a group of classmates, share the paragraphs you wrote for Question #1. Have each person in the group defend his or her interpretation of the text. Identify specific kinds of evidence that each person uses to support his or her conclusions about the text. What do you think this exercise suggests about the nature of textual analysis?

3. Using the text you described for Question #1 (or a different text), write a brief summary of the text. In a group of classmates, compare your summaries. What do you notice? What might this exercise suggest about summary? About the role of summary in textual interpretation?

9

# Reading Textual Analysis

The selections in this section include analyses of three very different kinds of texts: a classic short story by a great American writer, the film version of a best-selling novel, and graphic novels. Although the authors of these analyses have different purposes and different kinds of audiences, each essay exhibits the key features of effective textual analysis:

| A relevant topic worthy of analysis | • How does the writer establish the text(s) as worthy of analysis?<br>• Why should readers care about this text at this point in time?<br>• What is the context for the textual analysis? What is the writer's purpose in analyzing this text? |
| --- | --- |
| Complexity | • What does the analysis reveal about the text? In what ways does it illuminate the text?<br>• What claims about the text does the writer make on the basis of the analysis? Do these claims reflect an analysis of sufficient depth?<br>• How does the analysis enhance our understanding of the text? |
| Sufficient information and appropriate analysis | • What kinds of evidence does the writer provide to support his or her claims about the text? How persuasive is this evidence?<br>• How does the writer use summary of the text? Is the summary accurate and helpful?<br>• What specialized terminology does the writer use in analyzing the text? |
| Reasonable conclusions | • What conclusions does the writer draw about the text?<br>• In what ways are the conclusions well reasoned and supported by the analysis?<br>• How convincing is the writer's interpretation of the text? |

MindTap®

Read these textual analysis examples. Highlight and take notes online. Additional readings are also available online.

## Literary Analysis of "Hills Like White Elephants"
### by Diane Andrews Henningfeld

*Textual analysis in college courses often focuses on established works of literature. The following essay, which examines a well-known short story by Ernest Hemingway, is a good example of this kind of literary analysis. As the author, Diane Andrews Henningfeld, notes in her essay, Hemingway's story has been extensively studied by scholars and students of literature since its publication in 1927, and debates about the story's meaning continue today. Part of Henningfeld's rationale for choosing to analyze this story is that it has generated so much interest among readers over the years. Using what other critics have said as a starting point, Henningfeld focuses her analysis on an unusual blend of the comic and the tragic that she sees in Hemingway's story. It is a good idea to read "Hills Like White Elephants" before reading Henningfeld's essay, which, like any good literary analysis, might influence your own interpretation.*

......................................................

### Talking About This Reading

**Simranpreet Kaur (student):** I enjoyed this essay, but it was a little bit difficult following the analysis. I had to reread the piece a few times before I understood how the author came to her claims. I couldn't pick out the main ideas from the less important ideas, which made it difficult to understand at times.

**Bob Yagelski:** Simranpreet, your comment actually points to an important strategy for reading a complex analysis: identifying the writer's main points and supporting points. Doing so can help you understand the analysis and follow the writer's discussion. I would encourage you to apply this strategy whenever you are confused by a reading. (See Chapter 19 for more guidance in reading complex texts.)

......................................................

In 1927, Ernest Hemingway completed and published his collection of short stories, *Men Without Women*. The collection included several important stories, stories that have been closely examined by critics almost since the day of their publication. Among the stories in the collection, however, "Hills Like White Elephants" has become the most widely anthologized and the most frequently taught. The story continues to generate scholarly interest and heated debate among students.

"Hills Like White Elephants" is a very short story. Only about one thousand words, the story itself is comprised almost entirely of dialogue. Although there is a situation, there is no plot; although there are words spoken between the main characters, there is no resolution. The topic of their conversation, an abortion, is never even mentioned by name by either of the characters. In spite of the brevity of the story, and in spite of the absences created by the dialogue, scholars continue to produce pages and pages of critical commentary. Such critical interest at least suggests that the story is a rich, open text, one that invites reader participation in the process of meaning-making.

The story appears deceptively simple. A man and a woman sit at a table at a Spanish railway station, waiting for a train. They engage in a conversation, Hemingway seems to suggest, that has been going on for some time. The reader is dropped

*(Continued)*

in the middle of the conversation without context and must glean what information he or she can from the words the characters say. The setting of the story is contemporary with its writing; that is, although there is no definite mention of the date, it seems to be set sometime during the years after the First World War, but before the Spanish Civil War. In addition, the setting is narrowly limited both in time and space. The story is framed by the narrative announcement in the first paragraph that the "express from Barcelona would come in forty minutes" and by the Spanish woman's announcement near the end of the story, "The train comes in five minutes." Thus, all of the story takes place within the thirty-five minutes. In addition, the characters never leave the train station itself.

Interfoto/Personalities/Alamy Stock Photo

There are several important ways that critics have read "Hills Like White Elephants." Some concentrate on the structure of the story, noting the use of dialogue and the placement of the few short descriptive passages. John Hollander, for example, suggests that the story develops the way a film or play might develop and that the short descriptive passages read almost like stage directions. Other critics develop careful and complicated readings of the story based on word level analysis, examining the way that Hemingway uses allusion, simile, imagery, and symbolism. Some of these critics also include an examination of Hemingway's sources, connecting the story to T. S. Eliot's modernist masterpiece, *The Wasteland*. A more recent group of scholars concentrates on the use of gender-marked language in the story, looking closely at the different ways the American and Jig [the main characters in the story] use language to communicate. Still others try to use Hemingway's autobiographical manuscripts and letters to read parts of Hemingway's life into the story. However, the fact that so many critics read this story in so many ways does not mean that the story is flawed; it means, rather, that it is a text that invites participation. As Paul Smith argues, Hemingway does not tell the reader "how the characters arrived at their present condition, or how they will resolve their conflict; we do not need to be told, for the answers are embedded in what we so briefly do see and hear" (15). Although Smith seems to suggest in this statement that the "answers" are there for the reading, it is possible to arrive at a multiplicity of answers, using the same lines of text.

In an early review of the story, Dorothy Parker described the story as "delicate and tragic." Although it is unlikely that Parker meant to suggest that "Hills Like White Elephants" is a tragedy in the classical Greek sense of the word, it is possible to use her statement as an entry point into the story. An examination of both the comic and the tragic elements reveals how these ideas function in the story, and how modernism has transformed the ideas themselves.

To begin, it is important to make clear that the term "comic" here does not imply humor, or laughter. In this discussion, "comedy" does not refer to a television situation comedy that is designed to be funny. Rather, for the purpose of this discussion comedy is a shape that fiction can take. Comedy has its roots in the fertility rituals of spring. It celebrates marriage, sexual union, birth, and the perpetuation of society.

Comedy is not always light-hearted, however; it frequently carries with it pain, frustration, and near-catastrophe. The threat of death is always located in the underside of comedy. Ultimately, however, it is the triumph over death that gives comedy its characteristic shape.

Tragedy, on the other hand, has its roots in death and sterility. It announces the end of the line, the end of a family, the end of society. Its characteristic images are winter and wasteland. Modernism, the period of literature generally placed as beginning during World War I, reflects the culture's loss of history, tradition, and certainty in the face of the War's carnage, made possible by human-made technology. Modernism reduces the scope of the tragic in literature, focusing on smaller characters in more limited settings. Unlike the tragedies of the past, they no longer need to be about larger than life characters, trapped by their own tragic flaws. Rather, tragic movement can be seen in the alienation and isolation of contemporary life. Modernist tragedy tends to emphasize ironic detachment and T. S. Eliot's quiet, "not with a bang but a whimper" ending.

Close examination of "Hills Like White Elephants" reveals that Jig and the American are in a moment that teeters on the border between the comic and the tragic. They are at a moment of decision, one that will push them one way or the other. The landscape around them reflects both possible futures. On the one side of the station, the land is fertile and green. The water from the river nourishes new life. This is the comic landscape, the landscape of regeneration. On the other side of the station, the land is bleak and dusty, lacking in sustenance and life. The American, an essentially flawed character, fails to note the dichotomy of the landscape. His vision is limited by his own needs and desires. He lives in the perpetual "now," wanting only momentary pleasure, not lasting growth. The girl's pregnancy, a state that necessarily points toward the future, has upset his equilibrium in the moment. Acknowledging the pregnancy itself forces him to acknowledge the future. Strikingly, he never mentions the word "pregnancy" in the entire story, as if the mere mention of the word will both implicate and complicate his life.

Jig, on the other hand, seems highly aware of the precipice on which she stands. What she wishes for is the comic resolution, one in which the American will marry her, they will return home, and they will establish a family. She will participate in the birth of the next generation, and will focus her attention forward. However, she also realizes that what she wishes for is not likely what she will get. When she stands and walks to the end of the station, she observes the fertile valley of the Ebro in front of her, and she understands the connection between that landscape and the future she desires. As Barry Stampfl argues, "Jig indicates the truth about her relation with the American and about her feelings for her unborn baby by talking about landscapes" (36).

In some ways, this is a choric moment, that is, a moment when a detached observer makes a judgment about the characters and their actions. In this tiny story, Jig must play the part of her own chorus. At this moment, Jig stands outside herself and sees the larger situation. Looking out over the valley she says, "And we could have all this. . . . And we could have everything and every day we make it more impossible." It is as if she realizes that the comic ending is slipping away from her. She may be about to play a role in a modernist tragedy, a tragedy in which she finds herself, at best, isolated and alone, keenly aware of the absence of life in her womb. At its worst, she may find herself dying in an abortion clinic, surrounded by people who do not speak her language.

*(Continued)*

9

Unlike traditional comedies and tragedies, however, "Hills Like White Elephants" does not offer a recognizable resolution. Rather, the end of the story is inconclusive, the possible endings fragmented. For Jig, the longing for the fertile valley is both a longing for an Edenic past and the longing for progeny to carry on into the future. Neither of her choices offers the fulfillment of that longing, and she knows it. The American's glance at their suitcases covered with hotel labels signals his desire to remain in the permanent present, a present without past or future. Again, regardless of their choice, the man's desire will remain unfulfilled.

The story ends, the train still five minutes down the track. Frozen in the space between comic and tragic resolution, the characters remain, Jig and the American, the conversation ended. Although critics, academics, readers, and students may argue about what will "happen next," the truth is that nothing happens to the characters after the story ends. Hemingway leaves his characters as he found them, in the middle of something larger, outside the margins of the story. Jig and the American truly come to represent the lost generation at this moment. Without resolution, each isolated and alienated from the other, they remain in the no man's land of inconclusivity, the possibility of tradition and continuity represented by the fertile valley just outside of their reach.

## Works Cited

Hollander, John. "Hemingway's Extraordinary Reality." *Ernest Hemingway*, edited by Harold Bloom, Chelsea House Publishers, 1985, pp. 211–16. Modern Critical Views.

Smith, Paul. "Hemingway and the Practical Reader." *New Essays on Hemingway's Short Fiction*, edited by Paul Smith, Cambridge UP, 1998, pp. 1–18.

Stampfl, Barry. "Similes as Thematic Clues in Three Hemingway Short Stories." *The Hemingway Review*, vol. 10, no. 2, Spring 1991, pp. 30–38.

Source: Henningfeld, Diane Andrews. "Hills Like White Elephants." *Short Stories for Students*, Gale, 2002, go.galegroup.com/ps/i.do?&id=GALE%7CH1420022890&v=2.1&u=sunyo_main&it=r&p= LitRG&sw=w.

---

**EXERCISE 9C**    ANALYZING "HILLS LIKE WHITE ELEPHANTS"

1. How does Henningfeld's analysis relate to what other critics have written about "Hills Like White Elephants"? What do you think Henningfeld adds to the ongoing discussions of this famous short story?

2. What sources does Henningfeld consult in supporting her interpretation of "Hills Like White Elephants"? Does her use of these sources strengthen her analysis? Explain.

3. What did you learn about Hemingway's short story from this analysis? How does Henningfeld's analysis compare to your own interpretation of the story?

## Dangerous Illusions
### by Caetlin Benson-Allott

*When a novel is made into a film, what moviegoers see is not an exact representation of the novel but the director's interpretation of it. And such an interpretation can be fertile ground for literary critics, as in the case of the following essay by Caetlin Benson-Allott, a professor of English at Georgetown University. Benson-Allott analyzes the way director Gary Ross uses special digital effects—specifically, computer-generated imagery, or CGI—in his film adaptation of the best-selling novel* The Hunger Games. *As you'll see, Benson-Allott is interested in what Ross's use of CGI suggests about the filmmaker's interpretation of a key theme in the novel: the relationship between reality and illusion and the manipulation of our perceptions of reality by those in power. Benson-Allott devotes much of her analysis to several key scenes in the movie (and the novel) to raise questions about Ross's interpretation, which Benson-Allott suggests sends a disturbing message about the uses of illusion in contemporary life. In that regard, Benson-Allott's analysis of* The Hunger Games *movie, which was released in 2012, is also a larger argument about the need for humans to be vigilant in a world characterized by digital spectacles that, as she writes in the final paragraph of her essay, cease to amaze us.*

*You might wonder what makes an essay like this one, which was published in 2012 in a scholarly journal called* Film Quarterly, *different from a movie review that might appear in a newspaper or a film review website like* Rotten Tomatoes. *What distinguishes Benson-Allott's essay from such a review is the focus of her in-depth analysis on the filmmaker's interpretation of the complex themes explored in the novel. Although movie reviews often examine a film's themes and a director's use of special effects, they rarely offer the kind of sophisticated and detailed examination of a film's scenes that Benson-Allott presents in this essay. As you read, notice the way her essay exhibits the four important features of literary analysis. In the end, her essay is as much about the novel* The Hunger Games *as it is about the film version.*

· · · · · · · · · · · · · · · · · · · · · · · · · · · · · · · · · · · ·

### Talking About This Reading

> **Danielle Ewanouski (student):** I had a hard time following the organization of this essay and the ideas the author was trying to present. The author seemed to bounce around from one idea to another, and some sentences were too long and hard to follow.

> **Bob Yagelski:** As I note in the introduction to this essay, Danielle, the author presents a sophisticated analysis intended for other professional literary critics, not for novice readers. That might explain your difficulties with the essay, which probably have more to do with the complexity of her ideas and writing style than with the organization. One strategy is to summarize in a few sentences the main idea of each paragraph. Doing so will help you follow Benson-Allott's analysis and also recognize the logical organization of her essay.

· · · · · · · · · · · · · · · · · · · · · · · · · · · · · · · · · · · ·

We should have known from the moment the poster was released: when it comes to digital effects, the odds are never in our favor. In late January 2012, Lionsgate unveiled the final poster for *The Hunger Games* with Jennifer Lawrence as Katniss Everdeen looking . . . not quite human. In it, the working-class heroine who would inspire her country's huddled masses to rebel against an inhumane dictator has no pores, no freckles or blemishes, and preternaturally shiny hair and lips. Moreover, her features are almost contorted by an unreal mix of light and shadow. Unattached

*(Continued)*

shadows give "the girl on fire"' (as she is nick-named in the film) prominent cheek-bones and an aquiline nose, while minimal eye lights foster the illusion of an impassive facade. In January, I was tempted to dismiss this poster as just another instance of Photoshop run riot, but the film also foregrounds the destabilizing effects of CGI on our notions of bodily integrity. Gone are the novel's determinately manual prep team, who primp Katniss for her turn in the televised battle-to-the-death that gives *The Hunger Games* its title. The many manicures, leg waxes, and brow tweezes Katniss undergoes (and objects to) in Suzanne Collins's novel get a mere thirty seconds of screen time. Instead, the film focuses on image creation within the games, bringing the viewer into the control room where Head Gamemaker Seneca Crane (Wes Bentley) and his team use 3D computer models of the arena to engineer reality. Such digital wizardry never appears in the novel, but it may prompt the film viewer to reevaluate her experience of digital visual effects. Inside the control room, one sees a director and his team exploiting computer-generated terrors to subdue a national audience with images of physical violence. Yet despite unveiling the scene of production, *The Hunger Games* stops short of offering viewers a way out of the tyranny of the virtual that its narrative condemns.

Ross's movie emphasizes the digitally produced violence of the arena by cinematographically juxtaposing the Capitol's high-tech dangers with Katniss's low-tech life in District 12, a coal-mining province on the outskirts of her plutocratic nation. Opening montages present District 12 as downtrodden, impoverished, yet ecologically rich; although few in the district benefit from electricity and many of its children are starving, they have access to beautiful woods that offer Katniss both physical and psychic sustenance. Ross develops an aesthetic of underdevelopment for District 12 by cutting rapidly between indifferently focused, handheld shots of its residents, and although his cinematography is manifestly digital, its imperfections demonstrate a human touch. This artisanal technique is gone by the time Katniss arrives in the privileged, over-developed Capitol where she will be interviewed, trained, and marketed for the Games and their audience. Well-choreographed Steadicam and crane shots convey the precision and cruel indifference of the Capitol machine. This overly smooth aesthetic characterizes the ethos of Crane, his control room, and the Capitol's approach to spectacle.

The viewer first meets Crane during an advance interview with Games host Caesar Flickerman (Stanley Tucci). As the master of spectacle, Crane makes clear that the Games take place every year in an environment over which the Head Gamemaker has complete control. More than just movie studios, these arenas feature virtual skies that allow the Gamemakers to adjust both time of day and weather; cameras embedded in the landscape to let them film from any angle; and unlimited special effects that undermine previous distinctions between the virtual and the real. For example, when Katniss wanders too far from the other contestants, Crane orders up a spontaneous barrage of fireballs to drive her back. These blazing projectiles appear in Collins's novel as well, but only in the movie do we see a director deciding when and how to deploy them. We also hear the theory behind Crane's special effects tactics in new exchanges between Crane and President Snow (Donald Sutherland). Snow instructs Crane to manage his audience by offering them hope in limited doses: "A spark is fine as long as it's contained." During such scenes of direction and strategy, Crane becomes an avatar for Ross, since both men use computer-generated threats to imperil Katniss and thereby frighten viewers. This association gives Crane's digital world-making an additional allegorical significance, since it now seems to dramatize the conflation of illusion and materiality through which modern franchise filmmaking manages us.

In exposing how Crane and company terrorize the contestants, *The Hunger Games* distinguishes itself from most sci-fi and fantasy movies, which try to naturalize their CGI to help viewers believe in the fiction. That is, the control-room scenes reveal how *The Hunger Games* manipulates both its onscreen viewers and the audience in theaters, especially toward the end of the film. To hasten the Games' (and the movie's) climactic battle scene, one of Crane's assistants designs a "muttation," a monstrous dog with a humanoid face and ears. The muttation first appears as a 3D hologram, pacing and growling above a Gamemaker's monitor. The animal's behavior suggests a living beast waiting to be unleashed, but because it is rendered as a wireframe model, the muttation also displays its cyber origins. With its geometrics showing, this desktop creature neatly encapsulates the uncertain division between living beings and digital animation for contemporary film viewers, but after Crane approves the creation, its materialization further exposes the viewer's psychic vulnerability to CGI spectacles. Once the muttation manifests in the arena, it makes visible the epistemological double bind of CGI spectatorship, the way the viewer is called upon to recognize and appreciate the computer artistry (like Crane) and believe in its material existence (like Katniss). Yet the muttation corporealizes so quickly that the viewer may experience some incredulity: how did a digital hologram become a living, breathing monster in a matter of seconds? If she does, then she may also question what made the wireframe animation seem alive to her in the first place and what else the film is leading her to believe. One might say that in adding the muttation's scene of production, Ross takes Tony Kushner's advice from the "'Playwright's Notes'" for *Angels in America*: "It's OK if the wires show, and maybe it's good that they do, but the magic should at the same time be thoroughly amazing'" (Theater Communications Group, 2003 11). If so, the political effects are negligible, because *The Hunger Games* still captivates the viewer while showing her how she is held captive by computer-generated imagery; indeed, she is captivated by the same spectacles that give the diegetic Hunger Games their political potency.

In short, letting the wires show is not enough neither in the movie nor in the poster, which accentuates digital manipulation in a different way than but just as much as the film. One could argue that by making its manipulation of Lawrence's image so obvious, Lionsgate encourages viewers to recognize the digital divide between a star's image and her actual body, but the poster also proffers this composited visage as an idol, the face of a liberator. Some feminist bloggers have heralded *The Hunger Games* as a "'true lady-centric blockbuster franchise," as though that were an achievement for gender equality (Dodai Stewart, "'Racist *Hunger Games* Fans Are Very Disappointed," *Jezebel*, March 26, 2012). The narrative does celebrate a brave and audacious heroine, but there's more to a movie than its story. *The Hunger Games* takes us into a world in which digital horrors have cowed a nation, a world I think we already occupy. We may not cease to be amazed by digital spectacles, but we can ask what they're doing to us and maybe *The Hunger Games* could help us begin that process. Because we see the muttation hologram before it becomes fully rendered and real in the arena, we have an opportunity to recognize that such illusions are after us too.

Source: Benson-Allott, Caetlin. "Dangerous Illusions." *Film Quarterly*, vol. 65, no. 4, Summer 2012, www.filmquarterly.org/2012/06/summer-2012-volume-65-number-4/.

9

1. Benson-Allott devotes much of her analysis to a few scenes in *The Hunger Games*, which she summarizes in some detail. How effective did you find these summaries? To what extent do they contribute to the persuasiveness of her analysis? Do you think your answer to those questions depends upon whether you have seen (or read) *The Hunger Games*? Explain.

2. In paragraph 4, Benson-Allott refers to a scene in *The Hunger Games* in which the Gamemaker creates an animal called a "muttation"; she writes that this creation "makes visible the epistemological double bind of CGI spectatorship." What does she mean? How does her point about "the epistemological double bind" relate to her analysis of the film's interpretation of the novel?

3. What conclusions does Benson-Allott draw from her analysis of the film adaption of *The Hunger Games*? How does her analysis lead to these conclusions? Did you find her analysis persuasive? Why or why not?

## *Watchmen* and the Birth of Respect for the Graphic Novel
### by Karl Allen

*Writers often use textual analysis to explain a trend or examine the appeal of a specific work or genre. In this essay, Karl Allen explains the genre of graphic novels. At first glance, he seems to be offering an introduction to this increasingly popular kind of text, but his analysis of some of the most popular graphic novels actually leads to an interpretation of* Watchmen, *which is among the most influential graphic novels ever published. Allen's essay, which appeared on the website About.com in 2011, was written for a general audience, but his analysis is based on a careful examination of* Watchmen *as well as several other graphic novels in the same way that a literary critic might examine a more traditional work of literature. His essay suggests that effective textual analysis can be used to illuminate any kind of text.*

. . . . . . . . . . . . . . . . . . . . . . . . . . . . . . . . . .

### Talking About This Reading

**Sadman Sakib (student):** I couldn't quite understand the importance of this line: "But you also wish to avoid stores with names like 'Forbidden Planet' and 'The Dragon's Den.'" Why should stores with those names be avoided?

**Bob Yagelski:** Sadman, the key to understanding this line is the word *you*. Notice that in the opening paragraph (where this line occurs) Allen uses the second person (*you*) to address his readers directly, but who are those readers? Like all writers, Allen makes assumptions about his audience. In this case, he assumes his readers recognize Christopher Ware and Alan Moore. In other words, he assumes his readers are familiar with graphic novels and the stores where they can be purchased and will therefore understand his "inside" joke about those stores. This is a good example of how an audience can shape a writer's choices—and affect a reader's response.

. . . . . . . . . . . . . . . . . . . . . . . . . . . . . . . . . .

So you want to know more about graphic novels because you've read about Christopher Ware in *The New Yorker*, or you noticed that Alan Moore's labyrinthine *Watchmen* just made *Time Magazine*'s 100 best books in the English language list. But you also wish to avoid stores with names like "Forbidden Planet" and "The Dragon's Den"? You want to know what's good and what's bad. What's hot, what's indie, what's superhero, what's art, what's funny, what's dramatic, or simply what's going to be the next basis for a film? What follows is a highly condensed and thoroughly unfair portrait of a burgeoning genre with the briefest of glimpses at only a few representatives. It's only a start.

Let's look at *Watchmen* first. One of the reasons it's been proclaimed great by such disparate crowds as *Time Magazine* readers and comic book nerds alike is that it manages to spin so much depth into a medium that had been undervalued as a literary resource for so long. In other words, it surprised the hell out of everyone. This is a superhero comic book but Batman it ain't. Released in 1986 and 1987 in individual issues and then collected into a single volume (as is typical of most graphic novels) *Watchmen*'s superheroes are going through some existential angst as they reach their forties and they start to feel a little reticent about running around fighting crime in costume. Officially banned from public servitude, costumed superheroes are trying to get on with their lives after having been forbidden to wear their tights and underwear and utility belts. You'll recognize the skeleton of this plot as having been co-opted in various forms since *Watchmen*'s release, most notably in films like *Batman Begins*, where the notion of a costumed vigilante is treated in realistic terms, and also in *The Incredibles*.

Where Moore and artist Dave Gibbons take you is much bigger than that, though. *Watchmen* spans the 20th century in a world where Superman was released by DC comics and instead of spawning an industry it inspired otherwise normal people to create alternate identities for themselves and band together to fight crime. One of their partners in crime-fighting, The Comedian, is murdered at the beginning and as each of the former band of Watchmen reflect on their histories as superheroes we see their influence on world events, from the end of World War II through Vietnam onto the Cuban Missile Crisis and JFK's assassination and up to the book's own bizarre twist of an ending to the century.

Moore and Gibbons opened the door through which the comic book and graphic novel (also referred to occasionally as linear art or novel-length comics) would eventually enter the world of respected literature. However, it's doubtful that *Watchmen* would have made *Time*'s list in 1987. A lot has happened since then to pull *Watchmen* back into the forefront of *Time*'s consciousness. Artists working in varying forms of the medium have turned illustration into an art form in its own right and have done much to bridge the gap between literature and visual art.

*(Continued)*

9

Charles Burns, who has been doing commercial illustration since the mid-80's (and who has, incidentally, done a cover or two for *Time*), has also been hard at work on a graphic novel about a group of teens in the 1970's who are falling victim to an unexplained disease that changes their physical appearance. His bold and iconic artwork can be spotted on every cover of the literary magazine *The Believer* as portraiture of the different authors interviewed in each issue. Burns was made prominent through his association with Art Spiegelman who himself is best known for the great graphic-novel-to-mainstream-literature jumper *Maus*, about his father's experience in a concentration camp told in the guise of cats and mice.

There's also Daniel Clowes, whose book *Ghost World* was turned into a movie a few years ago; James Kochalka, who has been publishing his comic journals *American Elf*, several separate titles for both kids and mature; and Adrian Tomine, whose *Optic Nerve* series have been collected in various volumes over the years and whose work you might recognize from Weezer album covers and the 2002 *Best American Non-Required Reading* anthology—another literary crossover. More recently *Persepolis* and *Persepolis 2* by Marjane Satrapi have been released to critical acclaim- perhaps even more so from the literature world than the graphic novel community.

And then there's Christopher Ware. Oh boy, is there Christopher Ware! With his *Acme Novelty Library* which started in the early nineties, Ware soon became recognized as not merely a comics illustrator but as a supremely talented artist and writer whose work in the full-length *Jimmy Corrigan: Smartest Kid on Earth* placed him on a pedestal in not only the literature world but also in the visual art world, with his work appearing on several best-of-the-year book lists and in the 2002 Whitney Biennial. It's in *Jimmy Corrigan* that the worlds of comic books and novels truly collide. A coinciding history of milquetoast Jimmy meeting the father he never knew and his grandfather's relationship with his father, *Jimmy Corrigan* is (and this isn't said lightly) a work of unparalleled brilliance that ranks high in the annals of melancholy missives along with Thomas Hardy and in the sublime and subtle humor pantheon with Dickens.

Christopher Ware's art is reminiscent of early Bauhaus work in its intricately patterned geometrical structure and yet also contains a parody of the early Disney style character designs as well as a structure influenced by Herriman's early Krazy Kat newspaper dailies. Ware is also responsible for editing what is probably one of the best introductions to comic artists and the graphic novel in the *McSweeneys Quarterly* Issue Number 13 from 2003.

But what does all this have to do with *Watchmen*? It is, after all, a superhero story rooted in very traditional comic book style dialogue and illustration while the aforementioned are anything but. It's hard to say because the history of the graphic novel is being written while this is being read. It is beginning to look like *Watchmen* may get credited for creating a genre—or at least forcing old school denizens of literature to take notice of a form that has been discredited for so long—and still is by many. What is perhaps more important than *Watchmen* itself is *Time*'s placing it on its list of important literature. Certainly other books are better—even other graphic novels. But *Watchmen* is the one that first stood up, the first one that proclaimed a story with emotional depth and historical relevance could be told in words and pictures, and that perhaps, as the old maxim goes, those pictures told more than words ever could.

Source: Allen, Karl. "Watchmen and the Birth of Respect for the Graphic Novel." *About.com*, 2011, contemporarylit.about.com/od/graphicnovels/fr/watchmen.htm.

# Writing Textual Analysis

Imagine that a scholar visiting your campus gave a talk about the ongoing controversy surrounding the classic American novel *The Adventures of Huckleberry Finn* by Mark Twain. (See Focus: Revising *Huck Finn* on page 265.) Maybe you were assigned to read that novel in high school and have strong feelings about it. So you attend the visiting scholar's talk, which is followed by an intense question-and-answer session with the audience. The experience prompts you to weigh in on the controversy by writing a letter to the editor of your campus newspaper. Such a letter would be a good opportunity to use literary analysis.

Whether you have such an opportunity or have a specific course assignment that calls for literary analysis, keep in mind the main characteristics of analytical writing:

1. **A relevant topic worthy of analysis.** Identify the question or issue about the text that leads to your interpretation and explain why that question or issue is important:

   - What question or issue does this text raise for you? What specifically are you examining about the text?

   - Why is this question or issue important?

   - What does your interpretation offer to readers of this text? How might your interpretation relate to other interpretations of this text?

2. **Complexity.** Examine the text in sufficient depth to help readers understand your interpretation:

   - How carefully have you explored the text so that your interpretation is more than a simple evaluation of the text?

   - What does your essay offer readers beyond a summary of the text? Have you included summary of the text strategically to help readers understand your interpretation?

   - Does your interpretation avoid oversimplifying the text?

9

3. **Sufficient information and appropriate evidence.** Support your interpretation adequately:

- What evidence do you present to support your interpretation?

- Is your evidence sufficient to persuade readers that your interpretation is valid?

- Do you use appropriate terminology in presenting your evidence to support your interpretation?

- Do you summarize relevant passages from the text to help your readers understand your interpretation?

4. **Reasonable conclusions.** Present conclusions that grow reasonably out of your interpretation:

- What conclusions do you draw from your interpretation of this text?

- How do your conclusions relate to your interpretation of the text?

- In what ways do your conclusions present readers with a thought-provoking way of understanding the text you have analyzed?

Use the Ten Core Concepts described in Chapter 2 to help you develop an effective analysis of a text. Read this section in tandem with Chapter 3; each step described here corresponds to a step described in Chapter 3.

## Step 1 Identify a topic for textual analysis.

A friend once told me that Henry David Thoreau's book *Walden*, which was published in 1854, changed his life. When I asked him to explain, he told me that Thoreau's philosophy of simple living deeply influenced the way he thought about his own life. My friend's comment made me wonder why *Walden* seems to resonate with readers today. Such a question is often the starting point for textual analysis. We want to understand what a text means or why it affects us in a certain way. Sometimes, our interest in a text can arise from a controversy surrounding it.

So **begin by identifying a text that interests you or others:**

| Identify a text that interests you. | • Have you read a novel, story, or play that engaged you for some reason?<br>• Do you have a favorite poem?<br>• Have you seen a film or television show that you found puzzling or illuminating?<br>• Does the work of a particular writer, filmmaker, singer, or artist appeal to you?<br>• Have you encountered a text that seems especially important? |
|---|---|
| Examine a controversy about a text. | • What makes a novel like *The Adventures of Huckleberry Finn* controversial? What makes it great?<br>• Is the depiction of torture in the 2012 film *Zero Dark Thirty* inaccurate or misleading?<br>• Why do the *Harry Potter* novels appeal to so many readers?<br>• Does the hit TV series *The Walking Dead* glorify violence? |

Your course assignment might specify a text or a general topic for your essay. Here are some common examples:

- Choose a short story from the course textbook and develop an interpretation of it.
- Select three novels from the course reading list and discuss how they explore issues of social class.
- Using feminist theory, analyze gender roles in one of the assigned plays.
- Examine a major theme in Walt Whitman's *Leaves of Grass*.

Such an assignment provides a starting point for your analysis, but you must still define your specific topic and in some cases decide which text or texts to analyze. The best way to do so is to start with the texts that interest you or the aspects of a text that intrigue you.

Next, formulate a question. Whichever text (or texts) you choose, your analysis should start with a question:

- What does this text mean?
- Why is this text important?
- What does this text say about an important issue?
- How do these texts relate to each other?
- What questions do these texts raise for me?

At this point your question can be general and open-ended. You will refine it as you explore your topic and develop your interpretation. But your question is the starting point for your inquiry, so it should reflect your interests and your desire to understand the text or texts you will analyze.

Develop this question using Step #1 in Chapter 3.

**9**

## Step 2 | Place your topic in rhetorical context.

Consider what might interest other readers in the text you have chosen and the question you have developed:

| If you selected a text that interests you | • Why would this text or these texts be important to other readers?<br>• What might interest other readers about this text?<br>• What does your question (from Step #1) offer readers who might share your interest in this text or these texts? |
|---|---|
| If you selected a text that is the focus of controversy | • What interests you about this controversy?<br>• What interests you about what others have said about this text?<br>• Are you taking a side in the controversy? Why?<br>• Are you exploring a question that the controversy has raised for you? |
| If your course assignment specifies a topic | • What might interest your classmates about the question you formulated for Step #1?<br>• How does your question fit the assignment or relate to important course topics?<br>• How will your analysis contribute to your classmates' understanding of the text or texts you will analyze? |

Addressing these questions will help you identify a purpose for your analysis and develop an interpretation of the text or texts you are analyzing that will interest other readers.

With these considerations in mind, complete Step #2 in Chapter 3.

## Step 3  Select a medium.

Literary analysis is usually written in the form of a conventional academic essay. If you are writing in response to a course assignment, follow your assignment guidelines in developing your essay. However, if your assignment allows you to select a medium other than a conventional essay for your analysis, consider the medium that will enable you to present your analysis to your audience:

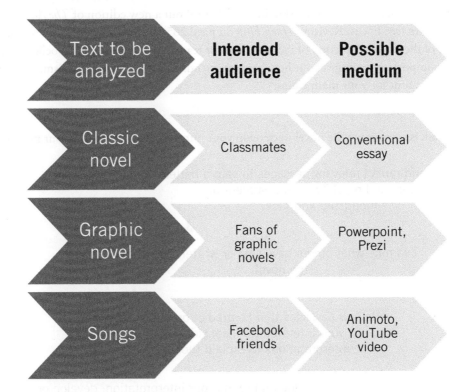

| Text to be analyzed | Intended audience | Possible medium |
|---|---|---|
| Classic novel | Classmates | Conventional essay |
| Graphic novel | Fans of graphic novels | Powerpoint, Prezi |
| Songs | Facebook friends | Animoto, YouTube video |

These are just possibilities. The point is to select a medium that will enhance your ability to present a complex textual analysis effectively to your intended audience. A multimedia program such as *iMovie* or *Photostory* that enables you to incorporate visual elements for an audience, for instance, might work well for an analysis of graphic novels or films. An analysis of poetry might be more effective if you were able to incorporate audio to illustrate how the poet uses sound or rhythm. (Always check with your instructor to see whether your choice of medium is acceptable.)

Follow Step #3 in Chapter 3 to help you decide on the most appropriate medium for your textual analysis.

9

**Step 4** **Develop your interpretation and identify your main claim.**

What will you say about the text or texts you are analyzing? The answer to that question is essentially your interpretation of the text or texts you are analyzing.

You might already have a good idea of what you want to say about the text(s) you have selected. For example, if you are interested in the debate about a new edition of *The Adventures of Huckleberry Finn* (see Focus: Revising *Huck Finn* on page 265), you might decide to examine the importance of the novel's depiction of race relations for readers today. Perhaps you believe that the novel has an important message about how genuine friendships can transcend racism. That could be the starting point for your **main claim:**

> Huck Finn *presents a vision of genuine friendship that transcends race.*

Now your task is to examine the novel to develop your interpretation and refine your main point:

Identify and reread relevant passages to gain a better understanding of Twain's treatment of friendship and race.

Examine what others have said or written about the novel.

Review passages that contradict or don't seem to fit your interpretation; consider alternative interpretations to explain those passages.

Develop and refine your interpretation; develop or adjust key points; eliminate unnecessary or weak points.

Adjust your main claim, if necessary.

If you do not yet have a good sense of what you want to say about the text(s), **begin with your question from Step #1.** That question might suggest a tentative claim, which you can develop, refine, or change as you explore the novel:

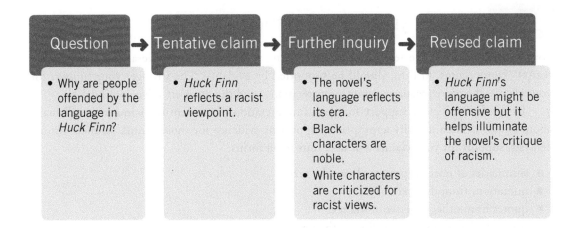

This step and the next one represent the main inquiry into the text(s) you have chosen to analyze. You might find that your ideas and opinions change as you proceed. Don't expect to know exactly what you will say at the beginning; part of the value of the process is the learning you will do as you examine the text(s) and develop your interpretation.

Your Guiding Thesis Statement, which you develop in Step #4 in Chapter 3, can serve as a summary of your interpretation and your main claim. In addition, consider the following questions as you work on your Guiding Thesis Statement:

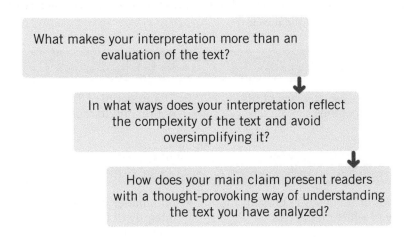

# Step 5 | Support your interpretation.

Your interpretation of the text(s) you are analyzing will be based on several claims about the text(s). Those claims, in turn, should be supported by evidence. The stronger your support for your claims, the more persuasive your interpretation—and the more effective your analysis.

To develop sufficient support for your interpretation, first identify claims you will make about the text. Then identify appropriate support or evidence for those claims. In most textual analysis, **support for your claims will take four main forms:**

- summaries of relevant passages from the text
- quotations from the text
- quotes from other analyses of the text
- reasoning based on your reading of the text

Let's return to the example of *Huck Finn*. In rereading the novel, you found two major scenes that you believe reveal the author's views about race relations. Your interpretation—that Twain saw beyond race to a person's fundamental character—is based on your reading of those scenes. You want to make two claims in support of your interpretation: (1) Twain was actually critiquing the racism he saw in his society by calling attention to its hypocrisy, and (2) the integrity of Twain's characters had nothing to do with race; "good" characters could be black as well as white, and many white characters were evil or stupid. The two major scenes will become important evidence to support these claims; you might also quote from several essays of literary criticism that generally support your view of the novel:

| Claims | |
|---|---|
| 1. Twain critiques racist views of his white contemporaries. | 2. The integrity of Twain's characters is not related to race. |

| Evidence | |
|---|---|
| • Summaries of scenes that present the hypocrisy of white characters<br><br>• Quotations from the text that highlight racism | • Summaries of scenes that show integrity of both black and white characters<br><br>• Relevant quotations from critics |

Keep in mind that in most textual analysis, there is no "proof" that a single interpretation is correct; rather, you are providing support for your claims about the text to make your interpretation more persuasive to your readers. Remember to use appropriate literary concepts and terminology—such as *theme* and *symbol*—to develop and support your interpretation. For example, to support your claim about Twain's critique of his racist contemporaries, you can use the common description of the raft in *Huck Finn* as a *symbol* of a colorblind refuge from racist society.

Step #5 in Chapter 3 will help you identify sufficient support for your interpretation. At this point, you are probably ready to write a complete draft of your project or move onto the next step before completing your draft.

## Step 6 Organize your textual analysis.

Unlike some other kinds of analytical writing that lend themselves to certain ways of organizing the essay, textual analyses rarely follow a straightforward organizational pattern. As the reading selections in this chapter illustrate, writers can take very different approaches to organizing their analyses. Ultimately, a writer must consider the intended audience and the purpose of the textual analysis in deciding how best to organize it. However, most essays of textual analysis will have some version of the following components:

- a rationale for analyzing the text(s)
- the main interpretation of the text
- claims about the text that support the interpretation
- support for the claims
- conclusions about the text on the basis of the interpretation

These five components can be used to develop a **basic outline for your textual analysis:**

1. **Introduction:** a statement of the focus of your analysis and the main question(s) about the text you are addressing in your analysis.

2. **Rationale:** your reason(s) for analyzing the selected text(s); the purpose of your analysis.

3. **Summary:** a strategic summary that highlights the important aspects of the text on which the analysis will focus.

4. **Interpretation:** an explanation of your interpretation of the text, including the main claims made about the text.

5. **Support:** your evidence to support your claims about the text.

6. **Conclusion:** the conclusions you draw about the text(s) on the basis of your interpretation.

Using such a basic outline requires you to make decisions about how to organize each main section of your essay. For example, you will still have to decide in which order to present your evidence for each of your claims. Step #6 in Chapter 3 offers additional help as you develop a structure for your essay.

**9**

## Step 7 | Get feedback.

Step #7 in Chapter 3 guides you through the process of obtaining useful feedback by focusing on the four main characteristics of analytical writing:

| A relevant topic worthy of analysis | • Has the writer provided compelling reasons for analyzing the selected texts?<br>• Does the writer have something relevant to say about these texts? Are the writer's claims clearly presented? |
|---|---|
| Complexity | • How thorough is the analysis of the text(s)?<br>• Has the writer examined the text(s) in sufficient depth?<br>• How does the writer's interpretation do justice to the text(s) and avoid oversimplifcation? |
| Appropriate and sufficient support | • What evidence does the writer present to support the interpretation of the text(s)? Do any sections need more support or stronger evidence?<br>• How does the writer use summary in the analysis? Are the summaries accurate and relevant?<br>• Does the writer use literary terms appropriately? |
| Reasonable conclusions | • Do the writer's conclusions grow logically from the analysis of the text(s)? Are the conclusions presented clearly and persuasively?<br>• What does the writer's interpretation add to our understanding of the text(s)? |

## Step 8 | Revise.

Follow the steps for Step #8 in Chapter 3 to revise your draft. Use the questions listed in Step #7 in this chapter to guide your revisions. Pay particular attention to the following:

- whether your interpretation is clear and thought-provoking and goes beyond an evaluation of the text you are analyzing;
- how you have used summary to help your readers follow your analysis and to provide support for your claims;
- what evidence you have used to support your claims; and
- how you have organized your draft so that your interpretation is presented clearly and logically to your readers.

## Step 9 Refine your voice.

Like all analytical writing, textual analysis is more effective if the writer's voice is strong and confident. Students sometimes try to sound academic in their literary analysis essays by relying too heavily on literary terminology or mimicking the writing style of professional literary critics. Such strategies usually weaken an essay. Instead, focus on developing a sound interpretation of the text that you have confidence in and that you explain as clearly as you can to your readers. That confidence will come through in your voice. For example, compare the different voices in Diane Henningfeld's essay (page 269) and Caetlin Benson-Allott's essay (page 273) in this chapter; their voices differ noticeably, yet each writer conveys confidence in her interpretation. Keep that in mind as you complete Step #9 in Chapter 3.

## Step 10 Edit.

Complete **Step #10 in Chapter 3**. Pay particular attention to specialized terms, and make sure your quotations from the text are accurate and correctly punctuated.

> ### WRITING PROJECTS | TEXTUAL ANALYSIS
>
> 1. Select a favorite story, novel, poem, film, song, or other literary work and write an essay for an audience of your classmates in which you offer your interpretation of that work and explain its appeal.
>
>    Alternatively, write an essay for a different audience—for example, readers of your hometown newspaper or your Facebook friends—in which you present your interpretation of your selected literary work and explain why those readers should care about that work.
>
> 2. Select two very different literary works—such as a Shakespeare play and several rap songs—that explore similar themes, and write an essay in which you present an analysis of how those themes are developed in each work.
>
> 3. Analyze the film version of a novel or play and draw conclusions about the director's interpretation of that work. Present your analysis in a multimedia format for an audience that you think would be interested in it.
>
> 4. Rewrite the essay you wrote for Question #1 or Question #2 in a completely different medium. For example, rewrite a conventional essay as a digital story using a program such as *Photostory* or turn it into a YouTube video or podcast.
>
> 5. Using social media such as Twitter or Facebook, ask for responses to the essay you created for Question #1. Do the readers who responded agree with your interpretation of the text? Why or why not? What have you learned about the text from their responses to your essay? Now consider what revisions you might make to your essay on the basis of these responses.

> ### MindTap°
> Request help with these Writing Projects and feedback from a tutor. If required, participate in peer review, submit your paper for a grade, and view instructor comments online.

## In this chapter, you will learn to

1. Define evaluation and understand its purpose and uses.

2. Identify appropriate rhetorical opportunities for evaluation.

3. Apply the four main features of effective analytical writing to sample evaluative writings.

4. Identify and apply the four common features of reviews to examples of evaluative texts.

5. Write an evaluation essay, applying the four features of evaluation and using the Ten Core Concepts from Chapter 3.

## MindTap®

Understand the goals of the chapter and complete a warm-up activity.

# Evaluating and Reviewing 10

**WE COMMONLY EVALUATE** the films, music, television shows, books, exhibits, and performances that entertain us and maybe even provoke us to think in different ways about important aspects of our lives:

- We tell a friend what we thought of a movie we enjoyed.
- We share opinions about whether a band's new recording is as good as its previous work.
- We recommend a new book we recently finished.
- We follow a debate on Twitter about whether a popular new video game reflects a trend toward more violent games.

No matter how brief, these conversations amount to informal critical evaluations. They are common forms of analysis that help us make sense of works or performances and place them in the context of what others think or say about them.

Perhaps just as often as we share views about films, books, or music, we also evaluate consumer goods: everything from smartphone apps to clothes to cars. With the rapid growth of online reviewing on consumer websites like Yelp.com and social media such as Facebook, more and more people are writing and reading reviews. As a result, reviews have become an ever-more important kind of analysis in our lives as citizens, consumers, and workers.

In academic settings, evaluation usually focuses more directly on the careful analysis of texts and is part of a discipline's inquiry into specific questions, problems, or ideas. For example, a historian might review a new study of the Pilgrims' settlement in New England that challenges prevailing beliefs about the way the colony was governed. A biochemist might evaluate grant proposals for studies of new blood pressure medications to determine which ones should be funded. Such reviews are a means by which scholars discuss and evaluate each other's work and thus contribute to their field's understanding of important issues, ideas, or developments.

Evaluative writing, then, plays a role in all aspects of our lives: in school, in the workplace, and elsewhere.

## Occasions for Evaluating and Reviewing

Writers are often motivated to evaluate something because of their own experience. For example, someone trying to decide where to have dinner might consult reviews of restaurants on an online review site. Afterward, that same person might write a review of the restaurant to add to what others have said about it. In this way, patrons engage in an ongoing conversation about restaurants and dining. Readers consult reviews to learn from the writer's experience and consider the writer's viewpoint about a topic of common interest. In this sense, writers of reviews and their readers share an implicit sense of purpose. In the case of restaurant reviews, for example, both writers and readers seek information and opinions to help them decide which restaurants to visit.

Rarely does a writer review something without readers in mind. In this regard, reviews and evaluations highlight the way rhetorical purpose informs a writer's work. As a writer, your reasons for writing an evaluation or review are likely to grow out of your sense of something's importance not only to you but also to others.

The same principle applies to evaluations and reviews written in academic settings. Academic journals in all fields contain articles that have been carefully reviewed by other scholars before they are published. In fact, reviewing manuscripts for possible publication is one of the most common kinds of scholarly writing. Many academic journals also regularly publish reviews of books in their fields. These reviews provide a forum in which scholars evaluate each other's work in their effort to advance their understanding of important topics in their fields. In addition, scholars routinely review proposals that seek grant funding for specific research projects. In these ways, evaluative writing is a crucial component of a scholar's effort to understand important issues, questions, or problems in his or her field.

College writing assignments routinely require students to evaluate texts, performances, or exhibits to deepen students' understanding of the concepts or information they are learning and to share insights about the subject matter. The evaluative writing required in such assignments engages students in careful analysis of their topics. For example, in reviewing a research article in sociology, students must apply their knowledge of research methods to evaluate the quality of the study; at the same time, they are learning more about the subject of the study itself. Similarly, students in an English course might be asked to review the film version of a classic novel they have been assigned to read; such reviews require students not only to think carefully about the subject matter of the film but also to apply the literary theories they are learning. In this sense, evaluative writing is not only an opportunity to express an opinion about whether something is effective or worthwhile but also an occasion to build and share knowledge.

---

**EXERCISE 10A**    **OCCASIONS FOR REVIEWING AND EVALUATING**

1. Think of a favorite film or TV show. If you were to write a review of it, what would you say about it? To whom would you address the review? What would be its purpose? In other words, what would you want that audience to learn from your review? Now find one or two reviews of the film or TV show. Compare the purpose of those reviews to your own sense of the purpose of reviewing this film or show. What conclusions might you draw about reviews?

2. Identify a current film you would like to see. Find several reviews of the film. In a brief paragraph, describe what the reviewers have said about the film. What did you learn from these reviews? In what ways might the reviews influence your desire to see the film and your expectations for the film?

3. Have you ever made a decision on the basis of a review? For example, did you decide to purchase a video game or an album after reading a review of it? If so, describe that experience. Explain what you learned from the review and how it influenced your decision. On the basis of this experience, what conclusions would you draw about the nature and purpose of reviews?

# Understanding Reviews and Evaluation

As the preceding sections of this chapter suggest, writers write reviews for many different reasons. Ultimately, the rhetorical situation determines what features a review should include and what makes for effective evaluative writing. Despite the great variety of forms that reviews can take, however, **reviews share four common features:**

- criteria for evaluation
- a summary or description of what is being evaluated
- a reason for the review
- something relevant to say

## Criteria for Evaluation

Whatever is being reviewed, the writer must have a set of criteria or standards by which to evaluate the subject of the review. To a great extent, the quality of the review depends on the validity of the criteria used for evaluation and whether readers agree with those criteria (see Focus: "What Criteria Should Be Applied?" on page 295). In a book review, for example, the reviewer will apply generally accepted criteria appropriate to the genre of the book. For example, reviews of novels will generally evaluate the effectiveness of the plot and the extent to which the novelist explores certain themes. Similarly, movie reviews often include evaluation of technical aspects of a film, such as cinematography and editing. These criteria or standards for evaluation are generally agreed upon and may have been established over many years. Sometimes, reviews are based on specialized criteria. For example, business or research proposals will usually be evaluated according to criteria that reflect the goals or needs of the program in question—say, a program for revitalizing small businesses in a rural region or a grant program to support studies of effective methods of teaching math. In such cases, the criteria reflect the specialized knowledge of the academic field or purpose of the program. But no matter how informal or technical, every review should be based on a standard or set of criteria, whether or not the writer explicitly states it.

## A Summary or Description of What Is Being Evaluated

Often, readers will not be intimately familiar with what is being evaluated, so reviewers must include a summary or description of the subject. For example, because movie critics often write reviews of movies before they are released to the general public, their reviews include a summary of the movie's plot so that readers can understand what the critic is evaluating. Similarly, book reviews include plot summaries under the assumption that many (perhaps most) readers will not yet have read the book being reviewed. How much summary or description to include depends on the nature and purpose of the review and what the intended audience can be expected to know about whatever is being reviewed. For example, a review in a campus newspaper of the latest recording by a popular musician would likely not include much background information about the musician because readers will already be familiar with him or her; a release by a new band, however, might include details about the band's musical style and history because many readers will probably know little about the band.

## A Reason for the Review

Evaluative writing is part of a broader effort to understand something or contribute to our collective knowledge. A good review should reflect that sense of purpose. Sometimes, the reason for a review is implicit and need not be stated. For example, we expect new movies to be reviewed because of the enormous popularity and cultural importance of film. The same can be said about certain books and musical works. But often a writer will provide a more specific reason for reviewing something. For instance, a reviewer might review several recent books about a controversial topic that has received a great deal of news coverage. A special anniversary—say, of an important historical event—might prompt a writer to review music, books, or exhibits related to that anniversary. The death of a famous actor might be the occasion for a review of films in which that actor starred.

## Something Relevant to Say

Even when they pass judgment on something, effective reviews usually have a point to make. For example, a writer reviewing a new book about the Vietnam War might advance a viewpoint about the U.S. involvement in a current war. A review of a fictional film about corruption in politics might make a statement about real-life politics. Although readers often read reviews to see whether the writer did or did not like a film, TV show, musical performance, exhibit, video game, or book, the most effective reviews have something more thought-provoking to offer. (The readings in this chapter include examples of reviews that make a larger point.) In this sense, a review is an occasion to explore a broader question or issue that goes beyond the subject of the review.

These four features usually appear in some form in most reviews, but writers must consider their intended audience and the purpose of the review as they decide what to include in a review.

Writers and readers can disagree about the evaluation of something, but reviews are more useful and persuasive when both writer and reader agree on the criteria being used for the evaluation. A novel, for example, will often be evaluated on the basis of its plot, the depth of its themes, and perhaps the style of writing; by contrast, a work of history will likely be judged on the basis of the quality of its analysis and the clarity of its storytelling. Fans of detective fiction will probably expect a reviewer to evaluate how well the writer of a detective novel builds suspense, but they are less likely to be concerned about whether the novelist's writing style is poetic. Reviewers, therefore, try to apply criteria that readers expect, even when those criteria are never explicitly stated. If the reviewer uses criteria that readers find irrelevant, inappropriate, or even unfair, they are more likely to reject the reviewer's evaluation of the subject. In writing a review, then, examine your rhetorical situation so that the criteria you develop for your review are likely to match your readers' expectations.

**EXERCISE 10B | UNDERSTANDING REVIEWS AND EVALUATIVE WRITING**

1. Select a favorite book, film, performance, or other subject and consider what criteria you might use in reviewing that subject. On what basis would you review that subject? What criteria would make sense for this kind of subject? What criteria do you think others who would be interested in the subject might expect? Are you aware of established criteria for this subject? Briefly describe these criteria.

2. Compare two or more reviews of a popular book, film, video game, or performance (ideally, one that you enjoyed). Examine the criteria that each reviewer used in evaluating the subject. Do the reviewers make their criteria explicit? Are those criteria similar across the reviews? If not, what differences in those criteria did you notice? What conclusions might you draw from this exercise about how reviewers select and apply criteria?

3. Using the same reviews you found for Question #2 (or a set of reviews about a different subject), compare the conclusions reached about the subject by the various reviewers. Do the reviewers agree about the subject? If not, what is the basis of their disagreements? Do you agree with any of the reviewers? Explain, citing specific passages from the reviews to support your answer. What conclusions might you draw from this exercise about the nature of reviews?

# Reading Reviews

Reviews come in a variety of forms and serve many different purposes for different audiences. The readings in this section reflect that variety. Each reading represents a common form of review: a review of a popular TV show, a video game review, and a book review. In each case, there is a specific occasion for the review: the publication of a book about an issue of current interest, the appearance of a new video game, and the end of a popular television series. As you read these selections, notice how each writer crafts his or her review for the rhetorical situation and uses the review to make a larger point that goes beyond an evaluation of the subject. Also consider the four main features of effective analytical writing:

| A relevant topic worthy of analysis | • How does the writer establish that the subject is worthy of a review?<br>• What is the context for the review? What is the writer's purpose in reviewing this text, show, game, etc.? |
| --- | --- |
| Complexity | • On what basis does the writer evaluate his or her subject? What criteria does the writer use for evaluation?<br>• Why are these criteria appropriate for the subject and rhetorical situation?<br>• In what ways does the review enhance our understanding of the subject? |
| Sufficient information and appropriate analysis | • What evidence does the writer provide to support his or her evaluation of the subject? How persuasive is this evidence?<br>• How adequate is the summary of the subject of the review? Does it help illuminate the subject? |
| Reasonable conclusions | • What conclusions does the writer draw about the text?<br>• Are the conclusions well reasoned and supported by the evaluation?<br>• What larger point, if any, does the writer make in the review? How compelling is this point? |

## MindTap®

Read these review examples. Highlight and take notes online.
Additional readings are also available online.

## What We Owe the MythBusters
### by James B. Meigs

*Sometimes a television show has an impact that goes well beyond entertainment. In the following essay, writer James B. Meigs argues that* MythBusters, *a popular reality show on the Discovery Channel from 2003 to 2016, did much more than entertain millions of viewers with quirky experiments; according to Meigs,* MythBusters *changed Americans' attitudes about science. In making his case, Meigs places the TV show in broader cultural and historical context and evaluates it not merely on the basis of its entertainment value but also for its educational value. In the process, he also makes a point about the importance of science education and comments on the state of science education in the United States. In this regard, his evaluation illustrates how reviews can serve a purpose beyond analyzing the subject of the review.*

### Talking About This Reading

**Melissa Whittington (student):** I didn't find this essay difficult to read, most likely because I am familiar with the show and I found it very interesting to see the experiments they would do.

**Bob Yagelski:** Sometimes we encounter a text that is easy to read because we are familiar with the subject and interested in the topic, as Melissa was with Meigs's essay on *MythBusters*. It's also possible that Meigs's writing style makes it easy for readers to follow his analysis. But the ease with which we read an essay should not lead us to conclude that the analysis is superficial. In this case, Meigs's main point is straightforward, but his analysis of the impact of *MythBusters* is actually complex.

When the reality TV show "MythBusters" debuted on the Discovery Channel in 2003, its producers weren't on a mission to transform science and education in America. They just wanted to entertain. In each episode, the hosts would try to debunk or confirm a few classic urban legends. Could a penny dropped off the Empire State Building really kill a person? Could eating a poppy-seed bagel actually make you test positive for heroin? The producers cast two San Francisco-based special-effects artists, Jamie Hyneman and Adam Savage, as hosts. The show was a surprise hit—pulling in as many as 20 million viewers a season—and it helped changed our culture.

Two weeks ago, Mr. Hyneman and Mr. Savage announced that the 14th season of "MythBusters," which begins in January, will be its last. It was a worthy run. Over the course of 248 episodes and 2,950 separate experiments, "MythBusters" taught a whole generation how science works and why it matters.

Americans have worried about the state of science literacy in our country since the days of Sputnik. Educators who want to improve our prospects in this field would do well to take a few pages from the "MythBusters" handbook.

When the show started, the image of science and engineering in mainstream culture was at a low ebb. NASA's Apollo glory days were long past, and the Columbia space shuttle disintegrated on re-entry just days after the show's premiere episode. There was no leading scientist able to connect with the general public the way the astronomer Carl Sagan had before his death in 1996. Even Bill Nye, "the Science Guy," had been dropped from the airwaves. And popular sci-fi movies of the era—"The Matrix," "Minority Report"—depicted science and technology leading us to bleak, dystopian futures.

*(Continued)*

Academic interest in science was in similar decline: Barely 20 percent of college freshmen were signing up for majors in science, technology, engineering and math, known as STEM fields—continuing a long downward trend.

"MythBusters" helped reverse that trend not by gussying science up, but by taking it seriously. "You can't underestimate the power of TV to give young people a lens to see science through," says the materials scientist and STEM evangelist Anissa Ramirez. "'MythBusters' helped viewers feel empowered to participate."

Too often, science is presented as a body of established facts to be handed down to obedient students. But "MythBusters" isn't about facts, it's about process: For every myth, the team has to figure out how to test the claim, then construct an experiment, carry out the tests and analyze the results. (Penny: false. Poppy seeds: true.) Every episode is an object lesson in the scientific method. Scientists had often been depicted in entertainment, but rarely had audiences seen people actually doing science.

Obviously, experiments staged for television can't have the rigor of peer-reviewed lab work. But "MythBusters" captures the underlying mind-set of science. At a time when "skepticism" too often means rejecting any ideas one finds politically unpalatable, "MythBusters" provides a compelling example of real scientific skepticism, the notion that nothing can be held true until it is confirmed by experimentation.

It's also good television. "MythBusters" is relentlessly entertaining partly because it channels the underlying suspense of science itself: The hosts don't know how an experiment is going to turn out any more than the audience does. And almost every test requires that the team build some sort of contraption: for example, a miniature Hindenburg to test the claim that it was the burning of the dirigible's paint, not its hydrogen, that destroyed the airship.

"The public doesn't often associate science with being deeply creative," Mr. Hyneman recently said. "We have pointed out how fun and creative and thought-provoking science and experimentation can be." The duo constantly hears from adult fans who were inspired by the show and are now working in science or engineering. "They say, 'You guys got me through high school physics,'" Mr. Savage said.

The MythBusters' delight in gonzo engineering also helped inspire the rise of the modern class of tinkerers known as "makers." When the show began, the idea that average people could build their own complex gadgets was a fringe notion at best. Today, more than 400,000 students worldwide gather to compete in FIRST Robotics competitions. Thousands of adults and kids attend Maker Faire festivals to show off their quirky inventions. "I feel really lucky that 'MythBusters' coincided with the whole D.I.Y. movement and contributed to it," Mr. Savage said. "I mean you've got 10-year-old girls building robots now!"

"MythBusters" didn't do all this alone, of course. American culture is embracing its inner nerd on many fronts today. The cult of Steve Jobs and our fascination with tech start-ups have played a part. So have fictional TV shows like "CSI" and "The Big Bang Theory." The astrophysicist Neil deGrasse Tyson has stepped into Carl Sagan's shoes, and "The Martian," which its star, Matt Damon, calls "a love letter to science," is one of the biggest films of 2015.

Martin Klimek/ZUMA Press/Newscom

Best of all, a study conducted by researchers at the University of California, Los Angeles, found that the number of college freshmen enrolling in STEM majors has climbed nearly 50 percent since 2005. If a few more kids today want to grow up to be Elon Musk or settle on Mars or cure cancer, we have Jamie and Adam partly to thank.

As "MythBusters" moves on to its afterlife of cable reruns, let's hope the show's example continues to resonate with educators and programmers. Science doesn't need to be cleaned up or prettified to be accessible; in fact, the best way to learn it is by getting your hands dirty.

---

### EXERCISE 10C  REVIEWING "MYTHBUSTERS"

1. Why does Meigs believe that *MythBusters* was such an important TV show? What evidence does he offer to support his claim about the need for the show? How persuasive do you find that evidence? Explain.

2. In paragraph 3, Meigs writes that educators who want to improve science education in the United States "would do well to take a few pages from the *MythBusters* handbook." What does he mean? What do you think that statement reveals about Meig's sense of the purpose of his essay?

3. What criteria does Meigs use to evaluate *MythBusters*? Are the criteria he uses appropriate? Why or why not? Cite specific passages from the essay to support your answer.

---

### Destiny
### by Trace C. Schuelke

*In 2015* Time *magazine published a brief article titled "Video Games Are One of the Most Important Art Forms in History." By the time those words were published, a debate about whether video games should be considered art had been raging for several years. The increasingly sophisticated graphics and complex story lines have prompted many critics to argue that video games are much more than games and in fact have many of the same qualities as other kinds of art, such as films or novels. Perhaps for these reasons the release of some video games can be as eagerly anticipated by fans as the appearance of a blockbuster movie. Destiny, a science-fiction online-only game, is one such game. Its release in 2014 was the largest launch of a video game up to that time. Gamers are also avid reviewers, and they used social media as well as online gaming sites to share their evaluations of* Destiny. *One of those reviews, which appeared on TeenInk. com in 2015, is reprinted here. As you'll see, the writer, Trace C. Schuelke, refers to "the hype" surrounding the release of the game, but the focus of his review is on the main elements that video gamers look for, especially graphics and story line, which become the criteria by which he evaluates the game. Schuelke also has something to say about the relationship between the popularity and quality of a game like* Destiny. *Despite its brevity, his review includes the main characteristics of evaluation and is a good example of how reviewers can take part in ongoing conversations about important cultural trends like gaming.*

*(Continued)*

### Talking About This Reading

**Aaron Toporovsky (student):** Why does there have to be plot or story line for a video game? People might just enjoy playing it.

**Bob Yagelski:** Aaron, your question is one that others have raised in the ongoing debates about whether video games should be considered art. (See the preceding introduction to this essay.) But it also underscores differences in how readers respond to a text. In this case, serious gamers are not likely to ask the question you pose, because they assume video games need story lines. As a gamer himself, Schuelke, whose intended audience is other gamers, makes the same assumption—which is why a good story line is one of the main criteria he uses in his evaluation of *Destiny*.

................................................

Imagine you're about to eat a pizza. Before you sink your teeth in, you're told that it will be perfect in all aspects; it was made by gourmet chefs, contains the best ingredients, and everyone agrees it's amazing. All you can think about is taking that first delicious bite. But when you do, you realize something awful: all the trimmings are there but the flavor is absent. "Destiny" is just that—a pizza without flavor. Sure, there's something to be said for its outer mechanics and features, but overall, it feels lacking.

Just in case there's anybody out there who missed the hype, "Destiny" is a first-person shooter produced by Bungie, the developers of the Halo series. The game centers around basic and understandable (albeit clichéd) plot points: the remnants of humanity are in danger, and you need to stop the bad guys from destroying everything.

While there are plenty of lackluster things about "Destiny," let's start on a positive note. This game has absolutely breathtaking visuals. Every set piece feels lovingly crafted and meticulously created; this game is sure to strike awe in those who load it up. In addition, the core mechanics are intuitive and fluid. Guns fire with snappy sound effects, vehicles control smoothly, and the central controls are mapped and coordinated near perfectly. As a whole, the game feels great, looks great, and controls with ease. So what makes "Destiny" so flavorless?

Without question, the biggest thing "Destiny" lacks is a cohesive story line. It's clear that immense time and effort were put into this product, but very little of the world is given backstory or reasoning, making the objectives empty and pointless. Sure, there are bad guys to shoot, but why? Sure, the environments on places like Venus are gorgeous, but why does Venus suddenly have plant life and a city on it? There are no answers, and as such, players feel as though the journey was meaningless. With repetitive mission objectives, lackluster boss encounters,

Destiny

a shallow earn-loot-through-challenges system, an underdeveloped character set, and an overall air of emptiness, this game is definitely not the fine dining experience so many were expecting.

Is "Destiny" a bad game? Not by any stretch of the imagination. If anything, it's an underdeveloped game that was massively overhyped and couldn't live up to expectations. There's no question that it's fun the first time around, but the longer you play, the more the flaws reveal themselves.

There's a saying that there's no such thing as bad pizza, and in the case of "Destiny," it's true. However, just because a pizza looks great, smells great, and is generally agreed to be great doesn't mean that it actually is.

Source: Schuelke, Trace C. "Destiny." *TeenInk*, Sept. 2015, p. www.teenink.com/reviews/video_game_ reviews/article/723331/Destiny/.

---

**EXERCISE 10D**   **REVIEWING "DESTINY"**

1. What are Schuelke's main claims about *Destiny*? What evidence does he provide to support those claims? Do you find that evidence sufficient? Why or why not?

2. How persuasive do you find Schuelke's evaluation of *Destiny*? If you have played the game, to what extent does your experience coincide with Schuelke's evaluation? If you have not played the game, has Schuelke provided enough information about this game and supported his claims sufficiently to persuade you that his conclusions are sound? Explain.

3. This review was published on a website for teens. In what ways do you think the style of this review is appropriate for that audience? How effectively does this writer address the rhetorical situation? Cite specific passages from the essay to support your answer.

---

## Review of *Thirteen Reasons Why* by Jay Asher
### By Bryan Gillis

*The following essay is an example of a conventional review of a novel. Like most such reviews, this one draws conclusions about the quality of the novel's plot and characterization. In this case, the reviewer, Bryan Gillis, evaluates a novel for adolescent readers called* Thirteen Reasons Why (2007), *by Jay Asher. What makes this review noteworthy is that it appeared in 2011 in a journal called* The Journal of Adolescent & Adult Literacy, *which is intended for scholars and other professionals interested in literacy. The purpose of the review goes beyond evaluating the quality of the novel as a work of literary art; Gillis also assesses the appropriateness of the novel for adolescent readers, thus helping his audience (educators, scholars, and other literacy professionals) determine whether the novel might be useful in their work with adolescent students. His review illustrates how audience and purpose can shape a writer's evaluation of a subject. Notice, too, that Gillis also assesses how effectively the novel addresses a relevant but difficult subject: teen suicide. In part, his purpose is to help his readers decide whether the novel might be an appropriate tool for them to use in helping teens understand this challenging subject. Finally, as you read, notice the brevity of this review. Many publications include numerous short reviews, such as this one, so that they can offer their readers reviews of many books rather than only a few longer reviews.*

(Continued)

### Talking About This Reading

**Sarah Gauthier (student):** I found the way the writer summarized the novel very useful. The summary was clear and helpful but didn't give away any details. I also liked the fact that the writer integrated into his review how the novel relates to the real world.

**Bob Yagelski:** As this chapter makes clear, strategic summary is one feature of effective reviews. Sarah's comment suggests why. Too much summary can weaken a review, and deciding exactly what to summarize isn't necessarily easy. Sarah obviously thinks that Bryan Gillis's summary of *Thirteen Reasons Why* is effective. She also reminds us why we read fiction: It can help us make sense of the "real" world.

. . . . . . . . . . . . . . . . . . . . . . . . . . . . . . . . . . . . . . . . . . .

Teen suicide is a hot-button issue. However, unlike abortion, casual sex, or freedom of speech, no one seems to be taking sides on this one. If you poll 100 people, all of them will tell you that they are against teen suicide. If you search teen suicide on the Internet, you will find sites that list reasons and prevention tips. Jay Asher, in his debut novel *Thirteen Reasons Why*, has taken the topic of suicide one step further. What if you really did know the reasons behind a young woman's suicide? What if, before she did it, she left behind audiotapes that explained all of the reasons why she decided to take her own life?

*Thirteen Reasons Why* tells the story of Clay Jensen, who receives a box in the mail from his now deceased friend, Hannah, containing seven cassette tapes. These seven tapes contain Hannah's voice on 13 recorded sides; one side for each person she wants to receive the tapes and each reason that Hannah perceived had something to do with her choice to commit suicide. Clay is not the first person to receive the tapes, nor will he be the last, and as we listen to the tapes with him, we not only learn about the events that Hannah thinks led to her decision, we learn about Clay, who initially doesn't understand how he could have possibly contributed to Hannah's decision.

The strength of *Thirteen Reasons Why* is the plotting. Readers discover right away that Hannah has already committed suicide. Still, her posthumous narration keeps readers engaged and guessing. The book is impossible to put down, because even though we know Hannah is dead, we want to know why she did it. Character development is also a strength. Asher makes us care about Clay. We want to know how and why he is involved in all of this. Readers won't get the entire picture until they have listened to the last tape. And the picture is quite surprising. No parental abuse stories, no creepy uncles, just a sequence of small incidents that, in Hannah's mind, were not handled properly and led to unmanageable circumstances.

Jay Asher has done a remarkable job of integrating Hannah's voice (via the tapes) with Clay's thoughts, responses, and memories to create an inventive and seamless dual narration. The author pulls no punches, including a descriptive and heart-wrenching (but necessary) hot tub scene that will leave you aching. After I finished reading *Thirteen Reasons Why* (in one sitting), all of those teen suicide websites filled with reasons and preventative measures seem rather ineffectual compared with the experience of reading Asher's story of a girl who felt she was left with no options. His message is clear: Stop being apathetic, pay attention, and, most important, be kind to one another.

*Thirteen Reasons Why* deals with some very serious subject matter and is probably most suitable for high school students and above.

Source: Gillis, Bryan. "Thirteen Reasons Why." *Journal of Adolescent & Adult Literacy*, vol. 54, no. 7, April 2011, pp. 542+.

**REVIEWING *THIRTEEN REASONS WHY***

1. How does Gillis establish the relevance of the novel he has chosen to review? How persuasive do you find his justification? Explain, citing passages from the text to support your answer.

2. Much of this review is devoted to a summary of *Thirteen Reasons Why*. How effective do you find this summary? To what extent do you think Gillis's summary contributes to his evaluation of the novel? Explain.

3. What conclusions does Gillis reach about *Thirteen Reasons Why*? In what sense do his conclusions relate to his audience's concerns and interests? To what extent do you think he achieves his purpose in this review?

# Writing Evaluations and Reviews

If you use social media, you most likely regularly read and share informal reviews of movies, concerts, TV shows, restaurants, and maybe even your classes. Such informal reviews can lead to a more formal evaluation. For example, you might find yourself following a debate on Twitter or Snapchat about a popular new movie that you have recently seen. Your desire to participate in such debates can lead to a decision to write a review for your campus newspaper or on social media.

Use the Ten Core Concepts described in Chapter 2 to help you develop such a review. Each step described in this section corresponds to a step described in Chapter 3. As you develop your project, keep in mind the main characteristics of analytical writing:

1. **A relevant topic worthy of analysis.** Identify the reason(s) for reviewing this text, performance, film, exhibit, game, music, or event:
   - What makes this subject appropriate for reviewing?
   - What is the occasion for reviewing this subject?
   - What is the purpose of the review?
   - Why would others be interested in an evaluation of this subject?

2. **Complexity.** Evaluate the subject in sufficient depth:
   - How thoroughly has the writer examined the subject? Does the review avoid oversimplifying the subject?
   - What criteria are used to evaluate the subject of the review? Are these criteria appropriate for the rhetorical situation?
   - What point does the writer make that will interest readers? Does the review go beyond a simple judgment about the subject of the review?

3. **Sufficient information and appropriate evidence.** Support your evaluation adequately:
   - What evidence does the writer present to support his or her evaluation? Is the evidence appropriate?
   - Does the review include a sufficient summary or description of the subject? How effectively is the summary used in the review?

4.  **Reasonable conclusions.** Present conclusions that grow reasonably out of your evaluation:
    ■ What conclusions does the writer draw from his or her evaluation of this subject? Does the evaluation lead reasonably to the writer's conclusions?

    ■ To what extent do the conclusions present readers with a thought-provoking way of understanding the subject?

    ■ Does the writer have a larger point to make? Is that point relevant and thought-provoking?

## Step 1 Identify a topic.

An effective review reflects a writer's interest in something and a desire to share an opinion about it with others who have similar interests:

■ Someone passionate about a specific kind of music is likely to have something to say about the work of an accomplished musician who plays that kind of music.

■ A new book by a famous author might prompt a strong reaction from a fan of that author.

■ A classic movie might provoke a film history buff to think differently about a current trend in film-making.

These examples suggest that evaluations grow out of our engagement with the things that matter to us.

### Start with Your own Interests or Passions

| Books | • Have you read a best-selling book that didn't meet your expectations? Or exceeded them? <br> • Have you read a provocative book about an important current issue that you care about? <br> • Is there a book that you think others should know about for some reason? |
| --- | --- |
| Music | • Has a favorite musician or band recently released a new recording? <br> • Have you noticed a trend in music that you feel strongly about? <br> • Is there a CD or album that you think is especially noteworthy for some reason? |
| Film and television | • Have you seen a film that you find especially important, enjoyable, or provocative? <br> • Do you watch a television show that you believe reflects an important social trend? <br> • Do you have an interest in the films of a specific director or actor whose work is noteworthy? |

| Art | • Have you visited a special exhibit of paintings, photography, or sculpture that is worth attention? |
|---|---|
| | • Does the work of a specific artist strike you as especially important for some reason? |
| | • Do you have an opinion about a trend you've noticed in photography or painting? |

| Performance | • Have you seen an especially powerful concert? |
|---|---|
| | • Have you attended a play that you believe is unusually good or provocative? |
| | • Do you have a favorite musician whose concerts seem different from his or her recordings? |

| Consumer items | • Do you have an opinion about an item you use for recreation (e.g., skis or snowboards, running shoes)? |
|---|---|
| | • Have you noticed an important trend in a specific kind of item (e.g., hybrid cars, smartphones, digital cameras)? |
| | • Have you played a new video game that you find exceptional? |

If you are required to review something specific for a course assignment (for example, an assigned book, a research article, a film), try to develop your review in a way that reflects your own interests. For example, an assignment in a criminal justice course might require you to evaluate how several popular television shows portray the criminal justice system. Although such an assignment constrains your choices, you might select specific television shows that you find interesting, which is likely to make the assignment more engaging.

## Consider Your Purpose

Once you have identified the subject you intend to review, consider why you are evaluating it: What is the purpose of your review? What do you hope to learn by evaluating this subject? Why is this subject worth reviewing? Identify your purpose as clearly as you can. (Your purpose might be specified by your course assignment.)

## Formulate the Purpose of Your Review as a Working Question

Let's return to the example of the criminal justice assignment. The purpose is to determine how selected television shows portray the criminal justice system. Your working question might be, "How accurately do these television shows depict the U.S. criminal justice system?" Here are additional examples:

■ If you are reviewing a book by a favorite author, your question might be, "How does this book compare to this author's previous books in terms of its themes and characters?"

- If you are reviewing several music recordings of a famous symphony, your question might be, "How well do these different performances capture the power of the composition?"
- If you are evaluating proposals for a marketing campaign for a new consumer product, you might ask, "What are the strengths and weaknesses of these proposals in terms of the likelihood that they would market this product effectively?"

Go to Step #1 in Chapter 3 to develop this question.

## Step 2 Place your review in rhetorical context.

As we have seen throughout this chapter, reviews are an especially effective way for writers and readers to engage in discussion about relevant works (films, books, performances, games) that matter to them. So think carefully about your audience as you develop your review:

1. **Identify an appropriate audience for your review.**
   - Who might be interested in your subject?
   - With whom would you like to share your evaluation of this subject?
   - Is the subject of your review likely to interest a specific group of readers or a more general audience?

Be as specific as possible. For example, if you are interested in reviewing a performance by a blues musician, you might wish to find an audience of other fans of the blues. (Your assignment might also specify an audience.)

2. **Consider what might interest that audience about the subject of your review.**
   - Why would your intended audience be interested in the book, film, exhibit, performance, event, or item you have chosen to evaluate?
   - What makes the subject of your review important to your intended audience?
   - What might you have to say about the subject of your review that would be useful or interesting to your readers?
   - What larger message do you hope your intended audience will take away from your review?

Addressing these questions will help you clarify the purpose of your review and develop your evaluation in a way that addresses the interests of your readers.

With that in mind, complete Step #2 in Chapter 3.

## Step 3 Select a medium.

Most reviews are written in conventional print format, but writers today have many options in selecting a medium that would be appropriate for different kinds of reviews.

If your review is part of a course assignment, follow your assignment guidelines. However, if you have a choice, consider the medium that would be most appropriate for the type of review you are writing and the audience you intend to address:

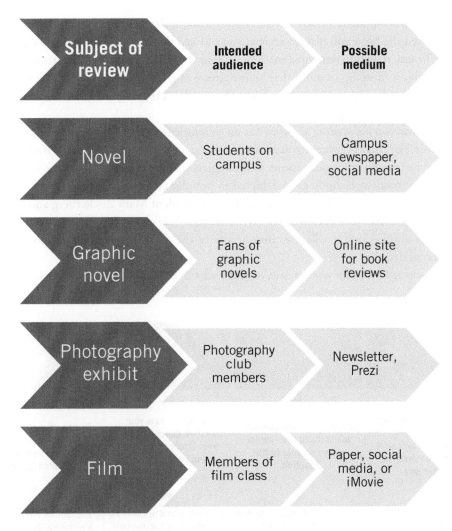

| Subject of review | Intended audience | Possible medium |
|---|---|---|
| Novel | Students on campus | Campus newspaper, social media |
| Graphic novel | Fans of graphic novels | Online site for book reviews |
| Photography exhibit | Photography club members | Newsletter, Prezi |
| Film | Members of film class | Paper, social media, or iMovie |

The medium you select should enable you to present your evaluation effectively to your intended audience but not limit your analysis of the subject. For example, a multimedia program such as iMovie might be a good choice for a video game review because it would allow you to incorporate scenes from the game. At the same time, an iMovie review might not be appropriate for an audience that typically reads reviews in print or on conventional newspaper websites.

Follow Step #3 in Chapter 3 to help you decide on the most appropriate medium for your textual analysis.

## Step 4  Develop the main point of your review.

A review that simply passes judgment on its subject does not offer much for readers. Explaining that you liked an action movie because the chase scenes are exciting, for instance, leaves your readers with only a superficial sense of the film. A good review should provide more.

At this point, you might already have an opinion about the subject of your review (for example, you enjoyed the book you plan to review; you disliked the concert; you were disappointed in the film). The task now is to develop a main point that not only justifies or supports your opinion about your subject (keeping in mind that your opinion might change as you explore the subject) but also goes beyond opinion to say something relevant about the subject. To do so, consider your rhetorical situation and the purpose(s) of your review.

Imagine that you are writing a review for an assignment in a communications course about popular media. For this assignment you are to review a popular film, book, or television show that focuses in some way on communications technologies; the general purpose of the assignment is to examine how modern technology is depicted in popular culture. You've selected the film *The Social Network* (2010), which tells the story of Harvard student Mark Zuckerberg and Facebook, the multibillion-dollar social media company he created. You chose this film partly because you enjoyed it but also because it tells the story of one of the most important technology developments in recent decades.

Having selected a film for your review, consider what main claim you will make about the film:

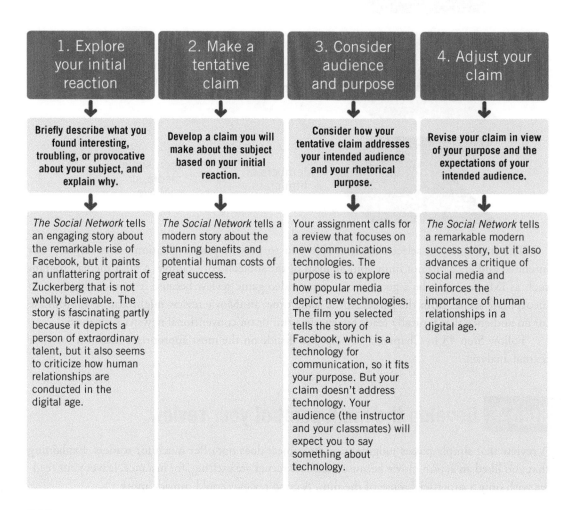

| 1. Explore your initial reaction | 2. Make a tentative claim | 3. Consider audience and purpose | 4. Adjust your claim |
|---|---|---|---|
| Briefly describe what you found interesting, troubling, or provocative about your subject, and explain why. | Develop a claim you will make about the subject based on your initial reaction. | Consider how your tentative claim addresses your intended audience and your rhetorical purpose. | Revise your claim in view of your purpose and the expectations of your intended audience. |
| *The Social Network* tells an engaging story about the remarkable rise of Facebook, but it paints an unflattering portrait of Zuckerberg that is not wholly believable. The story is fascinating partly because it depicts a person of extraordinary talent, but it also seems to criticize how human relationships are conducted in the digital age. | *The Social Network* tells a modern story about the stunning benefits and potential human costs of great success. | Your assignment calls for a review that focuses on new communications technologies. The purpose is to explore how popular media depict new technologies. The film you selected tells the story of Facebook, which is a technology for communication, so it fits your purpose. But your claim doesn't address technology. Your audience (the instructor and your classmates) will expect you to say something about technology. | *The Social Network* tells a remarkable modern success story, but it also advances a critique of social media and reinforces the importance of human relationships in a digital age. |

Whatever the subject of your review, follow these four steps to develop a tentative claim you will make in your review.

Your claim is the starting point for your Guiding Thesis Statement, which you should develop by completing Step #4 in Chapter 3.

 **Remember** Your claim is *tentative*. It can change as you explore the subject of your review and develop your evaluation of it.

## Step 5 Support your claim through your evaluation of your subject.

As noted earlier in this chapter, effective evaluation rests on specific criteria. The first step in developing an evaluation that will support your claim, then, is to identify the criteria by which you will evaluate your subject. The second step is to apply those criteria to analyze your subject.

 **Remember** This process is both systematic and exploratory. Although you are analyzing your subject according to certain criteria, you are also learning about it. You might even change your mind about your subject. So be prepared to adjust your claim as you develop your evaluation of your subject.

### Identify the Criteria for Evaluating Your Subject

The criteria for evaluating your subject depend upon the nature and purpose of your review and your rhetorical situation. Here are three examples:

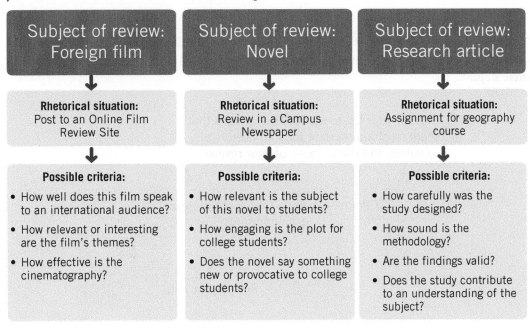

| Subject of review: Foreign film | Subject of review: Novel | Subject of review: Research article |
|---|---|---|
| **Rhetorical situation:** Post to an Online Film Review Site | **Rhetorical situation:** Review in a Campus Newspaper | **Rhetorical situation:** Assignment for geography course |
| **Possible criteria:** <br>• How well does this film speak to an international audience? <br>• How relevant or interesting are the film's themes? <br>• How effective is the cinematography? | **Possible criteria:** <br>• How relevant is the subject of this novel to students? <br>• How engaging is the plot for college students? <br>• Does the novel say something new or provocative to college students? | **Possible criteria:** <br>• How carefully was the study designed? <br>• How sound is the methodology? <br>• Are the findings valid? <br>• Does the study contribute to an understanding of the subject? |

In these examples, the criteria for evaluating the subject fit the rhetorical situation. If you are reviewing a novel for your campus newspaper, for example, you would consider whether other students at your college would find the subject of the novel relevant and the plot engaging. A review of a research article for a geography course would have more specific and technical criteria, as shown in the example. (See Focus:"What Criteria Should Be Applied?" on page 295.) It is also possible that your instructor will expect you to use certain criteria that have been examined in your course.

To determine the criteria that are appropriate for your review:

**Consider audience expectations:** What criteria will your readers likely use in evaluating your subject? What standards will they expect you to apply?

**Consider your purpose:** Which criteria will help you evaluate your subject effectively in view of the purpose of your review?

**Consider conventions for this kind of review:** What kinds of criteria are usually applied in this kind of review? (For example, What criteria do film reviewers typically use? What criteria do video gamers tend to use in reviewing video games?)

Now make a list of the main criteria you will use to evaluate the subject of your review. (You can list these criteria in the form of questions or statements or simply phrases.) Then complete these steps:

1. Review your list to identify the criteria that seem most appropriate for your rhetorical situation and the purpose of your review.

2. Eliminate criteria that seem irrelevant or less important.

3. Revise your list.

## Evaluate Your Subject

Now apply your criteria to the subject of your review. Determine how well your subject meets each of your criteria. Continue to explore your subject in order to develop your evaluation fully. For example,

- If you are examining how effectively a novel develops a specific theme, reread relevant passages where that theme emerges.
- If you are evaluating the methodology of a study described in a research report, reread the sections that describe the methodology and review the sections of your course textbook that discuss research methods.
- If you are evaluating the graphics of a new video game, replay portions of the game to examine the images more closely.
- If you are evaluating a director's technique in a new film, return to specific scenes that illustrate that technique.

Throughout this process, take notes and make necessary adjustments to your main claim.

Work your way through your list of criteria, developing your evaluation of the subject for each item on your list. Your goal is to explore your subject as thoroughly as you can so that you not only develop your evaluation adequately but also generate sufficient evidence to support each assertion you make about your subject. For example, if you decide that the novel you are reviewing does not adequately develop one of its main themes, you should identify passages in the novel that support that assessment. Similarly, if you find the cinematography of the film you are reviewing especially effective, identify specific scenes that illustrate what makes the cinematography effective.

Once you have explored your subject in this way, you should be ready to write a complete draft of your review. Step #5 in Chapter 3 will help you determine whether to move onto the next step before completing your draft.

## Step 6 Organize your review.

There is no standard way to organize a review; however, because most reviews share a few key elements, it is possible to develop a basic outline, adjusting the outline to fit the needs of your rhetorical situation and the medium of your review. (Obviously, some media, such as a multimedia program like iMovie, might require different approaches to organizing your review.)

Most reviews include a statement of the purpose or reason for the review, a summary or description of what is being evaluated, and criteria for evaluating the subject. These three elements can form the basic structure for your review:

I.  **Introduction:** includes a statement of the reason or purpose for the review as well as the occasion for the review.

II. **Summary/Description of Subject:** a summary of the book, film, play, or television show being reviewed; a description of the exhibit, performance, video game, or consumer item being evaluated.

III. **Evaluation:** analysis of the subject on the basis of the criteria being used for evaluation.

IV. **Conclusion:** conclusion(s) about the subject as a result of the evaluation.

Section III, which is the heart of the review, could be organized in a variety of ways depending upon the criteria you are using to evaluate your subject and the expectations for your specific rhetorical situation. For instance, let's return to the example of a review of the film *The Social Network* for a communications course.

Recall that the assignment asks for a review of a popular film, book, or television show that focuses in some way on new communications technologies. Your tentative claim is that *The Social Network* tells a story of remarkable success but also advances a critique of social media and reinforces the importance of human relationships in a digital age. Let's imagine that in developing your evaluation of the film to support that claim, you have identified three main criteria on which to base your evaluation:

- the effectiveness of the narrative about Mark Zuckerberg and Facebook
- the validity of the film's critique of technology and social media in particular
- the development of the film's main themes (especially the theme of the importance of human relationships)

Notice that these criteria do not include anything related to the technical quality of the film, such as cinematography, or the quality of the acting. That's because the purpose of your review is to examine what the film might reveal about technology, not to evaluate the film as an artistic work. Given that purpose, you might order your three criteria from least to most important, as follows:

1. the effectiveness of the narrative about Mark Zuckerberg and Facebook

2. the development of the theme about the importance of human relationships

3. the validity of the film's critique of technology and social media in particular

You might organize the third section of your review according to these three criteria. So a general outline for your review might look like this:

I. Introduction.

    A. Importance of *The Social Network*
    B. Purpose of review
    C. Statement of main claim about the film

II. Summary/Description of Subject.

    A. Basic summary of the topic and plot of *The Social Network*
    B. Summary of important relationships depicted in the film

III. Evaluation.

    A. Discussion of the effectiveness of the film's narrative of Zuckerberg's efforts to establish Facebook
    B. Evaluation of the film's depiction of key relationships
    C. Evaluation of the film's critique of technology

IV. Conclusion.

    A. Conclusion about the effectiveness of the film's narrative and its depiction of human relationships

    B. Conclusions about the film's critique of technology

Notice that your decisions about how to organize a review are driven by a sense of the rhetorical situation. Your review should be structured so that it addresses your audience and achieves your purpose. Step #6 in Chapter 3 provides additional guidance for deciding how to organize your project. If you haven't already completed a draft of your review, you should be ready to do so now.

## Step 7  Get Feedback.

Follow Step #7 in Chapter 3 to obtain useful feedback on your draft. In addition, ask your readers to consider the four main characteristics of analytical writing in their feedback on your review:

| A relevant topic worthy of analysis | • What is the purpose of the review? Is the purpose clear?<br>• What does the writer have to say about the subject of the review? Is the writer's point relevant?<br>• What context has the writer established for reviewing this subject? |
|---|---|
| Complexity | • How thorough and substantive is the evaluation of the subject?<br>• To what extent does the review go beyond a simple judgment about the quality of the subject?<br>• Does the writer's evaluation do justice to the subject? |
| Appropriate and sufficient support | • How effective is the writer's summary or description of the subject for the rhetorical situation?<br>• How appropriate are the criteria used for evaluating the subject? Are they applied effectively?<br>• How well does the writer's evaluation support the claim(s) made about the subject of the review? |
| Reasonable conclusions | • Do the writer's conclusions grow logically from the evaluation of the subject?<br>• How persuasive and thought-provoking are the writer's conclusions?<br>• What is the writer's larger point? |

## Step 8 Revise.

Follow Step #8 in Chapter 3 to revise your draft. Use the questions listed in Step #7 in this chapter to guide your revisions.

**Remember**

Revising is part of the process of exploring your subject and learning about it. As you complete Step #8 in Chapter 3, you might discover that you have to adjust your claim(s) about the subject of your review or delve more deeply into one or more sections of your evaluation.

## Step 9 Refine your voice.

Often, reviews are characterized by strong opinions about the subject. The effectiveness of a review therefore depends largely on how well your opinion about the subject you are reviewing is supported by your evaluation. But your voice is also an important component of your review's effectiveness. It should be confident, so that you sound authoritative without sounding unfair in your criticisms. It is not unusual for reviews to be weakened by a writer's dismissive, arrogant voice or negative tone (although some rhetorical situations might call for such a tone). Step #9 in Chapter 3 will help you avoid that problem.

Also, the readings in this chapter provide examples of reviews in which the writer's voice contributes to the effectiveness of the review. You might read other reviews of the subject you are evaluating to see how the writer's voice affects the review.

## Step 10 Edit.

Complete Step #10 in Chapter 3.

---

**WRITING PROJECTS**    **REVIEW AND EVALUATION**

1. Select a book you have read that you believe is important for some reason. Write a review of that book for a specific audience that would be interested in that book. Alternatively, select a film or television show for your review.

2. Identify a current controversy on your campus or in your region that relates to a larger issue of importance. For example, your campus might be considering allowing its security officers to carry weapons, a measure that has caused controversy at some colleges. Or your state might be considering new restrictions on drilling for natural gas because of environmental concerns. Once you've identified such a controversy, find several books or films related to the issue and write a review of them. The focus of your review should be on how these books or films might illuminate the controversy.

---

3. Visit several websites related to an activity or issue in which you are interested and review them for an audience who shares your interest. For example, many websites, such as WebMD and MayoClinic.com, focus on health issues for consumers; there are numerous websites devoted to almost any recreational activity, such as running, hunting, cooking, knitting, etc. Once you have selected the websites you intend to review, identify criteria for evaluating those websites that would be appropriate for your intended audience. Present your review as a website or blog post.

4. Write a review of a popular electronic device, such as the newest version of a best-selling smartphone, for an audience who would be interested in it.

5. Many people use websites when planning vacations. Using online resources such as TripAdvisor, investigate a trip you would like to take. Read reviews of the place you wish to visit and plan a three-night/four-day trip that includes travel, sightseeing, meals, hotel/resort stay, etc. Then write a synthesis of all of the reviews you found about the place you wish to visit.

## MindTap

Request help with these Writing Projects and feedback from a tutor. If required, participate in peer review, submit your paper for a grade, and view instructor comments online.

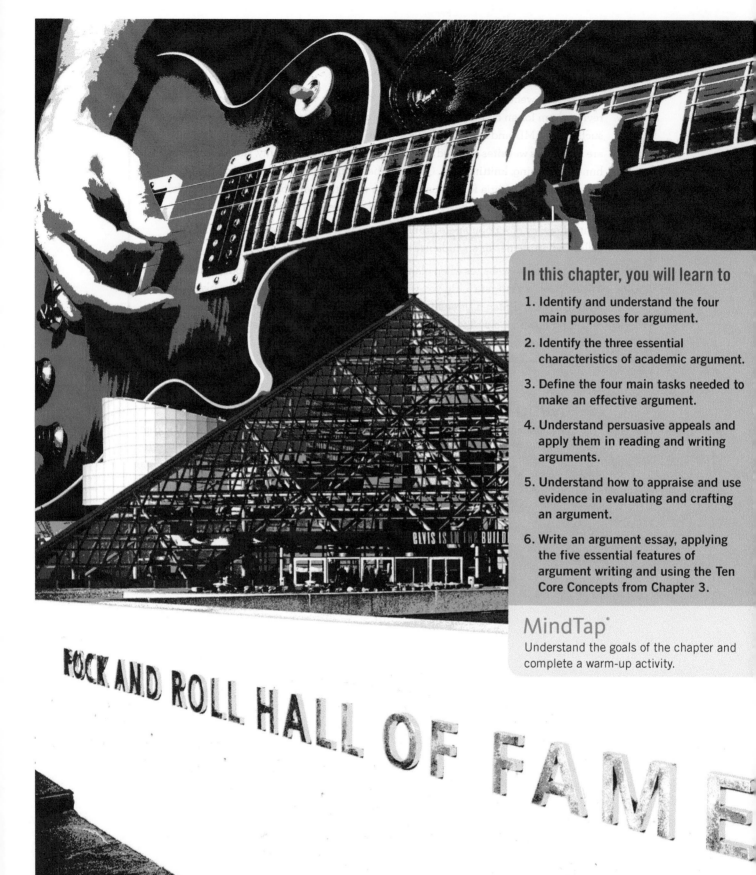

## In this chapter, you will learn to

1. Identify and understand the four main purposes for argument.

2. Identify the three essential characteristics of academic argument.

3. Define the four main tasks needed to make an effective argument.

4. Understand persuasive appeals and apply them in reading and writing arguments.

5. Understand how to appraise and use evidence in evaluating and crafting an argument.

6. Write an argument essay, applying the five essential features of argument writing and using the Ten Core Concepts from Chapter 3.

## MindTap®

Understand the goals of the chapter and complete a warm-up activity.

# Understanding Argument 11

**I HAVE A POLICY** in my classes allowing students to challenge their grades on any writing assignment. But I tell them that if they believe the grade is unfair, they must explain why and make a case for a higher grade. They must present some kind of evidence or reasoning that the grade they received does not reflect the quality of their writing for that assignment. It is not enough, I tell them, to claim that they should be rewarded for working hard on the assignment. Show me why the essay deserves a higher grade, I tell them. In other words, make a valid and convincing argument.

Even if you have never challenged a grade on an assignment, you probably make informal arguments to support a position, defend an opinion, oppose a plan, or convince someone to do something:

- to explain why a band should be honored by the Rock and Roll Hall of Fame
- to justify a decision to pursue a particular major or attend a specific college
- to express your support for a political candidate
- to convince a roommate to move to a different apartment
- to support your decision to use a certain kind of smartphone

We routinely engage in informal argumentation as we make decisions about important matters, small or large, in our lives.

You have probably also made more formal arguments that involve specific kinds of writing. In your college application essay, for example, you tried to convince the college admissions office that you deserved to be accepted into that school. Or perhaps you have posted messages to your college Facebook page in favor of a proposed new student center. In such cases, you are making an argument not only to take a stand on an issue (for example, to express support for the proposed student center because it will benefit students in a variety of ways and help create a better campus community), but also to achieve a goal or work toward a particular outcome (for example, to help make the proposed student center a reality). Argument, then, is not simply a matter of stating and supporting a position; it is also a way to participate in discussions about important issues, to address complicated situations, and to solve problems. It is a central part of how we live together.

In academic disciplines, argument is an essential means by which ideas are explored and understanding is advanced (see Focus: "Argument vs. Persuasion" on page 318). Writing effective arguments is an important component of college-level academic work.

Often, we make arguments to try to persuade someone to adopt a point of view, agree to a proposition, or take a course of action. But the goal of argumentation is not necessarily to persuade. Especially in academic contexts, argument is intended to advance understanding. Persuasion, by contrast, does not necessarily engage an audience in a dialogue about an issue; rather, persuasion is an attempt to convince the audience to think or feel a certain way. The distinction is similar to the difference between an advertisement intended to persuade consumers to purchase a specific product, such as this magazine ad for Nestlé, and one designed to present a point of view on an issue, such as this public service ad about plastic bottles. The Nestlé ad seeks to persuade consumers to purchase its brand of bottled water. By contrast, the public service ad can be seen as making an argument in favor of drinking tap water rather than bottled water, which, the ad suggests, contributes to environmental damage; if the ad seeks to persuade viewers to act in a certain way (that is, to drink tap water instead of bottled water), it does so by making a convincing argument that drinking tap water is a good idea, in part by educating the reader about the potential environmental impact of the plastic used for bottled water.

Last year, plastic bottles generated more than 2.5 million tons of carbon dioxide. Drink tap. Tappening.com.

# Occasions for Argument

We engage in argument for four main reasons:

- to solve a problem
- to assert a position
- to inquire into an issue or problem
- to prevail

## Arguments to Solve a Problem

In much argumentation, the parties involved address a problem in which they have a shared interest. Let's return, for example, to my course policy of allowing my students to argue for a better grade on a writing assignment. A student's purpose in making such an argument is pretty clear: he or she wants to earn a good grade and demonstrate the ability to write the kind of essay required by the assignment. By the same token, as the instructor, I have an interest in seeing that the student can complete the assignment successfully. I also want the grades I assign to motivate students to develop their writing skills. So our purposes overlap, and we both have a stake in a positive outcome to the argument. Ultimately, "winning" the argument doesn't necessarily help us achieve that outcome. The student's argument, then, is part of an effort to solve a problem: to assign a fair grade to an essay about which we seem to have different opinions. The argument for a better grade can result in our collaborative effort to reconsider how successfully the essay meets the assignment guidelines. In the process, the argument can be a way to help both of us better understand the essay so that it can be evaluated fairly.

The need to solve a problem is perhaps the most common occasion for making an argument:

- Members of a student organization decide whether to spend surplus funds on new equipment.
- Community residents debate whether to increase property taxes to build a much-needed new school building.
- Parents and school officials debate the best measures for increasing safety at their elementary school.

In each of these examples, the parties argue to solve a problem in which they all have an interest. The purpose of the argument is to achieve the best possible solution.

## Arguments to Assert a Position

Some situations call for arguments in which the primary goal is to assert and justify a position:

- in a meeting of a student organization that is considering whether to boycott local stores that sell goods produced in sweatshops
- in a class discussion about legalizing same-sex marriage
- in a debate about whether to invite a controversial speaker to campus
- in a public forum to discuss whether to arm campus police

In such situations, many voices may be heard. To make an argument that asserts your position effectively can contribute to a discussion of important issues and help you gain credibility as a thoughtful participant. Your argument can enhance others' understanding of an issue and influence what they think about it.

## Arguments to Inquire

In arguments about complex issues, writers often try to discover the best of many possible answers to the question or problem at hand. In such cases, the primary purpose of the argument is to understand the issue better:

- A debate about a new general education requirement enables both supporters and opponents to delve into broader questions about the purposes of a college education.
- In a controversy about whether law enforcement agencies should have access to private data on smartphones, participants examine the tension between privacy and safety.
- A proposal to moderate comments posted to a popular social media site leads to a debate about free speech and ethical behavior in online forums.

In such situations, writers make arguments as part of a careful inquiry into the issues. In this kind of argument, the writer's position emerges through that inquiry. Through the process of developing an argument, the writer discovers the most reasonable position for himself or herself. Others might reach a different conclusion, because different people can have different but reasonable positions about complex issues. Because the writer isn't trying to win the debate, he or she examines many different viewpoints before arriving at a conclusion. The goal is to understand the issue and make an effective argument to share that understanding with interested others.

## Arguments to Prevail

Sometimes there is a compelling reason for trying to win an argument, and the writer's primary purpose is to prevail over opposing points of view. Such cases often involve important and controversial issues that can have a big impact on those involved:

- Students make a strong case against allowing a controversial anti-immigrant organization to demonstrate on campus.
- Members of a law enforcement organization argue against the state's adoption of "stand your ground" self-defense laws, which they believe lead to more gun violence.
- A resident strenuously opposes a town bill restricting gas drilling on the grounds that it will deprive residents of much-needed income.

In such cases, the goal is not only to oppose something but to convince others to oppose it so that it doesn't happen. The writer of an argument in such situations believes strongly that his or her position is right.

Arguments to prevail should be undertaken with a strong sense of ethical responsibility (see Focus: "The Ethics of Argument"). Trying to defeat an opponent in an argument for the sake of winning serves little purpose and could have negative consequences for all parties. In some cases, however, the writer might conclude that the issue is such that the ends justify the means and making a forceful argument meant to prevail is not only ethical but also necessary.

---

### FOCUS   THE ETHICS OF ARGUMENT

Because argument has the power to persuade others to adopt a belief or take an action, often on matters of great importance, writers have a responsibility to engage in argumentation in an honorable manner. An argument should always be informed by a desire to seek truth or find a course of action that is morally justifiable—not to achieve self-serving, questionable, or illicit ends. A famous example of argument used for immoral purposes is Adolph Hitler's argument that anti-Jewish legislation in Germany in the 1930s was necessary to protect Germany from communism and to protect Jews from further persecution. But argument can be used for dubious purposes in much less dramatic contexts. For example, you might argue in favor of a proposed change in your major because the change will make it easier for you to graduate early, even though you believe that the change will weaken the curriculum and is probably not a good idea for most students. In such a case, you would be making an argument of questionable ethical merit. To make an ethical argument in such circumstances, you would have to acknowledge your own self-interest. In short, effective argument can be turned to honorable or questionable purposes, even in school assignments. Always consider whether the argument you are making is not only sound but also ethical.

---

These four purposes for argument can overlap, of course. For example, in an argument to prevail, the writer usually asserts a position, and it is often necessary to inquire before you can solve a problem. So an argument can address several purposes at once. But understanding these four main purposes can help you construct arguments that effectively meet the needs of specific rhetorical situations.

---

### EXERCISE 11A   EXPLORING OCCASIONS FOR ARGUMENT

1. Identify an issue or problem that you feel strongly about. It might be a national or international issue (a human rights issue, for example) or a local issue (a controversy on your campus or in your town). Write an informal statement explaining your position on the issue. Now consider three arguments you might make about the issue. Write a brief synopsis of each argument and explain why it matters to you.

2. Find an argument on a topic you care about in a newspaper, a blog post, a magazine article, a pamphlet, something you read in a course, or a YouTube video. Summarize the main argument. Now consider what makes the argument relevant to you and others. In a brief paragraph, describe what you believe was the writer's main purpose in making the argument.

3. Take the issue you wrote about for Question #1 or #2 (or identify another issue of importance to you) and imagine a situation in which you could write an argument on that issue for each of the main purposes described in this section (to solve a problem, to inquire, to assert, to prevail). In a brief paragraph for each purpose, describe the rhetorical situation (including the audience and the form of your argument).

# Understanding Argument in College

Argumentation in college is primarily about learning. As a student, you will engage in argumentative writing not only to sharpen your writing and thinking skills but also to understand your subject better. In fact, research indicates that a majority of writing assignments in college require argument of some kind. In some academic disciplines, such as economics and related social sciences, *most* writing involves argumentation, and many common forms of writing in college, such as proposals and lab reports, are actually specialized forms of argumentation.

Because argument is an essential part of the process by which scholars examine, share, debate, and promote ideas, information, and opinions about important topics or developments in their fields, it is a primary vehicle for advancing knowledge. Not surprisingly, then, academic argumentation often takes the form of arguments to inquire. An assignment in a philosophy course, for example, might ask students to take a position on a classic philosophical issue, such as the nature of reality or truth. In such an assignment, the goal isn't to prove a point but to inquire deeply into a complex question that philosophers have debated for centuries. In doing so, students learn what philosophers say about such questions as they develop their own ideas about those questions; at the same time, students learn how to engage in philosophical inquiry and argumentation.

Although the purpose of most academic argumentation is inquiry, arguments in different academic disciplines can have different characteristics. For example, a philosopher relies on logical reasoning to support a proposition about the morality of capital punishment, whereas a criminologist draws on crime statistics to make an argument about the impact of capital punishment on violent crime. Writing effective academic arguments requires understanding the conventions that govern argumentation in the discipline in which you are writing. Although a philosopher and a criminologist might each make an argument about the same subject (capital punishment), they will make different kinds of claims, use different kinds of evidence, and present their arguments in different ways.

Despite these differences, all effective argumentative writing shares **three essential characteristics**:

1. a clear main point that is relevant for the academic discipline in which the writer is writing

2. appropriate support for claims

3. shared assumptions or premises as a basis for the main argument

The following examples illustrate these essential characteristics.

In the opening paragraphs of an essay titled "Why We Won't See Any Public Universities Going Private," education scholar John D. Wiley introduces his argument by identifying a relevant problem (reduced state funding for public universities) and a solution that others have proposed (turning public universities into private ones). Wiley then clearly states his main thesis: that solution won't work.

> All around the country the story is the same: States are reducing taxpayer support for public higher education, offsetting those reductions with higher tuition. Using Wisconsin as an example, Table 15.1 illustrates the changes over the last 25 years. In some states, the changes have been even more dramatic; in others, less so. But the trend is essentially universal. Furthermore, the impacts of these changes vary, even within one

state. At UW-Madison (the flagship institution of the UW System), for example, state appropriations constituted 43.1 percent and tuition 10.5 percent of our budget in 1975. Today, those numbers are 19.5 and 15.7 percent, respectively. To make matters worse, nearly one-third of our state revenue comes to us with constraints requiring us to return it to the state for specific costs such as our share of the state utility bills, debt service, and mandatory payments to state agencies. Even if we were able to economize or find superior alternatives in any of those areas, we would not be able to reallocate the savings for other purposes. As a result, the state is providing only 13.5 percent of our base operating budget—the budget for hiring faculty and staff, and covering infrastructure and operating costs beyond debt service and utility bills. For the first time in the history of the institution, our students are contributing more to this portion of our operating budget than are the state taxpayers.

**TABLE 15.1** The Changing Mix of State Funding and Tuition at the University of Wisconsin (UW) System over the Last 25 Years

|  | 1974–1975 | 2004–2005 |
|---|---|---|
| State appropriations for UW-System per $1000 of personal income | $12.50 | $5.50 |
| State appropriations for UW-System as a share of total state spending | 11.5% | 3.9% |
| State appropriations for UW-System per FTE student (2004 dollars) | $10,600 | $7,400 |
| State appropriations for UW-System as a percent of UW-System budget | 49.50% | 26% |
| Tuition as a percent of UW-System budget | 12% | 21% |

Viewing these trends, many faculty, alumni, newspaper editors, and even legislators have urged us to consider "going private." By that, they have in mind that we could agree to forego all state support in our base operating budget and rely on increased tuition, coupled with some unspecified amount of additional student financial aid (what they assume to be "the private model" of high tuition and high financial aid) for ongoing operations . These views are often expressed in terms of a comparison: "You're way underpriced at a resident tuition of $6000/year. I'm paying three times that for my daughter's tuition at (at a private school), and the education she's getting is certainly not three times better. Even if you simply doubled your tuition, you would still be a bargain, and you would replace nearly all state funds. What's the problem?" Quite aside from political considerations (unwillingness of state to "let go" of prior investments and ongoing oversight), the larger problem is that the "private model," properly understood, simply cannot be scaled up to the extent required. It's a matter of simple arithmetic, and the numbers just don't work!

Source: Wiley, John D. "Why We Won't See Any Public Universities Going Private." *What's Happening to Public Higher Education?* edited by Ronald G. Ehrenberg, American Council on Education / Praeger, 2006, pp. 327–28.

In setting up his argument, Wiley makes two important moves. First, he places his argument in the context of ongoing debates about the rising cost of college. In doing so, Wiley establishes that his topic is one that his readers (other education scholars as well as policymakers and interested citizens) are likely to find relevant. Second, he supports his claims with evidence that his readers are likely to find appropriate and persuasive. Wiley claims that public support for higher education has diminished dramatically in the past three decades, and he cites statistical evidences to show the reduction in public funding for higher education, using Wisconsin as an example of a national trend.

Wiley's argument is a good example of an academic argument whose main purpose is to inquire into a complex and important issue. The next excerpt is also an argument whose primary purpose is to inquire into a complex educational issue—in this case, whether or not raising educational standards actually improves student learning. In making their argument, the authors address a well-established problem in education: the challenge of improving learning for all students. Specifically, they examine whether formative assessment—that is, assessment designed to help students learn rather than to measure how much they have learned—can result in higher educational standards for students. Like the previous example, this argument is addressed to an academic audience (education researchers) as well as a wider audience (policymakers, politicians, and the interested public). In this excerpt, which is taken from a longer essay published in a leading education journal called the *Phi Delta Kappan*, the authors introduce their main claims, summarize their argument, and explain the evidence they will present to support their claims:

> We start from the self-evident proposition that teaching and learning must be interactive. Teachers need to know about their pupils' progress and difficulties with learning so that they can adapt their own work to meet pupils' needs--needs that are often unpredictable and that vary from one pupil to another. Teachers can find out what they need to know in a variety of ways, including observation and discussion in the classroom and the reading of pupils' written work. . . .
>
> There is nothing new about any of this. All teachers make assessments in every class they teach. But there are three important questions about this process that we seek to answer:
>
> - Is there evidence that improving formative assessment raises standards?
> - Is there evidence that there is room for improvement?
> - Is there evidence about how to improve formative assessment?

In setting out to answer these questions, we have conducted an extensive survey of the research literature. We have checked through many books and through the past nine years' worth of issues of more than 160 journals, and we have studied earlier reviews of research. This process yielded about 580 articles or chapters to study. We prepared a lengthy review, using material from 250 of these sources, that has been published in a special issue of the journal *Assessment in Education*, together with comments on our work by leading educational experts from Australia, Switzerland, Hong Kong, Lesotho, and the U.S.

The conclusion we have reached from our research review is that the answer to each of the three questions above is clearly yes. In the three main sections below, we outline the nature and force of the evidence that justifies this conclusion. However, because we are presenting a summary here, our text will appear strong on assertions and weak on the details of their justification. We maintain that these assertions are backed by evidence and that this backing is set out in full detail in the lengthy review on which this article is founded.

We believe that the three sections below establish a strong case that governments, their agencies, school authorities, and the teaching profession should study very carefully whether they are seriously interested in raising standards in education. However, we also acknowledge widespread evidence that fundamental change in education can be achieved only slowly—through programs of professional development that build on existing good practice. Thus we do not conclude that formative assessment is yet another "magic bullet" for education. The issues involved are too complex and too closely linked to both the difficulties of classroom practice and the beliefs that drive public policy. In a final section, we confront this complexity and try to sketch out a strategy for acting on our evidence.

Source: Black, Paul and Dylan Wiliam. "Inside the Black Box: Raising Standards Through Classroom Assessment." *Phi Delta Kappan*, vol. 80, no. 1, 1998, p. 138.

Notice that the authors rest their main argument on the "proposition that teaching and learning must be interactive," a premise that their readers are likely to accept. In effective argumentation, writers must establish clear premises from which to make their arguments, thereby identifying key assumptions or beliefs that they share with their readers as a basis for their argument.

In the following section we will examine how to construct arguments that have these three essential characteristics to meet the needs of specific rhetorical situations.

---

**EXERCISE 11B** **EXPLORING ACADEMIC ARGUMENT**

For each of the following excerpts identify (a) the main point and (b) the evidence or support provided for the author's claims. The first excerpt is taken from an essay about gun control written soon after a gunman seriously wounded U.S. Congresswoman Gabrielle Giffords and killed others attending a political rally in Arizona in 2011. The second is from a report issued by an environmental organization about the growth of the local food movement. How well do you think the authors of each excerpt present and support their claims? Cite specific passages from the excerpts to support your answer.

*(Continued)*

1. Against the horrific backdrop of the Tucson, Arizona, tragedy, new gun control proposals are on the way. Some of our legislators will be tempted to apply Rahm Emanuel's aphorism, "Never let a good crisis go to waste." For example, Rep. Carolyn McCarthy, D-New York, wants to outlaw magazines with more than 10 rounds—even those already in circulation. She hasn't explained how a ban on previously sold magazines would deter anyone but law-abiding citizens.

    Still, the Supreme Court has suggested that sensible gun regulations may be constitutionally permissible. Sensible is not, however, what we have in Washington, Chicago, New York and other cities, where you can probably get a pizza delivery before a response from a 911 call. Police cannot be everywhere. . . . A regulation must be effective in promoting public safety, when weighed against reliable evidence that past restrictions have not lessened the incidence of gun-related crimes.

    Recall that Washington banned handguns for 33 years; during some of those years the city was known as the nation's murder capital. Killers not deterred by laws against murder were not deterred by laws against owning guns. Moreover, anti-gun regulations did not address the deep-rooted causes of violent crime— illegitimacy, drugs, alcohol abuse and dysfunctional schools—much less mental instability.

    In 2004, the National Academy of Sciences reviewed 253 journal articles, 99 books and 43 government publications evaluating 80 gun-control measures. Researchers could not identify a single regulation that reduced violent crime, suicide or accidents. A year earlier, the Centers for Disease Control reported on ammunition bans, restrictions on acquisition, waiting periods, registration, licensing, child access prevention and zero tolerance laws. CDC's conclusion: There was no conclusive evidence that the laws reduced gun violence.

    So much for the quasi-religious faith that more controls mean fewer murders. There are about 500,000 gun-related crimes annually in the United States. Further, Americans own roughly 250 million guns. Assuming a different gun is used in each of the 500,000 crimes, only 0.2% of guns are involved in crime each year. A ban on firearms would be 99.8% over-inclusive.

Source: Levy, Robert A. "Gun Control Measures Don't Stop Violence." *CNN*, Cable News Network, 19 Jan. 2011, www.cnn.com/2011/OPINION/01/18/levy.anti.gun.control/.

2. The system of long-distance food supply has now become the norm in much of the United States and the rest of the world. Apples in Des Moines supermarkets are from China, even though there are apple farmers in Iowa; potatoes in Lima's supermarkets are from the United States, even though Peru boasts more varieties of potato than any other country. Today, our food travels farther than ever before, often thousands of kilometers. The value of international trade in food has tripled since 1961, while the tonnage of food shipped between countries has grown fourfold, during a time when the human population only doubled. (See Figures 1 and 2.)

**FIGURE 1**

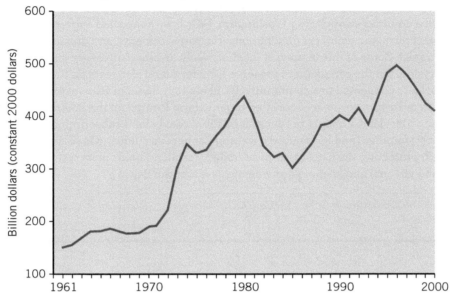

Value of World Agricultural Trade, 1961–2000

Source: Trade value and volume from United Nations Food and Agriculture Organization, FAOSTAT Statistics Database, at http://apps.fao.org, updated 4 July 2002.

**FIGURE 2**

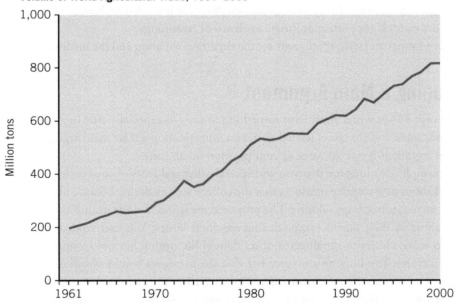

Volume of World Agricultural Trade, 1961–2000

Source: Trade value and volume from United Nations Food and Agriculture Organization, FAOSTAT Statistics Database, at http://apps.fao.org, updated 4 July 2002.

*(Continued)*

Understanding Argument in College **327**

But, as with many trends that carry serious social and ecological consequences, the long-distance food habit is slowly beginning to weaken, under the influence of a young, but surging, local foods movement in the Midatlantic and elsewhere. Politicians and voters in the counties surrounding Washington, D.C., have supported aggressive measures to protect farmland using tax credits, conservation easements, and greater emphasis on mass transit. Some of this interest is inspired by the desire to preserve the beauty of the countryside, but the campaign to preserve local farmland also rests on the assumption that farmers connected to a community are likely to farm more responsibly. Accokeek Ecosystem Farm, a seven-acre certified organic farm located on the Potomac River in southern Maryland, not only produces food for a weekly food subscription service for almost 90 families (and has started a waiting list because demand is so great), but plays a role in protecting the Chesapeake watershed (farmland holds more water than sprawling subdivisions) and keeping agrochemicals out of the Bay.

Source: Halweil, Brian. *Home Grown: The Case for Local Food in a Global Market.* World Watch Institute, 2002.

# Making Arguments

To make an effective argument you must examine the issue sufficiently so that you understand it well, which often requires research. You must also complete **four main tasks**:

- Develop a main argument that is appropriate for your rhetorical situation.
- Make an appeal that is likely to be persuasive for your intended audience.
- Support your claims with appropriate evidence or reasoning.
- Adopt a format and style appropriate for the rhetorical situation and the medium you are using.

## Developing a Main Argument

Core Concept #4—a writer must have something to say—is especially true in argument. As you explore your topic and the issues related to it, you must develop a clear main argument. However, your main argument is not the same as your position on an issue.

For example, let's imagine that you and several other residents of your college dormitory are concerned about new security measures that the college is considering because of recent incidents involving intruders in campus dorms. The proposed measures include prohibiting students from having visitors in their dorms except during specified hours. You and your dorm mates have decided to write a letter to the director of residential life urging her not to implement the new security measures. You hope to convince her that the measures would significantly restrict students' social activities without enhancing campus security. Your **topic**, then, is campus security. The **question** is whether the campus needs the proposed measures to improve security. You may be opposed to the proposed security measures, but that isn't your main argument; that's your **position**. You still need to identify the main argument you will make to reflect your position:

| Topic |
|---|
| Campus security |

| Problem or Question |
|---|
| Does the campus need new security measures for dormitories to protect students? |

| Your Position |
|---|
| Opposed to proposed campus security policies |

| Your Main Argument |
|---|
| Proposed security measures will restrict students unnecessarily without improving the safety of the dorms. |

Your main argument might evolve as you explore your topic and learn more about the issues at hand.

Keep in mind that your main argument is intended to help you achieve a specific goal. In arguing against proposed campus security measures, for example, you not only want to assert a clear position in opposition to the measures but you also hope to persuade the director of residential life to reconsider those measures and perhaps to make them less restrictive without compromising security. In addition, you hope your argument will win the support of other students who live in the dorms. So the argument must not only state the writer's opposition to the security measures; it must also present a persuasive case that those measures will not achieve the goal of improving security on campus, which is a goal that everyone—the students as well as the residential life director—supports.

---

**EXERCISE 11C**  **DEVELOPING A MAIN ARGUMENT**

1. Identify three issues that you feel strongly about. For each one, write a brief paragraph explaining your position on the issue and describing a main argument that you might make to support that position.

2. Find two or three arguments about the same topic—for example, arguments for or against gun control. Write a brief synopsis for each one that includes a statement of the writer's main argument. Compare the arguments, examining how each writer takes a stance on the issue and develops his or her main argument.

3. Think of two or three changes you would like to see on your campus or in your workplace. Now write a letter to your college president or your boss to argue in favor of these changes. Develop a main argument for each change you would like to see.

# Considering the Rhetorical Situation

An effective argument must meet the needs of the rhetorical situation. In opposing the proposed security measures for the campus dormitories, for example, you would develop your main argument and supporting claims in a way that takes into account the interests and positions of the intended audience—in this case, the director of residential life and other students on campus. As you develop your argument, then, identify what you know about your audience in that situation by addressing the following questions:

- **What is your audience likely to know about this topic or situation?** Although you can't know exactly what your audience knows, you can make reasonable assumptions to help you develop an appropriate argument. For example, the residential life director will certainly understand what is involved in keeping campus dorms safe and secure. You wouldn't have to explain to her how the restrictions would work, but she might not fully appreciate what they would mean for students.

- **What is the audience's interest or stake in the issue?** Your audience might not always have the same level of interest in the issue you're addressing, but identifying why they would be interested can help you develop potentially persuasive points and find common ground. For example, the residential life director obviously has a direct stake in the situation because she is responsible for the campus dorms. Other students also have a stake in a livable, safe campus. Those interests can help you decide how to develop and present your argument so that you address shared concerns and acknowledge common ground.

- **What does your audience expect?** The residential life director would probably expect a thoughtful letter that acknowledges the importance of safe dorms. She would be less inclined to take your argument seriously if you did not show a reasonable understanding of the situation or if you dismissed her concerns. She would also likely expect a well-written letter that has a respectful tone, even if it makes a strong argument against her position.

Exploring your audience in this way can help you identify claims that are likely to be acceptable to them as well as arguments they might reject.

Sometimes, a writer knows that some readers will almost certainly reject a specific argument, especially when the topic is controversial, such as gun control or same-sex marriage. Writing about such issues requires care in considering audience, and the writer should assume that some readers will be skeptical. But rather than dismiss the views of a skeptical or even hostile audience, consider their reasons for opposing your viewpoint and try to address their concerns in your argument.

**DO YOU HAVE TO WIN THE ARGUMENT?**

In theory, an effective argument persuades an audience to accept a proposition, adopt a position, or take a course of action. In reality, an argument can achieve its purpose without necessarily persuading readers to adopt the writer's position, especially when it comes to issues about which people have strong views. For example, imagine that your state legislature is considering a controversial ban on certain kinds of firearms. Citizens support or oppose the ban depending on their opinions about gun control. An argument against the ban is unlikely to change the minds of those who support it, but it might influence the discussion. Because both supporters and opponents agree that lowering crime rates is desirable, an argument that the ban is likely to reduce violent crime would probably interest all parties in the debate. The goal is to contribute to the debate and influence how others think about the issue.

**EXERCISE 11D** **CONSIDERING THE RHETORICAL SITUATION**

1. Take the paragraphs you wrote for Exercise 11C#1 and identify an appropriate audience for each argument. Briefly describe that audience and the most important characteristics that might influence the argument you would make for that audience.

2. Find a published argument that you agree with on a topic that matters to you and imagine rewriting it for a different audience. For example, if the argument was published in your campus newspaper, imagine rewriting it for a community website in your hometown. What changes would you have to make to that argument? Why?

3. Imagine writing an argument about a controversial topic for an audience who opposes your position. First, identify a topic that interests you and summarize your position. Next, summarize opposing positions. Finally, identify two or three arguments that might appeal to that audience, trying to find common ground on the issue.

# Making a Persuasive Appeal

Even if the main purpose of an argument is not necessarily to persuade readers, writers use persuasive appeals to strengthen an argument. Classical rhetorical theory identifies three modes of persuasion, or kinds of appeals:

- **Ethical**, or arguments based on the writer's or speaker's character
- **Emotional**, or arguments that appeal to the emotions
- **Logical**, or arguments based on reason and evidence

Most academic arguments rely on logical appeals, but even in academic arguments writers often employ all three modes of persuasion in some way.

## Ethical Appeals, or Appeals Based on Character

Writers often try to strengthen their arguments by presenting themselves as reliable and trustworthy experts on the topic at hand. For example, in making an argument about a proposed mental health policy, a psychiatrist might emphasize her expertise in working with patients suffering from depression, presenting herself as someone with the appropriate knowledge and experience to understand the issue. Sometimes, a writer will rest an argument on his or her good judgment or integrity, such as when a person presents himself as a nurturing parent in making an argument about child care regulations. In ethical appeals, then, the writer's character, expertise, identity, or experience is a primary reason that the argument is persuasive.

Ethical appeals are common in advertising. Corporations use celebrities to represent them or their products—for example, former basketball star Michael Jordan for Nike shoes (see Sidebar: "Ethical Appeals in Advertising"). The suggestion is that if a world-class athlete endorses this product, it must be good. Ethical appeals are also important in law and politics. Political candidates, for example, present themselves as loving family members or successful in business as a way to make their appeal to voters more persuasive. Conversely, candidates often question their opponents' credibility, suggesting that the opponent cannot be trusted to make the right decisions on important issues.

| SIDEBAR | ETHICAL APPEALS IN ADVERTISING |
|---|---|

This classic ad for Nike shoes focuses on an image of basketball star Michal Jordan's athletic prowess. What argument does the ad make? How might you describe its ethical appeal?

MICHAEL JORDAN 1
ISAAC NEWTON 0

Courtesy of the Advertising Archives

In the following passage, journalist Barbara Ehrenreich uses her own first-hand experiences to support her argument that life has become more difficult for low-wage American workers. As a college professor, Ehrenreich was an expert on issues related to the working poor, but her best-selling 2001 book *Nickel and Dimed: On (Not) Getting By in America*, in which she described her experiences trying to make a living by working at low-wage jobs, helped establish her as an authority for a larger audience. In this excerpt from a 2011 essay about how the so-called Great Recession of 2008 affected America's poor, Ehrenreich refers to her experiences as a low-wage earner to supplement the statistical evidence she presents:

> At the time I wrote *Nickel and Dimed*, I wasn't sure how many people it directly applied to—only that the official definition of poverty was way off the mark, since it defined

an individual earning $7 an hour, as I did on average, as well out of poverty. But three months after the book was published, the Economic Policy Institute in Washington, D.C., issued a report entitled "Hardships in America: The Real Story of Working Families," which found an astounding 29% of American families living in what could be more reasonably defined as poverty, meaning that they earned less than a barebones budget covering housing, child care, health care, food, transportation, and taxes—though not, it should be noted, any entertainment, meals out, cable TV, Internet service, vacations, or holiday gifts. Twenty-nine percent is a minority, but not a reassuringly small one, and other studies in the early 2000s came up with similar figures.

The big question, 10 years later, is whether things have improved or worsened for those in the bottom third of the income distribution, the people who clean hotel rooms, work in warehouses, wash dishes in restaurants, care for the very young and very old, and keep the shelves stocked in our stores. The short answer is that things have gotten much worse, especially since the economic downturn that began in 2008.

Source: Ehrenreich, Barbara. "On Turning Poverty into an American Crime." *The Huffington Post*, 9 Aug. 2011, www.huffingtonpost.com/barbara-ehrenreich/nickel-and-dimed-2011-ver_b_922330.html.

Here Ehrenreich tries to strengthen her argument by invoking her credibility as an authority on the working poor. She provides statistical evidence to support her claim that "things have gotten much worse" for poor Americans in the ten years since her book was published, but she also makes an ethical appeal on the basis of her experience and knowledge about this issue.

Ethical appeals are most effective when they meet the needs of the rhetorical situation, and writers will often present themselves strategically for an intended audience. For example, in making her argument for a general audience—say, readers of a large-circulation newspaper like *USA Today*—Ehrenreich might emphasize her experience in low-wage jobs to establish her credibility, but in an argument published in a scholarly journal she might rely on her academic credentials. (See Focus: "More on Ethical Appeals" on page 225 in Chapter 8.)

Although ethical appeals usually rest on the *writer's* character, writers sometimes try to strengthen their arguments by relying on someone else's expertise or character. In the following excerpt from an essay about school reform, columnist David Brooks rests part of his argument on the experience and expertise of the director of a charter school called the New American Academy:

The New American Academy is led by Shimon Waronker, who grew up speaking Spanish in South America, became a U.S. Army intelligence officer, became an increasingly observant Jew, studied at yeshiva, joined the Chabad-Lubavitch movement, became a public school teacher and then studied at the New York City Leadership Academy, which Mayor Michael Bloomberg and the former New York Schools chancellor, Joel Klein, founded to train promising school principal candidates.

At first, he had trouble getting a principal's job because people weren't sure how a guy with a beard, kippa and a black suit would do in overwhelmingly minority schools. But he revitalized one of the most violent junior high schools in the South Bronx and with the strong backing of both Klein and Randi Weingarten, the president of the teachers' union, he was able to found his brainchild, The New American Academy.

He has a grand theory to transform American education, which he developed with others at the Harvard School of Education.

---

Source: Brooks, David. "The Relationship School." *The New York Times*, 22 March 2012, nyti.ms/19eGqt6.

In this case, Brooks argues in favor of a specific approach to school reform in part because it is endorsed by Shimon Waronker, who, Brooks suggests, has the right experience to understand what is needed to make schools work. Brooks establishes Waronker's credibility as an expert whose approach is supported by several prominent people (for example, Joel Klein, the former chancellor of New York City schools), as someone who has studied at Harvard, and as a former an intelligence officer in the U.S. Army. In this way, Brooks uses an ethical appeal to support his main argument. Writers can also call someone's credibility into question to help support their argument. For example, in arguing against a proposed school reform endorsed by a politician, a writer might point out that the politician's previous school reform efforts have failed, thus undermining the politician's credibility.

You can use ethical appeals in these same ways. For example, if you are writing an argument about the minimum wage, you might use your own work experience to help support your claims. However, for most academic assignments, you will establish your credibility primarily by demonstrating your command of the issues and knowledge of your topic.

## Pathetic Appeals, or Appeals to Emotion

Appealing to readers' emotions is common in argument because it can be so effective. But because emotional appeals can be so powerful, they carry risk as well as potential reward.

Some arguments rely on emotions more than others do, but no argument is completely devoid of emotional appeal. Here is part of an essay about the disappearance of migratory songbirds in which the author's primary appeal is emotional:

Lately I have been sitting with the brooding knowledge that at least 7 million migrating songbirds were killed this spring running the gauntlet of 84,000 American communication towers that rise as high as 2,000 feet into the sky, braced by invisible guy wires that garrote the birds right out of the air.

This is actually just a fraction of the number of birds killed each year by running a collision course with human activity.

This spring has been more silent than ever. The traditional dawn chorus of birdsong has ebbed to a few lonely little souls, most belonging to non-migratory species like cardinals, bluejays, chickadees and sparrows.

They say that when Europeans first arrived on this continent, the migration of the passenger pigeons would literally darken the sky for minutes on end.

I have never seen a living passenger pigeon, and it seems that my grandchildren will not know what I mean when I talk about the dawn chorus of riotously busy, happy birdsong, any more than they will be able to imagine an apple orchard in full bloom buzzing with the diligent harvest of a million droning bees.

Knowledge like this makes me sick at heart. My rational side is aware that mourning is not productive, but another side of me knows that it is one of the special gifts of us humans to feel grief; to locate particular sadnesses in the larger landscape of suffering; and to use our sadness and anger at injustice as a lightening rod for change.

Other animals and birds feel grief as well, but you won't find the great community of birds gathering together to make plans to topple all the communication towers in North America.

No, the birds will go quietly, one by one, into the endless night of extinction.

Source: Browdy de Hernandez, Jennifer. "Stop the Holocaust of Migrating Birds." *Commondreams*, 29 Apr. 2012, www.commondreams.org/views/2012/04/29/stop-holocaust-migrating-birds.

In setting up her argument in favor of protecting migratory birds, many of which die in collisions with structures like towers and skyscrapers, Jennifer Browdy de Hernandez relies almost entirely on an emotional appeal. Her choice of language is intended to provoke sympathy and even outrage about the plight of migratory birds: "The traditional dawn chorus of birdsong has ebbed to a few lonely little souls"; the birds "run the gauntlet" of human construction and fly into guy wires that "garrote" them. By inciting readers' emotions with such language, Browdy de Hernandez tries to make readers more sympathetic to her argument. (Even the photograph that accompanies the essay, which depicts a beautiful bird singing its song, can evoke strong sympathies for songbirds.)

Often, emotional appeals are more subtle. In the following excerpt from an essay about the controversial Affordable Care Act that became law in 2010, U.S. Secretary of Health and Human Services Kathleen Sebelius strategically employs emotional appeals to make her argument more persuasive:

Two years ago, President Obama signed the Affordable Care Act. The President's health care law gives hard working, middle-class families security, makes Medicare stronger, and puts more money back in seniors' pockets.

Prior to 2011, people on Medicare faced paying for preventive benefits like cancer screenings and cholesterol checks out of their own pockets. Now, these benefits are offered free of charge to beneficiaries.

Over time, the health reform law also closes the gap in prescription drug coverage, known as the "donut hole." This helps seniors like Helen Rayon: "I am a grandmother who is trying to assist a grandson with his education. I take seven different medications. Getting the donut hole closed, that gives me a little more money in my pocket."

In 2010, those who hit the donut hole received a $250 rebate—with almost 4 million seniors and people with disabilities receiving a collective $1 billion. In 2011, people on Medicare automatically received a 50 percent discount on brand-name drugs in the donut hole. Over 3.6 million beneficiaries received more than $2.1 billion in savings—averaging $604 per person last year.

Source: Sebelius, Kathleen. "The Affordable Health Care Act: Strong Benefits to Seniors, Billions in Savings This Year." *The Huffington Post*, 29 April 2012, www.huffingtonpost.com/sec-kathleen-sebelius/the-affordable-care-act_b_1462694.html.

Here Sebelius appeals to her readers' sense of fairness by invoking sympathetic images—for example, of "hard working, middle-class families" and "a grandmother who is trying to assist a grandson with his education"—that are likely to make readers more inclined to consider her argument. Notice that Sebelius doesn't rely exclusively on emotional appeals, however; she also cites statistical evidence to support her claims. Her essay illustrates how emotional appeals can be woven effectively into an argument.

## Logical Appeals, or Appeals to Reason

Because reason is often assumed to be superior to emotion when it comes to argumentation, rational arguments are often considered more valid than openly emotional ones. Of course, reason can never be completely separated from emotion, and audiences rarely react to logical arguments in a way that is devoid of emotion. Nevertheless, logic is an essential component of argumentation, and even arguments that appeal to emotion or character usually incorporate reasoning. The most common forms of logical reasoning are *inductive reasoning* and *deductive reasoning*. (Patterns of organizing an argument based on inductive or deductive reasoning are reviewed later in this chapter; here the nature of inductive and deductive reasoning is discussed.)

### Inductive Reasoning

In induction, a conclusion is drawn from specific evidence. This type of reasoning is common in daily life. For example, you might have noticed more students riding bicycles and several new bicycle racks have been added to the campus. On the basis of this evidence you might reasonably conclude, or induce, that bicycles have become more popular.

Inductive reasoning is common in academic arguments, in which logical conclusions are reached on the basis of available evidence. The specific kinds of evidence and conventions governing inductive argument might differ from one academic discipline to another, but the basic approach is the same: reasoning from evidence.

Here's an example of a writer using inductive reasoning to make an argument about the value of a college education. In this excerpt from an essay titled "College Is Still Worth It," Mark Yzaguirre presents data about the impact of a college degree on a person's earnings and socio-economic status:

> Recently, the Pew Charitable Trusts came out with a report that supports what many of us have been saying to critics of higher education: While the system has its problems, by and large those with college degrees are better off than those without them, even during the recent economic turmoil.
>
> The Pew report makes several basic points that should be mentioned anytime someone claims that higher education isn't a good investment:
>
> - Although all 21–24-year-olds experienced declines in employment and wages during the recession, the decline was considerably more severe for those with only high school or associate degrees.
> - The comparatively high employment rate of recent college graduates was not driven by a sharp increase in those settling for lesser jobs or lower wages.

- The share of non-working graduates seeking further education did not change markedly during the recession.
- Out-of-work college graduates were able to find jobs during the downturn with more success than their less-educated counterparts.

These aren't trivial observations and they now have even more statistical support than before. The general economic benefits of getting a degree are still pretty clear. That doesn't mean that any college degree plan is a good one and any sensible approach to higher education, whether at the undergraduate or graduate level, should include a clear-eyed analysis of what one is likely to pay to and receive from a given school. . . .

It is simplistic and false to claim that more education always leads to more income or better job opportunities. It is also correct to point out that excessive student loan debt is a terrible burden that may not be justifiable for certain schools or fields of study. But that doesn't mean that it's good advice to tell young people who want to go to college and who are prepared to do so that they shouldn't do so because it's not worth the time or the price. Those with college degrees are still more likely to be employed than those without them and their prospects aren't bleak. While the phrase *caveat emptor* is a necessary one to consider in picking colleges and degree programs, the Great Recession shouldn't claim the idea that higher education is a ticket to a better future as one of its victims.

Source: Yzaguirre, Mark. "College Is Still Worth It." *The Huffington Post*, 16 Jan. 2013, www.huffingtonpost.com/mark-yzaguirre/college-education-worth_b_2483440.html.

Yzaguirre concludes that college is worthwhile on the basis of his evidence. He reasons inductively to arrive at that conclusion. Notice, though, that he qualifies his conclusion by saying that "it is simplistic and false to claim that more education always leads to more income or better job opportunities." In other words, the evidence allows him to conclude that, in general, college is worth the cost, but that evidence does *not* allow him to conclude that college is worth the cost for every student. Yzaguirre's care in drawing conclusions that logically follow from his evidence reminds us of one of the challenges of inductive reasoning: identifying evidence that isn't flawed, biased, or limited in some way. If the evidence is problematic, the conclusion will likely be questionable, rendering the argument weak, no matter how careful the reasoning.

## Deductive Reasoning

Deductive reasoning begins with a generalization, called a **premise**, and works to a conclusion that follows logically from that generalization. The premise is the foundation for the argument. Typically, deductive reasoning is effective when the issue involves a basic principle or belief. For example, arguments against capital punishment often rest on the principle that all human life is sacred. That principle becomes the major premise, and the argument is constructed logically from that premise:

**Major premise:** Taking a human life is immoral.

**Minor premise:** Capital punishment is the willful taking of human life.

**Conclusion:** Capital punishment is immoral.

Evidence can still be cited in support of the argument, but the strength of the argument rests on the truth or validity of the main premise and the reasoning that leads to the conclusion.

In the following example, writer Malcolm Gladwell challenges a widespread view of media with a deductive argument. Gladwell questions the claim that social media are the key factor in recent modern uprisings against unpopular governments, such as those that occurred in eastern Europe in 2009 and (after his article was published) in Algeria, Egypt, and Libya during the "Arab Spring" of 2011. To make his argument, Gladwell compares these revolutions to other activist movements,

including the famous "Freedom Summer" protests in Mississippi in 1964, in which three volunteers—Michael Schwerner, James Chaney, and Andrew Goodman—were murdered, many black churches were set on fire, and hundreds of volunteers were beaten, shot at, and arrested. "A quarter of those in the program dropped out," Gladwell notes. "Activism that challenges the status quo—that attacks deeply rooted problems—is not for the faint of heart." What makes people capable of this kind of activism? he asks. He then gets to the basis of his argument, which is his main premise: High-risk activism "is a strong-tie phenomenon." In other words, this kind of activism depends on a strong connection to the movement. Gladwell supports this premise by referring to a study of the Freedom Summer participants indicating that what kept people involved in such dangerous movements was their "degree of personal connection to the civil-rights movement." Then he works from this premise to argue that current movements that rely on social media are not the same as previous movements like the Freedom Summer:

> The platforms of social media are built around weak ties. Twitter is a way of following (or being followed by) people you may never have met. Facebook is a tool for efficiently managing your acquaintances, for keeping up with the people you would not otherwise be able to stay in touch with. That's why you can have a thousand "friends" on Facebook, as you never could in real life.
>
> This is in many ways a wonderful thing. There is strength in weak ties, as the sociologist Mark Granovetter has observed. . . But weak ties seldom lead to high-risk activism. . . .
>
> Boycotts and sit-ins and nonviolent confrontations—which were the weapons of choice for the civil-rights movement—are high-risk strategies. They leave little room for conflict and error. The moment even one protester deviates from the script and responds to provocation, the moral legitimacy of the entire protest is compromised. Enthusiasts for social media would no doubt have us believe that King's task in Birmingham would have been made infinitely easier had he been able to communicate with his followers through Facebook, and contented himself

with tweets from a Birmingham jail. But networks are messy: think of the ceaseless pattern of correction and revision, amendment and debate, that characterizes Wikipedia. If Martin Luther King, Jr., had tried to do a wiki-boycott in Montgomery, he would have been steamrollered by the white power structure. And of what use would a digital communication tool be in a town where ninety-eight per cent of the black community could be reached every Sunday morning at church? The things that King needed in Birmingham—discipline and strategy—were things that online social media cannot provide.

Source: Gladwell, Malcolm. "Small Change: Why the Revolution Will Not be Tweeted." *The New Yorker*, 4. Oct. 2010, www.newyorker.com/magazine/2010/10/04/small-change-malcolm-gladwell.

Gladwell bases his argument on deductive reasoning:

1. He establishes his main premise: High-risk activism like the Civil Rights Movement in the U.S. requires strong social ties to succeed.

2. He examines the recent activist movements that relied on social media to show that they do not display these strong ties. (This is his minor premise.)

3. He concludes that social media cannot be the vehicle for high-risk activism.

Although deductive reasoning can be effective in arguments about issues informed by fundamental values or beliefs, it can also be used effectively in many kinds of arguments, as Gladwell's essay illustrates.

---

**EXERCISE 11E**  **EXPLORING PERSUASIVE APPEALS**

1. Identify an issue about which you might write an argument. In a brief paragraph, summarize the main argument you would make and describe your intended audience. Now describe the appeals (ethical, emotional, or logical) that you think would strengthen your argument for that audience. For example, in an argument supporting anti-smoking laws, you might make an emotional appeal by describing the hardship caused by the death of the parent of young children from lung cancer; you might make a logical appeal on the basis of growing evidence that many serious health problems are linked to smoking.

2. Review the following passages and identify the ethical, emotional, and logical appeals in each.

a) Today introversion and extroversion are two of the most exhaustively researched subjects in personality psychology, arousing the curiosity of hundreds of scientists.

   These researchers have made exciting discoveries aided by the latest technology, but they're part of a long and storied tradition. Poets and philosophers have been thinking about introverts and extroverts since the dawn of recorded time. Both personality types appear in the Bible and in the writings of Greek and Roman physicians, and some evolutionary

*(Continued)*

scientists say that the history of these types teaches back even farther than that: the animal kingdom also boasts "introverts" and "extroverts, . . . from fruit flies to pumpkinseed fish to rhesus monkeys. As with other complimentary pairings—masculinity and femininity, East and West, liberal and conservative—humanity would be unrecognizable, and vastly diminished, without both personality types.

Take the partnership of Rosa Parks and Martin Luther King, Jr.: a formidable orator refusing to give up his seat on a segregated bus wouldn't have had the same effect as a modest woman who'd clearly prefer to keep silent but for the exigencies of the situation. And Parks didn't have the stuff to thrill a crowd if she'd tried to stand up and announce that she had a dream. But with King's help, she didn't have to.

Yet today we make room for a remarkably narrow range of personality styles. We're told that to be great is to be bold, to be happy is to be sociable. We see ourselves as a nation of extroverts—which means that we've lost sight of who we really are. Depending on which study you consult, one third to one half of Americans are introverts—in other words, *one out of every two or three people you know. . . .* If you're not an introvert yourself, you are surely raising, managing, married to, or coupled with one.

---

Source: Cain, Susan. *Quiet: The Power of Introverts in a World That Can't Stop Talking.* Crown Publishing, 2012, pp. 3–4.

b) Wal-Mart has become the poster child for all that's wrong with American capitalism, because it replaced General Motors as the avatar of the economy. Recall that in the 1950s and the 1960s, GM earned more than any company on earth and was America's largest employer. It paid its workers solidly middle-class wages with generous benefits, totaling around $60,000 a year in today's dollars. Today Wal-Mart, America's largest company by revenue and the nation's largest employer, pays its employees about $17,500 a year on average, or just under $10 an hour, and its fringe benefits are skimpy—no guaranteed pension and few if any health benefits. And Wal-Mart does everything in its power to keep wages and benefits low. Internal memos in 2005 suggested hiring more part-time workers to lower the firm's health care enrollment and imposing wage caps on longer-term employees so they wouldn't be eligible for raises. Also, as I said earlier, Wal-Mart is aggressively anti-union.

Wal-Mart's CEO in 2007 was H. Lee Scott, Jr. Scott was no "Engine Charlie" Wilson, who as GM's top executive in the 1950s saw no difference between the fate of the nation and the fate of his company. Scott has a far less grandiose view of Wal-Mart's role. "Some well-meaning critics believe that Wal-Mart stores today, because of our size, should, in fact, play the role that is believed that General Motors played after World War II. And that is to establish this post-World War middle class that the country is proud of," he opined. "The facts are that retail does not perform that role in this economy." Scott was right. The real problem—not of his making—is that almost nothing performs that role any longer.

> The rhetorical debate over Wal-Mart is not nearly as interesting as the debate we might be having in our own heads if we acknowledge what was at stake. Millions of us shop at Wal-Mart because we like its low prices. Many of us also own Wal-Mart stock through our pension or mutual funds. Isn't Wal-Mart really being excoriated for our sins? After all, it is not as if Wal-Mart's founder, Sam Walton, and his successors created the world's largest retailer by putting a gun to our heads and forcing us to shop there or to invest any of our retirement savings in the firm.
>
> Source: Reich, Robert. *Supercapitalism: The Transformation of Business, Democracy, and Everyday Life.* Knopf, 2007, pp. 89–90.

## Appraising and Using Evidence

No matter what kind of argument you are making, identifying and using appropriate evidence is essential for effective argumentation. Almost anything can be used as evidence: statistics, opinions, observations, theories, personal experience, anecdotes. The challenge is to determine whether a particular kind of evidence is appropriate for a specific claim in a specific rhetorical situation.

Consider the debate about the state of the U.S. Social Security system. For a number of years, economists, politicians, and financial experts have been debating whether Social Security will run out of money and what, if anything, should be done to prevent that. Experts disagree about the nature of the problem, and participants in the debate routinely cite statistics and factual evidence to support their competing claims. For example, here's an excerpt from a 2012 *USA Today* editorial arguing that Congress should take steps now to avoid a default of the Social Security Trust Fund:

> Self-proclaimed defenders of Social Security maintain that, because of the retirement program's large annual surpluses, it isn't in crisis. That argument is a red herring.
>
> For one thing, those surpluses, also known as the Social Security Trust Fund, have been spent and replaced with IOUs. For another, there aren't any more surpluses. This year, Social Security will collect $507 billion in taxes and pay out $640 billion in benefits. The difference will have to be borrowed, adding to the federal deficit.
>
> Even if you believe that the trust fund is more real than the tooth fairy, the picture is gloomy. This week, the trustees who oversee Social Security reported that if the government makes good on the IOUs by borrowing, taxing or cutting elsewhere, the main trust fund will run out of money in a little more than 20 years. At that point, income from the payroll tax will only be enough to cover 75% of expected benefits. The fund for Social Security's disability program will go bust even sooner, in 2016.
>
> Source: "Editorial: Fix Social Security." *USA Today*, 26 Apr. 2012, usatoday30.usatoday.com/news/opinion/editorials/story/2012-04-26/Social-Security-trustees-report/54562718/1.

The authors of this editorial provide what seems to be convincing evidence that Social Security will run out of money in two decades—for example, statistics showing that the Social Security Trust Fund pays out more than it takes in. They rest their argument on a report by the Fund's trustees, who express concern about the possible default of the fund. The question is whether this evidence actually supports the conclusion that the fund will run out of money. The expected deficit for one year, which they refer to in the second paragraph, does not necessarily mean continued deficits over twenty years. In addition, the trustees' prediction in the third paragraph depends upon the accuracy of their assumption about how much money the fund will need to cover benefits, which is a disputed figure.

In a rebuttal to this editorial, Max Richtman, the president and CEO of the National Committee to Preserve Social Security & Medicare, also cites the trustees' report, but he points to figures in that report that lead him to a different conclusion:

- The trust fund solvency date for Social Security has seen fluctuations many times in recent decades, from a depletion date as distant as 2048 in the 1988 report to as soon as 2029 in the 1994 and 1997 reports. This year's report is well within that range.

- Social Security will be able to pay full benefits until the year 2033. After that, there will be sufficient revenue to pay about 75% of benefits.

- There is $2.7 trillion in the Social Security Trust Fund, which is $69 billion more than last year, and it will continue to grow until 2020.

Source: Richtman, Max. "Opposing View: There is No Social Security Crisis." *USA Today*, 26 Apr. 2012, www.usatoday.com/news/opinion/story/2012-04-26/National-Committee-to-Preserve-Social-Security-Medicare/54561846/1.

Like the authors of the editorial, Richtman cites statistical evidence to support his claim but he reaches a different conclusion: "There is no Social Security crisis." Who is right?

This example illustrates that the use of evidence in arguments about complicated issues is itself complicated. In this case, the strength of the argument depends not only on the nature of the specific evidence provided but also on how that evidence is interpreted. Each side uses similar kinds of evidence but interprets the evidence differently.

In evaluating an argument, then, we have to appraise the evidence provided.

- **Is the evidence credible?** The evidence should be from a credible source. In the previous example, the source of the figures cited by the authors is a report by the trustees of the Social Security system, which lends those figures credibility. Had the authors cited figures from, say, an economist with little experience in fiscal issues related to social security, those figures could carry less weight.

- **Is the evidence appropriate for the argument?** Often, a great deal of evidence is available to support a claim, but the strength of that evidence will depend on how relevant it is to the argument. In this example, the authors could cite a wide variety of economic, financial, and historical statistics or information to support their claims about the fiscal viability of Social Security, but some evidence might be inappropriate for this argument. For example, a statement by a politician who is known to oppose Social Security as an unnecessary government program would be a weak kind of evidence to support the writers' claim that Social Security is running out of money.

- **Is the evidence applied appropriately?** Sometimes, evidence can be strong but used inappropriately. For example, the writers of the *USA Today* editorial note that "Social Security will collect $507 billion in taxes and pay out $640 billion in benefits." They use these figures appropriately to support their claim that such deficits make it more likely that the fund will run out of money. If, however, they cited these figures to argue that Social Security is already running out of money, they would be misusing these figures, since a deficit in a single year does not indicate that the fund is bankrupt.

- **Is the evidence interpreted in a reasonable way?** What a piece of evidence means is not always clear, and the same evidence can sometimes be used to support different claims. So writers must often explain what their evidence means. In this example, both Richtman and the editorial authors cite the same figure as evidence to support different claims—the date when the trustees expect Social Security to run out of money (what Richtman refers to as the "solvency date")—but they interpret this piece of evidence differently. The editorial authors assume that the date refers to a specific date when the fund will become insolvent; Richtman interprets the date as an estimate, noting that in the past the trustees have predicted different solvency dates. Part of the strength of each argument, then, rests on whether readers accept the authors' interpretation of the evidence.

- **Is important evidence missing?** Sometimes evidence that seems convincing becomes less so when other evidence is presented. Richtman, for example, notes that the Social Security Trust Fund has "$69 billion more than last year, and it will continue to grow until 2020." The authors of the editorial do not include the fund's growth in their argument, yet this figure seems to be important for estimating whether or when the fund might become insolvent. It is up to readers to decide whether that "missing" evidence weakens their argument and strengthens Richtman's claim.

Keep in mind that what counts as appropriate and persuasive evidence depends upon the rhetorical context. Personal experience might be acceptable to readers of a popular consumer magazine but not necessarily for a technical report on fuel economy for a government agency or for an essay in your Economics class. Consider your audience and purpose when determining what kinds of evidence are most appropriate and persuasive for your argument.

---

**EXERCISE 11F**  **APPRAISING EVIDENCE**

1. For each of the following passages, identify the claim(s) and the evidence presented in support of the claim(s). Then evaluate the strength of the evidence using the criteria discussed in this section. Excerpt A is taken from an essay by a political scientist challenging the assumption that voters act rationally when deciding which political candidates to support. Excerpt B is taken from from a book by an anthropologist examining what we can learn from traditional societies.

   a) Suppose that one scholar maintains that the average voter's belief about X is true, and another denies it. For their debate to make sense, *both* sides have to claim knowledge about (a) what the average voter believes, and (b) which belief is true. How can we get to the bottom of this sort of dispute?

   It is fairly easy to figure out what the average voter believes. High-quality surveys abound. The hard thing is figuring out how to "grade" the beliefs of the average voter—to find a yardstick against which his beliefs can be measured.

   *(Continued)*

The most straightforward is to compare voter beliefs to known fact. We can ask voters to tell us the fraction of the federal budget that goes to foreign aid, and compare their average answer to the actual number. Studies that use this approach find that the average voter has some truly bizarre beliefs. The National Survey of Public Knowledge of Welfare Reform and the Federal Budget finds, for example, that 41% of Americans believe that foreign aid is one of the two biggest areas in the federal budget—versus 14% for Social Security. The main drawback of this approach is that many interesting questions are too complex to resolve with an almanac.

Source: Caplan, Bryan. "The Myth of the Rational Voter." *Cato Unbound*, Cato Institute, 5 Nov. 2006, www.cato-unbound.org/2006/11/05/bryan-caplan/myth-rational-voter.

b) Traditional societies are far more diverse in their cultural practices than are modern industrial societies. Within that range of diversity, many cultural norms for modern state societies are far displaced from traditional norms and lie towards the extremes of that traditional range of diversity. For example, compared to any modern industrial society, some traditional societies treat elderly people much more cruelly, while others offer elderly people much more satisfying lives; modern industrial societies are closer to the former extreme than to the latter. Yet psychologists base most of their generalizations about human nature on studies of our own narrow and atypical slice of human diversity. Among human subjects studied in a sample of papers from the top psychology journals surveyed in the year 2008, 96% were from Westernized industrial countries (North America, Europe, Australia, New Zealand, and Israel), 68% were from the U.S. in particular, and up to 80% were college undergraduates enrolled in psychology courses, i.e., not even typical of their own national societies. That is, as social scientists Joseph Henrich, Steven Heine, and Ara Norenzayan express it, most of our understanding of human psychology is based on subjects who may be described by the acronym WEIRD: from Western, educated, industrialized, rich, and democratic societies. Most subjects also appear to be literally weird by the standards of world cultural variation, because they prove to be outliers in many studies of cultural phenomena that have sampled world variation more broadly. Those sampled phenomena include visual perception, fairness, cooperation, punishment, logical reasoning, spatial orientation, analytic versus holistic reasoning, moral reasoning, motivation to conform, making choices, and concept of self. Hence if we wish to generalize about human nature, we need to broaden greatly our study sample from the usual WEIRD subjects (mainly American psychology undergraduates) to the whole range of traditional societies.

Source: Diamond, Jared. *The World Until Yesterday*. Viking Books, 2012.

2. Identify an argument you might make about an issue that matters to you. In a paragraph, state your main argument and briefly describe the audience you would address. Now list several kinds of evidence to support your argument that would be persuasive for your intended audience. Briefly explain why each kind of evidence would be appropriate for your argument.

# Structuring an Argument

The most effective arguments are structured in a way that best meets the needs of the rhetorical situation, and writers generally adopt a format that presents their arguments clearly and persuasively to their intended audience:

- An argument about the influence of social media on peer groups for a communication course would likely be organized systematically around the main claims that can be made on the basis of available research.
- An essay for your campus newspaper in favor of the college's study-abroad program might be structured around your own study-abroad experience to make a case for the value of that program.
- A pamphlet supporting the legalization of medical marijuana might present several cases of patients who benefited from medicinal marijuana, with each case illustrating a main point in favor of legalization.

In each of these examples, the writer's decisions about how to structure the argument are shaped by the same basic factors:

- **Audience expectations.** Readers might be less skeptical about supporting the legalization of medicinal marijuana if the argument is presented in the form of the personal stories of patients whose lives were improved by the use of the drug.
- **Conventions governing argument in that rhetorical situation.** Academic arguments, such as a report on social media and peer groups in a communications course, usually follow accepted formats within the academic field. Other kinds of arguments, such as editorial essays for newspapers, tend to be less formally structured.
- **Purpose of the argument.** Structuring an argument around personal experiences and anecdotes, as in an essay arguing for the value of a study abroad program, might make the argument more engaging and persuasive to the intended audience (other students) and therefore be more likely to achieve the purpose of the argument (to assert a position about the issue).

As these examples illustrate, arguments can take many forms; writers should always assess the rhetorical situation carefully to determine how best to structure an argument. However, writers can also use one of four traditional ways of structuring an argument:

- classical arrangement
- Rogerian argument
- inductive reasoning
- deductive reasoning

## Classical Arrangement

Classical rhetorical theory defines a standard six-part structure for an argument:

1. **Introduction:** places the main argument in context and explains why it is important or relevant.

2. **Background:** a narrative of events or statement of the facts of the case that sets the stage for the argument.

3. **Proposition:** statement of the writer's position or main argument and an indication of the key points to be made in support of the argument.

4. **Proof:** the core of the argument, in which the writer presents his or her claims and evidence to support the main argument. Often, this section is arranged so that the strongest claims and evidence are presented first.

5. **Refutation:** consideration of opposing arguments, which can be rebutted or accepted to strengthen the main argument.

6. **Conclusion:** summary of the main points of the argument. Often, the writer will make a final appeal to the audience.

The advantage of this format is that it presents the argument in a clear, straightforward way. Using this format can help writers generate ideas for their argument and insure that nothing important is left out. Although the format might seem rigid, writers have flexibility in deciding how to organize each main section.

## Rogerian Argument

Based on the work of psychologist Carl Rogers, who advocated understanding and listening to resolve conflict, Rogerian argument is generally viewed as a means to negotiate differences and achieve social cooperation. Rogerian argument emphasizes resolution of the issue at hand, so writers make concessions rather than refutations. Like classically arranged arguments, Rogerian arguments have six main sections:

1. **Introduction:** presents the problem to be resolved and raises the possibility of a positive outcome.

2. **Summary of opposing views:** opposing views are stated as accurately and neutrally as possible.

3. **Statement of understanding:** the validity of opposing views is acknowledged. Without necessarily conceding that these views are always right, the writer seeks common ground with those who have opposing views.

4. **Statement of position:** the writer's position on the issue.

5. **Statement of contexts:** discussion of situations that illustrate the validity of the writer's position—in effect, providing support for that position to indicate that it can be acceptable even to those with opposing views.

6. **Statement of benefits:** an appeal to the self-interest of those with opposing views who might reconsider as a result of the writer's argument.

(Adapted from Richard Coe, *Form and Substance.* Wiley, 1981.)

Rogerian argument is most appropriate in situations in which people are deeply divided as a result of different values or perceptions and especially when conflicting parties seek a compromise. For example, an argument in favor of same-sex marriage presented in a Rogerian format would emphasize the common ground shared by those who hold strong, divergent opinions about the issue. Using a Rogerian approach in such a situation, a writer might highlight the desire for strong families, which is shared by those on either side of the debate. In such a case, pointing out the problems with opposing viewpoints is not likely to encourage those who hold such viewpoints to reconsider their position on the issue.

## Inductive Reasoning

Arguments based on inductive reasoning present a conclusion drawn from available evidence. When organizing such an argument, follow these guidelines:

- **Demonstrate the relevance of the topic.** The introduction presents the topic and explains why it is relevant to the intended audience.

- **State the main argument and claims clearly.** How clearly and carefully a writer presents his or her main argument can determine how convincing that argument is to the intended audience.

- **Arrange evidence so that it best supports the main conclusion.** Because some kinds of evidence are likely to be more compelling to the audience than others, you should assess how your audience is likely to respond to specific kinds of evidence and arrange that evidence in a way that will make the argument strongest, usually presenting the most compelling evidence first.

- **Interpret and analyze the evidence for the audience.** Although your evidence might be strong, you might have to explain why it is significant. For example, if you use an anecdote about an accident involving a student who parks her car on campus, explain what that anecdote means for your argument against the new campus parking restrictions. (See "Appraising and Using Evidence" on page 341.)

Because an inductive argument relies on evidence, this approach might be used most effectively when there is strong and abundant evidence to support a main argument or position.

## Deductive Reasoning

When constructing an argument on the basis of deductive reasoning, work backward from the main conclusion by following these steps:

- **Identify the conclusion.** Identify the main conclusion you want to reach in your argument. For example, let's say you support the idea of free college for all citizens and agree with politicians who advocate making public two-year colleges tuition-free for residents of the states where those colleges are located. So that's your conclusion.

- **Examine your reasons.** List your main reasons for your position, keeping in mind that some reasons will be more persuasive to an audience than others. For instance, you might believe that a college education is part of what it means to be an informed citizen and therefore strengthens democracy. That might be a valid reason for making two-year colleges tuition-free, but it might be less compelling than other reasons, such as the negative social and economic impact of the enormous debt that so many college students incur, which hurts families, communities, and the broader economy. Try to identify all the main reasons for supporting your conclusion.

- **Formulate the premise.** Your premise is the basic principle on which you will base your argument. Ideally, it should be a principle that your audience shares. Let's say your position on tuition-free college rests on your belief that all people have a right to a good education, regardless of their income level or social status. That's your premise. It will serve as the foundation for your argument:

  *All people should have access to a high-quality education in their quest for a healthy, happy life. Income and social status should not determine one's access to education. Therefore, college should be free for all citizens.*

You can structure your argument accordingly:

1. **Introduction:** State the problem.

2. **Main premise:** Present and explain the main premise on which the argument will be based. Also present the conclusion you will reach.

3. **Reasons:** Present the reasons for supporting the proposition. Address any counter-arguments that can weaken the main argument.

4. **Conclusion:** Restate the main conclusion in light of the evidence presented. Also remind readers of the main premise.

One benefit of structuring an argument in this way is that it encourages you to explore your subject carefully, which could lead to a stronger, more substantive essay.

# Features of Argument

Like other common forms of academic writing, argument is a form of inquiry. It is a vehicle for writers to investigate and understand a complex issue or problem and make a claim about that issue or problem to others who have a stake in it.

**Effective arguments have five essential features:**

1. **A clear main point.** In an effective argument, the writer communicates a clear main point related to his or her position on an issue. As we saw earlier in this chapter, the main argument is not the same as the writer's position on the topic. To state that you support online privacy protection is to take a stance on that issue; to make the case that online privacy should be protected because online communication is a form of constitutionally protected speech is to make an argument in support of that stance.

2. **A relevant purpose.** The purpose of any argument should be relevant to the rhetorical situation. For instance, an argument supporting leash laws to make your campus safer and cleaner would be appropriate for your campus newspaper or a student social media site, the audience for which would likely share your concerns about campus safety. However, the same argument for an assignment in a geography and urban planning course would have to place the issue of leash laws in the context of that field—for example, how land use laws and campus ordinances are intended to create livable public spaces. Even a carefully crafted and well-supported argument is unlikely to be effective if the topic is not relevant to the intended audience.

3. **Appropriate support for claims.** Sufficient and appropriate evidence to support claims is perhaps the most obvious feature of effective argument, but supporting a claim with evidence is not always straightforward. For example, statistical data showing that the average global temperature last year was the highest in five years might be true, but such evidence would be insufficient support for an argument that the earth is getting warmer. On the other hand, data showing a rise in global temperatures over several decades would be stronger evidence for a claim that the earth's atmosphere is getting warmer. In some contexts, such as economics, statistical data might carry more weight than expert opinion, whereas in other contexts, such as art history, the views of respected scholars might be more appropriate support for a claim than statistical evidence.

4. **Complexity.** Effective arguments explore their subjects in sufficient depth to avoid oversimplifying them. For example, it might seem obvious to argue that raising student test scores will improve learning, but a closer look might reveal questions about the reliability of tests or their impact on what students learn. In an effective argument, the writer should acknowledge such questions and address them in a way that reflects the complexity of the issue. Doing so will result in an argument that is stronger and perhaps more valid. It might also foster a deeper understanding of the issue.

5. **A persuasive appeal.** An argument can be based on appeals to reason, emotion, or character, but most arguments employ whatever appeals are appropriate for the rhetorical situation. Moreover, almost all arguments employ logic in some form. Not all reasoning is valid, however. In fact, logical fallacies and flawed reasoning abound in public debates about important issues in politics, education, technology, and culture. (See Focus: "Recognizing Logical Fallacies in Public Arguments" on page 395 in Chapter 13.) An effective argument leads readers logically to the conclusion that the writer supports, based on evidence and sound reasoning, even when the writer is appealing to readers' emotions or invoking character.

The following essay illustrates these features of argumentation. In this essay, which was originally published in *The New Yorker*, a magazine devoted to culture, politics, and the arts, Law professor Ekow N. Yankah makes a case against the increasingly popular idea that college athletes should be paid. His essay appeared in late 2015, just a few weeks after a major decision by a U.S. Appeals Court regarding compensation for college scholarship athletes, which Yankah refers to in his opening paragraph. This lawsuit, which came to be known as the "O'Bannon case," was originally filed by Ed O'Bannon, who played basketball for UCLA from 1991 to 1995 on an athletic scholarship. In 2009 O'Bannon sued the National Collegiate Athletic Association, or NCAA, which sets the rules for college sports, including how and whether scholarship athletes are compensated. The NCAA has long claimed that college athletes are amateurs and therefore should not receive pay for their sports performances. O'Bannon argued that college athletes should receive compensation when the universities they play for earn millions of dollars through the use of the players' images in video games, on television broadcasts, and on merchandise such as T-shirts. The high-profile case was controversial, in part because it challenged longstanding beliefs about college sports, which by 2009 had become a multibillion-dollar enterprise. As the case made its way through the legal system, it provoked intense debate among fans as well as coaches, university officials, and legal experts such as Yankah. After several decisions in lower courts, the case ended up in the United States Court of Appeals for the Ninth Circuit, which, as Yankah notes, handed down a mixed decision, asserting that the NCAA violated antitrust laws but also ruling that universities do not have to pay their athletes beyond the cost of attending college.

As you'll see, Yankah is not so much interested in the legal decision in the O'Bannon case as he is concerned about the broader question raised by O'Bannon's lawsuit: Should college athletes be paid? By the time Yankah wrote his essay in 2015, college sports, especially football and basketball, had become an even bigger business than when O'Bannon filed his lawsuit in 2009, and the question of whether athletes should be paid had become even more contentious. Yankah acknowledges the well-established arguments in favor of paying college athletes and concedes that athletes who play big-money sports are exploited, but he rests his own argument primarily on reason. He builds his case so that it leads logically to his conclusion that college athletes should not be paid for playing their sports. His reasoning is deductive. His main premise might be stated this way: Amateur athletics have great social and cultural value in their own right. His minor premise is that paying student athletes would undermine this value by emphasizing only the monetary worth of athletics. His conclusion, then, is that college athletes should not be paid.

Of course, in addition to his logical argument, Yankah also employs emotional appeals—for example, when he discusses his strong sense of connection to the athletic teams at the University of Michigan, which he attended. He also provides various kinds of factual evidence (inartistic proofs) to support his argument. In these ways, his essay, which was published in a popular magazine, illustrates the features of effective argument in academic contexts as well.

---

## MindTap®

Read this argument. Highlight and take notes online. Additional readings are also available online.

· · · · · · · · · · · · · · · · · · · · · · · · · · · · · · · · · · · · · · · · · · · · ·

### Talking About This Reading

**Dara Bordman (student):** I had some trouble following the organization of this essay. The author's main points sometimes seemed to be all over the place, and I didn't see a direct route from the beginning to the end.

**Bob Yagelski:** Dara, part of the problem might be that this author is making a deductive argument, which can be challenging to follow (see the introduction to this reading above). In such cases, it helps to identify the author's main premise, which he states in paragraph 4: that sports have educational value. That premise leads to his conclusion (also stated in paragraph 4) that paying college athletes would be a mistake. Knowing that can help you see how his other points fit into his argument.

· · · · · · · · · · · · · · · · · · · · · · · · · · · · · · · · · · · · · · · · · · · · ·

# Why N.C.A.A. Athletes Shouldn't Be Paid
## by Ekow N. Yankah

1   Two weeks ago, as Americans were settling into the harvest comfort of football Saturdays, the United States Court of Appeals for the Ninth Circuit issued a ruling in the antitrust suit against the National Collegiate Athletic Association. The decision drew blood on both sides. The court sided with the players in affirming that the N.C.A.A. is not immune to antitrust regulation, but simultaneously reversed a lower-court ruling that would have granted former athletes as much as five thousand dollars a year in deferred compensation—essentially back pay—for the use of their images in video games and other commercial ventures. At the same time, the court required that the N.C.A.A. increase scholarship payouts to cover the full cost of college attendance, thus making mandatory an option that the N.C.A.A. first permitted a few years ago.

2   These legal niceties did very little to address the deeper question of fairness. The N.C.A.A. ideal of amateurism in college athletics has come to border on farce. In the highest-revenue sports—football and basketball—the argument in favor of paying players is so searingly obvious as to seem undeniable. These athletes collectively generate tens if not hundreds of millions of dollars annually for their schools. Many college coaches are the highest-paid public employees in their states—a five-million-dollar salary is no longer eye-popping—and that paycheck doesn't include gifts from boosters, who will occasionally pay for a coach's house to make sure that he stays happy.

3   But this understates the exploitation. The athletes in major football and men's basketball programs are disproportionately black, many from poor and educationally disadvantaged backgrounds. For too many of them, the N.C.A.A. is the only game in town. In some dispiriting cases, the students are so unprepared that academic failure seems inevitable. In worse cases still, their scholarships are cynically undermined by the schools themselves. Coaches steer students into empty classes (what one recent report from the University of North Carolina at Chapel Hill characterized as a "shadow curriculum" [Crouch]) or supply so-called academic support that amounts to cheating. It hardly seems coincidental, then, that sports with less African-American participation, such as baseball and hockey, maintain robust minor-league systems without the national gnashing of teeth.

> **Appropriate Support for Claims**
> In the second and third paragraphs, Yankah uses factual evidence (about coaches' salaries) and an example (of a cheating scandal involving athletes at the University of North Carolina) to support his claim that college athletes are exploited.

4    And yet I believe that the drive to pay college athletes is a grave mistake—not because it misdiagnoses the disease but because it suggests that the only cure is to put the patient out of his misery. It fails, first of all, to recognize the value of sports as a part of education. This value can be seen in the countless student athletes, from gymnasts to softball players, who pour hours of work into training and competing with no hope of going pro. (Similarly, many of those in even the biggest sports show dedication long after it is clear that they will never be professionals.)

**A Clear Main Point**
At the beginning of the fourth paragraph, Yankah unequivocally states his position that college athletes should not be paid. From this point on, readers know Yankah's position and can focus on how he supports it.

5    This value is again revealed in the fact that many N.C.A.A. teams are vastly more popular than their professional counterparts. My beloved Michigan Wolverines pack the Big House with more than a hundred thousand spectators each football Saturday; the Detroit Lions, meanwhile, do not. (I know, I know—it's the Lions. That's why their stadium is smaller.) Minor-league arenas attract even fewer spectators. Fans are not only seeking athletic excellence as such—the biggest and fastest players in descending order. Our connection to the athletes is deeper. These student athletes walk the same halls, have the same professors, and sweat the same midterms that we did, however long ago. At the University of Illinois at Urbana—Champaign, where I once taught, the inscription on the statue of Alma Mater reads, "To thy happy children of the future, those of the past send greetings." It's easy to dismiss that sentiment as saccharine, but it gets at an important truth: we are embedded in our cultures and social groups, and we revel in their excellence.

**Persuasive Appeals**
Yankah's description of the scene at the stadium where his "beloved Michigan Wolverines" play can be seen as both an emotional appeal and an ethical appeal. The use of the term "beloved" in reference to a sports team reflects not only an emotional connection between fans and athletes but also his passion as a fan. At the same time, this passage helps establish Yankah's credibility as a sports fan.

6    Paying student athletes erodes that association. If a high-school football prodigy reported that he chose Michigan not for its academic quality, tradition, or beautiful campus but because it outbid all other suitors, a connection to the university's values would be lost. This is not naïve idealism. Auburn fans still bristle at accusations that Cam Newton auctioned them his services; prideful Michigan fans still smart over the sanctions surrounding Chris Webber, and over stinging comments intimating that he might just as well have attended a rival school. These episodes reveal what happens when college sports are

reduced to a market; that this occurs all too often already is no reason to surrender to it.

7   The law plays a critical role here, and the Ninth Circuit's ruling can be a constructive step. It recognizes that the N.C.A.A. is subject to antitrust regulation—unlike, say, Major League Baseball (Greenberg)—and refuses to put a monetary value on college sports. In the future, Congress could, through antitrust and commerce legislation, promote a more just landscape in college and professional sports. Professional leagues, in particular, could be encouraged to invest more seriously in their minor-league programs—the N.B.A. Development League is at least the right idea—and drop the relevant age restrictions. This would mean that the extraordinary few could go pro out of high school, and some other highfliers could enter the developmental leagues, paid whatever the market will bear. College sports might well lose some spectacular stars, but the stars alone were never really the point.

8   None of this would be easy to accomplish, of course, given the money that is at stake, and there would be casualties. Some of the players who might at least have been exposed to college would forgo it entirely. We might lose the story of the exceptional athlete, often poor and dark-skinned, who goes to school solely to play sports but then sees the world widen before him. Nor should we imagine that those who opt for the developmental leagues have made it; minor-league baseball and the lower tiers of European soccer remind us how thankless and poorly compensated (Pilon) such a life can be. But this is

**A Relevant Purpose**
In his opening paragraph and again in paragraph 7, Yankah refers to an important recent legal decision to establish both the timeliness and the relevance of his topic.

**Appropriate Support for Claims**
In paragraph 7, Yankah supports his claims about using antitrust laws to "promote a more just landscape in college and professional sports" by referring to examples from professional baseball and basketball. These examples are likely to be familiar to sports fans and also likely to be seen as credible and appropriate evidence by Yankah's readers.

**Persuasive Appeal**
When essays like this one appear in magazines or newspapers, the writers are generally identified in the byline. Readers who take the time to look at the byline will learn that Yankah is a professor at Cardoza Law School in New York City, which gives him credibility as someone well versed in the law. In paragraph 7, Yankah draws on his expertise to discuss some of the implications of the legal ruling he refers to in the opening paragraph. By implicitly reminding readers of his legal expertise, Yankah is strengthening his ethical appeal.

**Complexity**
In paragraphs 7 and 8, Yankah reviews some of the legal and financial implications of retaining the amateur status of college athletes. His discussion in this passage highlights some of the complexities of the question of whether these athletes should be paid. Yankah also acknowledges some drawbacks to the position he is advocating.

no less true for those who skip college to pursue music or theatre, and, more to the point, there is no reason to think that we wouldn't hear stories of intellectual discovery among slightly less athletically gifted athletes from the same streets. Even if we cannot save sports (or music, or theatre) from its high-risk nature, we can go some way toward making sure that a few elite college programs are not unduly feeding off it.

9    At sports bars, when I hear people dismiss these (or other) ideas for preserving college amateurism, I realize that it's not simply a question of their being overwhelmed by the practical difficulties involved. It is, rather, another manifestation of that corrosive American belief that anything that has value must also have a price. The recent ruling, though, hints at a path ahead, a way to cheer for our student athletes without being held hostage to money, exploitation, racism, or cynicism.

> **Persuasive Appeals.**
> In the concluding paragraph, Yankah reinforces his main logical appeal by restating his belief in the value of amateur athletics as more than monetary. Notice that he also makes a subtle ethical appeal by including an image of him visiting a sports bar, which reinforces his identity as a genuine sports fan. In addition, he uses the image of fans cheering for student athletes, who should not be "held hostage to money, exploitation, racism, or cynicism." This language helps make an emotional appeal to generate sympathy among readers for the athletes, whom Yankah claims to be supporting.

### Works Cited

Crouch, Ian. "The Price of Eligibility at UNC." *The New Yorker*, 24 Oct. 2014, www.newyorker.com/news/daily-comment/north-carolina-academic-scandal.

Greenberg, David. "Baseball's Con Game." *Slate*, 19 July 2002, www.slate.com/articles/news_and_politics/history_lesson/2002/07/baseballs_con_game.html.

Pilon, Mark. "Are Minor Leaguers Paid Legal Wages." *The New Yorker*, 20 Aug. 2015, www.newyorker.com/news/sporting-scene/are-minor-leaguers-paid-legal-wages.

Source: Yankah, Ekow. " Why N.C.A.A. Athletes Shouldn't Be Paid." *The New Yorker*, 14 Oct. 2015, www.newyorker.com/news/sporting-scene/why-ncaa-athletes-shouldnt-be-paid.

## 11

## Questions to Consider:

1. Yankah's essay might be seen as based on deductive reasoning (see the introduction to the essay on pages 349–350). Do you think this was an effective approach to making an argument about this topic? Why or why not? What might have been different about his essay if he had approached it inductively?

2. Using the criteria for appraising evidence described in this chapter (see page 341), evaluate the evidence Yankah uses to support his claims. To what extent does his use of evidence strengthen or weaken his essay?

3. What assumptions do you think Yankah makes about his audience? (Remember that his essay was originally published in the *The New Yorker*, a large-circulation magazine that reaches an international audience.) To what extent do you think his specific persuasive appeals reflect the general nature of that audience? Do you find his appeals persuasive? Explain. What might your answer suggest about the nature of persuasive appeals?

4. In general, how convincing do you find Yankah's argument? Explain, citing specific passages that you find especially effective or ineffective. On the basis of your response to this question, what revisions would you make to his essay?

MindTap®
Reflect on your your understanding of argument.

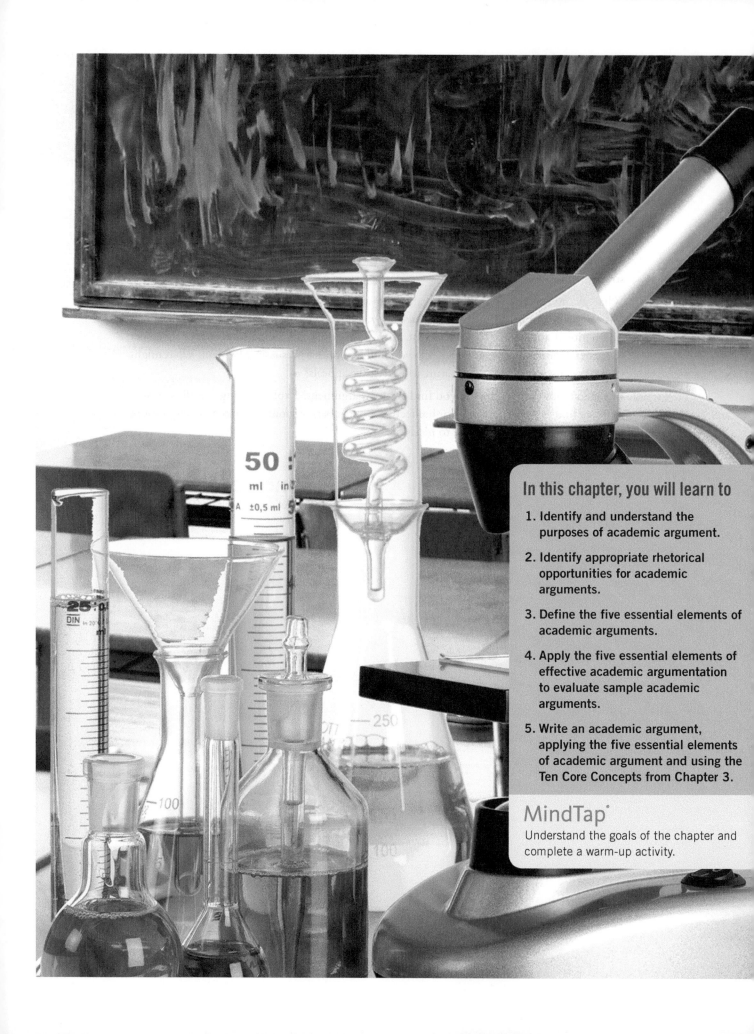

In this chapter, you will learn to

1. Identify and understand the purposes of academic argument.

2. Identify appropriate rhetorical opportunities for academic arguments.

3. Define the five essential elements of academic arguments.

4. Apply the five essential elements of effective academic argumentation to evaluate sample academic arguments.

5. Write an academic argument, applying the five essential elements of academic argument and using the Ten Core Concepts from Chapter 3.

MindTap®

Understand the goals of the chapter and complete a warm-up activity.

# Making Academic Arguments 12

RECENTLY, I WAS ASKED to participate in a panel discussion with several faculty members at my university. The panel was part of a colloquium featuring a special talk by a well-known researcher who studies how children learn to write. After finishing his presentation, the researcher answered questions from the panel members, some of whom challenged his stance on the issues he studies. In the ensuing discussion, the panel members and the researcher sometimes took different positions on the questions that were raised. Some audience members participated as well, posing questions for both the panel and for the researcher and offering their own views.

To a casual observer, the colloquium might have seemed like a discussion of intense disagreements among the participants, many of whom presented their views vigorously. In fact, the panel members, the researcher, and the audience were engaged in a common form of academic argumentation. The point of the discussion was not to convince anyone that the researcher or the panel members were right or wrong about the issues that were raised; rather, the point was to explore those issues so that everyone involved might gain a better understanding of them. In some ways, we all had the same goal: to understand writing better so that we could solve the problems we face in trying to teaching it effectively. We didn't all agree, but we presented our arguments as a way to advance our collective understanding.

Because the primary purpose of most academic arguments is to inquire into an issue, problem, question, event, or phenomenon, the writer presents a position that reflects his or her effort to understand the topic better. For example, an assignment in an organic chemistry course might ask students to identify an unknown substance. For several weeks the students conduct lab tests to determine important chemical properties of the substance and analyze the test results on the basis of what they already know about various chemical substances. At the end of the semester, the students submit a lab report in which they identify the substance, essentially making an argument using their analyses of their lab tests as evidence to support their conclusions about what the substance is.

In such assignments, students develop arguments by exploring their topics. Trying to "win" the argument in such situations makes little sense. The instructor in the chemistry course, for example, already knows what the substance is; he or she is interested in how the students apply their knowledge of chemistry to arrive at their conclusions. In that regard, their conclusions are perhaps less important than the process by which the students arrive at those conclusions. In such a case, an effective argument is largely a matter of how carefully the writer examines the topic and presents his or her position on the topic. In making the argument, students gain a better understanding of the topic and learn important lessons about the academic field—in this case, organic chemistry.

As this example shows, effective academic arguments are a means to deepen and share learning. That doesn't mean that academic arguments are not intense. Sometimes serious disagreements arise as scholars explore important issues and make arguments in which they present provocative or controversial claims. But most academic arguments never rise to such levels of controversy. Instead, arguments are vehicles for inquiry. For students, arguments facilitate learning. Reciting what historians think are the main causes of the Civil War for a history course is one thing; using what historians think to make an effective argument about the main causes of the Civil War is quite another. In making such an argument, you are engaged in genuine inquiry that contributes to your own understanding and perhaps your classmates' as well.

# Occasions for Academic Argumentation

There are many formal occasions for arguments whose purpose is to inquire into issues of importance in various academic disciplines or to the campus community. For example, students in a public policy class might debate various government responses to climate change. Faculty members in a foreign languages department might discuss whether to support a proposal to require all students to take two language courses. An ad hoc committee of students and faculty might hold an open forum in which they express their views about free speech in the wake of an incident that has caused racial tensions on campus. In such instances the participants address important questions and try to solve relevant problems through formal argumentation.

Academic arguments might also take place in less formal ways—for example, classmates working on a project for a philosophy course might defend their differing viewpoints about the usefulness of the assignment, or students in a biology class might debate whether a controversial kind of research should be conducted on their campus. All these examples demonstrate that argument is integral to how students and faculty confront questions or problems that are relevant to their academic work.

---

**FOCUS**     **THE DUAL AUDIENCE FOR ACADEMIC ARGUMENTS**

Many arguments written for college courses or other academic contexts assume a dual audience, even when the assignment seems to define a specific audience. When writing an argument for a college course, you are implicitly writing for a wider audience that will never read your argument: experts in the academic field you are studying. For example, in a psychology course you might be asked to write an argument defending a specific viewpoint about the growing use of medication to treat common behavioral disorders, such attention deficit hyperactivity disorder, in children. Your immediate audience is clear: the course instructor. But you are nevertheless expected to follow the conventions for argument in psychology as if your audience included psychologists. Part of the purpose of such an assignment is to help students understand how knowledge is made in the field and how ideas and information are exchanged and debated by scholars in the field. So when writing an academic argument, you are playing the role of an expert in an academic field and therefore you are expected to learn how to make an appropriate argument in that field.

---

What makes academic arguments different from arguments in other contexts, such as political elections, the opinion pages of newspapers, or popular blogs, is that academic arguments are always assumed to be part of the ongoing effort to advance knowledge and understanding in various fields (see Focus: "The Dual Audience for Academic Arguments" on page 358).

Academic arguments, then, are

- occasions for learning;
- opportunities to solve relevant problems; and
- invitations to participate in conversations about important issues in academic disciplines.

12

---

**EXERCISE 12A** | **OCCASIONS FOR ARGUMENT**

1. Identify an issue that interests you from one of your courses. Briefly describe the issue and why it interests you. Now, in a few sentences, identify two or three arguments you might make about that issue.

2. Take one of the arguments you identified for Question #1 and describe how you might make the same argument in a non-academic context—for example, on a social media site or in a letter to the editor of your local newspaper. In what ways might the arguments differ? What might account for those differences?

3. If you have attended a speech, lecture, presentation, or similar event in which a speaker made an argument, describe the situation and the argument that was made. What was the speaker's position? Did you agree or disagree with that position? Why or why not? What do you think you gained by listening to the speaker make his or her argument?

---

# Understanding Academic Argument: A Case Study

Academic arguments often address complex issues that require students to examine a subject—and their own perspectives about the subject—in depth. Such examination can deepen students' understanding of the subject. Sometimes, that journey of inquiry can be surprising—as some of my own students recently discovered.

The final project in one of the courses I teach requires the students, who are studying to become secondary school teachers, to resolve a dilemma involving an important issue in education. Working in small groups, the students are given a scenario that presents the dilemma; each group must propose and defend an appropriate solution to the dilemma. One of the scenarios involves a high school social studies teacher who ignites a controversy by asking his students to examine recent wars in which the U.S. has been involved, including the Vietnam War and the wars in Iraq and Afghanistan. The teacher assigns readings that present various arguments for and against each war and encourages his students to explore some difficult questions about the responsibilities of citizens and their government. The teacher, a military veteran, believes that the primary purpose of social studies is not to teach the facts of history but to prepare students for the challenges of citizenship in a democracy. He claims he does not promote a particular view about the wars studied in his course; instead, he wants to encourage his students to think carefully about what it means to be a citizen in a time of war. Many parents, however, see his teaching methods as anti-American and complain to the school administrators. These parents believe that social studies should not raise questions about American involvement in current wars but instead should promote a sense of patriotism among students. They demand that the teacher stop teaching lessons on the recent wars and be formally reprimanded.

The students in my course who were given this scenario found that developing a solution to the controversy turned out to be a much more complicated process than they had expected. They debated vigorously among themselves for several weeks about whether the teacher violated any rules of professional conduct and whether he was protected by his constitutional right to free speech. They argued about what rights the parents had in this situation. Their debates raised many hard questions: Who determines what the children should be taught in a social studies class? The school? The teacher? The state? What is the purpose of social studies education? Should students learn to question their government, or should social studies promote patriotism? Is it wrong to criticize the government when American soldiers are fighting and dying in a war? For that matter, what is the purpose of high school education? Who decides what should or should not be taught—and why?

TED ALJIBE/Staff/AFP/Getty Images

In the end, my students came to an uneasy consensus and developed a solution based on the argument that although social studies should promote critical inquiry, teachers have a responsibility to leave their own views out of the classroom so that their students are not influenced by the teacher's political beliefs. Here's how my students stated their thesis:

> *The teacher should be allowed to present the material on the Iraq war and other wars, but he should not disclose his personal opinion on this matter to his students.*

To support their position they presented an argument based on certain principles of education and citizenship. They cited decisions made in similar controversies, and they consulted position papers from professional organizations as well as the state standards for teaching history. In short, they explored their subject in all its complexity to make their case.

Not everyone in the group agreed with the argument made in the final paper, however. Here's what one student wrote in a reflection on the assignment:

*The final paper is not what I would have come up with on my own, and it isn't necessarily the product I would like it to be. There are parts of me in it, there are some parts I don't like as much, and there are contributions I didn't think of that make it better.*

Still, although the students disagreed about the main argument they presented in their final paper, they all valued the experience of developing that argument. Another member of the group wrote,

*It is important to note that, although our group did agree on many aspects of our scenario, we never actually reached a unanimous decision regarding the teacher's rights as an educator. While at first this seemed like an obstacle, I found that our differing viewpoints made for an excellent approach to creating a solution. Because we didn't all agree, we were able to consider many different sides of the situation that may have otherwise gone unnoticed.*

For this student, the arguments that group members made to one another in their effort to reach consensus contributed to their own learning. Yet another student was still exploring these questions in her final evaluation:

*After weeks of preparing and planning, our group was still unable to come up with one definitive answer. We came to a conclusion for the sake of the project, but on an individual level, we never agreed upon a final recommendation (only further pointing to the intricacies of our scenario). Although our group decided that the teacher should not disclose his personal opinion about the Iraq War or other wars, it seems virtually impossible to completely eliminate all judgment, especially when lessons and topics discussed in the classroom are based, to some degree, on the opinion of the teacher.*

For these students, argument was the vehicle for an in-depth inquiry into a complex set of questions. Although they were able to reach a consensus for their final paper, that consensus did not necessarily reflect the individual views of the group members. But that wasn't really important, because each member gained insight into the complicated issues at hand; each student deepened his or her own understanding as a result of the process of argumentation, regardless of whether they agreed with the conclusions presented in the final paper. Moreover, through their research, their debates among themselves, and the development of their argument in their final paper, they became part of a much larger conversation about important issues in education.

My students' experience underscores the main purpose of academic argumentation—to inquire into a topic in order to understand it better—and exemplifies the **essential elements of academic arguments**:

- **A clear main point.** Although academic arguments usually address complicated subjects involving social, cultural, political, historical, theoretical, or philosophical questions, writers nevertheless present a clear main point.

- **Relevance.** An effective academic argument addresses issues that others interested in the subject find relevant. Arguments contribute to academic inquiry when they address issues that matter to the academic field.

- **Appropriate support.** Academic arguments are characterized by specific conventions governing the kind of evidence or support that is considered appropriate and persuasive. Part of the task of writing an effective academic argument is understanding how to follow those conventions and use them to meet the needs of your specific rhetorical situation. (Also, see "Appraising and Using Evidence" on pages 341–344 in Chapter 11.)

- **Complexity.** Because curiosity, a willingness to question, and the desire to understand are hallmarks of academic inquiry, arguments that acknowledge the complexity of a topic are generally more effective than those that oversimplify the topic or reduce it to an either-or proposition. The most effective academic arguments delve deeply into their subjects and expose the complexity of the issues at hand.

- **Openness to ideas and alternative perspectives.** Arguments are stronger when they exhibit the writer's openness to other ideas and viewpoints, which reflects a desire to learn about the subject at hand. Dismissing or ignoring valid positions or claims simply because you disagree with them is likely to weaken your argument. On the other hand, addressing opposing viewpoints might enable you to develop counterarguments to strengthen your own argument.

You might notice that the first four of these elements are the same as four of the five essential features of argument in general that are discussed in Chapter 11 (see pages 348–349). That's because academic argument is more likely to adhere to the conventions of traditional argumentation than either arguments in public discourse (Chapter 13) or proposals (Chapter 14). Moreover, the fifth element discussed here (openness to ideas and alternative perspectives) reflects the main purpose of most academic argumentation, which is to understand the issue at hand and contribute to the academic field's collective knowledge about that issue. Neither arguments in public discourse nor proposals necessarily share that main sense of purpose.

One last thing to keep in mind about academic argument: Academic arguments also include persuasive appeals, which is one of the essential features of argument discussed in Chapter 11 (see pages 331–341). However, most academic arguments tend to reply on logical appeals (see page 336). As a result, it is usually less important for writers to explore persuasive appeals when they are writing arguments in academic contexts as compared to arguments in public discourse.

---

**EXERCISE 12B** | **UNDERSTANDING ACADEMIC ARGUMENT**

1. If you have ever written an essay for a class in which you had to make an argument, reflect on what you might have learned by writing that argument. What was the topic? What argument did you make? What do you think you learned about your topic—or about argument in general—by writing that essay? What do you think your experience suggests about argument as a way to learn?

2. The case study presented in this chapter describes a situation in which a group students collaborated to make an argument about a subject on which they didn't all agree. In a sense, writing their argument together was a process of negotiating differences and solving a problem they all faced, even though they disagreed. Think of a situation in which you or someone you know faced a similar challenge: having to work together with others to solve a problem about which they disagreed. In a few paragraphs describe that situation and how it was resolved. What role did argument play in that situation?

3. In a group of your classmates, share what you wrote for Question #2. Look for similarities and differences in these experiences. Try to determine what the points of disagreement were in each case. What do you think the experiences described in your essays suggest about solving problems? What might they suggest about argumentation?

# Reading Academic Arguments

The readings in this section illustrate the elements of effective academic arguments. As you read, be mindful of the fact that effective arguments in an academic setting are often very specialized yet still relevant to a larger, non-academic audience. Consider these questions:

| A clear main point | • What is the main argument?<br>• What is the author's main goal in making this argument? |
| --- | --- |
| Relevance | • Why is this argument relevant now?<br>• What is the context for this argument? What audience is addressed?<br>• What assumptions does the author make about the audience's interest in this topic? |
| Appropriate support | • What evidence is presented to support the author's claims?<br>• How persuasive is the author's support for the main argument?<br>• To what extent is the evidence appropriate for the topic and intended audience? |
| Complexity | • To what extent has the author explored this topic in sufficient depth?<br>• In what ways does the argument take into account possible complicating factors?<br>• How does the author avoid oversimplifying the issues? |
| Openness to ideas | • To what extent does the author consider alternative points of view on the topic?<br>• Has the author left out or misrepresented any important considerations that might complicate his or her position? |

## MindTap®
Read these academic argument examples. Highlight and take notes online. Additional readings are also available online.

## Crime and Punishment
### by Bruce Western

*Social scientists, law enforcement professionals, and lawmakers in the U.S. have long debated the question of how best to reduce crime. Soaring crime rates in the 1960s and 1970s pushed state and federal governments to adopt "get-tough" policies that increased prison terms for many crimes. As Bruce Western notes in the following essay, this approach resulted in a dramatic increase in prison populations in the U.S., which now has the world's highest rate of incarceration. Many politicians and law enforcement experts argue that this high rate of incarceration is the reason for the significant reduction in crime rates in the U.S. in the past several decades. Western, a professor of government at Harvard University, disagrees. In his essay, which appeared on the* Boston Review *website in 2012, he reviews statistical data complicating the view that high rates of incarceration are responsible for reducing crime. Instead, he argues, the U.S. can—and should—decrease its prison population without weakening the ongoing effort to fight crime. Western's essay is a good example of a strong but measured argument that relies on a careful analysis of evidence to address a complex problem that experts on all sides of the debate hope to solve.*

### Talking About This Reading

**Aaron Goldberg (student):** This reading was pretty clear cut in explaining this topic. But I was left wondering, what would be the best way to reverse the cycle of mass imprisonment that the author describes?

**Bob Yagelski:** Aaron, your question—which is an important one—implicitly addresses the matter of an author's purpose in an academic argument. We often expect an author to provide solutions in an argument about a difficult problem such as fighting crime. In this case, though, Western's main purpose is not to offer a particular solution but to argue against incarceration as the main way to reduce crime. He does point to solutions in paragraph 7, but we should remember that his purpose is not to argue in favor of them.

By the end of the 1990s, policymakers and police were celebrating the great American crime decline. Rates of murder, robbery, and rape had fallen across cities and suburbs, among rich and poor. Less appreciated perhaps is the continuing decline in crime in the 2000s. In every state fewer incidences of serious violence and property crime were reported to police in 2010 than in 2000. The murder rate is now the lowest it has been since the early 1960s.

Research on the 1990s traces the crime drop to better policing; to a subsiding crack trade, which, at its height in the late 1980s, unleashed a wave of murderous violence; and to increasing prison populations. However, some researchers find the apparently large effect of imprisonment controversial. Driven by tough-on-crime policy and intensified drug enforcement, prison populations grew unchecked from the early 1970s until the last decade, but crime rates fluctuated without any clear trend. By the early 2000s incarceration rates had grown to extraordinary levels in poor communities. Whole generations of young, mostly minority and poorly educated men were being locked up, leading to the United States' current status as the world's largest jailer, in both absolute and relative terms.

Prisons may have reduced crime a little in the short run, but at the current scale the negative effects of incarceration are likely to outweigh the positive. Commonplace incarceration among poor young men fuels cynicism about the legal system, destabilizes families, and reduces economic opportunities.

## DON'T THROW AWAY THE KEY

Between 2000 and 2010, the crime rate in the United States dropped by nearly 18.9%. Some observers credit that drop to rising rates of imprisonment. But crime rates in states that reduced incarceration between 2000 and 2010 fell just as much as the rates in states that increased their prison populations.

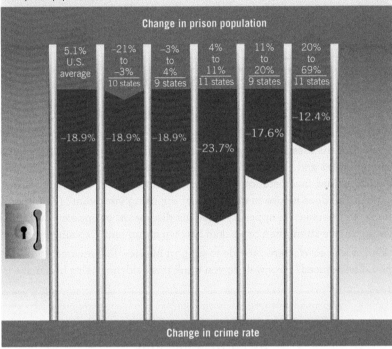

**Change in prison population**

| 5.1% U.S. average | −21% to −3% 10 states | −3% to 4% 9 states | 4% to 11% 11 states | 11% to 20% 9 states | 20% to 69% 11 states |

−18.9%    −18.9%    −18.9%    −23.7%    −17.6%    −12.4%

**Change in crime rate**

Source: Bureau of Justice Statistics and FBI Uniform Crime Reports. National Imprisonment Data includes Federal Prisoners. Data Assembled by Catherine Sirois, Harvard University.

Over the last few years, the rate of prison population growth in the states finally began to slow. (The growth in federal prisons has continued unabated.) As the political salience of crime declined and the cost of prisons ballooned, policymakers and the courts turned to alternatives to incarceration. Twelve states reduced imprisonment in the last decade. These states diverted more drug offenders to probation and community programs, and parolees were less likely to return to the penitentiary. All the states that reduced imprisonment also recorded reductions in crime. For instance, between 2000 and 2010, New York cut imprisonment by about a fifth, and the crime rate fell by about 25 percent.

States that raised their imprisonment rates averaged similar reductions in crime, though the declines show a lot of variation. Where prisons grew by more than 20 percent, crime fell by a little less than the national average. And in some places—such as Maine, Arkansas, and West Virginia—crime barely fell at all.

It seems clear, then, that ever-increasing rates of incarceration are not necessary to reduce crime. Although it's difficult to say precisely how much the growing scale of punishment reduced crime in the 1990s, the crime decline has been sustained even as imprisonment fell in many states through the 2000s.

These data are good news for governors who want to cut prison budgets. But cuts alone may not work. Policymakers should study cases such as New York and New Jersey. These states cut imprisonment while building new strategies for sentencing, parole and after-prison programs. *(Continued)*

The era of mass incarceration is not over, but there are signs of reversal. Given the social costs of incarceration—concentrated in poor neighborhoods—these are heartening trends. The last decade shows that public safety can flourish, even as punishment is curtailed.

Source: Western, Bruce. "Crime and Punishment." *Boston Review*, 1 Mar. 2012, www.bostonreview.net/bruce-western-crime-rate-prison-population-america.

---

## EXERCISE 12C   EXPLORING CRIME AND PUNISHMENT

1. How would you summarize Western's main argument? What makes his argument relevant now? How effectively do you think he establishes the importance of this issue?

2. Western begins his essay by describing a point of view about the relationship between incarceration rates and crime rates that he opposes. Why does he disagree with those who believe higher incarceration rates reduce crime? What kind of appeals (ethical, logical, pathetic) does he use in refuting that opposing viewpoint? (See Chapter 11 for a discussion of persuasive appeals.) Does his discussion of opposing viewpoints and counterarguments strengthen or weaken his own argument? Explain.

3. What evidence does Western provide to support his view that incarceration rates in the U.S. should be reduced? How well do you think this evidence helps him make is case?

## Fulfilling Her Mother's Dream
### by Patricia McGuire

*Debates about the value of a college degree are not new, but they intensified after the Great Recession of 2007-2009, which resulted in fewer job opportunities for college graduates at a time when student loan debt was increasing. These circumstances made the decision to attend college an even more difficult one for many students, especially those from low-income households, such as the one described in the following essay by Patricia McGuire. McGuire, the president of Trinity Washington College in Washington D.C., acknowledges the challenges of attending college for students like the ones at her school, but she also rejects the idea that the primary value of college is a better job and higher income. As she notes in her essay, graduates from her college do earn good incomes, but she believes the real value of their education cannot be quantified on the basis of salaries. Instead, she makes a more traditional case that college provides a variety of social and intellectual benefits that enable graduates to adapt to a changing workplace. She also argues that these benefits are particularly important for low-income students, who would otherwise have few prospects for a prosperous life.*

*McGuire's essay was published in 2013 in* The Huffington Post, *an online news site that reaches a wide audience, and although she is herself an accomplished academic, she tailors her argument to a general audience. For example, she employs various persuasive appeals that tend to be rare in academic argument. Nevertheless, her essay includes the essential elements of academic argument and illustrates how scholars engage in argument about issues of importance to people outside their academic fields.*

· · · · · · · · · · · · · · · · · · · · · · · · · · · · · · · · · · · · · · · · ·

### Talking About This Reading

**Imani Samson (student):** I had trouble with some of the language in this essay. For instance, I didn't understand what the author meant by expressions like "a socket wrench approach to collegiate learning as job training," or "broad-brush basing."

**Bob Yagelski:** Interestingly, Imani, these expressions are not the kind of specialized scholarly terminology that sometimes gives students trouble; rather, this is more vernacular language that the author used to address a non-academic audience. The expressions might be unfamiliar to you because they are not as common today as they once were, so try searching the Internet for them. Also, Step #4 of "A Strategy for Reading Scholarly Texts" in Chapter 19 (page 620) offers advice for identifying key terms that might help you make sense of these expressions.

· · · · · · · · · · · · · · · · · · · · · · · · · · · · · · · · · · · · · · · · · · ·

Her mother never made it past the second grade in her native Guatemala. But education was a relentless theme in her mother's daily lessons, a big dream for her children. This week, as Leticia (not her real name) enrolls as a freshwoman at Trinity Washington University, she fulfills her mother's lifelong dream for her daughter to go to college. Leticia now bears the hopes and dreams of her entire family for social advancement and economic progress.

Leticia's story is one of hundreds of similarly compelling life journeys among the women starting college at Trinity this fall, where we enroll a distinctively ambitious population of young women with serious life challenges, as well as older women and men who are resuming long-deferred dreams to finish college degrees. Our students are just like hundreds of thousands more women and men of all ages from challenging backgrounds who will start college all over the country this year. Some, like Leticia, are immigrants who have overcome unfathomable barriers of language, money, culture, violence, illness, discrimination and sheer fear to make it to opening day. Others, like my student Renee (also not her real name), grew up on the mean streets of far southeast D.C., coping with parental incarceration, drug use, hunger and homelessness while helping to raise siblings even while finishing high school and gaining acceptance to college.

But now, just as Leticia, Renee and so many students like them are celebrating the triumph of starting college this fall, in other quarters some very well-educated, well-off, elite pundits, tech savants and politicos are denouncing the whole idea of college as possibly not worth the time, effort and money (Biddle; Delbanco; Nelson). These are people who already received their college degrees but now seem hell-bent on discouraging others from doing the same. A relentless drumbeat of negativity about college right now, loosely grouped under headlines screaming, "Is College Worth It?", is a pernicious discouragement to the ambitions of rising generations of college students from the very populations that soon will be the majority in America (Matthews). Why is it that even as new populations of low-income African-American and Hispanic students enter higher education in even greater numbers, the new mantra of the elite commentariat is that maybe we need more job training, less Shakespeare and more socket wrenches?

To be sure, higher education has significant challenges that we must address quickly and with a genuine commitment to innovation. Some colleges and universities do cost too much, and some spend entirely too much time and money on the

*(Continued)*

wrong things—immensely expensive athletics programs, defense of scandals, feathering executive nests on the student dollar. We certainly should be accountable for our outcomes, and should not blink in the face of thoughtful scrutiny, which is not the same as broad-brush bashing. Scandals grab headlines and make for juicy exposes about colleges and universities. But those stories, however many newspapers they might sell (and I won't mention the fact that many of the critics hail from the print media industry, which has its own considerable challenges), must not be used as some kind of bizarre proof that all of higher education is a disreputable enterprise.

Some critics of higher education today advocate for replacement of classroom-based instruction with online learning, with the phenomenon known as the "MOOC" urged on us as a more cost effective (meaning "cheaper") solution to rising costs (McGuire). The MOOC—massive open online course—is a concept that has been with education for many years in other forms, e.g., books on tape, cassette recordings of famous lectures, etc. (Kolowich). Libraries as old as the Royal Library of Alexandria were probably the original MOOC. Broad access to learned lectures and treatises is a concept as old as Socrates arguing with his students under the proverbial tree about the need to liberate humanity from the caves of ignorance.

Like libraries, CD-Roms and other learning aids, MOOCs certainly have their place in the large reservoir of knowledge and learning tools. But unless we are willing to concede that all learning can be reduced to video illustrations—much as I turn to YouTube to learn how to fix my clogged bathroom drain (honestly, don't you want to be sure that your plumber or your brain surgeon received "live" instruction before performing their procedures?)—they are no substitute for the significantly transformative interpersonal experience of teaching and learning in classrooms and in co-curricular programming and personal exploration that colleges and universities provide every day.

Leticia, Renee and all of my students deserve better than MOOCs for their primary collegiate experience. They need and deserve the same kind of robust teaching, "live" faculty dialogue and richly supportive campus-based experience as my classmates in the Baby Boomer and subsequent generations have enjoyed.

For many if not most of us in the Boomer generation, college made us the success stories we are today—I would certainly not be Trinity's president today were it not for my own great education here and at Georgetown Law School. My parents did not go to college, but despite constant money worries, they set attending college as a high bar for their children, and the federal student loan program helped us along the way. In this small way, I can well understand and empathize with the great hunger of Leticia and Renee to prove that their families, too, can be part of the great American success story that includes earning college degrees as the ticket to economic and social success.

The earning power of a college degree is clear (Longley). College graduates earn more than twice the lifetime earnings of high school graduates, more than a million dollars and even more in many cases. At Trinity, where the median family income of our entering students is just about $30,000 in any given year, ten years after graduation more than 90% are employed with average salaries of about $65,000. Those who are not employed are in graduate school, caring for families or retired.

My students need and deserve more than a socket wrench approach to collegiate learning as job training. College graduates must know and be able to do far more than what the specific skill sets of any particular jobs require today. Who among us in the Class of 1974 learned the advanced technological skills we need for executive success today? We learned almost nothing about computers back then, but we did learn how to keep on learning, which may be the most important skill a good college will impart.

A great college education does not simply equip Leticia, Renee and others for success in this moment and to get first jobs, but rather, if we do it right, we will ensure their ability to be lifelong self-driven learners, to have the ability to keep learning, to discover new knowledge independently, to analyze and synthesize new material continuously, to write clearly and persuasively, to know how to use quantitative analysis effectively, even to create new knowledge through their own advanced intellectual powers. There's no "college scorecard" that can measure these kinds of outcomes with any justice to this kind of learning. And certainly no set of metrics can measure the way in which a great college education also engenders deep personal satisfaction by illuminating the joys of the aesthetic life in the humanities in particular, the place where knowledge and appreciation of great philosophy, art and literature are not mere sideshows but essential components of the intellectual and even spiritual fulfillment of truly learned people.

Leticia, Renee and all of my students entering Trinity this year have the right to make their families proud by earning that degree, even as I did so long ago. They will change the fortunes of their families by acquiring the learning and credentials that will ensure lifelong economic security. Their achievements will propel the achievements of their children. No evidence makes college more "worth it" than the improved conditions of families that results from making advanced education a priority across the generations.

By fulfilling the dream of her mother, Leticia is the hope of her family and should be the pride of our nation.

## Works Cited

Biddle, Sam. "Peter Thiel Just Paid 20 Kids $100k to Not Go to College." *ValleyWag*, 9 May 2013, valleywag.gawker.com/peter-thiel-just-paid-20-kids-100k-to-not-go-to-colleg-498525048.

Delbanco, Andrew. "Illiberal Arts." Review of *Is College Worth It?* by William J. Bennett and David Wilezol, and *College (Un)Bound*, by Jeffrey J. Selingo. *The New York Times*, 21 June 2013, nyti.ms/19rq6FE.

Kolowich, Steve. "The MOOC 'Revolution' May Not Be as Disruptive as Some Had Imagined." *The Chronicle of Higher Education*, 8 Aug. 2013, chronicle.com/article/MOOCs-May-Not-Be-So-Disruptive/140965/.

Longley, Robert. "College Degree Nearly Doubles Annual Earnings." *About News & Issues*, 15 July 2013, usgovinfo.about.com/od/censusandstatistics/a/collegepays.htm.

Matthews, Dylan. "Going to College is Worth It—Even If You Drop Out." *The Washington Post*, 10 June 2013, www.washingtonpost.com/news/wonk/wp/2013/06/10/going-to-college-is-worth-it-even-if-you-drop-out/.

McGuire, Patricia. "Got MOOC?" *HuffPost College*, 27 Nov. 2012, www.huffingtonpost.com/patricia-mcguire/got-mooc_b_2195053.html.

Nelson, Libby A. "The Bennett Hypothesis Returns." *Inside Higher Ed*, 20 June 2013, www.insidehighered.com/news/2013/06/20/bill-bennett-writes-new-book-whether-college-worth-it.

1. McGuire uses her own experience as well as her students' experiences as evidence to support her argument about the value of college. How effective do you find her use of experience as evidence to support her claims? Do you think this evidence is appropriate for her rhetorical situation? Why or why not? What other kinds of evidence does she provide to support her claims? Do you think this evidence is more or less effective than her use of own experience as evidence? Explain.

2. How would you characterize McGuire's tone in this essay? Is her tone appropriate for her subject matter? For her rhetorical situation? Do you think her tone strengthens or weakens her essay? Explain, citing specific passages from her essay to support your answer.

3. Identify the persuasive appeals that McGuire uses in her essay. Do you think her use of persuasive appeals is appropriate for her subject and intended audience? Why or why not? To what extent do you think her use of persuasive appeals is effective in supporting her argument?

## Mark Zuckerberg's Theory of Privacy
### by Michael Zimmer

*As more and more people share more of their lives online, the distinction between public and private is increasingly blurred. Nowhere is this tension between the public and private more evident than on Facebook, the giant social media platform launched in 2004 by a Harvard University student named Mark Zuckerberg. Almost immediately, Facebook faced criticisms about its policies regarding the privacy of its users' information. Today, as Michael Zimmer notes in the following essay, Facebook remains at the center of ongoing debates about what information should be private and who controls that information. That's because no other social media platform has as many users or as great an impact as Facebook. For Zimmer, a professor in the School of Information Studies at the University of Wisconsin at Milwaukee, the sheer size of its user base makes Facebook an important subject of study when it comes to understanding how social media can influence our views about privacy. Zimmer has carefully analyzed the public statements and writings of Zuckerberg, Facebook's founder and CEO, to understand Zuckerberg's own beliefs about privacy. As you'll see, Zimmer uses the results of his analysis as the basis for his argument about the impact of Facebook on privacy. In this regard, his essay is a good example of how a writer incorporates in-depth analysis into an argument—not only to strengthen that argument but also to understand the issue at hand more fully. In making his argument, Zimmer, whose essay was published in* The Washington Post *in 2014, raises complicated and difficult questions about how much control individuals can and should exert over their private information when they use social media platforms like Facebook.*

. . . . . . . . . . . . . . . . . . . . . . . . . . . . . . . . . . . . . . . . . .

### Talking About This Reading

**Reesha Jackson (student)** The thesis of this article seemed to change. At first, the author discussed the size of Facebook and its success. But the topic seemed to change to privacy and then to Zuckerberg's principles. At the end, the author seemed to focus on his own hopes about Facebook's policies.

**12**

. . . . . . . . . . . . . . . . . . . . . . . . . . . . . . . . . . . . . . . . . . .

Ten years ago, a 19-year-old Mark Zuckerberg sat at a computer in his Harvard dorm room and launched thefacebook.com. The goal, according to a 2009 Zuckerberg blog post commemorating Facebook's 200 millionth user, was "to create a richer, faster way for people to share information about what was happening around them" (Logan). If you believe the clumsy collegiate dating scenes in the movie "The Social Network," however, Zuckerberg's motivation for creating what has become the world's largest social networking platform was, at least in part, to meet girls.

He has definitely met the first goal. (He's also reportedly happily married, so the second one seems to have worked out for him, too.) Today, Facebook has more than 1 billion active users who, each day, share nearly 5 billion items, upload 350 million photos and click the "like" button more than 4.5 billion times. Facebook is the world's most popular social networking service and the second-most visited Web site. Only Google gets more visitors daily.

All that ubiquity challenges how we think about what should be private, and what we broadcast to our "friends"—a term that now includes anyone we happen to remember from high school, that temp job from a few years ago, or last night's party.

With every new product launch, from News Feed to the doomed Beacon advertising play, it seemed Facebook would wait for the inevitable negative reaction on privacy, then announce minimal changes without fundamentally altering the new feature. It would explain away the fuss with careful spin: "We are listening to our users," or "We look forward to your feedback." Each time, the people at Facebook reassured us all they really want to do is make "the world more open and connected."

In 2011, I found myself at Facebook's Palo Alto, Calif., headquarters for a gathering of the Future of Privacy Forum, a Washington-based privacy think tank. We met a number of Facebook engineers, advertising managers and public policy executives. All these Facebook employees were being asked about privacy concerns, in a room full of privacy advocates, but not one person ever uttered the word "privacy" in their responses to us. Instead, they talked about "user control" or "user options" or promoted the "openness of the platform." It was as if a memo had been circulated that morning instructing them never to use the word "privacy."

Sitting in that windowed conference room, with views into the open-plan office where dozens of Facebook employees were coding away, shaping this powerful social networking platform, I wondered: Does Mark Zuckerberg think anything should be private? Or does he think all information—photos, favorite movies, political views— wants to be publicly available for everyone, especially advertisers, to see? I didn't get a chance to ask him. Instead, I created the Zuckerberg Files, an archive of all the

*(Continued)*

public utterances of the Facebook creator. It includes blog posts, letters to shareholders, media interviews, public appearances and product presentations—nearly 100,000 words of the hoodie-ed wunderkind sharing his vision. We're just starting to analyze the archive, but already we can pull out three principles that appear to be at the core of Zuckerberg's philosophy of privacy.

### Information wants to be shared.

Updating the 1960s techno-activist slogan "information wants to be free," Zuckerberg clearly believes that "information wants to be shared," and that the world will be a better place if we start sharing more information about ourselves.

While comments from Zuckerberg in 2004 and 2005 point to a desire to simply position Facebook as a "really cool college directory," as the social network grew, so did his vision. In a 2006 blog post apologizing for the controversial rollout of the News Feed feature, Zuckerberg described his motivation this way: "When I made Facebook two years ago my goal was to help people understand what was going on in their world a little better." A focus on "helping people become more open, sharing more information" started to emerge in Zuckerberg's rhetoric by 2008. And by 2010, in an opinion piece in *The Washington Post*, Zuckerberg argued that sharing more information—your photos, your opinions, your birthday, for example—would make the world a better place: "If people share more, the world will become more open and connected. And a world that's more open and connected is a better world" (Zuckerberg).

### Privacy must be overcome.

In his initial public comments about what was then thefacebook, in a Feb. 9, 2004, article in the Harvard *Crimson*, when Facebook was only five days old, Zuckerberg bragged about the site's "pretty intensive privacy options" (Tabak). He also acknowledged that he hoped the privacy options would help to restore his tarnished reputation following student outrage over his earlier Web site, that hot-or-not-inspired Facemash—uproar that was well-depicted in "The Social Network."

From the start, Zuckerberg knew that privacy would be a significant factor in Facebook's success. He regularly mentions the site's "extensive privacy settings" in blog posts and interviews during the first few years of operation. But in many ways, Zuckerberg appears to view privacy as a barrier to the openness that his first principle demands.

This is most evident in a 2008 interview at the Web 2.0 Summit, when he noted, "four years ago, when Facebook was getting started, most people didn't want to put up any information about themselves on the Internet. . . . So, we got people through this really big hurdle of wanting to put up their full name, or real picture, mobile phone number" (Batelle). Later in this interview, Zuckerberg predicted that the amount of information people will share online will double each year, and the best strategy for Facebook is to be "pushing that forward."

### Control is the new privacy.

When Zuckerberg does talk seriously about privacy, he almost always cites control. Zuckerberg's apology for the launch of News Feed notes that his original vision for Facebook included the fact that users must "have control over whom they shared [their] information with." His response to backlash over a change in the site's terms of service in 2009 was aptly titled, "On Facebook, People Own and Control Their Information." That statement doesn't mention the word "privacy," but instead declares, "Our philosophy that people own their information and control who they share it with has remained constant" (Chan). In an interview with *Time* magazine in 2010 Zuckerberg declares: "What people want isn't complete privacy. It isn't that they want secrecy. It's that they want control over what they share and what they don't" (Stengel).

The problem with Zuckerberg's philosophy of privacy, of course, is that over Facebook's 10-year history, users' ability to control their information has largely decreased. Default settings lean toward making information public, and new advertising and third-party platforms are increasingly spreading users' information beyond their direct control.

On Feb. 18, 2004, only two weeks after Facebook's launch, Zuckerberg noted with surprise that the site had already attracted more than 4,300 users. It was nearly impossible to predict that 10 years later his creation would be used by more than 1 billion across the planet. And it would be foolish to try to guess where Facebook will take us 10 years from now. In an interview on the "Today" show, Zuckerberg reflected, "When I look back over the last 10 years, one of the questions that I ask myself is, 'Why were we the ones to help do this?' And I think a lot of what it comes down to is, we just cared more" ("Mark Zuckerberg"). Perhaps he does care more. I just hope he starts to care more about privacy as well in the next 10 years.

## Works Cited

Batelle, John. Interview with Mark Zuckerberg. *Sweet Speeches Alpha*. Sweetspeeches.com, 7 Nov. 2008, www.sweetspeeches.com/s/1845-mark-zuckerberg-web-2-0-summit-facebook-ceo-mark-zuckerberg.

Chan, Kathy H. "On Facebook, People Own and Control Their Information." *Facebook*, 16 Feb. 2009, 2:09 p.m., www.facebook.com/notes/facebook/on-facebook-people-own-and-control-their-information/54434097130.

Logan, Becca. "200 Million Strong." *Facebook*, 8 Apr. 2009, 6:27 a.m., www.facebook.com/notes/72353897130.

"Mark Zuckerberg on Why Facebook Succeeded: 'We just cared more'." Interview. *Today*, National Broadcasting Company, 31 Jan. 2014, www.today.com/money/mark-zuckerberg-why-facebook-succeeded-we-just-cared-more-2D12028484.

Tabak, Alan J. "Hundreds Register for New Facebook Website." *The Harvard Crimson*, 9 Feb. 2004, www.thecrimson.com/article/2004/2/9/hundreds-register-for-new-facebook-website/.

Stengel, Richard. "An Interview with Mark Zuckerberg." *Time*, 15 Dec. 2010, content.time.com/time/specials/packages/article/0,28804,2036683_2037109,00.html.

Zuckerberg, Mark. "From Facebook, Answering Privacy Concerns With New Settings." *The Washington Post*, 24 May 2010, www.washingtonpost.com/wp-dyn/content/article/2010/05/23/AR2010052303828.html?tid=a_inl.

12

# Writing Academic Arguments

You will encounter argument throughout your academic career: in class discussions of course topics, in assigned readings, and in writing assignments. In some cases, these arguments will relate to important issues that go well beyond your courses. For example, in an economics class you might read several scholarly arguments about the problem of student loan debt; at the same time, you might hear a guest on a television news show make an argument in favor of subsidizing student loans or read a blog on a newspaper website in which the writer argues against such subsidies. These examples underscore the central role argument can play in your college work as well as in your life beyond the classroom.

This section provides a framework for developing your own academic arguments using the Ten Core Concepts. Each step described here corresponds to a step in Chapter 3. As you develop your project, keep in mind the five essential features of argument that are explained in Chapter 11:

1. A clear main point. Present a clear main point related to your position on the issue at hand:
   - What is the main point you will make in this argument?
   - What purpose do you hope to achieve in making this argument?

2. A relevant purpose. Identify the relevance of your argument for your rhetorical situation:
   - What makes your argument relevant to your intended audience?
   - Why is your argument relevant now?

3. Appropriate support for claims. Support your claims with sufficient and appropriate evidence:
   - What evidence do you present to support your main claim and supporting claims?
   - What makes this evidence appropriate in the context of your rhetorical situation? Is your evidence sufficient to support your claims?

4. Complexity. Present your argument so that it reflects the complexity of your subject:
   - Have you explored the subject of your argument in sufficient depth and avoided oversimplifying it?
   - Have you considered complicating factors or alternative viewpoints on your subject?

5. **A persuasive appeal.** Use appropriate appeals to reason, emotion, or character to make your argument persuasive:

- What persuasive appeals have you employed in your argument?
- Are your persuasive appeals appropriate for your rhetorical situation?

## Step 1 Identify a topic for argument.

Begin with a question about a problem or issue that matters to you:

- Should government subsidize student loans to help make college more affordable?
- What, if anything, should be done about climate change?
- Are there situations in which free speech should be restricted?
- Should Americans give up some privacy rights for greater security against terrorism?
- Should transgender people have access to the bathrooms of their choice?

Make a list of four or five such questions.

**If your assignment specifies a topic,** follow your instructor's guidelines. But you might still need to identify a specific topic. For example, if your instructor asks you to select from a list of approved topics, select four or five topics from that list, turn each one into a question and proceed with this exercise. Or your assignment might call for an argument about a general subject, such as gender, in which case you can list four or five questions about topics related to gender—for example, should women be allowed to serve in front-line military combat units?

Now **select the one question from your list that is most interesting to you.** Consider the following:

| Your interest in the topic | The importance of the topic | Your opinion |
| --- | --- | --- |
|  |  |  |
| **Why does this topic interest you?** Consider what makes this topic worth exploring. It's best to make an argument about topics in which you have a strong interest. | **Why is this topic important?** Consider whether the topic fits your assignment, is relevant to the academic field for which you are writing, or is important to a larger audience. You don't want to devote time and energy to issues that don't seem important. For example, you might think hunting is fun, but is it worth making an argument about that? On the other hand, an argument about the importance of hunting in protecting wildlife relates to significant debates about conservation, wilderness protection, and the rights of gun owners. | **Do you have an opinion about this topic or a position on the issue?** Consider your feelings or attitude about the topic. What is your stance on this issue? Why do you feel the way you do? |
| **Do you have some special connection to this topic?** For example, as a college student you might have a keen interest in student loan policy; as a mountain climber you might worry about how climate change is affecting the mountainous regions where you climb. | | **Are you unsure?** At this point, it doesn't matter whether you have an opinion or stance. What matters is that the topic is important to you and others who might share your interests or concerns. |

Exploring these questions will help you decide whether to pursue the topic. If you decide that the topic you have chosen isn't appropriate, return to your list and select a different question. Once you have a question about which you want to make an argument, develop your question using Step #1 in Chapter 3.

## Step 2 | Place your topic in rhetorical context.

Effective arguments

- address an intended audience appropriately, and
- fit the rhetorical context.

In academic arguments, the audience is usually assumed to include scholars and students in the academic field in which you are writing (see Focus: "The Dual Audience for Academic Arguments" earlier on page 358), and the context is often assumed to encompass the broader effort to advance understanding in that field. For example, an argument in favor of federally subsidized student loans written for an economics course might be directed primarily at your course instructor and classmates, but it should be made in a way that is appropriate for a wider audience in the field of economics. In other words, the argument should be relevant in the academic field and meet the expectations of readers in the field.

With that in mind, return to your question from Step #1 and consider your audience and the rhetorical context for an argument about your question:

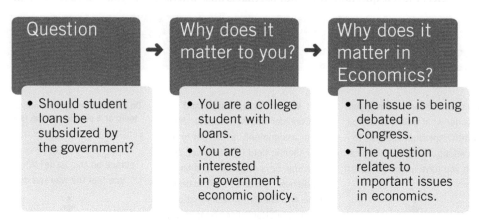

Using this procedure, explore the rhetorical context for your question, keeping notes as you do. Then, using your notes as a guide, complete Step #2 in Chapter 3.

## Step 3 | Select a medium.

Most academic arguments are presented in the form of a conventional paper, but if you have a choice, consider which medium will enable you to make your argument most effectively.

| If your course assignment specifies a medium | Use the medium specified in the assignment guidelines. | Focus on how to present your argument effectively in this medium. |

| If you have a choice of medium | Consider which medium best addresses your intended audience. | Consider how that medium enables you to present your argument effectively. |

**12**

For example, if you are making an argument about whether the federal government should subsidize student loans and you want to reach a wider audience of college students, consider writing your argument for a blog or another social media site that is popular among college students. (Be sure that such a medium is acceptable to your instructor.)

Complete Step #3 in Chapter 3 to help you decide on an appropriate medium for your argument.

## Step 4 Identify your main argument.

Your argument should grow out of the question you explored in Steps #1 and #2. Remember:

- Your main argument is not the same thing as your position on the issue, though it is related to your position. (See "Developing a Main Argument" in Chapter 11.)
- Your main argument might evolve as you develop it.

You might not know at this point exactly what your argument will be, but as you explore your topic, you will adjust and refine your argument. For now, the goal is to identify a clear main point as a starting point for developing an effective argument.

First, consider possible arguments you might make about your question. For example, here are some possible arguments to make about the question of whether student loans should be subsidized by the government (Let's assume you generally support subsidized student loans, given your own experience trying to pay for college.):

- The president should support subsidized student loans for college.
- Student loans should be subsidized by the federal government.
- Subsidized student loans provide economic benefits for individual students and society.

In assessing these statements as possible main arguments, consider which one best reflects your own interest. Also consider how each argument fits the rhetorical context. In this example, imagine that you are writing your argument for an introductory economics course:

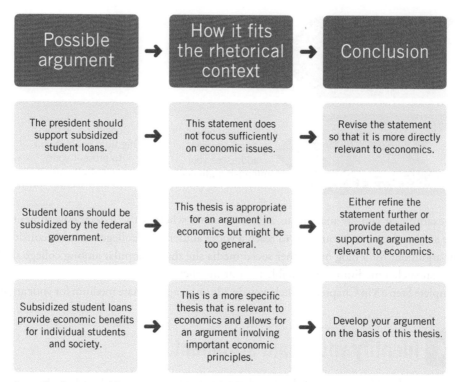

| Possible argument | → | How it fits the rhetorical context | → | Conclusion |
|---|---|---|---|---|
| The president should support subsidized student loans. | → | This statement does not focus sufficiently on economic issues. | → | Revise the statement so that it is more directly relevant to economics. |
| Student loans should be subsidized by the federal government. | → | This thesis is appropriate for an argument in economics but might be too general. | → | Either refine the statement further or provide detailed supporting arguments relevant to economics. |
| Subsidized student loans provide economic benefits for individual students and society. | → | This is a more specific thesis that is relevant to economics and allows for an argument involving important economic principles. | → | Develop your argument on the basis of this thesis. |

Make a list of a few possible main arguments that grow out of your question and consider how well they fit your rhetorical situation. On the basis of that analysis, select one statement that will serve as your main argument. By following Step #4 in Chapter 3 you will develop a Guiding Thesis Statement, which is essentially a more refined statement of your main argument.

## Step 5 Support your main argument.

As you develop a good sense of your main argument, you will also generate some ideas about your supporting arguments or claims. You have four main tasks at this point:

- Identify the arguments or claims you will make in support of your main argument.
- Begin to identify evidence or reasoning to back up each claim.
- Identify opposing arguments or complicating factors.
- Rebut those opposing arguments and address complicating factors.

Usually, completing these tasks requires research. As you move through this step, you will learn more about your topic, and as a result you might need to refine your argument and adjust your claims. Remember, be open to possibilities as you proceed.

Let's return to the example of an argument in favor of subsidized student loans. Here's your main argument as you have stated it at this point:

*Subsidized student loans provide economic benefits for individual students and society.*

To support that main point, you will need to show how students benefit economically from subsidized loans and demonstrate how society benefits as well. Let's imagine that you have learned that subsidized loans have lower interest rates than regular loans, which means lower costs for students. You suspect that lower interest rates mean fewer loan defaults, which is good not only for students but also for communities and for the banks that make the loans. One drawback to subsidized loans is that ultimately taxpayers pay for any loan defaults, but you believe that this potential drawback is outweighed by fewer defaults. Also, you consider it a benefit to society if more students are able to attend college, even though some people argue that government should not be involved in matters such as loans.

Now you need to develop these supporting arguments and claims and find evidence or develop reasoning to support them; you also need to address opposing arguments. To do so, follow these steps:

**State your main argument.**

Subsidized student loans provide clear economic benefits for individual students and society.

**List your supporting claims.**

| Subsidized loans mean more students can attend college. | Lower interest rates mean fewer defaults. | Lower default rates mean a healthier economy. |

**Identify possible evidence for each supporting claim.**

| Studies showing that such loans encourage more low-income students to attend college | Statistical evidence on student loan defaults | • Statements by respected economists<br>• Data on economic impact of loan defaults |

**Identify opposing arguments or complicating factors.**

| College isn't necessarily for everyone. | Lower interest rates mean lower profits on loans. | Subsidized loans amount to too much government interference in the loan market. |

**Answer opposing arguments and/or complicating factors.**

| True, but college should be available to those who want to attend. | Possibly, but that price is worth paying if more students attend college and fewer default on their loans. | Sometimes, strategic government interference is necessary if the potential benefits to society are worthwhile. |

12

Here are a few things to keep in mind as you develop support for your claims:

- **Follow the evidence.** Obviously, your evidence should support your claims, but your claims can change as you research your topic and look for evidence. You might find, for instance, that the available evidence does not support a claim. In this example, you might begin with a claim that lower interest rates result in fewer loan defaults, but your research indicates that the statistical data on this subject is mixed. So you might need to abandon or refine that claim. Don't make claims you can't support, which would result in a weaker (and perhaps unethical) argument. If you find evidence to support your claim, good; if not, adjust your claim.

- **Explore opposing arguments sufficiently.** Although it isn't always necessary or even possible to identify an opposing argument for each supporting claim, anticipating opposing arguments and identifying potential complicating factors can help you strengthen your argument. In this example, you might not have initially considered the argument that college isn't for everyone, but by identifying that opposing argument, you realize it is an important point to address. In doing so, you explore your topic more fully and make a stronger case for your position.

- **Remember that not all evidence is appropriate or persuasive.** As you find evidence to support your claims, determine whether that evidence is trustworthy, relevant to your topic, and appropriate for the rhetorical situation (see "Appraising and Using Evidence" in Chapter 11). A quotation from a politician about the value of college might be persuasive but less compelling than statistical evidence showing that college graduates enjoy higher employment rates and earn higher salaries than workers without college degrees.

Complete Step #5 in Chapter 3. You should be ready to write a complete draft of your project. Or you can move onto the next step before completing your draft.

## Step 6 | Organize your argument.

There are four standard ways to organize an argument (see "Structuring an Argument" in Chapter 11); which one you select will depend upon your rhetorical situation and the nature of the argument you are making.

For example, in making an argument against capital punishment, the kind of argument you make will help determine how best to organize it:

- An argument against capital punishment based on the belief that all killing is wrong is probably best organized as a **deductive argument**, since the argument flows from the basic premise that killing is wrong.

- An argument that capital punishment should be banned because it does not deter violent crime would likely involve various supporting claims that rest on statistical evidence (such as rates of violent crime in states with and without capital punishment); such an argument might be better organized using **classical arrangement**, which would allow the writer to incorporate the supporting claims more easily.

Keep in mind, too, that many academic disciplines have well-established conventions governing the form arguments take. For example, arguments in philosophy are often based on deductive reasoning. In many social sciences, such as economics or sociology, inductive reasoning is more common because the arguments rely on empirical evidence. So consider whether your argument is subject to expectations for a particular academic field.

To decide how best to organize your argument, take into account the following considerations:

| The rhetorical situation | • What structure would present your argument to your intended audience most persuasively?<br>• What expectations will your audience likely have regarding the form of your argument?<br>• How can you organize your essay so that your main argument is presented clearly to that audience?<br>• What are the conventions for structuring an argument within the academic discipline in which you are writing? |
|---|---|

| The nature of your argument | • Does your argument rest on a primary belief or principle (deductive reasoning)?<br>• Does it rely on conclusions drawn from evidence (inductive arrangement)?<br>• Does your argument include a number of complicated supporting claims and kinds of evidence (classical arrangement)?<br>• Is your purpose primarily to solve a problem or negotiate differences (Rogerian arrangement)? |
|---|---|

To illustrate, let's return to the previous example of an argument in favor of subsidized loans for college students.

## Consider the rhetorical situation

For most assignments, you will probably be expected to focus your argument on issues relevant to the academic discipline in which you are writing. For an economics course, for example, your argument should focus on the economic issues related to subsidized loans, such as how default rates might affect the financial well-being of individuals and businesses, the impact of government subsidies on interest rates, etc. You would be expected to present specific kinds of data to support claims about these factors. So an **inductive argument** (in which you draw your conclusion about subsidized student loans from appropriate evidence) or **classical arrangement** (which would allow you to incorporate many supporting claims and address opposing arguments) would be good choices for structuring your argument.

## Examine the nature of the argument

At this point in your project, you have identified several supporting claims for your main argument in favor of subsidized student loans. But you have also identified a fundamental principle on which to rest part of your argument: Governments should take certain actions for the common good. In this case, helping students attend college is in the public's interest. So you might consider a **deductive argument** based on that fundamental principle. However, such an approach might make it more difficult to incorporate the supporting claims you have identified; in addition, if you are writing for an economics course or another specialized academic audience in social sciences, a deductive argument might be less appropriate. So **classical arrangement** might be a better option, because it would enable you to incorporate your supporting claims and evidence as well as logical reasoning on the basis of a fundamental principle.

Here's a basic outline for an argument in favor of subsidized student loans using classical arrangement:

I. *Introduction*: explanation of the relevance of the issue of subsidized student loans in economics and to a wider audience.

II. *Background*:
   A. Discussion of why this problem is important
   B. Brief history of the problem of student loan debt
   C. Explanation of rising college costs
   D. Review of related economic issues

III. *Proposition*: statement of main argument that government should subsidize student loans because of the potential benefits both to individual students and to society in general.

IV. *Proof*: presentation of supporting arguments and evidence to support them.
   A. Subsidized loans allow more students to afford college.
   B. Lower interest rates mean fewer student loan defaults, which is better for communities, businesses, and individuals.
   C. Higher college attendance benefits individuals and communities.
   D. Lower default rates help keep the economy healthy, which benefits everyone.

V. *Refutation*: answers to opposing arguments and complicating factors.
   A. College attendance might not be for everyone, but subsidized loans help make college affordable for those who wish to attend.
   B. Although subsidized loans might mean lower profits for banks, the overall benefit to the economy is worth it.
   C. Although subsidized loans require government involvement in a free market, in this case government involvement results in greater benefit to the society as a whole.

VI. *Conclusion*: emphasize benefits of college attendance and the need for government assistance in helping students avoid loan debt and defaults.

If you were writing this essay for a different course or rhetorical situation, it might make sense to structure the essay as a deductive argument (see "Deductive Reasoning" in "Structuring an Argument" in Chapter 11). For example, if your essay were intended for a political science course, it might be appropriate to rest your argument on the principle that government should support public education in ways that benefit the society as a whole. In such a case, your essay might be more effective if you structured it as a deductive argument.

You can obtain additional guidance for organizing your essay by following Step #6 in Chapter 3.

## Step 7 Get feedback.

Feedback on your draft will be more relevant if your readers focus on the following sets of questions related to the features of effective academic argumentation:

| A clear main point | • What is your main point? Is it clearly stated? <br> • Is the purpose of your argument clear? <br> • How well is the focus of your main argument maintained throughout your essay? |
| --- | --- |
| Relevance | • What makes your topic relevant for your rhetorical situation? <br> • In what ways does your argument contribute to ongoing discussions of this topic? <br> • How do you address your argument to your intended audience? |
| Appropriate support | • What evidence or support do you provide for each of your claims? <br> • Can any claims be made stronger with additional or different support? <br> • Is your evidence appropriate for your topic and audience? |
| Complexity | • How does your argument reflect the complexity of your topic? <br> • Do you explore your topic sufficiently? <br> • How have you avoided oversimplifying the issues? |
| Openness to ideas | • Do you acknowledge other points of view on this issue? <br> • How well have you addressed complicating factors that might weaken your argument? <br> • Do you present opposing arguments fairly? |

Follow Step #7 in Chapter 3 to analyze your feedback and help you decide which revisions to make.

## Step 8 | Revise.

As you consider the feedback you received for Step #7, you might find that you need to do additional research to identify evidence to support your claims or address opposing arguments or complicating factors. That's OK. Remember, revision is an opportunity to deepen your understanding of your topic and strengthen your argument. It is also a chance to adjust and strengthen your persuasive appeals and make sure that your argument fits your rhetorical situation.

You can divide the task of revising your argument into three steps: (1) Review your draft using the questions listed in Step #7; (2) adjust your persuasive appeals; and (3) review each supporting argument or claim.

### 1. Review your draft using the questions listed in Step #7

Make sure you have addressed the key characteristics of academic argument:

- a clear main point
- relevance
- appropriate support
- complexity
- openness to other ideas

As you revise, keep your audience and sense of purpose in mind.

### 2. Adjust your persuasive appeals

To make an effective argument, not only must you have appropriate and sufficient support for your claims, but you must also present your case in a way that is likely to be persuasive to your intended audience. That means reviewing your draft to make sure that you have used ethical, emotional, and/or logical appeals effectively (see "Making a Persuasive Appeal" in Chapter 11). As we saw in Chapter 11, the appeals you use in making your argument depend in large part on your rhetorical situation. For example, you probably wouldn't make an exclusively emotional appeal in an argument about subsidized student loans for an economics course. But a carefully made emotional appeal might supplement an argument that is based mostly on a logical appeal.

### 3. Review each supporting argument or claim

Finally, determine whether you have made an appropriate persuasive appeal for each supporting argument or claim. Although you should now have evidence to support each claim, you can strengthen those claims with appropriate persuasive appeals.

Let's review a few claims in our hypothetical argument in favor of subsidized student loans. For each claim, consider the kind of appeal that might be most appropriate:

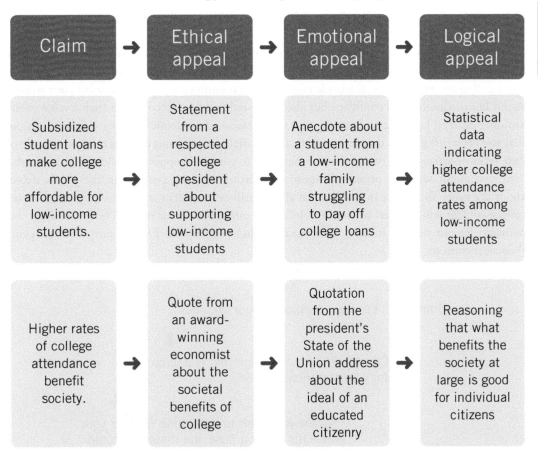

| Claim | → | Ethical appeal | → | Emotional appeal | → | Logical appeal |
|---|---|---|---|---|---|---|
| Subsidized student loans make college more affordable for low-income students. | → | Statement from a respected college president about supporting low-income students | → | Anecdote about a student from a low-income family struggling to pay off college loans | → | Statistical data indicating higher college attendance rates among low-income students |
| Higher rates of college attendance benefit society. | → | Quote from an award-winning economist about the societal benefits of college | → | Quotation from the president's State of the Union address about the ideal of an educated citizenry | → | Reasoning that what benefits the society at large is good for individual citizens |

In deciding which evidence to use and how best to present it, consider how each kind of appeal fits your rhetorical situation. Use appeals that will strengthen your argument—but only if they are appropriate for your rhetorical situation.

Follow Step #8 in Chapter 3 to make sure you have addressed all the essential aspects of your essay.

## Step 9  Refine your voice.

Voice is part of the means by which you establish credibility, which in turn strengthens your argument. Revise your draft with that in mind.

First, consider your purpose in making this argument, which will help shape your voice. Recall that Chapter 11 describes four main purposes for argument:

- to inquire into an issue
- to assert a position in an important conversation or debate

- to prevail over opponents
- to solve a controversial or complicated problem

Although these purposes can overlap, your primary purpose can determine how best to construct your voice.

For example, let's assume that your purpose in making an argument about subsidized student loans is primarily to understand this complex and important issue—that is, an argument to inquire. You are writing in an academic context (an economics course), so you want your voice to sound knowledgeable and confident but also measured and fair. To construct such a voice means avoiding charged language and writing in a straightforward academic style. By contrast, imagine that you are writing about the same topic in an editorial essay for your campus newspaper and you have recently learned that one of the U.S. Senators in your state opposes subsidized loans. In that case, you might see your primary purpose as asserting a strong position in the public debate about the issue. Your voice in that context should still be confident and knowledgeable, but as a college student who is faced with tuition bills, you might want your voice to be sympathetic and perhaps even provocative. In short, your voice should be appropriate for your purpose within your rhetorical context.

Review your draft and adjust your voice, if necessary:

Identify the primary purpose of your argument.

↓

Consider the kind of voice that is appropriate for your rhetorical context.

↓

Review your draft to determine whether your voice fits your purpose and rhetorical context.

Make necessary revisions to your draft. Then follow Step #9 in Chapter 3 to refine and strengthen your voice.

## Step 10 Edit.

Complete Step #10 in Chapter 3.

1. Identify an issue or controversy you feel strongly about. Ideally, it should be something that matters in your life—for example, a controversy over a proposal to eliminate your major at your college, or restrictions on the use of social media for certain kinds of activities on campus. Write an argument in which you take a position on this issue. Write your argument in a way that would be appropriate for both an academic audience and a wider audience. For example, if you write about a controversy about eliminating your major at your college, you might intend your argument for readers in an academic field such as education or philosophy as well as for a wider audience interested in educational issues.

2. Rewrite the essay you wrote for Question #1 in a completely different medium. For example, if you wrote an essay for a course, rewrite the essay as a multimedia presentation for a different audience or as a letter to a person at the center of the issue.

   Now compare the two arguments. What changes did you make in rewriting your argument for a different medium? In what ways (if any) did you have to adjust important elements of your argument, such as your evidence or your persuasive appeals? What might a comparison of these two arguments suggest about how argument is shaped by rhetorical context and medium.

3. Using the issue you wrote about for Question #1 or another topic, find three or four academic arguments about that issue or topic. In an essay intended for your classmates, summarize the arguments and then analyze them using the five main features of academic argumentation described in this chapter. Be sure to account for the rhetorical situation. On the basis of those features, decide whether the arguments are effective. Draw conclusions about what makes an argument effective.

## MindTap

Request help with these Writing Projects and feedback from a tutor. If required, participate in peer review, submit your paper for a grade, and view instructor comments online.

## In this chapter, you will learn to

1. Identify and understand the purposes of arguments in public contexts.

2. Identify appropriate rhetorical opportunities for making arguments in public discourse.

3. Define the four main features of effective arguments in public discourse.

4. Understand three common problems in public argument and identify them in sample arguments made in public contexts.

5. Apply the four main features to understand and critique sample arguments in public discourse.

6. Write an argument, applying the four main features of arguments in public discourse and using the **Ten Core Concepts from Chapter 3.**

## MindTap®
Understand the goals of the chapter and complete a warm-up activity.

# Making Arguments in Public Discourse

**SHOULD WOMEN BE ALLOWED** to serve in combat? Who should be the next president? Should colleges pay student athletes? We share opinions and debate matters big and small in every aspect of our lives: in our relationships, as citizens, at work and play. Debating these matters helps us understand issues we care about and consider what others think about them. In this way, everyday argument is part of how we make sense of the world, make decisions, and solve problems.

Expressing an opinion, though, is not necessarily the same as making a persuasive argument. Everyone voices opinions, and in most cases, such as a friendly debate about the latest Academy Awards, a weak or flawed argument has few serious consequences. But sometimes the arguments we engage in can have significant implications for our lives:

- Should a loved one have a recommended but risky surgery?
- Should you borrow money to attend college?
- Should your brother or sister join the military?
- Should you volunteer for a controversial political candidate?

In such cases, a careful argument can often result in a better decision or a workable solution to a problem. It is no accident that in business, politics, and community life, decisions about difficult problems and important issues are made on the basis of extensive discussions in which careful arguments are made:

- After listening to various arguments for and against building a new addition to the local high school, school board members vote on whether to levy a tax increase to pay for the new construction.
- The owners of a small computer software company exchange opinions with their staff about the risks and benefits of purchasing another software company.
- In deciding whether to support a new policy that would give the college access to information about students' online activities, a group of students and faculty listen to each other's positions and consider how the policy might affect privacy and online security at the college.

In these examples, arguments are presented as part of an effort to address a problem or make a decision. Making good arguments is no guarantee that the outcome will satisfy everyone. In fact, in decisions about important issues that will affect the participants, it is likely that some people will disagree with the outcome. But even they can serve their own interests by making good arguments, since the better their argument, the more likely they will influence how others think about the issue.

So arguments matter. Being able to make a sound, reasonable argument—and being able to recognize and refute flawed arguments—can help you better address the questions, problems, and challenges you face as a student, an employee, a consumer, and a citizen.

Making Arguments in Public Discourse  **389**

This chapter examines effective argumentation in public contexts, such as the mass media, social media, and other venues in which people present arguments about important issues or problems. We call these arguments "public" to distinguish them from more formal academic arguments (as described in Chapter 12). Although there is a great deal of overlap between academic argument and the kinds of arguments made in public contexts, there are important differences that will be examined in this chapter. Understanding these differences can help you make more effective arguments in a variety of rhetorical situations.

# Occasions for Public Argument

On September 17, 2011, several hundred people gathered at a park on Wall Street in New York City to protest the growing income inequality in the United States and what they perceived as the increasing control of the political process by wealthy individuals and corporations. The protesters remained there until November, when police evicted them. By then the protest, which was called Occupy Wall Street, had grown into what became known as the Occupy Movement. In cities throughout the U.S. and in many other nations, protesters set up camps in parks, squares, and other public places. Their slogan, "We are the 99 percent," focused attention on the gap in wealth between those Americans whose incomes place them in the top 1% of all Americans and everyone else (the 99%).

Not surprisingly, the Occupy Movement was controversial. Not only did it spark debate about income inequality and related issues, but it also influenced political discussions in the U.S., including the presidential primaries that took place in 2012. Income inequality became a focus of many national and regional political contests, and candidates debated fundamental questions about government's role in addressing problems such as unemployment and poverty. At the same time, the movement sparked countless arguments in a variety of forms in local newspapers, on blogs and websites, on Facebook, Twitter, and other social media, and in city council and town board meetings throughout the U.S.

---

**FOCUS**    **PUBLIC ARGUMENT VIA VISUAL MEDIA**

Controversies often spark a proliferation of images, videos, cartoons, and posters that circulate online. Cartoons like this one might be seen as engaging in public argument. One focus of the ongoing controversy over guns in the U.S. is the potential conflict between individual rights and legal restrictions on gun ownership intended to protect the public. Opponents of such restrictions sometimes argue that measures to control guns violate citizens' Constitutional right to bear arms. Consider how this cartoon presents a rebuttal to that argument. How would you summarize the implicit argument this cartoon makes?

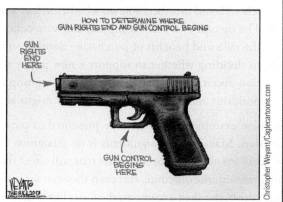

---

The Occupy Movement is a dramatic example of how people engage in argument to address complicated issues and problems that affect their lives as citizens, workers, consumers, and community members. But to make an argument in such debates isn't just a matter of voicing an opinion or responding to someone else's opinion; it is also an effort to help answer relevant questions and solve pressing problems. In this sense, argument plays a role in every aspect of our lives, even if we usually engage in argument in less dramatic ways:

- Residents of a neighborhood near a large shopping center use social media to voice support for or opposition to a town plan to build a new intersection near the shopping center to reduce traffic.
- A Peace Corps worker returns to the high school from which she graduated and presents a slide show to encourage students to consider joining the Peace Corps after they graduate.
- Homeowners write letters to their school district office arguing for or against a proposed policy regarding the use of bathrooms by transgender students.

These examples illustrate how prevalent argument can be in our daily lives.

---

## 13

**EXERCISE 13A    OCCASIONS FOR ARGUMENT**

1. Identify an issue about which you have a strong opinion. In a brief paragraph, explain the issue and why it is important to you. Also explain your position and why you hold it. Now identify two or three different audiences who share your interest in this issue. What argument might you make to each audience? What would be your purpose in making your argument in each case?

2. Find several arguments about an issue or problem that interests you. Try to find arguments about that topic that address different audiences in different media. Then compare the arguments. What similarities and differences do you see in them? What conclusions might you draw from these examples about why people engage in argument about topical issues?

3. Identify an issue about which you have had discussions with friends or classmates in which different viewpoints were debated. In a brief paragraph, describe the issue and why there was disagreement about it. Try to identify the main points of disagreement. Now consider how the arguments presented by you and your classmates or friends might have influenced your understanding of the issue. What do you think this situation suggests about the nature of argument in our daily lives?

# Understanding Argument in Public Discourse

The informal nature of most arguments in public contexts represents both opportunity and challenge for writers as well as readers. For one thing, the many different forms that public argument can take—from carefully developed newspaper op-ed essays to less formal blog posts to brief messages shared on social media to flyers and posters—can shape argumentation in different ways. The immediacy and brevity of social media sites, for example, call for different strategies of argumentation than the more fully developed arguments typically seen in traditional media, such as newspaper op-ed pages. Writers have many options for presenting their arguments but often have to adjust their strategies as they move from one rhetorical situation to another. For instance, a writer might be able to present less evidence to support a claim in an online forum as compared to a more formal essay, but an online forum allows a writer to link to other sites on the Internet as a way to provide evidence.

The purposes for argument in public contexts can also be less clear than for academic arguments (Chapter 12), which generally focus on understanding an issue, or proposals (Chapter 14), which often focus on solving a specific problem. Although popular arguments serve the four main purposes described in Chapter 11—to inquire, to assert, to prevail, and to negotiate differences and solve problems (see pages 319–321)—conflicting purposes often come into play at the same time. For example, Occupy Wall Street protesters might distribute flyers about the worsening economic inequality in the U.S. to assert their point of view about that issue. A politician might respond to the protest on his blog by making a vigorous argument intended to undermine the protesters' claims about economic inequality (an argument to prevail). At the same time, the leader of a community group might write a letter to the editor of the local newspaper to make a case for a compromise in the conflict that the protest has provoked (an argument to negotiate differences). And a concerned resident without a political agenda might post a response to a community social media site to make an argument that explores the complex reasons for income inequality in the U.S. (an argument to inquire). All these parties are involved in the same general discussion about the same general issue, but their goals and perspectives vary dramatically, diverging or overlapping in complicated ways and sometimes shifting focus rapidly.

In addition, writers advancing positions in public venues, such as blogs, newspapers, social media, television talk shows, and similar forums, rarely follow the rules of formal argumentation described in Chapter 11. Important features of argument, such as using credible and appropriate evidence to support claims, can vary dramatically from one rhetorical context to another. Statistical data that might be seen as compelling evidence of income inequality in, say, a paper for an economics course, might have little persuasive power in an argument presented on a social media site; moreover, in many public contexts, there is little expectation that assertions will be supported with solid evidence of any kind. Similarly, a powerful persuasive appeal in an academic argument might be ineffective in a public context. For example, the viewpoint of a prominent economist who is a Nobel Prize laureate might be used effectively as an ethical appeal in an academic essay; by contrast, the same appeal might fall flat for a public audience who associates that same economist with a liberal political perspective because he writes a column for a newspaper known for its liberal slant.

The complexities of public arguments can be magnified by online and digital media, which not only provide more venues for argument but also can influence the nature of argumentation in complex ways. As a result, writers and readers must be wary in presenting and evaluating arguments made in public contexts so that they recognize and avoid common problems in public argument, which are illustrated in the following example. In 2012, New York City Mayor Michael Bloomberg sparked a nationwide debate when he proposed a ban on so-called "super-sized" soft drinks. The proposal would have prohibited restaurants and similar establishments from selling soda and other sugary drinks in containers larger than 16 ounces. The proposal was intended to combat obesity, an increasingly serious public health problem in the United States. Not surprisingly, the proposal provoked a vigorous response from supporters as well as opponents. Jeff Halevy, a fitness instructor, wrote the following essay opposing the ban:

Last week, New York City mayor Michael Bloomberg unveiled his proposal to ban the sale of sweetened sodas in sizes larger than 16 ounces. While this proposal might intuitively seem like a stride in the right direction—who the heck needs more than 16 ounces of soda at a time anyway!?—I personally couldn't disagree more with the move. For one, the implementation is flawed, with 2-liter-peddling supermarkets and sugar-laden juices escaping the executioner's axe, and I also believe it will be a challenge to stem the actions of a motivated Big Gulp purchaser (two 16-ouncers should do the trick, right?).

But more fundamentally, I disagree with the move on a philosophical basis. We live in the age of corporate social responsibility, whereby we expect corporations to self-regulate themselves in the interest of the environment, consumers, and the world community. We in fact become outraged when we hear of a corporation that has violated what we believe to be its socially responsible actions; Wall Street, Apple, Nike and BP, to name just a few, have all drawn ire by violating this responsibility. It's easy to vilify corporations that, in their insatiable appetite for profits, have thrown their implicit social contracts out the window. But what about the individual, whose appetite, too, leads him to violate social trust?

I believe America is in a crisis now, not only of corporate or governmental social responsibility, but of *personal social responsibility*; we're uncertain of whether Wall Street or Uncle Sam has our best interest at heart, but just the same we should be looking at our neighbor. Our problem is not simply a matter of sugar, fat and salt; it is a matter of choice, behavior and education. We live in a country where we make sure our children are mathematically educated enough to figure out that two 16-ounce sodas will get them their Big Gulp fix, but where roughly **96 percent of them are not required to have daily physical education classes in school.** What exactly are we teaching them about behavior and choice?

Set aside what we're teaching young America, let's look at ourselves in the mirror. Most of us know what's healthy and what's not. I have had the privilege of meeting folks all over the country, and getting insight into their daily routines:

| | |
|---|---|
| John Doe | "What can I do to eat better? I feel like I eat okay but I'm already heavy and continue to gain weight." |
| Me | "Well, let's start with breakfast—what did you eat?" |
| John Doe | "I know what you're going to say. I probably shouldn't have had the sausage, egg and cheese on a bagel." |
| Me | "Bingo. So what could you eat instead?" |
| John Doe | "I guess I should have oatmeal, and maybe some fruit." |
| Me | "Well there's a big step in the right direction!" |

I cannot tell you how many conversations like this I've had over the years about food and exercise. We know what we're doing to ourselves, and most of us know how to change it. And in situations where additional warnings and information may be warranted, sure, I'm all for it; let's slap a warning label on soda, maybe even a picture of a diabetic amputee's leg—whatever it takes. Education is key.

However, our crisis isn't simply one of education. As I said above, it's one of personal social responsibility. Type 2 diabetes, in which insidious sugar sources like soda play a big role, costs this country in excess of $174 billion each year. Most Type 2 diabetics know that their lifestyles are unhealthy but do not take adequate action to prevent or reverse the disease. And who pays for it? How would we react to a corporation that did the very same? *(Note: This is NOT an attack on diabetics; I am merely illustrating a point.)*

And my point is simply this: Drinking soda, or better stated, our right to drink soda, is actually good for us. Isn't that what makes America great? We're the land of free choice. However, when government takes an arbitrary legislative potshot at the symptom, not the cause, of a problem, how much better off are we? Do we want to be hobbled by government making lifestyle choices for us, or empowered by government teaching and supporting better choices? I for one would much rather see legislation making daily physical education and nutrition classes mandatory for our students, ingraining better lifestyles and choices. And I'd love to see the Big Gulp yanked—not due to legislation, but due rather to poor sales from a healthy, educated consumer.

Source: Halevy, Jeff. "Would A Ban on Supersized Soda Help People Make Healthy Choices?" *The Huffington Post*, 4 June 2012, www.huffingtonpost.com/jeff-halevy/new-york-soda-ban_b_1563978.html.

Halevy leaves no doubt that he opposes the proposal to ban the sale of soft drinks in large containers. He presents several strong arguments against such a ban, including the claim, which he supports with evidence, that American students are not necessarily educated in ways that promote healthy lifestyles. He also rests his main argument on a fundamental principle that individuals, not governments, must bear responsibility for making healthy choices. The question of how to address serious public health problems such as obesity is a complicated and highly charged one, and Halevy contributes to the controversy by pointing out potential problems with the proposal to ban the sale of large containers of soft drinks. But Halevy's argument exhibits **three common problems with public argument:**

- **Missing or weak evidence to support claims.** Halevy makes several claims for which he provides no supporting evidence, including the claim that "most Type 2 diabetics know that their lifestyles are unhealthy but do not take adequate action to prevent or reverse the disease." He provides evidence that diabetes is a serious health issue, noting that it costs the U.S. $174 billion annually, but he doesn't explain the significance of that figure. How does that amount compare to costs associated with other diseases? Nor does he provide evidence that soft drinks are a significant factor in diabetes. It is possible that the consumption of soft drinks contributes to the rise in the incidence of diabetes in the U.S., but his assertion that such a link exists does not amount to evidence nor does the figure he presents support such a claim.

- **Flawed reasoning.** Halevy asserts that obesity in the U.S. is a matter of lifestyle, and he suggests that the problem might be addressed by requiring more physical education for American students. But his implicit claim that requiring physical education will lead to healthy lifestyle choices is flawed. He presents no evidence for the claim; moreover, although it is possible that physical education encourages healthier lifestyles, it does not follow logically that simply requiring students to engage in such activities will necessarily mean that they will make healthy choices in the future. There are too many complicating factors to show that a causal relationship exists between required physical education and a healthy lifestyle. (See Focus: "Causation vs. Correlation" on page 155.)

■ **Oversimplified or exaggerated assertions.** Halevy oversimplifies the problem in several ways. Notice, for example, how he uses his own experience as a fitness instructor to support his claim that "we know what we're doing to ourselves, and most of us know how to change it." His argument is that all we really have to do to combat obesity is "look in the mirror" and start making healthy choices. But the causes of obesity and related health problems are extremely complex, and many factors influence the lifestyle choices people make, including factors over which they have little or no control, such as socio-economic status. It is entirely possible that a person suffering from obesity knows about good nutrition but is unable to make certain healthy choices because of income or other circumstances.

This example illustrates the pitfalls of public argument. As a writer, take care to recognize when you might be making similar mistakes in constructing your argument; as a reader, be vigilant in evaluating a writer's claims and evidence.

---

**FOCUS** | **RECOGNIZING LOGICAL FALLACIES IN PUBLIC ARGUMENTS**

A logical fallacy is a flaw in reasoning. One of the most common fallacies is a *non sequitur* (which is Latin for "it does not follow"), in which a conclusion is reached that does not follow logically from the evidence or premise. For example, you might hear someone say, "Most people believe in God, so he must exist." It might be true that most people believe in

**Drone Strikes**

Obama, 2009: 51

Bush, 2001–2009: 45

God, but that fact does not mean that God exists. This kind of flawed reasoning is common in public argument, especially in political advertising, where it can often be difficult to identify. For example, during his presidency Barack Obama was criticized for his approval of the use of armed drones to attack alleged terrorists. In 2012, some advocacy groups distributed posters such as this one to highlight the claim that government has grown dangerously during Obama's presidency. But such an argument is logically flawed. Let's assume that the main argument of this poster can be stated as follows: "Government has become bigger and more dangerous under President Obama." The "evidence" for such a claim is that there have been many more

*(Continued)*

drone strikes in a shorter time period under Obama than under the previous president, George W. Bush. However, the number of drone strikes does not necessarily correlate to the size of government. There are many possible reasons for the increase in drone strikes under President Obama. For example, he might have authorized more drone strikes because he had better information about suspected terrorists than President Bush had. It is also possible that the increase in drone strikes reflects a different military strategy rather than an escalation. In other words, there are many possible conclusions that can be logically drawn from this evidence, but it does not logically support the conclusion that government has become bigger or more dangerous.

Such flawed reasoning can be subtle and difficult to identify, which makes it even more important to evaluate claims and reasoning carefully, both as a writer and a reader of public arguments.

---

**FOCUS    LINKING TO EVIDENCE ONLINE**

Essays such as Halevy's (on pages 393–394) that are published online often include hyperlinks to other websites that contain relevant information or opinions. This strategy, which is increasingly common in online writing, enables a writer to refer to evidence without having to incorporate it directly into the text. However, the strategy requires readers to follow the links if they wish to see the evidence and to evaluate the credibility of the website where the information is located. Whether linked online in this way or presented in traditional footnotes, evidence should always be carefully evaluated (see "Appraising and Using Evidence" in Chapter 11). The ease of access to such an enormous amount and variety of information online sometimes means that you have to take additional steps when evaluating sources (see Chapter 22). As a writer, always try to provide relevant, credible support for your claims, which means making sure of the credibility of any websites to which you link in an online essay.

---

Arguments that avoid these problems are likely to be more successful in achieving the writer's rhetorical purposes. Effective arguments in public discourse usually have the following four main features:

- **A clear main point.** Because arguments in public discourse tend to be about complicated subjects, it is important for writers to present a clear main point or position without oversimplifying the issue at hand. Issues worth arguing about can rarely be reduced to simple either-or propositions (e.g., standardized testing is good or bad; all tax increases are harmful or necessary); arguments with a clear main point that reflects the complexity of the issue are more likely to be persuasive (e.g., although standardized tests can provide useful information, schools should not rely on them to evaluate teachers; strategic, carefully designed tax increases can raise necessary revenue without weakening economic growth).

- **A relevant contribution.** By definition, public arguments focus on current issues that matter to writers and their readers. Effective arguments fit into ongoing debates about those issues, and writers who establish the relevance of their arguments are more likely to reach their intended audience. No matter the topic, writers should give their readers a compelling rationale that the topic is important and their position is worth considering.

- **Appropriate but accessible support for claims.** In many venues for public argument, it is not feasible for writers to present detailed evidence, extensive reasoning, or lengthy discussions to support their claims. So writers must present evidence succinctly and make it accessible to the audience. For example, a writer arguing in favor of a proposed gun control law in a letter to the editor of an online newspaper might have to summarize in a sentence or two the results of a relevant study of similar laws rather than present detailed statistical data from that study.

- **A reasonable effort to address opposing viewpoints.** Although ignoring, oversimplifying, or even ridiculing opposing viewpoints might appeal to readers who already share the writer's perspective, it is unlikely to appeal to readers who might not have strong views about the subject. An argument tends to be more effective if the writer acknowledges well-known counter-arguments and recognizes the legitimacy of reasonable or widely held opposing viewpoints. Doing so not only strengthens the writer's argument but also can enhance his or her credibility.

Of course, writers could ignore these features of effective argument if they believe doing so will make their arguments more persuasive for a specific audience. For example, a writer arguing against charter schools for an audience of educators who already oppose charter schools might see no value in acknowledging some of the benefits of charter schools, since he or she knows that the audience is unlikely to be swayed by such a discussion. In such a case, the writer must consider the rhetorical situation and decide whether it is ethical to ignore opposing arguments, even if including those arguments might not make the main argument more appealing to the intended audience. In other words, because writers often make arguments about complicated and highly charged topics, it can be easy to get away with questionable strategies. Whether it is right to do so is another matter, and every writer must decide whether to be ethical in making an argument. (See Focus: "The Ethics of Argument" on page 321 in Chapter 11.)

---

**EXERCISE 13B**  **UNDERSTANDING ARGUMENT IN PUBLIC DISCOURSE**

1. Find several arguments about the same topic in different media for different audiences. For example, you might find a newsletter, a post on a blog, and an essay in a large-circulation magazine such as *Time* about an issue that interests you. Identify each writer's main argument and the evidence supporting that argument, and evaluate the effectiveness of each argument using the characteristics of effective argument described in this chapter. On the basis of your evaluation, what conclusions can you draw about arguments in public discourse?

2. Evaluate the use of evidence to support claims in each of the following passages. (Each passage is an excerpt from a longer argument.) For each passage, identify the claim(s) and the evidence or reasoning presented to support those claim(s). How strong is the evidence for each claim? How logical is the reasoning? Does the evidence seem credible? How do you know? What conclusions can you draw about the uses of evidence in public arguments?

   a) Advocates of small-scale, nonindustrial [farming] alternatives say their choice is at least more natural. Again, this is a dubious claim. Many farmers who raise chickens on pasture use industrial breeds that have been bred to do one thing

*(Continued)*

well: fatten quickly in confinement. As a result, they can suffer painful leg injuries after several weeks of living a "natural" life pecking around a large pasture. Free-range pigs are routinely affixed with nose rings to prevent them from rooting, which is one of their most basic instincts. In essence, what we see as natural doesn't necessarily conform to what is natural from the animals' perspectives.

Source: McWilliams, James E. "The Myth of Sustainable Meat." *The New York Times*, 12 Apr. 2012, nyti.ms/1Bb4dEq.

b) The literature on fatherhood sends a stark message: All fathers are not equal. Breadwinners married to homemakers earn 30 percent more than those in two-job families and encounter favored treatment at work. One study found that fathers were held to lower performance and commitment standards than were men without children, presumably because respondents assumed that since a father "has a family to support," he will work hard. This study reflects the normative father, a breadwinner with a wife who is responsible for children and home. In contrast, a father who discloses that he has family care responsibilities faces job risks. One study found that men are often penalized for taking family leave, especially by other men. Another found that men with even a short work absence due to a family conflict were recommended for fewer rewards and had lower performance ratings.

Source: Williams, Joan C. "Let's Rethink Masculinity." *In These Times*, 6 Oct. 2010, inthesetimes.com/article/6510/lets_rethink_masculinity.

c) [Martin Luther King Jr.'s famous "I Have a Dream" speech] continue[s] to inspire a nation. But the Civil Rights Act did not spill forth from the mouth of King; it was the culmination of decades of community struggles, Congressional lobbying and judicial strategy. No speech, no matter how awe-inspiring, could have led a Southern Democrat in 1964, six weeks before his party's nominating convention, in the summer of a presidential election year, to sign the most important piece of civil rights legislation since Reconstruction. That unthinkable political act was made possible by a confluence of factors, including important shifts occurring within the Democratic Party. For example, in the 1958 midterm elections eleven racially liberal Republican senators were replaced by eleven racially liberal Democrats. The election did not alter total Congressional support for civil rights legislation, but it did shift the balance of power on race issues between the parties. For the first time, the party of Lincoln did not have exclusive claim on racial liberalism, and for the first time the Democratic Party's powerful Southern segregationist base was balanced against a progressive Northern force. This shift was just enough, when combined with the visible struggle of disciplined, nonviolent Southern resisters, to give Johnson the courage to act on civil rights.

Source: Harris-Perry, Melissa. "What Are Words Worth?" *The Nation*, 2 Sept. 2010, www.thenation.com/article/what-are-words-worth/.

$3.$ Find an argument with which you agree about a topic that interests you. In a brief essay, summarize the argument, identifying its main claims, evidence, and persuasive appeals. Explain what you think makes the argument effective. Why do you agree with it? What features of the argument make it persuasive for you? On the basis of your evaluation, draw conclusions about what makes a public argument persuasive.

# Reading Public Arguments

The following examples illustrate the main features of effective arguments in public contexts. In evaluating these arguments, consider how each writer supports the main argument with the intended audience in mind. Also, look for flawed reasoning (see Focus: "Recognizing Logical Fallacies in Public Arguments") and other common problems of public argument (see p. 395–396).

| A clear main point | • What is the main argument?<br>• How clearly does the author present the main point?<br>• What is the author's purpose in making this argument? |
| --- | --- |
| **A relevant contribution** | • Why is the argument relevant now?<br>• What is the context for this argument? What audience is addressed?<br>• To which ongoing discussions or debates does the author seek to contribute? What does this argument add to those discussions or debates? |
| **Appropriate, accessible support** | • What evidence is presented to support the author's claims? How strong is this evidence?<br>• What makes this evidence appropriate for the topic and intended audience?<br>• Does the author make the evidence accessible and understandable? |
| **Opposing viewpoints** | • To what extent does the author consider opposing viewpoints?<br>• Has the author oversimplified or misrepresented opposing viewpoints?<br>• Has the author avoided simple either-or propositions? |

MindTap®

Read these public argument examples. Highlight and take notes online. Additional readings are also available online.

# Trigger Warnings Don't Hinder Freedom of Expression:
## They Expand It
### by Lindy West

*As a college student, you are probably familiar with so-called "trigger warnings." As writer Lindy West explains in the following essay, trigger warnings are messages that let an audience know about disturbing content. The messages shown at the beginning of some films or TV shows warning viewers about nudity or violence in the film or show are a form of trigger warnings. Maybe you have taken courses in which the instructor gave such warnings—perhaps to alert students to racist language or graphic descriptions of sexual violence in an assigned reading. Such warnings might seem reasonable, but as West notes, they have also become controversial. She reviews the heated criticisms of trigger warnings that emerged in 2015, when her essay appeared in* The Guardian, *a British newspaper that is distributed internationally. These criticisms were made in response to policies regarding trigger warnings that were implemented on some college campuses, such as Oberlin College, which West refers to in her essay. Some critics claimed that such warnings "coddle" college students. West rejects such claims and makes it clear that she sees trigger warnings as healthy and appropriate. In making her argument in support of trigger warnings on college campuses, she actually addresses a much larger issue: freedom of expression. In that regard, her essay is part of a centuries-old conversation about a complex issue that affects all of us in some way. Her essay also illustrates the important role arguments in public contexts can play in addressing some of the most basic questions facing humans and the societies in which they live.*

. . . . . . . . . . . . . . . . . . . . . . . . . . . . . . . . . . . . . . . . .

## Talking About the Reading

> **Rainey McEwan (student):** Some readers may find it difficult to understand the author's reasoning for talking about trigger warnings in a more general sense in paragraph 6 and then jumping to society's views of women in paragraph 7.

> **Bob Yagelski:** Rainey, your comment underscores a big challenge writers face when making arguments about complex subjects in popular contexts (such as in newspaper op-ed essays like this one): sufficiently addressing the complexity of the subject in few words. In this case, the author makes a complex argument that trigger warnings are as much about gender bias as they are about free speech. That's a challenging argument to make, and she obviously had to condense her argument to make it fit the length restrictions of a newspaper essay.

. . . . . . . . . . . . . . . . . . . . . . . . . . . . . . . . . . . . . . . . .

Back in early July, comedian Jimmy Fallon tripped on a rug in his kitchen, caught his wedding ring on the counter as he fell, and suffered a gruesome injury called a "ring avulsion"—basically, a medical term for ripping your finger off. Fallon spent 10 days in intensive care and came close to losing the digit, which, unfortunately, most ring avulsion sufferers do. Explaining his massive white bandage when he returned to his late-night show weeks later, Fallon warned: "If you Google it, it's graphic. So don't Google it."

It's a perfectly ordinary thing to say—considerate yet mundane, a throwaway line that's also highly functional. It lets you know, efficiently and unobtrusively, that a Google search for "ring avulsion" will turn up disturbing photos of bloody finger stumps, which is useful because most people find it jarring to be unexpectedly bombarded with photos of dismembered human body parts. Some people faint at the sight of gore. Some vomit. Some panic. Some don't mind at all.

If Fallon were to actually show the images on TV, a quick, "Heads up, time to gird your loins/grab your barf bag/take a deep breath" would be basic human decency, and no one watching would think twice about it.

I keep returning to Fallon's little Google aside this week as I watch the internet devolve into bedlam over the supposed forthcoming doom caused by academic trigger warnings. A trigger warning, if you're not familiar with the term, is a note tacked on to a piece of media—whether it's a novel, blogpost or live event—letting the audience know about potentially disturbing content. Common iterations include "trigger warning: rape", "trigger warning: abuse" or "trigger warning: suicide." It gives the audience a modicum of control over if and how they engage.

Commonplace on social media and personal blogs, especially progressive communities on Tumblr, trigger warnings have begun finding their way into academia: some professors are voluntarily adding trigger warnings to their syllabuses, giving trauma survivors a chance to prepare emotionally before class. Some student groups have requested more widespread trigger warnings in their academic programs and, in one famous incident, a committee at Oberlin college suggested some potentially over-reaching guidelines that were then rejected. There are, undoubtedly, certain boundaries to be set regarding the utility and scope of campus trigger warnings, a line that I think all of academia is more than qualified to navigate.

The goal is not to keep challenging materials off syllabuses or allow students to meekly excuse themselves from huge swaths of the literary canon because bad words hurt their feelings; it's to increase engagement and increase accessibility by allowing students with trauma histories to manage their mental health. As Maddy Myers explained in a piece about trigger warnings and PTSD for geek culture blog The Mary Sue: "A trigger warning doesn't necessarily stop me from engaging with content, but it does help me prepare for what I might endure." Academia before trigger warnings didn't teach trauma victims how to be tougher (and, by the way, maybe we can leave students' psychiatric care to their psychiatrists?); it hindered their ability to engage in their own education. Attending to the needs of students with PTSD doesn't hinder academic freedom; it expands it.

Predictably, as with any cultural phenomenon associated primarily with young women (see also: vocal fry, pop music), campus trigger warnings have faced a swift, imperious and borderline unhinged backlash. The *Daily Beast* told college students to "grow up" and argued that they're "incapable of living in the real world." An *Atlantic* cover story recently described undergrads as "coddled," claiming rather hysterically: "A movement is arising, undirected and driven largely by students, to scrub campuses clean of words, ideas, and subjects that might cause discomfort or give offense." The authors then make a truly remarkable leap to accuse trigger warning proponents of engendering "campus culture devoted to policing speech and punishing speakers," as well as exacerbating mental health problems by shielding trauma victims from triggering texts that could serve as "exposure therapy."

It's a tidy way to link trigger warnings with the other progressive bogeyman du jour, political correctness, and all its sinister attendants: microaggressions, the supposed erosion of free speech, and the "right not to be offended." But all those concepts, when examined honestly, just boil down to treating marginalized groups with respect and humanity and striving to correct harmful imbalances. Thinking critically about the harmful assumptions inherent in, for example, the phrase "I don't see color" is not "[scrubbing] campuses clean of words." It's being a responsible human being.

*(Continued)*

Political correctness is, essentially, a family of suggestions: don't talk over people who have been historically silenced; demand and make way for diverse representation; trust people to be authorities on their own lives; be cognizant and careful with other people's trauma; listen, and be kind.

That's only threatening if you're part of the group being asked to scoot over and let those margins take up some real space. Odd that the anti-free-speech brigade isn't up in arms about announcements such as Fallon's—surely he, too, is "coddling" his audience, withholding valuable "exposure therapy" for avulsion victims and infringing on Google's free expression. It's almost as though, coded as feminine and largely associated with rape victims, the antipathy toward trigger warnings is about something else entirely.

The anti-trigger warning "coddled co-eds" narrative has a lot in common with the "false accusation" narrative used to derail discussions of on-campus rape. The first scoffs at people's attempts to cope with trauma once they've already been traumatized; the second undermines their efforts to avoid being traumatized in the first place. Both are symptomatic of our culture's deep investment in minimizing and normalizing sexual assault.

Maybe we can all get flippant and condescending about trigger warnings after we build a world where more than 3% of rapes lead to conviction, where we don't shame and blame people for their own victimization, where men don't feel entitled to women's bodies, and where millions of people aren't moving through life yoked with massive, secret traumas.

Political correctness isn't a new battleground in the culture wars—this conversation has been going on, with various targets, for at least three decades now—and it seems to function, encouragingly, as a side-effect of progress. It's the whimpering of the status quo. People hate trigger warnings because they bring up something most don't like to remember: that the world is not currently a safe or just place, and people you love are almost certainly harboring secrets that would break your heart. Even if it's unpopular, the fact that we're having that conversation at all is progress.

---

Source: West, Lindy. "Trigger Warnings Don't Hinder Freedom of Expression: They Expand It." *The Guardian*, 18 Aug 2015, www.theguardian.com/education/commentisfree/2015/aug/18/trigger-warnings-dont-hinder-freedom-expression.

### EXERCISE 13C ARGUING ABOUT TRIGGER WARNINGS

1. How would you summarize West's main argument in support of trigger warnings? How does she use opposing viewpoints to help make her argument?

2. Much of West's essay focuses on debates about trigger warnings on college campuses. As a college student yourself, how persuasive did you find her argument? To what extent do you think your own experience with trigger warnings has influenced your reaction to her essay?

3. How would you describe West's tone and voice in this essay? Do you think her tone makes her argument stronger? Does her voice contribute to her credibility? Explain, citing specific passages from the text to support your answer.

## American Wind Power
### by American Wind Energy Association

*The brochure reprinted here from a trade organization called the American Wind Energy Association™ illustrates how popular arguments can be made in alternative formats to advocate for a particular point of view or activity. The authors take advantage of the brochure format to incorporate visual elements into their argument, using color, layout, and other design features to enhance the presentation of their argument (see Chapter 20; also see "Analyzing Images" on page 228 in Chapter 8). The American Wind Energy Association™ advocates wind power, so the brochure's claim that wind power is good for America is no surprise; however, the brochure also makes a case in favor of government policies, especially tax incentives, that support the development of wind power. Notice that the brochure employs strategies that are commonly used in advertising, including emotional appeals. Being aware of these strategies can help you evaluate the effectiveness of the argument and influence your own reaction to the brochure. Also bear in mind that this brochure was available in 2012 when many Americans were debating the benefits and costs of alternative energy sources at a time of economic hardship; consider how the argument presented in the brochure fits that broader context.*

### Talking About the Reading

**Anna Garst (student):** "When the reading mentioned "tax incentives," I had a difficult time understanding what exactly those are. And the reading didn't explain what they are, so it wasn't very helpful."

**Bob Yagelski:** "Anna, you will often encounter unfamiliar terminology in your assigned readings in college. When that happens, I suggest two strategies. First, do your best to figure out what the term means in the context of the reading. If that doesn't work, try searching online. A quick search using the phrase *tax incentives* will lead you to several websites where you can quickly learn enough about that term to help you understand how it is being used in the pamphlet about American Wind Power."

### EXERCISE 13D ADVOCATING FOR WIND POWER

1. How would you state the main argument presented in this brochure? How clearly do you think that argument is presented? Do you think that argument would be more or less effective in a more traditional format, such as an essay? Explain.

2. What kind of evidence is presented in support of the claims made in the brochure? How credible is this evidence? How effectively do you think it is presented? On the basis of the evidence presented, what assumptions do you think are made about the audience for this brochure? Cite specific parts of the brochure to support your answers.

3. What are the main appeals made in this brochure (see "Making a Persuasive Appeal" in Chapter 11)? What do you think these appeals suggest about the intended audience for this brochure? Do you find these appeals effective? Why or why not?

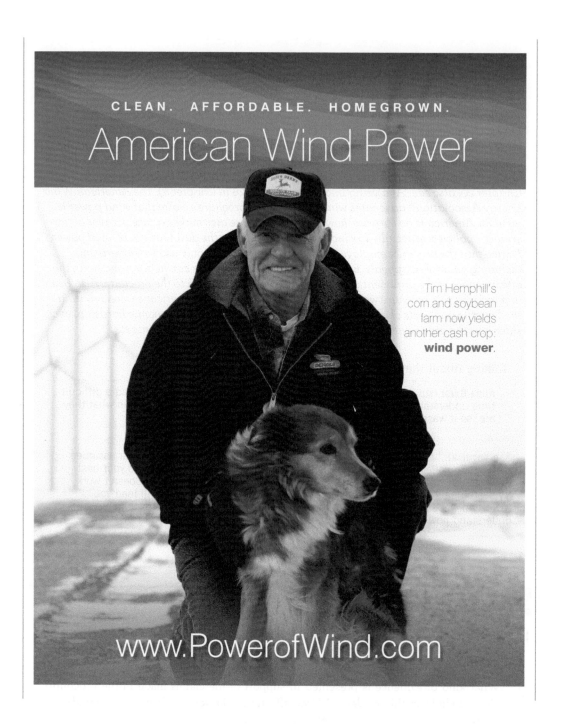

CLEAN. AFFORDABLE. HOMEGROWN.

American Wind Power

Tim Hemphill's corn and soybean farm now yields another cash crop: **wind power**.

www.PowerofWind.com

# Wind power is good for America

**that's why Americans want more of it.**

**Fifth-generation rancher Shaun Sims has tapped a new revenue stream he can count on: wind power.**
Evanston, Wyoming

**Mike Mayer's tire and oil shop got a big boost in business when developers began work on a local wind farm.**
Milford, Utah

**Thanks to the construction of a nearby wind farm, Judy Cleaves' bed & breakfast gained visibility and visitors.**
Weston, Maine

**Rural economic development fostered by a local wind farm helped build a new hospital, where Nancy Carter works.**
Milford, Utah

Wind power is good for the rancher who has a new source of steady income that helps preserve a way of life. It's good for the American manufacturer who produces one of the 8,000 components that make up a wind turbine. It's good for the family farmer who can now harvest the natural resource that blows across his land. And wind power is good for the rural school teacher who's been teaching in a trailer, but now educates students in a brand-new school built with revenue generated by way of the local wind farm development.

Wind is cost competitive with all other sources of new electricity. It bolsters America's economy through a supply chain of hundreds of manufacturing plants and over 2,500 companies investing in all stages of American wind power.

**Did you know that already, 20 percent of Iowa's electricity comes from wind power? In 2009 alone, the U.S. wind industry installed enough new capacity to power nearly 3 million homes.**

An overwhelming majority of Americans – well over 80% of all Republicans, Democrats, and Independents – want more wind power.

When you step back and look at the facts, it becomes clear that wind energy works for America.

**To learn more about what wind power can do for America.... and the federal and state policies that will unleash its potential.... please visit www.PowerofWind.com**

*(Continued)*

# Wind is Affordable

Wind power safeguards our families' checkbooks and creates opportunities for businesses large and small.

Wind is now one of the most cost-effective sources of new electricity generation. That's one reason wind accounts for 35% of all new electricity generating capacity since 2007.

Turbine prices and capital costs have dropped sharply in recent years. More efficient U.S.-based manufacturing is saving on transportation, and technology improvements are making turbines better and more efficient. Because of performance improvements over the years, a turbine with a nameplate capacity seven times larger than a typical turbine in 1990 can produce 15 times more electricity.

And the wind that turns the turbine blades costs nothing, locking in a predictable long-term cost of electricity for 20-30 years and protecting families and businesses from unexpected price spikes.

Alabama Power, a subsidiary of Southern Company, recently purchased its first wind power after the Public Service Commission

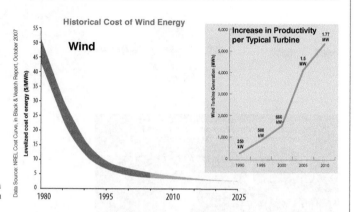

found that the "price of energy from the wind facility is expected to be lower than the cost the Company would incur to produce that energy from its own resource...with the resulting energy savings flowing directly to the Company's customers."[1]

In Colorado, Xcel Energy found that "by displacing natural gas with fixed priced wind energy, the Company has less exposure to

potentially volatile natural gas pricing."[2]

Market prices take into account the various incentives that all energy sources receive, and wind energy's is the federal Production Tax Credit. To stay affordable compared with other energy sources and their startup costs – already permanently incentivized over the last 90 years – U.S. wind power depends on Congress extending this single tax incentive.

# Wind is Homegrown

Wind energy has been one of the fastest-growing sources of new U.S. manufacturing jobs, even in the depths of the recession. Between 2005 and 2009, a period of relative policy stability never before seen by the industry, wind power grew at a fierce pace. Wind added 35% of all new electricity capacity between 2007 and 2010, neck and neck with natural gas as the top-two new electricity sources.

As a result of this market growth, today over 400 American manufacturing plants build wind components, including all the major turbine components, towers, and blades. Since 2007 over 100 wind energy manufacturing facilities have come online, been announced or expanded. Now over 60% of a U.S.-installed turbine's value is produced right here in America, according to a recent report from the U.S. Department of Energy. A 12-fold increase from just a few years ago. Some turbine manufacturers have already said they plan to make the vast majority of their components in America.

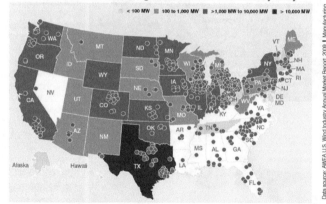

Unlike all too many products now produced overseas, the economics of wind power are such that components are best sourced domestically—that is, near the projects. The trend is expected to

continue—if long-term policies are put in place to signal the market stability enjoyed by other energy industries.

[1] Order, Alabama Public Service Commission, Docket 31653, Sept. 9, 2011
[2] Testimony, Public Service Company of Colorado, Sept. 19, 2011.

## Wind is Clean and Abundant

The United States boasts the perfect combination of massive electricity demand and a wind resource that is one of the best in the world. The wind power potential to be tapped is nothing short of amazing: 37 trillion kilowatt-hours of electricity annually—equivalent to nearly 10 times the country's existing power needs.[1]

Wind energy is already helping the nation meet America's electricity demand by powering the equivalent of over 9.7 million American homes. Today's wind farms produce enough electricity to power all of Virginia, Oklahoma or Tennessee. In Iowa existing wind projects could produce 20% of the state's electricity. Minnesota, North Dakota, Oregon, Colorado, and Kansas all receive more than 5% of their electricity from wind, and other states are following close behind with ever-growing wind power fleets.

According to the Bush Administration's U.S. Department of Energy report, "20% Wind Energy by 2030: Increasing Wind Energy's Contribution to U.S. Electricity Supply," wind can play a major role in meeting America's increasing demand for electricity, while producing multiple other benefits. Having 20% of the nation's electricity come from wind power is feasible with today's technology, the report found.

Moreover, the report found that installing more wind power would foster rural economic development, job creation, and energy price stability (by sidestepping fossil-fuel price volatility in addition to easing the pressure on natural gas prices). In the decade leading up to the 20% wind power benchmark, the U.S. wind industry could support roughly 500,000 jobs. It could also increase annual payments to rural landowners to more than $600 million in 2030.

**Wind provided 35 percent of all new U.S. electricity generation capacity, 2007-10**

  Coal    Wind
 Petroleum   Other Renewables
 Nuclear   Other
 Natural Gas

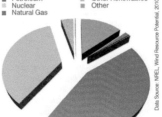

Data Source: NREL, Wind Resource Potential, 2010

Wind is a source of clean energy that has virtually no polluting properties or side effects. Each year, U.S. wind installations will save the nation over 20 billion gallons of water that would otherwise be withdrawn for steam or cooling in conventional power plants.

## A Lopsided Playing Field

Some people assume that wind power needs extra help from the government to compete. Since it's relatively new on the scene and boasts so many win-win attributes, are policy incentives really necessary? Only to level the playing field.

Fossil-fuel subsidies are – well, as old as fossil fuels. The Congressional Research Service notes that for more than 90 years, fossil fuel industries have taken subsidies via generous tax breaks. They are seldom debated or even heard of, because they are permanent. Examining the issue during the Bush Administration, the Government Accountability Office concluded that fossil fuels continue to receive nearly five times the tax incentives as renewable energy.[2] American taxpayers have already paid well over $500 billion to fossil fuel industries.[3]

Such strong policy support for old technologies like oil, gas, and coal during the last century succeeded in its goal:

**Fossil Fuels Enjoy Permanent Incentives 5x Those of Renewables**

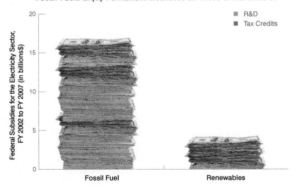

 R&D
 Tax Credits

Federal Subsidies for the Electricity Sector, FY 2002 to FY 2007 (in billions$)

Data Source: Government Accountability Office, October 2007

it helped create an abundance of affordable domestic energy, powering strong economic growth. Rising demand, volatile prices and national security concerns have since created a need for a more diverse energy supply.

[1] NREL, Wind Resource Potential, 2010
[2] Federal Electricity Subsidies (Government Accountability Office, October 2007).
[3] An Analysis of Federal Incentives Used to Stimulate Energy Production (U.S. Department of Energy, Pacific Northwest Laboratory Operated by Battelle Memorial Institute, December 1978) and Analysis of Federal Expenditures of Energy Development (Management Information Services, Inc (MISI)., September 2008).

*(Continued)*

## Predictable Policies Improve Investment

It's a wonder there's a U.S. wind industry at all, when you consider the lack of certainty companies have had to confront through the years. First, consider nearly 100 years of policy stability that has provided old techologies with a consistent environment in which to operate, plan, and grow.

Now consider wind power. The federal Production Tax Credit – the primary financial policy for the industry through the years – has been extended mostly in one- and two-year intervals, and even allowed to expire on occasion. The up-and-down nature of the industry is mainly the result of this short-term – and short-sighted – policy environment.

Wind has proven that it's a superior energy source. Why? Because it competes even on this uneven playing field. American wind installed 10,000 megawatts in 2009 – enough to power nearly 3 million homes. In recent years, it has gone head-to-head with natural gas for the leadership position in new power plant installations.

How did American wind power achieve such impressive numbers? Although it still operated with short-term policy,

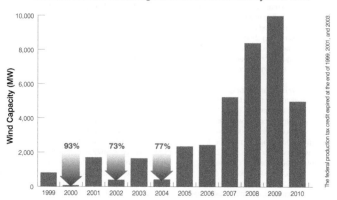

**Lack of consistent Market Signals Creates a Boom-Bust Cycle for Wind**

*The federal production tax credit expired at the end of 1999, 2001, and 2003*

there was a temporary period of stability for the industry. The PTC was extended for several years in a row without being allowed to expire. The frequent eleventh-hour extensions caused the industry some degree of stress as it began to establish a manufacturing base here; nevertheless, through its investments, the industry literally banked on Congress to act on long-term

policy. It's still waiting. One such policy is a national Renewable Electricity Standard, which would set targets for a certain portion of each utility's electricity mix to come from clean, renewable sources. Long-term tax policies, lasting more than just a few years, would also provide consistency and market certainty.

## America's Choice

Hands down, the American people support wind energy development. Recent polls consistently show that nearly nine out of ten voters – Republicans, Democrats, and Independents – believe increasing the amount of energy the nation gets from wind is a good idea. That's because wind power doesn't just generate electricity. It powers economic development. It adds a new source of steady income to family farmers' and ranchers' bottom line. It opens the doors of factories previously mothballed. It sends clean, home-grown energy to our homes and businesses, while protecting family budgets and small businesses from volatile price spikes. No wonder Americans want more wind power.

89% of American voters
84% of Republicans | 88% of Independents | 93% of Democrats
believe increasing the amount of energy the nation gets from wind is a good idea

Data Source: March 2010 survey by Neil Newhouse, Public Opinion Strategies. Anna Bennett, Bennett, Petts & Normington

To learn more about these Americans, and more about wind power,
go to **www.powerofwind.com**

## The Problem with Affirmative Consent
### by Alyssa Imam

*In November 2014, Rolling Stone, the well-known magazine of music and culture, published an article titled "A Rape on Campus," which described the experience of a student at the University of Virginia who claimed to have been raped at a fraternity house. As Alyssa Imam notes in the opening paragraph of the following essay, the* Rolling Stone *article provoked intense debate at that university, where Imam herself was a student. ("Grounds" in the first sentence refers to the University of Virginia campus.) The article also caused a nationwide controversy that intensified after it was revealed that the events described in the article never happened. For many colleges and universities, including the University of Virginia, the truth of the* Rolling Stone *article was less important than the problem it seemed to illuminate: sexual assault on campus. Concerns about what seemed to be an increase in sexual assault on college campuses in the past decade or so have prompted many institutions to adopt so-called "affirmative consent" policies, such as the one that Imam criticizes in this essay. These policies state that sexual activity requires the clear consent of two partners; otherwise, as Imam notes, seemingly acceptable sexual contact could be considered assault. Imam argues that these policies not only fail to address the problem of sexual assault on college campuses but also criminalize otherwise normal sexual behavior among college students. When she wrote this essay in 2015 for the University of Virginia student newspaper, Imam wrote from the perspective of a student who was directly affected by the University's affirmative consent policy. In that sense, her argument was a way for her to participate actively in a debate that had real consequences for her—and for her fellow students. As you read, consider whether her essay would persuade students on your own campus.*

### Talking About the Reading

> **Isaac Stillman (student):** I think this essay was far too brief. Sexual assault is a broad topic, so the essay should have gone into more depth.

> **Bob Yagelski:** You're right, Isaac, that sexual assault is a broad—and complicated— topic, but the question of how deeply a writer should delve into a topic is a complicated one that depends in large part on the rhetorical context. In this case, the author was writing an op-ed essay for a student newspaper, which likely had length restrictions that limited how much she could say. One strategy for dealing with such restrictions is to focus the argument narrowly, as this author does. Notice that her essay is not about sexual assault in general but specifically about affirmative consent policies.

After the *Rolling Stone* article "A Rape on Campus" came out last year, sexual assault became a heated topic around Grounds. The University has responded with steps such as asking students to complete a sexual assault module. More significantly, it adopted affirmative consent into its sexual assault policy. Naturally, the University needs to respond in some way, but affirmative consent is not the answer. In fact, the concept itself could have numerous problematic implications for how we view sexual assault.

One of the biggest problems with the "yes means yes" approach is that it oversimplifies sexual interactions, which by nature are much more complex than that policy would suggest. In fact, it does so to the extent that even an unwanted hug might be counted as sexual assault. The fact that this case would not logically constitute sexual assault for most people highlights the self-defeating characteristic of this policy: What purpose does a policy serve the community if we would generally classify so many interactions that violate it as unworthy of being reported, and possibly even silly? Furthermore, categorizing such interactions as sexual assault is dangerous because it trivializes attacks under more violent and traumatizing circumstances.

Affirmative consent fails to recognize that, while violent assault crimes are an ever-pressing issue, humans are still able to make mistakes concerning sex that (although they may regret them later) were not necessarily forced. The University website's Sexual Violence page describes affirmative consent as verbal or nonverbal, and states it can be obtained through "clear words or actions." The website also states consent is knowing, and that someone "should be able to clearly understand the who, what, where, when, and why they are consenting to anything sexual." This is an ambiguous guide at best, especially when placed in the context of the bar and college party scenes, where alcohol can impair one's judgment regarding what one is willing to do in the moment, and affect one's ability to both read and receive "clear" signs.

So, even when the partner correctly reads the other person's nonverbal, "clear" signs as consent, if that person later realizes otherwise, the interaction could be viewed as an assault.

Additionally, even if true affirmative consent is given, it can then be taken away if the other person goes further without a clear "No," since this view of consent requires it be given each time a deeper level of intimacy is reached. The concept of "checking in" with your partner is not only unrealistic when considering that few people's tastes involve a verbal confirmation that each level of intimacy is acceptable as it is reached, but also unfairly places most of the burden on the male counterpart (assuming this is a heterosexual relationship). If the man in the situation were to think consent was implied based on non-verbal signs from how the partner is reacting to the current level of intimacy and so tries to take it further, the woman should feel free to try and stop him. Since affirmative consent can include non-verbal signs, it results in even further blurred lines regarding consent, as shown in the guy's misunderstanding of her signs.

This is not to mention that in a culture where men are normally expected to make the move, this policy could result in us thinking it is also his responsibility to make sure that assault does not occur. In this way, while affirmative consent attempts to encourage both sides to seek consent from the other, in reality it could instead result in a double standard against men, criminalizing seemingly innocent, well-intentioned human contact and mistakes.

On the other hand, someone who maliciously intends to assault someone won't be deterred in his attempt to do so because of the implementation of affirmative consent. At the same time, the person attacked in violent cases such as these would not need this new policy in order for her experience to be considered an assault. While the burden of ensuring no assault occurs should not be placed on the victim's saying "no," it is also unfair to place it on the other partner to make sure there is a "yes." Affirmative consent oversimplifies the complex manner of sexual interactions and could change how sexual assault is viewed in negative ways.

Source: Imam, Alyssa. "The Problem With Affirmative Consent." *Cavalier Daily*, 16 Sep 2015, www.cavalierdaily.com/article/2015/09/imam-affirmative-consent-uva.

# Writing Arguments in Public Contexts

Arguments in public discourse are usually a way to work out difficult and often controversial questions that can affect our lives directly. Often, an argument about a specific problem is related to a much larger issue. For example, if you make an argument against a proposed security system on your campus, you are also participating in a larger, ongoing conversation about privacy.

This section provides a framework for developing such an argument using the Ten Core Concepts described in Chapter 2 and Chapter 3. Each step described here corresponds to a step in Chapter 3. You might notice that some of the steps are similar to those described in "Writing Academic Arguments" in Chapter 12. However, there are some important differences between academic arguments and arguments made in popular contexts; those differences are reflected here. In addition, as you develop your project, keep in mind the five essential features of argument that are explained in Chapter 11:

1. **A clear main point.** Present a clear main point related to your position on the issue at hand:
   - What is the main point you will make in this argument?
   - What purpose do you hope to achieve in making this argument?

2. **A relevant purpose.** Identify the relevance of your argument for your rhetorical situation:
   - What makes your argument relevant to your intended audience?
   - Why is your argument relevant now?

3. **Appropriate support for claims.** Support your claims with sufficient and appropriate evidence:
   - What evidence do you present to support your main claim and supporting claims?
   - What makes this evidence appropriate in the context of your rhetorical situation? Is your evidence sufficient to support your claims?

4. **Complexity.** Present your argument so that it reflects the complexity of your subject:
   - Have you explored the subject of your argument in sufficient depth and avoided oversimplifying it?
   - Have you considered complicating factors or alternative viewpoints on your subject?

5. **A persuasive appeal.** Use appropriate appeals to reason, emotion, or character to make your argument persuasive:

   ■ What persuasive appeals have you employed in your argument?

   ■ Are your persuasive appeals appropriate for your rhetorical situation?

## Step 1  Identify a topic for argument.

Begin with a question about a problem or issue that matters to you:

- What limits should be placed on individual freedom in the interest of national security?
- Should marijuana be decriminalized for medical uses?
- How should social media be used in college classrooms?
- What responsibility, if any, do individual citizens have when it comes to addressing problems associated with climate change?
- Should English be the official language of the U.S.?
- Why should college students be concerned about income inequality in the U.S.?

Make a list of four or five such questions. If there is a local issue that interests you, such as a current controversy in your town or on your campus, include it on this list.

Now select the question that you would most like to explore. Consider the following:

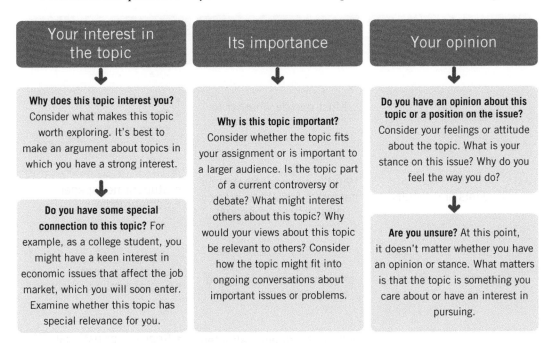

| Your interest in the topic | Its importance | Your opinion |
|---|---|---|
| **Why does this topic interest you?** Consider what makes this topic worth exploring. It's best to make an argument about topics in which you have a strong interest. | **Why is this topic important?** Consider whether the topic fits your assignment or is important to a larger audience. Is the topic part of a current controversy or debate? What might interest others about this topic? Why would your views about this topic be relevant to others? Consider how the topic might fit into ongoing conversations about important issues or problems. | **Do you have an opinion about this topic or a position on the issue?** Consider your feelings or attitude about the topic. What is your stance on this issue? Why do you feel the way you do? |
| **Do you have some special connection to this topic?** For example, as a college student, you might have a keen interest in economic issues that affect the job market, which you will soon enter. Examine whether this topic has special relevance for you. | | **Are you unsure?** At this point, it doesn't matter whether you have an opinion or stance. What matters is that the topic is something you care about or have an interest in pursuing. |

Addressing these questions will help you decide whether to pursue the topic. If you decide that this topic isn't appropriate or doesn't sufficiently interest you to sustain an argument, return to your list and select a different question. Once you have a question about which you want to make an argument, continue to develop your question using Step #1 in Chapter 3.

## Step 2 | Place your topic in rhetorical context.

Because the contexts for public arguments are so varied and sometimes very general, it can be challenging to identify with certainty the specific elements of your rhetorical context.

For example, imagine that the administration of your college has proposed installing security cameras in most public spaces on your campus, including the student center, the open areas outside the main classroom buildings, and the recreation fields where students often play Frisbee or study during good weather. The proposal was prompted by recent violence on other college campuses; however, some students and faculty members at your college object to the plan, expressing concern that instead of deterring crime, the cameras will invade students' privacy and be used to monitor student behavior. Some residents of the local community are also interested in the plan, because many of them come to the campus for various fine arts and sporting events, meetings, and other activities. Let's imagine that you agree with some of the criticisms of the plan, but you also share the concerns of the college administration about campus security. So the **main question** at this point is

*Should security cameras should be installed in public spaces on the campus?*

You are interested in developing an argument that makes a case for a middle ground that might address the concerns of all parties. As you develop that argument, examine your possible audiences:

| Possible audience | What is the audience's interest? | How can you reach this audience? |
|---|---|---|
| College administration | Must decide whether to install security cameras | • Letter <br> • Campus newspaper or social media site |
| Students and faculty | Will be directly affected by cameras; have both privacy and security concerns | • Student newspaper <br> • Social media |
| Community residents | Might sometimes be affected by cameras; care about issues on campus | • Local newspaper <br> • Social media or website |
| General audience (interested in security and privacy issues) | Will not be directly affected by cameras but care about larger questions of privacy and security | • Regional or national newspaper <br> • Online magazine <br> • Social media sites |

This graphic illustrates that the interests of your potential audiences overlap yet differ in some important ways. For example, students and faculty might worry about how their behavior could be affected by the new cameras. By contrast, a general audience (say, readers of a national blog or larger-circulation publication like *USA Today*) would not share that concern but might be very interested in the way your campus administration tries to address the conflict between security and privacy, which is an issue of national debate. It is possible that your argument might be written with all these audiences in mind. Ultimately, your interest in this topic and your audience's interests should overlap, giving your argument greater relevance.

With this in mind, return to your question from Step #1 and use this graphic to explore your audience and the rhetorical context for an argument about your question. Step #2 in Chapter 3 will help you examine your rhetorical context more fully.

**13**

## Step 3 Select a medium.

In selecting a medium for your argument, consider the advantages and drawbacks of each medium for specific audiences—keeping in mind that public arguments might appear in many different media. For example, using our hypothetical question about the proposal to install security cameras in public spaces on your college campus, compare the advantages and drawbacks of two possible media for the argument: an essay in the campus newspaper and a post on a social media site devoted to campus issues:

### Medium: Essay in Campus Newspaper

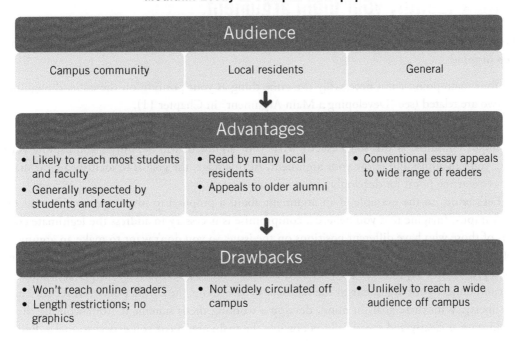

| Audience | | |
|---|---|---|
| Campus community | Local residents | General |

| Advantages | | |
|---|---|---|
| • Likely to reach most students and faculty<br>• Generally respected by students and faculty | • Read by many local residents<br>• Appeals to older alumni | • Conventional essay appeals to wide range of readers |

| Drawbacks | | |
|---|---|---|
| • Won't reach online readers<br>• Length restrictions; no graphics | • Not widely circulated off campus | • Unlikely to reach a wide audience off campus |

**Medium: Post on Social Media Site**

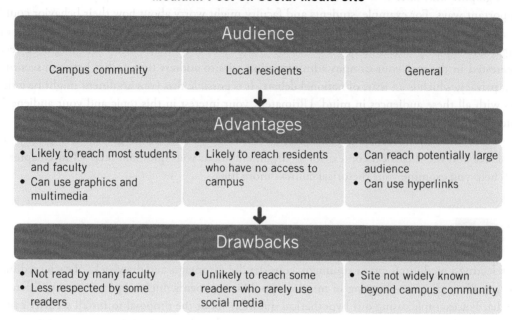

| Audience | | |
|---|---|---|
| Campus community | Local residents | General |

| Advantages | | |
|---|---|---|
| • Likely to reach most students and faculty<br>• Can use graphics and multimedia | • Likely to reach residents who have no access to campus | • Can reach potentially large audience<br>• Can use hyperlinks |

| Drawbacks | | |
|---|---|---|
| • Not read by many faculty<br>• Less respected by some readers | • Unlikely to reach some readers who rarely use social media | • Site not widely known beyond campus community |

Return to your main question and identify possible media for your argument. Evaluate each one in terms of its potential advantages and drawbacks for your intended audience, then complete Step #3 in Chapter 3 to help you decide on the most appropriate medium for your argument.

## Step 4  Identify your main argument.

The strength of your argument will rest in part on how clearly you can make your main point. Keep in mind:

- Your main point is not necessarily the same thing as your position on the issue, though the two are related (see "Developing a Main Argument" in Chapter 11).
- Your main point might evolve as you develop your argument.

You might not know at this stage exactly what your argument will be, but as you explore your topic, you can adjust and refine your argument. At this stage, the goal is to identify a clear main idea as a starting point for developing your argument.

Let's return to the example of an argument about a proposal to install security cameras on your campus. Imagine that you believe a compromise is necessary to address the legitimate concerns of those who have different positions on the issue, so you don't want to make an argument explicitly for or against the installation of the cameras; rather, you want to develop an argument that captures your support for the proposed cameras and your concern about privacy. You also want to connect your argument to the national debate about the conflict between security and civil liberty. With these goals in mind, develop a working thesis statement. Your working thesis should state as clearly and specifically as possible the main argument you expect to make. Refine your statement until it captures your main argument:

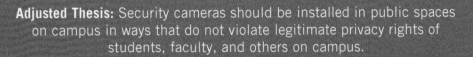

**Thesis:** The college should install security cameras in public spaces on campus.

| | |
|---|---|
| This statement reflects unequivocal support for the proposed security cameras. | The statement does not reflect your concerns about privacy and civil liberty. |

↓

**Adjusted Thesis:** Security cameras should be installed in public spaces on campus in ways that do not violate legitimate privacy rights of students, faculty, and others on campus.

| | |
|---|---|
| This statement reflects your position about the security cameras more accurately. | The statement still does not capture the larger conflict between security and civil liberties. |

↓

**Refined Thesis:** Institutions like colleges must carefully consider fundamental principles of civil liberty when taking measures such as installing security cameras in public spaces to protect the safety of students, faculty, and others who use their campuses.

| | |
|---|---|
| This statement captures the complexity of the issue and connects it to larger questions about security and civil liberty. | It also retains a focus on the local question about whether to install security cameras on campus. |

13

Notice that in developing your working thesis statement in this way, you are taking into account your rhetorical context and sense of purpose. In this case, you don't want to make an argument that is relevant only for your campus; you also want to connect the local question to larger issues that might speak to a more general audience.

Completing Step #4 in Chapter 3 will help you develop a Guiding Thesis Statement, which is essentially a statement of your main argument.

## Step 5 | Support your main argument.

At this point you will develop your main argument by identifying supporting arguments and claims and providing evidence and/or reasoning for each one. Often, completing this task requires research, so keep in mind that as you learn more about your topic, you might need to refine your argument and adjust your claims.

You have three main tasks at this point:

- Identify the claims you will make in support of your main argument.
- Identify evidence or reasoning to back up each claim.
- Address opposing arguments or complicating factors.

As you move through these steps, focus on developing your argument thoroughly. You might identify more claims and evidence than you will ultimately need, but later you can eliminate unnecessary claims or evidence.

Let's return to the example of an argument about security cameras on your campus. Here's your main argument:

*Institutions like colleges must carefully consider fundamental principles of civil liberty when taking measures such as installing security cameras in public spaces to protect the safety of students, faculty, and others who use their campuses.*

Consider possible claims you might make to support this main argument. First, you could claim that the college's concerns about security are valid, perhaps citing recent violence on other college campuses. You might also claim that security cameras can be an effective tool in preventing or responding to violent crime. In addition, you need to acknowledge the legitimate concerns about privacy and civil liberties. For example, you might cite evidence that security measures have led to violations of privacy rights in some cases. But you also want to show that such violations can be avoided, and you'll need some evidence for such a claim. Ultimately, you want to make the argument that civil liberties cannot be compromised because of security concerns, and that position might require logical reasoning to support. Develop each of these supporting and opposing arguments as follows:

## Main Argument

Institutions like colleges must carefully consider fundamental principles of civil liberty when taking measures such as installing security cameras in public spaces to protect the safety of students, faculty, and others who use their campuses.

## Supporting Claims

| | | |
|---|---|---|
| Colleges have reason to worry about campus security. | Security cameras in public places can be effective in deterring or responding to violent crime. | Security measures can be taken without seriously compromising privacy and civil liberty. |

## Possible Evidence or Reasoning to Support Claims

| | | |
|---|---|---|
| Recent incidents of violence on other campuses; the campus presents an opportunity for tragic violence | Statistical data showing positive impact of security cameras | Examples of other campuses using cameras with restrictions to protect privacy |

## Opposing Arguments or Complicating Factors

| | | |
|---|---|---|
| Tragic violence on a few campuses doesn't mean all campuses are at risk; overreaction could be worse than doing nothing. | Security measures have often resulted in the abuse of civil liberties. | Civil liberties are always in danger and must be protected, even if it means accepting some risk of violent crime. |

## Answers to Opposing Arguments and/or Complicating Factors

| | | |
|---|---|---|
| True, but colleges have a responsibility to prepare for unexpected tragedies. | Yes. That's why restrictions must be placed on the use of security cameras on campus. | Agreed, but protecting civil liberties and enhancing security are not mutually exclusive. |

As you develop supporting arguments and identify evidence to support your claims, keep the following in mind:

- **Present your argument fairly.** Avoid making misleading claims and misrepresenting opposing arguments. Instead, present your own claims and acknowledge opposing claims so that you don't oversimplify the issue. Although exaggerating or misrepresenting opposing viewpoints can win approval from those who might already agree with you, it can also lead to a weaker argument that is less persuasive for readers who might be undecided about the issue.

- **Be judicious in your use of evidence.** Remember that in public arguments, you might be limited in how much evidence you can provide to support your claims (see "Appropriate but accessible support for claims" on page 397). So be judicious in selecting and presenting your evidence, keeping in mind that you might not be able to cite sources with footnotes or provide lengthy explanations of your evidence. The rule of thumb is to present your evidence succinctly while making sure your readers know that the evidence is credible. For example, in an essay about ocean garbage, Usha Lee McFarling refers to studies to support her claims about the problems with plastic garbage that is dumped in the sea:

> A study released last month found plastic deep in the water column as well as on the surface, suggesting the ocean holds far more plastic than previously believed. A second study published this month indicates the amount of plastic in the Great Pacific Garbage Patch has increased 100-fold in the last four decades.

McFarling doesn't provide much information about these studies, but she notes that both studies are recent, which suggests that the studies' findings are still relevant. Given that her essay appeared on the opinion pages of a newspaper, she was not able to use footnotes to provide references for the studies. To strengthen the credibility of this evidence, she might have mentioned briefly where the studies were published and whether they are considered sound studies by other scientists. Apparently, she assumes that her readers will trust that she has reviewed the actual studies carefully to establish their credibility.

With these principles in mind, develop your claims and identify appropriate and sufficient evidence to support them. Also identify opposing claims and evidence or reasoning to address them. Step #5 in Chapter 3 will guide you in this task.

You should now be ready to write a complete draft of your project. If not, move on to the next step before completing your draft.

13

## Step 6  Organize your argument.

Arguments in public contexts tend to be more loosely structured than the four traditional ways of organizing an argument described in Chapter 11 (see "Structuring an Argument"). Writers in popular venues usually adjust the structure of their arguments to fit the needs of the rhetorical situation, including the medium and the expectations for form (if any). For example, an editorial essay might loosely follow a classical arrangement (see pp. 345–346 in Chapter 11) but eliminate the formal refutation of opposing arguments (which is Part V in classical arrangement). For a brief essay in a traditional format such as a newspaper, with limited space, this structure makes sense. The point is that you can adjust a format such as classical arrangement to suit your needs.

So use the four traditional ways to organize your argument as a guide rather than a rigid format, adjusting the structure of your argument to fit the needs of your rhetorical situation:

| The rhetorical situation | • How can you organize your essay to present your argument to your intended audience clearly and persuasively?<br>• What expectations will your audience likely have regarding the form of your argument?<br>• Are you writing within a rhetorical situation that has specific conventions for structuring an argument?<br>• In what ways might the medium in which you are writing restrict the structure of your argument? |
| --- | --- |
| The nature of your argument | • Does your argument rest on a primary belief or principle (deductive reasoning)?<br>• Does it rely on conclusions drawn from evidence (inductive arrangement)?<br>• Does your argument include a number of complicated supporting claims and kinds of evidence (classical arrangement)?<br>• Is your purpose primarily to solve a problem or negotiate differences (Rogerian arrangement)? |

To illustrate, let's return to the previous example of an argument about the proposed use of security cameras in public spaces on your college campus:

- **Consider the rhetorical situation.** Imagine that you have decided to present your argument in a blog post on a campus social media site. In many ways, your post would be similar to a traditional newspaper op-ed essay or even an academic essay. It will have to be relatively brief, though, and it should be clearly focused on the issue at hand (Should the campus install security cameras?). But your main argument addresses a complicated issue and connects it to the larger question of how to balance security with civil liberties. Given that complexity, using a form of classical arrangement might be a good approach to present your case effectively to a varied audience of students, faculty, and probably community residents. Classical arrangement would allow you to incorporate your several claims about security and civil liberties. On the other hand, since you are presenting what amounts to a solution that could appeal to people with different positions on the issue, Rogerian argument might also make sense.

- **Examine the nature of the argument.** Classical arrangement can be an effective approach to organizing an argument that includes several complicated claims and different kinds of supporting evidence. But you might consider arranging your post as an inductive argument, in which you are drawing conclusions from available evidence. In this case, the evidence might be the experience of other colleges with security cameras as well as statistical data about how security cameras reduce crime, and your main conclusion is that security measures must be undertaken carefully to avoid violations of civil liberty. An inductive approach will enable you to emphasize your evidence.

On the basis of this analysis, you have three options for organizing your argument: classical arrangement, Rogerian argument, and inductive reasoning. Select one of these approaches (or a different one) and develop a basic outline (see "Structuring an Argument" in Chapter 11). However you decide to organize your argument, the structure should be driven by your sense of how to present your argument most effectively for your rhetorical situation.

Follow these steps to analyze your situation and decide how best to organize your argument. You can get additional guidance for organizing your essay by following Step #6 in Chapter 3.

## Step 7 Get feedback.

Ask your readers to focus on two sets of questions about argumentation in popular contexts:

First, focus on the **features of effective argument in popular contexts:**

| A clear main point | • What is your main point? <br> • Is the purpose of your argument clear? <br> • Is the focus on your main argument maintained throughout your essay? |
|---|---|
| Appropriate, accessible support | • What support do you provide for each of your claims? <br> • Which claims might be made stronger with additional or different support? <br> • What makes your evidence appropriate for and understandable to your audience? |
| Relevant contribution | • How do you explain why your argument is relevant for your rhetorical situation? Do you place it in a context that makes sense to your readers? <br> • How does your argument contribute to discussions of your topic? |
| Opposing arguments | • How have you addressed opposing arguments? <br> • Do you present opposing arguments fairly and in a way that strengthens your own position? <br> • How have you avoided oversimplifying the issues? |

Next, focus on common problems in arguments in public contexts:

| Missing or weak evidence | • Do you provide sufficient evidence for each claim you make?<br>• Have you failed to support any claims?<br>• Is the evidence presented for any of your claims weak, misleading, or inappropriate? |
|---|---|
| Flawed reasoning | • Is your reasoning sound?<br>• Do you fall victim to any logical fallacies? (See Focus: "Recognizing Logical Fallacies in Public Arguments" on p. 395.)<br>• Do your conclusions follow logically from your evidence or claims? |
| Oversimplified or exaggerated assertions | • Do you oversimplify your topic or your claims?<br>• Does your argument do justice to the complexity of your topic?<br>• Do you make any exaggerated claims or assertions that need to be eliminated or revised on the basis of your evidence? |

Follow Step # 7 in Chapter 3 to analyze your feedback and help you decide which revisions to make.

## Step 8 | Revise.

As you consider the feedback you received for Step #7, you might find that you need to do additional research to identify evidence to support your claims or address opposing arguments or complicating factors. That's OK. Remember, revision is

- an opportunity to deepen your understanding of your topic and strengthen your argument, and
- a chance to adjust your persuasive appeals and make sure that your argument fits your rhetorical situation.

You can divide the task of revising your argument into three steps:

1. **Review your draft using the questions listed in Step #7.** Make sure you have addressed the four key features of effective argument in public contexts; also, eliminate any of the common problems in public arguments.

2. **Adjust your persuasive appeals.** Now is the time to review your draft to make sure that you have used ethical, emotional, and/or logical appeals in a way that strengthens your argument (see "Making a Persuasive Appeal" in Chapter 11). For example, the logical appeals made by Alyssa Imam in the essay reprinted in this chapter (see pages 410–412) are appropriate in an argument that examines an issue from a legal perspective, as her argument

does; however, if her argument focused on a specific case that in which a student was treated in a grossly unfair manner, she might have used an emotional appeal as well, which might resonate with her audience of college students. Review each of your supporting arguments or claims to determine whether you have made an appropriate persuasive appeal for that argument or claim given your rhetorical situation.

Let's return to our hypothetical argument about installing security cameras in public spaces on your campus; consider the appeals that might be appropriate for your main claims:

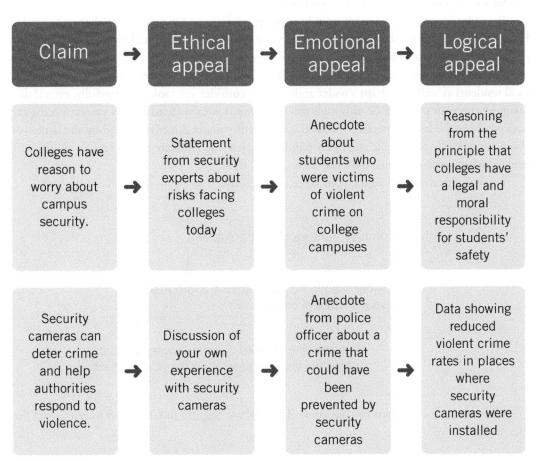

| Claim → | Ethical appeal → | Emotional appeal → | Logical appeal |
|---|---|---|---|
| Colleges have reason to worry about campus security. → | Statement from security experts about risks facing colleges today → | Anecdote about students who were victims of violent crime on college campuses → | Reasoning from the principle that colleges have a legal and moral responsibility for students' safety |
| Security cameras can deter crime and help authorities respond to violence. → | Discussion of your own experience with security cameras → | Anecdote from police officer about a crime that could have been prevented by security cameras → | Data showing reduced violent crime rates in places where security cameras were installed |

Notice that different kinds of evidence can be used to make different kinds of appeals. If we assume that all the evidence is valid and credible, then the decision about which evidence to use to support a claim should be a matter of determining which kind of appeal would be most effective for the rhetorical situation.

3. Finally, follow Step #8 in Chapter 3 to make sure you have addressed all the essential aspects of your essay in your revisions.

## Step 9 | Refine your voice.

The reading selections included in this chapter illustrate how varied a writer's voice can be in public argumentation. For example, compare the measured voice of Alyssa Imam (pages 410–411) to Lindy West's voice and her somewhat combative tone (pages 400–402), and consider how each voice fits (or does not fit) the topic and rhetorical situation. These examples underscore the point that an argument can be strengthened—or weakened—by the writer's voice. Keep that in mind as you review your draft with a focus on your voice.

Begin by considering your purpose in making your argument, which can shape your voice. For example, let's say your purpose in making your argument about installing security cameras in public spaces on your campus is to negotiate differences among the competing points of view in an effort to find a solution to a difficult problem. You want your readers (students, faculty, and local residents as well as perhaps a wider audience) to consider your solution carefully, even if they disagree with your position. So although you might want your voice to convey your concerns and passion about the issue, especially because as a student you are directly affected by the issue, you also want to sound reasonable and open-minded. Such a voice is likely to win respect among your readers, whatever their position on the issue.

Review your draft and adjust your voice, if necessary:

> Identify the primary purpose of your argument.

> Consider the kind of voice that is appropriate for your rhetorical context.

> Review your draft to determine whether your voice fits your purpose and rhetorical context.

Make necessary revisions to your draft. Then follow Step #9 in Chapter 3 to refine and further strengthen your voice.

## Step 10 | Edit.

Complete Step #10 in Chapter 3.

**1.** Identify an issue or controversy that you feel strongly about. Write an argument in which you take a position on this issue for an audience of people who have an interest in or connection to the issue.

**2.** Write an argument in response to an essay on a website or in a publication you regularly read. Write your argument for the same audience for whom the original essay was intended.

**3.** Rewrite the argument you wrote for Question #1 or Question #2 for a completely different audience or in a different medium. Then compare both arguments. What adjustments did you have to make in revising your argument? What conclusions might you draw about the role of audience and medium in constructing effective arguments in public contexts?

**4.** Think of an important experience you had that influenced your life in a significant way. Looking back on that experience, consider what larger issues the experience seems to involve. For example, if you encountered some kind of difficulty in school, you might consider your experience in light of debates about school reform or problems with education. Drawing on your experience, write an argument about an issue related to that experience. Identify an audience for whom your argument would be appropriate.

**5.** Review the argument you wrote for Question #1, #2, or #4 and identify the persuasive appeals (emotional, ethical, or logical) you used in your argument. Rewrite the argument, using different appeals to make your case. For example, if you relied primarily on an emotional appeal in the original essay, focus on a logical or ethical appeal in your rewrite.

**6.** Review several recent tweets on a current controversy that interests you. Identify tweets that reflect a position on the issue that you support. Now construct an argument on the basis of that tweet. Write your argument for an audience similar to the audience for the original tweet and adopt a medium that would reach that audience.

13

---

## MindTap®

Request help with these Writing Projects and feedback from a tutor. If required, participate in peer review, submit your paper for a grade, and view instructor comments online.

### In this chapter, you will learn to

1. Identify and understand the purposes of proposals.

2. Identify appropriate rhetorical opportunities for writing proposals.

3. Define the four main features of effective proposals and apply them to sample proposals.

4. Write a proposal, applying the four main features of effective proposals and using the Ten Core Concepts from Chapter 3.

## MindTap®

Understand the goals of the chapter and complete a warm-up activity.

# Presenting a Proposal 14

**A FRIEND ONCE COMPLAINED** to me about the writing skills of new employees at his engineering firm. Most are recent graduates from some of the most prestigious engineering schools in the U.S., with excellent academic records and relevant work experience but, according to my friend, poor writing skills. Few of them, he says, can write effective proposals, which is an essential skill in his line of work. Without persuasive proposals, his firm could not secure contracts for the large projects that earn them a profit. So my friend spends a lot of time helping new employees learn to write proposals.

Proposals, which are a special kind of argument, are essential in businesses like engineering firms, which compete with other firms for contracts. Proposals are common in many other contexts as well:

- Non-profit organizations write proposals to foundations or government agencies to secure funding for their work.
- Researchers submit proposals to obtain grants to support their research.
- Student leaders submit proposals to college administrators seeking permission to hold special events, such as concerts, on campus.
- Entrepreneurs pitch proposals for new businesses to potential investors.

As these examples illustrate, proposals are a specialized form of argument in which the primary goal is to convince someone to support a project, idea, or plan. Knowing how to write an effective proposal, then, can help you succeed as a student, a citizen, and a professional.

## Occasions for Writing Proposals

In a proposal, a writer uses argument not to take a stand or present a point of view but to convince a reader that a specific idea or plan is worthwhile. Proposals take many different forms, and writers in all kinds of situations—business, school, politics, and so on—use them in various ways. Although you might not have experience as a professional writer or businessperson, you have probably written some kind of proposal:

- for an independent study project in a high school or college class
- for a grant or scholarship application to support an activity or study
- to invite a business or foundation to sponsor a school trip or project
- to request permission from your school or church to have a dance or other special event

In such cases, the writer makes an argument that the project, event, trip, or activity is worthy of support.

Notice that these examples all describe very specific rhetorical situations with very specific and often small audiences. For example, a student writing a proposal for an independent study project addresses a teacher, principal, or faculty committee whom the student may know. Sometimes, however, a writer might wish to make a case for a specific course of action in a more public forum. In such instances, the writer is proposing not a project but a solution to a problem that is of interest to a larger audience. Shortly after the 2008 U.S. presidential election, for example, well-known writer Michael Pollan published an essay in the *New York Times* that was ostensibly addressed to President-Elect Barack Obama. In his essay, Pollan proposes several steps that the new president should take to promote local food production. He begins his lengthy essay by explaining why food policy should be a focus of the new president's attention:

> It may surprise you to learn that among the issues that will occupy much of your time in the coming years is one you barely mentioned during the campaign: food. . . . But with a suddenness that has taken us all by surprise, the era of cheap and abundant food appears to be drawing to a close. What this means is that you, like so many other leaders through history, will find yourself confronting the fact—so easy to overlook these past few years—that the health of a nation's food system is a critical issue of national security. Food is about to demand your attention.

Source: Pollan, Michael "Farmer in Chief." *The New York Times*, 9 Oct. 2008, nyti.ms/1Y2DDug.

Pollan goes on to describe the problems with the current system of food production and distribution, and he proposes a solution: to "resolarize" American agriculture. He argues that government policies should create incentives for farmers to give up their reliance on oil-based agriculture and return to more traditional techniques that rely on the sun. The result, according to Pollan, would be a healthy food supply, a healthier environment, and new economic opportunities for farmers.

Pollan's essay amounts to a proposal for a course of action. His proposal is not intended to seek approval or funding for a plan, as in a grant proposal, but to contribute to public discussions about solving a problem that affects a larger audience. This need to solve a problem characterizes proposals:

- A scientist submitting a grant proposal not only seeks funding for research but also hopes to generate new knowledge by answering a specific research question.
- A student proposing a research project for a class not only needs to complete an assignment but also wishes to explore a relevant topic.
- An entrepreneur pitching a business plan not only needs financial support but also wants to innovate in a specific kind of business.

In such cases, proposals are the best way for writers to meet the needs of the rhetorical situation and accomplish their goals.

Sometimes a proposal reflects a stance on an issue and becomes the focus of debate. One such example involves the practice of hydraulic fracturing, or "fracking," a technique to access oil or natural gas that is trapped in certain kinds of underground rock formations. In the past decade or so fracking became controversial as energy companies sought to tap large deposits of natural gas in Wyoming, Ohio, Pennsylvania, and New York. Opponents of fracking claim that it endangers water supplies and causes environmental destruction, leading to serious health problems for humans and wildlife. Proponents argue that fracking can be done safely to develop new energy sources. As new natural gas deposits were being developed, some communities restricted fracking and even banned the practice outright. In 2011, the government of New York was considering such restrictions, and lawmakers debated whether to implement a statewide ban on fracking or allow communities to restrict the practice. This poster reflects the position of those who supported the proposal to ban fracking in the state. It might be considered a succinct version of a more fully developed proposal for such a ban.

14

# Understanding Proposals

As a specialized form of argument, proposals have many of the same features that characterize other kinds of arguments, including a clear main idea and support for that idea (see Chapter 11). But because proposals focus on a making a convincing case for a plan to address a specific problem, they have **four main features** that other kinds of arguments typically do not have:

1. **A clear statement of the problem.** Because a proposal seeks support for a project or a plan of action, it must provide a statement of the problem that the project or plan of action will try to solve. The writer must clearly identify the problem to be addressed, explain why the problem needs a solution, and show why it should matter to the reader. Whether the proposal is a general one intended for a wide audience or a more specific proposal seeking grant funding, support for an activity, or approval of a proposed project, the writer must convince the intended audience that the problem is significant and worth solving.

2. **A description of the proposed project or plan of action.** The main section of most proposals is the description of the plan, project, or idea that is intended to address the problem. Effective proposals present their plans in sufficient detail to give readers a clear sense of what is being proposed. Formal grant or research proposals often follow very specific guidelines for describing the project, including a detailed description of the methods and techniques that the researcher will use in the project, but even in more general proposals, the proposed solution or plan of action should be clearly described.

3. **A compelling rationale for the proposed project or plan of action.** The key to a successful proposal is the rationale, which explains why the proposed project or plan of action will solve the problem identified in the proposal. The rationale is the writer's main argument for the project or plan. A good proposal not only makes a persuasive case that the problem is an important one but also establishes compelling grounds for supporting the proposed plan of action or project.

4. **Appropriate evidence.** Like all effective arguments, proposals should include appropriate and credible evidence for the writer's claims. Usually, in a proposal a writer makes two general kinds of claims: (1) claims about the problem being addressed, and (2) claims about the proposed solution. In both cases, the basic principles governing the use of evidence in argumentation apply (see "Appraising and Using Evidence" on page 341 in Chapter 11). The stronger the evidence, the more convincing the proposal will be.

The following example illustrates these features. This proposal was submitted by George Srour, the founder and director of a non-profit organization called Building Tomorrow (BT), which involves college students in fundraising for educational projects (such as building schools) in poor communities in sub-Saharan Africa. Building Tomorrow was seeking funding from a foundation called Echoing Green to expand its operations in Africa. (Included here are excerpts from the full proposal.)

While interning at the UN World Food Programme in 2004, I spent two months studying the effectiveness of the organization's school feeding program in Uganda. Behind the many faces I encountered were stories of poverty and disease headlined by the personal struggles of 11 and 12 year old children heading their family's households. I spent time in class under tree canopies with just some of the 2 million Ugandan children who have been orphaned by AIDS and learned that an education, while inaccessible for 42 million children in sub-Saharan Africa, is the best assurance of a brighter future for some of the world's most vulnerable children. From this experience grew Building Tomorrow (BT), an NGO encouraging philanthropy among U.S. students by engaging them in fundraising for educational infrastructure projects to benefit orphans and vulnerable children (OVCs) in sub-Saharan Africa. This organization is unique in two ways: • it creates one-to-one partnerships between U.S. colleges and sub-Saharan Africa communities, maximizing both fundraising and the initiative's educational impact on American students • by pursuing an "ownership" model for the African schools being built, it insures that they will be both sustainable and high in quality. BT began as a campaign entitled Christmas in Kampala (CIK) at The College of William & Mary in 2004. The goal of CIK was to raise $10,000 to replace a one room timber structure serving hundreds of OVCs I had visited during my UN internship. In just six weeks, $45,000 was collected to construct a three-story school which opened in April 2006 and currently serves 350 OVCs. From elementary students in the Bronx to seminary students in the Philippines, students around the world generously offered their support of CIK. BT's vision is to create a scalable model that promises brighter futures by exposing U.S. students to the world of social responsibility and philanthropy

**A compelling rationale:** The background about BT helps establish the effectiveness of its approach. Notice, too, the emotional and ethical appeals.

while equipping vulnerable children in the Third World with educational opportunities. BT believes that today's youth can be at the forefront of social change through a sustainable program built on solid cross-cultural partnerships.

The AIDS pandemic has single-handedly crippled the infrastructure of sub-Saharan African governments. UNICEF and UNAIDS estimate that 42 million children in this region alone are without access to primary education and the majority of the 15 million children who have been orphaned by AIDS receive no schooling. Uganda is the world's youngest country with over 50% of the population under the age of 15, a percentage that the country's Bureau of Statistics believes will continue to rise. Countries such as Uganda have initiated Universal Primary Education (UPE) programs, guaranteeing a free education to every Ugandan child, however the government simply does not have the means to provide children with even a basic classroom. Officials in the Wakiso District of Uganda, home to future BT schools, estimate that 55% of the district's 600,000 children do not have access to education. Furthermore, due to school, uniform and book fees, the expense of transport and unsafe conditions for young girls traveling long distances, the district's Minister of Education estimates the drop-out rate amongst children enrolled in P1 (1st grade) hit a new record of 80% during the 2005–06 school year. UNESCO estimates that the financial hardships incurred as a result of the HIV/AIDS epidemic will add $950 million to the cost of providing UPE across sub-Saharan Africa by 2015. According to Dr. Peter Piot, the Executive Director of UNAIDS, partnerships encouraging the collaborative efforts of local ministries and development NGOs are what is needed to reach vulnerable populations. By opening doors to new, accessible neighborhood classrooms, BT can help reduce the dropout rate, provide children with the opportunity to receive a valuable education, and be an instrumental partner in building a better tomorrow.

BT believes sustainable social change lies in creating one-to-one relationships that yield social capital as student communities establish and develop long-term connections with the communities they're serving. Most NGOs working in sub-Saharan Africa have turned to mass mailing and internet appeals to increase their donor base. BT sees greater long-term benefits in cultivating the philanthropic power of younger generations while fostering a culture of social responsibility.

**Problem statement:** The writer clearly establishes the seriousness of the problem and the need for the proposed solution.

**Appropriate evidence:** Here and elsewhere statistical data support the writer's claims.

This emphasis on grassroots mobilization empowers students to see and believe that they can be at the heart of positive change. Where aid organizations typically hire contractors to design building projects, BT creates opportunities for architecture and engineering students from participating universities to design our schools. Where school children are traditionally referred to clinics for health exams, BT arranges for U.S. medical students to offer basic services at no cost. BT's approach fosters a philanthropic culture among young generations while affording vulnerable children in the Third World life-altering educational opportunities.

BT has developed a new model in funding educational infrastructure development. Working with local officials, BT locates communities where at least 300 OVCs are without access to education. In these areas, BT offers a challenge grant equal to 75% of construction and land acquisition costs (est. $32,000–35,000), with the community providing the remainder through labor, materials and small contributions. An MOU detailing the expectations of all stakeholders is drafted and signed prior to project initiation. By involving all stakeholders, BT ensures long-term sustainability while involving the government in the provision of teachers and operating expenses in accordance with UPE. This differs from the approach NGOs such as World Vision use whereby a school is built on government land and wholly operated by the NGO. By not holding a land title, the NGO could lose control of the building should the land be seized. Furthermore, by shouldering all operational costs, the NGO commits itself for an indefinite amount of time to the financial needs of the school, creating further dependencies that stifle developmental growth. BT believes the community at large is essential in providing an education for the country's youth. Each BT school will be administered by a School Management Committee (SMC), comprised of lay leaders, teachers, parents, government officials and a BT liaison. This body, representing a diverse range of stakeholders in the educations field, allows the school to benefit from the technical expertise and insights of a group of individuals committed to educational excellence.

**Description of proposed plan:** Here and in the preceding paragraph the writer explains BT's approach to community action.

Source: "Proposal from Building Tomorrow to Echoing Green." *Grant Space*. Foundation Center, grantspace.org/Tools/Sample-Documents/Proposal-from-Building-Tomorrow-to-Echoing-Green.

In this proposal, the organization's case for funding rests in part on the seriousness of the problems it seeks to address. Notice how carefully the writer establishes the need for the kind of services provided by Building Tomorrow, citing a variety of statistical information to support the claims made about the extent of the problem and using both emotional and ethical appeals to strengthen his case. Notice, too, the great deal of detailed information both in the statement of the problem and in the explanation of how the proposed plan would help solve the problem. The writer makes it clear that he not only understands the problem to be solved but also has significant experience with this kind of work. This is a good example of a proposal using effective argumentative strategies to make a strong case for a proposed plan.

Proposals can appear in a great variety of formats. Often, the format is determined by the organization to which the proposal is being submitted, and writers should always follow any guidelines provided by the organization. If no such guidelines are provided, organize your proposal as you would any effective argument, keeping your audience and purpose in mind. Remember, too, that proposals often contain specialized features such as executive summaries and budgets, which are usually described in the proposal guidelines. (See Sidebar: "Writing an Executive Summary" and Sidebar: "Proposing a Budget.")

---

**SIDEBAR**  **WRITING AN EXECUTIVE SUMMARY**

An executive summary provides an overview of a proposal. Depending on the nature of the proposal and the requirements of the organization for which it is intended, an executive summary can be a few sentences or paragraphs or even as long as a page. The summary should convey the main points of the proposal in a way that draws the reader into the proposal itself. In this sense, the executive summary is more than just a condensed description of the proposal; it is part of the writer's effort to persuade readers that the proposal is worth supporting. Executive summaries should

- provide a brief but clear statement of the problem that the proposal addresses;
- highlight the key points of the proposal;
- mention points that are likely to be important to the reader;
- be as clear, succinct, and engaging as possible.

For proposals involving a request for money, a budget is usually required. The specific details of the budget are usually determined by the organization to which the proposal will be submitted, but generally budgets present a breakdown of how the requested funds will be spent. Follow any guidelines for the budget that are set by the organization. For example, if you are applying to a local philanthropic organization for funds to support a class trip, review the organization's website or other materials to determine whether there are specific requirements or restrictions for a budget; use the budget categories identified in those materials (e.g., travel, supplies, stipends). Often, budgets are accompanied by an explanation of these categories (sometimes called a "budget narrative"). For example, if you list a certain sum for travel expenses in your budget, you would include a few sentences explaining the purpose of the travel, the destination, and the specific costs (e.g., airfare, taxi fares, etc.). Your budget should make it easy for your audience to see exactly how you will use the money you are requesting.

**14**

## EXERCISE 14B  UNDERSTANDING PROPOSALS

1. Find an argument about a problem that interests you. The argument can be from a publication such as your campus newspaper, a blog, or some other source. Now consider a proposal that might address the problem described in the argument. First, clearly state the problem that your proposal would address. Then, in a brief paragraph, describe a plan or project that would address that problem, explaining why the plan or project would be a good solution to the problem.

2. Identify a problem that interests you from one of your college courses. How would you try to solve that problem? What kind of proposal could you develop for your solution? In a brief paragraph, describe a project you could do that would address that problem, explaining the need for the project. Imagine that the audience for your proposal is the instructor of the course.

3. Write an executive summary for each of the proposals included in the next section ("Reading Proposals"). In a group of classmates, compare your summaries. Identify differences and similarities and draw conclusions about effective summaries.

4. Using your idea from Question #2, consider an alternative medium that would be appropriate for the proposal given your intended audience: a multimedia presentation in a format such as PowerPoint, a video presentation, or another medium. Explain how you would adapt the proposal to that medium.

# Reading Proposals

The proposals included in this section reflect various forms and purposes. The nature of the proposal (e.g., a grant proposal vs. a proposal in an op-ed essay) and the rhetorical situation will shape its form and content, but all effective proposals include the main features described in the previous section. As you read the following selections, notice the different ways in which these main features are exhibited:

| Clear statement of the problem | • What is the problem to be addressed in the proposal?<br>• How effectively is the significance of the problem explained?<br>• How does the writer establish a clear need for a solution? |
| --- | --- |
| Description of proposed project or plan | • What solution does the writer propose to address the problem?<br>• How clearly is the proposed plan described?<br>• How persuasive is the description? |
| Compelling rationale | • What rationale does the writer provide for the proposed solution or plan?<br>• To what extent is the proposed solution or plan appropriate for the problem?<br>• How persuasive is the rationale for the plan or solution? |
| Appropriate evidence | • What evidence is presented to establish that the problem to be addressed exists and is significant?<br>• What evidence is presented to support the proposed solution?<br>• Is the evidence appropriate and sufficient? |

## MindTap®

Read these proposal examples. Highlight and take notes online.
Additional readings are also available online.

# University of California Student Investment Proposal
## by Fix UC

*In 2011, faced with an unprecedented budget crisis brought on by the economic downturn that began in 2008, the University of California system implemented drastic budget cuts and tuition increases. These financial measures were the latest and most dramatic of several years of budget reductions, and they pro-voked widespread protests by students and faculty. In response to the crisis, students on the editorial board of the* Highlander, *the student newspaper at the University of California at Riverside, began discussing a long-term solution to the crisis. Led by editor Chris LoCascio, the students spent nine months devel-oping a formal proposal that they presented to the University of California Board of Regents in 2012. The proposal, which generated a great deal of coverage in the media and was considered seriously by the University system leaders, was a radical one. Under its terms, students who attend UC schools would not have to pay tuition until after they graduated and began earning an income. As you'll see, the proposal addresses many details related to the complexities of college funding and reflects the extensive research that the* Highlander *editorial team did as they refined their plan. Although the proposal was written for the University of California Board of Regents, it was also a public document that became the focus of a larger movement to reform the way students at public universities in California pay for their education. The proposal was available on the website of an advocacy group called Fix UC (www.fixuc.org), which was founded by the students who developed the proposal. As you read, consider how the student authors of the proposal addressed their primary audience (the Board of Regents) as well as broader audiences interested in the matter of funding higher education.*

· · · · · · · · · · · · · · · · · · · · · · · · · · · · · · · · · · · ·

### Talking About This Reading

> **Thad Snyder (student):** The proposal didn't address issues that would arise between students if some students are paying upfront and some aren't. I don't think all the possible scenarios that would result from changing the tuition model at UC were addressed.

> **Bob Yagelski:** Thad, your comment points to a possible implication of the proposed tuition plan that the proposers did not address. The writers might have decided that this implication was not important enough to include in this very complex proposal. It might also be that they simply overlooked it. Your comment underscores the need for proposal writers to try to take into account the expectations of their intended au-dience when deciding what to include and what to leave out—which is not always easy to do.

· · · · · · · · · · · · · · · · · · · · · · · · · · · · · · · · · · · ·

An education from the University of California offers students an array of skills and opportunities that lead toward both a career and the overall enrichment of one's life. While the latter is an intangible and priceless benefit of graduating from UC, the path it sets individuals on toward a career can be measured by the income one earns from employment. The Student Investment Proposal aims to remedy this discrepancy by allowing students to attend UC with no up-front costs while maximizing revenue for the UC.

The University of California system represents the pinnacle of public higher edu-cation. But as it stands, the UC cannot sustain itself through another massive budget cut from the State of California. In order to meet the budget shortfall, students have been asked repeatedly to pay more to attend a UC suffering the loss of resources and

*(Continued)*

faculty members, essentially raising the cost on an education of lessening quality. The UC's dependency on the state leaves it at the will of financial ebbs and flows. Another budget cut like that of 2011 could fatally cripple the University of California.

In order to ensure a promising future, the University of California needs to reevaluate its current revenue system and pursue options that can support it indefinitely while still working to the advantage of students. This proposal outlines a stable and predictable plan toward growth and sustainability for the distant future.

Beyond its practical application as a real long-term solution to the University of California's current revenue system, one of the goals of the UC Student Investment Proposal is to encourage a shift in thought about the education students receive by attending the university, and their relationship with that university after graduation. Students will begin to think about the value of their education and its significance in the trajectory of their life from graduation to retirement. Therefore, the University of California will invest in the success of its students by providing the up-front costs for attending the university with the expectation that the investment will return once a student graduates and enters a career.

This proposal presents, in detail, a potential solution for the University of California. It is intended for consideration by UC regents as the groundwork for a new long-term funding plan.

## Outline

Under the proposed UC Student Investment Plan—Models A and B, graduates of the University of California pay a small percentage of their income, based on 5%, interest free, to the UC upon entering a career after graduation for twenty years of employment. Therefore, undergraduate students pay no fees up-front to the university, and attend school without the financial burden and risk of increased fees.

The current system of prepaid student fees will be dismantled in favor of the new investment plan. The Financial Aid system, including the Blue and Gold Plan, will also cease to exist, its funds being dedicated elsewhere.

Graduates of the University of California, as they begin participation in the new financial contribution program, will have access to extended alumni programs and benefits that help them stay involved with their campus into the future.

The amount of revenue entering the UC compounds annually with an additional graduating class paying into the system. Over time, the UC's annual revenue will exceed that which it currently receives from student tuition.

UC Student Investment Plan—Model B includes all provisions of Model A, but also incorporates caps on minimum and maximum income thresholds for contribution.

Graduates will not begin contributing to the UC until their income exceeds $30,000 annually. A high-income ceiling is also in place, so no income beyond $200,000 annually would be subject to percentage contribution.

## Implementation

In order to implement the new UC Student Investment Plan, the UC will change its current Blue and Gold program to incorporate the UC Student Investment Plan. A group of students on the Blue and Gold program whose entire cost of attending is covered by Blue and Gold (UC Return to Aid Funds) will serve as the initial population to enter the plan. These students will attend UC with no up-front costs, just as they would have before the UC Student Investment Plan, but would pay a percentage of their income to the UC upon graduating and entering a career. The revenue the UC would have otherwise not received is then used as capital to put more and more students on the plan, until the entire UC student body is attending with no up-front cost.

**Details**

Contribution will be enforced by a new department of the United States Internal Revenue Service in charge of collecting contributions from graduates of American universities, beginning with the University of California. This department, in conjunction with the UC, would maintain a database of graduates and arrange the regular contributions of graduates in-state, out-of-state and abroad. Other institutions could then use the infrastructure to implement their own similar funding systems.

Students who transfer into the UC system will pay 1% less of their income.

Students who drop out/transfer out of the system will pay a set amount upon leaving equivalent to the would-be annual tuition rate for their time spent in the system.

Contributions from students who die while attending the UC will be absorbed by UC Student Investment Plan.

Extended alumni benefits for UC graduates paying into the UC will include full career center and employment support. Because the UC will depend on the earnings of its graduates, it is in its best interest to ensure that graduates are in stable, high-paying jobs. The UC will use its tremendous network of graduate and private industry contacts to provide its graduates with job opportunities both upon graduating and afterwards.

Incentives, in the form of decreased percentages of contributions to the UC, will be in place for those who live and work within the state of California after graduation (0.5%), as well as for those who seek careers in the public sector (1%). Individual campuses may also offer incentives to academic and athletic high achievers as a means of recruiting, but with a cap on the amount of students who can receive these incentives per campus.

Out-of-state and international students pay an increase of 1%, with the same incentive option to stay and work in California.

Contribution waivers for emergency situations will be available.

Contribution rate at the time a student enters UC must remain unchanged for that individual's total contribution period. Changes in contribution percentage can only be applied to incoming students.

State of California investment in UC must not fall below 2% of the total state budget at any time. A decrease in state investment cannot go into effect until 10 years after UC Student Investment Plan is initiated, and can only be done in 0.2% annual increments.

Federal and state aid will continue to go directly to students for educational expenses.

The revenue collected from students of each campus will first cover that campus' budget. Additional funds enter a UC savings account, with some of those funds being saved for emergencies, and some being used for investing in bolstered K-12 programs.

Campuses will be encouraged to refrain from giving preferential treatment to departments and majors that lead students to more traditionally lucrative careers.

*(Continued)*

Campus fees will be covered by graduate contribution percentage. Each new referendum voted on by a student body will be reflected in a small increase in percentage for future incoming classes.

Student on-campus housing will be covered by UC Student Investment Plan, with a 0.65% increase in contribution percentage per year of housing, paid for the first ten years of the twenty year contribution period.

Studying abroad through campus programs will be covered, as long as it is done during the academic year and units taken fulfill full-time student status requirements.

### Benefits

To students: No financial burden on parents or students upon entering system and during college. Students will also not incur any debt upon graduation. Students financially contribute to the UC at a time when they are making money, as opposed to when they are not. The annual amount collected by the UC will always be within means, because the amount is set on percentage of income earned. The UC's extended alumni benefits will provide graduates with robust employment support.

To UC: Compounded revenue over time, increasing annually with each new class paying into system. Plan puts UC on path towards growth, stability and decreased dependency on fluctuating investment by state of California.

Source: "UC Student Investment Proposal." *Fix UC*, 28 Mar. 2012, www.fixuc.org/proposal/.

---

## EXERCISE 14C   PROPOSING A TUITION PLAN

1. What persuasive strategies do the authors of this proposal use to establish the need for their solution to the problem of rising tuition at the University of California campuses? How effective are these strategies?

2. Despite its brevity, this proposal addresses complicated financial problems and procedures. How effectively do you think the authors make the case that their approach will work? Do you think they take the complexity of the problem sufficiently into account in their proposal? Why or why not? Cite passages from the proposal to support your answer.

3. Aside from solving the problem of rising tuition at California's public universities, what purposes do you think the authors of this proposal were trying to achieve? To what extent do you think their proposal achieves those purposes? Explain.

1. What exactly is the nature of the problem that is identified in this proposal? How does Teillon establish that this is a significant problem? Were you convinced by her description? Why or why not?

2. What kind of evidence does Teillon present to establish the problem she proposes to address? How does she support her claim that Puppies Behind Bars can solve that problem? How effective is the evidence she provides? Cite specific passages from her proposal to support your answer.

3. What kinds of persuasive appeals does Teillon use in this proposal? How appropriate are these appeals given her rhetorical situation? How effective did you find these appeals?

## Puppies Behind Bars
### by Annie Teillon

14

*Grant proposals, like puppies, come in all varieties. Researchers seek grants to support their research, artists to support their art, and, as the following proposal illustrates, non-profit organizations to support their work. In this proposal, an organization called Puppies Behind Bars seeks funding from a philanthropy called the Planet Dog Foundation for a project titled Paws & Reflect, which uses volunteers and puppies to give homebound elderly people social interaction that they would otherwise not have. As the author of the proposal, Annie Teillon, an official with Puppies Behind Bars, explains, her organization brings puppies into prisons to help terminally ill inmates cope with their diseases. Paws & Reflect is a related program for homebound elderly people who are not incarcerated. As you'll see, this proposal does not include a formal problem statement. Instead, Teillon weaves the problem statement into her description of the work of the Puppies Behind Bars volunteers and the impact of that work on inmates and the homebound elderly. Through that description, Teillon identifies the problem her organization seeks to address. Puppies Behind Bars provides a solution to that problem. This proposal is obviously less formal than the Fix UC proposal (see p. 437), but it nevertheless includes the main features of an effective proposal.*

. . . . . . . . . . . . . . . . . . . . . . . . . . . . . . . . . . . . . . . .

### Talking About This Reading

**Tessa Brown (student):** It was a little confusing when the writer went back and forth talking about Puppies Behind Bars and Paws and Reflect. I understand that Paws and Reflect was established by Puppies Behind Bars, but when the writer discussed the volunteers, I was a unsure which program they were referring to.

**Bob Yagelski:** Tessa, your confusion highlights the importance of organizing a proposal (or any argument) so that readers can easily follow it. This proposal takes the form of a letter, so it doesn't have the usual sections (e.g., problem statement, rationale) that make a proposal easier to follow. However, you seem to grasp the main ideas. Reread the section about volunteers with those ideas in mind. That should help clarify the section for you.

. . . . . . . . . . . . . . . . . . . . . . . . . . . . . . . . . . . . . . . .

*(Continued)*

January 29, 2007


Ms. Kristen E. Smith
Executive Director
Planet Dog Foundation
322 Fore Street
Portland, Maine 04101

Dear Kristen:

In February 2005, when Puppies Behind Bars (PBB) set out to establish Paws & Reflect, our goal was to promote human interaction in the homebound elderly community by bringing our puppies on socialization visits to their homes. Two years later, this program has transcended even our wildest wishes, filling us with great pride and motivating us to do even more. Planet Dog Foundation was instrumental in allowing PBB to turn our dreams into reality and on behalf of all the staff, seniors, volunteers, puppies, and now inmates who are all deeply affected by this arm of Puppies Behind Bars, I thank you.

We have recently increased the number of seniors who receive visits twice monthly to thirteen which translates into 312 visits per year and hope to increase these numbers to fifteen and 360, respectively, by 2007 year end. One of our newest clients, Helen, is only 59 years old but has been suffering from Multiple Sclerosis for ten years. She has lost most muscular function in her limbs and has speech difficulty. She sits in a wheelchair, with her hands resting on an icepack to soothe the burning sensation that she constantly feels in her fingers. Fully cognizant and in dire need of companionship, Helen currently only interacts with her full-time caretaker who is dynamic and full of life but, only one person. Helen desperately wants a dog but the responsibility that comes along with a four legged friend is too much for her and her aide to handle. Paws & Reflect will be a perfect fit for Helen, who will begin to enjoy a new friendship with her PBB volunteer and the pups that will take part in the socialization visits. Helen, a woman who has lost all of her physical self, will experience companionship, pride in her ability to help socialize a working dog pup and she will have an event to look forward and reflect upon. We are thrilled to be able to offer her a new chapter in her life through Paws & Reflect.

Katie Losey, Director of Volunteers, has been the driving force behind the success of Paws & Reflect. She recruits PBB volunteers, works with elderly services organizations to find seniors interested in participating and coordinates training the volunteers, matching them with their senior partners and organizing weekend visits. Last year 30% of her time was dedicated to running Paws & Reflect and we expect even with increased client participation in 2007, her time should be allocated similarly due to a few changes she will put in place.

One challenge PBB has had to work through is that initially, in order to get the program off its feet, we recruited individuals even if they could not host a dog for the entire weekend and who were solely interested in taking the dog for a couple hour visit to the home of the senior. While we found five fantastic individuals, four of who are still with us two years later, their visits are only made possible by the participation of regular weekend sitters who agree to loan their dog for the senior visit. Initially, we did not foresee how much time would be involved in finding volunteers able to swap a dog for a few hours of their weekend time because of pre-scheduled weekend plans and logistical challenges due to Manhattan's geographic and transit constraints. To alleviate these scheduling dilemmas, we have decided that in the future, we will only recruit Paws & Reflect volunteers who can commit to taking the dog from the Manhattan Shuttle like any regular PBB volunteer and puppysit for the entire weekend. We will of course retain our initial Paws & Reflect volunteers for whom we will continue to find people willing to loan their PBB pup, but overall this will become a deviation from the norm. Katie will remain the sole staff member dedicated to Paws & Reflect and will continue to work to enhance the program and report regularly with PBB's President, Gloria.

As reported at mid-year, Puppies Behind Bars expanded the Paws & Reflect program to include visits at Bedford Hills and Fishkill Correctional Facilities, both of which house terminally ill inmates. The visits are carried out by inmate puppy raisers and their dogs twice weekly and the impact on the dogs, our puppy raisers, the terminally ill and the staff has been incredible. In a *Tell Tails* volunteer newsletter, Carl Rothe, PBB's senior instructor, writes, "It's not just the forlorn inmates in the RMU that are benefiting from the program. The puppy raisers are learning to communicate and work with others who are less fortunate than they. In this environment they are forced to look at and put the patient's needs and desires above their own. Additionally, they see results and progress of short term goals in their dog training. The puppies also benefit as the added socialization and exposure to, and working with, different types of people, helping to better prepare them for their future careers as working dogs."

True to PBB's credo that education is a key component of our work, Carl Rothe developed a course to teach inmates participating in the program how to react to, and interact with, the terminally ill; how to be good listeners; how to detect signs of stress in the people they are visiting as well as in their own dogs; and how to work with medical security staff. Puppy raisers involved in this program come back from their visits beaming with pride – in themselves as well as in their puppies. In the words of Wilfredo, a longtime puppy raiser for PBB, "I really do love going up there to the hospital to visit with the old guys. It makes me feel really good knowing that me and my dog put a smile on their faces."

It is clear that the impact of Paws & Reflect reaches many different populations on a variety of levels. Whether it's an elderly Manhattan resident, a terminally ill inmate, a volunteer or puppy raiser, Paws & Reflect creates common ground enabling people to engage with one another, take pride in their accomplishments and rise above their circumstances.

*(Continued)*

Planet Dog Foundation's grant of $2,500 accounted for 15% of our Paws & Reflect expenditures in 2006. We were able to secure the remaining financial needs from other foundations and individuals. In all, PBB was able to train potential volunteers, provide over 240 puppy socialization trips to seniors' homes, host a rooftop party to recognize the efforts of the seniors, provide holiday care packages for all homebound individuals, pay for the driver and gasoline to bring the puppies into Manhattan and develop the educational class for inmates interested in making visits to terminally ill patients living out their lives in prison. We expect our costs in 2007 to increase by $2,100 due to a salary increase for the Director of Volunteers (an increase of $1,800 over 2006) and inflated gasoline prices (an increase of $300 over 2006). My hope is that Planet Dog Foundation will raise its funding to $5,000 in 2007 to cover the increased costs of Paws & Reflect. We have already secured a grant from another foundation in the amount of $8,500 to be used for this cause as well.

Gordon T., a 91 year old man who receives visits from PBB volunteer Claudia, summed up his experience with PBB by saying, *"Paws & Reflect gives me an interest that I wouldn't have otherwise and for a man this is very important. The wives are always doing things – chatting, belonging to an organization – but the men are inclined to sit back and wither away. This gives me something to get up and look forward to on Saturday. Not just on Saturday, but the whole week!"* I have enclosed copies of two typed letters and a card that Gordon sent to Katie Losey, our Director of Volunteers, that further demonstrate the impact of Paws & Reflect on Gordon and his genuine, and deeply touching appreciation for his visits. I have also included photographs of Gordon and Claudia at the PBB rooftop party recognizing the seniors' volunteer efforts.

Again, I thank you for your past support. Your financial backing, the voluminous supply of collars, toys and dog beds and your words of encouragement are very much valued and appreciated by every one of us. I have enclosed a current budget for Paws & Reflect and please call me at 212.680.9562 if you would like any further information.

Warm regards,

Annie Teillon
Director of Development

**PUPPIES BEHIND BARS**
**PAWS & REFLECT Homebound Elderly Visitation Program**
**2007 Budget**
**30 visits per month / 360 visits per year**

| | |
|---|---:|
| Shuttle Driver Salary* | $936 |
| Gas & Tolls* | $2,067 |
| Insurance on Vans | $390 |
| Director of Volunteer (30% of salary) | **XXXX** |
|    Benefits | $2,970 |
| Supplies for Volunteers (including arts & crafts materials, dog food, toys) | $650 |
| Research, development and production of training materials | $2,000 |
| Senior Recognition Events (3 times per year) | $1,000 |
| Volunteer Training | $2,000 |
| **TOTAL** | **$28,513** |

\* 6.5% of transporation costs for Manhattan Shuttle allocated to Paws & Reflect

14

# Proposal to Reduce the National Drinking Age
## by Choose Responsibility

*In 1984, the United States Congress passed the National Minimum Drinking Age Act, which effectively set the minimum age to drink alcohol in the U.S. at 21. The law, which is often referred to as Legal Age 21, was intended to protect the health of young Americans by reducing underage drinking. It was also intended to help reduce alcohol-related traffic accidents and prevent public health problems among adolescents such as dropping out of school and suicide, which some studies show can be correlated with alcohol consumption. Whether the law achieved those goals is still being debated, and although the minimum drinking age of 21 remains in effect throughout the U.S., some critics believe it actually increases alcohol abuse among adolescents. Among those critics is Dr. John McCardell, former president of Middlebury College in Vermont. In 2004 McCardell wrote an essay for the* New York Times *in which he argued that "the 21-year-old drinking age is bad social policy and terrible law" and does not prevent underage drinking and alcohol-related problems on college campuses. Three years later, McCardell helped found an organization called Choose Responsibility, which advocates a minimum drinking age of 18 in the U.S. The following proposal for lowering the minimum drinking age was presented on the organization's website (chooseresponsibility.org). As you'll see, the proposal makes a vigorous argument that the current legal drinking age of 21 is ineffective and presents evidence that, it claims, shows how a minimum drinking age of 18 would more effectively address the problems that Legal Age 21 was intended to solve. As you'll see, the proposal includes two main parts: evidence that Legal Age 21 is ineffective and the specific components of a proposal to lower the drinking age to 18. As you read, pay attention to the argumentative strategies that are employed in the proposal, especially the use of evidence, and consider how effective they are in supporting the proposal's claims.*

............................................

## Talking About This Reading

**Ranae Hulse (student):** I did not have any problems with this reading, and I can see all sides of the issue. But I do wonder whether the authors truly believe that we can teach those aged 18 to 20 responsible alcohol use?

**Bob Yagelski:** Ranae, your question is one that the leaders of Choose Responsibility have probably heard often as they advocate for their proposal to lower the national drinking age. In fact, they probably welcome the question, because it offers them an opportunity to address a legitimate concern in a way that might make their proposal more persuasive to citizens. It also illustrates how a proposal like this one can provoke reasoned debate about important issues.

............................................

**Legal Age 21**

Most Americans know that the drinking age in our nation is 21. But many people don't know much more. Here are some facts:

- We don't have a national minimum drinking age—states are allowed to set the limit where they choose.
- Despite this, all states abide by Legal Age 21. Why? Because the National Minimum Drinking Age Act, which was passed in 1984, will withhold a percentage of federal highway funding from any state that chooses an age below 21.
- The US is one of only four nations worldwide with a drinking age as high as 21— we share this distinction with Indonesia, Mongolia and Palau.
- Legal Age 21 was only one of 39 recommendations offered in a comprehensive approach to fight drunk driving in the 1980s.
- These other measures—tougher DUI laws, increased enforcement, mandatory sentencing, mandatory seat belt usage, .08 legal BAC limit, and a massive public information campaign—have been extremely successful in both reducing the instance of driving under the influence and alcohol-related deaths on the road.

*The research shows that, by itself, Legal Age 21 has had very limited success.*

- The rate of traffic fatalities—in all age groups—began to decline in 1969, more than a decade before Legal Age 21 was adopted.
- From 1969–1975, when many teens could drink legally, the teen fatality rate decreased by 19%.
- Since 1992, there has been remarkably little statistical decline in the number of alcohol related traffic fatalities
- More lives have been saved in the last two years alone by safety belts and air bags than have been saved in the 22 years since the adoption of Legal Age 21.
- In 2002, according to a NHTSA study, the largest number of alcohol-related traffic fatalities occurred among 21 year-olds, followed by 22 and 23-year-olds. Twice as many 21 year olds as 18 year-olds were involved in alcohol-related traffic fatalities in that year.
- Legal Age 21 has *postponed* fatalities—not reduced them—because every claim of an 18, 19, or 20 year-old life "saved" as a result of Legal Age 21 is offset by the number of 21, 22, or 23 year-old lives lost.
- The number of drunken driving fatalities tracks *almost exactly, up or down, with the size of an age segment.* So, when there is a larger number of 16-20 year-olds, there is a larger number of drunken driving fatalities. When the number is smaller, the fatalities decline.
- Four factors have combined powerfully (and dramatically more than Legal Age 21) to the decline of driving fatalities associated with alcohol: safer cars, higher awareness by drivers of all ages, greater utilization of a "designated driver," and more vigorous law enforcement.

**Abridgement of the age of majority**

The drinking age is the lone exception to the legal age of adulthood in the US. 18 year-olds can vote, enlist and fight in Iraq, enter into binding contracts, marry, own businesses, serve in judgment on a jury and a host of other rights and responsibilities. In nearly all cultures, alcohol consumption is coincident with the legal age of

*(Continued)*

adulthood. Legal Age 21 is out of step with the generally accepted societal norm of alcohol as accompaniment to maturity and adulthood.

### Those who choose to drink are drinking more

Consider this: 90% of the alcohol consumed by 18-20 year-olds is consumed when the individual is engaged in a episode of heavy drinking (Institutes of Medicine, 2003). Especially when understood in terms of the effect of large quantities of alcohol on the developing brain, this is an alarming statistic. The 21 year-old drinking age has pushed young adult and adolescent drinking behind closed doors and away from supervision by parents, residence life staff, and other adult authority figures. Drinking that is not out in the open, and drinking that requires one to find a dark corner or travel to a remote location, is drinking that puts not only the drinker, but also the innocent citizen, at greater risk. The behavioral consequences of binge drinking are harmful, often destructive, and occasionally fatal. High schools, colleges, and military bases are forced to grapple with the devastating consequences of excessive drinking as it becomes the norm for young Americans.

### Marginalizes the role of parents

The 21 year-old drinking age ties the hands of parent and places them in an untenable position. They must either ignore the reality of alcohol consumption among young people and forbid their children from drinking or break the law by serving alcohol to their under-21 children. Neither option is acceptable to a responsible parent, or in a society governed by rule of law. Parents need to be re-enfranchised, again involved in the process of teaching their children how to make informed, healthy decisions about alcohol and its use.

### Breeds disrespect for law and causes ethical compromises

The consumption of alcohol by Americans under the legal drinking age is common and widespread. Yet few of the young people who choose to drink underage give more than a passing acknowledgment to the fact that each time they open a beer or mix a drink they are committing a crime. By banning an entire group of young adults from engaging in a behavior that is universally understood as a symbol of adulthood, the 21 year-old drinking age fosters rampant violation of and disrespect for law—one study estimates that only two in every 1,000 instances of underage drinking results in arrest or citation (Wolfson et al., 1995). In many ways the climate surrounding the 21 year-old drinking age is analogous to that during Prohibition in the 1920s—it is easy to see the culture of speakeasies, rum runners and bathtub gin mirrored in the keg parties, pre-gaming, and beer pong of today.

### Prevents adolescents from gaining access to alcohol

There is a significant body of research that suggests early initiation to alcohol leads to long-term alcohol problems. Thus, one of the arguments for the 21 year-old drinking age is that it prevents alcohol from reaching younger populations by making it illegal to purchase, possess, and consume. High school students, in particular, are better protected by the 21 year-old drinking age because their 18 year-old friends cannot buy and furnish alcohol to them (Johnston et al., 2006).

*However . . .*

- Perhaps this would be true if Legal Age 21 actually kept alcohol out of the hands of young teens. It doesn't—over the past two decades, the law has failed at actually preventing young people from drinking. In fact the average age of first drink has actually decreased since Legal Age 21 was implemented and has held steady around 14 years of age (Johnston et al., 2006). Under Legal Age 21 fewer young people are drinking, but those who choose to drink are drinking more and are drinking recklessly. This style of excessive, dangerous consumption has created a national epidemic of what is commonly called binge drinking, putting young people and innocent citizens at greater risk of alcohol poisoning, assault, sexual abuse, vandalism, and alcohol-related traffic accidents.
- It is unlikely that a lower drinking age would increase rates of life long alcohol abuse. Although a significant body of literature suggests that an early onset of alcohol use is correlated with alcohol abuse later in life, the same literature also indicates no significant difference in rates of alcohol abuse between those who start drinking at 18, 19, 20 or 21 (Chassin et al., 2002; DeWit et al., 2000). Those who begin to drink in early adolescence are more likely to end up with alcohol use problems later in life. In the majority of countries where the drinking age is 18 or lower, and often not enforced, drinking at young ages is not highly predictive of alcohol abuse later in life. It appears that the context in which one first consumes alcohol is as important, if not more important, as the age of initial consumption.

**Prevents drunken driving among 18-20 year-olds and the rest of the population.**

Advocates of the 21 year-old drinking age point to the fact that since the drinking age has been standardized at 21, drunken driving fatalities have decreased by 13% amongst 18-20 year-olds. Furthermore several studies that measured alcohol-related traffic fatality rates over the period in which the drinking age was changed to 21 from 18 preceding the standardization in 1987 and found a decline in drunken driving amongst the affected age group (Wagenaar and Toomey, 2002).

*However . . .*

This pattern of decline began in the early 1970s, years before passage of the National Minimum Drinking Age Act. During the 1980s and 1990s, legislative changes, increased law enforcement, tougher prosecution and punishment, highly visible advocacy, and public education were all components of the "war on drunk driving." Other legislative changes, such as mandatory seat belt laws, lower BAC limits, and stricter rules on automobile safety standards can also be credited. The decline in alcohol-related fatalities seen in the United States over the past two and a half decades is attributable to a combination of factors, including but not limited to safer vehicles, increased public awareness of the danger of drunk driving, use of designated drivers—a term that did not exist before the drinking age was raised—sobriety checkpoints, zero-tolerance laws for young drivers, and altogether more stringent enforcement of alcohol-impaired driving laws have led to the reduction seen in rates of drunk driving and related deaths. In fact, many of these improvements can be traced to the 39 recommendations presented by the Presidential Commission Against Drunk Driving in 1982 (Presidential Commission Recommendations). According to an analysis by NHTSA, safety belts and air bags have had a vastly greater effect in preventing fatalities than the 21 year-old drinking age; for example, in 2002 and 2003

*(Continued)*

14

alone, more lives on the road were saved by the use of safety belts and airbags than there were in the entire history of the 21 year-old drinking age (National Highway Traffic Safety Administration, 2005).

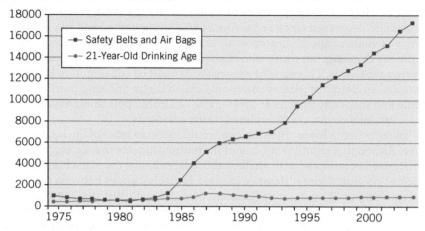

## Our Proposal

**Choose Responsibility** supports a series of changes to treat 18, 19, and 20 year-olds as the young adults the law otherwise says they are. Current drinking laws infantilize young adults. We should not be surprised, then, by infantile behavior from otherwise responsible adults.

We support a series of changes that will allow 18-20 year-old adults to purchase, possess and consume alcoholic beverages.

We propose a multi-faceted approach that combines education, certification, and provisional licensing for 18-20 year-old high school graduates who choose to consume alcohol. We envision an overarching program that combines appropriate incentive and reward for responsible, lawful behavior by adolescents, and punitive measures for illegal, irresponsible behavior.

### Waiver

The best venue for experimentation, innovation, and critical evaluation of the proposed program is at the state level; however, the National Minimum Drinking Age Act ties states to a minimum drinking age of 21 in order to avoid a 10% reduction in a state's federal highway appropriation. Choose Responsibility believes federal legislation should not penalize states who choose to participate in a pilot alcohol education program based on a minimum drinking age of 18. Thus, it is our belief that:

- States that present a plan for educating and licensing young adults that can maintain low levels of fatalities while lowering the drinking age ought to be granted a waiver of the 10% reduction penalty for a minimum of five years.
- States should create a mechanism to collect relevant data required to monitor the effects of the change in law.
- States should submit these statistics to Congress (or its designate), along with an analysis of the effects of the waiver from its inception, and may or may not request either an extension of the waiver.
- Individual state proposals must include the guidelines for eligibility and suspension of licenses proposed in the model program.

### Education

We recommend a new approach to alcohol education. Too often alcohol education either denies the reality of alcohol use amongst its subjects (Just Say No!) or is an intervention measure only after irresponsible alcohol use has been reprimanded (Court ordered alcohol treatment). We envision a program similar to Drivers' Education in that it will:

- Be taught by a certified alcohol educator, trained specifically to cover the legal, ethical, health and safety issues of the curriculum and skilled in dealing with young adults.
- Consist of at least 40 hours of instruction, with the most time spent in the classroom setting, supplemented by sessions of community involvement—DWI court hearings, safe ride taxi programs, community forums.
- Require a partnership between home and school.
- Entail a final examination that subjects must pass for licensing.
- Provide accurate and unbiased alcohol education for both drinkers and abstainers.

The alcohol education course curriculum must:

- Be a model for reality-based alcohol education.
- Involve collaboration between state, school, and home.
- Create a basis for responsible choices where alcohol is concerned, and wed those expectations of responsible behavior to a system of certification and provisional licensing for 18–20 year-olds.
- Be developed and implemented on a state-by-state basis.
- Provide accurate, truthful, and unbiased alcohol education. It will acknowledge the social reality of alcohol in American society, but it will advocate neither abstinence nor consumption. It will seek only to create a basis for responsible choices where alcohol is concerned.

Upon successful completion of the curriculum, each student of the program will receive a license, entitling him or her to all the privileges and responsibilities of adult alcohol purchase, possession, and consumption of alcohol.

### License

Like a driver's license, the drinking license—ideally an addition to a driver's license that can be electronically scanned to prevent falsification—is subject to adherence to the law. We advocate that:

- Any applicant for the license found to be in violation of a state's alcohol laws (for instance a Minor in Possession) prior to the age of 18 should be ineligible for licensing for a period of time to be determined by the state but for not less than 12 months for each violation.
- Any holder of the provisionary license will be suspended immediately upon citation for—and forfeited upon conviction of—any violation of a state's alcohol laws.
- In order to avoid public outcry over "blood borders" as occurred in the early 1980s when young adult drivers crossed state lines to purchase or consume alcohol in states with lower drinking ages, drinking licenses will be limited to use only in the state in which the young adult has declared residency, unless a state chooses to make them otherwise portable.

*(Continued)*

**References**

Chassin, L., Pitts, S.C. & Prost, J. (2002). Binge drinking trajectories from adolescence to emerging adulthood in a high-risk sample: Predictors and substance abuse outcomes. *Journal of Consulting and Clinical Psychology, 70*(1), 67–78.

DeWit, D.J. Adlaf, E.M., Offord, D.R. & Ogborne, A.C. (2000). Age at first alcohol use: A risk factor for the development of alcohol disorders. *American Journal of Psychiatry, 157,* 745–750.

Institutes of Medicine. (2003). *Reducing underage drinking: A collective ersponsibility.* Washington: National Academies Press.

Johnston, L.D., O'Malley, P.M., Bachman, J.G. & Schulenberg, J.E. (December 21, 2006). *Decline in daily smoking by younger teens has ended.* University of Michigan News and Information Services: Ann Arbor, MI. Retrieved January 15, 2007 from: http://www.monitoringthefuture.org

National Highway Traffic Safety Administration. (2005). *Traffic safety facts: 2004 Data* (DOT HS 809 905). Washington, DC: U.S. Department of Transportation.

Presidential Commission Recommendations. Retrieved January 20, 2005, from: http://www.ncadd.com/pc_recommendations.cfm

Wagenaar, A.C. & Toomey, T.L. (2002). Effects of Minimum Drinking Age Laws: Review and Analyses of the Literature from 1960 to 2000. *Journal of Studies on Alcohol.* Supplement 14, 206–221.

Wolfson, M., Wagenaar, A.C. & Hornseth, G.W. (1995). Law officers' views on enforcement of the minimum drinking age: a four-state study. *Public Health Reports, 110*(4), 428–438.

---

Source: *Choose Responsibility.* www.chooseresponsibility.org. Accessed 2 Aug. 2016.

## EXERCISE 14E  PROPOSING A SOLUTION TO UNDERAGE DRINKING

1. How would you summarize the main purpose of this proposal? What audience do you think the authors of the proposal are trying to reach? To what extent do you think this proposal is effective in achieving its purpose with that audience?

2. A great deal of evidence is presented in this proposal to support the two main claims that (1) the current minimum drinking age is ineffective in preventing the problems it is intended to prevent, and (2) reducing the minimum drinking age to 18 would actually solve those problems. What kind of evidence is presented to support those claims? How persuasive is this evidence? Explain, citing specific passages from the text to support your answer.

3. Why do you think the authors chose a website as the medium in which to present their proposal? Do you think the choice of medium is a good one in this instance? Explain. Would the proposal be more effective in a different medium? Why or why not?

# Writing Proposals

As we have seen, proposals are a specialized form of argument. Although they generally follow the principles of effective argumentation described in Chapter 11, they have special characteristics that make them somewhat different from academic arguments (see Chapter 12) and arguments in public discourse (see Chapter 13). They enable writers to take action on a problem. For example, imagine that you have a friend who has struggled to make the transition from high school to college, and you have some concrete ideas about how your school might support such students. A proposal could be an effective means of addressing that problem.

This section will guide you in developing an effective proposal. Each step described here corresponds to a step in Chapter 3. Also, refer to the five essential features of argument as explained in Chapter 11 as you develop your project:

1. **A clear main point.** Present a clear main point related to your position on the issue at hand:
   - What is the main point you will make in this proposal?
   - What purpose do you hope to achieve in making this proposal?

2. **A relevant purpose.** Identify the relevance of your argument for your rhetorical situation:
   - What makes your proposal relevant to your intended audience?
   - Why is your proposal relevant now?

3. **Appropriate support for claims.** Support your claims with sufficient and appropriate evidence:
   - What evidence do you present to support your main claim and supporting claims?
   - What makes this evidence appropriate in the context of your rhetorical situation? Is your evidence sufficient to support your claims?

4. **Complexity.** Present your argument so that it reflects the complexity of your subject:
   - Have you explored the subject of your proposal in sufficient depth and avoided oversimplifying it?
   - Have you considered complicating factors or alternative viewpoints on your subject?

5. **A persuasive appeal.** Use appropriate appeals to reason, emotion, or character to make your argument persuasive:
   - What persuasive appeals have you employed in your proposal?
   - Are your persuasive appeals appropriate for your rhetorical situation?

## Step 1 Identify a project for your proposal.

Proposals often begin with a project someone wishes to do:

- a scientific study of a particular phenomenon
- a community service initiative that seeks to improve a neighborhood
- a paper or project to fulfill an academic requirement

If you have such a project in mind, write a brief paragraph describing it. This paragraph will serve as a starting point for your proposal.

Sometimes, however, a proposal begins not with a project but with a problem that concerns or interests the writer: homelessness, climate change, the difficulties of making the transition from high school to college. In such cases, the proposal grows out of the writer's desire to address that problem.

If you do not have a specific project in mind,

1. Make a list of three or four problems or issues that interest or concern you.

2. Formulate a question for each problem.

3. Imagine a project or projects that might address each problem.

For example:

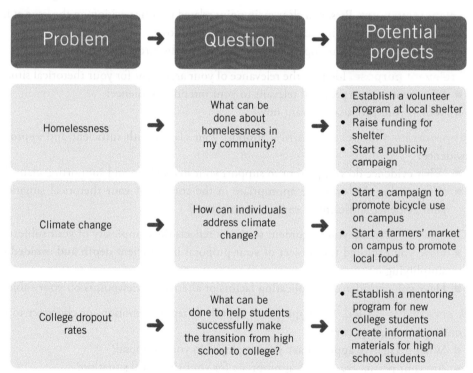

Notice that the question for each problem is formulated in a way that implies some kind of project. (Framing the question in terms of "how" can help.)

Now, identify the problem that is most interesting or important to you and describe a possible project to address it. Later, in steps 4 and 5, you will explore the problem more fully.

For example, let's imagine that you are concerned about how difficult it can be for some students to make the transition from high school to college. You know, for example, that a large percentage of college students do not make it to their second year, and you have read in the campus newspaper that the dropout rate at your own college concerns administrators. Moreover, many of your own friends felt unprepared for college-level work, even if they were successful students in high school. You also know that some advice you received from an older relative who had gone to college helped you avoid some of the struggles your friends were having, and you believe that other students would benefit from the kind of mentoring you enjoyed. So you decide that one possible way to address the problem would be a mentoring program to help new college students adjust to college.

In this way, identify a potential project. Step #1 in Chapter 3 will help you develop your idea for your project more fully.

## Step 2 Place your topic in rhetorical context.

Now identify an appropriate audience for your proposal. Depending on the nature of your project, your audience could be very specific (a course instructor, an office on your campus, or a community organization) or broader (students on your campus or residents of your community).

If your proposal is part of a course assignment or a program requirement (such as an honors thesis or capstone research project), follow the assignment guidelines to determine the audience for your proposal.

If your proposal is intended to address a problem beyond a course assignment or a program requirement, you will need to identify an appropriate audience for it. Consider the following:

- **Who would be interested in your project?** Who would support the kind of project you are proposing? Are there specific organizations or individuals who would have an interest in or connection to the problem you have identified? For example, a mentoring program for new students at your school would interest faculty and administrators who work with new students. In addition, there are offices on your campus that provide services for students or have responsibility for supporting students' social and academic activities; officials in those offices would have an interest in such a project.

- **Does your proposed project require permission or approval?** If so, your proposal might best be addressed to the person, office, or agency that must approve it. For example, if you are proposing to establish a mentoring program for new students on your campus, you will likely need permission from one or more campus offices or officials, such as the person in charge of campus residential life or perhaps the director of academic advising or student support services.

- **Do you need assistance to complete your project?** Determine whether you will need an official, an office, or a service to accomplish the goals for your project. For example, to establish a mentoring program for new students on your campus would likely require work that you could not do by yourself, such as identifying and training current students who can serve as mentors, connecting mentors with new students, securing meeting rooms, and publicizing the program so that new students can take advantage of it. Most likely you would need an office such as student support services to be able to do all these tasks and implement your proposal. In such a case, you would submit your proposal to the person in charge of that office. (Note that that person might be the same person from whom you would need to get permission for your project.)

14

- **Do you need funding for your project?** If your project cannot be completed without financial support, you will likely have to identify an agency or organization that provides funding for the kind of project you have in mind. For example, a mentoring program for new students would probably require funds to train mentors and publicize the program.

If your proposal is intended for a more general audience, you should identify the best way to reach that audience. For example, let's say you have decided that a mentoring program for new students is a good way to reduce dropout rates at your college but you don't want to be directly involved in such a program. You might write an essay for your campus newspaper or a similar forum in which you propose such a mentoring program.

Once you have identified an appropriate audience for your project, complete Step #2 in Chapter 3 to explore your rhetorical context more fully.

## Step 3  Select a medium.

The medium for a proposal is usually a conventional written document. However, as the proposal to lower the national age for drinking alcohol illustrates (see page 452), writers can take advantage of document design principles in various media (such as a website) to make their proposals more persuasive. Moreover, proposals that are presented in a group or public forum often take the form of a presentation medium such as PowerPoint. Proposals intended to promote a position on an issue (see Focus: "Proposals as Advocacy" on page 429) might be made in a medium that allows for the use of visual elements, but even in such cases a more conventional written document might also be required. So unless the rhetorical situation for which you are writing your proposal indicates otherwise, it is safe to assume that you should present your proposal as a conventional written document. If appropriate, consult the guidelines for your proposal from the organization, agency, or person to whom you will be submitting the proposal.

The exception is a proposal in the form of an essay intended for a more general audience. If you are writing such a proposal, select a medium that will enable you to reach your intended audience. For example, let's say you've decided to write a proposal for a more general audience about establishing a mentoring program for new college students. You want to argue that such a program would help address the difficulties many students have when making the transition from high school to college and therefore would help lower college dropout rates. You hope to reach several distinct but overlapping audiences: students and faculty on your campus as well as other college campuses, high school students and their parents, and perhaps a more general audience of readers interested in education issues. For such a proposal, you would have several possible media to choose from: your campus newspaper, a regional or national newspaper, a flyer, or an online forum such as blog or YouTube video. Compare the advantages and drawbacks of the available media.

Let's consider two possible media for your proposal: an essay in a regional newspaper and one posted on a social media site devoted to education issues:

**Medium: Essay in Regional Newspaper**

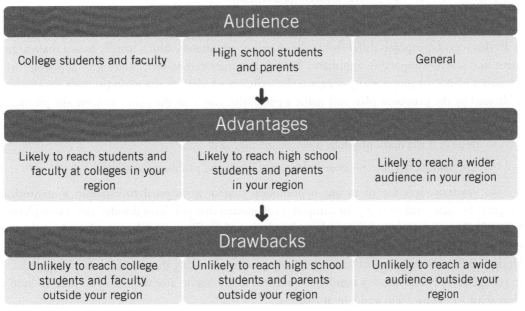

| Audience | | |
|---|---|---|
| College students and faculty | High school students and parents | General |

↓

| Advantages | | |
|---|---|---|
| Likely to reach students and faculty at colleges in your region | Likely to reach high school students and parents in your region | Likely to reach a wider audience in your region |

↓

| Drawbacks | | |
|---|---|---|
| Unlikely to reach college students and faculty outside your region | Unlikely to reach high school students and parents outside your region | Unlikely to reach a wide audience outside your region |

**Medium: Post on Social Media Site**

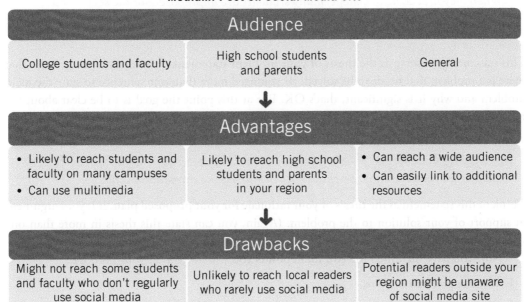

| Audience | | |
|---|---|---|
| College students and faculty | High school students and parents | General |

↓

| Advantages | | |
|---|---|---|
| • Likely to reach students and faculty on many campuses<br>• Can use multimedia | Likely to reach high school students and parents in your region | • Can reach a wide audience<br>• Can easily link to additional resources |

↓

| Drawbacks | | |
|---|---|---|
| Might not reach some students and faculty who don't regularly use social media | Unlikely to reach local readers who rarely use social media | Potential readers outside your region might be unaware of social media site |

After identifying and evaluating possible media for your proposal in these ways, complete Step #3 in Chapter 3 to help you decide on the most appropriate medium for your argument.

## Step 4 | Identify your main points.

Most proposals are written to convince a specific audience to approve a plan, fund it, or support it. In this regard, proposals differ from other kinds of arguments, which usually have a main argument and several supporting arguments but are not intended to seek funding or approval for a proposed plan. In a proposal, by contrast, the writer must identify the main problem that will be addressed by the proposed plan and make a persuasive case that the plan can solve the problem. So the task for the proposal writer is twofold:

1. to argue that the main problem is worth solving; and

2. to demonstrate that the proposed plan can address the problem effectively.

To illustrate, let's return to our hypothetical case of a proposal to establish a mentoring program for new students on your campus. Let's assume that you have decided (after completing Step #2) that your proposal should be submitted to the office of student services. In order for your proposal to be successful, you will have to convince the director of student services that the kinds of difficulties you and other students experience in making the transition from high school to college actually constitute a significant problem that deserves attention. So you need to have a clear sense of the problem and why it matters.

Begin by stating the problem and its significance as clearly as you can:

*When they first come to college, many students are unprepared for the social and academic challenges they face, which often leads to low grades or even dropping out of school.*

This statement can serve as the **thesis of your problem statement**. It is your main argument that there is a problem that needs to be solved. (If you need more than one sentence to state the main problem and why it is significant, that's OK. But at this point the goal is to be clear about the main problem your proposal will address. Later you will elaborate on the problem.)

Now state why your plan can help solve the problem:

*Struggling students can benefit from advice and support from a more experienced student who understands the challenges of making the transition to college.*

Think of this statement as the **thesis of your rationale for your proposed plan**. It is your argument in support of your solution to the problem. (Again, you can state this thesis in more than one sentence, but keep in mind that you will develop it more fully in subsequent steps.)

Now you have identified the **two main points** you will develop in your proposal:

1. why the problem matters;

2. why your plan is worth supporting.

Follow these steps for your proposal topic, keeping in mind that your two main points might evolve as you continue to develop your proposal. (If you are writing a proposal for a general audience, you still need to identify these two main points.) Step #4 in Chapter 3 provides additional guidance for developing your main points.

## Step 5 Support your main points.

Now that you have identified the two main points you will make in your proposal, you need to develop those points more fully, gathering sufficient information and evidence to support them. At this stage you have three tasks to complete:

1. develop your problem statement, which is your argument in support of your main claim that the problem you have identified should be addressed;

2. develop your plan to address that problem;

3. develop your rationale, which is your argument that your plan will address the problem.

Return to your two main points from Step #4 and develop your proposal by completing these three tasks:

| Develop your problem statement | • What exactly is the problem you want to address?<br>• What evidence is there that this problem exists?<br>• Why is this problem important? |
| --- | --- |

| Develop your plan | • What is your plan to address this problem?<br>• What are the components of this plan? What steps or activities does it involve? |
| --- | --- |

| Develop your rationale | • Why will your plan succeed in addressing the problem?<br>• What evidence do you have to support your plan as an effective way to address the problem? |
| --- | --- |

To illustrate, let's return to the example of a proposal to establish a mentoring program for new college students.

1. **Develop your problem statement.** Here's your main argument in your problem statement:

*When they first come to college, many students are unprepared for the social and academic challenges they face, which often leads to low grades or even dropping out of school.*

First, you'll need to establish that many new students do in fact struggle when they come to college. What does that mean exactly? You might begin with your own experience to illustrate these struggles, which might include adjusting to living with a roommate, meeting the academic standards of college-level studies, and being away from your support system of family and friends. You also have anecdotes from classmates who experienced similar problems. In addition, you might talk to campus officials about the extent of these problems on your campus, and you can search online for data showing the extent of these problems at other colleges. You also need statistics showing the dropout rate in college. In short, research the problem to find support for your main claim.

2. **Develop your plan.** Once you have made a case that this problem exists and is important, you need to describe in detail the plan you are proposing to solve the problem. You've decided that a mentoring program is a potentially effective way to support new students as they adjust to college. What would such a program involve? The main component is a group of experienced students who have already made the transition to college and succeeded in adjusting academically and socially. These students will need to be trained to mentor new students. The training might include workshops in which staff members from academic support services and the counseling center teach the student mentors about the difficulties of adjusting to college and how to support struggling students. Your plan should also include a way to publicize the program so that new students know it is available to them. You will need a rough schedule for implementing your plan. Will the mentoring take place over a semester? A full year? More than a year? How often will mentors meet with their students? By exploring these questions, you can develop a detailed, concrete description of your plan.

3. **Develop your rationale.** Finally, you need to make a case for this plan, showing how it will address the problem you've identified. Let's turn to the main point of your rationale:

*Struggling students can benefit from advice and support from a more experienced student who understands the challenges of making the transition to college.*

How do you know that the kind of mentoring program you're proposing will help struggling new students? Again, you can draw on your own experience, showing that having older relatives who experienced similar difficulties in college helped you overcome those difficulties. You can research similar programs at other colleges to show the impact of such programs. There might also be studies by educational psychologists and other professionals about such programs. In sum, explore possibilities to develop support for your claim that this plan will work.

As you complete these three steps, keep the following points in mind:

- **Use appropriate evidence.** As in any kind of argument, the evidence you present to support your two main points in a proposal should be credible, appropriate for your topic, and persuasive for your intended audience. (See "Appraising and Using Evidence" in Chapter 11).

- **Keep your audience in mind.** Try to anticipate what your intended audience will expect. For example, if you are submitting a proposal for a new mentoring program to the director of student services on your campus, you can assume that he or she will share your concerns about the struggles of new students, so you will want to provide sound evidence that those struggles exist on your campus. You can also assume that, as a campus official, the director will be concerned about dropout rates and similar problems, so providing data about those problems will likely strengthen your proposal. As you develop your support for your main points, then, identify the evidence and information that will most likely resonate with your audience.

■ **Include an executive summary and budget, if necessary.** Depending upon the nature of your proposal and the audience for whom you are writing it, you might need to include an executive summary and budget. Follow any guidelines provided by your intended audience in developing these components of your proposal. Remember that they are part of your effort to persuade your audience that your proposal is worth supporting. (See the Sidebars: "Writing an Executive Summary" and "Proposing a Budget" on pages 434 and 435, respectively.)

Step #5 in Chapter 3 provides additional guidance to help you develop support for your main points and your description of your proposed plan. You should now be ready to write a complete draft of your proposal. If not, move onto the next step before completing your draft.

**14**

## Step 6 Organize your proposal.

Few proposals follow the four traditional ways of organizing an argument described in Chapter 11 (see "Structuring an Argument" on page 345). Most proposals are organized according to the guidelines of the organization, agency, or person to whom the proposal is addressed. So the first step in deciding how to organize your proposal is to consult such guidelines. For example, if you are writing a grant proposal, it is likely that the foundation you are applying to expects you to follow a specific format.

If you do not have such guidelines, you can use a general format that includes the main components of a proposal:

I. **Introduction.** Briefly introduce the problem and describe the plan you are proposing. Your introduction should not only engage your readers but also lay the foundation for your main arguments in Parts II and IV.

II. **Problem Statement.** Describe the problem you will address, demonstrating its significance and providing evidence for your claims. Organize this section so that your strongest claims and evidence come first.

III. **Description of Your Plan.** Provide a detailed description of your plan to address the problem. Include a statement of the goals of the plan.

IV. **Rationale.** Explain how your plan will address the problem described in Part II, providing evidence to support your claims about your plan and its expected impact.

If you are including a budget, place it after the rationale. An executive summary (if you include one) should be placed before your introduction.

Your proposal should be organized in a way that will present your plan as clearly and effectively as possible to your intended audience. Remember that your goal is to convince them that your proposal is worth supporting. To achieve that goal, you want to make it easy for your audience to understand the problem you are addressing and the plan you are proposing. (See "Talking About the Reading" on page 400.) Step #6 in Chapter 3 provides additional guidance for organizing your proposal.

## Step 7 Get feedback.

Ask your readers to focus on the main **features of effective proposals** as they review your draft:

| Clear statement of the problem | • What is the problem you are addressing in your proposal? Is it clearly stated?<br>• What is the significance of this problem?<br>• How clearly have you established a need for a solution or plan of action? |
|---|---|
| Description of proposed project or plan | • Have you described your plan clearly and in sufficient detail?<br>• How clearly does your description explain how the plan will work?<br>• What, if anything, is missing from this description? Can anything be eliminated? |
| Compelling rationale | • How will your proposed plan succeed in addressing the problem?<br>• In what ways do you show that your plan is appropriate for the problem?<br>• How well does your rationale address the concerns of your intended audience? |
| Appropriate evidence | • What evidence do you provide to support your claims about the problem you have identified?<br>• What evidence do you provide to support your rationale for your proposed plan?<br>• Is this evidence sufficient? Is it persuasive? |

Step #7 in Chapter 3 will help you analyze your feedback and decide which revisions to make.

## Step 8 Revise.

As you consider the feedback you received for Step #7, remember that revision is an opportunity to develop your proposal more fully and adjust it to fit your rhetorical situation. You are still developing and strengthening your proposal.

Revising your proposal draft can be divided into three steps:

1. **First, review your draft using the questions listed in Step #7.** As you do, make sure each main component (problem statement, description of proposed plan, and rationale) is complete and persuasively presented.

2. **Second, adjust your persuasive appeals.** Like any argument, a proposal can be strengthened with appropriate persuasive appeals (see "Making a Persuasive Appeal" in Chapter 11). At this point, review your draft to determine whether you have made appropriate appeals:

   - **Consider your rhetorical situation.** In some proposals, certain kinds of appeals might be inappropriate. For example, a researcher submitting a grant proposal to fund a study of the impact of road construction on traffic patterns would not likely include emotional appeals to support his claims about the importance of his study. By contrast, the proposal from Puppies Behind Bars (see page 441) includes emotional appeals to help convince the reader that the program is worthwhile.

   - **Review your problem statement and rationale.** Determine whether the persuasive appeals you have made are appropriate for the problem you are addressing. Consider additional appeals that would likely be effective for your rhetorical situation. For example, here are some possible appeals you might make in support of your two main points in a proposal for a mentoring program for new college students:

| Main point | Ethical appeal | Emotional appeal | Logical appeal |
|---|---|---|---|
| Many students are unprepared for the academic and social challenges of college, which can lead to low grades or dropping out | Description of your experience with the problem as a college student | Personal anecdote illustrating a student's struggle to succeed in college | Reasoning to show that students' failure in college affects all of us in various ways |
| Struggling students can benefit from advice and support from experienced students who understand the challenges of making the transition to college | Quote from an expert about the importance of mentoring | Testimony from a student about how mentoring prevented her from dropping out | Results of a study showing the impact of mentoring |

Assuming that all the evidence is valid and credible, you should decide which kind of appeal would be most effective for the rhetorical situation.

3. **Finally, follow Step #8 in Chapter 3.** Make sure you have addressed all the essential aspects of your proposal in your revisions.

## Step 9 | Refine your voice.

As in most arguments, the writer's voice in a proposal should be appropriate for the rhetorical situation. Many proposals, especially for grants and research projects, call for a measured, objective, authoritative voice, as demonstrated in the proposal to lower the national drinking age (page 446). In other cases, such as the Puppies Behind Bars proposal (page 441), a less formal, more engaging voice can be effective.

First, review your rhetorical situation and consider the kind of voice your intended audience might expect. Then review your draft and adjust your voice, if necessary.

Step #9 in Chapter 3 will help you refine and strengthen your voice.

## Step 10 | Edit.

Complete Step #10 in Chapter 3.

---

### WRITING PROJECTS

1. Identify a problem that interests or concerns you. What is the nature of the problem? Why does it interest you? Consider what might be done about the problem. Then develop a proposal that addresses the problem. Write your proposal for an audience that has an interest in that problem. For example, if the problem involves safety in youth sports, you might write your proposal to the organization that sponsors youth sports in your community or to a local foundation interested in youth issues.

2. Rewrite the proposal you wrote for Question #1 as an essay for a general audience. Identify a specific publication or forum for which your essay would be appropriate.

3. Find an argument on a website or in a print publication about a problem that matters to you. Using that argument as a starting point, develop a proposal that would address the problem described in that argument.

4. Think of a problem that somehow figured into your own life. Drawing on your own experience, develop a proposal that describes a plan to address that problem. Identify an appropriate audience for your proposal.

## MindTap®
Request help with these Writing Projects and feedback from a tutor. If required, participate in peer review, submit your paper for a grade, and view instructor comments online.

14

## In this chapter, you will learn to

1. Identify and understand the purposes of narrative.

2. Identify appropriate rhetorical opportunities for narrative writing.

3. Understand the four main features of effective narrative.

4. Distinguish between two main kinds of narrative.

5. Understand and apply the main techniques for effective narrative.

## MindTap®

Understand the goals of the chapter and complete a warm-up activity.

# Understanding Narrative Writing

15

**READ THE OPENING PARAGRAPHS** of Chapters 2, 8, and 12 in this textbook, and you'll notice that they all begin the same way: with a story. That's no accident. Stories are an important way to convey information, explore ideas, and make sense of our experiences. We use them every day in many different ways:

- A classmate tells you a story about an experience with a professor who teaches a course you're thinking about taking.
- A patient tells a doctor the story of how he was injured.
- A business manager uses anecdotes in a report to her boss to explain the company's struggles to develop a new market for its products.
- A politician describes an event from her childhood to show voters that she understands their concerns.
- A relative tells you about a trip he took to another country.

Historians use narrative to organize and analyze the past to help us understand who we are and how we got here. Scientists use narrative to explain the natural world (see Sidebar: "Narrative in Science" on page 468). Most religious texts are narratives—for example, the parables in the Christian Bible, Zen koans, and the creation myths of Native American peoples.

Stories help us make sense of complicated events or phenomena. They give shape to our experiences. They turn the abstract (the pain of loss, for example) into the concrete (a story about losing a beloved relative). Through stories we impose order on the chaos of life. In fact, some scholars believe that narrative is as fundamental to human life as language itself. The influential scholar Jerome Bruner has written, "We seem to have no other way of describing 'lived time' save in the form of a narrative" (Bruner, Jerome. "Life as Narrative." *Social Research*, vol. 54, no. 1, Spring 1987, pp. 11–32.).

Narrative, then, might be understood as a tool by which we grasp reality. It is a way for novelists, memoirists, biographers, and journalists as well as scientists, philosophers, businesspeople—indeed, writers in *any* field—to explore and communicate ideas and do their work.

Although we tend to think of science as providing an objective description of the natural world, much of the writing scientists do has elements of narrative. In his revolutionary *On the Origin of Species*, published in 1859, which laid the foundation for the modern field of biology, Charles Darwin uses narrative techniques to help readers understand scientific principles and to explain how his theories emerged from his famous expedition to the Galapagos Islands off the western coast of South America:

> When on board H.M.S. 'Beagle,' as naturalist, I was much struck with certain facts in the distribution of the inhabitants of South America, and in the geological relations of the present to the past inhabitants of that continent. These facts seemed to me to throw some light on the origin of species—that mystery of mysteries, as it has been called by one of our greatest philosophers. On my return home, it occurred to me, in 1837, that something might perhaps be made out on this question by patiently accumulating and reflecting on all sorts of facts which could possibly have any bearing on it. After five years' work I allowed myself to speculate on the subject, and drew up some short notes; these I enlarged in 1844 into a sketch of the conclusions, which then seemed to me probable: from that period to the present day I have steadily pursued the same object. I hope that I may be excused for entering on these personal details, as I give them to show that I have not been hasty in coming to a decision.

In general, we use the term *fiction* to refer to stories that a writer makes up, whereas *nonfiction* is assumed to be an account of something that actually happened in real life. Fictional stories are not assumed to be accurate accounts of whatever the writer is describing but creations of the writer's imagination, even when the stories are based on real events. We know, for example, that the writer Herman Melville was a sailor on whaling ships, but we don't assume that his novel *Moby Dick* is an account of his actual experiences on those ships. Rather, it is a story he made up, based on his own sailing experiences and on a real event that he did not witness. So we call it fiction. By contrast, *The Wreck of the Whaleship Essex* by Owen Chase (1821) is a first-hand account of the sinking of a ship by a whale. Chase was a sailor on that ship, and he tells the story of what happened. His book is considered nonfiction. Although writers of both fictional and nonfictional narratives use similar techniques for storytelling, this textbook focuses on nonfiction narrative.

# Occasions for Narrative

One of my first professional writing assignments was a magazine article about rural health care. I was still in college and excited to have an opportunity to write something for which I would be paid. After several months of researching medical issues, interviewing doctors, and writing the article, I proudly sent my manuscript to the editor, thinking I was finished. All I had to do now was wait for the article to be published and cash the check I would receive from the magazine. A few weeks later, however, instead of a check, I received a long, detailed letter from the editor in which he described the many revisions he expected me to make. He explained that my article needed to be better adapted for readers of his magazine, and he included many suggestions for improving the piece, including deleting some of my favorite sections and adding new material that would require additional research. To say that his letter surprised me would be an understatement. I was deflated. It was like getting a bad grade on a course assignment. I had expected that writing the article would be similar to what usually happened when I wrote essays for my college classes: I would work hard, submit the essay, receive a grade (or a check), and move on. But now I began to realize that writing effectively was much more involved than that. The editor's comments were not like a teacher's grade; instead, they were part of a collaborative effort to create an effective article for the readers of that magazine. Eventually, I got over my disappointment, carefully reviewed the editor's suggestions, and set to work revising the article. Some months later, it was finally published, and I did receive my check. And I had to admit that the published article was much better than the one I originally submitted.

15

I have told this story many times—usually to my students. I tell it for several reasons: to illustrate the importance of revision and the collaborative nature of writing; to demonstrate the importance of experience in learning to write; to emphasize the role of audience. And right now I am telling the story again for another purpose: to make a point about the uses of narrative.

We use narrative for various purposes in many different contexts:

- You tell a close friend about the challenges of caring for a relative with a debilitating illness.
- A roommate tells you the story of how a longstanding relationship ended.
- A soldier returning from Afghanistan describes his experience in battle there.
- A mountain climber tells a fellow climber about what happened when she tried to climb an especially challenging mountain.
- An employee describes to her boss a difficult encounter with a customer.

In each of these examples, narrative helps both storyteller and listener make sense of what happened. And each of these situations might lead to narrative writing:

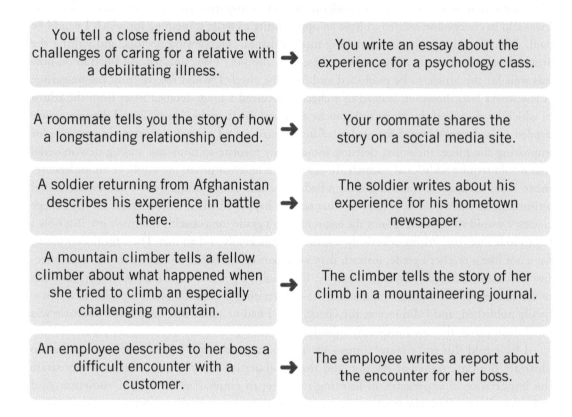

You tell a close friend about the challenges of caring for a relative with a debilitating illness. → You write an essay about the experience for a psychology class.

A roommate tells you the story of how a longstanding relationship ended. → Your roommate shares the story on a social media site.

A soldier returning from Afghanistan describes his experience in battle there. → The soldier writes about his experience for his hometown newspaper.

A mountain climber tells a fellow climber about what happened when she tried to climb an especially challenging mountain. → The climber tells the story of her climb in a mountaineering journal.

An employee describes to her boss a difficult encounter with a customer. → The employee writes a report about the encounter for her boss.

In such instances, narrative enables the writer to explore a complex and perhaps difficult experience and convey its significance to a reader. In writing a story, a writer not only describes what happened but can also examine *why* it happened and, perhaps more important, what it means. Writing about the challenges of caring for a sick relative, for example, can illuminate the importance of relationships in dealing with illness or reveal the joys of caregiving even when the experience is painful. Similarly, an employee's report describing a difficult encounter with a customer can help the company understand problems it might be having in customer relations. Writing about my experience with my rural health care article helps me continue to learn from the experience and convey what I've learned to you.

You have probably used narrative to find and share meaning in similar ways many times: in messages to your friends or relatives on social media, in your college admissions essay, in writing you have done for a class. Narrative, then, is a tool for living. The better you can tell a story in a piece of writing, the more useful narrative can be in all aspects of your life.

1. Think about the last time you told someone a story. What was the context? Why did you tell the story? What do you think you accomplished by telling the story? Write a few paragraphs describing this situation and explaining why you told your story. Now, in a group of classmates, share what you wrote. Try to identify commonalities in the reasons that you and your classmates told your stories. What do you think your respective experiences suggest about the uses of narrative in our lives?

2. Is there a story about an experience you had that you have told many times? If so, think about what makes that story important—to you and to others. Why do you tell that story over and over? To whom do you tell it? Do you tell it simply to entertain friends or relatives? Or does the story have greater significance to you?

3. Look over the front page of a newspaper or visit an online news source. Identify two or three reports that interest you. For each topic you identify, think of an experience you had that somehow relates to that topic. Now consider how you would tell the story of that experience to someone if you happened to have a conversation about that topic. What would you tell that person about your experience? Why?

# Understanding Narrative Writing in College

15

- In an economics class students are given statistical data about populations in the U.S., including percentages of various racial and ethnic groups, in different regions and during different time periods. The data also include employment figures, educational attainment statistics, and income levels. From this information students are asked to construct the "story" of a particular group in the U.S. during a specific time period.

- In an introductory geology course students write a memo to a specific audience (such as a government office or a town engineer) in which they explain current techniques for measuring seismic activity and determining the probability of an earthquake in a specific location. The memo includes a specific example of one town's experience in using these techniques to predict the possibility of earthquakes.

- An assignment in a psychology course requires students to write an essay about an experience in which their gender somehow played an important role. The stories are then used to examine how attitudes about gender can shape social relationships.

- Students in a zoology class make several field trips to a river near their campus, each time recording their observations of wildlife species that inhabit the river. In their final report for the class, the students describe the behaviors of the wildlife they observed, narrating what they saw the animals doing over time.

As these examples suggest, narrative writing is not only prevalent in college courses but also an important form of knowledge-making in academic disciplines. Narrative serves many different purposes and takes a variety of forms in different academic disciplines. The memo for the geology class, for instance, includes an example that tells the story of a place where earthquake prediction techniques were used; the zoology reports include passages that tell the story of what the students observed. To be an effective writer in college—and elsewhere—you need to be able to tell stories in ways that meet the needs of your rhetorical situation.

Before looking more closely at narrative writing in college, we need to distinguish between common forms of storytelling and the kinds of narrative writing reflected in the examples above:

- **Conventional narrative.** In conventional narratives, writers tell stories about something that happened—to themselves or to others—as a way to make sense of the experience and convey the meaning of the experience to an audience. Conventional narratives have the familiar features we traditionally associate with stories: a plot, characters, and descriptive writing; they often include dialogue. Memoirs, personal essays, and biographies are all forms of conventional narrative. Most novels and short stories are also conventional narratives. So are most movies, television dramas, and comedies.

- **Embedded or academic narrative.** Narrative is often used within another kind of text—for example, an analysis or an argument. In this "embedded" kind of narrative, writers tell a story to illustrate a relevant point, illuminate an idea, or support an argument (as I did at the beginning of the section titled "Occasions for Narrative"). For example, in an argument against decriminalizing marijuana, a writer might include the story of a person whose life was made difficult by the use of that drug. In such a case, the writer's primary purpose is not to tell an entertaining story that explores an experience but to use the story to make a point—for example, that using marijuana is risky.

Although you are likely to write some conventional narratives in college, much narrative writing in college courses tends to be embedded narrative, which is the focus of this chapter. (Conventional narratives are examined in Chapter 16.) The differences between these two categories have to do mostly with purpose. Conventional and embedded narratives share basic features, as we will see below, but as noted earlier, in an embedded narrative the writer's main purpose is not to tell an entertaining story but rather to make a specific point. In either case, an effective narrative should engage the intended audience and draw readers into the story, even when that story is embedded in another kind of text.

Narrative writing in college generally exhibits **four key features**:

- **A clear, narrow focus.** In academic writing, narratives tend to be narrowly focused on the event, experience, or phenomenon that the author is writing about to make a point. Unlike many conventional narratives, stories in academic writing usually do not include subplots that can make a narrative long and complex. In most cases, narrative in academic writing serves a very specific purpose, which is generally achieved through maintaining a narrow focus.

- **Brevity.** Most narratives included in academic texts tend to be brief. Often they take the form of anecdotes that are only a few paragraphs in length. Even when they are longer, they tend to be briefer than conventional narratives, which often try to bring readers deeply into the imaginative world of the story.

- **A basic structure.** Academic writers tend to tell stories in a straightforward way. Rather than using complex plots or manipulating chronological time, they structure their narratives to help readers follow the story and easily grasp the point of the story.

- **Succinct, purposeful description.** Whereas conventional narratives often include detailed, vivid descriptions of scenes or events, most narratives in academic contexts rely on succinct descriptions to convey a scene or point efficiently. Descriptions are used in a way that keeps the focus on the point and does not call attention to the writer's language.

Let's look at some examples that illustrate these features. In this passage from the introduction to an ethnographic study of Pueblo Indian schools, ethnographer Alan Peshkin begins his book-length study by highlighting what he calls the "dual-world existence" of Native American peoples, which is a major theme of his study. He uses a brief narrative to make his point:

> Disconcerted by the images of his people often held by non-Indians, Mateo Romero, a young Pueblo painter and Dartmouth College graduate, tried to set the record straight: "People think of Native American Indians in these noble, savage stereotypes. In reality, they're just human beings like everybody else." Being "like everybody else," however, is belied by the reality of lives shaped by these many objects of loss, but also by the recurrent mention by Pueblos of their dual-world existence and the resulting complications.
>
> In 1990, for example, Pueblo mother Bonnie Candelaria enrolled her daughter in a public school located outside San Felipe reservation, where she lived. Tribal authorities protested her decision to remove her child from the local reservation school and, thereby, from the influence of her tribe. Candelaria argued for her child's need "to learn to adapt to the world out there, rather than the world in here." It is debatable whether tribal authority established under the circumstances of tribal sovereignty as a nation-within-the-nation, extends to parental decisions about where reservation members send their children to school. That tribal authorities can even consider it a possibility indicates the magnitude of the issue of if and how children are to be socialized for Indian culture and community. Sam Montoya, Pueblo Indian and Bureau of Indian Affairs official, placed this issue in the perspective of the dual-world challenges and opportunities that confront his people:

>> Some people are waking up and saying we have to be more aggressive about protecting our way of life. We have existed here for hundreds of years … There is an awareness now that, yes, there is a challenge to these values. I'm not trying to say that any tribe is trying to shut out the outside world. They're trying to strike a balance between what they feel is unique … and the new opportunities provided by the other world. [quoted in Barringer 1990:B9]

**15**

Many Americans have grown up informed by and living to varying extents in two worlds. As generations pass, the distinctiveness of their subgroup culture diminishes, sometimes to the vanishing point. Indian cultures are decidedly different. In no other American group is there a Sam Montoya who can speak as he did after 500 years of culture contact between Indians and non-Indians.

Source: Peshkin, Alan. *Places of Memory*. Lawrence Erlbaum, 1997, pp. 2–3.

Notice that Peshkin doesn't tell the whole story of Bonnie Candelaria's efforts to find the right school for her daughter; rather, he tells just enough to illustrate his point about the challenges faced by Pueblo people as they navigate their "dual" existence. His narrative is not only brief but also narrowly focused so that his point is clear. (Brevity and a narrow focus are often evident in the kind of visual storytelling that is common in advertising. See Focus: "Telling a Story Visually.") Still, the story is engaging and likely to evoke emotion in a reader, even if it is not meant to entertain.

## FOCUS TELLING A STORY VISUALLY

In advertising, stories are often used to enhance the appeal of an ad. In this kind of visual storytelling, brevity and a tight focus are essential. In the same way, television commercials often tell a story, sometimes in as little as fifteen seconds. In this ad for Volkswagen cars, called "Young Darth Vader" (2012), a child dressed as the *Star Wars* character Darth Vader seems to use "the force" to control the new car in his family's driveway. In the one-minute ad, we eventually learn that the child's father is controlling the car remotely, which highlights Volkswagen's new technology:

AP Images/VW

Scholars also use narrative to explain *how* they conducted their research. Here's Peshkin again:

An American institution: it is Friday night. Indian High School's basketball team is playing a home game. Students, usually long gone for the weekend to their reservation homes, spill out of the school's several male and female dormitory buildings. They merge with the procession of cars and pickup trucks heading toward parking lots next to the gym. The gym is packed. Students, teachers, parents, and relatives mill about in the gym lobby, greeting friends, buying food and drink, anxious to return to their seats before the national anthem is sung. Then the game begins.

I have watched high school teams play basketball since my own student days. Never before had I seen a team play like Indian High School's varsity squad. They were quick, athletic, and relatively short—shorter than their opponents, who came from a non-Indian school in their non-public school athletic league. The home team won the game, but it was how they played the game that fascinated me: a full-court press. Their basic strategy literally overwhelmed their opponents. Indian High School players swarmed at both ends of the court. Sometimes I'd count the players on the floor, in disbelief that a legal five were able to do such damage. The result was one fine game in an overall winning season.

Many months later, I began my year-long contact with Indian High School and observed students at work in their classrooms. Regrettably, I saw no academic counterpart to this stellar athletic performance. Indian students take to and excel in the non-academic aspects of their school life. They acknowledge that they can and ought to achieve more academic success; they are disappointed that they do not.

About 1 month into my observations of Indian High School students in their classrooms, I decided that my initial fascination with the dual-world character of the student's lives—the one, their traditional, tribal, Indian, reservation world, the other, the mainstream American, dominant Anglo, non-Indian world—would be oriented to exploring why these students reacted as they did in their classrooms. From their school's many documents, I knew it had accepted as one of its main purposes helping students "to make fulfilling life choices." *Life choices* cover much ground. The choice of most interest to me—doing well in and with schooling—did not appear to be fulfilled.

15

Source: Peshkin, Alan. *Places of Memory*. Lawrence Erlbaum, 1997, pp. 4–5.

In this excerpt, Peshkin explains his perspective as a researcher studying the Pueblo community. You can recognize some familiar features of conventional narrative, especially the vivid but purposeful description of the basketball game, which helps readers imagine the scene he witnessed. But the description does not distract readers from his main point about the dual existence of Pueblo students. Like the previous excerpt, this one is brief and tightly focused. Peshkin doesn't get carried away by the story but uses the story effectively to convey an important idea in his research.

Sometimes, narrative is used more extensively to explore an idea or make a point. For example, the following essay, written by a professor of English, tells the story of the author's experience with her terminally ill father. Notice that the author uses features of conventional narrative, including plot and dialogue:

On the last day of his life, my father bought two scratch-off lottery tickets. We had just finished a lap through the Price Chopper, filling a cart with foods his urologist said he should eat during treatment for the metastasized renal cell cancer wreaking havoc on his body. The cancer was incurable, Dr. Petroski had told us, but not untreatable. I latched onto that word, to the possibility of prolonged life; I married myself to it. Only three days had passed since the terminal diagnosis, so I floated through these tasks with little sense of reality, a bride who keeps forgetting her new surname. Got cancer? Buy frozen veggies and V-8.

My father had everything wrong with him at this point. In the past week, he'd been hospitalized for anemia, and a colonoscopy had necessitated the removal of fifteen benign polyps. He had congestive heart failure, high blood pressure, and Type II diabetes. He had renal cell cancer (kidney cancer), which had spread to his lungs. And he had an enlarged prostate that forced him to wear a catheter, making trips to the grocery store—where he refused to be seated in a motorized cart—uncomfortable and embarrassing. Twice, the spout had fetched loose from the bag, spilling urine down the inside of his pants. He never really learned to attach the parts properly, and so walked with one hand pinching the tube that pinched his urethra.

As we puttered around the store inspecting nutrition labels, I thought of the words my father used to bark at me when I was a child: *Walk with a purpose*. My father was so irritated by dawdlers that he routinely shopped at night, sometimes the middle of the night, to avoid the elderly men and women who dominated the daylight hours, pushing walkers across the scuffed floor. Bluehairs, he called them, whisking me along as though the Price Chopper was downtown Manhattan.

Now, at age sixty-three and dying, my father crept along so slowly I had to keep stopping so as not to get ahead of him. I pretended to get caught up in the cereal aisle, affixing my eyes to the blurring boxes in search of heart healthy brands, because watching him walk made me want to sit down and wail. I stood always on the lip of a temper tantrum.

On our way out, me pushing the cart slowly enough to feel each pock in the tile, my father asked to stop at the scratch-off machines. He inserted a couple of dollar bills and gingerly, still pinching his catheter, fished a quarter out of his pocket.

"Here, hon," he said, handing me the tickets and coin. I scratched the film away to reveal sets of numbers and pictograms, and then handed the tickets back to my father. "I can't tell," I said.

He put his glasses on, a pair of Dollar General magnifying lenses, to study them. Then the corner of his mouth turned up. "Loser today," he said, "but winner in general."

\*\*\*\*

My father practiced a benign form of gambling—nothing addictive or financially threatening. Just the occasional opportunism. Still, his attraction to playing the odds was surprising for such an anxious, fretful man, a curio of his personality. Normally, my father was only interested in certainties, in facts. He obsessively memorized data, especially about sports and history. He loved trivia games. Guinness World Records. Quote books that allowed him to look up Winston Churchill's exact words to the woman who famously accused him of being drunk. ("Madame, you're ugly, but tomorrow I shall be sober.") We spent many a Thursday night watching *Jeopardy* together, and it wasn't uncommon for him to beat the actual contestants. As one of his friends wrote in the online guest book attached to my father's obituary: "He knew every worthless fact that never made him a dime."

But my father also suffered insomnia and panic attacks; he was a known pessimist, a fatalist, always sure that this winter would be unbearably bad, that his business would fail in the terrible economy, that he, a bachelor who'd lost the marriage odds with my mother, would be alone at the end of his life.

Yet he found the lure of possibility irresistible, believing that a set of numbers or a single correct answer could change everything someday. This, I've come to understand, was his version of hope.

****

Some people will have no truck with odds—they see the very opposite of hope in playing them.

In 1968, as the war gained momentum and more young men were hauled by the government out of their hometowns, my father's older brother, Freddy, volunteered for a second tour in Southeast Asia. My father had just turned eighteen and would be graduating high school in a few months. The draft was aptly called The Lottery, and the numbers assigned to young men like my father meant a whole different animal of possibility—the possibility of being shipped overseas to die. Freddy may have known that my father's nervous disposition wouldn't play well in combat.

To ensure that my father wouldn't be drafted, Freddy extended his own active duty. He was sent to Thailand as a supervisor at an air base that sent artillery-laden planes over Vietnam and Laos. The details remain cloudy, but one day, as Freddy made repairs to the bomb lift, he got caught in some rigging and was electrocuted. For the rest of his life, my father blamed himself for his brother's death.

On the day we learned of his cancer's metastasis, my father, mother, and I stood in the hospital lobby. "Why should I bother getting any treatment if it's just going to get me anyway?" my father said.

The automatic door behind us opened and closed, sucking out the heated air into a frigid November. My mother, his ex-wife of twenty-eight years, foraged in her purse for her gloves, perhaps contemplating taking a hit off her new electric cigarette. We were all exhausted from the slew of appointments that had led to this dismal news and this dismal place that smelled sharp and sweet, like rot. My mother stopped rummaging and looked at my father. "Danny," she said, sighing. "Okay, fine. It's up to you. You want to die? Do nothing. You want to live longer? Or at least try to? You got anything to live for?"

"Like what?" my father said. His winter coat hung like a vinyl box around his diminished frame. He had already lost thirty pounds.

My mother yanked on her gloves and cupped my shoulder. "Like your daughter? Like a future grandchild, maybe? Is that something you'd like to see someday, if you could?"

My father looked at the floor, ashamed. Even now, or perhaps especially now, he hated to disappoint my mother, to do anything that might push her goodwill away. "Yes," he said. "I would like that very much."

"Then stop acting like you have nothing to live for when we're *right here*."

It was the last argument my parents would ever have, and as usual, my mother won.

****

Recreational and problematic alike, gamblers are often driven dually by greed and generosity. They spend themselves on improbabilities for others. Back when I tended bar, like my father, at a place across town, one of the regular Quickdraw players routinely split half his winnings among the servers. At Close Quarters, the bar my father owned for twenty years until his death, the winners of sports pools (Superbowl, March Madness, World Cup, World Series) were tacitly expected to buy a few rounds, maybe even use the pot to throw a party for their losing comrades. Whenever those scratch-off tickets paid out, my father would take me out for an elaborate dinner, or, when I got older, give me money to help pay down my student loans. He loved having money for the sole purpose of spending it on others. Over the years, he used part of his tax return to buy my husband and me not one, but three toaster ovens, each one bigger and more expensive than the last.

"But this one's a Kitchenaid," he said when I questioned whether or not we needed the most recent toaster. "They're the best."

He even fantasized about winning. Particularly if he won a real jackpot—the New York Lottery, let's say. On late nights at Close Quarters, both of us drunk on beers and shots of blackberry brandy, wistfulness lining his face like cigarette smoke, he'd describe his imagined plans. First thing he would do was clear all of my mother's debts, he said, her mortgage and credit cards, and still more he would give her so she could retire and go to the bluegrass music festivals she loved, ride her horses, remodel her kitchen. I'm sure he pictured it many times—writing a check and presenting it to her, the way he did once when I was a kid, sending me home with five thousand dollars so she could put a new roof on our house.

"Hey," he would say, "somebody has to win, right?"

For my husband and me, my father said he would buy a house. One with an in-law apartment or a big, finished basement. That way, he could come to live with us when he got too old to care for himself, he said.

"I don't need much," he told us. "A TV and a bed, is all. And you."

Of all the riches he could fathom for his loved ones, what he desired most for himself was a family.

****

On the last day of his life, my father and I ran errands together. A doctor's appointment in the morning, then the Dollar General, then the Price Chopper. As I drove him home with his groceries, dud scratch-offs stuffed into his pants pocket, my father asked me again to tell him the odds of surviving his cancer. He knew I'd been researching nonstop since Dr. Petroski first discovered the kidney tumor, a bulge ludicrously visible on the CAT scan. I didn't, I couldn't, lie to him. These were facts. He had a right to know them.

"It's about 9%, Dad," I said, and then immediately had to qualify, for the single digit was shattering. "But remember, there are treatments. They can prolong your life." I hated the way we kept repeating the clinical language like we were studying for a quiz. None of us knew how to adapt cancer-speak for our own tongues, and the unfamiliar words in our mouths fed the impossibility of what was happening. If it didn't sound true, it couldn't be.

But it was.

In just a few hours, my father would call me in the middle of an acute coronary episode, the result of cancer's enormous stress on his body. "Please," he would say, choking a little into the phone, "just talk me through this, honey."

But I wouldn't. Instead, I would hang up and call 911, and then my husband and I would drive to my father's house to be with him. To answer questions about his medications. To watch, helpless, as the paramedics loaded him onto the ambulance. To ride with his dying body and listen to the wet, hollow sound of chest compression that would fail to revive him.

It would not be a peaceful death. I don't believe in such a thing. But he would not be alone.

As I explained the odds of his cancer survival, my father lit a cigarette and cracked the passenger side window of my car. My mother had bought him an electric cigarette like hers, and he promised to start using it that night. Another tiny gesture in the direction of hope, or maybe one of acceptance for the only absolute in life. The one unexceptional universal. My father and I had landed on a contended moment where we knew we were in this as a family, his dying. He told me he appreciated everything my mother and I had been doing for him. He told me I was the best daughter in the world.

Then he patted my hand across the console. "Well," he said, "somebody's got to be in that 9%, right?"

"That's true, Dad," I said. Somebody had to be.

---

Source: Monticello, Amy. "Playing the Odds." *The Nervous Breakdown*, 6 Apr. 2013, www.thenervousbreakdown.com/amonticello/2013/04/playing-the-odds/.

In this example, the author, Amy Monticello, devotes most of her essay to the story of her father's last days, but the essay is also about different ways in which human beings take chances in their lives. Notice that she tells the story much as any good storyteller might, using dialogue to give readers a sense of being there, creating tension to keep readers engaged, and following a basic plot to convey what happened. The drama created by the plot propels readers to the end of the essay, but along the way Monticello periodically pauses to comment on the gambles humans sometimes take in life. Although her essay has the main features of a personal narrative (see Chapter 16), it illustrates the ways in which narrative can be used in academic contexts to explore complex and important issues, such as the nature of risk in human life, that are the focus of academic inquiry.

# Telling Stories

Writing effective narrative is largely a matter of learning some basic techniques that enable you to take advantage of your natural ability to tell a story. This section offers advice about using effective narrative writing techniques to meet the needs of your rhetorical situation. In most academic writing, that means writing **embedded narrative** (see page 472); however, you will likely have occasion to write **conventional narratives** as well. The techniques described here will help you write both kinds of narrative.

# Maintaining Focus

Because stories often have so many different components—people, events, scenes, background—it can be easy to get off track. As we saw in the previous section, however, effective narratives keep to the point. The trick is to determine not what is relevant but what is *necessary* to your point.

The following two essays were written in response to the same assignment for an education class. The students were asked to tell the story of an experience that influenced them as a writer or reader. They were writing their stories for their classmates, all of whom were studying to be teachers. One student, Carrie, wrote about several unpleasant experiences she had as a young student:

> When I was in third grade I was supposedly so lucky to have been placed with my third grade teacher. I don't remember my teacher's name and barely remember what she looks like. She was young with a high pitched voice. She developed a writing lab in order to continue improving our newly developed reading and writing skills. Each week was a different piece of writing; we would develop drafts which would continue to evolve through the course. During these writing labs, we were designated to meet

with our teacher once a week to work one-on-one with her. One day my teacher told me, "You are just not a good writer." I don't remember the assignment or the rest of the conversation during that meeting; all I remember is that statement. I was embarrassed by my teacher in class and cried in front of my peers. The worst part was that I believed her.

Teachers make lasting impressions upon their students. As students, we don't remember every irregular verb in Spanish or memorize every area formula we were taught in math, but we do remember the teachers that taught those classes. We remember how the teacher made us feel, whether that feeling was pleasant or quite the opposite. Most often for students, negative experiences involved with learning have more of an effect than positive ones. The teacher can make a difference in the development of skill sets in an area of study; positive reinforcement can lead to motivation and success, whereas negative feedback can lead to resentment and disinterest in a subject. Even after this experience, I do not believe that I was completely shut off to reading and writing. I still really enjoyed reading and I learned a lot from the process of reading. Even as a third grader I understood the importance of literacy and being a literate person. However, writing did become less important. I did not want to be critiqued or humiliated. Thus my fear of writing began.

Before entering high school, eighth grade teachers recommend classes that fit a student's ability in a particular subject. I was recommended for honors history, science, and Italian. Honors English was the only accelerated class that I wasn't enrolled in. I went to my English teacher and asked her to recommend me. My teacher responded, "Why would you want to take honors? You're a terrible writer." She dismissed my question. Once again, I don't remember my teacher's name, I don't remember what she looked like, and I don't remember the rest of the conversation. I do remember her tone, what she said, and the way she made me feel. The worst part of this particular conversation was that I believed her.

I didn't like writing then and I still don't like writing because I don't think I'm good at it. As a result, I avoid writing. Instead of taking an English elective I take an extra science class. If projects allow for alternative approaches other than writing a paper, I would always opt out of the paper, eliminating the messy and overwhelming process of writing. Avoiding the practice of writing may explain the writer that I am today; I am unconfident in my writing. I feel that my thought process on paper is unorganized and hard to follow. Generally, people like to do things that they are good at. I think I can even go as far as to conclude that my uncomfortable feelings towards writing led me to choose my major. I chose science and mathematics because it involves reading and critical thinking to prove my knowledge rather than proving it through a piece of writing. I was never given encouragement to succeed in the process of writing as I was in other subject areas, and it's this fact that brought me to love chemistry.

Over the course of my development as a literate person I have grown as a student. I used to write to complete assignments (the night before they were due), caring little about the quality of writing I had produced but instead concentrating on minor details.

15

For instance, I would concentrate on whether the paper was long enough or whether my commas were correct instead of focusing on the more important questions that I ask myself now: Did I answer the question? Is this really what I want to say? How will my readers interpret this? I am still not confident in my writing; however, the attitude with which I approach writing and the process of writing is different. I know that I can create quality pieces of writing if I work at it. I have realized that writing is a process of revision, rewriting, and then revising.

Being literate is essential to being successful. Reading and writing differ from most skill sets; both are used in all disciplines of study. We see these skills in all professions. A scientist writes to share their research, politicians write to pass bills, and mathematicians read to understand and problem solve. Literacy in my life has been primarily through schooling. I understand that literacy in my life will turn into an everyday skill as a form of communication and expression. I will continue to work on developing as a professional teacher, improving my abilities and encouraging my students to do the same. My experiences also shaped my role and views as a teacher; constructive feedback is a lot more meaningful than negative criticism. As I evolve as a student, I see more importance in literacy. Overall, negative feedback I received about my skills in literacy as a young student has shaped a negative outlook on my ability to express myself in a written form. But I hope to instill and inspire my students to embrace and take an interest in literacy.

In this essay Carrie tells a disheartening story of how her early experiences with a few teachers shaped her self-image as a writer and affected her decisions about her college major many years later. That's the focus of her story. Notice, though, that in her final two paragraphs the focus shifts away from the story of her development as a writer and toward a discussion of the implications of her experience for her career as a teacher. Those final paragraphs are not irrelevant to her story, but they are probably unnecessary to convey her main point about the damage a teacher can do to a student's confidence as a writer. In fact, the focus of her story would probably be clearer if she eliminated those final two paragraphs.

Here's another essay written for the same assignment. In this case, the student, Nate, tells a story about coming to understand himself as a young man in part as a result of an experience he had with his grandfather; through that experience he learns something important not only about himself and his family but also about literacy:

I was never the one to be open about my feelings or personal life to others. However, this doesn't mean I never had feelings about life choices or events in my life. Despite growing up in a developed country and coming from a liberal family, I still felt it my duty to be strong for my family. My mother was born in Haiti, and my grandfather is particularly traditional about the gender role of men in the family. When I was born, my parents and I lived in my grandparents' house for about five years while my mom worked and my dad went back to college. As the oldest of two, I was seen by my grandfather as the man of the family, the one who must carry the proverbial torch when he passes.

My grandfather has always been quite fond of literature in general. Often I would catch him reading books on technology, our Haitian heritage, and even the manuals that come with electronic devices these days. As I grew up I never really read for enjoyment or fun. Instead, reading seemed like a chore or something I had to do. When I went to my grandparents' house, there was always some pseudo-philosophical discussion going on about life. I would always leave with some old world saying or an idea my grandfather would plant in my head. For my grandfather, getting me to think about the world in a different way was always his focus. This is why, according to my grandfather, it was less than ideal that I did not enjoy reading.

He tried different strategies to get me to read by quizzing me about what I was supposed to read. At one point my grandfather even paid me for each book I read. My grandfather would coerce me to carry around a pocket notebook to write down words I did not understand while reading in order to revisit them and build my vocabulary. However, in the off chance I actually did read, I would never share what I thought about that topic. It was engrained in my mind that I should not discuss my feelings with my family because I needed to be the foundation.

One day, much like any other day at my grandparents', I was speaking to my grandfather and actually started to discuss how I felt about a particular reading. I had read *The Black Jacobins*, which is a history of the Haitian Revolution. We discussed life back in Haiti and my ancestors, and out of nowhere my grandfather started talking about his father. My grandfather was young when his father died and was essentially forced to become the father figure in the household. As he cried, my grandfather detailed his struggle to get his siblings to focus on school and create a better life. It was the first time I had ever seen my grandfather cry, and to this day I am the only one in my family to ever see him cry.

I left the house confused as to what I just witnessed. There was a long period of time before I had another real conversation with my grandfather, and we never really discussed what actually happened to this day. However, as time passed I started to realize that it is okay to have emotions and not to be ashamed of my feelings. Gradually, I was able to become more personal with my writing in school and for myself. I started to write more music because music has been a large part of my life. It is particularly interesting to see my earlier musical endeavors because of how crude they were and how devoid of any feeling they really had.

It was quite a new experience to feel comfortable with my own emotions. I was always the type to think deeply about a topic that I was interested in. Now I was able to allow my thoughts to flow freely without restriction. In a sense, it was like my brain was full and instead of using the knowledge constructively, I just constantly allowed it to overflow. I had a clear mind and I flourished academically. Clubs started to look more enticing to join, and I was able to take an active role (often a leadership role) in many academic avenues.

Eventually I started having more in depth conversations with my grandfather about news, my life, academics, etc. I had countless conversations, debates, and lectures from my grandfather and they were so much more personal than ever before. He was able to cry on several occasions since then (although I can count them all on one hand), and I can remember each and every one of them.

15

It is in the reading and writing of people that we gain emotional understanding of others and ourselves. For my grandfather, literacy was a way to connect with me on a deeper level, a level that may have otherwise been hidden because of the strong and dominant male mentality. With his help I learned that literacy is much more than reading and writing; it is an emotional tether to others.

At first glance, Nate's story has much in common with Carrie's. Both writers tell about early experiences that shaped them as readers and writers and as human beings. Notice, however, that Nate's essay doesn't lose focus as he moves from his anecdote about the first time he saw his grandfather cry (paragraph 4) to his transformation as someone in touch with his own emotions. Whereas Carrie's essay drifts to a discussion of what her early experiences mean for her future career, Nate returns in his final paragraphs to his relationship with grandfather and how it has influenced his understanding of reading and writing, thus reinforcing the main point of his essay. Moreover, he discusses each subtopic in terms of this main idea about literacy and relationships. For example, in paragraph 5 he describes his interest in music but he does so in reference to his point about how his experience with his grandfather affected him as a person (rather than, say, in terms of his musical abilities or the power of music as a form of expression—both of which would be perfectly valid but not really relevant to his main idea). In this way, he maintains his focus on his main point, even though he covers a lot of ground in describing his relationship with his grandfather and his own development as a person.

Maintaining focus in a narrative, then, is a matter of

- **carefully selecting what to include and exclude, and**
- **presenting material in terms of the story's main point.**

You can use this approach in your own narrative writing:

> 1. State as clearly as you can the main point or idea you want to convey with your story.
>
> ↓
>
> 2. Review each section of your story (anecdotes, background information, etc.), and consider whether it is necessary to help convey your main point.
>
> ↓
>
> 3. Consider how each main section you have included contributes to the main point or idea of your story.

For example, imagine you are writing a college admissions essay about your experience in a musical production in high school. You want to convey to the admissions people that you have learned to work hard to overcome challenges in your life. In this case, you had to switch your role in the play just a few days before the first show because the student playing the lead role became ill. The director asked you to take that lead role, which you had only a few days to learn. Let's imagine, too, that the student who became ill was a close friend of yours with whom you had competed for the lead role. In fact, that competition led to an argument with your friend. Now you are taking your friend's part in the play.

So you have several important events or scenes to consider including in your essay: the auditions, your argument with your friend, being asked to take the lead role, and working diligently to prepare for the lead role in a very short time. What should you include?

First, state the main point of your story as best you can:

*Overcoming unexpected challenges often requires one to be dedicated, work hard, and believe in oneself.*

Now consider each main event or scene in terms of the two principles described above:

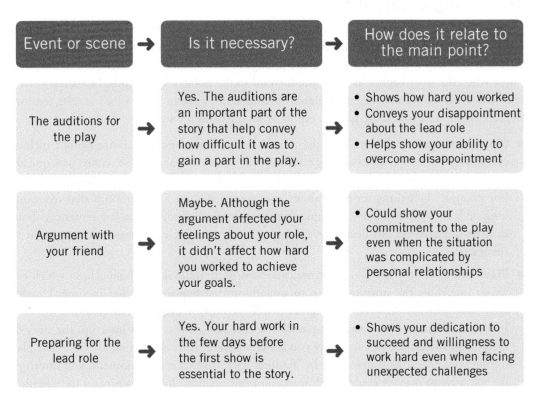

| Event or scene | Is it necessary? | How does it relate to the main point? |
|---|---|---|
| The auditions for the play | Yes. The auditions are an important part of the story that help convey how difficult it was to gain a part in the play. | • Shows how hard you worked<br>• Conveys your disappointment about the lead role<br>• Helps show your ability to overcome disappointment |
| Argument with your friend | Maybe. Although the argument affected your feelings about your role, it didn't affect how hard you worked to achieve your goals. | • Could show your commitment to the play even when the situation was complicated by personal relationships |
| Preparing for the lead role | Yes. Your hard work in the few days before the first show is essential to the story. | • Shows your dedication to succeed and willingness to work hard even when facing unexpected challenges |

Such an analysis will help you decide not only what to include but also how to keep it focused on the main point of your story. Following these steps will help you maintain the focus of your narrative, even when (like Nate's) it tells a multilayered story.

1. In a few paragraphs tell the story of an important experience you had. (Don't try to write a polished version of your story; just tell the story as thoroughly as possible.) Now review what you wrote to see whether you have included anything that isn't necessary. Using the technique described in this section, identify any passages that can be eliminated without losing important information.

2. Find a few stories posted by your Facebook friends or on another social media site you frequent. Use the technique described in this section to analyze whether the story is effectively focused. Identify revisions you might make to sharpen the story's focus.

# Structuring a Narrative

The most common way to structure a narrative is chronologically, in which the story is told from beginning to end without significant interruption. In a chronologically structured narrative, the writer tells the story in a way that mimics the passage of time, taking the reader back to the point in time when the story begins and working forward to the point when it ends. However, writers use several other well-established strategies for manipulating time in a narrative to create tension, heighten drama, and emphasize specific events or moments in the story:

- **Slowing the story down.** Even the most strictly chronological narrative cannot include everything that happened in a story, nor can it tell a story in real time. So writers pass quickly over less important parts of their stories and focus on the more significant moments or events. For example, in writing an essay about your experience on a soccer team that overcame long odds to win an unlikely championship, you might include only a few sentences about early-season matches but devote several paragraphs to a match that was a turning point in the season.

- **Flashbacks.** One of the most common narrative techniques is the flashback, in which the writer interrupts the story to return to something that happened earlier in time. Usually, flashbacks provide important background information or context. For example, in your hypothetical essay about your championship soccer season, you might interrupt the story to include an anecdote about an injury you suffered several years earlier that affected your play during your championship season. In "flashing back" to that earlier moment, you interrupt the narrative to provide readers with important information that helps explain the situation in the "present" moment of the story.

- *In medias res.* *In medias res*, which is Latin for "in the middle of things," is a common technique for creating tension or drama and drawing readers into the story. In this technique, the writer begins the story at a point just before the climactic moment but stops the story before reaching that moment to return to a point earlier in time, telling the story from that point to the end. For example, you might begin the story of your soccer season with the championship match, describing the hard-fought contest to give your reader a sense of that dramatic moment but not yet telling the outcome of the match. Instead, you stop short of describing that outcome and return to the beginning of the season, when your team was facing difficulties that made it unlikely for the team to win a championship. From that point, you tell the story up to the climactic moment during the championship match and then to the conclusion.

iStockphoto.com/Bob Thomas

- **Fractured narrative.** Sometimes a writer tells a story by moving back and forth in time. In this way, a writer highlights important moments but does not narrate those moments in chronological sequence. Instead, the writer might begin the story at some point in the middle, jump ahead to a point near the end, jump back to an earlier moment, and then back to an even earlier moment before returning to the present. An example of this approach is Jon Krakauer's *Into the Wild*, which tells the story of a young man named Chris McCandless who went alone into the Alaskan wilderness to try to live off the land. Krakauer moves back and forth between McCandless's childhood, adolescence, and adulthood as well as events that occurred after McCandless dies.

Using such techniques to manipulate time can sometimes distract readers from the main purpose of the narrative, which is why they are rarely used in academic writing. If you use these techniques, do so strategically to help bring out the main point of your narrative.

---

**EXERCISE 15D** **STRUCTURING A NARRATIVE**

1. In a few paragraphs tell the story of something important that happened to you. Tell your story in chronological order.

2. Restructure the story you wrote for Question #1 using one of the techniques described in this section.

3. Compare the two versions of the story you wrote for Questions #1 and #2. Evaluate each version. Which version do you think tells the story more effectively? Why? What conclusions might you draw from this exercise about narrative structure?

# Writing Purposeful Description

Effective description in narrative writing should convey a vivid sense of the place, person, thing, or event being described, but also serve a purpose in the narrative. For example, let's return to Alan Peshkin's brief description of a high school basketball game:

> An American institution: it is Friday night. Indian High School's basketball team is playing a home game. Students, usually long gone for the weekend to their reservation homes, spill out of the school's several male and female dormitory buildings. They merge with the procession of cars and pickup trucks heading toward parking lots next to the gym. The gym is packed. Students, teachers, parents and relatives mill about in the gym lobby, greeting friends, buying food and drink, anxious to return to their seats before the national anthem is sung. Then the game begins.

This paragraph vividly conveys the scene in the gym and the feeling of anticipation that Peshkin sensed as fans awaited the start of the game. His passage exhibits **two key features of effective description:**

- **Appropriate details.** Peshkin includes just enough detail for the reader to get a clear sense of what is being described. He succinctly describes the scene without going into great detail about the gym or the people. He doesn't describe the gym itself (the color of the walls or the kind of floor), leaving it to the reader to imagine a typical high school gym, nor does he provide details about the people he observed there. Adding such details is unnecessary because the focus of his description is on the sense of anticipation as the crowd gathers for the game. In fact, adding such details might distract readers and blur his focus.

- **Careful word choice.** Describing a scene vividly requires selecting words judiciously and avoiding "overwriting" the scene with unnecessary language, especially adjectives and adverbs. Careful word choice is the key to vivid description. For example, Peshkin writes that the students "spill out of the school's several male and female dormitory buildings," using the verb *spill* efficiently to convey an image of many students moving in a crowd from their dorms to the gym. Similarly, he writes that "they merge with the procession of cars and pickup trucks heading toward parking lots next to the gym." Again, he uses a verb (*merge*) to convey the sense of movement. The noun *procession* creates an image of a line of cars and trucks moving slowly, bumper to bumper, into the parking lot. Notice that he uses no adjectives or adverbs to create these images; rather, he carefully selects verbs and nouns that efficiently convey the scene and help readers imagine it. Adding details or descriptive language to this passage might actually make it less vivid, as in this version (the added words are in boldface):

Students, usually long gone for the weekend to their **distant** reservation homes, **excitedly exit** the school's several male and female dormitory buildings. They merge with the **slow** procession of **modest** cars and **well-worn** pickup trucks **crawling** toward **soon-to-be full** parking lots next to the **old** gym.

Almost all the added words here are adjectives (*slow, modest*) or adverbs (*excitedly*) that at first glance seem to bring concrete details to the description. But do they make the scene more vivid? More important, does that additional language help achieve Peshkin's purpose in describing this scene? Probably not. In this case, as is so often true in descriptive writing, less is more.

In describing something in your narrative writing, then, **follow these simple guidelines:**

- Include only as much detail as you need.
- Use appropriate details.
- Choose words that efficiently convey an image or scene.
- Avoid elaborate or "flowery" language.

---

**EXERCISE 15E**    **DESCRIBING A SCENE VIVIDLY**

1. In a brief paragraph describe a scene. It can be a place you frequent (such as a coffee shop or bus stop), an event (a basketball game, a concert), or some place that interests you for some reason. Describe the scene as clearly and vividly as you can. Now review your description. What details did you include? Why did you include them? Are they necessary? If so, why? Is anything missing from your description?

2. Rewrite the description you wrote for Question #1 so that it is only half as long. Now examine what you removed from the original description. Is the description more or less vivid now? Explain. What conclusions might you draw about descriptive writing from this exercise?

3. Working with a group of three or four classmates, select a place (as in Question #1) and write a description of it. Everyone in your group should describe the same place. Now compare your descriptions. What similarities and differences can you identify in your descriptions? What might this exercise suggest about descriptive writing?

**15**

---

## Showing and Telling

Writing instructors sometimes tell student writers, "Show, don't tell." That can be good advice, but what does it mean exactly?

In general, *showing* in narrative writing means conveying an idea or occurrence through description or action rather than explanation:

*Telling:*      She was afraid of what he might say.

*Showing:*    Her heart quickened, and she felt the knot in her stomach tighten as she waited for him to speak the words she didn't want to hear.

*Telling:*      The house was run down.

*Showing:*    The torn screen on the front door flapped in the breeze. Paint peeled from the windowsills. The porch steps, which looked like they hadn't been swept for months, creaked underfoot, and the porch sagged. A visible layer of grime covered the siding.

As these examples suggest, *showing* generally involves the use of details to convey the scene or action. Which version of each of these passages is preferable depends upon rhetorical context. In much narrative writing in academic settings, such *showing* is unnecessary, though it can sometimes be effective—as in Alan Peshkin's description of the high school basketball game (see pages 474–475). In such cases, adding details can make a passage more vivid—and often longer. But whether the added details improve the narrative is another matter. You have to decide whether *showing* in a passage is appropriate for your rhetorical situation.

When writing descriptive passages that are intended to *show* an action, scene, or event, **follow these two guidelines:**

- **Assess your rhetorical situation.** If you include description, be sure you describe the scene or event in a way that is appropriate for your rhetorical situation. For example, if you are writing a narrative for a psychology class about an experience with a school counselor, you might need to describe a meeting in which the counselor became frustrated and angry. Does that situation call for you to *show* the counselor's frustration by describing his face and mannerisms? If the purpose of the narrative is to examine the experience in terms of important concepts in counseling psychology, maybe not. For such a purpose, it might be sufficient just to state that the counselor became angry. By contrast, if you were writing about the same experience for a composition class, your purpose would likely be different, and you might want to describe the scene in a way that *shows* the counselor's anger.

- **Don't overdo it.** In academic writing, narratives tend to be succinct and focused, so writers should use *showing* carefully. But even in conventional narrative, students often try too hard to *show* and end up describing scenes or events with too much detail that can distract readers. To avoid that problem, carefully review any passages in which you are trying to *show* something and analyze whether the passage is necessary and whether you can condense it without weakening your description.

---

**EXERCISE 15F**    **SHOWING AND TELLING**

1. Write two or three statements about how you feel. For example, "I'm tired." "I am anxious about my upcoming interview." Then rewrite each statement in a way that *shows* the feeling expressed in that statement.

2. Take one of the passages you wrote for Question #1 and share it with two or three classmates. Ask them what feeling the passage shows. If they do not interpret the passage as you expected, revise it to try to convey the feeling more effectively.

---

# Features of Narrative

Effective narrative writing in academic settings has **four important features:**

1. **A clear, narrow focus.** Unlike conventional narratives, stories in academic writing usually do not include long, complex plots and many have no plot at all. Narrative in academic writing generally serves a very specific purpose, and stories are told in a way that achieves that purpose.

2. **Brevity.** Narratives written in academic contexts are usually briefer and more narrowly focused than conventional narratives, and they generally do not attempt to create the world of the story or the experience in the way many conventional narratives do. Depending upon the rhetorical situation and subject matter, narratives in academic writing will vary a great deal in length and style, but the general rule of thumb is to keep it short.

3. **A basic structure.** Narratives in academic writing usually follow a basic, chronological structure and rarely exhibit the more complex structures of many conventional narratives. Academic writers structure their narratives to help readers easily grasp the point of the story.

4. **Succinct, purposeful description.** Description in narratives in academic contexts is usually intended to convey a point quickly and clearly. Academic writers use language efficiently and rarely rely on elaborate diction in describing a person, scene, event, or thing.

The following essay by Amanda Giracca exhibits these features of effective narrative writing. A college writing teacher, Giracca is also an accomplished writer of creative nonfiction who focuses on environmental issues and travel writing. As she does in this essay, Giracca often uses her own experiences as subject matter for her examinations of how we interact with the natural world. In this essay, Giracca tells the story of butchering, cooking, and eating wild game, focusing on a specific meal she made from a squirrel. The real focus of her essay, however, is on humans' relationship with the food we eat. She explores her own experience with wild game as a way to examine complicated questions about the ethics of food consumption. In doing so, she reviews some of the history of our food production system and the changing relationship between humans and the natural world. Her story about preparing wild game for eating becomes the vehicle for her analysis of that relationship.

The essay reproduced here is a shortened version of the essay originally published in 2015 in *Aeon*, a magazine of science, philosophy, and society. As you read, pay attention to how Giracca uses her story to address her provocative questions about our ethical responsibility to the animals we consume as food. Consider as well the following aspects of her essay:

- **A clear, narrow focus.** Although this is a complex essay that examines several challenging questions, Giracca never loses her focus on her main topic: the ethics of food consumption. She explores a number of points related to that main topic, and her own story encompasses her experiences with hunting and wild game and how these matters figure into her relationships with her family. Despite these complexities, the focus of her story remains clear throughout.

- **Brevity.** This is not a short essay, but the narrative sections are relatively brief and tightly focused. In these sections, Giracca tells us about herself, her family, and her experiences, but she doesn't go into detail about her upbringing or other aspects of her life. Instead, she tells just enough of her story to contribute to her effort to address her questions about food consumption.

- **A basic structure.** Giracca follows a loose chronological order in telling her story, using flashback as a way to fill in important details and connect her present situation with her past experiences. The structure of her essay is sophisticated yet straightforward. It enables her to make her ideas and experiences accessible and allows readers to follow her story without getting lost in details.

- **Succinct, purposeful description.** This essay includes numerous descriptive passages, each of which is vivid but remains focused on a specific moment or activity. The descriptions convey a sense of the scene or event (e.g., preparing the squirrel for cooking) without losing focus on her larger questions about the ethics of food consumption.

### Talking About This Reading

**Davis Knutzen:** Organization was the main issue for me. I understood what I was reading and found the essay interesting, but there didn't seem to be a clear structure.

**Bob Yagelski:** Davis, even when a writer organizes a narrative chronologically, the structure can still be complex. In this essay, Giracca adopts a common strategy, especially in academic writing, loosely following a chronological structure, but interrupting the narrative to comment on food production and provide historical background and other relevant information. Those interruptions can make the narrative feel disorganized. However, if you keep the narrative thread in mind as you read those "interrupting" sections, you can more easily follow Giracca's overall discussion.

### The Art of Butchery
by Amanda Giracca

The skin did not come off like a sweater, as I'd been told it would. The falconer, Chris Davis, who had given me this squirrel, made it seem so simple—use scissors, he'd said, and snip horizontally into each side from the gaping hole where he'd gutted it, grab the corners of the soft fluffy pelt and pull up. Pull down. Voilà.

2    Out by the fire pit in my back yard on a late November evening, my fingers grew stiff and numb as I pulled at layers of epithelial tissue I could not see so much as sense, subcutaneous membranes of iridescent silver visible only when I shone my headlamp just right. I could see places where the talons of the hawk had punctured the muscle, bruising it. Little by little, I worked the rich gray pelt down and away from the purple muscles, snipped away the durable membranes, and turned the small mammal from one piece into two. Yesterday, when Chris had given me the squirrel, the eyes had been wide-open and filmy white. I was grateful that they'd shrunk to nearly closed overnight. I hardly noticed the face as I skinned, but I might have if it still had the demonic pale glare.

3    As it turns out, I wasn't even present for this squirrel's death. I'd gone out with Chris, who hunts with Harris's hawks. There was a good possibility that one of his hawks would catch a squirrel, and so I asked if I could keep it if that happened. But the hawks didn't catch any that day. Chris happened to have some in his van from the previous day's hunt, already gutted and without tails, which he'd given away as good-luck talismans.

4    As I butchered and prepared the squirrel for eating, I realized how much this follow-up work is often overlooked. The hunters in my family always emphasized the kill, the moments of being in the deep, silent woods, the story of the first buck snort, the chase, the final shot. Stories of sitting stock-still in deer stands, or crawling on hands and knees after a blood trail. During my childhood, if my brother or father got a deer, they gutted it and dragged it out of the woods and drove it home, hanging it from a maple tree in our backyard. For two days my father and brother would re-tell the story, the narrative itself slowly separating from the carcass dangling by rope. The animal would be an animal only in memory. Nobody talked about the stiffening carcass that slowly creaked in the wind.

5    Then, suddenly, the deer would be gone, reappearing days later as white parcels in our basement freezer, each stamped with the cut— roast, shank meat, tenderloin. Over the course of the year we'd open the parcels, the meat disappearing into us in the way of steaks, stews, and burgers. The story of the hunt would eventually fade too, except for the few that stood out—like the time my father started gutting one buck and it suddenly awoke, legs thrashing about. But usually, the animal, its meat and the memory of it, would just dissolve.

6    What was left out was the butchering. *Butcher*, as a profession, isn't exactly a title that many people aspire to anymore. Like so much else having to do with our contemporary diets, the art of butchering has become industrial, sterile, factory-line-style dismemberment that hardly seems to represent food.

7    My own desire to trap, skin, and eat a mammal—a rabbit, I'd always imagined it being—began after I spent several months living on a small meat farm in the early 2000s. Before that, I'd been a vegetarian college student, and before that an uninformed omnivore, a "normal eater" I suppose you could say. Except for the years that my father or brother shot a deer, our

**A Basic Structure**
In paragraphs 4 and 5, Giracca moves back in time from the present moment she described in the first three paragraphs to her childhood. Notice that from this point in the essay to the end she will move more or less chronologically, generally remaining in the "present" moment of her story with periodic flashbacks to fill in important information or to provide context. The structure of her essay might be seen as a version of *in medias res* (see pages 486–487). Structuring her essay in this way allows her to introduce her themes in an engaging and slightly dramatic way.

**A Clear, Narrow Focus**
In the opening paragraphs, Giracca begins her story about butchering, cooking, and eating a squirrel, but before getting too far into that story she introduces, in paragraph 6, one of the main themes of her essay, which is the dramatic change over the past century or so in how humans obtain their food. By doing so, she establishes her focus early in her essay.

15

meat came from the store in Styrofoam packages, tightly wrapped. The only time we ate meat that resembled the animal it came from was our roasted Thanksgiving turkeys.

8    College brought me out West. I remember driving by massive feedlots, where animal stench sticks with you for miles. It brought me into awareness: the ecological crisis of industrially-raised animals, the social injustice of that industry's employment tactics. So when I landed on a small organic farm back east, I was hesitant about meat. But it was clear that the small flock of sheep and the modest herd of beef cattle were not the destructive empires of the West and Midwest. Like any post-vegetarian, I relished, somewhat guiltily, the taste of meat again. But even on the farm, the butchering was done off-site at a slaughterhouse. We would round up pigs and load them into a trailer, and days later we'd pack frozen bricks of meat into the chest freezer, labeled with the farm's logo. Even then I wondered at the jobs of the people who worked at the slaughterhouse, how they'd chosen what I saw then as such unfortunate work. I couldn't help but wonder, who would want to do *that*?

9    A squirrel's body is a magnificent machine. Peeled, it resembles an outstretched frog, the muscle strong and sinewy, a deep purple-red. The ribs were strangely flat and flexible, not a sturdy cage like ours, but more like a set of curved reeds, made to fold together so the animal can squeeze into a tight space. I marveled at the acrobatic athleticism of this species as I prepared the animal for eating. It was my last look at the creature as a whole. I snipped it into quarters and then portioned off two medallions of meat from the midsection that weren't much more than thin flaps. I put the pieces into a bowl of red wine and onions to sit overnight.

**Succinct, Purposeful Description**
In paragraph 9, Giracca describes the squirrel's skinned body in vivid detail. Her brief description here extends the description in the first two paragraphs. In these passages, she uses description strategically to focus her readers' attention on the action or scene. These vivid but brief descriptions are integral to her story and help maintain her focus on the issues she is exploring—in this case, the ethical dimensions of killing and eating animals.

10    The next evening I removed the pieces, now a deep magenta. I pan-seared the meat, made a quick gravy in the pan. I added the wine marinade, several prunes and sautéed mushrooms. The meat cooked in this wine sauce until it was dark and tender, the sauce a rich brown. I served up two portions over rice, one for me, one for my boyfriend, Ben. When it came time to eat it, I'd almost forgotten that this was what it was about. But I ate. Every last piece of meat on my plate, even sucking meat off the bones. It tasted to me like rabbit. The meat was dark and what some might call gamey. It was unremarkable, a little dry. But when I was done I felt satisfied.

11    A common discussion among post-vegetarians, at least the hippie-ish, environmentally-minded ones in whose company I often find myself, is: If we are to eat the meat of an animal, should we hold ourselves responsible for its death? And really, the moral implications of slaughtering animals have plagued Western civilizations for centuries. It's hard to know how

much of our contemporary butchering practices have evolved for public health reasons, and how much because we are shamed by the act of large-scale killing.

12 The sociologist Amy Fitzgerald outlines the history of this evolution in her article, "A Social History of the Slaughterhouse: From Inception to Contemporary Implications." Fitzgerald cites the first public slaughterhouse dating back to 1662 in the United States, and in 1676 slaughterhouses in New York City were moved from the city's center to less densely populated regions. And it was in the early 18th century in both Europe and the US that these public slaughterhouses became preferable to private ones because they removed the "morally dangerous" work of animal slaughter from easy view.

13 If the first step was removing animal slaughter from the backyards and barns of civilians, out of the public eye, the second was the rise of factory-style meat processing. Fitzgerald draws on Upton Sinclair's famous novel *The Jungle*, which portrays lives of immigrant meat packers in Chicago's infamous Stock Yard. With the industrial revolution came mechanized production. Animal slaughtering is said to be the first "mass-production industry" in the US—Henry Ford partially adopted his assembly-line mechanisms from meatpacking factories. With mass-production came expendable employees and a culture of meat-factory ghettos on the city's edges where immigrants lived in destitution. It was a public health and human rights disaster.

14 The mid-20th century brought strikes and labor organizing, and, for a stretch of time, working in the meat industry was a lucrative job. But the power of unions diminished as the 20th century drew to a close. Instead of being outsourced to foreign countries as happened with other industries, the meat business relocated to the southern US, where unions were weak. Well-paying mid-century meat jobs had gone mostly to white men, but the new meat business employed minorities and immigrants. The work was increasingly industrialized, the positions less skilled, the workers once again as expendable and vulnerable as the characters in *The Jungle*.

15 In the past few decades, the world's meat consumption has risen, reaching a new peak in 2002 at 219 pounds per person, Fitzgerald says. Slaughtering methods have become more efficient and meat prices have actually dropped, reaching the lowest in 50 years. The number of meat-processing facilities has decreased, but the number of animals being processed has increased, meaning more animals in concentrated numbers, both living and dead, and more environmental health issues, such as toxically high manure levels. In today's most efficient factories, at least in the US, 400 cattle can be processed *per hour*.

**A Clear, Narrow Focus**
In paragraph 11, Giracca poses the question that drives her essay. Throughout the rest of her narrative, she maintains her focus on this question. Notice, however, that in the following paragraphs (paragraphs 12–22), Giracca pauses her story and reviews the history of the food production system in the United States. Although this history interrupts her narrative, it actually sharpens the focus of her essay, which is not her own story but the main question she poses in paragraph 11.

15

16   In the time it took me to skin, butcher and cook my squirrel, nearly 10,000 cattle were killed and processed in just *one factory*.

17   We live in what historian Richard Bulliet calls a new era of "postdomesticity"—people live far away, both physically and psychologically, from the animals that produce the food, fiber and hides they depend on. Yet they maintain close relationships with companion animals, often relating to them as if they were human. In *Hunters, Herders, and Hamburgers: The Past and Future of Human-Animal Relations*, Bulliet comments that people continue "to consume animal products in abundance, but psychologically, its members experience feelings of guilt, shame, and disgust when they think (as seldom as possible) about the industrial processes by which domestic animals are rendered into products and about how those products come to market."

18   We all know, or are, these people—the ones who'd rather buy our meat frozen, indiscernible from the animal it was, who brush off the family vegetarian at holidays with a *Don't ruin it for everybody else!*, who might cry when running over a squirrel on the way home from the grocery store.

19   Bulliet traces the recent divide, particularly in the US, to an obvious source: in 1900, 40 percent of people in the US lived on farms. By 1990, 2 percent did. In 1900, people were slaying animals in their backyards. Regulations had been put in place for the slaughter of animals to be sold at a market, hence the public abattoirs and slaughterhouses; but people who lived on remote farms and raised animals—a large percentage of the population—still did it themselves.

20   This meant exposure to blood and viscera and a solid understanding of what a skinned animal looks like; it meant knowing how meat is hewn from a carcass. It is easy to understand how this way of life afforded a better comprehension of what we eat and how it dies. What farm slaughter also exposed people to, says Bulliet, was how these animals not just died, but lived, including how they reproduced.

21   Children, who are naturally curious about sexual acts, would see animals copulating regularly. I remember this from the farm I lived on, how peculiar it could be—the way a grandmother cow would make no qualms about mounting her granddaughter, still a calf, when either was in estrus. I became more familiar with birth, with the prolapsed uteri of sheep, and the death that sometimes followed.

22   When this regular exposure to sex and death diminished in the US with the rise of industrial agriculture, Bulliet claims that in order to find another outlet for these curiosities, the US and other Western, postdomestic societies have developed a fascination with sex and blood. The 1960s was the era of free love, and the 1970s—the beginning of

**Brevity**

In paragraph 16, Giracca uses a single sentence to remind us that she is telling a story about butchering and eating wild game. This single sentence indicates that her own experience is part of the history she reviews in paragraphs 12 through 22. In this way, she underscores the point that our individual decisions about what and how to eat are all part of that history.

postdomesticity—saw an exploding porn industry. The 1970s and '80s brought slasher flicks such as *The Texas Chainsaw Massacre, A Nightmare on Elm Street*. It doesn't have so much to do with our degrading morals, but rather that fantasy has replaced our closeness to the visceral, the bloody.

23    I don't think my experience with the squirrel filled a primitive desire to get my hands bloody. Instead, the task involved me in death, in meat, in food. The way I see it, it's not that there's a *desire* for the blood and gore, but that we're hardwired to deal with the blood and gore, and when that innate machinery goes unused—as it does in a postdomestic society—humans are left with a gap, with something missing.

24    If I were to kill an animal, it would be difficult for my mind to wander elsewhere. I would want to be sure its death was swift. If I were tasked with punching holes into the heads of 400 animals every hour, there's the possibility that my mind would wander, that I would become desensitized, that death would come to mean something else entirely. But when involved in small deaths, in backyard slaughter and butchery, it seems to me the effect is the exact opposite of the fears that started to burgeon during the Enlightenment: the fear that killing animals would make men prone to violence. For me, butchering animals has made me more sensitive, more aware.

25    In the past few years, my father has taken to butchering his own deer. He didn't like the way the butcher did it. It was lazy cutting, he said. Halfway through shotgun season, I visited my parents to help them with the doe my father got, although I ended up watching more than helping.

26    It was a bitter cold day, and the skinned animal hung from a tree outside. My dad stood in his old camouflage jacket that he'd had since I could remember, the zipper long broken. He was working fast, and a little sloppily, because his hands got cold so quickly. I was barely out of the car when he said to me: "Let me show you how to cut the front shoulder." He pushed his knife through the meat, which made a peculiar hollow noise since it was partly frozen. When the hunk he wanted came off, we walked to the basement door. My mother opened it, and my dad put the meat on a length of wood he'd put across the washer and dryer; a strip of cardboard protected the dials from the mess.

**A Basic Structure**
In paragraph 25, Giracca resumes her story, but notice that the "present" moment is not the same time when she prepared her meal of squirrel but presumably some time later that year. The setting is different as well: instead of her own home she is now at her parents' home. This shift in time and place might seem complicated, but her anecdote about her father is consistent with her main focus on the ethics of food consumption. Moreover, Giracca structures her story so that this seemingly complicated shift in time and place is not confusing and reinforces her main themes.

**Succinct, Purposeful Description**
Like the opening paragraphs, which include description of the butchering of a squirrel, the final paragraphs of the essay contain vivid description of butchering, but this time of a much larger animal. The graphic descriptions in these related but distinct scenes helps Giracca bring her main themes into relief. In this regard, these passages illustrate how a writer can use description not only to help readers visualize a scene or an action but also to make a point.

15

27    He held his hands out to the side, and tipped his head towards my mother. "Hat," he said, and she pulled the gray knit cap from his head. Two patches of hair on either side of his head stood straight up, touching in the middle. "Glasses," he said, and she took off his glasses for him, placing them on top of the stand-up freezer. He consulted a book my mother had laid out on a drying rack. She had set up a card table with various sizes of Ziploc baggies and a sharpie.

28    "Now," he said, turning to the meat. "This must be the chuck roast and this the shoulder roast." The rest, he said, the smaller groups of muscles that made up the slender part of the leg, which, skinned, strongly resembled a human forearm, was shank meat.

29    As he began to cut, I flipped through the pages of the book. The chapter on skinning proposed a revolutionary method: poke a hole through the hide, tie one end of a rope to it, and the other end to your car bumper. Back up slowly. Zoop—off like a jacket. Something about this method seemed callous—one I probably wouldn't ever try.

30    Soon, the sight of blood and meat started to lose impact. My dad did all the work, cutting, separating, slicing away the silver skin. My mother held open the baggies, then labeled them, and put them on a shelf in the freezer below last year's meat—brisket and rib meat, some of which I went home with. Soon, it was like it was any old Sunday. A family gathered together, storing up the larder for winter.

**Brevity**
The final six paragraphs of this essay succinctly tell a story (about Giracca's father butchering a deer that he shot) that reinforces her main theme yet maintains her focus on the ethics of food consumption.

Source: Giracca, Amanda. "The Art of Butchery." *Aeon*, 24 Apr. 2015, aeon.co/essays/what-happens-when-carnivores-lose-their-taste-for-butchery.

## Questions to Consider

1. What do you notice most about Giracca's story of her own experiences? What do you take away from her story? To what extent do you think her story addresses her questions about humans' responsibility to the animals they consume as food? Explain.

2. In what ways do you think Giracca's examination of the ethics of food consumption would be different if she did not include her own story? Would it be more or less effective, in your view? Explain.

3. What do you think is Giracca's answer to the question she poses in paragraph 11? Do you agree or disagree with her? Why or why not? To what extent do you think Giracca's story affects your reaction to her examination of the ethics of food consumption? Explain, citing specific passages from her essay to support your answer.

MindTap®
Reflect on your understanding of narrative writing.

15

In this chapter, you will learn to

1. Identify and understand the purposes of personal narrative.

2. Identify appropriate rhetorical opportunities for personal narratives.

3. Define the four key characteristics and four main elements of effective personal narratives.

4. Analyze sample personal narratives.

5. Write a personal narrative, applying the four key features and using the Ten Core Concepts.

MindTap

Understand the goals of the chapter and complete a warm-up activity.

# Writing Personal Narratives 16

**I ONCE ATTENDED** a memorial service at which the eulogy was delivered by the grandson of the man who had died. Writing and delivering that eulogy was not an easy thing for the grandson to do, having just lost his beloved grandfather, whom he had known for all of his 29 years. But the grandson wanted to honor his grandfather. In his eulogy, he chose to tell the story of a day when he was much younger, about ten years old, and was helping his grandfather with some minor plumbing repairs in the basement of his grandfather's home. On the surface, it wasn't much of a story. The grandson told the grieving audience how his grandfather had carefully worked on the plumbing over many years. On the particular day that was the focus of his story, he listened as his grandfather explained in detail which pipes went where, the specialized tools he used, and the many plumbing problems he had solved over the years. The grandfather took great pride in the work he had done to this seemingly mundane and unglamorous part of his home, and that was the point of the grandson's story: His grandfather cared deeply about doing small chores that no one really noticed but that made his family's life a little easier. Nearly 20 years after that day in the basement, the grandson could still vividly remember his grandfather's pride in his work and his dedication to doing even a very minor job right. And the story he told in his eulogy allowed his audience to share in that long-ago moment.

When we write about our experience, we give it meaning. The grandson's story was a way for him to understand an important moment in his life. In this regard, personal narratives aren't simply stories about what happened to us; they are part of our effort to understand ourselves and our world and share that understanding with others. Writing an effective personal narrative, then, is not a matter of just reporting on something that happened; it is a process of getting at some truth or insight about what happened.

Writing about experience can be challenging, illuminating, and deeply satisfying—both for writers and readers. Learning to write effective personal narratives can help you not only improve as a writer but also appreciate and use the power of writing as a tool for understanding and learning.

## Occasions for Personal Narrative

Some rhetorical situations call for personal narrative: to honor an accomplishment, mark an anniversary, or celebrate a life. A politician giving a speech on Memorial Day might tell the story of a particular American soldier as a way to honor all soldiers and their sacrifices for their country. A minister's sermon at a wedding service might include a story of the newlywed couple's devotion to one another. If you wrote an essay as part of your college application, you might have told the story of an experience to make a point about something important that you learned or to illustrate important personal qualities you possess. In such cases, stories not only convey something relevant about the writer's experience but also often make a larger point about what that experience means.

Sometimes, writers write about their experiences as a way to enter ongoing conversations about important issues. In the following essay, journalist Jenna Levine tells part of her story as a college graduate saddled with student loan debt to make a point about the value of college in the United States. Levine graduated from college in 2007 at the start of the Great Recession, when jobs were difficult for many Americans to find and many college graduates had trouble paying off their student loans. Situations like Levine's helped provoke a heated national debate about the cost of college and the rise in student debt, which, as Levine indicates in her essay, prevented many graduates from being able to afford the basic costs of living. Levine's story illustrates how broad economic developments as well as national policies regarding matters like students loans can directly affect individual Americans. Her reference to Sallie Mae (in the fourth paragraph ), the large corporation that offers private student loans, is one that many college students will recognize, because so many American students pay for college by borrowing from that institution. In that regard, her story will be familiar to many readers, who might wonder about whether college is worth the cost. In questioning the value of her own degree, Levine becomes part of the ongoing conversation about education in the U.S.

> There was never a doubt in my mind that I would go to college. Where I grew up, college seemed to be the next natural step, a step I took for granted. I could have, and should have, chosen to go to the closest state college, which was Rutgers University, but I had this burning desire to work in politics. At 18 years old I thought I could change the world, and American University, which has one of the best Public Affairs programs in the country, was where I, with my one-track teenage mind, was desperate to go. I knew I couldn't afford to go to a private institution right away, so I opted to live at home for two years and attend my local community college.
>
> I heard about American University's Public Affairs program during my sophomore year of high school. I was informed by a senior at American that the education came with career-making internships. I genuinely believed that I would move out to Washington D.C., study hard, and the rest of my life would fall into place.
>
> I received my Associates Degree in Political Science in 2005, at which point I had already been accepted by American and filled out my FAFSA forms. I received word in June that I was only eligible for $1,500 per year in work study for financial aid. Apparently, my single mother, a New York City public school teacher, made too much money for me to qualify for more than that. Every little bit of financial assistance helps, but in comparison to the tuition of $19,000 due each semester plus housing, food and any other expenses, I knew that ultimately, that aid wouldn't take me far. Towards the end of June, I began to panic. I had been living at home for two years and working a full-time job, so that I could go to that school; I had to find a way to make it happen.

That's when I met the seductress, Sallie Mae. Sallie Mae, like a loan shark, was friendly and extremely eager to loan me the money I needed for my education; and, like a loan shark, they forgot to mention what would happen to my proverbial legs if I didn't pay up. Instead, Sallie Mae informed me that I could consolidate my various loans upon graduation; however, they did not mention that I couldn't consolidate *private* loans. I easily allowed the corporate giant to assure me, because I desperately wanted to believe I was making the right decision for my future.

I told my dream school "yes" and accepted the work study in early July. My parents offered to pay room and board, cutting about $10,000 off my bill, but the cost per year for American at the time was still a little over $38,000. My father co-signed for one Sallie Mae private loan of $30,000 while my mother co-signed for an additional $30,000 loan. My parents warned me about the interest rate and the risk I was taking, and I promptly ignored their concerns because at the time what I wanted for my future was far more important than the inevitable consequences. They allowed me to assure them, the same way Sallie Mae assured me, because they too wanted to believe in the life I intended to make for myself.

I took out one additional private loan of $18,000 to cover the rest of my expenses and continued to skip the fine print. My father's loan had a reasonable interest rate of 3.75%; however, my loan and my mother's loan were both at 9.75%. To top it all off, not all of my credits were accepted from my community college and I had to remain at American an extra semester. Due to this extra semester, I was forced to borrow an additional $15,000 with a 9.75% interest rate. Every time I signed that dotted line, I told myself, "I will consolidate once I graduate." I relied on the idea that I could reduce the interest, and would be well on my way to having a high paying salary. I was 20 years old, full of hope, and extremely naïve.

I didn't look at my loans again until the day I received my degree in December of 2007. The $93,000 my debt had started off at had ballooned to $120,000, and my repayment plan amounted to almost $1,400 a month on a salary that didn't materialize immediately. Due to the economic downturn, I couldn't find a job in my field that was willing to pay more than $30,000 per year. I knew there was no way for me to afford graduate school, so I started working in sales. I suddenly went from being a world-is-my-oyster graduate to feeling like that oyster shell was closing down on me.

While there are some silver linings to this story, the end of this tale is what a lot of Americans are facing today. My mother saved me by paying off her portion of the loan to reduce it to a reasonable interest rate. I now pay $350 per month for that loan, and have paid off $10,000. Sallie Mae, who did not in fact help me to restructure my interest rate, takes an additional $662 per month to cover the rest. Even though I have managed to pay my loans on time every month, to this day Sallie Mae has refused to consolidate the remaining $33,000 with the 9.75% interest rate.

I'm 26 years old and I always feel like I am looking down the barrel of a gun. I have had to turn down jobs that were perfectly suited for me, because the bottom dollar was not something I could survive on. I can't travel, I can't buy a new car, I don't know when/

**16**

if I will ever own my own home, and because I need to work two jobs to make ends meet, I can't volunteer for the causes that made me want to get into politics in the first place. All because of this $120,000 degree I can't afford to use.

Was it worth it to go to my dream school? I can honestly say even with all the wonderful friends I have made and experiences I have been lucky enough to have, that it wasn't. It *really* wasn't. While I still count my blessings daily, being young, healthy, and having the ability to work hard and pay this debt off over time, I would have preferred to go to a state school and not have these loans over my head.

If I could say one thing about the private American Education system and how it relates to me, it is that it took someone who wanted to change the world and forced them to focus on just surviving in it.

---

Source: Levine, Jenna. "$110,000 in Debt." *The Huffington Post*, 22 Feb. 2011, www.huffingtonpost.com/jenna-levine/jenna-levine-26-graduate-_b_823081.html.

Levine's story is a way to understand important economic developments that affect millions of people through the lens of one person's experience. In a sense, the story of her experience as one college graduate is a particular version of the larger story of education in the United States. The essayist E. B. White once advised writers, "Don't write about man. Write about *a* man." In this regard, personal narrative can be a way to tell a specific story that is part of a much bigger story. Levine tells her story as one person in order to say something about the challenges of affording college in the United States. In doing so, she addresses larger questions about education in general and specifically about the value of a college degree today.

Levine's essay demonstrates how personal narrative can be a way for writers to find common ground with their readers. In writing about our particular experiences, we identify common human concerns, hopes, fears, and joys. Sometimes, however, writers tell stories out of a need to make sense of an experience that puzzles, provokes, surprises, or troubles them. The motivation for writing the story isn't to make a point but to try to understand the experience. By telling the story of the experience, a writer can figure out what it means. Often, such personal narratives begin with a problem situation or a conflict that creates the need to understand: a teen struggling to deal with her parents' divorce; a son reconciling with his estranged father as a result of the father's terminal illness; an athlete trying to decide whether to continue competing after a serious injury; a grandson confronting the loss of his grandfather. In such situations, the writer might simply begin writing the story without really knowing what it means or whether it has a larger point. Something about the situation compels the writer to find a way, through the writing, to understand what happened. Usually, the writing leads to understanding—and often to a point that readers find compelling as well.

Personal narrative, then, emerges from a writer's need to:

- make sense of an experience
- connect that experience to others' experiences

Ultimately, the personal narratives you write should reflect your desire to understand your own experience—and perhaps discover something about human life as well.

# Understanding Personal Narrative

Personal narratives need not be about a momentous event. Any experience can be important enough to write about. What makes a personal narrative effective is how well the writer tells the story so that the significance of the experience is conveyed to the audience. Effective personal narratives usually have **four key characteristics:**

- **A focus on an experience that is important for some reason.** Stories matter to us because our experiences matter. Sometimes, an experience is significant for obvious reasons: losing a loved one, surviving a natural disaster, overcoming a great challenge such as military combat or a serious illness, discovering an uncomfortable truth about someone you admire. But more often writers focus their personal narratives on common experiences that reflect the happenings of our daily lives. What makes the experience appropriate for a personal narrative is that the experience matters to the writer.

- **Relevance.** Effective personal narratives focus on experiences that are not only significant to the writer but also relevant to readers. We might be interested in someone's story about a common kind of experience—say, learning to cook a new recipe or taking an important test in school or at a job—because we have such experiences ourselves. But even when telling the story of an unusual or unique experience, the writer must find a way to make that experience compelling and relevant to readers who might never experience something similar. The story of surviving a terrible automobile accident, for example, engages us because we know it might happen to us, and the writer can make it feel relevant to us even though something like that has never happened to most of us.

16

- **A compelling interpretation.** An effective personal narrative is not a simple recounting of an experience; it is the writer's interpretation of that experience. Through the narrative, the writer conveys a sense of the meaning of the experience to readers, and the effectiveness of the narrative rests in part on how compelling or valid the readers find the writer's interpretation. A narrative that describes a bad car accident might interest us to some degree, but a story about how the writer learned something about the fragility of human life by surviving a bad accident would probably be more compelling. What the writer makes of the experience helps determine how effective the story will be.

- **Engaging storytelling.** *How* writers tell stories can matter as much as *what* the stories are about. Writers use various techniques to tell stories in ways that keep readers interested and convey the meaning of the experience. (See Focus: "Four Elements of Effective Storytelling.")

---

**FOCUS**  **FOUR ELEMENTS OF EFFECTIVE STORYTELLING**

Although writers use many different storytelling techniques, most effective narratives have four main elements in addition to the four key characteristics described in this chapter:

1. **Plot.** The sequence of events that make up a story. A plot consists of what happened in a story. It is the basic framework within which other elements of the story must fit. It keeps the story moving from start to finish.

2. **Characterization.** The creation and development of characters in a story. Characterization is the process by which writers bring characters alive for readers. It encompasses description of the characters and their actions, dialogue, and impact on other characters.

3. **Sensory Appeals and Figurative Language.** The uses of language to convey a scene or action. Writers choose words and structure sentences strategically to describe sights, sounds, feelings, and action. They also use figures of speech to enhance descriptions and convey ideas (see Focus: "Common Figures of Speech" in Chapter 8; see also "Telling Stories" in Chapter 15).

4. **Setting.** Where and when a story takes place. Setting is often used to refer to the specific physical location of a story, but it also encompasses time and culture.

In-depth discussion of these elements is beyond the scope of this textbook, but a basic awareness of them can help you write more effective narratives.

---

These key features are evident in the following excerpt from a narrative about a famous mountaineering expedition to Annapurna, the world's tenth highest mountain, which is located in Nepal. In 1950, two legendary French climbers, Louis Lachenal and Maurice Herzog, climbed the peak and nearly died as they made their way back down to their base camp in a horrific storm. It was the first time any climber had reached the summit of one of the world's fourteen 8,000-meter peaks, despite more than twenty previous attempts by professional climbers. At the time, it was the greatest mountaineering accomplishment in history, and for decades afterward it was still hailed as one of the great achievements in the sport. Herzog's book about the expedition, titled *Annapurna*, became the best-selling mountaineering book of all time.

However, in 1996, David Roberts, an accomplished American mountaineer, learned some things about that famous expedition that called into question whether Lachenal and Herzog ever reached the summit. In his book *True Summit: What Really Happened on the Legendary Ascent of Annapurna*, Roberts tells the story of what he learned about that expedition. He begins his narrative with some background to show the impact of Herzog's book on him as an adolescent growing up in the shadow of the Rocky Mountains in Boulder, Colorado:

*Annapurna* hit me hard. By the time I read the book at age sixteen, I had started hiking up some of the inimitable "talus piles" of the Rocky Mountains—shapeless lumps of scree and tundra strung along the Continental Divide, peaks such as Audubon, James, Grays, and Torreys. It took stamina to push on at 14,000 feet, and judgment to descend in the face of a July lightning storm, but I knew what I was doing was a far cry from real mountaineering. Staring at a true precipice, such as the 2000-foot-high east face of Longs Peak, I felt an ambivalent longing: surely it took the competence and arrogance of the gods to inch one's way, armed with ropes and pitons, up such dark landscapes of terror.

*Annapurna* ratcheted that uncertain longing into full-blown desire. When I put down the book—swallowed in one sitting, as I recall—I wanted more than anything else in the world to become a mountaineer.

Over the decades, Herzog's narrative has had precisely that effect on an inordinate number of adolescents of both sexes. It might seem curious that a tale fraught with near-death, with fearful trials by storm and cold, and finally with gruesome amputations of fingers and toes turned black and rotting [from frostbite], should encourage any reader to take up the perilous business of climbing. Yet so exalted were the ideals that Herzog lyrically sang—loyalty, teamwork, courage, and perseverance—that rational apprehension was drowned in a tide of admiration.

Source: Roberts, David. *True Summit: What Really Happened on the Legendary Ascent of Annapurna*. Simon and Schuster, 2000, pp. 22–24, 27.

The experiences Roberts describes in this passage—and in his book—are not common, but he tells his story in a way that makes those experiences relevant even to readers who are not mountaineers but who can appreciate the ideals that motivate climbers like Roberts and Herzog.

16

Years after first reading Herzog's book, Roberts had a conversation with a French mountaineer named Michel Guerin about Herzog's book *Annapurna*, which Roberts believed was the greatest mountaineering book ever written:

> "Don't you agree?"
>
> It took a long moment for a wry smile to form around his cigarette; then he shook his head.
>
> "Why not?"
>
> I listened to the careful disquisition that spilled from Michel's lips, first in shock, then in dismay. It is a hard thing to have one's hero of forty years' standing dismantled before one's eyes.
>
> The essence of what Michel told me was as follows. *Annapurna* was nothing more than a gilded myth, one man's romantic idealization of the campaign that had claimed the first 8000-meter peak. What had really happened in 1950 was far darker, more complex, more nebulous than anything Herzog had written.

Roberts goes on to relate what he learned from Michel, which raised the possibility that one of the greatest mountaineering achievements in history had never happened:

> Listening late into the night to Michel's disquisition, I felt my shock and dismay transmute into something else. The true history of Annapurna, though far more murky and disturbing than Herzog's golden fable, might in the long run prove to be an even more interesting tale—one fraught with moral complexity, with fundamental questions about the role of "sport" in national culture, perhaps even with deep veins of heroism quite different from those Herzog had celebrated.

In these passages, Roberts not only sets the stage for his story but also begins to get at why this experience matters to him and why it might matter to others—that is, his interpretation of the experience. His story recounts his research into the 1950 Annapurna expedition and includes some of his own impressive mountaineering feats, but it also explores larger questions about truth, heroism, and the motivations for taking great risks. Ultimately, his story is about fundamental elements of human life. That's what makes this story, which describes uncommon human exploits, relevant to a wider audience. Roberts tells the story of something that happened to a few seemingly heroic men, but the story relates to concerns and questions that everyone has.

Roberts also tells his story in a way that helps keep readers engaged, using elements of effective storytelling (see Focus: "Four Elements of Effective Storytelling"). He creates a **plot** that takes readers through the night when he first learned potentially disturbing facts about the 1950 Annapurna expedition, he uses **characterization** to convey a sense of Michel, and he employs **sensory appeals and figurative language** to describe the experience. In addition, he invokes a **setting** to help readers better appreciate the moment.

Roberts' narrative illustrates how writers use specific storytelling techniques to help readers imagine the events being described and to provoke certain responses in their readers. It also demonstrates that personal narratives share the characteristics of all effective narrative writing described in Chapter 15:

- **Clear focus.** Notice that in these excerpts Roberts keeps his focus on the significance of the Annapurna expedition. Usually, the experiences we write about in personal narratives are multifaceted, and Roberts' experience is no exception. In such cases, it can be challenging to avoid following tangents or telling unnecessary anecdotes, but in effective personal narratives writers stick to the story.
- **Careful structure.** Effective narratives are structured to bring the experience alive for readers and maintain focus on the main story. Roberts uses a basic chronological format, periodically incorporating important background information. Such a structure helps maintain focus and keep readers engaged.
- **Vivid, purposeful description.** Effective personal narratives usually include descriptions of scenes, people, or events to help the reader imagine them. Notice that Roberts' brief descriptions convey a vivid sense of the moments he describes, but just as important, the descriptions support his interpretation of the experience.

---

**FOCUS** | **LITERACY NARRATIVES**

One form of personal narrative that has become increasingly popular in recent years is the literacy narrative. A literacy narrative tells the story of a writer's experience with reading and writing. For example, a writer might tell the story of being placed in a special reading class in elementary school; in telling such a story, the writer might examine the impact of that experience on his or her school performance, attitudes about literacy, or self-esteem. Sometimes, a literacy narrative tells the broader story of the writer's development as a reader or writer over time as a way to explore the factors that shaped him or her as a literate person. Often, when literacy narratives are assigned in college courses, the purpose is to examine the role of literacy in our lives and gain insight into the nature of literacy as a social practice.

Like other personal narratives, literacy narratives are based on the writer's experience. What makes a literacy narrative distinctive is that it focuses specifically on a writer's experiences with literacy. Nevertheless, an effective literacy narrative has the same features of effective personal narratives described in this chapter, and writers of literacy narratives use the same techniques described in this chapter and in Chapter 15.

**16**

---

**EXERCISE 16B** | **UNDERSTANDING PERSONAL NARRATIVE**

1. Find a personal narrative (maybe one assigned in a class or one you read in a newspaper, magazine, or blog) and analyze it in terms of the four main characteristics of effective personal narrative explained in this section. On the basis of your analysis, draw conclusions about the effectiveness of the narrative.

2. Read the three essays included in the next section of this chapter. Which of them most appeals to you? In a brief paragraph, explain why. What features of the essay engage

*(Continued)*

you? Does the subject matter interest you for some reason? On the basis of this analysis, draw conclusions about effective personal narratives.

3. With a group of classmates, share the paragraphs you wrote for Question #2. Compare your choices and the reasons for them. What conclusions might you draw from this exercise about personal narrative? What conclusions can you draw about the role of audience in effective personal narratives?

# Reading Personal Narrative

The three reading selections in this section illustrate the variety of form, style, voice, and perspective in personal narratives. Although each writer tells the story of a particular experience for a specific purpose, all three writers share their stories as a way to explore some aspect of being human. As you read these essays, be aware of the differences in the way these writers approach their subjects and tell their stories, and identify the similarities in the way these writers find meaning in their experiences. Also address these questions:

| An experience that matters | • What makes the experience described in the essay significant?<br>• Why does the writer tell the story of this experience? |
| --- | --- |
| Relevance | • In what ways might the experience described in this narrative be relevant to the intended audience?<br>• What makes the experience important to others? |
| A compelling interpretation | • What meaning does the writer find in the experience or event described in the narrative?<br>• To what extent does the writer's interpretation enhance the story? |
| Engaging storytelling | • How effectively does the writer tell her story?<br>• What storytelling techniques does the writer use?<br>• How well does the writer use these techniques? |

MindTap®

Read these personal narrative examples. Highlight and take notes online. Additional readings are also available online.

## The Balancing Act
## by Haley Lee

*Sometimes, our identities can be reflected in mundane things, such as clothes or hairstyles. In the following essay, Haley Lee describes her frustrations with chopsticks, a basic eating utensil that is part of her Chinese heritage. But in that seemingly simple matter of using chopsticks, Lee confronts the complexity of her identity as the daughter of a white American mother and a Chinese father. Her struggles with chopsticks mirror her struggle to accept that complicated identity.*

*As you read Lee's brief essay, notice how she focuses on one moment: a meal with her host family during her visit to China on a student scholarship. But that one moment—when she dropped a piece of fruit that she tried to eat with chopsticks—becomes the occasion for exploring the much larger challenge of understanding—and accepting—who she is. In this regard, her essay is an example of how a writer can tell the story of one moment or incident to examine complex themes that connect us as human beings. In the concrete details of that moment, such as the fruit lying on the floor, Lee introduces abstract ideas, such as identity and acceptance. Her brief essay, which was published in* The Best Teen Writing of 2014, *demonstrates that a writer does not need a lot of words to say a great deal. It also illustrates the power of even a very short narrative to help us understand the most challenging aspects of human life.*

· · · · · · · · · · · · · · · · · · · · · · · · · · · · · · · · · · · · · · ·

### Talking About This Reading

**Emily Clark (student):** I liked this essay and understood it, but I got bogged down in some of the vocabulary, especially at the beginning. That made it harder to get into the story.

**Bob Yagelski:** Emily, as explained in this chapter and Chapter 15, vivid, purposeful description is one of the key characteristics of effective narrative. In this case, the author focuses on a single moment, which she describes in detail in the first few paragraphs to take us into her experience. Sometimes, too much description can actually undermine the author's purpose, and as a reader, you must decide whether that's the case here. In other words, your difficulty with vocabulary in this essay might be an indication that the description is more vivid than purposeful.

**16**

· · · · · · · · · · · · · · · · · · · · · · · · · · · · · · · · · · · · · · ·

It began with a slice of cantaloupe. True, I managed to fake my way through dinner using a shallow serving spoon and the lip of my rice bowl as necessary crutches. But since clearing the other silverware from the table, my pretense of cutlery coordination had hastily started to deflate. Before I could gather my thoughts, the juicy truth tumbled out in melon form—

I didn't know how to hold chopsticks.

Thump.

The buzz of Chinese chitchat revved and then stalled. It was my first night with my host family on an NSLI-Y scholarship, a program that lists Mandarin proficiency and student ambassadorship as the end goals of a six week stay in Hangzhou. To my horror, visions of hand-eye coordination had trounced those twin specters of fluency and diplomacy by the time my portion of fruit clunked against the wooden floorboards.

Zigzagging under the table and now trailing a sticky rivulet, the orange crescent resembled too closely the arc of a mocking smile. I couldn't help grinning in

*(Continued)*

response, feeling helpless and a little ridiculous crouched on my knees. It was my host father who, after I collected myself and my dignity, spoke. "Do you want us to teach you how to use them?" He pointed to the instruments of my destruction, the chopsticks resting innocently against the broad-brimmed dessert platter.

Presented with this question now, "yes" seems like the obvious reply. At the time, I hesitated before answering. During childhood meals, I vacillated regularly between using chopsticks and a fork. The former promised dexterity and grace, the type of swanlike agility detailed by Amy Tan and wielded by Mulan. But in the end, the precision demanded by chopsticks proved too frustrating for me, and so the pair's pronged American counterpart, commanding in ease and in gleam, won my young heart.

Nobody judged me for choosing between utensils. In fact, at annual New Year's Eve dinners with my Dad's Chinese family, my grandma has more than once slid me a fork after watching oysters come back to life between my trembling chopsticks. My nebulous "Whasian" (half white, half Asian) status served as a ready-made excuse for my fumbling. So before my host father broached the subject, I lived for years believing my silverware scrimmages lay in the past. While I cannot claim to know what force compelled me

to nod in response to his offer, I do attribute my semi-mastery of chopsticks to his advice that followed:

"Relax your hand. The rest will come with practice."

My fingers slackened. I exhaled, relieved.

As a child, I let the fork triumph at chopsticks' expense. I reasoned that seeking refuge in my Mom's American influence would lead to a cleaner daily existence— fewer inquiries about the contents of my lunch box if I toted a ham and Swiss sandwich instead of sweet pork buns; fewer raised eyebrows when I told stories if I dubbed my grandma "Nana" instead of "Ngin Ngin." But as my grip loosened, I began to see that where I had staged a duel, there was no need for a dichotomy in the first place. My hands needed a lesson in pliability, but so did my mind.

Today, lowering my own pair of chopsticks into a bowl of instant ramen, I know that my host father was right: I must pursue the challenge of embracing silverware options and, ultimately, cultures. Being half Chinese doesn't justify hiding behind half commitments. It took a plunging cantaloupe wedge to dislodge my inertia, but since returning home I have successfully pinned tofu with chopsticks; I have started conversing with my grandma in Mandarin; I have begun to delve into literature on modern China. Although still a long way from achieving student statesmanship, I am enjoying savoring my fusion heritage. There is room for both a fork and chopsticks on my plate. And sometimes, I've learned, it's more fun to make a mess.

Source: Lee, Haley. "The Balancing Act." *The Best Teen Writing of 2014*, Scholastic, 2014, pp. 23–25.

1.  How would you summarize the main theme or point of Lee's brief story? What fundamental ideas about identity do you think she tries to convey to her readers?

2.  Assess Lee's use of storytelling strategies, especially plot, description, and dialogue. How effectively does she use these strategies to tell her story? Cite specific passages from her essay to support your answer.

3.  What do you think Lee's essay reveals about personal narrative as a way to understand ourselves?

## Some Thoughts on Mercy
### by Ross Gay

*In 2013, a man named George Zimmerman was acquitted in the shooting death of an unarmed teenager named Trayvon Martin. Outrage about the acquittal led to a movement that became known as Black Lives Matter, which organized protests throughout the United States against violence toward African Americans, including violence against African Americans by police. Through the Black Lives Matter movement, many African Americans expressed their fears and frustrations about police violence. The movement intensified the national debate about race relations—and racism—in the U.S. A few months after George Zimmerman's acquittal, college professor and writer Ross Gay published the following essay, in which he describes a seemingly innocuous encounter with a police officer. But as Gay tells the story, the encounter, which ended peacefully and without violence, was not at all innocuous; rather, it underscored the fear in which many African Americans live and the racism that can arise in commonplace activities, such as driving home from work, shopping, or taking a walk through a neighborhood. Gay's story is about his own experience of racism, but he tells his story as a way to give voice to experiences that, he tells us, are common to all African Americans. His essay thus illustrates how one person's story can be about much more than that one person.*

*Gay's essay is complex. He organizes it around the story of a single encounter with a police officer, but in telling that one story, he tells related stories about other moments or events, past and present, when he experienced racism and fear. In describing these experiences, Gay explores challenging questions about race in contemporary society, demonstrating how narrative can be a powerful vehicle for making an argument about important issues or problems. As you read, notice how Gay employs narrative techniques such as flashbacks to fill in background information and to help readers better understand the significance of his encounter with the police officer. His essay first appeared in* The Sun *magazine in 2013.*

### Talking About This Reading

**Nadia French (student):** This essay was not something that I could relate to, because I have never experienced discrimination like this author has. But I did find it interesting to read about his different experiences being followed by a security officer in the mall or pulled over by the police because of the color of his skin.

**Bob Yagelski:** Nadia, we can't help reading from the perspective of our own experience, which always shapes our response to a text. But a piece of writing can help us gain insight into experiences that we ourselves have never had—as Ross' essay seems to have done for you. That's one reason that narrative can be so powerful. If Ross is successful, then his story has made his experiences accessible to you.

*(Continued)*

16

I was in my garden, walking aimlessly with sickle in hand, taking swipes at the plantain that had erupted into tiny flower heads or at the blowzy red clover growing in tall thickets and slurped at by bumblebees. I walked with absolute freedom, barefoot behind the house I own, in the garden I had built with a joyful toil unlike any other I'd experienced: nibbling the blueberries and what were left of the strawberries; studying the bees and wasps that wove through the small forest of lavender; parting the dense foliage of the Nanking cherry bush to find the remaining tart fruits, beneath which the neighbor's cat slept. The beehive I had set up two weeks earlier between the brush pile and the gooseberries was busy, a cluster of bees gathered on the lip, one after another heading off to work, buzzing by my head on their way. There was no sign yet of the impending drought that would leave reservoirs so parched the soil would look like the surface of the moon, nor of the heat wave that would sear the lower Midwest for weeks with hundred-degree weather. It was a nearly perfect afternoon—cloudless, the sun warm on my shoulders, food in my garden and in my refrigerator, my bills paid—when I bent to tug free a head of new garlic to throw in with the potatoes and chard I'd planned for dinner, and my back seized up. It would be days before I could stand upright, let alone work in the garden, without pain.

I wasn't thinking of it, though it seems my body was: the seemingly insignificant run-in I'd had with the police the night before. For a black man any encounter with the police is tense, and that tension had found its way into my muscles, if not my mind.

I teach creative writing at Indiana University in Bloomington, and I had been in my office on campus until about eleven o'clock, working hard on my tenure file, trying to get a little breathing room before a guest came to stay for a few days. In my town, on an early-summer night at 11 PM, there's still a pleasant bit of activity on the street. So when the cop pulled me over, two local bars were crowded half a block away, their outside seating full to capacity, and the walking path was busy with pedestrians and cyclists.

I wasn't perturbed by the cop. I had made a decision in the recent past no longer to be afraid of the police. With their costumes, their hats, the boots worn by the "troopers," police are meant to make us feel scared, guilty, criminal (some of us more than others). There's a way in which they take up residence in our bodies (some of us more than others). When they appear behind us or in our line of sight, our heart rate accelerates, our breathing quickens, our muscles contract. We become acutely aware not only of what we were doing but also of what the cop might think we were doing.

But I had decided I'd try not to feel guilty when I next encountered the police. Why? First, because I am thirty-eight years old and generally law-abiding. Second, because it had occurred to me that when I paid my taxes, I was helping to pay police officers' salaries, and therefore this cop was actually my employee—though I wouldn't have said so to him. Third, I was tired of being afraid. So I'd decided to imagine the police in general—and this cop pulling me over in particular—as doing what I imagine a policeman should spend his time doing: making our community safer.

And so, for the first time in my life when a cop came to my car window, I looked him in the eye and asked as gently and openheartedly as possible if he could tell me why he'd stopped me. "After you give me your license and registration," he said. I handed them over, and he told me simply, "Your license-plate light is out." I'd had no idea there was such a thing as a license-plate light, and I told him as much, laughing to express my good-natured confusion and gratitude: *He wants to do me a favor.*

And he smiled—just for a second—then asked if I had any drugs in the car. When I said no, he asked if I had any guns in the car. When I said no, he asked if I'd been drinking. When I said no, he asked again, "You don't have any weapons or anything illegal in the car I should know about?" (Strange, you might think, for such questions to arise from a burned-out license-plate light.) And I said, looking straight ahead through the windshield, "No."

Probably any of you who are black or brown have a version of this story, if not a worse one. One friend of color, when I mentioned it to him, said, "I thought he was going to go toss the car and make you clean it up." Another friend's black father said, "Any time you meet the cops and don't go to jail is a good time."

The African American comedy duo Key and Peele have a skit in which President Obama is teaching his daughter Malia to drive. When she runs a stop sign, a cop pulls them over. Astonished and a bit embarrassed at having detained the president of the United States, the cop tells them they can go. But Obama, earnest as ever, says, "No, I want you to go ahead and treat us the way you would if I weren't the president." In the next shot we see Obama getting slammed on the hood of the car and handcuffed. It's funny. And not only black people laugh at such jokes. Everyone does, because *everyone knows*.

I recently realized that I've never, as an adult, driven past a car that's been pulled over without looking to see the race of its occupants. Part of every black child's education includes learning how to deal with the police so he or she won't be locked up or hurt or even killed. Despite my advanced degrees and my light-brown skin, I've had police take me out of my vehicle, threaten to bring in the dogs, and summon another two or three cars. But I've never been thrown facedown in the street or physically brutalized by the cops, as some of my black friends have. I've never been taken away for a few hours or days on account of "mistaken identity." All in all, this traffic stop the other night amounted to nothing. It was so nothing, in fact—so everyday, so known, so agreed upon, so understood—that I am embarrassed, ashamed even, by the scale of my upset, by the way this nonevent took up residence in my body and wrung me out like a rag. I didn't even get a ticket, after all. He just asked me some questions—questions I knew (we all knew, didn't we?) he had before he pulled me over. We say, "Yeah, that's just how it goes." Given what could've happened, I ought to be glad, right? I ought to get over it.

But it is also the familiarity of it all (black guy has unpleasant run-in with the cops) that makes my experience, and the many thousands like it, almost invisible— which makes the significant daily terror of being a black or brown person in this country almost invisible.

Having grown up in a largely white, working-class suburb of Philadelphia, I'm rarely shocked by racism. I've heard it all: "He's a nigger lover." "That nigger jumps real high." "You're not like those other niggers." "That girl's as tan as a nigger." In fact, when I meet people who say they haven't been around racism or anti-Semitism, I usually don't believe them. I remember in fourth grade a popular white kid with feathered hair and a slight overbite yelled, "Nigger!" after me as I ran to get on the bus. I dashed back to punch him before running again to the bus, and he yelled after me again, "Nigger!" It went on like this until I decided I'd better catch my bus. (The kid's best friend was Puerto Rican.) As a child, walking with a friend's little sister, I was chased down the block by a grown man who screamed, "Don't come around here with white girls, nigger!" while Mr. Miller, another white man and the father of two of my friends, held him back and apologized to me. Mr. and Mrs. Lee, a black couple, were sitting across the courtyard on their stoop, seething. When I learned from my Chinese American best friend the Cantonese word for "white

*(Continued)*

16

devil" (bukwai), I excitedly told a white buddy, as if to say, See, they have names for you too!—to which he rattled off an incredible litany of racial epithets for Asian Americans (though probably only about half as many as he had for black people).

Where I grew up, the white kids, some of whom were my close friends, told nigger jokes to my face or within earshot. I remember one redheaded, freckle-faced kid on the football team yelling across the locker room to one of the few black players, "The only thing I respect about you is your dick!" And even if they didn't make jokes, it might be that you couldn't go into their houses because you were black. Or your best friend's uncle might tell you to your face that black people are inherently lazy.

Not to mention what we all watched on TV and read in the newspapers. There were the "welfare queens" and "crack babies." There was the Rodney King beating and the trial and the ensuing riots. There were the Central Park Five, a group of black and Latino teens falsely accused of raping a white jogger, and that strange new word *wilding*, supposedly used by the suspects for their nonexistent crime spree. And there was the fact that nearly every criminal on the news—rapist, murderer, burglar, drug dealer—was black. Even if I wasn't consciously aware of it, I got the message.

I remember being thirteen and walking into a clothing store at the mall with a white pal. As we perused the racks, it didn't take long for me to realize the security guard was following me and was oblivious to my friend. So I gradually made my way to the back of the store while I glimpsed my pal up front stuffing a few hundred dollars' worth of merchandise into his backpack. If I was going to be profiled, I thought, at least my blond-haired buddy could get some new clothes out of the deal. I think we could have made a racket out of this, but we didn't.

At Lafayette College I played football on a scholarship, like most of the working-class kids on campus. One night I was having a conversation with two of my white teammates as we watched the Atlanta Falcons on Monday Night Football in their dorm room. Deion Sanders was on the sidelines, not dressed for the game due to an injury. He wore a jogging suit with a big gold chain and a crucifix that swayed beneath the lights. My teammates took the occasion to explain to me the difference between a "black person" and a "nigger." They categorized Sanders as the latter— mostly, it seemed, because of his clothes and his swagger. A "black person," in their minds, was someone like the Detroit Lions' Barry Sanders, whose humble attitude on the field appealed to them. Beginning the next morning I could swallow nothing for four days except water, and only a few sips if I bent over and twisted my head at a bizarre angle, looking back almost over my shoulder. I lost about twenty pounds—no small concern for a college tight end. The doctor diagnosed esophageal spasms and prescribed a muscle relaxant. I think the spasms were my body's revolt: You must not swallow this. But how could I not?

A friend of mine here at Indiana University, the late black writer and creative-writing professor Don Belton, came to my house one day looking especially weary. Don told me he had been at the bookstore, where a young white woman had asked if he needed any help, and he'd snapped, "Do I look like I need help?" I'm sure this behavior didn't make sense to the poor woman trying to assist him. Don thought he was being perceived as a criminal. "Can I help you?" twisted in his ear into "Are you stealing something?" I tried to tell him that I'd seen the clerks at that store ask everyone who walked in the same question. Don held his head in his hands. "I'm just so tired," he said.

I have my own catalog of similarly exhausting experiences: the janitor in my building on campus shouting, "How'd you get in here?" as I walked to my office one night, until I shook my key at him; the older white woman at the antique shop glaring at my pockets (one of which had a book in it), and my own halfhearted desire to allay her anxiety: *No, no, dear lady, I just need a chair. I just want a f\*\*\*ing chair.*

As a result of this, I've developed the habit of buying something in stores whether I want to or not, to put such possibly suspicious white people at ease. I'm behaving in response to what I imagine other people are thinking. After all, the janitor and the antique-shop clerk didn't say anything to me about the color of my skin. Just as the cop didn't say, "Since you appear to be of some African extraction, I would like to ask you if you have any drugs or weapons in the car." He just asked if I had any drugs or weapons in the car.

I've had to struggle not to absorb those stares and questions and traffic stops and newscasts and TV shows and movies and what they imply. I've been afraid walking through the alarm gate at the store that maybe something's fallen into my pockets, or that I've unconsciously stuffed something in them; I've felt panic that the light-skinned black man who mugged our elderly former neighbors was actually me, and I worried that my parents, with whom I watched the newscast, suspected the same; and nearly every time I've been pulled over, I've prayed there were no drugs in my car, despite the fact that I don't use drugs; I don't even smoke pot. That's to say, the story I have all my life heard about black people—criminal, criminal, criminal—I have started to suspect of myself.

As abolition became a real possibility in the nineteenth century, a mythology about black-male criminality was crafted by proponents of slavery, and that myth was then amplified after emancipation. Our current prison system, and the "drug war" that is responsible for that system's status as the largest in the world, actively cultivates the same story of a unique criminal blackness. I put "drug war" in quotes, because, as Michelle Alexander points out in her brilliant book *The New Jim Crow: Mass Incarceration in the Age of Colorblindness*, if there were a true War on Drugs, then "people of all colors, . . . who use and sell illegal drugs at remarkably similar rates," would be incarcerated at very nearly the same rate. But that's not the case.

Alexander's book is an incisive analysis of how the drug war has specifically targeted African American men, saddling huge numbers with ex-felon status, which makes employment, voting, housing, education, and more nearly impossible: in other words, effectively reinstating Jim Crow. Among her most striking observations is that in 1981, when President Ronald Reagan declared that he was "running up a battle flag" in the War on Drugs, fewer than 2 percent of the American public viewed drugs as the most important issue facing the nation. That figure jumped to 64 percent in 1989, thanks largely to a sensational (and racist) media campaign. She also points out that the police could make numerous drug arrests by raiding the fraternities and sororities at colleges, but for the most part they don't, because those students are not viewed as criminals: they're just kids who use drugs.

A few years back I was teaching a summer enrichment class for public-school students in Philadelphia who were almost all black, and I had a discussion about drug use with them. One outspoken child told me, and the class, "Mr. Ross, my name's not Sally; my name's Takeisha. I smoke weed." God bless this child and her weed. But what she didn't know, and won't until she makes some white friends or goes off to college, is that Sally probably smokes just as much weed as she does, or takes OxyContin, or snorts Ritalin, or uses cocaine or Adderall. Takeisha believed that she was different from white people in her habits. She believed she was a criminal, whereas her white counterparts were, well, white. I wish Takeisha and everyone else knew that people of all races use drugs. It's just that if you're black or brown, like the people in Takeisha's neighborhood, your drug

*(Continued)*

16

use is more often policed and punished. But the fantasy of black criminality continues. This, to a large extent, is what the drug war is about: making Takeisha—along with her teachers, her local shop owners, her neighbors, her city's police, her prosecutors—believe she's a criminal. It is, perhaps, the only war the U.S. has won in the last thirty years.

I shudder at the emotional and psychic burden we've laid on the young black and brown New Yorkers—so many of them children—being profiled in that city's "stop-and-frisk" program. One man featured in a *New York Times* video speaks with courage and dignity about having been stopped as a teenager "at least sixty to seventy times." Another, in a video made by *The Nation*, talks about having been roughed up for "looking suspicious" and called a "mutt." Eighty-seven percent of stop-and-frisk targets are black or Latino, though blacks and Latinos constitute only about half of New York City's population. How, when their city believes them to be criminal, do these young people escape believing the same of themselves?

Isn't it, for them, for us, a gargantuan task not to imagine that everyone is imagining us as criminal? A nearly impossible task? What a waste, a corruption, of the imagination. Time and again we think the worst of anyone perceiving us: walking through the antique shop; standing in front of the lecture hall; entering the bank; considering whether or not to go camping someplace or another; driving to the hardware store; being pulled over by the police. Or, for the black and brown kids in New York City, simply walking down the street every day of their lives. The imagination, rather than being cultivated for connection or friendship or love, is employed simply for some crude version of survival. This corruption of the imagination afflicts all of us: we're all violated by it. I certainly know white people who worry, Does he think I think what he thinks I think? And in this way, moments of potential connection are fraught with suspicion and all that comes with it: fear, anger, paralysis, disappointment, despair. We all think the worst of each other and ourselves, and become our worst selves.

Among the more concrete ramifications of this corruption of the imagination is that when the police suspect a black man or boy of having a gun, he becomes murderable: Murderable despite having earned advanced degrees or bought a cute house or written a couple of books of poetry. Murderable whether he's an unarmed adult or a child riding a bike in the opposite direction. Murderable in the doorways of our houses. Murderable as we come home from the store. Murderable as we lie facedown on the ground in a subway station. Murderable the day before our weddings. Murderable, probably, in our gardens.

We all exist, mostly unwittingly, in a world of illusions with all-too-real consequences. Too often we exist, as Ralph Ellison's narrator in *Invisible Man* says, as "phantom[s] in other people's minds." The title of poet Cornelius Eady's book *Brutal Imagination*, about the Susan Smith murders, says it all. Smith drowned her two children, then conjured (from her imagination) a black carjacker to explain their disappearance. The main speaker throughout *Brutal Imagination* is that black phantom, made of our culture's fears, just as we are made of each other's fears. Eady says in the poem "My Heart": "Susan Smith has invented me because/Nobody else in town will do what/She needs me to do." And later in the same poem: "Since her fear is my blood/And her need part mythical,/Every thing she says about me is true."

But what if we acknowledged those fears, regardless of how awful or shameful they are? What if we acknowledged this country's terrible and ongoing history of imagining its own citizens—indigenous, black, Japanese American, Arab American, Latino—as monsters? What if we acknowledged the drug war, and the resulting mass incarceration of African Americans, and the myriad intermediate crimes against citizens and communities as a product of our fears? And what if we thereby had to reevaluate our sense of justice and the laws and procedures and beliefs that constitute it? What if we honestly assessed what we have come to believe about ourselves and each other, and how those beliefs shape our lives? And what if we did it with generosity and forgiveness? What if we did it with mercy?

It seems to me that part of my reason for writing this—for revealing my own fear and sorrow, my own paranoia and self-incrimination and shame—is to say, Look how I've been made by this. To have, perhaps, mercy on myself. When we have mercy, deep and abiding change might happen. The corrupt imagination might become visible. Inequalities might become visible. Violence might become visible. Terror might become visible. And the things we've been doing to each other, despite the fact that we don't want to do such things to each other, might become visible.

If we don't, we will all remain phantoms—and, as it turns out, it's hard for phantoms to care for one another, let alone love one another. And it's easy for phantoms to hurt one another. So when the cop and I met that night, how could he possibly have seen the real me for all the stories and fantasies that have been heaped on my body, and the bodies of those like me, for centuries? And how could I see him?

Meanwhile he stood no more than three feet from me, and we looked each other in the eye. And when I gave him my license and registration, our hands almost certainly touched. And they almost certainly touched again as he gave them back.

Three weeks before that incident, I brought home my first box of bees. I'd picked them up from Hunter's Honey Farm, twenty miles up the road in Martinsville. Bees often come, as mine did, in a small screened box with a tin can full of sugar water that they drink from for the handful of days they're in transit. As instructed by the beekeeper, I removed three frames from my hive and set the entire box into the open space, where it fit snugly. Then I simply removed the tin-can feeder and began waiting for the bees—all nine thousand of them—to slowly walk out of the box. Ideally within three days they would be busy gathering nectar and making honey. I was hoping I could then open the hive, remove the box, replace the three frames, close the hive back up, and leave the bees alone.

Four days later I went back to the hive. I took off my shirt and wore my thinnest-soled shoes, so as to be both as close to the earth as I could and as vulnerable to the bees as they were to me. I was trying to convey to them my good intentions. I know it sounds crazy—my neighbor, a college kid, seemed to think it was, looking on from the farthest corner of her yard—but I knew it was right somehow. And though I'd assisted with a few beehives and had experienced thousands of bees flying in a constellation near my head and making their beautiful moan, I'd not done the handling of the frames myself, the real negotiating with the bees. On this day I would.

As I opened the hive, I saw that the bees had made substantial honeycomb on the hive lid, in addition to some on the box itself. I hadn't been told this might happen. Some people (my sweetheart is one of them) handle bees with ease and grace, singing lightly or talking to them: "Hey, girls, I'm gonna have to move you around a little bit. Excuse me." Some keepers almost dance with the bees while they do their work.

And some people, it is said, come to the hive angry or anxious or afraid, and the bees know this from far away. They can sense your fear, and they just might sting you for it—which was not reassuring to me as I lifted the box from the hive with what looked like a thousand bees clinging to it, still working on the comb they had been making. Nor was it reassuring when I needed to cut loose the comb they had built on

*(Continued)*

the hive lid, comb that I'd accidentally ripped apart when opening the hive, and that now prevented me from closing the hive back up.

Using a small kitchen knife to free the comb while asking the hundreds of bees as gently as possible to mosey out of the way, I became, despite my best intentions, as terrified as I've ever been in my life. The memory of every previous peaceful interaction with bees flew from my head, and rushing in came the image of the entire hive, all nine thousand, wrathful and swarming me. My hands were shaking, and the feeling of a bee landing on me, which had previously been pleasant, made my skin twitch like a horse's. And the song of the bees changed ever so slightly, climbing half an octave, as it does when they become anxious. And it took every shred of concentration just to hold steady and cut free the comb. And it took every shred of concentration as well not to weep.

What I wouldn't understand until after the frames were snugged back into the hive, the lid was on, and the comb was placed on a chair nearby (so the bees could haul its honey back inside) is just how afraid I'd been. I was on my knees, still on the verge of sobbing, helping the handful of bees who had gotten caught in the thick grass while I was working and were now struggling to find their way out. I gave my forefinger to each one, letting it crawl aboard, gather itself, and fly up to the hive while I whispered, "Climb up. You can do it, sweetie," the tiny needle of each stinger just kissing my flesh. And it was then I became fully aware of a vision I'd had while handling the bees.

I'd had it while the thousands of bees flew around me and the knife started shaking in my hand, and the possibility of the hive turning on me was all I could feel. I saw myself pouring gasoline on this hive that I loved and torching it. And I saw a billowing, and I felt such relief at their being no more. I saw cinders of the box and the sooty concrete blocks it sat on and the charred patch of grass beneath smoldering and the few bees not inside lost and circling in wider and wider loops. I saw myself standing with the pack of matches in my hand and the red fuel canister at my feet.

It is said, and I believe it, that bees can see inside you. And yet, and yet, the bees didn't attack. Not one sting. They didn't even warn me by coming toward my face. They didn't believe what I thought—what I imagined—was real. They knew inside me was a truth other than murder. They had mercy. And once the hive was all closed up, they went back to their business.

Source: Gay, Ross. "Some Thoughts on Mercy." *The Sun*, no. 451, July 2013, thesunmagazine.org/issues/451/some_thoughts_on_mercy.

---

**EXERCISE 16D**    **EXPLORING RACE**

1. What do you think is Gay's main point in telling the story of his experience with the police? To what extent do you think Gay's narrative makes an argument? How would you summarize that argument? How effectively does his story support that argument?

2. What do you think is the significance of Gay's anecdote about the bees? What does he mean when we writes that the bees "had mercy"? What does that have to do with his encounter with the police?

3. This is a lengthy essay. What storytelling strategies does Gay use to keep his readers engaged in his story? To what extent do you think these strategies make his narrative effective? Explain, citing specific passages from his essay to support your answer.

# Red Boat, Blue Sky
## by Edmund Jones

*At first glance, this essay tells a typical tale of youthful bravado in which a teenage boy takes an unnecessary risk and has a rather exciting, if brief, adventure. Edmund Jones looks back on a frightening but thrilling moment from his earliest days as a sailor—a foolish act on a small sailboat that could have had disastrous consequences. Although the story seems to be one that would appeal only to a specialized audience (sailors—or perhaps readers interested in sailing), it is also a coming-of-age story about an important moment in a boy's transition to adulthood. Jones' essay was published in* Sail *magazine in 2009, which means that he originally wrote it for an audience of other sailors who would understand the technical details of Jones' brief but potentially dangerous sail. (His intended readers would know, for example, that "sheets" refers to the ropes used to control the sails.) As you read, consider what makes his story interesting—and relevant—to a broader audience, including readers who have no interest in or experience with sailing.*

......................................................

## Talking About This Reading

**Blake Martin (student):** I wasn't sure about the moral of this story.

**Bob Yagelski:** Often, readers have a tendency to reduce a story to a single moral or thesis, but writers often tell stories about complicated aspects of life that resist being summed up in a single moral or thesis. Sometimes, a story can leave us wondering, as this one seems to have done for you, Blake. And that might be an indication that the writer has effectively explored the complexity of the subject. In this case, it might be that the experience Jones is describing has various "morals," and the best way to honor the complexity of the experience is to leave it open to the reader's interpretation.

......................................................

16

Summers in South Carolina could be unbearable before air conditioning became commonplace. That's why my family spent most of each summer at our lake cottage, and why I spent hours on, or in, the water.

One August morning the heat struck the cottage the instant the sun rose above the trees across our cove. A cool breeze ruffled off the lake, and I wanted to sail before it got too hot. My parents were asleep, so I slipped into the kitchen and had a quick bowl of cornflakes—a state-of-the-art breakfast in 1948. I carried the cotton sail for my boat, an 8-foot pram named *Red Boat*, to the dock.

Modern parents would be aghast. Where's the sunscreen? And the life jacket? And wasn't I going to tell anyone where I would be? At age 13 I was innocent of any such concerns. Wooden boats don't sink, I thought, so why worry?

Daily thunderstorms were routine on Lake Murray. While rigging the boat, I looked at the sky. A few popcorn-like cumulus clouds were forming already. As I pushed the boat across the sand, a water moccasin emerged from under the dinghy and wriggled toward the shallows.

Lake Murray is a large lake, shaped like a maple leaf, some 30 miles long. The lake itself had been created in the middle of the Depression to provide hydroelectric power, and there were few houses on its shores. The lake was empty as I glided through a light chop. I cleared the point and entered open water. The far shore was only 4 miles distant and my plan was to reach across the lake and back before the weather turned bad.

*(Continued)*

The light breeze was steady as *Red Boat's* bow wave made a happy chuckling sound. I sat crosswise on the floorboards, my back against the starboard side, feet propped up on the port gunwale. The sail was blinding white against the deep blue sky, and my only worry was those clouds.

On the far shore a meadow was a favorite camping spot for my family. I hoped to take a peek at it and then skeedadle. As I neared the shore, though, I could see the clouds growing like genies out of bottles. The closest one, just upwind, was the biggest, and it boiled rapidly upward. It looked like it was going to be a monster storm, and I hastily tacked and headed for home. But I'd gone too far—there was no way I could outrun it.

The cloud covered the sun and the warm breeze suddenly turned chilly. I looked back upwind and saw, beneath the jet-black underside of the cloud, a line of whitecaps heading toward me. Uh oh, here It comes. I had about three miles to go, but it looked like forever. Then a bolt of lightning lit the dark water followed immediately by a sharp crack. I shivered, knowing how close it had struck. And my mast was sticking up like a lightning rod.

As the whitecaps approached, I uncleated the mainsheet, getting ready to ease it quickly. Then, with a roar, the first gust was on me as I let it run all the way out, the manila line scorching my bare hand. The mainsail flogged as the boat heeled, the lee side dipping a few gallons before I got my weight onto the windward gunwale. A hard rain came with the wind, stinging my bare back like needles. I wished I'd worn a jacket.

I tried sheeting in just a touch and was thrilled as my ungainly little tub suddenly accelerated, almost hydroplaning on a broad reach. With a mixture of terror and excitement, I pumped the sheet as the gusts blasted through, luffing in the puffs and then trimming just enough to keep us racing toward home. It was a wild ride. My arm ached and my bare hand blistered as I worked the sheet. Despite my best efforts, I continually shipped water over the leeside. As I neared our cove, the boat was wallowing in the waves, but still moving fast. Curtains of rain made it hard to see the entrance.

Another lightning strike, even closer, made me instinctively sheet in more, trying to eke out as much speed as possible. At last I blew past the point and was in our cove, riding the half-submerged boat like a cowboy. I felt triumphant as the beach neared, yanking up the centerboard and pulling off the rudder as *Red Boat* ground onto the sand. I lowered the sail, turned the boat on its side to dump the water, and dragged it to safety.

Wearily, and still shivering, I stumbled up the walk and onto our screen porch. I wondered if I would be in trouble with my parents for doing something so foolhardy. My father sat there, drinking coffee. He tossed me a beach towel and said, "Dry off before you go in. Don't drip in the house."

I wrapped the towel around me and asked, "Did you see me sail in?"

"Yep. Looked like a real fun ride."

He didn't act like he'd been worried.

Then I noticed the binoculars. They usually sat on the mantle, but today they were on the table beside him.

"Want some coffee?" he asked.

I was surprised, but pleased. I'd never drunk it before—it's not for kids, my mother would tell me.

"Sure, I'll take a cup."

"Cream and sugar?"

I stood tall, like a young Masai warrior after killing his first lion. "Nope, just black."

Source: Jones, Edmund. "Red Boat, Blue Sky." *Sail*, vol. 40, no. 7, July 2009, p. 37.

1. How would you describe the lesson Jones learned from his experience? How does he convey that lesson through his story? What other lessons might he have taken from that experience? How might he have told his story differently to convey those other lessons?

2. How would you describe Jones' voice in this narrative? Do you think his voice helps make his story more or less effective? Explain, citing specific passages from the essay to support your answer.

3. Jones originally wrote this essay for an audience of other sailors. Evaluate his essay's effectiveness for a wider audience that would include readers who are not sailors. Do you think his essay is relevant to readers who do not share his interest in sailing? Why or why not?

# Writing Personal Narratives

We tell stories to find meaning in our experience. Sometimes, we can find meaning in everyday experiences, as Haley Lee does in her essay, "The Balancing Act" (see page 511). Sometimes, we write about unusually challenging experiences to try to understand them—for example, the loss of a loved one or a serious illness. This section will help you tell your story effectively in a personal narrative as you make sense of it and share it with your readers. Read this section together with Chapter 3. Each step described here corresponds with a step in Chapter 3. In addition, your project should be guided by the four main features of effective narrative, as described in Chapter 15:

1. **A clear, narrow focus.** Keep your narrative focused so that it describes your experience clearly and conveys a sense of its significance:
   - What is the main story you are telling in this narrative?
   - What is the purpose of telling this story?

2. **Brevity.** Make your story only as long as necessary to convey your experience clearly and effectively:
   - Does your narrative convey your experience fully?
   - Which parts of your experience are essential? What can you leave out without weakening your narrative?

3. **A basic structure.** Organize your narrative so that it tells the story of your experience clearly and in a way that engages your readers:
   - How effectively do you convey the chronology of your experience?
   - What narrative techniques do you employ to tell your story in a way that engages readers?

4. **Succinct, purposeful description.** Describe important moments, scenes, or components of your experience in a way that helps convey its significance:
   - Which moments, scenes, or components of your experience should be described to your readers?
   - What should your descriptions convey to your readers about these moments, scenes, or components of your experience?

16

## Step 1  Identify a topic for your personal narrative.

Any experience that matters to you can be the basis for a personal narrative, but there are **two basic sources for topics for a personal narrative:**

- an **experience** that was significant to you in some way and
- an **issue** of interest to you that somehow connects to your own experience

Explore each source for a possible topic for your essay.

## Make a List of Experiences That Were Important in Your Life

| A milestone | • Graduating from high school<br>• Earning a black belt in karate<br>• Becoming old enough to vote |
| --- | --- |
| An accomplishment | • Winning a championship in soccer or debate<br>• Earning academic honors<br>• Learning to swim |
| A challenge | • Dealing with a serious illness<br>• Moving away from home<br>• Surviving basic training in the military |
| A mistake | • Violating a rule or law<br>• Cheating<br>• Misjudging someone |
| An activity | • Gaming<br>• Hunting<br>• Running |
| A transition | • Going to college<br>• Moving abroad<br>• Joining the military |
| A decision | • Whether to take or quit a job<br>• Getting engaged<br>• Sharing a difficult secret |

## Make a List of Issues That Interest You and Connect with Your Own Experience

| A controversy | • **Gun control:** You might be involved in an effort to oppose arming your campus police force; a relative might have law enforcement experience; you might be a hunter. |
| An activity | • **Gaming:** You might be an avid gamer who is concerned about efforts to restrict the distribution of violent video games; you might have won a gaming competition. |
| Advocacy | • **Privacy:** You might have concerns about how your private data is being used online without your knowledge or permission; you might have been the victim of identity theft. |
| A trend | • **Social media:** You might be involved in an interesting project with social media; you might have had an unusual experience with social media. |

List three or four such issues. For each item on the list, identify a relevant experience and describe it in a few sentences. For example, you might be interested in the national debate about health care insurance because you have a relative whose illness placed your family at great financial risk. So on your list you would briefly describe that experience:

Issue: health care reform

Experience: My brother was diagnosed with a serious illness; his medical care nearly resulted in my parents declaring bankruptcy. The illness created great difficulties for the family.

## Identify the Experience That You Would Most Like to Write About

Review your two lists and select an experience that most interests you and that you would most like to explore in a personal narrative. Keep in mind that the experience you choose has to matter to you. If it doesn't matter to you, it is unlikely to matter to your readers.

Step #1 in Chapter 3 will help you further develop your topic.

## Step 2 | Place your topic in rhetorical context.

One of the key features of effective personal narrative is that the writer's story has to be relevant to readers in some way, even though the experience is the writer's alone. So at this point your task is twofold:

- Identify an audience for your narrative.
- Determine why that audience would be interested in your experience.

Let's say you have a younger brother who became seriously ill with a rare disorder, and you have decided to write about that experience. It was an extremely challenging time for you and your family that deeply affected your views about yourself, your family, and issues such as medical care. Consider the following:

| Who might be interested in my experience? | • People who have experienced serious illness<br>• People with concerns about health care<br>• Young people who have experienced serious illness in their families<br>• Parents who have had a child with a serious illness<br>• Medical caregivers |
| --- | --- |
| Why would they be interested in my experience? | • Anyone can experience serious illness in his or her family.<br>• Your experience might speak to readers' concerns about caring for family members and dealing with health care issues.<br>• Your story might illuminate how to confront these challenges. |

In this example, your potential audience would be quite broad, since everyone has to deal with illness at some point and everyone has family or friends they might have to care for. More specifically, your experience might interest people who have followed the debates about health care and medical insurance. Your story would potentially connect to all these readers in a variety of ways.

Explore your topic using these two questions to identify a potential audience and the relevance of your experience to that audience. Then complete Step #2 in Chapter 3 to explore your rhetorical context more fully.

## Step 3 Select a medium.

Today writers have a variety of options for choosing a medium for their stories:

- conventional print essays
- online media, including blogs and social media sites
- multimedia programs such as PowerPoint, Photo Story, and iMovie
- multimedia sites such as Flickr, Prezi, and Animoto
- video sites such as YouTube and GoAnimate

To decide on a medium for your personal narrative, consider these questions:

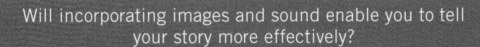

**Will a conventional print essay enable you to tell your story effectively?**

| **Yes:** Write a conventional print essay | **Maybe not:** Consider a different format |

↓

**Will incorporating images and sound enable you to tell your story more effectively?**

| **Not necessarily:** Write a conventional print essay | **Yes:** Consider a multimedia format |

↓

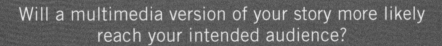

**Will a multimedia version of your story more likely reach your intended audience?**

| **Not necessarily:** Write a conventional print essay | **Possibly:** Consider a multimedia format |

16

Keep in mind that a conventional print essay can easily be shared via social media (posted on a blog or Facebook page). If you decide to tell your story in a multimedia or video version, Chapter 18 ("Telling Digital Stories") offers advice to guide you through the process. But you should still complete the remaining steps in this chapter to construct an effective personal narrative, no matter the medium.

Step #3 in Chapter 3 provides additional guidance to help you decide on the most appropriate medium for your argument.

## Step 4  Identify the main point of your narrative.

Your narrative tells the story of an experience, but what is the point of that story? You are telling your story for a reason, and you should be clear about your purpose. Otherwise, you run the risk of telling a story that might be engaging but does not say anything of substance to your readers. Your task now is to develop a clear idea of the main point you want to make by telling the story of your experience.

**Begin by stating as clearly as you can the idea, insight, or point you want your readers to take away from your story.** Try to capture this main point in a sentence or two. For example, let's return to the hypothetical story about your younger brother's illness. That trying experience helped you gain insight into yourself, your family, and the challenges of caring for someone you love who is seriously ill. It also taught you some hard lessons about the health care system. You would like to share these insights with readers. So you might state the **main point** of your essay as follows:

> *Caring for a very sick family member can bring out the best in us, even as it forces us to face some of our worst fears about ourselves and our own mortality.*

This statement can serve as your Guiding Thesis Statement, which can help you keep your story focused.

However, trying to boil down an experience as complex as caring for a seriously ill family member into a sentence or two can be tricky. You don't want to oversimplify the experience; rather, you want your story to capture the richness of your experience while remaining focused. So be open to possibilities. A key reason for writing about your experience is to understand it better. You might not be sure at this point what your experience means or what central ideas you will convey to your readers. That's OK. The process of writing about your experience will help you make sense of it.

In writing about a family member's illness, for example, you might find that you begin to remember your embarrassment about your own fears during that period of your life. Maybe you feel that you didn't quite live up to expectations as your family struggled with the challenge of such an illness. So it's possible that your story is not so much about the difficulties of caring for a sick family member as about the lessons you learned about yourself by facing hardship. If so, explore that possibility. As you develop your draft, be alert to such possibilities, even if they seem to deviate from your Guiding Thesis Statement. The more you explore your experience, the more you will learn about it. That learning might lead you to change the main point of your story.

As you clarify your main point and develop a Guiding Thesis Statement, you will gain a better understanding of your experience and a clearer idea of how you want to tell your story. Complete Step #4 in Chapter 3 to develop your Guiding Thesis Statement further.

## Step 5 | Support your main point.

We don't usually think about "supporting" the main point of a personal narrative in the same way that we support claims in an argument or assertions in an analysis; however, effective narratives include descriptions of events, background information, and explanations of important ideas or occurrences that help the reader understand the writer's experience and its significance. In other words, everything you include in your personal narrative should somehow contribute to telling your story effectively and conveying your main point to your audience.

If you have followed the first four steps here and the corresponding steps in Chapter 3, you should have either a Discovery Draft (see page 64) or notes and other material for your draft. The task now is to make sure you have the necessary material to tell your story effectively.

**Begin by considering what should be included in your narrative.** Review your Discovery Draft, notes, and other materials to determine whether you have included the essential information, scenes, events, and moments to convey your experience sufficiently to your readers. Address these questions:

- **What specific events or moments must be included for a reader to understand what happened?** For example, in your hypothetical essay about your brother's illness, you will probably need to include the moment when you learned of the diagnosis. Maybe there was also a time when a parent or other family member felt despair about the situation. You would likely include key scenes in the hospital or with specific doctors or other health care workers. Maybe you had an important conversation with your brother about what was happening. With your Guiding Thesis Statement in mind, make note of important and relevant scenes, events, and related material in this way. The goal is to identify anything about your experience that is essential for readers to know.

- **What background information will readers need to understand the experience described in the story?** For example, you will probably include information about your brother and your relationship with him. You might also need to provide information about where you live, your parents' financial circumstances, and so on. Consider anything that isn't part of the main story but is essential for readers to know in order to understand your experience.

At this stage, more is better, so if you're not sure about something, include it. You can eliminate it when you revise if you determine it isn't necessary.

You should be now ready to write a complete draft of your personal narrative. If not, move to the next step. But first complete Step #5 in Chapter 3, which provides additional advice to help you develop your narrative.

16

## Step 6  Organize your narrative.

How you structure your narrative will help determine not only how engaging readers will find your story but also how effectively you convey your main point.

In most personal narratives, the writer tells the story more or less chronologically. But as the examples in this chapter indicate, you have several options for structuring your narrative. Review the techniques for structuring a narrative that are described in Chapter 15 (pages 486–487). Your decision about how to structure your narrative should be based on the following:

- how to convey your experience vividly and completely to your readers
- how to incorporate background and related information

To develop a structure for your narrative, **follow this procedure:**

1. **Begin with a basic chronological structure.** Tell your story more or less in order from beginning to end. Tell it as completely as you can. Remember that this is a draft. You can eliminate unnecessary material and re-organize the story during revision.

2. **Start your narrative as close to the end of the story as feasible.** For example, in your hypothetical essay about your brother's illness, you could begin the story years before his diagnosis—when he was previously injured in a fall, for instance—but doing so might make your story too long. Alternatively, you might begin with the diagnosis and tell the story from that point, filling in necessary background where appropriate.

3. **Incorporate essential background information.** Even in a basic chronological story, you must find a way to incorporate background information. That usually means interrupting the story to explain something, fill in important facts, or include an important anecdote that occurred before the "present" story. There are several techniques for doing so: flashbacks, *in medias res,* and fractured narratives (see pages 486–487 in Chapter 15). Decide at which point in your narrative your readers will need specific background information or other material related to your main story, then use one of these techniques to work that information into the narrative. For example, in your essay about your brother's illness, you might include a scene in which you received the doctor's evaluation that your brother's condition could worsen. At that point, you might interrupt the narrative to explain relevant medical facts so that your readers understand the gravity of the situation. Alternatively, you might want to convey how difficult you found it to face your own fears at that point in the story, so you might include a flashback to an earlier time when your brother was healthy, using that scene to show how close you and your brother were and what might be lost as a result of his illness.

4. **Emphasize important scenes and passages.** Your narrative should focus on the most important moments or events in the experience you are writing about. Develop the passages about those events or moments so that they come through clearly and vividly. Devote less time to less important events or information. For example, you probably wouldn't need two or three paragraphs to describe the boredom of waiting in the hospital while your brother was undergoing tests. However, you might devote several paragraphs to the few moments when your family learned about the seriousness of your brother's condition.

5. **Make sure your introduction and conclusion establish and reinforce the focus of your narrative.** Your introduction not only draws your reader into your story but also establishes its focus as well as your tone and voice (see Focus: "Introducing Your Story" on page 331). Similarly, your conclusion should reinforce your main point and highlight an idea, image, or feeling that you want your readers to take away from your narrative.

---

**FOCUS** | **INTRODUCING YOUR STORY**

One of the most common mistakes student writers make in personal narratives is using what I call "life, the universe, and everything" beginnings. In other words, students start their narratives not with the story but with a kind of introductory statement that explains the significance of the subject of story. For example, here are the opening two paragraphs of a student literacy narrative (see Focus: "Literacy Narratives" on page 509):

> Today, literacy is essential for success. It is an ability that opens doors beyond school. We all have to create resumes and cover letters, no matter our future occupation. I did not always believe in the importance of reading and writing, but that changed drastically during my high school career.
>
> Before sophomore year of high school, I had never considered how beneficial reading and writing could be, not only for school, but for my development as a person. Going into 10th grade, I had never read an entire book. Up until that point, I had been able to get by on my ability to "do school." To "do school" is being able to follow directions and work within the teacher's instructions. It requires little creative thinking and even less actual ability because it is like following a recipe. I had been considered a good writer by my teachers. They also labeled me a determined student, which was false. In truth, I was lazy, and laziness became second nature because "doing school" was much easier than actually doing the work. Instead of truly reading, I was taking shortcuts just to complete the assignments. That all was about to change however.

Notice that this student delays the start of the story with an explanation of the importance of literacy. The opening paragraph sums up a main theme of the story and perhaps helps establish its focus, but it doesn't do much to draw readers into the narrative. This introduction would be more effective if the first paragraph was eliminated and the essay began with the second paragraph.

Remember that your introduction is your opportunity to bring your readers into your narrative and encourage them to keep reading. Often, the best way to accomplish these goals is simply to begin your story rather than introduce it with an explanation.

---

**16**

You can use these five steps to develop an outline. If you have already completed a draft, use these steps to determine whether you should adjust the structure so that your story is told more effectively.

Step #6 in Chapter 3 provides additional guidance for structuring your essay.

## Step 7 | Get feedback.

The most useful feedback on your draft is likely to come from readers who attend to **the key features of effective narrative:**

| A story that matters | • What is the significance of your experience?<br>• How does the narrative bring out the significance of the experience?<br>• What point does the story make? Is that point clear? |
|---|---|
| A relevant story | • What makes your experience important to others?<br>• How is the relevance of the story made evident to readers? |
| Interpretation | • What meaning do you find in your experience?<br>• How does the meaning of your experience come through in your narrative? |
| Engaging storytelling | • How is the story structured? Does the structure help convey the experience clearly?<br>• How do your descriptions help make your story vivid and contribute to your main point?<br>• What storytelling techniques have you used? Are they appropriate and effectively employed? |

Step #7 in Chapter 3 will help you analyze your feedback and decide which revisions to make.

## Step 8 | Revise.

There are three main issues to address in revising a personal narrative draft:

- telling an engaging story
- making sure the story conveys the main point or themes
- maintaining a clear focus

To address these issues, follow these four steps:

1. **Reread your draft.** Read from start to finish without stopping. Focus your attention on how effectively you tell your story. Address these questions:
   - Does the story keep your interest from start too finish? Are there sections that seem slow or tedious? Are there sections that seem too long or detailed?
   - Does the story make sense? Are the key events and essential background information included? Is anything missing?

2. **Review your draft using the questions from Step #7.** Focus on the first three sets of questions. Return to your Guiding Thesis Statement from Step #4:
   - Does your story convey the ideas in that statement?
   - Does each main section of your narrative contribute to those ideas?
   - Does your conclusion reinforce your main point?

3. **Evaluate how well your draft maintains its focus.** Determine whether your story conveys your main ideas and does not wander into irrelevant material. Follow the advice from Chapter 15 (see "Maintaining Focus" on pages 480–486):

State the main point or idea you want to convey in your story.

Review each section of your story (scenes, anecdotes, background information, etc.), and consider whether it is necessary to help convey your main point. If not, consider condensing or eliminating it.

For each main section you decide to include, consider *how* it contributes to the main point or idea of your story.

16

For example, let's imagine that in the draft of your hypothetical essay about your brother's illness, you have included several important moments from that your experience. Consider each one in terms of how it contributes to your main point:

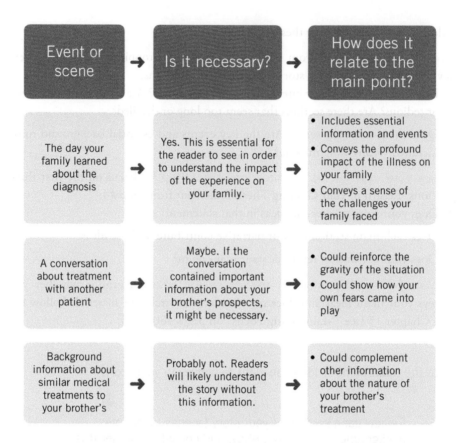

| Event or scene → | Is it necessary? → | How does it relate to the main point? |
|---|---|---|
| The day your family learned about the diagnosis | Yes. This is essential for the reader to see in order to understand the impact of the experience on your family. | • Includes essential information and events<br>• Conveys the profound impact of the illness on your family<br>• Conveys a sense of the challenges your family faced |
| A conversation about treatment with another patient | Maybe. If the conversation contained important information about your brother's prospects, it might be necessary. | • Could reinforce the gravity of the situation<br>• Could show how your own fears came into play |
| Background information about similar medical treatments to your brother's | Probably not. Readers will likely understand the story without this information. | • Could complement other information about the nature of your brother's treatment |

4. Review your introduction and conclusion. Make sure your introduction establishes the focus of the essay and draws readers into the story (see Focus: "Introducing Your Story" on page 531). Determine whether you conclude your story in a way that reinforces your main themes.

Follow Step #8 in Chapter 3 to make sure you have addressed all the main aspects of your essay in your revisions.

## Step 9 Refine your voice.

Although voice is important in any kind of writing, personal narrative often relies on the extent to which the writer's voice engages readers. The examples in this chapter reveal different ways a writer's voice can come through in a personal narrative. As you revise, listen carefully to your own voice to determine how well it contributes to the effectiveness of your narrative. Make sure your voice "sounds" right for the story you are telling and the point you want to make:

- Does your voice fit the story you are telling?
- Is it consistent? If not, in which passages does your voice get weak or change?

Step #9 in Chapter 3 provides additional advice for refining your voice.

## Step 10  Edit.

Complete Step #10 in Chapter 3.

---

**WRITING PROJECTS**  **PERSONAL NARRATIVE**

1. Identify an experience in your life that you believe has shaped you into the person you are today. In an essay, tell the story of that experience in a way that conveys the importance of your experience so that readers understand how it affected you.

2. Identify a general issue of interest to you that is also the subject of ongoing controversy—for example, gender roles, race relations, privacy, free speech, bullying. Write an essay about an experience you had that relates to that issue. For example, you might be concerned about bullying among adolescents. Your essay might tell the story of a time when you were confronted with bullying. Write your essay in a way that addresses a general audience who might share your concerns about the issue. Use your story to make a point about that issue.

3. Write an essay for an audience of your classmates about a time when you were faced with a difficult decision. Tell your story in a way that conveys what you learned from the experience.

4. Rewrite the essay you wrote for Question #3 for a different audience. Consider using a different medium to reach that audience. For example, if you wrote a conventional essay, consider using a blog or other social medium to reach a broader audience.

5. Adapt the story you wrote about for Question #1, #2, or #3 for a different medium. For example, if you wrote a conventional essay, consider a multimedia format, such as Prezi.

6. Using the experience you wrote about for Question #1, #2, or #3, tell the story of that experience in two or three Tweets. Now compare your "tweeted" story to the original. What are the main differences aside from length? What conclusions about effective storytelling can you draw from this exercise?

16

---

## MindTap®

Request help with these Writing Projects and get feedback from a tutor. If required, participate in peer review, submit your paper for a grade, and view instructor comments online.

---

www.youtube.com/

You Tube

Videos          Music          Shows

All Categories          Categor

Introducing: Teaching Channel
Teaching Channel showcases innovative and effective
teaching practices in America's sch...

Most Viewed Today

# Writing Informative Essays 17

**LOOK AROUND YOUR HOME** and you will probably find more informative writing than any other kind of writing:

- instruction manuals for your DVD player and smartphone
- cookbooks
- brochures from a local museum and government agency
- newspapers
- magazines

Go online and you'll find digital versions of all these kinds of texts—and more: instructional videos on YouTube, Prezi presentations, and other multimedia texts that convey information. Indeed, it is difficult to imagine going through a typical day without encountering a piece of informative writing or referring to some kind of informative writing in order to complete a task.

Some scholars believe that writing, as a technology for language, emerged from the need to convey information across space and time—for example, as a way to record the buying and selling of grain between two people so that information about the transaction is available to them or to others at a later date or in another location. Referring to writing systems that developed in Pre-Columbian America, Elizabeth Hill Boone has noted that writing "keeps and conveys knowledge, or to put it another way, . . . presents ideas" (Elizabeth Hill Boone and Walter D. Mignolo, eds., *Writing Without Words*, p. 3). In other words, informative writing is as old as writing itself.

Informative writing takes many different forms, but all informative writing has one essential characteristic: Its primary purpose is to convey information or ideas as clearly and effectively as possible. A DVD instructional manual should help the reader understand how the equipment should be operated and what to do if it doesn't work properly. A flyer from a health care agency provides information to help readers understand, identify, avoid, and perhaps treat a specific illness. In this sense, informative writing is often decidedly practical.

Although informative writing is usually distinguished from narrative, it can be understood as telling a story, albeit without the storytelling conventions of most narratives, such as plot or setting. A lab report, for example, is a way to tell the story of a lab experiment. A public service flyer might convey information in a way that tells a kind of story about a problem. As we will see in this chapter, though, informative writing often includes conventional narrative as a way to convey information or illustrate a point.

As a college student, you will be asked to compose various kinds of informative texts: research papers, lab reports, explanatory essays, flyers, multimedia presentations. To be able to create documents that convey information and ideas efficiently and effectively for various audiences is an essential skill for successful college writers. It is also a necessary skill in the workplace and other aspects of your life. This chapter will help you develop that skill.

# Occasions for Informative Writing

Not long ago, I took my car, which was more than seven years old, for inspection. The mechanic told me that the tires needed to be replaced. So I went online to gather information about tires: what to look for in a tire, what to avoid, how much I would have to spend, what safety issues to consider. Among the websites I visited were several that sold tires exclusively. In addition to a great deal of information about tires, these sites had forums where customers posted comments about tires they had bought. The comments often included detailed information about how the tires were used (e.g., mostly on highways or city streets, on sedans or sports cars, in snowy weather) and how they performed. Although these customers were writing in an informal context (an online discussion forum), many of their comments were actually sophisticated, if brief, informative essays that conveyed a lot of technical information. In addition, the test reports on these websites were carefully written informative essays describing how the tests were conducted and explaining the results for each tire that was tested. All this writing helped me make a decision about which tires would be best for my aging car.

My experience choosing tires underscores how often we turn to informative writing in our lives as consumers, citizens, and workers to share information, make decisions, and solve problems. You have probably had opportunities to write various kinds of informative texts, both formal and informal, that serve various purposes, from lab reports for a chemistry class to a how-to video about caring for a bicycle that you post on YouTube. Often, such informative texts are narrowly focused and serve very specific purposes. You might, for example, create a video about specific bicycle maintenance techniques for members of your campus bicycle club who ride on certain kinds of trails or roads. The purpose is to provide useful information for a specific audience who uses that information for a specific purpose.

At the same time, informative writing is about inquiry as much as it is about conveying information. When you write an informative text, you engage in a sophisticated process of discovery and learning, even if your rhetorical purpose is straightforward and practical. You have likely had this experience in your own informative writing:

- Writing a research paper about the uses of social media for political activism can help you understand social media and shape your views about activism.
- Writing a report about your volunteer activities for a scholarship application might reveal something about you as a community member that you had not previously realized about yourself.
- Developing a multimedia presentation about a campus organization you belong to can help you better appreciate the challenges facing that organization.

In each of these examples, the primary purpose of the informative text is to convey information to a specific audience, but the process of composing the text is more than just selecting, organizing, and presenting information for that audience. It is also a process of inquiry that can lead to sophisticated learning—about your subject, about your audience, about the world around you, and about yourself. In this sense, informative writing is as sophisticated as any other kind of writing you do. It is an important tool for living.

---

**EXERCISE 17A   EXPLORING OCCASIONS FOR INFORMATION WRITING**

1. Make a list of four or five activities or subjects about which you are knowledgeable or have experience. For example, you might play a musical instrument, compete in gaming competitions, work on a cattle ranch, or volunteer at a local retirement home. For each item on your list, imagine an informative document you might create for an audience who does not have your level of knowledge or experience with that topic. For example, if you volunteer at a retirement home, you might create a Prezi to explain what such volunteer work entails and the challenges and rewards of such work. If you work on a cattle ranch, you might write an essay for a general audience explaining the process of raising cattle.

2. Make a brief list of topics about which you are interested but have limited knowledge. Select one item from that list and find one or more informative texts about that topic. For example, you might be interested in learning about tea: where it grows, how it is cultivated, its different varieties, its history. Search online to find articles, websites, videos, or other documents that explain some aspect of that topic. Now evaluate those documents. Which were most helpful? Why? As a reader, what did you look for in the documents? On the basis of this exercise, what conclusions might you draw about informative writing? About how informative texts are used?

3. Think of a situation in which you had to explain a technical or specialized subject to someone who knew little about that subject. For example, maybe a friend asked you for help transferring a number from one phone to another. Or maybe you helped a teammate learn to do a proper header with a soccer ball. In a brief paragraph, describe how you explained the topic to the other person. How did you decide what information to share? What were the challenges of explaining the topic in that situation? Consider what conclusions you might draw from that experience about informative writing.

**17**

# Understanding Informative Writing

As the examples throughout this chapter suggest, informative writing is a broad category. Sometimes referred to as expository writing, it encompasses many different genres and forms. As noted earlier, informative writing is included in this section of this textbook devoted to narrative writing because it is a form of writing that tells a story about a topic, although not necessarily in the conventional sense of a story. Nevertheless, many kinds of informative writing include elements of conventional narratives, including the use of first person, description, and even action. **Effective informative writing has two distinctive features:**

- **Clear, engaging exposition.** In effective informative texts, technical information and complicated concepts are presented in ways that make them accessible to readers who might not be expert in the subject matter. The writer attempts to keep readers engaged, even when the subject matter is dense and challenging, and to explain complex material clearly and in ways that interest readers. (See Focus: "Presenting Information Visually" on page 544.)

- **A clear sense of purpose.** Informative writing is meant to inform, and the most effective informative texts convey information with a specific sense of purpose. Even when writers share their own experiences or present detailed technical explanations, their sense of their main purpose remains clear.

The following examples illustrate these features. In this excerpt from an article about his effort to restore his lost hearing, science writer Michael Chorost informs readers about the latest developments in hearing aid technology and cutting-edge medical procedures for people who have hearing impairments. Chorost uses the story of his own experience as a way to organize his article and present to his readers what he has learned about treatment for hearing problems. As a music lover, Chorost is especially fond of the classical composition *Bolero* by the composer Maurice Ravel. He begins his essay by telling the story of the moment when he lost his hearing altogether; this passage appears a few paragraphs into his article:

> And then, on July 7, 2001, at 10:30 am, I lost my ability to hear *Bolero*—and everything else. While I was waiting to pick up a rental car in Reno, I suddenly thought the battery in my hearing aid had died. I replaced it. No luck. I switched hearing aids. Nothing.
>
> I got into my rental car and drove to the nearest emergency room. For reasons that are still unknown, my only functioning ear had suffered "sudden-onset deafness." I was reeling, trying to navigate in a world where the volume had been turned down to zero.
>
> But there was a solution, a surgeon at Stanford Hospital told me a week later, speaking slowly so I could read his lips. I could have a computer surgically installed in my skull. A cochlear implant, as it is known, would trigger my auditory nerves with 16 electrodes that snaked inside my inner ear. It seemed drastic, and the $50,000 price tag was a dozen times more expensive than a high-end hearing aid. I went home and cried. Then I said yes.

Source: Chorost, Michael. " My Bionic Quest for Bolero." *Wired*, 1 Nov. 2005, www.wired.com/2005/11/bolero/.

Notice that Chorost provides information about the special medical procedure called cochlear implants by telling the story of his own experience. In other words, he is telling his own story primarily to inform readers about state-of-the-art medical treatments for hearing loss. As he continues with his story, he provides increasingly detailed information about hearing loss treatments and the challenges facing patients, like him, who have these treatments. In this passage, for example, he provides historical background to help explain the medical procedure he underwent:

For centuries, the best available hearing aid was a horn, or ear trumpet, which people held to their ears to funnel in sound. In 1952, the first electronic hearing aid was developed. It worked by blasting amplified sound into a damaged ear. However, it (and the more advanced models that followed) could help only if the user had some residual hearing ability, just as glasses can help only those who still have some vision. Cochlear implants, on the other hand, bypass most of the ear's natural hearing mechanisms. The device's electrodes directly stimulate nerve endings in the ear, which transmit sound information to the brain. Since the surgery can eliminate any remaining hearing, implants are approved for use only in people who can't be helped by hearing aids. The first modern cochlear implants went on the market in Australia in 1982, and by 2004 approximately 82,500 people worldwide had been fitted with one.

This passage looks more like what we might typically think of as expository writing, and it underscores Chorost's primary purpose of informing readers about hearing loss technologies. Notice that this information seems more important in the context of his own situation as someone who lost his hearing. In that sense, telling his own story helps readers better appreciate the information and "see" what it is like for a patient to have this treatment, as in this passage:

When technicians activated my cochlear implant in October 2001, they gave me a pager-sized processor that decoded sound and sent it to a headpiece that clung magnetically to the implant underneath my skin. The headpiece contained a radio transmitter, which sent the processor's data to the implant at roughly 1 megabit per second. Sixteen electrodes curled up inside my cochlea strobed on and off to stimulate my auditory nerves. The processor's software gave me eight channels of auditory resolution, each representing a frequency range. The more channels the software delivers, the better the user can distinguish between sounds of different pitches.

Chorost's use of the story of his own experience helps make his article more engaging and accessible to readers. Using his own experience to describe technical procedures helps make complex, abstract scientific concepts and medical treatments more concrete and therefore easier for readers to imagine and understand. Notice that although Chorost's article includes a great deal of information about his own experience, his focus remains squarely on the issue at hand: explaining hearing loss technology. No doubt Chorost's experience with his hearing loss treatments included many other moments or events that he might have included in this article, but he selected only the experiences and information that are directly relevant to his main focus on hearing-loss technology and treatment.

Here is an example of a more conventional kind of informative writing that exhibits these same features. In this excerpt from an article about the global water crisis, author Sandra Postel begins with an anecdote to introduce the scale and complexity of the problem and then provides background information before moving to her main discussion:

In June 1991, after a leisurely lunch in the fashionable Washington, D.C., neighborhood of Dupont Circle, Alexei Yablokov, then a Soviet parliamentarian, told me something shocking. Some years back he had had a map hanging on his office wall depicting Soviet central Asia without the vast Aral Sea. Cartographers had drawn it in the 1960s, when the Aral was still the world's fourth-largest inland body of water.

17

I felt for a moment like a cold war spy to whom a critical secret had just been revealed. The Aral Sea, as I knew well, was drying up. The existence of such a map implied that its ongoing destruction was no accident. Moscow's central planners had decided to sacrifice the sea, judging that the two rivers feeding it could be put to more valuable use irrigating cotton in the central Asian desert. Such a planned elimination of an ecosystem nearly the size of Ireland was surely one of humanity's more arrogant acts.

Four years later, when I traveled to the Aral Sea region, the Soviet Union was no more; the central Asian republics were now independent. But the legacy of Moscow's policies lived on: thirty-five years of siphoning the region's rivers had decreased the Aral's volume by nearly two-thirds and its surface area by half. I stood on what had once been a seaside bluff outside the former port town of Muynak, but I could see no water. The sea was twenty-five miles away. A graveyard of ships lay before me, rotting and rusting in the dried-up seabed. Sixty thousand fishing jobs had vanished, and thousands of people had left the area. . . .

The tragedy of the Aral Sea is by no means unique. Around the world countless rivers, lakes and wetlands are succumbing to dams, river diversions, rampant pollution and other pressures. Collectively they underscore what is rapidly emerging as one of the greatest challenges facing humanity in the decades to come: how to satisfy the thirst of a world population pushing nine billion by the year 2050, while protecting the health of the aquatic environment that sustains all terrestrial life. . . .

Observed from space, our planet seems wealthy in water beyond measure. Yet most of the earth's vast blueness is ocean, far too salty to drink or to irrigate most crops. Only about 2.5 percent of all the water on earth is freshwater, and two-thirds of that is locked away in glaciers and ice caps. A minuscule share of the world's water—less than one-hundredth of 1 percent—is both drinkable and renewed each year through rainfall and other precipitation. And though that freshwater supply is renewable, it is also finite. The quantity available today is the same that was available when civilizations first arose thousands of years ago, and so the amount of water that should be allotted to each person has declined steadily with time. It has dropped by 58 percent since 1950, as the population climbed from 2.5 billion to six billion.

Source: Postel, Sandra. " Troubled Waters." *The Sciences*, Mar.-Apr. 2000, pp. 16–24.

In this excerpt, Postel provides a great deal of information about the dire situation with the Aral Sea and about the global water crisis in general. Despite the complexity of her topic, all the information she presents, including the anecdote at the beginning, is directly relevant to her topic. In addition, note how carefully she organizes her discussion. After beginning with her anecdote about the Aral Sea, she includes relevant background information and then discusses several key points about the growing water crisis. In informative writing, a writer often works with a lot of material—as Postel does here—and must find a way to organize the text so that the material is presented logically to readers.

Postel's article also demonstrates the importance of clear explanations in informative writing. Often, writers must discuss unfamiliar or technical information or concepts in ways that readers can grasp. Here, for example, writer Rafe Sagarin explains a complex concept called "imaginative redundancy," which, he argues, can help us develop better security methods to protect against dangers such as terrorist attacks:

> What is more feasible is to look at "imaginative" redundancy built into nature. With this kind of redundancy, there are multiple problem solvers, but each employs different methods. This means that not only is there a backup if one system fails, but there is a different type of backup that won't fail in the same way against the next threat. And once again, this natural security system is found at every level of biological organization.
>
> For example, consider how the proteins that carry out the essential life functions are constructed. An RNA (a single-strand molecule that "complements" or matches the other strand of the double-stranded DNA molecule it was created from) provides the template for each type of protein based on thousands of combinations of four base molecules (the U, C, A, and Gs of the genetic code). The four base molecules are arranged in patterns of three molecules, known as codons, to make each of the thousands of amino acids that make up a protein. There are only twenty different types of amino acids but there are sixty-four possible codon combinations of the four letters that code for them (the 4 bases in 3 possible positions $= 4^3 = 64$). From a strict efficiency standpoint, this would appear wasteful. But from a natural security perspective it makes sense. The genome is under continual attack by "translational parasites" such as viruses, which essentially mimic the RNA template of their host in order to create proteins (or in the case of HIV, double-stranded DNA) to gain access to the cellular structure of their host. The virus version of RNA, and the codons that make up the RNA, must be a good match with the host in order to get the host to effectively produce viral molecules. By having many different ways to code for its own proteins, the host can avoid getting mimicked by the virus. It is a strategy essentially like regularly changing your computer password to avoid, among other problems, viruses.

Source: Sagarin, Rafe. *Learning From the Octopus: How Secrets of Nature Can Help Us Fight Terrorist Attacks, Natural Disasters, and Disease.* Basic Books, 2012, pp. 92–93.

As in Postel's article, Sagarin uses straightforward language to explain a technical scientific concept. Although the writer does use some jargon (such as "codon"), he explains it so that readers will be able to follow the discussion. To explain highly specialized subject matter to readers who are not specialists, writers rely on careful word choice, clear sentence structure, coherent paragraphs, and well-organized passages.

In addition to the two distinctive features described on page 540, the examples in this section demonstrate that most effective informative writing also exhibits three of the main characteristics of all narrative writing described in Chapter 15:

- **Clear focus.** Informative texts tend to be tightly focused, no matter how complex the subject matter. Even when they present a lot of information to readers, effective informative texts maintain a focus on the main point.

- **Careful structure.** Well-organized texts present information and ideas systematically and logically so that they are accessible and engaging to readers. In some ways, organizing an informative essay can be more challenging than organizing other kinds of essays because there is no conventional structure for writers to follow—as there is in conventional narratives (see "Structuring a Narrative" in Chapter 15) or arguments (see "Structuring an Argument" in Chapter 11).

- **Vivid, purposeful description.** Informative texts often include vivid description that helps convey important and complex information effectively to readers. Notice, for example, Chorost's careful description of his experience with his hearing-loss treatment or Postel's description of the Aral Sea. In each case, the descriptions help the writers accomplish their purpose in informing readers about their subjects.

| FOCUS | PRESENTING INFORMATION VISUALLY |
|---|---|

Often, the most effective way to present information, especially statistical information, is in visual form. Digital technologies make doing so easier than ever. Using graphs, charts, and similar visual elements not only enables a writer to include a lot of information efficiently in a text but also can make information easier for readers to understand. (See also Chapter 20, "Designing Documents.")

For example, here's a passage from the American Time Use Survey (ATUS), which is conducted by the U.S. Bureau of Labor Statistics. The ATUS provides information about how Americans spend their time. Consider whether this text would be more or less effective if the writer had not used graphics and had simply discussed the statistical data in textual form.

> The American Time Use Survey collects information about the activities people do during the day and how much time they spend doing them. For example, on an average day in 2014, Americans age 15 and over slept about 8.8 hours, spent 5.3 hours doing leisure and sports activities, worked for 3.6 hours, and spent 1.8 hours doing household activities. The remaining 4.5 hours were spent in a variety of other activities, including eating and drinking, attending school, and shopping.
>
> If this "average day" does not sound like a typical day in your household, it is because these numbers are for all persons in the U.S. age 15 and over, and for all days of the week combined. The information can be further analyzed by age, sex, employment status, day of the week, or presence and age of household children. Looking at information for certain groups in the population provides a more accurate picture of how each group spends its time. For example, the chart above shows how employed persons ages 25 to 54, who live in households with children under

18, spent their time on an average workday. These individuals spent an average of 8.9 hours working or in work-related activities, 7.7 hours sleeping, 2.5 hours doing leisure and sports activities, and 1.2 hours caring for others, including children.

**Time use on an average work day for employed persons ages 25 to 54 with children**

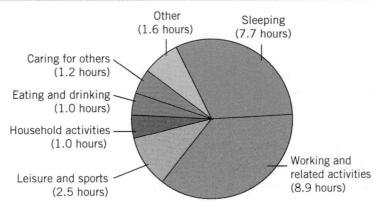

Other (1.6 hours)
Sleeping (7.7 hours)
Caring for others (1.2 hours)
Eating and drinking (1.0 hours)
Household activities (1.0 hours)
Leisure and sports (2.5 hours)
Working and related activities (8.9 hours)

Total = 24.0 hours

NOTE: Data include employed persons on days they worked, ages 25 to 54, who lived in households with children under 18. Data include non-holiday weekdays and are annual averages for 2014. Data include related travel for each activity.

SOURCE: Bureau of Labor Statistics, American Time Use Survey

Source: "Charts from the American Time Use Survey." *American Time Use Survey*, United States Bureau of Labor Statistics, 26 Oct. 2015, www.bls.gov/tus/charts/home.htm.

## EXERCISE 17B   UNDERSTANDING INFORMATIVE WRITING

1. Find an article, book, website, video, or other text that explains a topic of interest to you. For example, if you own a pet, find something about caring for that kind of pet. Evaluate how effectively that text explains the topic. What features of that text do you find helpful? What sections are confusing or unclear? On the basis of your evaluation, draw conclusions about what makes an informative text effective.

2. Search the Internet for two or three texts (articles, websites, etc.) that explain how to do something you have never done. For example, if you have never cooked an omelet, find texts that explain how to do so. Compare the texts you have found. Which one is most helpful in explaining the topic? What makes that text better than the others? What conclusions might you draw about informative writing on the basis of this comparison?

3. Using the texts you found for Question #2, compare how the writers organized the information. Why do you think each writer organized his or her text in that way? What do you find effective—or not—about the way each writer organized the text? What conclusions can you draw about structuring an informative text?

17

# Reading Informative Writing

Informative writing can vary tremendously in terms of format, style, and structure. The readings in this section reflect that variety. They also exhibit **the five main features of effective informative writing**, as discussed in this chapter and listed in this graphic. As you read these selections, compare the ways in which each author conveys information and helps his or her readers understand the subject matter. Be mindful of the audience each writer seems to be addressing and how the writer adjusts explanations to help make the material more accessible to that audience. Also consider these questions:

| Clear, engaging explanations | • What main information and ideas does the author present?<br>• How effectively does he or she explain technical or complex information? |
|---|---|
| Purpose | • What is the author's purpose in presenting this topic?<br>• Is that purpose clear?<br>• How does the author convey his or her sense of purpose? |
| Focus | • What is the main focus of the text?<br>• How does the author maintain that focus?<br>• How well does he or she incorporate relevant ideas and information without losing focus? |
| Organization | • How does the author organize the text?<br>• How well does the structure of the text help maintain the author's focus and keep readers engaged? |
| Description | • How effectively does the author describe important scenes, events, or processes?<br>• How do these descriptions help convey important ideas or information? |

## MindTap

Read these informative writing examples. Highlight and take notes online. Additional readings are also available online.

## Sculpting Identity: A History of the Nose Job
### by Tiffany Hearsay

*Plastic surgery, which is a sophisticated set of advanced surgical techniques for reconstructing specific parts of the human body, is now so commonplace in Western societies that we might rarely give it a second thought. In the following article, which appeared in* The Atlantic *magazine in 2015, writer Tiffany Hearsay asks us to look more closely at plastic surgery—in particular, the nose job—and what it might tell us about ourselves. Hearsay traces the history of modern plastic surgery from its beginnings during World War I to today, when, as she notes, millions of "cosmetic surgeries" are performed every year in the United States alone. More important, Hearsay invites us to consider what these now-common medical procedures reveal about our attitudes regarding important matters such as gender, body image, and beauty. In doing so, Hearsay demonstrates how informative writing can do more than convey information or explain a technical matter; it can also provoke us to examine important social developments and provide insight into who we are and how we live together in modern society. As you read, pay attention to how Hearsay uses narrative techniques to tell the story of the nose job and to invite her readers to consider challenging and perhaps uncomfortable questions about how they think about themselves as human beings.*

. . . . . . . . . . . . . . . . . . . . . . . . . . . . . . . . . . . . . . . .

### Talking About This Reading

**Sarah Eisenberg (student):** What I struggled with most in this reading was separating the author's opinion from historically factual narrative.

**Bob Yagelski:** Sarah, your comment reminds us that separating opinion from fact can be challenging. Often, when reading an article like this one, we expect an objective report about the subject. However, objectivity is a complicated ideal. Even if a writer avoids stating personal opinion, she will nevertheless make decisions about what information to include and exclude and how to present it. Those decisions can reflect the writer's opinion or bias about the subject. (See Focus: "The Ethics of Informative Writing" on page 558.) Even word choice can reflect opinion or bias—for example, "pro-choice" vs. "pro-abortion." Being sensitive to these nuances will help you become a more careful reader and better writer.

. . . . . . . . . . . . . . . . . . . . . . . . . . . . . . . . . . . . . . . .

All anxieties live in our bodies, but anxieties about our bodies feel particularly urgent. And since famous bodies are used to sell salve—cosmetics, waist-shapers, soft drinks—meant to soothe those anxieties, we're almost constantly embracing standards that even celebrities cannot maintain without intervention. Often, that comes in the form of cosmetic surgery.

Scores of Americans are remaking their bodies. According to the American Society of Plastic Surgeons, 15.6 million cosmetic procedures were performed in 2014 (ASPS). Plastic surgery sells norms of youth and beauty by offering consumers opportunities to recreate their appearance. It promises to fix socially undesirable physical features or delay the point at which we begin to show aging, a process framed by youth-centered culture as a slide into decrepitude, cultural irrelevancy, and death.

But these procedures entail an internal tension: Their results exist to be viewed, yet they are also meant to remain invisible, undetectable. The plastic surgeon is a sculptor who can remake the body in a way that looks natural while not betraying the

*(Continued)*

17

artifice of their work. However, they don't always succeed. It's when plastic surgery is invisible—think of Michael Jackson's infamous nose—that social fears of disfigurement manifest as revulsion.

***

The shape of the nose, in particular, is imbued with assumptions about one's character and place in society. Various efforts to fix undesirably shaped noses by way of plastic surgery have been employed over two millennia. In *Venus Envy: A History of Plastic Surgery*, Elizabeth Harken details one of the first recorded rhinoplasty procedures, performed in ancient India in the sixth century B.C. A flap of skin from the patient's cheek was repurposed to mold a new nose. However, it wasn't until a European syphilis epidemic in the late 16th century that cosmetic nasal surgery garnered much attention in the West. One of the unfortunate symptoms of advanced syphilis is soft-tissue decay, which affects the nose and leaves a gaping hole in the middle of one's face. Such a disfigurement carried the social stigma of disease and infection, even if the afflicted had lost their nose by another means. Different methods were employed to recreate noses. One of the most popular procedures involved taking skin from the patient's arm and grafting it to their face in an effort to make a new nose (or something resembling one, anyway).

Given its prominence on the face, even healthy noses can shame their bearers. The pseudoscience of physiognomy, which experienced a modern revival in the 19th century, claimed that the shape of the nose could tell you about a person's moral character. As Gabrielle Glaser explains in *The Nose: A Profile of Sex, Beauty, and Survival*, a straight nose signified refinement, while a "hawk" nose signified a cunning moral character. (This perpetration of this myth was not just pseudoscientific, but anti-Semitic as well.)

It was not until the late 19th century that plastic surgery began to gain popularity in North America. Americans wishing to cure themselves of socially undesirable features such as large noses, undistinguished jaw lines, or any features that did not conform to contemporary ideals of beauty could readily find a doctor who would cut and sculpt their face. These pioneers of cosmetic surgery included patients who went under the knife to remove racial signifiers. Procedures included making eyes, lips, and noses look less foreign, a dirty word in the early lexicon of American racism.

***

By the turn of the 20th century, advancements in war—poisonous gases, sniper rifles, and trench warfare—had made the jaws, lips, and noses of soldiers newly vulnerable. Facial injuries prompted surgeons to experiment with techniques to replace lost or damaged appendages. Soldiers such as John Bagot Glubb, who was also a scholar and renowned author, were offered surgery to fix facial disfigurements. Murray C. Meikle documents the mixed blessing of Glubb's fortune in *Reconstructing Faces: The Art and Wartime Surgery of Gillies, Pickerill, McIndoe and Mowlem*: "As most of my lower jaw had gone, I was shown albums of photographs of handsome young men and asked to choose the chin I would like to have."

Even with these medical advancements, plastic surgery could only do so much. During World War I, London General Hospital established the Masks for Facial Disfigurement Department. The Tin Noses Shop, as the soldiers called it, brought together American and European doctors and sculptors who worked to create individualized metallic masks, which then covered deformed or missing jaws, eyes, lips, and noses of wounded men. Though separated by a century, photographs of these men echo those of present-day celebrities with excessive or mask-like plastic surgery.

In his book *Making the Body Beautiful*, Sander L. Gilman argues that by the 1920s, the reconstructed faces of war veterans helped the public begin to accept cosmetic surgery. Although the benefits of medical advancements made in reconstructive surgery during the war were available internationally, plastic surgery began its boom in the United States during this time. The society that would later become the American Association of Plastic Surgeons was founded in 1921, right after the war and during the rise of a consumer culture that sanctions the exchange of money for beauty (and noses). The popularity of cosmetic surgery grew quickly, assisted by the normalizing presence of reconstructive procedures among veterans.

While modem war destroys noses by mishap, cultures have long employed nasal mutilation as a punishment. During the middles ages, a woman's hacked-off nose was a sign of disobedience or sexual promiscuity. In *A Social History of Disability in the Middle Ages*, the historian Irina Metzler explains that adultery was punishable by severing the nose in the Kingdom of Jerusalem of the 10th century. But even half a millennium earlier, the Vandal king Gaiseric "ordered his Gothic wife's nose and ears mutilated, having accused her of plotting against him" (23).

These atrocities are still committed. In 2010, Aesha Mohammadzai's nose-less face was featured on the cover of *Time* magazine under the warning, "What Happens If We Leave Afghanistan" (Baker). Mohammadzai's story is a harrowing account of life under Taliban rule. When she was 12, her father sold her to a Taliban fighter to pay off a debt. After she attempted to run away, her Taliban family cut off her nose and ears, leaving her for dead. She was rescued by aid workers, who then brought her to the United States.

Mohammadzai's post-Afghani life and the reconstruction of her nose have been widely covered in the press. CNN's Jessica Ravitz documented Mohammadzai's American integration, where she received a degree of public attention typically reserved for celebrities:

> In sunny Southern California, she bounced between lavish homes in gated communities. She was trotted out at a pricey gala dinner in Beverly Hills, where she debuted her prosthetic nose, a preview of what the surgery would do for her. She walked the proverbial red carpet, met Laura Bush and was honored by California's then-first lady, Maria Shriver. (par. 12)

When the time came for Mohammadzai to begin a marathon of surgeries, *The Daily Mail* updated its readers on reconstruction efforts, detailing the various procedures required to build her new nose. The techniques employed were similar to those used in ancient India: doctors used skin from her face to provide tissue for her new nose. Unlike celebrity body shaming or botched surgery rubbernecking, Mohammadzai's reconstructive process has garnered positive attention. Four years after the *Time* cover story, the media continues to document her progress. The tenor of this coverage harkens to Victorian freak shows, in which indigenous peoples from Britain's imperial conquests were displayed in Europe as primitive savages in need of saving. Media coverage of Mohammadzai similarly casts Western culture and technology as both civilizer and savior.

*(Continued)*

The aesthetic value assigned to a person's nose reflects historical and cultural beliefs on beauty, disease, race, war, and gender. The nose's prominence—projecting from the face for all to see in the flesh—turns out to make it a potent symbol, whether for the sake of consumer culture, ideals of beauty, the violence of war, or the power of the state.

## Works Cited

ASPS National Clearinghouse of Plastic Surgery Procedural Statistics. *2014 Plastic Surgery Statistics Report.* American Society of Plastic Surgeons, 2014, www.plastic-surgery.org/Documents/news-resources/statistics/2014-statistics/plastic-surgery-statsitics-full-report.pdf.

Baker, Aryn. "Afghan Women and the Return of the Taliban." *Time*, 9 Aug. 2010, con-tent.time.com/time/magazine/article/0,9171,2007407,00.html.

Gilman, Sander L. *Making the Body Beautiful.* Princeton UP, 1999.

Glaser, Gabrielle. *The Nose: A Profile of Sex, Beauty, and Survival.* Atria Books, 2002.

Harken, Elizabeth. *Venus Envy: A History of Plastic Surgery.* Johns Hopkins UP, 1997.

Meikle, Murray C. *Reconstructing Faces: The Art and Wartime Surgery of Gillies, Pick-erill, McIndoe and Mowlem.* Otago UP, 2013.

Metzler, Irina. *A Social History of Disability in the Middle Ages.* Routledge, 2013.

Ravitz, Jessica. "Saving Aesha." *CNN*, May 2012, www.cnn.com/interactive/2012/05/world/saving.aesha/.

Source: Hearsey, Tiffany. " Sculpting Identity: A History of the Nose Job." *The Atlantic*, 6 Sept. 2015, www.theatlantic.com/health/archive/2015/09/nose-job-history-plastic-surgery/403882/.

---

## EXERCISE 17C    TELLING THE STORY OF THE NOSE JOB

1. How would you describe the main purpose of this article? How effectively does the author accomplish that purpose? Explain.

2. In explaining the history of the nose job, Hearsay tells several stories, including that of an Afghan woman named Aesha Mohammadzai. What information about nose jobs and their role in contemporary Western culture is conveyed through the story of this one woman? How effectively do you think the story of that case informs readers about nose jobs and their significance in contemporary society?

3. Hearsay's essay includes a great deal of information about plastic surgery and about nose jobs in particular. How does Hearsay structure her essay so that this information is presented clearly to her readers? Did you find this information understandable? Why or why not? What might your answer to those questions suggest about you as a reader? About informative writing?

## Gamification: How Competition Is Reinventing Business, Marketing, and Everyday Life
### by Jennifer Van Grove

*In the following article from a popular online social media site, Jennifer Van Grove explains how gamification—the application of gaming design concepts to non-gaming activities or contexts—is being used by businesses, social scientists, and others to address problems or enhance certain processes. As Van Grove notes in her article, gamification is being used in a variety of ways to influence even the most routine everyday activities. She also notes that although the term gamification has only recently come into widespread use, the idea of applying gaming concepts to non-gaming contexts has been around for a while. Van Grove's article, which appeared on Mashable.com in 2011, was written for a general audience with an interest in technology, but in many ways her article is similar to the kinds of reports college students are often asked to write. In this kind of informative writing, the writer examines a trend, phenomenon, or development about which readers might be aware but have limited knowledge. The writer's goal is to inform the audience about the topic, going into sufficient depth to give readers a general understanding of it. As you'll see, Van Grove explains gamification in general and then looks more closely at specific ways in which the trend is affecting different aspects of contemporary life, including business and social relations. Pay attention to how she organizes her article to take readers on a kind of "tour" of the gamification trend.*

. . . . . . . . . . . . . . . . . . . . . . . . . . . . . . . . . . . . . . . . .

### Talking About This Reading

**Caleb Jablonicky (student):** The article mentions several companies and services that are unfamiliar to me, and it appears to assume some background knowledge—on the nature of "Foursquare," for example—while doing little to establish what a "gamification platform provider" might entail.

Bob Yagelski: Caleb, one challenge in writing about specialized subjects is determining how much background information or technical explanation to include. Those decisions are based on the writer's assessment of the rhetorical situation and intended audience. This article was published on Mashable.com, a website whose readers tend to be young and knowledgeable about media and digital technologies, so the author could reasonably assume they would be familiar with Foursquare and terms like "gamification platform provider." If you are not part of that audience, this article could be more challenging for you.

. . . . . . . . . . . . . . . . . . . . . . . . . . . . . . . . . . . . . . . . .

Can life, and all the menial or routine tasks that come with it, be transformed through game mechanics into an engaging, social and fun recreational activity? Such is the idea behind the emerging trend of "gamification."

Gamification is most often defined as the use of gameplay mechanics for non-game applications. The term also suggests the process of using game thinking to solve problems and engage audiences.

The word "gamification," much like the phrase "social media" a few years back, is being lobbed around in technology circles as the next frontier in web and mobile. Just as nearly every application, website, brand and marketer now employs social media in some capacity, so too will these entities gravitate toward game mechanics in the years ahead.

*(Continued)*

A recent Gartner report from April of this year suggests as much. Analysts predict that by 2015, more than 50% of organizations will gamify their innovation processes.

"By 2014, a gamified service for consumer goods marketing and customer retention will become as important as Facebook, eBay or Amazon, and more than 70% of Global 2000 organizations will have at least one gamified application," the Gartner report concludes.

Here we take a deeper look at the term, the trend, the mechanics and the real world implications.

## An Intro to the Gamification Trend

Gamification, as a concept, is far from a new idea.

"Companies have been using games in non-game context for a long time," says Gabe Zichermann, the author of *Game-Based Marketing* and the CEO of Gamification.co.

Zichermann cites the military, Hollywood and the hospitality sector—think airline frequent flier programs and hotel loyalty clubs—as three key industries utilizing game mechanics prior to the "coming out party" of gamification in 2010.

"What's changed over the past couple of years is the confluence of a few different factors," he says. Zichermann, like many others, specifically points to the success of startups such as Foursquare and Zynga as instrumental in embedding the idea into techie consciousness.

The second, and perhaps more significant factor, says Zichermann, is that once long-standing marketing techniques are now failing. "They're failing because people today are seeking more reward and more engagement from experiences than ever before," he explains. "The younger generation—the millennial generation and younger—is more game-attuned than previous generations."

Today's youth mandates a more engaging experience, he argues. "Gamification is required to bring those things into balance, and to make things engaging enough so people will pay attention to them and stay focused on them for a longer period of time."

The gamification trend is particularly hot in today's world because, should we follow this line of thinking, younger entrepreneurs are building applications and services for younger audiences who demand these features.

SCVNGR founder Seth Priebatsch agrees. "It feels like the next natural evolution of human-technological interaction to me," he says. "As we complete the social layer, we'll begin construction in earnest on the game layer."

## The Mechanics

The five most commonly used game mechanics, as identified by Zichermann, are as follows:

- **Points:** Points are everywhere, and they're often used in non-game apps as a way to denote achievement. Points also measure the user's achievements in relation to others and work to keep the user motivated for the next reward or level. They can even double as action-related currency. Health Month, for instance, uses points in an interesting fashion. The site asks users to set up weekly health-related goals and stick to them for an entire month. Each person starts with 10 "life points" and the goal is to end the month with at least 1 life point. The player loses a point every time he breaks a rule, but friends can help the player "heal" and earn back points.

- **Badges:** While badges have their origins in the physical world, Foursquare popularized the digital variety with its oh-so-clever set of real-life merit badges that range from easy (Newbie badges are awarded to users on their first checkin) to nearly-impossible to unlock (it takes 10 movie theater checkins to earn the Zoetrope badge).

- **Levels:** Zynga uses levels to make the seemingly mundane task of tending to crops all the more enticing, and LevelUp encourages mobile users to level up and get better discounts for becoming more loyal patrons.

- **Leaderboards:** Leaderboards rank users and work to motivate and encourage them to become players. Foursquare started with city-centric leaderboards, but now places the emphasis on ranking users against their friends. Earn a few points for a checkin, and Foursquare will show you which of your friends you've flown by on the leaderboard.

- **Challenges** These range from the simple to complex and often involve communal activity or group play. Priebatsch gamified his South by Southwest Interactive keynote with a group challenge that required all attendees to work together in rows. A proffered $10,000 donation to the National Wildlife Foundation was used to sweeten the deal.

### Game Design & Plug-and-Play Gamification Platforms

"At the start of any new market . . . you need to have these catalyzing technology platforms," Zichermann says.

He's speaking, of course, of gamification platform providers such as Bunchball, Badgeville and BigDoor. Businesses can use these platforms to add plug-and-play game mechanics to their websites and applications.

The platforms, in Zichermann's eyes, bring a scalable technology solution to market that makes it easier for companies to participate in the gamification trend, and it allows them build and deploy products faster.

Priebatsch, however, is a bit uncertain of these platform providers. "This sub-set of the trend has always confused me a little bit," he says. "I see a real difference between utilizing game mechanics to improve a core experience from the ground up, and what I call 'bolt-on gamification,' where you basically just tack a badge on to something and call it a day. That doesn't really work in my opinion."

The two do agree on the significance of game and product design. "[Platforms] don't obviate the need for good design," Zichermann says.

Game and product design, as Zichermann sees it, is an important science. Design, he argues, needs to be centered around the customer's needs and wants and should determine the mechanics that companies use.

Nike+, says Zichermann, is an example of a brand properly merging design with mechanics, mostly because Nike is always iterating on the product, he says. "Gamification isn't like doing an ad campaign—it requires ongoing maintenance."

Recycle rewards company RecycleBank is getting it right on the design front as well, he says. "They've had tremendous success by designing really compelling and interesting gamified systems that people can interact with to recycle more," he says. "They know their audience really well."

### Gamification & Real World Problems

Email overload, fitness phobia, diet and medication apathy. These are all real world problems and challenges that game mechanics can address.

(Continued)

17

Simple applications such as The Email Game and Health Month are meant to be stimulating and enjoyable tools to help people complete tasks they would otherwise dread.

"The game mechanics that I use are all about helping people feel less guilty about failure, since we've found that this is one of the primary obstacles to following through on a diet or fitness plan," explains Health Month creator Buster Benson.

"Games are one area of life where failure isn't taken personally. In games, failure is expected, and there's always a way to play again," he says. "Games help us appreciate the story of our failures and successes as an entertaining narrative rather than as a story about how you just aren't good enough for this or that."

Health Month users have been most responsive to the notion of being "healed" by friends when they lose their points. "By far, the most popular game mechanic is being able to 'heal' other players when they fall off the wagon," he says. "Social forgiveness and camaraderie are fairly untapped game mechanics, and yet really powerful."

One radical example of gamification in real life is changing the way people drive in Sweden. Kevin Richardson came up with a genius idea to get drivers to slow down: The Speed Camera Lottery.

"One troubling observation is the obscene amount of energy that goes to the one bad driver who speeds. Police, courts, fines, traffic school, points (the *bad* kind), increased insurance, and on and on," Richardson writes of the speed camera conundrum. "And where is the reward for people doing the *right* thing? What happened to that? Obeying the law is a pretty lonely endeavor."

Eventually, Richardson's thoughts materialized into an idea and he submitted the following to Volkswagen's Fun Theory contest. . . : "Can we get more people to obey the speed limit by making it fun to do? The idea here is capture on camera the people who keep to the speed limit. They would have their photos taken and registration numbers recorded and entered into a lottery. Winners would receive cash prizes and be notified by post. Better still, the winning pot would come from the people who were caught speeding."

Richardson's Speed Camera Lottery idea won the 2009/2010 challenge, and the idea has since been tested by the Swedish National Society for Road Safety in Stockholm. The result: A 22% reduction in driver speed in the first week after implementation.

"That's game thinking at its purist form," says Zichermann. "It gives people direction about what they should be doing in small, incremental positive ways."

One has to wonder, can anything be gamified? "Everything can be made more engaging and more fun by using game techniques," Zichermann argues.

Take cancer, a potentially awkward thing to gamify. "I don't presume to think that we can make having cancer into a purely fun experience," he says. "But, we have data to show that when we give cancer patients gamified experiences to help them manage their drug prescriptions and manage chemotherapy, they improve their emotional state and also their adherence to their protocol."

"You cannot gamify *anything*," Priebatsch says, taking a slightly different position. "Game mechanics can fix lots of problems and do lots of great things, but they are not a good fit for everything. Just like social is super powerful, but not a great fit for everything . . . everything has limitations and the beauty of both of these megatrends is that they're a great fit for more situations than not."

Source: Van Grove, Jennifer. " Gamification: How Competition Is Reinventing Business, Marketing, and Everyday Life." *Mashable*, 28 July 2011, mashable.com/2011/07/28/gamification/.

1. How effectively do you think Van Grove explains gamification and its applications? How well do her explanations convey the trend toward the uses of gamification in various walks of life? Explain, citing specific passages from the article to support your answer.

2. What makes this topic relevant to readers today? How does Van Grove establish the relevance of the topic? To what extent does her effort to establish the relevance of the topic also reveal her purpose in explaining gamification?

3. Van Grove does not rely on anecdotes or stories about her own experience to inform her readers about gamification. What storytelling techniques does she use? (See Chapters 15 and 16 for explanations of storytelling techniques.) Does her use of these techniques make her article more or less effective? Explain.

## What Honeybees Can Teach Us About Gang-Related Violence
### by Emily Badger

*One of the biggest challenges in informative writing is explaining a complicated idea or concept to readers who have little or no expertise in the subject. The following selection is an example of a writer meeting such a challenge. In this blog post from 2012 on* CityLab, *Emily Badger explains how a sophisticated mathematical model that anthropologists use to explain the behavior of social organisms such as bees can also be used to predict gang violence. As is often typical of blogs, Badger's writing is relatively informal, and her voice is almost personal, despite the sophisticated nature of her subject matter. But her post is an example of a very common form of informative writing in which a writer reports on a study or development from a technical field for an audience of readers who are not experts in that field. In that sense, her task is similar to one that college students often face: writing about a specialized subject in a field in which they themselves are newcomers. For example, if you have to write a report about a psychological personality test for an introductory psychology course, you are essentially doing what Badger has done: learning about a concept as a novice and writing about it in a way that will make sense to other novices.*

. . . . . . . . . . . . . . . . . . . . . . . . . . . . . . . . . . . . . . . . . . . . . . . .

### Talking About This Reading

**Luke Huddon (student):** The only difficult portion of this essay was in the beginning, where Badger states her thesis: "Those same spatial Lotka-Volterra competition equations that explain honeybee behavior appear to explain some territorial human behavior." Because this was the first mention of the mathematical elements, I was slightly confused.

**Bob Yagelski:** Luke, sometimes understanding a discussion of an unfamiliar subject requires patience and perhaps multiple readings. In this case, you encountered an unfamiliar but important term early in the article. One strategy for making sense of such a term is to read ahead to see whether the term is explained. Another strategy is to keep reading and then return to the section that confused you to see whether it make senses upon a second reading.

. . . . . . . . . . . . . . . . . . . . . . . . . . . . . . . . . . . . . . . . . . . . . . . .

*(Continued)*

17

Because she is not an expert in theoretical ecology or mathematical modeling, Badger relies on experts to explain the use of a specific kind of model to understand gang behavior. Notice that she quotes liberally from experts to explain the concepts and how they are used. She also includes graphics that help readers appreciate how mathematical modeling can enable researchers to "see" territorialism in animal species. Throughout her blog post, she keeps her language simple and her use of technical jargon minimal. She explains difficult concepts in relatively straightforward language. As you read, consider how effectively her explanations help you understand the concepts she is discussing.

There is a mathematical model in the field of theoretical ecology that describes how honeybees and chimpanzees and lions divide up space. In the grand competition for limited resources—i.e., dinner—bee colonies and prides of lions will generally create non-overlapping territories. Boundaries form between one group and the next, as the least bit of competition arises between them, and invariably that boundary sits smack in the middle between the beehives (or lion dens) on either side of it.

All of this sounds a little too simplistic to describe human behavior. As humans, we'd like to think that we rationalize our actions, that we fit them into more complex worldviews than a honeybee could ever contemplate (example: I believe in the importance of small businesses, therefore I shop at the local mom-and-pop corner store). But P. Jeffrey Brantingham, a professor of anthropology at UCLA, believes that human behavior is often far more predictable than we think. And as it turns out, those same spatial Lotka-Volterra competition equations that explain honeybee behavior appear to explain some territorial human behavior, too: specifically, that of rival urban gangs.

"Organisms all tend to have an anchor point for their activities, and gangs are no different."

Oftentimes, the way we use space is driven by the physical constraints of that space. When you need a gallon of milk, you don't drive to the grocery store five miles across town. You head for the nearest one, regardless of whether if it's a Food Lion or a Whole Foods. Social scientists, Brantingham says, tend to look at human behavior from the top-down, examining how people feel and think about such a situation. But in reaching instead for mathematical models, he and his colleagues look at human behavior (and particularly crime) from the bottom-up, examining the basic ways in which our behavior is constrained by physical space.

"If that's something that constrains humans, that's also something that constrains many other organisms," he says. "We're no different than hyenas or lions, or honeybees for that matter."

Honeybees and hyenas stake out territory over a pretty obvious scarce resource: food. But why might gangs do the same? Brantingham and colleagues Martin B. Short, George E. Tita and Shannon E. Reid suggest in a paper published online . . . in the journal *Criminology* that they're motivated by a similar limited resource: reputation.

"Ultimately, what's being competed for is your good name, or street credibility, your street rep," says Brantingham, who was the lead author of the paper. "If people recognize you as the toughest person around, then that has all sorts of benefits." (And, of course, more tangible benefits accrue from reputation, too.)

The authors used this mathematical model to identify the territories of 13 street gangs that operate in the Hollenbeck Policing Division of Los Angeles. (Random trivia: not all gangs are territorial by nature. Los Angeles and Chicago have predominantly territorial gangs; the gangs of Vancouver, British Columbia, on the other hand aren't

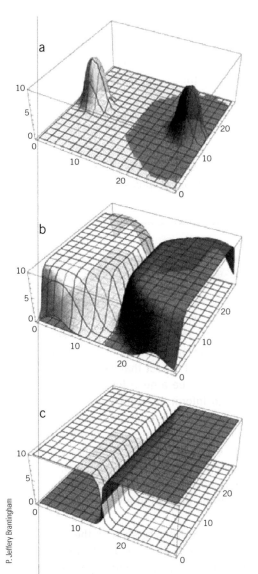

P. Jeffery Brantingham

particularly spatial.) The researchers identified anchor points of activity for each gang, relying on prior research: the home of a senior gang member, say, a street corner, or a neighborhood park.

"All people are like this," Brantingham says. "You have focal points around your house, or your community center. Honeybees have their hive. Hyenas have their den. And lion prides have their den. Organisms all tend to have an anchor point for their activities, and gangs are no different."

Using these anchor points, the mathematical model drew territorial boundaries between each gang. This is what the development of such territories looks like over time, starting from small densities of initial gang activity:

A mathematical equation obviously can't take into account the level of detail sociologists can collect on the ground, interviewing gang and community members, documenting graffiti and crime locations. But this theoretical model turned out to predict with pretty remarkable accuracy actual gang violence in Los Angeles. This model suggests most violence would occur not deep into gang territory, but on the contentious borders between gangs. The researchers overlaid actual crime data on top of their model—covering 563 violent crimes, between 1999 and 2002, involving these 13 gangs—and that's exactly what they saw.

Violent crime in this part of Los Angeles clustered along the theoretical boundaries between gangs produced by the same math equation that tells us how rival honeybees divvy up space. As a practical matter, this suggests police officers might want to focus their resources on these seams between gang territories.

This research also gives us a few other compelling clues about how gangs interact and what causes violence among them. The Lotka-Volterra equation suggests that, all things being equal, gangs will divide up space equally (and that may not mean along neat street boundaries). This process occurs when gangs experience more competitive animosity toward outsiders (other gangs) than among themselves. But, importantly, it takes very little competition to create these territories in the first place, or even to maintain them.

"Every time there's a gang-on-gang shooting, everybody talks about how there's an 'all-out gang war,'" Brantingham says. "But no, the numbers don't seem to suggest that."

Source: Badger, Emily. "What Honeybees Can Teach Us About Gang-Related Crime." *CityLab*, 26 June 2012, www.citylab.com/crime/2012/06/what-honeybees-can-teach-us-about-gang-related-crime/2377/.

17

1. How would you describe the focus of this blog post? Is it on theoretical modeling? Is it on explaining gang behavior? How does the author establish this focus? How well does she maintain it?

2. How clear did you find Badger's explanations of mathematical modeling and its uses in addressing gang violence? What makes her explanations effective—or not—in your view?

3. Badger includes some graphics in her post. How helpful did you find these graphics in explaining the concepts Badger is discussing? Would additional graphics have made Badger's explanations clearer? Why or why not?

## FOCUS     THE ETHICS OF INFORMATIVE WRITING

Although much informative writing might appear to be objective and not intended to persuade a reader, even the most seemingly straightforward informative writing reflects the writer's perspective and can thus convey a stance on the subject matter. The very choice of subject matter reflects a writer's perspective. For example, a writer's decision to write a report about the growth of alternative energy sources, such as wind farms, might reflect that writer's view that alternative energy is an important topic and that there might be a need for alternative sources of energy. Moreover, although a writer might seek to inform an audience about a topic in a neutral or objective way, the writer's stance will inevitably be reflected in the way the writer chooses to present information, which information to include or exclude, and what tone to adopt. For example, Jennifer Van Grove presents her explanation of gamification in a relatively positive way. Even though she is ostensibly explaining a process, how she presents information and her tone reflect her belief that the process is worthwhile. You can imagine a different writer with a less positive view of gaming describing the process in a very different way, even though the information would be the same.

Similarly, a writer might compose a report about a controversial topic, such as the use of hydraulic fracturing (or "fracking") to obtain natural gas, without mentioning the fact that the procedure is controversial. Another writer might write a report on the same topic that includes a discussion of the controversial aspects of the topic. Both reports might seem neutral because both writers explain the process and do not take an overt position on the issue, yet the reports reflect each writer's viewpoint about the issue. The first writer might be generally supportive of fracking and therefore not mention the controversy; the second writer, by contrast, might feel suspicious of fracking and thus include information about the controversy. In each case, the writer is making an ethical decision about how to present information to readers.

As a writer, you must decide whether information you present conveys an accurate and fair representation of the topic, regardless of your own views about the topic.

# Writing Informative Essays

Informative writing can be a powerful way for writers to convey information about matters of importance to them and to their readers. If you have the opportunity to inform an interested audience about something that matters to you—for example, volunteering for a political campaign or helping to create a community garden on your campus—the advice in this section will guide you through the process of developing an informative essay about that topic. Read this section together with Chapter 3. Each step described here corresponds with a step in Chapter 3. Also be mindful of these three features of effective narrative writing, as described in Chapter 15:

1. **A clear focus.** Keep your essay tightly focused on your main subject:
   - What is the main subject of this essay?
   - What is the purpose of explaining this subject?

2. **A careful structure.** Organize your essay so that it conveys information clearly and in a way that engages your readers:
   - How effectively does the structure of your essay convey essential and complex information?
   - To what extent does the structure of your essay help readers follow your discussion and remain engaged in the subject?

3. **Succinct, purposeful description.** Describe important scenes or events in a way that helps readers understand them and appreciate their significance:
   - Which scenes or events relevant to your subject should be described to your readers?
   - What should your descriptions convey to your readers about these scenes or events?

## Step 1  Identify a topic.

Informative writing grows out of a desire to share information with others about a topic that interests you. Often, we are asked to report on a topic that is assigned to us (such as in a class or at work). Sometimes, however, informative writing emerges from our own curiosity or experience. So begin by identifying:

- issues or topics about which you would like to know more
- activities or topics about which you are knowledgeable or have direct experience

17

| Topics you are curious about | Activities or subjects you have experience with |
|---|---|
| • A current trend (e.g., crowd sourcing)<br>• A controversy (e.g., individual liberty vs. national security)<br>• An important development (e.g., alternative energy)<br>• A concern (e.g., bullying)<br>• An activity that's new to you (e.g., dancing)<br>• A local issue (e.g., a new charter school) | • A hobby (e.g., painting or gardening)<br>• An experience that raised questions for you (e.g., an unfamiliar medical condition that someone you know developed)<br>• A topic you have expertise with (e.g., woodworking, politics, baseball)<br>• An important decision that others might share (e.g., going to college) |

1. **Make a brief list of possible topics in each category.**

For each item, jot down a few sentences about the topic: What do you know about it? What interests you about it? What do want to know or share with others about it?

2. **Select the topic that seems most promising to you.**

Remember that the topic you choose should be one that engages you for some reason: you're curious about it, you're passionate about it, it is important in your life in some way. Your genuine engagement with the topic is likely to result in a piece of writing that is also engaging for your readers.

Step #1 in Chapter 3 will help you further develop your topic.

## Step 2  Place your topic in rhetorical context.

Who will have an interest or stake in your topic? That is the primary question to address as you begin exploring your topic. So at this point your task is twofold:

a. Identify an audience for your informative text.

b. Consider your purpose in informing that audience about your topic.

In some cases, your topic might appeal to a wide audience. For example, an informative essay about the problem of bullying would likely interest readers of many different age groups, those who work with young people, and parents, among others. By contrast, some topics will interest a more specialized audience. For example, a report on developments in psychotherapy techniques for a counseling psychology course would likely be written for an audience with an understanding of counseling psychology. Remember, your topic must have relevance for your intended audience. Considering that relevance will help you write an informative text that engages your audience and effectively conveys information about your topic.

Imagine, for example, that you recently became involved in an effort on your campus to create a community garden. Let's say that the college has designated some land to be used for the garden, which will be open to both students and local residents. As a result of your involvement, you have begun to learn about a national movement to identify and grow rare varieties of common vegetables such as tomatoes. Although you have been gardening for several years, you have never heard of so-called "heirloom" vegetables. Some of the people who use the community garden, for instance, have planted several different varieties of heirloom tomatoes that vary dramatically in color and size and have different flavors compared to the tomatoes you are familiar with. Obtaining seeds for these varieties, however, is difficult, and you have learned that scientists as well as gardeners are interested in this movement as a way to preserve biodiversity. You decide you'd like to learn more about this movement and create an informative text to share what you learn with others. Consider the following:

| Who might be interested in this topic? | • Gardeners<br>• People involved with community projects<br>• Readers interested in science and issues related to biodiversity<br>• Students in certain science courses, such as botany or agricultural economics<br>• Readers interested in issues of sustainability and food |
| --- | --- |
| Why would they be interested in this topic? | • Gardeners might want information about obtaining and growing heirloom plants.<br>• People interested in science might be curious about the scientific aspects of the heirloom movement.<br>• Readers concerned about sustainability might see the movement as part of broader social and environmental developments. |

In considering your potential audience and their interest in your topic, you can see several possibilities for thinking about the purpose of your project:

- to convey practical information for gardeners and others interested in gardening
- to examine the movement in terms of broader developments related to sustainability and biodiversity;
- to explore technical matters related to raising rare varieties of vegetables.

As you develop your project, your sense of purpose will shape the information you decide to include and how to present it to your intended audience.

With this in mind, explore your topic using these two questions to identify a potential audience and determine the relevance of your topic to that audience. Then complete Step #2 in Chapter 3 to explore your rhetorical context more fully.

**17**

## Step 3 | Select a medium.

Which medium is best for your informative project depends upon your audience and your purpose.

Let's return to the example of an informative project about heirloom plants. Consider your audience and purpose in deciding which medium might be most appropriate for such a project:

| Potential audience | Local gardeners | People interested in sustainability | General |
| --- | --- | --- | --- |
| Purpose | To provide practical information about planting heirloom vegetables | To inform them about a movement that could contribute to sustainability | To inform them about an interesting gardening movement |
| Possible medium | • Brochure<br>• Article in local publication<br>• Blog post | • Newsletter article<br>• Post on relevant blog<br>• Video for relevant organization | • Newspaper article<br>• Blog post |

In evaluating the possible media for each audience, consider the capabilities of each medium. For example, a brochure enables you to use graphics, color, and other design features. By contrast, a conventional newspaper article would allow you to go into greater depth about your topic, which might be an advantage if you want to reach an audience of readers interested in sustainability issues. (If you are working on a specific course assignment, you should follow the guidelines for the assignment and select an approved medium.)

Step #3 in Chapter 3 provides additional guidance to help you decide on the most appropriate medium for your informative project.

## Step 4 | Identify the main point of your informative project.

In one sense, the point of any informative writing is to inform readers about a subject. But *why* should readers be informed about the subject? Your subject might interest you for some reason, but why would it interest readers? In other words, what makes this subject relevant to others? You need to answer these questions to determine the main point of your informative project.

**Begin by returning to the purpose of your project.** If you have followed Steps 1–3, you have already identified a purpose for your project. In our hypothetical example, we identified several possible purposes for an informative piece about growing heirloom vegetables, depending upon the intended audience. Let's imagine that you have decided to direct your project to an audience with a general interest in issues of sustainability and biodiversity. For Step #3 you expressed the purpose of your project as follows:

> *to inform readers about an important movement that could contribute to sustainability*

You can recast that statement of purpose into your **Guiding Thesis Statement:**

> *Raising heirloom crops is a growing movement that holds promise for efforts to increase sustainability and preserve biodiversity.*

This statement captures your sense of purpose and expresses the main point you will make in your informative piece. In effect, you will be informing readers about the heirloom gardening movement as a promising part of the larger effort to promote sustainable lifestyles.

Keep in mind that your Guiding Thesis Statement might change as you learn more about your topic and sharpen the focus of your piece. For example, you might learn that the heirloom plant movement is driven mostly by private citizens interested in gardening and by a few small farmers. If so, you would adjust your Guiding Thesis Statement to reflect that shift in the focus of your piece.

Complete Step #4 in Chapter 3 to develop your Guiding Thesis Statement further.

## Step 5  Support your main point.

Now that you have a good idea of the main point of your project, you can begin to explore your topic and gather sufficient information to inform your readers about that topic. Doing so involves three main tasks:

- Identify what you already know about your topic.
- Gather additional information about your topic.
- Eliminate unnecessary information.

### Identify What You Already Know

Review your Discovery Draft, notes, and other materials to collect the information and ideas you already have, including your own experiences with your topic. Include everything that seems potentially useful or relevant.

### Gather Additional Information

Review the materials you have generated so far to determine what additional information you need. At this point, you might have to do some research, especially if your topic is unfamiliar to you. Use appropriate resources, including online resources, people who might be knowledgeable about your topic, and printed materials you have access to (such as newspapers, books, flyers, etc.). However, rather than just looking for anything at all related to your topic, your research will be more efficient (and probably more effective) if you have an idea of what kind of information you need. So it's important to identify gaps in what you know or have already learned.

17

For example, let's say you have gathered the following information about your topic:

- how to raise certain types of heirloom plants
- the history of the modern movement to discover and preserve heirloom varieties of common vegetables (such as tomatoes)
- the challenges of finding heirloom varieties
- the benefits of raising heirloom vegetables

What else might your readers need to know about your topic? Given that your main point involves connecting the heirloom plant movement to the larger movement for sustainability and preserving biodiversity, you probably need some information about how raising heirloom plants contributes to a sustainable lifestyle and how it might address concerns about biodiversity. The more you research your topic, the easier it will be to identify issues or information that you should include in your project.

Review your materials in this way, keeping your main point and purpose in mind. If you identify gaps in the materials you have, look for appropriate information to fill those gaps. (Chapters 22 and 23 will guide you in identifying and evaluating source material.)

## Eliminate Unnecessary Material

Review your materials to determine whether any information you've collected can be eliminated without weakening your project. Keep in mind that some information might seem relevant but not be necessary. For example, through your research you might have learned about a person who has amassed an unusually large collection of heirloom tomato seeds and has become a supplier for gardeners seeking heirloom varieties. Although this information is interesting and relevant to your project, it probably isn't essential for readers to know in order to understand the heirloom movement and its potential role in fostering biodiversity.

Complete these three steps to develop your project and gather sufficient information to support your main point. You should be now ready to write a complete draft of your informative project. (If not, move to Step #6.) Step #5 in Chapter 3 provides additional advice to help you develop your project.

## Step 6 Organize your informative project.

Clear organization is one of the hallmarks of effective informative writing, but unlike some other forms of writing (such as argument), there are no well-established formats for organizing an informative text. Your main consideration is how to present information so that readers understand your topic. Follow these five steps:

1. **Begin with your main point.** Return to your **Guiding Thesis Statement** (from Step #4) and adjust your main point, if necessary, on the basis of what you have learned about your topic as you completed the first five steps. Ultimately, the way you organize your project should help readers grasp your main point.

2. **Determine which information or ideas are most important for supporting your main point.** Review the materials you developed for Step #5 (or review your rough draft) and identify the pieces of information and ideas that are essential for readers to know in order to understand your topic. Organize the information or ideas in order of descending importance, starting with the most important and moving to the least important.

3. **Identify supporting information or ideas.** Decide whether the supporting material should be placed *after* the essential material or incorporated into it. Decide on the basis of your sense of which approach would make the information easiest for readers to understand.

4. **Incorporate essential background information.** You have probably gathered background information that will have to be worked into your discussion. For example, in your hypothetical project about the heirloom plant movement, you might have relevant scientific information explaining biodiversity. Although that information isn't specifically about the heirloom plant movement, it is essential background so that readers understand how this movement can affect biodiversity. Decide where to fit this information into your project so that it is easy for readers to understand and doesn't interrupt the overall flow of your draft.

5. **Make sure your introduction and conclusion establish and reinforce the focus of your project.** Your introduction should introduce readers to your topic and convey a sense of your main point. Your conclusion should reinforce that main point. Also keep in mind that you want to present that information in a way that will engage your readers and draw them into your piece.

Use these steps to develop an outline. (If you have already completed a draft, you can use these steps to review it and determine whether you should reorganize your project.) Keep in mind that this outline is a guide and might need to be adjusted to reflect your sense of how best to convey your information to your audience.

Step #6 in Chapter 3 provides additional guidance for organizing your project.

17

## Step 7 | Get feedback.

Ask your readers to focus on **the key features of effective informative writing:**

| Clear, engaging explanations | • Does your draft present sufficient information and ideas about the topic?<br>• How clearly is technical information explained?<br>• How engaging are your explanations? |
|---|---|
| Purpose | • What is the main purpose of the text?<br>• Is that purpose clear?<br>• How does the text convey a sense of purpose so that readers understand the relevance of the topic? |
| Focus | • Is the text clearly focused? Is the focus maintained throughout the text?<br>• How are relevant ideas and information incorporated without weakening the focus? |
| Organization | • How does the organization of the draft help present information to readers? Is anything out of place?<br>• Does the structure of the text help maintain the author's focus and keep readers engaged? |
| Description | • How effectively does the author describe important scenes, events, or processes?<br>• Do these descriptions help convey important ideas or information? |

Step # 7 in Chapter 3 will help you analyze your feedback and decide which revisions to make.

## Step 8 Revise.

The most important consideration in revising your draft is making sure you have covered your topic sufficiently and conveyed information clearly so that your intended audience understands your topic and grasps your main point. Before revising, then, return briefly to Step #2 to remind yourself of your rhetorical context. Then follow these four steps:

1. **Review your draft using the questions from Step #7.** It is a good idea to return to your **Guiding Thesis Statement** from Step #4 and make sure your project conveys your main point.

2. **Evaluate how clearly your draft conveys information and explains your topic.** Clarity is a key feature of informative writing. Try to read your draft from the perspective of someone who doesn't have a background in this topic. Keep these questions in mind:

   - Have you conveyed ideas and information in a way that such a reader will understand them?
   - Are there any technical or complicated passages that might be difficult for readers unfamiliar with this topic to understand? If so, how can you make those sections more accessible?
   - What information might be missing that is essential for readers to know?
   - Have you included information that isn't essential and might blur the focus of your project, making it harder for readers to understand? If so, can you eliminate those sections without eliminating important information?

3. **Review the structure of your project.** Re-examine the way you have organized your project to make sure you present information in a clear fashion and effective order.

4. **Follow Step #8 in Chapter 3.** Make sure you have addressed all the main aspects of your essay in your revisions.

17

## Step 9 Refine your voice.

Your voice in your informative project will depend a great deal on your rhetorical situation (see Step #2). In informative writing, the most appropriate voice is often a measured, authoritative voice that doesn't call attention to itself. This is especially true if you are writing in the third person. However, if your project incorporates your own experiences and employs the first person, your voice might be somewhat less formal and more conversational (such as in the excerpts from the article by Michael Chorost on pages 540 and 541).

To help determine whether your voice is appropriate for your project, follow these two steps:

### Return to Your Guiding Thesis Statement

Remind yourself of your main point. Consider whether your voice in your revised draft seems appropriate for a project with this main point.

### Return to Your Rhetorical Context

Briefly revisit Step #2 to remind yourself of your audience and purpose. Will your voice likely engage your intended audience and help you achieve your rhetorical purpose? For example, in your hypothetical project about the heirloom plant movement, you have decided to address an audience interested in issues of sustainability and biodiversity. Such an audience is likely to see your topic as a serious one and will probably be put off by a voice that is very light and conversational. On the other hand, if you are writing an essay intended to inform a general audience about an interesting gardening movement, your readers are likely to expect your voice not to be overly serious and formal.

Follow these steps to help determine whether your voice "sounds" right for your subject matter, audience, and purpose. Step #9 in Chapter 3 will also help you refine your voice.

## Step 10 Edit.

Complete Step #10 in Chapter 3.

---

**WRITING PROJECTS** **INFORMATIVE WRITING**

1. Think of something you know how to do well that involves specialized knowledge or a skill that most people are unlikely to have. It could be an athletic activity, a hobby, or something similar. Develop an informative project that explains that process. Identify an appropriate audience and select a medium that is likely to reach that audience. For example, you might create a brochure for private computer users about how to protect a personal computer from hacking or viruses.

2. Think of an experience you had that led to a new understanding or insight. For example, maybe you witnessed an accident and learned something surprising about how emergency medical services work. Or you might have taken a trip and encountered unexpected problems that you could have avoided. Develop an informative project on a topic related to that experience. For example, if you witnessed an accident that made you wonder about how emergency medical services are organized and funded in the U.S., you might develop a report about emergency medical services. Incorporate your own experience into your project.

3. Identify a general issue of interest to you. It could be an ongoing controversy, a subject of current interest, or something that you have always been curious about. Explore that issue. On the basis of what you learn about it, develop an informative project. Identify an audience that might share your interest in the topic.

4. Rewrite the project you did for Question #1, #2, or #3 in a completely different medium. For example, if you write a conventional print report for Question #1, develop a multimedia or video version of that report.

---

### MindTap®

Request help with these Writing Projects and get feedback from a tutor. If required, participate in peer review, submit your paper for a grade, and view instructor comments online.

17

In this chapter, you will learn to

1. Identify and understand the purposes of digital storytelling.

2. Identify appropriate rhetorical opportunities for digital storytelling.

3. Apply the technical components of effective digital storytelling in both reading and writing digital stories.

4. Analyze digital stories by applying the three main characteristics of effective digital storytelling.

5. Create a digital story, applying the key technical components and the Ten Core Concepts.

## MindTap

Understand the goals of the chapter and complete a warm-up activity.

# Digital Storytelling 18

**DIGITAL STORYTELLING IS A POWERFUL NEW WAY** for writers to connect with readers. Using digital media, writers can incorporate sound, images, video, and special effects into their narratives to engage readers in ways that are not possible in conventional print media. Digital stories enable writers to participate in an increasingly multimedia world.

What is a digital story? For our purposes, *digital story* refers to narratives presented in a digital format that includes multimedia components such as photographs, video clips, and sound in addition to text. It is important to note that digital stories are not simple videos. Although digital stories might include video clips, the video clips are one component of the whole presentation into which the writer carefully integrates those clips with other images (such as still photographs), music, sound effects, and voice-over narration. Videos, by contrast, are usually composed entirely of video footage accompanied by sound. This distinction is important because the process of composing a digital video is not the same as making a video.

Composing a digital story encourages a writer to explore an experience in ways that can enrich storytelling. The digital format requires writers to think about elements that are not available in print formats—such as video clips, music, and other kinds of sound and graphics—and consider how these elements can be used to convey the writer's experience or ideas. Video and sound can make a story more engaging for a reader, but just as important, such elements change the way a writer composes a story. In addition to considering how matters like word choice and organization might influence a reader's response to a story, writers must consider the potential impact of images, colors, music, and similar elements on an audience. In digital media, images and sound become powerful rhetorical tools with which writers can meet the needs of a rhetorical situation, and writers must compose their stories with these elements in mind. They must go beyond words and anticipate how these other components can help make their stories more compelling for an audience. The process of creating a digital story, then, is not a simple matter of converting a written story into a digital format; it is a different process by which the writer explores his or her experience with different tools.

This is not to say that digital stories are better (or worse) than stories told in conventional print formats; both digital stories and conventional print narratives convey an experience to an audience. However, digital storytelling offers writers new opportunities for sharing their experiences and presents them with new challenges as well.

As someone living in this rapidly evolving digital age, you have probably used various media to tell a story:

- a Prezi presentation about a field trip you took for a biology course
- a video of a trip you took to a city you had never visited before
- a PowerPoint presentation about a community service project you participated in
- a blog post with photos and embedded video clips about your experience as an exchange student

These various media enable you to connect with readers in different ways to convey your story. Digital storytelling is likely to continue to grow in popularity and importance as new and ever-more sophisticated technologies become increasingly available to writers. This chapter will help you develop a better understanding of digital storytelling so that you can take advantage of its capabilities to meet your rhetorical needs.

# Occasions for Digital Storytelling

Not long ago I was browsing an online discussion forum devoted to sailing and came across a heated discussion about a video someone had posted to the forum. The video, which was about 30 minutes long, had been created by a young sailor in his mid-20s. It told the story of his experiences sailing an old sailboat with two friends. The narrator and his friends (two women about his age) found the boat deteriorating in a marina in south Florida. After working for several months to scrape together enough money, they bought the boat and then spent several more months repairing it to make it seaworthy. For the next year, the three friends lived aboard the boat and sailed along the southeastern coast of the U.S. and throughout the Caribbean, stopping here and there to earn extra money for supplies and to make additional repairs to the boat. The video told the story of their adventures. Through video clips, still photographs, and voice-over narration, the writer created a story about sailing through all kinds of weather to new places and making do with very little money and without the sophisticated navigation technology that mariners rely on today. Part of the point of the story was that if you seek adventure, you don't need much more than the desire for new experiences and the willingness to make do with what you have. It was an engaging story expertly told in a digital format.

The video sparked an intense response from some members of the discussion forum where it had been posted. Many of the participants in that discussion were older, having retired after long careers and now enjoying their later years by sailing. Some of these people objected to what they considered the irresponsible behavior of the three young people in the video, who knew how to sail but had limited experience sailing in coastal waters, which can be dangerous. Other participants defended the young sailors, admiring their adventurous spirit, resourcefulness, and problem-solving ability. They envied these young sailors the courage to follow their dreams in a little sailboat. The online discussion, which spanned a few weeks, wasn't really about sailing but about how to live. Participants shared their views about responsibility, happiness, and even the purpose of human life. They also shared their own stories—not only about sailing experiences but also about careers, families, dreams, and regrets. In many ways, the discussion was as compelling as the video itself.

That video revealed the power of digital media to tell a story. It was a well-crafted narrative that included carefully edited video footage, compelling still photographs, and an engaging voice-over narration. The story was engrossing not only because of the adventures it depicted and the narrator's provocative views about living but also because of the skillful use of imagery and sound. The intense debate in the online discussion forum suggests that the video deeply affected its audience. I don't know whether the young man who made that digital story followed the debate, but it seems clear from how carefully he composed his digital story that he felt a need to share it with other people interested in following a dream.

Of course, you don't have to have an adventure to tell a compelling digital story. Like any narratives about our own experiences (see Chapter 16), digital stories can be about any experience, no matter how mundane or common it might seem:

- A student creates a digital story for a criminal justice class about a family member's experience with the juvenile court system.
- A YouTube video tells the story of a family's vacation at a famous national park.
- The website of a community organization includes digital stories about the experiences of elderly residents of a historic neighborhood that is being renovated.
- Veteran teachers create digital stories about their professional lives to share with new teachers at the beginning of their careers.
- A college student creates a digital story about living at college to help new students adjust to life in a college dorm.

In these examples, writers use digital media to tell stories about experiences that matter to them and to others. Given the growth of digital media in recent years, digital stories can sometimes make it easier for writers to find an audience for their stories. For example, potential viewers might be more inclined to watch a digital story posted to an organization's website than to read the organization's newsletter because the digital story can be accessed and viewed so quickly and easily online.

In many cases, telling a story in a conventional print format might still be preferable, despite the advantages of digital storytelling. For instance, in Chapter 16 we used the example of a narrative about the experience of dealing with a family member who is diagnosed with a serious illness. Such a story can certainly be told in digital format, but it is a story that is also quite involved and multilayered, encompassing the person's health, sophisticated medical treatments, health insurance concerns, financial pressures, difficult decisions, and the impact of the experience on other family members. As a writer, you might decide that a conventional print story enables you to explore these many aspects of the story in greater depth than a digital story might allow, especially if you did not have relevant video footage or still photographs from that period of your life. In such a case, telling the story in digital format might not be a viable option. On the other hand, you might decide that the multimedia capabilities of a digital story enable you to tell your story in a different but equally compelling way.

18

Telling a story in digital format, then, is partly a matter of taking advantage of the media and materials available to you as a writer and deciding whether the format fits your rhetorical situation. Any experience that is important enough to share with others can be told in digital format if you have the necessary components, such as relevant video clips or photographs, to convey your story sufficiently to an audience. And in some situations, a digital format might be the best choice. For example, a student who belongs to a campus organization for business majors might create a digital story about her experience as an intern with a company that makes virtual reality software. Her digital story, which is intended for the organization's website, might include video footage showing her testing the software as well as graphics illustrating important elements of the software. In such a case, the availability of video, sound, and other multimedia elements enables the writer to convey her experience in ways that would be difficult or impossible in a conventional print format. For example, she can show video footage of the virtual reality test she experienced that might be challenging to describe in words.

Deciding whether to tell your story in digital format is partly a technical matter (Do you have relevant images? Do you have access to the right equipment?), but like any effective narrative, an effective digital story is one that meets the needs of a specific rhetorical situation. You can be a more versatile writer by learning how to craft digital stories and by taking advantage of digital media to achieve your rhetorical goals.

---

**EXERCISE 18A   OCCASIONS FOR DIGITAL STORYTELLING**

1.  Think of a recent experience you had that might best be conveyed to an audience as a digital story. What might you include in a digital story about that experience? What images or sound would be appropriate in telling that story? What advantages or disadvantages do you see in telling the story of that experience in digital form?

2.  Find one or two digital stories online. (A simple search for "digital stories" or "digital storytelling" should yield many links to sites where you can find digital stories.) After viewing the stories, imagine a print version of each story. In what ways might a print version of that same story be more effective? In what ways might it be less effective?

3.  If you have ever submitted a college essay or some other kind of application essay (such as for admission to a special sports camp or music workshop), consider how you might have converted that essay into a digital story. Would you have changed the story in any way? What advantages or disadvantages would a digital story have in such a case as compared to a conventional print essay?

---

# Understanding Digital Stories

At first glance, digital stories can seem straightforward: a narrator reading a story as images appear on the screen and music plays in the background. In fact, part of the appeal of many digital stories is that they can tell a story in simple terms with images, sound, and voice-over narration. But even the simplest digital story is actually a sophisticated combination of image, sound, and text that results from a writer's many careful decisions about what to include in the story and *how* to present it visually and aurally.

The following digital story illustrates the complexity of the decision-making that writers engage in as they design digital stories. "Good Will" tells the story of a daughter's decision about what to do with the many sweaters her mother has knitted over the years. On the surface, this four-minute video focuses on a few moments in the life of the narrator, Christi Clancy, as she drives to a homeless shelter to donate the sweaters. While on her way, she thinks about the sweaters and about her mother, whose impressive skill at knitting reflects her other qualities as a person. In the process of telling the story of her drive to the homeless shelter and her decision about whether or not to donate the sweaters, Clancy delves into her mother's sometimes difficult life and gains insight into her mother—and herself.

Here are the first few frames of Clancy's digital story along with the text of the voice-over narration. Keep in mind that each image appears on screen for several seconds to coincide with the narration. Also, some frames zoom in or out to highlight specific components of an image, and there is often a transition between images (for example, one image fades into another). All these design features contribute to the viewer's experience and enhance the story being told but cannot easily be represented on the pages of this textbook.

1.

[soft background music]
Narrator: I took some of the sweaters my Mom made to the homeless shelter.

2.

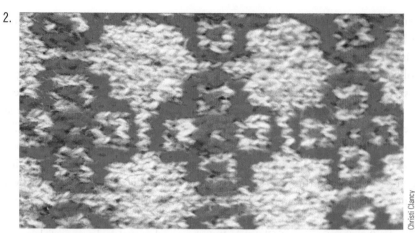

Narrator: I only wanted to take the ones that were too big, too itchy, too boxy, and too old.

3.

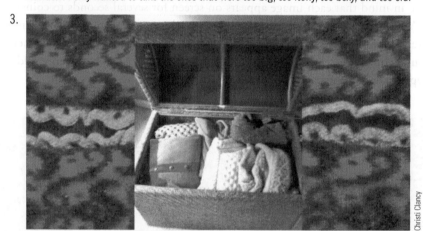

Narrator: I have so many sweaters that if you poked a hole in my house, yarn would burst out.

4.

Narrator: My mom doesn't just knit for me but for everyone else in our family. Last year alone she made 24 sweaters. Lately, all those sweaters have become a problem.

In these opening frames, Clancy sets up her story by telling us that she is on her way to the homeless shelter. She introduces her mother, provides a little background information, and, at the end of the fourth frame, introduces tension into her story: "Lately, all those sweaters have become a problem." Notice that this information is conveyed efficiently through the brief text of the voice-over narration. At the same time, the images enable viewers to see the sweaters without Clancy having to describe them (as she would have had to do in a conventional print narrative). In addition, the photograph in the third frame allows viewers to see what her mother and family look like. In these ways, Clancy carefully combines simple images with brief text to convey information and establish the focus of her story. In effective digital storytelling, the writer uses images and sound together with text to convey ideas and information, not to decorate the story.

In the next frame, Clancy begins to delve into her mother's character and explore her main themes of responsibility, resilience, and perseverance:

5.

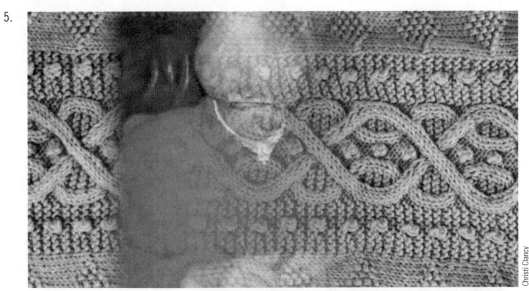

Christi Clancy

Narrator: When I asked my mom why she knits so much, she said that unlike most things in life, a sweater has a beginning, middle, and end. As someone who had to start her life over again, I'm not surprised by her answer. She's incredibly practical, paying herself a quarter for every load of laundry she does. We used to call her "Smart Pat," because her approach to conflict is just to get over things and move on.

18

Here, Clancy combines two still photographs to create an unusual image that represents the role of knitting in her mother's life and reinforces one of the story's main themes: resilience. This frame demonstrates how a writer can use simple still photographs to achieve a specific effect, convey information, and introduce or reinforce ideas.

In the next three frames (#6, 7, and 8), Clancy reveals that she herself does not knit, showing images of sweaters as well as photos of her and her mother and telling the viewer, "I tried a few times, but I get frustrated sometimes when I hit a snag." In this way, she establishes a contrast between herself and her mother, using knitting as a metaphor. Then in frame #9 she introduces a central part of her story: her family's difficulty with her father, who suffered from addiction and mental illness:

9.

Narrator: She's a problem-solver, but my dad was one problem she couldn't fix. He was handsome and charming—and a manic-depressive alcoholic.

10.

Narrator: Once he threw her down the basement stairs. Another time he told her to hide his gun because he was afraid he would use it.

11.

Narrator: She put my sisters and me in a plane in the middle of the night after that. She finished her Masters degree in speech pathology, and we started over in Milwaukee.

Notice that Clancy uses a single photograph in these frames, zooming in on specific components of the photograph as her narration tells the story of how her mother left her father and started a new life in another city. These frames illustrate **an important feature of effective digital storytelling: design features enhance the story without distracting from the ideas or themes.** In this case, Clancy zooms in on an image to emphasize the information she is conveying through her voice-over narration. The zooming doesn't merely catch the viewer's attention or make the image "snappy"; it contributes to the storytelling.

As this digital story illustrates, simple images can contain a great deal of information and introduce complex ideas if they are used carefully in conjunction with the narrative text. For example, notice how Clancy uses very basic photos in the next three frames to fill in more information and begin to reveal her own feelings about her mother's ability to care for her family:

12.

Narrator: She didn't make much money, sometimes not even enough for lunch.

13.

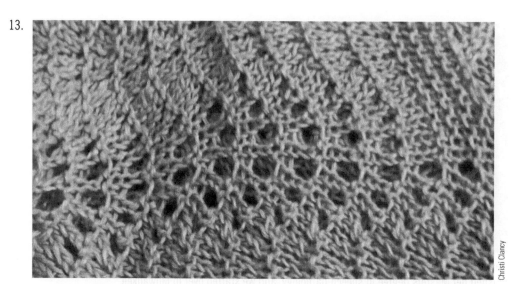

Narrator: But she could send me to school in a gorgeous hand-knit sweater that people would always compliment.

14.

Narrator: I loved the steady clicking sound of her knitting needles and the competent tap of her heels on the linoleum floor of the hospital when I visited her at work.

Clancy returns to images of the sweaters her mother made. She uses these images not only to show readers the quality of her mother's knitting but also to explore her themes and to keep her narrative clearly focused. Note also that in the 14th frame she includes a close-up photograph of her mother as a young woman. This photo not only provides readers with an accurate depiction of what her mother looked like at that time in her life, but it also shows her mother as happy and confident. This frame is another example of how a simple image can convey complex information and reinforce important themes in the story.

Clancy's repeated use of photos of her mother's sweaters also help move the story along by reminding us that she still has to decide what to do with all the extra sweaters. At the same time, as she displays more and more photos of those sweaters, she reinforces their importance to her as symbols of her mother's qualities and her own sense of identity as her mother's daughter. Using this same strategy of repeatedly showing images of the sweaters, Clancy continues her story, informing her audience that her mother is now retired and works part-time in a yarn store, still knitting and helping others learn to knit. Then Clancy returns to the problem at the center of her story: what to do with all those sweaters. Notice that she uses a photo of a sweater in the frame that depicts the moment of decision (frame #17):

16.

Narrator: I wonder if she knew we'd struggle with what to do with the sweaters she's given us.

17.

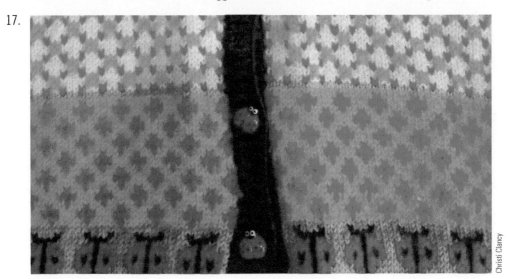

Narrator: Did she anticipate that we would experience a moment just like the one I was having in my car, trying to decide whether or not to let them go to strangers?

18.

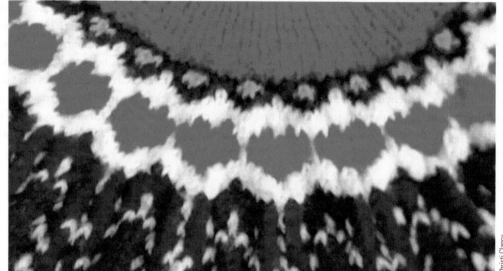

Christi Clancy

Narrator: I thought of a dream I once had of my dad, who died homeless on the streets of Denver when he was only 51.

Here again Clancy relies on images of her mother's sweaters to highlight the difficulty of her decision. The narration informs viewers of Clancy's struggle, while the images remind them of the beauty of the sweaters, which brings Clancy's difficult decision to the forefront: How could she part with such beautiful sweaters that were so expertly and lovingly crafted by her mother? That struggle intensifies when she remembers a dream she had of her father:

19.

Christi Clancy

Narrator: He came back to visit me. He was wearing a sweater my mom knit for him, but it had come unraveled.

20.

Narrator: He was dragging strings of yarn behind him that stretched back as far as I could see.

21.

Narrator: I couldn't donate them.

22.

Narrator: Every single stitch is a captured moment from her life, every sweater as much a part of her as her tissue. Knitting is her language.

18

23.

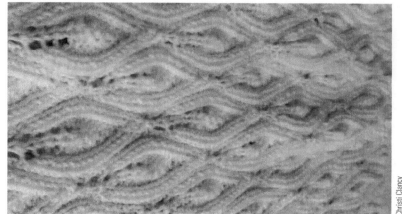

Narrator: I drove back home, but even now, months later, the sweaters are still in the trunk of my car. Maybe for her the sweaters have a beginning, middle, and end, but she goes on and on.

24.

Once again Clancy uses images to communicate ideas and reinforce themes. When she makes her decision (frame #21), she shows a photo of a sweater. In frame #22 she superimposes an image of her mother on that same sweater, reinforcing a main theme of her story and reminding us why she could not part with those sweaters. These are all very simple images, but Clancy uses them to convey complex ideas.

Clancy's story also demonstrates perhaps the most important feature of effective digital storytelling—and indeed of *all* narratives: It must tell a story that matters to the writer and be relevant to the intended audience. Clancy doesn't simply describe a difficult decision she had to make about whether to donate prized family possessions; rather, she tells the story of that decision in a way that explores complex themes of love and loyalty. Her story examines how a simple item such as a sweater can acquire important significance. In that regard, her story explores fundamental themes that her audience can relate to, whether or not they are interested in knitting.

Note, too, that the text of Clancy's narrative is spare, almost poetic. It conveys only what is essential to the story and works in conjunction with the images to provide necessary information for viewers to understand the story. Digital storytelling enables writers to use images and sound to communicate ideas and therefore to say more with less prose. As a result, writing the text of a digital story means choosing words carefully so that they complement the images rather than repeat information conveyed by the images.

**Effective digital stories, then, have three main characteristics:**

- **They tell a story that matters.** Like all effective narratives, digital stories relate experiences that matter to the writer and are relevant to viewers. A story that has little significance for an audience is unlikely to be any more compelling if told with images or sound. What matters most in a digital story is what matters most in any good narrative: It must tell a compelling story that connects with readers and conveys a relevant idea or point.

- **They use images, sound, and other multimedia elements to convey ideas and information.** The multimedia components of a digital story are more than illustration or decoration; they are essential elements that communicate information, convey ideas, and reinforce themes. Simply adding images or sound doesn't necessarily improve a narrative. Images, sound, and special effects must contribute to the story in some way; moreover, they should engage the audience without distracting from the point of the story.

- **They employ design elements to enhance the story.** Design elements such as transitions, zooming, color, and sound effects can be used to communicate ideas and reinforce themes in a story. A writer can make a gradual transition between two still photographs to suggest a connection between the images. Music can contribute to a certain mood that is appropriate for the story. In these ways, design elements help the writer tell a story and reinforce the writer's themes.

---

### EXERCISE 18B    EXPLORING DIGITAL STORIES

1. Think of an experience you might want to share in a digital story. Briefly describe one important moment or scene in that experience. Now image that brief description as one or more frames of a digital story. What images would you use? How would you revise your paragraph so that it is an appropriate narration to accompany those images? What sound would you include? On the basis of this exercise, what conclusions can you draw about the similarities and differences between composing digital stories and conventional print narratives?

2. Rewrite Christi Clancy's digital story "Good Will" as a conventional print narrative without the images, using as much of her narration as possible and adding whatever new text you believe is necessary to tell her story effectively. Now compare the original digital story to your print version of it. What do you notice in comparing these two versions? Which do you think is more effective in conveying her experience? Why? What does this exercise tell you about writing digital stories?

*(Continued)*

18

3. Compare how the authors of the two of the digital stories included in this chapter use the capabilities of digital media to tell their stories (see "Reading Digital Stories"). Analyze each author's use of images and sound. Evaluate the voice-over narration. On the basis of your comparison, what conclusions can you draw about composing effective digital stories?

# Managing the Technical Components of a Digital Story

The primary difference between a conventional print narrative and a digital story is technology. A writer telling a story in conventional print format generally does not have to consider matters of document design, such as layout, color, or graphics (except when using a medium such as a website or brochure that allows for such features); as a result, the writer can concentrate on the text. Telling a story in digital format, by contrast, requires a writer to think carefully about design, especially the use of images and sound. As the example in the preceding section of this chapter indicates, these features significantly affect the quality of the narrative and the reader's experience. As a writer, then, you must manage these **five technical components** when telling your story in digital format:

- a storyboard
- images
- sound
- narration
- transitions

## Creating a Storyboard

When composing a digital story, the writer creates a kind of script, usually called a **storyboard**, which is an outline of the digital story that includes information about images, sound, and design elements. A storyboard allows you to map out the story and to organize the multimedia elements. It enables you to "see" your entire digital story before you begin creating it with the appropriate software (see Focus: "Software for Digital Storytelling" on page 588).

Although you can find programs for creating storyboards, you can also use a word processing program to create a basic storyboard. To do so, simply create an outline with each main heading corresponding to a frame in your digital story. Each frame should include the following information:

- image (photo or video clip)
- audio (background music, sound effects)
- design (color, subtitles, special effects such as zooming)
- narration (the text of the story)

Let's imagine that you are creating a digital story about a study-abroad experience in Brazil. A basic storyboard for the first few frames would look like this:

I. Frame #1

- Image: photo of you and your host family
- Audio: Brazilian salsa music
- Design: title in standard font at bottom of frame
- Narration: "I thought I knew something about Brazil (pause) until I spent three months there as a high school senior."

II. Frame #2

- Image: panoramic photo of the city where you stayed
- Audio: Brazilian salsa music
- Design: pan across the photo
- Narration: "This is the Brazil I thought I knew: a sunny, busy place full of life and color."

III. Frame #3

- Image: split photo of shimmering beach and crowded barrio
- Audio: slow Brazilian folk music
- Design: zoom in and out of each photo
- Narration: "This is the Brazil I discovered: a land of contrast, of joy and hope alongside despair; a land of possibility."

A storyboard should contain this kind of information for each slide or frame in your digital story. You can also create your storyboard as a table to help you visualize your story:

| I. Frame #1 | II. Frame #2 | III. Frame #3 |
| --- | --- | --- |
| • Image: photo of you and your host family<br>• Audio: Brazilian salsa music<br>• Design: title in standard font at bottom of frame<br>• Narration: "I thought I knew something about Brazil (pause) until I spent three months there as a high school senior." | • Image: panoramic photo of city where you stayed<br>• Audio: Brazilian salsa music<br>• Design: pan across photo<br>• Narration: "This is the Brazil I thought I knew: a sunny, busy place full of life and color." | • Image: split photo of shimmering beach and crowded barrio<br>• Audio: slow Brazilian folk music<br>• Design: zoom in and out of each photo<br>• Narration: "This is the Brazil I discovered: a land of contrast, of joy and hope alongside despair; a land of possibility." |

**18**

Creating a storyboard is an integral part of the composing process. Many writers find it easiest to write their story as a complete text and then create a storyboard, revising the text of the story as they include the narration for each frame. Some writers prefer to compose the story as they develop the storyboard, considering appropriate images and sound as they write the narration. There is no right way. Do what works for you as a writer. The important point is that a storyboard enables you to develop your story as a multimedia presentation and helps you coordinate images, sound, design, and text.

Many different software programs and online sites can be used to create digital stories. One of the most widely used programs is *PhotoStory*, which is available free online. *Photostory* is easy to use and enables writers to incorporate still photographs and music into their digital stories. (Some versions of *PhotoStory* cannot accommodate video, however.) *PowerPoint* can also be used for digital storytelling. It includes a wide variety of special effects and allows the user to embed video and audio clips into a presentation.

Most personal computers have operating systems that include video software that can also be used for making digital stories. Microsoft Windows usually includes a program called *Moviemaker*. Apple computers have a similar program called *iMovie*. Both these programs are sophisticated tools that can be used to create digital stories, enabling writers to incorporate video clips as well as still images and sound; they also include many special effects and design features.

Increasingly, writers are using online resources to create their digital stories. *Flickr*, a social media site for distributing images, is one such resource. Podcasting, in which digital audio recordings are combined with photos or video clips, can also be used for creating digital stories.

If you have never created a digital story, it is probably best to use a basic program, such as *PhotoStory*, that is easy to learn. As you gain more experience with digital storytelling, you might find a need for more sophisticated digital tools. Your course instructor might provide resources for creating digital stories. You can also check with your college library.

## Using Images

Video clips, photographs, and other kinds of images are powerful tools for telling a story. They can communicate information, convey ideas, reinforce themes, emphasize a point, and evoke a feeling in an audience. Selecting and using images is one of the most important components of composing an effective digital story.

Many technical aspects of images are beyond the scope of this textbook, such as the composition of an image, image quality, camera angles, and so on. You can find resources about these topics online. (Also, see "Analyzing Images" in Chapter 8 and "Working with Images" in Chapter 21.) For our purposes, the most important considerations are what an image communicates to a viewer and how it contributes to your digital story. In selecting and using images, keep the following questions in mind:

- **What does this image communicate?** Some images provide information in a straightforward way. For instance, in our hypothetical example of a digital story about a study-abroad experience in Brazil, a photo of the host family enables viewers to see what the family members looked like; similarly, a video clip of the neighborhood where you stayed provides information to help viewers understand your experience there.

Images can also communicate ideas and introduce or reinforce themes in more subtle ways. For example, in Christi Clancy's digital story earlier in this chapter, the photos of the sweaters not only enable viewers to appreciate her mother's knitting skill but also convey important ideas about Clancy's relationship with her mother.

■ **How does this image contribute to the story?** An image should advance the story in some way, so consider the specific information or idea you want to convey or reinforce with a particular image. For example, a story about my grandparents might include an anecdote about a time they visited a religious shrine that was important to them. I might use this photo, taken in front of a fountain at the shrine:

Robert P. Yagelski

This photograph shows a specific location mentioned in my narration, but it also suggests the affection and warmth my grandparents felt for one another. Selecting this photo enables me to show viewers the place referred to in the narration and at the same time reinforce an important idea about my grandparents' relationship. By contrast, a common vacation photo, in which my grandparents were posing for the camera, might provide information about the location but would not necessarily convey anything important about their relationship. When selecting images for a digital story, then, consider not only the information you want the image to convey but also whether the image enables you to introduce or reinforce important themes.

■ **Is this image necessary?** Effective digital stories include only the elements that are essential to the story. If an image does not contribute to the story in some way, consider removing or replacing it. Avoid including images just because they are compelling unless they also move your story forward or enhance it in some way.

These same principles apply to *any* image: still photographs, video clips, sketches, cartoons, or paintings. Remember that you are telling your story by combining images with other media. Any image you use should contribute something important to your story. Also keep in mind that you can't always simply copy images from online sites and use them in your story. You must respect copyright laws (see Focus: "Intellectual Property Considerations").

---

**FOCUS** | **INTELLECTUAL PROPERTY CONSIDERATIONS**

Using images and music in a digital story can raise questions about copyright. If you created the images or sounds yourself, in general you own the right to use them in a digital story. However, if you obtained an image, video, or audio clip online, it might be subject to copyright restrictions and you might be unable to use it in your digital story without permission. If you wish to include images or audio made by someone else, you should determine whether you are allowed to use them or whether you need to obtain permission to do so.

In general, the fair use clause of U.S. copyright law allows students to use most images or music that belong to someone else as long as the image or music is used exclusively for a course assignment and will not be distributed to larger audiences or for profit. If you plan to post your digital story to a public website, you might not be protected by the fair use clause and you should probably obtain permission to use any images, videos, or audio clips that belong to someone else. Often, copyright information is included on the websites where you found image or audio. Check there first. You can also usually find good advice about copyright and intellectual property issues on the website of your campus library. If you're not sure about whether you need permission to use an image, video, or audio clip, check with your course instructor or a librarian.

Also, if you plan to use in your digital story an image you made of someone else (for example, a photo or video clip showing some friends), you should obtain their permission.

---

# Incorporating Sound

Most digital stories include background music that accompanies the voice-over narration. In effective digital stories, music helps establish an appropriate mood for the story, reinforces the writer's tone, enhances the image in some way, and evokes a certain feeling in viewers (joy, melancholy, excitement). In many digital stories, the same music plays throughout; in some stories the music changes to signal a shift in the story or reinforce an important moment in the narrative. In these ways, the sound you select can help convey your experience more vividly to your audience.

Digital stories can also include sound effects. For example, a story about an experience at a beach might include the sound of crashing waves in the background. Often, such sound effects can be used to emphasize an important moment in the story and make the story more vivid. But in selecting sound effects, be careful that they do not distract viewers and take away from the narration or the images.

When considering sound for your digital story, address these questions:

- **What mood do you want to convey?** Music is a powerful way to evoke feelings and set a mood. Consider the main point of your story and the nature of the experience you are sharing. If you decide to include background music, select music that fits your story and will help convey the appropriate mood to your audience. For example, a heartfelt and somber story, such as the one by Christi Clancy included earlier in this chapter, probably calls for soft, perhaps slightly melancholy music.

- **How can sound be used to convey relevant information or ideas?** In addition to setting a mood for your story, music or sound effects can also communicate information and ideas or supplement the images and text to highlight an important theme. For example, a story about your experience with a Hip Hop band might include clips of specific songs that were significant to you or your band members. Similarly, the lyrics of a song might reinforce an important idea in a story; for example, a segment about a difficult break-up in a long-term relationship might include a clip from a love song with lyrics that highlight the difficulty of the experience.

## Narrating a Digital Story

Effective voice-over narration is more than a matter of reading the text of your story. The narration must work in conjunction with images and sound to tell your story, explore your themes, and communicate your main points. In this regard, writing a digital story is different from writing a conventional print version of your story. Moreover, how you narrate your story will have an impact on your audience. In addition to your choice of words, your tone, pacing, and inflection can significantly affect the quality of your digital story and influence your audience's reaction to it. In narrating a digital story, then, keep these two main considerations in mind:

- **The text of a digital story works with the images and sound to present the subject matter.** The narration does not tell the whole story. Instead, the narration relies on images and sound to convey information and reinforce important themes. Writers don't try to include everything in the narration; they tell what is necessary, using images and sound where appropriate to communicate information and ideas. For example, there's no need to describe what someone looks like if you are including a photo of that person. Similarly, rather than describe an event or action, let a video clip or photograph show it. Use the narration to provide background information, ideas, and impressions that can't be conveyed through images or sound. The main thing to keep in mind is to include in the text only what you need. (To get a better sense of the difference between writing the narrative for a digital story and writing a conventional print narrative, complete Question #2 in Exercise 18B on page 585.)

- **The narration reflects an interpretation of the story.** Voice-over narration gives you the opportunity to use tone of voice, inflection, and pace in a way that fits your subject matter and reinforces important moments or ideas in your story. In this sense, your voice-over narration reflects your *interpretation* of your story, allowing you to highlight

18

important moments in the text, pause for emphasis, slow down or quicken your pace to match the action you are referring to, and evoke a certain emotion or mood with your tone of voice. As you prepare to record the voice-over narration for your digital story, consider these questions:

- What tone of voice is most appropriate for the subject matter of your story? What mood do you want to convey?
- What points in the narrative require emphasis? At such points, should you pause, change your tone, or inflect the words in some way (e.g., saying a word with a rising tone that indicates surprise or shock)?
- What pace of your narration feels appropriate for your subject matter? Should you slow down or speed up?

## Making Transitions

Most software programs for digital storytelling allow for various kinds of transitions from one slide or screen to the next (see Focus: "Software for Digital Storytelling" on page 588.). For example, you can dissolve one image into the next one, fade to black and then have the next image fade slowly into view, or cut abruptly from one image to the next. You can also use more dynamic transitions in which images rotate, wipe from left to right or top to bottom across the screen, or dissolve into specific patterns. It can be fun to experiment with transitions in this way, but transitions and other special effects can be distracting to viewers if they are overused or inappropriate for the subject matter. Like other components of effective digital storytelling, transitions should be used to reinforce ideas, emphasize a point, and help convey the story clearly to the audience.

When selecting transitions in your digital story, anticipate how each transition will help your audience appreciate your experience. Transitions should be engaging but not distracting. Ultimately, the goal is to take advantage of the technical capabilities of the software program you are using, not to show them off. In general, changing the style of transition too often can detract from your digital story. In this case, the rule of thumb often is less is more.

# Reading Digital Stories

The two stories included in this section illustrate the different ways in which writers can take advantage of the capabilities of digital media to convey their experiences to an audience. One of these digital stories is a personal narrative in which the writer explores an important experience. Such personal stories are common in digital storytelling, and this selection will help you understand why. In the other selection, the writer tells the stories of others, using digital media in a way that is typical of documentary filmmaking. Both of these digital stories exhibit the features of effective storytelling. As you read, pay attention to how each writer uses images and other multimedia components in combination with the narration to tell the story in a way that explores important themes. Consider these questions:

| A story that matters | • What is the main point of the story?<br>• What is the significance of the experience the author shares in the story?<br>• What makes the story relevant to the intended audience?<br>• What themes does the author explore in the story? |
|---|---|
| Images and sound | • What kinds of images are included?<br>• How do these images contribute to the story?<br>• How is sound incorporated into the story? How does sound enhance or detract from the main point of the story?<br>• How effectively does the voice-over narration convey the experience? |
| Design | • What design features does the author use?<br>• To what extent do these design features contribute to the story and help convey the main themes?<br>• In what ways do these design features enhance or detract from your experience viewing the story? |

## MindTap®
Read these digital storytelling examples and take notes online.

## Mountain of Stories
### by Nazbah Tom

*In this selection, college student Nazbah Tom tells the story of coming out to her parents. Tom's sexual orientation creates an obstacle between her and her family that she must find a way to overcome, but her decision to come out to them also reveals the power of love and teaches her an important lesson about acceptance. In this sense, her story explores themes that go beyond the challenges of confronting difference, whether that difference involves sexual identity or something else. Tom's story also explores other elements of identity. She is Navajo, and she draws on that sense of identity to help her accept other aspects of her identity. As you'll see, she incorporates into her story images of Mount Hesperus, a sacred place in Navajo culture, and even as she identifies herself as different from her family, their common identity as Navajo binds them together. In this regard, Tom learns something deeply important about her cultural heritage and her connection to her ancestral homeland.*

*In technical terms, Tom's story is relatively simple but exhibits expert use of multimedia components to make her story vivid and bring her themes into relief for her audience. You'll notice, too, that her narrative is spare, and she relies heavily on carefully selected photographs to do much of the storytelling, especially in the final frames. Nazbah Tom's digital story was published on the website of the Center for Digital Storytelling in 2012.*

*(Continued)*

18

## Talking About This Reading

**Kim Suyoun (student):** I couldn't pick out the main ideas from the less important ones because there wasn't enough background information about the author.

**Bob Yagelski:** Kim, in any narrative, determining how much background information to provide is one of the writer's biggest challenges. That challenge might be even bigger in composing a digital story because of the characteristics of the medium that are discussed in this chapter (see especially pp. 600–606). Because so much information can be conveyed through sound and visual elements, the writer has to be careful not to try to squeeze too much material into the story. In this case, though, perhaps the writer did not include sufficient background information for you to fully engage with her story.

Nazbah Tom

[traditional Native American music plays softly in the background.]

MARTIN GRAY/National Geographic Creative

Narrator: As I write my coming out letter to my mother, I look out from the wonder of my dorm room and see Mount Hesperus. I ask the mountain for strength to send this story. I send the letter.

Narrator: Three months go by without a word from my mother.

Narrator: An elder tells me, "Give your mother the same amount of time you gave yourself to accept who you are." . . .

Source: Tom, Nazbah. "Mountain of Stories." *YouTube*, 14 June 2012, youtu.be/ j_QNVfNXEgY.

1. What elements of conventional narrative does Tom use in telling her story digitally? To what extent do these elements help make her story more (or less) effective? (In answering this question, refer to the discussions of the elements of effective storytelling in Chapters 15 and 16.)

2. What important information about Tom and her family is communicated through the images in this story? How effective did you find Tom's selection of images? Explain, citing specific sections of the story to support your answer?

3. What do you think Tom's use of music contributes to this story? What important themes does the music reinforce?

## Common Ground
### by Scott Strazzante

*In this digital story, Scott Strazzante examines the impact of suburban sprawl on one family farm in Illinois, which is sold and then demolished to make room for a suburban housing development. Strazzante's story focuses on the experiences of two families, one of them the farmers who lost their farm, the other a young family who realizes their dream of owning their own home. Through these stories, Strazzante reveals the complexity of land development and the ways in which one person's loss is another's gain. His story invites viewers to confront difficult questions about how best to use the land.*

*"Common Ground" displays the full range of multimedia capabilities available to writers of digital stories. Strazzante uses photographs, subtitles, and music as well as video clips to tell the interconnected stories of these two families. His digital story is characterized by lengthy segments in which there is no voice-over narration. Notice, too, that Strazzante himself does not narrate this story. Instead, he uses the recorded voices of the two families to tell their stories and share their feelings about their situations. "Common Ground" was published by MediaStorm in 2008.*

. . . . . . . . . . . . . . . . . . . . . . . . . . . . . . . . . . . . . . . . .

### Talking About This Reading

**Julian Perez (student):** I found this reading to be emotional. The pictures made the reading more intense. Seeing the situation from the perspective of the families made the reading more interesting and real.

**Bob Yagelski:** Julian, your comment underscores the potential impact of the visual and audio elements of a digital story on the audience. As you suggest, Strazzante's digital story is powerful in part because the images he chose and the voices of the people in his story not only draw us into the narrative but also foster empathy for them. As a result, we feel deeply connected to the families we meet in the story. Your reaction to this story helps us appreciate this power of images and sounds to create certain effects on an audience.

. . . . . . . . . . . . . . . . . . . . . . . . . . . . . . . . . . . . . . . . .

COMMON
GROUND

SCOTT STRAZZANTE

Scott Strazzante

[piano music]

Scott Strazzante

Scott Strazzante

18

Voice of Jean Cagwin: We're watching all the buildings going down.

Voice of Jean Cagwin: The house was the last thing to go down. Didn't take long.

Scott Strazzante

Voice of Jean Cagwin: It was quite an emotional thing for Harold, because he lived there all his life.

Scott Strazzante

Voice of Jean Cagwin: But we knew it was time.

Scott Strazzante

Voice of Jean Cagwin: We just got in the truck and didn't look back . . .

Source: Strazzante, Scott. "Common Ground." *MediaStorm*, 29 July 2008, mediastorm.com/publication/common-ground.

18

# Creating Digital Stories

Although digital technology can be used to tell any story, digital stories can be especially effective when a writer wants to share an experience in which sound or the appearance of an object or a place are integral to the story—such as the mountain in Nazbah Tom's story (see page 593) or the sweaters in Christi Clancy's story (page 575). For example, maybe you had an important experience that involved playing a musical instrument, visiting another part of the world, or volunteering for a community organization or political campaign. This section will guide you through the process of creating a digital story to convey that experience to your readers.

Read this section together with Chapter 3. Each step described here corresponds with a step in Chapter 3. As you work through this section, keep in mind that the principles of effective narrative described in Chapter 15 apply to digital stories. Also, if your digital story is a personal narrative, review the advice on Chapter 16; if your digital story is an informative narrative, review Chapter 17. Finally, remember the three main characteristics of digital stories:

- Tell a story that matters.
- Use images, sound, and other multimedia elements to convey ideas and information.
- Employ design elements to enhance your story.

## Step 1   Identify a topic.

Like any effective narrative, a digital story tells a story that matters. Your story should be important to you but also relevant to your audience. To identify a topic for your digital story, consider

- an **experience** that was significant to you in some way;
- an **issue** that connects to your experience in some way;
- an **activity** or **subject** about which you are knowledgeable or have direct experience.

Explore each of these categories:

| A significant experience | An issue that interests you | Something you know about |
|---|---|---|
| • A milestone (e.g., graduating from high school, getting married)<br><br>• An accomplishment (e.g., winning a scholarship, earning academic honors, running in a marathon)<br><br>• A difficult challenge (e.g., moving away from home, losing a loved one, completing basic training in the military)<br><br>• A mistake (e.g., violating a rule or a law, cheating, misjudging someone)<br><br>• An activity (e.g., singing, hunting, rock climbing, running, rapping, gaming)<br><br>• A transition or turning point (e.g., going to college, moving abroad, joining the military, coming of age)<br><br>• A decision (e.g., whether to take or quit a job, choosing a college, whether to tell someone a difficult truth) | • A controversy (e.g., gun control: you might be involved in an effort to oppose arming your campus police force; a relative might have law enforcement experience; you might be a hunter)<br><br>• An activity (e.g., gaming: you might be an avid gamer who is concerned about efforts to restrict the distribution of some violent video games; you might have won a gaming competition)<br><br>• Advocacy (e.g., privacy: you might have concerns about how your private data is being used online without your knowledge or permission; you might have been the victim of identity theft)<br><br>• A trend (e.g., social media: you might be interested in the growth of a specific kind of social media that you regularly use; you might have had an unusual experience using social media) | • A hobby (e.g., playing drums, photography, gardening)<br><br>• A challenge that many others have faced (e.g., divorce, losing a job, struggling in school<br><br>• An experience that raised questions for you (e.g., an unfamiliar medical condition that someone you know developed, a cheating scandal at your school)<br><br>• A topic you have expertise in (e.g., politics, sports, skateboarding)<br><br>• An important decision that others might share (e.g., going to college, joining the Peace Corps) |

18

- **Make a brief list of possible topics in each category.** For each item, jot down a few sentences about the topic, describing the nature of your experience, what you already know about the topic, and what interests you about it. For example, if you had an enlightening experience on a church-sponsored trip, briefly describe the trip and what made it important to you. If you are a photographer, perhaps you had a specific experience in which photography helped you gain insight into yourself or someone else.

- **Select the topic that seems most promising to you.** Review your lists and select the experience that you would most like to share in a digital story. Remember that your digital story is likely to be more engaging for an audience if it tells a story that has significance for you.

**Step #1 in Chapter 3** will help you further develop your topic.

## Step 2  Place your topic in rhetorical context.

Many digital stories have wide appeal and are not necessarily intended for a specific audience. A story about struggling with one's identity, such as Nazbah Tom's, is likely to interest many people. At the same time, a story that focuses on a more specialized topic—such as competing in a motocross championship—might best be directed at a more specialized audience that shares an interest in that topic. Whatever the case, it is important that you have a sense of an audience for your digital story and why your story might interest that audience. So at this point your task is twofold:

a. Identify a potential audience for your digital story.

b. Consider why your story would interest that audience.

Let's imagine that you want to tell a story about learning how to play banjo from your grandfather. From a young age you spent many hours with him as he helped you learn the intricacies of the instrument and perfect your technique as a banjo player. Eventually you developed into a capable musician, and in your grandfather's later years you played with him at several public events, such as county fairs. During that time, you learned some things about your grandfather and your family's history that you had not known before. In the process, you came to understand your grandfather—and yourself—more deeply. So your story not only involves the challenge of learning to play banjo but also explores your relationship with your family and your own sense of identity. Now consider who might be interested in your story:

| Who might be interested in this topic? | • Banjo players<br>• Musicians<br>• People interested in music<br>• Readers interested in matters of family history<br>• Anyone interested in stories of coming of age |
|---|---|
| Why would they be interested in this topic? | • Musicians might be curious about how you learned to play and the role of the banjo in your life.<br>• Your story has general appeal because of its focus on family history and personal identity. |

Such a topic has broad appeal and would likely interest a potentially wide audience, including people who are not musicians. Notice that what is potentially engaging for an audience are the themes you might explore through your story. In other words, what makes the experience important to you—not only developing expertise as a musician but also gaining a deeper appreciation for your grandfather and yourself—is what will make it relevant for your audience. In this sense, the point of your story—not necessarily the specific subject matter—is what really matters.

With this in mind, explore your topic using these two questions to identify a potential audience and the themes that might engage that audience. Then complete Step #2 in Chapter 3 to explore your rhetorical context more fully.

## Step 3 Select a medium.

You have already selected the medium for your story, but you should consider how your finished digital story will reach your intended audience. If you are completing a course assignment, your instructor will likely have a way for you to submit and distribute your digital story. If so, follow those instructions. However, if you have no such guidelines, consider the possible forums for distributing your digital story:

- **YouTube.** This site is perhaps the most common vehicle by which people distribute videos, including digital stories. Many organizations now have their own YouTube channels (e.g., The Center for Digital Storytelling), and depending upon the nature of your story, one of those channels might be an appropriate venue for your story.

- **Social media.** Many people post videos and other multimedia files on Facebook, Instagram, and similar social media sites. You might consider distributing your digital story on such a site, either through your own page or by posting it to the page of an appropriate organization. For example, our hypothetical story about learning to play the banjo might be posted to the social media site of a relevant organization such as the American Roots Music Association.

- **Organization websites.** Many organizations include member forums for posting comments, stories, and multimedia files. Consider whether an organization focused on issues or subjects related to the topic of your story might be a good place to post it.

Although you have already selected the medium for your project, Step #3 in Chapter 3 will provide additional help as you consider an appropriate venue for your digital story.

## Step 4 Identify the main point of your digital story.

What do you want your digital story to say to your audience? That's the question you have to address at this point.

**Begin by stating as clearly as you can the main ideas you want your audience to take away from your story.** Try to capture these ideas in a brief paragraph. For example, in our hypothetical story about learning to play banjo from your grandfather, you might explore several themes involving relationships, family, and identity; you are also telling a story about meeting a challenge and dedicating yourself to developing a skill—that is, about perseverance and commitment. You might articulate these main ideas as follows:

*This is a story about the importance of a precious family relationship in shaping my sense of identity and teaching me important lessons about dedication and persistence in meeting challenges, whether those challenges have to do with learning a skill such as playing the banjo or overcoming difficulties in life. It is also a story about confronting some unpleasant realities about my own family but ultimately coming to appreciate the importance of my family, especially my grandfather, in my life.*

This statement can serve as your Guiding Thesis Statement and help you keep your story focused. However, be careful to avoid oversimplifying your experience by trying to boil it down into a brief statement. Part of the purpose of narrative is to explore the complexity of an experience and make sense of it. The meaning of your story should reflect the richness of your experience and complexity of the themes you are exploring. So keep these caveats in mind:

- **Your Guiding Thesis Statement should guide but not restrict you.** A Guiding Thesis Statement expresses the main ideas of your story, but you are still exploring your experience. Remain open to possibilities, keeping in mind that you are composing a digital narrative in part to understand your experience better. In writing about learning banjo from your grandfather, for example, you might discover feelings about your relationship that you weren't entirely aware of. You might remember parts of the experience that were important but not entirely positive. Exploring those aspects of the experience might shape your perspective and thus affect the meaning you convey to your audience. In short, your main ideas could change as you develop your story. Be alert to such possibilities, even if they take you in a different direction from the one reflected in your Guiding Thesis Statement.

- **Your Guiding Thesis Statement might change.** The more you explore your topic, the more you will learn about it, which might lead you to change the main point of your story. If so, adjust your Guiding Thesis Statement accordingly. Revise it as often as you need to as you are exploring your experience and developing your story.

Following this advice will help you develop the main ideas you want to convey through your story. Step #4 in Chapter 3 provides additional help for developing your Guiding Thesis Statement.

## Step 5  Support your main point.

Effective narratives include descriptions of events, background information, and explanations of important ideas or occurrences that help the audience understand the story. Everything you include in your digital story—images and sound as well as text—should somehow contribute to telling your story effectively and conveying your main ideas to your audience. The task now is to make sure you have explored your experience sufficiently to develop the material you need to tell your story effectively. Doing so involves **three main steps:**

   a. Identify what should be included in your digital story.

   b. Gather additional information.

   c. Develop multimedia components.

## Identify What Should be Included in Your Digital Story

Review your Discovery Draft (see Chapter 3), notes, and other materials to determine whether you have included the essential information, scenes, events, and moments to convey your experience sufficiently to your readers. Address these questions:

- **What specific events or moments must be included for a reader to understand what happened?** For example, in your hypothetical essay about learning to play banjo from your grandfather, you will likely include information about him, his banjo playing, and your own experience learning to play. You will also want to include relevant background information about your family as well as about your relationship with your grandfather. You might have experienced a particular challenge in developing the skill of banjo playing, or perhaps a specific event, such as a divorce or illness, affected your relationship in some way. Using your Guiding Thesis Statement to remind you of the main ideas you want to explore in your story, make note of any important and relevant scenes, events, and related information. The goal is to identify anything about your experience that is essential for readers to know.

- **What background information will readers need to understand the experience described in the story?** What else will your readers need to know that isn't directly a part of the experience you are describing? For example, will you need to explain anything about the banjo or the skill of playing it that is necessary for readers to understand your story? Consider anything that is essential for readers to know in order to understand the experience you are sharing.

At this stage, more is better, so if you're not sure about something, include it. Don't worry if your story seems to getting too long. You can eliminate unnecessary material when you revise.

## Gather Additional Information

Review your materials to determine whether you need additional information. Depending upon your topic, you might have to do some research. For example, in your hypothetical essay about learning to play the banjo, you might want to look into the history of the instrument because that was something your grandfather emphasized in learning to play. Or you might have to find out more about your grandfather's life—for example, what he did for a living as a young adult, how he learned to play banjo, and so on. Use appropriate resources to gather necessary information. (Chapters 21 and 22 provide advice for identifying and evaluating source material.)

18

## Develop Multimedia Components

By now you have probably identified some photographs, videos, or related materials that are relevant to your story. You might also have music or other sound effects in mind. At this point, you should focus on finding the images and sound to help you tell the story of your experience. In many cases, that means looking through old family photo albums, searching computer files for digital images, or reviewing videos you or others might have made. You can also search online for images you might need. (See Focus: "Intellectual Property Considerations" on page 590.) Some computer programs for digital storytelling include archives of images and sounds that you can use for your story. You might decide to make new photos, videos, or sound recordings for your digital story. The goal is to gather still and video images as well as music or sound clips that will enable you to tell your story effectively.

Again, more is better. If you find several photos of your grandfather as a young man, for example, but you only need one, keep all of them until you decide which one works best in your story. Try to find images for each of the main events, moments, or aspects of your experience that you identified early in this step.

You should be now ready to complete a draft of the text of your digital story. If so, write a draft of your story in textual form. You will use this draft as the basis for your storyboard in Step #6. Write as complete a draft as possible, following these guidelines:

- **Tell the whole story.** Include in your draft everything that is relevant. Incorporate all the material you have developed for this step. If something feels unnecessary, leave it out, but if you're not sure, keep it for now.

- **Don't worry about length.** You can condense and eliminate unnecessary materials during Step #8.

- **Write the story, not the voice-over narration.** The story draft is not necessarily the same thing as the voice-over narration. Eventually, you can use your draft as the basis for the narration, but for now, just tell your story as completely as you can.

- **Don't focus yet on images and sound.** As you write your draft, consider places for appropriate images or sound, but don't focus on those components yet. Rather, focus on telling your story completely and clearly. You will incorporate images and sound in the next step. At the same time, if an image seems especially important at a particular point in your draft, make a note about it at that point in the draft.

Step #5 in Chapter 3 provides additional advice to help you develop your project. Some writers prefer to "draft" their digital stories as a storyboard rather than writing a text of the story. If that approach works better for you, move to Step #6 before writing a draft of your story.

## Step 6 Organize your digital story.

Organizing your digital story involves **two main steps:**

- organizing the narrative itself
- developing a storyboard

Here we will concentrate on developing a storyboard. For guidance in organizing your story, see "Structuring a Narrative" in Chapter 15. (If your digital story does not focus on a specific personal experience but is an informative narrative, see Step #6: "Organize your informative project" in Chapter 17.)

Most digital stories tend to be organized chronologically. The digital stories in the previous section of this chapter, for example, are organized chronologically, though "Common Ground" does not always follow a strict chronological order. However, you can tell your story in any order that you think will make it engaging and accessible for your audience. If you have already written a draft of your story, review the draft to make sure you have organized your story in a way that conveys your experience clearly. (Step #6 in Chapter 3 can help you do so.)

Once you have decided how to organize your narrative, develop a storyboard. As noted earlier in this chapter, a storyboard is a kind of outline of your digital story that includes information about images, sound, special effects, and the voice-over narration (see pages 586–588):

- **If you have already written a draft of your story**, use your draft as the basis for an outline of your digital story.
- **If you have not written a draft of your story**, develop a detailed outline of your story.

Then follow this process to create a storyboard:

| Create an outline | Convert outline to single frames | Add images, sound, and narration |
|---|---|---|
| • Make a detailed outline of your story.<br>• Include each important scene, moment, or event.<br>• Include background information. | • Create a single frame for each heading and subheading in your outline. | • For each frame, include an image.<br>• Indicate background sound (for entire story or individual frames).<br>• Write voice-over narration for each frame. |

Once you have mapped out your digital story in a completed storyboard, you can add special effects: zooming, transitions, subtitles, colors.

For example, here's what the process might look like in our hypothetical digital story about learning to play banjo from your grandfather. Remember that your story explores themes of family identity, relationships, and important life lessons as well as developing the skill of playing a banjo.

**18**

The first few headings of your detailed outline might include the following:

I. Introduction

    A. Anecdote about playing banjo with your grandfather at a local fair

    B. Statement of the importance of your relationship with your grandfather

    C. Hint that learning to play banjo with your grandfather included difficult life lessons

II. Background about You and Your Family

    A. Basic information about your immediate family

        1. Family members

        2. Where you live

        3. Information about you

    B. Background information about your grandfather

        1. Biographical information about him (when and where he was born, where he lived, his working life)

        2. Information about his banjo playing

III. Learning to Play Banjo

    A. How you began learning banjo from your grandfather

    B. Difficulties learning to play

        1. Anecdote about wanting to quit

        2. Anecdote about learning difficult scales

Now convert your outline to single frames. Here's what the first headings in Part I of the outline might look like as frames:

Frame #1: Anecdote about playing banjo with your grandfather at a local fair.

Frame #2: Statement of the importance of your relationship with your grandfather.

Frame #3: Hint that learning to play banjo with your grandfather included difficult life lessons.

Continue in this fashion until you have a separate frame for each subheading.

**Finally, add images, sound, and narration.** Using your word processing program or digital storytelling software, add information about images, sound, and the voice-over narration for each frame:

| Frame #1 | Frame #2 | Frame #3 |
|---|---|---|
| Image: Photo of you and your grandfather playing banjo at a fair<br><br>Audio: banjo music (maybe a song you both liked)<br><br>Narration: "A few years ago I had the great joy of playing banjo with my grandfather in front of family, friends, and neighbors at a county fair. It was one of the last times we would play together, and it was a long journey to get there." | Image: Earlier photo of your grandfather showing you how to play a banjo<br><br>Audio: slower banjo music<br><br>Narration: "My grandfather taught me to play banjo when I was just seven years old. He taught me how to master the instrument, how to work hard to perfect my technique. He gave me the gift of his love for the banjo." | Image: same as frame #2<br><br>Audio: same as frame #2<br><br>Narration: "But I learned a lot more than how to play the banjo from my grandfather. I learned many important life lessons. And not all of them were happy ones." |

Proceed in this way to the end of your story. Once you have mapped out the story, add special effects to complete the storyboard. For example, for Frame #3 in this example, you might zoom in your grandfather's face to emphasize the point in the narration that you learned a lot of lessons from your grandfather.

As you develop your story board, you will likely discover a need to add or eliminate material and make adjustments so that your narration works together with the images and sound to tell your story. Don't hesitate to make such adjustments. It's part of the process of developing and refining your digital story. However, at this point don't worry too much about length. You will revise your digital story in Step #8, at which point you can condense it if necessary. Step #6 in Chapter 3 provides additional guidance for organizing your project.

Once you have completed your storyboard, you can begin creating your digital story using the software you have selected (see Focus: "Software for Digital Storytelling").

**18**

## Step 7 | Get feedback.

Show your digital story to a few trusted friends or classmates for their feedback. Ask them to focus on the key features of effective digital storytelling:

| A story that matters | • How effectively does your digital story convey the experience you are telling about?<br>• Does the story communicate a main idea or point that is relevant to your audience? To what extent does it explore your main themes?<br>• Is the story complete? Is it too long or too short? |
|---|---|
| Images and sound | • How do the images you've selected contribute to the story? Are they sufficient? Are there too many?<br>• Does the sound enhance or detract from the main point of this story?<br>• How effectively does the narration combine with the images to tell your story? |
| Design | • What design features have you incorporated into the story? How do they contribute to the story?<br>• In what ways do these design features enhance or detract from your experience of this story?<br>• Should any special effects be added or eliminated to enhance the quality of the story? |

Step # 7 in Chapter 3 provides advice for analyzing your feedback and deciding on possible changes to make to your digital story.

## Step 8 | Revise.

Revising your digital story draft involves addressing **two main concerns:**

| Narrative | How well have you told your story? | Review your narrative. |
|---|---|---|
| Technical | How effectively have you used multimedia? | Evaluate your use of images, sound, and effects. |

### Narrative: Review Your Story Using the First Set of Questions from Step #7

- How effectively does your story convey the experience you are telling about?
- Does the story convey a main idea or point that is relevant to your audience?
- Does the story sufficiently explore important themes?
- Is the story complete? Is it too long or too short?
- Is the story well organized? Are the frames in the proper order to tell the story clearly?

In addition, address the following considerations:

- **Review the feedback** you received to determine whether any sections of the story are confusing, incomplete, or unnecessary.
- **Make sure every frame contributes** important information or ideas.
- **Evaluate your opening frames** to make sure they engage your audience and introduce your story effectively.
- **Review your final frame** to see whether it reinforces your main ideas and leaves an impression on your audience.

### Technical: Review Your Story Using the Second and Third Set of Questions in Step #7

- **Images:** How do the photographs, video, and other images you've selected contribute to the story? Do they effectively convey the information, ideas, and feelings you intend? Are there unnecessary images that should be eliminated? Can any images be replaced with more effective ones?
- **Sound:** How does the background music enhance the story and reinforce important information, ideas, or emotions? Does it establish an appropriate mood for your story? Do the sound effects fit the story and help move it along?
- **Narration:** How effectively does the voice-over narration combine with the images to tell your story? Is the narration too wordy or too sparse? Is it clear? Is the tone of the narrator's voice appropriate for the story in each frame?
- **Design:** Are the transitions effective? Do they distract the viewer? If you have used subtitles, are they clear? Are they necessary? If you haven't, do you need them in any frames? Do any background colors or patterns you've used enhance or detract from the story?

**Review each frame** using these questions.

**Step #8 in Chapter 3** provides additional guidance for revising your digital story.

18

## Step 9 Refine your voice.

"Voice" can refer to two separate but related aspects of a digital story:

- the voice of the narrative itself (as explained in Chapter 2)
- the tone of the voice-over narration

Unlike voice in a conventional print narrative, which is conveyed exclusively through the words of the narrative, voice in a digital story is a combination of the narrative text, the images, and the sound as well as the tone of the voice-over narration. For example, the voice in Nazbah Tom's digital story included in this chapter (page 593) is created not only by the words of her narrative text but also by the photos she selected of Mount Hesperus, her family, and her partner. Scott Strazzante's digital story (page 575) has no voice-over narration. Instead, it includes the voices of the two families whose stories he tells as well as the piano and guitar music that plays while photographs are displayed. In that case, the music he selects helps establish the "voice" of the digital story.

To help determine whether your voice is appropriate for your project, **consider these questions:**

| Text | • To what extent does the text of your voice-over narration fit your story?<br>• Are your word choices appropriate for the subject of each frame?<br>• What makes the text "sound" right for the experience you are conveying? |
| --- | --- |
| Images | • How do the photographs, video clips, or other images help convey the right tone for your story?<br>• Are the images consistent in contributing to the voice of your digital story?<br>• Are any images out of place? |
| Sound | • How does the background music help create an appropriate mood for your story?<br>• Are the sound effects consistent with the voice you want to create?<br>• How do the pace and tone of the voice-over narration contribute to the overall impact of the story? |
| Design | • How do the special effects (zooming, transition, etc.) help create an appropriate voice for your story?<br>• Are the background colors and patterns consistent with the voice? |

Complete Step #9 in Chapter 3 for additional guidance in refining your voice.

## Step 10. Edit.

Complete Step #10 in Chapter 3.

---

**WRITING PROJECTS** | **DIGITAL STORIES**

1. Identify an experience you have had that has shaped you into the person you are today. Create a digital story in which you share that experience.

2. Take a personal narrative or an informative essay you have written and turn it into a digital story.

3. Identify a general issue of interest to you. It could be an ongoing controversy, a subject of current interest, or something that you have always been curious about. Create a digital story in which you explore that issue. Incorporate any experiences you have had that are relevant to your topic.

4. Create a digital story that focuses on an important person in your life. Focus your story on a particular aspect or event involving that person (as Christi Clancy does in her digital story about her mother, which appears in this chapter).

---

MindTap®

Request help with these Writing Projects and get feedback from a tutor. If required, participate in peer review, submit your paper for a grade, and view instructor comments online.

18

### In this chapter, you will learn to

1. Understand academic writing as sustained, specialized conversation about relevant topics.

2. Describe the four key components of academic conversations.

3. Apply a strategy for reading specialized academic texts.

4. Explain the purposes of summary, paraphrase, and synthesis in academic writing.

5. Understand summary-response writing as a specialized form of academic writing.

6. Write a summary-response essay.

## MindTap®
Understand the goals of the chapter and complete a warm-up activity.

# Working with Ideas and Information 19

**MANY STUDENTS THINK** of effective writing as a matter of crafting good sentences or using ornate language. My own students sometimes complain to me that they can't write well because they don't have big vocabularies. These complaints are understandable. Writing can be challenging, especially when the subject is unfamiliar to the writer. Most students genuinely want to learn to write well, and they worry about matters like word choice and punctuation. But when I hear such complaints, I always respond in the same way: Writing is ultimately about ideas. It is true that well-crafted sentences can make a piece of writing more effective, correct grammar can mean clearer prose, and having a good vocabulary can give a writer more options for choosing the right word. But those skills alone don't lead to effective writing. Without something relevant to say (Core Concept #4), a writer's well-crafted sentences, correct grammar, and impressive vocabulary mean little. And having something relevant to say means working with ideas and information.

This chapter is intended to help you manage complex material as both a writer and a reader. Because the subject matter in academic assignments can be challenging and unfamiliar, completing a writing assignment often requires learning to identify, explore, understand, and communicate complex ideas and information, often from specialized sources, in ways that follow special conventions, which sometimes vary from one academic discipline to another. To write effectively in academic contexts, then, students must be able to

- Read complex and often unfamiliar texts.
- Summarize and paraphrase those texts.
- Synthesize ideas and information from various sources.

These skills are essential components of the inquiry that you will engage in as a college student. Learning to apply them will enable you to participate in the ongoing academic conversations about important questions, problems, and ideas that you will encounter in your courses throughout the college curriculum. In turn, participating in those conversations can result in a better understanding of the subjects you are studying and improve your ability as a writer.

# Understanding Academic Writing as Conversation

I sometimes conduct workshops to help college professors learn to work more effectively with student writers in their classes. One of my favorite activities in these workshops is to ask the professors to summarize a short text on an unfamiliar subject, such as this excerpt from a technical guide to sailing:

> No matter how good the sails look, no boat sails well when they are pulling her over at extreme angles of heel. When a boat heels excessively, she slows down, develops severe weather helm, and wallows sluggishly through the water. She must be brought back upright by depowering the sails. If powering in light and moderate winds means to make the sails full at narrow angles of attack, depowering in winds stronger than about 15 knots (apparent) means to flatten sails and trim them wider. . . .
>
> The main sheet works quickest. When a gust hits and the boat begins to flop over, quickly ease out one or more feet of main sheet and keep it eased until she rights herself. Either the helmsman or a crew can cast the sheet off—the former when he first feels the drastic weather helm through the tiller or the wheel, the latter when he sees the helmsman begin to fight the helm. Even though the wildly luffing mainsail may seem to be wasted, the boat is sailing better because she's sailing on her bottom.
>
> The jib sheet may also be eased quickly in fresh winds to spill air from the jib. The jib sheet should be moved outboard in fresh and strong winds to decrease side force and increase forward force. It may also be moved aft to increase the amount of twist in the upper part of the sail, effectively spilling wind up high, where it exerts the greatest heeling leverage over the hull.

Source: Rousmaniere, John. *The Annapolis Book of Seamanship*. Revised edition, Simon and Schuster, 1989, p. 82.

If you have trouble understanding this text, you're not alone. So do the professors in my workshops. Because most of them are not sailors, they usually find this text confusing and difficult to understand. Not surprisingly, they have trouble summarizing it. As experienced academic writers, they are used to summarizing difficult texts, but summarizing this excerpt about the technical aspects of sailing stumps them. That's because despite their expertise in their academic fields, they are unfamiliar with specialized sailing jargon (such as *jib* and *sheet*), and they don't understand the concepts (such as *heeling force* and *weather helm*) and procedures of sailing (such as *easing a sheet* or *trimming a sail*).

If this excerpt from a sailing manual frustrates the professors in my workshops, it can also help them appreciate the challenges that their own students face when they are asked to write academic essays on subjects that are unfamiliar to them. Like the professors in the workshop who are unfamiliar with the language and concepts of sailing, most college students are newcomers to the academic subjects they study in their courses. Students in an introductory economics class, for example, might have a basic understanding of economics, but they are likely to have little knowledge of the specialized concepts and terminology that economists use and the sophisticated way that economists think about their subject. Yet those students will probably be asked to write in ways that are similar to economists. In other words, the students will be expected to participate like experts in the conversations that economists are always having about their subject—even though the students are novices and unfamiliar with those conversations.

As a college student, you might sometimes feel frustrated (like the professors in my workshop) as you try to make sense of assigned readings or meet the professor's expectations for writing. That's understandable. You are just beginning to learn about the subject itself and the rules for writing in that discipline. If you walk into a party or a meeting that is already under way and find people engaged in intense conversation, you have to listen for a while—and maybe ask some strategic questions—in order to figure out what is going on before you can join in. Much academic writing is like that.

Learning to write effectively in college, then, is partly a matter of understanding that **most academic writing is like taking part in a conversation**. To be part of that conversation, you must develop a sense of what is going on in each discipline you study—and in academic discourse in general. In other words, you have to acquire some relevant knowledge and develop the language necessary for participating in the conversations about important subjects in that academic field. You also have to learn *how* to participate in conversations about important subjects in that discipline—that is, you have to become familiar with the conventions of writing in that discipline.

Writing effectively in college requires understanding **four key components of academic conversations:**

- **Important concepts or ideas.** Academic fields are organized around certain kinds of questions and specific bodies of knowledge. Biologists, for example, examine questions about living organisms and how they function; to address these questions, they rely on knowledge developed through research and they draw on accepted theories, such as natural selection, to help them understand that research. Similarly, psychologists explore questions about how humans think and interact with each other, drawing on various kinds of studies and theories, such as behaviorism, to understand human cognition and social interactions. To write effectively in biology or psychology requires understanding the nature of the questions that scholars in those disciplines examine and becoming familiar with key concepts in those fields. In part, students gain this understanding simply by doing the assigned work in a course and learning the subject matter. But students are unlikely to be familiar with some of the less common concepts or ideas in academic fields if they encounter them in course readings or source material. For example, if you're reading a scholarly article in psychology, you might recognize references to *behaviorism* but not to *operant conditioning*, an important concept in behaviorism. Without a basic understanding of operant conditioning, you might find it difficult to follow the discussion in the article.

- **Specialized terminology.** Every academic discipline has specialized words or phrases, related to key concepts in that discipline, that scholars use in their writing. In fact, most professions do, too. Like sailors, people in just about any profession or activity you can think of—engineers, lawyers, accountants, electricians, nurses—use a specialized language to do their work. Sometimes this specialized language is criticized as jargon, but it is essential to the work scholars do in their disciplines. Just as knowing specialized terms on a sailboat allows sailors to operate the boat safely and effectively, knowing the terminology in an academic

19

field is often necessary for understanding scholarly texts in that field and can strengthen your ability to write effectively about relevant topics in that field.

- **Conventions.** Writing effectively in an academic discipline requires knowing not only what to say but *how* to say it. That means becoming familiar with some of the basic conventions of writing in that discipline. Conventions are common practices, such as how to introduce key ideas, when and how to cite sources, what is appropriate style, and how to organize a text. Although some basic conventions are followed in most kinds of academic writing, academic disciplines often have more specialized conventions that writers are expected to follow. For example, in many social science disciplines, such as psychology and economics, writers typically don't use direct quotations when citing a source; by contrast, in many fields in the humanities, such as history or English, direct quotations from sources are common and expected. In some disciplines, writers never use the first person, whereas in others the use of first person is common. As a student who is learning new disciplines, it is essential for you to be aware that these different conventions exist and to become familiar enough with the basic conventions to be able to understand the reading and writing you are asked to do in your classes.

- **Assumptions about the audience.** Because academic writers usually write for other experts in their disciplines, they can assume that their intended audience is familiar with the key concepts, specialized language, and conventions of the discipline. They also assume their audience shares their interest in relevant topics in that discipline. For example, anthropologists usually expect their readers to have an in-depth understanding of the complexities of culture and the main established theories for understanding how cultures develop and affect our lives. So they don't have to explain established concepts or theories, and they can assume that if they refer to an important study or figure in the field, their readers will not only recognize the reference but also understand its significance. As a newcomer to an academic field, you might not be part of the intended audience for specialized scholarly writing, which can make reading scholarly texts challenging. As a writer, part of your challenge is to determine what expectations you can reasonably make about your readers when it comes to the academic subject about which you're writing. For example, if you're writing an essay about ethical questions surrounding operant conditioning for a psychology class, you probably don't need to explain that concept, because you can assume your audience (your professor and other students in the psychology course) are familiar with it; however, if you're writing about the same topic for an introductory writing class, you will probably have to explain the concept and maybe even provide some history about it.

---

**EXERCISE 19A**   **UNDERSTANDING ACADEMIC CONVERSATIONS**

Here are the first three paragraphs of a scholarly article that was published in the *Journal of Experimental Social Psychology*. Read these paragraphs and answer the questions following them:

Individualism-collectivism is perhaps the most basic dimension of cultural variability identified in cross-cultural research. Concepts related to this dimension have been employed in several social science domains (cf. Triandis, McCusker, & Hui, 1990), and the individualism-collectivism dimension has come to be regarded as "central to an understanding of cultural values, of work values, of social systems, as well as in the studies of morality, the structure of constitutions, and cultural patterns" (Triandis, Brislin, & Hui, 1988). Several recent studies have suggested that individualism and collectivism are contrasting cultural syndromes that are associated with a broad pattern of differences in individuals' social perceptions and social behavior, including differences in the definition of self and its perceived relation to ingroups and outgroups (Markus & Kitayama, 1991), in the endorsement of values relevant to individual vs. group goals (Triandis et al., 1990), and in the pattern and style of social interactions (cf. Triandis, 1990).

However, little is known about the implications of these cultural differences for another social process that is fundamental to every culture: persuasion. Persuasive communications transmit and reflect the values of a culture. Persuasive messages are used to obtain the compliance that achieves the personal, political, and economic ends valued in the culture. Although social influence has always been a central arena of research in social psychology, little is understood about what differences exist in the types of persuasive appeals used in different cultures (see Burgoon, Dillard, Doran, & Miller, 1982; Glenn, Witmeyer, & Stevenson, 1977). Even less is known about the effectiveness of different appeal types in different cultures.

What types of persuasive appeals are prevalent in individualistic versus collectivistic cultures? And how do members of these different cultures differ in the extent to which they are persuaded by these appeals? This paper presents an exploration of these questions.

Source: Han, Sang-Pil, and Sharon Shavitt. "Persuasion and Culture: Advertising Appeals in Individualistic and Collectivistic Societies." *Journal of Experimental Social Psychology,* vol. 30, no. 4, July 1994, pp. 326–50.

1. Identify the key concepts or ideas discussed in this passage. (You can highlight them or make a list.)

2. What specialized terms or language do you see in this passage? Do you know what these terms mean? If not, to what extent does your lack of familiarity with these terms interfere with your understanding of the passage?

3. What conventions do these writers follow in this passage? For example, what conventions regarding writing style do they follow? How do they introduce and cite information or ideas from other sources?

4. What assumptions do you think these authors make about their audience? Who do you think their intended audience is? How do you know? Are you part of that audience? How do you know?

5. How well do you think you understand this passage? How much of your understanding of the passage is based on your knowledge of the topic and the academic discipline of social psychology? What do you think your experience with this passage suggests about participating in academic conversations as a college student?

**19**

# A Strategy for Reading Academic Texts

Academic writing assignments often require students to read various kinds of scholarly texts, which can be challenging to understand. Being able to make sense of difficult, specialized texts is an important part of engaging in the kind of inquiry that characterizes college-level study. Although it can also be frustrating when you struggle to understand course readings or scholarly sources you might find in your research, you can learn to make sense of even very complex, specialized scholarly materials. This section describes **a seven-step strategy for reading complex and unfamiliar texts:**

1. Skim to get the big picture.
2. Read the abstract, preface, or introduction.
3. Place the text in rhetorical context.
4. Identify key terms.
5. Use the structure of the text.
6. Review the bibliography.
7. Take notes.

This strategy will help you understand challenging texts even when you are unfamiliar with the subject matter. It is designed to help you read *scholarly* texts, which have certain features that others kinds of text, such as newspaper articles or blog posts, might not have. However, the principles that inform this strategy can be applied to reading *any* text. If a text you encounter does not have an abstract or bibliography (which most non-academic texts lack), simply skip that step in the process.

As you use this strategy, remember that reading a challenging text, like writing itself, is a process of inquiry. Just as effective writing might require numerous drafts, understanding a challenging text might require you to read it several times—or at least reread sections of it. Reading texts in this way is part of your effort to understand your subject matter more fully and, ultimately, to write more effectively.

## 1. Skim to Get the Big Picture

Before jumping into a text, especially one on an unfamiliar subject, try to get a sense of what you will encounter in that text. The best way to do so is to skim the entire text. If you are reading a scholarly article, read quickly through the abstract to get a general sense of the content of the article, page through the article to see the subheadings and main components of the piece, and check the bibliography to see what kinds of references the author cites. For a book, look at the table of contents, skim the preface and introduction, page through chapters that seem important, and browse the bibliography. Each of these strategies is discussed in detail below (see strategies #2, #5, and #6), but at this point the goal is simply to develop a sense of what the text is about and where you might encounter difficulties. Skimming helps you get oriented to the text so that you can anticipate what to expect.

# 2. Read the Abstract, Preface, or Introduction

Most articles in scholarly journals have short summaries, called *abstracts*, that usually appear after the title and name(s) of the author(s) but before the main text of the article. For books, the equivalent of an abstract is the *preface*, which is a short explanation of the book's subject and relevance, or the *introduction*, each of which are usually several pages long (though a preface is usually shorter than an introduction). Usually, an abstract of an article or the preface or introduction to a book will contain four important kinds of information about the text:

- the focus of the study described in the text
- the reason for the study
- how the study was conducted (the method)
- what the author(s) learned from the study (the findings or results)

For example, here's the abstract for an article titled "The Influence of Early School Punishment and Therapy/Medication on Social Control Experiences During Young Adulthood," by David M. Ramey, which was published in a journal called *Criminology*:

The use of suspensions and expulsions by American public school administrators has increased dramatically over the past 40 years. Meanwhile, a growing number of childhood misbehaviors have been diagnosed by doctors as medical conditions and are being treated with therapy or medication. As these trends develop at different rates for boys of different racial and ethnic groups, the connection between childhood and adult social control remains untested empirically. By using a prospective panel of 3,274 White, Black, and Hispanic males (15,675 person-years) and multilevel logistic models, I examine whether and how school punishment and/or the use of therapy or medication during childhood contributes to involvement in the criminal justice or mental health systems during young adulthood. The findings suggest that school punishment is associated with greater odds of involvement in the criminal justice system but not the mental health system. The use of therapy and/or medication during childhood is associated with higher odds of involvement in the mental health system but not the criminal justice system. Finally, although the relationship between school punishment and involvement with the criminal justice system is similar for White, Black, and Hispanic men, the relationship between medicalized social control during childhood and young adulthood is stronger for Whites than for non-Whites.

Source: Ramey, David M. "The Influence of Early School Punishment and Therapy/Medication on Social Control Experiences During Young Adulthood." *Criminology*, vol. 54, no. 1, Feb. 2016, doi:10.1111/1745-9125.12095.

From this abstract you can determine the following important information about this article:

- ***The focus of the study described in the article.*** The author conducted a study that examined "whether and how school punishment and/or the use of therapy or medication during childhood contributes to involvement in the criminal justice or mental health systems during young adulthood."

19

- *The reason for the study.* The first few sentences of the abstract refer to important trends in how schools deal with childhood behavior problems and explain that "the connection between childhood and adult social control remains untested empirically." That means that other researchers have not studied this connection but the author intends to do so.

- *How the study was conducted.* To conduct this study, the author used something called "multilevel logistic models." Without knowing exactly what that is, you can assume it is some kind of research method that you will probably learn more about in the article.

- *What the author learned from the study.* The last three sentences of the abstract briefly describe the main findings of the study.

For books, the introduction will usually include the same kinds of information, though often the author(s) will offer more detailed explanations.

Once you identify these main components in the abstract (or preface and introduction), you can look for them as you read the main text of the article or book, which can help you follow the text, even if you are unfamiliar with the subject itself.

# 3. Place the Text in Rhetorical Context

Core Concept #2 tells us that all texts must be understood within their rhetorical context (see Chapter 2), which includes the intended audience, the author's purpose for addressing that audience, and the circumstances surrounding the creation of the text, such as when the text was written. Most scholarly texts are intended for other scholars in the same academic field as the author (or related fields) and should be seen as part of specialized academic conversations. Understanding the rhetorical context, then, means identifying the academic conversation in which a scholar is participating. But you don't necessarily have to be familiar with that conversation to get a general sense of what the author is saying and why. **The opening sections of most scholarly texts follow a basic pattern** that you can recognize to determine the conversation in which the author is participating:

1. **Larger context.** The author refers to the larger context for his or her specific discussion.

2. **Problem.** The author identifies an unanswered question, unsolved problem, or previously unidentified issue within that larger context.

3. **Author's contribution.** The author introduces his or her specific contribution to the conversation about that unanswered question, unsolved problem, or previously unidentified issue.

This pattern is usually visible in the first few paragraphs of a scholarly article or the introduction to a scholarly book. If you can recognize the pattern, you can usually identify the general conversation in which the author is participating and the specific contribution the author is making to that conversation, even if you are unfamiliar with the academic field or subject.

The following excerpt, taken from an article published in a scholarly journal called *Criminology*, illustrates this pattern. Even without much knowledge of the field of criminal justice, you can use the pattern to help you place the article in rhetorical context and develop a general sense of the academic conversation in which this author is participating. These are the opening four paragraphs of the article:

> The proportion of school-aged males who have been suspended or expelled from school has increased dramatically over the past 40 years (Bertrand and Pan, 2011; Losen and Martinez, 2013). At the same time, a growing number of childhood misbehaviors have been defined by doctors as medically diagnosed conditions, including conduct disorder (Frick and Nigg, 2012), oppositional defiant disorder (ODD) (Frick and Nigg, 2012), and attention deficit and hyperactivity disorder (ADHD) (Barkley, 2002; Conrad, 2007). Moreover, evidence suggests that these trends are developing at different rates for boys of different racial and ethnic groups. As the proportion of Black and Hispanic boys suspended or expelled more than doubled between 1974 and 2010, the proportion of White boys removed from school remained relatively stable (Losen and Martinez, 2013). In contrast, Black and Hispanic boys are less likely than White boys to seek out and receive therapy or medication for behavior disorders (Bussing et al., 2012; Miller, Nigg, and Miller, 2009). Despite these developments, there has been limited research on the long-term consequences of either school punishment or the use of therapy and/or medication for child behavior problems.
>
> One possibility is that early experiences with school punishment and/or therapy and medication set the stage for involvement with different social control institutions later in life, including the criminal justice and mental health systems. By removing children from the classroom, school punishment disrupts academic progress and threatens long-term educational success (Arcia, 2006; Bowditch, 1993). Furthermore, the stigma attached to school punishment shapes future exchanges between boys and their teachers and principals, normalizing punishment and punitive social control early in their lives (Ferguson, 2001; Rios, 2011). Scholars have referred to this as a process of "criminalization" in which school punishment during childhood increases the risk of involvement in the criminal justice system during adolescence and adulthood (Hirschfield, 2008).
>
> Although school punishment may be an early risk factor for involvement with the criminal justice system, the long-term implications of early therapy and/or medication use

**1. Larger context.** The opening sentence identifies the broad conversation to which the author will contribute: the problem of school suspensions and expulsions. You can assume this is a topic of interest to other scholars in this field.

**1. Larger context.** Here the author further defines the larger problem: racial differences in how boys suspended or expelled from school are treated.

**2. Problem.** Often, scholars will identify the specific problem to be addressed by stating that "there has been limited research," as this author does, or "little is known about . . ."

**2. Problem.** In paragraphs 2 and 3, the author elaborates on the problem, referring to other studies that have examined it. These references identify the specific scholarly conversation—about addressing behavior problems in youth—in which this author is participating.

19

are less apparent. Although early-onset behavior problems increase the risk of incarceration in young adulthood (Fletcher and Wolfe, 2009; Hirschfield et al., 2006), this risk may in part be a result of a lack of treatment for specific disorders (Behnken et al., 2014; Hirschfield et al., 2006). If therapy or medication is successful in childhood, attempts to control behavior and temper during adolescence and young adulthood may instead involve the use of psychotropic drugs and psychoanalysis, establishing the mental health system as a primary social control institution (Conrad, 2007; Hinshaw and Scheffler, 2014). Scholars have referred to the process of identifying behavior problems in terms of mental health and using therapy or medication to control them as "medicalization" (Conrad, 1992). Importantly, because White and non-White boys have different experiences with school punishment and therapy or medication during childhood, there may be racial disparities in the processes of criminalization and medicalization across the life course.

**3. Contribution.** Here the author identifies his specific contribution to the conversation. In this paragraph, he elaborates on his effort to solve the problem he identifies in paragraphs 2 and 3.

In this article, I examine whether and how social control experiences of White, Black, and Hispanic males during childhood can set the stage for social control experiences during other stages of the life course. By using panel data from the National Longitudinal Survey of Youth—Child and Young Adult Surveys and multilevel logistic models, I answer two important questions about the relationship between criminalized and/or medicalized social control experiences across adolescence and young adulthood. First, does school punishment or the use of therapy and/or medication for behavior problems during childhood influence the odds of involvement in either the criminal justice or mental health systems during young adulthood? Second, is the relationship between childhood social control and adult social control different for White, Black, and Hispanic males?

**3. Contribution.** Scholars often identify their contributions by posing the specific question(s) they seek to answer in their text.

Source: Ramey, David M. "The Influence of Early School Punishment and Therapy/Medication on Social Control Experiences During Young Adulthood." *Criminology*, vol. 54, no. 1, Feb. 2016, doi:10.1111/1745-9125.12095.

By looking for the three main components of this pattern (context, problem, contribution), you can determine from the opening paragraphs that this article will try to answer two main questions about the impact of school punishment or therapy and/or medication on young white, black, and Hispanic males. You can also determine that the author's effort to answer these questions is part of a larger conversation about the long-term consequences of certain approaches to childhood behavior problems in the field of criminal justice. Having a general sense of the academic conversation that this author is participating in will help you make better sense of the rest of the article.

# 4. Identify Key Terms

One of the most challenging aspects of scholarly texts is the specialized language that scholars often use when writing about relevant topics in their disciplines. As we saw in the preceding section ("Understanding Academic Writing as Conversation"), specialized terminology is useful and often essential for understanding scholarly texts. As a student who is new to an academic field, you can't be expected to know all the specialized terms that experienced scholars use, so don't get discouraged if you don't understand such terms when you encounter them. Here is a basic strategy you can use to help you make sense of these terms.

1. **Identify important terms.** You can usually tell when a word or phrase is significant simply by noticing that the author repeats it often throughout the text. The first few paragraphs of a scholarly article usually include discussion of key terms (see "Place the text in context" on page 622). In addition, key terms are usually included in the abstract, preface, or introduction (see "Read the abstract, preface, or introduction" on page 621). Finally, subheadings sometimes include key terms (see "Use the structure" on page 627).

2. **Check to see whether the common definition applies.** Often, the dictionary definition doesn't convey the specialized meaning of a term within certain academic disciplines. If the dictionary definition doesn't seem to apply to how the author is using that term, chances are that the term has a more specialized meaning within the author's academic discipline. For example, the common understanding of the term *agency* is a business or government office that provides a specific service or function. However, in some academic disciplines, such as philosophy and sociology, *agency* is widely used to signify the ability or capacity of a person or a group of people to have control or power within a specific situation. In this case, the common meaning of the term would likely make little sense in a scholarly article in one of those disciplines.

3. **Use the context.** You can sometimes determine the meaning of a term by the way the author uses it. Read a few sentences that contain the term to try to figure out its meaning. Even if you can't determine the specialized meaning of the term, the way it is used can often give you some clues about its meaning and its significance.

4. **Find out more.** Search online to gain a better sense of the term's specialized meaning. (See Chapter 21 for advice about online searching.) Start with a general search engine, such as *Google*, but for some terms, especially those with common definitions (such as *agency*), you might need to use a specialized search engine, such as *Google Scholar*; a general scholarly database, such as *Academic Search Complete*; or a more specific database for the relevant academic discipline, such as *PsycInfo* for psychology or *philpapers* for philosophy. Usually, a quick search will yield enough information for you to learn what the term means.

For example, let's look at the passage in Exercise 19A (page 618), which is taken from an article in the *Journal of Experimental Social Psychology* in which the authors describe an experiment they conducted to understand how persuasion is influenced by culture. Here's part of that passage with some key terms highlighted:

> Individualism-collectivism is perhaps the most basic dimension of cultural variability identified in cross-cultural research. Concepts related to this dimension have been employed in several social science domains (cf. Triandis, McCusker, & Hui, 1990), and the individualism-collectivism dimension has come to be regarded as "central to an understanding of cultural values, of work values, of social systems, as well as in the studies of morality, the structure of constitutions, and cultural patterns" (Triandis, Brislin, & Hui, 1988). Several recent studies have suggested that individualism and collectivism are contrasting cultural syndromes that are associated with a broad pattern of differences in individuals' social perceptions and social behavior . . . .

- **Identify key terms.** The phrase "the individualism-collectivism dimension" seems to be especially important in this brief passage. Notice that the authors do not define this term, which indicates that they expect their readers to know what it is. That tells you that this is probably an established concept in the field of social psychology. So without knowing what the individualism-collectivism dimension is, you can already tell that it is an important, established concept in social psychology and therefore part of the larger conversations in the field.

- **Check to see whether the common definition of a term applies.** General online dictionaries, such as *Merriam Webster* (merriam-webster.com), are not likely to have a definition for the phrase *individualism-collectivism* or the *individualism-collectivism dimension*. But they will probably have definitions for *individualism* and *collectivism*, which are common terms. Knowing the meanings of those terms can help you gain a general sense of what the phrase *individualism-collectivism* means.

- **Use the context.** Although the term *individualism-collectivism dimension* is not defined in this passage, the discussion can give you clues to its meaning. For example, the third sentence seems to indicate that the term refers to contrasting qualities in how people perceive and act in social situations.

- **Find out more.** A Google search for the term *individualism-collectivism dimension* will likely identify links to scholarly publications in psychology, anthropology, and sociology as well as sources, like *Wikipedia*, that help explain the term. You can also do a basic search of a specialized database for psychology, such as *PsycInfo*, which will identify other scholarly texts containing this term. A quick review of some of these search results indicates that the *individualism-collectivism dimension* is an established concept in the field of social psychology that refers to the extent to which individuals are integrated into groups within a specific society or culture. That's all you really need to know to be able to understand how the term is used in this article.

Keep in mind that you don't need to try to become an expert. You need only to develop a sufficient understanding of key terms to be able to make sense of the text itself. In this case, for example, you could spend hours readings about the *individualism-collectivism dimension* and the theory that explains it, but all you really need to know at this point is what it means and that it is a well-established theoretical concept in the academic field of this author.

# 5. Use the Structure

Core Concept #6 emphasizes the rhetorical importance of the organization of a text, and academic texts, especially scholarly articles, often have a predictable structure that you can use to help you understand the content and find specific material. This structure usually includes **four standard components or sections** that serve specific functions:

- **Abstract:** a summary of the article that appears after the title and byline but before the main text. (see "Read the abstract, preface, or introduction" on page 621).

- **Statement of the problem:** An introductory section that identifies the specific problem or question that the author addresses in the article.

- **Review of the literature:** A discussion of scholarly texts that are relevant to the author's specific topic; this section places the author's contribution in the context of what other scholars have written about the subject.

- **Bibliography:** The list of texts that the author has cited (see "Review the bibliography" on page 627), which is called "Works Cited" in MLA style (see Chapter 24) and "References" in APA style (see Chapter 25).

In addition, scholarly articles that report on research usually include the following sections:

- **Method:** A description of the procedure the author(s) used to conduct the study. This section usually describes the location of the study (the research site), the participants who were involved in the study, the kinds of data collected, and how the data were analyzed.

- **Results:** An explanation of what the author(s) learned by conducting the study; sometimes called "Findings."

- **Discussion:** A section in which the results, or findings, are explained.

Note that all these sections are usually identified by **subheadings**, which you can easily see as you skim the article.

Knowing the purpose of each of these sections enables you to develop a quick sense of the contents of the article before reading each section more carefully. For example, reviewing the *Statement of the Problem* will tell you not only the specific problem or question the author is addressing but also how that problem fits into the relevant academic conversations. Similarly, if you're reading an article that reports on a study, you can go to the *Results* to find out quickly what the study revealed about the problem being addressed.

# 6. Review the Bibliography

Almost all scholarly articles and books include complete lists of all works cited by the author. In MLA style, this list is called the "Works Cited" (see Chapter 24); in APA style, it is called "References" (see Chapter 25). If you are reading a scholarly text on an unfamiliar subject, you are unlikely to recognize the specific works included in this list, but browsing the list can give you a sense of the focus of the article and the specific topics the author addresses; it can also help you identify the academic conversation in which the author is participating.

19

For example, here are several of the entries in the References list of an article titled "Neoliberalism as a New Historical Bloc: A Gramscian Analysis of Neoliberalism's Common Sense in Education," by Carlos Alberto Torres, which was published in 2013 in a journal called *International Studies in the Sociology of Education* (these entries are in APA format):

Apple, M. W. (2013). *Can education change society?* New York, NY: Routledge.

Baez, B., & Boyles, D. (2009). *The politics of inquiry: Education research and the "culture of science."* Albany, NY: New York Press.

Berman, E., Marginson, S., Preston, R., McClellan, B. E., & Arnove, R. F. (2007). The political economy of educational reform in Australia, England and Wales, and the United States. In R. F. Arnove & C. A. Torres (Eds.), *Comparative education: The dialectics of the global and the local* (pp. 252–291). Lanham, MD: Rowman and Littlefield.

de Sousa Santos, B. (Ed.). (2007). *Cognitive justice in a global world: Prudent knowledges for a decent life.* Lanham, MD: Lexington Books-Rowman and Littlefield Publishers.

Gadotti, M. (1996). *Pedagogy of praxis: A dialectical philosophy of education.* Albany, NY: SUNY Press.

Gramsci, A. (1980). *Selections from the prison notebooks of Antonio Gramsci.* (Q. Hoare & G. N. Smith, Ed. & Trans.). New York, NY: International Publishers.

Habermas, J. (1975). *Legitimation crisis* (J. J. Shapiro, Ed. & Trans.). Boston: Beacon.

Even if you don't know these works or recognize the authors, you can tell that these works all seem to deal with broad issues related to the purpose of education. You can also see that the list includes works about education in various nations, not only the United States. If you have taken a philosophy course, you might recognize the names *Gramsci* and *Habermas*, well-known 20th century philosophers, which tells you that this article might include discussions of philosophical concepts or arguments. (The title of the article confirms this conclusion.) This quick review of the bibliography can help you make sense of the article and place it in the context of broader academic conversations.

## 7. Take Notes

One of the best ways to understand a challenging text is to take notes as you read. You should take notes as you complete the preceding six steps in this strategy, but it is vital to make notes as you read more carefully through the text itself. Doing so not only will help you understand the text but also can be a record if you need to refer back to the text for a writing assignment or class discussion.

There is no right way to take notes. Use any procedure and technology that works for you. But however you take notes, your notes should include the following:

- **Key terms:** Underline or highlight important terms (see "Identify important terms" on page 625) or make a list of them and write down what they mean or what you have learned about them by following this strategy.

- **Important passages:** Identify passages that include material that you find especially important or relevant for your own purposes (such as a writing assignment or course exercise). Briefly explain why these passages seem important.

- **Questions:** Write down questions you have about anything you don't understand in the text or questions that the author raises for you about the subject.
- **Connections:** Note any connections you see in the text to your own ideas or to other texts you have read.

It's a good idea to keep a notebook devoted to assigned readings in your course or materials you are reading as part of your research for a writing assignment.

---

**EXERCISE 19B**    **READING ACADEMIC TEXTS**

1. Find a scholarly article on a subject of interest to you or select one you have found as part of your research for a writing assignment you are working on. Use the strategy described in this section to read that text. After you are finished, write a brief paragraph describing what you found most challenging about this text and what you found easiest to understand.

2. In a group of classmates, share the paragraphs you wrote for Question 1. What similarities and differences can you identify in your classmates' responses to this text? What conclusions can you draw from this experience about reading academic texts?

---

# Summarizing and Paraphrasing

Summarizing and paraphrasing are among the most important skills in academic writing. It is a rare writing task that does not include some summary or paraphrase:

- In an argument about capital punishment, the writer summarizes the main positions for and against capital punishment before defending a position on the issue.
- A chemistry lab report about campus air quality includes summaries of previous analyses of air quality.
- An analysis of housing density in a neighborhood near campus for a sociology class includes a paraphrase of a seminal study about the relationship between housing density and key socio-economic and demographic factors.
- In a literary analysis essay for an English literature course, a student summarizes the plots of several plays by Shakespeare and paraphrases a critic's evaluation of them.

These examples underscore not only how common but also how useful summary and paraphrase can be in academic writing. They also indicate that although students often need to summarize other texts, they might also need to summarize an argument, perspective, or theory that arises from multiple sources.

Usually, *summary* is distinguished from *paraphrase* (see Focus: "Summarizing vs. Paraphrasing"); in practice, however, the distinction is not always clear—or useful. For our purposes, distinguishing between summary and paraphrase is less important than understanding how to represent information and ideas from a source text accurately and how to credit the source appropriately. Accordingly, the advice in this section generally applies to both summarizing and paraphrasing.

19

Students are often confused by the difference between a summary and a paraphrase. That's understandable, because summary and paraphrase are very similar, and textbooks as well as online resources often contribute to the confusion.

**Paraphrase.** The Merriam-Webster Dictionary defines *paraphrase* as "a restatement of a text, passage, or work giving the meaning in another form." A paraphrase expresses the ideas or information from a source text in your own words. Usually, a writer paraphrases when the information and/or meaning of a source text is important but the original wording of that text is not. Sometimes writers paraphrase when the source text is specialized and difficult to understand. (When it is important to convey that original wording to readers, the writer should *quote* from the source text. See "Quoting from Sources" in Chapter 23.)

**Summary.** *Summary*, by contrast, is a condensed version of a source text that conveys only the main ideas or information from that text in the writer's own words. Writers summarize when they need to convey

- a key idea from a source text,
- a point of view expressed in a source text,
- the results of an analysis reported in a source text, or
- an argument made in a source text

*The main difference between a summary and a paraphrase is that a summary boils a source down into a brief passage (a sentence, a few sentences, or a paragraph), whereas a paraphrase restates the source text.* Both use the writer's own words, but the purpose of each is slightly different. In a summary, the writer conveys the main point or idea of a source text; in a paraphrase, the writer restates the source text to convey the information or ideas of that source text. Typically, a writer will *paraphrase* a passage from or portion of the source text but *summarize* lengthy passages or the the entire text.

Although summarizing seems to be a straightforward task, students encounter two **main problems when summarizing:**

- inaccurately representing the main point, idea, or information from the source text
- using too much of the original language from the source

For example, here's a passage from an article in which a law professor offers an analysis of the so-called "war on poverty" initiated by President Lyndon Johnson in the 1960s:

The commitment and symbolism of the "war on poverty"—and the energy and enthusiasm of those who fought it—were vital. For a brief period, the idea of conducting a war on poverty captured the nation's imagination. The phrase is surely one of the most evocative in our history. Yet the war's specific components were a tiny fraction even of the Great Society programs enacted between 1964 and 1968 during the administration of Lyndon Johnson, let alone those enacted during the New Deal and those added since, many during the presidency of Richard Nixon. And, even considering all these, we never fought an allout war on poverty.

Source: Edelman, Peter. "The War on Poverty and Subsequent Federal Programs: What Worked, What Didn't Work, and Why? Lessons for Future Programs." *Clearinghouse Review Journal of Poverty Law and Policy*, May–June 2006, p. 8.

The following summary misses the main point of the source text:

According to Edelman, the war on poverty captured the nation's imagination.

The source text does state that the war on poverty captured the nation's imagination, but the author goes on to argue that the U.S. never fought an "allout war on poverty." The main point of the passage is that, despite the popularity of the idea of a war on poverty, the federal efforts intended to alleviate poverty were a small part of total government social programs. This summary, although accurate to an extent, misrepresents the point of the source passage.

Here's a summary that better represents the point of the source text:

Edelman argues that although the idea of a "war on poverty" captured the country's imagination, programs focused on addressing poverty never amounted to more than a small part of President Lyndon's Johnson's Great Society programs and the social programs of other administrations.

Notice that this summary represents the source passage *as a whole* rather than focusing on one part of it.

It's possible that a brief summary like this would be insufficient, depending upon the nature of the writing assignment and rhetorical situation. For example, perhaps you are writing an argument in response to the source text, which means you would probably need to include a more complete representation of that source. In such a case, it's likely you would need to *paraphrase* the source passage. Here's a paraphrase that illustrates the very common problem of using too much of the original language of the source text (the passages that are taken from the source text are highlighted in orange):

The commitment and symbolism of the "war on poverty" were important. For a short time, the idea of a war on poverty captured the nation's imagination. But the specific components of the war were a tiny fraction of government programs enacted during the administration of Lyndon Johnson, not to mention those enacted before then and those added since. Even considering all these programs, an allout war on poverty was never really fought.

In this example not only are too many words and phrases taken verbatim from the source text, but much of the sentence structure is also reproduced in the paraphrase.

A more acceptable paraphrase transforms the source passage into the writer's own words while preserving the original meaning of the source text:

According to Edelman, the idea of a "war on poverty" was important for its symbolism as well as for the national commitment it reflected. But although this idea resonated with Americans for a time, the programs intended specifically to fight poverty were never more than a small part of total government social programs, whether those programs were part of Lyndon Johnson's Great Society, the earlier New Deal, or initiatives undertaken by Richard Nixon and subsequent presidents. As a result, Edelman states, a total war on poverty was never really fought.

19

This paraphrase borrows only essential phrases from the source text (such as "war on poverty") and restructures the passage so that the diction and syntax are the writer's own.

When summarizing or paraphrasing, follow these guidelines:

- **Accurately represent the main idea or point of the source text.** This is not simply a matter of including important information or ideas in your summary or paraphrase but also making sure that you convey the original author's intent or meaning.

- **Use your own language.** In many cases, this means finding appropriate synonyms for words in the source text, but it also means writing your own sentences rather than using the sentence structure of the source text.

- **Place quotation marks around important words or phrases from the source text.** If you reproduce key words or phrases from the source text, place them in quotation marks to indicate that the language is taken from the source text. In the previous example, the phrase *war on poverty* is placed in quotation marks not only because it is taken from the source text verbatim but also because it has become a phrase associated with a specific set of programs and and a specific period in history. (See "Quoting from Sources" in Chapter 23 for advice about how to quote appropriately from a source text.)

- **Cite the source.** Whether you are summarizing, paraphrasing, or quoting directly from a source text, you must cite that source properly to indicate to your readers that you are taking ideas or information from another text. (See Chapters 24 and 25 for information about citing sources.)

---

**EXERCISE 19C**   **PRACTICING SUMMARY AND PARAPHRASE**

1. Write a summary and a paraphrase of the following passage:

   Individualism-collectivism is perhaps the broadest and most widely used dimension of cultural variability for cultural comparison (Gudykunst and Ting-Toomey, 1988). Hofstede (1980) describes individualism-collectivism as the relationship between the individual and the collectivity that prevails in a given society. In individualistic cultures, individuals tend to prefer individualistic relationships to others and to subordinate ingroup goals to their personal goals. In collectivistic cultures, on the other hand, individuals are more likely to have interdependent relationships to their ingroups and to subordinate their personal goals to their ingroup goals. Individualistic cultures are associated with emphases on independence, achievement, freedom, high levels of competition, and pleasure. Collectivistic cultures are associated with emphases on interdependence, harmony, family security, social hierarchies, cooperation, and low levels of competition.

   Source: Sang-Pil Han and Sharon Shavitt, "Persuasion and Culture: Advertising Appeals in Individualistic and Collectivistic Societies." *Journal of Experimental Social Psychology*, vol. 30, no. 4, July 1994, pp. 327–28.

2. Revise the summary below so that it more accurately reflects the original passage:

**Original passage:** Prior to the official acceptance of the low-fat-is-good-health dogma, clinical investigators, predominantly British, had proposed another hypothesis for the cause of heart disease, diabetes, colorectal and breast cancer, tooth decay, and a half-dozen or so other chronic diseases, including obesity. The hypothesis was based on decades of eyewitness testimony from missionary and colonial physicians and two consistent observations: that these "diseases of civilization" were rare to nonexistent among isolated populations that lived traditional lifestyles and ate traditional diets, and that these diseases appeared in these populations only after they were exposed to Western foods—in particular, sugar, flour, white rice, and maybe beer. These are known technically as *refined* carbohydrates, which are those carbohydrate-containing foods—usually sugars and starches—that have been machine-processed to make them more easily digestible.

Source: Gary Taubes, *Good Calories, Bad Calories: Challenging the Conventional Wisdom on Diet, Weight Control, and Disease*. Alfred E. Knopf, 2007, pp. xix-xx.

Summary: Another hypothesis was proposed based on decades of eyewitness testimony from physicians and the observations that these "diseases of civilization" didn't occur in isolated populations until they were exposed to Western diets of refined carbohydrates. Refined carbohydrates include sugar, flour, white rice, and maybe beer.

# Synthesizing

In much academic writing, writers must do more than consult sources for relevant information. They must also bring together information or ideas from a variety of sources and synthesize the material into a coherent discussion that is relevant to the task at hand. Not only is synthesizing material from several sources an essential task in most academic writing, but it also lends depth to the writing. Consider this passage from *The Young and the Digital*, an analysis of the role of media in the lives of young people today:

> In years past, social scientists expressed serious apprehension about the media content, especially violent and sexual imagery, that's exposed to young children and teenagers. And though violent and sexual themes in media continues to be a serious topic of debate, a growing amount of attention is shifting to the proliferation of screens in homes and in young people's lives. There is rising anxiety about the sheer amount of time children and teens spend with media and technology. According to a 2006 study conducted by the Kaiser Family Foundation, kids spend between six and eight-and-a-half hours a day with media. Today, playtime for many young children usually involves time with a screen.

19

As they observe their parents' connection to mobile phones, BlackBerrys, laptops, and other electronic gadgets, many young children mimic those behaviors. We often hear, and for good reason, that young people are leading the migration to digital. But in many homes across America, parents are unwittingly teaching their kids to be digital. In the midst of the marketing and selling of the digital lifestyle, the American Academy of Pediatrics recommends that children's daily screen time be limited to one to two hours.

Tyler Olson/Shutterstock.com

Source: Watkins, S. Craig. *The Young and the Digital.* Beacon Press, 2009, p. 50.

In this passage, author S. Craig Watkins draws on several sources to make his main point about the increasing amount of time young people spend using digital media. Notice that Watkins cites two specific sources (a study by the Kaiser Family Foundation and a recommendation from the American Academy of Pediatrics), but the first few sentences of the paragraph provide an overview of an important development (the shift in attention from questionable media content to the amount of time children spend with media) that Watkins likely gleaned from several additional sources. In other words, Watkins is synthesizing ideas and information not only from the two sources he cites but also from other sources that he consulted while researching his topic. As this example suggests, synthesis can be extremely useful when a writer is working with complex subject matter and many different sources.

Effective writers follow **three basic guidelines when synthesizing ideas and information:**

- Keep larger goals in mind.
- Identify a main point.
- Use of source material that you need.

## Keep Larger Goals in Mind

When working with several different sources, especially in a longer project on a complicated topic, it can be easy to lose track of your reasons for consulting the specific sources you found. As you review sources and identify relevant information or ideas, remind yourself of the main goal of your project and identify how the section you are working on relates to that main goal. For example, the passage on page 633 from Watkins' book *The Young and the Digital* is taken from a chapter titled "The Very Well Connected: Friending, Bonding, and Community in the Digital Age," in which Watkins examines the increasingly central role digital media play in the social lives of young people. The passage focuses on the increasing amount of time young people devote to digital media, a point that supports Watkins' analysis that digital media have become one of the most significant factors in how young people manage their social lives. Notice that in synthesizing material from his sources to make his point about the time young people devote to digital media, Watkins also connects that point to his larger point about the social impact of digital media.

## Identify a Main Point

Source material is often varied and complicated, and when synthesizing this material you must identify what is relevant to the task at hand. In effect, you are managing information from different sources and connecting them to make a point. That task is easier for you if you keep focused on a main point. Here's an example in which a writer synthesizes information from several very different sources to make a point about the longstanding debates about vegetarianism:

> Debates about the efficacy of vegetarianism follow us from cradle to wheelchair. In 1998 child-care expert Dr. Benjamin Spock, who became a vegetarian late in life, stoked a stir by recommending that children over the age of 2 be raised as vegans, rejecting even milk and eggs. The American Dietetic Association says it is possible to raise kids as vegans but cautions that special care must be taken with nursing infants (who don't develop properly without the nutrients in mother's milk or fortified formula). Other researchers warn that infants breast-fed by vegans have lower levels of vitamin B12 and DHA (an omega-3 fatty acid), important to vision and growth.

Source: Corliss, Richard. "Should We All Be Vegetarians?" *Time*, 15 July 2002, p. 48+.

In this passage, the author draws on at least three separate sets of sources: (1) material about the 1988 controversy surrounding Dr. Benjamin Spock's recommendations about feeding young children a vegetarian diet; (2) the American Dietary Association's recommendations; and (3) nutritional studies of infants who were breast-fed by vegans. Although these sources all relate to the topic of the impact of vegetarianism on children, each has a different focus. The author brings them together to make a single main point, which is stated in the first sentence of the paragraph. The information from each source is clearly related to that main point. As a result, the author makes it easy for a reader to make sense of the information from these different sources.

## Use Only the Source Material You Need

When working with multiple sources, you might find a great deal of relevant material that is interesting and seemingly important. But don't overwhelm your reader by trying to synthesize information from too many sources at once. In the examples in this section, the authors select information from their sources carefully and use only what they need to make their points. It is likely that in each case the author had much more information than he used. Part of your task when working with sources is to evaluate the information you have gathered and select the material that helps you achieve your rhetorical goals. Synthesis can be a powerful tool in academic writing, but if you try to squeeze too much information from too many different sources into a passage, it is likely that your prose will be less clear and your discussion more difficult for your readers to follow.

19

Write a brief paragraph in which you synthesize the following information about the job market for college graduates:

> A Bachelor's degree is one of the best weapons a job seeker can wield in the fight for employment and earnings. And staying on campus to earn a graduate degree provides safe shelter from the immediate economic storm, and will pay off with greater employability and earnings once the graduate enters the labor market. Unemployment for students with new Bachelor's degrees is an unacceptable 8.9 percent, but it's a catastrophic 22.9 percent for job seekers with a recent high school diploma—and an almost unthinkable 31.5 percent for recent high school dropouts.

Source: Carnevale, Anthony, et al. *Hard Times: College Majors, Unemployment, and Earnings.* Georgetown University Center on Education and the Work Force, 2012, cew.georgetown.edu/wp-content/uploads/2014/11/Unemployment.Final_.update1.pdf.

> More than half of all recent graduates are unemployed or in jobs that do not require a degree, and the amount of student-loan debt carried by households has more than quintupled since 1999. These graduates were told that a diploma was all they needed to succeed, but it won't even get them out of the spare bedroom at Mom and Dad's. For many, the most tangible result of their four years is the loan payments, which now average hundreds of dollars a month on loan balances in the tens of thousands.

©zimmytws/Shutterstock.com

Source: McArdle, Megan. "The Coming Burst of the College Bubble." *Newsweek,* 9 Sept. 2012, www.newsweek.com/megan-mcardle-coming-burst-college-bubble-64671.

> [In 2011] about 1.5 million, or 53.6 percent, of bachelor's degree-holders under the age of 25 last year were jobless or underemployed, the highest share in at least 11 years. In 2000, the share was at a low of 41 percent, before the dot-com bust erased job gains for college graduates in the telecommunications and IT fields.

Source: Yen, Hope. "Half of New Grads are Jobless or Underemployed." Associated Press, 24 Apr. 2012. *NBCNews,* www.nbcnews.com/id/47141463/ns/business-stocks_and_economy/#.Vy-CLb7Vvf1.

> Underemployment also tends to be temporary for college graduates. Even after the recession hit, Pew found that annually, about 27 percent of BA's stuck in high-school level jobs transitioned to college-level employment. . . . Unemployment for college

graduates is higher than normal. Underemployment is more prevalent, though it's less severe than college critics portray, and perhaps no worse than during the Reagan days.

---

Source: Weissman, Jordan. "How Bad Is the Job Market For College Grads? Your Definitive Guide." *The Atlantic*, 4 Apr. 2013, www.theatlantic.com/business/archive/2013/04/ how-bad-is-the-job-market-for-college-grads-your-definitive-guide/274580/.

# Writing Summary-Response Essays

One of the most common forms of academic writing is the summary-response essay. A summary-response essay is a writer's direct engagement with another text: a scholarly article, a book, a film, a lecture, or some other kind of relevant document. In this regard, to write a summary-response essay is to participate directly in a relevant academic conversation, which is one reason why it is such a common assignment in college classes.

The specific form and content of a summary-response essay can vary depending upon the academic subject, but all summary-response writing serves the same basic purpose: to understand a text in sufficient depth so that you can respond in an informed way that contributes to an ongoing conversation about a relevant topic. For example, in an American history class, you might be studying the ongoing debates about the decision by the United States to use atomic weapons against Japan in World War II. Your instructor might assign essays by two prominent historians who have different perspectives on that decision and its moral dimensions. Writing a summary-response to one or both of those essays would enable you not only to delve more deeply into the historian's reasoning for his or her position but also to participate in this important and still-relevant debate.

Although summary-response essays are common in academic writing, they appear in various forms in popular media as well. Journalists, policymakers, business leaders, and experts in various professions will sometimes write essays in direct response to a book or editorial or magazine article as part of a conversation about important current issues or controversies. Such essays are different from reviews (see Chapter 10) in part because the purpose of a summary-response essay isn't necessarily evaluative. For example, in 2015, journalist Ta-Nehisi Coates published a book titled *Between the World and Me*, in which Coates, an African American, writes to his own teenage son about the history of racism in the United States and what it means to live as a black man in the U.S. today. The book, which won numerous awards, provoked an intense conversation about race in the U.S., and many prominent writers and political leaders wrote essays in direct response to Coates' book. Those essays, which took many different forms, might all be seen as versions of the summary-response essay. They enabled readers of Coates' book to engage in conversation about the important issues Coates raised.

As a college student, you will likely have many opportunities to write summary-response essays. Doing so is a way for you to become a more careful reader, a thoughtful participant in conversations about relevant matters, and a more effective writer.

**19**

# Features of Effective Summary-Response Writing

No matter what form they take, **effective summary-response essays have four essential characteristics:**

1. **Description of the focus text.** The writer's first task in a summary-response is to identify the text that is being summarized and responded to, which we will refer to as the "focus text." Typically, the opening paragraph of a summary-response essay includes the title and author of the focus text and a brief description that gives readers a sense of the rhetorical situation, including when and where the focus text was published, the author's purpose, and the intended audience. This is especially important if the focus text is a specialized article or book that is likely to be unfamiliar to the readers of the summary-response essay. For example, here's the opening paragraph of a summary-response essay written by a college student in 2012 on an important scholarly article that was published several decades earlier:

   In "Writing as a Mode of Learning," which was published in 1978 in the scholarly journal *College Composition and Communication,* eminent scholar Janet Emig discusses writing as a "mode of learning" that is ". . . not merely valuable, not merely special but unique" (122). Writing, according to Emig, is a process that needs to be more widely practiced in the classroom. Furthermore, writing is a particularly invaluable process to a teacher's classroom; it involves both practice and process, which is unlike other methods of communication. In 1978 educators were beginning to focus on the importance of writing as a tool for learning, and it was Emig's hope to raise awareness about this issue. Today, the advent of the newly-developed Common Core Standards will result in greater emphasis on writing in schools. But writing is a unique way of learning, one that *must* be incorporated into today's classroom, not simply for the reason that it is mandated by the state, but also because it is an effective vehicle for student learning.

   Notice that the writer of this summary-response essay provides enough information about the focus text for readers to understand why it was originally written in the late 1970s and why it is significant now. When you introduce your focus text, consider what your readers will need to know about that text so that they can place it in broader context and understand its relevance.

2. **Clear summary.** It goes without saying that an effective summary-response essay will include a clear, accurate summary that presents the focus text in a way that readers will understand, even when that focus text is complex and specialized. "Summarizing and Paraphrasing" on page 629 provides advice on writing effective summary, but keep in mind that your summary in a summary-response essay will depend in part on the nature of your assignment and rhetorical situation. Some summary-response assignments call for extended summary; others require brief, succinct summary. Consult your assignment guidelines and consider your rhetorical situation as you develop your summary. Always assume your readers are not intimately familiar with the focus text and be sure to summarize all the important components as if your readers have not read it.

3. **Substantive response.** In a summary-response essay, the response is more than the writer's opinion about the focus text. The writer must say something relevant about that text in a way that contributes to the ongoing conversation about the subject of the text (Core Concept #4). It

isn't enough for a writer to say he or she liked or didn't like something about the focus text. The response must explain *why* the writer found something about the focus text important, interesting, thought-provoking, questionable, or problematic in some way. In other words, in an effective response, the writer supports his or her claims about the focus text (Core Concept #5) and draws reasonable conclusions about the focus text on the basis of a careful analysis of that text.

For many students, providing a substantive response to the focus text is the most challenging aspect of writing a summary-response essay. That might be because the students are unfamiliar with the content of the focus text, especially if that text is a scholarly article on a specialized subject. In such a case, it is important to read the text carefully in order to understand it sufficiently. Use the "Strategy for Reading Academic Texts" (page 622) and keep in mind that writing your summary should also help you develop a better understanding of the focus text.

4. **Relevant purpose.** This characteristic is closely related to #3, a substantive response. Although the purpose of a typical summary-response assignment might seem self-evident (to summarize and respond to an assigned focus text), effective summary-response essays usually do more than simply analyze the focus text; they connect that text to broader, ongoing conversations about the subject of the focus text or related subjects. For example, let's return to the opening paragraph of the summary-response essay we looked at on page 649:

In "Writing as a Mode of Learning," which was published in 1978 in the scholarly journal *College Composition and Communication*, eminent scholar Janet Emig discusses writing as a "mode of learning" that is "...not merely valuable, not merely special but unique" (122). Writing, according to Emig, is a process that needs to be more widely practiced in the classroom. Furthermore, writing is a particularly invaluable process to a teacher's classroom; it involves both practice and process, which is unlike other methods of communication. In 1978 educators were beginning to focus on the importance of writing as a tool for learning, and it was Emig's hope to raise awareness about this issue. Today, the advent of the newly-developed Common Core Standards will result in greater emphasis on writing in schools. But writing is a unique way of learning, one that *must* be incorporated into today's classroom, not simply for the reason that it is mandated by the state, but also because it is an effective vehicle for student learning.

Notice that the writer states explicitly that the ideas of the author of the focus text should be applied to schools today. In other words, this writer's purpose is not simply to summarize and then respond to the source text but to use the summary-response as a way to make a larger point about the importance of a certain approach to writing in schools. When writing a summary-response essay, consider what purpose your essay serves and how it fits into ongoing conversations about the subject of the focus text.

To illustrate these features, let's look at a student's summary-response essay about a focus text titled "Internet Addiction Left My Brother Homeless," by Winston Ross, which was published in 2009 in *Newsweek*. The student, Avery Brahaum, wrote this essay in 2013 in the midst of ongoing national debates about the potentially damaging effects of spending too much time online, especially for young people. As you'll see, in his careful response, Avery reconsiders his initial rejection of the author's claims about the connection between Internet addiction and homelessness. In this

19

regard, Avery's essay illustrates Core Concept #1, that writing is an act of learning and discovery: By summarizing and responding thoughtfully to Ross' article, Avery learned something about addiction, which in turn influenced his own view of the problem.

## The Dynamics of Internet Addiction

In "Internet Addiction Left My Brother Homeless," Winston Ross claims that Internet addiction is a viable diagnosis. He bases this claim in part on the experiences of his brother, who, Ross tells us, is homeless due to his addiction to the Internet. The article, which was published in *Newsweek* magazine in 2009, focuses on how Internet addiction led to his brother's homelessness.

**1. Describe.** Avery identifies the title and author of the focus text as well as where and when it was published.

Although Ross' argument that an Internet addiction caused his brother's homelessness seems questionable, his article does show that Internet addiction is a valid affliction, and he raises important questions about what should be done to address a serious problem that many people might dismiss or overlook.

**4. Purpose.** Here Avery indicates that the purpose of his essay is to comment on an important problem that deserves attention.

Ross begins by reflecting on the belief that there is a non-substance addiction related to excessive Internet use. He provides various examples of how people can become addicted to the Internet, noting the most concerning effects of Internet addiction can be connected to people who are addicted to shopping, sex, and gambling. Specifically, Ross states "the Web may be dangerous for some people because it can feed or spur existing addictions, making gambling, shopping, and sex readily available to those who have already developed the compulsion to binge on those things."

Another effect of an excessive use of the Internet can be medical conditions, such as blood clots, that can result from sitting for a long period of time while playing games on the Internet, and effects on an individual's livelihood, such as a loss of their housing, employment, etc. Ross shares his personal story of his own brother's addiction to the Internet that has resulted in him being homeless. Ross relates how he and his brother were raised and questions how his brother could become addicted to the Internet when he did not, since they both were raised playing games often on the Internet. Ross' article expresses what appears to be his confusion over his brother's lifestyle and how his brother cannot make the appropriate changes to remedy his state of homelessness.

**2. Summary.** In paragraphs 3 through 5, Avery provides a clear, accurate summary of Ross' article, using quotations from the article to help convey a sense of its content and the author's argument.

Ross mentions a treatment program, named ReStart, which is a recovery center that helps individuals who are addicted to the Internet. Ross quotes Jerald Block, a clinical psychiatrist, as verifying that "compulsive computer use can be a difficult problem to treat." Block further notes that the "three most common methods of treatment is anti-depressants, treatment for ADHD, and extended retreats from the computer," and Ross notes that clients at ReStart engage in real activities, such as cooking, cleaning, and building things to take their focus away from the virtual reality they experience while on the Internet.

Ross goes on to assert that it is detrimental to remove Internet access from these individuals altogether and instead it is recommended that their use of the Internet be reduced and continue to taper off to a reasonable level. However, his article raises the question of whether there is any acceptable level of Internet use that would be recommended for someone who has an Internet addiction. As Ross states, this would be similar to giving a heroin addict "a gram of heroin to smoke per day." His article reflects on the various responses or treatment options recommended for Internet addicts and further addresses how difficult it is for an Internet addict to obtain employment that requires access to and use of the Internet.

As I considered the information provided in Ross' article, I did not at first see the connection between his brother's use of the Internet and his homelessness. I do agree that Internet addiction is a valid issue in our society and that it can contribute to issues in a person's life, but it did not make sense to me that one's use of the Internet would be the sole reason for his homelessness. Other issues, in addition to his Internet addiction, must have caused him to have such life problems.

But Ross provides information from various psychiatrists that persuaded me of the validity of a non-substance addiction—specifically, an addiction to the Internet—and I do believe that the use of the Internet can cause additional issues to those people who are already struggling with an addiction to sex, gambling, and shopping, since the Internet provides easy access to websites that support these addictions. The sources Ross quotes show how difficult recovery could be for an Internet addict and provide valid information on the action steps necessary to treat this type of addiction.

Other research on Internet addiction that I found supports Ross's conclusion that this type of addiction can have the same effects on a person as a substance abuse addiction, such as with drugs or alcohol. For example, writing in the *Christian Post* Reporter, Elton Jones notes that the negative effects of Internet addiction can cause changes in a person's

**3. Response.** Avery devotes about half of his essay to his response, which begins in paragraph 6. Sometimes, the response is longer than the summary. Consider your rhetorical situation and assignment guidelines when deciding how long your summary and response sections should be.

19

brain, such as are found in those who have a drug addiction. These research findings, which show how addictions can affect a person's financial status, employment, etc., help us understand how an individual who is addicted to the Internet can in fact become homeless. In a separate report on homelessness and addiction, Rhea Rosier notes that "the disease of addiction usually disrupts family relationships and relationships with friends, causes many people to lose their jobs, and addiction may exacerbate all their resources and cause them to lose their house." Rosier's article supports the need for specialized treatment for those with addictions and explains that addiction can be both a cause and a result of homelessness.

Ross' article led me to consider my own use of the Internet, as well as that of my family members, to determine if we use the Internet excessively. An Internet addiction is detrimental not only to the addict but also to family members who have to watch a loved one suffer while living on the streets, struggling to find money and food, and seeking out places where they can continue to support their addiction. In the end, Ross helps us see that Internet addiction and homelessness can be interrelated and that both issues must be addressed to allow individuals with an Internet addiction to become stable and healthy.

**3. Response.** Here Avery cites two sources that are not in the focus text to support his response. Not only do these sources strengthen his analysis of the focus text but they also add depth to his response.

**3. Response.** Avery's references to his own experience with the Internet give substance to his response and underscore the relevance of the focus text.

**4. Purpose.** Avery ends his essay by emphasizing the importance of the problem addressed in the focus text, which reinforces the purpose of his summary-response essay.

## Works Cited

Jones, Elton. "Internet Addiction Disorder's Effects Similar to Drugs and Alcohol." *The Christian Post*, 13 Jan. 2012, www.christianpost.com/news/Internet-addiction-disorders-effects-similar-to-drugs-and-alcohol-video-67143/.

Rosier, Rhea. "Homelessness and Addiction." Palm Partners Recovery Center, 19 Oct. 2012, blog.palmpartners.com/homelessness-and-addiction/.

Ross, Winston. "Internet Addiction Left My Brother Homeless." *Newsweek*, 7 Oct. 2009, www.newsweek.com/internet-addiction-left-my-brother-homeless-81273.

# Using the Ten Core Concepts to Write a Summary-Response Essay

In college, summary-response assignments often have very specific requirements, including which text you should summarize and respond to (the focus text), the format, and the length of the essay. If you are writing a summary-response essay as part of a course assignment, follow your instructor's guidelines. But whatever circumstances have prompted you to write a summary-response essay, this section will guide you through the process so that your essay meets the needs of your rhetorical situation.

## Step 1 | Identify a topic.

A summary-response essay begins with a focus text, and if you are completing a course assignment, your instructor might specify the focus text or provide you with a list of texts from which to choose your focus text. If so, choose a text that you find compelling for some reason—ideally, one that intersects with your own interests. If your assignment does not specify a focus text, consider the following:

| An interesting text | • Have you read an editorial or blog post that intrigued you or provoked you for some reason?<br>• Have you seen something posted on Twitter or Facebook that interests you?<br>• Have you encountered a course reading that sparked your curiosity? |
|---|---|
| An important trend | • Have you noticed an interesting or unusual trend among your peers or people in your age group?<br>• Have you seen news reports about an encouraging or troubling social or cultural development? |
| A controversial issue | • Is there a controversy on your campus that interests or worries you?<br>• Have you followed a controversial issue on social media or in mass media news reports? |

These questions can help you identify a focus text on a topic that matters to you. Step #1 in Chapter 3 provides additional guidance for identifying a topic.

## Step 2 | Place your topic in rhetorical context.

Most summary-response assignments are designed for a course. In other words, they serve specific rhetorical purposes in a course and are usually intended to be read by the course instructor and/or other students in the course to facilitate inquiry into course topics. If your assignment does not specify a rhetorical context but you are required to select a focus text from among your assigned course readings, you can probably assume that your primary audience is your instructor and your classmates. However, if you have selected a focus text of your own, consider the following:

- Who might be interested in the subject of your focus text?
- Why would they be interested in your focus text?
- What makes this subject and this focus text relevant now?

19

Answering these questions will help you identify a potential audience and a rhetorical purpose for your summary-response essay. Step #2 in Chapter 3 will help you explore that audience and purpose more fully.

##  Step 3 Select a medium.

Most summary-response assignments require students to write traditional academic essays that conform to the conventions of general academic style (see Chapter 26). If your assignment calls for such an essay, follow the guidelines carefully. However, if your instructor allows you to choose the medium for your project, consider which medium might be most appropriate for the rhetorical situation you identified in Step #2. Address these questions:

| Is your focus text a conventional print essay? | |
| --- | --- |
| **Yes:** Write your summary-response as a conventional print essay. | **No:** Consider a multimedia format if the focus text is a video or audio (such as a TED talk or podcast). |

| Will a multimedia project more effectively address your intended audience? | |
| --- | --- |
| **Not necessarily:** Write a conventional print essay. | **Possibly:** Consider a multimedia format for your summary-response project. |

Keep in mind that the medium should help you achieve your rhetorical goals. Select a medium with those goals in mind. Step #3 in Chapter 3 offers additional guidance for selecting an appropriate medium for your project.

## Step 4 Identify the main point of your summary-response project.

As we saw earlier in this chapter, one of the features of effective summary-response writing is a **substantive response** to the focus text, which is something more than your opinion about that text. In addition, effective summary-response writing usually has a broader purpose related to the subject of the focus text; in other words, part of your task at this point is to determine what you will say about the subject of the focus text to your audience that is relevant to them. **The main point of your summary-response essay, then, is twofold:**

1. What you will say about the focus text

2. What you will say about the subject of the focus text

These two aspects of your main point are closely related, but they are not necessarily the same. For example, in the summary-response essay titled "The Dynamics of Internet Addiction" on page 651, the writer makes two related but distinct main points:

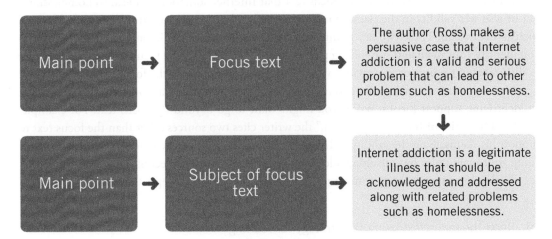

Main point → Focus text → The author (Ross) makes a persuasive case that Internet addiction is a valid and serious problem that can lead to other problems such as homelessness.

↓

Main point → Subject of focus text → Internet addiction is a legitimate illness that should be acknowledged and addressed along with related problems such as homelessness.

You can see that the writer's main point about the focus text (the article by Ross) leads to his main point about the larger subject of the focus text (Internet addiction).

As you begin developing your response, **address these two main questions:**

1. What will I say about the focus text?

2. What will I say about the subject of the focus text?

Try to answer each question in a sentence or two. It is possible to combine your answers to these two questions into a single main point. For example, we might state the main point of "The Dynamics of Internet Addiction" as follows:

> *Ross makes a persuasive case that Internet addiction is a valid illness that leads to other problems, and we should address it as such.*

However, at this stage, it is useful to keep these two main points separate, because what you say about the focus text and about the larger subject of that text are likely to evolve as you explore the text and develop both your summary and your response. Step #4 in Chapter 3 will help you develop your main point further.

## Step 5 Support your main point.

Because your support for your main points about your focus text arises from your summary of that text, **your first task at this point is to develop your summary.** Obviously, the first step in developing your summary is to read your focus text carefully. Follow the procedure described in "A Strategy for Reading Academic Texts" on page 622. As you draft your summary, follow the advice in "Summarizing and Paraphrasing" on page 629 and in "Features of Effective Summary-Response Writing" on page 648.

19

As you delve more deeply into your focus text and develop your summary, keep in mind the main point you identified in Step #4. Identify supporting points that enable you to elaborate on that main point. For example, in "The Dynamics of Internet Addiction," the writer expresses initial skepticism about the claim in the focus text that Internet addiction can lead to homelessness, but he also sees validity in the claim that Internet addiction is similar to other forms of addiction, such as alcoholism. These two key points support the writer's main point about the focus text. As you identify your main and supporting points, look for passages in the focus text that you can use to illustrate your points or to provide evidence for your claims about the focus text.

Next, return to the main point about the subject of the focus text that you identified in Step #4. In identifying support for this point, you might want to go beyond the focus text. For example, in "The Dynamics of Internet Addiction," the writer cites two sources other than the focus text to support his claims about the validity of Internet addiction as a legitimate illness. Consider strengthening your main point by consulting additional sources about the subject of the focus text.

To develop support for your main point, then, follow these six steps:

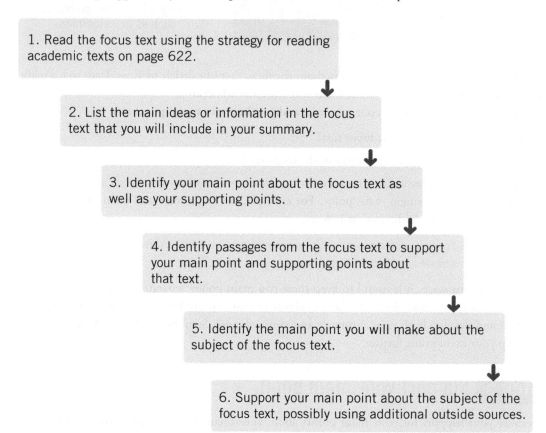

1. Read the focus text using the strategy for reading academic texts on page 622.

2. List the main ideas or information in the focus text that you will include in your summary.

3. Identify your main point about the focus text as well as your supporting points.

4. Identify passages from the focus text to support your main point and supporting points about that text.

5. Identify the main point you will make about the subject of the focus text.

6. Support your main point about the subject of the focus text, possibly using additional outside sources.

Step #5 in Chapter 3 provides additional guidance for developing support for your main point. You should now be ready to write a complete rough draft of your summary-response essay. If not, go to Step #6 to develop an outline.

## Step 6  Organize your summary-response project.

In general, organizing a summary-response project is usually more straightforward than organizing other kinds of academic texts because you can use the two main components—the summary and the response—as the basis for your project's structure. One approach is to integrate your response into your summary, summarizing each main idea from the source text and then responding to that idea before moving onto your summary of the next main idea, and so on. But the easiest way to organize a summary-response essay is to present your complete summary of the focus text and then your response, in that order. Of course, you still have to organize those two main sections, but you can follow this general outline to do so:

I.    Introduction
II.   Description of the Focus Text
III.  Summary
- A. Brief overview of focus text
- B. Summary of main components and ideas of focus text
- C. Additional points about focus text

IV.   Response
- A. Main response to focus text
- B. Supporting points
- C. Main point about subject of focus text.

V.    Conclusion

In developing an outline according to this format, keep the following in mind:

- Your introduction should place your essay in broader context and give your readers a sense of your purpose and your response without giving away the specific details of your response.
- Sometimes the introduction includes the description of the focus text, depending upon the overall length of the essay.
- The summary can be organized around the main ideas in the same order that they appear in the focus text.
- Include external sources to support your claims in your response, if appropriate.

As always, follow your instructor's guidelines. Step #6 in Chapter 3 provides additional guidance for organizing your project.

## Step 7  Get feedback.

When seeking feedback about your draft, ask your readers to focus on the main features of effective summary-response writing:

19

| Description of the focus text | • What is the focus text?<br>• Are the title and author of the focus text provided?<br>• What information about the focus text does the writer provide to help readers place it in context? |
|---|---|
| A clear, accurate summary | • How clear is the summary of the focus text?<br>• Does the summary include all main ideas or components of the focus text?<br>• Which sections of the summary are confusing, if any? |
| A substantive response | • What insights does the writer provide about the focus text?<br>• In what ways does the writer's response go beyond mere opinion of the focus text?<br>• What support does the writer offer for his or her claims about the focus text? How persuasive is this support? |
| A larger purpose | • What is the writer's larger point about the subject of the focus text?<br>• What makes this point relevant to the intended audience?<br>• What purpose does the summary-response serve? |

As always, review your reviewers' feedback carefully as you consider revisions. Step #7 in Chapter 3 offers additional guidance for getting feedback on your draft.

## Step 8 Revise.

Revising your summary-response project involves addressing **two main concerns:**

a. the clarity and accuracy of your summary of the focus text

b. the substance and relevance of your response

Review each of these main components of your project in turn. First, make sure your summary clearly and accurately conveys all important ideas and information from the focus text, which might mean rereading sections of the focus text. Then make sure your response reflects a genuine engagement with the focus text and a careful evaluation of it. Use the questions listed in Step #7 to do a complete review of your draft and identify potential revisions to strengthen your project.

Keep in mind that you might have to rewrite sections of your summary if your reviewers were confused by it, and you might need to do additional research about the subject of the focus text to give your response greater depth and substance. That's OK. Revision is part of the process of inquiry into the focus text and your response to it.

Step #8 in Chapter 3 will help guide your revisions.

## Step 9 Refine your voice.

If your assignment calls for a conventional academic essay, review your draft to make sure your writing is not inappropriately informal and meets the stylistic expectations for academic writing. (See Chapter 26 for advice on academic style.) At the same time, reread your draft to "listen" for your voice. Try to determine whether your voice conveys a sense of authority and strengthens your effort to convey your response to your intended audience. Make appropriate adjustments to strengthen your voice.

## Step 10 Edit.

Complete Step #10 in Chapter 3. Check any quotations you included from the focus text to make sure they are accurate and cited correctly.

---

**WRITING PROJECTS**     **REQUIRING SUMMARY-RESPONSE**

1. Find a scholarly article on a topic related to a current controversy that interests you. (You might need to use a database to find such an article; see Chapter 21 for guidance on using such databases.) For example, if you're interested in current debates about income inequality, you might find a scholarly article by an economist addressing some aspect of income inequality. Using the strategies described in this chapter, write a summary-response to that article in a way that connects it to the current controversy. Assume your audience is a general academic audience, including other students, who might share your interest in this controversy.

2. Find an op-ed essay or a blog post about the same controversy you identified for Question #1 (or a different controversy). Write a summary-response to that op-ed piece or blog post for a general audience.

3. Compare the essays you wrote for Questions #1 and #2. What differences and similarities do you see between them? What do you think the comparison of these two essays suggests about the nature and purposes of summary-response writing?

4. Recreate the essay you wrote for Question #1 or Question #2 in a different format—for example, a YouTube video or PowerPoint presentation. When you are finished, write a brief paragraph describing the adjustments you made to adapt your summary-response to a different medium.

19

MindTap®

Request help with these Writing Projects and get feedback from a tutor. If required, participate in peer review, submit your paper for a grade, and view instructor comments online.

### In this chapter, you will learn to

1. Define and analyze the audience and purpose of various document designs.

2. Identify the four key elements of document design.

3. Apply the four basic principles of document design when critiquing written documents.

4. Analyze three document design projects.

### MindTap®

Understand the goals of the chapter and complete a warm-up activity.

# Designing Documents

**RECENTLY** a friend of mine who works as a regional planner was asked to review a proposal. The proposal had been submitted to her organization by a consulting company that manages commercial and residential projects, such as strip malls, parks, and housing developments. The consulting company was seeking to be hired to create a development plan for the rural county where my friend works. It was a big proposal for a big project, and my friend had to evaluate it to help the county decide whether to hire the company to develop its regional plan. So she carefully studied the proposal, assessing the company's ideas for regional development as well as its ability to complete a good plan on time. The document was nearly 100 pages, with detailed analyses of issues like water flow, population density, and infrastructure (roads, bridges, and so on). My friend liked many aspects of the proposal, but her biggest complaint was that the document itself looked unprofessional. Although its analysis was sophisticated, with many graphs and tables, its design, she said, was amateurish. More important, she found it difficult to locate important information in the document.

This anecdote underscores the importance of design in many documents—not only in professional settings such as my friend's workplace, but in many other contexts as well:

- A campus group that trains volunteer mentors for first-year students creates a flyer to announce a meeting for new volunteers.
- A community organization that runs a food pantry develops a brochure to advertise its services to local residents.
- A college rugby club compiles an annual report, complete with photos and charts, for the campus athletic department.

And of course many college instructors expect students to include graphs, tables, and other visual elements in print reports and to make presentations using tools such as Prezi. In each case, a well-designed document is more likely to achieve its rhetorical purpose.

Because widely available technologies make it easy to create professional-looking documents, readers often expect more than well-written content. They want the content to be presented with appropriate graphics, attractive color schemes, and pleasing layouts. Such features are much more than ornamentation. The design of a document is a rhetorical tool that helps writers communicate ideas and information effectively to their audiences and helps convince readers that a document is worth reading. Effective document design also lends credibility to the writer. Today, knowing how to design a document well is an increasingly important part of being an effective writer.

Document design includes many sophisticated elements that are beyond the scope of this textbook, but this chapter will introduce you to basic concepts to help you develop the skills you need to design documents that will achieve your rhetorical goals. (You can find related information about visual design elsewhere in this book. See "Analyzing Images" in Chapter 8; Focus: "Presenting Information Visually" in Chapter 17; and "Using Images" in Chapter 18).

# Understanding Document Design as a Rhetorical Tool

Imagine that you want to raise awareness among students on your campus about alcohol abuse. Here's a public service poster from a university health center that does just that:

Source: Freidenberg, Brian M. *Did You Know?* Counseling Center, University at Albany, State University of New York, 2013.

What do you notice about this document? The authors certainly intend to catch your eye with the large yellow "98%" in the center of the page that contrasts with the darker background and the smaller text below it. Using color, layout, and font size strategically, they communicate a great deal of information with relatively few words. For example, they describe six different steps students can take to drink alcohol safely (using a designated driver, avoiding drinking games, and so on), and they identify the source of the information (a survey of students at that university). The layout of this information in a horizontal line of checked items at the bottom of the page sets it apart, making it more likely that you will read that information. And notice that the question in the upper left-hand corner of the document invites you into a kind of dialogue, a provocative way to entice students to read the entire document.

The authors of this poster have designed their document, first, to attract the attention of their intended audience (students at their university), and second, to communicate specific information efficiently to that audience. A more conventional document might be less effective in achieving these rhetorical goals, especially given how much information busy college students encounter in a typical day. For example, compare the poster to an email with the same information that might be sent to students as a public service announcement:

> Do you know that 98% of UAlbany students take steps to be safer in drinking situations? A random, anonymous survey of 1001 students conducted during spring, 2010, found that students take the following steps: using a designated driver, avoiding drinking games, pacing drinks to one or fewer an hour, eating before or during drinking, alternating non-alcoholic with alcoholic beverages, and choosing not to drink alcohol.

Which document is more likely to reach students? Which is more likely to grab students' attention? Which is more likely to be memorable to students?

Document design is a powerful way to make sure you reach an audience and convey ideas and information effectively. In designing your own documents, keep these points in mind:

- **Consider your audience.** The first step in designing a document is to identify the expectations of your intended audience and the rhetorical goals for your document. Who is your audience for this document? What kind of document are they likely to expect? What design features will appeal to them? A flyer announcing a campus farmer's market probably won't appeal to residents of a local retirement community if it has the flashy colors and provocative features of the public service poster on the previous page, which is intended for a much younger audience with very different tastes.

- **Consider your message.** Be clear about the ideas, information, or point you want to convey to your audience. What features will best help you convey your message? How might you use those features to emphasize key ideas and help readers find important information? For example, the large font and bright color of the figure "98%" in the poster on the facing page help emphasize the key point of the poster, which is that the vast majority of students on that campus try to use alcohol safely.

- **Avoid ornamentation.** Just as you should try to eliminate unnecessary information from a piece of writing, you should avoid design features that do little more than decorate your document. The images, graphics, font styles, colors, and layout you use should help you accomplish your rhetorical goals by communicating or emphasizing important ideas or information. If a design element doesn't help you accomplish your rhetorical goals, consider eliminating or changing it.

- **Make a good impression.** First impressions can influence how an audience responds to your document. If the design is effective, your audience is more likely to take your message seriously, and you are more likely to achieve your rhetorical goals. If your design is weak, you risk undermining your credibility, as happened to the authors of the poorly designed proposal in the anecdote at the beginning of this chapter.

---

**EXERCISE 20A    EXAMINING THE DESIGN OF DOCUMENTS**

1. Visit the websites of two or three restaurants in your town or neighborhood and review their menus. Compare the way the menus present information. How are the menus organized? How easy is it to find information about specific items that you might want to order? Which menu looks most professional? Now identify specific features that make each menu appealing or not: the colors, the layout of the pages, the use of images or graphics, and so on. Consider how these elements help you find the menu items you are looking for. What conclusions about document design might you draw from this exercise?

2. Compare the design of two or more textbooks that you are currently using for your classes (or textbooks you have used in the past). Select a representative page from each textbook and compare them. What do you notice about each page? Which pages do you find most appealing? Which are easiest to read? On the basis of this comparison, draw your own conclusions about which textbook has the most effective design.

---

# Principles of Document Design

The public service poster on page 662 demonstrates **four basic principles of document design:**

- **Contrast:** a pronounced difference in color, size, or other design elements that can be used for emphasis or to help readers navigate a document.

- **Repetition:** strategic repeating of text, color, patterns, or other features to emphasize information or ideas and show connections between content or sections of a document.

- **Alignment:** the layout of elements of a page or document in relation to each other and to the page borders.

- **Proximity:** the positioning of information or features next to one another to show connections or emphasis.

These four principles can guide your decisions about how to design a document to meet the needs of your rhetorical situation.

# Contrast

**Notice how the white text stands out against this black background.**

This light-colored text is more difficult to see against the yellow background.

These two examples illustrate the value of contrast—in this case, contrasting colors—to communicate or emphasize ideas and information. Contrast that is sufficiently strong, as in the top example, helps convey information more easily. Poor contrast can obscure information and make it difficult for readers to navigate a document.

**Writers use contrast for three main reasons:**

- **To emphasize ideas or information.** Notice, for example, that the color, size, and font of the phrase "to emphasize ideas or information" make it stand apart from the rest of this paragraph and give it greater emphasis. Contrasting images—say, of a crying baby and a smiling child—might be used to communicate an idea or point—for example, about the nature of childhood.

- **To organize a document.** Contrast is a common way to help readers navigate a document. For example, headings or subtitles that appear in sizes or colors that are different from the main text indicate to readers where different sections of a document begin and end. Icons can be used to indicate special information.

- **To establish a focus.** Contrast can be used to convey a sense of the focus or main idea of a document. In the poster on page 680, for example, the large contrasting type size for the figure "98%" helps focus the reader's attention on the point that most students use alcohol safely.

Contrast is commonly created with color and different font sizes or styles. For example, this 18-point font is immediately noticeable in a paragraph full of 12-point font. Similarly, you can use **a different font style like this** to set a title, subheading, or key sentence apart from surrounding text.

## FOCUS  UNDERSTANDING TYPOGRAPHY

Typography refers to letters and symbols in a document. It includes features such as *italics*, underlining, and **boldface** as well as the size and style of the font. You can use typography to make documents more readable, appealing, and easy to navigate. You can also use it to emphasize important ideas or information. Understanding a few basic concepts can help you use typography effectively in your documents.

*(Continued)*

**Serif and Sans Serif.** Fonts appear in two basic types: *serif*, which has small horizontal lines attached to the main lines of a letter, and *sans serif*, which does not.

$$\text{K} \qquad \text{K}$$

serif        sans serif

Although the uses of these styles can vary, serif fonts are considered more traditional and are generally used in formal writing (such as academic assignments), whereas sans serif fonts tend to be considered more contemporary. Serif fonts are generally considered easier to read and are therefore the best choice for long passages of text (as in a traditional academic paper).

**Font styles.** Writers can choose from hundreds of font styles, including common styles such as courier, arial, and garamond, as well as unusual styles, such as *lucida calligraphy* and Old English Text. Although it is tempting to use uncommon font styles, the rule of thumb is to select fonts that make your document readable. For most academic assignments, a traditional font such as Times Roman is preferable. Also keep in mind that different font styles take up different amounts of space.

**Font Size.** Fonts sizes are measured in points. The standard font size for most extended text is 12-point. Sometimes, larger font sizes, such as this 14-point font or this 18-point font, are used for titles and headings or in tables and charts. However, varying the font size too often can be distracting to readers, so select font sizes strategically and be consistent in sizing the fonts you use. For example, use the same font size for all extended text and another font size for all subtitles.

## Repetition

The careful repetition of specific features of a text—such as words, color, graphics, and font sizes or styles—can help make a document more readable and coherent. For example, the repetition of certain design features on the first page of each chapter of this textbook (such as color, the placement and style of images, the font size, and the layout of the page) enables you to identify the beginning of a chapter quickly and easily. In this same way, you already use repetition to help readers navigate your conventional print documents. For example, numbers in the same location on each page and subheadings separated from the main text are common features of essays or reports to help readers follow a document.

This use of repetition is so common that we might not even notice it, yet it can be used to communicate or emphasize important information very efficiently. For instance, the familiar repetition of the shape and color scheme of road signs tells motorists unequivocally that the signs contain relevant information, such as whether a traffic light or a pedestrian crossing lies ahead. (See Figure 20.1.)

**FIGURE 20.1** Standard Road Signs

© Nelson Marques/Shutterstock.com

In the same way, a writer might use the repetition of a color or font style to indicate that certain information is important. Notice the repetition of the color blue on the web page about maintaining health in college in Figure 20.2. Blue is used to signal main ideas: the page title ("College Health: How to Stay Healthy") and the questions that represent key points ("What can I do to stay healthy?" "What should I know about nutrition and eating well?"). Blue is also used to lend a sense of cohesion to the page; notice, for example, that the bullets are blue.

**FIGURE 20.2** Using Color to Organize Information on a Web Page

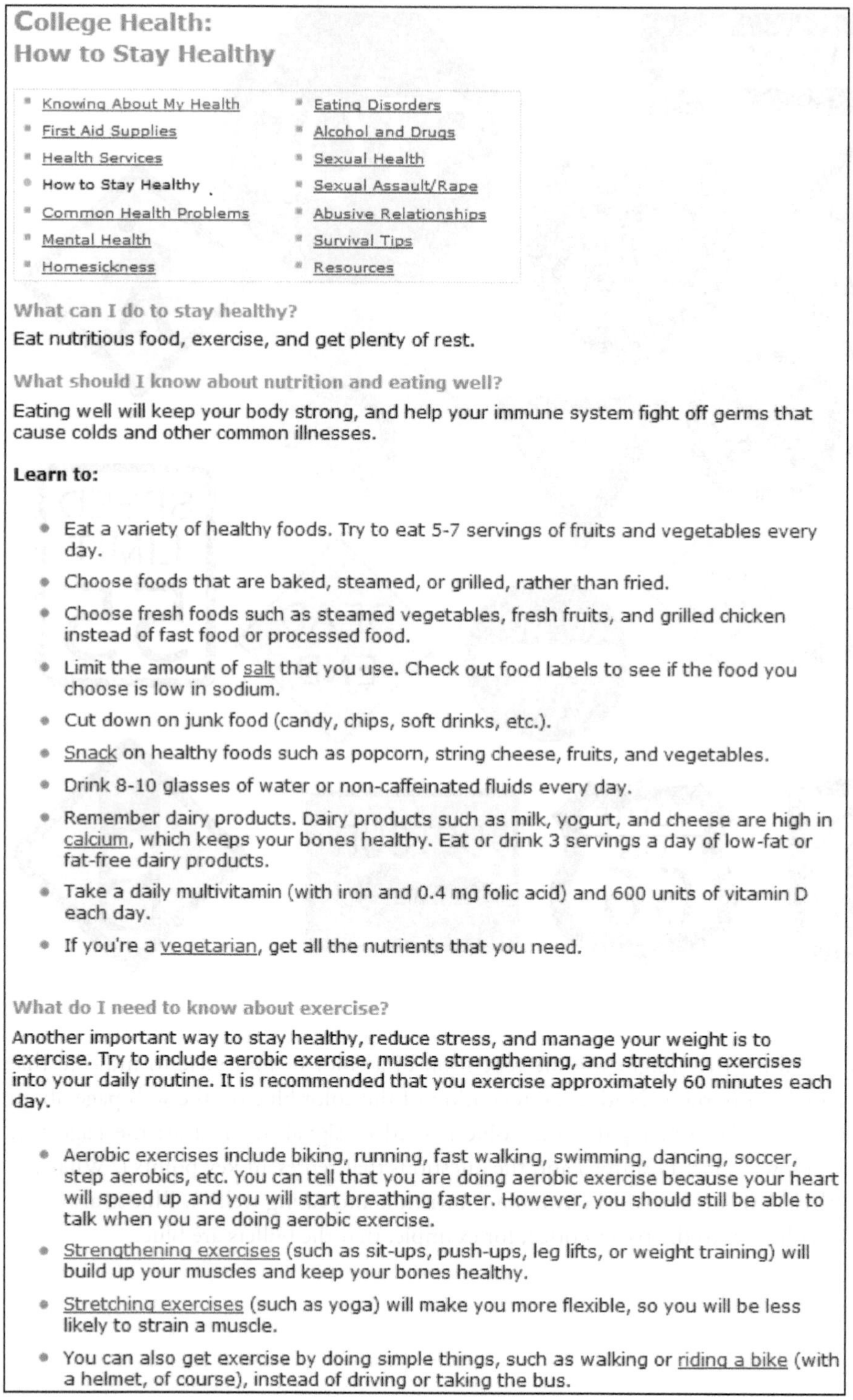

---

College Health:
How to Stay Healthy

- Knowing About My Health
- First Aid Supplies
- Health Services
- How to Stay Healthy
- Common Health Problems
- Mental Health
- Homesickness

- Eating Disorders
- Alcohol and Drugs
- Sexual Health
- Sexual Assault/Rape
- Abusive Relationships
- Survival Tips
- Resources

What can I do to stay healthy?

Eat nutritious food, exercise, and get plenty of rest.

What should I know about nutrition and eating well?

Eating well will keep your body strong, and help your immune system fight off germs that cause colds and other common illnesses.

**Learn to:**

- Eat a variety of healthy foods. Try to eat 5-7 servings of fruits and vegetables every day.
- Choose foods that are baked, steamed, or grilled, rather than fried.
- Choose fresh foods such as steamed vegetables, fresh fruits, and grilled chicken instead of fast food or processed food.
- Limit the amount of salt that you use. Check out food labels to see if the food you choose is low in sodium.
- Cut down on junk food (candy, chips, soft drinks, etc.).
- Snack on healthy foods such as popcorn, string cheese, fruits, and vegetables.
- Drink 8-10 glasses of water or non-caffeinated fluids every day.
- Remember dairy products. Dairy products such as milk, yogurt, and cheese are high in calcium, which keeps your bones healthy. Eat or drink 3 servings a day of low-fat or fat-free dairy products.
- Take a daily multivitamin (with iron and 0.4 mg folic acid) and 600 units of vitamin D each day.
- If you're a vegetarian, get all the nutrients that you need.

What do I need to know about exercise?

Another important way to stay healthy, reduce stress, and manage your weight is to exercise. Try to include aerobic exercise, muscle strengthening, and stretching exercises into your daily routine. It is recommended that you exercise approximately 60 minutes each day.

- Aerobic exercises include biking, running, fast walking, swimming, dancing, soccer, step aerobics, etc. You can tell that you are doing aerobic exercise because your heart will speed up and you will start breathing faster. However, you should still be able to talk when you are doing aerobic exercise.
- Strengthening exercises (such as sit-ups, push-ups, leg lifts, or weight training) will build up your muscles and keep your bones healthy.
- Stretching exercises (such as yoga) will make you more flexible, so you will be less likely to strain a muscle.
- You can also get exercise by doing simple things, such as walking or riding a bike (with a helmet, of course), instead of driving or taking the bus.

---

Source: "College Health: How to Stay Healthy." *Center for Young Women's Health*, 1 Feb. 2013, www.youngwomenshealth.org/collegehealth05.html.

## Alignment

Alignment is the primary means by which writers make documents easy to read and create a sense of unity on a page or screen. When you set margins for a report or essay and keep all the paragraphs justified to the left-hand margin, you are using alignment to make your document easier to follow.

Readers depend on conventions for alignment—such as justifying paragraphs to the left or centering titles—which standardize some elements of document design to avoid confusion.

Because of these conventions, most readers find it annoying to read text that is aligned to the right-hand margin. And notice how the insertion of columns in the middle of this paragraph makes it harder to follow.

Writers can use alignment to present information efficiently and in visually appealing ways. Notice how the columns at the top of the web page in Figure 20.2 make it easy for a reader to find the right link to other pages on that website. Notice, too, that the bullet points are all aligned in the same way: indented from the left margin. Such an alignment helps set off the main questions and makes it easier for readers to follow the text.

In some kinds of documents, including brochures, newsletters, and web pages, alignment is an essential tool for designing a page or screen that is both visually appealing and easy for a reader to navigate. When aligning elements on a page, consider how the placement of elements will draw a reader's eye and enable the reader to move comfortably from one element to the next.

## Proximity

Proximity creates cohesion and shows relationships among elements on a page or screen. Using this principle, you can create documents that are less cluttered and more efficiently organized, especially when you are combining text with visual elements.

Proximity can have a big impact on the appearance and effectiveness of a page. Let's imagine that you are part of a student organization that oversees all club sports on your campus, and you are creating a one-page flyer to inform students about the different club sports available to them. You might simply list all the sports:

Join a Club Sport!

| | |
|---|---|
| Softball | Swimming |
| Ski Team | Badminton |
| Bowling | Men's Baseball |
| Field Hockey | Equestrian |
| Fencing | Women's Ultimate Frisbee |
| Wrestling | Men's Ultimate Frisbee |
| Men's Soccer | Women's Soccer |
| Snowboarding | Ice Hockey |
| Men's Volleyball | Men's Lacrosse |
| Mixed Martial Arts | Women's Volleyball |
| Women's Rugby | Tae Kwon Do |

This unorganized list is visually aligned but tedious to read. To make it easier for students to make sense of the information, you can organize the sports by categories and place similar sports together:

Join a Club Sport!

<u>Co-Ed Sports</u>
    Badminton
    Bowling
    Equestrian
    Fencing
    Swimming
    Tae Kwon Do
    Ultimate Frisbee

<u>Winter Sports</u>
    Hockey
    Ski Team
    Snowboarding

<u>Men's Team Sports</u>
    Baseball
    Lacrosse
    Mixed Martial Arts
    Soccer
    Wrestling

<u>Women's Team Sports</u>
    Field Hockey
    Rugby
    Softball
    Soccer
    Volleyball

Simply by placing similar items together and adding space between the groups, you have organized the page in a way that makes it easier for a reader to find relevant information.

In more sophisticated documents that include images and graphics as well as text, the proximity of elements can significantly improve appearance and readability. For example, notice how many different elements catch your eye on this main web page from Yahoo.com. To make it easier for viewers to find information on a screen with so many elements, similar items are grouped together:

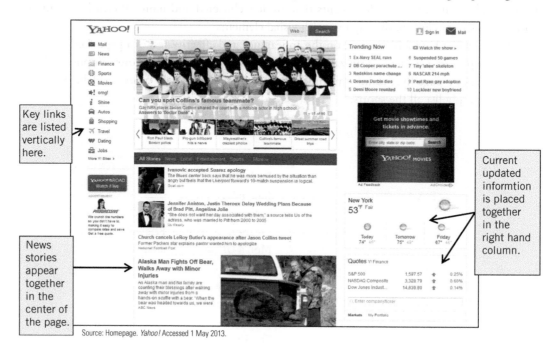

Source: Homepage. *Yahoo!* Accessed 1 May 2013.

Strategic use of proximity can make such a complex page even more readable. Here's a web page for an organization called Cross-Cultural Solutions, which sponsors international volunteer opportunities for students:

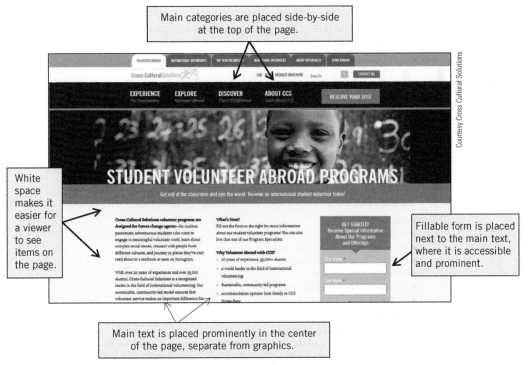

Main categories are placed side-by-side at the top of the page.

White space makes it easier for a viewer to see items on the page.

**STUDENT VOLUNTEER ABROAD PROGRAMS**

Fillable form is placed next to the main text, where it is accessible and prominent.

Main text is placed prominently in the center of the page, separate from graphics.

Source: "Student Volunteer Abroad Programs." *Cross-Cultural Solutions*, 2016, www.crossculturalsolutions.org/lp/student-volunteer-abroad-programs.

Careful grouping of similar items and the use of white space make this page appear clean and coherent, even though it contains a great deal of information. Notice, too, that repetition, contrast, and alignment make the page visually appealing and well organized. For example, the main links at the top of the page appear in similar font style and size (repetition) but in larger fonts than other text on the page (contrast), which makes them easier to find; the organization's tagline ("Get out of the classroom and into the world. Become an international student volunteer today!") appears in white font in a blue box, which makes it prominent and easy to read. In addition, all the main items are aligned vertically and horizontally, creating a balanced, cohesive, and unified page.

The most effectively designed documents, even relatively simple print texts, use all four design principles together. When deciding on the design of a document, follow three basic steps:

1. **Consider your rhetorical situation.** Who is your intended audience? What are your goals in addressing that audience with this document? What expectations might this audience have when it comes to the design of a document?

2. **Be clear about your message.** What is the central point you want to make with this document? What primary information do you hope to communicate?

3. **Apply the four principles of basic design.** How can you use contrast, repetition, alignment, and proximity to communicate your message effectively to your intended audience? How can you use these principles to make your document appealing and efficient?

Use the four basic principles of document design to evaluate this flyer from a public television station. The document is intended to help parents identify potential reading problems in their children. Assess how effectively the document uses design elements to convey its message to its intended audience.

# Ed Extras

Place your school name or logo here

*Helpful information about learning brought to you by Reading Rockets, Colorín Colorado, and LD OnLine*

## Recognizing Reading Problems

Learning to read is a challenge for many kids, but most can become good readers if they get the right help. Parents have an important job in recognizing when a child is struggling and knowing how to find help.

### What to look for:
- Difficulty rhyming
- Difficulty hearing individual sounds
- Difficulty following directions
- Difficulty re-telling a story
- Struggles to sound out most words
- Avoids reading aloud

### What to do:
- **Step 1: Meet with your child's teacher**
  Gather examples of your child's work that reflect your concerns. Ask the teacher for his/her observations and discuss what can be done at school and at home. Stay in touch with the teacher to monitor your child's progress.
- **Step 2: Meet with the principal and/or reading specialist**
  If your child's performance does not improve, meet with other professionals in the building to see if there are classes, services, or other interventions available.
- **Step 3: Get a referral for special education**
  If you have tried all interventions, request an evaluation. Talk to the principal to schedule this.
- **Step 4: Get an evaluation**
  A professional team—which may include a school psychologist, a speech-language pathologist, or a reading specialist—gives your child a series of tests and determines whether s/he is eligible to receive special education services.
- **Step 5: Determine eligibility**
  - If your child is found eligible for services, you and the school develop your child's Individualized Education Program (IEP), a plan that sets goals based on your child's specific learning needs and offers special services like small group instruction or assistive technology.
  - If your child is not eligible, stay involved and keep talking to the teacher about your child's progress. You can also turn to private tutoring for extra support.

**Check out the *Assessment* section for more information on identifying reading problems:**
**www.ReadingRockets.org/article/c68**

Visit our sister sites, ColorinColorado.org and LDOnLine.org, for more information about learning.

Reading Rockets, Colorín Colorado, and LD OnLine are services of public television station WETA, Washington, D.C. Reading Rockets is funded by the U.S. Department of Education, Office of Special Education Programs. Colorín Colorado, a web service to help English language learners become better readers, receives major funding from the American Federation of Teachers. Additional funding is provided by the National Institute for Literacy and the U.S. Department of Education, Office of Special Education Programs. LD OnLine is the world's leading website on learning disabilities and ADHD, with major funding from Lindamood-Bell Learning Processes.

Reading Rockets

Source: *Recognizing Reading Problems.* Reading Rockets / WETA, 2012, www.readingrockets.org/article/14541/.

# Working with Visual Elements

Many documents include photographs, charts, graphics, and other visual elements. Increasingly, college instructors expect students to incorporate such elements into conventional papers. However, visual elements should never be used simply as ornamentation; rather, they should be used in a way that communicates information, conveys important ideas, and enhances the effectiveness of the document.

This section provides advice on using two common kinds of visual elements:

- tables, graphs, and charts
- images

## Working with Tables, Graphs, and Charts

Many college assignments require students to work with quantitative information. For example, an analysis of the economic impact of college loan debt for an economics course will likely include various kinds of statistical data. Often, such data are most effectively presented in a table, bar graph, line graph, or pie chart. Contemporary word processing programs make it easy to create such elements in a variety of formats. However, the key to using such elements effectively is knowing what you want your readers to understand from the information you are presenting. Consider:

- **What is the nature of the information?** Numerical data can be easy to convert into a chart or table. Other kinds of information, such as directions for a procedure or a list of specific responses to a survey question, might not work as well in a graphical format. A chart or table should make the information easier for a reader to understand. Avoid using graphical formats if it makes the information more complicated or confusing.

- **What is the purpose of the information?** You present information for various reasons: to explain a concept, event, or development; to support a claim or assertion; to strengthen an argument; to illustrate a key idea or principle. The purpose can shape your decision about how best to present the information. For example, if you want to emphasize a specific set of statistics to support a central claim in an argument, using a graph or pie chart to present the data can make it more persuasive.

Tables, charts, and graphs have four basic elements:

- a title
- a vertical axis, called the $y$ axis
- a horizontal axis, called the $x$ axis
- the main body of data

Let's imagine you are writing a report on the benefits of a college education, and you wish to report the results of a survey of students who graduated in the past three years from three different departments on your campus. The survey was intended to learn about average starting salaries of graduates from your school. Numerical data such as survey results are commonly reported in the form of tables or graphs, but deciding how best to present that information depends on how you are using it in your report. If you are simply reporting the survey results to help your readers understand the average salaries of recent graduates, you might use a simple **table**. In this example, the *y* axis is used for the three different departments and the *x* axis for the three recent years; the main body of data is the starting salaries. The table would look like this:

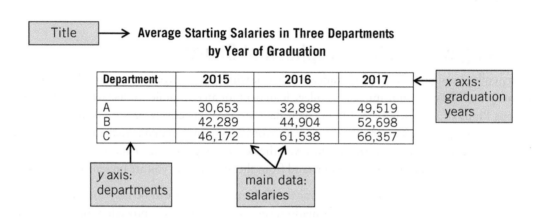

This table helps readers easily find the average salary for a specific department in a specific graduation year. Consider how much more tedious it is for readers to read an explanation of this information, which might look like this:

> The average starting salary for students who graduated from Department A in 2015 was $30,653; in 2016 it was $32,898, and in 2017 it was $49,519. For students who graduated from Department B in 2015, the average starting salary was $42,289; in 2016 it was $44,904, and in 2017 it was $52,698. Students who graduated from Department C in 2015 earned an average starting salary of $46,172; for 2016 graduates, the average starting salary was $61,538, and in 2017 it was $66,357.

Although presenting numerical information visually isn't always the most effective approach, in a case like this one, it is much more efficient than a verbal explanation.

A simple table might be too limited for presenting more complicated bodies of data, especially if you wish to compare information. Let's say that for an essay in which you argue for adjusting high school class schedules so that adolescents can get more sleep, you want to present information showing the different sleep patterns of different age groups; let's imagine you also want to show gender differences in sleep patterns to support your contention that those differences don't matter for adolescents. A **bar graph** is an effective means for comparing information. This graph shows average sleep times for people of different age groups; it also compares men and women:

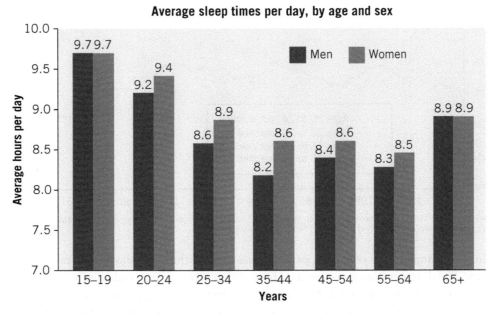

**Average sleep times per day, by age and sex**

**Note: Data include all persons age 15 and over. Data include all days of the week and are annual averages for 2014**

Source: "Charts by Topic: Sleep." *American Time Use Survey*, U.S. Bureau of Labor Statistics, 26 Oct. 2015, www.bls.gov/tus/charts/sleep.htm.

Here, the *y* axis is used for average hours of sleep per day and the *x* axis for age group.

If you wanted to show a trend or trajectory reflected in statistical information over time, a **line graph** might be a better option. For example, let's say you included in your essay about adjusting high school class schedules some data to show trends in employment rates for high school and college students over the past four decades; you want to show that employment rates for students currently in school have dropped. This line graph makes it very easy for readers to see those trends and compare the employment rates of students who are enrolled in high school or college to people of the same age who are not enrolled:

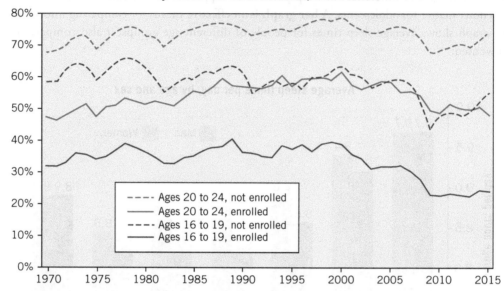

**Employment-population ratios in October of young people by school enrollment status, 1970–2015**

Legend:
- – – – Ages 20 to 24, not enrolled
- —— Ages 20 to 24, enrolled
- – – – Ages 16 to 19, not enrolled
- —— Ages 16 to 19, enrolled

Source: "Students Less Likely to Work in October 2015 Than in the 1980s and 1990s." *TED: The Economics Daily,* U.S. Bureau of Labor Statistics, 18 May 2016, www.bls.gov/opub/ted/2016/students-less-likely-to-work-in-october-2015-than-in-the-1980s-and-1990s.htm.

In this example, the *y* axis shows employment rate and the *x* axis shows the years from 1970 to 2015. The different lines represent data from different age groups and enrollment status. For example, you can see that in 1989 approximately 40% of young people between the ages of 16 and 19 who were enrolled in school were also employed, whereas only about 23% of these students were employed in 2015. By contrast, approximately 63% of students in this age group who were not enrolled in school were employed in 1989, but only 55% were employed in 2015. This seemingly simple line graph contains a great deal of information and enables readers to see trends in the data and to compare trends among different groups as well.

Tables, graphs, and charts can present information efficiently, but they also can be misleading. For example, let's say you want to show the percentage of four items in the budget of a student organization you work for: item A (11%), item B (42%), item C (5%), and item D (42%). In addition, you want to highlight item C, which is the smallest expenditure. Your pie chart might look like this:

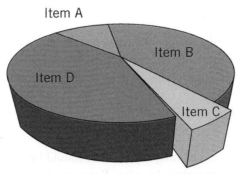

Item A

Item B

Item D

Item C

Source: "An Example of a Misleading Pie Chart." *Wikipedia*, 21 June 2012, en.wikipedia.org/wiki/Misleading_graph#/media/Misleading_Pie_Chart.png.

This three-dimensional chart, which makes it seem that you are looking at it from the side and slightly above it, is visually striking. Notice, however, that item C, which is only 5% of the budget, appears bigger than item A, which is 11% of the budget. Now here's the same information presented in a simpler, two-dimensional pie chart:

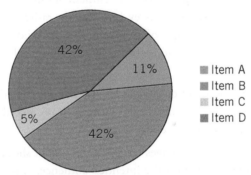

42%

11%

5%

42%

- Item A
- Item B
- Item C
- Item D

Source: "A Sample Pie Chart." *Wikipedia*, 21 June 2012, en.wikipedia.org/wiki/Misleading_graph#/media/Sample_Pie_Chart.png.

In this case, the simpler chart presents the information more accurately. Keep in mind that small changes in the design of a table, chart, or graph can dramatically affect the appearance of the information, sometimes making small differences appear much larger and thus conveying a misleading idea about that information. Although such strategies might seem effective in supporting a claim or point of view, they might also be ethically questionable. You should always use graphical elements in a way that presents information not only accurately but also ethically.

# Working with Images

For many documents, effective design includes the use of images, but simply incorporating images into a document isn't necessarily enough to improve its design. Using images effectively is a matter of making sure the images are appropriate for your document and help address your rhetorical situation.

When using images, follow the same basic principles that apply to document design in general (see page 654):

- **Consider your audience.** The images you select should be relevant to your subject matter and appropriate for your rhetorical situation. For example, a photograph of a car on a brochure about campus transportation services is probably a poor choice if the majority of students live on campus, do not drive cars to campus, and use the campus bus service. Moreover, consider whether the images you select might seem confusing or offensive to your audience. A photograph that might convey relevant information dramatically could also weaken your document if the image is considered inappropriate for some reason by your readers.

- **Consider your message.** Images in your document should reinforce important ideas or information. Ideally, images should convey information rather than just supplement written text. For example, a photograph of a specific location should enable the audience to gain an understanding of that location without a lengthy verbal description to accompany the image.

- **Avoid ornamentation.** Sometimes, images are used to enhance the appearance of a document, but too many images used only as decoration can become distracting for readers and therefore undermine the document's effectiveness.

- **Make a good impression.** Any images used in a document should contribute to the overall impression a document makes on the intended audience. A poorly selected image could weaken an otherwise effective document.

In addition to these basic principles, **consider how the content and perspective of an image fits your rhetorical situation.** For example, compare these two versions of the same photograph:

artcphotos/Shutterstock.com    artcphotos/Shutterstock.com

What is the difference between them? How does the potential impact of each differ? As this example demonstrates, simply "cropping" an image—that is, selecting a section of it and eliminating the rest—can dramatically change its impact and message. In this example, the version on the left might be appropriate for a report in a zoology class that includes descriptions of various kinds of raptors; the photograph could be used to show the size and color of a specific species of raptor. The cropped version on the right might be used to emphasize the extraordinary eyesight of raptors or to dramatize the fierce nature of a particular species. Your rhetorical purpose should dictate how you use an image and how you might alter it.

The **perspective** of an image can have a powerful effect on the message it communicates. Let's imagine you are writing an analysis of the social and economic impact of severe weather, such as a hurricane. This photograph dramatically conveys the devastating effects of the storm on property as well as the lives on local residents:

Jocelyn Augustino/FEMA

Notice that the perspective from which the photograph was taken (above and at a distance from the subjects) highlights the sense of vulnerability of the people in the photo, who appear small in comparison to the damaged homes surrounding them. This photo would be less effective in conveying these ideas if it were taken from ground level or from closer to the subjects. This photograph dramatically highlights the extent of storm-caused devastation and its impact on residents in a way that would be challenging to explain in words alone. At the same time, such an image can provoke strong emotions in readers and therefore can be used to influence readers—for example, to convince readers of the need to prepare for future storms or to contribute to a fund to help storm victims.

Like any other design elements, images should be placed strategically so that they convey their messages without undermining the overall appearance of a document. Images that are too large, for example, might distract a reader from other important information on a page. Images that are too small might not communicate important information clearly.

---

**EXERCISE 20C** **WORKING WITH VISUAL ELEMENTS**

1. Imagine you are writing an analysis of the impact of smartphone technology on college students for a general audience. For each of the following items, decide whether to present the information in a chart, table, graph, or in a written description; explain your reasons for your decision in each case:

   - The most common uses of smartphones among college students are surfing the Internet, texting, and playing games. 85% of students report using their smartphones for playing games much more often than for any other purpose.

   - In 2011 47% of college students reported owning a smartphone. In 2015 86% of college students reported owning a smartphone. In 2011, 35% of Americans owned smartphones. In 2015 64% of Americans owned smartphones.

   - Since 2008, sales of smartphones have increased by an average of 15% annually.

   - In 2015, 87% of college students reported that they used a laptop or notebook computer every week for their school work; only 64% reported using a smartphone for their school work. In 2014, 56% of college students reported using a smartphone every week for their school work.

2. Using some of the information in question #1, create a table, graph, and chart. (You can easily create these elements using a word processing program such as MS Word.) Use the same information for each graphic. Compare the table, chart, and graph. What are the differences in the way they present the same information? What advantages and disadvantages do you see to each kind of graphic?

3. Using the example from question #1, search online to find one or two images that you might use in your analysis of smartphones. Explain how you would use each image in your analysis. Justify your selection of images in terms of how they would help you accomplish specific rhetorical goals.

---

# Designing Documents: Three Sample Projects

This section presents three common kinds of projects that illustrate how the same basic design features can make different kinds of documents effective in meeting the needs of a rhetorical situation.

## Print Documents

For most college assignments you are likely to be asked to submit a conventional paper, whether in hard copy or in a digital form (such as a Microsoft Word file), but even conventional papers can be more effective when writers apply the principles of design. Whenever you submit a conventional paper for an assignment, be sure to follow the appropriate conventions for formatting, which include such elements as font size, the uses of underlining and boldface, and the format for citing sources. (See Chapters 24 and 25 for information about proper format for papers in MLA and APA style.) You can also use the design principles in this chapter to enhance even the most traditional kind of paper by making sure that your font sizes and styles are consistent and that you use features such as underlining strategically, avoiding ornamentation.

Sometimes, however, your rhetorical situation might call for a print document that is not a conventional paper—for example, a flyer, brochure, or memo. In such cases, applying the principles of document design can enhance the document's effectiveness, even when the document is relatively simple. For example, Figure 20.3 shows a one-page flyer with information for college students about getting proper sleep. The flyer was developed by a college health and counseling center and made available in print form as well as in PDF format on the center's website. It illustrates how even a basic print document can more effectively meet the needs of a rhetorical situation when design principles are carefully applied.

### 1. Consider the rhetorical context.

- The health and counseling center helps students deal with lifestyle and health problems common to college life. One such problem is insomnia. The center's goal is to inform students on its campus about the importance of proper sleep without overwhelming busy students with a lot of information.

### 2. Be clear about your message.

- The main point is to show that college students can use several easy strategies to avoid insomnia and get proper rest. Also, knowing the common causes of poor sleep can help students avoid sleep problems.

### 3. Apply the principles of design.

- The one-page flyer incorporates no images and only two small graphics, but it uses the principles of contrast, alignment, and repetition to convey a great deal of information efficiently and to reinforce the main point about getting proper sleep.

**FIGURE 20.3** College Health and Counseling Service Flyer

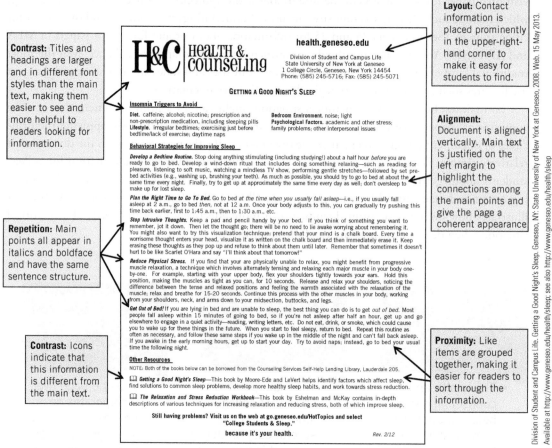

**Contrast:** Titles and headings are larger and in different font styles than the main text, making them easier to see and more helpful to readers looking for information.

**Repetition:** Main points all appear in italics and boldface and have the same sentence structure.

**Contrast:** Icons indicate that this information is different from the main text.

**Layout:** Contact information is placed prominently in the upper-right-hand corner to make it easy for students to find.

**Alignment:** Document is aligned vertically. Main text is justified on the left margin to highlight the connections among the main points and give the page a coherent appearance.

**Proximity:** Like items are grouped together, making it easier for readers to sort through the information.

Source: Cholette, Beth. *Getting a Good Night's Sleep.* Division of Student and Campus Life, State University of New York at Geneseo, 2012, www.geneseo.edu/webfm_send/5596.

# Prezi Presentation

College students today are routinely asked to make presentations as part of their assignments. Often, students turn to presentation software, especially PowerPoint, which enables a speaker to present information visually to an audience. Prezi is an online tool for making presentations that is similar to PowerPoint in that it enables a writer to convey information efficiently and in visually engaging ways on screens or "slides." (See Sidebar: "Using Prezi.") Like PowerPoint, Prezi also allows the writer to embed images, sound, and video in a presentation. However, there are **two important differences between Prezi and PowerPoint:**

- PowerPoint presentations usually supplement the presenter's spoken words. By contrast, Prezi presentations are generally intended to be viewed online rather than presented in person by the author. However, increasingly students use Prezi in place of PowerPoint to supplement their oral presentations.
- Unlike PowerPoint, which requires you to present information sequentially from one slide to the next, Prezi is a dynamic tool that enables you to arrange text and images on a single screen according to an organizing theme or metaphor; a viewer clicks arrows to move from one place on the screen to another to follow a story or access information. Each individual screen in a Prezi presentation is therefore a section of the whole presentation rather than a discrete slide, as in PowerPoint.

Despite these differences, the same principles for designing an effective PowerPoint show apply to Prezi. The best presentations

- are well-organized,
- have a coherent visual theme,
- do not overwhelm the viewer with text,
- take advantage of the visual capabilities of the presentation tool, and
- apply the principles of design.

---

**SIDEBAR**    **USING PREZI**

Although there are differences between Prezi and PowerPoint, learning to use Prezi is no more difficult than learning to use PowerPoint. To use Prezi, you must create a Prezi account (visit prezi.com). The Prezi website includes a great deal of information and advice for using the tool and taking advantage of its multimedia capabilities.

---

Here's an example of a Prezi presentation that meets these criteria and uses design principles effectively. The author, Hayley Ashburner, created this presentation for an assignment in a writing class at the University of North Carolina at Wilmington. The assignment called for students to tell their own literacy histories and show how their experiences fit into larger cultural and historical contexts. Hayley's narrative focused on her journey from her birthplace in South Africa to a new home in Australia and the impact of that journey on her literacy and use of technology.

| 1. Consider the rhetorical context. | 2. Be clear about your message. | 3. Apply the principles of design. |
|---|---|---|
| • Hayley's presentation was intended for students in her writing class, but because it would be available online at prezi.com, it might also be viewed by a much broader audience. Her primary purpose was to tell her literacy history in a way that was consistent with the expectations of her course, but she also wanted her story to resonate with viewers outside her class who might simply be interested in her unique experience. | • Hayley's main idea was that her experiences growing up in two different cultures shaped her as a person and as a reader and writer. She wanted to explore how her experiences affected her sense of herself and her uses of literacy and technology in her life. | • Hayley developed her presentation so that a viewer could follow her journey as a person who grew up in two different cultures. She relied on the principles of proximity and alignment to make her presentation engaging and to organize her journey into a coherent story. |

Here's the main screen of Hayley's presentation, titled "African Dreams":

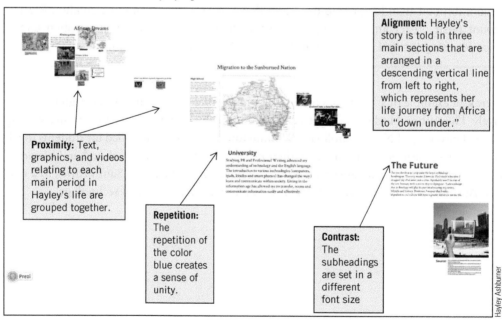

**Alignment:** Hayley's story is told in three main sections that are arranged in a descending vertical line from left to right, which represents her life journey from Africa to "down under."

**Proximity:** Text, graphics, and videos relating to each main period in Hayley's life are grouped together.

**Repetition:** The repetition of the color blue creates a sense of unity.

**Contrast:** The subheadings are set in a different font size

Hayley Ashburner

A viewer navigates the presentation by clicking arrows that appear at the bottom of the screen. Here's what a viewer sees after the first three clicks:

1. The first click emphasizes the title, "African Dreams":

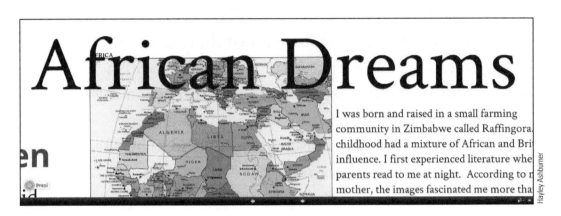

2. The next click zooms in on a map to show Hayley's birthplace:

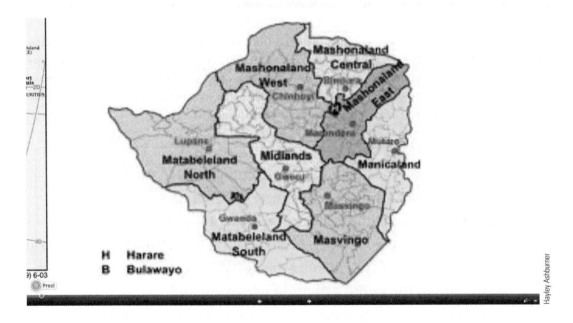

3. The next click highlights text describing Hayley's early years:

I was born and raised in a small farming community in Zimbabwe called Raffingora. My childhood had a mixture of African and British influence. I first experienced literature when my parents read to me at night. According to my mother, the images fascinated me more than the words. My brothers and I were exposed to a variety of music by my parents and encouraged to perform in community plays.

Throughout her presentation, which included thirty-five separate screens, Hayley combines carefully written text with images and video clips to keep her audience engaged and to make her story coherent. Her selection of these elements also reflects her effort to communicate her main point about the influence of culture on her. The text in this screen, for example, explains how various media helped her become familiar with Australian culture:

Television, phones, radio and computers helped my family adjust to life in Australia. The internet offered a cost effective way to communicate with friends and family back in Zimbabwe. Whilst, local television and radio exposed us to Australian culture, lifestyle and events. Listening to the radio, watching television and communicating with new peers changed the way I spoke. "Ya" became "yeah", "Chum" became "Mate" and "That's tight" became "hell good!" It also advanced my taste in music.

The next few clicks take the viewer through two embedded videos that illustrate her evolving taste in music:

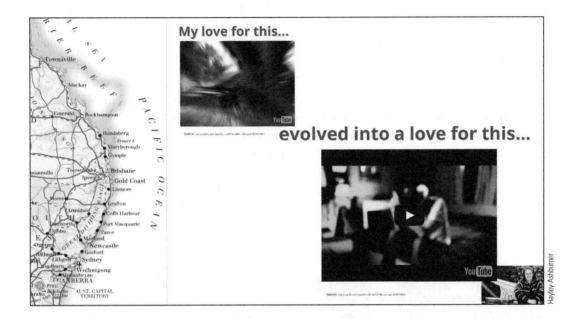

Clicking the video on the left starts a video clip with music that Hayley listened to in South Africa; clicking the right-hand video starts music that she listened to in Australia. Using sound and video in this way, she conveys to the viewer a deeper sense of her experience. The proximity of these videos and the contrast between them highlight the change in her musical tastes over time and communicates a sense of her development as a person growing up in two different cultures.

(You can view Hayley's complete presentation at http://prezi.com/c1q2bitx009e/literacy-narrative/).

## Designing a Website

Websites are an invaluable means by which organizations and individuals establish a presence and communicate information to various audiences. Web authoring software (e.g., Dreamweaver) can make it easy to create a sophisticated website, but the use of basic design principles is what makes a website rhetorically effective. The most effective websites are:

- **Clean and uncluttered.** Too much text and too many images can make a website feel messy and difficult for visitors to find information. A website should not overwhelm visitors. Use relevant graphics that convey important ideas or information, and keep text limited and easy to read.

- **Easy to navigate.** Websites are tools that should be easy for visitors to use. The design should enable visitors to find information easily and quickly. Even extensive websites with many separate pages can be designed so that visitors don't get lost or confused as they seek specific information.

- **Coherent.** Appealing websites have a consistent appearance that unifies the various pages and gives the entire site a feeling of coherence. Color schemes, font styles, and graphics tend to be consistent from one page to another, which can give the site a sense of focus and make it easier for visitors to find what they are looking for.

Following these guidelines and applying the principles of design can give a website a professional appearance and enhance its ability to address its intended audience. This website was developed for the Capital District Writing Project, a non-profit organization in upstate New York that promotes effective writing instruction in schools and provides services to teachers, students, and communities to help improve writing. The main page of the website is shown in Figure 20.4. Notice how clean and uncluttered the page appears. It also has a coherent visual theme, with two main colors and consistent font styles and sizes, that is applied to all individual pages on the site. Significantly, the page is designed so that various audiences—teachers, school administrators, and parents—can get a sense of the organization's purpose and find the specific information they need.

| 1. Consider the rhetorical context. | 2. Be clear about your message. | 3. Apply the principles of design. |
|---|---|---|
| • The organization serves teachers, students, and schools in its region. Its website is intended to convey a sense of its mission to those audiences and to provide relevant information about its services. It must compete with many other organizations that are involved in education. | • The central point of the main page of the website is that the organization is an important resource for teachers and administrators interested in improving writing, teaching, and learning in their school districts. | • The main page of the website uses contrast, alignment, and proximity to convey its message and highlight important information contained on the website. It presents a clear and professional image through its strategic use of image, layout, and color. |

**FIGURE 20.4** Website of the Capital District Writing Project

**Proximity:** Similar items are grouped together. This *navigation bar* places all important links together, making it easy for visitors to find the pages they need.

**Alignment:** Text is aligned in vertical columns. The *navigation bar* near the top of the page and the links at the bottom are aligned horizontally to set them apart from the main text.

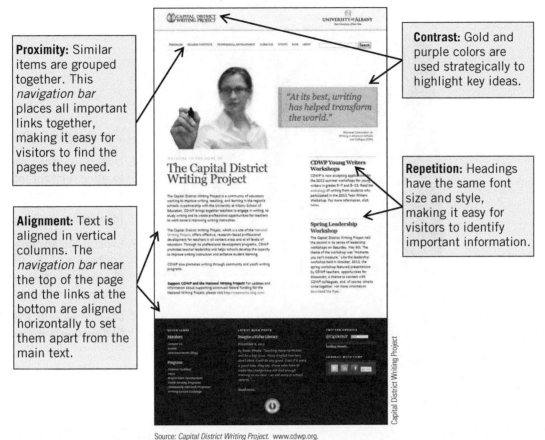

**Contrast:** Gold and purple colors are used strategically to highlight key ideas.

**Repetition:** Headings have the same font size and style, making it easy for visitors to identify important information.

Source: *Capital District Writing Project.* www.cdwp.org.

Notice that the main elements on this page are easier to find because of the strategic use of white space between them. Also, the single image of a teacher writing reflects the organization's purpose without distracting a visitor. The navigation bar includes links for specific audiences.

MindTap

Reflect on what you know about the principles of effective document design.

### In this chapter, you will learn to

1. Understand the importance of locating relevant information from a variety of sources.

2. Identify six main types of sources.

3. Explain the advantages and limitations of the three main kinds of search tools and use these tools to locate appropriate source material.

4. Develop an effective strategy for finding relevant source material.

## MindTap®

Understand the goals of the chapter and complete a warm-up activity.

# Finding Source Material  21

**RECENT STUDIES INDICATE** that research-based writing, which has always been a mainstay of academic writing, is becoming ever more common in the assignments students encounter in their college courses. So being able to work effectively with sources is essential for successful college writing. This chapter will guide you in learning how to locate relevant information from a variety of sources.

## Understanding Research

While I was still in college, I made a road trip with a friend that took me through the Badlands of South Dakota, a remote, sparsely populated, and starkly beautiful region of pastel-colored hills, mesas, and prairies etched with countless canyons and dry creek beds. As we drove along a desolate stretch of Interstate 90, we passed one of those large green exit signs. Under that sign someone had attached another sign: a weathered plank with hand-painted red letters that read, "Doctor wanted." The sign surprised us and made us wonder: Were the residents of that isolated area really so desperate for medical care that they took to posting hand-painted signs on the Interstate? Was their situation common in rural areas? Was medical care scarce for Americans who lived in such areas? I had never really thought about what it might be like to live in a remote area where things that I took for granted—like medical care—might not be available.

When I returned from my trip, I contacted a cousin who is a family doctor and told him about the sign. He explained that providing doctors for remote rural areas was a longstanding challenge in the U.S. that was complicated by rising health care costs and the growing use of expensive medical technology. I was intrigued and wanted to know more. I contacted a magazine editor, who expressed interest in an article on the topic. At that point, I had a topic, an interesting and relevant experience, some basic information, and a lot of additional questions. I also had a goal: to inform the readers of the magazine about a little-known problem in American health care. I was ready to learn more. I could now begin my research.

As my story suggests, research should begin with a question or problem that you want to address—one that matters not only to you but also to a potential audience. Core Concept #1 tells us that writing is a process of discovery and learning (see Chapter 2). Research is an integral component of that powerful process of inquiry. Research is not the *reason* for writing. Rather, you conduct research to explore and understand your subject. In this regard, finding sources is a purposeful activity: The sources help you achieve your rhetorical goals.

So the most important thing to remember about working with sources is that it isn't about the sources. In other words, your focus should be, first, on the purpose of your project and how it fits your rhetorical situation. So start there:

- What are you writing about and *why*?
- What are you trying to accomplish with a particular writing project?
- What do you need to know in order to accomplish your rhetorical goals?

By the time you're ready to begin consulting sources, you should already have begun exploring your subject and have a sense of your intended audience and the purpose of your project. Your rhetorical goals should guide your research—not the other way around.

---

**SIDEBAR** — **DON'T START LOOKING FOR SOURCE MATERIAL TOO SOON**

A common mistake students make in research-based writing is moving too quickly to the process of finding sources. After receiving an assignment, the first thing they do is go online to search for information about a possible topic before they have begun to develop some idea of what they will say about that topic. As a result, what they find, rather than their rhetorical purpose, guides their project. In such cases, the resulting project is often a compilation of source material rather than a genuine inquiry into the subject.

To avoid that mistake, follow the steps in Chapter 3 and don't focus on looking for source material until you have begun exploring your topic and have a good sense of your rhetorical situation. It's certainly OK to peruse source material to get ideas about a topic, but if your research is purposeful rather than haphazard, finding sources will be part of the process of inquiry that writing should be.

---

Doing research today is a kind of good news–bad news proposition. The good news is that students have ready access to an astonishing amount and variety of material online so that they can quickly find information on almost any conceivable topic. The bad news is that having access to so much information can be overwhelming and make it difficult to distinguish useful information from erroneous or dubious information. Following a few simple guidelines will enable you to take advantage of the wealth of material available to you and avoid the common pitfalls of finding useful and reliable sources.

The key to finding appropriate sources is threefold:

- determining what you need
- understanding available sources
- developing a search strategy

The remainder of this chapter is devoted to examining these three aspects of finding relevant source material.

# Determining What You Need

To make your research efficient and successful, it's best to identify the kinds of information you need. Otherwise, your searches are likely to be haphazard and time-consuming. Follow these basic steps:

1. Consider the purpose of your project and your intended audience.

2. Generate questions you will probably need to address.

3. Identify possible sources of information to address those questions.

To illustrate, let's look at three writing assignments that call for research:

- a literacy narrative requiring you to analyze your own experiences as a young reader and writer in terms of available research on literacy development;
- an argument in favor of abolishing the electoral college in U.S. presidential elections;
- a history of your neighborhood focusing on the period since the end of World War II.

## 1. Consider Your Purpose and Audience

| Literacy narrative | • To gain insight into your own literacy experiences<br>• To understand literacy development in general<br>• To share this learning with students in your writing class |
|---|---|
| Argument against electoral college | • To illuminate problems with the current election system<br>• To propose an increasingly popular solution<br>• To educate other students about this issue<br>• To encourage other voting citizens to consider this solution |
| History of your neighborhood | • To understand important developments in your neighborhood's past<br>• To understand how the past affects the present<br>• To share these insights with other students of history and neighborhood residents |

# 2. Generate Questions You Might Need to Address

**Literacy narrative**
- What important childhood experiences shaped you as reader and writer?
- What role did literacy play in your life as an adolescent?
- What influence did your family have on your writing and reading habits?
- What does research indicate are the key factors that affect literacy ability?

**Argument against electoral college**
- How exactly does the electoral college work? Why was it developed?
- What are the main criticisms of the electoral college?
- What problems have occurred in past elections?
- What solutions have others proposed? What concerns do critics have about these solutions?

**History of your neighborhood**
- What key economic, political, and social developments occurred in your neighborhood since WWII? What changes have taken place in that time?
- How do these developments relate to broader developments in your region or the nation?
- What problems does the neighborhood face today? How are those problems related to past developments?

# 3. Identify Possible Sources to Answer Your Questions

**Literacy narrative**
- Family members; former teachers
- Relevant artifacts from your childhood (school papers, books, letters)
- Scholarly articles and books about literacy development
- Published studies of childhood literacy

**Argument against electoral college**
- Reference works on political science and elections
- Articles in political journals, newspapers, and newsmagazines
- Blog posts, public affairs websites
- Materials from political watchdog groups

**History of your neighborhood**
- Archived newspaper articles
- Documents from local historical society or state museum
- Op-ed essays in local newspapers, websites, blogs
- Interviews with local leaders and residents

These examples illustrate **four important points about finding sources:**

- **The kind of information you need and the possible sources for that information depend on the nature of your project and rhetorical situation.** For example, the literacy narrative assignment requires looking into your past experiences with writing and reading but also requires finding specialized information about literacy development that is most likely available only in academic publications. Moreover, because the narrative is intended for an academic audience, the instructor will probably expect you to consult scholarly sources. By contrast, the argument about the electoral college is intended for a more general, less specialized audience. It addresses a topic that has been discussed in a variety of contexts, including academic journals as well as the popular press and social media. Given that rhetorical situation and the more general appeal of the topic, some relevant sources will probably be less specialized than those for the literacy narrative assignment.

- **Identifying what you don't know will help you find the right sources for what you need to know.** By starting the research process with questions that you need to answer, you will quickly identify what you don't know about your topic, which will help you identify what you *need to know*. For example, for the argument against the electoral college, you might already have a sense of the problems with the current election system, but you might have little knowledge of the history of that system or what experts and others have said about it. Similarly, for the neighborhood history, you might know a lot about the present economic and political situation in your neighborhood but little about how it came to be that way. Posing questions about your topic helps you identify such gaps in your knowledge and point you to possible sources of information to fill those gaps.

- **Some projects call for original research.** Two of these three examples point to the possibility of students doing their own *primary research* (see Focus: "Primary vs. Secondary Research"). For the neighborhood history project, for example, students might interview residents and local leaders as well as examine archived documents in a local historical society or museum. For the literacy narrative assignments, students might interview family members and former teachers and use documents such as old school papers. These original sources will be supplemented by *secondary sources*, such as academic journals, newspapers, books, or websites.

- **Research begets research.** The more you learn about your topic, the more questions you are likely to have. That's as it should be. For example, in researching the history of your neighborhood, you might discover that the closing of a local factory after World War II left many residents out of work, which led to an exodus of young people to other towns and states. Learning about that development might lead to questions about the basis for the local economy, which in turn might lead you to look at sources (e.g., economic data) that you had not previously considered. Similarly, in reading a journal article about childhood literacy for your literacy narrative, you might encounter a reference to a study about the relationship between literacy development and social class. That study in turn might prompt you to reexamine your own literacy development in terms of your socio-economic background. As you proceed with your research, you will learn more about your topic, which will probably mean that you will begin to understand better what you need to know to complete your project.

Scholars usually distinguish between two kinds of research:

**Primary research** is firsthand investigation. It involves conducting experiments, collecting various kinds of data (such as through surveys, interviews, or observation), or examining original documents (such as manuscripts, public records, or letters) or artifacts in libraries or museums. If you interview someone, design and distribute a survey, conduct a laboratory experiment, or analyze data that have not been previously published, you are conducting primary research. Most college students do not engage in primary research, although some college assignments require such research.

**Secondary research** is based on the work of others. It involves investigating what other people have already published on a given subject—in other words, finding information about a topic online, in books, in magazine or journal articles, and similar sources. Most of the research college students do is secondary research. The advice in this chapter generally assumes that you are doing secondary research.

# Understanding Sources

The main challenge in research-based writing is finding the right sources that have the material you need to meet the rhetorical goals for your project. Understanding the different kinds of available sources will help you meet that challenge. In this section we will examine **six main types of sources:**

- books
- scholarly journals
- magazines and newspapers
- reference materials
- websites
- social media

Some of these types of sources, such as websites, appear only online; others, however, might appear both online and in traditional print form (see Focus: "Print vs. Online" on page 687). For example, *The New York Times* is still published every day as a print newspaper, which you can find on the newsstand at a convenience store or in your library, but it also is available online at the *Times'* website, where you can access the same material that appears in the print newspaper in addition to other content, such as blogs and videos, that is not available in print form. Unless otherwise noted, the discussion in this chapter assumes that most source material you find in your research can be found both in print and online. However, given the wealth of online resources and the fact that so many traditional materials now appear in digital form, most of your source material is likely to be available online or in some digital format (such as a library database). In other words, less and less research involves traditional print sources.

## 21

Only a few years ago the difference between a traditional print source, such as a book or a magazine, and online resources, such as websites, was pretty straightforward, and searching for print materials as compared to online resources involved different search tools and procedures. However, the distinction between print and online resources has become increasingly blurred as many traditional print sources become available online or disappear altogether. Most print newspapers and magazines now have websites where online versions of print articles are available in addition to other materials, such as social media and videos, that do not appear in print form. Similarly, many scholarly journals make articles available in both print and online form, and many journals now do not appear in print format at all but are available only online. In addition, many books are now available online through services such as Google Books and Project Gutenberg, although access to many books online is partial or limited because of copyright restrictions. Moreover, the main tools for finding resources—search engines and databases (see pages 693–695)—can be accessed online with a computer, tablet, or smartphone, which means that most research required in college classes is conducted online, and students do not need to search physically for materials in a library as frequently as in the past—if at all.

As a result of these developments, students today can use various devices to gain relatively easy (and often instant) access to an astonishing variety and quantity of information and potential source material. However, although access to source material is easier today than in the past, finding the right source material is more complicated today, and much of the material available online requires more careful scrutiny than traditional print materials available in a library (see Chapter 22).

# Books

In this instant-access digital age, books can seem archaic. It can be easy to find up-to-the-minute information on media websites, quickly get facts about a topic by using a search engine like Google, or instantly access information about a subject on a reference website like Wikipedia. Getting information from a book, on the other hand, requires you to go to the library (or bookstore) and physically page through the book to find what you need (unless you are using a tablet, which enables you to search the contents of a book digitally). Nevertheless, printed books continue to be stable sources of information compared to many online resources, which can change without notice or even disappear, making it difficult or impossible for readers to access or verify the information. The extensive process of producing a book requires writers and editors to consider the relevance of the content over a longer term than is necessary for much online material. Unlike websites, which can be revised and updated constantly, books are likely to remain in print for years before being revised or updated. In general, that means that if you cite information contained in a book, readers who want to track it down will likely be able to do so.

In addition, books—especially scholarly books—often contain the best of what is known about a subject, even when the book is several years or even decades old. That's partly because scholarly publishers generally do not publish with an eye toward what is trendy or popular; rather, they often look for material that includes well-established knowledge and important new developments in a particular field. As a result, scholarly books often reflect the state of knowledge that an academic field has generated over many years, even when the subject is current and changing. This does not mean that books are always accurate or unbiased (see Focus: "Detecting Bias" in Chapter 22); sometimes a new development in a field will significantly change or even invalidate previous thinking about an important subject in that field, and like trade books (that is, books that are published commercially and for profit), scholarly books can reflect a particular perspective or school of thought. But by and large, scholarly books and many trade books can be credible, stable sources of information.

In general, then, if you need well-established information in a field, consider searching for that information in books. For example, let's return to our earlier example of an argument about the electoral college system in United States presidential elections. You can easily find current newspaper articles and blog posts expressing various viewpoints about the electoral college, but you can gain a deep understanding of what scholars have said about this system and its development in American politics by consulting scholarly books. A quick search of your library catalog might yield several titles like this:

Belenky, Alexander S. *Who Will Be the Next President? A Guide to the U.S. Presidential Election System*. Springer, 2013.

Edwards, George C. *Why the Electoral College is Bad for America*. Yale University Press, 2004.

Shaw, Daron R. *The Race to 270: The Electoral College and the Campaign Strategies of 2000 and 2004*. University of Chicago Press, 2006.

These works, all published by scholarly presses, are likely to include in-depth analyses and historical background about the electoral college that can help you understand how it works and become familiar with the questions experts have raised about it. Notice that one of these books (*Who Will Be the Next President?*) is relatively new and therefore likely to contain more recent scholarly developments. But although the other two titles are older, they are likely to reflect established scholarly thinking about this subject, which is a longstanding issue in American politics. This example illustrates the usefulness of books, even when up-to-the-minute information and opinion might be available from newspapers or social media.

## Scholarly Journals

If you search your college library's periodical holdings, you will discover that there are thousands of scholarly journals devoted to every academic subject and their many subspecialties. For example, in 2016 the library of the State University of New York at Albany listed 511 scholarly journals in the field of general biology and an additional 766 journals in subspecialties such as genetics, microbiology, and immunology. Taken together, these journals reflect the most up-to-date knowledge in biology and its subfields. Every academic field, no matter how small or specialized, has its own scholarly journals. In addition, some prestigious journals publish articles from many related fields. The journal *Science*, for example, publishes articles from all fields of science.

As a general rule, scholarly journals are considered reputable, dependable, and accurate sources of information, ideas, and knowledge. Most scholarly journals are *peer-reviewed*, which means that each published article has been evaluated by several experts on the specific subject matter of the article. By contrast, articles in trade and popular magazines are usually reviewed by an editor (or sometimes by an editorial team); they are generally not evaluated by an outside panel of experts. Consequently, articles that appear in scholarly journals are generally considered to meet rigorous standards of scholarship in their respective fields. If your research leads you to material in a scholarly journal, you can usually be confident that it is credible.

The challenge facing most student writers, however, is that scholarly articles are written by experts for other experts in their respective fields. These articles can often be difficult for a novice (as almost all students are) to understand, and students can find it hard to assess whether the material in such articles fits the needs of their project. If you find yourself in such a situation (and you probably will at some point), use the following strategies to help you decide whether the material in a scholarly article is useful to you:

- **Apply the strategy for reading academic texts in Chapter 19 (see page 620).** The strategy described in Chapter 19 will help you make sense of even the most specialized scholarly articles.

- **Ask a librarian.** Librarians are trained to understand the characteristics and nuances of many different kinds of source material. If you're not sure about whether a specific scholarly article is relevant for your project, ask a librarian.

- **Search the internet.** Often a scholarly article is part of a larger body of work by the author(s) and others in a specific field. If you find an article that seems relevant but you're not sure whether it contains material that you need, do a quick Internet search using the subject or title of the article and/or the authors' names. Such a search might yield links to websites, such as the authors' university web pages, that are less technical and contain information that can help you decide whether the scholarly article is useful for your project.

## Magazines and Newspapers

For many topics—especially topics related to current events—magazines and newspapers provide rich sources of up-to-date information. But there are many different kinds of magazines and newspapers, and their quality and dependability can vary widely. Here are the main categories:

- **Trade magazines.** Trade magazines and journals are specialized periodicals devoted to specific occupations or professions. Many are considered important sources for information and opinions relevant to those occupations or professions. *Automotive Design and Production*, for example, publishes articles about the latest technology and news related to the automobile industry. Other well-known trade journals include *Adweek, American Bar Association Journal, Business & Finance,* and *Publishers Weekly.* Although most trade publications do not peer-review the articles they publish, they nevertheless can provide reliable information and important perspectives on subjects related to their professions.

- **Popular magazines.** This very large category includes numerous publications on every conceivable topic, but the main feature that distinguishes popular publications from trade or public affairs journals is that popular magazines are intended for a general, non-specialist audience. *Sports Illustrated*, for example, a popular magazine, might publish an article about the top track and field athletes competing in the Olympic Games, whereas *Track & Field News*, a trade publication, might include technical articles about the latest training techniques used by world-class sprinters to prepare for the Olympics. Popular magazines tend to value the latest news and often cater to specific segments of the general population (for example, *Seventeen Magazine* targets teenage girls) in an effort to attract advertising revenue. Although they vary widely in quality and dependability, they can be an important source of information, depending upon the nature of your project. However, some college instructors consider many popular magazines less credible sources than either trade or scholarly publications, so check with your instructor to determine whether to use such magazines as sources for your project.

- **Public affairs journals.** A number of periodicals focus on politics, history, and culture and publish carefully researched articles, often by well-known scholars and other experts. Many public affairs journals have developed reputations as respected sources of the most knowledgeable perspectives on important political, economic, and social issues. Some of these journals have been publishing for many decades. Among the most well-known public affairs journals are *The Atlantic, National Review*, the *Nation*, and *Foreign Affairs*.

- **Newspapers and newsmagazines.** Daily and weekly newspapers and weekly or monthly newsmagazines are general sources for the most up-to-date information. Among the advantages of these publications for researchers is that they tend to be accessible, intended for a wide audience, and publish material on a wide variety of topics. Like popular magazines, newspapers and newsmagazines can vary significantly in quality, focus, and dependability. In general, well established newspapers, such as *The New York Times, The Washington Post, The Guardian*, and the *Los Angeles Times*, and newsmagazines, such as *Time* and *Newsweek*, tend to have rigorous editorial review and often employ fact-checkers to verify information they publish. However, like all sources, these publications are subject to bias, no matter how objective and thorough they might claim to be (see Focus: "Detecting Bias" in Chapter 22). They might be dependable and well respected, but they also represent various points of view. Don't assume that because something is published in a reputable newspaper or newsmagazine, it is free from bias.

Depending on the nature of your project, any of these kinds of publications can provide useful material, but it is important to be aware of the differences among them so that you can better judge the appropriateness of a specific source.

## Reference Materials

Reference materials, such as encyclopedias, statistical abstracts, dictionaries, atlases, and almanacs, are large compilations of general or specialized information. If you need statistical information about employment rates in the U.S., for example, you can search the *Statistical Abstract of the United States*. In the past, these materials were available as large, multivolume book sets that you could usually find in a library. Today, most traditional reference materials are available online, often through your college library's website. Venerable reference resources such as *Encyclopedia Britannica* are now available online along with more recently developed resources such as *Wikipedia*. In addition, there are now many digital reference materials, such the *Gale Virtual Reference Library*, that do not appear in print form; often, you can access these resources only through paid subscriptions, but many college libraries make them available to their students.

# Websites

Because the Internet contains an almost inconceivable amount of material, it can be a boon for researchers, but the sheer amount of available information online can also be overwhelming and confusing. Businesses, government agencies, media outlets, individuals, and organizations of all kinds maintain websites that can be excellent sources of information for researchers. For example, if you are looking for information about standardized testing in K–12 schools, you can search the website of the U.S. Department of Education; you can visit the websites of state education departments, school districts, and related government agencies; and you can consult the websites of the many not-for-profit organizations and advocacy groups devoted to education issues, many of which provide a wide variety of information on education-related issues. Similarly, for-profit organizations that provide education services maintain websites that can also be useful sources. In addition, the websites of media organizations devoted to education issues, such as *The Chronicle of Higher Education*, can be excellent resources. It's safe to say that with careful searching you can almost always find relevant websites that provide useful and reliable information, no matter what subject you are researching.

At the same time, all websites are not created equal when it comes to the usefulness and credibility of information they contain. We will examine how to evaluate source material in Chapter 22, but for now it is important to be able to distinguish among **five basic categories of websites:**

- **News organizations.** As noted earlier, all major newspapers and newsmagazines, such as *The New York Times* and *Newsweek*, maintain extensive websites, which are usually carefully managed and contain information that is reviewed by editors. News organizations such as NBC, PBS, and Fox also maintain extensive websites, as do smaller, lesser known news outlets such as regional newspapers. In general, these websites can be extremely useful sources of information that is generally trustworthy and up-to-date.

- **Public agencies.** Government offices, such as the U.S. Department of Labor or state departments of transportation, maintain websites that provide services to citizens but also contain relevant information. For example, the U.S. Department of Labor website offers statistical data about employment and wages; state education departments provide data about school graduation rates, testing, and funding. Often, these sites contain specialized information that is trustworthy and cannot be found elsewhere.

- **Advocacy groups.** Organizations that represent various perspectives on countless social, political, environmental, economic, education, and health issues maintain their own websites, which, like those of government agencies, can be useful sources of specialized information. Websites for well-known political advocacy groups, such as People for the American Way and the Family Research Council, as well as issue-oriented organizations, such as Greenpeace and the National Rifle Association, can be important sources as well, depending upon the subject of your research, but using these websites requires understanding the organizations' purposes and perspectives and their potential biases (see Focus: "Detecting Bias" in Chapter 22). The same is true of websites maintained by organizations devoted to sports, hobbies, and leisure activities, such as dancing or hunting.

- **Business.** Today, it is a rare business that does not have an online presence. Although most websites maintained by businesses are used to advertise and sell their products and services, they can sometimes contain useful information that might not be available elsewhere. For example, the website for West Marine, a large company that sells products for boaters, includes informational web pages and videos on subjects of interest to boaters, such as repairing boats or maintaining engines.

- **Private individuals.** Anyone with access to the Internet can launch a website on any subject that interests them. These websites sometimes contain useful information and often include insights about the subject from the person who maintains the site. For example, someone with experience and expertise in photography might maintain a website that includes helpful descriptions of various techniques for taking photographs. Such sites can be worth visiting, depending upon the nature of your research project, but because most private individual websites undergo no review of their content, they require scrutiny to make sure you can trust the information you find there. Approach them with skepticism.

## Social Media

Social media, such as Facebook, Twitter, and Snapchat, have become important sites for debate, discussion, and the exchange of information. Many blogs have become as important and respected as the most reputable journals as sources of ideas, opinions, and information, and services like Tumblr and Facebook can be useful sources for some kinds of information. Often, such sites contain up-to-date perspectives and information because they are constantly revised to reflect current developments. They also reflect the often overtly biased (and sometimes problematic and offensive) views of the people who use them, so carefully evaluate information and ideas you find on any social media site before using it in your research project.

As always, the nature of your project and your rhetorical situation will dictate which sources are the most relevant. For many academic writing tasks, some sources will be considered inappropriate. If you're not sure whether a specific source is appropriate for your project, check with your instructor or a reference librarian.

## Locating the Right Sources

Given the wealth and variety of available resources, how do you find the information you need? There are **three primary tools for finding the right source materials** for your project:

- library catalogs
- databases
- online search engines

# Library Catalogs

A library lists all the materials it holds in its online catalog, which is usually easily accessible from the library's home page. In addition to listing books held by the library, the library website typically enables you to access other resources maintained by the library, including its reference collections; periodicals (scholarly journals as well as newspapers and magazines); audio, video, and digital media holdings; government documents; and special collections (such as local historical materials or manuscripts from a well-known author). If you are searching for books on your subject, the library online catalog is the best place to start. But the library website is also a good place to start your search for other materials as well. Get to know what is available on your college library's website. It will serve you well in your research.

# Databases

Databases are listings of published materials that enable you to locate articles in scholarly journals, trade journals, or popular newspapers and magazines. Some databases provide only citations or abstracts of articles in the periodicals they list; some also provide direct access to the full texts of the materials they list. The most popular databases, such as *Academic Search Complete*, are general and interdisciplinary, indexing a wide variety of materials from all subject areas. However, many databases are specialized and index only periodicals relevant to their subject. For example, *MedLine* indexes periodicals and related materials on medicine, nursing, dentistry, veterinary medicine, the health care system, and pre-clinical sciences.

Chances are that you will need to search several different databases for many of your college writing projects, so it makes sense to become familiar with the databases available through your college library. Among the most widely used databases are the following:

- **Academic Search Complete.** Multidisciplinary scholarly database, part of the *EBSCOhost* Research Databases, that includes thousands of full-text periodicals in the social sciences, humanities, science, and technology.

- **JSTOR.** Scholarly database that provides access to full-text articles from many different journals in a variety of academic disciplines.

- **Article First.** General database that indexes the content page of journals in science, technology, medicine, social science, business, the humanities, and popular culture.

- **Google Scholar.** Multidisciplinary scholarly database that lists citations for articles, papers, books, and related scholarly documents in all major academic disciplines.

- **LexisNexis Academic.** Extensive databases providing citations and full-text articles from newspapers, magazines, and many different periodicals in law, business, biography, medicine, and reference.

- **WorldCat.** General database that includes citations for any materials held by a library.

- **Scopus.** General database that indexes abstracts and provides access to the contents of thousands of international journal titles as well as conference proceedings, book series, scientific web pages, and patents, with a focus on science, technology, and medicine.

Keep in mind that although some databases (such as *Google Scholar*) are freely available on the Internet, others are available only through a subscription or license (e.g., *Academic Search Complete*). If your library has a subscription to these databases, you can usually access them by signing in through your library's website.

## Search Engines

Search engines are websites that search the Internet for available materials. Typically, search engines return a list of links to websites and other web-based resources, which you must then visit to find the material you're looking for. Google is the most popular search engine, but there are many other search engines, including specialized search engines that focus on specific subject areas, such as automobiles, business, computers, or education. Among the most commonly used general search engines are Yahoo, Bing, and Ask.com.

Although these three kinds of resources overlap, in general you can use them as follows:

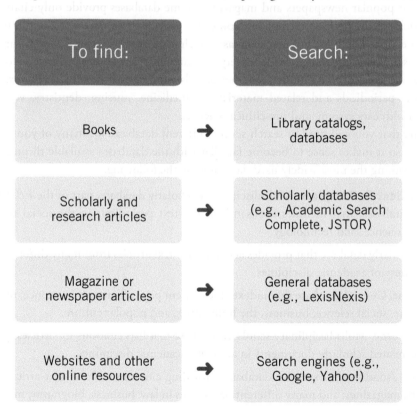

Of course, you can use an Internet search engine such as Google to find references to books, scholarly articles, and newspaper and magazine articles, but if you limit your search tools to

Internet search engines, you might miss important resources, especially if your topic is specialized and your assignment is academic in nature. (See Focus: "Databases vs. Search Engines.") It's best to use these three basic kinds of online resources in combination to be able to identify the most useful sources for your project.

---

**FOCUS  DATABASES VS. SEARCH ENGINES**

Both databases and search engines enable you to find relevant materials very quickly; however, there is an important difference between them: Databases contain materials from publications and other sources that have been screened, usually by an editorial team that applies specific criteria (such as whether a journal is peer-reviewed), whereas search engines rely on sophisticated algorithms that automatically and rapidly search millions of websites to find content related to your search terms. Unlike databases, search engines look only for content and typically do not screen the results of searches, which means that you often have to work harder to sort through and evaluate the references returned by a search engine (see Chapter 22). When you search a database such as *Academic Search Complete*, you are searching only the contents of that database, which is likely to include certain kinds of materials, such as scholarly journal articles or books, that have been evaluated and selected by experts in that field; when you use a search engine like Google, you are actually searching the entire Internet.

If you find a citation in a specialized database, it is likely to be related to the specific subject area and from a source that has been evaluated by the editors of the database. By contrast, search engines return links to *any* site or resource related to the search term, no matter what the source of that site.

Knowing these differences between databases and search engines will help you decide how to use each search tool and how to evaluate the sources you find with them.

---

# Developing a Search Strategy

Understanding the many different sources available to you and knowing which search tools to use still isn't quite enough for successful research. For example, your library catalog lists thousands of book titles, but how do you even know whether searching for a book makes sense for your project? Similarly, a search engine such as Google can point you to thousands of links related to a certain topic, but what will you look for among those many links? How do you know which ones to pursue? You will more likely find what you need if you develop a general search strategy that focuses on the kinds of information you need for your project and takes advantage of all potential sources to find that information rather than limiting your search to one set of resources, such as online materials or scholarly journals.

To illustrate, let's return to our earlier example of an assignment to write a research-based argument in favor of abolishing the electoral college in U.S. presidential elections (see "Determining What You Need" on page 683). We identified the purpose of the project as follows:

- to illuminate problems with the current election system
- to propose an increasingly popular solution to this problem
- to encourage other voting citizens to consider this solution

Let's imagine further that you are writing this essay with several overlapping audiences in mind: classmates in your writing course, other college students, and voting citizens. So your audience is both general and academic. You have become interested in the topic because you have heard many young people of voting age express apathy about the recent presidential election, partly because the popular vote does not directly elect the president. You have also read several op-ed essays about this issue, some of which have called for abolishing the electoral college.

After reading about the electoral college online, you have decided you support the idea of replacing it with a system in which the national popular vote directly elects the president. However, you need to learn more about how the electoral college works as well as the various arguments for and against that system.

Here's the list of questions you have identified as a starting point for your research:

- How exactly does the electoral college work? Why was it developed?
- What are the main criticisms of the electoral college?
- What problems have occurred in past elections?
- What solutions have others proposed? What concerns do critics have about these solutions?

And here are some potential sources you have identified for addressing these questions:

- reference works on political science and elections
- articles in political journals, newspapers, newsmagazines
- blog posts, public affairs websites
- materials from political watchdog groups

How should you proceed?

When you have a general idea about what you might want to say about your topic (in this case, that the electoral college should be replaced with a national vote for U.S. Presidential elections) but limited knowledge of the subject, a good search strategy is to start broadly and narrow your search as you learn more about your topic and refine your main point (Core Concept #4). That means beginning with general searches of the major categories of resources—library catalogs, databases, and search engines—and then searching for more specific materials as you identify questions or subtopics that you need to explore, using the appropriate search tools at each stage. In our example the process might look like this:

**1. General search for materials on your topic:**
- Library catalog for books
- General database (e.g., LexisNexis)
- Search engine (e.g., Google)

**2. Narrower search to explore specific issues and questions:**
- Specialized databases (e.g., Worldwide Political Science Asbtracts, Google Scholar)

**3. Targeted search to fill gaps and find alternative viewpoints:**
- advanced search of relevant database (e.g., LexisNexis, Google Scholar) and search engine

# 1. Do a General Search for Materials on Your Topic

Recall your questions about the electoral college:

- How exactly does the electoral college work? Why was it developed?
- What are the main criticisms of the electoral college?
- What problems have occurred in past elections?
- What solutions have others proposed? What concerns do critics have about these solutions?

These should guide your general searches. You need basic information about the electoral college, its history, and the criticisms of the system. You also need information about proposed solutions. Search the three main kinds of resources for relevant materials.

## Library Catalog

Libraries have different kinds of search mechanisms, but most allow users to do **keyword searches** of their catalogs for subjects or titles of books and related materials in their collections. In this case, you could use *electoral college* as a subject keyword. In 2016, a search using these keywords yielded 71 books in the library of the State University of New York at Albany. Here's what the first page of the results screen looked like:

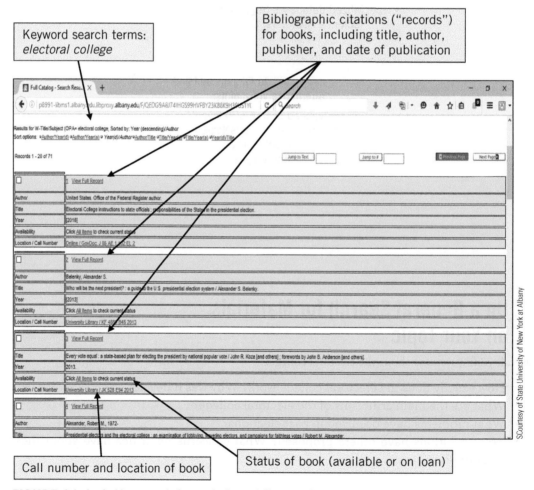

**FIGURE 21.1** A Keyword Search in a Library Catalog

This screen shows the first three of 71 total "records," which provide bibliographic information about each book as well as its call number so that you can locate it in the library. You can also click a link to check on the status of each book (whether it is out on loan, when it is due, etc.). Although search screens can differ noticeably from one library to another, they will all have these key components, including complete bibliographic information about the book (author, publisher, date of publication) and the status of the book (whether it is available for loan, where it is located in the library).

Review the search results to see which books seem most likely to contain the information you need about the electoral college. Some of the books listed in this sample search will likely provide general information about the electoral college:

*Who Will Be the Next President? A Guide to the U.S. Presidential Election System* (2013), by Alexander S. Belenky

*After the People Vote: A Guide to the Electoral College* (2004), edited by John C. Fortier

*Electoral College and Presidential Elections* (2001), edited by Alexandra Kura

Some specifically address the controversy about the electoral college and proposals to reform it:

*Every Vote Equal: A State-Based Plan for Electing the President by National Popular Vote* (2008), by John R. Koza et al.

*Enlightened Democracy: The Case for the Electoral College* (2004), by Tara Ross

*Why the Electoral College is Bad for America* (2004), by George C. Edwards

Some might be too specialized for your purposes:

*Electoral Votes Based on the 1990 Census* (1991), by David C. Huckabee

Based on the information in the search results, select the books that seem most useful and visit the library to review them. (You might also do an online search to find additional information about each book before visiting the library. For example, a Google search of the book's title and author will often yield descriptions of the book, reviews, and related information that can help you determine whether the book is worth borrowing from the library.)

## General Databases

Search one or more general databases using the same or similar keywords. A good place to start is *LexisNexis Academic*, which indexes many different newspapers and magazines as well as other kinds of materials; it also indexes more specialized journals.

Like many databases, *LexisNexis Academic* has a basic search screen and an advanced search screen. Begin with a basic search of the news using your keywords *electoral college*. Notice that this database allows you to select categories of sources (news, legal, companies, etc.). In some cases, it might make sense to narrow your search to one such category; in this example, however, a broader search is appropriate:

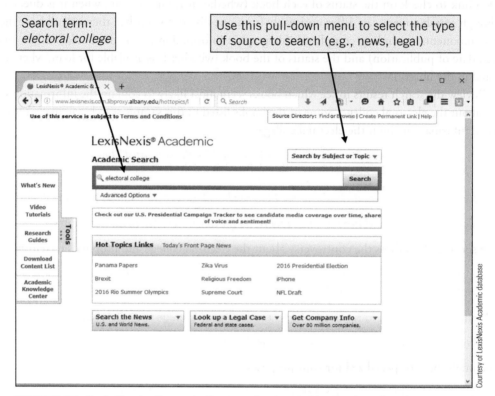

**FIGURE 21.2** A Basic Search Screen in *LexisNexis Academic*

This search of "news" returned 999 entries. Here's the first screen:

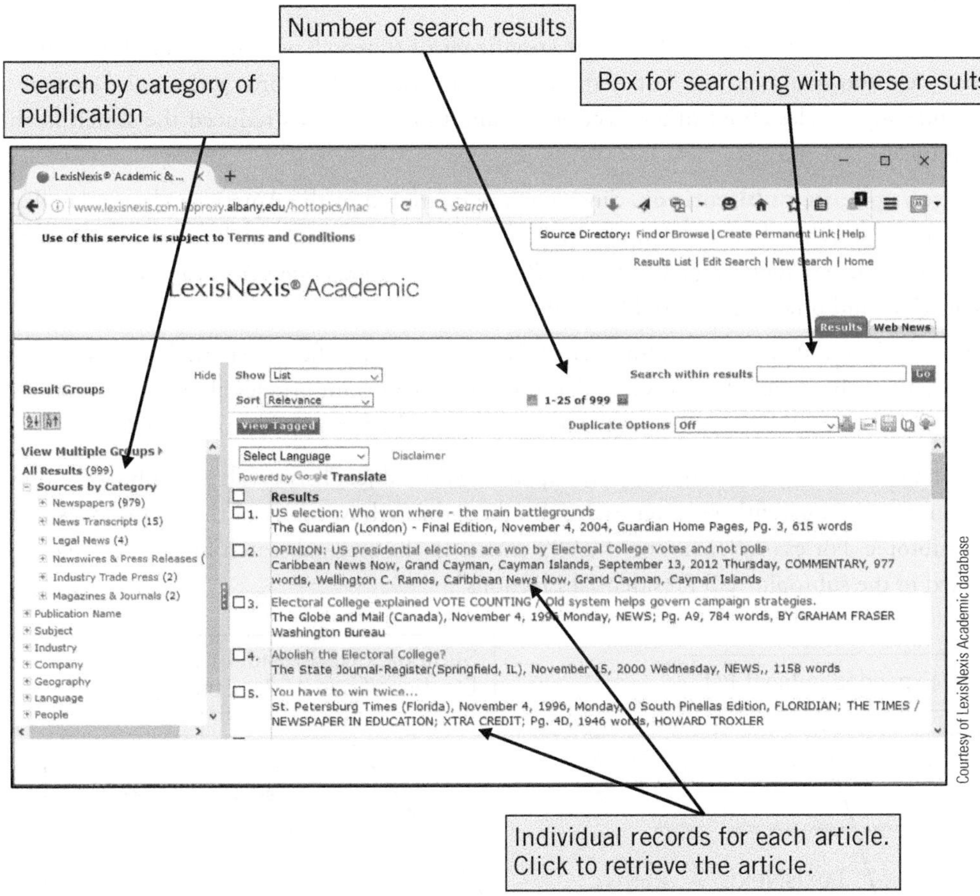

**FIGURE 21.3** Search Results for "Electoral College" in *LexisNexis Academic*

Databases have very different search screens, and it might take some time to become familiar with the ones you are using. However, all major databases allow you to specify the parameters of your search (e.g., by publication type, date, author, title, keywords, and so on) so that you can search broadly or be more strategic. Moreover, they all provide the same basic information about the sources that are returned in a search, which in this example are called "records." Usually, that information includes the author, title, publication, and date of the entry. Sometimes the entry will include an abstract or summary of the source. You can use this information to review the entries and decide which ones to examine more closely.

Obviously, the 999 records returned in this sample would be too many to review, but you can **narrow your search** in several ways:

- **Search within the results.** Use more specific terms to search within the results of searches that yield too many entries. For example, you can use the keywords *presidential election* to exclude any articles about other elections. Using those keywords reduced the search in this example to 744 records.

- **Search specific publications.** Since you are interested in the American electoral college, you might search only American newspapers. You can limit your search further by searching only major newspapers (e.g., *Washington Post, The New York Times*). You can do the same for magazines and other types of publications.

- **Specify dates.** If you want to find materials related to a specific time period, you can specify the dates of the materials you want. For example, if you want articles about the 2000 Presidential Election, you might search for materials published from 1998 through 2001.

Notice that you can also search by subject. Expanding the subject list reveals a number of subtopics. The numbers in parentheses after each subtopic indicate how many of the 999 records relate to that subtopic. For example, among the 999 entries in the original search in this example, 467 are related to the subtopic "US Presidential Elections":

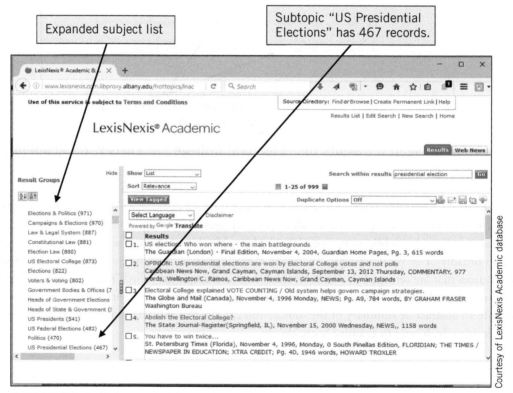

**FIGURE 21.4** Using a Subject List to Search in *LexisNexis Academic*

You can use the subject categories to narrow your search further by clicking on the subject "US Presidential Elections" and search the 467records within that category. In this way you can find sources that are more likely to be relevant to your specific topic.

As you gain experience, you will become more efficient in finding the materials you need. In the meantime, **when searching databases, follow these guidelines:**

- **Experiment with keywords.** Sometimes, it takes several different combinations of search terms before you begin to see the search results you want. In our example, the search term *electoral college* returned good results, but depending upon what you are looking for, you might have to try various other search terms: *elections, popular election, presidential elections, election controversies*, and so on.

- **Use several search strategies.** Sometimes, a basic keyword search gets you right to the materials you need. More often, you will have to try different search strategies to narrow your search to manageable numbers and to find the most relevant materials. If various keyword searches don't yield what you need, try subject searches. Try various searches within your search results. Don't rely on a single approach.

- **Use different databases.** Different databases have different search options and will return different results. Although most databases allow for refined or advanced searching, each database has its own interface with its own peculiarities. So the same keywords are likely to yield different results in different databases. In this sample search, for example, using the same keywords (electoral college) with the *Academic Search Complete* database will turn up some of the same sources but also different sources. You might also find some databases easier to use than others. Be aware that it can take some time to become familiar with the characteristics of each database, so if you have trouble finding what you need in a specific database, ask a librarian or your instructor for guidance.

## Internet Search Engines

Having searched your library catalog and one or more databases, you can expand your search to include online materials using a general search engine such as Google or Yahoo!. Remember that search engines will return many more entries than a library catalog or a database, so you might have to adjust your search terms to keep the search results manageable. In our sample search you might begin with general search terms, such as *electoral college*, but be aware that such general searches will usually yield enormous numbers of results. A search of Google using those terms in 2016 yielded more than 3 million items, for instance. That kind of result isn't surprising when you remember that Google is searching the entire Internet for anything (websites, documents, etc.) that contains those two words. So try different strategies for narrowing your search. For instance, placing those terms in quotation marks (see Sidebar: "An Important Tip for Searching Databases and Search Engines") reduced the results by half. That's still an unmanageable number, but you can review the first few pages of search results to determine whether any of the links might be useful.

After reviewing the first several pages of search results, narrow your search using different search terms, such as *electoral college presidential election, electoral college controversy, history of electoral college*. Each of these terms will yield different results. Review each set of results for materials that seem promising. Continue to narrow your search so that the results are not only relevant but manageable.

As you proceed with these three kinds of general searches, you will gather relevant information and gain a better understanding of your subject, which can help you search more strategically for additional materials.

---

**SIDEBAR**    **AN IMPORTANT TIP FOR SEARCHING DATABASES AND SEARCH ENGINES**

You can search databases and search engines more efficiently by using quotation marks strategically. Placing search terms in quotation marks tells the search engine to look for exactly those words in exactly that order. For example, if you search for *online privacy*, your search will turn up sites with both those words as well as sites that have either one word or the other; however, placing that term in quotation marks ("*online privacy*") will yield only sites containing the phrase *online privacy*, which is more likely to point to relevant sources. Experiment with different combinations of search terms, with and without quotation marks, to find the most useful sources.

---

# 2. Narrow Your Search to Explore Specific Issues and Questions

Your general search should yield enough information for you to begin to identify specific issues, questions, and subtopics that you need to explore further. The searches thus far in our example have yielded a lot of information about the electoral college, how it works, its history, criticisms of the system, and proposals to reform it. Although much of that information is general (e.g., books and websites explaining the electoral college), some is more specialized (e.g., analyses of specific elections in which the popular vote did not elect the president; scholarly critiques of the system). Given that your intended audience is both general and academic, you might now look more closely at what scholars and other experts have to say about the pros and cons of the electoral college.

- **Examine the references in the books you have found.** Most books contain bibliographies or works cited pages that can point you to additional sources. The references in those bibliographies often include citations of relevant scholarly articles. Make a list of citations that seem promising, and use your library catalog or a general database to track down the sources that seem most relevant.

■ **Search specialized databases.** Your library website will list available databases. Find one or more that relate specifically to your subject. In this example, you could search general scholarly databases, such as *JSTOR, Academic Search Complete*, or *Google Scholar*, as well as databases specific to political science or the social sciences, such as *Worldwide Political Science Abstracts* or *Social Sciences Abstracts*. Given the nature of your project (which is intended for a general academic audience rather than a more specialized audience of readers in political science), it makes sense to search a general scholarly database, such as *JSTOR*. If you were writing your argument for a political science course, it might make more sense to search the databases specific to that field, such as *Worldwide Political Science*.

---

**SIDEBAR** | **USING BOOLEAN OPERATORS WITH DATABASES AND SEARCH ENGINES**

Boolean, or logical, operators are words that command a database or search engine to define a search in a specific way. The most common Boolean operators are *AND, OR*, and *NOT*. Understanding how they work can help you search the Internet and databases more efficiently:

■ *AND* tells the search engine to find only sources that contain both words in your search. For example, if you entered *sports AND steroids*, your search would likely yield sources that deal with steroids in sports and would not necessarily return sources that deal with steroids or sports in general.

■ *OR* broadens a search by telling the search engine to return sources for either term in your search. Entering *sports OR steroids*, for instance, would yield sources on either of those topics.

■ *NOT* can narrow a search by telling the search engine to exclude sources containing a specific keyword. For example, entering *steroids NOT sports* would yield sources on steroids but not necessarily sources that deal with steroids in sports.

In addition, keep these tips in mind:

■ You can use parentheses for complex searches: (*sports AND steroids*) NOT (*medicine OR law*); this entry would narrow the search to specific kinds of sources about sports and steroids that did not include medical or legal matters.

■ With most search engines you can use Boolean operators in combination with quotation marks to find a specific phrase. For example, "steroid use in sports" would return sources that included that exact phrase. (See Sidebar: "An Important Tip for Using Databases and Search Engines" on page 704.) Using this strategy allows you to narrow your search further: ("*steroid in sports*") AND ("*steroid controversies*"). Such a search would find sources that include both phrases in the parentheses.

■ Generally, you should capitalize Boolean operators.

Let's imagine that after reviewing the materials you found in your general searches, you want to know what scholars say about the implications of the electoral college for modern elections. You can search *JSTOR* for relevant scholarly articles. Here's the opening screen:

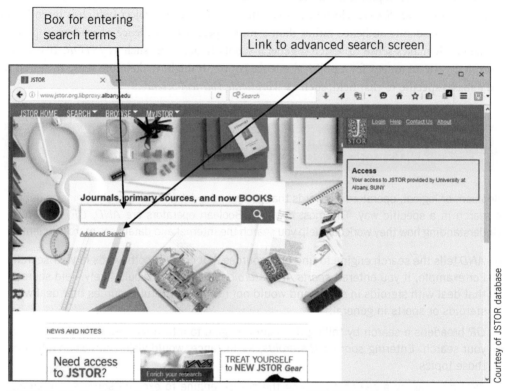

**FIGURE 21.5** A Basic Search Screen for the *JSTOR* Database

A general search using the search terms *electoral college* is likely to yield too many results (in this case, such a search returned more than 33,500 articles in 2016), so an **advanced search** would make more sense. Here's part of the *JSTOR* advanced search screen:

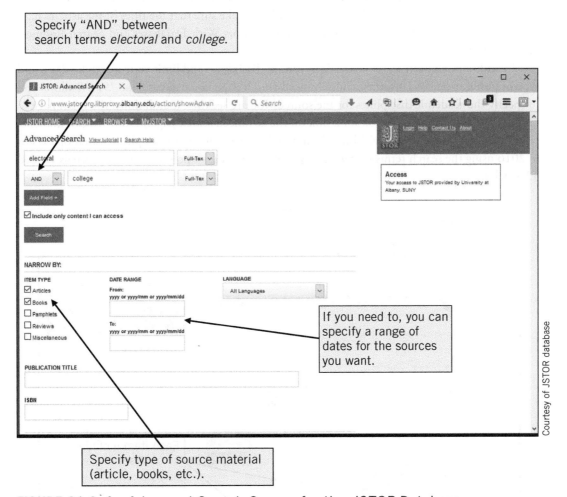

**FIGURE 21.6** An Advanced Search Screen for the *JSTOR* Database

Such an advanced search screen allows you to limit your searches in various ways to increase the likelihood that the results will be useful. For example, using the drop-down menu next to each search term, you can specify that the search terms appear in the article titles rather than the body of the articles, making it more likely that the focus of the article will be relevant to your needs. Also, you can use the *Boolean operator* "and" to make sure that the titles of the articles have *both* search terms (see Sidebar: "Using Boolean Operators With Databases and Search Engines" on page 705).

In addition, you can search journals in certain disciplines and limit your search by dates and type of publication. Usually, the main advanced search page in a database like *JSTOR* allows you to specify the academic disciplines for the sources you are seeking. (Scroll down the main page to find the list of disciplines or look for a link on the advanced search page.) Doing so can dramatically narrow your search and yield much more relevant results. For example, a search of *JSTOR* in 2016 using the search terms *electoral college* only in the title of political science journals yielded 42 articles:

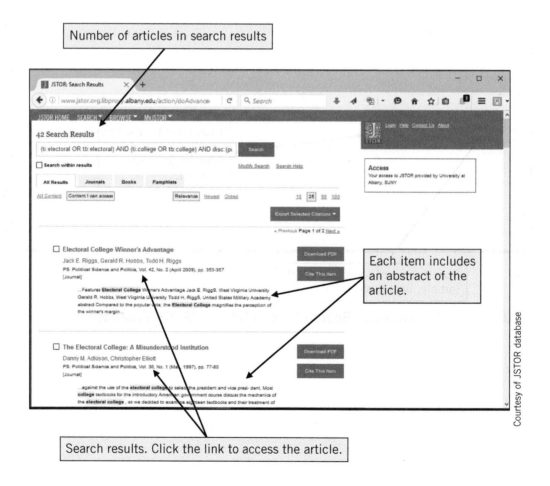

**FIGURE 21.7** Search Results for "Electoral College" in the *JSTOR* Database

Notice that *JSTOR* search results include all relevant bibliographic information (author, title, journal, date, etc.) for each result as well as an abstract, which can help you decide whether to review the full article. If you wanted to narrow your focus to more recent elections, you could modify your search to include only articles published since 2002. Such a search returned 11 articles in 2016.

At this point, you have probably narrowed your search enough to begin reviewing specific articles. Browse these results to find articles that seem most relevant for your needs. In this example, if you scrolled through the 11 items that your final search returned, you would find an article titled "Why the Electoral College is Good for Political Science (and Public Choice)," by Nicholas R. Miller, published in 2012 in a journal called *Public Choice*. If you click the link for that entry, you'll access the article:

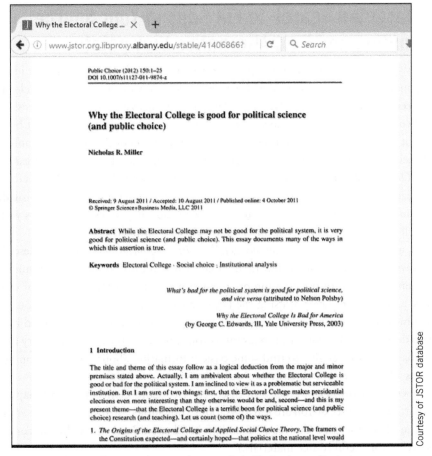

**FIGURE 21.8** Accessing a Journal Article in a Database

A quick review of the abstract and the opening paragraph reveals that the author doesn't argue for or against the Electoral College system for presidential elections in the U.S. but instead focuses on some of the implications of that system, including its impact on the academic field of political science. That focus might not be relevant to your project, but the article seems to provide important background information and might offer an unusual perspective on the issue.

Like general databases, specialized databases can differ noticeably, and you might have to experiment with several databases to become familiar enough with their search screens to conduct effective searches. But all databases have features such as those in this example that allow you to target your searches by entering specific parameters (type of publication, dates, subject terms, and so on). No matter which databases or search engines you are using, you can apply these same basic strategies to make your searches successful. As always, consult your librarian for help, if necessary.

## 3. Do a Targeted Search to Fill Gaps in Your Source Information and Find Alternative Viewpoints

As you narrow your search further, more specific questions might arise or you might identify subtopics that you hadn't previously considered. For example, in reviewing scholarly articles about the role of the electoral collect in recent U.S. presidential elections, you might come across references to legal challenges to the electoral college, a topic that seems relevant to your project but one that you might not have previously encountered. At this point, if you decide you need more information about such a specialized topic, you can return to the databases that you have already searched (such as *JSTOR*) and do an additional search focused on legal challenges to the electoral college system; you can also search specialized databases, such as *Westlaw Campus*, which provides access to legal decisions. The goal at this stage is to identify any specific issues or questions you need to explore as well as gaps in the information you have already gathered.

Keep in mind that *a search is not necessarily a linear process*. The strategy described here assumes you will be continuously reviewing the materials you find. As you do, you might need to return to a general search for information on a new topic that seems important. For example, as you examine arguments in favor of using the popular vote to elect the president, you might discover that some experts have concerns about the wide variety of voting systems used by different states. If you decide that this concern is relevant to your project, return to your library catalog or a general database or search engine to find some basic information about the regulations governing the way states allow citizens to vote.

Remember that writing is a process of discovery (see Core Concept #1 in Chapter 2), and research is part of that process. You are learning about your subject matter to achieve your rhetorical goals. (The advice for Core Concepts #2 and #5 in Chapter 3 can also help you conduct more effective searches for useful source materials.)

> ## MindTap
> Practice research skills that you have learned in this chapter, receive feedback, and reflect on your learning.

WIKIPEDIA
The Free Encyclopedia

English
5 209 000+ articles

Русский
1 332 000+ статей

日本語
1 025 000+ 記事

Español
1 273 000+ articulos

Deutsch
1 935 000+ Artikel

Français
1 779 000+ articles

Italiano
1 293 000+ voci

Português
930 000+ artigos

中文
892 000+ 條目

Polski
1 178 000+ hasel

## In this chapter, you will learn to

1. Evaluate source material in terms of rhetorical purpose.

2. Determine the trustworthiness of a source.

3. Understand and apply the concepts of credibility, reliability, and bias when evaluating potential source material.

## MindTap®

Understand the goals of the chapter and complete a warm-up activity.

# Evaluating Sources 22

**FINDING INFORMATION** for your project is one thing. Deciding whether a source is appropriate, credible, and reliable is another. Given the enormous variety of available sources, evaluating the materials you find can be challenging, but it is an integral part of research.

When evaluating sources, you need to address two main questions:

- Is the source trustworthy?
- Is the source useful for your purposes?

Answering the first question involves understanding the nature and purpose of the source itself. For example, a newspaper article about a political campaign and a campaign flyer can both be useful sources, but they are very different kinds of documents with different purposes. The purpose of a newspaper is to provide readers information about important and relevant events—in this example, a political campaign. A political campaign flyer, by contrast, is intended to present a candidate in the best possible light to persuade voters to support that candidate. Both documents can provide accurate information about the candidate, but the information they present must be considered in terms of their different purposes. The campaign flyer, for instance, might emphasize the candidate's record of voting against tax increases, whereas the newspaper article might explain that the candidate's vote against a specific tax increase resulted in reduced funding for a special program for disabled military veterans. Both sources are technically "true," but each presents information from a particular perspective and for a specific purpose.

As a writer evaluating sources for a project, you have to sort through these complexities to determine how trustworthy a source might be and whether it suits your own rhetorical purposes. The advice in this chapter will help you do so.

## Determining Whether a Source Is Trustworthy

Evaluating source material requires understanding the different kinds of sources that are available to you. (Chapter 21 describes the characteristics of various kinds of sources.) It helps to develop a sense of the main similarities and differences in the general categories of sources you are likely to consult:

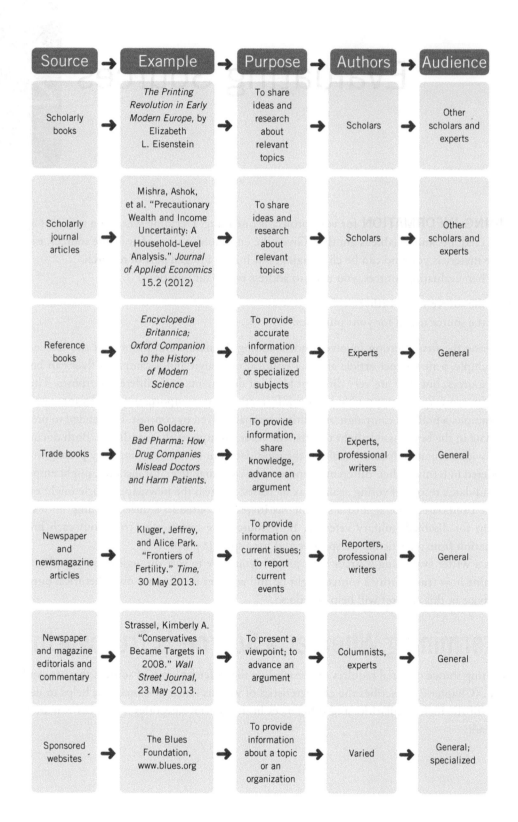

| Source | Example | Purpose | Authors | Audience |
|---|---|---|---|---|
| Scholarly books | *The Printing Revolution in Early Modern Europe,* by Elizabeth L. Eisenstein | To share ideas and research about relevant topics | Scholars | Other scholars and experts |
| Scholarly journal articles | Mishra, Ashok, et al. "Precautionary Wealth and Income Uncertainty: A Household-Level Analysis." *Journal of Applied Economics* 15.2 (2012) | To share ideas and research about relevant topics | Scholars | Other scholars and experts |
| Reference books | *Encyclopedia Britannica; Oxford Companion to the History of Modern Science* | To provide accurate information about general or specialized subjects | Experts | General |
| Trade books | Ben Goldacre. *Bad Pharma: How Drug Companies Mislead Doctors and Harm Patients.* | To provide information, share knowledge, advance an argument | Experts, professional writers | General |
| Newspaper and newsmagazine articles | Kluger, Jeffrey, and Alice Park. "Frontiers of Fertility." *Time,* 30 May 2013. | To provide information on current issues; to report current events | Reporters, professional writers | General |
| Newspaper and magazine editorials and commentary | Strassel, Kimberly A. "Conservatives Became Targets in 2008." *Wall Street Journal,* 23 May 2013. | To present a viewpoint; to advance an argument | Columnists, experts | General |
| Sponsored websites | The Blues Foundation, www.blues.org | To provide information about a topic or an organization | Varied | General; specialized |

A glance at this graphic reveals that different kinds of sources can be very similar in some respects (e.g., their intended audiences) but very different in others (e.g., their primary purpose). Having a general sense of the characteristics of these categories of sources can help you evaluate information from specific sources and determine its usefulness for your project.

Source materials within any of these general categories can also vary in terms of three important considerations when it comes to trustworthiness: credibility, reliability, and bias.

## 22

## Credibility

Credibility is the extent to which a source is respected and can be trusted. It refers to your sense of whether a source is reputable and dependable and the information found there generally reliable. The credibility of a source can arise from a reputation built over time. Well-established newspapers, magazines, and publishers are usually considered credible sources because of their record of publishing certain kinds of reliable, accurate information and their demonstrated commitment to high standards of integrity. Scholarly publications, for example, are generally considered credible because they tend to be peer-reviewed and because of their commitment to holding their authors to high standards of quality and accuracy. The fact that an article published in a scholarly journal has likely been carefully evaluated by established scholars can give readers confidence that the article meets high standards for accuracy and integrity.

Credibility can also be a function of a writer's general approach to the subject matter: his or her tone, the level of fairness with which subject matter is treated, how carefully he or she seems to have examined the subject, and so on. For example, if you notice a writer making easy generalizations or drawing dubious conclusions about a complicated subject, you might be skeptical of the writer's credibility when it comes to that subject. Consider the following passage from a post on AlterNet, a website devoted to politics and culture that is well known for having a left-leaning political slant. The writer, who was an editor at AlterNet at the time, was reporting on a newspaper survey of recent Harvard graduates regarding their career choices after college. As the editor of an established news website, she might be seen as a credible professional source for information about current political, economic, and cultural issues, but the website's political perspective might also affect what information is included in the piece and how it is presented:

> Wall Street's propensity to ravage the economy, launder money, and illegally foreclose on families with no harsher punishment than a slap on the wrist seems to have irked some of the nation's brightest. Either that or the shrinkage of jobs in the finance sector is turning them off. According to a survey by the student newspaper the *Harvard Crimson*, Harvard graduates are just saying "No" to Wall Street, with some of them looking instead to put their smarts to work making America a better place.
>
> The paper reports that about a third of new graduates plan to work in finance, with 15 percent working on Wall Street and 16 percent doing consulting. In 2007, before the recession, 47 percent of

This description of Wall Street, which is at least debatable, is presented as fact, reflecting the writer's bias.

The writer provides no information about how the survey was conducted or whether its results are credible.

Harvard grads went onto work in finance and consulting, a number that fell to 39 percent in 2008, and 20 percent in 2012.

As the Huffington Post noted, it looks like the financial crisis may have triggered a change in the aspirations of the nation's brightest, prompting millennials to prefer work in industries where they can contribute to social good, like health and tech, although many of them, no doubt, want to score big in tech. At the same time, Wall Street is laying off more employees than it hires, so grads' reasons for career shifts may be more pragmatic than idealistic.

> This sentence calls into question the writer's own conclusions about the graduates' aspirations.

Source: Gwynne, Kristen. "Even Harvard Grads Don't Want to Work on Wall Street Anymore." *AlterNet*, 29 May 2013, www.alternet.org/even-harvard-grads-dont-want-work-wall-st-anymore.

This passage illustrates that inaccurate information, such as the results of the survey referred to in this passage, can be presented in a way that reflects a certain political perspective on the issue at hand. This writer seems eager to draw a specific conclusion—that the behavior of Wall Street firms has "irked some of the nation's brightest" college graduates—that isn't necessarily supported by the evidence she presents: Although the survey results, which are reported in the second paragraph of the passage, indicate a decline in the percentage of Harvard graduates seeking employment in finance, the reasons for that decline are unclear.

This example illustrates that skepticism can be healthy when evaluating source material. In this case, given the rhetorical situation (that is, the writer is writing for a left-leaning website whose readers would very likely be critical of the financial firms on Wall Street), although the writer could be considered credible as a professional journalist, the way she approaches her subject should make you look carefully and critically at the information she presents. So be judicious in deciding how you use any information from this source. You might, for example, use the figures from the student survey to show that college graduates' career decisions have changed in recent years, but you might reject the writer's conclusions about the reasons for that change.

**In determining the credibility of a source, consider the following:**

- **Author.** Who is the author? Do you know anything about his or her background? Is the author an expert on the subject at hand? Does he or she have an obvious agenda with respect to this subject?

- **Publication.** What is the source of the publication? Is it a scholarly book or journal? A trade magazine? A sponsored website? What do you know about this source? What reputation does it have? Is it known to have a particular slant? Is it associated with a group that espouses a particular point of view on the subject?

- **Purpose.** What is the purpose of the source? To what extent might the purpose influence your sense of the trustworthiness of the information in the source? For example, is the author presenting a carefully researched analysis of a controversial topic—say, gun control—as in a scholarly journal article, or is the writer vigorously arguing against an opposing perspective on that topic for an audience of people who share the writer's views, as in an op-ed essay on a sponsored website? Having a sense of the purpose of the source and the rhetorical situation can help you determine how skeptical to be about the information contained in the source.

- **Date.** How recent is the publication? Is it current when it comes to the subject at hand? For some kinds of information, the date of publication might not matter much, but for many topics, outdated information can be problematic.

## Reliability

Reliability refers to your confidence in the accuracy of the information found in a source and the reputation of a source for consistently presenting trustworthy information. In general, credible sources gain a reputation for publishing accurate information over time. For example, major newspapers and magazines, such as the *Los Angeles Times* and the *The New Yorker*, usually employ fact checkers to verify information in articles they are preparing to publish; respected publishing houses usually edit manuscripts carefully to be sure they are accurate, and scholarly publishers employ expert reviewers to evaluate manuscripts. These practices usually mean that material published by these sources tends to be consistently accurate and trustworthy, so they gain a reputation for reliability. By contrast, many popular news outlets emphasize breaking news and sometimes publish information quickly before it can be verified. Often, such publications are not subject to the kind of rigorous editorial review that characterizes scholarly publications, which can result in inaccuracies and weaken your confidence in their reliability.

Because you are not likely to be an expert on many of the subjects you write about in college, you often won't have a sense of the reliability of a particular source, so you will have to make judgments on the basis of the nature of the source and its credibility. **Follow these guidelines:**

- **Choose credible sources.** In general, if you have a choice of sources, use those that you know or believe to be credible (see "Credibility" on page 715). Sources with reputations for credibility are more likely to supply reliable information. In general, scholarly publications, reference works (such as encyclopedias), well-established newspapers or magazines, and respected government agencies or non-governmental organizations (such as the Centers for Disease Control or the American Heart Association) tend to be safe bets as sources for your research.

- **Consult multiple sources.** Using multiple sources on the same topic can help you avoid using unreliable information. If you have information that is consistent across several sources, including sources you consider to be credible, that information is more likely to be reliable as well.

Determining whether a source is trustworthy is usually not an either-or proposition. Even credible and reliable sources might have information that isn't accurate or is inappropriate for your purposes. Your decisions about the trustworthiness of a source, then, should be guided by your rhetorical situation as well as by your own growing understanding of your subject. As you gain experience in reviewing unfamiliar sources, you will begin to develop a sense of what to look for and what to avoid when determining whether information from a source can be trusted. Such decisions about source material must also be made with an understanding of the potential bias of a source, which is discussed in the following section.

# Understanding Bias

Bias is a tendency to think or feel a certain way. It is the inclination of a source to favor one point of view over others that might be equally valid—the privileging of one perspective at the expense of others. Bias is sometimes thought of as prejudice, though bias is not necessarily a negative quality. One might have a bias in favor of cats rather than dogs as pets, for example. In this textbook, bias generally refers to a source's perspective or slant.

It is important to understand that *all sources are biased in some way*. We tend to think of some kinds of source material, such as encyclopedias and other kinds of reference works, as objective or neutral. But even a venerable reference such as the *Encyclopedia Britannica* can be said to have certain biases. For example, the kind of information that is considered appropriate for inclusion in *Encyclopedia Britannica* reflects a set of beliefs about what kinds of knowledge or information are relevant and important for its purposes. Although such a reference work tries to be comprehensive, it inevitably excludes some kinds of information and privileges others. For instance, extremely technical information about the rhythms of Hip Hop music might be excluded from an encyclopedia, even though more general information about that musical form might be included. The decisions the editors make about what to include and what to exclude in the encyclopedia represent a bias, no matter how open-minded the editors might be.

Bias, then, is not necessarily a negative quality in a source, but it is essential to recognize bias in any source you consult so that you can evaluate the usefulness of information from that source. Some kinds of sources are transparent about their biases. Scholarly journals, for example, tend to make their editorial focus and purpose clear. Here is a statement of the editorial policy of a journal titled *Research in the Teaching of English*, published by a professional organization called the National Council of Teachers of English (NCTE):

> *Research in the Teaching of English* publishes scholarship that explores issues in the teaching and learning of literacy at all levels. It is the policy of NCTE in its journals and other publications to provide a forum for open discussion of ideas concerning the teaching of English and language arts.

Scholarly journals often provide such descriptions of the kinds of articles they seek to publish; they might also provide explanations of the processes by which manuscripts are reviewed. These editorial policy statements help make the biases of a journal explicit.

Many sources, even credible and reliable ones, are not so transparent about their biases. For example, although many readers consider newspapers to be trusted sources of information, many newspapers have well-established points of view. *The New York Times* is generally considered to have a liberal bias, whereas *The Washington Times* is usually thought to reflect a more conservative viewpoint. However, if you did not already have a sense of such biases, you might find it difficult to determine them. Here, for example, is the description that *The New York Times* provides of its editorial board:

The editorial board is composed of 16 journalists with wide-ranging areas of expertise. Their primary responsibility is to write *The Times's* editorials, which represent the voice of the board, its editor and the publisher. The board is part of *The Times's* editorial department, which is operated separately from *The Times's* newsroom, and includes the Letters to the Editor and Op-Ed sections.

Source: "*The New York Times* Editorial Board." *The New York Times*, 2 May 2016, www.nytimes.com/interactive/opinion/editorialboard.html.

Although this statement explains that the editorial department is separate from the newsroom at *The New York Times*, which might give readers confidence that the newspaper's reporting is not influenced by its editorial opinions, the statement does not describe a particular political slant or perspective. You would have to examine the newspaper more carefully—and probably over time—to gain a sense of its political bias.

Such examples underscore the important point that even the most credible and reliable sources will have biases; however, a bias does not mean that a source is untrustworthy. Rather, bias influences the kind of information a source might contain and how that information is presented, even when the information is trustworthy. For example, like major newspapers, major public affairs magazines are usually considered to have either a liberal bias (e.g., *The Nation*), a conservative bias (e.g., the *National Review*), or other bias (e.g., libertarian). Those biases mean that each magazine is likely to focus on some issues as opposed to others and to examine issues from a particular perspective. For instance, the *Nation* might publish an argument in favor of a proposal to increase the national minimum wage, reflecting a liberal perspective on the government's role in economic matters. The *National Review*, by contrast, might publish a critique of the same proposal, reflecting a conservative bias in favor of less government intervention in economic matters. Both articles might contain reliable and accurate information, but the information is presented in a way that reflects the political bias of the publication.

Often, the bias of a source is much more subtle and difficult to detect. For example, advocacy groups often try to appear objective in their treatment of certain issues when in fact they have a strong bias on those issues. For example, an environmental advocacy group might oppose the development of a large wind farm in a wilderness area. Its website might seem to be a neutral source of information about various kinds of energy, including wind power, but its opposition to large wind farms means that its treatment of wind power is likely to focus on the disadvantages of wind power and the harmful impact of wind turbines on wilderness areas. In such a case, even though the information on the website might be accurate, that information might also be incomplete or presented in a way that paints a negative picture of wind power. (See Focus: "Detecting Bias" on page 720.)

**When evaluating a source for bias, consider these questions:**

- Does this source reflect a particular perspective or point of view?
- Does this source represent a specific group, political party, business, organization, or institution?
- Does the source seem to have an agenda regarding the subject at hand?
- To what extent is the bias of this source evident? Are there blatantly slanted statements? Do you notice questionable information? To what extent does this bias seem to affect the trustworthiness of the information it presents?

Many sources that appear at first glance to be neutral or objective on a particular issue or subject might actually have a strong bias. The website shown below, for example, contains information about education reform but is sponsored by an organization that advocates a particular perspective on school reform in favor of charter schools and related movements that are controversial. Notice that nothing on the this web page conveys a sense of the organization's strong views about specific kinds of education reforms; instead, the language is neutral ("CER has created opportunities that give families choices, teachers freedom and students more pathways to achieve a great education") and seemingly nonpartisan ("Join us in our fight to make *all* schools better for *all* children"). The information on such a site can be useful, but it is important to understand that it is being presented from a particular point of view. In this case, you might find accurate information about charter schools, but you are unlikely to find studies whose results are not flattering to charter schools.

To detect bias in a source, try to identify its purpose and its perspective on the subject. Use the questions at the bottom of page 719 to evaluate the source and identify its potential bias regarding the subject. Also, read Focus: "Tips for Evaluating Online Sources" on pages 721–722.

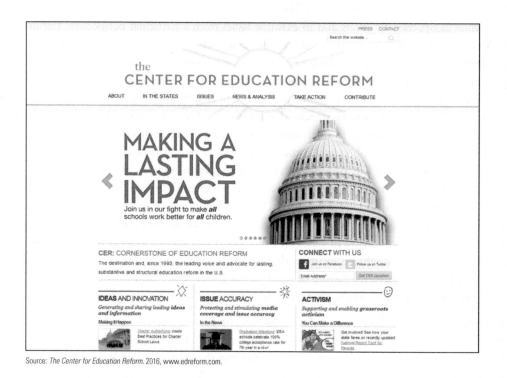

Source: *The Center for Education Reform.* 2016, www.edreform.com.

*All* sources should be evaluated for trustworthiness, but different sources can present different challenges when you are trying to determine trustworthiness. **Use the following questions to guide you as you evaluate specific sources:**

## Books and Articles

- **Who published this article or book?** (scholarly press, trade publisher, respected newspaper or magazine, professional organization, non-profit organization, government agency, advocacy group, business)

- **Who is the author?** (Is the author's name provided? Is the author an expert on the subject?)

- **What is the purpose?** (to share information or knowledge, to advocate for a point of view)

- **Does the source have a reputation for reliability?** (Is the source known to have a bias or slant? Is the source generally considered credible?)

- **When was it published?** (Is the date of publication indicated? Is the book or article current or outdated?)

## Websites and Social Media

- **Who sponsors the site?** (a news organization, business, political organization, advocacy group, non-profit foundation, government agency)

- **What is the purpose of the site?** (to inform, to advertise or sell a product, to promote a point of view)

- **What are the contents of the site?** (Does it include relevant information? Does it have advertisements? Does it seem to contain accurate information? Are the sources of information indicated?)

- **Is the site current?** (Is the site regularly updated? Are the web pages dated? Is the information current?)

---

**FOCUS** | **TIPS FOR EVALUATING ONLINE SOURCES**

Although the advice in this chapter applies to all kinds of sources, you can follow additional steps to help you determine the trustworthiness of online sources, especially websites:

- **Read the "About" Page.** Many websites have pages titled "About" or "About Us" that provide useful information about the authors, purpose, and sometimes the history of the site. Sites sponsored by advocacy groups and non-profit organizations often include information about their boards of directors or administrators. Such information can help you evaluate the trustworthiness of a site and determine the extent to which it might be biased. For example, a site of an organization that seems to advocate green energy but whose board of directors includes mostly business leaders from large energy companies might have a bias in favor of large business interests. By contrast, the site of a clean energy advocacy group whose directors are members of well-known environmental organizations might be less likely to support business interests when it comes to energy issues.

*(Continued)*

Determining Whether a Source Is Trustworthy **721**

- **Look for a Date.** Most websites sponsored by legitimate organizations indicate the date when the website or individual web pages were updated. Many organizations, especially respected media organizations, update their websites daily. However, some websites are not actively maintained and can be available on the Internet many years after they cease to be updated or revised. If you cannot find dates on a website or if the only dates you find are well in the past, be wary of the material on that site.

- **Check the Links.** Many websites contain pages with various kinds of resources, including links to related websites sponsored by other organizations. Often, those links reflect a website's own biases and can help you determine whether the site is biased in a way that should concern you. If these links are not active, it indicates that the site is not well maintained—another reason to be skeptical about information you find there.

# Evaluating Source Material for Your Rhetorical Purposes

Once you have determined that information from a source is trustworthy, you must still decide whether it is useful and appropriate for your project. It isn't enough to determine whether a source is credible and reliable or to identify its biases; you must also evaluate the information in terms of your own rhetorical situation and especially in light of the purpose of your project.

To illustrate, let's imagine two related but different kinds of writing assignments:

- an analysis of the ongoing debate about health care reform in the United States
- an argument about the impact of the Affordable Care Act (ACA), often called Obamacare, which became law in 2010

Suppose that the analysis is for an assignment in a writing course that requires students to examine public debates about a controversial issue; the audience includes other students in the course as well as the instructor. The argument is intended for the student newspaper on your campus. Both pieces require research. Let's imagine that for each assignment, you want to understand how the current debates about health care coverage in the United States are influenced by the controversy that occurred when the Affordable Care Act was being implemented in 2011 and 2012. In your search for information about that controversy, you found the following three sources from 2013:

- a blog post from the website of *Forbes* magazine
- a blog post from a website called California Healthline
- an article from AlterNet

Let's consider how the different rhetorical situations for these two assignments, with their different audiences and purposes, might shape your decisions about whether and how to use information from these sources:

## Obamacare Will Increase Health Spending by $7,450 for a Typical Family of Four
by Chris Conover
*Forbes.com*, 23 Sept. 2013

**22**

It was one of candidate Obama's most vivid and concrete campaign promises. Forget about high minded (some might say high sounding) but gauzy promises of hope and change. This candidate solemnly pledged on June 5, 2008: "In an Obama administration, we'll lower premiums by up to $2,500 for a typical family per year.... We'll do it by the end of my first term as President of the United States." Unfortunately, the experts working for Medicare's actuary have (yet again) reported that in its first 10 years, Obamacare will boost health spending by "roughly $621 billion" above the amounts Americans would have spent without this misguided law.

$621 billion is a pretty eye-glazing number. Most readers will find it easier to think about how this number translates to a typical American family—the very family candidate Obama promised would see $2,500 in annual savings as far as the eye could see. So I have taken the latest year-by-year projections, divided by the projected U.S. population to determine the added amount per person and multiplied the result by 4.

Simplistic? Maybe, but so too was the President's campaign promise. And this approach allows us to see just how badly that promise fell short of the mark. Between 2014 and 2022, the increase in national health spending (which the Medicare actuaries specifically attribute to the law) amounts to $7,450 per family of 4.

Let us hope this family hasn't already spent or borrowed the $2,500 in savings they might have expected over this same period had they taken candidate Obama's promise at face value. In truth, no well-informed American ever should have believed this absurd promise. At the time, Factcheck.org charitably deemed this claim as "overly optimistic, misleading and, to some extent, contradicted by one of his own advisers." The *Washington Post* less charitably awarded it Two Pinocchios ("Significant omissions or exaggerations"). Yet rather than learn from his mistakes, President Obama on July 16, 2012 essentially doubled-down on his promise, assuring small business owners "your premiums will go down." He made this assertion notwithstanding the fact that in three separate reports between April 2010 and June 2012, the Medicare actuaries had demonstrated that the ACA would *increase* health spending. To its credit, the *Washington Post* dutifully awarded the 2012 claim Three Pinocchios ("Significant factual error and/or obvious contradictions.")

As it turns out, the average family of 4 has only had to face a relatively modest burden from Obamacare over the past four years—a little over $125. Unfortunately, this year's average burden ($66) will be 10 times as large in 2014 when Obamacare kicks in for earnest. And it will rise for two years after that, after which it hit a steady-state level of just under $800 a year....

Obamacare will not save Americans one penny now or in the future. Perhaps the next time voters encounter a politician making such grandiose claims, they will learn to watch their wallet.

Source: Conover, Chris. "Obamacare Will Increase Health Spending by $7,450 for a Typical Family of Four." *Forbes*, 23 Sep. 2013, www.forbes.com/sites/theapothecary/2013/09/23/its-official-obamacare-will-increase-health-spending-by-7450-for-a-typical-family-of-four/#244a2e122c62.

The Affordable Care Act contains a number of provisions intended to incent "personal responsibility," or the notion that health care isn't just a right—it's an obligation. None of these measures is more prominent than the law's individual mandate, designed to ensure that every American obtains health coverage or pays a fine for choosing to go uninsured.

But one provision that's gotten much less attention—until recently—relates to smoking; specifically, the ACA allows payers to treat tobacco users very differently by opening the door to much higher premiums for this population.

That measure has some health policy analysts cheering, suggesting that higher premiums are necessary to raise revenue for the law and (hopefully) deter smokers' bad habits. But other observers have warned that the ACA takes a heavy-handed stick to smokers who may be unhappily addicted to tobacco, rather than enticing them with a carrot to quit.

### Possible Pain Lies Ahead for Tobacco Users

Under proposed rules, the department of Health and Human Services would allow insurers to charge a smoker seeking health coverage in the individual market as much as 50% more in premiums than a non-smoker.

That difference in premiums may rapidly add up for smokers, given the expectation that Obamacare's new medical-loss ratios already will lead to major cost hikes in the individual market. "For many people, in the years after the law, premiums aren't just going to [go] up a little," Peter Suderman predicts at Reason. "They're going to rise a lot."

Meanwhile, Ann Marie Marciarille, a law professor at the University of Missouri-Kansas City, adds that insurers have "considerable flexibility" in how to set up a potential surcharge for tobacco use. For example, insurers could apply a high surcharge for tobacco use in older smokers—perhaps several hundred dollars per month—further hitting a population that tends to be poorer.

### Attitudes on Smoking Help Inform Policy

Is this cost-shifting fair? The average American tends to think so.

Nearly 60% of surveyed adults in a 2011 NPR-Thomson Reuters poll thought it was OK to charge smokers more for their health insurance than non-smokers. (That's nearly twice the number of adults who thought it would be OK to charge the obese more for their health insurance.)

And smoking does lead to health costs that tend to be borne by the broader population. Writing at the Incidental Economist in 2011, Don Taylor noted that "smoking imposes very large social costs"—essentially, about $1.50 per pack—with its increased risk of cancers and other chronic illness. CDC has found that smoking and its effects lead to more than 440,000 premature deaths in the United States per year, with more than $190 billion in annual health costs and productivity loss.

As a result, charging smokers more "makes some actuarial sense," Marciarille acknowledges. "Tobacco use has a long-term fuse for its most expensive health effects."

But Louise Norris of Colorado Health Insurance Insider takes issue with the ACA's treatment of tobacco users.

Noting that smokers represent only about 20% of Americans, Norris argues that "it's easy to point fingers and call for increased personal responsibility when we're singling out another group—one in which we are not included."

As a result, she adds, "it seems very logical to say that smokers should have to pay significantly higher premiums for their health insurance," whereas we're less inclined to treat the obese differently because so many of us are overweight.

This approach toward tobacco users also raises the risk that low-income smokers will find the cost of coverage too high and end up uninsured, Norris warns. She notes that tax credits for health coverage will be calculated prior to however insurers choose to set their banding rules, "which means that smokers would be responsible for [an] additional premium on their own."

### Alternate Approach: Focus on Cessation

Nearly 70% of smokers want to quit, and about half attempt to kick the habit at least once per year. But more than 90% are unable to stop smoking, partly because of the lack of assistance; fewer than 5% of smokers appear able to quit without support.

That's why Norris and others say that if federal officials truly want to improve public health, the law should prioritize anti-smoking efforts like counseling and medication for tobacco users. And the ACA does require new health insurance plans to offer smoking cessation products and therapy.

But as Ankita Rao writes at *Kaiser Health News*, the coverage of those measures thus far is spotty. Some plans leave out nasal sprays and inhalers; others shift costs to smokers, possibly deterring them from seeking treatment.

Some anti-smoking crusaders hope that states will step into the gap and ramp up cessation opportunities, such as by including cessation therapy as an essential health benefit.

"The federal government has missed several opportunities since the enactment of the ACA to grant smokers access to more cessation treatments," the American Lung Association warned in November. "Now, as states are beginning implementation of state exchanges and Medicaid expansions, state policymakers have the opportunity to stand up for smokers in their states who want to quit."

Source: Diamond, Dan. "The Premium Conundrum: Do Smokers Get a Fair Break Under Obamacare?" *California Healthline*, 23 Jan. 2013, californiahealthline.org/news/the-premium-conundrum-do-smokers-get-a-fair-break-under-obamacare/.

### How's Obamacare Turning Out? Great If You Live in a Blue State, and 'Screw You' If You Have a Republican Governor
#### by Steve Rosenfeld
*AlterNet* 25 May 2013

Obamacare implementation is becoming the latest dividing line between blue- and red-state America, with Democrat-led states making progress to expand healthcare to the uninsured and the poor—and Republican-led states saying "screw you" to millions of their most vulnerable and needy residents.

*(Continued)*

The latest sign of the Republican Party's increasingly secessionist tendencies comes as Obamacare passed a major milestone in California, which late last week announced lower-than-expected healthcare premiums for its 5.3 million uninsured, less than many small businesses now pay in group plans.

"Covered California's Silver Plan . . . offers premiums that can be 29 percent lower than comparable plans provided on today's small group market," the state's new insurance exchange announced Thursday, referring to the least-expensive option of four state-administered plans and posting this price comparison chart.

In contrast, the refusal by red-state America to create these health exchanges, which would be more local control—a supposed Republican value—and to accept federal funds to expand state-run Medicaid programs for the poor, means that about half the states are turning their backs on their residents, especially millions of the poorest people.

The federal government plans to step in later this summer and offer uninsured people in recalcitrant red states the option of buying plans via federally run heath care exchanges. But the poorest people can't afford that, meaning the refusal to expand Medicaid programs will leave them in the cold. They will see ads selling new federal healthcare options that will be unaffordable for them.

*The New York Times* reports that local healthcare advocates in red states are predicting a backlash once Obamacare is rolled out and the poor realize that they cannot take advantage of it because Republicans are blocking it. However, that does not change the bottom line in state-run Medicaid programs: the GOP is again penalizing the poor.

### Progress in Blue States

Meanwhile, in blue states, there have been surprising developments in the cost of Obamacare for those people who currently are uninsured. There, the bottom line is insurance premiums are hundreds of dollars a month lower than what employers are now paying for their workers under existing group plans.

California, with 5.3 million uninsured adults, is the biggest state to release cost estimates for Obamacare. Its lower-than-expected estimates are in line with announcements in Washington, Oregon, Maryland and Vermont. The actual prices will be known after insurers file rate documents in coming weeks.

Source: Rosenfeld, Steven. "How's Obamacare Turning Out? Great If You Live in a Blue State, and 'Screw You' If You Have a Republican Governor." *AlterNet*, 25 May 2013, www.alternet.org/news-amp-politics/hows-obamacare-turning-out-great-if-you-live-blue-state-and-screw-you-if-you-have.

All three sources are relevant to both assignments, but are they useful? To answer that question, first determine whether each source is trustworthy by addressing the three main aspects of trustworthiness described in this chapter:

1. Is the source credible?

2. Is the source reliable?

3. What is the bias of the source?

# Is the Source Credible?

As we saw earlier (see pages 715–719), the credibility of a source depends on several important factors: the author, the nature of the publication, the purpose of the publication, and the date. Review each source accordingly:

## Is the source credible?

| Blog post on Forbes.com | Blog post on California Healthline | Article on AlterNet |
|---|---|---|

### Who is the author?

| Chris Conover: researcher at Duke University, scholar at American Enterprise Institute | Dan Diamond: managing editor of health blog, contributor to *Forbes*, a business magazine | Steve Rosenfeld: reporter for AlterNet, author of *Count My Vote: A Citizen's Guide to Voting* (2008) |
|---|---|---|

### What is the nature of the publication?

| Blog post on the website of a major business news magazine | Blog post on the website of a non-profit foundation devoted to health care reform | Article on a website devoted to politics and culture |
|---|---|---|

### What is the purpose of the source?

| To advocate for a position on health-related issues | To examine issues related to health care | To share information and ideas with audience interested in political issues |
|---|---|---|

### When was it published? Is it timely?

| 2013. Yes. The debate about Obamacare was intense in 2013 and continued through the 2016 presidential election. | 2013. Yes. The debate about Obamacare was intense in 2013 and continued through the 2016 presidential election. | 2013. Yes. The debate about Obamacare was intense in 2013 and continued through the 2016 presidential election. |
|---|---|---|

Addressing these questions will help you develop a better sense of the nature of each source, which will help you determine its credibility. Evaluating these sources in comparison to each other also reveals some important differences among them. For example, AlterNet covers all kinds of newsworthy topics, whereas the California Healthline focuses only on health issues and can therefore be assumed to have more in-depth and extensive coverage of issues like the Affordable Care Act; the Apothecary, a blog on the website of *Forbes* magazine, addresses health-related issues from a business perspective.

If necessary, you can find more information to answer each of these questions about these sources. For example, you can look for more information about each author. Visiting a website like Amazon or Alibris might enable you to learn more about Steven Rosenfeld's book *Count My Vote*, which could give you insight into his background and his perspective on political issues. Similarly, you could visit the website of the American Enterprise Institute, a well-established conservative think tank, to learn more about Chris Conover's perspective. You could also find more information about the sponsor of the California Healthline to determine whether the site could be considered a credible source of information.

As noted earlier in this chapter, credibility can also be a function of a writer's tone, fairness, and general approach to the subject. With those criteria in mind, you might note that the general tone of the *Forbes* blog post toward the Affordable Care Act is negative, and the language of the AlterNet article is explicitly dismissive and disrespectful of a conservative viewpoint. These characteristics should make you a bit more skeptical about these two sources. Nevertheless, both sources seem to have accurate information about the topic of health care reform, even though they present that information from a decidedly partisan perspective.

Let's say that after examining each source in this example, you have determined that all three sources can be considered credible, despite your reservations about the AlterNet article and *Forbes* blog post. Next, try to decide whether the source is reliable.

## Is the Source Reliable?

Reliability generally has to do with your confidence that a source has established a record for accuracy and credibility. In this example, both *Forbes* magazine and AlterNet represent perspectives that are consistent over time. Both sources are respected by their constituencies. You are aware of their respective political leanings, and you can judge the reliability of information from each site in the context of those perspectives (see "What Is the Bias of the Source" on page 729). For example, you expect *Forbes* magazine to be skeptical about the Affordable Care Act because it favors business and tends to oppose large government programs; by contrast, you expect articles on AlterNet to be supportive of the ACA and critical of conservative resistance to it. Neither source is surprising in this regard. In other words, each source is reliable in terms of its political perspective and generally reliable in the kinds of information it presents.

The reliability of the blog post from the California Healthline is less clear, mostly because it is a less well known and more specialized source. To gain a better sense of its reliability, you should investigate further. For one thing, you can check the "About Us" page on its website. Here's what you will find:

Source: "About Us." *California Healthline*, 2016, californiahealthline.org/about-us/.

This description provides the important information that the California Healthline is sponsored by an organization called California Health Care Foundation but is published independently by a national health care research and publishing organization called Kaiser Health News. That information lends credibility to the site because it suggests that the publication is nonpartisan and lacks a particular political or ideological agenda. In addition, a quick Internet search would reveal that this news service has been in existence since 1998, which strengthens your confidence in its reliability as a source of health care information. Finally, the author of this blog post seems to be an established observer of health care and business matters. Notice that, like Chris Conover, this author also writes for *Forbes* magazine, a leading and well-respected business publication. All these facts can give you confidence that this is a reliable source for information about health care issues.

This analysis enables you to conclude that all three of these sources can be considered reliable.

## What Is the Bias of the Source?

You have established your sources as credible and reliable, but their usefulness to you will also depend on the extent to which they are biased.

You have already determined that *Forbes* magazine and AlterNet reflect conservative and left-leaning political biases, respectively. What about the California Healthline? Your review of its "About Us" page led you to conclude that it is credible, reliable, and probably politically nonpartisan, but even if it does not reflect a political bias, it might reflect other kinds of bias. It makes sense to look more closely at this source.

The "About Us" page indicates California Healthline is sponsored by a nonprofit organization called California Health Care Foundation. Here's how the organization describes itself on its website:

> The California Health Care Foundation (CHCF) is dedicated to advancing meaningful, measurable improvements in the way the health care delivery system provides care to the people of California, particularly those with low incomes and those whose needs are not well served by the status quo. We work to ensure that people have access to the care they need, when they need it, at a price they can afford.
>
> CHCF informs policymakers and industry leaders, invests in ideas and innovations, and connects with changemakers to create a more responsive, patient-centered health care system.
>
> CHCF supports the testing and evaluation of innovative approaches to improving care. We also commission research and analysis that policymakers, clinical leaders, payers, consumers, and the media depend on to better understand California's complex delivery system, in service of three overarching goals: improving access to coverage and care for low-income Californians, ensuring high-value care, informing decision makers.

Source: "About CHCF." *California Health Care Foundation*, 2016, www.chcf.org/about.

This explanation tells you that the foundation is not a political group and supports health care reform through research and analysis. But on the same web page you also find the following statement:

> The Affordable Care Act (ACA) has helped millions of Californians get coverage through Medi-Cal and Covered California. Yet many people struggle to get the care they need, when they need it, at a price they can afford. Drawing upon expertise in Medi-Cal, public policy, commercial and safety-net health plans and providers, and emerging service delivery and IT innovations, CHCF seeks to expand access.

From this passage you could reasonably conclude that the organization is supportive of the Affordable Care Act. That conclusion doesn't necessarily call into question the information on the California Healthline site, but it does suggest that the Healthline is likely to cover the Affordable Care Act closely and is not likely to be consistently critical of it. In other words, articles and blog posts on the site are likely to reflect a bias in favor of expanded health care reform, including the ACA.

You can examine the biases of your three sources in more depth by addressing the four sets of questions listed on page 719:

| To what extent is the source biased? | | |
| --- | --- | --- |
| Blog post on Forbes.com | Blog post on California Healthline | Article on AlterNet |

↓

| Does the source reflect a particular viewpoint or perspective? | | |
| --- | --- | --- |
| Yes, a generally conservative viewpoint | No obvious political or ideological perspective | Yes, a left-leaning political point of view |

↓

| Does the source represent a specific group or organization? | | |
| --- | --- | --- |
| Yes, website is hosted by *Forbes* magazine. | Yes, sponsored by a nonprofit foundation that supports health care reform. | No, the site is an independent, nonprofit news entity. |

↓

| Does the source have an agenda regarding the subject? | | |
| --- | --- | --- |
| Yes, generally opposed to federal health care reform initiative | Yes, supports health care reform | Yes, generally supportive of the Obama administration's reform efforts. |

↓

| To what extent is the bias of the source evident? | | |
| --- | --- | --- |
| The critical stance toward the ACA is noticeable | Bias in favor of health care reform is implicit | Overt bias in favor of Obama administration and against its conservative opponents |

At this point you should have a good sense of the biases of your three sources.

# How Useful Is the Source?

Now that you have carefully evaluated your sources, you can examine their usefulness for your rhetorical purposes. Recall that both your hypothetical assignments—the analysis and the argument—are about health care reform in the United States, but their purposes and intended audiences differ, which will influence your decisions about whether and how to use the sources you have evaluated.

Let's imagine that your analysis is an effort to answer this question:

*Why does the debate about the Affordable Care Act continue to be intense and confrontational so many years after it became law?*

You want to understand some of the reasons for the sustained and vitriolic nature of this debate and what it might reveal about public debates in general. You are writing your analysis primarily for your instructor and other students in your class. For your argument, let's imagine that you want to make the case that the ongoing debates about the Affordable Care Act are relevant to college students. For this piece, your audience is broader than for your analysis: students and faculty who read your campus newspaper.

We can sum up the rhetorical situations for these two pieces of writing as follows:

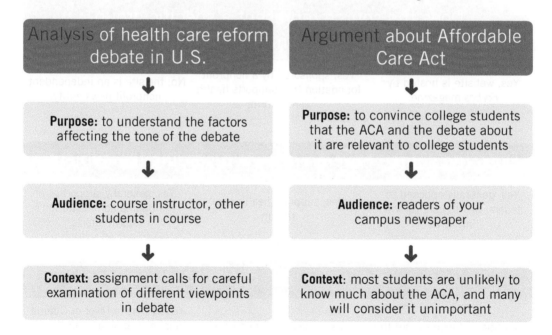

Analysis of health care reform debate in U.S.

**Purpose:** to understand the factors affecting the tone of the debate

**Audience:** course instructor, other students in course

**Context:** assignment calls for careful examination of different viewpoints in debate

Argument about Affordable Care Act

**Purpose:** to convince college students that the ACA and the debate about it are relevant to college students

**Audience:** readers of your campus newspaper

**Context:** most students are unlikely to know much about the ACA, and many will consider it unimportant

With these factors in mind you can examine how each of the three sources you found might fit into these two assignments:

- **Analysis Assignment.** For your analysis of the debate about the Affordable Care Act, you might use the article from AlterNet and the *Forbes* blog post as examples of more extreme positions in the debate. In this case, you don't need to worry much about the accuracy or reliability of the sources, because you would be using them as examples of how conservative and left-leaning viewpoints emerge in the debate about health care reform. Your analysis would require you to identify clearly the political perspectives represented by each source and how those perspectives influence the way each source represents the Affordable Care Act. For example, you might examine the numbers included in the *Forbes* blog post to show that the author presents only data that cast the ACA in a negative light. Similarly, you might evaluate the specific language used in the AlterNet article to refer to Republican or conservative positions— for example, "secessionist" and "recalcitrant"—and the unsupported claims that "the GOP is again penalizing the poor." For your purposes it would not be necessary to decide how accurate the information in each source is; you are simply analyzing *how* the sources present the information, not the information itself, so the overt biases of the sources is not a problem.

- **Argument Assignment.** For your argument, by contrast, you would likely need to present accurate information about the Affordable Care Act and the problems it is intended to address, especially in terms of how it might affect college students. You want to convince your audience that the debate about health care reform is one they should pay attention to. In this case, some of the information from the California Healthline blog post is likely to be useful in arguing that the debate matters to college students. For example, the author notes that the law is "designed to ensure that every American obtains health coverage or pays a fine for choosing to go uninsured." That fact should be important to college students, many of whom will need new health care insurance once they graduate. If you include that quotation in your argument, you will need to be confident that it is accurate. Your evaluation of this source should give you that confidence, but you can also look for other sources that could corroborate it. At the same time, the information included in the *Forbes* blog post and the AlterNet article might also be useful, but given your rhetorical purpose, you would have to take into account the obvious biases of those sources as you decide whether to use specific information. For instance, the author of the AlterNet article identifies differences in how individual states will enact the Affordable Care Act. Those differences could be important to college students because they could affect the kind of health insurance that is available to them in one state or another. However, you might be more skeptical of the author's claim that "Republican-led states [are] saying 'screw you' to millions of their most vulnerable and needy residents." Given the author's political perspective, which makes him more likely to be critical of Republican policies, it would be sensible to verify such a claim before using it in your own argument. Moreover, you would want to avoid undermining your argument by relying on sources whose political views might alienate some of your intended readers.

These examples illustrate how the rhetorical situation can influence your decisions about how to use the source material you find in your research. Obviously, you should evaluate *all* source material in terms of credibility, reliability, and bias. But how your evaluation will affect your decisions about using source material will ultimately depend upon the rhetorical goals you hope to achieve with your intended audience.

> ## MindTap®
> Practice research skills that you have learned in this chapter, receive feedback, and reflect on your learning.

# Using Source Material 23

**STUDENT WRITERS** sometimes have less trouble finding the source material they need for their projects than they do using that material effectively in their own writing. The challenge many students face is resisting the tendency to rely too heavily on source material so that it doesn't take over the student's own writing. Using source materials effectively, then, is partly a matter of keeping in mind the purpose and main point of your project. The most important guideline to follow when using any source material is to focus on your own ideas and the point *you* are making. The source material you cite should support *your* thinking and should not become the focus of your writing. (See Core Concept #4: "A writer must have something to say.") So it is important to be able *integrate* source material into your writing rather than simply reproduce information from a source. This chapter describes some basic strategies for using your source material strategically and maintaining control of your own writing.

## Quoting from Sources

In academic writing, there are three main ways to integrate source material into your own prose:

- summarizing
- paraphrasing
- quoting

Summarizing and paraphrasing are discussed in Chapter 19 (see pages 629–632). In this section we will examine how to quote sources appropriately.

To integrate source material smoothly into your writing, **follow four basic guidelines:**

- Quote only what you need and when necessary.
- Reproduce the original text accurately.
- Be concise.
- Make it fit.

### Quote Only What You Need and When Necessary

Writers quote from a source when the rhetorical situation dictates that it is important to include information or ideas *as stated in the original language of the source.* If you are consulting a source for specific information and don't need the exact language of the source, summarize or paraphrase the source passage. (See Chapter 19 for advice about summarizing and paraphrasing.) Sometimes, however, the original wording of the source is necessary to make or emphasize a point. In such cases, quoting can enhance your writing.

For example, imagine that you are writing an analysis of the debate about what should be done to address global climate change. One of your sources is *Field Notes From a Catastrophe*, in which author Elizabeth Kolbert reviews scientific data indicating that climate change is an increasingly serious problem. Here are two passages that you consider important and want to include in your analysis:

> All told, the Greenland ice sheet holds enough water to raise sea levels worldwide by twenty-three feet. Scientists at NASA have calculated that throughout the 1990s the ice sheet, despite some thickening at the center, was shrinking by twelve cubic miles per year. (52)

> As the effects of global warming become more and more difficult to ignore, will we react by finally fashioning a global response? Or will we retreat into ever narrower and more destructive forms of self-interest? It may seem impossible to imagine that a technologically advanced society could choose, in essence, to destroy itself, but that is what we are now in the process of doing. (189)

Source: Kolbert, Elizabeth. *Field Notes From a Catastrophe*. Bloomsbury Press, 2006.

The first passage contains important information about shrinking glaciers, which scientists consider a sign of climate change that could have a significant impact on coastal communities. The second passage is taken from Kolbert's conclusion, where she makes a plea for action to address climate change. Here's how you might use these passages in your analysis:

> Scientists have documented the decline of glaciers and arctic sea ice over the past several decades. For example, the Greenland ice sheet, which contains enough water to increase global sea levels by 23 feet, is shrinking by 12 cubic miles per year (Kolbert 52). To many scientists, the loss of glacial and sea ice is one of the most worrisome indicators that climate change is accelerating, and some argue that humans must act now to avoid potentially catastrophic impacts on human communities in the coming decades. Elizabeth Kolbert expresses the concerns of many experts: "As the effects of global warming become more and more difficult to ignore, will we react by finally fashioning a global response? Or will we retreat into ever narrower and more destructive forms of self-interest? It may seem impossible to imagine that a technologically advanced society could choose, in essence, to destroy itself, but that is what we are now in the process of doing" (189).

Notice that the first passage from the source text (p. 52) is cited but not quoted. Although the information in that passage is important, the wording of the source text is not. The second passage (p. 189), however, is quoted, because Kolbert's wording conveys her point more effectively than a summary or paraphrase would.

This example illustrates the need to be judicious in deciding whether to quote or summarize and cite your source. In making that decision, always consider the purpose of your project and the impact you wish to have on your audience.

# Reproduce the Original Text Accurately

Quotation marks indicate to a reader that everything inside the quotation marks is exactly as it appears in the source text. So whenever you are using a quotation, make sure that you have accurately reproduced the passages you are quoting. Although this advice might seem obvious, misquoting is a common problem in student writing that can lead to misleading or inaccurate statements. For example, let's imagine you are writing an essay about childhood obesity and you want to use the following quotation from a study of the link between childhood obesity and cancer:

> In conclusion, overweight in 1,110,835 male adolescents, followed for 40 years, was found to be related to a 42% higher risk of developing future urothelial cancer. Our results should be viewed in terms of the growing global epidemic of obesity, especially childhood and adolescent obesity, in the last few decades as well as the increasing incidence of bladder cancer in the developed world.

Source: Leiba, Adi, et al. "Overweight in Adolescence Is Related to Increased Risk of Future Urothelial Cancer." *Obesity*, vol. 20, no. 12, Dec. 2012, pp. 2445–450.

A misplaced quotation mark or incomplete quotation could significantly change the meaning of this statement:

> According to a recent study, overweight adolescents are 42% more likely to develop urothelial cancer in their lives. The study's authors caution that their results "should be viewed in terms of the growing global epidemic of obesity, especially childhood and adolescent obesity, in the last few decades as well as the increasing incidence of bladder cancer" (Leiba et al. 2449).

In this example the writer failed to include the phrase "in the developed world" at the end of the quoted statement. Although everything else included in the quotation marks is accurate, the quoted statement is now misleading. The authors of the original study specifically noted the increase in bladder cancer *in the developed world*. Because the quotation in this example omits that phrase, a reader could misinterpret the quoted statement to mean that bladder cancer is increasing in *all* nations, not just in so-called "developed" nations.

As this example indicates, even a minor mistake in quoting from a source could result in erroneous or misleading statements.

# Be Concise

One of the most common problems students have when quoting from a source is wordiness. Often, students use unnecessary words to introduce a quotation. Here's an example:

> In the article "New Teachers" by Neil Postman and Charles Weingarten, they state, "One of the largest obstacles to the establishment of a sound learning environment is the desire of teachers to get something they think they know into the heads of people who don't know it" (138).

Technically, there is nothing wrong with this sentence, but the writer could introduce the quotation more smoothly with fewer words:

> In "New Teachers," Neil Postman and Charles Weingarten state, "One of the largest obstacles to the establishment of a sound learning environment is the desire of teachers to get something they think they know into the heads of people who don't know it" (138).

> In their article, Neil Postman and Charles Weingarten state, "One of the largest obstacles to the establishment of a sound learning environment is the desire of teachers to get something they think they know into the heads of people who don't know it" (138).

> Neil Postman and Charles Weingarten state, "One of the largest obstacles to the establishment of a sound learning environment is the desire of teachers to get something they think they know into the heads of people who don't know it" ("New Teachers" 138).

Here are a few more examples:

**Wordy:** Janet Emig, in her work "Writing as a Mode of Learning," argues that "writing serves learning uniquely because writing as process-and-product possesses a cluster of attributes that correspond uniquely to certain powerful learning strategies" (122).

**Better:** According to Janet Emig, "Writing serves learning uniquely because writing as process-and-product possesses a cluster of attributes that correspond uniquely to certain powerful learning strategies" ("Writing as a Mode of Learning" 122).

**Wordy:** "Nobody Mean More to Me than You and the Future Life of Willie Jordan" is an essay written by June Jordan that analyzes Black English as a language "system constructed by people constantly needing to insist that we exist, that we are present" (460).

**Better:** In "Nobody Mean More to Me than You and the Future Life of Willie Jordan," June Jordan analyzes Black English as a language "system constructed by people constantly needing to insist that we exist, that we are present" (460).

The rule of thumb is to be concise and include only the necessary information about the source. If you're not sure how to introduce a quotation, use one of the standard approaches to introducing a quotation. (See Focus: "Four Common Ways to Introduce Quotations in Academic Writing" on page 739.) Keep in mind that if you have a bibliography or works cited page (which you should if you are using sources), you need to give your readers only enough information in your text to be able to find the citation in your bibliography or works cited page.

## FOCUS | FOUR COMMON WAYS TO INTRODUCE QUOTATIONS IN ACADEMIC WRITING

If you pay attention as you read academic prose and scholarly writing in books and journals, you will notice four common patterns that writers use to introduce quotations from source materials. You can use these patterns to make your own use of source material more effective and help give your own prose a more scholarly "sound":

1. In [title of source], [name of author] states (argues, asserts, claims, suggests), "[insert quotation]."

   In *Contemporary Philosophy of Social Science*, Brian Fay argues, "Knowledge of what we are experiencing always involves an interpretation of these experiences" (19).

2. According to [name of author], "[insert quotation]."

   According to Brian Fay, "Knowledge of what we are experiencing always involves an interpretation of these experiences" (19).

3. [Name of author] states (argues, asserts, claims, suggests), "[insert quotation]."

   Brian Fay argues, "Knowledge of what we are experiencing always involves an interpretation of these experiences" (19).

4. "[Beginning of quotation]," according to [name of author], "[rest of quotation]."

   "Knowledge of what we are experiencing," Brian Fay argues, "always involves an interpretation of these experiences" (19).

You can use all four patterns to vary the way you introduce quotations and therefore avoid making your prose sound repetitive.

# Make It Fit

Core Concept #9 ("There is always a voice in writing, even when there isn't an I") underscores the importance of voice in academic writing, no matter what the specific writing task might be. Many students weaken their voices by failing to integrate quotations and source material smoothly into their writing.

For example, in the following passage, the student discusses ideas for education reform proposed by the authors of a source text:

In the article "New Teachers" by Postman and Weingartner, there are several explanations as to why change is not an option for some teachers. The biggest problem is, "Where do we get the new teachers necessary to translate the new education into action? Obviously, it will be very difficult to get many of them from the old education. Most of these have a commitment to existing metaphors, procedures, and goals that would preclude their accepting a 'new education'" (133). Older teachers have no use for the "new education." This article focuses mainly on how teachers can be trained to translate this "new education" to their students.

In this example, the student relies too heavily on the source and does not allow her own voice to emerge. Part of the problem is wordiness, but also notice that the quotations from the source text tend to overpower the student's own writing style. Compare this passage to the following one, in which a student also writes about the possibility of education reform and draws on the work of a well-known education theorist. Unlike the previous example, in this case the student effectively integrates references to and quotations from the source text while maintaining her own voice:

> One of a teacher's main objectives in the classroom should be to equip students with cognitive and metacognitive skills so that they are mindful of the world around them. This process of critical thinking is an essential practice that students must not only understand but also be able to utilize in order to become knowledgeable, empowered individuals. In "The Banking Concept of Education," a chapter from the larger work entitled *Pedagogy of the Oppressed*, however, Paulo Freire discusses something *more* than providing students with critical thinking skills in school. He encourages teachers to raise students' awareness about themselves and society, so that they are able to work towards the broader idea of social change; this is what he calls "critical consciousness" (35). According to Freire, it is the responsibility of the teacher to instill in his/her students a sense of agency, fostering the potential and possibility for change. Without knowing that they have the capacity to transform society, Freire argues, students will become passive members of society; change, therefore, will never be possible. With this argument, Freire places great responsibility on the shoulders of those who work within the education system. But can educators really take on this role?

In this passage the student maintains control of the material. The paragraph includes summary, paraphrase, and quotations from the source text, but the main point of the paragraph is the student's own. (See Focus: "A Strategy for Integrating Source Material Into Your Writing" on page 741.) Moreover, the voice of the source never takes over, and the student's voice remains strong.

As you work with source material, remember that even when your assignment calls for a review or critique of a source text, the analysis and conclusions about that text are yours. So work the source material into your own writing—not the other way around.

Chapter 26 provides advice for writing clear, cohesive paragraphs. Sometimes paragraphs become incoherent because the student loses control of the source material. Use the advice provided in this chapter to avoid that problem. You can also follow a basic structure for your paragraphs when you are integrating source material into a paragraph:

1. **Topic Statement:** Introduce the subject of the paragraph and provide context for the source material to follow.
2. **Source Material:** Summarize, paraphrase, or quote from the source.
3. **Takeaway:** Comment on the source material to connect it to your topic statement.
4. **Parenthetical Citation:** Cite the source using MLA or APA format (see Chapters 24 and 25).

The sample paragraph on page 740 illustrates this structure:

> One of a teacher's main objectives in the classroom should be to equip students with cognitive and metacognitive skills so that they are mindful of the world around them. This process of critical thinking is an essential practice that students must not only understand but also be able to utilize in order to become knowledgeable, empowered individuals. In "The Banking Concept of Education," a chapter from the larger work entitled *Pedagogy of the Oppressed*, however, Paolo Freire discusses something *more* than providing students with critical thinking skills in school. He encourages teachers to raise students' awareness about themselves and society, so that they are able to work towards the broader idea of social change; this is what he calls "critical consciousness" (35). According to Freire, it is the responsibility of the teacher to instill in his/her students a sense of agency, fostering the potential and possibility for change. Without knowing that they have the capacity to transform society, Freire argues, students will become passive members of society; change, therefore, will never be possible. With this argument, Freire places great responsibility on the shoulders of those who work within the education system. But can educators really take on this role?

**Topic Statement:** The student establishes the focus of the paragraph and provides context for the source material.

**Source Material:** The student paraphrases and quotes from the source.

**Citation:** Using MLA format, the student properly cites the source of the quoted phrase.

**Takeaway:** The student connects the source material to the Topic Statement and poses a question about the material to provide a transition to the next paragraph.

23

# Additional Guidelines for Quoting from Sources
## Punctuate Complete Quotations Correctly

When including a complete quotation from a source in your writing, use quotation marks and final punctuation marks as follows:

**Direct Quotation:**

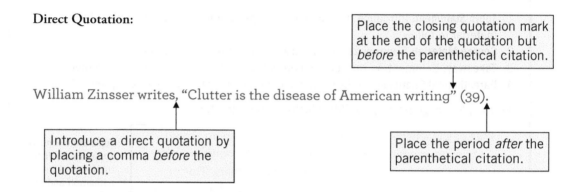

Place the closing quotation mark at the end of the quotation but *before* the parenthetical citation.

William Zinsser writes, "Clutter is the disease of American writing" (39).

Introduce a direct quotation by placing a comma *before* the quotation.

Place the period *after* the parenthetical citation.

**Indirect Quotation:**

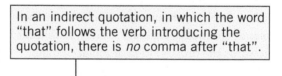

In an indirect quotation, in which the word "that" follows the verb introducing the quotation, there is *no* comma after "that".

William Zinsser believes that "[c]lutter is the disease of American writing" (39).

The capital C is made lowercase because an indirect quotation does not begin with a capital letter (unless the first word of the quotation is a word that is always capitalized, such as a name or proper noun). The brackets indicate that the letter C is capitalized in the original source.

You can also introduce a quotation with a colon:

Zinsser makes a provocative point: "Clutter is the disease of American writing" (39).

However, the colon is *not* a substitute for a comma in a direct quotation. In this example, a complete sentence precedes the colon. In the example above for a direct quotation, the quotation actually completes the sentence and makes it grammatically correct.

## Insert Quoted Phrases When You Don't Need an Entire Statement

Sometimes you want to quote only a word or phrase from a source rather than an entire sentence or passage. In such cases, integrate the phrase into your sentence, using quotation marks to indicate the quoted words and citing the source properly with a parenthetical citation:

> The economist E. F. Schumacher argued that "work and leisure are complementary parts of the same living process," and therefore should not be considered separate from one another (55).

In this example, there is no need for commas around the quoted phrase because it is used as part of the sentence.

This sentence requires a comma after the quoted phrase because of the coordinating conjunction "but".

> The economist E. F. Schumacher argued that "work and leisure are complementary parts of the same living process," but he also acknowledged that few people in industrialized societies understand work and leisure in this way (55).

## Use Ellipses to Indicate Missing Words from a Quotation

If you quote a passage from a source but omit part of that passage, you can indicate that something is missing by using ellipses—that is, three periods, each followed by a space:

**Original Passage from Source:**
> To my mind, voyaging through wildernesses, be they full of woods or waves, is essential to the growth and maturity of the human spirit.

**Quotation with Missing Words:**
> Despite his ordeal at sea, in which he survived alone in a life raft for 76 days, Steven Callahan still believed in the value of wilderness experiences. "To my mind," he writes," voyaging through wildernesses . . . is essential to the growth and maturity of the human spirit" (234).

In this case, the writer decided that the phrase *be they full of woods or waves* in the original source was unnecessary and therefore omitted it; the ellipses indicate to a reader that words are missing at that point in the quoted passage.

## Use Brackets to Indicate a Modified Quotation

If you have to modify a quotation in order to fit it into your sentence, use brackets to indicate changes you have made to the source material:

**Original Passage from Source:**

> I have focused on two people, one familiar, the other less so: Plymouth governor William Bradford and Benjamin Church, a carpenter turned Indian fighter whose maternal grandfather had sailed on the *Mayflower*.

**Modified Passage in Quotation:**

> In his provocative history of the Pilgrims, Nathaniel Philbrick "focuse[s] on two people, one familiar, the other less so: Plymouth governor William Bradford and Benjamin Church, a carpenter turned Indian fighter whose maternal grandfather had sailed on the *Mayflower*" (xvii).

In this example the writer has changed the original verb *focused* to *focuses* so that it fits grammatically into the sentence. The brackets indicate to a reader that the s at the end of "focuses" is not in the original text.

# Avoiding Plagiarism

Plagiarism is the use of others' words or ideas without giving credit or presenting someone else's words or ideas as your own. It is tantamount to intellectual theft. It goes without saying that plagiarism is unethical. It is dishonest as well as unfair to your classmates, your instructor, and the plagiarized source. It is also a squandering of an opportunity to learn or make something new and useful through your academic work.

Because plagiarism is such a serious breach of ethical standards, it can have serious consequences. In the most extreme cases, plagiarism can result in lawsuits, penalties, or fines. Most colleges and universities have strict codes of student conduct that often include severe sanctions for students caught plagiarizing, including failing an assignment, failing a course, and even expulsion from school.

Plagiarism can include the following:

- **Failing to cite the source of a quotation or idea that isn't your own.** If you take information, an idea, or special language (a phrase, sentence, or lengthier passage) from a source and do not cite it properly using MLA or APA format, you are indicating to a reader that the material is your own. That's plagiarism. Any ideas, information, or quotations you use from a source must be cited properly in your own text to indicate that those ideas, information, or quotations are not yours.

- **Including a passage from a source text without using quotation marks.** Quotation marks around material that you have taken from a source indicate that the words were taken verbatim from that source and are not your own. If you use language from a source but do not place the passage in quotation marks, you are plagiarizing, *even if you cite the source.*

- **Submitting someone else's work as your own.** Obviously, you are plagiarizing—and blatantly cheating—when you submit writing that someone else has done as if it is your own. This includes purchasing a paper online from so-called "paper mills" and submitting it to your instructor as if you wrote it yourself. It also includes asking a classmate or friend to write something for you and then submitting it as if it is your writing.

In most cases, these forms of plagiarism are intentional. Sometimes, however, students plagiarize unintentionally—often because they misunderstand the nature of academic research or rely too heavily on source material instead of using sources to support or extend their own ideas. To illustrate this problem, let's return to an example of a summary of a source passage from Chapter 19. This passage is taken from an article in which a law professor offers an analysis of the so-called "war on poverty" initiated by President Lyndon Johnson in the 1960s:

> The commitment and symbolism of the "war on poverty"—and the energy and enthusiasm of those who fought it—were vital. For a brief period, the idea of conducting a war on poverty captured the nation's imagination. The phrase is surely one of the most evocative in our history. Yet the war's specific components were a tiny fraction even of the Great Society programs enacted between 1964 and 1968 during the administration of Lyndon Johnson, let alone those enacted during the New Deal and those added since, many during the presidency of Richard Nixon. And, even considering all these, we never fought an allout war on poverty.

Source: Edelman, Peter. " The War on Poverty and Subsequent Federal Programs: What Worked, What Didn't Work, and Why? Lessons for Future Programs." *Clearinghouse Review Journal of Poverty Law and Policy*, May-June 2006, p 88.

Here's a summary of that passage from a student essay:

> The commitment and symbolism of the "war on poverty" were important. For a short time, the idea of a war on poverty captured the nation's imagination. But the specific components of the war were a tiny fraction of government programs enacted during the administration of Lyndon Johnson, not to mention those enacted before then and those added since. Even considering all these programs, an allout war on poverty was never really fought (Edelman 8).

The bright blue phrases in this summary indicate material that was taken verbatim from the source text. This highlighted material comprises a majority of the summary: 42 of the 72 words in this summary are taken from the source exactly as they appear in that source. That means that the summary is made up mostly of language from the source text, not the student's own words. Notice that even though the student has cited the source properly, he or she has used no quotation marks to indicate that the highlighted phrases were taken verbatim from the source text and are not the student's own words. An instructor might interpret this summary as plagiarism, because the student has not used quotation marks to indicate that most of the language is taken verbatim from the source text.

One solution in such a case is for the student simply to use quotation marks to indicate that the phrasing is taken from the original source. However, in a case like this one—in which the *ideas* from the source, *not* the original language of the source, are important—using quotation marks for all the quoted phrases would result in a cumbersome passage:

> "The commitment and symbolism of the 'war on poverty'" were important. For a short time, "the idea of a war on poverty captured the nation's imagination" (Edelman 8). But "the specific components" of the war were "a tiny fraction" of government programs "enacted during the administration of Lyndon Johnson," not to mention those enacted before then and those added since (Edelman 8). "Even considering all these" programs, "an allout war on poverty" was never really fought (Edelman 8).

There is simply no need to quote phrases like "the specific components" and "a tiny fraction," and the excessive quoting in this passage is distracting to a reader.

Avoiding plagiarism in a situation like this one (which is common in academic writing), is best accomplished by summarizing the source passage carefully so that the summary reflects the student's own words:

> According to Edelman, the idea of a "war on poverty" was important for its symbolism as well as for the national commitment it reflected (8). However, although this idea resonated with Americans for a time, the programs intended specifically to fight poverty were never more than a small part of total government social programs, whether those programs were part of Lyndon Johnson's Great Society, the earlier New Deal, or initiatives undertaken by Richard Nixon and subsequent presidents. As a result, Edelman states, a total war on poverty was never really fought (8).

Notice that the student writer's voice is strong in this passage, and although the student is drawing his or her ideas primarily from the source text, the student is using his or her *own* words and does not allow the language of the source text to take over this summary.

The best way to avoid plagiarism is to apply the Ten Core Concepts in your writing and follow the advice presented in Chapters 21, 22, and 23 for finding and using source material. If you focus on what *you* have to say in your writing, you are much less likely to plagiarize. In addition, **follow these guidelines:**

- **Use sources to support or extend your own ideas.** As noted earlier, if you focus on making and supporting your main point (Core Concepts #4 and #5), you are less likely to fall victim to unnecessarily borrowing from a source or unintentionally presenting ideas from a source as your own.

- **Summarize and paraphrase carefully.** As the example in this section illustrates, you are more likely to plagiarize inadvertently if you don't sufficiently understand the functions of summary and paraphrase, so review the advice for summarizing and paraphrasing in Chapter 19. Because academic writing so often requires you to work with source material, being able to summarize and paraphrase appropriately is essential, and developing those skills will help you avoid plagiarizing.

- **Integrate source material into your own writing.** Following the advice in this chapter will help you present source material appropriately. Apply the appropriate strategies for quoting from sources to make it clear to your readers when the material you are presenting is taken from a source and when the language is your own.

- **Credit your sources.** Follow the conventions for citing sources that are explained in Chapters 24 and 25. Use APA or MLA format correctly (or use another format approved by your instructor). Be sure to cite sources correctly so that there is no confusion about whether the material you are presenting is yours or taken from a source.

- **Take careful notes.** When you are researching a topic, keep accurate notes about the sources you have consulted so that you know where you found the material you are using and have the correct information for citing the sources. If you are using online sources, it is a good idea to bookmark the pages from which you have taken information.

- **When in doubt, cite your source.** The rule of thumb is that you must cite any material you take from a source that is not considered to be "common knowledge," which generally means facts, information, or ideas that most people might know. For example, you wouldn't need to cite Charles Darwin as the originator of the idea of natural selection, since that fact is widely known. However, determining what is common knowledge and what isn't can be difficult and subject to interpretation. If you're not sure whether to cite a source for information or an idea that you have taken from a source, cite it to be safe.

> ## MindTap®
> Practice research skills that you have learned in this chapter, receive feedback, and reflect on your learning.

**In this chapter, you will learn to**

1. Identify the appropriate types of sources that require formal documentation.

2. Identify the two main components of MLA style: in-text citations and a Works Cited list.

3. Create in-text citations in MLA style for a variety of sources.

4. Create Works Cited entries in MLA style for a variety of sources.

## MindTap®

Understand the goals of the chapter and complete a warm-up activity.

# Citing Sources Using MLA Style 24

**THE PURPOSE OF CITING SOURCES** is to be as clear as possible in showing where your information comes from. Citing your sources according to established style guides not only credits the source for the material you are using but also provides your readers with sufficient bibliographic information to judge or even find your sources for themselves. In general, you must document the source of

- a direct quotation,
- an idea or opinion that is not your own,
- visual materials, such as photographs, maps, or graphs, that you did not create,
- multimedia content, such as videos or audios, that you did not create, and
- information (a fact or statistic) that is not general knowledge.

In most academic writing today, writers use the Modern Language Association (MLA) style guide when they are writing in the humanities: literature, languages, performing and visual arts, history, classics, philosophy, and religion. This chapter explains how to cite sources using MLA style. (APA style, which tends to be used in the social sciences—psychology, sociology, education, economics, anthropology, geography, and political science—is explained in Chapter 25.) The guidelines in this chapter are based on the *MLA Handbook*, 8th ed.

## Two Main Components in MLA Style

MLA style uses in-text parenthetical citations to document sources. There are **two main components to in-text parenthetical citation systems:**

1. **In-text citations.** Parenthetical citations, which appear in the body of your writing, indicate to a reader that information you are presenting is taken from another source.

2. **A Works Cited List.** The Works Cited list is a separate section at the end of your document that includes bibliographic information for every source you cited in your document.

Let's imagine you are writing an essay about the cultural significance of heavy metal music and you want to refer to a specific analysis of so-called death metal music in a book by Natalie J. Purcell titled *Death Metal Music: The Passion and Politics of a Subculture*. On page 188 of that book, Purcell makes a point about the philosophical function of death metal music that you want to include in your essay. Using MLA style, you would cite your source as follows:

> Death metal music performs a genuine philosophical function by examining the dark side of human nature (Purcell 188).

If you mention the author's name in your sentence, you do not need to include it in the parenthetical citation:

> Critic Natalie Purcell considers death metal a "philosophical response, whether conscious or subconscious, to terrifying questions about nebulous human nature" (188).

The information in parentheses indicates to readers that the idea about the philosophical function of death metal is taken from page 188 of a work by Purcell. Readers can then consult your Works Cited page, where they will find the following entry:

> Purcell, Natalie J. *Death Metal Music: The Passion and Politics of a Subculture.*
>     McFarland, 2003.

Each in-text citation in your document must have a corresponding Works Cited entry to give your readers the means to find and read the original source themselves.

---

**FOCUS** | **FOOTNOTES, ENDNOTES, AND CONTENT NOTES**

Traditionally, footnotes or endnotes were used to document sources. Strictly speaking, a **footnote** appears at the foot of the page, and an **endnote** appears at the end of the paper. However, the MLA now recommends that writers use parenthetical, or in-text, citations of the kind described in this chapter. Traditional footnotes are used not for documenting sources but for additional explanation or discussion of a point in the main text. These notes are called **content notes**.

---

# Creating In-Text Citations in MLA Style

MLA style, which reflects the conventions of the humanities, emphasizes the author and the author's work and places less emphasis on the date of publication. When citing a work parenthetically, the author's last name is followed by a page number or range of pages. There are particular situations in which somewhat different information is given in parentheses, but *the general rule is to provide enough information to enable a reader to find the source in your Works Cited page.* You do not need to include inside the parentheses information you have already provided in the text. For instance, if you start the sentence with the author's name, you do not need to include the author's name in the parentheses.

---

**FOCUS** | **FIND THE IN-TEXT CITATION MODEL YOU NEED**

A. Work by one author (page 751)

B. Work by multiple authors (page 751)

C. Work by a corporate author (page 752)

D. More than one work by the same author (page 752)

---

## A. Work by one author

If you were citing information taken from page 82 of a book called *The Printing Revolution in Early Modern Europe* by Elizabeth L. Eisenstein, the parenthetical citation would look like this:

> The widespread adoption of the printing press in the 16th century helped standardize the major European languages (Eisenstein 82).

If you used Eisenstein's name in your sentence, the citation would include only the page reference:

> Elizabeth Eisenstein examines how the widespread adoption of the printing press in the 16th century helped standardize the major European languages (82).

There is no punctuation between the author's name and the page number. Note that the parentheses are placed *inside* the period at the end of the sentence. Also, the abbreviation *p.* or *pp.* is not used before the page reference in a parenthetical citation in MLA style.

## B. Work by multiple authors

When citing a work by two authors, include both authors' names in the citation (or in your sentence). For example, if you wanted to quote from page 2 of *Undead TV: Essays on Buffy the Vampire Slayer*, by Elana Levine and Lisa Parks, you could do so as follows:

> We might consider how the hit television series *Buffy the Vampire Slayer* "dramatizes the travails of its title character but uses its metaphorical representations of life and death, good and evil, comedy and tragedy to speak about the power struggles inherent in many people's everyday lives in the Western world" (Levine and Parks 2).

or

> Elana Levine and Lisa Parks assert that *Buffy the Vampire Slayer* "dramatizes the travails of its title character but uses its metaphorical representations of life and death, good and evil, comedy and tragedy to speak about the power struggles inherent in many people's everyday lives in the Western world" (2).

If you are referring to a work by more than two authors, list only the first author's name followed by the Latin phrase *et al.* (which means "and others"). For example, if you were citing information from page 79 of a journal article titled "Empirical Foundations for Writing in Prevention and Psychotherapy," by Brian A. Esterling, Luciano L'Abate, Edward J. Murray, and James W. Pennebaker, the parenthetical citation would look like this:

> Studies have shown that writing has therapeutic benefits for some patients (Esterling et al. 79).

Note that there is no comma after the name of the author.

## C. Work by a corporate author

A "corporate author" is an organization, committee, or an agency (rather than an individual or group of individually named authors). When citing a corporate author, use the same format as for a single author. For example, if you were citing a study by the Center for Research on Educational Outcomes, you would do so as follows:

> According to the Center for Research on Educational Outcomes, in 37 percent of charter schools, students had math scores that were lower than their public school peers (3).

You could also include the corporate author in the parentheses; omit any initial article:

> In one recent study, 37 percent of charter schools had student math scores that were lower than in public schools (Center for Research on Educational Outcomes 3).

## D. More than one work by the same author

If you cite more than one work by the same author, you need to distinguish among the works by using a shortened form of the title of each work you cite. For example, if you were quoting from two different books by Paulo Freire, *Pedagogy of Hope* and *Letters to Cristina*, your parenthetical citations might look like this:

> Freire emphasizes the crucial role of hope in the struggle for change. Acknowledging that hope "seldom exists apart from the reverses of fate" (*Letters* 14), Freire argues that the "dream of humanization . . . is always a process" (*Pedagogy* 99).

The shortened titles (*Letters* and *Pedagogy*) enable a reader to find the specific references in the Works Cited list. Also note that because it is clear from the context that both works cited are by the same author, the author's name does not need to be placed inside the parentheses. If the author's name is not included in the text itself, include it inside the parenthetical citation:

> Hope is a crucial element in the struggle for change. We should acknowledge that hope "seldom exists apart from the reverses of fate" (Freire, *Letters* 14) and remember that the "dream of humanization . . . is always a process" (Freire, *Pedagogy* 99).

Note that a comma separates the author's name from the shortened title, but no comma appears between the title and the page number.

### E. Work without an author listed

If you cite a work without an author listed, include a brief version of the title in parentheses. For example, if you cited information from page 27 of an article from *The Economist* titled "Carrying the Torch," you would do so as follows:

> The sports management industry in Great Britain received a significant boost in business as a result of the 2012 Olympic Games in London ("Carrying" 27).

### F. Entire work

When you refer to an entire work, include only the author's name, either in your sentence or in parentheses. No page numbers are needed.

> Cheryl Sandberg discusses the reasons women are still not adequately represented in leadership positions.

If you do not mention the author's name in your sentence, cite it in parentheses:

> For many reasons, women are still not adequately represented in leadership positions (Sandberg).

### G. Quotation within a cited work

When using a quotation from one source that you have found in another source, you must show that the quotation was acquired "secondhand" and was not taken directly from the original source. In such cases, use the abbreviation *qtd. in* (for "quoted in") to indicate that you are taking the quotation from a second source rather than from the original text. For example, let's say you were reading a book called *Literary Theory* by Terry Eagleton that included a quotation by Sigmund Freud. If you wanted to use Freud's quotation in your essay, you would cite it as follows:

> Even Freud acknowledged the central importance of economics in human relations, famously stating, "The motive of human society is in the last resort an economic one" (qtd. in Eagleton 151).

In this instance, you are signaling to readers that you read Freud's statement in the book by Terry Eagleton. Your Works Cited page must include an entry for Eagleton's book but not Freud's original text.

### H. Work in an anthology

Name the author of the particular work, not the editor of the entire anthology, in your citation. For example, if you were citing a story by Nathan Englander that appears in the anthology *The Best American Short Stories 2012*, edited by Tom Perrotta and Heidi Pitlor, you would not need to mention the editors of the anthology:

> Nathan Englander plays off Raymond Carver's famous story title in his short work "What We Talk About When We Talk About Anne Frank."

The entry in your Works Cited page, which would list Nathan Englander as the author of the story, would also include the editors' names.

## I. Electronic sources

When citing electronic sources, follow the same principles you would use when citing other sources. However, there are many different kinds of electronic sources, which might not include the same kinds of information that are available for a print book or journal article. For example, online sources, such as websites, often do not have page numbers. If the online source has numbered paragraphs, provide the number of the paragraph in which you found the information or quotation you are citing:

> (Martinez, par. 8)

Note that a comma is placed after the author's name.

If page numbers or paragraph numbers are not available, include sufficient information for readers to find the source in your Works Cited list, such as the author's last name or a brief title:

> (Martinez)

## J. Long quotations

In MLA style, a long prose quotation is defined as one that takes more than four lines in your paper. Quotations of more than three lines of poetry are considered long, and any amount of quoted dialogue from a play is treated as a block quotation. These quotations should be indented one-half inch from the left margin as a block quotation—*without* quotation marks. The entire block should be double-spaced, and no additional space should be used above or below the block quotation. In this example, the writer introduces a long quotation from an author named Sharon Crowley:

> Sharon Crowley offers contemporary scholars a radical inspiration from ancient times:
> I can see no reason why contemporary teachers cannot develop theories of composition that are fully as rich as those developed in ancient times. Much thinking remains to be done, and I do not doubt that enterprising teachers of composition will do it—because there is a place for composition in the university, and that place does not depend on Freshman English. (265)

The page number for the quotation is included in parentheses at the end of the block quotation. Notice that the parenthetical citation is placed *after* the final period of the block quotation. If the author's name does not appear in the main text, include it in the parentheses.

## K. Work in more than one volume

If you use more than one volume from a multivolume work in your paper, indicate the volume and page number in each citation. The volume number is followed by a colon. In this example, page 236 in volume 3 of a work by Trieste is cited:

> (Trieste 3: 236)

If you cite only one volume, however, you can provide the page number only. In your Works Cited entry, list the volume number.

# Creating a Works Cited List in MLA Style

Each source you cite in your text must correspond to an entry in the Works Cited list. In general, in entries that appear in a Works Cited list, MLA style emphasizes **nine core elements** that appear in some version in most entries, whether that entry refers to a traditional print text, a digital format, or another kind of nonprint source (like a work of art):

1. **Author:** The creator of the source you are citing.

2. **Title of source:** The title should be for the *specific* source (e.g., the title of a poem or article you are citing, *not* the title of the book in which the poem appeared or the magazine where the article appeared).

3. **Title of container:** The larger source that contains the specific source (e.g., the book of poems that contains the specific poem you are citing or the magazine that contains the article you are citing).

4. **Other contributors:** Others who contributed to the source, such as editors or translators.

5. **Version:** The specific version of the source, such as the revised edition of a book.

6. **Number:** The number indicates the place of the source in a sequence, such as the volume and issue numbers for scholarly journals or the episode number of a television series.

7. **Publisher:** The organization that produced the source, such as the publisher of a book or sponsor of a website.

8. **Publication date:** The date when the source was made available to a public audience.

9. **Location:** The location of the source, such as page numbers for a print source or a URL or DOI for an online source. (See Focus: "What is a DOI?" on page 756.)

Each entry in your Works Cited list should include these core elements, if available. Note that some entries might refer to containers within larger containers. For example, if you found a journal article through a database like *ArticleFirst*, the specific source you are citing is the title of the article; the journal is container #1, and the database is container #2. In such an entry, include relevant information about the larger container—such as its title and the source's location within it—and place any information about container #2 *after* all information about the source itself and container #1, separated by a period. The rule of thumb is to include information that will help your readers locate the specific source.

To create a Works Cited entry, then, follow this basic procedure:

- List core elements 1 (author) and 2 (title of source).
- List core elements 3-9 that provide information about the *first* container.
- List core elements 3-9 that provide information about the *second* container.

The examples in this chapter illustrate this procedure.

*DOI* stands for digital object identifier. A DOI is a unique string of numbers that identifies an electronic publication and enables you to access that publication online. It is more stable than a URL (or web address), which can change or be deleted. MLA style recommends using a DOI in a Works Cited entry, in place of a URL, if a source has a DOI assigned to it. (If there is no DOI, use the URL.)

Many scholarly journals now include DOIs for online publications. Usually, the DOI appears on the first page of the article and has the descriptor "doi." A DOI looks like a string of numbers, like this: doi: 10.1080/09243450600565795. See an example of a Works Cited entry that includes a DOI on page 762.

Your list of Works Cited should appear at the end of your project, beginning with a new page. Organize the Works Cited list alphabetically according to the authors' last names (or, if the work includes no author, the first main word of the title). In MLA style, follow these rules:

- Capitalize the first word, the last word, and every important word in titles and subtitles. Do not capitalize prepositions (such as *on* and *to*), coordinating conjunctions (such as *and* and *but*), or articles (*a, an, the*) unless they begin the title or subtitle.
- Italicize the titles of long works such as books, periodicals, and websites.
- Place the titles of shorter works, such as articles, stories, and online postings, in quotation marks.
- Italicize the titles of most containers, such as magazines, television shows, or databases.
- For sources (such as journals and magazines) that have a publication date that includes a month (Apr. 2016), abbreviate all months except May, June, and July.
- For websites or other online sources (such as databases), include a URL or a DOI (digital object identifier) if one is available for your source. Do not include *http://* or *https://* as part of the URL in your citation.
- For the publication date of online sources, list the day, month, and year, if available. If there is both an original publication date and a more recent "last modified date" mentioned on the site, then use the most recent date in your citation.
- For online sources that have no publication date listed, include the date you accessed the site at the end of your citation. Format the access date as follows: day month year (for example, Accessed 17 Oct. 2016).
- Double-space citations but do not skip spaces between entries.
- Use hanging indents for entries in the Works Cited list.

***BOOKS***

1. Book with one author (page 758)
2. Book with two or more authors (page 758)
3. Two or more books by the same author (page 758)
4. Anthology with an editor (page 759)
5. Works in an anthology (page 759)
6. Book with an author and an editor (page 759)
7. Book with a translator (page 759)
8. Book by a corporate author or without an author listed (page 760)
9. Introduction, preface, foreword, or afterword written by someone other than the author of the work (page 760)
10. Subsequent editions of a book (page 760)
11. Work in more than one volume (page 760)
12. Book in a series (page 760)
13. Encyclopedia entry (page 760)
14. Sacred text (page 761)

***PERIODICALS***

15. Article from a scholarly journal (page 763)
16. Article from a weekly or monthly magazine (page 763)
17. Article from a daily newspaper (page 764)
18. Editorial (page 764)
19. Letter to the editor (page 764)
20. Review (page 764)

***OTHER SOURCES***

21. Website (page 765)
22. Web page (page 765)
23. Blog (page 766)
24. Podcast (page 766)
25. Interview (page 766)
26. E-mail (page 767)
27. Film (page 767)
28. Television or radio program (page 767)
29. Sound recording (page 767)
30. Online video (page 767)
31. Social media (page 768)
32. Advertisement (page 768)
33. Art (page 768)
34. Government publication (page 768)

Note: The directory of in-text citation models appears on pages 750–751.

24

# Books

Here is the general format for an entry for a book in the Works Cited page:

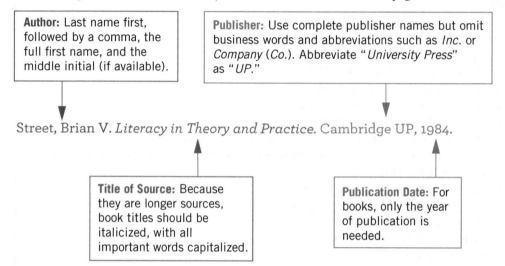

Author: Last name first, followed by a comma, the full first name, and the middle initial (if available).

Publisher: Use complete publisher names but omit business words and abbreviations such as *Inc.* or *Company* (*Co.*). Abbreviate "*University Press*" as "*UP.*"

Street, Brian V. *Literacy in Theory and Practice.* Cambridge UP, 1984.

Title of Source: Because they are longer sources, book titles should be italicized, with all important words capitalized.

Publication Date: For books, only the year of publication is needed.

Note: For online books, include the name of the site or database where the book is located and the URL.

### 1. Book with one author

> Fineman, Howard. *The Thirteen American Arguments: Enduring Debates That Define and Inspire Our Country.* Random House, 2008.

> Lockhart, Charles. *Gaining Ground: Tailoring Social Programs to American Values.* U of California P, 1989, ark.cdlib.org/ark:/13030/ft2p300594/.

In the second example, the URL is included at the end of the citation because the work was accessed online.

### 2. Book with two or more authors

> Stewart, David W., and Dennis W. Rook. *Focus Groups: Theory and Practice.* SAGE Publications, 2007.

If there are two authors, list both authors' names. Notice that only the first author is listed with the last name first.

For books with three or more authors, use the abbreviation *et al.*:

> Wysocki, Anne Frances, et al. *Writing New Media: Theory and Applications for Expanding the Teaching of Composition.* Utah State UP, 2004.

### 3. Two or more books by the same author

When you are listing two or more books by the same author, you do not repeat the author's name for each entry. Instead, use three hyphens and a period in place of the author's name for the second, third, and subsequent entries by the same author. Also, list the entries in alphabetical order by the book title.

Freire, Paulo. *Letters to Cristina: Reflections on My Life and Work.* Routledge, 1996.

---. *Pedagogy in Process: The Letters to Gineau-Bissau.* Seabury Press, 1978.

---. *Pedagogy of the Oppressed.* Translated by Myra Bergman Ramos, Continuum, 1970.

### 4. Anthology with an editor

McComiskey, Bruce, editor. *English Studies: An Introduction to the Discipline(s).* NCTE Publications, 2006.

Hill, Charles A., and Marguerite Helmers, editors. *Defining Visual Rhetorics.* Lawrence Erlbaum Associates, 2004.

Use the description *editor* for a single editor and *editors* for multiple editors. Place the description after the editor's name, which is followed by a comma.

### 5. Works in an anthology

Dittrich, Luke. "The Brain That Changed Everything." *The Best American Science and Nature Writing,* edited by Mary Roach, Houghton Miffin Harcourt, 2011, pp. 46-68.

Notice that the page numbers for the article are provided, preceded by the abbreviation *pp.* Also, the description *edited by* appears before the editor's name (Mary Roach).

If you cite two or more articles (or other short works) from the same anthology, use a shortened form of the citation for each one, and then cite the entire anthology according to example #4 above. Here are two abbreviated citations as well as a citation for the complete collection that these abbreviated citations refer to:

Bhattacharjee, Yudhijit. "The Organ Dealer." Roach 1-14.

Dittrich, Luke. "The Brain That Changed Everything." Roach 46-68.

Roach, Mary, editor. *The Best American Science and Nature Writing.* Houghton Mifflin Harcourt, 2011.

In this example, readers would know that the articles by Yudhijit Bhattacharjee and Luke Dittrich are included in the anthology *The Best American Science and Nature Writing*, which is edited by Mary Roach.

### 6. Book with an author and an editor

Thoreau, Henry David. *Walden.* Edited by Jeffrey S. Cramer, Yale UP, 2004.

The author's name is placed first. The editor's name is placed after the title, preceded by the description *Edited by.*

### 7. Book with a translator

Tsunetomo, Yamamoto. *Hagakure: The Book of the Samurai.* Translated by William Scott Wilson, Kadansha International, 1979.

The description *Translated by* appears before the name of the translator (William Scott Wilson).

### 8. Book by a corporate author or without an author listed

> *The Condition of College and Career Readiness 2015.* ACT, 2015, forms.act.org/research/
> policymakers/cccr15/pdf/CCCR15-NationalReadinessRpt.pdf.

List the group or organization as the author. If no author or organization is listed, then omit the author and begin the entry with the title of the book. Also, if the group or organization that authored the publication is also the publisher or sponsor for the publication (as in the example above), then start the citation with the title of the work and list the group or organization (in this example, ACT) *only once*, as the publisher.

### 9. Introduction, preface, foreword, or afterword written by someone other than the author of the work

> Zelazny, Roger. Introduction. *Do Androids Dream of Electric Sheep?* by Philip K. Dick,
> Del Rey Books, 1968, pp. vii-x.

In this example, Roger Zelazny wrote the introduction to the book *Do Androids Dream of Electric Sheep?* by Philip K. Dick. Include the page numbers of the introduction (or preface, foreword, or afterword) after the date of publication.

### 10. Subsequent editions of a book

> Creswell, John W., editor. *Qualitative Research and Design: Choosing Among Five
> Approaches.* 2nd ed., SAGE Publications, 2007.

Use the abbreviation *ed.* for "edition."

### 11. Work in more than one volume

> Milton, John. *The Prose Works of John Milton.* John W. Moore, 1847. 2 vols.

### 12. Book in a series

> Pedersen, Isabel. *Ready to Wear: A Rhetoric of Wearable Computers and Reality-Shifting
> Media.* Parlor Press, 2013. New Media Theory.

This citation is similar to a citation for a book (see example #1 on page 758) except that the name of the series (New Media Theory) is placed after the date of publication and followed by a period. It is not italicized or placed in quotation marks.

### 13. Encyclopedia entry

The format for entries for encyclopedia articles is similar to articles in anthologies or edited collections.

> Sockett, Hugh. "The Moral and Epistemic Purposes of Teacher Education." *Handbook
> of Research on Teacher Education,* edited by Marilyn Cochran-Smith et al., 3rd ed.,
> Routledge, 2008, pp. 45-66.

This example shows an article written by Hugh Sockett that appeared in the encyclopedia *Handbook of Research on Teacher Education*, edited by Marilyn Cochran-Smith and others. If no author is listed for the specific article, then begin with the title of the article. Even when you are citing an encyclopedia or other reference work in which the entries or articles are organized alphabetically, you should include page numbers at the end of the citation.

If you accessed the encyclopedia article through an online database, include the name of the database (*Oxford Reference*, in the example below) as the second container (set in italics) followed by a comma and then the URL followed by a period:

> Lacey, Alan. "The Meaning of Life." *The Oxford Companion to Philosophy*, edited by Ted Honderich, 2nd ed., Oxford UP, 2005. *Oxford Reference*, www.oxfordreference.com/ view/10.1093/acref/9780199264797.001.0001/acref-9780199264797-e-1423#.

### 14. Sacred text

> *The Bible*. King James Version, American Bible Society, 1980.

Insert the name of the version you are using after the title (King James Version, in this example). Include names of editors or translators, if any, before the version information.

24

---

**FOCUS** | **CITING WIKIPEDIA AND OTHER ONLINE REFERENCES**

Many instructors have policies regarding the use of *Wikipedia* and similar online references, so check with your instructor before using such resources in your research. In MLA Style, if you cite information taken from such sources, the format is similar to the format for citing a web page (see example #21 on page 765):

> "Ultramarathon." *Wikipedia, The Free Encyclopedia*, 9 Aug. 2016, en.wikipedia.org/ w/index.php?title=Ultramarathon&oldid=733648256. Accessed 16 Aug. 2016.

In this example, because there is no author, the entry begins with the title of the article, followed by the name of the website in italics (*Wikipedia, The Free Encyclopedia*), the date when the entry was last modified, and the permanent URL for this specific entry. If the publisher or the sponsor of this site (Wikipedia, in this example) is essentially the same as the title of the website, it is not necessary to include a publisher's name in the citation.

If a site offers a permanent link or a stable URL for an article or entry or posting (as Wikipedia does), it is preferable to use that URL in your citation, rather than copying the URL from your browser. Stable URLs or permalinks are a more reliable way for readers to locate your sources.

---

# Periodicals

Here is the general format for an article from a scholarly journal that was located in a database (in this example, *JSTOR*):

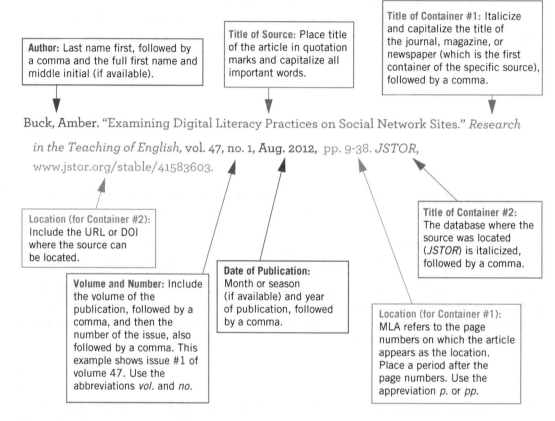

**Author:** Last name first, followed by a comma and the full first name and middle initial (if available).

**Title of Source:** Place title of the article in quotation marks and capitalize all important words.

**Title of Container #1:** Italicize and capitalize the title of the journal, magazine, or newspaper (which is the first container of the specific source), followed by a comma.

Buck, Amber. "Examining Digital Literacy Practices on Social Network Sites." *Research in the Teaching of English,* vol. 47, no. 1, Aug. 2012, pp. 9-38. *JSTOR,* www.jstor.org/stable/41583603.

**Location (for Container #2):** Include the URL or DOI where the source can be located.

**Volume and Number:** Include the volume of the publication, followed by a comma, and then the number of the issue, also followed by a comma. This example shows issue #1 of volume 47. Use the abbreviations *vol.* and *no.*

**Date of Publication:** Month or season (if available) and year of publication, followed by a comma.

**Title of Container #2:** The database where the source was located (*JSTOR*) is italicized, followed by a comma.

**Location (for Container #1):** MLA refers to the page numbers on which the article appears as the location. Place a period after the page numbers. Use the appreviation *p.* or *pp.*

If you found a print version of this source and you did not use a database, the entry would appear without the title of the database or the URL (or DOI), as follows:

> Buck, Amber. "Examining Digital Literacy Practices on Social Network Sites." *Research in the Teaching of English,* vol. 47, no. 1, Aug. 2012, pp. 9-38.

Note: If a scholarly journal article has a DOI, use that instead of a URL in your citation:

> Torres, Carlos Alberto. "Neoliberalism as a New Historical Bloc: A Gramscian Analysis of Neoliberalism's Common Sense in Education." *International Studies in Sociology of Education,* vol. 23, no. 2, 2013, doi: 10.1080/09620214.2013.790658.

This example shows a scholarly journal. **For magazines and newspapers:**

- Omit the volume and issue number.
- Include the day, month (abbreviated), and year for the date of publication, if available, and use this format: 11 Apr. 2016.

### 15. Article from a scholarly journal

> Mayers, Tim. "One Simple Word: From Creative Writing to Creative Writing Studies." *College English*, vol. 71, no. 3, Jan. 2009, pp. 217-28.

If you accessed this article online via a database such as *JSTOR, LexisNexis, InfoTrac, or Academic Search Complete*, the citation would appear as follows:

> Mayers, Tim. "One Simple Word: From Creative Writing to Creative Writing Studies." *College English*, vol. 71, no. 3, Jan. 2009, pp. 217-28. *JSTOR*, www.jstor.org/ stable/25472320.

Note that this citation begins with complete print source information, including page numbers, followed by the title of the database (*JSTOR*, in this example), in italics, and a URL provided for this article in the database.

However, if you accessed this same article via the journal's website (instead of a database), the citation would appear like this:

> Mayers, Tim. "One Simple Word: From Creative Writing to Creative Writing Studies." *College English*, vol. 71, no. 3, Jan. 2009, www.ncte.org/library/NCTEFiles/ Resources/Journals/CE/0713-jan09/CE0713Simple.pdf.

In this case, a URL is included *in place of* page numbers.

### 16. Article from a weekly or monthly magazine

> Lasdun, James. "Alone in the Alps." *The New Yorker*, 11 Apr. 2016, pp. 34-39.

If you accessed the article online through a database such as *Academic Search Complete*, include the italicized title of the database followed by a comma and then the URL provided for the article in the database (as in the example at the beginning of this section on page 762).

However, if you found the article through the magazine website, cite it as follows:

> Lasdun, James. "Alone in the Alps." *The New Yorker*, 11 Apr. 2016, www.newyorker.com/ magazine/2016/04/11/hiking-the-via-alpina.

In this case, the URL of the magazine website replaces page numbers.

Note that this example shows a weekly magazine (*The New Yorker*). If you are citing an article in a magazine that is published monthly, use the identical format with only the month and year for the date.

### 17. Article from a daily newspaper

> Kepner, Tyler. "Grand Home of a Larger-Than-Life Team." *The New York Times*, national
> ed., 21 Sept. 2008, p. N1.

Note that the page number includes the section in which the article appeared—in this example, section N, page 1. Also, if available, include the edition (in this example, *national ed.* for "national edition") before the publication date.

If the article is accessed online through a database, include the complete print source information as listed in the database. Then list the italicized title of the database, followed by a comma and then the URL:

> Kepner, Tyler. "Grand Home of a Larger-Than-Life Team." *The New York Times*, 21 Sept.
> 2008, p. SP1. *General OneFile*, go.galegroup.com/ps/i.do?id=GALE%7CA185353770&v=
> 2.1&u=nysl_me_wls&it=r&p=GPS&sw=w&asid=fb14c17410255fa0f73229b423492e88.

If you accessed the article through the newspaper's website, cite it as follows:

> Kepner, Tyler. "Grand Home of a Larger-Than-Life Team." *The New York Times*, 20 Sept.
> 2008, nyti.ms/1SK9RCi.

List the publication date as listed on the website (this may sometimes be slightly different than the print publication date) and the URL. Some sources, such as *The New York Times*, offer a permanent URL for their articles (nyti.ms/1SK9RCi in the example above); if available, include this kind of permalink in your citation instead of copying the URL from your browser.

### 18. Editorial

> Kayyem, Juliette. "A Rainy Day Fund Doesn't Work if It's Always Raining." Editorial.
> *Boston Globe*, 23 May 2013, www.bostonglobe.com/opinion/2013/05/22/another-
> disaster-and-yet-relief-stays-same/R6DsCQCr8xhg0vZOUzlRcL/story.html.

The term "Editorial" appears after the title of the article, followed by a period. In this online example, there is no edition or page number because the article was accessed through the newspaper's website.

### 19. Letter to the editor

> Tamor, Sarah. Letter to the editor. *The New York Times*, 7 Apr. 2016, nyti.ms/23hYMDi.

Note that because this source was located online at the newspaper's website, there is a URL in place of page numbers.

### 20. Review

> Uglow, Jenny. "The Saga of the Flaming Zucchini." Review of *Consider the Fork:*
> *A History of How We Cook and Eat*, by Bee Wilson. *The New York Review of Books*, 6
> June 2013, www.nybooks.com/articles/2013/06/06/saga-flaming-zucchini/.

Notice that the name of the author of the review is placed first. The name of the author of the work being reviewed follows the title of the work being reviewed, preceded by the word *by* (in this example, "by Bee Wilson").

If the review does not have a separate title (like "The Saga of the Flaming Zucchini" in this example) omit that part of the citation. For publication information, use the format for the kind of source you used (e.g., newspaper website or monthly magazine).

For film reviews, include the name of the director of the film, placed after the title of the film and preceded by the description *directed by*:

> Sharkey, Betsy. "*Before Midnight* Finds Its Couple in a Dark Place." Review of *Before Midnight*, directed by Richard Linklater. *Los Angeles Times*, 24 May 2013, articles .latimes.com/2013/may/24/entertainment/la-et-mn-before-midnight-20130524.

## Other Sources

### 21. Website

When citing an entire website, include the author, editor, or compiler of the site (if available), followed by the title of the site in italics, the name of the organization sponsoring the site, the publication date (if available), and the URL:

> *Feirstein Graduate School of Cinema*. Brooklyn College, CUNY, www.brooklyn.cuny.edu/ web/academics/schools/mediaarts/schools/feirstein.php. Accessed 30 Sept. 2016.

In this example, there is no author, so the entry begins with the title of the website (*Feirstein Graduate School of Cinema*). Also, if a site has no publication date or is revised and updated often, as in this example, include a date of access at the end of your citation.

### 22. Web page

For a web page, include the name of the author (if available), the title of the page in quotation marks followed by the italicized title of the website, the name of the sponsoring organization (if available), the date of publication, and the URL:

> Vandervort, Don. "Water Softener Buying Guide." *HomeTips*, 22 Apr. 2016, www.hometips.com/buying-guides/water-softener-systems.html.

If the sponsoring organization or publisher of the site is the same as the title of the overall website, then do not include the sponsoring organization in your citation. In the example above, "HomeTips" is both the name of the sponsoring organization and the name of the website, so it is listed only once in the entry (as the title of the site).

The citation for a web page by a corporate author (such as an organization or business) is similar in format:

> Writing Center at the University of Wisconsin-Madison. "Writing Cover Letters.'" *The Writer's Handbook*, U of Wisconsin-Madison, 29 Aug 2014, writing.wisc.edu/ Handbook/CoverLetters.html.

Notice that the name of the agency or organization (Writing Center at the University of Wisconsin-Madison) appears in place of an author's name. In this example, *The Writer's Handbook* is the website where the web page ("Writing Cover Letters") is located; the University of

Wisconsin-Madison is the sponsoring organization. Note that if no publication date is available, include the date when you accessed the web page at the end of the citation.

For a web page without an author, the citation appears like this:

"Dodging Bombs and Building Trust in Yemen." *UNWomen*, 24 Mar. 2016, www.unwomen.org/en/news/stories/2016/3/dodging-bombs-and-building-trust-in-yemen.

The title of the web page ("Dodging Bombs and Building Trust in Yemen") appears first, followed by the italicized title of the website (*UNWomen*), the date of publication, and the URL. In this example, because UNWomen is both the name of the website and the name of the sponsoring organization, the name of the sponsoring organization is omitted.

### 23. Blog

Villaespesa, Elena. "Data Stories Centralized: A Digital Analytics Dashboard." *Digital Underground*, Metropolitan Museum of Art, 29 Oct. 2015, www.metmuseum.org/blogs/digital-underground/2015/data-stories-centralized.

Include the author (if known), the title of the blog entry (in quotation marks), and the title of the blog (in italics). Next, list the sponsor of the website. Note that according to the MLA guidelines, the articles *the* and *a* are excluded from the name of a sponsoring organization or publisher in citations; so, in this example, "The" is omitted from The Metropolitan Museum of Art. Also, remember to include the date of the blog entry and the URL.

### 24. Podcast

Davies, Dave, narrator. "Do Voter ID Laws Prevent Fraud, or Dampen Turnout?" *Fresh Air*, National Public Radio, 15 Aug. 2012, www.npr.org/2012/08/15/158869947/do-voter-id-laws-prevent-fraud-or-dampen-turnout.

Begin with the performer's or author's name, followed by the title of the podcast in quotation marks, the italicized name of the program or series that the podcast is part of, the sponsor of the program, the date of the original broadcast, and the URL.

### 25. Interview

For an interview that you conduct yourself, include the name of the person you interviewed, a description (Personal interview), and the date of the interview:

Gallehr, Don. Personal interview. 19 Apr. 2010.

For a published or broadcast interview, include the name of the person who was interviewed and the title of the interview, if available, placed in quotation marks. Add the name of the interviewer if relevant. Be sure to include the publication information and the URL if it is an interview you found online. For example, in this entry, the interview was published on the website *City Pages:*

Pollan, Michael. "A Coffee Date with Michael Pollan." Interview by Keane Amdahl, *City Pages*, 7 May 2013, www.citypages.com/restaurants/a-coffee-date-with-michael-pollan-interview-6615340.

### 26. E-mail

Yagelski, Robert. "A Summary of Key Revision Ideas." Received by Laura Ross, 28 Mar. 2016.

List the name of the person who wrote the e-mail first, followed by the subject line of the e-mail message in quotation marks, the name of the person who received the e-mail, and the date the message was sent.

### 27. Film

*The Great Gatsby*. Directed by Baz Luhrmann, Warner Bros. Entertainment, 2013.

If you are discussing a film in a general way, place the title of the film first and omit the names of directors or performers. Include the company primarily responsible for distributing the film and the date of the film's original release. If you are discussing the work of a particular person connected with the film, include that person's name with a description in your citation. The example above emphasizes the work of the director of the film.

If you accessed a film online, your citation would also include the name of the site or service where you accessed the film (such as *Hulu* or *Netflix*), and a URL for the film.

### 28. Television or radio program

"Second Sons." *Game of Thrones*, season 3, episode 8, Television 360, 2013.

If you are citing an episode or program in a general way (as in this first example), include the title of the episode, the series title (in italics), and the season and episode numbers. Depending on your rhetorical emphasis, you will also want to include either the production company and the year the episode was produced (as in the first example), *or* the distribution company and the date that the episode originally aired (as in the second example below).

If you are citing the work of a particular character or other person connected with the episode or program, include that person's name with a description in your citation. In this second example, the series creators and the work of a particular actor in the episode are emphasized:

"Second Sons." *Game of Thrones*, created by David Bebioff and D. B. Weiss, performance by Peter Dinklage, season 3, episode 8, Home Box Office, 19 May 2013.

### 29. Sound recording

Rollins, Sonny. *Saxophone Colossus*. Prestige, 1987.

When citing an entire album or collection, begin with the name of the artist(s), followed by the title of the album or collection, the recording company, and year of issue.

To cite a specific song, include the song title, in quotation marks, after the name of the artist:

Rollins, Sonny. "You Don't Know What Love Is." *Saxophone Colossus*, Prestige, 1987.

### 30. Online video

Welch, Kiera. "Useful Knots to Know: Ten Most Useful Knots." *YouTube*, 4 Dec. 2015, youtu.be/JGXQIrRraLA.

24

Include the name of the author of the video, if available. If the video was posted by someone other than the author, use the following format:

"Led Zeppelin: Whole Lotta Love." *YouTube*, uploaded by Brian Silva, 23 Sep. 2013, youtu.be/uiLKT5rPHBA.

In this example, the creator of the video is not included. Begin with the title of the video in quotation marks, followed by the container (*YouTube*). Include the name of the person who uploaded the video preceded by the phrase *uploaded by*. Then list the date when the video was uploaded followed by the URL.

### 31. Social media

@MalalaFund (Malala Fund). "#FACT: Increasing the number of girls completing 12yrs of edu by 1% could boost a country's economic growth by 0.3%." *Twitter*, 24 June 2016, 11:29 a.m., twitter.com/MalalaFund/status/746379764814974978.

For a short untitled message, like the tweet in this example, include the full text of the message in quotation marks as the title in your citation. Include both the date and time the message was posted, and the URL for the specific message.

Metropolitan Museum of Art, New York. "What can be learned from unfinished films, from works that arrive to us as fragments?" *Facebook*, 9 May 2016, 7:48 p.m., www.facebook.com/metmuseum/posts/10153693407457635.

For an online posting on a social media site (*Facebook*, in this example), include the name of the author of the post, the title of the post (or the first sentence of the post if there is no title, as in the example above), and the name of the social media site. List the date and time of the post, followed by the URL for the post.

### 32. Advertisement

"Nike." Advertisement. *Adweek*, 27 Mar. 2013, www.adweek.com/adfreak/nikes-new-tiger-woods-ad-says-more-about-us-him-148172.

Notice that this entry includes a description of the kind of source it is (advertisement). Otherwise, the entry is similar to a web page entry.

### 33. Art

Cave, Nick. *Soundsuit*. 2011, Museum of Modern Art, New York.

Cite the artist first and then the title of the work. Next, include the date when the work was created followed by the name of the institution where the art is housed and the city. If you found the art in a print source, follow the appropriate format for publication details.

### 34. Government publication

United States, Department of Transportation. *Bridge Management: Practices in Idaho, Michigan, and Virginia*. Government Publishing Office, 2012.

For government documents, the name of the nation or state appears first, followed by the agency (Department of Transportation, in this example) and the title of the publication (*Bridge Management*). Also include the publisher (Government Publishing Office) and the date of publication (2012).

If you accessed the publication online, include the URL:

United States, Department of Transportation. *Bridge Management: Practices in Idaho, Michigan, and Virginia.* Government Publishing Office, 2012, www.fhwa.dot.gov/asset/hif12029/hif12029.pdf.

# Sample MLA-Style Research Paper

The following essay by Matt Searle, written for a writing class at Emerson College, follows MLA guidelines for formatting a research paper. Matt's essay is a causal analysis (see Chapter 6) that explores the potential impact of digital technologies on literacy and cognition. He addresses the question, What effects are the rapidly growing uses of digital technologies having on how we read and think? As you read, notice how Matt examines this question from various angles, taking into account what different experts think and what research has shown. Notice, too, how Matt carefully documents his sources using MLA style.

For research papers, MLA recommends placing your name, the title of your paper, and other relevant information (such as the date, the course number, and the instructor's name) on the first page, as Matt has done, rather than on a separate title page. If you are required to use a title page, center this information on the page.

When formatting a paper in MLA style, remember to

- Use one-inch margins.
- Use a legible font, such as Times Roman, set at 12 points.
- Double-space the text throughout the document (including the title and Works Cited page).
- Double-space between the heading and the title and between the title and the main text on the first page.
- Indent paragraphs one-half inch.
- Number all pages, including the first page, in the upper-right-hand corner.
- Place your last name before the page number on each page. (If you are using a program such as Microsoft Word, you can use the header function to create a running head that includes your name and the page number on each page.)
- Include the Works Cited list on a separate page at the end of the document.

Searle 1

Matt Searle

Dr. John Dennis Anderson

Evolution of Expression

20 October 2015

Anxieties Over Electracy

Over the course of the past decade, technology has shaped the way society accesses and absorbs information. In *Internet Invention: From Literacy to Electracy*, Gregory L. Ulmer argues that our culture is transitioning from traditional literacy to a type of "electracy" afforded by the digital age. However, this transition has been met with resistance by those who fear the changes it will bring. Concerns involving the superficiality of internet reading, loss of memory, and depletion of traditional literary skills have been brought to the forefront of the debate about literacy and electracy. As the internet continues to rewire our brains and becomes a ubiquitous presence in our world, we must take the time to fully understand its impact.

One of the primary criticisms of electracy, defined by Ulmer as being to digital media what literacy is to print, is that it causes superficial understanding (*Internet* xii). Just as Johann Gutenberg's invention of the printing press increased freedom of thought and public expression, the advent of the internet has increased the availability of information. Those who welcome this influx of data subscribe to a philosophy that Adam Gopnik has coined "Never Better-ism," a belief in the internet's potential to create a new utopia. However, there are others who are as skeptical as the "Never-Betters" are optimistic. In a well-known article titled "Is Google Making Us Stupid?," writer Nicholas Carr expresses the belief that digital literacy leads to a depletion of textual analysis and cognition. Citing his own inability to read lengthy articles without skimming and an increasing lack of patience with text, Carr claims that the internet leads to ADD-like behavior. He contends that we are no longer "scuba divers" of information—that is, we no longer critically assess what we read (57). Furthermore, internet users often feel the need to hop around to various sites rather than focus on one in particular. Though some believe this habit of "power browsing" stimulates creativity, internet critics such as Carr worry that our culture will be permanently unable to perform in-depth analysis (59). Carr cites the research of Maryanne Wolf, a developmental psychologist, to highlight this concern:

> Wolf worries that the style of reading promoted by the Net, a style that puts "efficiency" and "immediacy" above all else, may be weakening our capacity for the kind of deep reading that emerged when an earlier technology, the printing press, made long and complex works of prose commonplace. When we read online, she says, we tend to become "mere decoders of information." Our ability to interpret text, to make the rich mental connections that form when we read deeply and without distraction, remains largely disengaged. (59)

With newspapers such as *The New York Times* attracting readers by adding abstracts for every three pages and online journalists peppering their articles with hyperlinks, the medium is gradually adjusting to our changing behavior (61).

While the criticisms lodged by Carr and others towards electracy may seem extreme, some research suggests that the internet is shaping the way we think. Human brains are extremely malleable as neurons often break old connections and form new ones. Just as reading Chinese text from right to left is not a natural talent, electrate reading is very much a learned skill. Rather than following the typical linear progression of alphabetic literacy, numerous hyperlinks and a virtual cornucopia of information encourage a "zigzag" approach to reading (Rich A27). Thus, the question is not whether the internet is affecting the way we think, but whether it is modifying the brain in a positive fashion. It is possible that our neurological transition to electrate thinking is a natural progression in our mental development, but anxiety still exists over electracy's permanent effects. For example, studies have shown that the internet can have a serious impact on memory (Johnson).

According to MLA style, you must set off as a block quote any quotation that is four lines or more from your source text, as Matt does here. Indent the block quote one-half inch from the left-hand margin. Notice that the page reference is placed in parentheses *after* the period of the final sentence of the block quote.

For this citation, Matt includes the author's last name (Rich) followed by the page reference, indicating that Matt is citing information from that specific page of the source text.

For this citation, Matt includes only the author's last name (Johnson) because he is citing the entire source text rather than a specific page from that text.

**24**
MLA

Because websites such as Google easily provide the answers to our questions, some consider it no longer necessary to attempt to memorize information. In this way, we as a culture tend to "outsource" our memories to electronics rather than use our brains for retention (Johnson A7). In one study, three thousand people were asked to remember the birthdate of a relative; only forty percent of people under thirty years old were able to answer correctly as compared to eighty-seven percent of people over the age of fifty (Thompson). Even more staggering was the fact that fully a third of youths were able to recite their phone number only after checking the phone itself (Thompson).

This loss of recall seems to be directly linked to electracy, as further studies have shown that people are more likely to remember information that they believe will be deleted. According to neuroscientist Gary Small, "We're ... [u]sing the World Wide Web as an external hard drive to augment our biological memory stores" (qtd. in Johnson A7). However, as with any neurobiological development, there are some psychological benefits. With less of our brain used for memory storage, we can free up our gray matter to be used for brainstorming and daydreaming. Some experts promote the idea that intelligence is not truly about knowing information, but instead knowing where to find it. University of Pittsburgh psychology professor Richard Moreland has labeled the perceived need to retain all information "maladaptive" (qtd. in Johnson A7). Thus, skeptics of electracy must consider both the positive and negative aspects of the transition.

The question of whether electracy will supersede traditional literacy has also become an issue in recent years. Children between the ages of eight and eighteen have increased their internet usage from an average of forty-six minutes per day in 1984 to an hour and forty-one minutes per day in the present (Rich A16). At the same time, only one-fifth of seventeen-year-olds read for fun every day, a statistic that some critics argue seems to correlate with a drastic

The abbreviation *qtd. in* (which means "quoted in") in this citation indicates that the quotation by Gary Small in this sentence was taken not from the original text by Small but from the text by Johnson.

drop on critical reading test scores (Rich A16). Proponents of internet reading claim that it is simply a new type of literacy that allows its users to create their own beginnings, middles, and ends. Reading online can also allow those who have learning disabilities such as dyslexia to read in a more comfortable environment and format (Rich A17).

Another argument against electrate skepticism is that the internet encourages reading amongst those who would not normally read otherwise. For example, giving internet access to low income families who may struggle to buy books has been shown to increase overall reading time (Rich A16). With ninety percent of employers listing reading comprehension as very important (Rich A16), it is essential that future generations be able to comprehend the information they take in. This means that while electracy may have a place in our culture, where it belongs is still unclear. Groups such as the Organization for Economic Cooperation and Development plan to add electronic reading sections to aptitude tests, but these actions have been scoffed at by many (Rich A17). The experts that fear our transition from literacy to electracy are aware that only the reading of traditional literate texts has been proven to cause higher comprehension and performance levels (Rich A16). Therefore, electracy opponents do not necessarily want to dissolve the medium, but simply do not want it to replace what is currently known as reading.

Ulmer does not see the internet as destroying our literate abilities, but rather building on them in what he calls a "society of the spectacle" (*Internet* xiii). In Ulmer's vision, imagination and visualization can be used in combination with critical thinking in order to solve problems: "What literacy is to the analytical mind, electracy is to the affective body: a prosthesis that enhances and augments a natural or organic human potential" ("Gregory Ulmer-Quotes"). For Ulmer, electracy is an apparatus that is to be used for future generations, which is why he labels *Internet Invention* as a new

Notice that Matt cites the source text by Rich repeatedly in these paragraphs. Normally, if you are citing the same text repeatedly, you don't need to include a citation in each sentence. However, because Matt is taking information from different pages of the same source text, he includes numerous in-text citations to indicate to readers specifically where in the source text this information appears.

Matt does not include a page number in this citation because his source is an online source without page numbers.

24
MLA

generation textbook (*Internet* xiii). Ulmer's convictions are reflected by others who support the movement towards electracy. These thinkers point out that when literacy first began, it also caused cynicism, but it ultimately became the widely accepted norm. Indeed, it seems that the advent of new technologies has always made people uneasy and stirred fears that the capacities of the human brain may either be replaced or diminished. However, as Ulmer sees the situation, technological progression is both a natural and welcome development. We may no longer be able to think in a purely literate and literal sense, but as Michigan State University professor Rand J. Spiro puts it, "[T]he world doesn't go in a line" (qtd. in Rich A16). If we as a culture can harness the potential of the internet, perhaps Ulmer's vision can come to fruition.

The world is constantly evolving as new technologies and philosophies begin to dominate the cultural landscape. With the internet a ubiquitous presence in the lives of almost all human beings, becoming fluent in what Greg Ulmer has dubbed electracy is integral. Fears that the internet causes superficiality, rewires our brains, and decreases literacy have been corroborated by studies, but that does not mean that the internet is without benefits. By understanding its effects and using electracy to build off our literate knowledge, we can determine where this skill fits within our society.

Works Cited

Carr, Nicholas. "Is Google Making Us Stupid?" *The Atlantic*, July-Aug. 2008, pp. 56-63.

Gopnik, Adam. "The Information: How the Internet Gets Inside Us." *The New Yorker*, 14 & 21 Feb. 2011, www.newyorker.com/magazine/2011/02/14/the-information.

Johnson, Carolyn Y. "Memory Slips Caught in the Net." *The Boston Globe*, 15 July 2011, pp. A1+.

Rich, Motoko. "Literacy Debate: Online, R U Really Reading?" *The New York Times*, late ed., 27 July 2008, pp. A1+.

Thompson, Clive. "Your Outboard Brain Knows All." *Wired*, 25 Sept. 2007, www.wired.com/2007/09/st-thompson-3/.

Ulmer, Gregory L. "Gregory Ulmer-Quotes." *European Graduate School*, 2011, www.egs.edu/faculty/gregory-ulmer/quotes/.

---. *Internet Invention: From Literacy to Electracy*. Longman, 2002.

Begin the Works Cited List on a new page after the main text of the essay. Center the term *Works Cited* at the top of the page. Note that there is no extra space between the term *Works Cited* and the first item in the list. The items are listed alphabetically by author's last name or the title (if no author is listed).

**24**
MLA

Matt follows the MLA guidelines for each item in his Works Cited list, as explained in this chapter. Notice that each item in the list is formatted with a hanging indent of one-half inch.

MindTap®
Practice documentation skills that you have learned in this chapter and receive feedback.

## In this chapter, you will learn to

1. Identify the types of sources that require documentation.

2. Identify the two main components of APA style.

3. Create in-text citations in APA style for a variety of sources.

4. Create References list entries in APA style for a variety of sources.

### MindTap®

Understand the goals of the chapter and complete a warm-up activity.

# Citing Sources Using APA Style

25

**THE PURPOSE OF CITING SOURCES** is to be as clear as possible in showing where your information comes from. Citing your sources according to established style guides not only credits the source for the material you are using but also provides your readers with sufficient bibliographic information to judge or even find your sources for themselves. In general, you must document the source of

- direct quotations,
- ideas or opinions that are not your own,
- visual materials, such as photographs, maps, or graphs, that you did not create,
- multimedia content, such as videos or audios, that you did not create, and
- information (a fact or statistic) that is not general knowledge.

In most academic writing today, writers use the American Psychological Association (APA) style guide when they are writing in the social sciences: psychology, sociology, education, economics, anthropology, geography, and political science. This chapter explains how to cite sources using APA style. (MLA style, which tends to be used in the humanities—literature, languages, performing and visual arts, history, classics, philosophy, and religion—is explained in Chapter 24.) The guidelines in this chapter are based on the *Publication Manual of the American Psychological Association*, 6th edition (2009).

## Two Main Components in APA Style

APA style uses in-text parenthetical citations to document sources. There are **two main components to in-text parenthetical citation systems:**

1. **In-text citations.** Parenthetical citations, which appear in the body of your writing, indicate to a reader that information you are presenting is taken from another source.

2. **A References List.** The References list is a separate section at the end of your document that includes bibliographic information for every source you cited in your document.

Let's imagine you are writing an essay about the cultural significance of heavy metal music and you want to refer to a specific analysis of so-called death metal music in a book titled *Death Metal Music: The Passion and Politics of a Subculture*, by Natalie J. Purcell. On page 188 of that book, Purcell makes a point about the philosophical function of death metal music that you want to include in your essay. If you were using APA style, you would cite the source as follows:

> Death metal music performs a genuine philosophical function by examining the dark side of human nature (Purcell, 2003, p. 188).

or

> Critic Natalie Purcell (2003) considers death metal a "philosophical response, whether conscious or subconscious, to terrifying questions about nebulous human nature" (p. 188).

The entry in the bibliography would look like this:

> Purcell, N. J. (2003). *Death metal music: The passion and politics of a subculture.* Jefferson, NC: McFarland.

Each in-text citation in your paper must have a corresponding References entry so that your readers can find and read the original source themselves.

---

**FOCUS** | **CONTENT NOTES**

The American Psychological Association recommends that writers use parenthetical, or in-text, citations of the kind described in this chapter when documenting sources (rather than traditional footnotes or endnotes). Writers can also use **content notes** for additional explanation or discussion of a point in the main text. APA discourages the use of such notes unless they are essential to the discussion. If you do use content notes, APA format requires them to be placed on a separate page titled "Footnotes" that appears at the end of the document. Indicate the presence of a content note in your main text by using a superscript number. For example, if you wanted to include a content note related to the following sentence in your main text, place the superscript number at the end of the sentence:

> Some research suggests a correlation between literacy and higher-order cognitive skills.[1]

The corresponding footnote would appear at the end of your main document on the Footnotes page:

> [1] The correlation between literacy and cognition has been seriously questioned by many scholars, notably Sylvia Scribner and Michael Cole in their well-known study *The Psychology of Literacy.*

---

# Creating In-Text Citations Using APA Style

The APA style for citing sources reflects the conventions of empirical research. Because research tends to build on previously conducted studies and because the relative currency of research is important, APA emphasizes the author's last name and year of publication in in-text citations.

APA style also requires that in-text citations include page number(s) for material quoted directly from a source. However, direct quotation in APA style is not as common as paraphrase and summary.

**25**

### A. Work by one author

If you were citing information taken from a book called *The Printing Revolution in Early Modern Europe* by Elizabeth L. Eisenstein, published in 1983, the parenthetical citation would look like this:

> The widespread adoption of the printing press in the 16th century helped standardize the major European languages (Eisenstein, 1983).

Note that there is a comma between the author's name and the year of publication. As always in APA style, you could use Eisenstein's name in your sentence, and include only the year of publication in the parentheses immediately following the name:

> Eisenstein (1983) examines how the widespread adoption of the printing press in the 16th century helped standardize the major European languages.

### B. Work by multiple authors

APA has several rules for citing works by multiple authors.

- **Work by two authors.** When citing a work by two authors, use both authors' names in the citation or in your sentence. If authors are named in parentheses, use an ampersand (&) to join them; however, if you name the authors in your sentence, use the word "and." For example, if you wanted to quote from page 2 of the introduction to *Undead TV: Essays on Buffy the Vampire Slayer*, by Elana Levine and Lisa Parks, published in 2007, you could do so as follows:

> The hit television series *Buffy the Vampire Slayer* "uses its metaphorical representations of life and death, good and evil, comedy and tragedy to speak about the power struggles inherent in many people's everyday lives in the Western world" (Levine & Parks, 2007, p. 2).

Note that a comma is placed after the second author's name and another comma is placed after the year of publication.

If you use the authors' names in your sentence, cite the quotation like this:

> Levine and Parks (2007) assert that *Buffy the Vampire Slayer* "uses its metaphorical representations of life and death, good and evil, comedy and tragedy to speak about the power struggles inherent in many people's everyday lives in the Western world" (p. 2).

Place the date in parentheses immediately after the authors' names. The page reference should be placed in parentheses at the end of the sentence.

- **Work by three to five authors.** If you are referring to a work by three, four, or five authors, list all the authors' names the first time you cite the work. For example, if you were citing a journal article titled "Empirical Foundations for Writing in Prevention and Psychotherapy," by Brian A. Esterling, Luciano L'Abate, Edward J. Murray, and James W. Pennebaker, the parenthetical citation would look like this:

> Studies have shown that writing has therapeutic benefits for some patients (Esterling, L'Abate, Murray, & Pennebaker, 1999).

If you cite the same work again, list only the first author's name followed by the Latin phrase *et al.* (which means "and others"):

> The therapeutic benefits of writing include lower blood pressure and higher self-esteem (Esterling et al., 1999).

Note that there is no comma between the name of the author and the abbreviation *et al.*, but a comma is placed before the date of publication. Also note that there is no period after *et*, but there is a period after *al*.

- **Work by six or more authors.** When citing a work by six or more authors, use the first author's last name followed by the phrase *et al.* For example, if you cited a 2008 book co-written by Mark Smith and eight additional authors, the citation would appear as follows:

> Researchers have found that many mammals mate for life (Smith et al., 2008).

If you included the name of the author in your sentence, the citation would look like this:

> Smith et al. (2008) found that many mammals mate for life.

### C. Work by a corporate author

A "corporate author" is an organization, committee, association, or agency (rather than an individual or group of individually named authors). When citing a corporate author, use the same format as for a single author. For example, if you were citing a 2012 study by the Center for Research on Educational Outcomes, you would do so as follows:

> According to the Center for Research on Educational Outcomes (2012), 37 percent of charter schools had math scores that were lower than their public school peers.

You could also include the corporate author in the parentheses; omit any initial article:

> In one recent study, 37 percent of charter schools had math scores that were lower than their public school peers (Center for Research on Educational Outcomes, 2012).

### D. More than one work by the same author

If you cite more than one work by the same author, you need to distinguish among the works by including the publication date of each work you cite. For example, if you were citing two different books by Paulo Freire—*Pedagogy of Hope*, published in 1994, and *Letters to Cristina*, published in 1996—your parenthetical citations might look like this:

> Some reformers emphasize the crucial role of hope in the struggle for change. They argue that hope is part of the process of improving human existence (Freire, 1994), but they also acknowledge that hope "seldom exists apart from the reverses of fate" (Freire, 1996, p. 14).

25

The dates indicate that information was taken from two different texts by the same author; the dates also enable a reader to find the specific works in the References list.

### E. Two or more works cited within one set of parentheses

List the works alphabetically, separated by a semicolon, as they appear in your References list:

> (Harden, 2012; Raine, 2013)

### F. Works by authors with the same last name

Include the author's first and middle initials (if given) in all in-text citations to avoid confusion.

> B. Brown (2013) and S. T. Brown (2011) found that weather patterns have changed significantly in the past decade.

### G. Work without an author listed

If you cite a work without an author listed, include a brief version of the title, either in parentheses or in the main text. Here the title of the article "Carrying the Torch" is shortened to "Carrying":

> The sports management industry in Great Britain received a significant boost in business as a result of the 2012 Olympic Games in London ("Carrying," 2012).

In in-text parenthetical citations, titles of articles and web pages are placed in quotation marks; titles of books are italicized or underlined.

**H. Online source**

When citing online sources in in-text parenthetical citations, follow the same principles you would use when citing print sources. However, there are many different kinds of electronic sources, which might not include the same kinds of information that are available for a print book or journal article. For example, websites don't usually have page numbers. In such cases, provide the number of the paragraph in which you found the information or quotation you are citing, using the abbreviation *para.*:

> (Martinez, 2000, para. 8)

If page numbers are not available or paragraph numbers are not feasible, include sufficient information for readers to find the source you are citing:

> (Madoff, Bradley, & Rico, Results section).

If the heading is too lengthy to cite, then use a shortened title. For the long heading "Genetic Variations Link Found in Bipolar Twins Separately Adopted," you could use the first several words:

> (Bico & Marley, 2013, "Genetic Variations Link Found," para. 3).

According to APA style, if you do not have reliable page numbers or paragraph numbers, leave them out of the parenthetical citation:

> (Martinez, 2000)

**I. Quotation within a cited work**

When using a quotation from one source that you have found in another source, you have to show that the quotation was acquired "secondhand" and was not taken directly from the original source. In such cases, indicate the original source in your text and the secondary source in parentheses. For example, let's say you were reading a book called *Literary Theory* by Terry Eagleton that included a quotation by Sigmund Freud that you wanted to use in your essay. You would cite the Freud quotation as follows:

> Even Freud acknowledged the central importance of economics in human relations, famously stating, "The motive of human society is in the last resort an economic one" (as cited in Eagleton, 1983, p. 151).

Note the phrase *as cited in* in the parenthetical citation. In this instance, you are signaling to readers that you read Freud's statement on page 151 of the book by Terry Eagleton.

**J. Long quotations**

In APA style a long quotation is defined as one than contains more than 40 words. These quotations should be indented one-half inch from the left margin as a block quotation—*without* quotation marks.

> LeVine et al. (1994) describe the child care practices of the Gusii people of Kenya in regard to cultural assumptions:
>
>> Gusii mothers are devoted to the welfare and development of their infants, and their sense of what is best for them is framed in terms of indigenous cultural models that

assume high infant mortality, high fertility (but with protective birth-spacing), and a domestic age-hierarchy in which young children acquire useful skills and moral virtues through participation in household food production. (p. 2)

The page number for the quotation is included in parentheses at the end of the quotation. Include the abbreviation *p.* for "page." Notice that the parenthetical citation is placed *after* the final period of the block quotation. If the author's name does not appear in the main text, include it in the parentheses.

### K. Work in more than one volume

If you cite a multivolume work in your paper, indicate the range of the years of publication:

(Trieste, 1999–2002)

If you cite only one volume, provide the year of publication for that volume only. In your References entry, you will list the volume number.

### L. Personal communication

Personal emails, letters, interviews, conversations, and other private communications are not retrievable by others and so are not listed in the References. In the in-text citation, provide initials and last name for the correspondent, provide an exact date, and use the label "personal communication":

(L. L. Fothergill, personal communication, October 5, 2013)

## Creating a References List in APA Style

Each source you cite in your text must correspond to an entry in your bibliography, which is called the References list in APA style. Your list of References should appear at the end of your document, beginning with a new page. Organize the References list alphabetically according to the authors' last names (or, if the work includes no author, the first main word of the title). In APA style, follow these rules:

- Capitalize only proper nouns and the first word in the titles and subtitles of books, chapters, and articles.
- Capitalize all important words in the names of journals, newspapers, and magazines.
- Italicize the titles of books and longer works; also italicize titles of journals, magazines, and newspapers.
- Do *not* italicize or place in quotation marks titles of shorter works, such as journal articles.
- For both print and electronic sources, provide the DOI if available. (See Focus: "What Is a DOI?" on page 788.) If there is no DOI for an online source, include the URL.
- Double-space entries but do not skip spaces between entries.
- Using hanging indents of one-half inch for entries in the References list.

# Books

Here is the general format for an entry for a book in the References list:

**Date of Publication:**
The year of publication appears in parentheses followed by a period.

**Title of the Book:**
Italicized. Only the first word of the title and subtitle and any proper nouns are capitalized.

**Place of Publication:**
Include both the city and the state.

Street, B. V. (1984). *Literacy in theory and practice.* New York, NY: Cambridge University Press.

**Author:** Last name first, followed by a comma, the first initial, and the middle initial (if available).

**Publisher:** Do not abbreviate "University Press." However, shorten other names, and omit words such as *Publisher*, *Inc.*, and *Co.*

However, for books that are accessed online, the publisher and place of publication are eliminated and replaced by the URL (web address) or DOI where the book was found:

**25**

**Authors:** Last name first, followed by a comma, the first initial, and the middle initial (if available). Note that the same form (last name followed by initials) is used for the second and subsequent authors.

**Date of Publication:**
The year of publication appears in parentheses followed by a period.

**Title of the Book:** Italicized. The first word of the title and subtitle are capitalized; proper names (*Lord Keynes*, in this example) are also capitalized. All other words appear in lowercase.

Buchanan, J. M., and Wagner, R. E. (1977). *Democracy in deficit: The political legacy of Lord Keynes.* Retrieved from http://www.econlib.org/library /Buchanan/buchCv8.html

**Online Location:** Indicate that the work was accessed online with the phrase *Retrieved from.* Include the URL (web address) where the book was accessed online. If the publication has a DOI (see Focus: "What Is DOI?"), replace the URL with the DOI and replace the phrase *Retrieved from* with *doi* in lowercase followed by a colon. Do not place a period after the URL or DOI number.

### 1. Book with one author

> Fineman, H. (2008). *The thirteen American arguments: Enduring debates that define and inspire our country*. New York: Random House.

> Cowles, J. T. (1937). *Food-tokens as incentives for learning by chimpanzees*. Baltimore, MD: The Johns Hopkins Press. doi: 10.1037/14268–000

### 2. Book with two or more authors

> Stewart, D. W., Shamdasani, P. N., & Rook, D. W. (2007). *Focus groups: Theory and practice*. Thousand Oaks, CA: SAGE.

> Buchanan, J. M., & Wagner, R. E. (1977). *Democracy in deficit: The political legacy of Lord Keynes*. Retrieved from http://www.econlib.org/library/Buchanan/buchCv8.html

The second example shows a book accessed online. Eliminate the publisher and place of publication and include the URL where the work was accessed. If a DOI is available, use that instead of the URL (as shown in Focus: "What Is a DOI?" on page 788).

Notice that an ampersand (&) is used in place of *and* before the name of the last author. If there are more than six authors, follow the sixth name with *et al.* (meaning "and others").

### 3. Two or more books by the same author

If you cite two books by the same author or by the same set of authors whose names are given in the same order in both books, arrange them by publication date in the References list. List the earlier work first.

> Freire, P. (1970). *Pedagogy of the oppressed*. (M. B. Ramos, Trans.). New York: Continuum.

> Freire, P. (1996). *Letters to Cristina: Reflections on my life and work*. New York: Routledge.

> Freire, P. (2004). *Pedagogy of hope: Reliving* Pedagogy of the Oppressed. New York: Bloomsbury.

If the works were both published in the same year, alphabetize the works by title, (excluding *A* and *The*) and then assign letter suffixes (a, b, c, and so on) after the year, as follows:

> Harvey, D. (2003a). *The new imperialism*. Oxford, UK: Oxford University Press.

> Harvey, D. (2003b). *Paris, capital of modernity*. New York, NY: Routledge.

### 4. Anthology with an editor

> Hill, C. A., & Helmers, M. (Eds.). (2004). *Defining visual rhetorics*. Mahwah, NJ: Lawrence Erlbaum.

Use the capitalized abbreviation *Ed.* for *editor* and *Eds.* for *editors*; place the abbreviation in parentheses followed by a period.

### 5. Work in an anthology

> Olson, C. (1973). Projective verse. In D. M. Allen & W. Tallman (Eds.), *The poetics of the new American poetry* (pp. 147–158). New York: Grove Press.

Note that the page numbers of the specific work are placed in parentheses after the title of the anthology (and before the period); use the abbreviation *pp.* for "pages."

### 6. Introduction, preface, foreword, or afterword

> Zelazny, R. (1968). Introduction. In P. K. Dick, *Do androids dream of electric sheep?* (vii-x). New York: Del Ray.

In this example, Roger Zelazny wrote the introduction to the book *Do Androids Dream of Electric Sheep?* by Philip K. Dick. Include the page numbers (in parentheses) of the introduction after the title of the book.

### 7. Book by a corporate author or without an author listed

> Center for Research on Education Outcomes. (2009). *Multiple choice: Charter school performance in 16 states.* Stanford, CA: Stanford University.

If no author or organization is listed, begin the entry with the title of the book. Place the year after the title.

### 8. Translated book

> Tsunetomo, Y. (1979). *Hagakure: The book of the samurai.* (W. S. Wilson, Trans.). Tokyo, Japan: Kadansha International.

Place the name of the translator and the abbreviation *Trans.* (for *translator*) in parentheses, separated by a comma. Note that the abbreviation is capitalized. Also, the name of the translator appears with the first and middle initials first, followed by the last name.

### 9. Subsequent editions of a book

> Creswell, J. W. (Ed.). (2013). *Qualitative research and design: Choosing among five approaches* (3rd ed.). Thousand Oaks, CA: SAGE.

**25**

### 10. Work in more than one volume

> Milton, J. (1847). *The prose works of John Milton* (Vols. 1–2). Philadelphia, PA: John W. Moore. Retrieved from http://app.libraryofliberty.org/

### 11. Encyclopedia article

The format for entries for encyclopedia articles is similar to articles in anthologies.

> Sockett, H. (2008). The moral and epistemic purposes of teacher education. In M. Cochran-Smith, S. Feiman-Nemser, & D. J. McIntyre (Eds.), *Handbook of Research on Teacher Education* (3rd ed., pp. 45–65). New York, NY: Routledge.

If no author is listed, begin with the title of the article. The rest of the citation is the same.

### 12. Government publication

> United States Department of Transportation. (2012). *Bridge management: Practices in Idaho, Michigan, and Virginia.* Washington, D.C: Government Publishing Office.

For government documents, the name of the nation or state appears first combined with the agency (Department of Transportation, in this example).

If you accessed the publication online, indicate the URL:

> United States Department of Transportation. (2012). *Bridge management: Practices in Idaho, Michigan, and Virginia.* Washington, D.C.: Government Publishing Office. Retrieved from http://www.fhwa.dot.gov/asset/hif12029/hif12029.pdf

# Periodicals

Here is the general format for an article from a scholarly journal:

**Author:** Last name, followed by a comma, the first initial, and middle initial (if available).

**Title of Article:** Only the first word of the title and subtitle (if there is one) should be capitalized. Do *not* place titles of articles in quotation marks.

**Title of Periodical:** Italicize and capitalize the title of the journal, magazine, or newspaper. Place a comma after the title.

Buck, A. (2012). Examining digital literacy practices on social network sites. *Research in the Teaching of English, 47*(1), 9–38. Retrieved from http://www.ncte.org/journals/rte/issues

**Date of Publication:** Year of publication appears in parentheses followed by a period. For newspapers and magazines, place a comma after the year and include the month as follows: (2012, April).

**Volume and Issue Number:** Include the volume of the publication in italics followed the issue number in parentheses (which is not italicized). This example shows issue #1 of volume 47. Place a comma after the closing parenthesis.

**Pages:** The page numbers on which the article appears followed by a period. If the article does not appear on continuous pages, separate the page numbers with a comma.

**Online Location:** If you found the article in print, end the citation with the page numbers. If you found the article on a website or through an online database, indicate that by including "Retrieved from" followed by the URL (web address). If there is a DOI, use that in place of the URL and replace the phrase "Retrieved from" with "doi" in lowercase followed by a colon. Do not place a period after the URL or the DOI.

---

**FOCUS | WHAT IS A DOI?**

DOI stands for digital object identifier. A DOI is a unique string of numbers that identifies an electronic publication. It is more stable than a URL, which can change or be deleted. APA style requires that, when available, the DOI be included in an entry on the References page, as shown in the example in this Focus box. Use the DOI in place of the URL.

Many scholarly journals now include DOIs for online publications. Usually, the DOI appears on the first page of the article; in this example of an article published in the scholarly journal *School Effectiveness and School Improvement*, the DOI appears at the very bottom of the page. The entry in the References list would look like this:

Ross, J. A., and Gray, P. (2006). Transformational leadership and teacher commitment to organizational values: The mediating effects of collective teacher efficacy. *School Effectiveness and School Improvement, 17*(2), 179–199. doi: 10.1080/09243450600565795

Notice that there is no period following the DOI.

*School Effectiveness and School Improvement*
*Vol. 17, No. 2, June 2006, pp. 179–199*

Routledge
Taylor & Francis Group

# Transformational Leadership and Teacher Commitment to Organizational Values: The mediating effects of collective teacher efficacy

John A. Ross* and Peter Gray
*Ontario Institute for Studies in Education, University of Toronto, Ontario, Canada*

Transformational leadership researchers have given little attention to teacher expectations that mediate between goals and actions. The most important of these expectations, teacher efficacy, refers to teacher beliefs that they will be able to bring about student learning. This study examined the mediating effects of teacher efficacy by comparing two models derived from Bandura's social-cognitive theory. Model A hypothesized that transformational leadership would contribute to teacher commitment to organizational values exclusively through collective teacher efficacy. Model B hypothesized that leadership would have direct effects on teacher commitment and indirect effects through teacher efficacy. Data from 3,074 teachers in 218 elementary schools in a cross-validation sample design provided greater support for Model B than Model A. Transformational leadership had an impact on the collective teacher efficacy of the school; teacher efficacy alone predicted teacher commitment to community partnerships; and transformational leadership had direct and indirect effects on teacher commitment to school mission and commitment to professional learning community.

## Introduction

Previous research has demonstrated that transformational leadership contributes to valued teacher outcomes. For example, teachers in schools characterized by transformational principal behavior are more likely than teachers in other schools to express satisfaction with their principal, report that they exert extra effort, and be more committed to the organization and to improving it (Leithwood, Jantzi, & Steinbach, 1999). Few studies of the relationship between principal behavior and teacher outcomes have examined the mechanisms through which leadership impacts

*Corresponding author. OISE/University of Toronto, Trent Valley Centre, Box 719, Peterborough, Ontario, K9J 7A1, Canada. Email: jross@oise.utoronto.ca

ISSN 0924-3453 (print)/ISSN 1744-5124 (online)/06/020179–21
© 2006 Taylor & Francis
DOI: 10.1080/09243450600565795

### 13. Journal article with one author

> Mayers, T. (2009). One simple word: From creative writing to creative writing studies. *College English, 71*(3), 217–228.

If you accessed this article via the journal's website or from another online resource, the citation would look like this:

> Mayers, T. (2009). One simple word: From creative writing to creative writing studies. *College English, 71*(3), 217–228. Retrieved from http://www.ncte.org/journals/ce/issues

If a DOI is available, include it in place of the URL:

> Desimone, L. M. (2009). Improving impact studies of teachers' professional development: Toward better conceptualizations and measures. *Educational Researcher, 38*(3), 181–199. doi: 10.3102/0013189X08331140

The abbreviation *doi* is in lowercase and followed by a colon. Do not place a period after the DOI number.

*Note*: APA style does not require that you include the name of the database if you accessed the work through an online database such as *Academic Search Complete*.

### 14. Journal article with multiple authors

*For a work with two authors:*

> Bowles, S., & Gintis, H. (2002). *Schooling in Capitalist America* revisited. *Sociology of Education, 75*(1), 1–18.

In this example, part of the article title is capitalized and italicized because it includes the title of a book (*Schooling in Capitalist America*).

*For a work with three to seven authors:*

> Esterling, B. A., L'Abate, L., Murray, E. J., & Pennebaker, J. W. (1999). Empirical foundations for writing in prevention and psychotherapy: Mental and physical health outcomes. *Clinical Psychology Review, 19*(1), 79–96.

*Note*: For a work by more than seven authors, include the first six authors' names, as in the previous example, and use an ellipses in place of the remaining author names. Include the final author's name after the ellipses.

### 15. Magazine article

> Lasdun, J. (2016, April 11). Alone in the Alps. *The New Yorker*, 34–39.

This example shows an article that appeared in a weekly magazine that was published on April 11, 2016. Cite an article from a monthly magazine in the same way, but eliminate the specific day, as follows: (2016, April). Note that for magazine articles, the abbreviation *pp.* (for "pages") is *not* used.

If you found the article through the magazine website or other online resource, cite it as follows:

> Lasdun, J. (2016, April 11). Alone in the Alps. *The New Yorker*, 34–39. Retrieved from http://www.newyorker.com

### 16. Newspaper article

> Kepner, T. (2008, September 21). Grand home of a larger-than-life team. *The New York Times*, p. N1.

Include both the day and month of publication for daily newspapers. For the month of publication, do not use an abbreviation; write the month out in full. Note that the page number includes the section in which the article appeared (in this example, Section N, page 1). Also, for newspapers, include the abbreviation *p.* (for "page) before the page number.

If you accessed the article through the newspaper's website, cite it as follows:

> Kepner, T. (2008, September 21). Grand home of a larger-than-life team. *The New York Times*, p. N1. Retrieved from http://www.nytimes.com

### 17. Editorial

> Fighting 'Patent Trolls.' [Editorial]. (2013, June 6). *The New York Times*, p. A22.

Notice that the word *Editorial* is capitalized, placed in brackets, and followed by a period.

### 18. Letter to the editor

> Griffey, D. (2013, July). The price is wrong. [Letter to the editor]. *Money*, p. 10.

### 19. Review

> Krugman, P. (2013, June 6). How the case for austerity has crumbled. [Review of the books *The alchemists: Three central bankers and a world on fire; Austerity: The history of a dangerous idea;* and *The great deformation: The corruption of capitalism in America*]. *The New York Review of Books*. Retrieved from http://www.nybooks.com

## Other Sources

### 20. Website or web page

If you are citing a website, you can simply include the location of the website in your in-text citation without including an entry in your References list. For example, if you are citing the website for the BBC, your in-text citation would look like this:

> The BBC is one of the most respected international news organizations (http://www.bbc.org).

25

If you are citing a specific web page, cite it as you would an article from a journal, including the following information, if available: author's name, the date of publication (in parentheses), the title of the document or web page, and the online location. A citation of a specific web page from the BBC website would look like this:

Davies, E. (2016, April 1). The world's loudest animal might surprise you. Retrieved from http://www.bbc.com/earth/story/20160331-the-worlds-loudest-animal-might-surprise-you

In this case, you are citing a web page titled "The World's Loudest Animal Might Surprise You," by Ella Davies, which appeared on the BBC website. Notice that the host website (BBC) does not appear in the citation. Also, the month of the publication is not abbreviated. If you can't find a date of publication, use the abbreviation *n.d.* (for "no date").

The citation for a web page by a corporate author (such as a government agency or business) is similar in format:

The Writer Center at the University of Wisconsin-Madison. (2014, August 29). Writing cover letters. Retrieved from https://writing.wisc.edu/Handbook/CoverLetters.html

Notice that the name of the agency or organization (*The Writing Center at the University of Wisconsin-Madison*, in this example) appears in place of an author's name.

For a web page without an author, the title appears first followed by the date (in parentheses):

Dodging bombs and building trust in Yemen. (2016, March 24). Retrieved from http://www.unwomen.org/en

## 21. Blog

To cite a blog post, include the following information, if available: author's name, the date of publication, the title of the blog post, and the online location:

Villaespesa, E. (2015, October 29). Data stories centralized: A digital analytics dashboard [blog post]. Retrieved from http://www.metmuseum.org/blogs/digital-underground/2015/data-stories-centralized

Notice that the description *blog post* is placed in brackets *after* the title of the post but *before* the period. The name of the blog itself (in this example, *Digital Underground*) does not appear in the citation.

If you are citing a comment someone posted in response to a blog, the format is similar. However, include the abbreviation *Re:* before the title of the blog post to indicate that the comment was posted in response to that blog post. Make sure that the date is the date of the *comment* and not the date of the original blog post. Also, include the URL for the comment; however, if the comment appears on the same page as the blog post itself and does not have a unique URL, use the URL for the blog post, as in this example:

Kendzior, A. (2015, November 3). Re: Data stories centralized: A digital analytics dashboard [blog post]. Retrieved from http://www.metmuseum.org/blogs/digital-underground/2015/data-stories-centralized

### 22. Podcast

> Davies, D. (Narrator). (2012, August 15). Do voter ID laws prevent fraud, or dampen turnout? [Audio podcast]. *Fresh air*. Retrieved from www.npr.org

Begin with the name of the most relevant contributor. The contributor's title—*director*, *host*, *executive producer*, or (as in this example) *narrator*—appears next, capitalized and in parentheses, followed by a period.

### 23. Interview

Personal, telephone, and e-mail interviews are cited only within the text since they are not retrievable by other researchers. See example L on page 783.

### 24. Film, video, DVD

> Luhrmann, B. (Director). (2013). *The great gatsby* [Motion picture]. United States: Warner.

For videos, DVDs, filmstrips and similar media, use the same format, noting the medium in brackets after the title but before the period.

### 25. Television or radio episode

> Martin, G. (Writer), & MacLaren, M. (Director). (2013, May 19). Second sons [Television series episode]. In D. Benioff & D. B. Weiss (Executive producers), *Game of thrones*. New York, NY: HBO.

Include the writer and director and original broadcast date of the specific episode you are citing. List the episode title ("Second sons" in this example) with the description (Television series episode). Then provide the series information including the producer's name, the series title, and the city and name of the network.

### 26. Music recording

> Kuhn, J. (2013). *All this happiness* [CD]. New York, NY: PS Classics.

### 27. Advertisement

> Nike [Advertisement]. (2013, March). *Adweek*, 14.

In this example, the page number (14) appears after the title of the publication (*Adweek*).

### 28. Social media

The format of citations for social media content—including posts to Facebook, tweets, Snapchat, etc.—is similar to the format for blogs (see example 21 on page 792). Follow these guidelines:

- Include, if available, the following information: author's name, the date, the title of the post or message with the type of media in brackets, and the source.
- Include the full title of the post or tweet or message up to the first 40 words.
- If the item has no title (for example, a photograph), include a description of the item in brackets.
- If the author uses a screen name (such as on Twitter), include the screen name in brackets after the author's name; if only the screen name is available, do not use brackets.

Here are citations for references to Facebook posts, which are called *status updates*:

Mathieu, P. [Paula]. (2016, May 6). Say no to lawn chemicals [Facebook status update]. Retrieved from https://www.facebook.com/paula.mathieu.3/posts/10206279302762083

The Metropolitan Museum of Art, New York. (2016, May 9). What can be learned from unfinished films, from works that arrive to us as fragments? [Facebook status update]. Retrieved from https://www.facebook.com/metmuseum/posts/10153693407457635

The second example shows a corporate author (*The Metropolitan Museum of Art*). For a tweet, format the citation as follows:

Gates, B. [BillGates]. (2016, May 6). How the world is helping young African women fight HIV: b-gat.es/1NZlqbn vis @MJGerson [Tweet]. Retrieved from https://twitter.com/BillGates/status/728584639238049792?lang=en

Notice that the author's screen name (BillGates) appears in brackets after the author's name.

# Sample APA-Style Research Paper

In the following essay, which was written for an introductory writing class at Emerson College, Duncan Gelder follows APA guidelines for formatting a research paper. Duncan examines differences between the generations, focusing on the ways in which different generations use new technologies and how those technologies relate to the way people think. He makes an argument that the differences between generations are not caused by technology but are a function of the values of each generation. Duncan's essay is a good example of an argument to inquire (see Chapter 5). His goal is not to "win" an argument about why generations think differently; rather, he makes his argument as a way to understand this complex question and share that understanding with his audience.

Duncan adheres to the APA guidelines in formatting his paper. First, he includes a title page with the title and his name centered on the page. APA does not require information on the title page other than the title, author's name, and the institutional affiliation, but if the course instructor requires his or her name, the course name, and a date, omit the institutional affiliation and replace it with the information required by the instructor, as Duncan has done. Notice that the title page is numbered and includes the same running head ("Generations") as the rest of the paper.

Second, Duncan includes an abstract, which is a summary of his paper. According to APA style, abstracts should not exceed 250 words. Notice that the word "Abstract" is centered one inch from the top of the page.

When formatting a paper in APA style, remember to

- double-space the entire document;
- use one-inch margins;
- indent paragraphs one-half inch;
- include the title at the start of the paper (on the third page, after the abstract), centered above the main text;
- use a running head with a shortened version of the title, in capital letters, on the left side of the page and the page number on the right side (include the running head on every page of the document).

The Generations That Influence Technology

Duncan Gelder

Professor Betsy Milarcik

WR 101 14 Introduction to College Writing

November 26, 2015

25

Abstract

Some experts believe we are witnessing a shift in cognitive styles between the Baby Boomer generation and younger generations as a result of the emergence of new technologies and the growing role of media in the lives of young people. However, in the past century, it has not been the technology and appliances that separate one generation from another; instead, the generation's needs and values at the time determine what innovations are prevalent for them.

The Generations That Influence Technology

How often does a person hear someone use the cliché phrase "back in my day. . ." followed by a long-winded explanation of how things used to be? Differences in generations is a common theme through much of the discussion about today's technology. According to N. Katherine Hayles (2007), "we are in the midst of a generational shift in cognitive styles" (p. 187). She believes that an "obvious explanation for the shift. . . is the increasing role of media in the everyday environments of young people" (189). However, in the past century, it has not been the technology and appliances that separate one generation from another; instead, the generation's needs and values at the time determine what innovations are prevalent for them.

A look back to the beginnings of the idea of "modern" technology, the Industrial Revolution in the 19th century, reveals that there are correlations between the ideas of that generation and the increase in technological innovations. The United States was going through major changes at the time. Increasing numbers of people who were willing to work quickly and for cheap were immigrating into the country. Owners of the factories and mills that dominated the era's industry wanted to ensure that this new surplus of workers were doing the work they were supposed to do. The capitalists who owned these businesses created the factory setting and the major technologies, such as the steam engine, that drove industrial growth (Backer, 2012). In a way, Hayles' (2007) idea of hyper attention comes into play during this era as well. Hyper attention, according to Hayles, is characterized partly by "switching focus rapidly between different tasks" (p. 187). The factories could take care of the steps of production from start to finish in one huge building. The technologies that were designed were, in a way, a mechanical form of hyper attention. This is really where our modern idea of capitalism began as well, with the wealthy starting businesses and buying out their competitors. Major monopolies became common during this generation because the upper class were not content with just owning one factory; they needed to own all of the factories and have the biggest hold on their sector of the industry, which is just another large-scale form of hyper attention among the wealthy. The attitudes, both of the workers being accountable for their work and the capitalists wanting to do as much as possible in a shorter amount of time, shaped what technology was prevalent and created the need for the innovations in the first place.

The way in which generational attitudes affected the technology of the era continued on as the industrial revolution began to fade. With two major world wars taking place, the country found itself in need of weapons and military technology. The unified attitude of the country forced these generations to come up with new innovations that would help protect our country. Aircraft and other forms of war transportation were made to be more efficient and able to withstand harsher conditions, bombs were perfected, and boots and uniforms were mass produced; the generations that were affected by these major wars fueled the need for new innovations that would help them succeed. The women, many of whom were not able to fight overseas, turned to other ways to assist the country; they began to build and assemble all of the parts needed by the soldiers. The first World War coincided with the women's suffrage movement, a major point in generational attitudes (National Women's History Museum, 2007). These women wanted to prove that they were equal to men, but not all of them were able to operate undercover overseas or as switchboard operators. So they turned to the factories and began to find new ways of creating wartime innovations that would prove to be instrumental in winning these two major wars.

When the Second World War ended, the generation known commonly as the "Baby Boomer" generation was born as soldiers were now coming home from war and families were complete once again. The country was now focused on family life. Children were born, couples were together again; the home was the most important value during this era. Because there was need for products to be tailored to the consumer again, instead of for the military, many companies found that they needed to create products for the home life. This was the generation of appliances and at-home technology. The housewives that women were now expected to be meant that the women who had been hard at work during the war were now faced with the need to find power and freedom. Here again the idea of hyper attention comes into play. Women, who were the ones who took care of the house and were unable to work due to social inequalities, were now faced with monotonous, time-consuming household tasks. They needed new and unique innovations to make housework faster, giving them less work to do. Thus came the major changes in appliances and at-home technology, with faster washing machines and stronger vacuums being invented and updated as quickly as they were released. The Baby Boomer generation, which focused on family life more than any other idea, influenced what technology and innovations were available and invented during this era. Women were not housewives because they had washing machines available; the washing machines were available because of the strong social inequalities that required women to find ways of coping with the new work they had at home. The invention of the birth control pill during this era was another example of an innovation being influenced by the ideas of the generation. Many women were looking for freedom from the household life. The birth control pill was invented to give them a chance to live their lives without being burdened by children (Walsh, 2012).

The same correlations between values and technology are evident. We live in a time when social equality is a common theme. Women have broken away from the housewife stereotype and are now working to try to break the glass ceiling in the workplace. The racism and prejudice towards people of color is being challenged, a change best symbolized by the election and re-election of our country's first African American president. Gays and lesbians are fighting to receive equal rights. The country is in the midst of a new emphasis on uniqueness and individual rights. And because of this emphasis, technology has adapted to become more customizable for each and every person. Netflix allows us to watch the shows we want to watch. Smart phones allow us to download any app we choose. The current generation is fueled by the need for individualism and customization, and our technology reflects that. Our "hyper attention" is not so much a product of technology; the human need to be entertained and to move forward influences the technology that is a major part of our day-to-day lives. Technology, in a way, is the result of hyper attention. It isn't the technology that influences us; it's us that influences the technology.

### References

Backer, P. R. (n.d.). *The cause of the industrial revolution.* Retrieved October 28, 2015, from http://www.engr.sjsu.edu/pabacker/causeIR .htm

Hayles, N. K. (2007). Hyper and deep attention: The generational divide in cognitive modes. *Profession*, 187-199.

National Women's History Museum. (2007). *Clandestine women: Spies in American history.* Retrieved from http://www.nwhm.org/online--exhibits/spies/12.htm

Walsh, K. T. (2010, March 12). The 1960s: A decade of change for women. *U.S. News & World Report.* Retrieved from http://www .usnews.com/news

25

## MindTap®

Practice documentation skills that you have learned in this chapter and receive feedback.

## In this chapter, you will learn to

1. Identify five stylistic strategies that are integral to effective academic writing.

2. Analyze the style strategies of various academic writing samples.

3. Apply the five stylistic strategies to your own writing.

4. Explain four basic principles of academic inquiry.

5. Understand and apply the three characteristics of effective paragraphs.

## MindTap®

Understand the goals of the chapter and complete a warm-up activity.

# Composing with Style  26

**BY THE TIME** they enter college, most students have developed the ability to write grammatically correct sentences, use proper punctuation, form verb tenses appropriately, spell correctly, and so on. Of course, *all* students, even the most successful writers, make mistakes and sometimes have trouble remembering certain rules of formal writing (such as when to use a semi-colon rather than a comma). But for the vast majority of students, learning to write effectively in college is not about learning these "basics." For most students, the main challenge is learning to write effectively in an appropriate academic style and conveying complex ideas and information clearly in the kind of authoritative voice that college instructors expect—in other words, learning to write like a scholar.

Chapter 19 offers guidance for working effectively with complex ideas and information in your academic writing assignments. This chapter will help you develop an effective academic writing style by focusing on stylistic strategies necessary for writing the kind of prose expected in academic settings. These strategies correspond to the Ten Core Concepts described in Chapter 2. For example, developing an effective and appropriate voice in academic writing (Core Concept #9) requires understanding and applying the stylistic conventions of academic writing, which are explained in this chapter. Similarly, achieving your rhetorical purpose (Core Concept #2) requires being able to write clear, appropriate prose that conveys your ideas effectively to your intended audience. If you can't do these tasks well, your writing is likely to be less effective, no matter how compelling your point or how sound your ideas.

Although learning to write effective academic prose encompasses many skills, you can learn to develop an appropriate academic writing style by focusing on **five essential stylistic strategies:**

- developing an academic writing style
- writing effective paragraphs
- framing
- introducing
- making transitions

The more effectively you apply these skills, the more you are likely to learn from your writing—and the better your writing is likely to be.

## Developing an Academic Writing Style

A few years ago my son, who was a first-year college student at the time, complained to me about a comment a professor had written on his paper in a political science class. The assignment required students to use a certain theory to analyze a recent political event. My son was keenly interested in the topic, had read the assigned readings carefully, and understood the theory, but he had very little experience writing about such specialized topics. He tried his best to write prose that sounded like the scholarly articles he had been assigned to read. In other words, he tried to write like a scholar of political science. He worked hard on the paper and was confident that his analysis was sound. His professor agreed but nevertheless criticized the paper, calling it a parody of bad academic writing. In the professor's view, there was nothing wrong with the analysis my son had written; the problem was with *how* it had been written.

In trying to write like a scholar, my son was using unfamiliar language in a style he had not yet mastered. The professor's comment that the paper sounded like a parody of bad academic writing was unfortunate, but in a sense it was accurate. My son had not yet developed the skills a writer needs to write in an appropriate academic style about such a sophisticated topic. So it was inevitable that he would make some mistakes. After all, like just about every new college student, he was on unfamiliar terrain. Although he knew the material, he didn't have the experience and the tools to convey that material effectively in appropriate academic style.

## Learning to Write Like a Scholar

My son was like a novice skier trying to descend an expert slope for the first time: The novice knows how to ski but his skills are not developed enough to tackle the more challenging slopes. So although he can descend an easy slope with smooth, controlled turns, on the expert slope his turns are sloppy, he loses control now and again, and he looks like a complete beginner. My son was venturing onto the expert slopes of a challenging kind of academic analytical writing without the experience and skill to negotiate that slope smoothly; as a result, his prose was full of sloppy turns and slightly out-of-control sentences.

This story underscores three important lessons for effective academic writing:

- *How* **you write affects** *what* **you write.** To complete most academic writing tasks successfully requires more than having something relevant to say (Core Concept #4); it also requires saying it well. In academic writing, that means adopting an appropriate style and presenting your ideas in a way that meets the expectations of your audience. Academic audiences expect writers to know how to summarize relevant information and other points of view, to quote properly from appropriate sources, to synthesize ideas clearly, to write coherent paragraphs about complicated subject matter, and to place their arguments or analyses in the context of the larger academic subject within which they are writing.

- **Good writing isn't necessarily always good writing.** Core Concept #2 ("Good writing fits the context") reminds us that what counts as good writing always depends upon the rhetorical situation. In college-level academic writing, students must learn to fit into the ongoing conversations about the subjects that are the focus of the academic disciplines they are studying (see "Understanding Academic Writing as Conversation" in Chapter 19). Sociologists examine how human societies function. Anthropologists explore culture. Biologists describe the living world. Scholars and researchers in every field engage in continuous conversations about specialized topics by reporting the results of their studies, proposing hypotheses, debating conclusions, and raising questions. This is the nature of academic discourse, and students must eventually learn to write in ways that enable them to become part of that discourse. Good academic writing is writing that fits into the relevant academic conversation.

■ **Practice might make perfect, but it also means making mistakes.** My son was trying to write like a scholar without yet having mastered the skills of scholarly writing. So he made mistakes. His professor did not recognize that those mistakes were actually a sign of growth. My son was stretching just beyond his ability as a writer, and ultimately he learned from those mistakes, in the process gaining valuable experience and insight into academic writing. Like the novice skier trying to ski down the expert slope, my son was advancing his skills by challenging himself to go beyond his present level of ability. Through practice, he eventually acquired those skills and was able to write effective academic prose—but not without mistakes. Just like that skier, when you try to do something that is beyond your skill level, you'll stumble and fall, but by practicing you will eventually master the necessary skills and avoid those early mistakes. You'll make it down the expert slope smoothly. So expect some stumbling as you develop the specialized skills described in this chapter. If you struggle, it doesn't mean you're a "bad" writer; it just means you haven't yet developed the specialized skills needed to write effective academic prose.

As you work on your writing assignments, these lessons will help you keep your mistakes in perspective, enable you to understand and build on your strengths, and identify aspects of your writing that need improvement.

# Principles of Academic Inquiry

The conventions of academic writing reflect the fact that writing is central to academic inquiry. Developing an effective academic writing style is partly a matter of learning to use language in a way that reflects **four basic principles of academic inquiry.**

### Qualify Your Statements

Academic writers must back up what they say (Core Concept #5). Often, that means avoiding unsupported generalizations and qualifying your statements. For example, in casual conversation or informal writing, it's acceptable to say something like this:

> Drivers just don't pay attention to speed limits.

In academic writing, which values accuracy and validity, such statements usually need to be qualified, depending on the rhetorical context:

> Drivers *often seem to* ignore speed limits.

> *Many* drivers ignore speed limits.

> Studies show that a *most* drivers *sometimes* exceed speed limits.

The italicized words in these examples make the statements "more true." If you can't support a statement with evidence, then qualify it so that it is valid.

## Be Specific

Academic audiences value specificity, and good writers avoid vagueness. Here's an example of a vague statement from a student essay:

> In order for education to work, things need to change.

Such a statement seems reasonable enough, but it doesn't quite hold up under scrutiny. What does it mean to say that education must "work"? What "things" must change? And what kinds of "changes" are necessary? Often, vague terms like *things* are a sign that a statement itself might be vague. Even if this statement appears in a longer paragraph explaining those "things" and "changes," such a statement is weak by the common standards of academic writing. We might revise it as follows:

> If schools are to solve the problems that prevent students from obtaining a sound education, both administrative and curricular reforms should be implemented.

Notice that in this statement the writer avoids vague terms and tries to be more specific about what it means for schools to "work." Specificity isn't always possible or even desirable, but often vagueness can weaken your writing. (By the way, you'll notice that the revised sentence employs the passive voice, which many teachers discourage. See Focus: "Active vs. Passive Voice" on page 808.)

These examples illustrate that strong academic writing is partly a result of careful word choice, which should reflect your effort to make valid, accurate, and clear statements.

## Give Credit

Giving credit in academic writing is not just a matter of citing sources properly (which is discussed in Chapters 23–25); it is also a matter of using appropriate language to signal to readers that you are using source material or referring to someone else's ideas. For example, here's a student referring to a source in a paper about education reform:

> The article states that money spent on schools can do little to improve educational outcomes.

Technically, there is nothing wrong with this sentence, but it is an awkward way of introducing information or referring to material taken from a source. For one thing, it isn't the article but the author who makes a statement. That might seem to be a minor point, but minor revisions can make this sentence stronger by bringing it into line with the conventions of academic prose:

> The author claims that money spent on schools can do little to improve educational outcomes.

> According to this author, money spent on schools can do little to improve educational outcomes.

These versions make it clear that the assertion being made is attributed to the author of the source, not to the writer of this sentence; they also sound as though the writer is in better command of the source material, which conveys a sense of authority.

In general, unless the assertion is yours, credit the author or source for the assertion. Because academic writing is essentially a matter of participating in ongoing conversations, crediting a source for a statement not only indicates who deserves credit for the statement but also helps place your own writing in the context of the larger academic conversation in which you are participating. It shows that you are part of that conversation.

## Use Specialized Terminology Judiciously

A common complaint about academic writing is that it is full of jargon. The complaint assumes that jargon is bad; however, when used properly, jargon—or specialized terminology—is not only useful but essential. All academic fields have specialized terminology that refers to important ideas and concepts within those fields. In education, for example, *pedagogy* refers to a teacher's instructional approach and the beliefs about teaching, learning, and knowing that inform that approach. It would be difficult to convey that concept efficiently and clearly without that term. Equivalent terms using common language, such as *instructional approach*, don't quite capture the complexity of the concept. *Pedagogy* might sound like jargon, but it is an efficient term that conveys important ideas to readers and reflects the writer's familiarity with the field. The challenge for student writers is to become familiar enough with such terminology so that it becomes a tool for effective writing rather than a distraction for the reader.

In the following passage, for example, the writer discusses the increasing socio-economic inequality in higher education:

> At the same time that family income has become more predictive of children's academic achievement, so has educational attainment become more predictive of adults' earnings. The combination of these trends creates a feedback mechanism that may decrease intergenerational mobility. As children from higher socio-economic strata achieve greater academic success, and those who succeed academically are more likely to have higher incomes, higher education contributes to an even more unequal and economically polarized society.

This passage contains terms that are widely used in academic discussions about poverty, education, and education reform: for example, *academic achievement* and *intergenerational mobility*. These terms have specialized meaning in fields like sociology, education, political science, and public policy and therefore can be useful for writers in those fields. Not only do these terms convey important ideas efficiently to a reader, but they also signal that the writer is knowledgeable about the subject. At the same time, such terminology can make a passage dense and difficult to follow. Some careful revisions (which are highlighted in the passage below) to reduce wordiness can make the same passage clearer without eliminating necessary terms:

> At the same time that family income has become more predictive of children's academic achievement, so has educational attainment become more predictive of adults' earnings. The combination of these trends could decrease intergenerational mobility. As the children of the rich do better in school, and those who do better in school are more likely to become rich, we risk producing an even more unequal and economically polarized society.

Source: Adapted from Edsall, Thomas. "The Reproduction of Privilege." *The New York Times*, 12 Mar. 2012, campaignstops.blogs.nytimes.com/2012/03/12/the-reproduction-of-privilege/?_r=0.

In this revised version, some specialized terms (e.g., "higher socio-economic strata," "greater academic success") are replaced with more common language ("rich," "do better in school"), but key terms (*academic achievement* and *intergenerational mobility*) are preserved. Replacing those key terms with common language would result in a lengthy passage that might not be clearer.

For example, *intergenerational mobility* refers to the process by which children do better economically than their parents; in other words, children attain a higher socio-economic status than their parents. Explaining that idea in a sentence or two would unnecessarily lengthen the passage. If this passage were intended for a general audience, then it might be necessary to define the term or replace it entirely; for an academic audience, however, the term enables the writer to keep the passage shorter while at the same time making an important point. It also suggests that the writer is part of the ongoing academic conversation about this topic.

The rule of thumb is to use language that communicates your ideas clearly to your intended audience:

- Use appropriate terminology to communicate specialized ideas, but make sure you understand the terminology.
- Replace confusing terms or unnecessary jargon with common words if you can do so without undermining your point or changing the meaning of the passage.

Following these guidelines will help you write prose that is both clear and sophisticated.

## FOCUS  ACTIVE VS. PASSIVE VOICE

Popular writing guides, pundits, and many English teachers warn students to avoid the passive voice and use active voice in writing. The prevailing belief is that using the active voice strengthens your prose, whereas the passive voice weakens your writing by making it unnecessarily wordy and vague. Like most such "rules," that one is misleading. Remember Core Concept #2: "Good writing fits the context." Although it might be true that in many contexts the active voice makes for better writing, the passive voice is not only acceptable but also essential in academic writing. In some cases, the passive voice is actually preferable because it can change the focus of a statement to emphasize a point or idea. To illustrate, let's return to the example on page 806:

> If schools are to solve the problems that prevent students from obtaining a sound education, both administrative and curricular reforms should be implemented.

The main point of this sentence is that school reform is needed. Notice that in the main clause ("both administrative and curricular reforms should be implemented"), the use of the passive voice ("should be implemented") places the emphasis on *reforms* (which is the subject of the clause). Revising the sentence to place the main clause in the active voice changes that emphasis. Here's how that sentence might look in the active voice:

> If schools are to solve the problems that prevent students from obtaining a sound education, they should implement both administrative and curricular reforms.

Is this version clearer, more succinct, or more valid than the original sentence? Not necessarily. Notice that in the revised version the subject of the main clause is now "they" (presumably referring back to "schools"), which shifts the emphasis of the statement slightly. In this case, the passive voice enables the writer to keep the emphasis on the need for school reform—which is the main point of the sentence—not on *who* will accomplish the reform—which is an important and related topic but not the focus here. So the use of passive voice in this example does not weaken the writing; rather, it allows the writer to maintain the appropriate focus. If the writer's focus happened to be on a specific entity responsible for education reform, the active voice might be more appropriate. For example, let's assume that the writer was discussing reforms that only elected politicians could enact. In that case, the subject would be clear and the active voice more appropriate:

> If schools are to solve the problems that prevent students from obtaining a sound education, elected officials should undertake several reforms.

The passive voice should be used judiciously. Excessive or inappropriate use of the passive voice can weaken your writing. Often, active voice results in more concise prose, but as this example illustrates, writers can use the passive voice as an important tool for emphasis and clarity.

---

**EXERCISE 26A  PRACTICING ACADEMIC STYLE**

Using the advice for academic writing style in this section, revise the following statements so that they are clearer and appropriately supported or qualified. For each item, imagine an appropriate rhetorical context and indicate how that context would shape your revisions. (For example, for item (a) you might imagine that statement in an argument supporting gun control for a criminal justice course.)

1. We need better gun laws to make our communities safer. Otherwise, we'll just have more and more violence.
2. Poverty-stricken Americans of low socio-economic status will be adversely affected by legislative actions that facilitate the attainment of citizenship by undocumented residents.
3. Smartphones are convenient but they are making everyone dumber because people rely on them rather than on their own minds.

**26**

---

# Writing Paragraphs

By the time they enter college, most students have had many hours of instruction in writing correct sentences and paragraphs. Yet new college students often struggle to write effective paragraphs that convey complex ideas clearly and coherently. Part of the problem is that the subject matter in college writing is often new and sometimes challenging, and students have to learn how to write clearly about unfamiliar ideas, concepts, and information. But students can also improve their writing by learning how to create more effective paragraphs, no matter what subject they are writing about.

Effective paragraphs in academic writing have **three key characteristics**. They are

- **Well developed.** A paragraph should cover its topic sufficiently. Often, that means elaborating on key points, ideas, or facts and including examples. Under-developed paragraphs tend to be superficial and suggest that the writer has not explored the topic in sufficient depth.

- **Coherent.** Coherence refers to the extent to which the paragraph retains a focus on a main idea or point. In a coherent paragraph, all the sentences relate clearly to one another and communicate ideas or information relevant to the main point. Usually, but not always, a strong paragraph also has a clear topic sentence that states the main point and establishes the focus of the paragraph.

- **Cohesive.** Cohesion means that the statements, ideas, and information in a paragraph are explicitly linked together. To a great extent, cohesion is a function of the use of specific words and phrases that indicate to a reader that statements are connected: *similarly, by contrast, also, therefore, on the other hand, moreover, in addition*, and so on. Writers also achieve cohesion by repeating key words or phrases.

## Writing Well-Developed Paragraphs

The key to writing a well-developed paragraph is making sure the topic of the paragraph is sufficiently explained or examined and the main point adequately supported. When necessary, elaborating on a point and illustrating it with examples also contributes to paragraph development. Here's an example of an under-developed paragraph from an essay about the relationship between poverty and educational achievement:

> The culture of poverty is defined by Paul Gorski as "the idea that poor people share more or less monolithic and predictable beliefs, values and behavior" (32). This is not true. Later studies show that a culture of poverty does not exist. This belief was constructed from data collected in the early 1960's showing that certain behaviors, such as increased violence and failure to foresee or plan for the future, were common among poor people. The original study portrayed stereotypes of poor students, not a culture of poverty.

In this paragraph the student tries to explain the idea of "the culture of poverty," relying on a source for information about the origins of that idea and how it has been interpreted. The author of that source, Paul Gorski, argues that the idea of a culture of poverty is actually a misunderstanding of a particular study of poverty; he cites subsequent studies that invalidate the whole idea of a culture of poverty. The student attempts to communicate Gorski's position. However, although the student defines the term *culture of poverty*, the complexity of that idea and the problems associated with it are not sufficiently explained. The student writes that the idea "is not true" and that studies show it "does not exist," but the lack of explanation makes it difficult for readers to understand the problems with the original study and how the data were interpreted. In short, the paragraph is insufficiently developed to communicate this complicated information.

In situations like this one, in which the writer is trying to convey complex ideas and information in a single paragraph, the solution is to elaborate on key ideas to make sure they are explained sufficiently to the reader. In this case, the student must provide more information about the origins of the idea of the culture of poverty, how it was misinterpreted, and how it was invalidated:

> The culture of poverty, according to Paul Gorski, is "the idea that poor people share more or less monolithic and predictable beliefs, values and behavior" (32). The idea emerged

from a 1961 book by Oscar Lewis that reported on ethnographic studies of several small poor Mexican communities. Lewis's data indicated that those communities shared fifty attributes, such as frequent violence and a failure to plan for the future. From this small sample, he concluded that all poor communities share these attributes, which reflect a culture of poverty. The idea that "people in poverty share a persistent and observable 'culture'" (32–33) became popular among scholars trying to understand poverty. However, numerous later studies revealed great differences among poor communities and called the very idea of a culture of poverty into question. According to Gorski, these subsequent studies make it clear that "there is no such thing as a culture of poverty" (33). Gorski concludes that "the culture of poverty concept is constructed from a collection of smaller stereotypes which, however false, seem to have crept into mainstream thinking as unquestioned fact" (33).

In this developed version, the writer elaborates on specific points, such as how Lewis arrived at the idea of a culture of poverty and how the idea was subsequently challenged. The writer also uses quotations from the source text to provide additional information about this topic, which makes it much easier for a reader to grasp the main idea and supporting points.

Longer is not always better, of course, but when you are writing about complex ideas in academic contexts, under-developed paragraphs can result in superficial and sometimes confusing prose.

## Achieving Coherence

In effective academic writing, paragraphs are not only sufficiently developed but also clearly focused and organized. In a coherent paragraph:

26

- The writer is in control of the subject matter and takes the reader deliberately from beginning to end.
- All the sentences contain relevant information.
- The discussion follows a clear and logical progression.

Often there is a topic sentence, but even without one, the main point of the paragraph is clear.

Students sometimes lose control of a paragraph when they are writing about complicated, abstract, or unfamiliar ideas and aren't sure what information to include or how to organize that information. In the following example, a student tries to explain what he believes is a basic principle of social life: competition. However, he struggles to make the main point of the paragraph clear and to present his ideas about competition in an orderly way:

Our society is based on competition. It is natural for all of us to compete. Probably cheating is caused by our desire to succeed in competition. The first place we experience competition is at home when we cry to be held by our parents. We compete with their busy schedules to get their attention. Our next major competition is school, where we are all compared with other students. Until this time we only know that the time we spend with our parents is limited, but if we exert ourselves we get what we want. Being compared with other students is when we first realize that we compete for others' time and compliments. As children we only know that we need to get someone's attention to achieve what we need. We find that most competition is based upon being recognized.

Although the paragraph has a general focus on competition, the main idea seems to shift. The opening sentence suggests that the paragraph is about the central role competition plays in human society, but the final sentence suggests a somewhat narrower point: that competition arises from the need to be recognized. In addition, the third sentence is irrelevant to the main point about competition, and the paragraph isn't well organized.

To address these problems, the first task is to identify the main point of the paragraph. Stating that point in a topic sentence can help, but the topic sentence does not have to be at the beginning of the paragraph. Let's assume that the writer wants to make the point that competition arises from the human need to be recognized. That can serve as a topic sentence. We want to keep the focus of the paragraph on that main point. We also want to order the sentences so that the reader can follow the discussion easily from one supporting point to the next. Here's a revised version:

> Our society is based on competition, and it is natural for all of us to compete. But why? Competition, it seems, arises from a basic human need to be recognized. We first experience competition very early in our lives when we cry to be held by our parents, actually competing with their busy schedules for their attention. For the first years of our lives, we learn that the time we spend with our parents is precious but limited, so we exert ourselves to get the attention we need. Our next major competition occurs in school, where we are compared with other students. We are still seeking the time and attention of others, but now we realize that we must compete with other students to be recognized. Every stage of our lives is characterized by different versions of this competition to fulfill our basic need for attention and recognition.

In this version, much of the original language is retained, but the focus on the main idea has been sharpened by adding a clear topic sentence ("Competition, it seems, arises from a basic human need to be recognized"), eliminating unnecessary material (the sentence about cheating), rewriting some sentences so that they relate more clearly to the topic sentence, and reorganizing the paragraph. The paragraph is now more coherent, which makes its main point more evident to the reader.

Coherence can be difficult to achieve, but following these three steps can help make your paragraphs more coherent and effective:

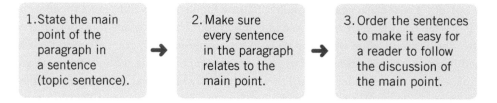

1. State the main point of the paragraph in a sentence (topic sentence).

2. Make sure every sentence in the paragraph relates to the main point.

3. Order the sentences to make it easy for a reader to follow the discussion of the main point.

# Achieving Cohesion

Cohesion refers to the extent to which statements, ideas, and information in a paragraph are related and explicitly connected to one another. In concrete terms, cohesion is a measure of how well the individual sentences in a paragraph are linked together so that the reader can see the relationship between the ideas or information in one sentence to those in another sentence. If a writer does not make those relationships clear, the paragraph becomes harder for a reader to follow. Even a coherent paragraph (that is, one in which all the sentences relate clearly to the main topic of the paragraph) can lack cohesion. Fortunately, **cohesion can usually be achieved in two main ways:**

- by the strategic use of certain "linking" words and phrases (e.g., *also, similarly, by contrast, in addition, then, therefore*, etc.); and
- by the repetition of key words and phrases.

Here's a paragraph that is coherent but not cohesive. Like the example in the section on developing a paragraph (page 810), this example also addresses the idea of "the culture of poverty" and draws on the same source. In this case, the paragraph retains its focus on the main topic, which is Paul Gorski's explanation of the concept of the culture of poverty, but the paragraphs lacks cohesion that would help a reader follow the writer's discussion more easily:

In "The Myth of the 'Culture of Poverty'" (2008), Paul Gorski examines the concept of the "culture of poverty" and how it relates to education. Numerous case studies and academic articles as well as first-hand experience are discussed. Research shows that the culture of poverty doesn't exist. Many teachers have a preconceived notion that a culture of poverty is responsible for creating unmotivated students and uninvolved parents. He goes into great detail about the bias of educators, which leads them to promote a "culture of classism" that results in an unequal education for those living in poverty. Gorski suggests several ways that teachers can better address the needs of poverty-stricken students and avoid the problems associated with bias in education.

Compare this paragraph with the following one, which has been revised to make it more cohesive. The key revisions are highlighted. Orange highlighting indicates the repetition of key words or phrases; blue highlighting indicates a linking word or phrase.

In "The Myth of the 'Culture of Poverty'" (2008), Paul Gorski examines the concept of the "culture of poverty" and how it relates to education. Gorski draws upon numerous case studies and academic articles as well as the first-hand experience of a classroom teacher to explain the origins and interpretations of this concept. In addition, he cites research to show that the culture of poverty doesn't exist. Gorski points out that many teachers have a preconceived notion that this "culture of poverty" is responsible for creating unmotivated students and uninvolved parents (2). He carefully examines this bias, which, he argues, leads educators to promote a "culture of classism" that results in an unequal education for those living in poverty (3). Gorski also suggests several ways that teachers can better address the needs of poverty stricken students and avoid this "culture of classism" and its damaging effects on poor children.

26

Notice how simple linking words (e.g., *also*, *this*) and careful repetition of key phrases (e.g., "culture of poverty") create connections among the sentences and enable the reader to follow the discussion more easily. Students sometimes mistakenly believe that repeating words and phrases is a mark of poor writing, but as this example illustrates, strategic repetition actually makes the passage more cohesive and therefore strengthens the writing.

---

**EXERCISE 26B   WRITING EFFECTIVE PARAGRAPHS**

Using the advice in this section, revise the following paragraph to make it more coherent and cohesive. Also, revise the sentences so that they reflect a more effective academic prose style:

> Religion is a man-made device that has allowed people to find a meaning in life. Whether it is monotheism or polytheism, or whether it is mixes of various beliefs regarding a creator, idols, or an overall power, people revert to some form of belief for solace. Spiritualism, which is not the same as religious faith, is on the rise. Studies routinely show that Americans are much more religious than most other nations. As religions grow, cultural aspects come into play, and it is the spiritual and physical actions that tend to dictate societal and personal beliefs. Some people want to hold onto traditional values. Many traditional values and actions have faded in religions, especially in mainstream, secular society. Judaism, among other religions, has become secularized, except for some sects. The same is true of many Christian denominations.

---

# Framing

You might have heard an instructor comment about "framing" an argument, analysis, or discussion:

> *Be sure to frame your argument clearly.*

> *Frame your analysis of the new health care law in terms of the ongoing debates about the role of government in citizens' lives.*

> *Try to frame your discussion in a way that makes it relevant for your readers.*

In these statements, "framing" means placing your project in a context that gives it relevance or significance for your audience. It is a technique for putting into practice Core Concept #2: "Good writing fits the context." All writing must fit into a specific rhetorical situation that includes an intended audience and a context for communicating with that audience. It is part of a writer's task to show his or her audience why the topic at hand is important and meaningful. "Framing" is a term used to describe a technique for doing that.

For example, in the following passage, the authors—three biologists—frame their argument about "eusociality" in terms of an ongoing debate in their field:

> For most of the past half century, much of sociobiological theory has focused on the phenomenon called eusociality, where adult members are divided into reproductive and (partially) non-reproductive castes and the latter care for the young. How can genetically prescribed selfless behaviour arise by natural selection, which is seemingly

its antithesis? This problem has vexed biologists since Darwin, who in *The Origin of Species* declared the paradox—in particular displayed by ants—to be the most important challenge to his theory. The solution offered by the master naturalist was to regard the sterile worker caste as a "well-flavoured vegetable," and the queen as the plant that produced it. Thus, he said, the whole colony is the unit of selection.

Modern students of collateral altruism have followed Darwin in continuing to focus on ants, honeybees and other eusocial insects, because the colonies of most of their species are divided unambiguously into different castes. Moreover, eusociality is not a marginal phenomenon in the living world. The biomass of ants alone composes more than half that of all insects and exceeds that of all terrestrial nonhuman vertebrates combined. Humans, which can be loosely characterized as eusocial, are dominant among the land vertebrates. The "superorganisms" emerging from eusociality are often bizarre in their constitution, and represent a distinct level of biological organization.

Source: Nowak, Martin A., et al. "The Evolution of Eusociality." *Nature*, vol. 466, no. 26, Aug. 2010, p. 1057.

In this passage, the authors place their specific argument in the context of a problem that evolutionary biologists have long confronted in their efforts to test Darwin's theories—a problem that they state as a question: "How can genetically prescribed selfless behaviour arise by natural selection, which is seemingly its antithesis?" In this way, the authors show how their argument (which is captured in their statement in the second paragraph that "eusociality is not a marginal phenomenon in the living world") is relevant to biologists by connecting it to a recognized problem in the field—in other words, by *framing* it in terms of that recognized problem.

Here's another example, this one from a scholarly article reporting on a study of college students' use of digital media. In this passage, the author cites evidence of the increasingly important role that social media play in the lives of young Americans:

According to the Pew Internet and American Life Project, as of August 2011, 83% of 18–29 year-olds used a social network site (Madden, 2012). Their interactions on these sites were also purposeful, as Pew reports that this age group is most concerned with online identity management: 71% of them have changed the privacy settings on the sites they use (Lenhart, Purcell, Smith, & Zickuhr, 2010). Living a "literate life in the information age" (Selfe & Hawisher, 2004) increasingly means learning to navigate these spaces, managing one's identity and online data, and considering complex issues of privacy and representation. Using ethnographic case study data, this article examines how one undergraduate student integrated his use of social network sites into his everyday literacy practices to represent his identity. I approached this case study with three research questions: 1) How does this writer integrate social network sites into his everyday literacy practices? 2) How does this writer use those literacy practices to represent his identity for multiple audience groups on social network sites? 3) How does this writer negotiate site interfaces to represent his identity and communicate with others?

Source: Buck, Amber. "Examining Digital Literacy Practices on Social Network Sites." *Research in the Teaching of English*, vol. 47, no. 1, Aug. 2012, p. 10.

26

Here the author frames her own case study of a college student in terms of larger social and technological developments in contemporary society—specifically, the growing importance of social media and the emergence of practices that people of a certain age-group engage in to manage their online identities. She cites other research (from the Pew Center and by other scholars—in this case, Selfe and Hawisher) to establish the importance of social media and place her own study in the context of these important developments.

Both these examples illustrate how authors use framing not only to introduce readers to the subject matter but also to identify why their arguments or analyses are relevant. By framing their discussions, these authors explicitly connect their arguments or analyses to larger debates or conversations that matter to their readers and show how their own arguments or analyses fit into those conversations.

Framing typically happens in the introduction to a piece, but a writer might see a need to frame a segment of a piece of writing, especially in a longer essay or report that might contain several sections. For instance, in an analysis of the economic impact of a proposed tax on gasoline, the writer might include a section presenting a specific kind of cost-benefit analysis using a new economic model. In such a case, the writer might frame that section in the context of, say, an ongoing debate about whether certain kinds of taxes hurt the average consumer or benefit the economy as a whole.

When framing an argument, analysis, or discussion, use these questions to guide you:

- What makes your argument, analysis, or discussion relevant to your intended audience? Why would my audience be interested in this topic?
- To which larger debates, conversations, or arguments is your topic related? How might you connect your topic to those larger debates, conversations, or arguments?
- What makes your topic important or relevant now? How can you show your readers that your topic is important and timely?

These questions can make it easier for you to frame your discussion in a way that makes it relevant for your readers and enables them to place it in a larger context.

---

### EXERCISE 26C  PRACTICING FRAMING

1. Imagine an argument you might make about a current issue that interests you. Using the bulleted list of questions on this page, describe briefly how you would frame this argument. In your answer, identify your intended audience and a purpose for your argument.

2. Using your answer for Question #1, reframe your argument for a different audience.

3. In a brief paragraph, describe how the authors of the following passage frame their research in this introduction to their series of studies about "Millennials" (that is, people born between 1981 and 2000):

   Generations, like people, have personalities. Their collective identities typically begin to reveal themselves when their oldest members move into their teens and twenties and begin to act upon their values, attitudes and worldviews.

America's newest generation, the Millennials, is in the middle of this coming-of-age phase of its life cycle. Its oldest members are approaching age 30; its youngest are approaching adolescence. Who are they? How are they different from—and similar to—their parents? How is their moment in history shaping them? And how might they, in turn, reshape America in the decades ahead? The Pew Research Center will try to answer these questions through a yearlong series of original reports that explore the behaviors, values and opinions of today's teens and twenty-somethings.

Source: Keeter, Scott, and Paul Taylor. "The Millennials." *Pew Research Center*, 10 Dec. 2009, www.pewresearch.org/2009/12/10/the-millennials/.

# Introductions

An introduction is a kind of roadmap to your paper: It tells your readers where you plan to go and why. In most forms of academic writing, the introduction not only presents the topic of the paper but also conveys a sense of why the topic is relevant and what the writer will say about it.

Below are four examples of introductions, each illustrating a common approach to introductions. The first three examples are from student essays: one from a paper written for an economics course, the second from a course on the history of modern China, and the third from an introductory psychology course. The fourth example is from an article by Deborah Tannen, a professor of linguistics at Georgetown University. Notice that, regardless of the approach, each introduction clearly establishes the focus of the paper and conveys a sense of the writer's main idea. Notice, too, how each introduction establishes the tone and style of the paper.

## Getting Right to the Point

One of the most common mistakes students make when introducing an essay is saying too much. Often, the most effective introductions are those that get right to the point and move the reader quickly into the main body of the paper. Here's an example:

### The Legalization of Prostitution

Prostitution is the "contractual barter of sex favors, usually sexual intercourse, for monetary considerations without any emotional attachment between the partners" (Grauerhold & Koralewski, 1991). Whenever this topic is mentioned, people usually shy away from it, because they are thinking of the actions involved in this profession. The purpose of this paper, however, is not to talk about these services, but to discuss the social, economic and legal issues behind prostitution.

Source: "Comments on an Economic Analysis Paper." *WAC Student Resources*, Coe Writing Center, 2001, www.public.coe.edu/wac/legalization.htm.

26

This brief introduction quickly establishes the focus and main purpose of the paper. It also places the topic in the context of general perceptions of prostitution and clarifies that the writer will be examining that topic from a different angle. This is a good example of a writer efficiently introducing a topic. As this writer demonstrates, sometimes the best approach is the one that uses the fewest words.

## Focusing on Context

This next example, from a history paper about the impact of Mao Zedong on modern China, illustrates how an academic writer can use techniques from narrative writing to introduce a topic and at the same time establish a context for the topic. This introduction begins with a brief description of the birthplace of Mao Zedong as a way to dramatize the main point of the paper that Mao "remains the central, dominant figure in Chinese political culture today." The second paragraph provides background information so that the reader can better appreciate Mao's significance to modern China, while the third paragraph establishes the focus of the paper, which examines Mao's enduring legacy in contemporary China.

### Mao More Than Ever

Shaoshan is a small village found in a valley of the Hunan province, where, a little over a century ago, Mao Zedong was born. The first thing heard in Shaoshan is the music, and the music is inescapable. Suspended from posts towering over Mao's childhood home are loudspeakers from which the same tune is emitted over and over, a hit of the Cultural Revolution titled "We Love You, Mao."

The Chinese people were faced with an incredibly difficult situation in 1976 following the death of Mao Zedong. What was China to do now that the man whom millions accepted as the leader of their country's rebirth to greatness has passed away? China was in mourning within moments of the announcement. Although Mao rarely had been seen in public during the five years preceding his death, he was nevertheless the only leader that China had known since the Communist armies swept triumphantly into Peking and proclaimed the People's Republic twenty-seven years earlier. He was not only the originator of China's socialist revolution but its guide, its teacher, and its prophet.

Common sense foretold of the impossibility of erasing Communism and replacing Chairman Mao. He departed the world with his succession and China's future uncertain. With his death, historians and reporters around the world offered predictions of what was to become of China. They saw an instant end to Maoist theory. Through careful examination of Chinese life both under and after Mao, it is clear that the critics of 1976 were naïve in their prophecies and that Mao Zedong still remains the central, dominant figure in Chinese political culture today.

Source: "Comments on an Economic Analysis Paper." *WAC Student Resources*, Coe Writing Center, 2001, www.public.coe.edu/wac/Nordmann.htm.

In this example, the writer establishes the context by "telling the story" of Mao's enduring influence on China. This approach is common in the Humanities (history, literature, etc.).

## Using a Reference Point

Another common approach to introductions in academic writing is to use an established idea, point of view, development, text, or study as a reference point for the topic of the paper. In this example from a paper written for a psychology course, the writers begin by referring to a study of the anxiety people experience while waiting in hospital waiting rooms.

### Sitting Comfort: The Impact of Different Chairs on Anxiety

Kutash and Northrop (2007) studied the comfort of family members in the ICU waiting room. They found that no matter the situation, waiting rooms are stressful for the patients and their families, and it is the nursing staff's job to comfort both. From this emotional distress many family members judged the waiting room furniture as "uncomfortable" and only talked about it in a negative context. From this study we have learned that there is a direct relationship between a person's emotional state and how that person perceives the physical state he or she is in, such as sitting in a chair. Is this relationship true in reverse as well? Can the way a person perceives his or her present physical state (such as sitting in a chair) affect his or her emotional state? This is the question that the present study sought to answer.

Source: Baker, Jenna, et al. "Sitting Comfort: The Impact of Different Chairs on Anxiety." *Schemata*, 2011, www.lycoming.edu/schemata/documents/Psy110GroupPaper_Final.pdf.

Here the writers cite a previously published study that raises a question that is relevant to readers interested in psychology: "Can the way a person perceives his or her present physical state (such as sitting in a chair) affect his or her emotional state?" That question clearly establishes the focus of the paper. One advantage of this approach is that the question sets up the expectation that the writer will answer the question. In this way, the writer gives the audience a clear sense of what will follow.

## Telling an Anecdote

Using an anecdote to introduce a topic, which is common in many different kinds of writing, can be effective in academic writing as well. In this example, linguist Deborah Tannen shares an anecdote to illustrate the problem she will address in her article. Notice how she uses the anecdote to establish the focus of her paper and encourage the reader to continue reading.

---

**Sex, Lies and Conversation**

I was addressing a small gathering in a suburban Virginia living room—a women's group that had invited men to join them. Throughout the evening, one man had been particularly talkative, frequently offering ideas and anecdotes, while his wife sat silently beside him on the couch. Toward the end of the evening, I commented that women frequently complain that their husbands don't talk to them. This man quickly concurred. He gestured toward his wife and said, "She's the talker in our family." The room burst into laughter; the man looked puzzled and hurt. "It's true," he explained. "When I come home from work I have nothing to say. If she didn't keep the conversation going, we'd spend the whole evening in silence."

This episode crystallizes the irony that although American men tend to talk more than women in public situations, they often talk less at home. And this pattern is wreaking havoc with marriage.

Source: Tannen, Deborah. "Sex, Lies and Conversation: Why Is It So Hard for Men and Women to Talk to Each Other?" *The Washington Post*, 24 June. 1990, p. C3.

---

Using an anecdote can be very effective, but students sometimes devote too much time to the anecdote, which can make it more difficult for readers to see where the paper might be going. If you use this approach, keep the anecdote brief and follow it up with a few sentences indicating why you're sharing the anecdote and what it means—as Tannen does in her second paragraph.

# Transitions

Earlier in this chapter we noted that in effective academic writing, paragraphs must be coherent and cohesive (see pages 811–812). The same is true for an essay or other kind of document as a whole. Your sentences can be clear and your paragraphs coherent and cohesive, but if you don't connect them to one another, your essay is likely to be more difficult for your readers to follow. The main tool for keeping your essays coherent and cohesive is the transition, which is why writing effective transitions is an essential skill in academic writing. Fortunately, it is a skill that is easy to develop.

What exactly is a *transition*? It is a device to get your reader from one paragraph—or section of your document—to the next. Transitions amount to signposts that keep your readers oriented and enable them to know where they are in your text. If you have written an effective introduction that tells your readers what to expect in your text, transitions signal to your readers when they have reached each main section.

It is important to remember that you don't need a transition between every paragraph in a document. Often, the connection between paragraphs is clear because the subject matter of one paragraph clearly relates to the subject of the next. However, transitions are usually necessary

- when there is an important shift in the focus of discussion from one paragraph to the next, or
- when moving from one main section of a document to another.

The section on "Achieving Cohesion" in paragraphs (page 813) describes two strategies for writing cohesive paragraphs that can be used to write effective transitions between paragraphs to create more cohesive essays:

- using linking words or phrases (e.g., *first, second, in addition, then, therefore, that*) and
- repeating key words and phrases.

In addition, a third important strategy is to set up your transitions by letting a reader know what to expect in a section or in your entire document. For example, your introduction might explain that your essay will address four key questions. When making the transitions between the four main sections of your essay, you can refer back to those questions to remind your reader what will follow.

The following passage from a student literacy narrative illustrates these common strategies for transitions between paragraphs. In this slightly humorous narrative about the student's experience in a college writing class, the writer explains the first few weeks of the class. Notice how the transitions help keep the narrative coherent and enable the reader to follow the story more easily. (Key transition strategies are highlighted in blue.)

**26**

1   Prior to college I had never had a true intensive course. My high school English classes consisted mostly of reading assigned literature, with the occasional plot summary, known as a book report, thrown in for variety. Never had a teacher of mine critiqued papers with anything more in mind than content, unless it was to point out some terrible structural flaw. That changed when I enrolled in college and found myself in a required course called Introduction to Academic Writing.

> The introductory paragraph establishes the focus of the narrative. The final sentence in particular conveys a sense of what will follow.

2   Introduction to Academic Writing was designed in part to eliminate from the writing of incoming students any weaknesses or idiosyncrasies that they might have brought with them from high school. Run-on sentences, incoherent paragraphs, and incorrect

> This paragraph begins with a repeated phrase (*Introduction to Academic Writing*) that clearly links it to the last sentence of the preceding paragraph. Also, the final sentence of this paragraph sets up the transition to the next paragraph.

footnoting were given particular emphasis. To address these issues, the professor assigned a great deal of work. Weekly journal assignments and multiple formal essays kept us very busy indeed. And then there were the informal in-class essays.

3    The first such essay took place on the second day of classes so that our professor could evaluate each student's strengths and weaknesses. Before accepting our work, however, she had us exchange papers with one another to see how well we could spot technical flaws. She then proceeded to walk around the room, interrupting our small-group discussions, and asked each of us what we thought of what we had read. It was not a comfortable situation, though the small size of the groups limited our embarrassment somewhat.

> The writer uses linking words (*the first such essay*) to make the transition to this paragraph. The same strategy is used for the transition to the following two paragraphs (*This unique brand; Eventually*).

4    This unique brand of academic humiliation was a palpable threat in class, which consisted mostly of students with little confidence in their writing abilities. Most of them seemed to be enrolled in majors other than English, and they viewed this remedial writing course as a painful, albeit necessary, endeavor. Our professor sympathized, I believe, and for the most part restricted her instruction to small groups and one-on-one sessions. But the in-class writing exercises were a daily hardship for the first few weeks of the semester, and I think most of us dreaded them.

5    Eventually, we were deemed ready for the first formal essay, which was a kind of expository writing in which we were to select an academic subject of interest to us and report on that subject to the rest of the class. Most of the students seemed wary of the assignment, because it was the first one in which we were given a choice of topic. All the in-class essays were on assigned topics. So the first source of anxiety was the uncertainty about which topics would be acceptable.

Although this example is narrative writing, which is less common than other forms of academic writing, its strategies for effective transitions are the same strategies used in analytical and argumentative writing. For example, here's a passage from a psychology research report published in a professional journal. The style of this passage reflects the formal writing typical of the social sciences, yet the transition strategies the authors use are the same as those in the passage from the student narrative essay above.

1    The Action-to-Action (ATA) model of Norman and Shallice (1986) has three subcompo-
nents: *action schemas, contention scheduling,
and a supervisory attentional system* (SAS).

> This paragraph establishes the expectation that the authors will discuss these three key concepts in turn, thus setting up the transitions in the following paragraphs.

2    Action schemas are specialized routines for
performing individual tasks that involve well-learned perceptual-motor
and cognitive skills. Each action schema has a current degree of activation that may be increased by either specific perceptual "trigger" stimuli
or outputs from other related schemas. When its activation exceeds a
preset threshold, an action schema may direct a person's behavior immediately and stereotypically toward performing some task. Moreover, on
occasion, multiple schemas may be activated simultaneously by different trigger stimuli, creating error-prone conflicts if they entail mutually
exclusive responses (e.g., typing on a keyboard and answering a telephone
concurrently).

3    To help resolve such conflicts, the ATA
model uses contention scheduling. It functions rapidly, automatically, and unconsciously
through a network of lateral inhibitory connections among action schemas whose response
outputs would interfere with each other (cf.
Rumelhart & Norman, 1982). Through this network, an action schema (e.g., one for keyboard
typing) that has relatively high current activation may suppress the activation of other
potentially conflicting schemas (e.g., one for
telephone answering). Contention scheduling
allows task priorities and environmental cues to be assessed on a decen-
tralized basis without explicit top-down executive control (Shallice, 1988).
However, this may not always suffice to handle conflicts when new tasks,
unusual task combinations, or complex behaviors are involved.

> In the first sentence of paragraph 3, the authors use two sets of repeated words or phrases along with a linking word (*such*). The first repeated word (*conflicts*) links this paragraph to the preceding one. The second repeated phrase (*contention scheduling*) links this paragraph to the first paragraph and reminds the reader that the discussion has moved to the second of the three main concepts mentioned in that paragraph.

4    Consequently, the ATA model also has an
SAS. The SAS guides behavior slowly, flex-
ibly, and consciously in a top-down manner. It
helps organize complex actions and perform
novel tasks by selectively activating or inhibit-
ing particular action schemas, superseding
the cruder bottom-up influences of contention
scheduling and better accommodating a person's overall capacities and
goals. For example, one might expect the SAS to play a crucial role during
switches between unfamiliar incompatible tasks that are not ordinarily
performed together.

> Like the previous paragraph, this one demonstrates two transition strategies: linking words (*Consequently* and *also*) and a key repeated term (*SAS*).

Source: Rubinstein, Joshua, et al. "Executive Control of Cognitive Processes in
Task-Switching." *Journal of Experimental Psychology: Human Perception and
Performance*, vol. 27, no. 4, 2001, p. 764.

**26**

The best time to strengthen the transitions in a piece of writing is during revision (Core Concept #8). Step #8 in Chapter 3 includes revising to improve your transitions. At that point in the process of revision, review your entire draft, focusing only on transitions. As you do so, keep the following **guidelines for effective transitions** in mind:

- **Set up your transitions.** An effective introduction will convey a sense of the main parts of your text. Your transitions from one main part to the next should refer back to the key terms you use in your introduction. In addition, you can make transitions more effective by letting the reader know what will follow in each main section. In effect, write a brief introduction to each main section—as the authors did on the previous page.

- **Use linking words or phrases.** As the examples in this section demonstrate, there are many common words and phrases that writers use to signal a transition from one point or topic to the next or from one main section of a document to the next. Here's a brief list of some of the most common linking words and phrases:

  next

  then

  also

  in addition

  similarly

  on the other hand

  therefore

  consequently

  first, second, third, . . .

  finally

  at the same time

  sometimes

- **Repeat key words or phrases.** The examples included in this section illustrate how writers repeat key words or phrases to link one paragraph to the next and to signal to readers that they are making a transition from one point to another. Select these words and phrases carefully so that you can keep your writing cohesive without being repetitive. Repetition in itself is not a weakness in writing, but unnecessarily repeated words or phrases can make your prose tedious and distracting for readers.

**PRACTICING TRANSITIONS**

Add transitions to the following passage to make it more cohesive and easier for a reader to follow:

Writing developed as a visual means of communication, and a long, continuing history of close incorporation of visual elements in many different text forms has been maintained. Illustrated manuscripts, calligraphy, and tapestries are but a few of the art forms in which distinctions between word and form are blurred to the point of meaninglessness. Olson (1992) reminds us, "The calligraphic (meaning 'words written by hand') form incorporates all the elements of a painting—line, shape, texture, unity, balance, rhythm, proportion—all within its own unique form of composition" (131).

The distance between the visual and the verbal forms of information practiced in verbal-based classrooms is highly artificial. Shuman and Wolfe (1990) draw what they see as "two pertinent conclusions": (1) Early composition that was used as a means of preserving and transmitting ideas and information through the ages took the forms of singing and drawings. (2) Early alphabetic writing was an art form that may have had less to do with composing the content of what was to be communicated than with the art form itself. "Obviously, connections between language and the arts have roots deep in antiquity" (2).

Olson explores connections between writing and art. She notes that the "Greeks chose to represent each spoken sound with a symbol (or letter). Just as speech developed out of the imitation of sound, writing developed out of the imitation of forms of real objects or beings. At the beginning of all writing stands the picture" (130).

Currently educators are interested in interdisciplinary approaches at all levels, primary through postsecondary. It is a particularly opportune moment to attempt instructional approaches that bring together art and writing.

---

Source: Hobson, Eric. "Seeing Writing in a Visual World." *ARTiculating: Teaching Writing in a Visual World*, edited by Pamela B. Childers et al., Boynton/Cook, 1998, pp. 3-4.

**26**

MindTap
Practice style strategies that you have learned in this chapter and receive feedback.

## In this chapter, you will learn to

1. Apply the three steps for avoiding style, grammar, and usage errors to sample paragraphs.

2. Apply grammatical rules for correcting common sentence-level problems to sample sentences.

3. Apply the grammatical rules for correcting common pronoun errors to sample sentences.

4. Apply the rules for effective word choice and style to sample sentences and paragraphs.

5. Apply all grammatical rules for the seven required uses of commas to sample sentences.

## MindTap®

Understand the goals of the chapter and complete a warm-up activity.

# Avoiding Common Problems in Grammar and Usage

**CORE CONCEPT #10** —"Good grammar is necessary, but it doesn't necessarily mean good writing"—underscores a reality about writing that eludes many people: "Good" writing and "correct" writing aren't necessarily the same thing. In fact, as noted elsewhere in this textbook, the complexity of writing and the importance of rhetorical context make it impossible to define "good" writing in a way that applies to all circumstances. What counts as good writing in one situation might look like poor writing in another. The same principle applies to the rules for "correct" writing. Rules that must be followed in one situation can be ignored in others. For example, using the first person ("I") is perfectly fine in an op-ed essay for the campus newspaper but usually inappropriate in a chemistry lab report.

At the same time, the widespread belief that good writing is also correct writing is powerful, both in academic settings and in American culture generally. Many people see one's grammar usage as a reflection of character, and they interpret errors in writing as signs of laziness, sloppy thinking, and even stupidity. Of course, a punctuation error doesn't mean a student is lazy or stupid, and such attitudes about "good grammar" ignore the complexity and rhetorical nature of writing. Nevertheless, these common attitudes influence how readers respond to a writer's words. What that means for you is that it is important to follow the conventions of writing so that you avoid errors that can interfere with the clarity of your prose and weaken your credibility as a writer.

As every student writer knows, rules for usage, punctuation, and spelling can be confusing and often seem capricious. One teacher might take off points for an "error" that another teacher ignores. How can student writers produce clear, effective, "correct" writing when the rules often seem so vague and relative? This chapter is intended to help answer that question.

Despite the confusing nature of many rules for grammar and usage and despite the variability with which these rules are applied by teachers and others, there are some basic principles of grammar and usage that apply to most writing situations. Moreover, in academic writing, certain conventions for style and usage are widely followed. In addition, research has identified the kinds of errors students tend to make in their writing. The advice provided in this chapter is based on prevailing conventions of academic writing as well as research on writing quality and error.

This chapter is not a comprehensive guide to grammar and usage. Instead, it explains the most important principles of grammar and usage in academic writing and offers advice for avoiding the most common errors. If you follow this advice, chances are that your writing will have fewer errors. Moreover, the strategies described in this chapter should help you grasp important rules for writing and gain a better understanding of the conventions of writing.

# Strategies for Avoiding Errors

Let's start with two important points:

- **You already know most of the important rules of grammar and usage.** If you've made it to college, you are already a competent writer, and you have a working knowledge of most of the basic rules of writing, including punctuation, spelling, verb tense, and so on. This is true even if you can't actually state the rules you apply in your writing. For example, you might know that a comma belongs in a certain place in a sentence without knowing exactly why a comma belongs there. The point is that you have a good foundation for strengthening your grasp of the conventions of writing. You can build on that foundation by identifying the rules you do know and learning the ones you should know—which this chapter will help you do.

- **You can't learn all the rules of grammar and usage.** Nobody can. I've been writing professionally for three decades, I've written textbooks (like this one) for writing courses, and I've been a consultant for various kinds of writing tests, yet I still need to check handbooks and style guides to clarify a rule or learn one that I didn't know. Sometimes I even find that I was mistaken about a rule I thought I knew. If someone who does this kind of thing for a living can't know all the rules, it makes little sense for student writers to expect to learn them all. The fact is that you already know most of the important rules, and the ones you still need to clarify or learn are probably relatively few in number. Focus on identifying those.

These two points should help reduce your anxiety about grammar and usage. Students often tell me that they "have bad grammar" or that they know they "need better grammar." What they really need—what most student writers need—is to build on what they already know about grammar to increase their confidence as writers and determine what they should know in order to avoid the errors that might be weakening their writing.

To accomplish these goals, follow these three steps:

1. Identify the errors you make in your writing.

2. Learn the rules related to those errors.

3. Practice.

Following these steps will help you become more aware of specific problems with grammar and usage in your writing and strengthen your understanding of the conventions of written English in general.

1. **Identify the errors you make in your writing.** What kinds of errors do you routinely make in your writing? What kinds of problems do your instructors point out in your writing? Once you pinpoint the specific errors you tend to make, you can begin to work on avoiding them. Although this approach might seem daunting, especially if your instructors often return your papers full of red ink, the challenge is probably not as great as you think. Research suggests that most students tend to make the same errors repeatedly in their writing. If you can identify and eliminate those errors, you will significantly improve your writing.

2. **Learn the rules related to those errors.** Once you have a sense of the errors you tend to make in your writing, use this chapter (perhaps in conjunction with a comprehensive grammar handbook) to understand the rules related to those errors. If you're like most students, most of the errors you make are probably minor, such as missing or misplaced commas or incorrect apostrophes. It's quite possible that you make those errors because you either misunderstand the appropriate rule or convention or never learned the rule or convention in the first place. In addition, college-level academic writing is governed by conventions that you might not have learned in high school, so you might need to learn some new rules. Understanding the principles of usage and the grammar conventions that apply to the errors you make will help you avoid those errors.

3. **Practice.** The best way to improve as a writer is to practice writing. The same is true for learning to avoid errors. If you want to eliminate errors from your writing, you have to practice identifying and correcting those errors in your writing. You can do so in two general ways:

   - **First, consult handbooks or style guides** that have exercises for applying the specific rules related to the errors you tend to make. Doing such exercises will sharpen your ability to identify and correct those errors and strengthen your knowledge of specific rules of usage and grammar. (A quick Internet search will yield many websites devoted to this kind of grammar practice.)

   - **Second, practice editing your own drafts** in a way that focuses specifically on the kinds of errors you tend to make. If you follow the procedure in Chapter 3 when you are working on a writing project, include in Step #10 an additional step that focuses on the specific errors you have identified as common in your own writing. If you make such a step a routine part of your practice as a writer, you will eventually begin to notice that fewer and fewer errors appear in your finished projects.

The rest of this chapter focuses on the problems that research indicates college students tend to make in their writing. The errors you commonly make in your own writing are probably the same errors most college students make, and the usage and syntax problems that can make your sentences unclear are very likely the ones described here.

# Coordination, Subordination, and Parallelism

The structure of a sentence—what teachers often call *syntax*—is more than a function of rules for usage and grammar. It is also a means of conveying relationships and emphasizing words, phrases, and ideas. The elements of a sentence must fit together syntactically, but the syntax should also match the intended meaning so that the structure of the sentence not only is grammatically correct but also helps convey the writer's ideas.

The many complexities and nuances of syntax are well beyond the scope of this chapter, but you can improve the clarity of your prose by avoiding common problems in three areas of syntax: coordination, subordination, and parallel structure.

# Coordination

*Coordination* refers to the use of similar or equivalent grammatical constructions to link ideas or show relationships between generally equal ideas or information. Writers use coordinating conjunctions (*and, but, so, yet, or*) to show such relationships between elements of a sentence:

The celebration was joyful **but** subdued.

> The coordinating conjunction *but* indicates a roughly equal relationship between the two adjectives *joyful* and *subdued*.

> independent clause

The day was short, **and** the night was long.

> The coordinating conjunction and links the independent clauses.

It is important to note here that using different coordinating conjunctions can change the relationships between the coordinate elements:

The day was short, but the night was long.

In this example, *but* changes the relationship between the first clause ("the day was short") and the second ("the night was long"). Although this point might seem obvious, using coordinating conjunctions carefully and strategically to convey specific or precise ideas about the relationships between elements of a sentence is a hallmark of effective academic writing. For example, consider how the choice of *and* or *but* in the following example affects the relationship between the first clause ("Life can be a constant struggle") and the second ("death is final"):

Life can be a constant struggle, and death is final.

Life can be a constant struggle, but death is final.

In both sentences, the clauses are still coordinate, but replacing *and* with *but* changes both the relationship between the clauses and the emphasis of the sentence—which is turn affects the meaning conveyed by the sentence. In the first sentence, the two clauses have equal emphasis and can be seen as two equal statements of the human condition. We might interpret the sentence as follows: Let's recognize the two important realities about human existence that life is hard and death is final. In the second sentence, however, the use of *but* shifts the emphasis to the second clause, which alters the meaning of the entire sentence. We might state the meaning this way: Yes, life is hard, but death is final. The implication might be something like this: Because death is final, live life to the fullest, no matter how hard it can be.

This example illustrates how the choice of a single coordinating conjunction, even in a seemingly straightforward sentence, can significantly affect the ideas conveyed by the sentence. In this sense, coordination can be a powerful tool for writers. Notice that greater emphasis is usually attached to the final element in a coordinate relationship.

Students commonly make two mistakes in using coordination in their writing: They use the wrong coordinating conjunction (usually *and* when *but* or *so* is more appropriate), and they use too much coordination:

Shifts in climate patterns have resulted in more frequent severe weather in many regions, and local governments are struggling to develop more effective emergency services.

coordinating conjunction

independent clause

In this example, there is nothing grammatically incorrect about the sentence, but the conjunction *and* does not quite convey the cause-effect relationship between the first and second clauses of the sentence. If the writer wanted to show that local governments are struggling to develop effective emergency services specifically as a result of changes in several weather patterns, *but* might be a better choice to link the two main clauses:

Shifts in climate patterns have resulted in more frequent severe weather in many regions, but local governments are struggling to develop more effective emergency services.

As you revise your drafts for style, usage, and grammar, it is a good idea to pay attention to your use of coordinating conjunctions so that you can identify sentences in which the coordination does not convey the specific ideas or relationships you intend. If you notice that you are relying on *and* to link elements of a sentence—especially main clauses, as in this example—it is often a sign that you might need to adjust some of your sentences by using a different conjunction.

27

# Subordination

*Subordination* refers to the use of elements in a sentence to show hierarchical relationships or relationships among ideas that are not equal. Subordination is indicated through the use of dependent clauses and is signaled by the use of *subordinating conjunctions*. The most common subordinating conjunctions are *if, although, because, before, after, since, whether, when, whereas, while, until,* and *unless*; writers also commonly use *than* and *that* to indicate subordination. Here are some examples:

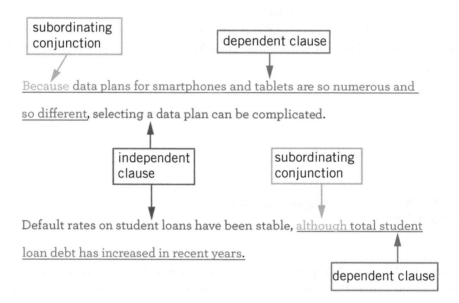

In these examples, the information or ideas in the dependent clauses is subordinated to the information in the main independent clause. Writers can use subordination to emphasize the ideas in the independent clause and indicate the relationship between those ideas and the less important ideas in the dependent clause.

Notice that although the ideas in the independent clause receive emphasis, you can use the order of the clauses to adjust the relative emphasis of each clause. Consider how reversing the order of the clauses in the second example can change the emphasis on each clause and subtly influence the meaning of the sentence:

> Default rates on student loans have been stable, although total student loan debt has increased in recent years.

> Although total student loan debt has increased in recent years, default rates on student loans have been stable.

In both versions of this sentence, the main emphasis is on the independent clause; however, because the dependent clause comes last in the first version, there is slightly greater emphasis on the information in the dependent clause than in the second version. In this way, you can use subordination strategically to direct your readers' attention to specific ideas or convey a more precise sense of the relationship between the ideas in each clause.

Students often use coordination where subordination would be more effective. Consider this sentence:

> Genetically modified foods can have significant risks for farmers, but such foods can be less expensive for consumers.

The use of the coordinating conjunction (*but*) in this sentence results in equal emphasis on both independent clauses. Although the sentence is perfectly acceptable in this coordinate form, the writer can use subordination to emphasize one or the other independent clause:

> Although genetically modified foods can have significant risks for farmers, such foods can be less expensive for consumers.

> Although genetically modified foods can be less expensive for consumers, such foods can have significant risks for farmers.

In these two versions of the sentence, the emphasis is noticeably stronger on the ideas in the independent clause than in the coordinate version of the sentence, which gives more or less equal weight to the ideas in both clauses.

## Parallel Structure

In general, sentences should be written so that words and phrases have the same form, especially if used in a series. Varying the form of words or phrases in a sentence can result in awkward prose:

> The protest movement was a failure for three reasons: weak organization,
>
> excess ego, and having unclear ideas.

The third item in this series ("having unclear ideas") takes a different form (a participle) from the first two items ("weak organization" and "excess ego"), which are nouns, making the sentence awkward.

Make the series parallel by changing the form of the third item so that it is consistent with the form of the first two:

> The protest movement was a failure for three reasons: weak organization, excess ego, and unclear ideas.

Sometimes two verb constructions in the same sentence take different forms and upset the parallelism of the sentence:

**It is easier** to get lost in the past **than** planning the future.

> *Than* creates a comparison between two verb phrases: *to get lost in the past* and *planning for the future*; however, the verb phrases take different forms: an infinitive (*to get*) and a participle (*planning*).

Simply make the forms of the two verb phrases consistent:

**It is easier** to get lost in the past **than** to plan the future.

> The two verb phrases now have the same form (infinitive); as a result, the sentence is parallel.

# Common Sentence-Level Problems

Most student writers have a grasp of the basic rules of sentence structure, but sometimes writers stumble when trying to write academic prose. Usually, the sentence-level problems that result are of the three main types discussed here.

## Run-On or Fused Sentences

A run-on occurs when two or more independent clauses are joined without proper punctuation or linking words:

Often, the easiest solution is adding the proper punctuation mark (usually a period or semi-colon):

At first I was resentful. I wanted my old life back.

All this hate needs to disappear; we've been fighting each other for far too long.

Sometimes, adding linking words or rewriting the sentence is a better option:

At first I was resentful, and I wanted my old life back.

We've been fighting each other for far too long, so let's eliminate the hate.

In many cases, run-on sentences result from an effort to write a complex sentence that contains several ideas:

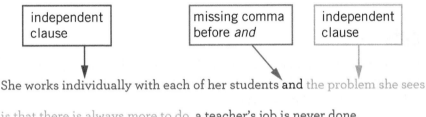

In this example, three independent clauses are fused without proper punctuation. To correct these errors, the writer has several options:

■ **Insert correct punctuation:**

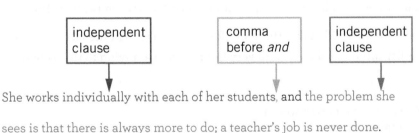

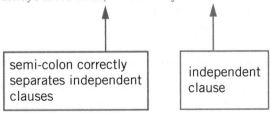

- **Break up the sentence into two or more shorter sentences:**

  She works individually with each of her students, and the problem she sees is that there is always more to do. A teacher's job is never done.

- **Rewrite the sentence:**

  Working individually with each of her students, she sees that there is always more to do, because a teacher's job is never done.

  Working individually with each student means that she always has more to do. A teacher's job is never done.

Which option is best depends on the context within which this sentence occurs and the effect you want to have on your audience.

# Fragments

A sentence fragment is an incomplete sentence, often lacking either a subject or a main verb. Sentence fragments often occur when a period is placed incorrectly between a dependent clause or phrase and the main clause of the sentence:

Her parents decided that there wouldn't be time to visit the last college on her list.

Although she was still very interested in applying to that school.

> **Sentence fragment:** The conjunction *although* makes this a dependent clause that must either be revised or appropriately attached to the independent clause with correct punctuation.

> **Correct sentence:** This independent clause correctly has a subject and verb to make it a complete sentence.

This error can be corrected by using the proper punctuation between the two clauses:

Her parents decided that there wouldn't be time to visit the last college on her list, although she was still very interested in applying to that school.

> Replacing the period with a comma correctly attaches the dependent clause to the independent clause.

This error can be also corrected by rewriting the sentence fragment to make it an independent clause:

Her parents decided that there wouldn't be time to visit the last college on her list. Still, she remained very interested in applying to that school.

Sometimes fragments occur when a phrase, such as a prepositional phrase or an appositive, is incorrectly set off from the main clause by a period:

There was one thing he loved about that old house. The ivy-covered brick.

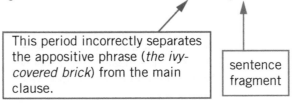

This period incorrectly separates the appositive phrase (*the ivy-covered brick*) from the main clause.

sentence fragment

In this case, the error can be corrected by using the proper punctuation (either a comma or a colon) or by rewriting the sentence slightly:

There was one thing he loved about that old house: the ivy-covered brick.

What he loved about that house was one thing, the ivy-covered brick.

The one thing he loved about that old house was the ivy-covered brick.

## Misplaced and Dangling Modifiers

In general, phrases and clauses that modify a word should be placed as close to that word as possible. When a clause or phrase modifies the wrong element in a sentence, readers will find that sentence unclear, difficult to follow, or grammatically incorrect.

Here is an example of sentence with a misplaced modifier:

When quoting the teachers at the working-class school, the tone of

the writer is negative and seems critical of teachers' efforts.

Grammatically, this clause modifies the subject of the main clause (*tone*). But the sentence doesn't make sense, because it is not the tone that is doing the quoting but the writer.

Address the problem by rewriting the sentence:

When quoting the teachers at the working-class school, the writer adopts a negative tone and seems critical of teachers' efforts.

In this revised sentence, the modifying clause (*When quoting the teachers at the working-class school*) is placed close to the noun it modifies (*writer*).

27

Sometimes, the problem is that the misplaced modifier can change the meaning of the sentence:

Tad only played tennis on Wednesday.

> With the adverb *only* placed here, the sentence means that the only thing Tad did on Wednesday was play tennis.

Simply move the modifier:

Tad played tennis only on Wednesday.

> Moving the adverb *only* changes the meaning of the sentence. Now it means that Tad played tennis only on Wednesdays rather than on other days.

The same problem can occur when a modifying phrase is placed too far from the noun it modifies:

Chaz spent the rest of the night playing video games, having finally turned in his assignment.

> Placed here, the phrase *having finally turned in his assignment* modifies the phrase *playing video games* rather than the subject of the sentence (*Chaz*).

Clarify matters by moving the phrase:

Having finally turned in his assignment, Chaz spent the rest of the night playing video games.

Here is another very common version of the same problem; however, in this case, the intended subject of the main clause is replaced by an indefinite pronoun (*it*), which makes the sentence awkward and confusing:

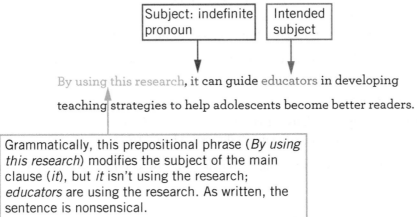

There are two basic ways to address this kind of dangling modifier:

- **Rewrite the sentence to make the intended subject the grammatical subject:**

    By using this research, educators can develop curriculum and teaching

    strategies to help adolescents become better readers.

    The pronoun *it* is deleted and the intended subject (*educators*) is now the grammatical subject of the sentence.

- **Change the modifying phrase into the subject of the sentence:**

    The phrase *using this research* is now the subject of the sentence.

    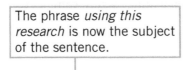

    Using this research can help those in the educational field develop

    curriculum and teaching strategies to help adolescents become

    better readers.

27

# Common Pronoun Errors

There are many different kinds of pronouns, which means that there are many opportunities for incorrectly using pronouns. However, most pronoun errors are of two kinds: (1) lack of agreement between the pronoun and its antecedent and (2) a missing or vague antecedent for the pronoun.

**There are three basic principles governing the uses of pronouns:**

1. The pronoun must be in the correct *case* corresponding to its function in the sentence.

2. Every pronoun (except indefinite pronouns) must have an **antecedent**—that is, the noun to which the pronoun refers.

3. The pronoun must agree with its antecedent in number and gender. (If the antecedent is singular, the pronoun must also be singular; if the antecedent is female, so must the pronoun be.)

If you apply these principles, you are unlikely to make the most common kinds of mistakes with pronouns.

## Incorrect Pronoun Case

*Case* refers to the form of a pronoun that reflects its specific function in a sentence: subject, object, or possessive:

**He** is an excellent dancer. (The pronoun *He* is the subject of the sentence and therefore correctly in the subjective case.)

Jose and **me** went swimming yesterday. (*Me*, which is the objective case of the first-person pronoun *I*, is incorrect because it is being used as a subject. The correct form of the pronoun is *I* in this instance.)

The dance club gave **he** and **I** an award for best dancer. (The pronouns *he* and *I*, which are in the subjective case, are incorrect because they are being used as indirect objects of the verb *gave*. They should be in the objective case: *him* and *me*.)

He brought **his** dancing shoes. (The pronoun *his* is possessive and is therefore used correctly in the possessive case.)

Most students are able to identify the proper case of pronouns. In academic writing, however, students sometimes lose track of the proper case when writing lengthy, complex sentences.

# Lack of Pronoun-Antecedent Agreement

This error is usually easy to avoid if you identify the antecedent; however, this kind of pronoun error is common in part because the wrong pronoun often "sounds" right:

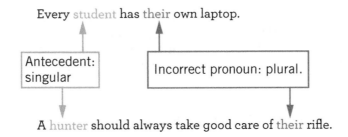

Every student has their own laptop.

Antecedent: singular

Incorrect pronoun: plural.

A hunter should always take good care of their rifle.

Correct these errors either by changing the pronoun or rewriting the sentence:

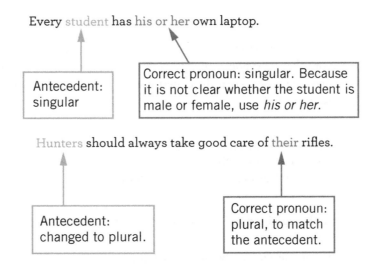

Every student has his or her own laptop.

Antecedent: singular

Correct pronoun: singular. Because it is not clear whether the student is male or female, use *his or her*.

Hunters should always take good care of their rifles.

Antecedent: changed to plural.

Correct pronoun: plural, to match the antecedent.

Making sure that the pronoun agrees with its antecedent can be tricky when the antecedent is an **indefinite pronoun** (e.g., everyone, anyone, anybody, someone):

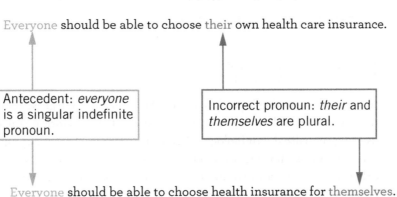

Everyone should be able to choose their own health care insurance.

Antecedent: *everyone* is a singular indefinite pronoun.

Incorrect pronoun: *their* and *themselves* are plural.

Everyone should be able to choose health insurance for themselves.

Common Pronoun Errors  **839**

Again, correct the errors by changing the pronoun or rewriting the sentence:

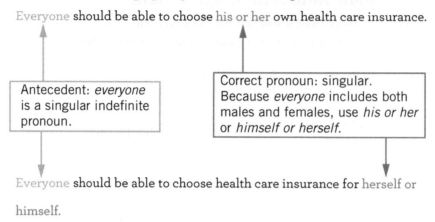

Everyone should be able to choose his or her own health care insurance.

Antecedent: *everyone* is a singular indefinite pronoun.

Correct pronoun: singular. Because *everyone* includes both males and females, use *his or her* or *himself or herself*.

Everyone should be able to choose health care insurance for herself or

himself.

## Vague Pronoun Reference

Usually, the antecedent is the noun closest to the pronoun. Sometimes, however, the antecedent can seem to refer to more than one noun. In this example, technically the antecedent for the pronoun *he* should be *Steve*, because *Steve* is the closest noun to the pronoun. But a reader might assume that *he* refers instead to *Bob*.

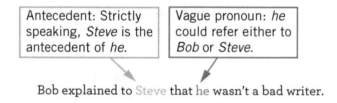

Antecedent: Strictly speaking, *Steve* is the antecedent of *he*.

Vague pronoun: *he* could refer either to *Bob* or *Steve*.

Bob explained to Steve that he wasn't a bad writer.

In such cases, rewrite the sentence to clarify the antecedent:

Bob explained to Steve that Steve wasn't a bad writer.

Bob said to Steve, "You're not a bad writer."

According to Bob, Steve wasn't a bad writer.

# Word Choice and Style

An effective style in academic writing is partly a matter of careful and strategic selection of words, not only to craft clear sentences but also to meet the needs of the rhetorical situation. Sometimes that means using specialized terminology (often called "jargon") that is appropriate for the subject—say, economics or psychology. More often, though, writers must make choices among words that have slightly different shades of meaning to convey precisely what they want to say to their readers. Consider the differences in the following statements:

The audience was **interested** in the speaker's argument.

The audience was **engaged** in the speaker's argument.

The audience was **fascinated** by the speaker's argument.

The audience was **enthralled** by the speaker's argument.

Although all of these sentences generally mean that the audience listened to the speaker, each sentence conveys a different sense of the impact of the speaker's argument on the audience. Selecting the verb that conveys precisely what you want to convey about that impact is part of what it means to write effective prose.

Students tend to make three errors when it comes to word choice:

- making imprecise word choices
- using the wrong word
- confusing similar words

## Imprecise Word Choices

The best word choice is always shaped by the rhetorical situation—especially the writer's sense of the audience's expectations and the appropriate style—as well as by the writer's own preferences. However, students sometimes rely too much on general words when more specialized or specific words would be more precise:

The mayor gave a **great** speech to the residents after their town was hit by the hurricane.

Words like *great, good, bad,* and *awesome* are overused and vague, even if their general meanings are clear. In this example, the writer conveys a positive sense of the mayor's speech but not much more than that. Consider these alternatives:

The mayor gave a **comforting** speech to the residents after their town was hit by the hurricane.

The mayor gave an **encouraging** speech to the residents after their town was hit by the hurricane.

The mayor gave an **emotional** speech to the residents after their town was hit by the hurricane.

Which of these choices is best will depend on the specific meaning you want to convey to your readers and the context of the text in which the sentence appears, but any of these choices conveys a clearer, more precise description of the mayor's speech than the original sentence. As these alternative examples show, a single word can significantly improve a sentence.

**27**

# Wrong Word

Studies show that one of the most common errors in student writing is the use of the wrong word or word form; however, those same studies do not identify specific words that students routinely misuse (other than the ones discussed in the next section). That might be because of the richness of the English language and the idiosyncrasies of each of us as writers. In other words, all writers sometimes use the wrong word, but we all make different versions of this error. You might have trouble remembering the correct form of a specific verb, while your classmate struggles with a different kind of word that you find easy to use. This variability does not allow us to make generalizations about specific errors in word choice that are common in student writing, and it underscores the need to become aware of the errors that you tend to make, as noted in the first section of this chapter.

# Confusing Similar Words

Words that look and sound alike but have very different functions can sometimes confuse writers and lead to common errors. In such cases, the best approach is simply to learn the correct uses of these words and any rules related to their usage. Being aware that these words are often the source of errors is also important. You can be vigilant in using these words and focus on them when editing your drafts.

The three most commonly confused sets of words are *their, there,* and *they're; affect* and *effect*; and *then* and *than.*

- **Their/there/they're.** Each of these words has a very different function:

  *Their* is a plural pronoun.

  > The players put on **their** uniforms.

  > Voters never seem to be able to make up **their** minds.

  *There* is an adverb denoting place; it can also be used as a pronoun.

  > We don't want to go **there**. (adverb)

  > **There** are three reasons to support this candidate. (pronoun)

  *They're* is a contraction for *they are.*

  > They told us that **they're** not going on the field trip.

  > Although the peaches are inexpensive, **they're** not very fresh.

A common mistake is using *their* in place of *they're*:

The students can't explain why their unhappy with the new class.

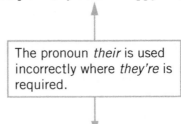

The pronoun *their* is used incorrectly where *they're* is required.

Although the workers are tired, their planning to finish the job.

To avoid this mistake, replace the word (*their, there, or they're*) with the words *they are*. If the sentence makes sense, then you must use the word *they're*.

Another common mistake is using **there** in place of **their**:

The children forgot to bring there towels to swimming class.

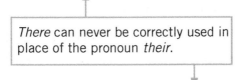

*There* can never be correctly used in place of the pronoun *their*.

When it began to rain, the workers covered up there tools with plastic tarps.

- **Affect/effect.** Although both these words can be either nouns or verbs, *affect* is most often used as a verb meaning to act upon, whereas *effect* is most often used as a noun to mean an impact, result, or consequence:

The heavy rains will probably **affect** the harvest.

Seemingly, he was not **affected** by the long hours and lack of sleep.

The weather always **affects** our vacation plans.

Growing up in a small town had a big **effect** on me.

Historians have long debated the **effects** of the industrial revolution.

What is the **effect** of the new regulation?

The two most common errors involving these terms are using *effect* as a verb when *affect* is required and using *affect* as a noun when *effect* is required:

**27**

Hot weather doesn't effect me.

> *Effect* is incorrectly used as a verb where *affect* should be used.

The farm was not effected by the drought.

The police returned his personal affects.

> *Affects* is incorrectly used as a noun where *effect* should be used.

The economist could not anticipate the affects of the hurricanes.

Be aware that *affect* can be used as a noun and *effect* as a verb, although these uses are much less common than those explained above. As a noun, *affect* refers to an emotional state or feeling:

The patients lacked **affect** in their expressions.

The woman had a joyful **affect**.

The criminal displayed a disturbing **affect**.

When used as a verb, *effect* means to cause something to happen or to bring about:

The reformers sought to **effect** significant change in the way schools are run.

The farmers were successful in **effecting** an increase in commodity prices.

- **Then/than.** The easiest way to distinguish between these two common words is to remember that *then* generally refers to time, whereas *than* is always used in comparisons:

I'll go to the bank, and **then** I'll go to the grocery store.

The book's influence has been much greater **than** the author could ever have imagined.

We were much more optimistic back **then**.

She liked the green sweatshirt better **than** the blue one.

The most common mistake with these two words occurs when *then* is used in place of *than*:

I have always been a better athlete then my sister.

> Because a comparison is being made, *then* is incorrect and *than* must be used.

He wanted to visit Europe more then anything.

To avoid this error, remember that you can never use *then* in a comparison such as in these examples; in such cases, *than* is *always* required.

Here are some other commonly confused words:

- **Accept/except.** *Accept* is a verb meaning to receive something. *Except* is generally used as a preposition:

  She was happy to **accept** the award.

  Everyone **except** the boss received a raise.

- **Advice/advise.** The easiest way to avoid confusing these words is to remember that *advice* is a noun meaning guidance, whereas *advise* is a verb meaning to give guidance or advice. Another handy trick for avoiding this confusion is to remember that you can give advice but you can never give advise.

  My lawyer always provides me with good **advice** when I'm trying to make a decision involving legal matters.

  The lawyer will **advise** a client about the best way to handle a legal problem.

- **Complement/compliment.** *Complement* can be used as a noun or a verb; it means to complete or add to. A *compliment* can also be a noun or verb; it means to praise.

  The blue hat nicely **complemented** his tan suit.

  I paid him a **compliment** on his blue hat.

- **Lie/lie/lay.** These often-confused words have very different meanings and functions. The irregular verb *lie* means to recline or place your body in a prone position and takes three forms: *lie, lay, have lain*. The regular verb *lie* (which takes the forms *lie, lied, and have lied*) means to tell a falsehood. The regular verb *lay* (which takes the forms *lay, laid, and have laid*) means to place something or put something down. Most often students use *lay* when they should use *lie*:

  **Incorrect:** She likes to **lay** down on the sofa after lunch to take a nap.

  **Correct:** She likes to **lie** down on the sofa after lunch to take a nap.

  **Incorrect:** He **laid** down on the sofa to take a nap.

  **Correct:** He **lay** down on the sofa to take a nap.

  **Incorrect:** Before he finished his paper, he had **laid** down on the sofa to rest.

  **Correct:** Before he finished his paper, he had **lain** down on the sofa to rest.

  **Incorrect:** She commanded her dog to **lay** down.

  **Correct:** She commanded her dog to **lie** down.

  **Incorrect:** He **lied** the baby down in the crib. He lay the baby in the crib.

  **Correct:** He **laid** the baby down in the crib.

27

- **Past/passed.** *Past* is a preposition meaning gone by or a noun meaning a time period before the present. *Passed* is the past tense of the verb *pass*, which means to go by.

  He drove **past** the accident.

  He **passed** by the accident

  The accident occurred in the **past**.

- **To/too/two.** These three words that sound similar have very different functions. *To* is a preposition. *Too* is an adverb. *Two* is a noun or adjective.

  She ran **to** the finish line.

  He gave his car **to** his friend.

  She wanted a new car, **too**.

  He, **too**, was interested in running the race.

  There were **too** many runners in the race.

  There were **two** runners who did not finish the race.

  **Two** is better than one.

- **Through/threw.** *Through* is used either as an adverb or preposition. *Threw* is the past tense of the verb *throw*.

  He went **through** the tunnel.

  She **threw** a rock into the tunnel.

  Only **through** hard work can you succeed.

# Common Punctuation Errors

## Missing Commas

Missing commas where they are required are among the most common errors student writers make. This section reviews the rules for seven required uses of commas:

1. before a coordinating conjunction
2. after an introductory element
3. before a quotation
4. around nonessential elements
5. in a series
6. between coordinate adjectives
7. to set off nouns of direct address, *yes* and *no*, interrogative tags, and interjections

If you become familiar with the rules for these ~~five~~ seven uses of commas, you will avoid these common errors.

1. **Before a coordinating conjunction (for, and, nor, but, or, yet, so).** In most cases, a comma should be placed *before* a coordinating conjunction (such as *for, and, nor, but, or, yet, so*) that connects two independent clauses:

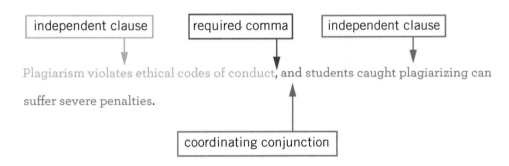

Plagiarism violates ethical codes of conduct, and students caught plagiarizing can suffer severe penalties.

The weather promised to turn stormy later that afternoon, so we took along rain jackets.

Every student is potentially affected by tuition increases, but students who rely on loans might suffer the most because they will end up borrowing more money to pay for their educations.

There is one important exception to this rule: No comma is needed before a coordinating conjunction that joins two very short sentences:

I was tired and I slept well.

2. **After an introductory element.** A comma should be placed after an introductory clause, phrase, or word in a sentence:

**Introductory clause:**

When students are satisfied with their own writing, they are often eager to share it with classmates.

**Introductory phrase:**

Worried about his car, Brian decided not to drive the long distance back to his apartment.

Despite her misgivings, she signed up for the backpacking trip.

**27**

**Introductory word:**

> Furthermore, I was starting school that fall.

> Ultimately, they found what they were seeking.

> Traditionally, conservative teachers have never questioned the principle of school governance by part-time citizens.

Notice that in this last example, the comma changes the meaning of the sentence. Without the comma, "traditionally" modifies the subject (teachers), and the sentence means that teachers who are traditionally conservative have never questioned the principle of school governance by part-time citizens. However, with the comma, "traditionally" modifies the main verb (questioned), and the sentence means that conservative teachers have traditionally not questioned the principle of school governance by part-time citizens.

3. **Before a quotation.** Direct quotations of complete sentences must be preceded by a comma:

> John Lennon once said, "Life is what happens to you while you're busy making other plans."

> Audre Lorde wrote, "It is not our differences that divide us. It is our inability to recognize, accept, and celebrate those differences."

4. **Around nonessential elements.** Use commas to set off elements of a sentence that are not essential for understanding who or what is being discussed. Nonessential elements include appositives, modifying phrases or clauses, transitional words or phrases, or parenthetical words or phrases.

**With appositives:**

> When my second brother was born, we switched rooms so that the boys could share the larger room and I, the only girl, could have the small room for myself.

In this sentence, the phrase "the only girl" is an appositive modifying the pronoun "I" and must be set off by commas.

**With nonessential (non-restrictive) modifying phrases or clauses:**

In the following sentences, the highlighted words are nonessential clauses or phrases that must be set off by commas. (In these cases, removing the highlighted words does not change the meaning of the main sentence, which is why they are called "nonessential.")

> The car, which was brilliant red, was stuck on the side of the road.

> David, seeing the gathering clouds, quickly ran for shelter.

> Hungry and cold, the stray cat hid under the back porch.

**With transitional words or phrases:**

What is interesting, though, is that they never realized what they were doing.

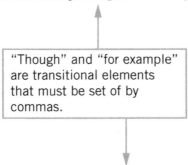

"Though" and "for example" are transitional elements that must be set of by commas.

Her most recent novel, for example, examines unconventional families.

**With parenthetical words or phrases:**

Parenthetical phrases or words are like "asides" or related but nonessential comments: They are not necessary, and removing them does not affect the meaning of the main sentence.

Jasmine heard the comment and, understandably, left the room.

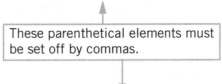

These parenthetical elements must be set off by commas.

Jerry believed that everyone, except maybe people with debilitating illnesses, should have to work.

5. **In a series.** Place a comma after each item in a series, whether those items are words, phrases, or clauses. (In these examples, the different items in each series are shown in different colors.)

Students were told to bring a pencil, paper, and an eraser.

The tired sailors found themselves struggling to stay on schedule, worried about the condition of their boat, and hoping for better weather.

The triathletes were wondering whether to emphasize swimming, running, or bicycling in their workouts

Only a few days after the hurricane, power was restored, stores reopened, and people returned to their homes.

**Note:** The preceding sentences all contain **the Oxford Comma**, also known as the series *comma*, which is placed after the second-to-last item in a series and before the coordinating conjunction (*and, or*). The Oxford Comma is typically expected in academic writing; however, it is rarely used in popular writing. For college writing assignments, I recommend using the Oxford Comma unless instructed otherwise.

6. **Between coordinate adjectives.** Coordinate adjectives are adjectives that are equal and reversible, so that their order does not affect the meaning of the phrase. Usually, if adjectives can be connected by "and," they are coordinate and should be separated by commas:

> PJ Harvey's album *To Bring You My Love* is full of dirge-like, erotic vocals.

> These two adjectives (*dirge-like* and *erotic*), which modify the noun *vocals*, could be reversed without altering the meaning of the phrase or the sentence, so they must be separated by commas.

> The juicy, ripe, sweet peach is one of the best tastes of summer.

> The adjectives modifying the noun *peach* could be reversed without altering the meaning of the phrase or the sentence, so they must be separated by commas.

Compare the previous two examples with this one:

> He bought seven red apples.

In this case, no comma separates the adjectives *seven* and *red* because the two are not equal. *Seven* modifies the entire phrase *red applies*. The adjectives *seven* and *red* are cumulative. They cannot be logically reordered or be connected with *and:* For example, we would not say, "seven and red apples" or "red seven apples." Commas should *not* be used to separate cumulative adjectives.

7. **With nouns of direct address, the words *yes* and *no*, interrogative tags, and mild interjections.** Names and other terms used in direct address must be set off by commas:

> Mike, turn it up. (direct address)

> No, I won't turn it up.

> You're not going to turn it up, are you? (The phrase "are you" is an interrogative tag.)

> Look, take it easy. (The word "Look" is an interjection.)

# Unnecessary Commas

Maybe because there are so many rules governing the uses of commas, students often place commas where they are not needed. Two kinds of unnecessary commas are among the most common punctuation errors: commas that incorrectly separate sentence elements and commas placed around essential (or restrictive) elements.

■ **Separating sentence elements.** Commas should not be used to separate essential elements in a sentence, such as the subject and verb, compound words or phrases, and necessary phrases or clauses, unless those essential elements are separated by other elements that must be set off by commas. Here are some examples of unnecessary commas:

> This comma incorrectly separates the two parts of a compound verb (*is* and *keeps*) with the same subject (*she*) and should be deleted.

She is meticulous, and keeps her equipment stored carefully in its original boxes.

If an element that must be set off by commas, such as a nonessential phrase, were included between the essential elements, then be sure to use commas around that element:

She is meticulous, almost to a fault, and keeps her equipment stored carefully in its original boxes.

In this example, the phrase *almost to a fault,* is a nonessential (non-restrictive) element that modifies the pronoun *she* (which is the subject of the sentence) and therefore must be set off by commas. (See "Around nonessential elements" on pages 877–879.)

> This comma incorrectly separates the infinitive phrase (*to increase their power*) from the main clause of the sentence (*nations are taking land*).

The European nations are taking land from weaker nations, to increase their power.

■ **With an essential (restrictive) element**

An element that is necessary for the intended meaning of a sentence should not be set off by commas. In many cases involving restrictive elements, the use of commas changes the meaning of the sentence.

**27**

> Because the relative clause (*who receives the most votes*) indicates a specific candidate and is essential to the meaning of the main clause, it should *not* be set off by commas. These two commas should be deleted.

The candidate, who receives the most votes, will win the election.

The Democratic Party supports quotas, which are consistent with the ideal of equality.

> This comma is essential to the meaning of the sentence. With the comma, the sentence means that *all* quotas are consistent with the ideal of equality. Without the comma, the sentence means that the Democratic Party supports *only those quotas* that are consistent with the ideal of equality.

## Comma Splices

A comma splice, sometimes called a comma fault, occurs when a comma is incorrectly used to separate two independent clauses. The commas in the following sentences are incorrect:

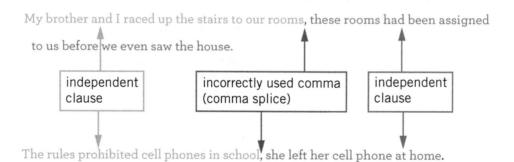

My brother and I raced up the stairs to our rooms, these rooms had been assigned to us before we even saw the house.

| independent clause | incorrectly used comma (comma splice) | independent clause |

The rules prohibited cell phones in school, she left her cell phone at home.

In many cases, there are several ways to correct a comma splice. Often, the simplest way is to replace the comma with a period or semi-colon:

My brother and I raced up the stairs to our rooms. These rooms had been assigned to us before we even saw the house.

The rules prohibited cell phones in school; she left her cell phone at home.

Sometimes, rewriting the sentence is a better option:

> My brother and I raced up the stairs to the rooms that had been assigned to us before we even saw the house.

> My brother and I raced up the stairs to our rooms, which had been assigned to us before we even saw the house.

> The rules prohibited cell phones in school, so she left her cell phone at home.

> Because the rules prohibited cell phones in school, she left her cell phone at home.

# Incorrect Use of Semi-Colons

The semi-colon might well be the most misunderstood and misused punctuation mark. Learning a few basic rules can help you avoid misusing semi-colons and, more important, learn to use them strategically to strengthen your writing.

The semi-colon has three main functions:

1. to separate two independent clauses whose subjects are closely linked:

> With writing, the audience is usually absent; with talking, the listener is usually present.

> Apples in Des Moines supermarkets can be from China, even though there are apple farmers in Iowa; potatoes in Lima's supermarkets are from the United States, even though Peru boasts more varieties of potato than any other country.

> Protecting the health of the environment is a prudent investment; it can avert scarcity, perpetuate abundance, and provide a solid basis for social development.

2. to separate elements in a series when those elements include other punctuation marks:

> Present at the meeting were the board president, John Smith; April Jones, treasurer; Molly Harris, secretary; and Josh Jordan, who was filling in for an absent board member.

> If you plan to hike in the mountains in winter, you should always carry proper clothing, especially dependable rain gear; extra food and water; matches, a lighter, or a portable stove for cooking and for melting snow for water; and a tarp for shelter.

3. to separate two independent clauses that are linked by a conjunctive adverb, such as *however, therefore, moreover, nevertheless,* and *consequently*:

> The students planned to attend the opening night of the play at the campus theater; however, when they arrived for the show, they learned that it was sold out.

> Although many colleges do not use standardized test scores when evaluating applicants for admission, most colleges still require applicants to submit SAT or ACT scores; therefore, high school students who wish to attend college should plan to take either the SAT or the ACT or both.

There are other uses for the semi-colon, but if you learn to use the semi-colon in these three main ways, you will avoid the most common mistakes that student writers make with this punctuation mark.

**27**

- **Semi-colon instead of a colon.** One of the most common mistakes students make is using a semi-colon instead of a colon to introduce a sentence element, such as a series:

> The semi-colon should *never* be used to introduce a series. The correct punctuation mark here is a colon.

The mud was horrendous, and it got onto everything; our clothes, our skin, our hair.

He argued that the U.S. is too dependent on one kind of energy source; oil.

> In this example, either a colon or a comma would be correct, but a semi-colon is incorrect.

- **Missing semi-colon.** Another very common error occurs when the writer neglects to use a semi-colon with a conjunctive adverb (e.g., *however, therefore, nevertheless, consequently*). When two independent clauses are joined by a conjunctive adverb, a semi-colon must precede the conjunctive adverb, which is followed by a comma. In such cases, a comma preceding the conjunctive adverb is incorrect:

The internal resistance of the battery was found to be lower than it was in

the other circuit, however, it still resulted in a significant difference in voltage.

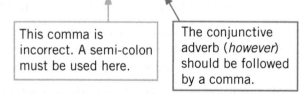

> This comma is incorrect. A semi-colon must be used here.

> The conjunctive adverb (*however*) should be followed by a comma.

# Incorrect Use of Apostrophe

Apostrophes can be confusing because they are used in several very different ways. The two main functions of apostrophes are

- to indicate possession; and
- to indicate omitted letters, especially in contractions.

If you understand these functions, you should be able to avoid the most common mistakes student writers make in using apostrophes.

- **Missing or incorrect apostrophe to indicate possession.** An apostrophe followed by the letter *s* indicates possession or ownership for most **singular nouns**:

> John's car
>
> the student's book
>
> the government's role
>
> Thomas Jefferson's signature
>
> the musician's instrument
>
> the tree's shadow

The most common violation of this rule occurs when a writer neglects to use an apostrophe where it is necessary to show possession:

> She remembered to bring her husbands jacket when she left the house.

> In this example, *husband* is possessive and should have an apostrophe before the *s*: *husband's*.

In most cases, this rule also applies if the singular form of the noun ends in *s*:

> New Orleans's mayor
>
> the dress's hem
>
> progress's risks
>
> the witness's memory

Note that **possessive pronouns** (*mine, yours, hers, his, theirs, ours, its*) *do not* have an apostrophe:

> If you don't have a bicycle, you can use **mine**.
>
> The horse had a scar on **its** left foreleg.

To form **the possessive of a plural noun that already ends in *s***, use an apostrophe at the end of the word *without* an additional *s*:

> the birds' nests
>
> the ships' destinations
>
> the cowboys' horses

**27**

However, if the plural form of a noun does not end in *s*, use an apostrophe followed by an *s* to indicate possession:

the children's scarves

women's rights

the sheep's pen

Note that in these examples, the nouns are already in their plural forms, and the apostrophe does not make the nouns plural; rather, the apostrophe designates possession.

■ **Missing apostrophe in a contraction.** An apostrophe is required in a contraction, such as *isn't, can't, doesn't,* or *won't.* In contractions, the apostrophe stands for a missing letter or letters: *isn't* for *is not; can't* for *cannot; doesn't* for *does not; won't* for *will not.*

He couldnt see what was right in front of him.

*Couldn't*, the contraction for *could not*, requires an apostrophe between the letters *n* and *t*.

■ **Confusing *its* and *it's*.** *Its* and *it's* are two very different kinds of words: *its* is a possessive pronoun and *it's* is a contraction meaning *it is*. Students often confuse the two and, as a result, misuse them. To avoid this very common error, you need to **remember two rules.**

- *its* is a possessive pronoun and therefore does not have an apostrophe;
- *it's* is the contraction for *it is* and therefore must always have an apostrophe.

**Use this simple strategy:**

1. Replace *its* or *it's* with *it is* in the sentence.
2. If the sentence makes sense with *it is,* then *it's* is the correct word.
3. If the sentence doesn't make sense with *it is,* then *its* is the correct word.

Here's how it works:

**Example 1**

**Sentence:** The dog became extremely aggressive whenever anyone approached **it's** cage.

**Strategy:** Replace *it's* with *it is*: The dog became extremely aggressive whenever anyone approached **it is** cage.

**Result:** The sentence does not make sense with *it is,* so *it's* must be replaced with **its**: The dog became extremely aggressive whenever anyone approached **its** cage.

**Example 2**

**Sentence:** He is putting a jacket on because **it's** very cold outside.

**Strategy:** Replace *it's* with *it is*: He is putting a jacket on because **it is** very cold outside.

**Result:** The sentence make sense with *it is*, so *it's* is correct.

**Example 3**

**Sentence:** The sailboat was distinctive because of the loud color of **its** sails.

**Strategy:** Replace *it's* with *it is*: The sailboat was distinctive because of the loud color of *it is* sails.

**Result:** The sentence does not make sense with *it is*, so *its* is correct.

## Incorrect Use of Colons

The colon is a kind of "pointing" mark of punctuation; it calls attention to the words that follow it. A colon is commonly used to introduce a list or series, a quotation, or an appositive.

**To introduce a list or series**

By the time she was twenty, my grandmother Virginia knew how to play several musical instruments: piano, fiddle, guitar, banjo, and mandolin.

The protest movement was a failure for three reasons: weak organization, excess ego, and unclear ideas.

**To introduce a quotation**

Rainier Maria Rilke has unusual advice for young poets: "Love the questions themselves."

Among Thoreau's best known statements is a line from *Walden*: "The mass of men lead lives of quiet desperation."

**With appositives**

As my father once told me, there is only one way to do things: the right way.

The gymnast had only one goal: a gold medal.

Notice that when a colon precedes a complete sentence, the first word after the colon *must* be capitalized; however, if the word or phrase following the colon does not make a complete sentence, the first word following the colon is *not* capitalized.

**27**

# Index

periodicals, 788–791. *See also* Periodicals, APA style for citing
rules for, 783
Refutation, 346
"Reign of Recycling, The" (Tierney), 164–168
Relevance
of academic arguments, 361, 363, 374, 383
of arguments, 342, 348, 353
of arguments in public discourse, 399
of personal narratives, 505, 510, 532
Reliability of sources, 717, 728–729
Repetition in document design, 654, 656–658, 672, 679
Research, 681–686
audience and, 683
primary *vs.* secondary, 686
process of, 696
purpose of, 683
questions in, 684, 696
sources for, 696–697. *See also* Source material
understanding, 681–682
Research paper
in APA style, sample of, 794–799
defined, 129
in MLA style, sample of, 769–775
Review. *See also* Evaluating and reviewing
APA style for citing, 791
criteria for evaluations, 293, 295
MLA style for citing, 764–765
reason for, 294
relevancy of, 294
summary or description in, 293–294
"Review of *Thirteen Reasons Why* by Jay Asher" (Gillis), 301–303
Revision, 47–49
of academic arguments, 384–385
in action, 79–83
in applying Core Concepts, 107–115
of arguments in public discourse, 422–423
of causal analysis, 178–179
of comparative analysis, 212
of conclusions, 82, 113–115
of content, 80, 107–111
of digital storytelling, 610–611
*vs.* editing, 48
of evaluating and reviewing, 314
of form, 81, 111
of Guiding Thesis Statement, 71, 95
of informative essays, 567
of introduction, 82, 113–115
of literary analysis, 288
methodical, 49
overview of, 47–48
of personal narratives, 532–534
prioritizing list of, 82
as process of discovery and meaning making, 49
of proposal, 463–464
of rhetorical analysis, 260
of rhetorical situation, 81, 113
of summary-response essays, 648–649
of transitions, 822
writer and, 49
Rhetorical analysis, 214–261
audience and, 216–225, 229–230, 246, 249–252, 260
basic, 218–220

claims or assertions in, 251, 253–257, 258, 259, 260
classical rhetorical theory, 221–227. *See also* Appeals
complexity of, 233, 246, 254, 259
conclusions in, 233, 246, 259
of Declaration of Independence, 239–245
defined, 215
editing, 261
of eulogy, 234–236
evidence in, 221, 233, 246, 253–255, 256, 257, 258, 259
examining rhetorical situation, 220
feedback in, 259
framework for, 218–227, 253, 257–258
of images, 228–232. *See also* Visual analysis
information in, 233, 246
main point or idea in, 217, 254–255
medium, 250–251
occasions for, 215–217
organizing, 255–258
outline for, 256–258
outside sources for, 255
of poster, 217
of public service announcement, 237–239
purpose in, 218, 219, 220, 226, 229, 230, 233, 250, 251, 253, 257, 258, 259, 260
questions in, 217
reading, 231–245
revising, 260
rhetorical context in, 249–250, 252–253, 255, 257, 260
stylistic analysis in, 225–227
support for, 253–255
topic for, 246, 247–250
understanding, 217–220, 227
voice in, 260
writing, 246–261
"Rhetorical Analysis of a National Health Service of England Public Service Announcement," 237–238
"Rhetorical Analysis of the Declaration of Independence: Persuasive Appeals and Language, A" (Stover), 239–245
Rhetorical context
in academic arguments, 376, 378
academic texts in, 622–625
in action, 65–67
in applying Core Concepts, 92–93
in arguments in public discourse, 414–415
audience and, identifying, 65, 92
in causal analysis, 170
in comparative analysis, 202
considering, 66, 84, 92–93
in digital storytelling, 602–603
Discovery Draft and, 67, 93
evaluating and reviewing in, 306
examining, 65–67, 92–93
form and, 73, 101
in informative essays, 560–561, 568
in literary analysis, 282
medium, 93–94
in personal narratives, 526
in Prezi presentation, 674
in print documents, 671
of proposal, 455–456
questions in, 66, 93
revising, 81, 113

in rhetorical analysis, 249–250, 252–253, 255, 257, 260
summary-response essays in, 643–644
in supporting claims, 140, 142
voice and, 84, 116
in websites, 678
Rhetorical question, 227
Rhetorical situation, 27–31
in academic arguments, 345, 381
argument in, 330–331, 345
in arguments in public discourse, 420
audience and, 29
culture and, 29
in document design, 652–654, 661
in evaluating sources, 722–733
form or genre and, 28–29, 43, 46
good writing, studying, 31
in images, 668–669
overview of, 27–28
purpose and, 28, 46
triangle metaphor and, 27–28
writer and, 30–31
Roberts, David, 507–508
Rogerian argument, 346–347
Rosenfeld, Steve, 725–726, 728
Rough draft
organizing, 73
outline and, 73, 175–176
purpose of, 25–26
revising, 48, 76
writing, 76
Run-on or fused sentences, 832–834

**S**

Sacred text, MLA style for citing, 761
Sans serif font, 565
Scenes in personal narratives, 530
Scholarly journals, 688–689
Schuelke, Trace C., 299–301
Science, narrative writing in, 468
*Scopus*, 693
"Sculpting Identity: A History of the Nose Job" (Hearsay), 547–550
Search engines, 694–695
Boolean operators used with, 705
Internet, 703–704
Search for hidden meaning, explication *vs.*, 264
Search strategies for finding source material, 695–710
Boolean operators, 705, 708
general search, 697–704
guidelines for, 682
keyword searches, 698–699
narrower search, 697, 704–710
purpose of project and, 696
questions in, 696–697
targeted search, 697, 710
Sebelius, Kathleen, 335–336
Secondary audience, 249
Secondary research, 686
Self, understanding through writing, 17–18
Semi-colon, 853–854
functions of, 853
instead of colon, 854
missing, 854
Sensory appeals in storytelling, 506, 508
Sentence-level problems, 832–837
fragments, 834–835
modifiers, misplaced or dangling, 835–837
run-on or fused sentences, 832–834

# Using *Writing: Ten Core Concepts*
## to Meet WPA Outcomes (v3.0)
### An Instructor's Guide

By Joe Creamer
SUNY Albany

## Table of Contents

## Using *Writing: Ten Core Concepts* to Meet WPA Outcomes (v3.0)

When the Council of Writing Program Administrators (WPA) first began discussing an outcomes statement for first-year writing, the goal was to help collegiate writing programs outline national expectations for students who have completed a first-year composition course. In addition to being a standard for assessment, it also outlined a set of common objectives to establish professional accountability for collegiate writing courses across the country. The four WPA outcomes draw attention to "common knowledge, skills, and attitudes" that are representative for students completing first-year composition courses.

The purpose of this instructor's manual is to highlight how *Writing: Ten Core Concepts* addresses these outcomes both in content and approach and to serve as a guide for instructors who are incorporating the WPA outcomes into their day-to-day teaching, assignment design, and course assessment practices. Different parts of the book speak to the outcomes in a unique way, lending flexibility to instructors using the book as an assessment tool.

The information that follows details the WPA outcomes and identifies assignments, readings, and class activities in *Writing: Ten Core Concepts* that may help you meet primary course goals. Lastly, it's worth noting that many of these outcomes overlap in effective writing assignments. So although suggestions are often linked to specific outcomes, they do not exist independently of any single outcome and are often appropriate for overall assessment of the WPA outcomes.

| WPA Outcomes | *Writing: Ten Core Concepts* |
|---|---|
| ■ Rhetorical Knowledge | ✓ Chapters 1 to 5, 11, 15 |
| ■ Critical Thinking, Reading, and Writing | ✓ Chapters 5 to 23 |
| ■ Processes | ✓ Chapters 4 to 18 |
| ■ Knowledge of Conventions | ✓ Chapters 5 to 27 |

For a full copy of the WPA statement, visit: wpacouncil.org/positions/outcomes.html. The most current "WPA Outcomes Statement for First-Year Composition (v3.0)" was adopted on July 17, 2014.

## The WPA and *Writing: Ten Core Concepts* Approach: A Quick-Start Guide

### Suggestions for Assessing Rhetorical Knowledge

*Writing: Ten Core Concepts* offers a unique approach to first-year composition by focusing on ten foundational practices that every writer must know. These flexible concepts are applied throughout the three main parts of the book, each of which focuses on a major genre: analysis, argument and narrative.

| Rhetorical Knowledge | *Writing: Ten Core Concepts* |
|---|---|
| By the end of first-year composition, students should<br><br>■ Learn and use key rhetorical concepts through analyzing and composing a variety of texts.<br><br>■ Gain experience reading and composing in several genres to understand how genre conventions shape and are shaped by readers' and writers' practices and purposes.<br><br>■ Develop facility in responding to a variety of situations and contexts calling for purposeful shifts in voice, tone, level of formality, design, medium, and/or structure.<br><br>■ Understand a variety of technologies to address a range of audiences.<br><br>■ Match the capacities of different environments (e.g., print and electronic) to varying rhetorical situations. | Chapter 1:<br><br>✓ First-year students often claim that they will not need to write very much in college or in their intended field. In this chapter, students begin to see the powerful ways that everyday writing can impact their lives and their society.<br><br>Chapter 2:<br><br>✓ The Ten Core Concepts are outlined in this chapter; many of these concepts address rhetorical knowledge directly. Core Concept #3 discusses the best medium for the rhetorical situation.<br><br>Chapters 5, 11, 15:<br><br>✓ In addition to explaining the main features of analysis, argument and narrative, respectively, these chapters include an annotated sample reading with questions for discussion.<br><br>Chapters 6-10, 12-14, 16-18:<br><br>✓ Each of these assignment chapters tackles subgenres within the main category. For example, in the argument portion, academic arguments, popular arguments and proposals are discussed. The Ten Core Concepts are applied step-by-step to these genres, including such concepts relevant to rhetorical knowledge as context, main point, support for claims, purpose, writing as social practice, and voice. |

**Individual Assessment:** At the beginning of the term, challenge the students' basic rhetorical knowledge by assigning the students to find, read, and bring in to class an academic journal article (or you could provide one for the students). You can limit the scope to the theme of your course or to the students' majors. Ask the students to write a short summary of the article focusing on how the author's point of view is being conveyed. Ask the students to record whether or not the essay was effective in influencing their understanding of the topic and why/why not. This can be submitted to the instructor for feedback, shared with the rest of the class, shared in small groups, or shared in a combination of the three. By asking students to choose a piece of writing and to analyze the rhetorical situation, you will begin pushing them to work closely with a text to understand a writer's purpose and audience. Return to this assignment throughout the semester, adding new genres and different types of texts to the discussion. As a final project, ask students to write a rhetorical analysis essay. Students could use "Writing Rhetorical Analysis" in Chapter 8 (page 246) as a step-by-step guide. A sample prompt for a rhetorical analysis essay follows:

> After you've completed the final draft of your essay project, please develop a brief but intensive rhetorical analysis. In a two-page essay, describe the rhetorical moves in your argument: various support strategies, counterarguments, concessions, etc. The goal is not to re-argue your point or sum up your essay, but to describe the machinery of argument, to analyze its rhetoric.

**Course Level Assessment:** At the end of the term, students should showcase their work from throughout the semester in a portfolio; this can be an electronic file or a physical collection of their essays complete with drafts. Ask students to write a letter introducing their portfolios and the work they've completed in various genres. The letter should craft an argument that addresses the objectives set forth in the Rhetorical Knowledge outcome. Students should use examples from their portfolios as evidence.

# Suggestions for Assessing Critical Thinking, Reading, and Composing

Through contemporary readings and writing samples, *Writing: Ten Core Concepts* asks readers to identify the importance of writing, research, and communication in every aspect of their lives while at the same time teaching students to think, read, and write with a critical perspective.

| Critical Thinking, Reading, and Writing | Writing: Ten Core Concepts |
|---|---|
| By the end of first-year composition, students should<br><br>■ Use composing and reading for inquiry, learning, critical thinking, and communicating in various rhetorical contexts.<br><br>■ Read a diverse range of texts, attending especially to relationships between assertion and evidence, to patterns of organization, to the interplay between verbal and nonverbal elements, and how these features function for different audiences and situations.<br><br>■ Locate and evaluate (for credibility, sufficiency, accuracy, timeliness, bias, and so on) primary and secondary research materials, including journal articles and essays, books, scholarly and professionally established and maintained databases or archives, and informal electronic networks and Internet sources.<br><br>■ Use strategies—such as interpretations, synthesis, response, critique, and design/redesign—to compose texts that integrate the writer's ideas with those from appropriate sources. | Chapters 5–23:<br><br>✓ Core Concept #1 states that "Writing is process of discovery and learning." Like all the core concepts, this point is integrated throughout all the assignment chapters as "Step 1," where short writing tasks are suggested to generate ideas and deepen inquiry. Exercises and discussion questions following every reading allow students to inquire as they read.<br><br>✓ Chapters 5 to 18 discuss how analysis, argument and narrative are forms of inquiry about oneself and the world. They include opportunities to develop intellectual skills common to these genres, such as using a theoretical lens and deploying narrative in academic writing.<br><br>✓ Each assignment chapter (6–10, 12–14, 16–18) asks students: what do you have to say? (Core Concept #4) These chapters provide genre-specific help in formulating a main idea or thesis for the essay.<br><br>✓ Chapters 19 to 23 focus on skill development, including summary, paraphrase, quotation, and source synthesis, as well as locating and evaluating sources. |

**Individual Assessment:** Ask small groups of students to research, design, and implement a PowerPoint presentation introducing a rhetorical tool (such as an appeal, allusion, or form of evidence). This collaborative learning exercise combines critical thinking, reading, and writing skills, as well as various methods for research and presentation, allowing students to effectively communicate course knowledge to a peer audience.

**Course Level Assessment:** At the end of the term, assign an argument essay that presents a particular position on a topic. This project asks students to find outside examples. Or, you can make this an in-class essay with pre-chosen texts. This final assignment builds on the critical thinking, reading, and writing skills demonstrated in the individual presentations and assesses the retention and translation of genre knowledge beyond an individual assignment.

# Suggestions for Assessing Processes

*In Writing: Ten Core Concepts,* Core Concept #7 explains, "Writing is a social activity," while Core Concept #8 discusses revision. By returning to these concepts throughout the book, students realize the many ways that good writing is the result of a collaborative process.

| Processes | *Writing: Ten Core Concepts* |
|---|---|
| By the end of first year composition, students should<br><br>■ Develop a writing project through multiple drafts.<br><br>■ Develop flexible strategies for reading, drafting, reviewing, collaborating, revising, rewriting, rereading, and editing.<br><br>■ Use composing processes and tools as a means to discover and reconsider ideas.<br><br>■ Experience the collaborative and social aspects of writing processes.<br><br>■ Learn to give and act on productive feedback to works in progress.<br><br>■ Adapt composing processes for a variety of technological modalities.<br><br>■ Reflect on the development of composing practices and how those practices influence their work. | Chapters 4 to 18:<br><br>✓ Each of the assignment chapters (6–10, 12–14, 16–18) guides students through the writing process, including Steps 7 (Seeking feedback) and Step 8 (Making revisions). In addition, each assignment chapter includes Step 9, "Refine your voice," which guides students through a series of questions and considerations for strengthening their voice and ensuring it is appropriate for the rhetorical situation.<br><br>✓ Chapter 4 allows students to see a fellow student's entire process as she develops her essay from invention through multiple revisions.<br><br>✓ Electronic media are discussed in Chapter 18, which is devoted to digital narratives, while exercises throughout the assignment chapters ask students to consider the best medium for their specific rhetorical context.<br><br>✓ "Focus" sidebars throughout *Writing: Ten Core Concepts* invite students to think about their previous writing experiences and products. This process of metacognition helps students begin to think of themselves as writers making decisions that will affect their readers. |

**Individual Assessment:** Implement regular oral and written reflections throughout the writing process and at the end of each writing assignment. Ask students to assess the writing process and the roles they played with their teacher and peers throughout the review. Reflections can be completed as in-class writing, discussion, or formal writing assignments.

**Course Level Assessment:** Use writing portfolios to track process and assess progress in your writing class. Students should complete written "Reflection" assignments after each project. At the end of the course, ask students to use their drafts, projects, and reflections to write a piece of commentary examining the writing process throughout the term. Students can comment on any or all parts of the process, from invention to reflection, and should use their individual writing projects and reflections for research and development.

# Suggestions for Assessing Knowledge of Conventions

| Knowledge of Conventions | Writing: Ten Core Concepts |
|---|---|
| By the end of first-year composition, students should<br><br>■ Develop knowledge of linguistic structures, including grammar, punctuation, and spelling, through practice in composing and revising.<br><br>■ Understand why genre conventions for structure, paragraphing, tone, and mechanics vary.<br><br>■ Gain experience negotiating variations in genre conventions.<br><br>■ Learn common formats and/or design features for different kinds of texts.<br><br>■ Explore the concepts of intellectual property (such as fair use and copyright) that motivate documentation conventions.<br><br>■ Practice applying citation conventions systematically in their own work. | Chapters 6-10, 12-14, 16-18:<br><br>✓ Each assignment chapter teaches the conventions of that genre, while noting the range of possibilities available depending on the rhetorical context.<br><br><br>Chapters 19- 27:<br><br>✓ These chapters cover the full range of issues regarding information literacy, including locating and evaluating sources, source synthesis, and document design. The final chapters cover MLA and APA Style, explain academic citation conventions, highlight helpful moves for integrating quotations as scholars would, and emphasize ways to avoid plagiarism. They also offer a correctly cited sample paper for each method. The last two chapters focus on the most common errors students make with grammar, usage and style, but do not attempt a comprehensive review. |

**Individual Assessment:** Conduct a writing workshop that puts the knowledge of conventions in the hands of the students. As a class, read the "Step 7": Get Feedback" and "Step 8: Revise" sections of one of the assignment chapters (for example, Chapter 12, page 383–385). Discuss the "Get Feedback" questions as a class, and use your personal course emphases on writing conventions and documentation to guide the discussion. From there, ask students to complete a peer workshop in pairs, using the "Get Feedback" questions to assess their partner's work.

**Course Level Assessment:** As a final project in conventions, ask students to write a short assessment of their final argument essay using the comments about developing an appropriate academic voice in Chapter 12, "Refine your voice," (page 385–386). They could include this in their final portfolio.

# Adopting WPA Outcomes for Assessing Your First-year Writing Course

## The Big Picture: An Overview of Outcomes-based Assessment in Your Course

1. **Determine what you want to assess:** Assessing writing is a difficult task worthy of many arguments in the composition world; however, using the WPA outcomes makes the instructor's job a bit clearer. In adopting the WPA outcomes for first-year composition, you are starting with a general idea of the knowledge that students should have when exiting your first-year writing course. Although writing can be a subjective discipline, the WPA agrees that there is specific knowledge students *should* be working toward, and in an outcomes-based education, this knowledge is assessable. With that in mind, outcomes such as rhetorical knowledge and processes move from abstract ideas to concrete objectives that can be evaluated using writing assignments from *Writing: Ten Core Concepts*.

2. **Write and establish course objectives:** These objectives will probably be a combination of the WPA outcomes with your specific program and course goals. Think about what skills or knowledge of writing your school's population of students *should* have when they leave your course. How is this knowledge similar to or different from the five WPA outcomes? Where do they overlap? Where are there conflicts? How might you compromise to work with the WPA outcomes? Writing course objectives is not an easy task; however, the clearer you can be with what you want to accomplish, the easier it will be to use *Writing: Ten Core Concepts* to meet those expectations.

3. **Design assignment sequences:** After you have determined course objectives, think about how you might achieve those objectives. What needs to happen in and out of class for you to reach these goals? Ask yourself which objectives the larger writing projects will address. Plan shorter assignments to meet remaining objectives, as necessary.

## Taking Action: Using Outcomes as Pedagogy for Lesson Plans

Now that you've established the big-picture goals, you can create lesson plans based on your outcomes-based pedagogy. What follows are sample lesson plans for use with the "Ideas for Writing" prompts in Chapters 2 through 13 in *Writing: Ten Core Concepts*.

## Working with Students

When dealing with assessment, it is easy to get caught up in the outcomes and objectives, but it is important not to forget whom this assessment directly affects: the students. Explaining the course objectives at the start of the semester, and frequently returning to these goals, will help students comprehend how each assignment works to further their knowledge in the course. Students often misinterpret writing assessment as one teacher's subjective grade on a finished paper. However, putting an emphasis on the WPA outcomes as an education in writing that students should develop and acquire throughout the first year will help to diffuse the misconception that students need to write assignments "for the instructor" because "each instructor grades differently." Adopting a clear set of objectives based on the WPA outcomes and showing how *Writing: Ten Core Concepts* can help students develop this knowledge is one way to turn that subjective point of view into a more tangible and objective evaluation process.

## Sample Student Assignment Handout

One way in which to effectively convey outcomes to students is to translate your weekly lesson plans into detailed assignment sequences that explain the course objectives and tasks for each writing project. This is illustrated in the following model.

| English 110: Intro to Writing Week One: An  Week 1: |
| --- |
| Introduction to the Writing Process<br><br>■ Objective: To gain an understanding of the writing process students will<br>■ Develop a writing project through multiple drafts.<br>■ Develop flexible strategies for drafting, getting feedback, revising, rereading, and editing.<br>■ Use composing processes and tools as a means to discover and reconsider ideas. Experience the collaborative and social aspects of writing processes.<br>■ Learn to give and act on productive feedback to works in progress.<br>■ Reflect on the development of composing practices and how those practices influence their work. |
| Day 1: Students should arrive to class already having read Chapter 1. Discuss why we write, the topic of Chapter 1. Do the "Exercise" on pages 13–15 as a class. Homework: Complete "Exercise 1D" on page 21 in Chapter 1. Students should come to the next class with the completed assignment and be prepared to share their writing with a small group of peers, and students should be ready to continue working with this piece to develop it into a personal narrative. Students should also read Chapter 15. |
| Day 2: As students arrive to class, resume the same groups from the previous class meeting. Students will share their writing sample to the rest of the group. Using the prompts in Chapter 16's "Step 7: Get feedback" (page 532), students will begin to revise their essays. This will take up the entire class period. Homework: Students should revise their essays for submission at the next class meeting. Drafts and notes should be included in the submission for review. This further emphasizes the importance of working through the writing process. |
| Day 3: In Chapter 15, using the readings as samples or models, students will work to further refine their essay. Discuss effective features of personal narratives and how the author's used these features. Remember that as you move through the remaining sections of the chapter, writing throughout the process is essential; a notebook must be kept so that all drafts and notes can be reviewed as part of the assessment process. Before the class is dismissed, peer review partners will be assigned. Homework: Final draft of essay. |

## Daily Exercises from *Writing: Ten Core Concepts* that Work with WPA Outcomes

| WPA Outcomes | *Writing: Ten Core Concepts* |
| --- | --- |
| Rhetorical Knowledge | Chapters 1–2, 5, 11, and 15 provide an explanation of the features and conventions of writing, including analysis, argument and narrative writing. Chapters 1 and 2 include "Practice This Lesson" activities, and Chapters 5, 11, and 15 include exercises as well as questions that accompany annotated professional readings. |
| Critical Thinking, Reading, and Writing | Short composing activities throughout Parts 1–5 offer students opportunities to better understand key concepts. Also, all reading selections in Chapters 5–18 are followed by questions for discussion and writing. |
| Processes | Assignment chapters (6–10, 12–14, 16–18) walk the student through a ten step writing process based on the Ten Core Concepts, adapted for each genre. |
| Knowledge of Conventions | Chapters 5, 11, and 15 offer exercises on the conventions of analysis, argument and narrative, while Chapters 19-23 have exercises to hone specific writing skills, such as summary, paraphrase, synthesis, etc. |

## Sample Lesson Plan: Making Academic Arguments

- WPA Outcomes for Assessment: Processes and Rhetorical Knowledge
- Outcomes-based Course Objective: Writing is a process requiring multiple drafts, research, and collaborative critiques to communicate a message to an audience.
- Task: Making Academic Arguments, *Writing: Ten Core Concepts*, Chapter 12

| | Objectives | Tasks from *Writing: Ten Core Concepts* |
| --- | --- | --- |
| Week One | ■ Knowledge and conventions of academic arguments<br>■ Working draft of the project | ✓ Read: Chapter 11, "Understanding Argument;" Chapter 12, "Making Academic Arguments," pages 316–387;<br>✓ Discuss: The "Exercises" throughout Chapter 11.<br>✓ Write: Choose one of the "Writing Projects" at the end of the chapter<br>✓ Homework: Begin drafting topic chosen during class for argument essay |
| Week Two | ■ Further exploration of academic arguments<br>■ Awareness of writing processes<br>■ Revision methods | ✓ Read: Chapter 12, "Making Academic Arguments," page 357–387; Bruce Western "Crime and Punishment," page 364–366; Patricia McGuire, "Fulfilling Her Mother's Dream," page 366–369; Michael Zimmer, "Mark Zuckerberg's Theory of Privacy," page 370–373<br>✓ Discuss: The "Exercises" after each reading; "Steps 2 through 5: "Rhetorical Context, Medium, Main Argument, Support Main Argument" |
| Week Three | ■ Revised assignment<br>■ Peer review<br>■ Knowledge of genre in a new context | ✓ Read: Chapter 12, "Making Academic Arguments," page 357–387.<br>✓ Discuss: "Step 7: Getting Feedback" Peer review of drafts<br>✓ Write: Revise drafts<br>✓ Homework: Revise drafts for submission for grading |

## Evaluating Multiple Purposes and Genres

*Writing: Ten Core Concepts* connects academic writing with real-life situations and topics in which students will need strong and effective written communication skills. Yet, with such varied forms of writing, the question of evaluation often looms in the classroom, as both students and teachers try to negotiate how to grade items from personal exploratory essays to more formal research-based argument essays with the same set of guidelines. Translating the WPA outcomes into a rubric for evaluation is one way to tackle this issue. Instead of grading each rhetorical mode only by its conventions and mechanics, instructors can construct a rubric that assesses all written projects on the same composition plane. Depending on course and assignment design, rubrics can be focused and personalized to meet instructor goals, while still addressing the WPA outcomes—and also assessing the independent genre projects.

## Single Outcome Rubric

| Rhetorical Knowledge Rubric | excellent | above average | meets standards | insufficient |
|---|---|---|---|---|
| Attention to Audience | | | | |
| Responds to Rhetorical Situation | | | | |
| Knowledge Of Genre Conventions | | | | |
| Appropriate Use of Language and Tone | | | | |

## Multiple Outcomes Rubric

| Grading Rubric for Argument Writing Assignment | Comments |
|---|---|
| Rhetorical Knowledge: demonstrates a rhetorical awareness through | |
| audience appeal, writing persona, genre knowledge, and context | |
| Critical Thinking, Reading, and Writing: uses research for communicating, synthesizing ideas, and integrating multiple perspectives | |
| Processes: demonstrates evidence of critique and large-scale revision through a peer-review and self-evaluation process | |
| Knowledge of Conventions: employs a knowledge of genre conventions, formal mechanics, and style | |

## E-Portfolios, WPA Outcomes, and *Writing: Ten Core Concepts*

Electronic portfolios are an increasingly popular method of assessing student work not only for single courses, but also for long-term measurements over a student's educational career. Likewise, for a two-semester course or a multi-course assessment program, e-portfolios can be useful for collecting data and tracking the progress of groups and individuals. Using e-portfolios in coordination with the WPA outcomes and *Writing: Ten Core Concepts* will require the same representative sample of student writing that would accompany a print portfolio. The difference and perks of e-portfolios come in the convenience and organization of the various assignments (no more large stacks of folders to carry) and also in the critical connections that students can make, linking texts and peer commentary to revisions and reflections via the functions of electronic folders.

E-portfolios allow students to easily retain writing projects from all steps in the writing process to access them for later analysis and assessment. The writing assignments in *Writing: Ten Core Concepts* begin with invention and lead students through multiple drafts and critiques to a final essay. In addition to a representative sample of writing, students could also include a reflective letter, revised writing assignments, a case study of a single writing assignment, peer commentary, or commentary on collaborative learning. Asking students to design and complete a written analysis of the e-portfolio to show knowledge of rhetoric; critical thinking, reading, and writing; processes; and conventions requires the same critical approach used in the ten step processes of Chapters 6 through 18. This culminating assignment applies all of the elements that have been introduced throughout the course and emphasizes the importance of the writing process while allowing students to showcase their work. In addition, e-portfolios raise student awareness of the idea that a "finished" draft does not mean the writing is done. When asked to compile a portfolio, the writing is reborn, revisited, and redefined through the organization and rewriting involved in the e-portfolio project. Suddenly the documents become part of a public and professional presentation of their writing identity.

# 10 Core Concepts

**1**   *Writing is a process of discovery and learning.*    The act of writing is rarely a straightforward, linear process, and it often takes you to places you didn't expect.

**2**   *Good writing fits the context.*    The writer, the subject, and the audience are the context that will determine how well a piece of writing does its work.

**3**   *The medium is part of the message.*    You can express your ideas in a wide variety of ways depending on the tools and technology you use.

**4**   *A writer must have something to say.*    Having a clear, valid main point or idea is an essential element of effective writing.

**5**   *A writer must support claims and assertions.*    Not only must you have something relevant to say, but you must also be able to back up what you say.

**6**   *Purpose determines form, style, and organization in writing.*    Every kind of text is governed by general expectations regarding its form, which helps it fulfill its purpose in a given context.

**7**   *Writing is a social activity.*    Writers share drafts; they write for specific audiences; and they draw on socially constructed conventions to accomplish their purposes.

**8**   *Revision is an essential part of writing.*    Adding, deleting, and moving material is integral to the writing process: writers keep rewriting until their message is clear to readers.

**9**   *There is always a voice in writing, even when there isn't an I.*    Distinctive writing results from being able to "hear" the writer's voice or personality in the word choices and sentences the writer uses.

**10**   *Good writing means more than good grammar.*    A perfectly correct essay can be a perfectly lousy piece of writing if it does not fulfill its purposes and meet the needs of its audience.